18.95
4.4

D1552518

Prophecy and Politics

Socialism, Nationalism,
and the Russian Jews,
1862–1917

Published under the auspices of the
Research Institute on International Change
Columbia University
and the
Russian Institute
Columbia University

PROPHECY AND POLITICS

Socialism, Nationalism,
and the Russian Jews,
1862–1917

JONATHAN FRANKEL

*Department of Russian Studies and
Institute of Contemporary Jewry,
The Hebrew University of Jerusalem*

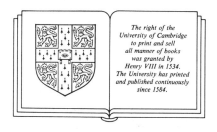

The right of the
University of Cambridge
to print and sell
all manner of books
was granted by
Henry VIII in 1534.
The University has printed
and published continuously
since 1584.

CAMBRIDGE UNIVERSITY PRESS

CAMBRIDGE

LONDON   NEW YORK   NEW ROCHELLE
MELBOURNE   SYDNEY

Published by the Press Syndicate of the University of Cambridge
The Pitt Building, Trumpington Street, Cambridge CB2 1RP
32 East 57th Street, New York, NY 10022, USA
296 Beaconsfield Parade, Middle Park, Melbourne 3206, Australia

© Cambridge University Press 1981

First published 1981
First paperback edition 1984

Printed in the United States of America

Library of Congress Cataloging in Publication Data
Frankel, Jonathan.
Prophecy and politics.
1. Jews in Russia—Politics and government.
2. Socialists, Jewish. 3. Labor Zionism.
4. Jews in the United States—Politics and government.
5. Russia—Ethnic relations. 6. United States—Ethnic
relations. I. Title.
DS135.R9F73 947'.04924 80-14414
ISBN 0 521 23028 4 hard covers
ISBN 0 521 26919 9 paperback

Illustrations have been reproduced from the following sources: Central
Zionist Archive—Figures 1, 22, 24, 30; YIVO Archive—Figures 2, 3, 4,
17, 18, 21, 34; Bund Archive—Figures 5, 10, 11, 12, 13, 14, 15; Archive
and Museum of the Jewish Labor Movement—Figures 19, 20, 23, 25,
26, 27, 28, 29, 31; Byron Collection, Museum of the City of New
York—Figure 32; Jacob A. Riis Collection, Museum of the City of New
York—Figure 33.

TO
MY PARENTS

Contents

CONTENTS

Preface

This book has long been in preparation. My first sally into the field was my Ph.D. thesis, which took up the years 1957–61. I returned to the subject late in 1972 and completed the body of the book six years later. Remnants of the thesis, rethought and rewritten from scratch, are incorporated here in Part II (Chapters 4–7).

Over these extensive periods I have received help and encouragement, often far beyond the call of duty, from a very large number of people – academic colleagues, librarians, archivists, editors, secretaries, typists, photocopy workers. I remember the innumerable acts of goodwill and the work well done with feelings of deep gratitude. Unfortunately, I can only mention a small percentage here by name.

In the Cambridge years, I was guided wisely and generously by my teachers and friends: E. H. Carr, D. J. V. Fisher, Charles Wilson, Moses Finley, Maurice Cowling, and Betty Behrens. Denys Page, the late Master of Jesus College (where I was appointed a Fellow for the years 1960–3) also gave me his unflagging support in those early stages, as did Chimen Abramsky and Isaiah Berlin. Indeed, the idea of this work, which took shape in my mind while aboard ship on the Mediterranean in the summer of 1956, was perhaps first implanted by the report of a lecture in which Sir Isaiah discussed the Russian roots of the Yishuv.

As a Senior Fellow at Columbia University, I have invariably been made to feel at home. Both the Russian Institute and the Research Institute on International Change (now RIIC, formerly RICA) made it possible for me to work intensively on the book during extended visits. Those colleagues – Alexander Dallin, Zbigniew Brzezinski, Marshall Shulman, Robert Belknap, and the late Henry Roberts – who had the onerous task of directing those remarkable institutions have ensured throughout that the working conditions there would be congenial and the intellectual atmosphere open, stimulating, and very often exciting. At Columbia, too, I have always been able to turn for professional advice to my friends Joseph Rothschild, Alexander Erlich, and Marc Raeff. Sonya Sluzar (for many years the assistant director of RICA) invariably ironed out the various technical problems that arise even in the best run institutions. Louise Luke, at one time the editorial assistant at the Russian Institute, taught me the little I know about problems of editing. I also owe much to Lynn Solotaroff, who now holds that post, maintaining the same open-door policy.

At the marvelous library of the YIVO Institute I could count on the unflagging concern of Dina Abramowicz and her staff. And a few blocks away in Manhattan, at the Bund Archive, Hillel Kempinsky is in no way to be outdone in his determination to track down the most obscure publication. Many consultations with David Roskies and Miles Cohen of the Jewish Theological Seminary, Neil Jacobs of YIVO, and Hanna Maschler of the Hebrew University helped me to grapple with the complexities of transliteration and the rendition of names. My research in New York was facilitated by grants from the Littauer Foundation and the Memorial Foundation for Jewish Culture, which made it possible to extend my stay in 1973–4.

In Jerusalem I have been fortunate to have the close friendship and constant advice of fellow historians Ezra Mendelsohn, Israel Getzler, and Lloyd Gartner (the latter of Tel Aviv University). My two departments at the Hebrew University – the Institute of Contemporary Jewry (so devotedly built up over the years by Moshe Davis) and Russian Studies – have always given me every possible encouragement during this rather protracted enterprise. My sincere thanks are likewise due Shmuel Ettinger whose active and wide-ranging interest in it dates back to its beginnings.

Gratitude is tempered with much sadness when I recall the encouragement that I received throughout from Jacob Talmon, who (with Professor Ettinger) supervised my work when I came to Jerusalem as a visiting student in 1959. I came to admire him not only as a passionately involved historian who painted on a truly broad canvas but also as a public figure possessed of unflinching civic courage. Over the last years, I would sometimes join him on his afternoon walks and we would discuss history, our daughters (who are of much the same age), and the issues of the day about which he was, of late, pessimistic although never without hope. He died on 16 June 1980.

Various people have been good enough to read the manuscript in whole or in part: Mitchell Cohen, Shmuel Ettinger, Alexander Erlich, Rafael Frankel (my brother), Lloyd Gartner, Israel Getzler, Israel Kolatt, Ezra Mendelsohn, Matityahu Mintz, Marc Raeff, and Steve Zipperstein. My parents and my wife have done likewise and, what is more, have helped in the thankless task of editing. It goes without saying that while the latter-day improvements are thus primarily due to others, the flaws that remain are purely my own responsibility.

In 1978, Yehuda Slutsky assured me that he would like to read over the manuscript. His death shortly thereafter carried away a man held in great affection for his generosity and kindness, and in the highest regard as historian of Russian Jewry and the Yishuv. Author of major studies in his own right, editor of *He-avar* and the multivolume history of the Hagana, he made a unique contribution.

My parents have followed the genesis and growth of this book with remarkable patience. It is dedicated to them. Last but not least, I wish to thank my wife, Edith, who, despite all rational indications to the contrary, never gave up hope. I feel that this is now her book no less than mine.

Some technical details must be mentioned. The system of transliteration from Yiddish is based on the YIVO system as formulated in Uriel Weinreich's dictionary; from Russian on that of the Library of Congress; and from Hebrew on that used by the *Encyclopedia Judaica*. However, in the case of Russian and Hebrew, I have introduced modifications in order to avoid diacritical marks and other usages that are not required by the specialist, but that could deter the general reader. In accord with this line of reasoning, the silent *shva* is not noted (e.g., *kvutsa*) except where its omission could confuse the English reader, and there it is signified by "e" (e.g., *tehiya*).

Surnames are in most cases transliterated from the Russian form. However,

PREFACE

where a different usage is highly familiar (e.g., Jabotinsky) or where the particular individual was active primarily in an English-speaking country (e.g., Schlossberg), that spelling has been preferred. First names normally appear in the form most appropriate to the cultural-political context in which the individual was active (e.g., Jacob De Haas, Yaakov Rabinovich, Iakov Lvovich Rozenfeld, Yankev Binyomin Salutsky). In a few cases, the standard English rendering has been preferred (e.g., Chaim, Zvi). Variant spellings in common use are cross-referenced in the Index.

Finally, it should be noted that foreign-language words and terms generally have not been italicized if they are included in *Webster's Third New International Dictionary.*

Jerusalem
June 1980

J.F.

Glossary

The following entries are not comprehensive but refer to the specific meaning of terms as used in the text.

AFL   The American Federation of Labor (1886).

Ahdut Ha-Avoda   Lit. United Labor; founded 1919, the leading Jewish socialist party in Palestine in the 1920s.

AJC   The American Jewish Committee (1906).

AJRC   The American Jewish Relief Committee (1914).

aliya [aliyot]   Jewish immigration to Palestine; the First Aliya is usually dated 1881–1903, the Second Aliya, 1903/4–1914.

Am Olam   Lit. "the eternal people"; the movement founded in Russia to establish Jewish farming colonies in the USA (1881).

artel   A group of laborers or craftsmen in Russia organized on a cooperative and often egalitarian basis.

Bar Giora   A clandestine, paramilitary group formed by Poale Zion members in Palestine (1907).

Bei zhidov!   A common slogan in the pogroms was: "Beat the Jews and save Russia!" ("Bei zhidov, spasai rossiiu").

Bezalel   A school for arts and a center for craft manufacture established in Jerusalem (1906).

Bilu   The Palestine-oriented youth movement (1882); an acronym from "Bet Yaakov, lekhu ve-nelkha"; "House of Jacob come, let us go" (Isaiah 2:5).

Black Hundreds   *Chernosotentsy;* members of the vigilante, Russian nationalist groups and movements formed, 1905, to combat the revolution; encouraged pogroms.

B'nai B'rith   Lit. "Sons of the Covenant"; a major Jewish fraternal and service organization founded in New York, 1843. Until 1933: the Independent Order of B'nai B'rith.

boyar   A member of a noble order in medieval Russia.

xiii

GLOSSARY

Bund, the	Der algemeyner yidisher arbeter bund in rusland un poyln (The General Jewish Labor Union in Russia and Poland); founded 1897; in 1901 its name was changed to read: "in Lithuania, Poland and Russia."
buntarstvo	Rebelliousness; the ideology (associated with Bakunin) favoring mass peasant uprising.
Cantonists	*Kantonisty;* Jewish children and youth inducted into the Russian army under Nicholas I; from age eighteen they still had to serve another twenty-five years.
Cherny Peredel	Cherny peredel: partiia sotsialistov federalistov (The Black Repartition: the Party of Socialist Federalists); advocated agitation among the peasantry with the aim of agrarian revolution (1879).
Chernoperedelets [Chernoperedeltsy]	Member of the Cherny Peredel.
chinovnik	A government bureaucrat (usually pejorative).
Credists	A term used by Lenin to describe supporters of Economism (q.v.); it was derived from "The Credo," a title ironically assigned by its critics to a memorandum by E. D. Kuskova (1898).
Duma	*Gosudarstvennaia duma;* the parliament created in the wake of the 1905 revolution; four Dumas were elected 1906–17.
dunam	One thousand square meters, approximately a quarter of an acre.
Economism	The theory that the labor movement in Russia should concentrate on economic issues (wages, hours) avoiding political activity (hence, Economist) – terms used by Plekhanov and others against the majority in the Union Abroad (q.v.).
ekspropriatsiia	Lit. "expropriation"; a term used by revolutionaries to describe robbery for party purposes.
ekstern	Usually an ex-yeshiva student not permitted to enter a Russian high school who chose to study the curriculum privately in the hope of passing the matriculation exams.
Erets-yisrael (Yid: *erets-yisroel)*	The land of Israel, Palestine.
ESDRP-PZ	Evreiskaia sotsial-demokratischeskaia rabochaia partiia-poale tsion (The Jewish Social Democratic Party-Poale Zion) (1906).

GLOSSARY

Evsektsiia	Evreiskaia sektsiia; the Jewish section of the Communist Party in Soviet Russia, 1918–30.
Ezra	The Hebrew name (abbr.) for the Hilfsverein der deutschen Juden (The Relief Organization of the German Jews) (1901).
Fareynikte	Fareynikte yidishe sotsyalistishe arbeter partey (The United Jewish Socialist Labor Party), formed by the merger of the SERP and the SSRP (1917).
FAZ	The Federation of American Zionists (1898).
Fellakh[y] (Russ.)	Fellah [felaheen]; a peasant or agricultural laborer in the Arabic-speaking areas of the Middle East.
Folkspartey	The Jewish People's Party (Evreiskaia narodnaia partiia) (1906).
franc	A french franc (pre-1914) was worth approximately U.S. $0.20.
galut (Heb.)	The Exile or Diaspora (pejorative).
Gegenwartsarbeit (Germ.)	The direction of party efforts toward the attainment of immediate and concrete, as against long-term or final, goals.
genosn	The term for "comrades" used in the mainstream Jewish labor movement in the USA (from the German Social Democratic usage, Genossen).
gimnaziia [gimnazii] (Russ.); *gimnasya [gimnasyot]* (Heb.)	A high school with an emphasis on the humanities; hence, *gimnazist[y]*, a student therein.
goles (Yid.)	See galut.
Group, the	The Group for the Liberation of Labor (Gruppa "osvobozhdenie truda"), established by Plekhanov and associates when they proclaimed allegiance to revolutionary Marxism (1883).
guberniia [gubernii]	An administrative area in the tsarist empire. European Russia (i.e., excluding Poland and the Caucasus) was divided into some fifty such provinces.
haluka	The traditional system for the distribution of charity (mainly contributions from abroad) within the Jewish community in Palestine, particularly in Jerusalem.

GLOSSARY

Hanuka

The eight-day festival of lights, commemorates the Maccabean victory of 164 B.C.E. over Antiochus of Syria.

Ha-Poel Ha-Tsair

The Young Workers party (in full: Histadrut ha-poalim
ha-tseirim be-erets yisrael) (1905).

Ha-Shomer

The Watchman; an organization formed in Galilee to take
over guard duty in the Jewish colonies (1909).

Hasid

An adherent of Hasidism, a popular religious movement
inclined to mysticism; strongest in Podolia, Volhynia,
Congress Poland, and Galicia.

Haskala

The enlightenment movement in the Jewish world (particularly in Hebrew).

"Ha-tikva"

The song adopted by the Zionist movement – unofficially
in 1905, formally in 1933 – as the Jewish national anthem.

HEAS

The Hebrew Emigrant Aid Society (1881).

hectare

Gektar; approximately two and a half (2.471) acres.

heder [hadarim]

An elementary school conducted in Yiddish to teach the
Hebrew Bible, commentaries, etc.

heym, der

Lit. "home"; used by new immigrants in the U.S. to describe the Old Country.

Histadrut

Ha-histadrut ha-klalit shel ha-ovdim ha-ivrim be-erets
yisrael (The General Jewish Labor Federation in Palestine)
(1920).

hora

A vigorous circle dance (primarily of Roumanian origin),
very popular among the pioneers in Palestine.

Hovev Zion

Lit. a lover of Zion (Palestinophile); a member of the
proto-Zionist movement (Hoveve Zion) formally founded
1884.

humash[im]

The Pentateuch (or Five Books of Moses); a term used in
Aron Liberman's correspondence as a code-word for his
paper, *Ha-emet.*

ICA

The Jewish Colonisation Association, founded by Baron
Maurice de Hirsch (1896).

ILGWU

The International Ladies Garment Workers Union (1900).

intelligent

Member of the intelligentsia; in tsarist Russia implied a
commitment to political opposition.

Iskrovtsy

Members of the RSDRP who supported *Iskra* ("The
Spark"), the journal founded by Lenin and his associates
(1900).

JSF	The Jewish Socialist Federation, a subsection of the SP (1912).
kabalistic	Pertaining to the most influential system of Jewish mysticism, the Kabala.
Kadets	*Kadety;* members of the Constitutional Democratic Party (1905).
kahal	See kehila.
Kasrilevka	A shtetl created by Sholem Aleichem; implies extreme provincialism and economic insecurity.
kassa [kassy]	Mutual-benefit associations formed by the workers; served as strike organizations and as the quasi-trade union basis of the Bund.
kehila [kehilot]	The umbrella organization of the Jewish community in a given place, responsible for charity and other common interests.
kibush ha-avoda	Lit. "the conquest of labor"; the attempt of the Russian-Jewish youth to substitute themselves for the Arabs as wage workers in the Jewish colonies in Palestine.
klal-yisroel politik	See *kol-yisroel politik.*
kolel	A roof organization for the traditionalist Jewish immigrants from a particular country or area; most common in Palestine, but also established elsewhere.
kol-yisroel politik	Politics based on the idea of Jewish unity as against the politics of the class struggle.
kopek	*kopeika;* one-hundredth of a rouble.
kruzhok [kruzhki]	A group of intelligentsia or workers, usually clandestine, for political education or revolutionary organization; hence *kruzhkovshchina:* a preference for this form of revolutionary action.
kulak	Lit. a "fist"; denoted the upper stratum of peasants who lent money or rented out land, livestock, and implements to the poorer peasantry.
kvutsa [kvutsot]	A cooperative or communal labor group in Palestine (after 1911 increasingly for purposes of settlement).
landslayt	Compatriots, particularly from the same area, town, or shtetl.
landsmanshaftn	Immigrant societies formed for purposes of mutual aid (welfare, burial, etc.); the members originated from the same town or area in Eastern Europe.

LSDRP	The Latvian Social Democratic Labor Party (1904).
Litvakes (Yid.)	Lithuanians; here, Lithuanian Jews.
magid[im]	A popular preacher (usually itinerant); addressed synagogue congregations, often on contemporary issues; relied heavily on biblical and other popular religious tales or themes.
Mapai	Mifleget poale erets yisrael (The Palestine Labor Party) (1930).
mark	The German Imperial mark (pre-1914) was worth approximately U.S. $0.25.
maskil[im]	An adherent of the Haskala (q.v.)
melamed [melamdim]	A teacher of the Hebrew language and basic religious texts, particularly in a heder.
meshchanin [*meshchane*]	A member of the *meshchanstvo:* the petty bourgeoisie (usually pejorative: Philistine, narrowly materialistic).
mir	See *obshchina.*
moshav ovdim (or moshav)	A smallholding settlement, incorporating some cooperative principles, in Palestine.
muzhik [i]	A Russian peasant.
narod	Lit. "the people," more specifically the peasantry and laboring masses: hence *narodnichestvo,* agrarian populism; and *narodnik,* populist.
Narodnaia Volia	*Partiia "narodnoi voli"* (The People's Will Party); agrarian, terrorist, committed to the overthrow of the tsarist regime and to the reorganization of the state (1879).
Narodovolets [Narodovoltsy]	Member of the Narodnaia Volia.
Nili	A pro-British espionage group led by Aaron Aaronsohn, founded 1915 (an acronym from "Netsah yisrael lo yeshaker"/"The strength of Israel will not lie." I Samuel 15:29).
numerus clausus	The quota system imposed on the entry of Jews into Russian high schools and universities (1887).
NWC	The National Workmen's Committee on Jewish Rights in the Belligerent Lands (1915).

obshchina	The Russian peasant community, which in many areas involved the periodic repartition and equalization of land holdings.
OK	*Organizatsionny komitet;* the committee established in March 1902 to prepare the Second Congress of the RSDRP.
Okhrana	Lit. Security; denotes generally the tsarist departments responsible for combating subversion.
OPE	Obshchestvo dlia rasprostraneniia prosveshcheniia mezhdu evreiiami v Rossii (The Society for the Dissemination of Enlightenment among the Jews in Russia); initially, it sought to increase knowledge of the Russian language, but from the 1890s it became more a focus for the conflicting claims of Yiddish and Hebrew.
ORT	Obshchestvo remeslennogo i zemledelcheskogo truda sredi evreev v Rossii (The Society for [the Advancement of] Craft and Agricultural Labor among the Jews in Russia) (1880).
OZE	Obshchestvo okhranenii zdorovia evreiskogo nasileniia (The Society for the Health Protection of the Jewish Population) (1912).
pan[y]	A member of the Polish gentry.
Poale Zion	Lit. The workers of Zion: initially, a general term for labor Zionist groups; from 1906 applied specifically to the ESDRP-PZ and its affiliated parties abroad.
podpolshchik	A member of the revolutionary underground.
pogromshchik[i]	An instigator of, or active participant in, the anti-Jewish riots (pogroms).
polkovnik(Russ.)	A colonel.
polu-intelligent	A man whose formal education was in the heder and yeshiva but who was an autodidact in Russian culture.
Polyakn (Yid.)	Poles; here Polish Jews.
pound	A pound sterling (pre-1914) was worth approximately U.S. $5.00.
PPS	Polska Partja Socjalistyczna (The Polish Socialist Party) (1892–3).
PPSD	Polska Partja Socjalno-demokratyczna Galicji i Śląska Cieszyńskiego (The Polish Social Democratic Party of Galicia and Teshchen Silesia); the allied party of the PPS in Galicia, founded 1891; until 1897 known as the Galician Social Democratic Party.

GLOSSARY

praktik — A party member concerned with organization.

Proletariat — A Polish revolutionary party (in full: Międzynarodowa Socjalno-Rewolucyjna Partja Proletariat) (1882).

PSD — The Polish Social Democratic movement (see SDKP).

PSR — Partiia sotsialistov revoliutsionerov (The Party of Socialist Revolutionaries) (1902).

Rabochedeltsy — Members of the Social Democratic faction associated with the "Economist" journal *Rabochee delo* ("The Workers Cause"), 1898–1902; see Economists.

raznochinets [*raznochintsy*] — A member of the intelligentsia who was not of noble or gentry origin.

rebbe — Usually, a Hasidic rabbi.

referat — A formal lecture usually opening an ideological debate in which the lecturer (referent) had to face a full-scale critique (*kontr-referat*).

rossiiskii [*rossiiskaia,* fem.] — Russian, adj.; a term implying association with Russian territories as opposed to *russkii,* which suggests an identity with (or membership in) the Great Russian nation.

RSDRP — Rossiiskaia sotsial-demokraticheskaia rabochaia partiia (Russian Social Democratic Labor Party) (1898).

rouble — a rouble (pre-1914) was worth approximately U.S. $0.50; until 1897 it was worth about U.S. $0.80.

Russkii [*russkaia,* fem.] — See *rossiiskii*.

SDKP — Socjaldemokracja Królewstwa Polskiego (The Social Democratic [Party] of the Kingdom of Poland) (1894), later the SDKPiL.

SDKPiL — Socjaldemokracja Królewstwa Polskiego i Litwy (The Social Democratic [Party] of the Kingdom of Poland and Lithuania) (1900).

sech — A Cossack center; in modern times, the Cossacks combined arable farming with military duty as cavalry soldiers.

Sefer [Sifre] Torah — The scrolls containing the Five Books of Moses; kept in every synagogue.

Seim — A representative assembly or parliament (from the Polish, Sejm) (see SERP).

GLOSSARY

SERP	Evreiskaia sotsialisticheskaia rabochaia partiia (The Jewish Socialist Labor Party) (1906); its members were often referred to as the ES or as Seimisty (see *Seim*).
Shekhina	The Divine Spirit; the presence of God in the world.
shtadlonim (Yid.)	Influential Jews whose task it was traditionally to intercede with the governmental authorities on behalf of the Jewish community; in modern times used pejoratively to condemn policies of intercession (*shtadlones*) as opposed to those of power or public protest.
shtetl [shtetlkh]	A small town in eastern Europe.
shul	Yiddish term for synagogue.
Soiuzniki	See Union Abroad.
SRs	Socialist Revolutionaries (members of the PSR, q. v.).
SSRP	Sionistsko-sotsialisticheskaia rabochaia partiia (The Zionist Socialist Labor Party), usually known as the SS (1905).
stikhiia, stikhiinost	Elemental or spontaneous forces, naturally determined and uncontrolled by conscious or voluntaristic factors.
Talmud Torah	A school for the basic study of the Bible and rabbinic literature; usually communally supported, and larger than a heder.
tefilin	Phylacteries; small leather boxes containing Biblical passages worn by Jews during the morning weekday prayers.
teoretik	A party ideologist and theorist.
troika (Russ.)	Lit. a carriage and three horses; used to describe a three-man team, often a leadership trio.
Trudovik[i]	A member of the labor faction or party in the Duma; formed primarily to represent peasant interests (1906).
TsK	Initials indicating central committee (both Heb. and Russ.); used, e.g., in the Bund and RSDRP.
ukaz[y]	An official edict of the tsarist regime.
Union Abroad, the	The Union of Russian Social Democrats Abroad (Soiuz russkikh sotsialdemokratov zagranitsei) (1895); hence *Soiuzniki*.
Union for Equal Rights, the	The Union for the Attainment of Full Rights for the Jewish People in Russia (Soiuz dlia dostizheniia polnopraviia evreiskogo naroda v Rossii) (1905).

GLOSSARY

Valtovshchina	The ideological trend associated with Lesin (A. Valt) in Minsk (1894).
UHT	The United Hebrew Trades (1888).
verst	*Versta;* 1.06 kilometers.
Vozrozhdenie	Lit. "rebirth"; the name of a revolutionary and Jewish nationalist journal and movement (1903); hence, Vozrozhdentsy.
yahudim	A derogatory term used by Yiddish-speaking immigrants to describe the established Jews in the West (specifically those of German origin).
yeshiva[yeshivot]	A school for advanced Talmudic study.
yeshiva bokher	A student in a yeshiva (q. v.).
Yishuv	The Jewish people in Palestine; the "old Yishuv" describes the traditional, religiously observant community established in the period before 1881.
zemskii sobor	The Russian national assembly or parliament of the sixteenth and seventeenth centuries; Slavophile and other political theorists hoped to revive it in a modern form.
zemstvo[zemstva]	Organs of local self-government in tsarist Russia; elected, but with a restricted franchise (1864).
zhid[y]	Jew (pejorative).
Zione Zion	Lit. Zionists of Zion; those Zionists who rejected the East Africa project (1903–5) and remained loyal to the Palestine orientation.
ŻPS	Żydowska Partja Socjaldemokratyczna (The Jewish Social Democratic Party); the counterpart of the Bund in Galicia (1905).
Zusammenbruchstheorie (Germ.)	The crisis theory; the thesis that socialism would result from the cataclysmic decline of capitalism.

Introduction

The history of European Jewry over the last two hundred years divides into three periods or, to be more exact, has followed three distinct but overlapping patterns of development. The original mode of Jewish life as it existed throughout most of Europe in the early eighteenth century was still medieval. Juridically defined as a separate community in the hierarchy of different orders and estates, assigned specific economic functions, possessed of its own languages (Yiddish and Hebrew) and laws (those administered by the rabbinical authority), the Jewish people from the Rhine to the Dnepr formed a highly conservative (albeit not unchanging), inward-looking, and self-contained entity.

A new historical process, which drove an ever wider breach through the walls of this medieval community, was set in motion under the combined impact of the Enlightenment—known in the Jewish world as the Haskala—and the various governmental acts of emancipation. The idea of one law for all and equality before that law was carried eastward by the French armies of the revolution and Napoleon; and even though that program was not fully carried out anywhere in central or eastern Europe, no state there failed to implement it in part.

Increasingly, throughout the early and mid-nineteenth century, a sharply contrasting way of life emerged in the Jewish world alongside the old. Speaking the vernacular rather than Yiddish, regarding himself as an equal citizen in his land of birth, narrowing the idea of Judaism to a religion rather than a nationality, and reforming the religion to fit this concept (or simply discarding it as outmoded), the modern Jew adapted himself to the changing times. It was assumed that Europe as a whole was moving inexorably along the trail already pioneered by revolutionary France and by the United States of America; that the future promised total emancipation, equal opportunity for all, and the steady acculturization of minority groups. The trend was toward liberalism in politics, individualism in thought and as a way of life, laissez-faire and industrialization in economics: in short, toward westernization.

However, it is the third, the postliberal, pattern in modern Jewish life with which this book is concerned—not 1789, but 1881; not emancipation, but the failure of emancipation; not the absorption of the Jews in the West, but their savage exclusion in the Russian Empire of Alexander III and Nicholas II. In general terms, this is a study of the political response to the crisis of Russian Jewry in the period 1881–1917, a crisis that was marked by a population explosion, chronic underemployment (and unemployment), poverty; by periodic waves of pogroms and governmental harassment; by a massive emigration which carried the east European Jews in hundreds of thousands—and eventually millions—to new centers all over the world.

INTRODUCTION

To a great extent, the experience of German (and Austrian) Jewry anticipated that of the Russian Jews. There, too, reaction and virulent antisemitism followed the revolutionary periods of 1789–1812 and 1848–9. There, too, the steps taken toward civil equality were subject to sudden reversal. After 1848 Jews emigrated in enormous numbers from Germany, too (particularly to the United States). But the Jewish people in Russia had been molded far less completely by the emancipation era and, with the reversal of 1881, it moved, as it were, directly from a preliberal to a postliberal stage of development, from medieval community to projects for national revival, from a religious to a social and secular messianism.

It was the intelligentsia (in the prerevolutionary Russian sense of that term) that played the crucial part in creating the postliberal politics and ideologies. And this work concentrates specifically on the role of the Russian-Jewish intelligentsia as a new leadership stratum within the Jewish people. The intelligentsia did not replace the established authorities – whether theocratic or plutocratic – which had hitherto reigned supreme in Russian and world Jewish affairs, but it emerged parallel to them, possessed of its own alternative philosophical attitudes, culture, and way of life. It was created as a political force by the prolonged Russian-Jewish crisis, and its politics and ideology were stamped by that crisis.

The sudden and drastic reversal in attitudes that marked the emergence of the new ethos was summed up brilliantly by Lev Pinsker in 1882 with his slogan, "self-emancipation." Contained in this term was the conviction that the Jewish question could not – and would not – be solved by the grant of equal rights from above nor by a return to the status quo ante of traditional Judaism, but had to be won by total change, collective action, political planning, and organization. With liberalism and individualism pronounced a failure, the radical and collectivist ideologies – nationalism and socialism – naturally came into their own.

In many ways, the politically active and conscious intelligentsia that after 1881 became a new force in the Jewish world can be best understood as one of the branches of the Russian (and Russified) intelligentsia. Certainly, it developed under the continuous influence of Russian oppositional politics.

Thus, in organizational terms, its most characteristic creation was the political party, small in number but fiercely committed to its own particular ideology. Again, as in the Russian revolutionary movement, the party ideologies were marked by strong elements of messianism or utopianism, on the one hand, and populism ("all for the people and by the people"), on the other. A narrow leadership stratum was thus in constant search of a mass base. Last but not least, the intelligentsia, which created the Russian-Jewish politics of the postliberal era, shared the outlook of the Russian intelligentsia as a whole. There was the same glorification in the role – in part freely chosen, in part forced upon them – of outsiders, youthful rebels, standing against the existent and condemning it in the name of future salvation. There was the same ascetic strand, with its pride in self-sacrifice, its reckless defiance of objective difficulties, its determination to translate thought into action, dream into reality.

But there was another side to the coin. That section of the intelligentsia that chose to work in the Jewish world differed in important ways from its Russian (and Russified) counterpart. First, after 1881, it enjoyed far easier access to the Russian-Jewish masses than did the intelligentsia as a whole to the Russian *narod*.

Faced by a bitterly hostile government and environment, forced in large numbers to leave their homes and motherland, often penniless, the Russian Jews were much more ready (albeit sporadically and inconsistently) to accept the socialists and the nationalists as their spokesmen and leaders. Where the rabbis could easily be dismissed as belonging to an irretrievable past, and the bankers and magnates as tied to a hopeless and fickle present, there the radical youth alone remained to promise the days of the Messiah.

Second, the involvement of the Russian-Jewish intelligentsia in Jewish politics was never confined to the Russian Empire but, on the contrary – from the time of Aron Liberman – was clearly international in scope. Wherever the Russian Jews migrated in large numbers, they were accompanied or followed by the socialists and nationalists of the various and rival camps. And, while competing among themselves, these immigrant politicians were, nevertheless, soon ready to challenge the established Jewish leadership in their new countries. One political subculture came into being in Vilna, Minsk, Belostok, the East End of London, and the Lower East Side of New York. Its lingua franca was Yiddish; its economic base, the clothing industry and the sweat shop; its politics, the running dispute and constant interaction between socialist internationalism and Jewish nationalism; its organizational expression, the Yiddish press, the public meeting, the trade union, the ideologically committed party, and (where relevant) the armed self-defense unit. A further outpost of this Russian-Jewish subworld was created in the Palestinian colonies, but there – lacking the mass environment – the intelligentsia (or *poluintelligentsiia*) developed its ideologies and institutions in a Hebrew-speaking and agricultural context. Successful political innovations on the Lower East Side were adopted in the Pale of Settlement and vice versa. The politically involved youth passed restlessly from one center to another, spending years now in Russia, now in London, New York, Galicia, or Palestine. The Borochovs, Litvaks, Brenners, Medems, Goldfarbs, and Ben Gurions were nothing if not peripatetic; and yet, moving across three continents, they always remained within the same Russian-Jewish environment.

Finally – and this is the central theme of the book – the dilemmas of the intelligentsia working in the Jewish world were to a great extent qualitatively different from those facing the Russian intelligentsia in general. Psychologically, it found itself grappling with a double alienation – at once estranged from, and drawn to, the ways and problems of their own nationality, on the one hand, and a Russian or universalist political philosophy, on the other. How far was it legitimate to return to the old world without betraying the new? Was Russian or Yiddish or Hebrew the rightful language of the Jewish future? At what point did nationalism become chauvinism or obscurantism? And when did internationalism degenerate into "cosmopolitanism," a desertion from one's own people in its hour of need?

The search for an identity both Jewish and socialist, national and international, was not unique to the Russian-Jewish intelligentsia. It was revealed in all its pathos in the life of Moses Hess, a German socialist and (ultimately) a Jewish nationalist. But Hess turned to the preliberal Jewry of eastern Europe for the fulfilment of his proto-Zionism, and it was only in Russia that his experience eventually became that of an entire sociological stratum.

Politically, the crucial choice had to be made between two totally different (and on the surface at least) contradictory strategies – between revolution and exodus (organized emigration and colonization). But beyond that were other choices. Did loyalty to the Russian revolution exclude the need for Jewish political organization, for national rights? Did a commitment to a territorialist solution logically exclude participation in Russian revolutionary politics?

In the context of prerevolutionary Russia, these were unique political issues. To find a parallel one has, perhaps, to turn to black history in the United States, which likewise has been torn between integration and separatism, territorialism and cultural autonomism, organized emigration and violent opposition to the state. A nonterritorial and oppressed national minority inevitably has to grapple with political options significantly different from those of majority and territorial nationalities.

What is to be traced here, in sum, is the search over two generations and three continents for a Jewish solution to the Jewish question – a solution both universal and particular, of the future and yet rooted in popular reality, socialist but also national, scientific and nonetheless messianic.

I

The preparty stage

The year 1881–2, as a major watershed in modern Jewish history, looms large over what came after. In that year the problem of Russian Jewry was first revealed in something of its true magnitude and menace; the vision of the exodus caught the popular imagination and at the same time became an issue of wide-ranging political debate; and Jewish nationalism became a significant political force. These developments in turn made possible the gradual emergence (first in the emigrations, later in Russia) of the Jewish socialist movements that sought a synthesis between socialism and Jewish nationalism or, at the very least, between internationalism and the cause of Jewish auto-emancipation.

But for all the centrality of 1881–2, it should not blind the observer to what had gone before. It opened a new era in the sphere of political action but not in that of political thought. Highly articulate theories of Jewish socialism had been formulated long before the assassination of Alexander II. There was no constituency of any significant size ready to adopt these ideologies. They were not written in response to any widely perceived imperatives. They were, rather, the work of men in the wilderness, seeking to bridge the inner gulf between their instinctive loyalties to the Jewish world in which they had grown up and their commitment to the avant-garde, revolutionary world. This anticipation in miniature of the future has its own intrinsic and independent importance. Moreover, in the post-1881 period, these thinkers were gradually "discovered" and (in the case of Hess, for example) exerted an influence unthinkable during their own lifetime.

In sum, this section illustrates both the autonomy of ideology and also its total dependence as a force for change on the sociopolitical context. A seed in isolation can encapsulate life, but it can only grow in the right soil.

CHAPTER I

Dilemmas of the messianic conscience
Moses Hess and Aron Liberman

Moses Hess and Aron Liberman were the first "Jewish socialists," the first to argue that Jews should form an independent unit in the fight for international socialism. In 1862, Hess – successively mentor, comrade, party opponent, and finally part-time ally of Karl Marx and Friedrich Engels – published the case for the establishment of a Jewish socialist state in Palestine. He thus anticipated by almost forty years the next major statement of socialist Zionism, that presented in 1898 by Syrkin, who saw himself as in some sense his heir. Liberman presented his theories of Jewish socialism in Lavrov's revolutionary journal *Vpered!* during the years 1875–6. If Hess was the first drawn to the maximalist pole of Jewish socialism, then Liberman was the first to explore its minimalist counterpart. Jewish socialists, he contended, should not put forward any national demands and yet they should organize the Jewish workers as an autonomous unit within the movement, be it the Russian party or be it the Socialist International.

However, what makes a study of Hess and Liberman important here is not that they were first in the field, nor even that they had a marginal influence on later developments, but that their own lives are of intrinsic interest to the historian of Jewish socialism. In their biographies can first be seen the type of inner tension that was to constitute a basic characteristic of Jewish socialism.

On the one hand, they were drawn powerfully to the assumption that socialist internationalism as applied to the Jews meant assimilation. Negatively, they were repelled from Judaism as a medieval religion and from Jewish life as dominated by trade or, at least, by traders. Positively, they were attracted to socialism as a movement of new men who were fighting the past and already living in the future, in a new world undivided by outmoded ethnic barriers. But, for all that, neither could surrender himself totally to this logic. They felt restraints, counterpressures, that hundreds of other socialists of Jewish origin at that time did not.

Reared in boyhood and youth on Biblical, rabbinical, and later forms of Hebrew literature, both found themselves moved by the parallels between the prophetic and apocalyptic elements in their national tradition and those in contemporary socialism. More specifically, Liberman was bound by the power of place. He was the product of the culturally autonomous life led by the Jews of Lithuania, complete with their two national languages and literatures (Hebrew and Yiddish), their developed sense of collective responsibility, their emerging political groupings. He came to the Russian revolutionary movement as a citizen of what Vera Zasulich would later dub ironically "the Minsk-Vilna Fatherland." As against this, in the political and psychological development of Hess was demonstrated the power of pride – pride in the Jewish "nation" as he came to call it. For some twenty years he repressed this emotion but, at a particular juncture, it swept over him, carrying him back to, and beyond, the ideology of his early manhood.

Thus each in his own way felt compelled to question the meaning of internationalism as applied to the Jewish issue. Seeking, even (in the case of Liberman) demanding, the approval of the socialist leadership, accepting its legitimacy, they nonetheless deviated from its norms. They found themselves becoming reluctant heretics. In so doing, they anticipated what was perhaps the major theme in the history of Jewish socialist ideology at least until 1914.

Moses Hess

Early writings, 1837–1841

In 1837 Moses Hess, then twenty-five years old, published his first book, *The Sacred History of Mankind*. This work has been described by Auguste Cornu as marking the "transition from a Jewish ideology to a socialist ideology."[1] It is true that this was the first socialist work to be written and published in Germany, but Cornu was wrong to describe the socialist element as excluding the Jewish. In his writings of 1837–41 (not all of which were published at the time), Hess, in fact, assigned a role of critical importance to the history of the Jews. Only from late in 1841 did he begin to see his socialist commitment as being in conflict with his profound interest in what he had hitherto chosen to call his "Jewish nationality."

It is no exaggeration to say that everything Hess ever wrote, from his *Sacred History* to his posthumously published *Dynamic Theory of Matter*, was inspired by his faith in the socialist millennium. But Hess took his socialism for granted – it was an axiom, a given – and so the transition to, or structure of, the future society seldom held his attention. Throughout he concentrated on what he saw as the essential preconditions of socialism.

Like every new religion – and Hess described socialism as just that – it needed a revelation of the new truth. And, in turn, philosophical truth had to be translated into ethical terms. Most difficult, the new ethics had to be absorbed by and so transform mankind. Thus, as a socialist, Hess was led to explore ceaselessly two basic fields of interest: philosophy and nationality. Without philosophy there could be no socialism, because freedom was an integral element of Hess's socialism. In his view, no man could be free unless he understood the laws governing nature and society. But the actual task of transforming abstract truth into social truth belonged to the nations of the world. Socialism could only become reality when adopted and implemented by national states.

In consequence, from the late 1830s until his death, Hess was gripped by an intense interest in the major nations of Europe. His book of 1837 concentrated on the relationship of Germany and France. Germany was to contribute to socialism the religious spirit, the philosophical truth; France, with its proven revolutionary energies, the element of ethical social commitment. One nation was the more passive, the other more active; the one contemplative, the other practical; Germany a nation of the spirit, France of the will. If the German genius could merge with the French, the millennium was assured.

Jewish history was vital to Hess's presentation. Only in the Old Testament, he

7

argued, could be seen – albeit in embryonic, partial, and instinctive form – an example of what mankind was about to experience universally, totally, and consciously. This was a bold assertion but it was central to the argument of *The Sacred History*. Psychologically it was understandable enough. Until his late teens, Hess had been given an intensive Jewish education of the traditional kind with its heavy emphasis on the Talmud and Bible, and later rabbinical commentaries. At the age of five, when his parents moved to Cologne, he had been left behind in his grandparents' house in the Jewish quarter of Bonn to receive the thorough Jewish education befitting a boy whose maternal grandfather and paternal great-grandfather were both rabbis.[2]

His secular education, which was informal and consisted largely of an intensive immersion in modern philosophy, did not lead to a simple or violent reaction against his earlier Jewish training. Rather, he found himself thrown into a profound spiritual crisis. Dissatisfied with orthodox Judaism, he was nonetheless unable to find any ready-made substitute. In a letter of 1831 to a friend, Hess, then twenty-two years old, described the "immeasurable revolution which has taken place within me and raged for a good two years. . . . And I suffered a lot in that time, in so many ways I could have become its victim; the struggle was hard; always new dangers, always new reinforcements, finally victory – the free, the natural, the true!"[3]

The Sacred History was evidently the result of some six years of such battling for a personally tenable philosophical position. It was written, as Edmund Silberner aptly puts it, in "a kind of prophetic trance."[4] Given the autodidactic, private, and inspirational origins of his first work, it was hardly surprising that in it the Jewish past loomed so large. This was the history that had been absorbed most deeply into his consciousness.

In *The Sacred History*[5] can already clearly be seen what was perhaps the fundamental characteristic of Hess's approach to philosophy and politics. He sought monistic solutions to the problems of being and becoming, but he also sought room within the monistic framework for a mass of seemingly contradictory elements. Of all modern thinkers, the one who probably influenced him most was Rousseau; in him Hess recognized his own passionate need to find the ultimate meaning of life together with his own respect for the complexity and variety that characterize that life.

He rejected what he described as the one-sidedness of Hegel and Schelling, although he readily acknowledged his debt to both. Hegel was wrong to describe Nature as inferior to Man, as "alienated Spirit," just as Schelling erred in reducing the historical and philosophical to the natural and the poetic. The divine force, Hess argued, was immanent equally in nature and society, in the world of unchanging instinct and in the ever unfolding world of human consciousness. "The sacred," Hess wrote,

> is to be found exclusively neither in faith nor in knowledge, neither in Schelling's blissful sensibility nor in Hegel's religion of intellectual ideas, neither in the static nor the dynamic, neither in the past nor the future – but in both together, not with the one absorbed into the other but with both existing in peace side by side. They thus form true life.[6]

This view of the world, Hess argued, had inspired the Hebrew Bible. Mankind, nature, and the cosmos were seen as equally the creation of God and as such each was possessed of its own independent but interrelated value. Man felt himself an integral part of this world and had no need for another idealized world, for a heaven. No barrier divided the spiritual life from the physical. The real was understood to be permeated by the ideal and the present to hold within itself the seeds of a perfected future. Of course, all this was understood poetically, prophetically. God was feared as an authoritarian father figure demanding obedience, not offering freedom. And yet, at its own primitive level, here was an integrated view of reality – the polar opposite of both the dualistic asceticism dominant in medieval Christian thought and of Hegel's exaggerated idealism. Taken up again by Spinoza at the higher level of speculative and universal thought, this philosophy was destined to remake the world. Once mankind understood that life itself is God and that life in turn is conceived and maintained by love it would have to create its own heaven here on earth.

In outline, *The Sacred History* followed the same three-stage progression followed by Hegel: a first period marked by innocence and instinctive unity, an intermediate period characterized by fragmentation and conflict but also by new heights of spiritual awareness, and a final era of reintegration at the level of full consciousness. But while Hegel saw the Greek polis as typical of ancient history, Hess chose the Hebrew state for this role. And while Hegel dealt only with historical experience, Hess argued that it was possible to extrapolate the future from the past. Hegel found in history "the cunning of Reason," a logic hidden from contemporary man; Hess confidently argued that the laws of history like those of nature were open to discovery. "Mankind," he wrote, "is like man, a natural phenomenon; it develops like everything in nature according to an eternal and necessary law."[7]

The logical unfolding of events that Hess discovered in the pre-Christian history of the Jews became for him the standard pattern, which had inevitably to repeat itself at successively higher levels in the two post-Christian periods. Thus, *The Sacred History* traced the Biblical parallels in medieval history. The first period opened with Adam, natural man emerging from Eden, and his immediate descendents; a society of the "free and the equal," just becoming aware of God the Father. The middle period likewise opened with the exceptional individual, with Christ, the "God-Man," with the recognition of the fact that God exists within man and with the disciples determined to carry this truth to the entire world. (Christ, Hess wrote, "broke through the narrow bounds of nationality as the young man breaks away from the bonds of family and strives for . . . universality and eternity.")[8]

But in each case early promise was corrupted by over-rapid growth, competition, and greed. And then came the period of destruction and rejuvenation. In the Bible there was the great Flood; in the Christian era the same task fell to the barbarian invasions sweeping over the Roman Empire. On the ruins new societies were slowly created – societies that sought to build the religious concept into the state. Thus King David, in building Jerusalem, represented the culmination of a process which had started with Moses, just as the Hildebrandine Papacy (symbolized by the Crusades and conquest of Jerusalem) was the climax of a process initiated by

Gregory the Great. From the peaks only descent was possible, and the Babylonian exile was paralleled by that of Avignon (both of seventy years' duration). Yet the political decline was accompanied by a new spiritual ferment. Post-Maccabean Palestine witnessed a proliferation of sects (Sadducees and Pharisees being only the most prominent), and a turmoil of messianic expectations. The same process repeated itself in Europe before and after the Reformation, when Lutherans, Calvinists, and the many break-away churches confidently prophesied the millennium.

This pattern, argued Hess, was now going through its third and final cycle. In the modern epoch the role of Adam and Christ had fallen to Spinoza. While they had been respectively "natural man" and "God-Man," he was man pure and simple.[9] He had developed a philosophy that was speculative and rational and yet embodied within itself the prophetic insights of Judaism and the mystic truths of Christianity. ("The speculative spirit is as poetic as philosophic, as prophetic as mystic, as real as ideal.")[10] The French Revolution was the new flood, Napoleon the modern Attila. Everything, Hess insisted, pointed to the conclusion that the era of the New Jerusalem was imminent. This messianic society, this sabbath of history,[11] would, like the kingdoms of David and Hildebrand, be based on an alliance of state and religion – the socialist creed; would, like the ancient Jewish state, combine national cohesion with the goal of social equality; and would, like the medieval church, be universalist, striving for a community of states.[12] But now, at last, the growth of citizens to full self-consciousness and the abundance of goods ensured by the rational use of technology would permit the ideal to become the real.[13]

However, there was a basic paradox in Hess's relationship to the Jews. On the one hand, there was his conviction that Jewish history had been of archetypal importance, holding human potentiality embryonically within itself. (He even discerned a significance in the fact that Mohammed had a Jewish mother and that Spinoza was born of Jewish parents.)[14] But when he had to define the present and future role of the Jewish people he became hesitant, self-contradictory.

Despite his often critical attitude toward Hegel, he tended to accept his view that a world-historical nation could only appear on the stage of history once. The future belonged to France, Germany, and (Hess added in 1841) also to England. A threatening question mark hung over Russia; but the Jews, surely, had had their day. And Hess frequently described the Jewish people as a kind of walking corpse:

> Where truth reigns there is life; . . . where the lie reigns there is death. Life now sundered may carry on for some time, but God is no longer its essence. History furnishes us . . . with two major and cautionary examples. We are terrified when we behold them as if we had seen some nocturnal spirits. Both have long since fallen into the grave. One can still be seen like some cloud up in the skies; the other like a rigid corpse. We mean the Jewish people – the spirit without a body; and the Chinese, a body without a spirit.[15]

From this perspective, of course, the natural conclusion was that the sooner the Jewish people disintegrated the better. And in his book of 1841, *The European Triarchy*, Hess gave seemingly his implicit approval to the concept of assimilation. "Thanks to the widespread intelligence of all the [Christian] denominations in Germany," he wrote there, "thousands of educated Jews – perhaps in greater numbers than in all Europe put together – would without any hesitation marry outside their religion and educate their children not in their religion."[16]

Nonetheless, at this stage he did not make an explicit commitment to the assimilationist solution. A potent combination of resentment and pride held him back. He was angered by the legal inequalities that still existed in Germany and that, for instance, forbade Jews to marry outside their faith. Only baptism could bring equality. Moreover, whatever logic demanded, it could not have been easy for him psychologically to eliminate from his vision of the future this, his own nation with its remarkable past. Thus, tentatively, Hess sought for some function, however marginal, to justify the survival of the Jewish people. Even if it were dead, perhaps its ghostlike existence was necessary:

> Judaism has embraced within itself all aspects of the ancient consciousness of God just as Christianity has within it all the contradictions of the modern consciousness of God. Judaism like Christianity has thus to be recognized as the underlying principle of the historical process. Jews, therefore, must exist as the thorn in the flesh of Western mankind.
>
> Just as the East needs a Chinese Wall so as not to be disturbed in its stationary existence, so the Jews are the fermentation within Western mankind, from the beginning called upon to represent the principle of movement . . . [Since Christ] they have wandered like a ghost through the world of the living . . . and they can neither die nor be resurrected.[17]

Or, as he wrote elsewhere: "Its enemies cannot destroy it because a ghost cannot be touched. Its spirit has penetrated this world; and soon the world will witness a new stage worthy of its old mother . . . the old law will once again be resurrected in a perfect light."[18]

For one brief moment, in 1840, Hess went much farther. Because of a passing but wounding disillusionment with Germany, he felt himself forced to consider the possibility of a national rebirth for the Jews. Until the Franco-Prussian War of 1870 – when Hess seems finally to have despaired of Germany – he was held in the grip of a profound love-hate relationship with that country. In his scheme of things, it had a crucial function to perform in the redemption of mankind. But in 1840 he felt the German people had betrayed him; they did not react with an outcry of indignation against the sudden, startling accusation that Jews in Syria had been murdering gentiles in order to bake their blood into Passover bread – the notorious, much publicized and long-drawn-out case of the Damascus Blood Libel.[19]

In the face of the brazen antisemitism of the German patriotic school, the followers of Arndt and Jahn, and the apathy elsewhere, Hess definitely decided that the Jews had to rally to their own defense. In a manuscript unpublished at the time, Hess argued that the Jews in trying desperately to make themselves into Germans had simply laid themselves open to constant humiliation:

> Did not the German Jews fight in the War of Liberation? Were they not Teutomaniacs and ready to smash the French? Did we not chant but yesterday with Nikolaus Becker "They Shall Not Possess It, the Free German Rhine"? Did I myself not commit the unpardonable stupidity of sending a musical version of the "German Marseillaise" to its author? . . . I forgot then

that the Germans after the War of Liberation not only discriminated against the Jews, their erstwhile comrades in arms against the French, but even persecuted them with the frequent cries of "Hep, Hep" . . . The German is not at all anxious to assimilate any foreign elements and would be perfectly happy if he could possess all his fatherland for himself.[20]

Given this situation, the only honorable, the only rational course was to identify fully with one's own people:

The nations may tolerate us and even grant us emancipation, but they will never respect us as long as we place the principle *ubi bene, ibi patria* above our own great national memories . . . It is not the old-type of pious Jew that is most despised but the modern Jew . . . who denies his nationality while the hand of fate presses heavily on his own people. The beautiful phrases about humanity and enlightenment which he employs as a cloak to his treason . . . will ultimately not protect him from the judgment of public opinion . . . In vain, he hides behind his geographical and philosophical alibi . . . Mask yourself a thousand times over, change your name, religion, and character, travel throughout the world incognito . . . and still every insult to the Jewish name will strike at you.[21]

But what could such a commitment to the Jewish people mean in practical terms? He had already expounded his belief in the profound importance of the Jewish past. Yet he was also – and much more – a man possessed by the future, and the future, he had decided, belonged to a socialism to be organized by national states. Logically, if the Jewish people *per se* were to play an active – rather than a passive – role in the new era, then they would have to reestablish their own national state. In fact, Hess followed this logic up to and including support for a Jewish return to Palestine. "I myself," he later wrote,

was momentarily inclined to return to the hope – long since abandoned by the Jews – of giving the scattered members of the Jewish people room to reunite in a real part of this world . . . I was deeply embittered by the brutal mood of the mob – that of the East and that of the West – which found expression on the Continent in connection with the Damascus Case and was already willing to support the orthodox, religious wish of the Jews.[22]

However, he hastened to explain, he had rapidly been "cured forever from this error." First, on closer examination, he had come to the conclusion that those English politicians who were advocating a Jewish return to Palestine did so out of purely short-term commercial motives.[23] ("After all, the English know how to profit from everything.")[24] Much more important, Hess concluded there was absolutely no demand from within the Jewish people to transform a pious hope into a real policy.[25] "How," he asked, "can the political rebirth of a people be realized without its own free and powerful will – and this will is here totally lacking."[26]

Although Hess here wrote in retrospect rather banteringly of this episode, it was clearly a turning point in his life.[27] Hess had arrived at the conclusion that the Jews had only one collective goal: equal rights, emancipation. And here the Jews were dependent on the peoples of Europe. The Jewish people as such could not escape its passive role. In *The European Triarchy* of 1841, Hess placed the responsibility for the Jewish fate firmly in the lap of the European and particularly the German states: "He who wishes to study the barometric level of spiritual freedom must examine the relationship of the state to its Jewish subjects. To oppose the Jews is to risk nothing. On the contrary, by intolerance toward the Jews one makes oneself popular with the Christians, in other words: beloved to the Christian mob."[28]

What this meant politically was that the Jewish intelligentsia had to throw in its lot with those forces in Germany which were fighting for more rationality and equality, more justice, more freedom. In fact, this was the raison d'être of *The European Triarchy:* a passionate argument in favor of Germany allying itself with the progressive powers of Europe – France and England – rather than with Russia, the favorite of many on the German right. (Given the chance, he wrote, Russia would "strive to create a Slavic World Empire on the ruins of Roman-German Europe.")[29] Optimistically, though, he predicted that rapid industrialization was leading inevitably to a social revolution in England, a revolution which would immensely strengthen the Left in France and Germany.

In sum, Hess in the years 1837–41 felt bound by a dual commitment: loyalty to the Jewish past and loyalty to the future still being formed within the womb of German radical thought. "The point is quite simply this," he wrote in 1841, "we Germans are the most universal, the most European people of Europe."[30]

Activist, 1841–1851

From late 1841 to 1845 Hess paid little attention to the Jewish people, and from 1846 to 1859 virtually none. Explaining this volte-face in later years, Hess wrote that his feelings of 1840 for "my unfortunate, slandered, despised and dispersed people" had "unfortunately been immediately stifled in my heart by the greater pain which the suffering of the European proletariat evoked in me."[31]

However, this retrospective explanation much oversimplified what was in reality a complex process. Not until the mid-1840s did Hess come to view the industrial proletariat as the one class exclusively destined to carry through the communist revolution. On the other hand, he had identified himself with the working poor in general since the mid-1830s. But if until 1841 he had assumed that a critical loyalty to the Jewish past reinforced his socialist vision, after 1841 he no longer did so.

The initial shift in Hess's position resulted, it would seem, from the drastic change which transformed his way of life in 1841. Until the publication of his *European Triarchy,* he lived a rather isolated existence. Without a profession, without even a high school diploma, he had felt driven to accept a position in his father's large grocery business in Cologne. He had few friends and those he had, such as Berthold Auerbach, tended like himself to combine an interest in German politics and culture with a concern for Jewish affairs. As if anxious not to cause any violent disruption in his routine, he even published his books anonymously.

But, in marked contrast to *The Sacred History,* his new book attracted public attention. Here, after all, Hess had deliberately set out to apply his general principles to issues of immediate interest; at one level, he joined Cieskowski in urging the Left Hegelian school to move away from purely critical idealism and to make "a positive transition from German philosophy to action"[32] and, at another level, he expounded far-reaching solutions to topical problems in the relationship of state to church and Germany to Europe. The authorship of the book became an open secret and Hess was suddenly much sought after.

In mid-1841 he was invited to join those planning the establishment of a new liberal journal in Cologne. He rapidly emerged as the most enthusiastic member of the initiating group and when the paper, the *Rheinische Zeitung,* appeared in January 1842, he became in practice (although not in name) the chief editor. The paper followed a radical political line and attracted as contributing editors most of the leading Young Hegelians, among them Bruno Bauer and Max Stirner, Arnold Ruge and Ludwig Buhl, Friedrich Engels and Karl Marx.[33]

As a paid editor, Hess found himself liberated from irksome financial dependence on his father. Catapulted into literary and political prominence, he became almost overnight a leading figure in what he tended to call a "party" and perhaps more accurately should be called a movement. This movement – the Young Hegelians or, more broadly, Young Germany – was determined to subject German attitudes and institutions, political and religious, to an unrelenting barrage of radical criticism.[34] For Hess, this was an intoxicating experience. In his two books he had argued that thought must be translated into action, that the present must yield to the future, that the ideal permeate the real. Now, as he saw it, he had a remarkable opportunity to play an active role in this process.

Jewish history and even the Jewish issue – political emancipation – lost their unique importance for Hess as he found himself transported from his private corner to this public stage, and the logic of this new situation asserted itself at once. First, there was the Braunfels incident. Hess had assured his friend, Ludwig Braunfels, of a place on the editorial board of the *Rheinische Zeitung.* But on 10 October 1841 Hess wrote to warn him of a probable change of plan; the initiating group was very anxious not to provide any grounds for the suspicion that the paper could be dominated by Jews. "You indeed have been baptized but you are still a baptized *Jew* and *one* Jew on the paper [they say] is enough."[35] Hess acquiesced and, not surprisingly, Braunfels felt that he had been wronged. To Auerbach he complained that Hess "told me a hundred times: 'if they will not have you, then I will quit myself.' (This he has forgotten to say at the decisive moment). This behavior is cowardice and because of its motive has still worse a character. This is how the philosopher behaves in the face of mob prejudice."[36]

Once the paper was functioning it campaigned for equal civil rights for all subjects of the Prussian state, and in a number of articles Hess denounced the Prussian government for its persistent denial of equal status for the Jews and its plan to compensate them by strengthening their corporate organizations. Where equality had been granted as in France or Norway, he wrote, the Jews surrendered all forms of national and other separatism.[37] This overtly assimilationist approach was new. He had only implied support for it in *The European Triarchy* and had at once qualified that support by stating that the Jewish people were anyway doomed to survive.

In a letter to Auerbach on 27 July 1842, Hess justified his role as editor of the *Rheinische Zeitung* and its policy of treating the Jewish question as strictly secondary:

We represent an entirely new and certainly very radical line ... fear cannot make us change our convictions nor distort them ... our paper has created an upsurge in the whole of Germany and you must be proud of that. Just look at what we have achieved for the Jews – and we have the satisfaction of knowing that in everything for which we have fought we have always followed the one single principle: we cannot be accused by anybody of inconsistency or of having a special preference for this or that – otherwise this charge would certainly have been leveled against our fight for the Jews; but nobody ventures to do that because our principle is so obvious throughout and to everybody.[38]

It is possible that this insistence on firmly subordinating the particular to the universal further exacerbated the relations between Hess and Auerbach. Certainly, by the autumn of 1842 Hess was writing in one letter to his old friend that by now he stood "far from Judaism" and in another that he felt their relationship was deteriorating fast "not because of some chance or minute superficialities but because of our realization that mutual divergence exists in our *inner* life."[39] Hess's rapid estrangement from the Jewish community alienated him at the same time from those such as Auerbach who remained attached to it.[40]

But more was probably implied in this reference of 27 September 1842 to a fundamental divergence of attitudes, for at this time Hess was already thinking out a more radical formulation of his philosophical assumptions. In one way, of course, he was from the first the most extreme member of the group associated with the *Rheinische Zeitung;* as its only socialist (or communist) he had taken it upon himself to radicalize his colleagues. So, for instance, in a letter to Auerbach, Hess mentioned that in 1842 "Engels came to Cologne from Berlin. We spoke about current problems and he – a revolutionary from Anno I – left me as a fully pledged communist."[41] And Marx's declaration in the *Rheinische Zeitung* of 16 October 1842 that communism should be fought not by guns but by debate and that he intended to subject it to a "thoroughgoing criticism" was clearly a response to socialist material smuggled into the paper by Hess.[42]

On the other hand, when it came to the philosophical premises underpinning his political standpoint Hess was in danger of falling behind the avant-garde. His optimistic tendency to assume that present-day contradictions could be smoothly reconciled in the latter-day unity did not accord well with the increasingly mordant, all-embracing, "confrontationist" criticism developed by the Hegelian Left. Influenced by the writings of Bauer and Feuerbach and by personal contacts with Marx, he began to radicalize his own philosophical position. As early as September 1841 Hess described the twenty-four-year-old Marx as

the only *real* philosopher now living ... think of Rousseau, Voltaire, Holbach, Lessing, Heine united in one person – I say, united not mixed up – and you have Dr. Marx ... As for his leanings and philosophical outlook, he goes further not only than Strauss but than Feuerbach and this last is saying a lot ... I have always wanted such a person as my teacher in philosophy. Now for the first time I feel what a bungler I am in true philosophy. But, patience, I can still learn something.[43]

As long as he was an active editor of the *Rheinische Zeitung,* Hess had little time for philosophical reformulations, but in October 1842 Marx took over the chief editorship and early in December Hess left for Paris as the paper's French correspondent. In the summer of 1843 three articles of his appeared in *Einundzwanzig Bogen aus der Schweiz,* a collection of radical essays published by Julius Frobel in Switzerland in order to bypass the German censorship, and they demonstrated that Hess had come to look at the world from a sharply new perspective. Where earlier the past and present had been justified in terms however relative and critical as the path to the future, Hess now argued that they were barriers to that future and should be thrown down. He held in his hand the axe provided by Bauer and Feuerbach, whose radical critique of religion was becoming more total with every new publication in the period 1840–3.[44]

In his two books of 1837 and 1841 he had described human development as the unfolding realization that God is immanent in man and nature, that man and God are one. He had written history in theological terms. But in 1843 he insisted that belief in God crippled man. All absolutes – whether "the Life Idea, the Eternal Law, Absolute Spirit, World Spirit, God or whatever one can call, exactly, or inexactly, the General and Eternal" – had been created not by men but by willing slaves, too ignorant, too poor for freedom.[45] To recognize God was to acquiesce in a fatal dualism in all spheres. Man's longing for the good had been surrendered to the priesthood; his ability to rule himself vested in kings. The church was cherished as spiritual; the flock despised as materialist. The state was revered as altruistic and rational; the citizens left to their egoistic free-for-all.

This division had no doubt been necessary in the past, but now church and state had a vested interest in perpetuating a dualistic and anachronistic view of the world. Faith in God (or *Geist* or the Life-Force) demanded disbelief in man, and disbelief in man legitimized the status quo: "The theological consciousness is an enormous lie, the principle of all the enslavement (and the domination) to which our species is subject so long as the Life-Idea seems to man to be external, so long as he does not recognize the self-conscious act . . . The lie of religion and politics must be wiped out with one blow and mercilessly."[46] Feuerbach's atheism, which made man whole and therefore free, had to be united in one system with Proudhon's anarchism, which demanded that there be no ruler and ruled, only equals.

Given this militant root-and-branch criticism of God, religion, and state, Hess could hardly maintain his sympathetic attitude to the Jewish Bible. His few references to it nearly all sought to expose its unhealthy view of man's relationship to God. While Adam had previously been a hero of man's emerging consciousness, he had now become a symbol of man's self-humiliation. "The Bible itself," Hess wrote, "that venerable document which stands at the root of our religion and politics, and which leads us with great naiveté into a theological cul-de-sac, permits Adam to hear the voice of an external and higher being only after the Fall."[47]

The Hebrew Jehovah was merged by Hess with Moloch, a god who demanded human sacrifice. "Everywhere," Hess wrote,

> human sacrifice lends service to God and the state its basic theme. The "Absolute Spirit," which celebrates its realization in the "state," is an imitation of the Christian God who permitted the crucifixion of his first-born Son,

who found satisfaction in martyrdom and built his church over one martyr, "on this rock." The Christian God is an imitation of the Jewish Moloch-Jehovah, to whom the first born was sacrificed in order to "appease" him. Later, in the justemilieu period of the Jews, money replaced the first born who was "redeemed" and cattle were sacrificed in place of men. The original sacrifice was everywhere man ... And so, in a figurative sense, he has remained and still is, so long as religion and politics maintain themselves.[48]

From exposing the centrality of human sacrifice in the Jewish past it was only one step to exposing that same element as the essence of contemporary Jewish life. This particular progression, though, was first made (in print, at least) by Marx in his "On the Jewish Question," his attack on Bruno Bauer.

In earlier years, Hess rather than Marx could have been expected to respond to Bruno Bauer's biting criticism of the demands for Jewish emancipation – after all, much of what Bauer said in his articles of 1842–3 sounded like a direct attack on the ideas central to *The Sacred History*.[49] For instance, where Hess had praised those ancient Jewish laws that had (in his words) "divided up possessions equally and sought to maintain their equal division,"[50] Bauer dismissed them as unworkable, as "so many arithmetic fantasies."[51] Where Hess had described messianism and Prophecy as remarkable manifestations of human potentiality, Bauer saw in them only a form of escapism: "What kind of truths are those which, being divine and eternal should be valid now, come into their own in the future only!" While Hess had seen the survival of the Jewish people, albeit in ghostly form, as inevitable, even necessary, Bauer saw it as a perversity – a meaningless attachment to a "chimerical nationality," an obstinate refusal to join those "historical nations which are capable of making history."[52]

In 1837 Hess could have replied in historical terms; in 1840 in national terms; in 1841 in the name of liberal state principles; but, by 1843, as we have seen, he had rejected theological history, Jewish national indignation, and the idea of the state in all its forms. He avoided a direct confrontation with Bauer, even though his essays published in mid-1843 did in fact anticipate the main theses of Marx's "On the Jewish Question." Thus, first, Hess accused Bauer (albeit without naming him and in one sentence only)[53] of exploiting the ideal of a universal humanism in order to deny modest but rational reform now:

The rationalist politicians ... want their "rational state" [*Vernunftstaat*], which is a fiction ... but in reality they do not want liberal principles – and so we have no reason to be surprised when one of these Hegelians (political rationalists) asserts, for instance, that Protestants, Catholics, and Jews have no right to be put on an equal basis in the state because they cannot be "rational" citizens so long as they are not men, i.e., atheists but still only Protestants [Catholics, Jews] etc.[54]

And, at the same time, Hess argued that anyway the *Rechtsstaat* or *Vernunftstaat*, even in its most republican forms such as the United States, had "negated itself by its own dialectic ... It ... sets out to give the people sovereignty but insofar as it is called upon to guarantee personal freedom, personal property, it must – as the unity or generality of the various individuals – put itself over and against them. The people that seeks to rule itself divides against itself into rulers – domination – and ruled – slavery."[55] Thus, like Marx after him, Hess declared it was absurd to deny the Jews political emancipation in the modern state, which ruled over innumerable particularist groupings, and it was no less absurd to expect human emancipation – the fulfillment of mankind's potential – from this state, however liberal it might be.

Marx, elsewhere in 1844, acknowledged his debt to the essays published by Hess in the *Einundzwanzig Bogen*, calling them one of the only "original and substantive contributions"[56] to German socialist thought, but at the same time his attack on Bruno Bauer carried him beyond the Hess of 1843. In essence, he presented his conclusions on the Jewish question by standing Bruno Bauer's theses on their head, following the same technique that he was then developing in his critique of Hegel's *Philosophy of Right*. This meant that he accepted the validity of Bauer's factual judgments on the Jewish people but explained those facts not in theological but in socioeconomic terms. What counted was not Jewish belief but Jewish practice as a people of traders and usurers. If Jewish law was fictional, as Bauer described it, then this was because it was "a religious caricature of the morality and the law with which the world of property in general clothes itself." If the Jewish people, as Bauer said, "cannot create a new world," it was because it reduced everything to "practical needs," to "private property." If the Jewish nationality had survived it was because "the materialistic spirit of Judaism has kept itself alive in Christian society and achieved there its highest expression." Marx thus concluded that "the emancipation from usury and money, that is from practical, real Judaism, would be the self-emancipation of our time."[57]

Even though this defense of Jewish emancipation revealed a deep contempt for the Jews – deeper perhaps than Bauer's – Hess did not dissent.[58] Nothing if not an enthusiast, he was caught up in the excitement of forging the ideological path from, as he put it, theology to anthropology and from anthropology to socialism. And he, too, had come to see the Jewish people, like the Christian church, purely as a manifestation of man's profound self-alienation: spiritual, political, and economic. The ancient cult of blood had been translated into the modern cult of gold, one form of human sacrifice had been substituted for another, and the Jews had played a major role in this entire process. Clearly, Hess was here applying the transformational method to his own concepts of 1837.

Thus, his works published in 1845, including his influential essay "On the Nature of Money,"[59] contain references to the "rich Jewish or Christian-German money wolf";[60] and to the fact that "the discovery of money and the alphabet belongs to the Phoenicians, the same people who invented the *Jewish God*."[61] "Judaism," we read in "On the Nature of Money,"

> which in the natural history of the social animal-world had the world-historical call to develop mankind into a beast of prey has now completed its mission. The mystery of Judaism and Christianity is openly revealed in the modern Jewish-Christian world of shopkeepers. The mystery of *Christ's blood*, like the mystery of the *ancient Jewish blood-worship*, here finally appears revealed as the mystery of the beast of prey. In ancient Judaism the Blood Cult was a prototype only; in medieval Christianity it was developed theoretically, idealistically, logically – i.e., man really consumed the alienated

blood of mankind, but only in imagination, the *blood of the God-Man*. In the modern Jewish-Christian shopkeeping world this impulse and drive of the social animal-world appears not *symbolically* or mystically but most *prosaically*.[62]

Hess had stood on its head his original concept of history, including that of the Jews; and this meant, among other things, that he had finally exhausted every reason, whether positive or negative, for interest in the Jewish people. In the years 1845–51 it really was true that he became absorbed by "the greater pain which the suffering of the European proletariat evoked in me." In this period, he acted less as pure ideologist, more as revolutionary agitator.

Early in 1845 he together with Engels was to be found addressing a series of workers' meetings in Elberfeld – meetings that aroused considerable popular interest. ("One speaks of nothing here but communism, and every day we gain new supporters," wrote Engels to Marx.)[63] And in the same month, February 1845, Hess in a letter to Auerbach expressed his disappointment that his old friend had chosen to remain a sequestered poet and aesthete: if "you had come with me into the hovels of the unfortunate and discovered the terrible secrets of deprivation you would perhaps have presented them better than Sue."[64] The police put an end to the public meetings. But Hess (at first together with Engels) then began to publish a popular newspaper of socialist leanings, the *Gesellschaftsspiegel*. The first biographer of Hess, Theodor Zlocisti, noted that with this paper he became the first man in Germany "to begin systematically and stubbornly to organize and arouse the proletariat – not with economic theory but with concrete actions in industry."[65]

Hess's break with Marx alienated him still further from the sphere of philosophical exploration. Late in 1845 he, together with his common-law wife, Sybille Pesch, had joined Marx and Engels in Brussels, where as a trio they worked on joint projects. As part of one plan, Hess had translated two socialist works into German, one of them significantly Buonarroti's *Conspiration pour l'Égalité dite de Babeuf*. He also wrote some chapters for their monumental (and long unpublished) cooperative work, *The German Ideology*.[66] But when Marx broke with Wilhelm Weitling in March 1846, Hess found himself unable to give his full support to Marx and Engels. "You are too 'divisive,' I perhaps by nature too much an 'appeaser . . . ,' " he wrote to Marx in May 1846. "With you personally I may still have much to do; with your party, nothing."[67] Ironically, having become a firm disciple of Marx's new socioeconomic doctrine, he now found himself politically excommunicated from Marx's inner circle. In the winter of 1847–8, Engels in Paris was actively undermining Hess's hitherto dominant influence among the German socialists there. "How the mighty have fallen," Engels sarcastically reported on the Hess who "was once the world-shattering high flier."[68]

In these years, Hess was so absorbed in the revolution – in awaiting it, agitating for it, predicting its course, urging it on – that his breach with Marx and Engels evidently did not break his morale. So, for instance, he proved himself a gifted writer of agitational literature. Twice he produced communist versions of the catechism, one in 1844 and one in 1849 or 1850, and both were impressive in their brilliantly controlled but unmistakable fervor.[69]

Late in 1847 he produced a three-part article entitled "The Results of a Proletarian Revolution" that anticipated the main arguments of *The Communist Manifesto*, in particular, the belief in the international nature of the coming revolution and the key role assigned to England in that revolution. But Hess adopted a more extreme position than Marx and Engels. While they thought in terms of a two-stage revolution – with the democratic bourgeoisie leading the first stage – Hess anticipated a direct proletarian victory that, starting in England, would sweep across Europe. ("When the storm from the West comes, the waves of the proletariat rising from the deep will break together foaming over the monarchy, the aristocracy and the bourgeoisie . . . We leave the German bourgeoisie to its own fate.")[70]

Robespierre and the Jacobins, of whom Hess had been very critical in the past, were now held up as models: "A revolution, as St. Just has already said, is not made with rosewater, least of all a revolution of the proletariat . . . Which gentlemen will complain about 'tyranny,' 'dictatorship,' 'terror,' etc.? The gentlemen bourgeoisie, the same counterrevolutionaries who will have provoked that 'terror.' "[71] Hess's *Red Catechism for the German People* even became a symbol of the extremism of the German communists – it was produced as a major piece of evidence in the trial of the revolutionaries held in Cologne in 1852. (Typical of the *Catechism* was the eleventh question, "What does the red flag mean?" and its answer: "The permanent revolution up to the final victory of the working classes in all civilized lands: the Red Republic.")[72] When the League of Communists split in 1850, Hess joined the more incendiary camp of Willich and Schapper in opposition to that of Marx and Engels.

In his reply of 1850 to Alexander Herzen's *From the Other Shore*, Hess revealed most fully his state of mind in the years of revolution. He criticized Herzen for being too much the philosopher, too little the apostle. (In 1843, ironically, he had attacked Weitling for the exact opposite.)[73] "As apostles of the new Evangelism," he wrote,

> we must feel a kindred spirit with the apostles – rather than with the philosophers – of all times. If we no longer believe in the Christian God or the God of Robespierre, nevertheless, our entire life and aspirations are far more apostolic than philosophic . . . The spiritual attitude . . . chosen by the "apostles" of our time, e.g. an August Willich or a Barbès, is to seek out martyrdom as the ordeal by fire for their beliefs. This is *Schwärmerei* if you like but a *Schwärmerei* justified by history and motivated by life.[74]

Old crossroads, new routes, 1860–1875

As fate would have it, Hess was not among those communists arrested in the wake of the 1848 revolutions. He left France in 1849 and spent the next four years – at times in hiding – in Switzerland and Belgium. He considered emigrating to the United States, and many of his friends did so; but eventually, in 1853, he received permission to return to Paris. Convinced that the revolutionary wave had spent itself he promised to forgo all political activity. For the next five years he became a student of the natural sciences, attending lectures, reading avariciously, admiring particularly the new "materialist" works of Moleschott and Büchner.

He was possessed, as always, by the urge to find the unifying law and logic underlying the apparently divergent and contradictory. In a long article of 1856–7, Hess suggested that all spheres of the universe – cosmological, geological, biological, and social – were governed by what was ultimately the same process of cyclical change, that the constant flux concealed an underlying tendency toward equilibrium, toward a balancing out of centrifugal and centripetal, of production and consumption, of death and reproduction.[75] Mankind, he argued, was moving toward an equilibrium at a new and higher level; rational methods of production and consumption would eliminate the need for the existing domination by race and class. "Karl Marx, the genius, who founded the positive science of society," he wrote, "[was right]. Ethics today are only a socioeconomic problem."[76]

In 1860 Hess began working on his third full-scale book, *Rome and Jerusalem*, and it was published in mid-1862. The first indication of his new line of thought had come in one of his articles in the Geneva paper *l'Espérance* on 22 April 1860. "After the liberation of Italy," he wrote, "will come the turn of the Eastern nations and among them even the ancient people of Israel."[77] But nothing could have prepared those who knew him for the book itself which, in the main, they greeted with anger and disbelief.

Up until this point, after all, Hess had followed a path which was already sociologically familiar and was to repeat itself on a large scale in eastern Europe.[78] Alienated from a traditional Jewish middle-class home, he had been swept into the avant-garde movement of his time – had become atheist and communist, anarchist and internationalist. And even when the revolutionary tide of 1848 had ebbed, his new scientific interests had carried him forward into the most up-to-date realms of speculative materialism. Arnold Ruge, indeed, could not resist noting in his spiteful but perceptive way that "Rabbi Moses Hess as always is chasing after the newest fads, thus ensuring for himself the support of History."[79]

But with *Rome and Jerusalem* Hess had adopted a totally idiosyncratic stance. Philosophically, the book was highly old-fashioned; and, as for its politics, the socialists were bound to regard them as a throwback to the Middle Ages. What, then, had prompted Hess to write this book?

As the title itself suggests, the immediate inspiration for *Rome and Jerusalem* was supplied by the rapid emergence in the years 1859–60 of a unified and independent Italy. "With the renaissance of Italy," we read in the preface, "begins the rise of Judah." Specifically he wrote that "ever since the Italian War of Liberation I discovered a real relationship between my race studies and the modern national movement . . . ; these studies convinced me that all racial dominance will disappear and that nations will be reborn. First of all, it was my own Jewish people which – since that time – began to fascinate me more and more."[80]

But *Rome and Jerusalem* for Hess represented far more than a commentary on, and advocacy of, the reemergence of the classical nations. The personal, fragmented, often emotional form in which the book was put together gave it a unique place among his works. It was the closest he came to writing his confessions. Yet it was still more than that. In its concept of world history it recalled his first book of 1837. In its discussion of relations between Germans and Jews, it contained a long quotation from one of his unpublished manuscripts from 1840. In short, it is hard to escape the conclusion that Hess was reaching back across twenty years of his life. Always open to new discoveries, his own past now came to him as the latest, and perhaps the most startling, of them all.

Edmund Silberner, in his definitive biography of Hess, has noted that nowhere did *Rome and Jerusalem* repudiate explicitly, still less logically, those long-held philosophical positions which it repudiated implicitly: "In the past, he had so thoroughly scorned the priests and the church-goers of all religions that one cannot but wonder where he later found the courage to praise in all seriousness any religion whatsoever."[81] This paradox, though, provides a key to *Rome and Jerusalem*. Once he surrendered to a new idea—or, in this case, to an old idea rediscovered—Hess was like a man possessed. He was then interested only in what he would be able to say about the morrow and not the slightest in what he had said yesterday.

Hess had, in effect, decided to go back to the crossroads of 1840 and follow the path he had then rejected. Such a decision, by its very nature, had to be the result of an inner struggle. Hess explained this himself in *Rome and Jerusalem:*

> A thought which I believed to be forever buried in my heart has been revived in me anew. It is the thought of my nationality.... For a number of years this half-strangled thought stirred within my breast and clamored for expression. I lacked the strength to swerve suddenly from my beaten track, which seemed to be so far from Judaism, to a new path which unfolded itself before me in the hazy distance.[82]

His return to a line of thought so long neglected must certainly be explained first of all by the fact that from 1853 Hess had been thrown back entirely on his own inner resources. In the 1840s his thought had developed within three concentric circles: the movement, Germany (or, more specifically German humanism), and Europe (or, at least, revolutionary Europe). For Hess in the Paris of Napoleon III, none of this was left.

Louis Napoleon's coup d'état in December 1851 had marked for Hess the final defeat of the revolutionary wave of 1848. Although the apocalyptic note was to reappear from time to time in his writings, his faith in the all-encompassing revolution, proletarian and communist, seems to have faded away in the 1850s. And, as in the prerevolutionary period, the interrelationship of nations came to dominate his thought on the preconditions necessary for socialism. In his "Epilogue" to *Rome and Jerusalem* Hess stated that "the race struggle is primary, the class struggle secondary.... With the cessation of race antagonism, the class struggle will also come to a standstill. The equalization of all classes of society will necessarily follow the emancipation of all the races, for it will ultimately become a scientific question of social economics."[83]

As for Germany, all his long-standing fears of Teutonic chauvinism were fanned to new heights by the widespread support in that country for Austria in its war against the Italians and the French. In one letter of 1859, Hess wrote that "the Germans have no modern patriotism as have the Swiss, the French, and the English: its patriotism is reactionary race fanaticism. They forget that the anthropological mission of the Germans—racial regeneration—is finished." In another letter he predicted, as he would again in 1870, a general European coalition which would finally destroy German hopes for the military domination of the continent: "Then we shall see ... what will become of those millions of 'German swords' which are now being brandished. It will come to this in the end, mark my words."[84]

Finally, the movement which had absorbed him totally from 1841 to 1851 had disintegrated in the 1850s, its members in prison, across the Atlantic or (like Hess in Paris and Marx in London) secluded in their studies. But, perhaps still worse, looking back on those years Hess could not shrug off memories of the ugly political feuds, of the bitter infighting and invective which had formed an integral part of the experience. There had been the increasingly harsh break with Marx and Engels – for example, when they had arrived in Cologne in May 1848, Hess, who was there planning the *Neue Rheinische Zeitung,* promptly left for Paris. And in the mid-1840s there had been the public exchange of abuse with Arnold Ruge, his close associate and flat-mate in Paris in 1843. In his book of reminiscences published in 1846,[85] Ruge had referred to him ironically and frequently as "The Rabbi" or "the Communist Rabbi"; and he had mocked him ironically for being both a Jew and yet not Jewish ("you are a Christian who would like to pass as a Jew.")[86] "With other nations," we read in *Rome and Jerusalem,* "there is strife only between the various parties, but the Germans clash even when they belong to the same party. The members of my own party have made me loathe the aspirations of the Germans and by their actions caused me to go [prematurely] into exile."[87] He noted that even antisemitism had been employed as a debating weapon: "I have experienced it personally ... even with my own party members. In personal controversy, they always make use of the 'Hep' weapon and in Germany it is always effective. I have made it easy for them to use this weapon by adopting my Old Testament name, Moses."[88]

A rare insight into Hess's frame of mind in his politically quiescent years can be gained from the letter to Berthold Auerbach on 30 April 1856. "It is impossible," he wrote,

> to give you a conception of what I have lived through inwardly and outwardly for the last fourteen years. But I can tell you this much – the emotional storm in my soul has now calmed down and I am now tending to move in a direction which could appeal to your poetic and so anyway more harmonious temperament ... A sad feeling comes over me when I think that in all the many years since our ways parted nobody has understood me or felt with me as you did. Why in the storm of passing time have we been so separated – why? Because I was too fanatic – the entire fault was mine! Now that I have become calmer I see it myself.[89]

The spirit of independence needed to write *Rome and Jerusalem* surely was forged in these years of isolation, recollection, and study. But by temperament, Hess was simply not suited to an exclusively philosophical role and the actual decision to embark on this new venture was again born amid inner storm.

The Franco-Austrian War in Italy gave Hess the chance to reengage in politics because all his natural sympathies were, in this case, with Napoleon III. He even helped compose an open letter of support to the emperor. He observed the events of 1859 in a mood of rising exaltation. Thus, in a letter to Semmig, he wrote that "the movement which is now beginning – and in comparison with which 1848 was child's play – will go its own way.... The French troops are already in Italy, the entire Italian people will rise up, the Austrians will be smitten out of Italy and then *adieu* to all the monarchistic foundations of Europe and *adieu* to the diplomatic balance of power [game]."[90]

It is apparent from a letter of May 1859 that Hess still excluded the Jews as a factor in the new era. The future, he there suggested, belonged only to racially mixed nations such as the North American or French and not to the "relatively unmixed" such as the German or the Jewish.[91] The decision to advocate the reestablishment of a Jewish state was therefore sudden. That it was essentially inspirational is confirmed by the following passage in *Rome and Jerusalem:* "Whenever I stand at a new turn in my life, there appears an unhappy woman who imparts to me daring and courage to travel the unknown road.... Your infinite sorrow, expressed on the death of one you loved, brought forth my decision to step forth, as a champion of the national renaissance of our people."[92]

If, as Edmund Silberner argues convincingly, the reference is to Josephine Hirsch, then Hess's decision can be traced to around February 1860 (the month when Emilie, Josephine's sister and Hess's sister-in-law, had died).[93] He was reestablishing ties with his family, his youth, his early ideas.[94]

In 1840 Hess had contemplated but rejected the idea of Jewish resettlement in Palestine; Hegel had argued that "world-historical nations" appear on the stage of history but once, and Jewish indifference to plans for such a return had simply confirmed Hegel's thesis. In the intervening years, though, Hess had extended his list of chosen nations to include not only France and Germany but also England, later North America, and finally Italy – a nation that by Hegel's standards had long since departed the historical stage. The Jews could easily fit into this group, which had grown larger as his faith in Germany wavered. Essentially this was a subjective choice and his references to ethnographical research were most unconvincing: the relatively unmixed blood he ascribed to the Jewish people was used to prove them moribund in 1859 and the opposite in 1862.

Once he had predicted the rebirth of a Jewish state, Hess felt compelled to alter the historiographical scheme of *The Sacred History,* even though surprisingly few basic changes were made. The tripartite historical division leading up to the present messianic age remained in its original form (except that it was reinforced by reference to geological and cosmological parallels).

If there were life in the nation once thought to be a ghost, if (like "the germs of corn in the graves of Egyptian mummies") it had retained the power of regeneration, then medieval history had to appear in a new light. The barbarians, who had been described as a rejuvenating force, were now seen simply as brutal conquerors. The medieval Christian era, which had been considered the seedbed of modern German idealism, was still described as "a long step forward toward the goal" but in much more grudging tones. (Hess's rage at German and Papal opposition to the Italian Risorgimento made itself felt here.) "Christianity," he concluded, "is, after all, a religion of death, the function of which ceases the moment the nations reawaken into life.... Christianity and Islam are both only inscriptions on the tombstones erected by barbaric oppression on the graves of the nations."[95]

By the same logic, a greater emphasis was now placed on the fundamentally

Figure 1. Moses Hess 1812–1875.

Jewish nature of the ideas expounded by Christ – as distinct from the church – and by Spinoza. Hess quoted approvingly Graetz's thesis that Jesus had believed not "in the immortality of the soul . . . in heaven [but] in the resurrection of the just and the pious on earth as the beginning of . . . the messianic era." As for Spinoza, he shared the belief of "Moses and the Prophets [that] life as the ethical or, more exactly, as the sacred, sprang from the conception of God as the one and only essence of an existence which otherwise would be void and transitory."[96]

As always, though, history was for Hess subordinate to the future, its instrument. Thus, his entire book really revolved around the one idea. The seeds of life hidden deep within the Jewish people could only start to take root, to grow, eventually to bear fruit if planted securely in the ancestral soil. He could not contemplate any other form of national, nonterritorial regeneration because, in his eyes, the Jewish contribution to mankind lay precisely in the combination of national state and national religion, formal law and social ethics, politics and prophecy.

And he was therefore determined to prove what he had denied twenty years before—that the Jewish people had the will to recolonize Palestine. Probably (as frequently with Hess, whose empiricism was honored mainly in the breach) the conclusion had preceded the search for evidence. But the fact remains that by the time *Rome and Jerusalem* was published in mid-1862 it included a remarkably prescient estimate of the potential forces which could guarantee the success of resettlement.

First, Hess noted, there had been a crucial shift of opinion among the Jews of the Western countries. The tide of wholesale and rapid assimilation—"perhaps the greatest danger that ever threatened its [Judaism's] existence"—had turned. He noted that in Germany and France Jewish writers such as Kompert and Weill were now choosing to write about Jewish subjects; that in Melbourne, Australia, a large public meeting had been held to discuss the first steps for the "Jewish settlement in Palestine"; that Graetz and his school wrote Jewish history as national history; and that in France an organization, l'Alliance israélite universelle, had been established to aid Jews throughout the world in the struggle for equal rights and against persecution. This awareness of a common fate would surely induce "enlightened Jews to labor for the political regeneration of our people." The colonization effort could expect leadership, "talent and capital" from the Jews of the West.[97]

But the colonists would come from the East. "In Russia, Poland, Prussia, Austria and Turkey there live millions of our brothers who believe seriously in the restoration of the Jewish Kingdom. They have preserved the very kernel of Judaism, that is, Jewish nationality—more faithfully than our Western Jews." Many would willingly become workers in Palestine given the economic development of that country. From the first, the workers should organize on a cooperative basis, in "societies of agriculture, industry and commerce on the Mosaic, i.e., socialist principles."[98] (Arguing that the Hasidim already lived "in a socialistic fashion insofar as the house of the rich is always open to the poor," Hess hoped for an alliance between them and "the national movement.")[99] National pride and social justice would reinforce each other. "The masses," he wrote, "are never moved to progress by mere abstract conceptions; the springs of action lie far deeper than even the socialist revolutionaries think. With the Jews . . . all political and social progress must necessarily be preceded by national independence . . . The social man needs for his growth a wide, free soil: without it, he sinks to the status of a parasite."[100]

While he had doubted England in 1840, Hess was now ready to seek support from the French government. His Francophile loyalty seems never to have faltered throughout his life and he hoped that the Jews, like the Italians, would gain from the French interest in the Mediterranean. France was then active, of course, in the construction of the Suez Canal. The French, he concluded, "will help the Jews to found colonies which may extend from Suez to Jerusalem and from the banks of the Jordan to the Mediterranean."[101]

As once with his *Sacred History*, so now with *Rome and Jerusalem*, Hess was euphorically confident that it would make an extraordinary impact. In a letter of 15 May 1862 he wrote that he was "being assured by competent sources that my manuscript will produce a radical (firstly, a spiritual) revolution in Judaism. Translations in Hebrew, French, English and Italian will be prepared."[102] In reality, the first translations, all into Hebrew, were not published until decades later – extracts translated by S. I. ("Shay") Hurvich appeared in *Ha-magid* in 1888–9 and the full version came out in book form in Warsaw in 1899.[103]

Yet, at the same time, Hess was fully aware that his book could only annoy his old friends. On one side were those like Auerbach who believed in a community which was Jewish by faith and German by patriotic allegiance. He could not forgive Hess his new line and accused him of "arson." "Yes, I admit it," he wrote, "I am a German Jew (however laughable or disgraceful you may find it), as good a German, I believe, as can be ... For me it is not a matter of indifference that one talks of a Fatherland and a mother tongue."[104] On the other side were the socialists, most of whom apparently did not even read the book. One who did, Johann Philipp Becker, referred to it derisively: "Mr. Hess who, very forgivably, is deeply in love with his Jewish nationality – which has been assigned by Providence the mission of liberating mankind from spiritual darkness – seems to forget that his race does not in the long run have the stuff in it to remain a nation."[105]

But Hess had steeled himself against such reactions. In a letter enclosed with part of the manuscript which Hess sent to Becker in May 1862 he wrote frankly: "Of course, you will be able to accept little of what is in it and perhaps you will smile at my efforts on behalf of the Jewish nationality ... [Yet] I have presented my entire self here as I am and at last have given air to my repressed heart."[106]

With the decision to go back to his earliest writings – to knit his ideas together in a new way – Hess had liberated himself from the pressures to conform. In the 1830s he had been an outsider anxious to get in; later he had become an insider. Now, in the 1860s, he felt free to develop his own intuitions, to commit himself to more than one cause, to retain an ideological independence.

Not only in his historiographical but also in his socialist thinking, he tended to return to his positions from before 1841. An enthusiastic supporter of Lassalle, and a successful socialist agitator in Germany in 1863, he once again looked to the existing state as a potential source of reform. As in the 1830s, he considered revolution possible but not inevitable. In the late 1860s he became a prominent member of the International, attacking Bakunin as a new embodiment of the Russian danger he had always feared,[107] and yet at the same time, firmly criticizing the concept of worker dictatorship once dear to him, still dear to Marx. "The entire younger generation of workers, " he wrote in 1868, "is fully cured of the theory of worker dictatorship which necessarily always conceals within it an individual dictator."[108]

But he was also active in the Jewish world, writing articles on history and politics, urging men prominent in French life to found a Jewish colonization corporation for Palestine. In the feuds between the rival camps of Jewish theology, he identified himself, although not uncritically, with Graetz's Breslau school; he even translated the third volume of Graetz's history into French under the title *Sinai et Golgotha*.[109] Jewish orthodox practice was justified in Hess's eyes not as divine revelation, not as eternally valid, but as a necessary form of national self-preservation in exile; and he devoted great energy, both in *Rome and Jerusalem* and after, to attacking reform Judaism as overrationalistic, as a threat to the national existence.

In his colonization campaign, he found himself increasingly at odds with the wealthy and powerful men who, at one time or another, promised support. Disillusioned with Henri Dunant (the founder of the International Red Cross and onetime enthusiast for a Jewish Palestine), Hess wrote to a friend that "we Jews must rely on ourselves, that is the best."[110] But he spoke with increasing sharpness, too, of the Jewish leadership, a leadership that had not taken up his colonization plans and satisfied itself with the establishment of one agricultural school, Mikve Yisrael, in Palestine. Hess stopped contributing to the journal of the Alliance israélite universelle and in 1870 he published a bitter attack on the Jewish plutocracy in Graetz's *Monatsschrift für Geschichte und Wissenschaft des Judentums:*

> It is to put it mildly an unpardonable weakness when those who act as the defenders of Judaism . . . try to prettify everything to do with Jewish history and the Jewish race. There has been in fact only a small kernel in Judaism to which should be ascribed everything great and holy in the Jewish spirit. No doubt that kernel had a healthy influence on the surrounding masses. But there has always been – and still is today – an egotistical, acquisitive and crass class which hunts wealth and favor. This class . . . has earned the Jews since ancient times and not without reason the mistrust of the nations . . . The Prophets of old did not flatter their wealth and influence. On the contrary, they prophesied the most terrible days for all Israel because of them and their sins . . . The true representatives of Judaism are obliged to tell the truth to those who seek wealth and domination and to liberate our brothers from a solidarity which in every way can only be pernicious.[111]

In this passsage we hear the voice of Hess, already a sick man, a few years from his death in 1875. ("I did not recognize [Hess]," wrote Bakunin in 1869, "so old have we both become.")[112] He was angry but not in despair. Eventually, others would renew his attempt to combine socialist and Jewish messianism. After all, Hess had not arrived at it easily; as later for others, it was a psychological necessity.

Aron Liberman

Hess died a natural death at the age of sixty-three, not a major figure but respected in the small circles where he was well-known. Prominent French and German socialists spoke at the funeral ceremony in Paris; Graetz and Marx paid him tribute in letters to his widow. Liberman committed suicide at the age of thirty-five in the town of Syracuse, New York; he died in total obscurity. Hess achieved a certain serene maturity; Liberman found himself remorselessly sucked down into despair.

This contrast should probably be explained less by their differing temperaments than by differences of status, time, and place. Thus, as perhaps the first socialist ideologist in Germany, Hess could never bring himself to recognize anybody in the movement, not even Marx, as more than primus inter pares. But Liberman quickly came to see himself as no more than a middle-ranking officer in the army of the

Russian revolution, and this meant that he was chronically dependent on the revolutionary leaders, in need of their approval, in fear of their criticism.

A product of German thought in the 1830s, Hess tended to return again and again to the idea that socialism could only develop within the framework of the national state. His dilemma had been to decide how he – a German socialist, a member of the European avant-garde – could possibly demand a Jewish state. In the Russia of the mid-1870s, though, the concept of revolutionary class war, not of the proletariat against the capitalists but of all the exploited against their exploiters, had become so predominant that the issue of nationality was now seen as at best secondary and at worst dangerously divisive. The socialists of the 1840s and 1850s, Lavrov explained, had been "the artists of the revolution [who had] . . . only the haziest idea of the . . . ground on which they were fighting," and had even turned for aid to the existing regimes. But by now the revolutionaries realized that exploitation of the have-nots by the haves "is the *basic* evil of the existing order, the evil which draws all the minor symptoms after it."[113] Given this doctrine of the social revolution – one, indivisible, and international – Liberman had to watch his every move lest he overstep the line dividing orthodox populism from heterodox nationalism.

Not the philosopher but the apostle – the activist, the martyr – had represented the ideal type for Hess. In practice, though, he had reconciled himself to the intermediate role of prophet, involved in yet detached from the world. Like Marx, he never fully emancipated himself from the belief that to think was in itself to act and again, like Marx, he was therefore ready to accept an unearned (albeit inadequate) income from bourgeois sources. But Liberman joined a revolutionary movement which demanded that the individual cast off all ties with the existing order, that he prove his dedication to the people day in, day out. The hallmark of Russian socialism, Lavrov wrote, was the "enormous significance it assigned to personal conduct, to 'living one's life according to nature and truth.' "[114] Thus Liberman felt under constant compulsion to produce tangible results, to prove that his strategy would work on the battlefield and that he, too, was ready to go to the front line.

The maskil

In July 1875 Aron Liberman had to flee Vilna[115] following a police search, and in August he reached London, where he joined the Russian revolutionaries grouped around Peter Lavrov's journal, *Vpered!*. Liberman had been a member of the clandestine circle in Vilna which included Aron Zundelevich and Vladimir Yokhelson, who later would both play an important role in the terrorist Narodnaia Volia. Revolutionary socialists had gained a significant following in Vilna, and since the early 1870s that city had become a key link in the smuggling of illegal publications into Russia.[116] In a raid of April 1876 the police rounded up some fifty-five Jewish youngsters in that city – a sizeable number considering that the total number of revolutionaries apprehended throughout the empire in the period 1873–7 was just over a thousand.[117] But what distinguished Liberman from others in the group was that he was not just a socialist. He also had an established reputation by 1875 as a Hebrew publicist, as a maskil, and this fact was undoubtedly of crucial importance in his development.

"The Haskala" was the term used by the Jews of East and Central Europe to describe their form of the Enlightenment (or Aufklärung). As with the Enlightenment in general, it was not a homogeneous movement but rather a broad concept which covered an entire spectrum of differing groups and ideas. Nonetheless, underlying the enormous variety there was a lowest common denominator, a general agreement that Jewish life had to adapt itself to the modern world, intellectually through an educational revolution and economically through "productivization," a radical change in Jewish occupational patterns.[118] Beyond this was conflict.

In 1874 Liberman had sketched out his own position as a maskil in a fictional work published in three installments by the Hebrew periodical, Ha-shahar. It was entitled "The Crux of the Matter" and signed with a pseudonym.[119] The work was composed of a series of visions, scenes from the netherworld and scenes of this world as seen from the next. Liberman was drawn to the fantastic and grotesque in literature (probably under the influence of Gogol), and he was to return to this form again in 1877. In all probability, though, he chose this literary device primarily as the easiest way to smuggle his sociopolitical ideas past the Russian censorship: Ha-shahar was published in Vienna but most of its approximately one thousand subscribers were to be found in the Pale of Settlement and it had to select its contents accordingly.[120]

Liberman's satire in this piece was directed partly at the familiar and long-hated targets of the Haskala as a whole. At one point, for instance, the devil exulted in the hopeless economic situation that forced great masses of Jews to become peddlers or beggars living from hand to mouth. "There are no technical schools in all the various places where the Jews live and for years to come there shall be none." And when, at last, some Jewish philanthropist would establish such a school, it would no doubt be outside the Pale of Settlement. Again, for the teachers of the traditional Jewish school (the heder), Liberman had nothing but contempt: "Among the thousands of melamdim you won't find more than two or three who know à thing about education and how to explain subjects to pupils in good taste... How long will these mosquitoes buzz about the heads of our children without anyone taking any notice?[121]

But Liberman also took a clear stand on the issues which divided the Haskala against itself. He did not conceal his contempt for the concept of Enlightened Despotism, a concept which since the 1830s had appealed strongly to the maskilim in Russia as it had in an earlier age to the French philosophes. Thus the government decision of 1873 to close its rabbinical seminary in Vilna and to replace it by a teachers' institute was presented in Liberman's work as part of the devil's plot to stifle all independence among the students (independence here meaning variously an interest in modern Hebrew literature or an urge to enter the universities). He also rejected the idea central to the thinking of many maskilim, that wealthy Jews could lead the movement for change. The Jewish bourgeoisie was bitterly lampooned whether for its self-indulgence ("if I did not satiate myself, the hungry artisans would lack for bread; the more I insist on heavy work for poor pay, the more I strengthen their physiques"), whether for its charity (given "in order to cloak their sins and ... from the money they make out of the poor.")[122]

On the nationality issue, the survival of the Jewish people, Liberman took if anything an even stronger stand. He placed himself in total opposition to those who (again since the 1830s) had seen the modern as the negation of the national. He dismissed contemptuously the rabbis of "the new kind who despise their own people and who have an attitude alien to everything deep-rooted in Israel." He rejected out of hand the governmental attempts initiated by Nicholas I to impose alien education on the Jews ("schools that teach your children about your Holy Law . . . and how to reform your faith"). He condemned angrily those communal authorities which had hunted down Jewish boys from among poor families or neighboring areas in order to fill the recruitment quotas for a near-lifetime service in the army: "There are those who argue that . . . the government was only seeking to test the attitude of the Jews and that the people then managed to reveal its nature by going beyond the call of duty in carrying out the law . . . And the rabbis. Why were they silent? . . . This is our eternal shame."[123]

No all-embracing solutions were presented but suggestions emerged. The Jews should organize their own modern schools that would teach Russian and mathematics while also providing a first-class knowledge of the Hebrew language. Otherwise, modern Hebrew literature and publishing, which were fighting to survive, would soon fade away and the "maskilim would turn to the corrupted form of German spoken" by the Jews – that is, to Yiddish. "Will you never learn" (this was surely Liberman speaking through one of his characters), "will you never learn that you must breathe into your child the Hebrew spirit so that he will learn to love his people from birth?"[124]

With this publication, Liberman had taken his stand as a member of that branch of the Haskala which sought to combine political and social protest with a Jewish patriotism, the attitudes of Russian populism with those of Peretz Smolenskin, founder and editor of *Ha-shahar*. This group of writers, most of whom published in *Ha-shahar*, included Y. L. Levin (or Yehalel), Dr. Yitshak Kaminer (soon to become Akselrod's father-in-law), Zvi Ha-Cohen Shershevsky, Eliezer Dov Liberman (Aron's father), and also, more peripherally, S. Y. Abramovich (better known as Mendele Mokher Seforim) and Moshe Leb Lilienblum.[125] Liberman's satirical work was received enthusiastically within this circle, and henceforward he was frequently described as the most talented Hebrew stylist among the younger generation of writers. The term "Hebrew Socialists" aptly described the inclinations of at least some of this group in the mid-1870s – particularly Levin and Kaminer – but none except Liberman was associated actively with the Russian revolutionary movement.

Maskil and revolutionary

Thus when he arrived in London Liberman clearly felt that it had fallen to him to speak for the Russian-Jewish people among the revolutionaries and for Russian revolutionary populism among the Jews. Swept along by the potentialities of this new situation, he was in a euphoric mood in the late summer and early autumn of 1875. On the one hand, he had with him a plan to bring out a bilingual socialist journal (in Hebrew and Yiddish). While on his way to England, he had been promised support from a group of Russian-Jewish students in Berlin who were socialistically inclined but also (in a couple of cases) had rich families back in Mohilev on whom they could draw for funds. They had even spoken in Berlin of founding a Jewish Section of the International.[126]

Figure 2. The Berlin group of socialists (1875 or 1876). Seated from left: (2) Grigorii Gurevich: (3) Khasia Shur; (4) Aron Liberman; (6) Gerasim Romm. Standing: (1) Maksim Romm; (3) Aron Zundelevich.

His first letters from London were written in an exalted tone. In one (written in Hebrew), he exhorted his younger brother to abandon his settled existence and he composed a new version of the Ten Commandments for his benefit: "Fight against everything old and cast off all the nonsense inherited from your fathers" (the third commandment); "Work in order to justify your right to live; work in order to be complete in body and soul" (the fifth); "Don't say what is mine is mine and what is yours is yours but say everything is everybody's" (the seventh). Again, another letter called on Levin to abandon all liberal hopes in the tsar: "for the sake of mankind in general and for the sake of [the People of] Israel in particular – Israel, which will only be saved in the days of the Messiah and after the War of Gog and Magog."[127]

On the other hand – and even more encouraging – Liberman was welcomed by Lavrov and began to work in the *Vpered!* office, both as journalist and typesetter. *Vpered!* was the leading Russian revolutionary journal of the period and enjoyed considerable prestige in radical circles. Liberman no doubt owed this opening to the fact that Lavrov adopted a relatively flexible attitude toward national problems. Although a confirmed internationalist and active supporter of Marx in the International, he was still a populist[128] and, as such, argued that the revolutionaries had to work within a strictly national environment:

> The *national* question, in our opinion, must disappear entirely in view of the important tasks of the social struggle. [But] nationalities form the real and

unavoidable basis on which every social process takes place. One has to work in a *given* place, in a society speaking a *given* language and formed in a *given* culture. [Otherwise] the goal of social action will take on an entirely abstract character.[129]

Elsewhere, Lavrov wrote of Uvarov's trilogy – Autocracy, Orthodoxy, *Narodnost* (Nationality) – that only the last retained its validity: "not a *narodnost* which hates Germans, Poles, *Zhidy* [Yids], but a *narodnost* as the shared unity of individuals all of whom possess equal rights."[130]

Lavrov was in fact willing to give Liberman the chance to spell out his ideas. This editorial policy, remarkable for its lack of dogmatism, was demonstrated immediately on Liberman's arrival. On 1 September 1875 *Vpered!* carried an article, "From Vilna," unsigned but clearly written by him. Here he developed many themes familiar from his work in *Ha-shahar,* except that now they were capped by an openly revolutionary program.

Thus, once again, Liberman stressed the idea of Jewish national solidarity – or, more exactly, solidarity among the Jewish masses. In attacking the regime of Alexander II he not only enumerated a variety of measures adopted against the Jews (the wholesale dismissal of Jewish employees from the railway service, discriminatory methods of army recruitment), but he also spoke out for the heder and for separate military units. "Will not a new decree," he asked apprehensively, "soon come into force which will close the hadarim, thus in an indirect way forbidding Jews to teach their children Hebrew?"[131] Again, he complained that in the army even the Tatars had their own units but not the Jews. "They have somebody to speak out for them albeit a 'sick man' [the Turkish sultan] . . . but we have nobody to depend on, neither the state, nor the various Gintsburgs, Poliakovs, Varshavskys, etc., whose interests are diametrically opposed to those of the people."[132]

"The only hope for the people," he wrote, *"is in social revolution."*[133] Here he developed a theme that clearly held him in its grip at this point: the belief that Jewish history and teaching had prepared this people and its natural spokesmen for revolutionary socialism:

> Socialism is not alien to us. The community [obshchina] is our existence; the revolution – our tradition; the commune – the basis of our legislation as quite clearly indicated by the ordinances forbidding the sale of land, by those on the Jubilee and sabbatical years, on equal rights, fraternity, etc. Our ancient Jewish social structure – anarchy; the real link between us across the surface of the globe – internationalism. In the spirit of our people, the great prophets of our time such as Marx and Lassalle were educated and developed . . . And persecution? It cannot be worse for the people than now; we, the propagandists, are invulnerable. Did not our ancestors go through all the horrors of torture by the Inquisition and go to the stake for their convictions; so how can hard labor frighten us today, we who are pursuing much higher goals?

At this point, a counterbalancing note appeared, that of the internationalist:

> The Russian people is suffering; the same force which is trampling us with its feet is strangling them with its hands. Who can remain indifferent to such a

sight? How can one calmly eat a piece of bread when one knows that the rye has grown from ground manured with the peasants' blood . . . ? The Russian muzhik is our brother; for us socialists there is no nationality, no racial division; all of us living in Russia are Russians [russkie]; we have the same interests, the same ways. We Russians! Let us unite against the enemy.

Governmental policies, he was sure, would boomerang: "The Russian government . . . is making large efforts to russify us and we are russifying – but not in its spirit and it will not rejoice in our russification. Our youth too is awakening."[134]

Here, in this first article published abroad, Liberman had surely formulated his political philosophy as he himself conceived it, without fear of the Russian censor and without pressure from the editors of Vpered! However complicated the sentiments (if all were becoming Russian why the passionate anxiety to nurture Hebrew?), they nonetheless reflected Liberman's own duality as maskil and revolutionary, admirer of Smolenskin and Lavrov.

However, very soon, by early 1876, Liberman had modified his stand, had toned down his euphoric appraisal of Jewish history and religion. As Lavrov later recalled it, Liberman had had "the idea of using the tradition of messianism interpreted in a socialist sense but he soon abandoned this plan in favor of socialist propaganda in the usual form."[135] Lavrov did not explain this changed line but a number of factors had apparently combined here.

In some émigré circles, Liberman's article produced a furor. Thus a Ukrainian revolutionary in Dragomanov's group wrote an angry letter of protest to Smirnov, the assistant editor of Vpered! "It is not right," he argued,

> to see a division along class lines among the Jews. The Jews in Russia are not a nation but an entire class, which lives exclusively at the expense of the petty-bourgeois population. The weight of their exploitation is great and their harmfulness unlimited . . . If we find it possible to preach revolution, and only revolution, against the nobles [pani], how can we defend the Jews? . . . We cannot have any faith in the laughable "Yiddish International" nor in the sympathies of the Yids for the revolution.[136]

Lavrov clearly resisted the logic of this attack; throughout 1876 he continued to publish Liberman's articles on the Russian Jews, and he gave his official support to Liberman's efforts to organize the Jewish workers in London. But, at the same time, he and Smirnov must have argued in favor of a less mystical or messianic approach. In a letter to Smirnov from mid-1876, Liberman referred specifically to "the arguments at the beginning of my stay here." And he added that "there is nothing left of them now."[137]

Liberman simply did not have the self-confidence to maintain his original position and exaltation. As he explained to Smirnov, as long as he had remained in Russia he had had "quite a high opinion" of himself. "On the one hand, the lack of morality, parasitism and rapaciousness . . . aroused in me contempt for my surroundings; on the other, true education is still so lacking among the Jews . . . that I even felt the superiority of a more all-rounded education."[138] But once he had come into contact with the Vpered! circle, he came to realize that he lacked "system, a systematic presentation, and I am afraid that that cannot be acquired or at least not everybody can acquire it." True, he considered himself even now "one of the best stylists in the Hebrew language, but style alone is not enough for a writer."[139]

What was more, he feared that he had not as yet sufficiently transformed his own lifestyle:

> After I came to know the social activists I saw and realized that I did not have an ounce of morality in me . . . I remember, for example, that I believed that if I earned my bread "honestly" . . . I had by this alone proved my honor even though I was completely bourgeois and even now I cannot get away from that and become a worker.[140]

Liberman was working in the *Vpered!* press, but clearly this was not enough to calm his conscience. The fact is that even as a revolutionary, Liberman maintained many of the personal habits he had acquired in Russia as a *pater familias* (he had left behind a wife and children), teacher, business agent, and maskil. Vinchevsky has described Liberman as he knew him in 1880 – and that was after he had spent some two years in prison:

> With his neatly kept beard, his sharp dark eyes – somewhat strained but penetrating – his firmly built forehead, he looked like the type of *intelligent* who lets the world know that "one can be a man of sense and still keep one's fingernails clean" (as Pushkin says). He not only kept his nails clean but also the words that came out of his mouth . . . However hungry he was, he did not like to eat without a table cloth (a clean one) or without his own sharp knife which he himself had polished.[141]

The arguments advanced by Lavrov and Smirnov were almost certainly reflected in the article published by Liberman in the *Vpered!* of 15 February 1876. Where earlier he had written to inspire national pride in the Jewish reader and so win him over, he now insisted that the *intelligent* was duty-bound to reflect only the popular will. "If we were political revolutionaries, he wrote,

> there would be no need to find out if the people is suffering and if it feels its miserable situation . . . ; guided exclusively by our own personal interests, we would try to draw the people after us, we would try to *rouse* discontent in them in the name of who knows what, would choose the factor most likely to throw the masses into our arms regardless of any other considerations – we would choose, for instance, even such a flexible and special principle as that of nationality, which today is exploited by politicians in different ways. But we are *social* revolutionaries, we create nothing, don't force anything on anybody; we have been called to life by the dissatisfaction of the people . . . ; all our activity consists of giving *clear expression* to this dissatisfaction and of *directing* it to its fundamental causes.[142]

Here, surely, was to be heard the voice of Lavrov and his circle of "Propagandist Populists." Their viewpoint was, in a sense, paradoxical. They idealized the *narod* and yet distrusted it; believed in its values but also anticipated the possible corruption of those values; depended on it to overthrow the tsar but feared that it would permit a new dictator to take his place. "The people," Lavrov wrote, "really is a

God-Sufferer (*Bog-stradalets*), but a God who does not know his own omnipotence."[143] The propagandists had to reveal to the people its true nature – its socialist potential – and not pander to its passive whims. They were to lead, advise, guide, but not become leaders.

Clearly, Liberman felt that he had been challenged, that now he had to argue and then prove that there was a revolutionary potential immanent within the Jewish masses – a potential that was not dependent on, and could be divorced from, any specifically national or religious traditions. Even in theory, let alone in practice, this was no easy task. Liberman was never again to return to the optimistic, liberated mood of August and September 1875.

In his articles published in *Vpered!* in the winter of 1875–76, Liberman argued that the Jewish masses were trapped in a spiral of economic decline. Drawing on his first-hand experience of the area, he described the situation in sober, detailed, and factual terms, the more impressive because in such contrast to his earlier satiric and messianic styles. He examined the situation in the small semiurban centers (the *mestechko* or shtctl) and in the towns; among Jews, Poles, Germans, and Lithuanians; in the fields, the factories, the workshops. He explained the effects of the journeyman and apprenticeship systems; of the fourteen – eighteen-hour day; of child and woman labor; of piecework and the flat rate; of the unbelievably crowded and sordid living space; of the all-pervading credit-system which linked every class in hierarchical dependence.

"The urban population of the Lithuanian towns and townlets," he summed up,

> is, in general, extremely poor. The artisans are in decline, industry is only beginning to develop (except in Belostok and its surroundings), trade is not flourishing, despite the predominance of the Jewish element. It consists of exporting timber and unfinished agricultural products, in which Lithuania is not particularly rich, and of importing salt, herrings, and an insignificant quantity of other commodities. Only speculation, usury, and the exploitation of the rural and urban proletariat have reached the fullest possible development.[144]

The people, he argued, was becoming aware of an impending crisis: "Up to a point, it realizes that if things carry on as usual then the future will be still worse; . . . it foresees the time when many will no longer have a place in this world of ours, when neither skill nor industriousness will be able to save man from death by hunger." Of course, urban workers could not be reached by propaganda designed for the peasants of "the Russian interior" and the correct approach would have "to approximate to that of western Europe." It was also true that often the workers were "too crushed, too devoured by need and work" to strike back at their employers. Nonetheless, his final conclusion was that "*the soil for social-revolutionary propaganda and agitation is ready among us.*"[145]

For the immediate future, though, the main hope lay in the fact that the Pale of Settlement had to be regarded as a first class reservoir of revolutionary propagandists. He described with what fascination the youth seized on every socialist pamphlet smuggled from abroad –

> true, at first, out of curiosity, then because of the novelty of the world-view . . . , but then they begin to take it seriously, find in some places a

36

rational answer to the questions which are torturing them . . . and in the end
they give themselves up entirely to the cause, breaking their ties with their
past . . . even though their new action is in direct conflict with their personal
happiness, . . . their old world and personal habits.[146]

Surely, here we find a reference to Liberman's own personal experience.

Only those who still lived within the Jewish world could undertake to found a
revolutionary movement within that world. All his animus against the russified
Jewish intelligentsia surfaced here. "In contemplating action among the Jewish
population," he wrote,

one must not be guided by the views of those socialists among the youth at
the institutions of higher learning who have left the Jewish environment . . .
They do not know their own people [plemeni] . . . They themselves never
tried to draw near to the people; on the contrary, they tried to keep as far
away from it as possible in order to seem as European as possible . . . Nevertheless, they claim to know the Jewish people excellently and therefore
never try to verify their view of it.[147]

As against the university students were those young Jews "who are close to the
workers and have not broken their ties with the people." The reference was in the
first place to students in the yeshivot, of whom Liberman held high hopes but also
perhaps to those in the Teachers' Institutes in Vilna and Zhitomir. "Once they go
over to socialist work this youth provides the most fiery champions of the cause
and will take the socialist message also to elements in other nationalities to whom
they are mostly quite close." At this point, Liberman took the opportunity again to
stress his abandonment of his messianic strategy: "All that is needed is to work on
them sufficiently and step-by-step to destroy their worship of the old and the
traditional leaving them only with love for their own people—that is, for those
close to them."[148]

For all the modification implicit and explicit in Liberman's new approach, he
was not willing to abandon the idea that the revolutionaries working among the
Jewish workers should form their own organization even if within some broader
international framework. However tentative the tone, the import was clear:

Now the question must be how to create trust between the different nationalities. I personally do not undertake to decide that . . . My personal opinion
is that propaganda must begin by uprooting national pride and exclusiveness, but the most suitable way of doing this is to conduct preparatory work
in each nationality separately. The propagandists will take their stand on the
international character of the movement. And the circles of fully conscious
socialists in each nationality will come together and federate or, finally, unite
together.[149]

Propagandist, 1876–79

With his article in Vpered! no. 27, Liberman had formulated his program, and now
he had to test it against reality. This he sought to do in three ways: through his
manifesto to the Jewish youth in Russia, through his work among the Jewish

immigrant workers in London, and finally, through his socialist journal published in Hebrew, *Ha-emet* (The Truth).

The manifesto was published in Russian and Hebrew in some thousands of copies, smuggled into Russia (by Yokhelson and perhaps others), and distributed there. It was also printed in *Vpered!* on 1 August 1876.[150] The manifesto was issued in the name of an ostensible Union of Jewish Social Revolutionaries, though all the signs suggest that it was the work of Liberman alone.[151] However, that Lavrov and Smirnov gave their approval is evident from the editorial statement in *Vpered!* wishing "our Jewish comrades success in their new undertaking, which is an integral part of the general movement of the worker-socialists of our time."[152]

Although the manifesto was addressed primarily to the yeshiva students, it made no appeal to Jewish messianism or national pride. It was based strictly on class lines. The Jewish bourgeoisie – whether commerical, professional, intellectual, or rabbinic – was condemned out of hand as a stratum of blood-sucking exploiters astride the back of the Jewish working people. ("The intellectual development of which you are so proud was bought with our labor, our suffering, our blood.") Not satisfied to exploit the Jewish poor alone, it had extended its plundering to other nationalities and thus enflamed inter-ethnic tensions: "Because of you, race and religious hatred flamed up . . . Because of you, thousands of our brothers, sons of the people, were destroyed . . . Because of you, curses are thrown down on the entire Jewish people, a suffering and impoverished people which more than the masses of other [nationalities] is the victim of your plundering."[153]

The Jewish youth, "the young intelligentsia, still not entirely corrupted by the present social structure," had only one way out: "Down with careers! Down with the worship of treason, down with the worship of money and power! Throw off the past and join the working people and its friends. To it alone belongs the future. Outside it is only destruction and death."[154] What Liberman was hinting at here was an idea widely held in his circle of radical maskilim in Russia. In their correspondence, they frequently stressed their fear that pogroms would follow the expected revolution, and they argued that only if the Jewish masses placed themselves firmly in the revolutionary camp might this danger be averted. Or as Y. L. Levin put it early in 1876 (in deliberately cryptic language for fear of the censor's eye): "Let this people open its eyes and let it see what the times demand in order that it might unite with all its brothers and not be cast down. If only we could tell this people what will be in the end of days in order that it may not be thrown into the same grave as the evil-doer and not die with the lords."[155]

Nonetheless, the manifesto received a highly critical reception from the maskilim. It was too extreme, they felt, too much ahead of its times, divorced from reality. ("Until the Jew has learned to understand himself and his own," wrote Levin, "he will not thank us at all, but will call us rogues and traitors. And so I could not use the manifesto.")[156] Grigorii Gurevich of the Berlin group in later years could not remember ever having seen it.[157] But, in contrast, Vinchevsky recalled that he had read it in Kovno at the home of the Port family (radical maskilim), and that it completed his conversion to socialism ("a process which had begun . . . with Chernyshevsky's *What Is To Be Done?* and other such works").[158]

If the effect of the manifesto was marginal, Liberman's efforts to organize the immigrant workers ended in definite failure. According to plan, the organizational campaign was to develop in two stages. The committed socialists would first form their own group; then this inner core would initiate a general trade union among the workers in the clothing and tailoring workshops of the East End (Liberman believed that there were 55,000 Jewish immigrants in London, some ten times the actual number).[159] On 20 May 1876 the Hebrew Socialist Union was set up: there were ten founding members, among them Lazar Goldenberg (who like Liberman worked in the press of *Vpered!*) and Isaac Stoune (who in the 1880s was to aid Vinchevsky in his Jewish socialist projects in London).[160] The Union held twenty-six meetings, reached a total of thirty-eight members on its books, and conducted its proceedings in Yiddish – the language in which Liberman, as secretary, also kept the minutes.[161]

The statutes (composed by Liberman in Hebrew) followed the same strictly class lines as his manifesto. There was the same attack on "the capitalists, the rulers and the clerics who have taken all the rights of men and all the wealth of the world to themselves"; and the same insistence that "salvation can come to us Jews only through the salvation of all mankind." The Union would therefore seek "to unite in fraternal union with the fellow workers of other nationalities"; but, as in Liberman's article of 15 February, the statutes came out explicitly for the principle of autonomous Jewish socialist organizations and propaganda "in every place possible." In an internal discussion on 21 October, Liberman expressed the view that as England was "the only place where we can come out openly, our Union serves as a banner for the Jewish socialists elsewhere, a proof that we exist."[162] Like the manifesto, the statutes were published in *Vpered!* with an enthusiastic editorial endorsement.[163]

It was at the second stage of the plan that unexpected trouble developed. On 26 August a public meeting was called. An invitation printed in two thousand copies had been distributed in advance, the audience ran into the hundreds, and Liberman was one of the speakers. What he said was consistent with the position he had adopted since the winter. So, for instance, he chose the occasion to repeat his theory that the "Jewish plutocracy [*geldaristokratye*] is the basic cause of the persecutions to which even today Jews are subjected, particularly in eastern Europe." He then went on to attack the leaders of the London synagogues as part of the exploiting class (giving as an example the £3 10s 0 which even a poor couple had to pay to be married). "He drew a parallel," reads the report "between the state and the Jewish community [*gemaynde*] and said that it is in the hands of the workers to create ... a workers' republic in their internal affairs and that they should not let themselves be dominated by any 'authority'."[164] At this juncture, somebody in the audience (described as "a bourgeois") jumped up, demanded the right to speak, claimed to represent the Chief Rabbi (Dr. Adler), and in no time succeeded in unleashing tumult ("uncontrollable noise"). The meeting broke up in chaos and rumors immediately began to spread that the socialists were Christian missionaries.[165] Only eighty workers signed up for the new trade union.

The two subsequent meetings were declared "closed" in an attempt to exclude bourgeois trouble-makers, but nonetheless, the first was again disrupted by hecklers (with a synagogue official, a *shamash*, in the lead). It now became apparent that Liberman had fallen hard between two stools. In mid-September the new trade union met and the workers there declared themselves totally independent of the Hebrew Socialist Union. His comrades readily placed the blame for this development on Liberman's public speech. As one leading member put it: "We socialists are much hated in the city and for that the fault lies in the meeting where Liberman ruined the whole thing." So bad did things become that gossip in the East End held Liberman "guilty of the arrests in Vilna" and people were saying that "the situation of the Jews here could get worse too through socialist intrigues and interfering in politics."[166] By November, the trade union acting alone had succeeded in recruiting some three hundred members.

Ironically, while Liberman's anticlerical and revolutionary rhetoric had antagonized the mass of immigrant workers, his insistence on a separate Jewish organization aroused opposition within the Union. George (Hirsh) Saper, a founding member, maintained a constant barrage of criticism. He argued in favor of an "educational union" which would encourage Germans as well as Jews to join and, as its name implied, would concentrate on a select group of workers.[167]

As early as July, Liberman had to reject Saper's demand to hold a public meeting on the traditional day of mourning for the destruction of the Temple. While Saper had argued that "we know only our own cause which, at the same time, is that of all mankind and no more," Liberman had replied that

> so long as the social revolution has not come, so long does political freedom have a great significance for the Jewish people – the Ninth of Av is the day we lost our independence and our people has mourned the fact until today, for more than eighteen centuries. It must have value enough that we can postpone the meeting for a few days.[168]

But while Liberman had enjoyed a position of strength in the summer, by the autumn he was on the defensive. He was even accused to his face of "thinking only of himself and of how to make himself important."[169] On 21 October he resigned as secretary and, even though he continued to attend meetings, the union now went into rapid decline. Before the end of the year it had disintegrated.

At the same time, in an unrelated but no less wounding development, Liberman's position in the *Vpered!* circle had become untenable. Liberman had long been disliked by such key members of the journal's technical staff as M. I. Yantsin and N. Kuliabko-Koretsky. (In June, Liberman had written that he would tolerate Yantsin "so long as he does not transfer his antipathy for me personally to all the Jewish people.")[170] As against this, though, Liberman had apparently been able to rely for a long time on a large measure of good will from Lavrov and Smirnov. By late 1876, however, Lavrov was in the process of withdrawing from editorial control, Smirnov was on bad terms with the workers in the press, and they – organized on a cooperative basis – were left to make their own decisions. Liberman was told or, in a variant account, chose to leave.

To make matters worse, Goldenberg and Liberman had infuriated Smirnov (then in Heidelberg) by signing a telegram of good will dispatched to the Berne congress of the Bakuninists held at the end of October. How, demanded Smirnov, could Jewish socialists take a stand on this issue as if they were Russians? In his reply, Liberman argued that the socialists of a given country formed one fraternity even if they had to work in different languages:

That I have tried to publish a paper [in a Jewish language] . . . is far from being nationalism. It would be another matter if I had dreamed of the victory of the synagogue over the Roman curia or of winning Palestine by balls of gold or of lead . . . You know very well that I hate Juda-*ism* just like any other national or religious *ism* and I say this openly . . . I am an internationalist . . . but I am not ashamed of my Jewish origins and I love, among all the oppressed, also that section of mankind which the prevailing national and religious principles mark off as Jews. But I say again I do not love all [Jews] but only the suffering masses and those persons capable of joining them . . . And I regard myself as a *Russian* socialist not by nationality but by the territory on which I work, by the place in which I was born, the country which I know even better and by the interests of that country which attract me always more . . . Believe me I do not want *to take pride in my Jewishness,* not from the religious or historical angle (that you must believe) and not even from the racial aspect. I recognize only men and class, no more.[171]

Despite this double setback in London, Liberman still had one hope to sustain him. He had arrived in England with the idea of bringing out a socialist journal in Hebrew (perhaps also in Yiddish), and although the scheme had had its ups and downs, it was near to realization at the end of 1876. Since the summer he had been given firm pledges of financial support from the Berlin group, and in January 1877 he was in the German capital laying final plans for the journal. If necessary, he wrote to Smirnov, he was ready to smuggle himself into Russia to raise supplementary funds. His letters from this period reflected a feeling of isolation and a desperation to succeed in his venture. "I will carry on," he wrote in one letter, "regardless of how others treat my work . . . as a partisan if not as a member of any party. Once I have torn myself away from the present system, I cannot return to it; I cannot, sir; better to die." In a later letter he told Smirnov that he resented warnings about the dangers of going to Russia: "If I do not do that of which I am capable and as much as my strength permits, then I am really a superfluous man. What would I do then."[172]

But funds, minimally sufficient, did come through.[173] In March 1877 Liberman, now in Vienna, was able to print a *Prospectus* of the journal, and the first issue of *Ha-emet (The Truth)* was finally published in May. It was planned that *Ha-emet* enter Russia legally, avoid an outright ban by the censors, and be financed by subscriptions – a scheme clearly derived from the successful experience of Smolenskin's *Ha-shahar,* which was also printed in Vienna and, as already noted, had published much socially radical material. Liberman was counting on the fact that, at this juncture, the censors who examined Hebrew material were far from fanatic in their search for revolutionary or socialist propaganda and would let almost anything through as long as it was veiled in even slightly ambiguous terms.

This scheme was ingenious, and in the three issues of the journal that appeared, Liberman was able to present all his basic ideas. (Exploiting the journal's official policy of total anonymity, he in fact wrote nearly all the material himself.) There were detailed attacks on capitalism and wealth. In an article on the Jewish immigrants in London he drew a vivid contrast between the magnificent buildings in the West End and the conditions of unemployment and starvation in the East End:

"These are not people standing for sale in the London market but machines of flesh and blood called 'hands,' and happy are those 'hands' which find a buyer . . . because, as bad luck would have it, these machines have stomachs which demand food."[174] Political liberty alone was worthless – this was a recurring theme: "Freedom only gives people *rights* and rights are worth . . . something only to those who can use them." The only solution was the communal control of resources: "Private wealth and communal wealth are two contradictory phenomena and the one can only grow at the expense of the other."[175]

He presented his ideas on revolutionary organization in a piece that, like that of 1874, took the form of a vision. It was written in the language and style of a classic kabalistic work and described the Jewish revolutionaries as the thirty-six righteous men of mystic legend who, in order to deceive Satan, "have sometimes to appear in the world as evil men," but who are really "acting according to the secret law from on high, . . . gathering strength to fight the war of good against evil, life against death, truth against falsehood, the war of the sacred against the profane – until the Divine overthrows the Satanic."[176]

In articles on Machiavelli and Darwin he placed the blame for wars and conflicts between men on the fanaticism of false absolutes and ideologies, meaning, primarily and by clear implication, the established religions. There is, he wrote, "no absolute good, or absolute evil" but, as Machiavelli put it, "ruthlessness is good in every place where it serves the people . . . on condition that it is pursued undeviatingly."[177] For his part, Darwin had demonstrated that conflict within a given species is abnormal; that, indeed, only "unity and brotherhood among all mankind" could enable the maximal use of natural resources.[178] And international brotherhood meant in turn (as he explained in yet another article) that "we Jews do not have a special culture different from the culture of the people among whom we live . . . Everybody knows that in wars Jew fights against Jew and links, if they ever existed, are broken."[179] Still less could there be a bond linking the Jewish rich and the Jewish poor – "these are different people far removed the one from the other."[180]

As a vehicle of what can be called "legal socialism," *Ha-emet* undoubtedly enjoyed a measure of success. The group of radical maskilim in Russia were genuinely thrilled to see a journal in Hebrew dedicated to the cause of major social change. Of the piece about the thirty-six righteous men, Y. L. Levin – who was not easy to please – wrote that "it is a work of art and even now I still kiss every word."[181] In another letter, using their code language, he wrote that "there are many indigent boys here and it would be a really holy deed to teach them the Torah free of charge and if I get the *humashim* I will give them to the boys."[182] Kamensky, another member of the group, wrote that he had shown Abramovich (Mendele Mokher Seforim) both the *Prospectus,* which had "made an enormous impression on him," and the first issue, "which is in agreement with his own views."[183] They made real, although largely unavailing, efforts to raise funds for the journal; and wrote frequently to encourage Liberman. "We share in your troubles, our brother," wrote Kaminer in July 1877. "You will go through trials; stand up to them, my brother, stand up to them all. If you wish it, you can do it! I wish you great strength, a renewal of the soul."[184]

That the paper did make a deep impression among the radical maskilim was demonstrated, too, by Lilienblum's decision to contribute his remarkable parody on Elisha Ben Avuya to it,[185] and by Vinchevsky's publication in 1878 of a new periodical as its successor (likewise socialist, legal, and Hebrew). Defending Liberman there against Smolenskin's attack, he wrote that his had been the first modern Hebrew journal "to turn its back on the vanities of the war against Hasidism and against the religious reformers, [to repudiate] the new hypocrisy and sycophancy which everybody calls the Haskala. He presented the truth naked before all."[186] Again in Kremenchug, Spivakovsky, then sixteen years old, was shown a copy by German Rozental and under its influence joined a revolutionary circle.[187]

But for Liberman such a modest degree of success was hardly enough to compensate for the fact that, by its very nature, this enterprise, like his earlier attempt at Jewish trade unionism, placed him under intolerable cross fire. In the Jewish radical world it was widely felt that his anticlericalism and internationalism were formulated in a deliberately provocative and counterproductive manner; while Smirnov tended to view the entire enterprise as possibly nonsocialist and nationalist.

Of course, there was nothing surprising in Smolenskin's outraged response to Liberman's statement that hitherto modern Hebrew journalism had "found nothing else with which to busy itself than questions of religion and nationality and other similar vanities in which every normal man has long lost interest."[188] But Liberman was startled when the student group in Berlin panicked at his radicalism and criticized his "haste": "First find subscribers, friends and supporters and carry through your program stage by stage. One can mix a spoon of vinegar into the water but why a full portion of poison from the start?"[189] At another juncture, Kaminer asked angrily: "Why touch on matters of religion? This is not the time! This is not the place! And this is not the goal."[190] When Liberman hinted at support for intermarriage, Kaminer wrote that "if you molest even with a word or a hint the faith and ordinances of Israel . . . you and all who are with you will be lost."[191]

Again, he was warned repeatedly that a purely negative line, couched in a difficult Hebrew, could make only the weakest impact. Where, asked Kaminer, was the positive ideal? ("Without an ideal you won't win the enthusiasm of our youth, who do not know for what they are directed to fight, do not know the shape of the new home for the sake of which they have to destroy the old.")[192] Shershevsky wondered whether Liberman was not obliged to lower "his view to that of the readers (if there are any)" and whether Liberman was justified in writing "everything for those readers who themselves are writers."[193]

Yet, simultaneously, Liberman had to take into account the fact that Smirnov, speaking in the name of the *Vpered!* group, was constantly questioning his socialist orthodoxy. Why, Smirnov asked in March 1877, was a socialist paper being presented to the tsarist censorship? Liberman had to explain that he only intended the paper to be legal in its early stages: "Now, *The Truth* has to group around itself all the sympathies from different strata, penetrate everywhere, carry out its own propaganda, arouse our young writers and give them a place where they can pour out their boiling rage . . . And when it will have become a necessity for our youth then we shall jump over the barriers of the censorship."[194]

Why, Smirnov asked, had he chosen Hebrew rather than Yiddish, the language of the masses? Liberman explained this too: "As soon as it became a question of a legal paper, then we had to choose Hebrew. Yiddish is anathema to the regime because of its [policy] to russify the Jews – Yiddish publications from abroad meet insurmountable obstructions regardless of their contents . . . [Besides] in Russia you won't find a town or townlet where there are not people who understand Hebrew."[195]

Was the paper, Smirnov questioned, fully socialist? Liberman had to admit that it did not "present the s. r. program clearly and explicitly" but its socialist features would easily be discovered under the mask. He certainly did "not intend to play with religious socialism and depend on the Talmud or the Bible." If he mentioned them it would be to stress "the unsuitability of their ideals for our times"[196] (On this issue Liberman had come a long way in two years.) The journal was designed

> to penetrate among our yeshiva students . . . and arouse them, prepare them; it must take that Jewish stronghold which the iron Nicholas I could not overcome (because he did not know how) and then use that stronghold for the work of destruction. I am sure it will succeed because now there are among the propagandists many who have decided to remain "seminarists" fully in outer appearance, with their long coats and side-curls and they will penetrate everywhere. They don't even need expenses. They are used to sleeping on a bare bench in the school and going from place to place on foot, etc.[197]

This letter was written in March before the journal had begun to appear. When it finally did come out and as he began to receive reports on its contents, Smirnov became ever more critical. (As a Russian, he of course could not read it himself.) In a letter of October 1877 Liberman wrote that "you condemned the paper so decisively that I was left with nothing to say in its defence." Ironically, he added, he was being attacked in the Hebrew press "for communism, nihilism, for my wish to destroy the Jewish national spirit, for atheism, etc." He concluded: "In a word, all attack me, all Jewish parties from the obscurantists to the progressives. And I am fated to be rejected by my own comrades too."[198]

By the time Liberman wrote this letter, the last number of *Ha-emet* had been published. The fourth was ready for publication but was never printed. Faced by the combination of financial pressures and criticism from all sides, Liberman did not have the will to persist in this enterprise, so long planned and in which such hope had been invested.

Trapped

On 17 February 1878 Liberman was arrested in Vienna. He had been recently involved in smuggling socialist publications into Russia but – after nine months in prison awaiting trial – he was eventually sentenced to only one month's imprisonment for living in Austria under a false name (A. Freeman). He was deported from Austria and in January 1879 arrested by the German authorities. He was brought to trial again in Berlin together with Grigorii Gurevich and Moisei Aronzon, accused of setting up an illegal and subversive organization. The archive of *Ha-emet* had been confiscated by the Austrian police and the evidence of Liberman's international socialist connections was presented in the Prussian trial. He was sentenced to imprisonment for nine months and, on his release, went to London in January 1880.[199]

There he tried to pick up the threads of his former life. This time he had a disciple and an ally in Vinchevsky, who had been arrested in Koenigsberg and deported to England in November 1878. (Bismarck's antisocialist legislation had come into force in October.) Together they set up – again as in 1876 – a socialist core organization (with many of the same members as in 1876) and a worker organization (The Jewish Workingmen's Benefit and Educational Society).[200]

But Liberman could not settle down to the routine life of a minor labor leader in the immigrant East End, where at most there were a few hundred potential recruits. His attention was drawn more to Russia. There the Narodnaia Volia was riding high on its terrorist wave and among those involved were Liberman's old comrades, Zundelevich, Yokhelson, and Lazar Tsukerman. From his few letters to Smirnov which survive from this period it is clear that Liberman was strongly attracted to the idea of joining the terrorist party. In fact, on 19 May 1880 he wrote that "A few days ago I received a letter from there which decided me to leave for Russia . . . I am only waiting for money and I promised to leave within two days of my getting the necessary expenses for the journey. I have joined the Narodnaia Volia group and the matter is finally decided."[201]

It is hardly clear why Liberman did not go.[202] But there is no doubt that he was profoundly worried by the problem of whether or not the Narodnaia Volia was in reality a socialist organization. A number of revolutionaries of Jewish origin were attracted to the terrorist party precisely because they believed – with Zheliabov – that what Russia needed before all else was political liberty, a liberal constitution. Lev Deich even described Zundelevich, for instance, as "one of the first Social Democrats in Russia."[203] Another Narodovolets, Abram Magat, wrote to his sister in 1879 that "I see two-and-a-half million people in slavery and say . . . one must fight for their freedom."[204]

Liberman, however, had long committed himself heart and soul to the concept of the social revolution in Russia: a revolution which would bypass, leap over, the "political" or bourgeois stage. Could it be, he asked Smirnov, that the Narodnaia Volia was simply repeating past errors, that "with us it is still 1848 or 1789?"[205] In his last letter to Smirnov, written on 27 May 1880, he referred to himself as "Daniel" (presumably because of the censorship). This letter expressed perplexity, desperation:

> Daniel can grant that the Narodnaia Volia is not a socialist but a constitutionalist party. At least, he could read this out of your letters; if this is so . . . does real socialist activity exist in the motherland; . . . is such activity possible under given circumstances; finally, can he personally work for the cause in Russia? . . . You know that Daniel is, of course, a Jew; even if he regarded a constitution as desirable he cannot have any particular wish for a constitution in Russia . . . As a Jew he is a cosmopolitan; no country can tie him to any particular patriotism and if he wants to enjoy a constitution he can do it in England or, if you like, in America. But Daniel is not a constitutionalist . . . He is a socialist . . . a socialist Jew . . . ; but he is in no way a Jewish nationalist; he is an internationalist who wants nothing more than the disap-

Figure 3. Liberman (standing) and Zundelevich.

pearance of all national divisions... For socialism, for a pure workers' popular socialism, denying... any aristocracy (including its most dangerous form, "the aristocracy of thought"), against every division of people by nationality and against the division of the world into separate territories – for such a socialism I am ready to give my head, but only for this and not for something else... No, I was and will never be a political revolutionary, never! Now what, in your opinion, is the Narodnaia Volia?[206]

Vinchevsky has described in vivid terms how distraught Liberman was becoming at this time. He had fallen hopelessly in love with Vinchevsky's cousin Rachel – a love which she in no way reciprocated. She was a married woman with a growing daughter and a husband who was more absent than present. In the summer of 1880 she left with her daughter for the United States. According to Vinchevsky, she was literally trying to run away from Liberman's overwhelming attachment. But he followed her to America.

On 18 November 1880 he came to her home in Syracuse. He had only been there a few hours when he shot himself. He left a note: "Adieu world. He who has nothing but troubles must die. I ask that nobody judge me unless he is in my place." This last sentence was an adaptation of the classical Hebrew saying in the *Ethics of the Fathers*, "Do not judge your neighbor until you are in his place."[207]

Conclusion

Hess and Liberman were unusually clear examples of men thinking a generation ahead of their time. Seeing in Hess the "first religious socialist in Judaism," Martin Buber in 1944 even wrote that "today almost seventy years since his death the Zionist movement has not yet really caught up with him."[208] (Buber thus went farther than Herzl, who had noted in his diary of 1901 that "everything we are trying to do he has already said.")[209]

Both died in obscurity (dignified in the one case, tragic in the other), and their intellectual biographies had to be unearthed in stages as if by a protracted archeological dig. But by 1903, as noted by Edmund Silberner, the German Social Democrats directed by Karl Kautsky were waging a successful competition with the Zionist movement for possession of Hess's archive, then still in the hands of his widow. And, following the 1905 revolution, Bundists undertook to research the life of Liberman, requesting information from Zundelevich and other revolutionaries who had worked with him some thirty years before. With growing knowledge came a measure of recognition. In 1903, "Father of German Social Democracy" was inscribed, at the initiative of the local party, on Hess's tombstone in Cologne. It survived the Nazi period, and in October 1961 he was reburied by the Sea of Galilee in the cemetery of the first kibbutz pioneers. In 1935 Liberman's remains were brought from Syracuse to the New York cemetery of the Jewish socialist fraternity, the Arbeter Ring, where he was reburied next to the grave of Vinchevsky.

How is the historian to explain the phenomenon of what can be termed premature ideologies? Curiously enough, possibly hinting inter alia at his relationship to Liberman, Vinchevsky discussed this question in 1878, when he wrote that "significant people, men of outstanding talent, live tens or hundreds of years before the time when men will follow in their footsteps ... Their words sound fantastic to their contemporaries ... Among those few who move in their shadow are usually young people, those who belong to the coming generation."[210] Implied here was the idea that the man of genius can only gradually gather disciples who, in turn, can only gradually disseminate his ideas.

Such an explanation could well be applied to the development of Marxism but is hardly applicable to Hess or Liberman. They were men of outstanding intelligence but no more than many contemporaries, as they were the first to admit. Furthermore, Hess had no followers, and Liberman had only a handful of disciples, or at least successors – primarily of course Vinchevsky himself.

Paradoxically, perhaps their extreme isolation in their own day could explain their success in anticipating the thoughts of a later period. Their ideological development was, before all else, intensely subjective. Auerbach was very perceptive when he wrote to Hess in response to *Rome and Jerusalem* that "you world reformers are really strange saints, you take the stages of development of your personalities and your momentary thought processes very easily for the development of the actual period and real world."[211] Eager to submerge themselves in the socialist movement, they were unable to do so permanently (in the case of Hess) or completely (in the case of Liberman). They were thus forced back on their own individuality, on their own personal ideologies, program, plans. They produced answers to their own questions and, in so doing, reinforced their initial isolation.

Insulated from objective conditions – or from what contemporaries regarded as such – they pursued truths which were political in intent, private in fact. When the objective conditions, or at least collective perceptions, changed, as they did in the Pale of Settlement after 1881, the questions which had once concerned them alone became those asked by entire groups.[212] And the same questions then produced similar responses.

Thus, to avoid the charge of nationalism, Liberman fell back on a strictly "objective," anticlerical, class-oriented theory of Jewish socialism and so condemned to instant failure his appeals to the Jewish working masses and yeshiva students. But it was just this logic that later became central to the ideological evolution of the Bund. Again, by dividing his time between his socialist and proto-Zionist campaigns, Hess was unable to work effectively in either, but it was this clear-cut division of functions – albeit in rationalized form – which Syrkin would later advocate as the only one tenable for the socialist Zionists.

Parallels could be drawn with the intense individualism of a Rousseau (whose posthumous status changed so radically as the classical Europe gave way to the romantic) or of a Radishchev (who was only discovered gradually by post-Decembrist Russia). Some of Dostoevsky's contemporary heroes or anti-heroes – in search of faith, plagued by doubts, wrapped up in themselves, yet somehow foreshadowing major political realities – are surely also relevant here. Hess and Liberman, after all, both lived according to the norms of political romanticism.

CHAPTER 2

The emergence of the new politics

The Russian-Jewish crisis, 1881–1882

A revolution in modern Jewish politics took place in Russia during the years 1881–2. The inner turmoil engendered by the pogroms starting in April 1881 reached a climax in the months from January to May 1882, when the Jewish people appeared to be living in expectation of an imminent and massive emigration. The image of a new exodus, a going-out from the land of bondage to a promised land, came to dominate, however momentarily, every aspect of Jewish public life in Russia.

The far-ranging enthusiasm for an exodus represented a profound reversal of deeply held attitudes. For the literary intelligentsia – those perhaps two-score writers whose articles now filled the Jewish press in Russia – it meant that what had been considered mythic was now seen as practical, even necessary. That eastern Europe would sooner or later follow the West in granting the Jews equality, although not necessarily fraternity, had long been accepted by them as an unquestioned axiom. In the first months of 1882 this belief remained only as the article of faith of a die-hard minority. The startling new question was whether in its policy to the Jews Russia did not represent the historical norm and the liberal policies of Europe and North America a temporary aberration.

For the student youth, the upsurge in favor of exodus from Russia necessitated an even more traumatic upheaval. Profoundly influenced by the norms of Russian revolutionary populism, they felt compelled to translate the ideological metamorphosis of 1881–2 from thought into action. If the Jewish masses had now to be seen as a suffering *narod* – in itself an unheard-of idea for the vast majority – if its salvation required migration and resettlement across the seas, then surely it was their task, the task of the repentant sons, to pioneer the way. The year 1881–2 thus witnessed a Jewish "going to the people," closely analogous to and in part consciously modeled on that of 1873–4, when the Russian students had left in their hundreds for the villages.

It is less easy to judge the impact of the exodic vision on the great mass of the some three million Jews then estimated to be living in the Russian Empire. But innumerable eyewitness reports make it clear that not only in southern Russia, the scene of the pogroms, but also in the northwest wildly exaggerated rumors of grandiose emigration schemes swept from place to place; that spontaneously in almost every town of any size societies were founded for the colonization of Palestine; that some thirty to forty thousand Jews (many of them penniless) left Russia in the period from mid-1881 to mid-1882 – a manifold increase over the previous annual average;[1] and that Jews in large numbers were ready at that moment to put their trust in anybody, be it repentant students or self-styled emis-

49

saries of the Alliance israélite universelle or Laurence Oliphant, who appeared to hold a solution to the national crisis.

Jews in eastern Europe had last been gripped thus by expectation of an exodus in the years 1665–6, when Nathan of Gaza had pronounced Shabbetai Zvi the Messiah come to lead his people back to the Holy Land. And if many religious Jews now rejected the wave of political activism, it was partly because of the fear entrenched since then of false prophets, premature messianism, attempts to force the hand of God.

But does this upheaval, however great, warrant the term revolution? The historians Y. Leshchinsky and E. Cherikover both warned against the view that the years 1881–2 ushered in revolutionary change over the long run. Thus Leshchinsky pointed out that large-scale Jewish emigration from Russia to the United States began not in 1880 but in the 1870s, over fifty thousand Jews having gone to America from the Russian Empire in that decade. He also noted that Jewish migration within the empire, particularly from the northwestern to the south and southwest (Bessarabia, New Russia, and the middle Dnepr regions), had been a permanent feature of the nineteenth century and did not cease in 1881. Migration, whether within or beyond the frontiers, was caused primarily by deep-rooted socioeconomic trends, by what Leshchinsky termed "immanent" as against "political" factors. In particular, the population explosion – an increase from one-and-a-half to over five million during the nineteenth century – combined with the economic stagnation of Lithuania, White Russia, and the northwestern Ukraine to sustain constant population movement. "The emigration to America," he concluded, "was essentially a part of the same migratory and laborizing process which was taking place [inside Russia] on an even greater scale."[2]

For his part, Cherikover noted that the swing against cosmopolitanism and toward Jewish nationalism in various forms (including in one or two instances even the demand for the resettlement of Palestine) had gained momentum rapidly from the mid-1870s. And in contrast, assimilationist and internationalist impulses reasserted themselves strongly after 1882. "The ideological crisis of the Jewish intelligentsia," concluded Cherikover, "was felt *before* the pogroms and, on the other hand, the turn to nationalism was not characteristic of *all* the Russian-Jewish intelligentsia."[3]

However vital such qualifications are, the fact remains that at the strictly political level, as distinct from long-term economic or social trends, the period 1881–2 must be considered of revolutionary significance. True, the quasi-messianic programs then advanced proved impracticable and had to be ignominiously modified or even abandoned. True, the apocalyptic euphoria was very short-lived and soon gave way to depression in the emigrationist camp and to renewed self-confidence among its russifying opponents. But, nonetheless, the political impact of that year was to prove long-lasting and profound.

Before 1881 Jewish politics had been purely auxiliary, and men such as Hess, Liberman, or Eliezer Ben Yehuda had been the exception. Emancipation was expected to result from the decision of the Russian government. The only question therefore was how the Jews could hasten a favorable decision. Debate revolved around the related issues of education (how far should they proceed with Russification), religion (how far should they modify long-standing traditions), advocacy (should the Jewish press adopt an apologetic or accusatory stance), and philanthropy (should Jewish public funds go to educational or socioeconomic goals; to publishing, teaching, and students or to land colonization and workshops).

Now, after 1882, a rival concept took permanent hold: Jewish politics should strive to be autonomous. The most influential slogan to emerge from the crisis was that made famous by Lev Pinsker – self-emancipation. The goal should no longer be adaptation to the environment but rather the creation of an environment radically new.

The Jewish politics of pre-1881 had been elitist. Revolving around issues of philanthropy, education, and advocacy, they involved alliances between elements in the plutocracy and in the established Jewish intelligentsia. This was true of the leading cultural organization (OPE), of the economic organization (ORT), and of the Jewish press. After 1882, the concept if not always the practice of the open and mass organization took hold. Party politics, nationalist on the one hand and socialist on the other, now gradually emerged as a permanent aspect of Russian-Jewish life.

Increasingly, until 1881 politics had concentrated in St. Petersburg, where the Russian-language newspapers and journals were published, where OPE and ORT had their offices. After 1882 the balance shifted to Kiev, Warsaw, Belostok, Vilna, Kovno, Moscow, and Odessa (which now regained much of the avant-garde role it had played in the 1860s). Moreover, a new, global, dimension was added. The influx of Russian Jews into London, New York, and, on a small scale, Palestine created satellite communities where ideas brought from Russia struggled to survive in alien environments. Every successful experiment in the Russian-Jewish centers there – the East End, the Lower East Side, or the environs of Jaffa – could and often did influence politics in the mother country (the *heym*).

This chapter, then, will seek to answer three related questions. What new forces were brought to the fore by the crisis of 1881–2? To what extent, and how, did the new political formations survive the period of crisis itself? And, in particular, what was the impact of this crisis on the ideological development of the radical Jewish intelligentsia, its relationship to socialism and nationalism?

Crisis and Response, 1881

New political forces

It was in the Russia of 1881 that, for the first time in nineteenth-century Europe, the Jews had to face antisemitism not simply as a permanent inconvenience but as an immediate threat to their established way of life, as an explosive force, as a dynamic rather than static phenomenon.

On 15 (27) April a pogrom broke out in Elizavetgrad. It raged virtually unchecked until, on the third day, the armed forces finally intervened. Starting from 17 April, violently destructive attacks were launched by the local peasants against the numerous Jewish agricultural settlements (established during the reign of Nicholas I) in the surrounding areas. Less than two weeks later, Kiev became the scene of a pogrom; for days on end entire neighborhoods were looted and largely destroyed by crowds estimated at over four thousand. April also saw pogroms in such towns as Kishinev, Yalta, and Znamenko, and early in May the wave of destruction reached Odessa.[4]

It has been estimated that by the end of the year pogroms had taken place in over two hundred towns and villages. In all, during 1881, some forty Jews were killed, many times that number wounded, and hundreds of women raped. Moreover, in the northwest, where there were no pogroms, the summer of 1881 witnessed a series of enormous fires which destroyed large sections in the Jewish neighborhoods of such cities as Minsk, Bobruisk, Vitebsk, and Pinsk. Thus tens of thousands were suddenly rendered homeless and penniless.

The Russian press, led by such nationalist papers as Aksakov's *Rus,* Suvorin's *Novoe vremia,* and the *Kievlianin,* generally described the pogroms as the natural and justified rebellion of the long-suffering indigenous population against merciless exploitation by an alien element. When Jews called for the punishment of those responsible, these papers described the demand as an affront to the Russian people, an attempt to turn brother against brother. Papers such as *Nedelia,* which had been considered liberally inclined toward the Jewish population, now remained silent or in some cases even joined the hunt. Given the strict surveillance of the press which then existed in Russia, the ever more virulent attacks were considered to enjoy at least the passive approval of powerful governmental figures.[5]

Here was a crisis of unprecedented proportions in modern Jewish history. But just because it was so unfamiliar, the initial response from within the Jewish community was hesitant, even routine. Thus, when the established leadership in St. Petersburg began to collect relief funds late in April, the sums donated were hardly more than symbolic. (The railway magnate S. S. Poliakov reportedly gave 1,000 roubles and the banker A. Zak a mere 500.)[6]

At the other extreme, the large group of Jewish students at Kiev University who were linked to, or at least in sympathy with, the revolutionary movement, frankly welcomed the pogroms. "We were convinced," explained a member of the group not long afterwards, "that all the Jews were swindlers . . . [that] we belonged to the Russian people, were educated on its tunes, grew up on its literature."[7] Abe Cahan in his memoirs was to recall that in his revolutionary *kruzhok* in Vilna the response had been similar: "We regarded ourselves as 'men,' not as 'Jews.' Jewish concerns had no appeal to us. There was one cure for all the ills of the world – socialism. That was the fundamental law of laws for us. To say that the pogroms did not interest us is an understatement."[8]

Writing to friends from Kiev on the morrow of the events, Yehuda Leb Levin expressed his conviction that the socialists had incited the pogrom there.[9] This widespread estimate goes far to explain the attitude of both the Jewish socialist youth and the St. Petersburg leadership. They were at one in regarding the pogroms as simply another round in the life-and-death struggle between the government and the revolutionaries, the conflict which had led to the assassination of Alexander II on 1 March 1881. This view was confirmed by no less an authority than Alexander III himself, in an audience he granted to a deputation of prominent Jews led by Baron Gintsburg at Tsarskoe Selo on 11 May. The pogroms, he told them, were caused by "the anarchists" and the government would certainly not tolerate them.[10]

David Gordon's *Ha-magid,* a weekly published across the frontier in East Prussia, greeted the tsar's statement with relief.[11] Commenting on it, another Hebrew paper reported the common belief that the authorities had been slow to put down the violence only for fear that to do so would be to follow the plans of the socialists, to provoke a revolution.[12] Nor were these views entirely illusory. Documents from the archives of the ministry of interior, published after 1917, tended to confirm that the pogroms had surprised the tsarist authorities – in the main, at least – and that initially they suspected socialist responsibility.[13]

The tendency to assume that the anti-Jewish eruption was a transient phenomenon was somewhat shaken in mid-May when the chief procurator of Kiev, General Strelnikov, took up a favorite theme of *Novoe vremia,* asking rhetorically in court why the Jews did not make use of the fact that "while the Russian border to the east is closed to the Jews, that to the west, on the other hand, is open."[14] But, even then, the dominant tendency remained to wait and see. Both Aleksandr Tsederbaum and Y. L. Levin actually expected a decisive turn for the better to result from the replacement of Loris Melikov as minister of the interior by Count N. P. Ignatev, whom they regarded as friendly to the Jews.[15] And *Russkii evrei* could write as late as June that the current crisis would surely lead the government to recognize the danger in legal discrimination against the Jews, of outlawing them, as it were. "The work of those whose task it is to deal with a solution to the Jewish question," the paper concluded, "has been made significantly easier by the latest events."[16]

In general, then, the initial response followed a traditional pattern. Given the assumption, rooted in long experience and common sense alike, that the fate of the Jewish people in Russia ultimately lay only in the hands of the government, a waiting policy was understandable. But coming from those who were expected to initiate an effective response, such a policy of dependency was bound to create a leadership vacuum. In times of crisis, if the established leaders fail to exert their authority, then new forces can emerge. This process unfolded among the Russian Jews only fitfully during the year 1881; it developed with full force in the early months of 1882.

Essentially, the new types of leadership came from two distinct sociopolitical groupings. First, there were those (both students in the *gimnazii,* universities, and colleges and also the self-taught *polu-intelligenty*) who had hitherto regarded themselves as disciples of Russian thought in its various revolutionary and populist forms. Second, there were the writers and journalists who had access to the Jewish papers and journals, in particular to the Russian weeklies *(Razsvet, Russkii evrei,* and *Nedelnaia khronika voskhoda),* to the three Hebrew weeklies *(Ha-melits, Ha-magid,* and *Ha-tsfira),* and to the two influential monthlies *(Voskhod* and *Ha-shahar).* In the 1870s (as described above) individuals drawn from these two separate worlds had sought to form an alliance grounded on an ideology which can be variously described as "Hebrew socialism" or "Jewish populism." Liberman, Vinchevsky, and Tsukerman, on the one hand, and Y. L. Levin, Lilienblum, and Kaminer on the other, did work together for a short time, but their venture had remained throughout the work of a few, a peripheral enterprise. In 1881–2, the role of the populistically inclined Jewish youth and that of the nationally oriented Jewish writer were both to become central.

"The going to the people": 1881

The way in which circumstances propelled the youth to the center of the stage was demonstrated most clearly in 1881 in Elizavetgrad and Odessa. This process, as it unfolded in Odessa, was described in detail shortly afterwards by an active participant, M. I. Rabinovich (who would later become well known as a novelist and short story writer under the characteristic name of Ben Ami, "a son of my people"). His account appeared in the émigré journal, *Volnoe slovo*, which was edited by M. P. Dragomanov, the Ukrainian radical and populist.

As he told it, when the news of the Elizavetgrad pogrom reached Odessa, a meeting of Jewish students was called. Some thirty students came and they decided to take immediate steps toward the organization of self-defense. They envisaged the recruitment of able-bodied youth in every Jewish neighborhood, the acquisition of arms, and the necessary training. As a first step, they called public meetings in the synagogues of the city for the night of Saturday, 2 May. (That the students in Odessa reacted initially so differently from those in Kiev can perhaps be explained by the fact that a pogrom had taken place in Odessa in 1871 and, although an isolated event, had made a lasting impression on the local population.)

The students went to the synagogues in pairs and explained their plan to the assembled crowds. According to Ben Ami's account, those who spoke in Yiddish (then called "the Jargon") enjoyed the greatest success, especially when they were able to include some popular Biblical or Talmudic aphorisms. "This," he wrote,

> was the first "going to its people" on the part of the educated Jewish youth, driven by a deeply tragic moment. . . . The mere idea that here educated persons, whom the masses had come to regard with pride but also as beyond their reach, were thinking of them – this alone raised their fallen spirits, raised their feelings of human dignity. . . . Everywhere, absolutely everywhere, the youth met only the most profound gratitude and – more important – absolute trust and the promise to do everything that the youth would propose . . . To this day I see before me the picture of a venerable, almost seventy-year-old man who after I had said my words of encouragement, came to me, laid his hands on my head to bless me but could not say a word and burst into tears.[17]

In fact, the pogrom in Odessa began on the following day – Sunday, 3 May – before any counteraction could be organized. But spontaneous attempts at resistance were made and false rumors spread around the Jewish areas that the student committee was directing the self-defense. Students did join in, albeit individually, and some of them were rounded up by police with other Jews found resisting the *pogromshchiki*. According to the report submitted by Count Dondukov-Korsakov, the acting governor general of Odessa, there were among the five hundred people arrested some one hundred and fifty Jews who, as he put it, "were preparing for an open battle with the Christians."[18] Among those he mentioned by name were the students Mordekhay Grech (who was soon to play a leading role in socialist politics in New York) and Khavkin (who according to the report was linked to the revolutionary party, Cherny Peredel). All those arrested were put on ships and kept out at sea for two weeks. Subsequently, some twenty-six of the Jewish prisoners were charged with the illegal possession of revolvers.[19] In his account, Ben Ami emphasized that none of those arrested had revealed to the authorities the existence of the student committee.[20]

There was a direct transition from the hasty attempt to organize self-defense to the formation of the emigration movement in Odessa. Late in May, a group was set up to establish an agricultural commune in the United States. Central figures in this project were S. Bailey, M. Herder, H. Sabsovich (who were among those arrested during the pogroms), Ben Ami himself, and above all, Monye Bokol. From Ben Ami's description of Bokol, it emerges that he had originally been a teacher, a melamed, in a heder in a small town near Odessa. Falling under populist influence, he decided that he should earn his living only through manual labor, and he apprenticed himself in a workshop in Odessa. Possessed, according to all accounts, of a magnetic personality, he had gathered around himself by early 1881 a group of enthusiasts, both Jews and Russians, who had made up their minds to set up a farming commune in southern Russia.[21]

With the pogroms, however, Bokol's group rethought its goals. The concept took on a more Jewish orientation: The universal was now to be realized through the particular. Ben Ami quoted Bokol as saying that perhaps the Jews "are destined to show the world that life can be established on the basis of the highest truth and justice."[22] The name adopted by the group, Am Olam, clearly emphasized its new position. Am Olam (The Eternal People) was the title of the booklength essay published by Smolenskin in 1872, which had become the manifesto of the nationally oriented wing of the Haskala movement during the later 1870s.[23]

The Odessa Am Olam group developed a three-point program for its planned colony in America. Its land would be held in common, distribution would go to each member according to his needs, and money would be set aside to buy new lands "for other Russian Jews."[24] It was in this latter clause that the more national emphasis now came to expression.

Although the leadership was drawn from the student intelligentsia and demi-intelligentsia, the majority of the group were "artisans, simple workers and small traders."[25] This willingness of working people unfamiliar with socialist thought to follow the populist intelligentsia provoked considerable comment at the time. After all, the peasants had given short shrift to the narodniki of the original "going to the people" in the summers of 1873–4 (a fact meanwhile rendered into satire by Turgenev in his novel, Virgin Soil). Thus I. Rombro[26] (an active member of revolutionary circles in Russia during the late 1870s and now an émigré in Paris) could write in early 1882 that however much the Jewish masses were accused of

the purest materialism – by their nature they are always and everywhere prone to a very high level of pure idealism. That same Chaim who is apparently ready to sell himself for a penny can . . . enter a state of exalted wonderment, is even ready to weep, when you describe to him a Jewish colony planned to be set up in America, even though it is communal, some kind of New Icaria. In this sad and unfortunate time for him he is so excited by this fascinating new life of which he had never heard until now that he is ready to leave his homeland and emigrate to America.[27]

In his memoirs, Abe Cahan recalled the "religious enthusiasm" of "artisans and traders who lived not badly in Russia [and now] sold everything to join the parties which were going to establish a new Jewish life in America."[28]

In selecting new members for the group, Bokol actually preferred candidates from the *narod* as against those from the intelligentsia. Ben Ami, himself a fully fledged *intelligent*, endorsed this policy. "The dictatorial instincts of the youth," he wrote, "can ruin the best cause. This must be taken into account by that section of the Jewish youth which has recently started to draw near to its own masses. Those masses will in no way tolerate a dictatorship . . . they will submit easily and voluntarily to a true friend."[29]

During the summer of 1881, the leaders of the Odessa Am Olam traveled around southern Russia spreading their message and winning recruits. At this time, too, Ben Ami was sent abroad in search of the financial backing needed by the group to reach the United States and establish their commune; specifically, he was expected to win the support of the Alliance israélite universelle in Paris. The advance party, about seventy people, left Odessa in November, crossed the frontier into Galicia, and found itself stranded in the town of Brody for weeks on end.

It had been preceded by a similar but independent group from Elizavetgrad. Less is known about the origins and ideology of this second movement, but, as in Odessa, it had emerged in direct reaction to the pogroms. It was led by German Rozental, a russified *intelligent*, not apparently socialist but certainly influenced by the agrarianism central to populist thought. He arrived in the United States on 4 (16) August 1881.[30] The rest of the group, twenty-six families, left Russia in October and their arrival in Breslau was reported by Dr. Landsberg (a local rabbi) on 10 November 1881. Their intention, he wrote, was "to found communally an agricultural colony in America."[31] They were carrying with them a Sefer Torah that they had bought in Brody, a fact suggesting a more traditional orientation than that of the Odessa group.

A letter sent in November 1881 from one of the emigrant groups (almost certainly the Elizavetgrad party) described its goals:

> We are going to a new country not to find gold . . . but to devote our mental and physical efforts to honorable and useful work . . . Our goal is very broad and complex: it is not simply that a small number of people should be able to live honorably and securely . . . Our goal is to broaden our society with a constant flow of new forces so that in case of a repetition of misfortune our brothers . . . would know that across the ocean is a handful of people to whom they could turn for advice . . . Our labor will be purely agricultural, using scientific methods.[32]

Both the Odessa and Elizavetgrad groups carried the hallmarks of the Russian populist movement: faith in the simple folk, agrarianism, communalism. Indeed, if it had not been for the crisis situation, Bokol's fraternity would probably have developed along lines similar to those followed by the Spiritual-Bible Brotherhood established by Jacob Gordin in Elizavetgrad at the beginning of 1881. This brotherhood advocated the creation of farming communes to be settled jointly by Jews and Stundists (Russian dissenters). Its ideology combined Christianity and Judaism, the Old and New Testaments, and it harshly rejected rabbinical authority,

Jewish tradition, and ordinances such as circumcision. The Spiritual-Bible Brother-hood was soon followed by a similar experiment in Odessa: Priluker's New Israel. In normal times these experiments could have anticipated a sympathetic hearing from the radical youth, and they were in fact welcomed by Dubnov (later the famous historian, now a struggling young journalist).[33] But the temper of the times was changing rapidly, and for the most part the Russian-Jewish intelligentsia – young and old – turned bitterly against them. They were accused of seeking (like the Karaites) to win from the Russian government those equal rights denied to the Jews collectively. Reform of Jewish religious practice, argued Ben Ami, would be accepted by the masses only if based on the Talmud and sanctioned by the estab-lished rabbis ("authoritative hands").[34]

At this stage, the populist ethic was compelling the "sons" to return to, and lead, the Jewish *narod*. That same spontaneity which had marked the original going to the people could now be discovered in the speed with which the groups of Bokol and Rozental organized themselves, formulated their ideologies, and left Russia. It was only when they reached Austria that they had to come into contact with the wider Jewish world, that they had to begin negotiating with the powers-that-be – the Alliance and other such bodies – for transportation costs, land, and capital investment.

The literary intelligentsia as pressure group, 1881

Therein perhaps was to be found the major difference in 1881 between the populist-oriented youth and the literary intelligentsia. The former, beginning with the Odessa and Elizavetgrad emigration groups, were action oriented and thus caught up from the first in microcosmic but concrete problems. The latter were concerned with the macrocosmic. Where, they asked, was the leadership required by the Jewish people in Russia in its time of crisis? What historical forces would determine the future of that people? The literary intelligentsia thus gradually came to play a dual role: a political pressure group and political claimant to power in the Jewish world and a debating circle where rival sociohistorical theories were advanced, criticized, and revised.

What first provoked a group of writers to intervene forcefully in the Jewish politics of 1881 was the low-key response of the St. Petersburg magnates to the April pogroms; no political action was initiated and the sums of money collected were absurdly small. In 1879, when a case of blood-libel in Kutaisi had thrown the Jewish leadership in St. Petersburg into momentary confusion, the banker Abram Zak had stepped into the breach and paid for the dispatch of lawyers to defend the accused.[35] But now nobody made a move.

Exasperated, a trio of young writers – the journalists Mordekhay Ben-Hillel Ha-Cohen and S. Z. Lure, and the poet S. Frug – decided to force the hands of the Jewish leadership. All three worked for the weekly *Razsvet*, which was pub-lished in St. Petersburg, and so, although only in their early twenties, they had some familiarity with public life in the capital. They drew up a list of the men prominent in Jewish affairs and sent them invitations to an emergency meeting which was to take place at a stated time in the home of Baron Gintsburg. Simultaneously, they wrote a letter to Gintsburg in the name of "The Society."

He was told of the meeting and given a three-part program that he was expected to present to it.

When the guests arrived at Gintsburg's home they found the police at the door taking names; any unauthorized assembly was enough to arouse suspicion in the charged atmosphere of the times. But the meeting took place and, even more surprisingly, the program was largely adopted.[36] As proposed, a delegation did meet with the tsar (in the following week, on 11 May). Fund raising now moved into a higher gear, and the idea of a conference to be composed of delegates from all the major Jewish communities in the empire was accepted in principle, although no date was fixed.

In his memoirs, M. Ha-Cohen stated that the possibility of organized Jewish emigration from Russia was first raised at this meeting and was there sharply rejected. Of this discussion, he recalled that "it would be almost true to say that the Jewish leaders in the capital were more afraid of the idea of emigration from Russia than of the pogroms ... In their eyes emigration meant a declaration of bankruptcy for the Jews in Russia."[37] The truth of the matter is, though, that at that very early stage emigration had hardly become a matter of major controversy. Voices were raised in May calling for Jewish colonization in Palestine[38] but the tone was still tentative and other issues clearly had priority. The attitude of the new tsar was considered still an unknown quantity and of decisive importance. Thus it is probable that Ha-Cohen was writing here with the benefit, and bitterness, of hindsight.

However, by the summer, July and August 1881, emigration was becoming the central issue. The cause of this shift of interest was straightforward enough. A sociopolitical chain reaction had been set in motion in April. Large population movements had been started by the pogroms. In Kiev, for instance, in late April there were numerous reports of a mass flight from the city; ten or twelve extra carriages had to be coupled onto every train leaving for Berdichev and Belaia Tserkov.[39] In turn, according to secret governmental reports, the population flows served to increase popular excitement through the south and contributed to new outbreaks of destruction in the region: In the months of June and July, respectively, there were large-scale pogroms in Nezhin and Pereiaslav. The prolonged turmoil, for its part, brought trade in southern Russia almost to a halt. On 30 May, T. S. Morozov wrote secretly in the name of the Moscow business community to Ignatev urging him to do everything in his power to halt the pogroms because the major trade fairs were being canceled throughout the south and huge quantities of food were piling up in the Moscow warehouses.[40] The spreading economic chaos made it all the more difficult to employ the refugees or even to provide them with enough food to keep them from starving. This spiral of violence, flight, and disruption was exacerbated by the popular tendency to blame the catastrophe on the Jews themselves. Emboldened by the failure of the government to take an effective stand, in word or deed, against the pogroms, the zemstva now joined the press in calling for a halt to Jewish competition in various areas of trade and education or, as they put it, to prevent the Jews from exploiting the local population. Some petitions even demanded that the Jews be totally evacuated – expelled – from their areas.[41]

But despair and fear alone would not have led the Jewish intelligentsia to weigh seriously the idea of organized and mass emigration. The refugee problem would have remained a localized and philanthropic issue if it had not been for the intrusion of another element: hope. Historians are generally agreed that revolutionary attitudes can emerge only when objective needs are matched by subjective expectations. In the summer of 1881, this extra dimension was added by the policies, real and rumored, of the Alliance israélite universelle in Paris.

As an organization established specifically to act in defense of the Jews attacked anywhere in the world, the Alliance found itself groping for some suitable response, beyond the mere dispatch of relief funds, to the developing crisis. The July issue of its monthly bulletin announced two lines of action. First, the Alliance was planning to send two representatives to Russia to examine the situation in situ. Second, it was studying the possibility of aiding a selected group of able-bodied Russian Jews to emigrate.[42] As noted in its publication, the Alliance in the years 1870–1 (following the famine in Lithuania) had paid for the passage of over five hundred Jews to settle in the United States.[43] A familiar concept, it was now easily revived. In its bulletins from July to September, the Alliance discussed the emigration issue. It made very clear that it saw a future for mass Jewish settlement neither in Palestine (it was too infertile and poor) nor in Spain (which had just announced an open-door policy for the return of the Jews) but only in the United States, "a vast, rich and free land where all who wish to work can find a living."[44] Experience, it stated, has shown that "every emigrant capable of work draws after him, given a certain time, members of his family and friends"[45] and creates a self-perpetuating process.

The Alliance explained that it was thinking of an extremely strict selection process, very limited numbers, and a well-ordered system that would not begin for some months and would stretch over many years. But the actual effect of its plans was at total variance with its intentions. Plans that were tentative and modest in Paris were blown up to gigantic size as if by a distorting mirror as they reached the Jews in Russia. Thus, early in August both *Razsvet* and *Ha-melits* published a letter (allegedly sent by the Alliance to seventy-five would-be emigrant families) in which able-bodied young men were promised a free passage to the United States.[46] The Alliance was later to deny the authenticity of this leter,[47] but, meanwhile, rumor was doing its work and word was spreading that aid would be forthcoming to those who left Russia. In August the first reports began to come in of a large-scale movement of penniless Jews across the frontier into Galicia. Late in the month, Dr. Schafier, the delegate of the Alliance, who was on his way to Russia, received a telegram en route diverting him to Galicia, where he found some five hundred refugees marooned in the town of Brody.[48]

By now, a full-scale confrontation in Russia between those Jews favoring organized emigration and those opposed to it had become unavoidable. The plans – more imagined than real – of the Alliance had provided the casus belli, and the first rounds were fired off in the Russian-Jewish press during the summer. In late July, two St. Petersburg weeklies *(Russkii evrei* and *Ha-melits)* carried editorial attacks on the whole idea of organized emigration. Both papers emphasized that under existing conditions such an enterprise would certainly be illegal and that the initiative therefore lay not with the Alliance but with the government. So far, its stand on the issue was unknown. Second, voluntary emigration could under no conceivable circumstances become large enough to lessen significantly the size of the problems of the Jewish population living in Russia. ("And let us suppose that 60,000 or 100,000 Jews leave – what is such a number compared with the three million Jews living on Russian soil?")[49] Thus, the two papers concluded, the relatively small sums which might be raised would be more rationally spent on trying to put Jewish life on sounder socioeconomic foundations; the pogroms had, if anything, increased the need for technical education and for agricultural colonies in Russia.

These arguments were further developed in the following issues of these two weeklies. The policy suggested by the Alliance of selecting only the strong and the young, thus leaving behind the weak and the elderly, wrote Aleksandr Tsederbaum in his *Ha-melits,* could only add fuel to the fires of Russian antisemitism (lending credibility to the argument that young Jews always sought to evade their military and other obligations to the state).[50]

An article in *Ruskii evrei* (probably by the mildly nationalist L. O. Kantor) suggested that the emigrationist enthusiasm was an obsession primarily of the youth, which, having staked all its hope on the progressive forces in Russia, had now been thrown by its sudden disappointment into a state of shock:

> With a kind of desperation, exasperation, it [the youth] destroys its previous ideals; it does not have the strength to bear this heavy disappointment; it cannot shrug off these ceaseless insults to our national honor, these brutal and shameless cries – "You are superfluous, you are a burden to us; you are three million superfluous mouths who are eating up our wealth." But in the heat of the moment it does not notice that it is only harming itself and serving our enemies.[51]

How could the Jews themselves accept the arguments of the most violent Judaeophobes, who were the first and most enthusiastic advocates of a mass exodus? Too, by emigrating, the youth might save itself from insult, but "can it attain this same salvation for the people [*narod*], for the masses who have had . . . to bear on their shoulders all the consequences of the ferocious excesses in the south?"[52] Massive resettlement overseas could not be financed; and even if transported to a new country, how would unskilled Jews knowing only Yiddish or Russian be able to survive in an alien society?

Rejoinders were not slow in coming. On 19 August G. Bogrov published a reply to Kantor entitled "What Is To Be Done?" *(Chto delat)* and he followed this up with a supplementary letter. On 21 August Dubnov published an article in *Razsvet* in which he developed arguments almost identical with those of Bogrov.[53] Both these writers – Bogrov from the older generation, Dubnov from the younger – were known for their hostility to romanticism, their demands that Jewish life and religion be totally modernized, and their stand on the emigration issue therefore served to emphasize the extent of the ideological upheaval then already in progress.

Emigration, they suggested, could somewhat alleviate the immediate crisis. "When a man is drowning or burning, our religious code ignores all the strict Sabbath ordinances and our people in southern Russia is now in just such a dangerous situation."[54] But, they argued, far more than the immediate crisis was involved. There was no solution in the strictly Russian context for the enormous economic problems of the Jewish people.

Land settlement in Russia was not an answer. The annual expenditure of ORT was a derisory ten or twelve thousand roubles a year. Besides, the many agricultural colonies already established earlier in the century had been among the first targets of the pogroms. The greater the success of the settlements, the greater would be the outcry against Jewish land-grabbing. On the other hand, an emigration policy would be supported by Jews in the West and would thus have a solid financial basis. Even if the Jews in Russia were granted equal rights, their economic situation would still continue to deteriorate steadily. The population growth, wrote Bogrov, was so explosive that every year it was becoming more difficult for the mass of Jews to keep body and soul together. A constant stream of emigration would ease the pressure on the limited resources and so benefit those left behind; and it would simultaneously enable many Russian Jews to become independent farmers overseas, a calling they would "learn better in a strange land than in the place where they were born and where they have become used to believing (why not admit it) that bread grows, and is even baked, of itself."[55]

The conclusion, as stated by Dubnov, was clear: "The active elements of Russian Jewry can and must, to a considerable extent, lead in the organization of emigration."[56] Here was the concrete program of what by August was already becoming a new political coalition. The newspaper articles have to be seen as only one aspect of the campaign then being organized to bring pressure to bear on the established leadership in St. Petersburg.

As it took shape in the summer of 1881, the emigration camp was centered in the provinces, within the Pale of Settlement. Those on the spot were naturally drawn by the sight of extreme need to the advocacy of extreme measures. Moreover, those at a distance from the capital and rooted in the quasi-autonomous life of the provincial Jews were less absorbed by the day-to-day nuances of government policy. There, many were attracted to the idea of organized emigration just because it represented a way in which the Jews could help themselves.

The literary intelligentsia played a crucial role in the formation of this coalition. Situated in cities throughout the Pale of Settlement, closely linked to the editors of the Jewish journals abroad and in the capital, the writers were able to bring a measure of unity to what otherwise would have remained isolated initiatives. In this liaison effort, the Hebrew writers (Lilienblum in Odessa, Fin in Vilna, A. S. Fridberg in Grodno, S. P. Rabinovich in Warsaw, Levin in Kiev) formed a central core. They maintained ties with Peretz Smolenskin, the editor of *Ha-shahar* in Vienna, and with David Gordon, the editor of *Ha-magid* in Lyck (East Prussia). In the capital, the group of young writers associated with *Razsvet* (Ha-Cohen, Lure, Frug, Rozenfeld the editor and publisher, and momentarily Dubnov) constituted an important link in this chain, although, as relative newcomers who wrote predominantly in Russian, they kept throughout something of a separate identity.

In their own localities, the writers worked together with those in the Jewish world who were determined to do something to cope with the emergency. So, for instance, in Kovno were the famous, learned, but independent Rabbi Yitshak Elhanan Spektor and his active assistant, Rabbi Yaakov Halevi Lifshits. Most important, in Kiev there was the relief committee, organized since the spring of 1881 under the leadership of Dr. M. Mandelshtam, a lecturer in medicine at the university. In the crisis of 1881–2 Mandelshtam was to emerge as a highly articulate spokesman and effective organizer. In Kiev, too, was recruited Lazar Brodsky, the sugar magnate (and, inter alia, the employer of Y. L. Levin). Acting as go-between with the Western world was Dr. Rülf, a rabbi in Memel (East Prussia), who now devoted all his energies to the cause of the Russian Jews.[57]

In a letter of 29 August 1881, A. S. Fridberg summarized the dilemma then facing the emigration movement. To collect money by means of an open and public appeal was illegal and therefore impossible. But to undertake a secret fund-raising collection across Russia, as at first contemplated, would be relatively ineffective. Therefore, they were hoping for a governmental decision to legalize organized Jewish emigration.

It was to seek such legislation that a five-man delegation from Kiev, headed by Lazar Brodsky, went to St. Petersburg in August. The group went with the strong backing of Count Dondukov-Korsakov. But, according to Fridberg's report, Ignatev, on hearing the delegation's request, "jumped up and swore that as long as he were there such a policy would never be allowed."[58] The meeting with the tsar, which Ignatev had promised to arrange, failed to materialize.

That a group from the provinces would attempt to approach the government directly, bypassing the Jewish establishment in St. Petersburg, was a highly unusual step. According to Ha-Cohen, this initiative was seen as a direct challenge in St. Petersburg and forced Baron Gintsburg to seek official permission for the long-awaited conference of Jewish representatives.[59] Permission was granted and telegrams sent out inviting two delegates from each of the major centers throughout the empire, and the list of those invited was drawn up by Baron Gintsburg and his advisers.

It was widely assumed that the conference would adopt a pro-emigration stand. After all, hitherto in 1881, the St. Petersburg leadership had tended to yield under pressure. The London *Jewish Chronicle* reported that, at the very least, the emigration question would be "examined in all its bearings,"[60] and Fridberg wrote off urgently to Smolenskin and Levin urging them to bring pressure to bear on the conference: "Now when the leaders of our people are assembled to seek ways of improving the situation, all the publishers and writers among us should send off letters requesting—insisting forcefully—that they use all means to attain governmental permission for emigration."[61] The conference opened on 31 August.

It was just at this time that Dr. Schafier arrived in Brody. Hitherto, the leadership of the Alliance, like that in St. Petersburg, had confined itself to raising and transmitting relief funds to the victims of the pogroms and fires. Its statements on emigration had been tentative. But now it, too, would have to make far-reaching political decisions.

In the summer issue of *Ha-shahar*, Smolenskin had anticipated this moment and sought in a long editorial article to persuade the Alliance to opt in favor of Palestine rather than America as the center for Russian-Jewish colonization.[62] At this stage, the basic political division in Russia was between those for and those against emigration in general; the division between *Palestintsy* and *Amerikantsy* was still secondary. But for Smolenskin, writing in Vienna and aware that the Alliance was already toying with emigration schemes, the decisive problem from the first was "whither?"

Smolenskin, in his influential editorial "How to Bring the Redemption," now developed the case for Palestine in the broadest possible context.[63] He described Jewish history from Biblical times as a constant struggle by the mass of the people to impose its concept of justice on its ruling class. In the period of the ancient Jewish state, the rich had resented the demands imposed upon it by the Mosaic law – demands which forced them periodically to release their slaves, to judge the poor and weak fairly, to leave the gleanings on their fields. There had thus developed the paradoxical situation among the Jewish people that the poor had been the patriots, the rich the potential traitors. Only with the fall of the Temple and the Dispersion was the rule of Mosaic law firmly established: "The rich did not return to lording it over the poor because the kingdom and government of Israel were gone and the Law and religion were its kingdom . . . ; and only those expert in the Law were lords over Israel."[64] But – and here was his point – since the Enlightenment, "false prophets" had reemerged to pander to the whims of the rich, to tell them that they could find salvation by breaking away from the people and its laws.

The Jews, he insisted, constituted a nation and philanthropy would be worse than useless unless it served their national interests. To send the Russian Jews to America was to expose them to incredibly harsh economic conditions, especially for new settlers on the land. But even supposing that the individuals could benefit, the nation could not. "It is a personal way out . . . which will not save or help those – more than two million – on the verge of starvation."[65] Besides, there was no guarantee that antisemitism would not eventually become a force in the United States.

Settlement in Palestine, on the other hand, would be the first step to regaining it as a national territory. "In every land where Jews go," he wrote, "they will always be a minority . . . and will do not what is good for them but what the majority regards as good for itself. . . . But this is not so in Palestine. If large numbers of Jews go there they will be the majority and will decide how things should be and will be able to help their brethren in other countries."[66]

The Alliance would be judged by how it acted in this time of crisis. "The money which has been and will be taken from Jews as a collective is only meant for the Jews as a collective, for those ready to settle in Palestine, and you cannot on your honor touch a penny of it for anything else."[67] It would be treason for the Alliance to allow itself to be guided by "famous bankers who . . . simply want to send the poor to a distant land in order that they themselves can be left in peace."[68]

Rather, the Alliance should call a conference of reliable spokesmen, trusted rabbis and members of the literary intelligentsia, in order to ascertain what the Jews in Russia themselves wanted. "What advice," he asked, "can be gained from emissaries who may be sent to Russia, for they do not know that vast land nor the situation of the Jews in it? . . . The Alliance should call people from Russia, not send them there."[69]

If the Alliance were to persist in its initially negative stance toward Palestine, it would unleash an internecine struggle among the Jews themselves. The natural leaders of the people, "its sages and writers,"[70] would fight for Palestine settlement even against the Alliance: "They will rise up against you in word and deed and you will cause a terrible war among us which [as in the time of Haskala] . . . will pit son against father, daughter against mother and will banish peace from every home and community."[71]

For many years, Smolenskin had worked closely with the Alliance, which had at times subsidized his journal and employed him as a special emissary to study conditions in eastern Europe. His description of the Alliance as potential traitor therefore has to be seen as yet another sign of major political upheaval.

Some political decisions, September–December 1881

Thus, by the autumn of 1881 the established Jewish leadership in St. Petersburg and Paris could no longer avoid making vital political decisions. In Brody, from September on, hundreds of new and destitute refugees were arriving every week. The colonization groups from Elizavetgrad and Odessa reached Brody in the months of October and November respectively and sought support. In Russia, an influential section of the literary intelligentsia, and many provincial leaders, were demanding from St. Petersburg a centrally organized and nationally motivated emigration policy. Abroad, Smolenskin insisted that the Alliance be guided by representatives of the Jewish people in Russia.

The St. Petersburg conference of Jewish representatives, which met early in September under the chairmanship of Baron Gintsburg, decided almost by default against the emigration thesis.[72] Many had assumed that this would be the major topic of dicussion, but, as explained by the report in the *Jewish Chronicle,* it was "entirely ignored in order not to excite the opposition of the Government."[73] It became apparent that the organizers of the conference saw in it primarily the most effective way of petitioning the regime, in the cause of equal rights or, at the very least, of communal security against violence. Hopefully, the tsar would receive a delegation from the conference. Of the chairman, the *Jewish Chronicle* wrote that "while possessing the *suaviter in modo* he has not to so great an extent the *fortiter in re* [and] hence the discussions wandered from the subject."[74]

In fact, however, the government dealt the conference a death blow. That the conference had received official sanction had generally been regarded as a hopeful sign. But while it was in session the delegates were thunderstruck by disastrous news – they received word of a memorandum authorized on 22 August and sent to the provincial governors by the ministry of the interior three days later.

The memorandum called for the establishment in each guberniia of commissions drawn from the local population to examine the causes of the pogroms and to recommend remedies. Representatives of the Jewish communities were to be invited to join the commissions.[75] But, in general, the memorandum judged the issue in advance and blamed the Jews for the pogroms, "recognizing the detriment caused to the Christian population of the Empire by the activity of the Jews, their tribal exclusiveness and religious fanaticism." Governmental efforts over a twenty-year period to bring about "a fusion of the Jews with the rest of the population," the memorandum declared, had not solved the problem, which had to be seen as essentially economic, "the exploitation [by the Jews] of the indigenous population and mostly of the poorer classes."[76] Thus, in effect, the commissions were called upon to recommend in which ways further to restrict Jewish economic life. Many delegates at the St. Petersburg conference saw here a transparent invitation to further pogroms and, at the very least, the memorandum signaled a change in government policy—initially it had feared revolutionary exploitation of mob violence, now it sought to ride the anti-Jewish wave itself.

Given this policy, it came as no surprise that Alexander III declined to meet with a Jewish delegation nor that permission was refused for the establishment of a standing committee to represent the Jewish people vis-à-vis the government. Delegates returned home in a mood of foreboding, aware that the conference had achieved nothing and that the government had given the St. Petersburg leadership a deliberate slap in the face.

Meanwhile, the Paris Alliance was moving to deal with the refugee problem. Under the direction of Isidore Loeb, its chief official, and on the advice of Charles Netter (for many years involved with the agricultural school at Mikve Yisrael near Jaffa), the Alliance refused adamantly to consider Palestine as a possible center for refugee settlement. Contacts were made with the Board of Delegates of the Union of American Hebrew Congregations in New York, which agreed to supervise the reception of refugees sent to the United States.[77] At the beginning of September, the Board of Delegates started a public fund for that purpose (the treasurer was De Witt J. Seligman of the well-known banking family).[78] At the same time, Dr. Schafier administered the dispatch of the first forty-six refugees sent from Brody at the expense of the Alliance.[79]

According to the understanding between the Alliance and the New York Board, five hundred Russian Jews were to be sent initially to the United States, a figure that followed logically from the conception of a highly selective and gradual emigration process.[80] But throughout the autumn the flow of destitute arrivals at Brody increased enormously. Writing from there on 13 October, Charles Netter (who had arrived a week earlier to help Schafier) stated that three thousand refugees had come since the beginning of September: "For every sixty people we process per day, a hundred newcomers arrive."[81] He himself was working for sixteen to eighteen hours a day; crowds of supplicants—mothers with their babies, children, families—pushed into his hotel ready to waylay him when he emerged at six in the morning and when he returned late at night. In one letter he wrote in desperation that it had taken him an hour to push through the crowd to the office and that in the crush he had literally been lifted off his feet several times. Rumors, exaggerated or false, of the plans of the Alliance were bringing ever greater numbers to Brody. "We must not fool ourselves," he wrote in his letter of the thirteenth, "the movement is only beginning . . . I would like all those who are hesitating to spend twenty-four hours here. The cause will be won!"[82]

By this time some two hundred and fifty Russian Jews had been sent to America. Under Netter's supervision, from 22 October to 20 November another thirteen hundred were sent in seven parties.[83] But the very scale of the operation proved its undoing. In his letter of 14 October Netter himself had written—in marked contrast to his letter of the previous day—that "at all costs the emigration must be stopped until we have dealt with those already on the lists."[84] When the sudden influx hit New York, the reaction there was equally panic-stricken. By mid-November the New York Board was demanding an immediate halt to the project. *The American Hebrew* of 2 December wrote that "the Alliance has been cabled to, and written to, but it seems that the emigration has virtually gone beyond their control. The Alliance is willing to furnish funds but they cannot limit the emigration."[85] Ten thousand dollars had been sent from Paris to supplement the some sixteen thousand already spent by the New York Board.[86] But, contrary to the newspaper report, the Alliance had yielded to the barrage of telegrams and (as stated in the December issue of its bulletin) had "committed itself formally to the Board in New York not to send any groups of Jews to America."[87] When Netter left Brody on 28 November, there were still over three thousand refugees there. They were encouraged to return to Russia. Money for travel expenses was made available and by January there were a mere one hundred remaining.

The impotence of the St. Petersburg conference and the extremely modest goals set itself by the Alliance both served to expose the high degree of illusion which had prevailed until then among those writers and public figures who supported the idea of organized emigration. That in time of crisis the Jewish people could unite on a common platform had been proved false. That the Jews in the West, who raised the funds, would let their use be decided by the Jews in the East had likewise been revealed as wishful thinking. These visions would recur periodically in Jewish politics over the coming decades and would continue to prove illusory, at least until 1948.

In contrast to the frustration of the literary intelligentsia – Smolenskin and Fridberg, Bogrov and Dubnov – the Odessa and Elizavetgrad groups of young colonists enjoyed (at least initially) a striking success. There was, of course, irony here. Men like Monye Bokol had no knowledge of the Jewish establishment in the West. Nonetheless, they had a number of advantages working in their favor.

They arrived in Brody with a concrete and limited plan: the establishment of agrarian colonies. Moreover, the fact that they had simply taken their fate into their own hands and left Russia presented the Jewish authorities in the West with something of a fait accompli. The Elizavetgrad group associated with German Rozental came in time to be included in the lists drawn up by Netter and were sent on their way to America at the expense of the Alliance.[88] But the Odessa group reached Brody too late and could well have been forced to return to Russia. Yet the combination of its youth and its agrarianism appealed to various individual leaders in the Jewish communities in the West, particularly to Dr. Landsberg (the rabbi of Liegnitz) and to Professor Bernstein (of the Alliance in Berlin). These men raised the funds necessary to send the first group of the Odessa Am Olam, some sixty-five in all, to New York in December.[89]

Once in the United States, these same factors continued to work in their favor. The Elizavetgrad group was dispatched immediately to Louisiana to settle land acquired for them largely at the expense of the organization just formed to deal with the sudden influx of Russian Jews, the Hebrew Emigrant Aid Society. Capital was also raised in New Orleans. The group was initially put up in a hotel in that city, where they were feted and were able to participate in a Hanuka celebration. It was, read one report in the Russian-Jewish press, "probably the first time that the streets of New Orleans rang with the melancholy but resounding melody of 'Down the Mother Volga.' "[90] Almost at once, the advance guard moved on to their land, a forty-hour trip up the Mississippi, on Sicily Island. The statutes of the settlement, officially entitled The First Agricultural Colony of Russian Israelites of the State of Louisiana, were drawn up on 28 December 1881 and published in *Russkii evrei* on

12 (24) February 1882. Until all the debts were paid off, the land and inventory were to be communally owned.[91] M. A. Kursheedt of the Hebrew Emigrant Aid Society even considered the colony to be established on "communistic" foundations,[92] but this was an exaggeration; the land was to be divided and worked individually.

The Odessa group coming later had a somewhat harder time of it but they too received land in the space of a few months. The group had approached the well-known socialist, Sergei Shevich, who translated their colonization proposal from Russian for the benefit of his comrade, Alexander Jonas, the editor of the German Social Democratic weekly in New York, *Volkszeitung*. He was impressed enough to introduce the leader of the group to Professor Adler, the founder of the Ethical Culture Society, whose enthusiasm for agrarian communes was widely known. In fact, according to the group's report, Jonas and Adler were finally won over when they learned that "we also want to set ourselves up only on a cooperative basis, that since the beginning of October we have been living from a communal budget, that we are determined to work only in farming."[93] Michael Heilprin, a leading figure in New York Jewish affairs and a veteran of the 1848 uprising in Hungary, also came to their aid, and by April 1882 they could announce in the Russian-Jewish press that New Odessa was to be founded in Oregon, that they would be setting sail for Portland and traveling via the Isthmus of Panama.[94]

The statutes of their planned colony were also published in *Russkii evrei* and were considerably more radical than those of the Elizavetgrad group. In New Odessa, common land ownership was established in perpetuity. Hired labor was totally forbidden. Trading was prohibited "except for the sale of products produced by personal labor." There was to be compulsory secular education for all children over six. Moreover, while members were permitted to farm plots of land individually, many of the group committed themselves to live on a fully communal – a "family" – basis. Within the commune "every member works according to his capacity and abilities and receives as far as possible according to his needs." The individual had no right to "refuse obligations placed on him by the 'family' " and all important decisions would be decided by simple majority vote at the general meeting. The only exception was the voting of members into or out of the commune, which required a two-thirds vote (new members were also subject to a one-year probationary period).[95]

The colony was planned initially for a membership of thirty to sixty people. But it was assumed that it would expand rapidly and perhaps reach a total membership of two thousand. Certainly, in the initial stages, the boldness of the action-oriented youth had paid dividends.

The emigration fever, January–May 1882

The negative decisions taken in the autumn of 1881 – the rebuff from the St. Petersburg conference and the refusal of the Alliance to continue the dispatch of Russian Jews to America after November – did not lead, as they might logically have done, to disillusionment with the emigration idea. On the contrary, the enthusiasm for a mass exodus from Russia reached its climax in the first four or five months of 1882.

Despite the setbacks, those factors which had produced the initial interest in an exodus continued to exert their influence, but with a redoubled force. Statements from leading government officials were becoming more threatening; the attacks against the Jewish people in the Russian press (whether on the patriotic right or the revolutionary left) more hysterical; the pogroms (even though less frequent) more far-flung and violent. Against this background, the vision of an exodus to the ancient homeland, or alternatively to the New World, shone all the brighter. The failures of 1881 were dismissed by most as merely temporary, a belief strongly reinforced by the constant reports of new and now much better organized efforts in the West to support the Jews in, and the refugees from, Russia. The feeling grew that despite, or even because of, the failure of its established leaders to act, the Jewish people in Russia was organizing itself politically, was taking its fate into its own hands. Mass excitement fed alike on rumor and reason, hope and despair.

Toward a mass exodus

As generally predicted and feared, the memorandum sent out by the ministry of the interior on 25 August 1881 ushered in a new phase in government policy. The local commissions provided an open and officially inspired platform for the expression of popular resentments and ethnic hatreds. It is true that, in a few cases, their final reports were relatively moderate (the Pale of Settlement which restricted Jewish settlement to their areas was, after all, often resented by the non-Jews who lived within it). But, in general, their conclusions reflected the now official line, which argued that if only for the sake of public order, the Jewish role in economic life had to be severely restricted. On 19 October a governmental committee was set up in the capital to receive the local reports and to propose appropriate remedies.[96]

Thus, until the publication of the Temporary Regulations on 2 May 1882, the Jewish population was held in suspense waiting for the legislative outcome of all this activity. Ignatev did nothing to calm the Jews. He granted frequent audiences to Jewish leaders but he offered no concrete solutions, preferring general speculations that could easily be read as threats. His frequent reference to the possibility of Jewish settlement in those areas of Central Asia recently acquired by Russia aroused especial alarm. It was feared that the government might expel Jews from western Russia, from all the villages, perhaps, or from all the border districts or from even more broadly defined areas, and send them to Turkestan. Large-scale expulsion in the autumn of 1881 from Orel, Tambov, Kiev, and Dubno lent credence to these fears. Those Jews, in particular S. S. Poliakov or Rabbi Shvabakher of Odessa, who took the Central Asian colonization project at its face value found themselves bitterly attacked. ("We do not have the rights of an animal," said Mandelshtam to Poliakov in April 1882 at the second Jewish conference, "and suddenly they let us go to Tashkent – no doubt only to finish us off there altogether.")[97]

Ignatev's statements on emigration from Russia created endless confusion. He would never permit organized emigration, he said in mid-1881. But early in January 1882 he indicated that perhaps he would do just that, and a few weeks later he again appeared to contradict himself.[98] Besides, he said, he thought it in the interest of the Jewish people that migration be directed to Palestine rather than America. Of course, as he said to Orshansky in January, emigration could only continue at all if "entire families move," if "among the emigrants there are no young people who have not fulfilled their military obligations," and if it be understood that those leaving automatically forfeited Russian citizenship.[99] This was interpreted to mean that it was desirable for Jews in large numbers to leave Russia but that the government preserved its right to arrest them at the frontier if it so chose. Those who sought to find an explanation for these contradictory, and often eccentric, statements generally concluded that Ignatev was hoping to be bought off by the St. Petersburg magnates. He was widely reported to have asked Baron Gintsburg to his face for a bribe of one or two million roubles – an offer which was not taken up.[100]

Provided with clear official sanction, the Russian press, led by *Rus* and *Novoe vremia*, no longer let a day pass without attacks on the Jewish population. To charges of economic exploitation there was now increasingly added the accusation that the Jews were guilty of international conspiracy to dominate the world. This theory was not new; Iakov Brafman had assiduously disseminated it throughout the reign of Alexander II, particularly in his *Kniga kagala* (The Kahal Book), first published in 1869, but it now became a major theme in the press campaign. The Alliance israélite universelle was described as the spider at the center of the conspiratorial web, Hebrew as its secret language, and the remnants of Jewish self-government, the kahal, as its local manifestation in the Russian empire. Jewish spokesmen, rabbis and writers, sought to refute these charges by detailed evidence, but confidence in the power of facts to convince was fast disappearing. An awareness was dawning that even in modern times a national minority could be helpless in the face of attacks from within the majority nationality, attacks backed by paranoia and patriotism at its most primitive, by narrowly defined economic self-interest. Commenting on the ceaseless demands that the Jews be excluded from many branches of the economy, even *Russkii evrei*, which throughout sought to maintain a calm rationality, revealed a mood of desperation:

> What can the Jews do then? Let them do what they want. Let them flee from Russia. Let them die of hunger. Let them cover the plains of North and South America with their corpses. From the point of view of Mr. Samarin [in *Novoe vremia*] it is unpatriotic to worry about what the Jews, the aliens [*inorodtsy*], will live from.[101]

Against this background of incitement, from the regime and the press, it caused no surprise that pogroms flared up sporadically during the latter half of 1881. In November, the arrival of the famous French actress, Sarah Bernhardt, sparked off disturbances in Odessa, where the word had spread that she was a Jewess. Her carriage was stoned; Jewish homes were looted. But nothing that had happened hitherto prepared anybody for the news of the massive pogrom in Warsaw in mid-December. Some fifteen hundred homes, shops, and synagogues were sacked before the troops intervened. Hitherto, the outbreaks of violence had been regarded as a purely south Russian phenomenon; but if they had now reached Warsaw – the most European of cities in the empire – no Jew could feel safe.[102]

The most destructive and bloody episode of the entire period was, however, still to come. On 29–30 March 1882, a pogrom raged in the largely Jewish town of Balta in Podolia. It had long been anticipated, and a rudimentary self-defense organization had been formed under the leadership of Eliezer Mashbir, a young teacher in the city (who came originally from Mohilev). But the police intervened to disarm the few groups which tried to defend themselves. Some five thousand peasants poured into the city to join in the pillage and by the second day all but thirty Jewish homes had been looted or destroyed. Some forty Jews had been killed, maimed, or seriously wounded.[103]

In short, fear – of the known and still more of the unknown – had become a central factor in Jewish life in Russia by the end of 1881. But in itself fear would not have won over a large part of the Russian-Jewish intelligentsia to the idea of a mass exodus. At work here was also the widespread belief that positive factors existed which could make organized emigration a realistic alternative.

First, because the numbers were so small and the time-span so short, large-scale emigration and settlement had hardly been put to the test in 1881. Reports reaching Russia from the first wave of organized emigrants (the fifteen hundred sent by the Alliance to America in 1881) tended initially to be optimistic. As already noted, those seeking to establish colonies had been assigned land. Others were tided over by the American-Jewish welfare organizations until they could find work. A report sent from New York and published in *Russkii evrei* in December 1881 stated that skilled artisans were earning up to fifty dollars a week; and that the unskilled were being sent to "special agricultural farms where for a year they will receive clothing, food, will learn farming skills and the English language . . . It is enough to see the happiness of these people, who have suffered and are now being looked after, to weep tears of joy with them."[104]

Nothing had happened, either, to disillusion those who believed that Palestine was the most suitable destination. As yet no large numbers of emigrants had attempted to settle there. The fast-burgeoning schemes had in no way been measured against reality. In this sense, the refusal of the Alliance to send any Jews to Palestine, other than a few children destined for the Mikve Yisrael school, served to increase its hold on the imagination. The negative estimate of the Alliance was more than counterbalanced by the knowledge that a number of highly placed Englishmen, not even Jews, regarded a return to Palestine as an eminently practical scheme. In particular, Laurence Oliphant's plan for Jewish settlement on the east bank of the Jordan, as presented in his book of 1880, *Land of Gilead,* was taken as eyewitness proof that here was no utopia. In 1882 Oliphant was to find himself drawn personally into the maelstrom of Russian-Jewish politics.

True, the Alliance had backed away from its emigration projects in November 1881. But it soon became apparent that this decision signaled not so much the end of the campaign in the West on behalf of the refugees (and Russian Jews in general) but rather a pause for regroupment. Two new organizations now emerged, the Hebrew Emigrant Aid Society in New York and the Mansion House Relief Fund in London, and they, rather than the Alliance, aroused the greatest expectations in early 1882.

The Hebrew Emigrant Aid Society (HEAS) of the United States was founded at a meeting held in New York on 27 November 1881. Its initial goal was simply to create a full-time staff to handle the wave of immigrants sent by Charles Netter from Brody. Jacob Schiff was only persuaded to support the establishment of the society when it was pointed out that large numbers of Russian Jews were stranded miserably at the Castle Garden disembarkation point with nobody to help them; volunteer aid had proved inadequate. Ironically, the HEAS was founded at the very moment when the Alliance had decided to halt further emigration. Far from declaring itself redundant, however, it immediately began to initiate a major immigration scheme of its own.[105]

In its plan, the society suggested that initially ten thousand Russian Jews be settled on the land in the United States at a total cost of one million dollars. Armed with this proposal, Moritz Ellinger, an ex-coroner of the City of New York, was sent as the emissary of the society, first across the United States to found local branches and then early in January across the Atlantic to raise money.[106] A report, first published in October 1881,[107] that Baron Hirsch (the Austrian-Jewish banker) was prepared to donate immediately one million francs for the resettlement of the Russian Jews overseas, had apparently inspired the idea that very large sums could be raised in Europe for agricultural colonization. From January until March, Ellinger toured western Europe advocating the plan to the local Jewish communities.

The American project reflected both the long tradition of agrarianism associated with the settlement of the West – the hope was expressed that the immigrants would emulate the large groups of Mennonites who had come as farmers from Russia in the 1870s – and also the contemporary capitalist faith. Ellinger said of the HEAS plan that "this matter is [not] . . . a great charity; it must be conducted as a great business."[108] For its part, the British counterpart of the HEAS, the Mansion House Committee, was the product of a political crusade, that explosion of public outrage so favored by high Victorian England.

British Jewry reacted slowly to the events in Russia. Apart from desultory fund-raising,[109] the Jewish leadership had done little else than make periodic representations to Her Majesty's Government (questions were raised in Parliament by the president of the Anglo-Jewish Association, the Baron Henry de Worms, and a delegation went to see the Foreign Secretary, Lord Granville, in May).[110] As Gladstone was adamantly opposed to taking any steps which might exacerbate relations with Russia, these measures were necessarily ineffectual. It was only on 6 November that a joint conference of members of the Board of Deputies and the Anglo-Jewish Association met to discuss the crisis and form a committee to take any measures it deemed necessary. (Sir Nathaniel de Rothschild was the chairman of the Russian-Jewish Committee and Dr. A. Asher its secretary).[111]

Even then, apart from periodic meetings of the committee held in camera, no visible steps were taken for at least another two months. This inaction became the source of growing criticism among the Jewish public in England, where the arrival of Russian immigrants en route from Brody to Liverpool and hence to North America had aroused considerable interest. In particular, pride was expressed at the fact that there was a "vast difference between the real Russian Jew of Kiev, Odessa and Elizavetgrad and the Polish Jew with whom we are brought in contact at our local Board of Guardians . . . He stands erect, has no mannerisms at all, dresses entirely in a European manner . . . They [are] blacksmiths, bricklayers, masons."[112]

Such reports were important in reassuring the British Jews, who tended to share the opinion frequently expressed in the editorials of the *Jewish Chronicle* that the migration of "the raw unfledged Polak,"[113] of "the swarm of Polish Jews" was the root cause of antisemitism in Rumania, in Germany (where "they vex the soul of Professor Treitschke")[114] and indeed throughout the world.

In Britain the most articulate statements and impassioned plea for united action by the Jews of the West came in a series of articles published under the pseudonym Jurisconsultus. Those Jews, argued Jurisconsultus, "who occupy the highest place, social and official, in each country should . . . combine for the Defence of the Jewish People." Unfortunately, he added, there was a widespread

> notion that it is not wise for the Jews to obtrude themselves, even for defensive purposes, upon governments, or peoples, or public opinion or the press . . . But I beg to remind you that the Jew is quite as conspicuous when he crouches as when he stands erect . . . Sir, the Jews of Russia are at this very hour living under sentence of death . . . But it is the Jews of France, of Italy, of Austria, of Germany and of England, above all, who are on their trial.[115]

Early in 1882 the tempo of protest, stimulated by the Warsaw pogrom, began to quicken. In the second week of January, the *Times* published a long, two-part article analyzing the nature and scope of pogroms and the role of the tsarist government.[116] (The material had been supplied by the Russian-Jewish Committee, which proceeded to publish it as a separate brochure). The article in the *Times* stimulated a growing demand for a series of public protest meetings, a demand advanced most vociferously by the Jews of Birmingham. (At a meeting in that city on 22 January, it was stated that the London leadership was "too much rocked in the cradle of luxury. . . It was not London that passed the Reform Bill. It was Birmingham that told the Lords in no mistakable voice that they would have either reform or revolution.")[117]

Finally, on 1 February 1882 a large public meeting under the chairmanship of the Lord Mayor of London did assemble in the Mansion House. The list of speakers and the oratory were both suitably impressive. Among those who addressed the gathering were the Bishop of London, Professor Bryce, Lord Shaftesbury, and Cardinal Manning. All went to great pains to stress that the meeting in no way intended hostility either to the Liberal government or to the Russian state. But, they declared, the voice of conscience could not remain mute in the face of atrocities wherever they were committed. (There were still those who hoped that Gladstone would abandon his passivity and display, at least in some measure, the fervor he had invested in defense of the Bulgarians only a few years before.) As described in the *Jewish Chronicle,* it was "the fullest, most enthusiastic and one of the most influential of public meetings which the Mansion House officials remember."[118] Similar public meetings were held in the month of February in most of the major cities across the country, and the British press was suddenly filled with articles roundly condemning the pogroms.

The Mansion House Relief Fund had been launched at the meeting and quickly reached impressive figures; by mid-February a sum of £50,000 had been raised.[119] (This in turn stimulated the creation of an ad hoc committee in Paris headed by Victor Hugo and Baron Alphonse de Rothschild, which soon collected 800,000 francs).[120] The Mansion House funds were administered by an ad hoc committee which was usually chaired by the Lord Mayor or Cardinal Manning but was mainly attended by leaders of the Jewish community (the Chief Rabbi, Dr. Adler, A. Asher, J. Sebag, I. Seligman, and Samuel Montagu). Its first important decision was taken in mid-February: Laurence Oliphant (who had volunteered his services) was to be sent to Galicia in order to examine the situation of the refugees there, to select those suitable for dispatch to the United States, and to recommend what should be done with the remainder.[121]

In Russia itself it was possible to follow the activities of the Hebrew Emigrant Aid Society and the Mansion House Committee through the frequent reports in the local Jewish press. Additional publicity was given to the British protest movement by such papers as *Novoe vremia*, which struck out angrily both at the meddling foreigners abroad and at the Jews at home (who were blamed for disseminating slanders against their native land).

The inevitable effect of the initiatives launched in New York and London, once news of them reached Russia, was to stimulate a new stampede of destitute refugees toward the frontier. As with the Alliance in 1881, this had hardly been the intention of the new committees. Oliphant had instructions to select only small groups of people suited to agricultural or other physical labor. But the numbers speak for themselves. In January 1882 there were about one hundred refugees left in Brody; in March there were reportedly some fourteen hundred there; by 1 May there were about six thousand; and by the end of the month more than double that. In fact, seven thousand were believed to have arrived in the first week of May alone. Refugees were reported to be sleeping thirty or forty in a room, crowded together in synagogues, or in the streets.[122]

This flow of people, far larger in size than that of 1881, fed on the intrigue and rumors which so easily flourished among the ill-informed and desperate sections of the population. Self-styled emissaries of the Alliance circulated from town to town selling false travel and settlement arrangements. Agents of the Atlantic shipping companies were thought to be actively spreading mythical stories. Reports from Zhitomir spoke of a widespread belief there in the "imminent expulsion of all the Jews" from Russia.[123] " 'Emigration', 'to emigrate', 'America,' etc. – these words and concerns," wrote the Zhitomir correspondent, "have caught up all sections of our population, starting with the rich and educated and ending with the poorest types of artisan."[124] In April, S. P. Rabinovich could report that a sizeable number of people were leaving his city, too, even though the local Jews, as he put it, "have always been ready to think that there is no salvation outside Warsaw."[125] From Odessa, it was reported that the young people preferred to leave for the United States married rather than single and that one hundred and seventy-five weddings had been performed there in one day.[126] (In his memoirs, Abe Cahan was to recall that this phenomenon carried over to Brody, where a contrapuntal note to the overcrowding and undernourishment was provided by the constant wedding celebrations).[127]

Faced with the rush across the frontier into Galicia, the Western organizations, particularly the Paris Alliance and the Mansion House Committee, had to decide between two possible courses of action. They could stand firm on the principles enunciated by the Alliance late in 1881. A select group of refugees would be sent to the United States and settled there in full cooperation with the New York Hebrew Emigrant Aid Society. The remainder would meanwhile be provided with the minimal aid required to keep body and soul together until they could be repatriated to

Russia. This was (and remained throughout) the position of the French and American committees.[128] As against this, the Mansion House Committee was initially strong in its opposition to returning refugees to the Russia of Ignatev and of Balta. Therefore, it found itself committed, faute de mieux, to the dispatch of the refugees to the United States.

An international conference held in Berlin on 23–24 April to iron out a united policy produced an agreement on the technical division of functions between the local committees: Vienna was to be responsible for the selection of suitable emigrants; Berlin for their transportation to England; London for their travel to the United States and for liaison with the American end of the transit chain; New York for their reception and distribution in America; and Paris for researching the possibility of settling Russian Jews in countries other than the United States.[129] It is not necessary to read far between the lines to see that this arrangement represented a takeover by the Mansion House Committee and a retreat to the sidelines by the Alliance in Paris.

For weeks before this conference met, Laurence Oliphant had been in Brody, selecting emigrants and sending them on their way to America. He was joined there on 26 April by Dr. Asher and Samuel Montagu, who with the aid of the Jewish committees in Brody and Lemberg established a selection machinery to speed up the whole process. By June 1882 three trains a week, each carrying about three hundred refugees, were leaving Brody en route to the North Sea ports.[130] All in all, from April until the end of June, the Mansion House Committee sent some eight thousand Jews at its expense to the United States.[131] But, of course, this was not a static process. The more who were sent, the more came.

The literary intelligentsia in a leadership role

The inaction of the traditional Jewish leadership in St. Petersburg – standing in such marked contrast to the bustle of activity in the West – thrust the literary intelligentsia increasingly onto the center of the stage. Where earlier the writers had sought to pressure others into making decisions, they now initiated, or tried to initiate policies of their own.[132]

That the initiative was passing out of the hands of the St. Petersburg magnates could be discerned immediately after the September conference in the capital. When Rabbi Yitshak Elhanan Spektor returned from the conference to Kovno with detailed knowledge of the Ignatev memorandum, he was persuaded by his assistant that the time had come to alert public opinion abroad to what was happening. Spektor's initial thought was to consult with Baron Gintsburg, Poliakov, and Bakst, but the failure of the conference had undermined their authority. Instead, he turned to those writers with whom he was in contact throughout the Pale of Settlement – Levin, Lilienblum, Fridberg, S. P. Rabinovich – and asked them to supply him with detailed accounts, backed by eyewitness evidence, of the pogroms in their areas. At frequent intervals reports were now written up and smuggled in various ways, sometimes through Dr. Rülf in Memel, to Dr. Asher in London. (The first letter, which included the text of the Ignatev memorandum of 22 August, was printed in Hebrew in the traditional form of a rabbinical legal opinion.)[133]

In his memoirs, Y. L. Levin recalled how he had used the contacts of the Kiev relief committee to collect the accurate information required. It was this and similar material which alerted the Jewish leaders in the West to the change in governmental policy and eventually formed the basis for the two-part article in the London *Times*. (Or, as Dr. Asher put it in a Hebrew letter to the Kovno rabbi: "We have blown the shofar across the land and its sounds have been heard on high.")[134] The truth of the *Times* articles was vigorously denied by the tsarist government, both in the official *Journal de St. Pétersburg* of 22 January 1882 and also by a special press representative sent to London. And at Asher's request, a mass of additional facts (on the number of rapes, on the openly hostile role of the authorities during the pogroms) were collected in the south, relayed to London, and there published.[135]

Their success in arousing public opinion, especially in Great Britain, undoubtedly surpassed the expectations of those who had initiated the scheme, and the writers thus had grounds for their belief that they, with Spektor, had been the first to take any effective action in the crisis. (As they wrote to Baron Gintsburg in April 1882: "The voice of the congregation of Israel . . . came to our ears: 'Save us! Help us!' And there was no savior and there was nobody to help."[136] It had fallen to them alone to alert the outside world.)

This episode by its nature went unpublicized at the time and has received little attention since (neither Dubnov nor Gessen mentioned it in their histories). As against this, the attempt by the weekly *Razsvet* to bypass the traditional leadership in St. Petersburg and build up its own base of support in the provinces was of necessity a highly public development. As such it constituted a key factor in the political turmoil of early 1882.

On 16 January, Ignatev received for an interview Dr. Ilia Orshansky, a well-known figure in the Jewish community of Ekaterinoslav who was now to join the staff of *Razsvet*. What the minister of the interior said to him, as Aleksandr Tsederbaum was quick to point out, was in no particular way new.[137] Since September he had been telling Jewish leaders that "the western frontier is open for the Jews" and that the Pale of Settlement would "be preserved inviolate" except for the possible colonization of "sparsely populated areas."[138] Orshansky asked him to permit "the Jewish intelligentsia in Russia . . . to come to the aid of the poverty-stricken population and to take the lead in resettlement [*pereselenie*] both outside Russia and within the empire,"[139] but on this issue Ignatev would not commit himself.

What rendered this interview sensational was not so much its content as the decision taken by the editor of *Razsvet* to publish the news of it immediately in a special supplement. Hitherto, interviews with Ignatev had been either kept entirely secret or, at most, reported through mere hints in the press. The sudden transmission to the Jewish people at large of information hitherto known definitely only to a few – words addressed, as it were, directly from Ignatev – had a shock effect. Later, many came to see *Razsvet*'s decision to rush the interview off the press as the most decisive cause of the subsequent mass move to Brody.

But *Razsvet* had chosen this course deliberately enough. The time had come, it wrote in a series of editorials, to treat the current events for what they were – a major crisis – and to seek the instruments required to deal with it: the full legalization and organization of emigration. A committee representative of the Jewish people in Russia should be established to control the flow of emigrants and to select the country most suitable for mass resettlement. Such decisions should be taken by the Jews in Russia, who were personally involved, not by those in the West.

The attempt by *Razsvet* to direct events met with a rough reception. Predictably enough, it was violently opposed by Gintsburg, Poliakov, and their respective circles of advisers, who launched a systematic attempt to undermine the paper.[140] Predictably, too, given the existence of fierce journalistic rivalry, the initiative was greeted with scepticism by the other Jewish weeklies in the capital. *Russkii evrei* even wrote that "we have, it would seem, already suffered enough from various false messiahs."[141] But doubts about the wisdom of establishing an emigration committee also came from less expected quarters. Within the emigration camp itself there were those who argued that such a committee might well fall under government domination (the Jews had no machinery for selecting a representative body and the tsarist bureaucracy was notoriously rapacious); and the government, capriciously reversing itself, could well exploit the existing laws in order to punish those involved in fostering emigration. As Lilienblum put it caustically in a letter to Y. L. Levin on 20 March 1882, if the government were ever to obtain a list of would-be emigrants it "would collect all those people and send them forcibly to Turkestan, because nothing is impossible these days."[142]

But the *Razsvet* group (Rozenfeld, Ha-Cohen, Orshansky) were deeply convinced that their case was strong, that the Russian-Jewish people had a right to information and leadership. They saw themselves as the champions of the people against the oligarchs. "We had thought," wrote Orshansky, "that an entire people are not children and that nobody among us has the right to decide whether or not the Jews be informed of their position at any given moment."[143] In its editorial of 1 February *Razsvet* formulated its challenge boldly:

> Only the provinces can and must decide whether the Jews have to fear the words "emigration" and "emigration committee" or not, and only they can decide which is better – a secret, disorderly emigration of a mass of half-starving people . . . or [one] that is conducted openly, that collects funds publicly, supports the indigent and directs the emigration in the direction – and to the extent – which are desirable.[144]

By taking this stand, *Razsvet* became the center and the symbol of the fast-spreading resentment against the St. Petersburg magnates. In a letter to Akselrod, a Kiev student could write in February that the Russian-Jewish people was now divided into two warring camps – the one led by *Razsvet* was for emigration, the other, represented by *Russkii evrei* and Baron Gintsburg, was "bourgeois" and against it. "Actually," he added, "Gintsburg would like the mass of Jews to emigrate but he would like it done in his way, secretly, so that he could declare his loyal feelings and attachment to Russia and so gain equal rights."[145] *Razsvet*, wrote Moshe Aizman a few months later, was in the national camp together with the new youth parties (Am Olam, Bilu) and with such writers as Lilienblum while ranged against them were the "cosmopolitans" in the form of *Russkii evrei*, *Voshkod*, the Alliance in Paris, and Bogrov, who had early come out against the plan for an official emigration committee.[146]

In an article in *Razsvet* significantly entitled "The Capital and the Provinces," a correspondent from Kharkov asked in April why "that section of the Jewish intelligentsia and of the Jewish masses which consider regulation of the emigration absolutely necessary" could not simply take over the leadership itself.[147] He pointed out that in a large number of towns – Kremenchug, Kharkov, Suvalki, Kiev, Simferopol, Konoton, Balta, Vladimir-Volynskii – groups of Jews, sometimes entire communities, had banded together to despatch emissaries to Palestine in order to examine the possibilities for settlement there or even to buy land. These spontaneous initiatives, he wrote, showed that the provinces represented an independent political entity. Drawing on them, it would be possible to assemble a conference of "true popular delegates."[148]

However, by far the most explosive article in this confrontation, that of Y. L. Levin, was published not in *Razsvet* but in *Ha-melits* of 9 March 1882. In it he revealed how that same populist passion, a contempt for the wealthy and mighty, which had made him the ally of Liberman and the Russian revolutionary movement in the 1870s, could now appear unchanged in the service of a cause more national than social.

"There were days," he wrote, "when we were tied to our 'aristocrats' and saw them as leaders of the people . . . In all times of trouble, we turned to them . . . ; in our eyes they were like the nurse to the infant and in their eyes, too."[149] But now they, the traditional leaders, were fighting the emigration cause in the name of a higher loyalty to the motherland, to Russia. They refused, he insisted, to see that emigration for the masses was now a matter of necessity, not of choice:

> We, the masses of the people . . . have loved our land more than you, we have made greater sacrifices for it. Our sons spilled their blood on the battlefields of our country; we carried a heavier load of taxes . . . ; we were like nails driven into our land and we knew no other . . . ; day in, day out we strove to draw near to the indigenous population but, look, they are attacking us with crowbars . . . We are leaving because we are forced to.[150]

Orshansky had done nothing more than his duty in telling the truth to the people and yet

> the men of power are ganging up on him; they see in him a hindrance to their own position and are shouting: "Who put you at the head? Who empowered you to talk?" – because they, the aristocrats, had not anointed him . . . But Orshansky is not from above the people but from within the people . . . and so he can speak in its name.[151]

He concluded on a harsher note still: "Get you away from the people! Let our brothers in distress see that they have nobody to rely on but themselves."[152]

That Aleksandr Tsederbaum should have published such an incendiary article was remarkable but understandable. The months of March and April saw the emigration fever reach its high point and Tsederbaum, who had the reputation of being a trimmer, was yielding to what he felt to be the overwhelming force of an aroused public.

Each of the two camps sought to prove that it had public opinion on its side. The St. Petersburg leadership was convinced that at all costs the Russian-Jewish people must refute the charge of disloyalty. In the St. Petersburg synagogue on 18 January, Dr. Drabkin, the widely respected rabbi, told the large mass of people there assembled that the minister of the interior was requesting that the Russian Jews publicly protest against "the British intervention" on their behalf, that they reaffirm their allegiance to tsar and country. Fierce arguments broke out in the synagogue, with the students vehemently opposed to acquiescence and the older people largely in favor.[153]

Thus, apparently, began the war of the petitions and letters. Word went around that the agents and supporters of Baron Gintsburg in the provinces were collecting signatures to a memorandum to be presented to Ignatev rejecting the emigration concept. On the other side, collective letters – to Drabkin, to the Jewish press – were drawn up accusing the St. Petersburg leadership of cowardice or worse.[154] In contrast to the similar effort of August 1881, the literary intelligentsia did not have to carry the project on its shoulders alone; on the contrary, the lead was now taken by the students. "We have decided," read the letter from Akselrod's student friend in Kiev, "to explain to the people [narod] all the devious calculations of Gintsburg and so hinder his plan and also to protest officially against it (via a letter from the students to the press)."[155] And another letter from Russia sent shortly afterwards to the Jewish Chronicle spoke of the "profound impression" made "by an appeal which a number of students and young authors have addressed to the influential Jews in Russia. They brand in scathing language the selfish conduct of many wealthy Jews and impress upon them the necessity of affording their poorer brethren the means of seeking new and peaceful homes in Palestine."[156]

The news in March that the St. Petersburg leadership was planning to call a select group of notables to a second conference similar to that of September 1881, but now with the emigration question as central to the agenda, produced a further flurry of letters. M. M. Dolitsky, the young and emotional Hebrew poet, circulated a petition in protest: "The representatives . . . are not our [the people's] delegates and so of course we will not recognize them as our intermediaries in the question of emigration. And just as we oppose the way in which it is organized so we will oppose the action that is taken."[157]

Under pressure from Lilienblum, who held to a moderating stance throughout, Levin, Fridberg, S. P. Rabinovich, and other writers decided to address a private appeal to Baron Gintsburg couched in relatively calm language, although the accusatory note remained clear enough. "Today," they wrote in their letter of 10 April,

> when statesmen like Shaftesbury and General Grant, great scientists like Tyndall and Darwin, spiritual leaders like Manning and Farrar have decided unanimously that we have no hope except emigration, now when a mighty spiritual turnabout has taken place among the idealistic youth . . . and they are seeking new lands, returning to their people and their God, when the sons are returning to their fathers . . . , when our brothers are leaving in their hundreds and thousands . . . now when the people fears that it has no future in this country, when the rule of law has given way to mob law . . . , now we see once again that its leading figures have not followed the people but have buried their faces in the sand. They are not ready to fight for the survival of the people.[158]

This collective letter was composed as the tide was in full flow. On 14 March 1882, Y. Y. Levontin, a student in Moscow, could write to his brother Zalman David, then already in Palestine, in the following terms:

When we were in Kremenchug [in 1881] could we imagine that the Palestine idea would be taken up by all our people? Then I was still torn in two directions. But if only you could read all that is now written in *Razsvet*. All the people is in a state of agitation, it will not rest until it has left Russia. There is no town large or small without its people ready to leave for Palestine or America ... without its committees, its colonization projects, fundraising, bureaus, programs.[159]

In this highly charged atmosphere it is not surprising that those opposed to the emigration movement found themselves at times threatened with physical force. In Kharkov, a youth group committed to the cause of Palestinian colonization demanded financial contributions on pain of death.[160] A letter from Minsk to Y. L. Levin described how twenty Jewish farmers from the neighboring area who were about to leave for Palestine had appeared to demand support from the richer Jews in the town and were threatening to "smash all their windows, to cast mud at them in the streets, to stone them, attack them, loot them." Levin's young correspondent added hopefully: "If only this really happens and they [the rich] suffer total defeat."[161]

This upsurge of collective enthusiasm within the Jewish world, combined as it was with intolerable pressures from without, was bound to produce a mixed reaction – self-doubt, anger – from those under attack. L. O. Kantor, the editor of *Russkii evrei*, became very defensive, pointing out in correspondence with his friends among the Hebrew writers that his paper had throughout supported the idea of individual as against organized emigration.[162] And his paper even published a report from the provinces on the widespread resentment there at the fact that the delegates to the April conference were "not elected by the Jewish population but in most cases are designated by the Petersburg millionaires."[163] In contrast, G. M. Rabinovich, one of the proprietors of the paper, refused to give ground and attacked the more extreme forms of pressure as so much empty bombast. "Some supporters of emigration," he declared at the second St. Petersburg conference,

threaten us with internal disturbances ... But, gentlemen, fortunately we do not have a *narod* in its fashionable sense, meaning the antipode and rival of the intelligentsia, although, unfortunately, and to our shame, among us are beginning to appear *narodniki* who would very much like to arouse in the people a distrust for the educated class ... [But] our masses are extremely sober and generally literate; therefore they are completely unsuitable material for various uprisings and disturbances.[164]

The St. Petersburg magnates remained unmoved by the turmoil, and the outcome of the second conference, held in mid-April, was similar to the first. However, on this occasion, votes were taken and formal resolutions carried. The conference rejected totally "the idea of organized emigration as being inimical to the dignity of the Russian body politic and to the historic rights of the Jews in their present fatherland."[165] And it called on the government to grant the Jews equal rights, to

79

suppress the pogroms more vigorously, and to find means to compensate the victims. (The concept of Jewish colonization in Central Asia transmitted from Ignatev by Poliakov was acrimoniously rejected.)

A small group of those attending, again led by Mandelshtam of Kiev, voted against the resolution condemning the emigration idea. But there was no chance that the hand-picked conference (almost half the delegates were from the capital) would oppose the combined opinion of Gintsburg, Poliakov, and others who could claim inside knowledge of governmental intentions. Whether because of its conservatism (or inertia), divided counsels, fear of foreign opinion, or pressure from mercantile interest groups – or, most probably, a combination of all these factors – the regime was not ready to come out openly in favor of organized emigration. The result of the conference was thus a foregone conclusion.

It was condemned out of hand, of course, by the emigration camp. *Razsvet* described "the touchingly harmonious orchestra of the provincials overawed by the wisdom of the capital,"[166] and another critic wrote later in the year that "it was reminiscent of the Russian *zemskii sobor* under the tsars of the sixteenth and seventeenth centuries – when those boyars who lived in Moscow were *all* invited while from the provinces only two were sent from each town."[167]

But the time was long past when criticism alone would suffice. Clearly the rebels now had to prove their mettle and substantiate their claim that theirs was the voice of the people. And in a letter of 6 May 1882, Y. Y. Levontin could inform his brother in Jaffa that Rozenfeld, the proprietor of *Razsvet*, was in fact trying to arrange a rival conference which would provide the emigration movement with the organizational direction it clearly required.[168] Another source reported more specifically that Rozenfeld was "planning to call a congress somewhere in the provinces to unite the existing *kruzhki*, to create a joint-stock [colonization] company. And at that point, in his view, emigration should begin."[169]

This latter report came from Odessa at the end of May; Rozenfeld was there en route to Constantinople. The purpose of his journey was to observe at first hand the quasi-diplomatic negotiations being conducted with the Turkish government in the cause of Jewish settlement in Palestine. Rozenfeld's mission was financed by a group in Moscow and he was accompanied by Moisei Kamensky, who was mandated by a group in Kremenchug to purchase land in Palestine on its behalf[170] (this was the Kamensky who had provided Liberman with financial support for his *Ha-emet*).

Although a number of prominent personages were in contact with the Turkish government on the Palestine issue – Edward Cazalet was trying to negotiate an agreement combining railway concessions with Jewish settlement – the attention of the Russian Jews was almost exclusively fixed on Laurence Oliphant, and it was mainly to see Oliphant that Rozenfeld had considered it necessary to leave Russia at so crucial a juncture. The fact that even before the pogroms Oliphant had advocated a Jewish return to Palestine, that he knew that country intimately, that he was a prominent explorer and well connected in British governmental and royal circles, that he had been the first representative of the Mansion House Committee to reach Brody and review the transport of the refugees to the United States, that at the same time he was known to regard Palestine as a preferable long-term alternative, and finally that in May he had proceeded to Constantinople, where he was actually negotiating with the Turkish government for the grant of large areas in Palestine for Jewish settlement – all this was known in Russia and had made an enormous impression.

Unlimited hopes were placed in Oliphant's ability to negotiate a pact with the Turkish government. There was a widespread belief that Turkey was in such serious financial straits that it would be more than willing to sell Palestine for a negotiable sum of money. In a letter of 10 May, David Gordon even suggested to Y. L. Levin that Oliphant himself was "ready to spend all his own capital for the good of settling Palestine and for the Jewish people."[171] And a report in *Russkii evrei* stated confidently that Oliphant was going to Turkey "to gain self-rule and a national militia for the Jews."[172] When Rozenfeld and Kamensky set sail on the *Rossiia* en route to see Oliphant, a crowd of two thousand people came to see them off at the pier in Odessa. M. L. Lilienblum was among those in that city who met with Rozenfeld before he left. He, too, despite his deep vein of scepticism, believed briefly that Oliphant would be "the Messiah for Israel."[173]

In Constantinople, Oliphant found himself besieged by an increasing stream of Russian Jews. Some came to seek his opinion on the emigration issue. Others were en route to Palestine. By May 1882, hundreds of families had sold their belongings and set sail for that country. He was also inundated by letters. One such letter, typical of many, came from a group of *Palestintsy* in Nikolaev. "We, the people," read this statement, "are for you and follow you! We will follow you down into the depths of the sea and into the barren desert knowing that you, like God's fiery column of old, will lead us to the [promised] land . . . Yes, sir, this is our faith and faith makes miracles!"[174]

Rozenfeld did not return to Russia until July 1882. His plans for a conference representative of the emigration camp remained unchanged, but the situation he found on his return was very different from the one he had left in May.

The literary intelligentsia in its prophetic role

The emergence of the literary intelligentsia as a major force in Jewish politics in 1882 can, then, be explained in functional terms. The traditional leadership, the St. Petersburg "oligarchy," had been cut off from the ultimate source of its authority, the tsarist government. At the same time, political parties had as yet not become a recognized force in the Russian Jewish world. As in similar contexts in modern European history – Mazzini and his circle during the 1840s, Masaryk in World War I, the Petöfi Club in 1956 – the literary intelligentsia was thrust into a political role.

Yet, ultimately, its authority, its influence, would stand or fall not on its organizational ability but on the way in which it analyzed the political crisis, explained its historical meaning, and offered long-term solutions to it. The existence of an influential Jewish press had provided it with a forum in which to take on the prophetic role.

Provided with this opportunity the writers divided, broadly speaking, into three different categories. There were those who saw the crisis as an opportunity, the prelude to the long-awaited return of the Jewish nation to its ancient homeland; there were those who discovered in it, above all, a profound threat, a threat that could ultimately endanger the existence of the Jewish people; and there were those who saw it as an essentially transient phenomenon, the significance of which should not be recklessly exaggerated. Some donned the prophetic mantle; others felt it forced upon them; still others shunned it.

In the first category, Peretz Smolenskin remained throughout the most prominent figure. As described above, he had first made his plea for a Jewish return to Palestine in the summer of 1881. Prior to that date he had argued that to talk in these terms was premature and irresponsible. Against the young Eliezer Ben Yehuda he had written early in 1881 that while "the *hope* of redemption" must be retained, "the redemption itself is still far distant from us."[175] The cultural and ethical – not the political – tradition of the Jews had always constituted the core of the national heritage: "Everybody who loves his people will say that its law and its spirit are dearer to us than our land . . . We lived in our own country for only eight hundred years and not always at peace together and for the main part we lusted after idols and polluted the land."[176] To try to "rebuild the ruins of Zion and Jerusalem," he had then written against Ben Yehuda, was to seek to "build a tower on a roof before the house is built. You want to go to your own country. Good! But who will go with you?"[177] This apolitical stance was rooted in his conviction that the Jews – misled by the early optimism of the Mendelssohnian or Berlin Haskala, intoxicated by the awards of assimilation – would reject all plans for a collective effort to colonize Palestine.

But, as he saw it, the reality had changed abruptly in mid-1881. Now the Jews of western Europe were planning the systematic resettlement of the refugees overseas. This fact suggested an entirely new potentiality, the idea of treating Palestine not as an abstract hope but as a place "to settle our brothers . . . [as] a *refuge* for all in distress."[178] In eastern Europe, too, the situation had altered sharply; the idea that adaptation to the environment would win acceptance had lost its grip. "In this one year," he wrote in mid-1882, "thousands and tens of thousands have rooted out of their hearts false ideas planted there for eighty years."[179]

Thus, in the space of a few months, a profound scepticism had given way to the wildest hopes and estimates. Later in the summer of 1881 Smolenskin could write: "The House of Rothschild is with us and if they so wish they can work miracles overnight, for with a mere fifth of their wealth they could buy the country [Palestine] and resettle in it all the hungry and all those thirsting for salvation."[180] This theme reappeared constantly in his writings in this period. Instead of the fifteen hundred Jews sent to America late in 1881, fifteen thousand could have been sent to Palestine. And if ten thousand Jews were sent to America in the spring of 1881, up to one hundred thousand could have been settled in the Holy Land.[181] And with the sum total collected in the West on behalf of the Russian Jews – estimated at "more than six million francs" – "the Alliance could have bought more than half the country and settled there those who were persecuted."[182] That this, in his eyes, extraordinary opportunity was utterly wasted induced in him a mood of terrible bitterness. Above all, he placed the blame on Charles Netter, who, using his intimate knowledge of the country, had asserted in letters to the press early in 1882 that Palestine was totally unsuited – climatically, economically, socially – for mass colonization by the Jews. Even when Smolenskin heard that Netter had died (probably, in part, from exhaustion) at Mikve Yisrael in October

1882, he did not relent: "His death cannot absolve him from the errors and the evil by which he sinned before his people . . . Let those who listened to his advice . . . [know] that his sin shall be remembered for ever and ever."[183]

Smolenskin's belief that a return to Palestine could be engineered "overnight," if only the Alliance or the Rothschilds wished it, stemmed from his reading of Jewish history. The mass of the people had always retained their integrity; the leaders had frequently chosen to betray their nation. Herein had been the root of disaster in the past and the choice between salvation or further catastrophe therefore lay squarely with the Jewish leaders in the West. In Smolenskin's thought, the national will emerges as the one major force determining the fate of the nation.

These assumptions – that inner factors were of central importance, that external factors such as antisemitism were secondary and that as a historical nation with its own destiny the Jews must repossess its historical land – were all reminiscent of Hess. Indeed, Smolenskin has been accused on occasion of plagiarizing *Rome and Jerusalem*, with which he was familiar.[184] But there was a paradox here. Smolenskin, rejecting Hess's idealized view of the ancient Hebrew kingdoms and his related thesis that Jewish ethics divorced from the territorial state were bound to atrophy, had until mid-1881 not seen a return to Palestine as an urgent necessity. However, now that he had changed his stance he emerged as far more utopian than Hess, who had never argued that the nation could return to Palestine at will. *Rome and Jerusalem*, after all, had assigned a key role in Palestinian resettlement to the ambition of France as an upcoming power in the Middle East.

In the summer of 1881, the messianism that then permeated Smolenskin's writings was still an isolated phenomenon. But by the winter of 1881, and particularly in the spring months of 1882, it had gained a strong hold. It made itself evident in the mushrooming of Palestinian colonization societies, in the movement of hundreds of families to Palestine, in the Oliphant cult, and a number of writers now joined Smolenskin both stimulating, and stimulated by, the popular mood.

For example, there were three articles published in *Ha-melits* in December and January by the young Belostok poet, M. M. Dolitsky. Smolenskin's article, "How to Bring the Redemption," he wrote, had inspired him: "Read that article again and you will see that every word, every word, is written in his blood, in the blood of your brothers."[185] If only the Jews would unite their forces, he insisted, "there will be enough money not only to buy from Turkey all the Jordan Valley . . . but also to rebuild there a thousand towns now laid waste and to maintain our brothers until they have established themselves."[186] By sending the refugees to America, the Jews in the West were "severing limbs from the body of Israel – and they will not even have a Jewish burial place."[187] The only destination could be Jerusalem. ("Naked and barefoot we left her, naked and barefoot we shall return.")[188]

Then, again, there was the young writer from Nikolaev, Moshe Aizman, who in an article published in May 1882 described the coming resettlement of Palestine in romantic terms as the escape of the people from an overdeveloped militaristic society to the pastoral values of the desert. "We have nobody to depend on," he wrote,

> but on the strength of the people itself. The people in its masses must turn its
> back on the rich and the great who have chosen assimilation . . . There [in

the land of our fathers] we will not bow down to European civilization with
its belief in force: there we will carry the principles of semitic civilization
among the Arab tribes, our relations. And that means a holy civilization –
wisdom and morality, love of man and peace. Ishmael is our brother . . .
After the ingathering of the exiles the Lord will send us the one Messiah and
he will come to Mount Zion to remake the world.[189]

At this time even the poet Y. L. Gordon, who regarded the Palestine project with
instinctive irony and who was closely linked to Baron Gintsburg, wondered if after
all he could not discern "the footsteps of the Messiah and the beginning of the
Redemption."[190] (Later he would recall that "for a moment we were like unto
dreamers.")[191]

The upsurge of emotionalism, the instinctive attempt to grasp at hope in the
midst of despair, to interpret the crisis as the prelude to the messianic coming,
made a central strand in the history of the period. But it was not the only one.
There were those who found themselves increasingly repelled by what they saw as
the abandonment of reason. L. O. Kantor, as the editor of *Russkii evrei* – rejecting,
as he put it, "the universal slogan" that "whoever disagrees with us is a traitor to
his people"[192] – sought doggedly to distinguish reality from myth. In the spring of
1882, his editorials argued that it should be possible in the immediate future to
settle some thousands of Jews in Palestine but that the great majority of refugees
would have to go, as hitherto, to the United States, where alone they would find
work. The debate of *Amerikantsy* against *Palestintsy* was therefore absurd and also
a form of self-indulgence, because while so much effort was going into the debate,
little was being done for the many who were starving: "There has been such a
growth of strategists mapping out in broad outline grandiose plans of campaign
that there are no simple soldiers left."[193]

For his part, the young Dubnov, who had been among the first to advocate
emigration, now expressed a mounting scepticism. In July 1882 he began to publish in *Voskhod* his study of "Shabbetai Zvi and Pseudo-Messianism in the Seventeenth Century."[194] Writing of a period two hundred years before, it was as if he
were also describing his own day; now as then, he was suggesting, objective pressures had driven the Jews to seek refuge in unreason, escapism, to find a "false
messiah."

The similarities between the two years, 1665–6 and 1881–2, were certainly
striking enough. What Gershom Scholem writes of the former year could have been
written of the latter:

> In that deeply agitated year . . . the movement possessed mass strength of
> great proportions: the most diverse elements joined together. There devel-
> oped a movement of penitence which was regarded as a kind of final effort
> to draw closer to the Messianic redemption . . . All too easily perspectives
> became distorted as the frenzied proclamation of a redemption about to
> begin was accompanied by all the phenomena of a mass movement.[195]

And yet it was, and would be, highly misleading only to dwell on this analogy. A
crucial difference (not, of course, the only one) lay in the fact that increasingly in
1881–2 the Russian-educated youth was moving to the political forefront. And

they, for the most part, were not receptive to the overtly messianic schemes developed by Smolenskin, Dolitsky, and Aizman (who all wrote in Hebrew).

When embodied in poetry, the exodic myth did certainly have an extraordinary influence. The most famous poem of the time – that published by Frug in *Razsvet* in January 1882, which took as its theme the biblical verse, "Speak unto the children of Israel that they go forth"[196] – stirred deep emotions and was mentioned constantly at the time and later in memoirs. But in prose the prevailing taste was different. A generation which had devoured the writings of Chernyshevsky, Dobroliubov, Pisarev, Mikhailovsky, and Lavrov sought in its mentors neither mysticism nor scepticism but a world-view that combined, or appeared to combine, scientific method, the laws of history, and ethical imperatives. That is why neither Smolenskin (who won a following in the 1870s) nor Dubnov (who would come into his own in the early 1900s) but Lilienblum was the most effective publicist during the crisis of 1881–2.

Strongly influenced since his youth by the iconoclastic utilitarianism of Pisarev, Lilienblum sought even now to minimize the romantic element in his thought. Writing of the Jewish revolt in the year 66–70 C.E., for instance, he argued that "we should have done well ... to surrender to Titus for then – remaining in our own land until a better time, until the fall of the Romans – we would very probably have come into our own as did many other peoples which had been enslaved to Rome and would now be a nation of fifty or sixty million."[197] Of the contemporary crisis, he wrote that if there were no chance of gaining political independence in Palestine, then it would be preferable to direct the Jews to the United States ("a country where railways and canals spring up overnight").[198] The future Jewish state, he insisted, could legitimately use English or German rather than Hebrew as its official language. ("Why," he asked of Ben Yehuda, "does he have to be more patriotic than our forefathers [who spoke Aramaic]?")[199] And it should establish a modern capital on the lowlands of Palestine ("We do not need the walls of Jerusalem, nor the Jerusalem temple, nor Jerusalem itself").[200]

Lilienblum adopted this irreverent stance to what he regarded as secondary questions in order to throw all the emphasis on what he saw as the primary issue. In his article published in *Razsvet* on 9 October 1881, "The General Jewish Question and Palestine," he advanced the proposition that the current crisis was not a transient deviation from the norm but symptomatic of an emergent trend, not a throwback to a barbaric past but a premonition of the future. "We are accustomed to think," he wrote there,

that the medieval afflictions suffered by the Jews have long since passed forever, that German antisemitism is only a creature thought up by Bismarck for political ends, that our pogroms are a direct result of the fact that the Jews do not enjoy equal rights, etc., and that therefore when Bismarck achieves his goals and when the Russian Jews attain equal rights ... this entire disaster will go away, the XIX century will come into its own ... But if one considers that every phenomenon has deep roots in the life and history of the society ... from which it grew then perhaps we will come to a different, albeit quite bitter, conclusion.[201]

The fact had to be faced, he argued, that as a national minority, distinct both biologically and culturally, the Jewish people existed everywhere only on sufferance. Historically, the Jews had been tolerated where they had a distinct – a separate – function to fulfill in the economy of the country. In eastern Europe for centuries they had served as an intermediate stratum between the nobles and peasants. But when the caste barriers began to break down as society became more fluid and complex, so the Jews increasingly found themselves in direct competition with members of the majority nationality. Competition produced resentments and resentments provided fertile soil for antisemitism.[202]

In advancing this thesis, Lilienblum had not simply cast doubt on the central assumption which had motivated two generations of maskilim in Russia. He had reversed it entirely, stood it on its head. The belief had been that the more useful the Jews became to society, the more they would win acceptance. Now Lilienblum argued that the opposite was true. To be useful at any level meant to be successful and success was dangerous. Every Jew who had work when a native did not, every Jewish merchant with a fine house, every Jewish professor aroused envy. And the envious were not impressed, for example, by "the fact that the Jews have contributed a great deal to science . . . and so he cries 'Out with the foreigner!' "[203] Throughout the 1870s Lilienblum had been in the forefront of those maskilim who had advocated the principle of "productivization" and called for the establishment of Jewish agricultural colonies. But now he wrote: "It would seem that there cannot be anything more useful than science and agriculture. But no! . . . The moment the 'aliens' took them up, the furious cry went out, 'Beware, the Jew is coming!' . . . After all, Jewish colonists and artisans suffered the most from the pogroms."[204]

To follow this logic was to conclude that the greater the emancipation, the greater the danger; the more the modern world advanced, the less secure the situation of the Jews. Although Lilienblum had been profoundly affected by the pogroms in Russia – he himself had lived through the May outbreak in Odessa – his general argument owed at least as much to the recent emergence of the organized antisemitic movement in Germany under the leadership of Stöcker, the chaplain to the imperial court. The instant and widespread success of this movement (in May 1882 the First International Anti-Semitic Congress would meet amid considerable publicity in Dresden) was taken by Lilienblum as clear proof that the Jews were faced by a phenomenon that was not local but universal, not contingent but necessary.[205] It was true, he granted, that the Jews in England, France, and Italy lived in peace, but they owed that privilege only to the fact that hitherto they had escaped notice. There were, after all, relatively few Jews there. And, further, public attention had been long distracted by major national issues: the frequent revolutions in France, the Risorgimento in Italy, the rapid expansion of British industry and empire. With time, those countries too could be expected to follow "the normal track"[206] already taken by Germany, Hungary, Roumania, and Russia. "Many," he noted,

> have been asking with horror, "Have the Middle Ages returned?" In my opinion, yes! . . . And in this, there is nothing surprising. Has the stranger been permitted into the family in the XIX century? Will he be in the XX and XXI centuries? Human nature in general does not change . . . [although] our

definitions [do]. In the Middle Ages the sign of an "alien" was religion and now it is nationality.[207]

Under these circumstances, to seek to evade the mounting danger by assimilation was neither honorable for the individual nor possible for the collective.

There were two practical conclusions to be drawn. First, the Jews had to have their own sovereign state, and here Palestine was the obvious choice. To that country, he argued, "we have a historical right which has not been destroyed nor forfeited by the loss of independence – a fact proven by the peoples of the Balkan Peninsula. That is why Palestine has an enormous advantage over transoceanic America, which is also alien to us."[208] Second, the goal must not be just resettlement of Palestine but rather a general evacuation, "in such a way that in the course of one century the Jews can almost totally leave hostile Europe and move to the land of our fathers."[209]

In his memoirs, Mordekhay Ben Hillel Ha-Cohen stated that it was Lilienblum's article which tipped the balance in the *Razsvet* editorial board toward Palestine and against America.[210] As the months passed, it became apparent that his general ideological stance was becoming that of an ever wider circle. This fact is easily explained. Lilienblum had embodied in a sociological (or quasi-sociological) law the emotion predominant among the Jewish *intelligenty* in Russia at that moment. Above all, they felt spurned, humiliated. They had not rejected Russia, Russia had rejected them. They had not returned to the Middle Ages, Russia had. It was this image of the guest become outcast which Lilienblum had raised, as it were, to the level of science.

The ideological turnabout among Russian Jews has been described as a "reevaluation of values." But that was not the dominant note. The Jewish *intelligenty* (most, not all) felt that they had remained true to values which others had renounced.[211] It fell to Lev Levanda, the veteran advocate of Russification, to express this general thought perhaps the most bluntly of all. "Our best people for the last thirty years," he wrote in *Russkii evrei* on 1 January,

> have done everything in their power to advance a *merging* in which they saw the most reliable cure for all our ills and for the sake of which they were ready even to give up our traditions and social peculiarities... And this development had gone so far and so fast and so deep that it appeared to be close to success. But what can one do if those with whom one so wants to merge shun the merger... with crowbars and clubs in their hands...? It is not with joy that many of us are now devoting ourselves to the most unheard-of plans. Even the dreamer... who dreams of an independent Jewish state does so, we believe, only because people and events are driving us into the kingdom of darkness... If events changed he would join the chorus that would be singing: I am a Russian [*russkii*] and love my land.[212]

In his readiness at least to consider America as a possible alternative to Palestine, Lilienblum had simply anticipated the profound doubt on this issue which gripped a large section of the Jewish intelligentsia in the autumn and winter of 1881–2. Smolenskin's total commitment to the historic homeland did not constitute the norm. The idea of selecting a sparsely populated area in the United States and concentrating Jewish settlement there exerted a powerful attraction. With a population of sixty thousand, it was widely publicized, a territory could become an equal state within the Union and the Jewish people would thus come into possession of a self-governing unit.

What made America preferable at first for so many was not simply that it had such an enormous economic and absorbtive capacity. At least as much weight was assigned to the fact that the United States, in marked contrast to Ottoman Palestine, stood squarely in the mainstream of Western culture and politics. Y. L. Levin, in a letter to *Ha-magid* in October 1881, pointed out that in America the Russian Jews would be equal citizens in an enlightened country; in Palestine they would be subjects of the sultan with few chances of being anything else. At the most, "after a long period of many years we will become one of the small principalities"[213] which, as in the Balkans, would have to fight in order to win even modest independence. In the United States, wrote Y. L. Gordon in March 1882, the Russian Jews could become members of the modern world and like the children of Israel during the forty years in the wilderness would "learn the law of life, slough off their limited ways, their slavery, and become free men worthy of entering their own land."[214]

L. Zamenhof, the young Warsaw writer and future creator of Esperanto, emphasized in his article of January 1882, "What Finally Is To Be Done?" that the new Jewish settlers in Palestine would find themselves tyrannized by the fanatically religious Jews already entrenched in Jerusalem and would eventually have to face demands for the rebuilding of the Temple or even the renewal of sacrifices. "On the chaos which will be unleashed in Palestine on the first day of its liberation," he suggested, "one could write entire books."[215] Possessed of their own self-governing territory in the United States, on the other hand, the Jewish people would be genuinely free to chart a national political course, to choose among a number of options. Here, indeed, was probably the first clear statement of the ideology that would later be known as territorialism. "If," wrote Zamenhof,

> it emerges that we have to be cosmopolitans then of course on our [American] territory we will not be deprived of the possibility but will gain the *right* to preach fraternity between men. If it turns out that we need Palestine . . . then it will not be lost to us . . . but will be much more accessible because we will have much greater strength and a more powerful voice than now. If you are afraid that those who settle [in America] . . . will become too attached to their new motherland, then do we not have enough people to settle two national homes?[216]

It is certainly true that opinion swung rapidly over to Palestine and against America in the early months of 1882. The writers just quoted – Levanda, Levin, Gordon, Zamenhof – all changed their positions almost overnight and became supporters of the Palestine cause (Gordon only momentarily, the others permanently). They were undoubtedly swayed by the evidence of a great upsurge of popular support for a return to the ancestral homeland, but there were other arguments advanced to explain the turnabout. First, there was the fear, central to Lilienblum's thesis, that the Jews carried persecution, as it were, on their backs. In his article of May 1882 explaining his reversal, Y. L. Levin asked what guarantee there was that the Jewish immigrants to the United States would not meet the same fate as the

Chinese, who had been subjected in that country to physical violence and to hostile restrictions on further immigration.[217] Many refugees, wrote A. S. Fridberg, will inevitably become peddlers in the United States and, as such, arouse local hostility.[218] Besides, it was widely argued, there was nobody in the West prepared to encourage the plan for concentrated Jewish settlement. On the contrary, the tendency there manifestly was to diagnose the sickness as that of individuals – displaced persons – and not as that of the nation as a whole. And the cure prescribed was therefore to scatter the refugees far and wide.

Countertheses were also marshaled in direct rebuttal of the anti-Palestine theses. So long as Palestine was under Turkish rule, wrote Lilienblum, the fanatically orthodox Jewish sects would not have the power to impose their views on the new arrivals. Therefore the shape of the future society would be decided not only by the veterans already there but also by those, including free-thinkers, still to come. It was thus premature to talk in terms of a kulturkampf.[219] Again, the fact that Palestine was "uncultivated and poor" was described in *Razsvet* as a positive advantage. Almost deserted, it awaited the Jews to come to work it: "What use is it for us that the banks of the Rhine, for example, are wonderfully cultivated when . . . they belong to the Germans! . . . Only people used to getting everything ready-made . . . can speak against Palestine . . . because of its unworked land."[220] Finally, the fact that the country was so small was likewise presented as an advantage; the settlers could not scatter to the winds but would automatically be forced to coalesce into a national unit.

Lilienblum and others who shared his outlook went to considerable pains to differentiate themselves from the more romantic wing of the Palestine camp. In response to Moshe Aizman's demand that the Jews renounce the culture of Europe for that of the Arab East, Lilienblum could write scathingly: "There are many among us in general, who, after the pogroms, let out their fury at the Haskala in all its aspects and argue that we have to return to the ways of our fathers in the Dark Ages. It is hardly necessary to say that this is . . . so much froth on the ocean."[221] And another critic went even farther: "We have lived to hear from [Aizman and others] words worthy of Aksakov and his school, which pours out abuse against the West and all its Enlightenment."[222]

Of course, in the eyes of Dubnov or Kantor the Palestinian ideology, whether presented by the romantic Smolenskin or the utilitarian Lilienblum, remained an irrational delusion. They themselves were ready to endorse the idea of establishing some Jewish colonies in Palestine but they insisted that when the debates were over the vast majority of Russian Jews would still be living in Russia. And their problems would have to be solved in Russia or not at all. From this fundamental reality there could be no escape except into fantasy. ("It is a shame, truly a shame," Dubnov would write in 1883, "that many youthful forces are spent entirely on something which deserves only such forces as are commensurate with its results, i.e., an extremely small quantity.")[223]

Nevertheless, it is essential for the historian to emphasize the real differentiation that existed within the emergent Palestinian camp. It was through the writings of Lilienblum, Levin, and their school that the new movement could exert a powerful influence on the socialist and radically inclined youth. As presented by them, Palestinophilism was founded less on national romanticism and more on national necessity, less on religious or quasi-religious faith and more on sociohistorical analysis.

The youth parties

The aspect of the emigration movement which most impressed contemporary observers in early 1882 was the increasing participation of the Russian-educated youth, particularly the students. It had generally been assumed until 1881–2 that Russification logically involved alienation from the Jewish world (and that undoubted exceptions only proved the rule). The spectacle of the returning sons therefore aroused widespread wonderment.

It is true that the participation of the student youth in the emigration politics of early 1882 basically followed the pattern already observed in the previous year. But there were differences, mainly quantitative but also qualitative. The Odessa and Elizavetgrad groups had been founded in 1881 as an ad hoc response to the pogroms in those cities. They were small in number, dominated by one or two forceful personalities, composed more of artisans than students, self-absorbed. In 1882 the student involvement took on the dimensions of a general sociological phenomenon unrelated to the actual outbreak of pogroms, to the presence of charismatic leaders, or other purely local conditions. If in 1881 Monye Bokol and German Rozental had been involved in the politics of the sect, in 1882 Mints, Belkind, and Aleinikoff were clearly groping their way toward the politics of the party – a permanent and interurban organization, a considerable membership, an ideological platform.

Although the Odessa students had initiated (in Ben Ami's terminology) the first "going to the people" in May 1881, those in Petersburg and Kiev made a far greater public impact with their similar actions in January and February 1882. In this, the second "going to the people," the students appeared in the synagogues not in pairs but en masse to express symbolically their solidarity with the Jewish people in a time of trial. The occasion for these demonstrations was the day – Monday 18 January in St. Petersburg, Monday 1 February in Kiev – adopted by the local Jewish communities as a moment for fasting and public prayer. In their military-type uniforms, the mass of students and *gimnazisty* stood out clearly in the synagogues, which were crowded beyond capacity for the occasion.

Writing in his memoirs of the scene in the St. Petersburg synagogue on 18 January, M. Ha-Cohen suggested that it constituted the type of event "which intrinsically may not have any special significance, and which if used frequently becomes meaningless but which at the right moment and under the right conditions becomes a powerful factor . . . of almost historic importance."[224] Certainly it made a powerful impression on those present. In a letter written immediately afterward to Smolenskin, the young journalist S. Z. Lure recalled that the high point of the service was the address by Rabbi Drabkin, who took as his theme the verse from the book of Exodus: "The enemy said, I will pursue, I will overtake, I will divide the spoil."[225] "My pen," Lure wrote,

> shakes in my hand as I remember the impression which these words made on
> those present in the synagogue. One cry, as it were, broke from the hearts of

all those there, a cry which quickly became a roar of anguish that almost
brought down the synagogue walls . . . There was not an eye which did not
shed tears . . . Rabbi Drabkin had to stop for ten minutes until those present
could overcome their weeping.[226]

Those minutes, Ha-Cohen suggested later, were "valuable minutes worth more
than entire years."[227]

The parallel action in Kiev was planned at a meeting held on 29 January in a
private apartment. According to a contemporary report, one hundred and eighteen
students were present, almost the total Jewish student body then at Kiev University.[228] It was decided that speeches in Russian and Yiddish be prepared in advance
for the demonstration. And some poems on the current crisis, composed by one of
the students, were printed in a large number of copies for distribution there. "The
presence of the students in the synagogue," wrote Akselrod's Kiev correspondent,

> their sincere, warm and yet fiery speeches, the poems – brought tens of thou-
> sands of Jews to the synagogues and, for lack of space, people had to stand
> in the street . . . The police could not help noticing, of course; the demon-
> stration was rather successful and the governor general called in the rabbi
> and rebuked the censor for permitting the poems to be printed.[229]

Caught up on this wave of collective excitement, growing numbers of the youth
began to think in terms of emigration not merely as a conceptual solution to the
collective crisis but as an immediate personal decision. The question of America as
against Palestine became for them all-consuming. And the clash between the emigrationist intelligentsia (represented above all by *Razsvet*) and the St. Petersburg
oligarchy associated with Baron Gintsburg took on the most concrete significance;
on its outcome could hang the fate of their numerous colonization projects. The
constant meetings and discussions stretched far into the night, and the issues,
political in their general significance, became matters of conscience at the individual level – a fact clearly reflected in the letters and diaries that have been preserved
from those months.

The first question that faced the enthusiasts of the new cause was whether it
demanded that they themselves leave Russia at once to join the projected colonies. In letters from December 1881 and January 1882 to his cousin, Zalman
David Levontin, M. Ha-Cohen argued that the students should not aim to become pioneers immediately but should first complete their education, gain some
experience of life, study the past and present of their own people. In St. Petersburg, he explained, the student *kruzhok* (Ahavat Zion) was gathering once a
week to analyze the crisis in all its theoretical implications. At a meeting disguised as a birthday party, held late in December, over five hundred young men
and women had attended. There, "Yiddish suddenly became a spoken language"[230] and only Jewish poems and songs had been heard. He saw this as-
tounding turnabout as sufficient in itself for the time being. "From the bottom of
my heart," he wrote, "I thank the Lord that the pogroms came in order to
breathe life back into these dry bones."[231] Besides, he asked, "what would we
gain if we succeeded in having ten or twenty students leave their studies and
books . . . and plod after a plow in the fields of Bethlehem?"[232]

However, Levontin was unpersuaded. He himself had decided as far back as August 1881 that there had to be pioneers and that he would be one of them. For months he traveled around southern Russia seeking others who might want to join him in forming a colony, on a private land-holding basis, in Palestine. On 30 January 1882 he could write to Ha-Cohen from Odessa on the eve of his departure for Jaffa, "I have never said 'Go!' but rather 'Arise, let us go up!' "[233]

In the heat of the moment, ideological positions were adopted and discarded with lightning speed but often with life-long consequences. A diary of the time, that of Chaim Khisin, a student in Moscow, recorded the turmoil almost day by day. An entry from 10 February 1882 recorded the following soliloquy:

> I have begun to be driven by a sharp, merciless question: "Who are you?" . . . I try to convince myself: "Do I really *have to be somebody?*" But I cannot get away from the question . . . "Of course, I am a Russian," I reply and feel that it is not true. On what do I base that answer? Only on my *own* sympathies and dreams. But fool, don't you see that to your ardent love, they respond with insulting and cold contempt? . . . No, first of all and unwillingly, I am a Jew . . . [But] my Judaism does not give me any satisfaction. What, apart from memories, does it give me? With what can I fill my existence? . . . My God, why are we refused the love and sympathy of those around us?[234]

The entry of 2 March recorded a new turn: "Nothing is left but to emigrate. But the question remains – to where? Some are for Palestine; others are for America."[235] On this point, surely, there could be no doubt about the choice. America, the land of freedom, justice, and fertile soil, was clearly preferable to Palestine, which was barren, in the Turkish grip, and boycotted by the Jewish philanthropists of the West: "So I shall go to America and only to America . . . collecting a suitable group of people we shall set up an agricultural colony."[236]

But the entry for 12 April records a "complete reversal"[237] in his plans. A young acquaintance, Yehiel Chlenov, a Moscow *gimnazist,* had convinced him with the aid of one of the articles in *Razsvet* that it was Palestine – compact, underpopulated, near-by – which had the decisive advantage. On 17 April he noted the fact that his Moscow group of young *Palestintsy* had made contact with the larger group in Kharkov, soon to take the name Bilu. By 27 June he was in Odessa, a party member en route to Jaffa.[238]

Of course, Khisin was an extreme case in his willingness to throw himself totally into so reckless an enterprise. But his feverish search for an all-embracing cause which would solve his own personal identity crisis as well as the collective crisis of the Jewish people, and his eagerness to translate his new creed into personal action, were characteristic of those months. Z. D. Levontin, who had arrived in Jaffa in January 1882, was from the first inundated with excited letters from would-be pioneers requesting him either to confirm or deny the feasibility of a national return to Palestine. "The eyes of the people," Y. Y. Levontin reported from Moscow in February, "are turned to you . . . And if the enterprise is impossible or very difficult then tell the people honestly and let it go to America because there, too, people say that we can found a Jewish state."[239] Writing from Elizavetgrad on 6 February 1882, another correspondent set forth his criteria for resettlement. There

92

could be no dependence on the existing, orthodox Jewish community in Palestine: "We must create a new civilization and create everything new."[240] There had to be an answer to the problem of the refugees and the poverty-stricken strata in general:

> We must concern ourselves only with the masses who are many and poor and depend on their hands to make a living. They must have the means to eat and feed their children on the day they arrive in the land of their fathers or in America and cannot under any circumstances wait a year or two until their fields bear crops ... This is the question of the stomach and all admit that this question takes precedence over the question of the nation.[241]

Finally, there had to be large-scale capital investment in Palestine, sums which would have to come from the Alliance israélite universelle. Thousands, this letter concluded, were waiting for Levontin to pass judgment.

If many of the Palestinophile youth had originally opted in favor of America, the reverse was also true; many of those who joined the youth groups going to America in May and June 1882 had actually intended to go to Palestine. In his reminiscences, Dr. Raevsky (Shamraevsky) described how he had gone to Brody as "an ardent *Palestinets*"[242] and how, together with Yaroslavsky (later the well-known American anarchist, Yarros) and others, he had done everything he could to "turn the stream of emigration from the west to the south, to Palestine."[243] And Dr. Spivak (Spivakovsky) recalled how he, too, in Brody "had been occupied day and night with thundering propaganda [on behalf of Palestine]."[244] But, as Raevsky put it, "instead of our diverting the stream of emigration, the stream carried us with it."[245]

The ease with which the individual could suddenly be swept off his feet by the power of the emigration current is strikingly illustrated by the case of Abe Cahan. In the spring of 1882 Cahan was in flight from the police, who had obtained information about his links with a *kruzhok* of the Narodnaia Volia in Vilna. His own intention was to go to Switzerland, pursue his studies as best he could (he came from a poor family), join the revolutionary colony there, and perhaps return to Russia at some stage as a *podpolshchik*. But in Mohilev he chanced upon a (or even the) leading figure in the Bilu: Yisrael Belkind, "an activist of the new type," in Cahan's words, "an idealist, almost 'one of us.' "[246] Quickly realizing that Cahan as a militant internationalist would not consider going to Palestine, Belkind argued that at least he should join the Jewish youth going to America rather than the Russian revolutionaries in Switzerland.

As Cahan recalled the conversation, Belkind asked him why he should consider giving his life "for that Russian people which is making pogroms against us ... If you want to serve the socialist cause, why go to Switzerland? Why not America?"[247] Belkind described to him in detail the plans of the *Amerikantsy,* and the young Cahan, isolated from comrades and family, became an immediate convert. "Before me," he recalled,

> there formed a fantastic picture of communistic life in distant America, a life where there was no "mine" and "thine," where all were brothers and sisters. Earlier I had believed that all this would be realized in the future; now it would become reality at once and I would take part in its realization ... Belkind, the *Palestinets,* made me into an *Amerikanets.*[248]

From Mohilev Cahan proceeded to Brody (crossing the frontier at night with the aid of smugglers), and in June 1882 he left for the United States attached to the Am Olam group from Balta.

It was in this situation (the release of hitherto untapped youthful energies, ideological turmoil) that the new colonization parties took shape. There were three major organizations – the Bilu, the Kiev Am Olam, the Odessa Am Olam – as well as a host of smaller groups. Each of the three larger organizations had its own distinctive character reflecting something of the wide variety of attitudes then prevailing among the emigrant youth.

From what little is known of it, the Odessa Am Olam seems to have remained true to the principles laid down by Bokol's group in the previous year. Thus Oregon, where New Odessa was being established, was declared their destination by the some three hundred emigrants, members of the Odessa Am Olam, who passed through Cracow on 29 May en route from Brody to the United States.[249] Once in New York, it was the Odessa group which became linked most closely to William Frey, the veteran Russian émigré whose devotion to Comte's positivism, to nonviolence, and to vegetarianism had long earned him a reputation close to secular sainthood. In his memoirs, Abe Cahan describes how a number of the immigrants including Bokol fell under Frey's influence: "For some months," he recalled, "vegetarianism became 'the height of fashion' in the Russian colony."[250] Frey's decision to join the Oregon colony (he would spend some years in New Odessa) served to underline the persistence of a strongly internationalist (or at least Russian, as against Jewish) element in the Odessa Am Olam. The fact that Frey had been a member – together with the well-known revolutionaries Nikolai V. Chaikovsky, G. A. Machtet, and V. K. Debogory-Mokrievich – of the agricultural commune in Cedar Vale, Kansas, in the years 1875–7 also provided an ideological link between the Russian *Amerikantsy* of the 1870s and the Jewish *Amerikantsy* (both groups had been shaped by the same utopian and agrarian elements in populist thought).[251]

In Kiev, the Am Olam developed independently from the Odessa movement. A product apparently of what has been described above as "the second going to the people" in February 1882, it developed a stronger nationalist tendency than the organization in Odessa. Indeed, in April 1882 it was moving clearly in favor of settlement in Palestine. A letter dated 14 April 1882 from Y. L. Levin in Kiev to Dr. Asher in London reported that "if at first America was the idea [of the Am Olam] and they devoted all their energies to it . . . now they [are ready to support Palestine] if only they are assured that their . . . effort will not be in vain."[252] A memorandum sent on 28 April from the Kiev Am Olam (The Russian Jewish Emigration Society, as it was officially called) spoke of "the gigantic movement in favor of Palestine which has seized almost the entire Jewish people in Russia."[253] At the same time, it insisted on firmly linking national to social goals. "Above all," it stated,

> [we must] try not to bring into the new country, the promised land, the scourge of the old civilization, large private land-holding and the system that goes with it – the most terrible exploitation of the landless proletariat. The agrarian question is one of the most terrible and to carry it to the new land,

to plant in it the seeds of the old world, is to condemn ourselves to failure. This is particularly important for the first colonies which in their structure must serve as a model and example for those who follow. Do not forget that the renaissance must be not only national but also economic. Our times have put economic goals to the fore ... The first colonies [must be based] on cooperative principles, the only wise and suitable ones, especially in a new country.[254]

Interestingly enough, the memorandum came out in diametrical opposition to Bokol's preference for artisans as the most reliable pioneers: "It is essential that in the first Palestinian colony, the *intelligenty* and educated element should predominate as much as possible. Remember what a struggle there will be with the orthodox, how firmly we will have to stand so as not to be turned backwards."[255] The first to be sent would have to be carefully selected and financed by the movement regardless of their possible lack of private means.

With this coherent ideology, with well over a hundred members, with a recognized leader in Nicholas Aleinikoff and with close links to similar groups in other cities, the Kiev Am Olam was regarded as a major reinforcement by the Palestinian camp. Thus, on 10 May 1882 David Gordon could write to Y. L. Levin asking him "to tell the members of the Am Olam society that they should restrain themselves a little, that they should do all they can to unite as one, create an organization and wait a little time until land is bought [in Palestine]."[256] But such expectations proved misplaced. The Kiev Am Olam decided against any delay and crossed the frontier into Galicia in May. Possibly they did not initially consider this step as a final choice in favor of America, but in Brody the representatives of the Western aid committees consistently withheld funds from those preferring Palestine. At the end of May, the Kiev Am Olam, a group one hundred and twenty strong, left for the United States. Following the example of the Elizavetgrad group in October 1881, the Kiev party carried with it a Sefer Torah, which was held aloft at the railway stations where they halted en route and were greeted by enthusiastic local reception committees. The Sefer Torah, recalled Cahan, was regarded "not as a religious sacred object but as a national standard."[257]

Both the Odessa and Kiev Am Olam made contacts with the philanthropic committees in Germany and Austria and received financial aid. The Kiev group arrived in America with a capital sum of $2,000,[258] and there they were given another $1,000 raised by Michael Heilprin.[259] Their plan was to send an advance guard to select a suitable site for their colony in the West and, meanwhile, they went to work in New York in factories or in the docks. Some of their members also went to work the farmlands recently purchased by the Hebrew Emigrant Aid Society at Vineland, New Jersey. In a report from New York in October 1882, Abe Cahan wrote that both the Kiev and Odessa Am Olam were waiting for "the large-scale aid from Europe" which they had been promised.[260]

Unlike the Am Olam parties, where socialism and nationalism were held in varying types of balance, the third major youth party, the Bilu, was essentially nationalist in its ideology. It is true that of its two major leaders, I. Belkind and M. Mints, the latter was and remained a socialist. (Vladimir Dubnov's description of him in late 1882 as an "ex-socialist" was almost certainly incorrect.)[261] But until

1883 his socialist leanings did not leave any clear mark on the direction of the movement, unless its proclaimed goal of establishing a "central colony ... which will be the property not of individuals but of the organization as a whole" is understood as a veiled reference to communal principles.[262]

The Bilu was the creation of students at Kharkov University who (like the founders of the Kiev Am Olam) first came together to discuss concerted action after going to synagogue on the day of communal fasting. Fourteen students, led by Yisrael Belkind, decided to form a group open only to those willing to commit themselves at once to go as pioneers to Palestine. They originally took the name *Dabyu*, formed from the words, "Speak unto the Children of Israel that they go forth."[263] As noted above, knowledge of the movement spread rapidly (reaching Khisin in Moscow and Cahan in Mohilev by the spring of 1882). Groups from other cities were encouraged to join the movement and many did so. At its height, in April–May 1882, it was variously estimated to have had between three and five hundred members.[264]

But even though large numbers were taken into the movement, the original Central Bureau (situated first in Kharkov and from April in Odessa) sought throughout to keep firm control. Centralism was considered essential in order to regulate the flow of emigration to Palestine. First, as a student from the Kharkov group explained, there was the need to prevent a mindless flight by the masses to Palestine:

> Earlier the people [*narod*] was afire with impatience and wanted to emigrate, without delay. But the Kharkov circle succeeded in persuading it to wait meanwhile until they [members of the circle] go in advance to prepare the way for it there somehow. The *narod*, understanding full well that the student youth not only is not going from necessity but is even sacrificing a great deal on its behalf, has complete trust in them.[265]

Second, the Central Bureau took it upon itself to decide which pioneer groups should go and when: "All the circles which join us must be ready to start moving at the moment they receive instructions from the Central Bureau."[266] Khisin's diary shows that this idea was taken seriously – the Moscow group received its instruction to leave on 17 June and less than a week later some of its members were already in Odessa.

The messianic strand which ran through much of the thinking in early 1882 was also discernible in that of the Bilu. Thus, initially the party displayed an unlimited trust in the power and influence of Oliphant. It was with the greatest expectations that in May two delegates, Mints and Y. Berliavsky, were sent to Constantinople to confer with him. They drew up a memorandum for him which explained the ideology of the movement (following Lilienblum, it stated that "we need a home ... because everywhere we are *aliens*")[267] and everything was considered to depend on his decision. "The memorandum," the Central Bureau declared in a letter of 5 June, "is expected to be examined by Oliphant today, and tomorrow or the day after there will be the final result."[268]

But when Oliphant eventually met with them it was only to explain that because of strained Anglo-Turkish relations he could in fact "for the moment give no moral or material help."[269] That this was a shattering psychological blow to the movement could hardly be concealed. ("Man proposes, God disposes," as the spokesmen in Constantinople put it.)[270] Yet the impetus built up over the previous months now proved sufficient to prevent immediate collapse and to prompt new initiatives.

For their part, Mints and Berliavsky decided to stay in Constantinople to pursue the diplomatic course independently. As the months passed, they gained access to high government circles and persuaded themselves that the Bilu would be provided with a large land grant for their proposed model settlement. "One has to be here oneself," they wrote late in 1882, "intervene personally, go, request, write, and only in this way can one hope to obtain land."[271]

At the same time, the leadership agreed that an advance guard should proceed at once to Palestine even without a land grant, and on 24 June the first group, led by Yisrael Belkind, landed in Jaffa. This decision was described by the Central Bureau as a desperate attempt to focus popular attention on Palestinian colonization: "We are beginning to lose credibility in the eyes of the masses . . . We have to show that we do not believe in the possibility of a bearable existence in Russia . . . that now, as before, we are ready to sacrifice ourselves for a great and holy idea – the rebirth of our people."[272]

Although few in number, they drew satisfaction from their ability to adapt to work on the land at the agricultural school at Mikve Yisrael. "The Director, Mr. Hirsch," Belkind wrote in November, "who at first regarded Russian Jews in an unfriendly way and as incapable of working under the sun . . . is [now] convinced that we do not lag behind the Arabs and to some extent even surpass them."[273] (They were paid one franc a day for their labor.) "Our ultimate goal . . . ," Vladimir Dubnov wrote to his brother Shimen on 20 October, "is, with time, to gain Palestine and to return to the Jews that political independence which they lost two thousand years ago. Do not laugh. It is not a chimera."[274]

The revolutionary socialists

The political upheaval within the Jewish world was so intense that it even produced a crisis of conscience among the revolutionary socialists. In the 1870s, the internationalism (albeit in Russian form) proclaimed as their creed by the socialists had assured their movement a position of prestige in the eyes of many Jews. Thus, as described above, nationally minded maskilim such as Y. L. Levin, Y. Kaminer, and M. L. Lilienblum saw in revolutionary socialism an exemplary attempt to bring together in one brotherhood the working masses of the various nations within the empire. The premise underlying this judgment was that the Jews had to adapt their way of life to their social environment by all the means available. These same maskilim could, therefore, also support the establishment of ORT, the philanthropic organization founded in 1880 with governmental permission by Poliakov to further agricultural and technical skills among the Russian Jews. At two opposite political poles, the Lavrovs and Poliakovs had won legitimacy in their eyes by acting in what was considered the interest of the Jewish masses.

But the crisis of 1881–2 necessarily undermined the authority of the groups most clearly identified with Jewish adaptation to Russian life. The mounting hostility manifested by the tsarist government to the Jewish people undercut the prestige and self-confidence of Baron Gintsburg, S. S. Poliakov, and the St. Petersburg "oligar-chy" in general. A parallel process could be observed also at the other extreme. The fact that two major revolutionary parties in Russia showed clear signs of sympathy with the pogroms raised the gravest doubts in radical Jewish circles – and indeed among party members – about their professed internationalism.

At the time, the full extent of the conflict and doubts that plagued the party leadership, particularly the socialist émigrés, was not generally known. But docu-ments published in the 1920s both in the Soviet Union and abroad revealed unmista-kably that in early 1882 the émigrés had been brought to a state of utter confusion by the pogroms, the response of the revolutionaries in Russia, and the emigration fever among the Jewish youth. The episode involving Pavel Borisovich Akselrod (and, through him, Lev Deich, Petr Lavrov, Vera Zasulich, and Georgii Plekhanov) is the best documented and will be discussed in some detail. However, this incident was not an isolated case but rather symptomatic of the widespread self-questioning, rethinking, and sudden reversals then prevalent among the revolutionaries, espe-cially among those of Jewish origin.

What made the situation in 1881–2 so difficult for established revolutionaries such as Akselrod and Deich (who were Jews) and Lavrov and Plekhanov (who were not) was the fact that they suddenly found themselves subject to scathing criticism in the émigré and student colonies abroad; in sharp disagreement with the policies of their own parties in Russia; and last but not least, unable to agree among themselves on a correct solution to the ideological problems raised by the pogroms.

Even though the attitude of the revolutionary organizations in Russia, as it came to expression in proclamations and articles in the underground press, was hardly uniform, there could be no doubt that it was predominantly sympathetic to the pogroms and still more to the *pogromshchiki*. The most extreme example was the proclamation of 30 August 1881 addressed by the executive committee of the Narodnaia Volia "To the Ukrainian People." This remarkable document contained such passages as these:

> It is difficult for people to live in the Ukraine and, as time passes, the harder it becomes . . . The people in the Ukraine suffer worst of all from the Jews. Who takes the land, the woods, the taverns from out of your hands? The Jews. From whom does the muzhik, often with tears in his eyes, have to beg permission to get to his own field, his own plot of land? – the Jews. Wherever you look, wherever you go – the Jews are everywhere. The Jew curses you, cheats you, drinks your blood . . . It was not always like this in the Ukraine, not in the time of our grandfathers and forefathers. All the land then be-longed to the muzhik; there were neither *pany* nor Jews . . . But [now] as soon as the muzhiki rise up to free themselves from their enemies as they did in Elizavetgrad, Kiev, Smela, the tsar at once comes to the rescue of the Jews: the soldiers from Russia are called in and the blood of the muzhik, Christian blood, flows . . . You have begun to rebel against the Jews. You have done well. Soon the revolt will be taken up across all of Russia against the tsar, the *pany,* the Jews.[275]

Of this proclamation the Soviet historian S. S. Volk wrote in 1966 that "it was disavowed by the majority of members of the executive committee and had no serious consequences."[276] But this is to underestimate the role of the document. True, there is no evidence to suggest that the proclamation provoked further violence; by September the first wave of pogroms had already somewhat spent its force. And it is also true that it was only decided to publish it after considerable discussion in the executive committee (which by mid-1881 had anyway been terribly weakened by constant arrests). Yet the fact remains that it was printed in two thousand copies on the party press, distributed to the provincial centers, and in Elizavetgrad even reprinted on the local hectograph. (On the other hand, Vera Figner apparently had the copies which reached Odessa destroyed.)[277] The crucial factor was that the author of the proclamation, G. G. Romanenko, a member of the executive committee, had actually become accepted as the party's expert on Ukrainian affairs because he had been born and educated in the south.

Dissent from his unqualified incitement to further pogroms came only in private letters. Tikhomirov, for instance, stated in one letter late in 1881 that "I was very much against it [the proclamation] but it is already an accomplished fact."[278] In contrast, Romanenko was able to restate his position in an unsigned and therefore official article which appeared in the October issue of the party journal. The hatred for the Jew, this article stated, was justified because it resulted not from "his religion, of course," but from his exploitation of the people.[279] The roaming crowds which destroyed and plundered were "just like the sans-culottes at the time of the Great [French] Revolution except that with us the terror is not limited to the large towns but spreads across the countryside."[280] Moreover, the intervention of the armed forces had stirred the crowds to still greater determination and revolutionary fervor. It concluded,

> Do you remember one of the stories of the French Revolution from Taine? One of the crowd throws himself on the corpse of a woman who has just been trampled to death by the enfuriated mob. He tears open her breast, drags out her heart and with exaltation sinks his teeth into it. But should Robespierre, Danton, St. Just and Desmoulins have abandoned their role and obligations in French history because of the excesses of the people enraged by oppression? . . . We have no right to react with indifference, still less with hostility, to a true popular movement . . . Elemental forces will erupt, the horrors of the French Revolution and the Pugachev rebellion will repeat themselves.[281]

In a note to this article, the August proclamation was specifically mentioned as an example of correct agitational tactics.[282]

The belief that the pogroms had to be understood as the first stage of the revolution was not confined to the Narodnaia Volia. Thus, the author of "A Letter from the South" published in the leading journal of the rival party, the Cherny Peredel, in September 1881 could declare that "I personally regard the rout of the Jews as the prelude to a more serious and purposeful popular movement."[283] As evidence he noted the belief widely held in the villages that "after the expulsion of the Jews (some want to send them to the Amur, others to Egypt, others more extreme simply to drown them in the Dnepr), the tsar will order the distribution of the land among the muzhiki."[284] Further, he suggested, the prestige of the socialists had been boosted by the general conviction that they were responsible for the pogroms and so they were now in an excellent position to lead a popular uprising.

Certainly, as against the tendency to legitimize or even incite the pogroms, there were socialist statements published in Russia that expressed a different line of thought. The proclamation issued in Kiev by the South Russian Union of Workers in the midst of the April pogrom was one example. "Our own merchant or factory owner," read this proclamation,

> plunders and destroys the worker worse than the Jew [zhid] . . . So how can one leave such a bloodsucker in peace and, at the same time, plunder a Jew who, perhaps, finds it no easier than one of us to keep body and soul together by the hardest work, as an artisan or a laborer? If we are to hit out then let us hit out at every plundering kulak.[285]

And in the worker paper, Zerno, published by the St. Petersburg section of Cherny Peredel, an article appeared in June 1881 which developed the same argument. "Why," it asked,

> did they [the pogromshchiki] beat only Jews? Yes, you, brothers, look closely at the Jews themselves and you will see that not all by far are rich, not all are kulaks. There are many poor among them who earn their bread by the sweat of their brow, who are squeezed by the kulaks and masters no less than you . . . Understand that all workers of whatever religion and nation must unite, must work against the common enemy.[286]

But even these two documents reveal clear signs of inner confusion. Thus, the Kiev proclamation opened with the statement that "one should not hit the Jew [zhid] because he is a Jew and prays to his own God – there is, after all, one God for everybody – but because he plunders the people, sucks the blood of the workingman."[287] Moshe Mishkinsky has argued convincingly that this document, certainly written in haste, reflected deep-rooted ideological divisions.[288] This, beyond doubt, was the case with the article in Zerno, which similarly accompanied its call for brotherhood with a bitter attack on Jewish exploitation: "The Jew owns the bars and taverns, rents land from the landowners and then leases it out to the peasant at two or three times the rate, he buys wheat on the field, goes in for money lending and charges percentages so high that people call them simply 'Yiddish' rates".[289] Here it is known that, when the original article – a full-blooded defense of the pogroms – reached the underground press in Minsk, the typesetters (all three were revolutionaries of Jewish origin) refused to print it. One, I. Getsov, hastened to St. Petersburg and persuaded the author to rewrite it in large part.[290]

If knowledge of the socialist publications in 1881 had been confined to revolutionary and governmental circles, their immediate impact would have been limited. But in fact rumor of their existence and import spread rapidly, although not always accurately. On the morrow of the Kiev pogrom, Levin wrote to Lilienblum and others that the proclamations, which he himself had seen, provided direct evidence of socialist responsibility,[291] an apparent exaggeration given the double-edged tone of the one known document. A more careful report in the Jewish Chronicle of 16 December 1881 suggests that by then there was a remarkable awareness of revolutionary attitudes. "At the outset," wrote the correspondent in Lyck, it was believed that the *Judenhetze* was provoked by the Nihilists. This belief was a groundless one ... But things have altered, and now the Nihilists in their proclamations likewise recommend the populace to persecute the Jews. This change of front has naturally produced a veritable panic for as soon as the Nihilists set themselves against the Jews their lives are no longer safe.[292]

Avrom Lesin recalled in his memoirs what an impression it had made on him as a young child to hear of the stand taken by the revolutionaries. "I kept asking myself: can it be that men who are capable of such dedication should break into the homes of strangers and scatter the feathers from the pillows and rob and murder?"[293]

That the revolutionaries in Russia generally welcomed the pogroms was in reality not surprising. The inherent tendency of revolutionary populism to idealize the *narod* was here reinforced in varying degrees by Bakunist *buntarstvo* (the ideology of the peasant jacquerie) and by Tkachev's or even Nechaev's Jacobinism (the justification of the means by the ends). Moreover, the struggle – literally for life or death – against the tsarist regime, the constant depletion of the ranks by arrests, and the failure of the assassination of Alexander II to shake the regime inevitably drove many revolutionaries to read an apocalyptic meaning into the pogroms.

But for the leading revolutionaries abroad – Plekhanov, Zasulich and Deich in Geneva, Akselrod in Zurich, Lavrov and Kropotkin in London – the entire turn of events produced by the pogroms was disastrous. In the émigré colonies they found themselves thrown onto the defensive, subject to the severest attacks by many of the students, and faced by a formidable, a tried-and-tested, critic in the veteran Ukrainian radical and revolutionary, M. P. Dragomanov.

That Dragomanov had long concerned himself with the Jewish question in the Ukraine now enabled him to argue that while he had foreseen and tried to forestall the current crisis, the Russian revolutionary leadership throughout had buried their heads ostrich-like in the sand. It was in the mid-1870s that he had first suggested a working arrangement between his Ukrainian-oriented group and the Jewish socialists led by Liberman. Despite the unbridled attacks on Liberman by such Ukrainian revolutionaries as Sergei Podolinski, Dragomanov had believed that such a rapprochement was logical and had, in fact, arranged for a leading Ukrainian revolutionary to meet secretly with Y. L. Levin in Kiev in 1877 to discuss the issue.[294] In 1880 he, together with two other Ukrainians (A. Liakhotsky and M. Pavlik), had come out in print in support of an alliance between the Ukrainian and Jewish working masses in southern Russia. (Their statement came in the form of an addendum to a manifesto, "From a Group of Socialist Jews," originally drafted, it seems, with the participation of Lazar Tsukerman, a one-time comrade of Liberman who in 1879 was working as a typesetter for Dragomanov's journal, *Hromada*).[295]

The manifesto itself praised Liberman's "serious effort to organize socialist literature for the masses in the 70s,"[296] but argued that its use of Hebrew rather than Yiddish had doomed it to failure. At a time when "everywhere literature in the simple folk-language is coming to life"[297] the future clearly belonged to Yiddish, and they, "the group of Jewish socialists," therefore pledged themselves to publish revolutionary literature in that language. In their endorsement, Dragomanov's trio suggested that a third of the Jews in the Ukraine had to be categorized as workers who should therefore unite with the Ukrainian people. It was essential to break down barriers between the two peoples and so prevent indiscriminate attacks on the Jews during the coming revolution – "bloody scenes that would be far more unjust than those of the seventeenth and eighteenth centuries."[298]

At the time, this initiative had constituted no more than an ephemeral sensation in the émigré colony in Geneva. With Tsukerman's departure to work in the St. Petersburg press of the Narodnaia Volia, there were no Jewish activists of stature to defend it.[299] At a public debate in 1880, the concept advocated by Dragomanov of a Jewish socialist organization based on Yiddish was attacked and mocked by such leading figures in the Russian revolutionary movement as Nikolai Zhukovsky and Lev Deich. ("Only the extraordinary efforts of the chairman," Dragomanov later wrote, "prevented the meeting from ending in a major scandal. Speakers from the Russian and Polish parties – especially those of Jewish origin – reacted with particular venom.")[300]

But in late 1881 and early 1882, of course, the tables were turned. The arrival in Switzerland of young populists such as Ben Ami and H. Sabsovich, who were associated with the Am Olam movement, provided concrete proof of the new orientation among the Jewish youth within the Empire. And, at the same time, the growing evidence that the Narodnaia Volia and Cherny Peredel had welcomed, were even inciting, the pogroms undermined the prestige of the "internationalists" (now vulnerable to the accusation of being de facto chauvinists) and enhanced that of the "nationalists" (the Jewish and Ukrainian populists, who could now claim to represent genuine internationalism).

The available records do not permit the historian to trace in detail this new confrontation as it developed in all the various Russian colonies abroad, although it is known, for example, that in London Y. A. Finkelshtein (the founder of the Vilna *kruzhok* in 1872) was so infuriated by Kropotkin's statements on the pogroms that he moved toward the Palestine movement;[301] and that in Zurich, Grigorii Gurevich was prominent in the circle of Russian-Jewish students who there subjected Akselrod to relentless criticism.[302] But, as against this, and thanks to the many articles devoted to the subject by Dragomanov and Ben Ami in the journal, *Volnoe slovo,* it is possible to form an almost complete picture of the attack then being advanced against the Russian revolutionary leaders in Geneva.

The fundamental error of the Russian revolutionary movement in the 1870s, argued Ben Ami and Dragomanov alike, lay in the fact that it had legitimized, encouraged, the alienation of the Jewish intelligentsia from its own *narod.* "While within the Russian intelligentsia, particularly the student youth," Ben Ami wrote, "there has developed a powerful drive to join 'the little brother,' the mass of 'gray people' . . . among the Jewish intelligentsia . . . the exact opposite drive has developed – to get as far away as possible from the Jewish masses, to break all connections with them."[303] The socialists of Jewish origin, Dragomanov declared, were "pleased with their emancipation from the Jewish world and [in many cases] would be glad to forget its existence."[304]

This paradoxical development, they suggested, had led to a number of negative results. Dragomanov, as the spokesman of a radical Ukrainian nationalism, insisted that the influx of uprooted and russified Jewish *intelligenty* into the ranks of the

Russian parties had inevitably strengthened their centralistic tendencies, their blindness to the vast local differences which distinguished the various peoples living within the empire. "The socialists and *narodniki,* cut off from their own people," he wrote, "were even less capable than others of linking up with the non-Jewish popular masses and so they only strengthened the 'general-Russian,' i.e., alienated [*bezpochvenny*] element in the Russian [parties]."[305] There was an aversion to visualizing the masses in their concrete, national context.

His frequent attempts (dating back to Zurich in 1873) to discuss the issue publicly, Dragomanov wrote, had long convinced him "that the Russian socialists and populists, particularly in their press, simply did not want to undertake an examination of the Jewish question[306] ... some because of their ability to make do with abstract propositions (or their habit of doing so); some because of their fear of raising questions painful to many."[307] Falling back on the common assumption that the Jewish problem would be solved by the granting of equal rights, they had ignored the fact that "Russia is not Switzerland or even Germany – in the western parts of Russia there are at least 3,000,000 Jews. That is an entire nation [*natsiia*]."[308] And nations could not simply be ignored.

Ben Ami went a step farther. The flight of the intelligentsia, he wrote, inevitably suggested to outside observers that "the Jewish masses were therefore something so disgusting that the best Jews themselves seek to get away from them."[309] And instead of refuting this view, the Jewish *intelligenty* usually confirmed it, anxious as they were "to earn the passionately desired compliment that they were in no way similar to [the mass of] Jews."[310] Ben Ami thus made the implicit accusation that by cutting themselves off from their own people, the Jewish *intelligenty* had contributed if not directly to the pogroms, then at least to the sympathetic reception given those pogroms in liberal and socialist circles.

Of course, even in the first months of 1882, there remained fundamental points of disagreement between Dragomanov and Ben Ami. In particular, while Ben Ami, in tune with the current mood, was a passionate advocate of Jewish emigration, Dragomanov dismissed the plan as so much fantasy. With a natural increase of 120,000 per annum, the Russian-Jewish population could not be significantly reduced by emigration projects even if the Rothschilds and their ilk were ready to contribute huge capital sums. "Millions of people," he stated, "do not emigrate."[311] Those Ukrainian *narodniki* who were counting on a general Jewish exodus would serve the interests of their cause more effectively by demanding the abolition of the Pale of Settlement and "the carefully organized transfer of Jews from the western part of the empire to the eastern."[312]

Meanwhile, such disagreements were overshadowed by their common rejection of the thesis that for the Jewish socialist internationalism meant Russification. The Jewish intelligentsia was duty-bound to organize the Jewish laboring class using the language – Yiddish – it understood best. In May 1882 Dragomanov could write of Ben Ami that he "was one of the type which the masses in southwest Russia, not only Jewish but also Christian, now need most, i.e., that type of person who is educated but has not cut himself off from his own 'dark' masses and insists on the need of those with education to go to their own *narod..*"[313]

It was no doubt criticism of the type here described, taken up in Zurich by the students around Gurevich (his friend from Mohilev and Berlin days),[314] that reduced Pavel Borisovich Akselrod by early 1882 to a mood of self-mortification. He accepted the validity of the case made against the Russian revolutionary leadership (of which he was a member), and made up his mind to rectify the situation, to recognize the Russian-Jewish question as a major issue in its own right, to apply the principles of socialist internationalism fearlessly and publicly to the current crisis.

Early in 1882 (probably in February) he began writing a brochure on the subject which he hoped or even assumed would be accepted as a statement of their collective policy first by Plekhanov, Deich, and Vera Zasulich (the exiled leadership of the Cherny Peredel) and, subsequently, by the executive committee of the Narodnaia Volia. In short, he sought not simply to state a personal position but to attain the official repudiation of what he held to be the major errors perpetuated by the two parties in Russia in 1881. For their part, the trio in Geneva agreed that Akselrod should draw up such a statement in draft form for their collective perusal. During the spring months of 1882 he apparently drew up more than one version of the brochure, "On the Tasks of the Jewish Socialist Youth," but only one manuscript has survived.[315]

Akselrod opened with a personal statement:

> It is probable that many of the Russian-Jewish socialists, before they set foot on the revolutionary path, dreamed of devoting their energies to the cause of the social and national rebirth of the Jewish people. But, as is well known, all – or, at least, all those who developed under the influence of Russian literature – cast off these thoughts regarding the Jewish masses at the first moment that the blinding light of socialist ideas penetrated their minds. I still remember how, reading the book of Lassalle, I felt a kind of shame at my concern for the interests of the Jewish people. What significance could a handful of Jews have in comparison with the universal interests that were the concern of socialism . . . After all, strictly speaking, the Jewish question does not exist and the only question is the liberation of the working masses of all nations, including the Jewish . . . Would it not be senseless and criminal to devote one's efforts to the Jewish people, which is no more than a single element in the vast population of the Russian Empire![316]

But, in reality, Akselrod now suggested, "the cosmopolitan idea of socialism" had not necessarily demanded this conclusion. It would have been at least as logical for such socialists in Odessa, Kharkov, or Kiev to organize revolutionary groups among the Jewish working population and at the same time to have retained the "closest connection . . . even as active members" with (or within) the general Russian movement.[317] Liberman had taken this stand, but his "attempt to organize propaganda among the Jews . . . was not supported by the active elements among the Jewish socialists and so led to no serious results."[318] Now the full measure of that error stood revealed. Given "ten years of systematic propaganda among the Jews" and close ties between the Jewish and Russian worker circles, it might well have been possible

> to weaken significantly the one-sided, ugly-nationalistic character of the "anti-Jewish pogroms," to prepare elements which, at least in a few cases,

could have diverted the crowd from attacking the poor and directed them, if not against the centers of popular exploitation in general, then at least against the rich Jews.[319]

As it was, left to "the natural course of things," the laboring masses had become the major victims of the pogroms. And this sight of

> indiscriminate destruction and violence against tens of thousands of Jewish families . . . [together with] the cynical hounding of the Jews as a *nation* by a significant section of the Russian press – in a word, a host of ugly phenomena symptomatic of a purely medieval attitude . . . has finally opened the eyes of the Jewish–socialist intelligentsia to its mistake.[320]

Akselrod then proceeded to analyze the Jewish problem in Russia and to suggest the action socialists should take in relation to it. The crucial fact, he maintained, was that the Jews in Russia constituted "a nation"; that this nation occupied "a completely exceptional position" and was "hated by the vast majority of the most varied strata of the Christian population."[321] Thus, "it is not this or that category of Jews which earns . . . destruction but all who are linked by blood to the Jewish people, all the *zhidy* to a man, as a nation."[322]

Up until this point it could have been a Lilienblum writing. But when he sought to trace the roots of this phenomenon, Akselrod followed a line of thought strikingly similar to that of Dragomanov. Hatred for minorities, in this case the Jews, was not rooted in national or racial instincts, not in an immutable and universal human nature, but rather was the product of a particular socioeconomic structure, a historically determined environment. Thus, with Dragomanov, he noted that a far higher percentage of Jews were engaged in nonproductive occupations in the south and southwest, where the pogroms had been concentrated, than in the northwest. Even a starving tavern-keeper (such as his father) was, as a middleman, inevitably regarded as an exploiter by the peasants. "However great the poverty and deprivation suffered by the Jewish masses . . . the fact remains that, taken overall, some half of them function as a nonproductive element, sitting astride the neck of the lower classes in Russia."[323]

For socialists, Akselrod urged, the conclusions were clear. As a result of "the class antagonism which exists among the Jews no less than among other nations" they could only ally themselves with the Jewish working masses and could not concern themselves with "the national renaissance of Jews or the establishment of a Jewish state."[324] They could, however, legitimately join the emigration movement to the United States in order to take part in the attempts "to convert the mass of émigrés into a productive class, on the one hand, and to fuse them with the local population, on the other."[325]

In contrast, as long as Russia remained bereft of fundamental freedoms there could be no systematic attempt there to transfer the Jews to productive branches of the economy. And because of the primitive level of "the peasant masses and even the urban *meshchanstvo*" it would likewise be absurd to work for an immediate merger of the Jews and Russians. ("It can be positively stated that, on average, the Russian Jews stand higher in their mental and political demands.")[326] All that could be done, therefore, by those socialists who remained in Russia was to create revolutionary organizations among the Jewish population, link those organizations to the general movement, and by propaganda seek to prevent further pogroms (or, if worst came to worst, to ensure that only the Brodskys, the Poliakovs, and Gintsburgs fell victim to the onslaught).

Grigorii Gurevich had by now become a passionate *Palestinets,* and Akselrod, too, as revealed in his correspondence with Lev Deich, planned initially to include in his brochure support for Jewish settlement in Palestine. In 1924, writing to Lesin, Akselrod recalled how, early in 1882, he had argued that " 'because of historic tradition . . . Palestine could be for the Jews a true fatherland,' their 'own little state' where they would feel at least as much the political masters and equal citizens as the Letts, the Finns, or the Poles in those Russian provinces which were theirs historically."[327]

At Akselrod's request, Vera Zasulich even took a list of questions on the practicability of the Palestine scheme to the well-known geographer and socialist Élisée Reclus. And even though Reclus declared it "a country unsuited for migration and settlement where the Jews could only live by trade and exploitation,"[328] Akselrod persisted in his support of Palestine into April. Thus, in a letter of 21 April, Deich could complain that "we, as socialist internationalists, should not . . . recognize special obligations toward 'co-nationals' [*so-plemenniki*] and so your siding with the Judaeophile *Razsvet* [*sic*] on the question of Palestinian settlement doesn't please us."[329] Deich (at one with Dubnov on this issue) argued that in Palestine the Jews would "become frozen still further in their prejudices" and eventually, in a few generations, return to Europe even less suited to blend into modern life. "Once the Jews are emigrating," he concluded, "then let them go to America where they will merge with the local population."[330] Judging from the surviving version of the brochure, Akselrod eventually decided to modify his position here along the lines urged from Geneva.

But Palestine was not the only issue which made it difficult for the trio to accept the brochure. In particular, they objected to Akselrod's opinion that the low cultural level of the Russian peasant and urban masses made thought of Jewish assimilation with them ridiculous. Unlike Akselrod, who had already been profoundly influenced by the German Social Democratic movement, Plekhanov, Deich, and Vera Zasulich were too close to their original Bakuninism to accept so disparaging a view of the Russian *narod.* The brochure, wrote Deich, should describe "the real revolutionary movement" to the Jews; call on them "to cooperate in winning political freedom"; and "advise them to work toward a merger with the other nationalities of the Russian state and not to remain isolated."[331]

As there seemed little chance of agreement on Akselrod's draft, it was suggested that perhaps Lavrov would agree to write an alternative version, but he proved very reluctant to do so. "I must admit," Lavrov wrote on 14 April,

> that I consider it an extremely complex question and, practically speaking, for a party seeking to draw near to the people and rouse it against the government also in the highest degree difficult. To solve it on paper and in theory is very easy; but in view of the existence of popular passions and the necessity of the Russian socialists to have the people wherever possible on their side it is quite another matter.[332]

And in a footnote to this letter, Deich added:

> The Jewish question is now in reality, in practice, almost insoluble for the revolutionaries. What, for example, should they do now in Balta where they are beating up the Jews? To defend them means, as Reclus says, "to call up the hatred of the peasants against the revolutionaries who not only killed the tsar but also defend the Jews." Of course, it is an obligation to seek equal rights for [the Jews] ... but that, so to speak, is activity in the higher spheres; and to conduct pacificatory agitation among the people is very, very difficult for the party.[333]

Throughout, Akselrod insisted that, one way or the other, a public stand had to be taken to rebut the view that Romanenko represented the revolutionary movement. If all else failed, he considered having the brochure published at his own (or Gurevich's) expense. But Deich insisted that he accept the decision of the majority as binding. The small group of Chernoperedeltsy was then engaged in complex negotiations for unification, or at least close collaboration, with the Narodnaia Volia, and Deich argued that any show of internal division was bound to weaken its bargaining position. Akselrod replied angrily that even the German Social Democrats did not demand "the suppression to such an extent of individual views in deference to party and personal ties."[334] However, Deich was not impressed. What was required was "the tightest unity, terrible solidarity."[335] "Do not think," he wrote again, "that [the Russian-Jewish situation] has not pained and confused me, for example; but, nonetheless, I remain always a member of the Russian revolutionary party and do not intend to part from it even for a single day, for this contradiction, like some others, was not created by the party."[336]

In May 1882 negotiations were still proceeding, and Akselrod had not given up hope that somehow the socialist internationalists would take a public stand against the pogroms and in favor of a Jewish "going to the people."

After-effects

The fever ends

In its historical sense, the term "revolution" is most commonly understood to mean an abrupt and long-lasting form of change. Thus, the Hildebrandine, scientific and industrial – no less than the Puritan, American, and French – revolutions have long become established in the historical lexicon. Conversely, dramatic and sudden upheavals (Peter the Great's reforms, the uprisings of 1848, the Paris Commune) are frequently denied the title because they represented perhaps a less pronounced watershed. Thus, whether the crisis of Russian Jewry in 1881–2 should be termed a revolution in modern Jewish politics must be judged not simply by the dimensions of the immediate political eruptions – which were clearly extraordinary – but also and primarily by its long-term results. And this, as already noted above, is a controversial historiographical issue.

Certainly, the immediate fate of the emigration movement in 1882 was anticlimactic and led most contemporary observers to feel that they had just lived through a high fever, that they were now in a period of lethargy and weakness and that gradually life would return to its normal routine. The objective developments which had given impetus to the exodic movement came to an abrupt halt in the summer of 1882. The chain reaction that had hitherto sustained the accelerating excitement now began to work in reverse.

The key throughout had lain with the tsarist government, and in May and June, Russian Jews discovered signs of a sharp change in official policy. On 3 May 1882, the so-called Temporary Regulations were issued. Historians (Dubnov and Cherikover, for instance)[337] have tended to describe the governmental decisions in blackest terms, and, of course, it did signal the beginning of a new anti-Jewish era in tsarist legislation. But, in reality, it was greeted at the time with quiet relief. The Regulations made it illegal for urban Jews to settle or acquire land in the shtetlkh or villages. This could only be seen as a reprieve given the widespread fear which had existed until then that there could be a massive transfer of the Jewish population to Central Asia or a general expulsion from the rural areas (which was what Ignatev had originally proposed to the Council of Ministers).[338]

Then, on 30 May, Ignatev was replaced by Count Dmitrii Tolstoy. And almost at once – on 9 June – he issued a circular to the provincial governors in which he insisted unequivocally that pogroms in any shape or form be prevented. "The government," it declared, "will prosecute every kind of violence against the Jews . . . ; any sign of disorders will unavoidably result in the immediate prosecution of all officials who are responsible for keeping public order."[339] Even though this was an internal memorandum, news of it soon became public and by 30 June an editorial in *Russkii evrei* could note the general belief that the era of violence was over.[340] In a letter of early June, Y. Y. Levontin noted wryly that in Russia, as against Europe, everything was upside down – the Jews had to rely on such archconservatives, reactionaries, as Tolstoy and Katkov while the "liberals" had emerged as among their most merciless opponents.[341]

The introduction of Tolstoy's new policy coincided with the crumbling, the collapse even, of the schemes which had been developed for large-scale emigration to and settlement in America and Palestine. In the months of May and June, the Mansion House Committee was sending up to nine hundred Jews per week to the United States. But for all its panache, this campaign could not last.

As early as March 1882, M. A. Kursheedt (managing secretary of the HEAS) had sent the following telegram to London: "Only young unmarried refugees should emigrate hither. Send neither families nor farmers."[342] At that stage, London had rejected this plea, arguing that they were all faced by "a natural flow of emigration" and that the most which could be done from Europe was "to prevent the emigrants arriving destitute on your shores."[343] A memorandum, circulated in April among members of the Mansion House Committee and somehow leaked to the press, suggested that the New York Committee be circumvented altogether and the Russian Jews supplied with through tickets to various towns throughout the United States. It was on this basis that the huge migration was now organized.[344]

For a time, London ignored the increasingly irate letters arriving from New York and Paris. "This could be a true calamity for the Jews in the United States," declared a letter of 15 May from the Alliance, "for their own situation could be compromised."[345] And on 9 June Kursheedt wrote: "It is no more than justice to

American Israelites not to send hither 'convoys' of incapable people . . . It is unwise and unendurable that America should by your act be made to provide for such unfortunate cases."[346] From London the constant reply was that thousands of destitute refugees could not be left callously to their fate. The Jewish press in the two countries joined in the confrontation. The HEAS, the *Jewish Chronicle* declared on 30 June, "provides employment only for those who could obtain it without their help and they advocate wife desertion and renunciation of primary religious observances."[347] And, for its part, the *American Hebrew* stated bluntly on 23 June: "All emigration for the present *must* be stopped."[348]

In this contest of wills, the London committee could not win except in the very short run. The American economy in mid-1882 was entering a recession and there were not enough jobs for the unskilled arrivals. In many cases all that stood between them and starvation were the charitable efforts of the Jewish communities in the various cities where they appeared. In New York so many hundreds of immigrants gathered daily around the HEAS offices that policemen were stationed permanently at the door to keep the crowds under control, a step not easily understood nor forgiven by people newly arrived from tsarist Russia. In Cincinnati the Jewish committee suddenly found itself called upon to cope with a trainload of two hundred and fifty immigrants who had arrived without advance notice, ragged and famished – supplied with through-tickets and checks in Europe, they did not have the ready cash to eat en route from New York.[349] In Philadelphia, the leader of the community, Moses Dropsie, felt compelled to announce that some immigrants were being returned to Europe because the pressure had become intolerable.[350] Given these enormous day-to-day financial pressures, the plans for large-scale land purchases and colonization were inevitably assigned a low priority, crippled at birth.

Reports published in the Russian-Jewish press from the immigrants were now, in contrast to 1881, frequently marked by a note of desperation. The only aid to be expected from the American Jews, one new arrival wrote, was the constant advice, "Help yourself!"[351] Russian Jews should be warned to stay away. Another correspondent blamed the Jewish intelligentsia in Russia for encouraging this hopeless venture and declared that "it is the duty of the Russian Jews who have stayed in their homeland to aid their unfortunate brothers to return to their burnt-out homes."[352] News of the removal of Ignatev encouraged many to seek to go back to Russia, and by July the newspapers could describe how hundreds of Jews were arriving from America at the Russian border only in many cases to be denied reentry there.

At the same time, it had become apparent that the more Russian Jews were sent to the United States, the more arrived in Brody in the hope of joining the convoys. Close to nine thousand refugees were to be found in Brody in mid-July,[353] even more than the total sent on since April. Under these circumstances, the Mansion House Committee decided late in June to reverse its stand totally and halt the transportations. In early August, a conference representative of the main European aid committees was held in Vienna and the British delegate proposed that all the thousands of Russian Jews stranded in Galicia be repatriated. Even though this proposal was rejected as too extreme, the great majority of refugees were now returned speedily to Russia.[354]

"Reviewing the work done," the *Jewish Chronicle* wrote on 15 September 1882, "we can surely feel proud of the part taken in it by England."[355] An American commentator declared that historians in the future would record that in the crisis "no people on earth have done more in work and in money than the Jewish inhabitants of the United States."[356] But in Russia, the mood was one of extreme deflation. Editorials in *Razsvet* spoke of Jews "starving or dying in New York [and] Brody,"[357] of the severely exacerbated "problem of our proletariat"[358] in Russia, and of the impossibility of large-scale Jewish colonization in the United States. *Russkii evrei* could not refrain from a certain schadenfreude:

> Thousands of emigrants are returning to Russia having gone hungry in Brody for many months . . . ; hundreds are returning home even from America. We ask those who until recently argued for emigration at any cost to consider how productive was the expense of transporting the latter . . . across the Atlantic. In a word there can no longer be any doubt that emigration cannot serve as a possible way out for the suffering.[359]

If the American campaign had been forced to a standstill in the summer of 1882, the Palestinian alternative proved itself even less suited to pass the harsh test of reality. The general assumption that the Turkish government would welcome large-scale Jewish settlement in Palestine was gradually revealed in the months of May and June to be false. When, early in May, a notice was posted at the Turkish Consulate in Odessa announcing that, by order of the sultan, Jews would not be permitted to immigrate to Palestine, the news was greeted with consternation, not despair. Laurence Oliphant and other influential men of the world were in Constantinople and were expected to dispel such misunderstandings.

But, as noted above, by mid-June Oliphant himself had given up hope of an early diplomatic triumph at the court of the sultan. However much inclined to religious mysticism, he still saw the situation for what it was and di ' not hesitate to transmit his assessment to the Russian Jews. As the result of the Egyptian crisis, he informed his Russian-Jewish contacts, it had become impossible for Englishmen such as Cazalet and himself to exert any positive influence in Constantinople. His advice to the Bilu was to wait in Russia for a period of months until the situation clarified itself (advice that was rejected). Even though in all his letters he expressed his faith that in the near future circumstances would change, that the Jews would soon leave "their present slavery" as they had once "been liberated from Egypt,"[360] there could be no doubt of the crushing impact made by his negative reports.

Already in May, a denunciation of Oliphant sent from one of the many observers in Constantinople, the writer Iosif Rabinovich, had been published in the Russian-Jewish press. Oliphant, he declared, had neither influence nor money; he was not the long-awaited savior, not "the English Bar-Kochba," but a false pretender, a "Bar Koziba," one of "the false prophets who have led the Jews astray."[361] A letter to Z. D. Levontin at this time warned that the messianic mood could thus easily end in total despair:

> The Jewish people which has always tended to rely on authority, today too depends on one "great man" or another . . . And so it is in this instance: much has been staked on Oliphant and people believed him because the

papers said that he is a great man, wise and knowledgeable, an "authority." And if somebody else comes along and reveals a flaw in him, they will lose heart and not know what to do.[362]

With the evaporation of hope in Oliphant, the Palestine movement found itself face to face with grim realities. Hundreds of poor families who had scraped together the means to sail for Palestine now found themselves stranded in Jaffa or Constantinople. The Alliance was slow to come to the aid of these Jews, who had therefore to suffer terrible want in the late spring and summer of 1882. Grigorii Gurevich, who had gone to explore Palestine for himself, was severely shaken by his encounter with these starving families who, as he wrote, had "fled, without any doubts, with their wives and children to Jaffa." When asked why they had taken this step, "all gave one answer – our newspapers told us to go to Palestine; we read that Mr. Oliphant promised to help us; that [Z. D. Levontin's] Jaffa committee was setting up colonies."[363] Another observer now noted that many of the emigrants had hoped "to become rich quickly and easily," and that "the emigration, like every popular movement, had brought to the surface much that is vile and many pathological phenomena which pass unnoticed in the normal circumstances of life."[364] Eventually, the Alliance supplied the sums necessary to evacuate and disperse the impoverished families,[365] but, as Sokolov's journal Ha-tsfira noted, the idea that Palestine could serve in the foreseeable future as a refuge for mass migrations had been thoroughly discredited.[366]

Under the stress of frustrated expectations, the spokesmen for the movement took to attacking each other. The leaders of the Bilu in Constantinople, Mints and Berliavsky, denounced Rozenfeld of the Razsvet as a windbag who was not prepared to assure their party any concrete aid. They, in turn, found themselves dismissed by Lilienblum and Kamensky as "hot-headed schoolboys unknown to anybody,"[367] and the Bilu itself now split in half. The efforts of Mints and Berliavsky in Constantinople to make a diplomatic breakthrough were renounced by the advance-guard in Palestine as escapist fantasies. "Everybody will realize," Belkind wrote to Razsvet, "that those who are actually working in Palestine . . . constitute the Bilu and not those who are building castles in the air in Constantinople."[368]

Later in 1882, Zeev (Vladimir) Dubnov, a member of the Bilu, could write to his brother: "All our youth was watching us, they expected very much from us – and now what? The mountain has given birth to a mouse – squabbles, quarrels, pettiness and finally a split."[369] The sums of money freely promised the Bilu by wealthy wellwishers in the heady days of the spring did not materialize in the more somber period that followed, when, it was noted, the young Palestintsy were perhaps altogether too radical and utopian in their social outlook. "We [Russian Jews] . . . ," wrote the correspondent of the Jewish Chronicle in mid-August, "have learned a great deal [too much] from the Russian Nihilists, whose principles the advocates of colonization of Palestine appear to have taken as their model."[370]

On his return from Constantinople in July 1882, Rozenfeld found that the enthusiasm for a founding conference of the Palestinian camp had dramatically waned. The fact that Count Dmitrii Tolstoy had come out not only against the pogroms but also, in a circular of 21 June (at Poliakov's urging),[371] against Jewish emigration had raised awkward questions about the political advisability and safety of such a conference. Letters from the *Razsvet* circle now complained that "in the provinces many have been lulled or calmed down – or pretend to be calmed down – by the ostensible changes in government policy";[372] that "Tolstoy's circular on emigration has frightened many, raised the hopes of others and generally loosened the anyway weak link which existed before among the emigrationists."[373] Plans for the conference, envisaged in many variants for the summer of 1882, were soon abandoned, and another victim of the new mood was *Razsvet* itself. The interest in it went into sharp decline, a trend strongly encouraged by the St. Petersburg magnates, who (in Flekser's words) used "all means in order to discredit that messianically inclined journal."[374] Early in 1883, *Razsvet* had to close down, bankrupt.

The euphoria had given way to depression. Grigorii Gurevich in his report on Palestine concluded that "the nature and life of the East will dictate its conditions to us, not we to it. And what an enormous struggle is required, what gigantic work . . . And the pioneers ready to sacrifice themselves in such a barren struggle of life and death are hardly to be found."[375] "The immediate renewal of the Holy Land," concluded Pinsker, was out of the question; but the American movement had failed too. What a difference, he wrote, there was between the Biblical exodus and the one they had just been forced to witness:

> A few barracks [for the refugees] and a few thousand free tickets . . . And then a few shipments for the return back; and, yes, also a few thousand bitter disappointments, and the power of the popular movement which promises a new life is beginning to weaken. There is quiet all around and our philanthropist brethren in the West can return to their serene calm.[376]

But it was left to the leading Hebrew poet of the time, Yehuda Leb Gordon, to summarize most succinctly the mood of the time. "You ask what we are?" he wrote. "We are not a nation, nor a congregation; we are a herd."[377]

With the general change of mood and, in particular, with Grigorii Gurevich's report – not so much negative as despairing – from Palestine, Pavel Borisovich Akselrod gradually ceased to press his demand that the Russian socialists take a public stand on the Jewish issue. He was still absorbed by the problem in the late spring[378] but, thereafter, he lapsed back into a long silence.

The sudden end of the euphoria doubtless contributed to the rapidly widening gap which opened up in the summer of 1882 between Dragomanov and Ben Ami. During the spring, Dragomanov had clearly seen the upsurge of the youth parties such as Am Olam as proof that his concept of an alliance between Jewish and Ukrainian populism was not only logical but also practical. He shared with Ben Ami a belief in a Jewish "going to the people," a revulsion against Russification, a respect for the particularity of every nationality and of every folk-language and had eagerly sought out this common ground. But, as the months passed, as intractable realities reasserted themselves, so the divisions of opinion between the two came to overshadow all else.

For Ben Ami, the Jews had to be seen as a nation of victims, a minority persecuted throughout the centuries and now, with cruel injustice, held responsible for the results of that persecution. For Dragomanov, the simple fact was that, whatever the reasons, the Jews in the Ukraine provided the bulk of the kulak class and only a minority—less than one third—could be considered economically productive. Ben Ami held it to be the first duty of every revolutionary to condemn the wanton pillage of innocent working people. For Dragomanov, the interests of the Ukrainian masses had to take priority.

What finally turned a difference of emphasis into an open clash were the differing assessments of Romanenko's well-known proclamation of 31 August 1881.[379] "This proclamation," Dragomanov wrote in July 1882, "describes in essence correctly the status quo in the relationship between the Jews and the Ukrainian people," even though it had erred seriously in its failure to mention the class of working Jews.[380] Dragomanov's comment was too much for Ben Ami. The pogroms, he insisted, were simply a manifestation of irrational and despicable national passions, and to explain them in socioeconomic terms was in effect to justify them. It was the Jewish farming settlements which, above all, had been "destroyed with an incomprehensible frenzy, the agricultural equipment smashed to smithereens, the cattle taken away or killed in the most barbaric way . . . And these vile, base acts met almost no criticism . . . [Now] Dragomanov sees the [Romanenko] proclamation as an encouraging phenomenon with only a minor reservation."[381] To blame the Jews in Russia for the fact that most were not farmers "makes one's blood boil with anger." Jews, after all, had been forbidden traditionally to own land, a law still in force. "It is shameful to . . . chain a man up and then blame him for not moving from where he is."[382] But Ben Ami's indignation simply alienated Dragomanov further: "The Jewish nation," he wrote in September, "constitutes in its majority not only a separate stratum but a parasitic stratum."[383] The Jewish workers had not proved their class consciousness by deeds; on the contrary, they clearly "dreamed of joining the ranks of the exploiters." "Should not the appeal for worker and proletarian solidarity be directed first of all to the Jewish proletariat or, at least, not to the Ukrainians alone?"[384]

It was from this point (mid-September 1882) that *Volnoe slovo* (Dragomanov's journal) began to publish a series of highly favorable articles on the First International Anti-Semitic Congress then held in Germany. At least, read one such article, "the antisemites in central Europe, unlike almost the entire press and public opinion [there], believe that the anti-Jewish disorders [in Russia] were caused . . . by the acts of the Jews themselves . . . and this fact shows how strong is the force of their conviction, their independence of character, their moral bravery."[385]

The failure of the leading Russian socialists abroad to announce in print their opposition to the pogroms, combined with the increasingly anti-Jewish position of Dragomanov, left statements such as Romanenko's as the official position of the Russian revolutionary movement. The significance of this became apparent in mid-1883 when the Narodnaia Volia—again in its major journal—chose to defend a pogrom which had then broken out in Ekaterinoslav. Romanenko had long since been arrested but the thesis he had defended in 1881 was now repeated:

The *narod* . . . attacks the Jews not as Jews but as *zhidy*, i.e., as exploiters . . .[386] The Jews, as Karl Marx once explained so well, being an unfortunate and long persecuted people, have become highly nervous and receptive; they reproduce in themselves as in a mirror (not a normal, but a distorting mirror) all the defects of the surrounding society, all the sores of a given social structure so that when anti-Jewish movements begin one can be sure that concealed within them is a protest against the entire order.[387]

Looking at the year of the "exodus" in the light of its immediate aftermath it was possible to believe that it had produced no substantial change. But, in retrospect – with the aid of hindsight – it is possible to see that this was not the case.

Ten years later

The energies generated by the crisis of 1881–2 would clearly dissipate themselves if they were not soon directed into stable organizational channels. It is the institutionalization of radical change that distinguishes the political revolution from the political upheaval. The dramatic and spontaneous has to be translated into the routine; the messianic and utopian into the constructive; the charismatic into the administrational. That such a transition could be made appeared highly doubtful in the latter months of 1882. It is necessary to move forward at least a decade, to take the years 1890–2 as a vantage point, in order to distinguish the ephemeral effects from the permanent.

Two political movements which emerged from the crisis of 1881–2 had established themselves, proved their viability, during that ten-year period. They were, on the one hand, the proto-Zionist movement – the Hoveve Zion in Russia, the colonies in Palestine – and, on the other, the Jewish labor movement in the United States, particularly in New York. Both these movements had developed not in accord with the blueprints sketched out in 1881–2 but through a complex process of trial and error, of adapting the ideal to the real.

Compared with their millennial aspirations, their rhetorical self-definitions, their achievements were absurdly modest. Seen against the background of Jewish politics in the pre-1881 era, what they had accomplished was remarkable. They had become the first political movements, as distinct from pressure groups, philanthropic organizations, ideological sects, and newspaper campaigns, in modern Jewish history.

Sprung from the same seedbed – the emigrationist ideology of 1881–2 – these two movements had to develop under highly divergent circumstances and soon reached a point of violent opposition the one to the other. Thus, the division within the Jewish world (which would become increasingly important until 1933) between a socialist camp virulently hostile to the Zionist idea and a nationalist wing committed to it can be traced back to the late 1880s.

That the idea of Palestinian settlement could be translated into viable political terms in this period is a historical phenomenon which almost defies rational understanding. Following the experiences of 1881–2 it was clear that arrayed against it were the overt hostility of the Turkish government, the tried and tested antipathy of the established Jewish leadership in the West and in Russia itself, the proven impossibility of absorbing mass immigration into Palestine, and the by now well-documented difficulty of any colonization effort in that country – given the bureaucratic arbitrariness of Turkish officialdom, the speculative land prices, and the harsh and complex agricultural conditions.

This apparent hopelessness of the Palestinian cause led Lev Pinsker to give a territorialist rather than a Zionist slant to his influential analysis of the post-crisis situation, *Auto-Emancipation,* published in the latter half of 1882. The Jews, Pinsker wrote, should not adhere blindly to the ancestral homeland but should select rationally a territory where they would be granted access to fertile soil and political autonomy.

If nonetheless the Palestinian idea took root, it was because of the grim, the fanatical, determination of a small body of men. Those few settlers who had actually gone to Palestine in 1882, and who subsequently insisted on staying there against heavy odds, prevented their cause from simply withering away. This was particularly true of the Bilu group and of the colonists who under the leadership of Zalman David Levontin had established the settlement of Rishon Le-Zion in 1882 (although the Roumanian Jews who set up Zikhron Yaakov and Rosh-Pina in that same year also attracted a measure of attention).

By their presence in the country they had moved their idea from the plane of theoretical strategy to that of concrete needs. They had demonstrated their will to lay the foundations of the colonization enterprise and had thus transferred the responsibility for success or failure to the Jews in Russia and elsewhere, who would have to raise the requisite capital sums. Their own desperate plight lent weight to their demand that others commit themselves. Given their access to the Russian-Jewish press and their knowledge of the Jewish world, the Bilu and Levontin's group were well equipped to exploit this bargaining position.

The first important breakthrough came when an emissary from Rishon Le-Zion[388] succeeded in October 1882 in gaining access to, and winning the sympathy of, Baron Edmund de Rothschild in Paris. Rothschild's decision to make an initial grant of 25,000 francs to that colony – in particular, to six of the founding families that were left without any means – proved to be the beginning of a lifetime involvement in the cause of Palestinian settlement. He not only invested increasingly large sums in buying land, developing vineyards, building houses, and supplying livestock and equipment but also sent out overseers and agronomists to ensure that modern methods of farming be introduced. By the late 1880s all the settlements (except Gedera) were receiving capital investments from him: Rishon Le-Zion, Zikhron Yaakov, Rosh Pina, Petah Tikva, Ekron, Yesud Ha-Maala, and Wadi Hanin (Nes Ziona).[389]

But Rothschild was drawn into this enterprise only gradually, and at no time did he agree to finance the entire colonization effort. The Bilu throughout (and for a period the settlers in Petah Tikva) were entirely dependent on the ability of Jews in Russia to raise funds. This simple but important fact provided the primary raison d'être for the development and consolidation of the Palestinophile movement in Russia.

Throughout 1883 a core group within the Bilu party worked as day laborers at the agricultural school in Mikve Yisrael. Some dozen members of the Bilu had decided to settle as colonists in Rishon Le-Zion, but those at Mikve Yisrael insisted that, as always planned, the party should found its own colony. Their persistence gradually won over supporters, among them the well-known Russian-Jewish writer and public figure, Yehiel Mikhael Pines, then resident in Jerusalem. Pines agreed to help the Bilu find and purchase a tract of land on the condition that the money required be forthcoming from Russia. In a letter of late 1883 to S. Fin in Vilna, Pines defended the youth party against those, such as Levanda, who saw it as irresponsible and arrogant. "The members of the Bilu," he wrote,

> were the first to move and in their moving they drew others after them. [They] took decisive action. Without thinking about it very long, they left their country, the land of their birth, their homes, their schools, gave up their peace, their promising futures and went just like that to the land of our fathers. Our rich gentlemen said to them: "Go and we will send moneys." They went and our rich gentlemen forgot about them ... Do you abroad know what kind of work they have to do? Work in Mikve Israel under *Hirsch*. Dear sirs! If you had been in Palestine ... that short answer would be enough in itself to understand all the hard labor, all the poverty and pressures which the Bilu have had to suffer in body and soul.[390]

In a letter of 1 May 1884 David Gordon wrote to S. P. Rabinovich supporting this same point of view: "All this will be to our shame for all our lives. All the Jews of Russia could not establish a colony for these youngsters we so value ... What right do we have to shout at Hirsch and Erlanger if our strength is only in words."[391] Eventually, in 1884, the money was raised to enable Pines to make his land purchase, and late in the year the first nine Bilu members moved to Gedera (or Katra, as it was then more commonly known).[392]

In November 1884, the founding conference of the Palestinophile movement was finally held in Kattowitz, the conference first planned by Rozenfeld two and a half years earlier. It met abroad in order to give it an international appearance and avoid entanglements with tsarist officialdom but it was essentially a Russian-Jewish enterprise. The constituent societies had, in the main, existed since 1882, and the goal of the new organization – known officially as the Moses Montefiore Memorial Fund in Palestine – was therefore to turn a loose and unofficial federation of independent *kruzhki* into a centralized and representative movement. In this it was partially successful. As the elected president of the organization, Lev Pinsker gradually proved able to impose his leadership upon it. Funds were channeled through a central budget and the decisions of the periodic conferences (held in Kattowitz in November 1884, in Druskeniki in 1887) were recognized as binding on the members. In 1890 the movement (now entitled the Society for the Support of Jewish Farmers and Artisans in Syria and Palestine and commonly known as the Odessa Committee) even gained a measure of legal recognition from the tsarist regime. Able to raise between 20,000 and 50,000 roubles per annum, it helped prevent the collapse of Petah Tikva and Gedera at critical moments.[393]

It was nominally made up of some one hundred branches with a membership of about fourteen thousand, but these figures were more impressive on paper than in fact. Active organizations existed only in Moscow, Odessa, Warsaw, Belostok, Vilna, Rostov, Poltava, Minsk, and Kovno. The one major journal which supported it, Tsederbaum's *Ha-melits*, had a circulation of a mere fifteen hundred. What strength the movement had lay in the fact that it had brought together in permanent form remnants of the emigrationist coalition of 1881–2. In the leadership of the movement were represented members of the literary intelligentsia (Pinsker and Levanda from those who wrote in Russian; Lilienblum, S. P. Rabinovich, and S. Fin from the Hebrew writers); important figures from the provincial communities (M. Mandelshtam from Kiev and such rabbis as Mohilever of Belostock and Spektor in Kovno); and finally an impressive group of student activists most of whom had been swept into politics during the crisis period (M. M. Ussishkin, Yehiel Chlenov, Vladimir Temkin, Yaakov Maze, Abram Idelson, and Meir Dizengof). Among the masses the movement continued to command attention, and itinerant Palestinophile preachers (magidim) were often enthusiastically received in the synagogues of the Pale of Settlement. But it could certainly not be considered a mass movement.

It represented just one foot of the tripod on which the Palestinian cause now rested; at the other two corners stood respectively the few hundred settlers in Palestine and Rothschild in Paris. That it had become a permanent aspect of Russian-Jewish life, its first political movement, can only be explained by the power of the national idea in moments of collective adversity. Palestine was so rooted in the group consciousness that despite all objective difficulties, it could exert a powerful magnetic attraction once the existing way of life was seriously threatened. Pinsker, who had started out in 1882 from a territorialist standpoint, recognized this fact, the instinctive pull to the ancestral homeland, and decided that if self-emancipation were to be achieved it would have to be through a return to that country which commanded the most general recognition.

Once he had made this decision he gave himself to it unstintingly, even though he was throughout the last ten years of his life (he died in 1891) a very ill man. In a letter of 26 November 1886, he wrote to Levanda enumerating the obstacles standing in the path of the movement and then added:

> But does it follow from all this that we should give up? I personally do not think so. I knew before that we were undertaking a burdensome, long-drawn-out and almost impossible cause. But I believed in the wisdom of our undertaking and I wanted to believe in the energy and determination of our people which was at least bound to equal the energy and determination of its persecutors.[394]

If the obstinate faith in a full-scale national revival prevented the collapse of the Palestinophile movement in Russia, the strength of the populist idea made possible the emergence of organized Jewish labor as a force in New York. It was among the new immigrants to the United States that the concept of a "going to the Jewish people" first made a major and lasting impact.

By 1890–2 the immigrant socialists had demonstrated beyond a shadow of doubt that it was possible to organize a mass following in New York and that the key to success lay in a combination of trade unionism and popular journalism. On 9 October 1888 a federation of unions, the United Hebrew Trades, had been established by the socialists. At first a skeletal organization (its only two constituent organizations were the typesetters and the theater choristers), it grew by leaps and bounds over the next two years. By early 1890 there were twenty-two unions in the UHT with some six thousand members. At a conference held in October 1890, twenty-seven unions and socialist organizations from New York were represented with an estimated membership of close to fourteen thousand members. The

UHT was able to send Louis Miller to the founding Congress of the Second International held in Paris in 1889 and Abe Cahan to the Second Congress in Brussels in 1891.[395]

Early in 1890 the UHT took the initiative in organizing the Operators and Cloakmakers Union (No. 1) and delegated to it three of its members: Joseph Barondess, Bernard Weinstein, and M. Schach. In May of that year, the cloakmakers declared a strike and some eighty-five hundred workers participated in the long-drawn-out conflict, the first strike of its scale on the Lower East Side. The young Joseph Barondess emerged as the leader of the union and at the age of twenty-one briefly found himself perhaps the best-known socialist leader in the Jewish immigrant world. By August, most of the demands presented by the union – higher wages, shorter hours – had been accepted by the employers and the strike was finally called to a weary, but successful, halt.[396]

On 7 March 1890 the first number of the Yiddish weekly, *Di arbeter tsaytung*, had appeared. To a large extent, it was the work of the same men who had founded the United Hebrew Trades; Louis Miller (Bandes) and Morris Hilkovich (Hillquit) played a central role in both undertakings. But it was Abe Cahan who from the start gave the new journal its distinctive character, even though the official editor-in-chief was Philip Krantz (Rombro), who had been imported for that position from London. Cahan insisted that the journal aim at a mass circulation, and he wrote innumerable articles in popular language – a style and vocabulary very different from the heavily Germanized and stilted forms hitherto used in Yiddish journalism. The circulation of the new socialist paper soon reached the unheard-of figure of over eighty-five hundred, and it exercised real influence among the immigrant masses.[397] "Thanks to *Di arbeter tsaytung*," wrote Cahan in his memoirs, "everything suddenly took on a different look. The unions began to grow and that in turn increased everybody's interest in *Di arbeter tsaytung* ... We were in the center of every union action ... [as] speakers, agitators, and organizers."[398]

But the movement made its most spectacular impact through its public demonstrations. Early in March 1890 some four thousand Jewish workers marched through the streets of New York carrying flags in commemoration of the Paris Commune. On May Day of that year some nine thousand Jews paraded through the Lower East Side, past hundreds of tenements decorated with red banners, to Union Square, where they joined the other (non-Jewish) demonstrators. There were three platforms (one for Yiddish, one for German, and one for English). Abe Cahan was reported to have declared in his oration that this is "the beginning of the great revolution which will overthrow the capitalist system."[399] On Labor Day the number of marchers was estimated at fifteen thousand. And the public celebration held in Cooper Union for the first anniversary of *Di arbeter tsaytung* was so well attended that many thousands had to be turned away. "The enthusiasm of the audience," Cahan recalled, "was indescribable ... Almost every word he [Louis Miller] said was greeted with hurrahs and with thundering applause."[400] The only cause for regret, Krantz wrote of these demonstrations, was that the long-suffering brethren in Russia could not witness them, could not partake in this "hope for a speedy Redemption."[401]

Although the spectacular growth and enthusiasm of 1890 was not maintained in subsequent years, a successful formula had been found and it proved itself time and again in the coming decades. The socialists were not able to acquire a mass political following at this stage nor could they ensure themselves a stable union membership. The tendency to join unions during the periods of full production only to abandon them during the periods of "slack" was extremely deep-rooted. For insurance against sickness or for burial, the mass of Jews tended to look not to the labor movement but to *landsmanshaftn* or other general orders, and the burden of additional union dues was widely resented. The fluid and fragmented structure of the sweatshop system, with its constant influx of new immigrants and exodus of veterans into more profitable or tolerable forms of employment, did not lend itself to the maintenance of permanently powerful unions. But however unevenly and sporadically, the combination of unionism and journalism did provide the real bridge between the small socialist circles and the immigrant masses.

The idea of a "going to the Jewish people," as already noted, was not new and certainly not unique to America. It had been ably advocated by Liberman in England and Russia in the mid-1870s. It had been taken up again by Dragomanov and the Geneva circle in 1880. Akselrod had made it the central theme of his unpublished brochure of 1882 as did Ilia Rubanovich (a revolutionary exile then living in Paris), in an important article of 1886 in *Vestnik narodnoi voli*: The pogroms, he wrote there, have "made the youth more sensitive to the sufferings of the people and the people more receptive to revolutionary ideas. This could well serve as the basis for the independent activity of the Jewish masses."[402] In 1887 a group of students in Zurich went a step farther, creating the Jewish Workers Library, which published a Yiddish translation of Shimen Dikshtein's famous agitational brochure, *What Do People Live By?*

In London in the mid-1880s renewed attempts were made by the Russian-Jewish socialists then living there to organize the immigrant workers. A series of socialist journals were published, with Vinchevsky again taking the lead as in 1878, and unions were periodically organized among the clothing workers in the East End of London. For a few years London was even considered the hub of the emergent Jewish labor movement, and its socialist journal, *Arbeter fraynd*, enjoyed a following in New York.[403] However, the decision of its editor, Philip Krantz, to move to America in 1890 symbolized the new status acquired by New York and the relative decline of London. He was soon followed by other leading Jewish socialists in England: Morris Vinchevsky, B. Feigenbaum, and M. Baranov.

The fact that the Jewish labor movement first became a real political force in New York rather than elsewhere was due to a complex conjunction of factors involving the intelligentsia, the workers, and the entire sociopolitical environment.

So long as the Russian-Jewish radical youth was under the direct influence of the revolutionary elitism represented by the Narodnaia Volia, it could not devote itself unreservedly to the organization of a mass movement. Thus, throughout the 1880s, the Jewish revolutionaries active in Russia itself made no concerted effort to reach the Jewish working class within the Pale of Settlement. This fact is not to be explained by a revulsion from all revolutionary action. On the contrary, in the 1880s far more Jews entered the movement than in the 1870s. If in the years 1873–7 there were a mere 63 Jews among the 1,054 revolutionaries identified by the Okhrana, in the years 1884–90 there were 579 Jews among a total 4,307.[404]

The sharp increase in the Jewish student population (in 1876 there were 247 Jewish students, in 1886 the number had risen to 1,856);[405] the persistently hostile attitude of the tsarist government and, in particular, the imposition of a harsh numerus clausus on entry to schools and universities in 1887 – all combined to encourage this rise.

For its part, the Narodnaia Volia in its last publications in the years 1885–6 finally repudiated publicly and sharply its original attitude toward the pogroms and so eased the path for those many young Jews who sought to identify themselves with it. In its journal published in September 1884, the editorial stated bluntly that while "protest is vitally important . . . we are in no way obliged and even do not have the right to lower our revolutionary idea before the people by participating in acts which by conscience and conviction we do not recognize as wise or just."[406] Rubanovich was given access to the *Vestnik narodnoi voli* to make the same point: "It is not fear of heavy sacrifices . . . but simply the interests of the cause, the interests of the laboring masses which sternly demand that the conscious activists do not lower themselves to the unconscious impulse of the mass . . . but rather raise it up by criticism and organization."[407]

This line of argument would henceforth become the accepted doctrine of the Russian revolutionary movement, populist and Marxist alike, in its relationship to the pogroms. Together with the loosening hold of the exodus as an alternative force of attraction, this fact ensured that the crisis of 1881–2 did not permanently alienate the Jewish youth from the general revolutionary movement. Certainly, as far as Russia in the 1880s was concerned, Cherikover was right to warn against overestimating the long-term effects of the "reevaluation of values."

Among the emigrant student youth, however, the ideological development was less straightforward. True, the fascination exerted by the revolutionary heroism of the Zheliabovs and Perovskaias was enormous. No subject was more popular for lectures, articles, and discussions than the history of the Narodnaia Volia. Every year on 1 March a meeting was held in the New York socialist colony to commemorate the martyrs responsible for the assassination of Alexander II. In general, there was a strong tendency among the immigrant youth to see themselves as Russian revolutionaries in exile. For twenty years, the social event in New York was always the New Year's Ball, "with Russian songs, socialist speeches, with toasts for the Russian freedom fight, with cheers for the martyrs of Schlüsselberg and Siberia."[408] Until 1886, a series of socialist clubs which were essentially revolutionary *kruzhki* transferred to American soil were set up in New York: the Russkii Rabochii Soiuz (The Russian Labor Union) in 1884, the Russkii Progressivny Soiuz (The Russian Progressive Union) in 1886, and the Labor Lyceum in 1885, which, despite its name, specialized in Russian lectures and debates.

This attachment to the Russian revolutionary tradition, as it had crystallized in the 1880s, undoubtedly goes far to explain the powerful grip exerted by anarchist (as distinct from Social Democratic) doctrine on the immigrant intelligentsia in London and New York. The refusal of the anarchists to compromise with the existing order, to take part in elections or parliaments, to grant the possibility of real improvements until the social revolution, naturally attracted the Russian-Jewish radicals, who were accustomed to see politics in terms of ruthless and manichean conflict. Unlike the Jewish revolutionaries in Russia in the 1880s, the immigrant anarchists in London and New York were ready enough to employ Yiddish in order to reach the masses. And this, at least in part, was the result of the crisis of consciousness of 1881–2. But they were profoundly reluctant to make any further concessions to popular sentiment as it existed among the workers. Thus both in England and America, the Jewish anarchists insisted on organizing balls and feasts during the most sacred fast day – Yom Kippur – an act well calculated to polarize community feeling and leave them in a small minority. Their support, however theoretical, for the use of violence and bombs even in the parliamentary West inevitably had a similar result.

In London this alienation was inevitable; by the end of the 1880s it was becoming obvious that England objectively did not provide soil suitable for a mass movement among the Yiddish-speaking workers. First, there was the purely quantitative factor; over a million Russian Jews went to America between 1880 and 1910, while in that period a mere tenth of that number settled in England. Second, there was no tradition of multi-ethnicity in English life and there were no precedents for large-scale political organizations based on a foreign language. The frequent attempts to organize a mass following in the East End – although occasionally spectacular – all proved short-lived. Under these circumstances, it was natural enough that the anarchist and social-revolutionary hold on the immigrant socialists in London should maintain itself throughout the 1880s and 1890s. As the doctrine of a sect rather than a movement, it had a raison d'être. In fact, the two main socialist institutions in the East End, the *Arbeter fraynd* and the Berner Street Club, both ended up in the years 1890–1 as strictly anarchist organizations. Thus, at the time that Philip Krantz went to New York to become editor of *Di arbeter tsaytung*, the anarchist leader, Shoel Yanovsky, crossed the Atlantic to London to become editor of the *Arbeter fraynd*.[409]

While the objective situation in London tended to keep the immigrant socialists in isolation, in New York it had the opposite effect. The radical youth, who had arrived in large numbers in 1881–2, found themselves under constant pressure to modify imported doctrines and attitudes. On the one hand, the agricultural colonization effort lost its momentum after 1883. True, this was a gradual rather than a sudden process. Michael Heilprin (working through his Montefiore Agricultural Aid Society) was able to devote all his energies to that cause as soon as the immigrant transports ceased in mid-1882. Colonies were founded, or aided, by his society in Oregon, South Dakota, New Jersey, and Kansas.[410] A report sent to *Russkii evrei* in December 1882 sounded a somber but optimist note: "To the idea there have remained loyal only those who are really ardently dedicated to it, who have made up their minds to abandon the pursuit of alluring, glittering illusions and devote themselves entirely to planting among the Jews . . . a class of peaceful farmers."[411] At the same time, Abe Cahan could write that "the Am Olam and the Odessa party – however much suffering they have had to bear – are still persisting along their own path."[412] But the colonization movement in the United States lacked staying power. One by one the colonies disintegrated. In 1887 even the most publicized of the settlements, New Odessa, Oregon, was abandoned and the settlers returned to New York. Russian-Jewish farming settlements maintained themselves only in New Jersey (in the Vineland area), but the role of the intelligentsia there after the mid-1880s (with the notable exception of Sabsovich) was negligible.[413] The total isolation of most of the colonies, scattered as they were at lonely points across North America, served to wear down the morale of the beleaguered colonists.

The clear failure of the agrarian dream was paralleled by a growing disillusionment among many of the youth with what they now came to see as the excessive romanticism of the anarchist ethos. As they became more familiar with American politics they came to resent the anarchist rejection of elections and the representative system. The hard-fought campaign of Henry George in 1886 for the mayoralty of New York aroused enormous interest on the Lower East Side and made the doctrine of boycott particularly unpalatable. Even the widespread sympathy for the Haymarket martyrs executed on 11 November 1887 could not counteract the growing attraction of the Social Democratic viewpoint.

Marxism, in its Social Democratic form, reinforced the one idea imported from Russia which had a chance of taking root in American soil – the populist impulse, the "going to the people." This strand in the thinking of the immigrant intelligentsia had throughout acted as a counterweight to revolutionary elitism. It is significant that the two key elements in the Jewish labor movement as it was to develop in the United States – unionism and propaganda (or "enlightenment") – emerged as the first wave of mass immigration was still arriving in July 1882. Attempts to use the new arrivals from Russia to break the rail and dock strikes then in progress in New York led to the intervention of the radical youth, who explained to them what an "American strike" was. "On 12 July in the evening," Petrikovsky reported, "four hundred Jewish emigrants working on the piers marched along Broadway ... to St. Peter's Hall to a meeting called by Jewish agitators ... Speeches held in Russian and the Jewish jargon explained the significance of the strikes, the necessity for an international struggle of the workers against capitalist exploitation."[414] On 13 July hundreds of Jewish workers together with newly arrived Italians signed up in the Strike Union. "Imagine," continued the report, "eight hundred people gesticulating energetically, slapping one another in a friendly way on the shoulder, shaking hands and trying to show by mimicry that they are brothers, that the interest of the one is the interest of the other."[415]

It was early in July, too, that the Propagande Fareyn was established with the goal of bringing socialist lectures in Russian, English, German, and Yiddish to the new immigrants. Bernard Weinstein in his memoirs recalls having helped Abe Cahan in printing and distributing the five hundred handbills in Yiddish that announced the first meeting, devoted to the theme "When Will the Persecution of the Jews Stop?" The handbill stated inter alia that "the persecution of our brothers in Russia, Germany, and Hungary ... can take on ever-wider dimensions if we do not find out its causes and ... so work to prevent it."[416] Among the speakers was the well-known Social Democrat Sergei Shevich, who followed the general theme of the meeting in warning of the dangers involved in scabbing.

The Propagande Fareyn enjoyed considerable popularity during the remainder of 1882 and it was there that Abe Cahan first made his mark as an agitator; coming from Lithuania he had a better command of Yiddish than most of his comrades, who came from southern Russia. It was followed in later years by similar organizations, the most important of which was the Yidisher Arbeter Fareyn, active from

1885 to 1887.[417] This latter organization encouraged the creation of two socialist (although privately sponsored) journals in Yiddish, *Di naye tsayt* and the *Nyu yorker yidisher folks tsaytung*.

The increasingly popular Marxist – or more accurately, Social Democratic – doctrine legitimized, gave a historical sanction, a sense of purpose, to this type of activity, which had hitherto been regarded as rather gray and mundane. Through Marxism it was possible to explain the failure of agrarian communalism (a utopian illusion) and the dangers of anarchist terrorism (premature violence). It shifted attention to the urban proletariat, permitted electoral activity, and emphasized the central role of trade unions.

Moreover, the fact that the German immigrants in New York had already developed a well-organized Social Democratic movement provided the Russian Jews from the first with a precedent, an example and aid. Thus, the United Hebrew Trades was not only modeled on the Vereinigte Deutsche Gewerkschaften, not only adopted its title (with the appropriate modification), but also received from it some initial financial subsidies. The Socialist Labor Party, founded in 1876, was essentially an immigrant party ("One could have thought," as Abe Cahan put it, "that the Americans were the foreigners and the Germans the natives"),[418] and it welcomed the establishment in 1887 of the new Russian-Jewish branches (the eighth, which used Yiddish, and the seventeenth, which used Russian).[419]

It was this pull of Social Democracy, combined with the now spontaneous flow of Russian-Jewish immigrants at the rate from 1885 of at least twenty thousand per annum, which swung the balance against the potential isolationism of the intelligentsia and toward the mass action of 1888–92. Here the quantitative reinforced the theoretical.

Given the fact that the Palestinian and Jewish socialist movements had both effectively originated in the emigrationist fever of 1881–2, and that both shared originally a common faith in agrarianism, "the people," and the necessity of solving the Jewish question, it would not have been illogical to expect a modus vivendi, cooperation, or even a synthesis to have developed between them. And particularly in the years 1882–5 there were many who advocated such a development. It is true that Akselrod permitted Deich to talk him out of his Palestinian notions and that Grigorii Gurevich lost much of his enthusiasm for the Middle East after visiting it. But this was by no means the universal reaction.

Yankev Aba Finkelshtein (or Apolon Valentin Litvinov), the founder of the Vilna *kruzhok* of 1872, was both socialist and *Palestinets* in London during the 1880s, and in 1890 he made the first translation of Pinsker's *Auto-Emancipation* into English.[420] Philip Krantz, writing under his real name of Y. Rombro, publicly committed himself to the Palestinian cause in the early 1880s even though he was an ex-Narodovolets and an active socialist. At that juncture, his populist faith was broad enough to embrace both socialism and nationalism. In 1884 he could write that "the colonization of Palestine realizing in a new . . . way the age-old ideals of Israel, must be the exclusive responsibility of the entire Jewish people [*narod*]."[421]

The same dual position was adopted by Elyohu Volf Rabinovich, who had collaborated with both Liberman and Vinchevsky in their Hebrew socialist journals of 1877–8. In a letter to Y. L. Levin sent from London on 13 April 1883, he set forth his hopes and his doubts. He favored the Palestinian plan, he wrote, because "this idea is one of the two ways leading to a solution of the Jewish question" and because he identified himself with "every nation fighting for its freedom."[422] But he was not totally convinced. There were too few *Palestintsy* who shared Pinsker's belief in the need for a modern state where state would be separated from religion, and the movement was therefore possibly leading toward a "theocracy."[423] "How many youth," he wondered, "are there like the Bilu?"[424] Again, if the Jews simply created another class-ridden state, as had the Italians and Germans, the effort would hardly be justified: "Can we speak to the poor among our people calling on them to tear themselves from their parents and loved ones and send them to a waste land . . . where we know that they will not reap the harvest which they sowed in tears?"[425]

Levin (who, of course, had also been active in Liberman's enterprise) replied from Kiev with an open letter in which he hinted that there was a chance of Palestine being built up on a socialist (or at least populist) basis. "It is," he wrote, "very hard to change existing institutions in an old country but a new society can be treated on true and just foundations."[426] However, he continued, this was not the crucial issue. Even though England, for instance, was suffering from an unprecedented problem of pauperization and proletarianization,

> would you not rejoice to see the Jews settled in their own country, happy and blessed with a tiny fraction of the blessings enjoyed by England? The question of poverty in general is one thing; the question of a nation which is outlawed and plundered is another . . . Let God grant that we settle in Palestine . . . and then every man will have the duty to ask there the question asked in all countries – the question of property and labour.[427]

In 1884 E. V. Rabinovich joined Morris Vinchevsky in establishing in London the first radical Yiddish journal to have appeared anywhere in the world, *Der poylisher yidl*. Even though Vinchevsky was never a *Palestinets*, he was willing at this stage to publish favorable albeit small notices on the founding of colonies in Palestine ("it is time that our brothers in Palestine should fulfill the saying, 'Eat your bread in the sweat of your brow' ");[428] on the Kattowitz Conference; and on the establishment of the Palestinophile journal in Vienna ("we naturally wish the enterprise the utmost success").[429] As the editor, Vinchevsky advocated a populism which included both labor solidarity and national solidarity. "We regard the Jews," read the first editorial, "as man, as Jew and as worker."[430] It was a cause for the greatest regret, he wrote elsewhere, that the Jews lacked "the unity that is to be found among the Irish, the Poles and other oppressed nations. They unite to gain a goal, we unite [as in 1882] to help one another in time of trouble."[431]

Above all, as its name suggested, the journal saw itself as the organ of the immigrant worker. It defended his tongue – "a kind of old restitched German patched on one side with Russian, Polish, and Lithuanian and, on the other, with Hebrew tape but nonetheless a language like all languages."[432] And it defended his honor. The Western Jews, he wrote,

> are cleverer than us, talk more carefully, have a handkerchief for their noses, a white shirt on their backs, and are called "papa" and "mama" rather than

"tate" and "mome" by their children . . . [But] when it is said that the Jew hates to work, that he is a bloodsucker and exploiter . . . who brings this slander on the Jews – the Polish Yidl or the Portuguese, English, and German Jews [Yude]?[433]

Never before had the attitude which would later become known as "folkism" – Jewish populism – appeared in so unadulterated a form.

If the socialists were at this point inclined to give Palestinophilism the benefit of the doubt, there were also *Palestintsy* actively committed to socialism. As already noted, the most conspicuous member of this class was M. Mints, a founding member of the Bilu. From 1882 to 1884 Mints led that faction in the party which demanded innovative and large-scale rather than piecemeal and miniscule measures. He stayed on in Constantinople for a year seeking to gain an official land grant from the Turkish government.

When in 1883 he finally joined the group in Palestine, he, together with Berliavsky and others, insisted on the necessity of the Bilu establishing its own model colony. A blueprint was drawn up for a central settlement of three hundred members which would be the property of the Bilu party. It would only accept unmarried people under twenty-five years of age. A member would have to pledge himself to remain for a lengthy period, during which he would "renounce both the possession and the acquisition of private property."[434] At the same time, he would study agricultural and technical skills and learn "the language of the country [Arabic] and to know the people in it, with all their physical and spiritual characteristics so that he learn how to live with, rather than fight, them."[435] At the end of the three years, the Bilu organization would help the individual member acquire land and establish himself in a constituent colony. Although their plan was not explicitly socialist, it bore the imprint of attitudes current in the Russian radical milieu: communalism, immersion of the self in the cause, internationalism.

Hopelessly frustrated in his attempts to implement the plan, Mints with five others left Palestine in April 1884 and, after a period in Europe, he went to New York. There he became one of the founders and editor of the *Nyu yorker yidisher folks tsaytung,* the influential and only socialist paper in Yiddish to appear regularly in that city from 1886 to 1889. While refraining from an openly Palestinian position, the paper made a direct appeal to Jewish national consciousness and pride.[436]

At the time of Hanuka, describing Judas Maccabaeus as a man whose "only ideal was to liberate the downtrodden Jewish people and to break the chains of their slavery,"[437] it declared that labor was now enslaved by capital and needed the Maccabean spirit to liberate itself. Attacked in established Jewish circles for its socialism, it replied that this was a natural choice because "we are Jews and share the pains of the people [folk], all its bitter sufferings of past and present."[438] It was inevitable that

a new life and a free(?) country call forth new demands . . . After so many centuries of keeping silent, the old spirit of freedom is awakening in Itsik – that spirit inculcated in him by our holy Prophets!

Let the fiery speech of Isaiah ring in your ears . . . The ideas of socialism were not alien to him [Isaiah] and are not in contradiction to Judaism.[439]

By the late 1880s, however, such an ideological stance was becoming a definite anachronism. To unite the national and the international, the historical and the contemporary, the particular and the universal – the Jew and the man, as Vinchevsky had put it – had become a problem that was losing its legitimacy. Monism was supplanting dualism; polarization replacing synthesis. This shifting of positions, reversal even, was due to factors at work in both the Palestinophile and the Jewish socialist movements.

Thus, for its part, the Palestinophile movement in Russia showed itself ready to make any sacrifice in its effort to sustain the few settlements already established in the ancestral land. And as what the settlers most urgently needed was financial aid, in practice, this meant permitting those who paid the piper to call the tune. Originally, Pinsker had thought in terms of a genuinely popular movement: "Despite the indifference of our monied barons and their hangers-on," he had written to Levanda in 1883, "this idea must throw down roots in the people [narod] – slowly, but surely and steadily."[440] But as the need for funds became predominant, this goal was inevitably neglected. Thus, Pinsker's Auto-Emancipation was translated into Hebrew, the language of the essentially middle-class maskilim, but not into Yiddish, the language of the lower classes, of the great majority. "It is vitally necessary ... ," Yampolsky wrote from Rostov to Pinsker in 1884, "that [our] idea penetrate the ordinary people [sery narod] . . . but the masses have for some reason been forgotten."[441]

In Palestine itself the price paid for sheer survival was, if anything, even higher. Baron Edmund de Rothschild had very definite ideas about what could and could not be permitted in the new colonies. He had a romantic image of small-scale farmers, simple people devoted to orthodox religious practice, dressed in Arab or Turkish style. The supervisers whom he put in charge of the colonies were expected to keep tight control over all aspects of life there.

Rothschild's conception could not be reconciled with that of the Biluim, who (although for the most part not socialists) were convinced that their duty was to act as the core of a modern, secular, and political movement. He rejected out of hand the ambitious blueprints of Mints and his faction who, in 1884, dismissed as day laborers at Mikve Yisrael, left Palestine. Those who remained were ready in principle to adopt a pragmatic and low-key strategy. They felt that Mints had advocated "stupid fantasies and sweeping, prophetic plans."[442] His departure, B. Lifshits wrote in mid-1884, was proof of the fact that "only true Jews educated and inspired at the real spring of pure Judaism" had the tenacity to hold out in Palestine, that "a man of a different type would ... , in the last resort, be picked up by some wave and carried off to another shore of the Black Sea or the Atlantic."[443] But even the pragmatists found it well-nigh impossible to adapt to the conditions laid down by Rothschild.

In 1883 Yisrael Belkind, who had settled with other Biluim in Rishon Le-Zion and had clashed with the overseers there, left it rather than have Rothschild cut off funds from the entire colony. In 1887 this pattern repeated itself. In this case, the decision by the overseer (Ossovetsky, a young Russian Jew, recruited by Netter at Brody in 1882) to expel the leader of the day laborers in Rishon Le-Zion (Mikhael Halperin) led to a bitter clash with the entire colony. Ossovetzky was even accused of shooting at a number of the settlers, and he certainly called in Turkish troops to restore order.[444] In the wake of this dispute, the colonists were ordered by the Rothschild administration to seek permission every time they wished to hire a given worker or take in a staying guest. Rather than comply, three of the founding members (Yosef Feinberg, Yehuda Leb Khankin, and Levi Yitshak Aizenband) eventually chose to leave the colony.

Rothschild and his staff in Paris were convinced that they were faced by a form of Russian nihilism, a view strongly reinforced by the fact that in 1887 the director of Mikve Yisrael, Hirsch, did receive a threatening letter in the name of a secret society of the pioneers in Palestine calling itself Emet. In Paris they spoke of "the revolutionaries in Rishon,"[445] of "the free-thinkers," of "the so-called *intelligenty*"[446] who were sabotaging constructive efforts. And in general, Eliezer Ben Yehuda, who had settled in Jerusalem, shared this assessment. "The experience of four years," he insisted in articles and letters,

> has shown us that Judea will not be built by *intelligenty* whose . . . only thought is to be free . . . In the colonies they are a total disaster . . . The colonies will be built up by people who are used to thinking the day long only of how by the sweat of their brow to bring bread to their homes and who know nothing of anything else, not of liberty, freedom, etc.[447]

If it had not been for the combined efforts of Pinsker, Pines, and Lilienblum, the Biluim could not have remained as a group in Palestine. Lilienblum, acting as Pinsker's secretary, was unwavering in his support of the young colonists who had aroused Rothschild's ire. In letters from Odessa to Pinsker, who in 1884 was traveling in Europe, he wrote that

> they are people who settled in Palestine in the name of an idea, fled the knout – and suddenly – here is a still more terrible knout . . . [448] Is it not laughable to regard people . . . as free-thinkers, as socialists [just because] they do not wish to be servile slaves . . . True, every baron has his fantasies but it is sad when fantasies are translated into fact.[449]

For his part, Pinsker was able to channel funds periodically to Gedera, the settlement of the Bilu that was boycotted by Rothschild. But even in Gedera the few remaining Biluim were not free to live as they chose. Religious zealots in Jerusalem reported back to Russia that they were free-thinkers and so turned the leading rabbis in the Palestinophile movement (Mohilever, Eliasberg, and Berlin) against them. Pinsker, in a clash with Mohilever and the head of the Volozhin Yeshiva (Naftali Zvi Yehuda Berlin), had to use all his authority to sustain his view that "it is not for us to put teachers, overseers, guardians over them as over children."[450] But at the same time he wrote to the group in Gedera appealing to them to maintain voluntarily the traditional religious observances for the sake of the general cause: "As the pioneers [*halutsim*] of the Yishuv who sacrificed the joys of youth for the sacred idea, you must in the future, too, put the general interest of the Yishuv first."[451] Pinsker's letter had its effect. Most of the small group in Gedera, ranging between one and two dozen, agreed, as Pines reported, to take on "the yoke of the Torah."[452]

Faced by this development of Palestinian colonization – quantitatively negligible, administratively confined, economically dependent, politically more and more conservative – the ideologists of the movement fell back on one of two defensive lines. Asher Gintsberg (better known as Ahad Ha-Am, "one of the people"), expounded in the late 1880s and early 1890s an argument very reminiscent of Smolenskin in the 1870s. The national rebirth had to start in the sphere of ideas, attitudes, and self-awareness rather than in that of practical politics and economics. The Palestinian colonies, a community of sturdy, independent agriculturalists, could serve as an example, a spiritual center, if only mass settlement were recognized as utopian for the foreseeable future. "The economic aspect of the Jewish question," he wrote in 1891, "must find its answer in America while its spiritual aspect . . . can only be fulfilled, if at all, in Palestine."[453]

To others, notably Lilienblum and Ussishkin, this approach implied an admission of failure. Rather than adapting their ideology to reality, they preferred to explain their setbacks as transient, caused by a conjunction of difficulties which could not last indefinitely. "The work of the Hoveve Zion," Lilienblum wrote to Ussishkin in 1887, "is only the beginning of that real effort which awaits the arrival of better days – days which it is not in our power to bring speedily."[454]

The high price paid for survival, the widening gulf between expectation and achievement, alienated all but the most stubborn Palestinophiles, particularly, of course, the radicals, the socialists, the youth. Ilia Rubanovich, who had been associated since 1883 with the small Evreiskoe Rabochee Obshchestvo (The Jewish Labor Society)[455] in Paris and who argued in favor of a Jewish revolutionary organization in Russia, was perhaps the first to develop in detail the left wing case against Palestinophilism. In the *Vestnik narodnoi voli* of 1886 (edited by Lavrov, who was then also living in Paris), he insisted that the Palestinian movement was ideologically unsound, politically naive and, from a socialist standpoint, potentially dangerous.

Against Pinsker and Lilienblum he argued that antisemitism could not rationally be regarded as a permanent phenomenon rooted in the nature of man as a social being. "These," he wrote, "are essentially mystical and fantastic views which prevent the examination of the real conditions of life, which stand outside time and place; and which therefore cannot be subjected to rational argument."[456] Modern economic forces – "international plundering"[457] – were already breaking down the barriers between nations, uniting labor against capital on a world scale. "The essence of contemporary history," he concluded, "is not the *national* but the *class* struggle."[458]

The failure of the Palestinian movement to achieve its goals, he argued, was no random development. Real problems could not be solved by resorting to the "legend of the Messiah formed under different historical conditions,"[459] to "childish dreams fed by the belief, which still lives on among the dark masses, in the hour of Redemption."[460] The Palestinophiles had taken

> the feverish condition prevailing among the Jews after the pogroms for the upsurge of national identity; the enforced move of a few thousand families for the beginning of a [national] transmigration. And arming themselves with their pens they have started – on paper, of course – the triumphant procession to the Holy Land of our forefathers.[461]

They had ignored the deep roots which the Jews had thrown down in the lands of their birth, their ties to the local language, customs, and economy. They had ignored the inhospitability of Palestine as a land of mass settlement. The Turks could hardly be expected to sell their own territories, and even if they did,

> what is to be done with the Arabs? Would the Jews expect to be strangers among the Arabs or would they want to make the Arabs strangers among themselves? . . . [462] The Arabs have exactly the same historical right and it will be unfortunate for you if – taking your stand under the protection of international plunderers, using the underhand dealings and intrigue of a corrupt diplomacy – you make the peaceful Arabs defend *their* right. They will answer tears with blood and bury your diplomatic documents in the ashes of your own homes.[463]

The Palestine movement, Rubanovich wrote, had placed its hopes in the Jewish masses, in the proletariat, but they would be guided in the last resort by actualities, not by dreams. Nonetheless, the danger remained that the propagation of myths might distract the proletariat "from the real struggle in the life around it, isolate it artificially from the Russian masses."[464]

Typically enough – this, after all, was a period of transition and genuine self-questioning – Rubanovich was not prepared to denigrate totally the concrete achievements in Palestine. "One can rejoice," he wrote, "that outside Russia a few . . . Jewish agricultural colonies have been created which – as with the Irish emigrants [in North America] – can help their fellow Jews in Russia conduct the real struggle."[465] But the fact remained that the settlement of "a few thousand families [cannot be] a solution for a population of three million."[466] The only way out lay in the overthrow of the tsarist regime, in a massive land distribution, and in the correction of other social inequities. "Is it necessary to say," he asked in conclusion, "that the interests of the Jewish proletariat are at one with the interests of the revolution?"[467]

Interestingly enough, Pinsker had addressed himself to this last point in his opening address at the Kattowitz conference. "Whether in the near future," he said there, "a war of life and death will be declared (rightly or wrongly) against the property system . . . one thing is certain – the Jews will be the first if not the only victims of that threatening revolution as, to an extent, they have already become in consequence of its distant approach alone."[468] But Rubanovich had an answer here, too. A major revolution, he argued, is not a time for national hatreds, but rather a moment when "age-old, narrow, egoistic feelings . . . make way for the fraternal solidarity of all the laboring people."[469]

Rubanovich had maintained a nonabusive tone throughout, but his theme was now taken up by others with much greater stridency. Thus, if *Der poylisher yidl* had been marginally sympathetic to the Palestinian cause, its successor in London, the *Arbeter fraynd,* soon adopted a sharply hostile stance. This change of front is probably to be explained by the fact that Elyohu Volf Rabinovich was not associated with the new venture; that its main editor, Philip Krantz (Rombro) was an ex-*Palestinets* who presumably was now seeking to expunge his past error; and that Vinchevsky, who was active in the new journal as in the old, had long resented the hold of the Palestinian idea on many who had once been his closest comrades.[470]

An important article in the new journal noted in mid-1887 that "there are many people who used to call themselves socialists and have now become nationalists and argue that they can still be socialists . . . [that] once the Jews have their own country they will be able freely to develop social ideas and cooperate with other peoples."[471] But, insisted the author, this was to forget the crucial fact that "the origin of nations is betrayal, robbery and murder, . . .[472] [that] socialism is actually the contradiction of nationalism."[473] The Palestinian movement was no exception. It, too, had become the tool of the exploiting class: "You, dear socialist-Palestinians . . . are slaves of the Jewish capitalist robber-bands who want to buy a piece of land in Palestine in order to bring poor Jewish workers there and then suck their blood."[474]

The thesis expressed explicitly here that socialism and nationalism were contradictory concepts rapidly became the accepted orthodoxy not only among the Jews in the Russian revolutionary parties – something clearly to be expected – but also among those who were now founding the Jewish labor movement. The growing hold of militant internationalism on this emergent movement was caused by a number of factors. First, as noted above, there was the growing alienation from the Palestinian movement, which was increasingly linked to the middle class, the rabbis, and an unadulterated nationalism. Then, equally important, there was the developing and ever sharper division within the Jewish labor movement between the anarchist and Social Democratic wings. Both these doctrines proclaimed an uncompromising internationalism and discouraged ideological eclecticism or experimentation. Basing their claims to authority on fixed scientific laws, they encouraged rigidity of thought and a clear-cut logicality based on a monistic view of history. Both doctrines saw the class conflict as the single issue which dominated and determined all else.

Finally, the fact that the Jewish labor movement had taken root first in England and the United States (which were essentially mono-cultural societies) discouraged speculation on the national question. It is true that in the United States the Socialist Labor Party was organized in practice as a federation of different linguistic branches, but this was universally regarded as a transitional phase; eventually the immigrants or their children would become English-speaking and old ethnic-cultural distinctions would be wiped out.

To a great degree, the Jewish socialists in England and America came to see it as their duty to aid the immigrant workers to integrate fully into their new societies, most specifically into the existing trade unions and labor organizations, but also into the world of modern secular thought in general. As long as they were fulfilling this, their pedagogical or cultural function, the socialists could usually count on widespread popular interest. As lecturers and journalists, they had a far easier task than as party political or even trade-union leaders. The American observer of the Lower East Side, Hutchins Hapgood, was thus taking too one-sided a view when he wrote that "socialism as it is agitated in the Jewish quarter consists in a wholesale rejection, often founded on a misunderstanding, of both American and Hebraic ideals. The socialists harp monotonously on the relations between capital and labor."[475] In their militant internationalism, their secularism, and their faith in science, the socialists were not only endowing the immigrants with a strongly critical consciousness, but were also hastening their integration into English or American life.

There was here, of course, much that was paradoxical. The more "Jewish" the socialist movement became – the more it went over entirely to the use of Yiddish, the greater its following on the Lower East Side, the deeper its influence there – the more internationalist it became; and the more internationalist its doctrine, the more it was held necessary to break down all historically and culturally conditioned barriers. Socialist internationalism and Americanization thus easily complemented each other. And insofar as the Social Democratic wing implicitly endorsed this equation it gained in popularity over the more alienated anarchists. To take one example, in June 1890 Abe Cahan could write in *Di arbeter tsaytung* that "the Declaration of Independence is a holy revolutionary act of freedom which cost streams of blood and the Constitution of the United States is an honest, pure document."[476]

Thus, by the early 1890s, the adaption of ideology to reality had produced a Palestinian movement thoroughly nationalist in its outlook and a Jewish-socialist counterpart dedicated to militant internationalism, albeit in a Yiddish-speaking environment. Nevertheless, even at that stage there were countervailing potentialities concealed within each of these two movements.

Within the Palestinian camp, the discipline and conservatism imposed by Rothschild with the aid of rabbinical forces in Russia and Palestine was throughout threatened (however marginally) by the persistent flow (or, more accurately, trickle) of young migrants into the new colonies. Their Workers Union (Agudat Poalim) had been the initial cause of the explosion in Rishon Le-Zion in 1887. They were not encouraged to go to Palestine by the Russian organization, which became increasingly wary of any immigrant who could not bring with him a capital sum of at least three thousand roubles. But they continued to go and to demand a recognized role in the development of the Yishuv. Writing of his visit to Palestine in 1891, Ahad Ha-Am commented on the existence of what he termed the workers party (*mifleget ha-poalim*) and its demands for land grants. "In time," he wrote ironically, "we shall be witness to an unprecedented sight – the question of property and labor where property has still not harvested any of the fruits of labor."[477]

Within the Jewish labor movement in the West, unadulterated internationalism was threatened potentially both by the populist tradition and by the still unbroken threads tying the immigrants to their land of origin, the *heym*. Thus, an article of 1892 in *Di fraye velt* (the journal published by the social revolutionary group of Vinchevsky, Baranov, and Feigenbaum in London) could state explicitly that in order to reach down into the Yiddish-speaking masses

> one must be a Jew and not be ashamed of it, one must be a bit of a nationalist, a Jewish patriot – naturally not . . . a Palestine patriot. You must be at one with all socialists who preach internationalist ideas while remaining national (not nationalistic). Have you ever heard of an English union which calls itself "international," etc.? Among Jews it has become the fashion to call all unions international . . . almost as though this would change their long noses or Minsk mannerisms.[478]

Nor was this the purely idiosyncratic view of its author, C. Liberman. A resolution of the group stated that while "remaining internationalist . . . [we] recognize that our task is to work among Jews as long as they are differentiated by their language and ways of life from other nations."[479]

When Abe Cahan came as a delegate of the UHT to the Brussels congress of the Second International in 1891, he explained that his organization had "nothing to do with religion or nationality" and that its name was adopted "only because of the language spoken by all its members." But he also introduced a resolution which would have had the congress strongly condemn antisemitism. In his speech he stated that while within the socialist camp there could be no Jewish question, that was no reason for the movement to ignore it. "The Jews," he said, "are persecuted, hounded; they have been made into a special class. This class wants to fight and asks for its place in the ranks of Social Democracy . . . The Russian press constantly attacks the Jews and asserts that we are hated even by the worker-socialists. I want you to declare that this is not true."[480] In fact, the congress, in its unseemly haste to avert a long debate on the subject, condemned not only antisemitism but also "philosemitism" and Cahan was so embarrassed that he chose to take refuge in silence. He made no mention of the episode in his report to *Di arbeter tsaytung*. (Ironically, it was left to the journal of Plekhanov, Akselrod, and Zasulich – *Sotsial-Demokrat* – to condemn the pusillanimity of the congress.)[481] Yet the fact remained that it was the delegate of the bourgeoning American Jewish labor movement who had first raised the issue of European antisemitism at a congress of the International.

These, however, were minor themes in the early 1890s. Polarization and doctrinal monism – nationalism on the one hand and internationalism on the other – had become the dominant tendencies. It would take yet another historical turn to produce a reaction against this, the prevailing trend.

II

The party ideologies until 1907

During the revolutions of 1905–7, those movements that combined revolutionary socialism and Jewish nationalism came into their own. In their many varied and rival forms, they now achieved an unprecedented popularity within the Pale of Settlement. There, they even overshadowed general Zionism, on the one hand, and revolutionary "assimilationism," on the other. This moment of ascendancy had been long in the making, for the ideological and political tributaries that finally merged into the floodwaters of 1905 had their origins largely in the 1880s and 1890s.

The most important of the "synthetic" movements was, of course, the Bund, but from the time of the Kishinev pogrom in 1903 there were Zionist and territorialist movements that sought this same synthesis. These were the movements that raised such veteran ideologists as Syrkin and Zhitlovsky (who had been advocating socialist nationalism since the 1880s) to leadership positions.

In the years 1905–6, they formed into a number of political parties that, while competing with each other, sought to outflank the Bund and to develop a line that would be more nationalist but also more revolutionary. They, too, committed themselves increasingly to Marxism, to scientific determinism, to the class-war doctrine. Borochov, who had been born in 1880, was representative of this all but irresistible, quasi-religious flow of belief among the youth, while Syrkin and Zhitlovsky with their populist and voluntarist credo, came to be regarded as ideologically anachronistic.

Thus, while Part One was concerned with a major historical turning point, here the emphasis is on a long-drawn-out, historical process; on the interaction over time of the rival thinkers, groups, and parties; on their development and metamorphoses; and ultimately on the political education of a new generation of Jewish youth in the Pale of Settlement.

CHAPTER 3

The politics of Jewish liberation

1905–1906

The pull of the revolution: 1881–1882 and 1905–1906

"I do not know how others number the years. But I count them from 1905."[1] This was the opening line of a prose poem written in 1936 by Dovid Einhorn (then in Paris) in tribute to his friend Borekh Vladeck (then in New York). Born in White Russia in the same year, 1886, these two men had been less than twenty when the revolution began. But this did not prevent them (both members of the Bund) from reaching a very considerable measure of fame in the period 1905–6, the one as a poet, the other as an orator of the revolution. Extreme youth became, if anything, an asset in these years when natural talent, however untutored and be it organizational, intellectual, oratorical, or literary, was suddenly in enormous demand.

"We are now living through a *Sturm und Drang* period," Iulii Brutskus wrote in March 1906, "similar to that experienced by the German Jews one hundred years ago in the time of the French Revolution and Napoleon I."[2] Born in 1870, Brutskus belonged to an earlier generation than Vladeck and Einhorn. Moreover, he was not a socialist but since his student days had been Palestine-oriented, first as a Hovev-Zion and then as a Zionist. To those of his school of thought and his generation, the revolutionary years presented exceptionally complex problems, but for them, too, it was a time when the tempo of life sharply accelerated, when major political and ideological decisions brooked no delay, when the future of Russia and Russian Jews was seen to hang in the balance. Political activity in the Russian-Jewish world became so much more intense at this moment than in the preceding years that contemporaries, regardless of age or ideology, felt that they were living through a tense drama.[3]

As in the period 1881–2, popular expectations rose beyond all measure. Once again, the spark of hope set fire to the dry timber of poverty and misery which – impervious to efforts by the Zionists and the Bund – continued to weigh down the daily lives of the majority in the Pale of Settlement. The messianism concealed in modern secular ideology once more merged with the messianism implanted in the popular consciousness by religious teachings and folk traditions to produce an apocalyptic mood. And the extreme volatility of Russian-Jewish politics – the rapid transition from expectancy to euphoria and then to despair – was illustrated anew.

But while in 1881–2 the hope had been for liberation through a national exodus, now it was for liberation through revolution. Then the debate had been whether and how to organize a collective escape from Russia. Now the issue was in what form the Jewish people should participate in the Russian insurrection. In 1881–2 all eyes followed the mass emigration, the colonization parties, the plans

גניזת ספרי התורה הנקרעים

Figure 4. Preparing for the ritual burial of the vandalized Torah scrolls after the Kishinev pogrom. The date given is 6 August 1903.

of the Jews in the West to deal with the emergency. Now the attention of Jews abroad was drawn to events in Russia.

This sharp contrast between the political mood of 1905–6 and that of 1881–2 is, on the face of it, paradoxical. The sociological, or more exactly the sociopolitical, factors which had earlier inspired the ideology of emigration were again present in the later period. In fact, they now reappeared in larger dimensions.

The pogroms in the first year of Alexander III had involved primarily the wholesale destruction of property. In comparison, those which took place in the years 1903–6 saw a steep escalation of violence and frequently involved loss of life.[4] According to contemporary estimates, and to take just the most extreme examples, forty-seven Jews were killed in the Kishinev pogrom of 6 April 1903, twenty-nine in that of Zhitomir at the end of April 1905, one hundred in Kiev on 10 July, sixty in Belostok on 1 August, eight hundred in Odessa on 18 October, and two hundred in Belostok on 1 June 1906.[5] Another, usually more cautious, source estimated that six hundred and ninety pogroms occurred in the last two weeks of October alone.[6]

Now, as then, the pogroms were matched by a startling jump in the rate of emigration. Thus, Jewish emigration from Russia to the United States rose according to standard estimates from 37,011 in 1900 to 77,544 in 1904; 92,388 in 1905; and 125,234 in 1906.[7] And in the West, the Jewish communities once more responded to the wave of pogroms by the organization of special relief funds and political protest actions. Here, too, the reaction was reminiscent of 1881–2, albeit on a larger scale; American Jewry now took the lead, the sums of money collected were greater, and the demonstrations more popular.

Yet however inescapable the impression of déjà vu, however marked the parallels with the events of twenty-five years before, the undeniable fact remains that at the level of politics and political ideology the attitude of the Russian Jews was in radical contrast to that of the earlier generation. The differing response was certainly not due to ignorance of the events of 1881–2. Of course, most of the younger leaders had not even been born then and they saw that period as past history. But the older generation, those now in their forties or fifties, could not avoid discussing what for many of them had been the most memorable episode of their own youth.

Thus, for instance, in November 1905 at the Second Congress of the Union for Equal Rights, Ahad Ha-Am could recall "the proclamations calling for Jewish pogroms put out by the Narodovoltsy in the 1880s,"[8] a statement which, according to the protocol, produced "a stir among the delegates"[9] and an angry response from M. A. Krol. A veteran Narodovolets himself, Krol argued that "if we are to start digging into the history of the parties and going through their dirty linen we could come up with details more shocking."[10]

In his famous (or, for the Left, notorious) series of articles, "The Lessons of the Terrible Days" (published in December 1905), Dubnov dwelt at some length on the parallel between the two periods, emphasizing that governmental hostility to, and deep-rooted popular hatred for, the Jews were little changed:

> In 1881, the anti-Jewish pogroms were officially called (by the minister, N. P. Ignatev) "popular justice" and in 1905 they are officially included in the series of "patriotic demonstrations" conducted under the national flag and the tsar's portrait. Then, they were justified by imaginary economic factors and now by political factors – revenge for the revolutionary activity of the Jews. The motives have changed and so has the practice . . . it has changed for the worse . . . ; before, there was governmental inaction; now it cooperates . . . in organizing the pogroms. Before there were pogroms but since 1903 there has been murder and massacre . . .
>
> And what of the people? . . . Those thousands and tens of thousands of workers, peasants, *meshchane*, and *raznochintsy* who across the length and breadth of Russia, from Odessa to Tomsk broke Jewish heads, tore out children's eyes, raped women and cut them to pieces, burnt, plundered, stole . . . were they all just making a counterrevolution? No, they were doing what their fathers and brothers did in years past and will do again given favorable circumstances.[11]

But Ahad Ha-Am and Dubnov certainly did not intend to argue that the dictum *plus ça change, plus c'est la même chose* should also apply to contemporary Jewish politics. These two veteran publicists were not exempt from the general mood of the time. They felt that the fate of the Jews was going to be decided by the outcome of the revolution and that they had to participate in the Russian political power struggle. They were less optimistic than the younger generation, and indeed than most of their contemporaries. They felt that the Jews should first do what they could to safeguard their own minimal national interests, but they were certainly not advocating that the Jewish people stand aside during the revolution. Dubnov summed up his own attitude thus: "From the terrible experience of the last quarter of a century Russian Jewry has developed an irreconcilable hatred for the despotic regime . . . [12] From the tortured heart of the people has been wrung a Carthaginian oath that the struggle against what still remains of the regime will not cease."[13]

The simple fact is that contemporaries (even a Dubnov or an Ahad Ha-Am) considered the differences between 1905 and 1881 to be of far greater weight than the similarities. First, the intervening years had witnessed the long-drawn-out agony of emigrationist politics. Originally, the plans for an exodus had assumed a chain reaction in which the mass flight from Russia would produce large donations of capital from the Western Jews; the capital would be employed to settle the refugees on a select territory; the colonization would lead to self-government, eventually to statehood; and this in turn would provide all Jews uprooted from their native lands with a secure home. But the parts of which this logical construct was composed had remained obstinately separate in reality.

Capital had been raised in the West but it was dispersed in a variety of directions: agricultural settlement in the Argentine, Brazil, New Jersey; modern and technical education for the Jews in the Middle East, North Africa, Galicia, Rumania, and Russia itself; aid to the emigrants who chose to make their own way to the West and required assistance. With a share of this money, colonization in Palestine had consolidated itself but at a level so modest that it was clearly irrelevant to the immediate political and economic plight of the Jewish people in eastern Europe. Again, mass emigration had become a permanent phenomenon but it followed a pattern more accurately foreseen by the Alliance than by Lilienblum or the Am Olam. It had emerged as a self-generating sociological force directed not to a select territory but to centers all over the Western world and, above all, to the great cities of New York, London, Philadelphia, Boston, Chicago.

However, even this massive outflow of people was proving insufficient to change radically the basic pattern of life among those who stayed behind or even to put an end to the rapid growth in absolute terms of the Jewish population in the Russian Empire. So desperate did the situation appear that, following the Kishinev pogrom in 1903, Herzl felt compelled to propose the acceptance of Uganda as a center for the concentrated and mass settlement of Jews (to be used at least as long as entry to Palestine was restricted).[14] As a result, in July 1905, the world Zionist movement at its Seventh Congress held in Basel split in two, with the territorialist and the Palestinophile wings going their separate organizational ways. Coming as it did at the height of the Russian revolution, this schism brought home in a peculiarly dramatic form the fact that the emigration movement had so far failed to produce results in any way commensurate with its goal of national self-liberation; that for the foreseeable future close to six million Jews would continue to live in the Russian Empire and that for them the outcome of the revolution was therefore crucially important.

But emigration was only one of the factors now perceived very differently in the light of changing circumstances. Even more important was the fact that Russian politics and society had clearly taken on a new shape during those twenty-five years – and never before had this change appeared so total as in 1905 (particularly up until October).

During the first year of Alexander III, the Jews felt utterly isolated, deserted. Government and revolutionaries alike had shown themselves ready to condone, exploit, and even encourage pogroms. The press and the *zemstva* had acted as vehicles for a popular and peculiarly ugly form of antisemitic incitement. And those Russians who disagreed had tended toward silence.

Since then the government had indeed raised hostility to the Jews to the level of a calculated policy, sealing the Pale of Settlement still tighter, expelling thousands of families from Moscow and other cities in the midst of winter, closing the doors to middle and higher education against all but a small percentage of the youth. But in this aspect of its policy, the regime could no longer count on general approbation from the educated and articulate strata of society. Opposition to the regime, largely silenced under Alexander III, had risen steadily during the reign of his son, and the more hostile to the Jews official policy became, the more socialists and liberals tended to associate antisemitism with reaction.

The argument that the pogroms had only played into the hands of the regime had in the years 1884–6 been clearly formulated, as a kind of last will and testament, in the final publications of the Narodnaia Volia. Thereafter, this theory became axiomatic in the thinking of the oppositional forces, whether the liberal constitutionalist camp (grouped from 1902 around the journal *Osvobozhdenie*), the revived populist movement (formed from 1902 into the Party of Socialist Revolutionaries), or the proletarian-oriented Social Democratic movement.[15]

This was the theme that Plekhanov chose to develop in an article published in *Iskra,* in May 1903, following the news of the Kishinev pogrom. In 1881, he recalled, the Narodnaia Volia had supported the pogroms and this had been "the *view not simply* of an individual Narodovolets [but] . . . *the official view, as it were, of the Narodnaia Volia party.*"[16] (In evidence, he quoted at length from the relevant article of the party journal of October 1881 and referred to the Roma-nenko proclamation.) The pogroms, in reality, had not sparked off a revolution but had produced "national prejudices even in those sections of our population to which they had hitherto been foreign. It can be said without any exaggeration that *the psychological consequences of the Jewish pogroms . . . have continued to harm our socialist movement throughout all the last twenty years.*" Fortunately, the socialists had learnt from the "cruel mistake" of that time, and the Social Demo-cratic party could be relied upon to "do absolutely everything in its power to fight against the antisemitic 'riots.' "[17]

There were manifold layers of irony, both conscious and unconscious, in the way that Plekhanov elaborated his argument. Ostensibly just a reaction to the Kishinev pogrom, it was also intended to cause maximal embarrassment to the Party of Socialist Revolutionaries, which proclaimed itself heir to the Narodnaia Volia; less obvious but also implicit was the rebuke to the Bund. Apart from the dubious taste involved in using the Kishinev pogroms (condemned by all the contemporary oppo-sitional movements) in order to score points off rival parties, there was the fact (then unknown to the public) that Plekhanov himself, for fear of antagonizing the Narodnaia Volia, had actively discouraged Akselrod from publishing his critical brochure on the subject in 1882. But all this only served to underline the truth of

Plekhanov's basic theme – that to view the pogroms as an instrument of revolution rather than reaction was a thing of the past; that, as the title suggested, "Times Change."

Increasingly, the Russian-Jewish intelligentsia tended to draw what was or appeared to be the only logical conclusion from this realignment of attitudes and forces. Whatever the social roots of antisemitism, its adoption as an instrument of concerted governmental policy left the Jews no choice but to hope and work for the victory of the opposition, and in 1905 that meant the victory, at least partial, of the revolution. The events of the first nine months of that year, the use of armed forces to protect *pogromshchiki,* the increasing participation of the soldiers themselves in the pogroms, the role of both Jewish and non-Jewish socialists in the self-defense efforts – all tended to drive home this same message.[18] True, the eruption of massive anti-Jewish violence immediately following the Manifesto of 17 October undermined confidence in the revolution and revolutionaries. But it also served to commit the Jewish leaders and a large part of their following still more irrevocably (despite their frequent misgivings) to the opposition side.

In a series of editorials in the Zionist weekly, *Khronika evreiskoi zhizni,* which was only marginally left of center, Abram Idelson discussed this commitment in anguished terms. Thus, on 28 October he could write:

> For us Jews, the immediate gathering of a Constituent Assembly is undoubtedly the most desirable development – only the revolutionary storm which would precede the meeting of the Constituent Assembly can tear out by the root the age-old and giant trees of state antisemitism. But at the same time our tragic position between the hammer and the anvil makes us tremble at the thought of what price we will have to pay for that final victory.[19]

Even after the failure of the December uprising in Moscow, Idelson continued to feel that the Jewish people had made its choice and there could be no backing out:

> Our position in the struggle has in practice already been defined. As a nation suffering more than others from reactionary legislation and the arbitrariness of the police, we – as represented by the most conscious elements of our people – stand on the side of the liberation movement in its struggle against the old order ... For us, the stimuli in this struggle are national honor and basic, vital, interests.[20]

Idelson belonged to the Palestinophile generation recruited during the early 1880s and was therefore neither a revolutionary nor a youthful enthusiast. Here he was simply giving expression to the view prevalent among the Jewish intelligentsia as a whole. In the crisis of 1881 there had been no room for the Jewish people as an active force in Russian politics; now, in the crisis of 1905, the Jews felt that there was no escape from the Russian arena, that they had no choice except to participate.

It has to be remembered, after all, that the pre-October enthusiasm for – and post-October loyalty to – the revolution came as the climax of a largely subterranean process which had gradually gained momentum over the previous fifteen or twenty years. In 1881 nobody had seriously anticipated the series of blows which would fall on the Jewish people after the assassination of Alexander II. The response throughout had carried the clear imprint of bewilderment and improvisation.

In contrast, the revolution had long been expected by Russian Jews. Since the mid-1880s, the constant and accelerating flow of its youth into the socialist movements had created innumerable ties between the Jewish people, or considerable sections of it, and the revolutionary cause. First, there were the bonds of family and kinship. Not only the poor or obscure but also many of the leading figures in Russian-Jewish life had sons and daughters, grandsons or nephews, actively involved in the underground movements. Aleksandr Tsederbaum, prominent maskil in the 1860s and 1870s, and *Palestinets* since the 1880s, was the grandfather of a number of important revolutionary Social Democrats: Iulii (Martov), Sergei (Ezhov), Vladimir (Levitsky), and Lydiia Kantsel (later the wife of Fedor Dan).[21] The same was true of another influential *Palestinets,* Klonimos-Volf Vysotsky, the Moscow tea magnate, whose grandchildren included A. R. Gots, Mikhail Gots, and I. I. Fundaminsky, all leading Socialist Revolutionaries. The chief rabbi of Moscow was the father of Osip Minor. By 1900 some 30 percent of the political arrestees in the Russian Empire were Jews.[22]

All this did not justify the official assumption, made explicit by both Pleve and Witte in the years 1903–6, that the established leaders of the Jewish community had the power if they wished to bring their youth to heel.[23] The Jewish people at this stage in its history was unified neither organizationally nor ideologically. At most, such demands could encourage some of the highly conservative elements in the community to act more diligently (out of fear of pogroms and governmental reprisals) as informers for the authorities. In general the position adopted by Pleve was counterproductive. Unable to prevent the influx of the educated youth into the revolutionary movements, the Jews nonetheless found themselves identified collectively with them. Even orthodox Jews deeply hostile to socialism, even Zionists naturally inclined to passivity in Russian politics, tended increasingly to sympathize with their young relatives in the revolutionary underground.

In a private memorandum sent to Theodor Herzl in June 1903, Chaim Weizmann, following a visit he had just made to Russia, sought to describe the dimensions and importance of this revolutionary recruitment from within the Jewish world:

> Almost all those now being victimized [by the police] in the entire Social Democratic movement are Jews, and their number grows every day. They are not necessarily young people of proletarian origin; they also come from well-to-do families and, incidentally, not infrequently from Zionist families. Almost all students belong to the revolutionary camp; hardly any of them escape its ultimate fate ... It is a fearful spectacle, and one that obviously escapes west European Zionists, to observe the major part of our youth – and no one would describe them as the worst part – offering themselves for sacrifice as though seized by a fever.[24]

As the result of this process, the alienation of the socialist from the Jewish world was becoming less complete. Even those who joined general Russian revolutionary movements had not necessarily made a permanent break with the specifically Jewish milieu. Men like Martov, Zhitlovsky, An-sky, and M. B. Ratner, though active members of the Russian Social Democratic or Social Revolutionary parties, played central roles in the development of Jewish politics (organizationally and still more ideologically) at various stages during the years 1890–1905. While in the late 1880s the revolutionary youth (with one or two exceptions) had been totally cut off from the Jewish people, the intervening years had produced a more complex reality. The relationship had now to be seen as a continuum in which the opposite poles had absolutely no contact – except for a profound and mutual hatred – while in the center there was no longer a clear dividing line.

Increasingly, the central section of this continuum came to be dominated in the years before 1905 by the Bund, which stood as it were with one foot in the Russian revolutionary camp and the other in the Jewish world. Founded officially in 1897, the Bund (or, to use its full title, the General Jewish Labor Union in Lithuania, Poland, and Russia) traced its organizational origins back to the early 1890s. A movement specifically created to organize the Jewish proletariat as a revolutionary force, it came over the years to embody the idea of active resistance by Jews qua Jews against the tsarist regime. It preached day-in, day-out that the Jewish masses could reach salvation only through a general Russian revolution, that the Jewish proletariat and intelligentsia had to make their own contribution to that revolution, through solidarity, disruption, and eventually insurrection. Working within the cities and towns and even the shtetls of the Pale of Settlement, it had brought the concept of the revolution into the very heartlands of the Jewish world long before 1905.

Against the background of the Russian autocratic system, in which oppositional or even trade-union activity (unless under police supervision) was subject to harsh repression, the success of the Bund inevitably became the object of almost legendary respect. It is probably true to say that its highly conspiratorial form of inner organization only served to heighten the outer impression it gave of enormous reserves of strength – an impression not always shared by those within the movement. Thus, early in 1903, Prince P. D. Sviatopolk-Mirsky, the governor-general of the northwestern region, could write in a memorandum to St. Petersburg that

> with the gradual extinction of Polish domination and the gradual pacification of the Poles, there arose very serious movements among the local Jewish population ... The Jewish political organization, the Bund, acts with enormous energy, is rapidly strengthening its ranks and having created ... a fighting detachment [*boevaia komanda*] has become almost omnipotent. Proclamations ... are distributed in thousands of copies; workers' strikes ... are organized ... ; the peaceful loyal section of the workers is intimidated ... Strikes, street demonstrations during which red flags are hoisted, demonstrations in theaters, resistance to the authorities occur primarily in ... [such centers as] Vilna, Grodno, Kovno, Belostok, Brest, Smorgon Krynki, and others.[25]

Or, to take another example, Weizmann, who in late 1901 could write that the Bund's "*sozialpolitische Bedeutung* within Jewry is still negligible,"[26] had to grant by mid-1903 that "our hardest struggle everywhere is conducted against the Jewish Social Democrats (the *Jüdischer Arbeiterbund* of Russia and Poland),"[27] that "this movement consumes much energy and heroism and is located within the Jewish fold," and that in consequence "children are in open revolt against their parents."[28]

The long years of preparation – by the Bund, by Jews acting as individual mem-

Figure 5. A Bund self-defense group in Pinsk, 1905.

bers of the Russian and Polish socialist parties – meant that when the revolution came it was seen by large sections of the Jewish people as part of the natural order of things: revenge for twenty-five years of humiliation and victimization, and the long overdue entry of Russia into Europe. When the mass pogroms came in October 1905 the tendency of the intelligentsia was therefore to interpret them as a particularly bloody and horrifying battle in the war for Russia's future, the price which had to be paid for Jewish self-liberation. While in 1881–2 the Jewish people had stood unprepared, now it had an entire generation of youth to defend it (even if only symbolically in many cases) against attacks, to fight for its rights, to uphold its honor. This was the answer given to Dubnov, Jabotinsky, and others who insisted that following the pogroms the Jews should concentrate more on organizing a united, national front and less on general participation in the revolution.

"The solution for us [the Russian Jews] is totally clear," said M. A. Krol at the congress of the Union for Equal Rights in November 1905.

> There was a time when the situation of the Jews in Russia appeared completely hopeless, that was the beginning of the 80s – terrified by the pogroms, downtrodden, humiliated . . . but this position did not last long. Brought to despair, the Russian Jews decided to take their fate into their own hands; the Jewish revolutionary proletariat appeared on the scene and it threw a proud challenge to the violence and malevolence of the Russian regime . . . The position of the Jews in Russia has been changed in the most basic way; thanks to the selfless struggle of the Jewish proletariat, the Jews have begun to be taken seriously and the Council of Ministers yielded to the pressure of

Jewish public opinion and granted Jews the right to vote, not wanting "to introduce new inflammable material among the Jews."[29]

This same basic theme was developed by S. An-sky (also a veteran of the revolutionary populist movement from the 1880s) in his series of articles replying to Dubnov. An-sky suggested that the three waves of pogroms—1881–2, 1903, and 1905–were indeed caused by the same factors. "The pogroms of all three periods," he wrote, "were simulations–some more, some less successful–of a spontaneous movement, while, in actuality, they were all organized by the government with the single goal of putting out the revolutionary fire with Jewish blood."[30] What had changed, however, was the Jewish response:

> The Kishinev pogrom ... met a new Jewish people, very sensitive to its human dignity, holding an enormous store of militant energy within itself ... In everybody, and before all else, there emerged the thirst for revenge ... The poet Bialik with the power and clarity characteristic of him expressed the popular mood following the Kishinev pogrom in his "Masa Nemirov."[31] The culminating point of the tragedy for the poet is not the physical suffering and its horror but the unending insult to human dignity ... And the lesson drawn by the people from the pogrom was the exact opposite from the 80s. Instead of the cry–"Back!"–back from universal human culture, back from the revolution, there came the cry to combat– "Forward!" [*Vpered*!]; "To arms!" for the defense of life ... The revolutionaries who twenty years earlier were considered enemies of the people–bringing down on it the vengeance of God, the tsar, and the people–emerged now as its most reliable champions.[32]

Forms of Jewish participation in the revolution

The reaction of the Jews to the revolution of 1905, then, came more as a culmination than a break, was characterized not by radical discontinuities but by a sudden increase in tempo and scale. However, these changes of magnitude did transform if not the nature then certainly the structure, balance, and mood of Jewish politics. Quantitative change became qualitative.

. Thus, during the previous fifteen years the socialist youth had sought with considerable although uneven success to organize the Jewish workers in the revolutionary movement (primarily in the Bund). But by mid-1906 the claim could seriously be made that "the Jewish revolutionary socialist organizations have gathered under their flag almost the entire Jewish proletariat, have established their leadership over it, and enjoy the trust of broad strata of the Jewish population."[33] There was no doubt an element of hyperbole here. Statistics suggested that there were in the entire Russian Empire close to four hundred thousand Jewish wage-earning workers, and of these, in mid-1906, less than a quarter were members of the socialist parties.

As against this, though, it must be remembered that over one hundred thousand members of this wage-earning group were classified as unskilled laborers (*chernye rabochie*) and were largely unorganizable;[34] that the power of the socialists was not evenly distributed geographically and that, as a result, in key cities such as

Vilna a majority of the Jewish proletariat was probably organized in the revolutionary parties; that the direct influence of the socialists extended through many channels over large numbers of the population outside the party ranks; and that, in consequence, in the last months of 1905 the concept of the "hegemony of the proletariat" was considered an appropriate description of the actual situation in a number of largely Jewish cities.[35]

Shimen Dimanshtein (in 1905 a revolutionary active for the Bolsheviks among the Jewish workers in Lithuania, and in the Soviet Russia of 1918 the first people's commissar for Jewish affairs) would later recall the popular enthusiasm in the following terms: "In the period of the 1905 revolution there was an enormous desire to be organized . . . it was enough for any group of intelligentsia to appear with a red flag for it to gather round itself for a time a considerable number of people who wanted – regardless how – to join the revolution."[36]

Parallel to and interacting with the mobilization of the workers was the increasing militancy of the youth, now acting collectively and openly rather than as hitherto, individually and secretly. A report from a prominent St. Petersburg *intelligent* who traveled through the Pale of Settlement in the autumn of 1905 described how in Jewish high schools, the pupils were "demanding participation at the teachers' meetings where the choice of new students is discussed";[37] how in the Mohilev agricultural school, the youths were suddenly refusing to do their practical work such as weeding the fields, and how in numerous other ways the influence of the "extreme parties"[38] was leading the youths to ignore all established authority (not only external, but also internal, within the Jewish world itself).

However, granted the general upsurge of political energy, it should be stressed that the degree and the forms of participation in the revolution were not uniform throughout. Both chronologically and geographically the political mood, the degree of commitment, and the modes of action varied enormously. The reasons for this variation were complex, but an underlying pattern emerged rather clearly.

Where the classic revolutionary motivations – liberty, equality, fraternity, and nationality – merged and reinforced each other, the enthusiasm of the Jewish masses could reach remarkable heights. But where they clashed, when the urge for social equality came into conflict with the movement for political liberation, when – even more – cooperation between ethnic groups was overshadowed by interethnic tensions, then the euphoria did not develop at all, subsided rapidly, or took on highly sectarian forms. Where all the disparate forces of discontent united, the dam of traditional restraints, fears, and suspicions was smashed down; but, even then, the onrushing barrage of floodwater easily dissipated itself the moment unity was lost.

In the early stages of the revolution, fraternity (in the specific sense of interethnic or international cooperation) was crucial in forming revolutionary attitudes. An examination of the reports sent in from local organizations of the Bund in January and February 1905, for instance, reveals that the militancy of the Jewish workers rose or fell sharply in accord with the degree of non-Jewish involvement.

This no doubt resulted in the first instance from strictly practical considerations. Living in cities of mixed population, Jewish workers could act most effectively only in unison with Poles, Russians, or Latvians. This was doubly true because Jews were not employed on the railways or in the post and telegraph offices and were represented poorly in the large factories; hence, a general political strike could not be totally successful anywhere if they had to act alone.[39] Again, over and beyond this was the eternal fear, never absent in the years 1905–6, that any revolutionary action might develop – or be converted – into a pogrom. The international solidarity of the proletariat had to be seen quite literally as a matter of life or death.

Strikes were initiated by the Bund in some sixty cities in January 1905 as its response to the mass shootings in St. Petersburg on Bloody Sunday.[40] Where the participants saw that the non-Jewish workers had also come out on strike, a mood of intense excitement prevailed. "The strike is general," wrote the Vilna correspondent of the Bund's *Poslednie izvestiia* on 19 January. "The factories, plants and workshops, printing shops, bakeries, etc., are all at a standstill. There are no papers and no bread."[41] The same was true in Kovno: "We now have a general strike of the Jewish and Christian workers. Some fifteen thousand people, it is said, are on strike. Yesterday all the shops were closed, the electricity was off."[42] From Dvinsk the report read: "The strikes are engulfing new towns every day. Our turn has come . . . For two days now I have not been working: the organization of the strike demanded an enormous lot of time and work."[43]

In Lodz and Warsaw, where the Jewish population constituted large minorities rather than a majority, the general participation in the strikes, the joint action by Poles and Jews, was doubly impressive because so unusual. "There is not one large factory working," it was reported from Lodz on 15 January. "From today the small workshops have begun to close . . . And today there is absolutely no work being done in the whole town . . . In Warsaw events are developing so fast that they tell us clashes have taken place between the workers and the armed forces. No newspapers are coming out there either."[44]

The most tense reports, though, came from Riga where Latvian, Russian, and Jewish workers were all involved:

> There is a revolution here! There is fighting in the streets. Many comrades have been killed or wounded. Like lava, crowds of thousands flow from one end of the town to the other . . . Ilia Epstein has been killed . . . This is already the third day that the shops are closed and the papers have not come out. The work is desperate, feverish. Every day proclamations are printed in 8,000 copies . . . Twelve demonstrations were held on one day. A proletarian army of 25,000 under the red flag is moving about the town.[45]

A later despatch spoke of eighty-seven demonstrators killed and two hundred and fourteen seriously wounded.[46]

In those towns where the Polish and Russian workers remained uninvolved, the tone was totally different. "The Jewish workers here," read the report from Bobruisk, "are not very conscious and organized – the failure of the strike among the Christian workers led to a fall in their spirits . . . The weaker the strike became, the less its influence on 'society' and the intelligentsia."[47] (The police, it emerged, had placed guards at the gates of the large factories in order to prevent agitators from reaching the Russian labor force.) From Brest-Litovsk (likewise a town with an absolute Jewish majority) the story was the same: "[We] had no possibility of organizing the Christian workers: and there is no organization here which can do so successfully . . . in the town all the talk was of the strike. The people were in a panic . . . they feared a pogrom."[48] There were similar despatches from Zhitomir and Minsk; in the latter town the soldiers ran riot, looting the stores and shouting "Bei zhidov!"[49]

However, in the first nine months of 1905 the pattern of Riga rather than that of Brest or Bobruisk more often prevailed and dominated the public consciousness. Thus, by far the most dramatic and effective actions by the Jewish masses took place in large cities with truly mixed populations and would hardly have been conceivable if the revolutionary mood had not been general and tangible. This was true of the great funeral march, thirty thousand strong, organized by the Bund in Warsaw on 2 April which ended with the armed forces shooting into the crowd, followed by a general strike on 5 April in the entire Jewish section of the city.[50]

It was true even more of the events in Lodz and Odessa in the summer, during the "June Days," as they came to be called. On 5 June in Lodz a demonstration, in which the supporters of the Bund and the Polish socialist parties merged, was fired upon and two days later some fifty thousand people marched in the funeral procession. A general strike was called on 10 June, and that night barricades were raised in the Jewish Quarter and elsewhere in the city. Pitched battles were fought with the cavalry all during that night and into the next day.[51] Contemporary estimates reported about 561 people killed (of whom 341 were Jews) in the fighting in Lodz.[52] "I cannot but emphasize," *Iskra*'s correspondent wrote in the city on 11 June,

> the great respect in which – over the past year and especially the recent months – Christian Lodz holds the Jews. The heroic conduct of the Jews in the clashes with the police and the army units arouses admiration everywhere . . . Legends are circulating about yesterday's battle between the Jews and the Cossacks on the Wschodnaja – legends which describe the Jewish workers as some kind of Samsons.[53]

In Odessa, armed clashes between workers and police flared up on 14 June after a strike had been proclaimed jointly by the Bund and the Mensheviks. "The mood was such," read the report in *Poslednie izvestiia*,

> that, throughout, those who attacked were not the Cossacks but the workers . . . there were cases when the workers, pursuing the police, broke down the gates behind which the police were hiding . . . In their fury they struck such fear into the police that often it was enough to show them a revolver to make them flee. Our organization can consider this Tuesday its day of triumph . . . Almost only Jewish workers took part in the clashes on this day and members of our organizations played a role everywhere.[54]

On the following day, the fifteenth, the S.S. *Potemkin Tavrichesky* under the control of its mutinous crew sailed into the port of Odessa, lending the uprising new confidence. A report sent to *Iskra* on that day declared that "Odessa port is in the hands of the [revolutionary] Black Sea flotilla . . . there is reason to hope that we will succeed in taking control of the entire town, in forming our own army, our own government."[55] This, of course, was one of many cases of counting chickens before they were hatched. The Odessa uprising was quickly suppressed as the port and surrounding area were destroyed by a fast-spreading fire and as the Cossacks systematically cleared the streets of resistance. In this case, too, hundreds of people lost their lives.

Nevertheless, summing up the recent events, the liberal Jewish paper *Voskhod*, known hitherto for its cautious and modulated tones, could write:

> Never before, perhaps, has the Christian population in the Pale felt, in such solidarity with the Jews, the entire weight of administrative oppression ... The horrors of Odessa and Lodz are utterly remarkable in their scale; the most somber pages of modern human history pale before them. The violent official measures not only proved totally impotent but uprooted all the faith of the population in the local government, i.e., destroyed morally all governmental power.[56]

Given this rising confidence in a united front of the oppressed nationalities and classes, it was not surprising that the persistent outbreak of pogroms was interpreted, at least until October, as the final thrashings of a dying political order. This was true even when the political threat posed the revolutionary movement by this problem was too great to be ignored. So, for example, on May Day, 1905 (18 April in Russia), the Bundist organizations generally chose, for fear of anti-Jewish outbreaks, to celebrate the occasion by a strike rather than by street demonstrations. Despite this caution a major pogrom still occurred in Zhitomir ten days later.

Yet this sequence of events was seen as confirming the revolutionary prognosis. The Bundist paper, *Poslednie izvestiia*, noted first that the prolonged efforts by right wing and governmental forces to organize a general wave of pogroms had failed, a failure which demonstrated that "passive resistance by the surrounding population against the persecution of the Jews [was at work] and that significant changes have taken place in the consciousness and psychology of the Russian popular masses." Second, the Jewish self-defense had proved its courage in Zhitomir (as well as in Melitopol) and, what was more, Russians had fought side by side with Jews against the *pogromshchiki*. "The times of Kishinev," concluded the paper, "have gone for ever. Since Kishinev everything has changed."[57]

Or as Litvak would put it looking back from the end of the year: "In Zhitomir there was no pogrom but a war."[58] Of May Day itself Litvak then recalled not the apprehension, nor the caution, but the confidence and the unanimity: "The towns were as quiet as on Yom Kippur and as joyfully festive as on Pesach. Even western Europe has never witnessed such a holiday [*yontev.*]"[59]

In these, the early months of the upheaval, it was not only the national or ethnic factor which (as it seemed to contemporaries) had been successfully mobilized by the revolution. The egalitarian drive also reinforced the appeal of the insurrectionary cause. The developments of 1905 are normally described as primarily an aborted political revolution in the cities paralleled by an incipient social uprising in the countryside. But this estimate, although broadly correct, should not lead one to overlook the social and economic unrest running deep in the urban areas.

As the control of the governmental administration declined during 1905, so the relative power of the socialist parties increased. In the autumn months, there were frequent reports, for instance, of the revolutionaries in the Jewish areas imposing early (or earlier) closing time on the shopkeepers (in order to shorten the working hours of their employees); of their forcing merchants to take on extra, although unwanted, assistants (in order to cut down unemployment); of their forcibly exacting "taxes" from the richer members of the community.[60]

Moreover, by no means all the strikes during the revolutionary period were "political;" on the contrary, economically motivated strikes were more common and waged with greater effectiveness than ever before. Describing developments in Grodno, for instance, Akimov wrote that "the strike movement of 1905 generally raised wages 25 percent: in individual cases it varied from 10 percent to 60 percent."[61] Working hours were reduced to nine or ten per day.

One (not particularly sympathetic) observer even described the Bund at this time as "a philanthropic institution . . . a society for aid to the Jewish poor."[62] But this critic admitted elsewhere that it was precisely because the Bund concerned itself with economics, "strikes and patronage" (as well as with politics) – with all Jewish affairs "up to and including charitable organizations and Talmud Torahs" – that it had become "the sole representative not only of the proletariat but of Jewry as a whole."[63]

Chemerisky made basically the same point in his humorous account of the streets (*birzhes*) where the party organizers and workers assembled in the evenings in what were essentially nonstop and perambulating meetings:

> The entire town [Lodz in May 1905] knew about the *birzhes*; everybody knew the activists. People used to come for every different reason: questions of divorce; a dowry; business partners who had fallen out; a speculator who himself had been outwitted; a young woman who had been deceived; a quarrel in the family; maids with complaints against the ladies of the house – all used to come and one could hardly escape them by telling them that they should rather go to the rabbi.[64]

Nothing succeeds like success, and as long as the socialists could juggle effectively keeping all the balls – self-defense, interethnic cooperation, economic action, the fight for political democracy – up in the air, they had an inspirational effect on those around them. The urge to stand up to the authorities, to insist on one's rights, proved infectious.

A despatch from Pinsk in late September illustrates just how far this process had gone by then. Following the shooting of two policemen by persons unknown, the chief of police called a meeting of leading personages, Jews and Christians, to discuss the fast-deteriorating situation. "I assure you, gentlemen," he reportedly said, "that if another assassination attempt is made against the police, I will personally come at the head of a force and we will shoot out the Jews."[65] Far from intimidating his audience this statement unleashed a barrage of criticism. A local pharmacist spoke out against "the conduct of the lower police ranks and of the Cossacks – they are savages, wild beasts, and treat the public absolutely inhumanly. And it is not surprising if they are paid back in their own coin."[66] Another Jewish spokesman argued that

> the questions occupying us at this meeting now involve all of Russia and Russia has already come to its own decision, as everybody knows. The movement . . . takes on a more intensive form in the border areas because

Figure 6. A Bund self-defense group in an Odessa cemetery with three fallen members. The sign in Russian reads: "Long live freedom."

[there] the nationalities feel the burden of the regime on their backs to a greater degree than do the Russians [*korennye*] . . . Its dimensions are still more imposing in the Pale of Settlement because the Jews there are deprived of their rights in the most terrible ways. Equality for the Jews . . . equality between all nationalities, other conditions—freedom of speech, of the press, of association and assembly, the inviolability of the person—are the only means to restore order; everything else is only a miserable palliative.[67]

The despatch ended by noting that everybody in Pinsk was eagerly awaiting the anticipated resignation of the chief of police.

This incident, in itself no more than a vignette, was symptomatic of the first phase of the revolution, a time of rising confidence in the future. When the Manifesto was issued on 17 October promising the basic freedoms, the inviolability of the person, the power of legislative veto for the coming state Duma, and a broader franchise, hope appeared on the verge of fulfillment. But for no group in Russia would the fall from triumph come so suddenly as it did for the Jews.

In dozens of cities and towns, the victory celebrations on 18 and 19 October provided both the pretext for and the initial object of anti-Jewish pogroms. In Minsk, Governor-General Kurlov ordered the troops to fire into the enormous crowd which had gathered on the Station Square to celebrate the news. One hundred people, nearly all Jews, were reportedly killed and four hundred wounded.[68] In Odessa alone, the number of dead and wounded was alleged to have reached six thousand. Again, on those two days, there were heavy casualties as the result of pogroms in Kiev, Kherson, Ekaterinoslav, Kishinev, Nezhin, Novosylkov, and Simferopol. "Since the days of Bogdan Khmelnitsky," wrote Litvak, "the Jews have not suffered through such bloody days."[69]

"We are standing on a volcano which has already engulfed tens of thousands of Jewish victims and the crater of which is still active," wrote Dubnov. "We have suffered such an economic disaster that our masses – impoverished even before this – will not recover for many decades."[70] Massive destruction on this scale might have been expected to put an instant end to organized Jewish involvement in the political life of the country. But, in reality, that was not the result, or perhaps it would be more exact to say, not the immediate result.

The period from 17 October 1905 to July 1906 was one of powerful cross-currents. While the pogroms served to depress the popular mood, the October Manifesto and subsequent increase in political freedoms acted as a heady stimulant. Facts, which drove many out of the public into the private sphere, goaded others to seek revenge against the regime. It was a time when the revolution had great power both to repel and attract, when political fragmentation and polarization existed side by side with efforts to build broad political organizations and coalitions. It was a time of both spreading confusion and limitless hope.

The belief in fraternity, in ethnic brotherhood, which had had so inspiring an effect from January until 17 October, could of course not survive the subsequent experience in anything like its original messianic form. It was not just that the pogroms were frequently carried out – under police or army protection – with the massive participation of workers and peasants. It was also that the Russian revolutionary parties with one or two notable exceptions rarely intervened to fight the October pogroms. This was variously explained as the result of indifference, betrayal, or organizational passivity and weakness. But whatever the reason, the fact was undeniable and damaging.

There could be no doubt that the revolutionary fever among the Jewish masses now declined sharply. "The pogroms," wrote An-sky in March 1906, "acted for the Jews as a kind of terrible memento mori holding them back from rapid and explosive forward movement."[71] The mass demonstration or march, tens of thousand strong, now became a thing of the past in the Jewish world. When in December a strike was called jointly by the Bund, the SRs, and the RSDRP in Dvinsk, the Jewish masses did come out to the last man – in itself an impressive show of solidarity – but their interest waned sharply as soon as it became clear that the railway workers were still at work. "People began to say openly among the masses," recalled Leyb Blekhman, "that there was no point in maintaining the strike any more. The Jewish workers in Dvinsk could not and would not make the revolution in Russia."[72]

In the main, the Jewish intelligentsia, which was committed to the belief that the pogroms were a lost battle in a war about to be won, found this more sceptical mood among the mass of the Jewish people deeply disturbing. "There is no doubt," read the editorial in Voskhod on 30 December 1905,

[that] the cause of the recent pogroms – from Kishinev to October – is primarily political . . .[73] But that is not how the Jews understood the horrors of the bloody days in the localities. The masses do not think logically. They are guided by impressions . . . These pogroms, coming *now* at the height of the

Figure 7. THE REACTION: "We have to put it out—either with water or with blood."

(The pogromschiki, *carrying a flag labeled "The Union of True Russian Hooligans," are trying to douse the sun of freedom. The actual name of the organization was the Union of True Russian People,* Soiuz istinnykh russ-kikh liudei. *This and the following two cartoons are reproduced from* Der bezim *[The Broom], a satirical supplement to* Der fraynd. *They are all from no. 47 [26 February/11 March 1906].)*

Russian revolutionary struggle, on the day of the triumph of Russian freedom, confused, discouraged and disappointed the Jews who had thrown themselves with such enthusiasm into the struggle for freedom—the freedom through which they had expected immediate escape from all evils . . . Jewish impotence and alienation were again underlined, and faith wavered in those steps to political freedom already undertaken.[74]

The October debacle dispelled much of the mystique which had hitherto clung to the established socialist organizations, first and foremost the Bund, and this in turn undercut their ability to control the fever of unrest and social change within the Jewish world. Thus, egalitarianism, which until October 1905 had largely reinforced the general upsurge of protest and insurrection, now developed a dynamic of its own – the leveling urge increasingly served to fragment rather than unite.

Symptomatic of changing realities and perceptions was the publication late in December of an attack by Iulii Brutskus on the socialists, who he argued were willfully unleashing chaos in the Pale of Settlement. He wrote that in Warsaw (which he saw as typical in this respect of the main centers of Jewish life) the masses "do not distinguish between robber bands and organized anarchists because both indulge in robbery: the masses do not distinguish the anarchists from the PPS, the Zionist Socialists or the Bundists because under all these flags money is extorted at revolver point, violence is used against peaceful citizens and even murder is committed in the economic struggle."[75] He placed direct blame on "the childish and terroristic activity of various local representatives."[76] But he also stated that in his view the top socialist leaders were not acting firmly enough to maintain discipline. As against this, the liberal and non-Zionist *Voskhod* argued that the central committee of the Bund was having difficulty in exerting direct control over all its local organizations and that it was therefore premature to accuse it (as the Warsaw *Ha-tsfira* had done) of deliberately "cultivating bandit instincts among the youth."[77] This issue would later (in August 1906) become a point of controversy at the Seventh Congress of the Bund, with some delegates complaining that the party central committee had not done enough to organize "normal expropriation" and others, most notably Virgily, that it had not "fought energetically against the expropriation tactic."[78]

Beyond doubt, though, was the fact that everyday life was becoming more dangerous and anarchic. The use by the authorities of Cossack units to patrol the cities produced a state of almost constant violence. At the same time, the rising flow of weapons to the revolutionary parties, made possible in large part by funds raised for Jewish self-defense units, provided local groups of all kinds with an almost unlimited power to intimidate and to extort (or "expropriate") funds and economic concessions from employers and property-owners.

A direct consequence of this deterioration and, in turn, a further cause of its acceleration was the reemergence of what were widely called the "Jewish Black Hundreds" (a term that lacked the precise organizational connotations of its Russian counterpart and was applied loosely to any group ready to take action against the revolutionaries). Such action commonly took the form of lockouts, coordinated attempts to bar the socialists from the synagogues (where they sought to address the public), and the transmission of information on oppositional activity to the authorities. Indicative of the new conditions was a report from Bobruisk late in December describing how at a public meeting of leading citizens, Jews and non-Jews, the majority (fearing a pogrom) had resolved to send a delegation to the governor in Minsk requesting him to return the chief police officer to their town.[79]

The descending spiral of chaos and reaction, anarchy and Black Hundreds, revolution and pogroms took on its most extreme form in Belostok. This textile center, with a population of some sixty-five thousand of whom over forty-eight thousand were Jews and the remainder mainly Poles, had long been considered one of the most incendiary centers of revolutionary activity and a stronghold of the Bund. In 1905 it had twice (in June and again in August) witnessed major clashes between workers and the armed forces in which the latter had shot dozens of people and (here the Cossacks were responsible) run riot in Jewish areas of the city. Late in 1905 and in the first half of 1906, it witnessed a process of rapid fragmentation at every level – social, political, and national.

A despatch from Virgily in December reported the establishment in the city of a new society (Agudes Yahudim) by "our Jewish Black Hundreds."[80] Its aims were still not fully defined but would no doubt include strike-breaking, hobbling the revolutionaries as much as possible, and also, perhaps, fighting "the expropriation tactics of the local anarchists and 'young social revolutionaries.' "[81]

Ironically, this latter problem increasingly worried the Bund itself in 1906. An editorial in *Folks-tsaytung* on 26 February argued that anarchism was the movement of the desperate Jewish lumpen-proletariat and described Belostok as its springboard in Russia."The home [of anarchism]," it stated, "is the Jewish ghetto, the Jewish Pale, and the atmosphere it breathes is that of the rising revolutionary fire. The first nest of Russian anarchism was Belostok. It spread only in the Pale and there only among the Jewish population . . . In Paris, in London, and other places where Jewish emigrants have settled, anarchism has also taken root."[82]

But, apart from the anarchist problem, the Bund was also faced by the employment issue which in Belostok periodically (and again in 1906) raised the tensions between the Jewish and non-Jewish workers to a fever pitch. The specific issue was whether the Jewish weavers in a given factory should be allowed to transfer from the handlooms (about to be discarded) to the new steam looms, a function normally reserved for Poles and Russians. By late February 1906, the bitterness was so great that the Bund threatened force in order to ensure that the Jewish workers not be replaced. A leaflet was issued calling on the non-Jewish weavers to renounce their "mad, criminal plan" and stating that "the Jewish workers will not permit you to use violent means against them."[83] The Bund actually introduced its combat unit [*boevoi otriad*] into the conflict, which dragged on for months until in April a compromise was finally patched up.[84]

When one of the worst pogroms of the period hit Belostok in June (some nine hundred Jews were killed or wounded), the atmosphere was so embittered that the Bund felt compelled to assign a share of the responsibility to other parties. Thus, the frequent bomb-throwing – in the eyes of the local anarchists a manifestation of *die Propaganda der Tat* – was blamed for having provoked the anti-Jewish outbreak. "Among the Jewish working masses," stated the Bundist paper on 22 June, "there is a terrible, burning hatred . . . for the anarchists who with their senseless tactics created the atmosphere [conducive to the pogroms]."[85] The two major socialist parties (the PPS and PSD) also stood accused – in their case, for having neglected to conduct effective propaganda among the Polish workers (preferring to propagandize the Jews, who were more receptive).[86] But the most damning accusation of all was reserved for the "so-called anarchists or simply hooligans of the anarchist school [who actually] took part in the pogrom."[87]

Nonetheless, the Belostok experience should not be seen as typifying the opposition movement during the immediate post-October period. Rather, it represented the most extreme development of the divisive and self-destructive potentialities inherent in that movement. Elsewhere revolutionary energies were not infrequently funneled into more constructive channels. There were enormous variations from city to city and area to area. Where pogroms had not occurred (as in Dvinsk, for instance) or where they had proved ineffectual (as in Vilna or Riga), the progress of fragmentation was less dramatic than in such cities as Belostok and the loss of impetus less precipitate than in such cities as Zhitomir. Following the pattern of 1881–2 (and anticipating that of 1918–20), Lithuania and Latvia were barely touched by the pogroms, which were nearly all concentrated in the Ukraine.

But, over and beyond this factor, there were internal forces at work which permitted the established revolutionary and oppositional leaderships to maintain and consolidate mass political mobilization at a suprisingly high level even after October.

First, with the decline of fraternity as an immediate goad to action, the relative importance of nationality increased. In organizational terms, this meant above all renewed preparations for armed self-defense against further pogroms. Here, as so often in the Jewish politics of the post-Manifesto period, there was an element of paradox. In purely practical terms, the experience of late October had been disastrous for Jewish self-defense. The relative success enjoyed by the defense units in the Zhitomir pogrom of April 1905 was now rarely repeated. In dozens of the small centers of Jewish life there was no self-defense or it was not activated. In some of the large cities, most notably in Odessa, Kiev, and Riga, armed groups (predominantly but not entirely Jewish) put up a heroic stand. But they now faced large army detachments and in some cases were wiped out to the last man. Analyzing what had gone wrong, commentators pointed out that the self-defense forces in any given town were nearly always split along party lines; that they had rarely obtained the best weapons (Browning or Smith and Wesson) but had had to make do with inferior guns which often fired off accidentally;[88] and that large quantities of arms had been seized by the police before the pogroms even began. However, Jabotinsky was stating a widely held opinion when, going beyond such technical issues, he wrote that against regular army units "the Bund and all the Jewish socialist parties together are as weak and helpless ... as [we] in the Union for Equal Rights."[89]

Yet the conclusion most frequently drawn from this experience was that, however great its limitation, self-defense remained a necessity. Jabotinsky again stated a general view when he wrote on 10 January 1906 that at least "self-defense and the revolutionary struggle raise the spirit of the Jewish people."[90] Bitterness and fury against the regime had been fanned by the pogroms to a white heat, and these emotions found a natural outlet in the self-defense units of the Jewish socialist parties.

Symptomatic of this fact was the central role assigned self-defense by the three new socialist parties that were founded during the revolutionary years: the SSRP, the SERP, and the ESDRP-PZ. According to the official party statistics, for instance, of the sixteen thousand members who belonged to this latter party at its height in 1906, fully half were organized in fighting units. The SERP reported a smaller figure in self-defense – three thousand – but of these one hundred were killed during the fighting, three hundred wounded, and about one thousand arrested.[91] Similar statistics are not available for the SSRP, but it was generally recognized as the strongest of the three parties in this sphere (as in most others). "Self-defense," stated the journal of the SSRP in July 1906, "is becoming more and more a necessity for the Jewish population."[92]

This assessment followed the Belostok pogrom in which (on 1 June) close to four hundred men in armed units successfully defended many of the side streets (although not the main thoroughfares) of the Jewish Quarter.[93] Of this episode Litvak wrote at the time in the Bundist *Folks-tsaytung:*

> When the *pogromshchik* is met by death at every door, at every window . . . then he knows that the pogrom is a war in which you can not only kill but also be killed. That frightens the hooligans; it frightens the police; it delays . . . the soldiers. At stake are our lives – and still more our honor and human dignity. We must not let ourselves be slaughtered like oxen.[94]

But to describe the post-October months in terms of frustration, anarchy, and violence alone would be a definite distortion. For many Jews, as for other Russian subjects, the truly significant event of October remained the Manifesto, the further retreat by the regime from the autocratic system. The 17 October was seen as the latest, the most significant, but by no means the last in a series of milestones – the ukazy of 12 December 1904, 18 February, and 6 August – that marked the road leading to a constitutional monarchy or a democratic republic or even beyond.

Not until the dispersal of the Second Duma on 3 June 1907 would the regime finally set clear and narrow limits to the liberties now wrung from it. In the interval, and particularly in the first months following the Manifesto, the new freedoms, however ill-defined and uncertain, however dangerous to those who made use of them, nonetheless exerted a powerful attraction.

Even for the socialists, who now lived half within and half without the law, the new era revealed organizational horizons hitherto undreamed of. The trade union movement which had existed only in embryonic form during the previous fifteen years now came into its own. Membership was no longer considered to carry with it the previous dangers of arrest, imprisonment, and penal exile. Offices were opened and recruitment conducted quite openly.[95] Proletarian clubs devoted to cultural, educational, and political ends similarly emerged into the daylight. But the extent of the change was revealed most dramatically by the appearance of a legal press, not only socialist but revolutionary. Throughout 1906, the Bund published its newspaper in Vilna (*Der veker,* later the *Folks-tsaytung*) a few times a week. The weekly of the SSRP (*Der nayer veg*) and the paper of the SERP (*Folks-shtime*) were also published in that city. "In November 1905," recalled Anna Rozental (who had then just returned from Siberia), "Vilna was boiling like a kettle. Every day new trade unions held their founding meetings and workers clubs were opened . . . It was feverish work."[96] It was in 1906 that Avrom Lesin – then in New York for over ten years, a well-known poet and the editor of *Di tsukunft* – seriously considered returning to Russia in order to work in the Bundist press.[97]

This sudden, albeit uncertain, transition to legality had a direct impact on party organization. Those socialist groups that had not formally coalesced into country-wide parties now hastened to do so – the Poale Zion founded the ESDRP in February 1906 and the Seimists the SERP in April. No group could afford to lag behind in the fierce competition for membership and influence. But the established organizations, most notably the Bund, also could not escape change. Leyb Blekhman has described his shock when, arriving in Dvinsk in November 1905, he found that all the time-honored conspiratorial rules had already been set aside.[98]

The drive for democratization and openness in the party could no longer be easily resisted. Never before (and never again) would the Bund in Russia conduct so open an ideological debate as it did – on the issue of party reunification – in its press and in its local committees during the spring and summer of 1906. Representatives of both sides published innumerable articles in which no blows were spared. (The paper of the SSRP was also open to harshly outspoken controversy.) Again, the fact that the workers were now forming their own clubs and trade unions on an elective basis brought pressure to bear on the parties to introduce the same principle in place of the system (established de facto) of nomination from above and cooption. "The organization," Litvak wrote in *Der veker* on 29 December 1905,

> must be built from below up, not from above down. The organized members of the Bund have in the last year become so political, they have so clear a conception of the events happening around them that one can already entrust them with a say in party life . . . The organization cannot remain underground any longer. It cannot hide its representatives. The broad masses know the agitators. From all sides, from the farthest corners, people now turn to the lower institutions and even to the [city] committees with all kinds of demands and requests . . . The party lives in the street.[99]

Probably the most exhilarating aspect of political life in the post-October period was the free speech now permitted to a far greater degree than before. In an age before radio or television and in an area where political speaking and even Yiddish theater had hitherto been banned, the open public meeting now enjoyed an extraordinary appeal. "Meetings, *referaty,* and lectures," noted Litvak early in January, "have become daily occurrences."[100] When in the winter the weather was too cold for open-air gatherings, synagogues and churches served continuously as meeting halls. Fame was now in the reach of those with oratorical abilities. The young Bundists – Vladeck, Groser, Maksim Klevansky, Max Goldfarb – were in enormous demand because they could hold the attention of mass audiences of thousands. Vladeck even acquired the nickname of the "young Lassalle." Others, such as Liber and Litvak, were required to deliver ideological *referaty* or conduct debates against the spokesmen of other parties. Jabotinsky's emergence as the leading Zionist figure of the period was largely due to his power as a public speaker, and the same was true of Borokhov's role in proletarian Zionism. "It was a struggle," Shazar recalled,

> for the hearts and minds of every Jewish youth and maid in every city and every shtetl. Then the gift of oratory and rhetoric and the art of public appearance were the weapons without which no movement could carry through its mission to the people . . .[101] [The people were seeking] the buds of the long-awaited spring, the signs of the revelation of the Shekhina.[102]

Thus, the meeting, debate, conference, and congress, long the dominant interest of the student colonies abroad, were now transferred to Russia and above all, perhaps, to the Pale of Settlement. This was the time, as one observer later put it, "When the political theoreticians hastened back to Russia in order to apply their theories to practice."[103]

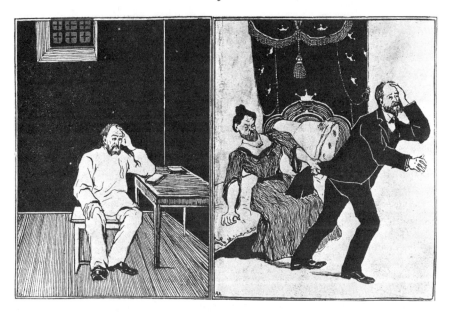

Figure 8. POTIPHAR'S WIFE WITH JOSEPH – A NEW VERSION. (*Captions from right to left.*) (1) 18 October 1905: "Trust me!" (2) 18 December 1905: Trapped!
(*Nicholas II is depicted as Potiphar's wife.*)

In this new era of semi-open politics, however, the socialists were in many ways at a disadvantage. In comparison with those of the Zionists and liberals, their meetings were more frequently disrupted by the police, their newspapers more often closed down, their members more liable to arrest. Thus, Jabotinsky could speak freely in many cities where the socialists did not dare debate him publicly. Or, again, the Union for Equal Rights could hold its Second Congress openly in St. Petersburg in November 1905 before an audience of some two thousand – an event widely reported in the Jewish press – while the socialists still had to hold their congresses secretly in Russia or alternatively (as is the case of the Bund) abroad.

More serious from the socialist point of view was the fact that in the election to the First Duma, held in April 1906, the workers in the Pale of Settlement were nearly all disenfranchised. This meant that while they had to choose between a symbolic campaign or a boycott, the nonsocialist groups organized in the Union for Equal Rights could run candidates with a good chance of success.[104] Understandably – in line with the great majority of socialist groups in Russia but as opposed to the Mensheviks – all four Jewish socialist parties chose to boycott the elections.

But, in this case, the powerful urge of the Russian Jews to participate in politics acted against the socialists. As one Bundist put it with some bitterness: "Not one other people in Russia took so strong a part in the elections to the Duma as the Jews . . . The Jewish bourgeois [*balbos*] was drawn to the new, unfamiliar Duma as a groom to his beloved bride."[105] When the results were all in, it emerged that twelve Jewish deputies had been elected, five of whom were Zionists (eight supported the Kadets and three the Trudoviki).[106] Of course there were no representatives of the Jewish socialist parties in the Duma.

Interparty rivalry and ideological adaptation, 1905–1906

In the Jewish world, then, the Russian revolution of 1905 was dominated almost totally in its initial stages by the Bund. It began the year of upheaval as a long-established party with a coherent ideology, a relatively efficient albeit skeletal organization, and firm roots in a section of the Jewish working class. It had its hidden printing presses in Russia on which it published newspapers and proclamations in Yiddish (the latter in very large quantities). Its paper abroad came out more than once a week during 1905 and was regularly smuggled into Russia. As an underground movement – its members and followers sent off in their hundreds and thousands to prison and exile – it had always inspired a degree of awe in certain Jewish circles beyond the working class itself, most notably among the educated youth and intelligentsia in the Pale of Settlement. But its prestige had grown still more when it entered the field of self-defense in 1903 and when the pogroms broadened and hardened the hostility of Russian Jewry to the regime.

Until the foundation of the Socialist Zionist Labor Party (SSRP) in February 1905, there were no other revolutionary parties in the Jewish world, only scattered groups. Thus, in December 1904, when there was still no sign of exceptional unrest in the Jewish communities of the Pale of Settlement, the central committee of the Bund alone could take the lead and issue a proclamation in close to a hundred thousand copies calling for all-out war on the regime. "The order of the day," it declared excitedly,

> is the liquidation of the Autocracy. Mighty blows, which nobody can parry, will drive the decrepit monster into the abyss ... The sun will shine joyfully on this great land where the heavy chains of political oppression still clank, where the dark shades of violence move, and the muffled groans of the victims – of millions who have been destroyed – can be heard. That will be the sun of freedom. The slave will give way to the citizen.[107]

Only the Bund had prepared systematically and long for this moment, and now it moved naturally and easily to the center of the stage.

What this meant in party terms was that the scales which had been balanced between the Bund and the Zionist movement now tipped sharply against the latter. The Palestinophile movement, of which Herzlian Zionism was the latest extension in Russia, had been in existence ten years longer than its Social Democratic rival; it possessed able leaders and articulate spokesmen; it had the establishment of some dozen colonies in Palestine to its credit and it could count on widespread, historically rooted (although ill-defined) sympathy from broad strata of Russian Jewry. But it entered the revolutionary year in a state of disarray.

Herzl had died in 1904, leaving behind a world movement divided between those for and those against his Uganda proposal: between those demanding immediate action in some measure commensurate with the socioeconomic and political plight of the Jewish masses in eastern Europe and those advocating dogged loyalty to the

Palestinian idea. Almost to a man, the established leaders of Russian Zionism—Ussishkin, Temkin, Chlenov, Kogan-Bernshtein, Weizmann—came out passionately for Palestine. They succeeded in carrying a majority of the Russian movement with them, but the price was high. Many took the categorical rejection of Uganda and every other territory except Palestine as a victory for Ahad Ha-Am and a posthumous betrayal of Herzl, an admission, conscious or not, that Zionism could do nothing to solve the Jewish question in its concrete Russian form.

This decision antagonized in very large part that section of the youth which had hitherto inclined to Zionism. Thus, even before the revolution the Zionists in Russia felt that their movement had entered a period of crisis and decline. "The old ones are dying," Weizmann wrote to his fiancée while on a visit to Pinsk in March 1904, "and the young ones have not arisen to succeed to Zionist tradition, but have disintegrated and gone to pieces. There is no leading thread, there are no leaders. Uganda and Kishinev, the bloody reality of the everyday life of the Jews in the Pale, weigh heavily on everything, everything, everything . . . It's sad, Verusik, terribly sad."[108] And Jabotinsky could report that everywhere he went in 1904 he was asked whether Zionism had simply drained away during that year.[109]

The rapid political change of 1905 accelerated this decline (at least in the pre-October period). Nothing in the ideology or practice of Palestinophilism or Herzlian Zionism had prepared the movement to take an active part in Russian politics. (In this respect its attitude had always differed from that of the Palestinian movement in Galicia to the political life of the Austro-Hungarian Empire). Late in the day, in 1901, it did decide to concern itself partially with local problems but what it envisaged were such projects as credit associations, cooperatives, and educational institutions rather than opposition to the regime. Living permanently in a twilight zone between legality and illegality, the Zionist movement in Russia always went out of its way to stress its noninvolvement in politics, its emigrationist and cultural objectives. The only exception to this rule came after the Kishinev pogrom, when self-defense became of increasing concern to Zionist groups.

Not until May 1905 did the Zionist leadership in Russia, its Actions Committee, break its silence and issue a statement in favor of radical change in Russia. And even this statement, although bold in tone—"We regard the rights given by a country not as a privilege but as the inalienable possession of everybody living in the country"[110]—did not contain any specific program other than a general demand for political and national equality. The Zionists had been thrown onto the defensive by the revolution. At a time of the here and now it could not be otherwise for the movement of the "has been," the "will be," and the "there." At a time when the crucial issue was (or was perceived to be) the mobilization of tens of thousands out on the streets, the settlement of a few hundreds more in Palestine was bound to appear irrelevant. Wherever it turned, the established Zionist leadership found the ground slipping from under its feet. A report in a journal of the movement in April 1906 spoke of the difficult crisis through which Zionism had lived during the last year and stated bluntly that "many groups have disintegrated, many have sunk into a deep sleep."[111] The Zionists were left with the choice between isolation and adaptation; and most, although not all, chose to adapt, to improvise.

So, for example, Ussishkin and Idelson (as will be described more fully below) actively encouraged pro-Palestine groups in the Poale Zion movement to create their own party. They thus tacitly acknowledged that during the revolutionary period the established Zionist Organization had largely lost its appeal to the youth and the working class. There was the obvious risk that the new pro-Palestine party, avowedly socialist, Marxist, and committed to the revolution in Russia, would move out of the orbit of the world Zionist movement. And, indeed, within a few years the Russian Poale Zion would decide to boycott the Zionist congress. But in the years 1905–6 Ussishkin could see no other way of saving some remnants among youth and labor for the Palestinian cause.

Another aspect of the revolution which presented the Zionists with a complex dilemma was the necessity to think in terms of mass propaganda, mass education, and mass culture. Clearly Zionists could not compete in the new era of growing political consciousness unless they made far greater use of Yiddish. But this demanded a sharp reversal in Zionist theory and practice. In the ideological sphere, the Russian Zionist movement had (at least until 1902) become increasingly committed to Hebrew as the language of Jewish history (linking the present to all the past generations) and of Jewish nationhood (linking Russian Jews with all Jews throughout the world regardless of local cultural differences). In this respect, guided by Ben Yehuda and Ahad Ha-Am, Russian Zionism had come under the domination of a trend of thought which can be traced back to the Smolenskin wing of the Haskala. At the same time, in practice, the Zionist Organization conducted much of its everyday business in Russian or even in German.

In the years 1905–06, however, there could be no escaping the fact that Yiddish was the language of the moment and (it was increasingly assumed) also the language of the future. The confident expectation that the state was about to be democratized stirred passionate interest in plans for universal, publicly financed, and modern schooling among the Jewish population. And the belief that such education should be organized in the mother tongue of the great majority of the children gained new adherents day by day, for it seemed to meet alike the demands of democracy, utility, and nationality. "The hero in the Jewish drawing room of Petersburg," wrote one commentator in February 1906, "is now the Jargon. It is the topic of conversation for both young and old."[112]

The established organizations in Russian-Jewish life which had hitherto neglected Yiddish now came under heavy attack from the left. Thus, An-sky could point out angrily that none of the leading modern Hebrew poets, neither Lebenson, nor Yehuda Leb Gordon, nor Bialik, had been translated into Yiddish. No Jewish organization had undertaken to translate even the Bible into the language of the people, "leaving that task to the Christian missionaries."[113] This failure, he concluded, could not now just be forgiven and forgotten: "Before you Zionists— whether of the spiritual or the material school–take it upon yourselves to demand something from the Jewish masses, it is permissible to ask whether you have fulfilled any kind of duty to those masses."[114]

Equally vulnerable to criticism was the oldest Jewish cultural organization in Russia, the OPE. By a curious twist of fate, this society, which had been founded by Baron Gintsburg as an instrument of Russification from above in 1863, provided in 1906 a platform for those demanding the democratization of the Russian state and of Jewish life, the replacement of Russian and Hebrew by Yiddish as the main pedagogical language. Every congress and conference of the society in 1905 witnessed the stormiest scenes, in which a central role was played by veteran socialists and radicals. "A wave of liberation," Bramson said at a special conference of OPE in February 1905, "has suddenly swept into these normally musty walls."[115] "The Kiev section of OPE," M. B. Ratner declared in September, "must become the cultural center of Jewry in the southwest; it must set out to meet the needs of the Jewish masses, must take part in its liberation from the thousands-year yoke – a liberation ... which will come in the immediate future."[116]

It was no coincidence that An-sky, Ratner, and Bramson (or Krol, who was also active in OPE) were all linked to the Russian populist movement; the enthusiasm for Yiddish was to be explained, partially at least, by the enduring hold of *narodnik* or folkist sentiment on the intelligentsia in pre-1914 Russia. Palestinophilism of course had also drawn inspiration from this theme in Russian thought. And many Zionists now found it possible to involve themselves in the movement for the democratization of OPE and the plans for mass education in Yiddish. Among Ratner's allies in Kiev, for instance, were such veterans of early Palestinophilism as Grigorii Gurevich and Dr. Maks Mandelshtam (both now Zionists). But not all in the pro-Palestine camp were ready to accept the current trends.

The correspondence of Yosef Klausner, then editor of the near-bankrupt Hebrew monthly, *Ha-shiloah*, reveals the bitterness felt at that time by many in or close to the Ahad Ha-Am school of thought. Of Dr. Vortsman (the editor of the Zionist journal, *Di yidishe tsukunft*, published in Warsaw since late in 1904), he wrote in February 1905 warning Ussishkin:

> True, he is a Palestinian Zionist but his "Palestinianism" does not spring like yours or mine ... from the recognition that it is impossible to sever the *historical* connection between the people and the land. No. No. For him, the historical connection is nothing. He regards the Jargon as our national language ... and says quite clearly that we can sever the link between the people and the Hebrew language, and what gives Palestine [*erets-yisrael*] the advantage over Hebrew [*sfat-yisrael*]? ... He considers Palestine a better territory than Uganda, and if the opposite proves itself – if we are offered a really better country – he will throw over Palestine.[117]

Of himself, he wrote in May 1905: "How terrible it is that after I have devoted all my powers and strength to Hebrew literature I *have* to write Russian because there is no alternative."[118] In a letter of January 1906 he complained that "we do nothing for Palestine and even our Zionist official papers deal only with the question of galut. Hebrew is being pushed aside more and more by the Jargon."[119]

Threatened by the rapid erosion of their support, by inner dissension and self-doubt, the Zionists in Russia were unable to enter the revolution as a united body with a single and coherent program. But this was not a case of total disintegration. Many of the Zionist leaders sought to adjust to, and master, the fast-changing realities. Of those who opted for this course, perhaps the most conspicuous were Ussishkin, Jabotinsky, Idelson, and Shmarya Levin. But it is a remarkable fact that even Ahad Ha-Am became deeply absorbed in the issues of the moment, in the question of Jewish tactics in the Russian revolution.

During the years 1905–6, the Zionists tended to ally with the forces of political and ideological liberalism in the Jewish world. This alliance can variously be seen as a coalition of one-time enemies against a new and common threat; of the center against the Left; of the middle-aged against the young; of the threatened against the threatening. Of course, to every rule of this type there are many exceptions. Jabotinsky, the most visible Zionist leader in the years 1905–6, was then only twenty-five years old, considerably younger than, for example, Zhitlovsky, Syrkin, M. B. Ratner, Litvak, or Noyakh Portnoi, who played leading roles in the socialist camp. Nevertheless, it is clear that the division between the nationalist and the liberal that had been so central to the crisis of 1881–2 had become largely a thing of the past, and insofar as it persisted was temporarily subordinated to the other priorities.

The leaders of liberalism in the Jewish world – Vinaver, Sliozberg, and Gruzenberg – were now ready to concede the value of national rights for the Jewish people in Russia, while the emigrationists admitted the necessity of involving themselves in Russian politics. Challenged from the left, undercut by the new generation, they naturally sought each other out. The Union for Equal Rights, founded in Vilna in March 1905, was the joint creation of liberals and Zionists. Its program demanded both political and national equality for the Jews in Russia.[120]

In the early stages of the revolution, the Union inevitably played a rather subdued role. Centered on St. Petersburg, it found it difficult to put down roots in the Pale of Settlement. By late in the year it still had only seven thousand members.[121] A speaker for the Union who toured the provinces in the autumn of 1905 discovered that little was known there about the organization. His attempts to stir up enthusiasm for the elections to the Bulygin Duma (then planned but later aborted) were constantly hindered by the socialist youth. "In Orsha, as in many other cities of the Pale," he wrote, "a crowd of youths came in during the prayers, closed the doors, placed an armed guard at them, and announced that violence threatened anyone taking part in the elections."[122]

What the Union did do at this stage was to provide an organizational and ideological framework for all the political forces in the Jewish world which had not been swept into the socialist camp. As such, it joined the federation of (mainly professional) organizations, the Union of Unions, which demanded (at public meetings, through petitions and resolutions) that Russia be restructured as a parliamentary democracy.[123] A minority (Ahad Ha-Am was its most articulate spokesman) argued that the Union for Equal Rights was acting too much as an auxiliary to Russian liberalism and not enough as a national pressure group, that it should constantly draw attention to the discriminatory laws against the Jews, and that, apart from this one issue, it should essentially let the Russians run their own revolution. However, this was very much a minor theme in the pre-October period.

Following the wave of pogroms, the character and role of the Union for Equal Rights began to change. There was a subtle but nonetheless perceptible shift in the internal balance of forces. The Zionists now began to assert an ideological leadership which they had earlier yielded almost uncontested to the liberal wing. They were the first group that tried to draw radical conclusions from the eruption of anti-Jewish violence, to propose a new course.

At the Second Congress of the Union in November, they brought in a resolution calling in principle for the early election on the basis of universal suffrage of a Jewish National Assembly in Russia. The time had come, they argued, for the

Figure 9. THE CONGRESS OF THE UNION FOR EQUAL RIGHTS [*Dergraykher*] IS COMING. "Before you get yours, I'll get mine!"
(The worker carries a banner labeled "Workers, Unite!" and is threatening the leaders of the Union for Equal Rights, which was popularly known in Yiddish as "the Attainers" or "the Getters" [Dergraykher] from its full title: the Union for the Attainment of Full Rights for the Jewish People in Russia. On the chair, Vinaver is reaching for a ministerial seat, while Shmarya Levin is reaching for Palestine.)

Jewish people to organize itself as one political unit, to arrive at a final concept of national self-government in Russia, and to draw up its concrete proposals for presentation to the Russian Constituent Assembly (then considered imminent). It was not that the Jews should despair of the revolution but that they should organize as a national force within it. In advancing this view, Ussishkin even hinted (through his reference to Dashevsky) at support for the use of organized terrorism against the regime:

There are three forms of struggle against the enemy, said Jacob, the Patriarch – to pay, to beseech, and to fight . . . Now only one form of struggle is possible but in order to fight we need to unite and to organize the popular forces. Until now, apart from Dashevsky, there were no Jewish revolutionary heroes, there were only Jewish revolutionaries. But we need Jewish fighters [bortsy] . . . We must send out a call to all the Jewish people and bring together a Jewish Popular Assembly [vseevreiskoe narodnoe sobranie].[124]

Dubnov emerged as a passionate advocate of the National Assembly both at the November congress of the Union and in his *Voskhod* articles, which is predictable, in that since the late 1890s he had been advocating the concept of Jewish autonomy in Russia and indeed could be considered to have introduced it into contemporary politics.

It was Jabotinsky, however, who took up the idea with the greatest persistence, passion, and brilliance. In formulating and advocating the case for the National Assembly, and even more so in denouncing its opponents, Jabotinsky now first came into his own as a political leader. In his oratorical genius, in his love of debate and the public limelight, in his youth, his journalistic verve, his penchant for grandiose ideological pyrotechnics, he alone in the Zionist camp had the virtuoso qualities needed to learn and master the music of the times.[125]

As he presented it, the National Assembly would become the linch-pin of Jewish politics in Russia. It was the natural response to the bitter experience of the late October days. It would permit the Jewish nation to formulate and defend its own interests at a time of inner and outer confusion. "Our mood," he said at the November congress, "can clearly be characterized by two words – weakness and perplexity . . . Our main and first task is [therefore] to meet together, to clash with one another, to receive directives from the entire Jewish people."[126]

The Assembly, he insisted, should be seen not only as a response to the present crisis but also as the logical expression of a growing sense of national unity. "The Jewish people," he wrote in February 1906, "is instinctively striving toward so-called 'self-determination' – to full freedom for many-sided, national, organizational action."[127] To give this popular impulse political form was simply to obey the imperatives of the general struggle for liberty. "This Russian revolution," he argued, "will be the height of deception if it fails to give all the peoples of Russia the possibility to make their own history freely. To remind the nations of that, to call on them not to wait it out but to take their own fate into their own hands – means to join the first ranks in the struggle for liberation."[128] In presenting the concept of national politics – a concerted implementation of the national will – as his first principle, Jabotinsky had taken up an excellent position from which to defend the Zionist case and assault its opponents.

Aware of this fact, the liberal wing in the Union for Equality sought at the November congress and in *Voskhod* to belittle the idea of a National Assembly, arguing that it meant "to weaken and loosen the link between Jewry and the general Russian liberation movement"[129] and to indulge in utopian escapism. It would be absurd, insisted *Voskhod,* to expect from the Jews, "a disorganized people . . . not united by any defined beliefs or concrete goals . . . ,what one could not expect from a more organized [people]."[130] But such skepticism simply provoked Jabotinsky to sharp and angry retort. The Jewish liberals, who now cast doubt on the proposals of others, had as yet not formulated a clear national program of their own:

> Yes, gentlemen, it was twenty-five years ago – twenty-five years – that you should have worked out your national programs. Now it is already late . . . These gentlemen . . . can be for a National Assembly or against, praise the Zionist tactics or condemn them. It is all the same for us, for them, for the whole world. Epochs of revolution, such as that through which the Jewish people is now living, always throw overboard a certain number of unnecessary elements who for a certain time will manage to keep swimming above water but can neither help nor hinder.[131]

However, the clash with his liberal allies was of secondary importance at this time. Jabotinsky's advocacy of the National Assembly, and in particular, the polemical use to which he put that idea, was aimed primarily against the socialists. "His favorite slogan," Shmarya Levin recalled, "was – 'Make the bear come out and fight,' "[132] and at this time he understandably saw the Bund, the dominant force on the left, as his bear.

It was typical of the period that, in attacking the socialists, Jabotinsky tended to adopt their historico-philosophical modes of thought and even their vocabulary. He, too, spoke of the inevitable unfolding of historical necessities; of the logical development from revolution to Jewish national autonomy in Russia and from autonomy as a penultimate stage to final and maximal goals. This ideological framework was shared by all the Jewish socialist parties in 1906. More specifically, Jabotinsky adopted the incrementalist or quasi-evolutionist approach to revolution and territorialism first advanced in coherent ideological form by the Vozrozhdentsy in the years 1903–4. In fact, the following remarkable passage, written by Jabotinsky in December 1905, reads, on first acquaintance at least, as if it had come straight out of their journal:

> The future development of our nation from the ghetto to the national state will come not by way of degeneration, not by way of mounting despair, but by way of constant regeneration [vozrozhdenie], by way of the strengthening and consolidation of the national organism . . . In various parts of our Diaspora, under the influence of historical necessity, the Jewish masses organize in juridically autonomous units, with an inevitable . . . tendency to full and absolute self-government. Under the influence of this historical necessity, these groups merge in one great unit, and in place of our present, mythical "world Kahal" . . . there will be created a really united Jewry, a nation among the nations.[133]

What was missing here, and throughout, was the factor of class difference and class warfare, which, in many permutations and in varying degrees, was central to all socialist ideologies in that period. Jabotinsky proclaimed himself not a class but a national politician (a kol-yisroel politiker) and argued that "general national interests" increasingly overshadowed mere "class interests."[134] In the specific context of the post-October days this meant that the Jewish people should concentrate on their own inner organization first and act in the general revolutionary movement only as a rear-guard. "The Jewish revolt," he wrote in January 1906, "was terrifying to the government as long as the Russian heartland was silent and was only terrifying because it was a match which could set the Russian heartland afire. But now when all Russia is ablaze, who remembers the match, who takes it into account?"[135] Standing beyond or above class, his movement had the right and duty to take the lead in the politics of national unity. "We Zionists," he concluded, "consider ourselves not a party but the spokesmen of the entire Jewish people."[136]

In narrow political terms, the decision of Ussishkin and Jabotinsky to emphasize the centrality of the National Assembly was undoubtedly profitable. It enabled the Zionists to participate in the feverish political debate not as outsiders but as pacemakers. They could now reemerge as a coherent force in Russian-Jewish politics. Their resolution on the Assembly was carried by a majority at the November congress of the Union for Equal Rights. Again, acting within the framework of the Union, they played a major role in the elections to the First Duma – a policy which (as reflected in the electoral returns) paid handsome dividends. True, the more old-fashioned observers within the Zionist camp, while conceding that there was perhaps no choice, still remained highly sceptical. "You have done well," Klausner wrote to Ussishkin in January 1906.

> That is, you *had* to act thus for he who turns his face against the waves goes under. In *these* times, that is a great rule . . . If "something is better than nothing," then this something is the Jewish National Assembly. Perhaps we will save some little Hebrew nationalism from this destruction and desolation . . . [But] most of the Zionists with Jabotinsky at their head are ashamed of the fact that the Zionists did not work in the revolution until now and they are overanxious to prove themselves. The Zionist tasks will not be done by the non-Zionists and if *we* don't do them either who will? . . . And this nationalism to which, as Zionists, we are giving ourselves heart and soul – what is it? Will we really be doing something great if we preserve a Jargon-Russian-Bundist-territorialist Judaism?[137]

Such reservations, however, were rarely voiced in public. Backed initially, although not throughout, by Ussishkin (who dominated the organization of Russian Zionism) and by Idelson (who edited its major journal), Jabotinsky emerged uncontested in 1906 as its leading spokesman and ideologist. This fact was acknowledged at the congress of the movement held in Helsingfors in December 1906. The platform adopted there endorsed the idea of "one organization of the Jewish people for autonomous national action," the "participation of the Zionists in the liberation movement of the territorial nations in the Russian state," and the unification of Russian Jewry on the basis of "juridically guaranteed self-government in all matters pertaining to the Jewish national existence."[138] Here, essentially, was a retroactive vote of confidence in Jabotinsky.

However, looked at in a broader political perspective, the balance sheet was less obviously positive. After all, when the idea of the National Assembly was first raised at the November congress of the Union, its advocates hoped (or professed to hope) that it would soon gain general acceptance in the Jewish world, including support from the left. The autonomist concept had been adopted by the Bund as early as 1901 (when it was still taboo to Zionists and liberals) and had meanwhile been endorsed by most, although not all, the other Jewish socialist groupings. "In the last resort," Jabotinsky said, "the Bund will undoubtedly come in – such leading party organizations submit to the demands of the workers and the idea of a [Jewish] Constituent Assembly will produce an enthusiastic echo among them."[139]

But this judgment was thoroughly erroneous. There was no reason to assume that all the political forces in the Russian-Jewish world would readily accept a strategy which had been initiated by the Zionist leaders and which in all likelihood would strengthen the Zionist movement. Jewish national assemblies based on forms of general suffrage would finally meet in 1918, both in the United States and in the independent Ukraine, but they proved to be the cause of bitter debate and recrimination. The idea (although not the reality) is perpetuated today in the American, and the World, Jewish Congress movements, but they remain minority and Zionist-oriented organizations. Jewish unity, which has to a great degree become a political fact of life in the non-Communist world since 1948, expresses itself through loose, ad hoc links between existing organizations rather than through the direct elective principle.

In the winter of 1905–6, the political trends were not running predominantly in favor of a National Assembly. It was central to Jabotinsky's position that the Jewish socialist parties and groups had already made their major contribution to the Jewish revolution, that the final victory over the Autocracy would be won in the interior of the country, and hence that the time had come to shift the emphasis from sporadic, partisan, and quasi-military warfare to the ordered presentation of national demands, to the institutionalization of Jewish national politics, to participation in the liberation movement as a collective entity.

But to the great majority of the politically active youth, to the socialists of all kinds, this basic thesis was utterly unacceptable. In late 1905 and the early months of 1906, the revolution absorbed their entire lives. For some it was social revolution, for others political; for some the internationalist theme was all-important; still others saw the revolution as primarily a national war, providing the Jews with a chance to defend their collective honor and to take revenge against the regime responsible for the pogroms and the endless humiliation.

The socialist groups were occupied in collecting arms and in organizing combat or self-defense units, trade unions, clubs, strikes, newspapers, meetings. They saw themselves as preparing actively for the decisive confrontation with the old regime which they were confident would come in the immediate future. The policies of the Union for Equal Rights appeared to them as a diversion, a gesture of contempt for what they were doing. When all forces should have been directed to arming and financing the Left, the Union was advocating a National Assembly and calling for participation in the elections to the blatantly nonrepresentative Duma. All the anger of the front-line troops for those living comfortably in the rear now came to divide the socialists of all denominations from the Union for Equal Rights.

Looking back from the summer of 1906, Jabotinsky ascribed the rejection of his program by the Left to the specific political situation which had prevailed in December and January, "when the dreams of proletarian dictatorship were still . . . [floating] in the air."[140] But this was too narrow an explanation. The truth is that a profound generational and situational gulf divided the socialist from the nonsocialist world. The youth were inclined to see the revolution as its arena and could not accept the fact that in the post-October days the middle-aged and middle-class (albeit represented by the youthful Jabotinsky) increasingly seized the political initiative. Thus, in April 1906, following the elections of the twelve Jewish deputies to the First Duma, Olgin could describe them and their triumphant supporters, "the liberal bourgeoisie," as "gray-haired children who have not grown up,"[141] and Syrkin wrote somewhat later that

> among no other people has the bourgeoisie been as passive during the revolution as among the Jews and in no other place did it have the ability to pluck the fruits of the revolution so much or so thoroughly as in the Jewish street . . .[142] The electoral movement has been taken into their hands by the pillars of the community, the rich, the orthodox, the bourgeois assimilator and the bourgeois Zionist.[143]

The fact that the Left in the Jewish world remained throughout fragmented into innumerable parties in no way lessened its collective hostility in the post-October period to both the Zionist and liberal wings of the Union for Equal Rights. On the contrary, the growing fury of interparty rivalry among the socialists only accelerated their alienation from the center. The themes of national liberation and socialist revolution reinforced each other to intensify extremism. No party was willing to yield to another as the most radical champion of the Jewish masses in all spheres.

Thus, the territorialist SSRP constantly argued that it was no less socialist than the Bund but that the Bund was betraying Jewish national interests. In turn, the Bund argued the reverse, that it was the first in self-defense and other spheres of national action and, at the same time, the only truly socialist party in the Jewish world. The Palestinian-oriented socialists and the Seimists were equally reluctant to yield the maximalist crown in any sphere to their rivals. "In these times," it was noted in *Folks-tsaytung* in March 1906, "in order to have success with the Jewish working masses one must paint oneself red."[144]

Interestingly enough, Jabotinsky himself realized that the mounting nationalism on which he based his own plans was matched by a concurrent pull to the left. "Whoever has observed our proletarian trend," he wrote on 30 December 1905,

> cannot but have noted a definite order of rank, almost a hierarchy. The complexity of the Jewish question has forced each of these parties to violate the Social Democratic program with heretical points of a more or less national character, and the greater the extent of the heresy in a given party the more it feels a kind of spiritual depression . . . Each party tries to justify itself before that which is less heretical but at the same time lords it over that which is more heretical and here it willingly goes in for exaggeration, as the result of a simple and innocent calculation – the more you abuse your lowly neighbor for his heresy, the more you demonstrate to your superiors your own orthodoxy.[145]

Jabotinsky was confident that this was an ephemeral phenomenon and that the reverse trend, toward national unity, would prevail. But this was not to be. As one of the liberal leaders pointed out perceptively at the November congress of the Union for Equality, the political party was at that point clearly emerging as the dominant institution in Jewish life. ("What is happening now – and what is bound to happen," said M. M. Margolin, "is differentiation by parties.")[146] This trend was, of course, not new but it was greatly accelerated by the intermingling of hope and confusion, messianism and despair, that characterized the post-October period.

The party at that time provided an organizational outlet for long-pent-up energies now released; a fraternal brotherhood in which the youth could merge with the workers; a romantic world of self-defense and combat units; and an ideological map showing the way step by step from present distress to future salvation.

The Galician parallel

As has often been observed by historians, the impact of the revolution did not stop at the frontiers of the Russian Empire.[147] A little-studied but striking example of this fact is provided by the development of Jewish politics in Galicia. The analogous social structure, the similar linguistic pattern, the common historical origins, the geographical proximity, and the almost open frontier all facilitated a rapid transmission of political ideas and fashions during the years of upheaval from Russian to Galician Jewry. To some extent – in the case of Jabotinsky's form of Zionism – there was also a reverse influence.[148]

In Galicia, the history of modern political movements among the Jewish population had followed a somewhat different course than in the Pale of Settlement, but during the revolutionary period they ran remarkably parallel to those unfolding in Russia. The Zionists became almost totally immersed in local politics, the emigrationist socialists moved sharply to the left, and the internationalist socialists at work in the Jewish world moved to more nationalist positions.

As in Russia, these apparently contradictory trends all resulted from the sudden rise in radical political consciousness among far broader strata of the Jewish population than hitherto – "a mass movement, deep and stormy,"[149] as one contemporary observer put it. There was the same fierce competition among the existing political groups to mobilize mass support, the same tendency to promise both national and social liberation, to arouse maximalist expectations.

In party terms, this meant that the Zionists in December 1905 came out for Jewish national autonomy in Austria-Hungary; that they decided to compete in the elections to the Reichsrat and that they succeeded (in 1907) in having a number of their candidates elected (including Adolf Stand from the Brody constituency). A territorialist faction broke away in 1905 from Poale Zion and the latter party itself drew apart from the general Zionist movement, voted to seek membership in the Socialist International, and came under increasing pressure from its left wing to adopt a strictly Marxist program. (As one disgruntled observer put it in 1906, the party had "significantly moved from its previous position and had begun to move toward the proletarian Talmudism [coming] from Russia, where rootless abstractions, the 'rabbincial' approach, and casuistry often take precedence over real life.")[150] Finally, an influential group split away from the "internationalist" Polish Social Democratic Party (the PPSD) to form an independent Jewish socialist party avowedly modeled on the example of the Bund;[151] and for its part, the PPSD fought back by creating a largely autonomous "Jewish section" within its own organization.

The parallel between the Jewish experience in the Pale of Settlement and that in Galicia reinforces the argument that the revolutionary years witnessed one of those explosions of mass activity that—as, for instance, in the Europe of 1848—was neither exclusively social nor political, national nor international; that could not be unified by any one movement; and that easily fragmented and exhausted itself.

CHAPTER 4

The Bund

Between nation and class

The role of ideology in the history of the Bund

This chapter is a study of the ideology that by 1905 had come to be known as
Bundism. It deals primarily with the origins and development of that ideology
rather than with its impact.

That Bundism exerted enormous influence on Jewish political thought is not in
doubt. Although Dubnov and Zhitlovsky were the first to advocate the idea of
autonomism (or extraterritorial self-government), the Bund alone took it up at an
early stage (in 1901) and thus lent it real weight. It was adopted in the years 1905–6
by nearly all the Jewish parties in Russia and in 1918 (as "national rights") by the
leaders of American Jewry. Via this route it found its way in 1919–20 into the
Paris Peace Treaties, which dealt with the newly independent states of non-Soviet
eastern Europe. Jewish autonomism was explicitly rejected by the Bolshevik regime. However, the related concept also first (but not exclusively) developed by the
Bund – a Jewish nationality expressing itself through the Yiddish language and a
secular proletarian Yiddish culture – was absorbed, albeit temporarily, into official
Soviet thinking in the 1920s.

If the external influence of Bundist ideology is beyond dispute, the same cannot
be said of the role played by the ideological factor in the evolution of the Bund
itself, in its history as a revolutionary and Social Democratic movement. True, a
coherent theory of party historiography was early developed by Bundist spokesmen
and has been largely accepted by historians since then. Nevertheless, there were
members of the movement itself, Ben Tsiyon Hofman (Zivion) being the most
outstanding example, who dissented from the majority view, and in recent years
Moshe Mishkinsky has remapped early Bundist history, drawing attention (to take
just one example) to the crucial importance of Gozhansky's previously neglected
Letter to the Agitators.[1] It is the purpose of this study to extend the scope of this
reexploration, specifically to examine emergent Bundist nationalism in the evolving
context of Russian-Jewish politics and ideology until 1907.

In broad strokes, the established historiography of early Bundism can be summarized along the following lines. Starting in the late 1880s, so the argument goes, the
revolutionary intelligentsia in Russia (including the socialist *kruzhki* in Vilna and
Minsk) were increasingly making the transition from populism to Marxism. Initially this ideological transformation did not involve any change in the way in
which the revolutionaries ran their movement. The basic organizational unit was
the revolutionary circle, the *kruzhok;* the major effort went into "propagandiz-

ing"–or educating–small groups of workers; and all activity was conducted in the utmost secrecy.

However, a number of factors coalesced to force a sharp break in the development of the Vilna Social Democratic movement, starting from the year 1892. On the one hand, Marxist ideology demanded that its adherents think in terms not of individuals and elites but rather of classes and specifically of the wage-earning proletariat. From this perspective, it made no sense to concentrate all efforts on propaganda circles that sought to produce a few fully fledged conscious socialists drawn from the working class. As Plekhanov put it in an influential brochure of 1892, "A sect can be satisfied with propaganda in the narrow sense of the word; a political party never . . . A propagandist gives *many* ideas to one or a few people but an agitator gives *only one* or *only a few* ideas to a mass of people . . . History is made by the masses."[2]

On the other hand, the urban labor force itself was becoming increasingly restless under the yoke of the incredibly long working hours and low wages. There had been a number of strikes among the clothing workers in Vilna, Belostok, and other cities in the Pale of Settlement during the 1880s.[3] As the Jewish proletariat expanded–a result of deepening capitalist relationships and accelerating urbanization–so the workers tended, however haphazardly, to organize for the defense of their elementary economic interests. In particular, primitive strike and other mutual-benefit funds (*kassy*) were established with greater frequency.

Thus, evolving socioeconomic realities acting from below reinforced the self-questioning prompted by recently assimilated Marxist theory to produce the difficult but crucial change of tactics from "propaganda" to "agitation." What this meant in practical terms was that the proletarian recruit to the revolutionary movement would now be expected to devote his efforts primarily to organizing his fellow workers; to coordinating demands for higher wages, shorter hours, and better sanitary conditions in the workshop; and above all to preparing for and, when the time came, leading strikes.

The transition to the policy of economic agitation was under way by 1892, and it formed the central theme of the speech of one of the four workers who addressed the May Day meeting that year in the woods outside Vilna. At that early stage too, an archaic law, which dated back to the time of Catherine II and limited the length of the working day, was already being invoked to provide the new strategy with a legal cover. "In order that we should be united and not scattered," said Fania Reznik, a clothing worker,

> we must organize frequent *skhodki,* workers' meetings. Everybody must do all he can to set up and spread *kassy.* We must organize strikes. For strikes, too, we must have *kassy* which provide our only means of support at such a time. To strike! The word alone frightens us. Through it we could lose our jobs altogether . . . [but we must take the risk.] A worker instead of working twelve hours a day, as is established by law, now works for fifteen to seventeen hours.[4]

The changeover to the new strategy did not go unopposed. Many of the workers who had previously been organized in propaganda circles fought bitterly against a policy which shifted the emphasis away from the education of the few to mass organization. Avrom Gordon (Rezchik), an engraver, led this opposition, which persisted in Vilna at least until 1895 and reemerged elsewhere in subsequent years. But – and this is a recurrent theme in the dominant historiography – the opposition was doomed to failure because it represented too narrow a stratum (or as I. Trunk put it in the four-volume *History of the Bund*), "a kind of worker elite which had mentally divorced itself from the working masses . . . and had begun to see the hard life of the workers not as a social evil which had to be fought in an organized way . . . but as a fatal curse from which each individual as such had to try to liberate himself."[5] Cut off from the revolutionary intelligentsia and the proletariat alike, the worker opposition was doomed to wither away.

Once launched, the agitation movement developed its own momentum. It was provided with a conceptual underpinning in the brochure *On Agitation*, written in 1894 by Arkadii Kremer with the aid of Martov. Organized at first only to fight for immediate and readily understood economic interests, the working masses, Kremer argued, would be forced inexorably by the highly restrictive political system into a revolutionary confrontation with the Autocracy.

The new strategy caught the imagination of an ever-widening circle of Social Democrats not only in the northwest but throughout European Russia. The constant migration from the overcrowded and economically underdeveloped Lithuania and White Russia to such rapidly developing cities as Belostok, Lodz, Ekaterinoslav, and Kiev, and the centrality of Vilna as a major link in a far-flung system for the import and distribution of illegal literature throughout Russia, as well as its importance as a hub of the intelligentsia with its Jewish Teachers Institute and high schools – all facilitated the rapid dissemination of what was frequently called the Vilna Program. The creation in November 1895 of the St. Petersburg Union for the Liberation of the Working Class (led primarily by Martov and Lenin) and its subsequent role in a series of massive strikes constituted only the most dramatic example of the general trend.

For the Jewish working class, the move from propaganda (or *kruzhkovshchina*) to economic agitation, so it is traditionally argued, necessarily meant not only a tactical but also a linguistic metamorphosis. A movement that sought to organize not tens but hundreds or even thousands in a given city had to go over to the use of Yiddish, the language of the masses, in its everyday work. This was not a sudden change. At the May Day Rally of 1892, three of the four workers spoke in Russian (with Fania Reznik among them). But with the expansion of the movement the demand for literature, lectures, and revolutionary songs in Yiddish grew apace.

In turn, this meant that the *polu-intelligentsiia*, ex-yeshiva students who had a better command of Yiddish than Russian, moved into key positions in the revolutionary hierarchy. Without them, the growing output of revolutionary material, papers and brochures, in Yiddish would not have been possible. Moreover, the *polu-intelligenty* took the lead in running the movement's Jargon Committee in 1895 and in its subsequent efforts to commission the writing and legal publication not only of basic educational material but also of belles-lettres in Yiddish. Thus, Y. L. Peretz and Dovid Pinsky, now emerging as leading Yiddish writers, were aided and encouraged to a great degree by the Jewish Social Democratic movement with which they increasingly identified themselves. Mass politics and Yiddish literature moved together.

In May 1895, Martov, who had been active since 1893 in the revolutionary leadership in Vilna, analyzed the progress made by the movement. His lecture, delivered to some forty worker-agitators, was published in 1900 and was entitled *A Turning Point in the History of the Jewish Labor Movement* (in Russian) and *A New Epoch in the History of the Jewish Labor Movement* (in Yiddish). Martov's central thesis was clear and strongly presented. "Our movement," he said there,

> has become first more democratic and, second, more materialist . . . The object of our activity . . . is not the worker-*intelligent* who is divorced from his environment by his mental abilities, his need for education, but the average worker of the masses with his average needs, average morality, and average level of development. The materialist character of our movement today . . . consists of the fact that all our hopes and expectations depend not on a faith in the omnipotence of our ideas . . . but . . . on the needs of the masses.[6]

But in becoming more democratic and more mass-oriented, Martov continued, the movement had inevitably become more national in character:

> [Previously], relegating the Jewish working-class movement to second place, we tended to scorn the realities of its existence, and this attitude found expression in the fact that we conducted our work in the Russian language[7] . . . [But] life has forced us to change our tactics . . . While we tied all our hopes to the general Russian movement we – without even noticing it ourselves – raised the Jewish movement to a height not yet attained by the Russian one . . . Having placed the mass movement in the center of our program we had to adapt our propaganda and education to the mass, that is make it more Jewish.[8]

What was now required was to recognize the logic dictated by experience, to translate the unconscious gains made hitherto into a conscious organizational program for the future:

> *The goal of the Social Democrats working in the Jewish sphere [should be] to create a separate Jewish labor organization which would lead and teach the Jewish proletariat in the struggle for economic, civil and political liberation.*[9]

It will be suggested below that Martov's speech should not in fact be considered a major turning point in the history of the Jewish labor movement. Although it summed up brilliantly the case for the formal establishment of an autonomous Jewish proletarian movement, anticipating by two-and-a-half years the actual creation of the Bund in September 1897, it was in this respect neither original nor decisive. As against this, however, it did certainly represent the first clear exposition of what was to become the dominant line of thought in Bundist historiography.

What Martov had done was to describe the emergence of the impressive Jewish labor movement in Vilna – capable of running strikes and an embryonic trade-union organization, linked informally to numerous other centers in the Pale of Settlement – as though it were the creation of unconscious historical forces. Once the agitation movement had been launched (the necessary result of the materialistic and democratic outlook) "life" had guaranteed its subsequent success and forced the leadership to adopt a more national policy based on the Yiddish language and on a demand for Jewish civil equality. Thus, the national orientation was presented not as a controversial issue but as a fact, a datum, a verdict already pronounced by history. The Vilna movement (like the British Empire) had been created in a fit of absentmindedness.

Martov's thesis was to reappear time and again in the thinking and self-analysis of the Bund. The tendency was to argue that as the movement put down roots in the proletariat, expanded in size, and became more democratic so it inevitably produced a more national program. The development of the Bund was perceived to have followed a clearly evolutionary path with pressure from below – from the masses – forcing periodic adjustments in the ideological superstructure. Martov's speech, the creation of the Bund in 1897, the adoption of a tentative national program by the Fourth Congress in 1901, the break with the RSDRP in 1903, the adoption of a full national program in 1905, and the reunion (on satisfactory terms) with the RSDRP in 1906, all marked stages in this process of growth. It followed directly from this perception of an organic development that ideological debate and internal dissension, however strident at times, had to be seen as temporary growing pains which lacked long-term significance.

In order to illustrate the persistence of this line of thought, it is worth quoting a number of leading figures in or associated with the Bund. "The amazing vitality of the Bund" wrote Pavel Rozental (An-man) in 1901, "is easily explained: [its] secret . . . lies in the fact that the aims of our movement spring from the conscious and real interests of the working proletariat, that the Bund has embraced the broad masses and not a group of ideologues."[10] In a pamphlet of 1902, Vladimir Kossovsky stated that "insofar as the Jewish workers' movement has become a *mass* movement, it must inevitably become not only international but national too."[11]

Writing in the *Folks-tsaytung* in June 1906, Ezra Rozin argued that "only with the growth of a mass movement . . . only in the period 1899–1901 when the Bund came to express the aspirations of broad strata of the awakening Jewish working masses . . . only then did our present concept of the proletariat and its organization emerge."[12]

"The national program," Olgin wrote in an article for *Di tsukunft* in 1907, "developed together with the development of the Jewish proletariat . . . As life became richer, more complex, as the masses began more and more to recognize the special character of their movement . . . so it became ever more essential to work out a positive national program."[13] And Avrom Lesin expressed the same idea except with an ironical touch in his recollections written in the late 1930s: "The leaders of the Bund did not lead but were always led and it was life itself that directed them. The Bund only absorbed that which had reached maturity."[14]

However, the view of a logical progression in which the shift to a mass movement forced the transition first to agitation in Yiddish, then to a more Jewish orientation culturally and politically, and finally (and gradually) to a full-fledged national program has not been the monopoly of Bundist spokesmen and writers. It has had a profound influence on most of the non-Bundist historians who have written about the movement in the pre-1914 period, including the author of this work.[15]

If there are grounds for questioning the dominant historiographical theory, it is not because new facts have come to light but rather because it is possible to regard long-established knowledge from relatively unfamiliar vantage points. More attention and greater weight can be assigned alternatively or cumulatively to the comparative history of the Jewish labor movements throughout the world, to the attitudes as recorded by contemporaries of the Jewish proletariat itself, and to the role of factions or groupings within the Bundist organization.

Among the many contributions made by Elyohu Cherikover to the study of Jewish socialism was the emphasis which he placed on its worldwide character. Although not the first to stress this aspect of the subject (priority must go to Herts Burgin's history published in New York in 1913 or even perhaps to the theoreticians of the Poale Zion and territorialist movements during the period 1905–7), Cherikover provided it with documentary underpinning. In the many volumes which he prepared for the YIVO Institute in Warsaw, Vilna, and New York he published material, often by then very rare, that clearly proved the value of the comparative approach.

The Cherikover publications illustrated that by the early 1890s the idea of a Jewish labor organization, based on the Yiddish language, had gone far to establishing its popularity if not its legitimacy throughout the socialist world. The ability of the Russian-Jewish socialists in London – and much more spectacularly in New York – to create a self-supporting Yiddish press and Yiddish-speaking trade-union movement inspired growing respect. Nothing succeeds like success, and in the years 1891–5 socialists throughout eastern Europe sought to repeat what had been achieved in the East End and the Lower East Side.

The Yiddish-speaking socialist movement in Lithuania and White Russia would prove to be the most viable of the new initiatives, but in the same period parallel experiments were launched in Congress Poland, in Austria-Hungary, and in Roumania. What united all these groups was their proletarian orientation, usually of a clearly Social Democratic or Marxist character, and their eagerness to use Yiddish at least as the language of mass agitation.

Thus, Y. M. Pesakhzon has described how in 1892 (or 1893) a group of young Social Democrats in Warsaw produced a May Day manifesto (printed on a hectograph) in Yiddish.[16] In July of that year a similar group in Lemberg (the major city of eastern Galicia) organized a Jewish Labor Party which succeeded in bringing out a number of issues of a Yiddish journal, *Di arbeter shtime*.[17] Again, in 1893, an autonomous Jewish socialist organization called Lumina was set up in Jassy, the capital of the Moldavian section of Roumania, and it too, in 1896, began to publish an organ in Yiddish, *Der veker*.[18]

In short, wherever there were large Yiddish-speaking populations, the attempt was made, at least in the major city of the area, to create a labor movement. These experiments were directed at proletarian populations which in many ways were sociologically alike – they shared a common language, a similar historical background, and a parallel economic structure (based primarily on domestic and workshop manufacturing). But, in fact, the Jewish socialist efforts fared very differently in different countries. Of particular interest to us here is the fact that there was no direct correlation between the creation of a mass movement and the crystallization of a more nationalist program.

It has been noted that in England and in the United States the general trend had been away from the Jewish national orientation which colored the socialism of the emigrant youth in 1882 and toward a militant internationalism. As the Yiddish-speaking movements grew larger, so their ideologies became less national. This trend could be explained, of course, by the special circumstances facing the emigrant in the English-speaking countries, where assimilation (or at least acculturation) was possible and encouraged by numerous economic and cultural incentives.

But, as against this, account has to be taken of the fact that the Galician experience paralleled that of Jewish socialism in the West. The Jewish Labor Party founded in Lemberg in 1892 had adopted a clearly national position, advocating a federal structure for the socialist movement. "There is an erroneous opinion here in Galicia," its journal stated,

> that one can unite all nations and languages – i.e., the Polish, the Ruthenian, and the Jewish under the Polish flag . . . [but] in order to propagandize the great masses of Jewish, Ruthenian, and Polish workers it is essential to take and enlighten each linguistic group, each people, separately. The Polish organizations and papers in Galicia should educate their own workers, the Ruthenians their own, and the Jews theirs; and each should have control of its own affairs. Beyond that, there should be a High Committee composed of representatives of all the parties. The High Committee should decide when these various independent parties should act together . . . This kind of unification is called a federative union.[19]

However, Yiddish-based socialism in Galicia did not develop along these lines. On the contrary, the Galician Social Democratic Party (from 1897, the PPSD), a section of the Austrian Social Democratic Labor Party, quickly gained the initiative. Encouraged by its leader, Ignacy Daszynski, (who demanded in 1892 that the Polish socialists "consider the Jews like every other nation, i.e., give it the same rights),"[20] the Galician Social Democratic Party showed considerable flexibility on the Jewish issue. From 1893 it brought out its own paper in Yiddish, *Der arbeter,* and it acquiesced in a degree of de facto autonomy for the socialists grouped around the journal. The Jewish Labor Party opposed to the official Social Democratic party and sympathetic to emergent Ukrainian socialism, died a speedy death; and an independent party was not revived until 1905.[21]

The Roumanian case provides an example of yet another type of development. There, Jewish socialism developed as the result of a schism which gradually divided a group of Jewish Social Democrats in Jassy from the party leadership in Bucharest. The leaders of the movement were unwilling to risk its electoral fortunes by coming out openly for the abolition of Jewish civil inequalities. The rift became a full-fledged schism in July 1895. On the one hand, Diamandy, one of the Bucharest leaders, could now write that "it is absolutely impossible, quite mad, to believe that the Jews, establishing their own party, can win political rights here in our country."[22] On the other hand, the Lumina group in Jassy took up an increasingly national stance. "You Jewish workers," stated *Der veker* in 1896, "who were born and educated in Roumania, who pay taxes, who become soldiers, you have no rights in this country, you are considered aliens . . . You must fight with all your might for political equality with the Roumanian inhabitants of the country. You must demand political rights for the oppressed Jewish people."[23] Another article later in the year followed up this theme:

> Although we are internationalists and say that all peoples without distinction of nation or religion must be fraternally united, still we do not reject pure nationalism. Just because we are international Social Democrats, we do not cease to be Jews. The man who cannot find his way to love and make sacrifices for his own people, the people from which he sprang, will never be idealistic enough to sacrifice himself for others.[24]

Surveying the experience of the Jewish labor movement in these various centers — London, New York, Lemberg, Jassy — it is hard to escape the conclusion that politics rather than sociology determined ideology. More specifically, where there was an established socialist party ready to permit or even encourage the autonomy of a Yiddish-speaking section, as in Galicia or the United States, there the internationalist (in effect the assimilationist) tendency won out. However, where the Jewish socialists felt betrayed by the dominant party, as in Roumania, a reverse process was set in motion.

Developments in Congress Poland (which will be described more fully below) tend to confirm this hypothesis. Suffice it to say here that in Warsaw the PPS followed a vacillating line, in theory recognizing agitation in Yiddish while neglecting it in practice, and that this vacillation was reflected in the attitude of the socialists involved in the Jewish sphere. Half-in and half-out, they were unsure whether to opt for schism, for open conflict with the PPS, or for a subordinate status that would perhaps develop eventually into full autonomy within the party.

What all this suggests is that if it is possible to discern a "natural" or dominant trend through the comparative approach — and this is doubtful — then it is toward a socialism national in form but internationalist (or integrationist) in content. Nevertheless, it is also possible to approach the problem of Bundist history, and specifically its ideological development, from a sociological standpoint. The dominant historiographical theory rests after all on the assumption that in becoming a mass party the Bund had to become more national, had to develop a program that offered specific and immediate answers to the Jewish question. It is taken for granted here that the Jewish masses were nationally inclined, but put in so undifferentiated a form this is a misleading overgeneralization.

Certainly, there were enormously powerful national impulses at work within the mass psychology of the east European Jews. Cut off from the surrounding population by language, culture, ethnic type, and religion, the average Jew retained a strong sense of separate identity. Everywhere a second-class citizen — if not de jure then (as in Galicia) de facto — he naturally saw his only security in group solidarity. Forced to choose between narrow, often narrowing, economic opportunities and migration, he was easily swept away by dreams of a collective return to Palestine, of a Jewish territory, or of full political self-government in his land of birth.

The meteoric rise of Theodor Herzl to the status of folk hero — commonly known as the "King of the Jews" — attests to this fact. His visit to Vilna in August 1903, even though it followed his unpopular audience with Pleve, brought out sensational crowds who followed him wherever he went.[25] "Every oppressed people," Shmarya Levin wrote of the Herzl phenomenon,

has its messianic dream. But the Jewish people . . . had developed that dream
to a supreme form . . . In the double darkness of its inner being – for its outer
life was dark too – it wove the legend of its liberator and from time to time in
history – at long intervals it is true – there were men who came forward to
claim that legend as their own . . . To Herzl, the modern, the perfect European aesthete, we must apply the legend in order that we may understand his
power.[26]

But the Herzl mystique was not the only form taken by this latent national
instinct. The hope of a new exodus reappeared periodically after 1881: in 1891–2
when Baron Hirsch first raised his Argentinian scheme, and again in 1903–4 when
the East African project was under consideration. "The Jewish masses in London,"
Weizmann wrote to Ussishkin in October 1903, "are in the throes of an African
fever, but they are so unenlightened that tomorrow they might be just as easily
fired with enthusiasm for America and the day after for Palestine."[27]

However, at this point in his letter, Weizmann drew what he saw as the logical
conclusion: "If this is the so-called voice of the people that our Africans speak so
ferociously about, one can ignore it with a clear conscience."[28] This comment, of
course, throws an entirely different light on the question of the influence exerted by
the masses on the politically active intelligentsia. The volatility of mass nationalism,
with its momentary enthusiasms erupting out of and subsiding back into prolonged
periods of apathy, deprived it of the power to make a sustained political impact.

This was particularly true in Russia, where until 1906 there were no elections
and where the mass of the people therefore had no effective way of making their
will felt. When the intelligentsia spoke of the masses, the reference in reality was
usually not to the millions or hundreds of thousands but rather to the few thousands who were politically active. Only in the years 1905–6, as described above,
did this situation momentarily change.

For the Bundist (and proto-Bundist) movement, this fact was expressed in the
distinctions made variously between the petty-bourgeois and the proletarian
masses; between the proletariat as a whole and the "organized" proletariat; and
still more narrowly between the organized workers and the conscious (or "propagandized") proletarians. While the petty-bourgeoisie – self-employed artisan, small-
scale employer, shopkeeper – was usually depicted as traditionally minded and inclined to nationalism, the proletariat was more often described in the opposite
terms. In fact, though, this distinction along class lines was over-schematic. The
rapid rise in 1905–6 of three socialist parties with boldly nationalist programs
demonstrated clearly that the Jewish working class was by no means immune to
the appeals of national slogans. A more meaningful distinction can be made between the organized proletariat (led by its "conscious" members) and the Jewish
masses as a whole. Those workers who had long been members of Bundist-led
organizations, the embryonic trade unions or, still more, the political and propaganda circles, constituted a clearly differentiated stratum. They tended towards
militant secularism and antinationalism.

It has to be remembered that, for the average worker, the commitment to the
socialist movement usually meant a violent break with religious belief and practice,
a passionate faith in the new doctrine, particularly in its scientific and internation-

alist underpinnings. And, in turn, this emotional reaction against deeply rooted tradition was reinforced by considerations of a strictly practical nature. Internationalism and scientific socialism translated into mundane terms meant learning a major European language (Russian or Polish) and receiving a basic education in natural history, arithmetic, and political economy. Thus, the socialist movement was often seen as a stepping-stone into the modern world, a first move on the road to emigration or to setting up as an independent master craftsman or contractor.

When writing of their immediate proletarian following – not in ideological generalizations but in concrete terms – the socialist intelligentsia tended to stress its openness, its mobility (both upward to the middle class and outward to America), its passion for modernity. In his retrospective essay on the Jewish labor movement, Litvak even selected the internationalism of the proletariat as one of its central characteristics. "The striving for education," wrote P. Libman in 1914, "often takes abnormal, hardly desirable, forms in the Jewish worker. One of the leaders of [our] movement . . . has remarked, for instance, that in every Jewish worker is concealed an *ekstern*."[29] In the same year Ester Frumkina could complain that the Bundist plans for education in Yiddish aroused little interest in the proletariat:

> Can one say that the Jewish working-masses throw themselves *spontaneously* into the fight for the Yiddish language as the language of education? Can one say that they are ready to make sacrifices so that their children be educated in Yiddish? Can one say they feel the oppression of the Russian school in a hundredth, in a thousandth degree that it is felt by the Polish or Georgian masses?[30]

Litvak explained this phenomenon as the result of the status of the Jews as an "extra-territorial minority."[31] Speaking at the Fifth Congress of the Bund, Liber was more specific, ascribing the "assimilationist tendencies . . . of the Jewish proletarian [to the fact that he] strives for knowledge and does not find it in Yiddish [publications]. The tragedy is that instead of acquiring real learning he has to spend his time on Russian grammar."[32] Perhaps the most interesting comments on this subject, however, were made by An-sky in an article published in 1906:

> Apart from their ignorance of our national culture . . . there are many other reasons why our Jewish working masses . . . so willingly adopt an internationalist point of view . . . One must not forget that the Jewish worker . . . has to break the fetters of religious tradition, has to fight in a sphere where religion is the only form and expression of nationalism, has to hear . . . the abuse – "Goy! Convert! Traitor!" . . . Thus . . . he carries with him . . . a deep hostility to those foundations which in his mind are intimately linked to nationalism. Then, emerging onto the broad stage of sociopolitical life, he meets the [Zionist] party, which has gained a monopoly on Jewish nationalism . . . and was the first to state in the sharpest form the incompatibility between class and national politics, thus alienating the masses not only from Zionism but also from nationalism. Finally, it appears to me, the internationalist idea is in a general way congenial to the Jewish spirit. It is not by chance that the Jewish people – the first adherents of one God – then gave mankind the teacher of Christianity, who declared that there is "neither Hellene nor

Jew" and, finally, produced the most impassioned advocate of internationalism, Marx.[33]

The analysis, as developed so far, forces one to consider another aspect of
Bundist history. If the worldwide trend of Jewish socialism was toward militant
internationalism, if this same tendency was observed in the proletariat organized
by the Bund in Russia, then why did that party develop slowly but steadily – until
1905 – in a nationalist direction? How did it become the first Jewish party to
adopt the idea of national autonomy?

In order to answer this, the central question, it is essential to reexamine another
aspect of Martov's thesis: his organizational assumptions. Martov spoke of the
movement's becoming constantly more "democratic." Insofar as this term was
often applied by the socialist intelligentsia to any movement enjoying support by
the people, by the masses (the *narod*), then Martov was correct. Starting from the
early 1890s, the Vilna movement (discounting ups and downs) did gain an ever
larger popular following. However, in the more specific sense, that implying
greater control by the rank and file over the leadership, Martov's term was certainly not appropriate.

On the contrary, between 1892 and 1904 the leadership of the movement
steadily emancipated itself (above all in the ideological sphere) from control from
below. In 1906 this trend was reversed, and the Bund began to move rapidly
toward a representative system complete with open debate in the party press,
factional rivalry, and local committees elected by the membership. These developments revealed the democratic potentiality concealed within the Bundist movement; but, nonetheless, in the prewar period they constituted the exception rather
than the rule.

The defeat of the worker opposition in the years 1892–5, the creation of the
Bund in 1897 complete with a central committee in Russia and a committee
abroad, and the reorganization of the movement in the years 1902–3 all represented steps towards greater centralization. When he wrote his first history of the
Russian Marxist movement in 1904, Vladimir Akimov described the Bundist organization as being based on a mixed constitution, combining election from below
with nomination from above. Even he, however, made a number of reservations in
stating this opinion. First, he was convinced that what he called "the break-up
period" (the division in 1902–3 of the economic or trade – union base from the
revolutionary or political committees) had resulted in a reduction, both formal and
real, in rank-and-file influence. Thus, the trade councils themselves, the *fakhovye
skhodki*, were now nominated from above. Second, he admitted that even where
the elected principle was nominally enforced it had in fact atrophied to a great
degree. Specifically, he noted that where in theory the agitators' council elected the
local or urban committee, in practice it "rarely makes use of this right because a
committee is elected for an indefinite term, and as its individual members are
arrested it is replenished by cooption."[34]

As the movement was increasingly financed from without, that is, by funds sent
by sympathizers in the United States, so the immediate recipients of this money (the
committee abroad and the central committee) inevitably gained in power. Local
party newspapers disappeared. And the professional revolutionaries appointed by

the TsK grew in number and influence. In 1905 Akimov had the opportunity to observe the Bundist organizations at first hand in Riga, Grodno, Lodz, and Warsaw. Enormously impressed by the power of the movement – "the heart in the social organism of the Jewish proletariat" – he nonetheless felt compelled to revise his views of its internal structure.[35] "I became convinced," he wrote, "that during the previous years the electoral rights of the subordinate organizations of the Bund had finally disappeared and that the whole organization is constructed from above[36] . . . [In fact] the Bund represents a rare example in the international movement of a *mass* organization reared from above."[37] Coming from the man who had probably done more than anybody else to publicize the essentially democratic nature of the Bund, this judgment must carry great weight.

In sum, then, whether observed from the comparative, sociological, or organizational angle, Bundist ideology turns out to have developed not inexorably as a superstructure reflecting the realities of the mass base but rather as a result of specific political contingencies. Although the trend was toward a more national ideology, this was not an inevitable tendency; it was pushed forward amid harsh and often bitter political infighting and was even reversed (albeit temporarily) in 1906.

The decision-making process in the ideological sphere – at least when it came to the nationality question – was until 1906 almost entirely confined to the highest echelons of the organization. Essentially, the long-drawn-out development of the Bundist program reflected attempts by the leaders to define the nature and role of the movement; and, even more perhaps, to define their own place in history and politics. In contrast to Palestinophilism, which created the movement after the ideology, the Vilna Social Democrats developed their ideology in the process of building a movement. The problem of self-definition, the unending search for identity, was endemic to this process.

Among Bundist publicists it was Zivion alone perhaps who, albeit in scattered form, gave clear recognition to this fact. To take just one example, this is how he explained the central decision of the Fourth Congress in 1901 to endorse the concept of Jewish national autonomy:

> The national question was brought to the Bund more from abroad than from within the country. The Bundist intelligentsia which was studying in Germany, Switzerland, and Austria, where at that time all possible questions were discussed in the Russian "colonies", was particularly interested in the national question which was debated more than any other in their clashes with the Zionists or simply with the nationalists. It was the Bundist intelligentsia abroad which placed the national question on the agenda of the Bund.[38]

Here, as in other similar passages, Zivion rightly stressed that the ideological development of the Bund took place not in isolation but within a broader context: It formed an integral chapter in the history of the Russian-Jewish intelligentsia. The doubts so central to that development were those of a distinct stratum in modern Jewish life – *intelligenty* torn between the people of their origin and the new frontiers of internationalism, between the concrete past and hypothetical future, between the populist ethic and scientific socialism. The dilemmas that had been highly idiosyncratic when observed in Hess and Liberman reappeared as the dilemmas of the Bundist leadership, and indeed of the entire generation of Jewish socialists involved in the 1905 revolution.

If the issues were general, however, the particular course followed by the Bund was unique. One must remember that among the Jewish socialist organizations that emerged in various countries during the 1880s and 1890s, the Vilna group was the only one not to grow in the shadow of an established socialist movement. In the United States, Galicia, and Moldavia, and to a lesser extent in England, the Yiddish-speaking groups had to adjust to an existing framework. But the Russian Social Democratic movement had neither the strength nor the will in the 1890s to impose a pattern on the Vilna group. The Russian organization was small, and until 1898, it lacked any kind of framework. Moreover, the memory of the socialist debacle during the pogroms of 1881–2 undoubtedly had an inhibiting effect on the founding fathers of Russian Marxism, Plekhanov's Group for the Liberation of Labor, and in consequence they permitted the Jewish movement to grow unhindered and uncriticized (at least publicly).

Thus, the Vilna group was exposed to and buffeted by various ideological cross currents. In the Russian-Jewish world it found the idea of self-liberation – of a Jewish solution to the Jewish question – firmly established in the form of Palestinophilism. As against this, the Russian-Jewish emigrations in England and America offered the Vilna Social Democrats the example of a Yiddish-speaking socialism which, in the name of international fraternity, rejected the very concept of national politics.

At the same time, the proto-Bundists could not escape the influence of the Polish socialist movement. Although unable to persuade the Lithuanian-Jewish socialists that they were Polish, it did force them to question the assumption that they were Russians. Beyond this, the bitter disputes between the PPS and the Polish Social Democrats provided the Vilna group with two opposing interpretations of the socialist doctrine. The PPS demonstrated that socialism could be seen not as the negation but as the fulfillment, the most effective form, of national liberation; while, for its part, the PSD insisted that on the contrary, proletarian internationalism was totally incompatible with national demands.

Developing under such conflicting pressures, the Vilna group found itself torn throughout its history between two different conceptions and strategies. On the one hand, there was the belief that the class principle was all-embracing, that the Jewish workers owed their allegiance to the all-Russian and world-proletarian movement, that they should divide off as sharply as possible from the rest of the Jewish people and should merge (first politically but, over time, also culturally and linguistically) with the proletariat of Russia as a whole. This line of thought demanded that the Jewish movement keep its autonomy within strictly technical limits and make every effort to create a united Social Democratic movement representative of the proletariat of the entire Russian Empire.

As against this, the alternative concept assumed that the Jewish proletariat had to defend its particular as well as its universal interests, that it had to fight not only against tsarism in general but also specifically against the anti-Jewish policies of the regime, and that it was therefore the avant-garde in the national struggle, the leading champion of Jewish rights. Standing on the extreme left wing of the Jewish people, pursuing the economic struggle against Jewish capital, the proletariat was thereby mobilizing forces for the war against tsarism. As the most oppressed group in the nation, the workers had the most to gain from its liberation. Translated into strategic terms, this view demanded the full-blooded support of the national claims up to and including self-determination; the encouragement of opposition forces in the nonproletarian strata of the Jewish people; and, if necessary, the assertion of organizational independence from the Russian Social Democratic movement.

It was possible to find support for both points of view in Marxist doctrine. *The Communist Manifesto* – the work of Marx and Engels most influential among the early Russian Marxists – lent itself to ambiguous interpretations on this issue. The *Manifesto* certainly emphasized the declining importance of nationality in the age of expanding capitalism. "National differences and antagonisms between people are vanishing more day by day, owing to the development of the bourgeoisie, to freedom of commerce, to the world market, to uniformity in the mode of production."[39] But, as against this, there were other passages which suggested that the proletariat had to pursue its goal in a national framework. "The proletarian movement," reads the *Manifesto*, "is the independent movement of the majority in the interest of the immense majority ... Though not in substance, yet in form, the struggle of the proletariat with the bourgeoisie is at first a national struggle."[40] Elsewhere it states: "Since the proletariat must first acquire political supremacy, must rise to be the leading class of the nation, must constitute itself *the* nation, it is, so far, itself national, though not in the bourgeois sense of the word."[41] Marx and Engels, of course, were not referring to nationalities living within a multinational state but to the compact nations of western Europe.[42] However, this did not deter some of their disciples in the Jewish socialist movement from adapting the concept of the proletariat as a national class to their own experience.

Either strategy, if pursued consistently, could have paid its own dividends. The one policy would have prevented the bitter feuds over the national question that divided the Bund from the Russian Social Democrats in the period 1901–6. The alternative line could conceivably have established the Bund as the most powerful political movement in the Russian Jewish world, permanently overshadowing the Zionists and territorialists.

In practice, however, the Bund steered a middle and often erratic course between these two poles. At each extreme of the movement were well-defined groups which demanded a clear-cut decision, but the majority of the leadership was unwilling to come down fully or permanently on either side. For socialists reared on Russian culture and the traditions of the Russian revolutionary movement, it was almost unthinkable to break entirely with that movement, but to give up the idea of true autonomy for the revolutionary Jewish proletariat was equally repellent.

Logically, such a situation pointed to one outcome: a schism in the Vilna movement. The same ideological dilemma, after all, produced two schisms in the Polish movement, that between the PPS and PSD starting in 1893, and that between the left and the right wings of the PPS starting in 1906. The Russian Social Democratic Labor Party split between Mensheviks and Bolsheviks in 1903, and the Poale Zion divided into three feuding parties in the years 1905–6.

However, the Bund remained intact until the years 1919–21, when, like all the Social Democratic movements in continental Europe, it fragmented under Communist pressure. The dominance in the Bund of the *praktiki* over the *teoretiki* lay at the root of this organizational unity. It can be said that if the Mensheviks developed along the lines of Puritan sectarianism (dividing into feuding factions) and the Bolsheviks as a quasi-military hierarchy (at least in theory), then the Bund was comparable to a close-knit family where emotional loyalties outweigh antagonistic beliefs.

The result of this situation – ideological tension combined with organizational unity – was that enormous efforts had to be invested in patching over, playing down, and even denying the existence of dispute and disagreement. In fact, the popularity of Martov's historiographical theory can no doubt be explained to a large extent by the fact that it enveloped the highly inflammable national issue in a wrapping of historical materialism. Medem's theory of "neutralism" later served a similar function.[43]

Divided ideologically, the Bundist leadership was, to a large degree, forced to improvise in its strategy. It was at its strongest where it could move into a political vacuum, where it could act as unrivaled path-finder. Thus, it played a dominant part in founding the RSDRP in 1898, in establishing the concept of Jewish national autonomy in the period of 1895–1901, and in organizing the Jewish masses in the revolution of 1905. In contrast, strong organizational and ideological competition, when coming from the "internationalist" Left, aggravated its own internal dissensions and so threw it onto the defensive. Bound together in conspiratorial brotherhood, the leadership could never cut the Gordian knot, could never finally decide whether its first duty lay with the international proletariat or with national liberation. In this respect, perhaps, it reflected more faithfully than any other movement the divided soul of the modern Jewish intelligentsia.

The new program, 1893–1895

In fact, there was a turning point in the ideological development of the Vilna movement, but it coincided neither with Martov's speech of 1895 nor with the turn to economic agitation in 1890–1. It came in the year 1893. The new program was carried through not with the support of the organized workers but against their almost unanimous opposition. It involved not an evolutionary process in which practice gradually forced ideological adaptation but rather an abrupt and far-reaching change of course, which embraced both practice and theory (or rather a variety of theories).

Available sources do not permit the historian to pinpoint the exact moment when the new policy was debated and adopted. Martov placed it early in 1894; but Pati Srednitskaia and Avrom Gordon in their separate memoirs both referred to 1893 as the crucial year. So, furthermore, did the first official history of the movement published in 1900.[44] Although Martov's autobiography carries the ring of authenticity, it is possible that he was simply less well informed than the others; he did not come to Vilna until June 1893 and was only drawn into the central revolutionary group toward the end of the year.

Despite the problem of dating the change of policy, the sources agree on what it meant in immediate organizational terms. Essentially, the "new program," as it was called, demanded that the established order of values and priorities be stood on its head. Hitherto, the Vilna organization, as it had developed from the mid-1880s, had been structured as a pedagogical hierarchy – workers selected from the rank and file progressed upwards through a series of study circles. Starting with lessons in the fundamentals of Russian language, natural history, political economy, and even arithmetic and anatomy, they advanced to lessons on Darwinism and Marxism. Eventually, if they succeeded, they were given free access to the classics of Russian socialism and radicalism. To enable workers to become "conscious Social Democrats" was the immediate objective of the system.

Now, in 1893, it was decided to relegate this educational process to second place and to treat the recruitment of a mass proletarian following as primary. In practical terms, this meant that only those workers who proved themselves to be effective and dedicated agitators would be permitted to advance up the educational ladder. More, the Russian language would have to yield first place to Yiddish. Only if the agitators themselves heard the basic lectures in Yiddish would they be able to pass on the information easily and quickly to the rank and file. Only if the movement now obtained and produced an increasing number of books, brochures, and leaflets in Yiddish could it reach out to a broad mass following.

Just how profound a break was involved here can be judged by the reaction of the workers. There were a few hundred workers organized in *kruzhki* or *kassy* in Vilna at that time,[45] and they, in turn, came into contact with broader circles at their places of work. As awareness of the new program spread, it was rejected with increasing vehemence by the great majority of the workers involved.

Avrom Gordon, who became the leader of the opposition, would later recall the development as he remembered it. At first, he wrote, "the masses – apart from some two dozen workers in the highest circles – had no concept of the 'new program' around which for months an internal struggle was being waged."[46] But, eventually, he heard from a member of this inner circle what was happening. As he remembered the conversation, he was told:

> The whole movement is in danger. The *intelligenty* are now introducing their new program which is based on a few brochures in Yiddish . . . ; they are destroying all culture in the movement! For several months now the highest workers' circles have been refusing to allow this. In order to put an end to this situation, the *intelligenty* last Saturday prepared in advance to get it through the three upper circles. Aleksandr [Kremer] was at two himself and the workers – against their will – had to vote for it. At the third there was Liuba . . . and she did not get it through. It has been postponed . . . till Aleksandr can come . . . You see, he will arrive with his sharp tongue and beat everybody down and all will give way. Then everything will collapse.[47]

Gordon suggested that the workers fight back in the name of democracy ("As the program affects the entire mass, the *intelligenty* and a handful of workers have no right to introduce it by force").[48] There now followed a period of one to two years that by all accounts was marked by open and bitter conflict. Gordon succeeded in uniting the workers' movement against the leadership. He, with his own group of supporters, gave speeches in workshops and at meetings, distributed leaflets, forced the *intelligenty* into debates. Gozhansky, who was one of the two main architects of the new policy (Kremer being the other), later recalled that when they came to speak they "often remained alone in an empty room. The workers left the meeting because they believed that we wanted to lead them blindly."[49] Martov described how, as a result of this split, their "entire work was disorganized"[50] and Pati Srednitskaia (Kremer's wife) wrote that of the workers "only a small handful, only individuals, remained with the organization."[51] Even in his contemporary brochure, *On Agitation,* Kremer admitted that of "the worker Social Democrats, the majority" were opposed to the intelligentsia.[52]

What could have driven the leadership into so desperate a conflict with their own following? The standard answer, that the reordering of priorities formed an integral part of the economic agitation program, is hardly adequate. Here, chronology becomes of vital importance. Available evidence suggests clearly that the Vilna movement had begun to place heavy emphasis on strikes, strike funds, and *kassy* at least as early as 1891.[53] Timofei Kopelzon, one of the veteran leaders, even claimed that "the strike movement – led by the organization – began in 1888."[54] The use of Yiddish in the movement was also not new in 1893. Brochures in that language had been employed since 1888 at least. It was used in classes to explain Russian texts, and some Russian material was translated into Yiddish and distributed long before 1893.[55]

But none of this had thrown the movement into chaos. True, Avrom Gordon had been opposed throughout to the agitation movement, arguing that the Jewish proletariat, based as it was on declining domestic industry, could only lose by constant strikes. At the May Day meeting in 1892, he had attacked the *intelligenty* for seeking quick results at all costs. But on that issue he had failed to rally any support. On the contrary, as he himself described, he was excluded from the movement following his speech, was boycotted by his fellow workers, and even considered suicide. Only a substantially new element introduced into the situation in 1893 permitted Gordon to turn the tables.[56]

During its prolonged debate against the worker opposition, the Social Democratic leadership produced a number of statements in defense of their policy. Three of these have survived: Gozhansky's *Letter to the Agitators,* Kremer's *On Agitation,* and Martov's speech of 1895. Although each of these professions of faith carries a strongly individual stamp, taken together they do reveal what the underlying issue in that embittered conflict really was.

Put in the baldest terms, the leadership had decided to recognize the labor movement in Vilna as an end in itself – as an autonomous political factor. Hitherto, the Social Democrats had regarded their own labor organization as a recruiting ground for the revolutionary proletariat rather than as a branch of it. In Lithuania, there were no really large factories, no heavy industry, and therefore no modern proletariat of the type envisaged by Marxist theory. What Vilna could provide were workers fully trained and experienced as revolutionaries. "Those who first founded revolutionary circles in Vilna," Kremer recalled, ". . . only wanted to produce a few more developed workers, bring them to socialist consciousness, prepare them as agitators for Russia, for the industrial centers, for the Russian working class."[57] In 1893 this entire approach was consciously abandoned by the leadership.

Paradoxically, the recognition of the Jewish working class in Vilna and the northwest region as an equal branch of the international proletariat led of necessity to the conflict between the intelligentsia and the workers. Previously, the movement had acted as a way of escape for the worker from the old environment into a completely new world with a new language (Russian), a new culture (Russian libraries), a new faith (socialism), a new peer group (the intelligentsia), and ever widening horizons (the international socialist movement). But, as now envisaged, the movement was to become that of the Jewish working class with Yiddish as its language, the local workshop as its focal point, and "trade unionism" – or *kassy* and economic strikes – as its major form of activity. Gordon recalled the issue in these terms:

> Would the movement remain a solid and powerful socialist movement for Russia as a whole, or would it become an empty swindle confined to the cramped Jewish street with pogroms and disgrace . . . The workers could not and would not permit their whole ideal and their entire faith – to which they had devoted their best years with so much impassioned energy – to be shattered at one blow.[58]

But the architects of the new program had committed themselves to it and were determined to fight the issue through to a decisive conclusion.

Two different types of argument were employed by the leadership. First, there was the strictly socioeconomic line of attack. It recurred in all three documents, was probably acceptable to the entire leadership group, and therefore should be seen as the lowest common denominator in the thinking of the intelligentsia.

In his *On Agitation,* Kremer chose to frame his argument in terms of sociological realities and economic determinism. At issue, he suggested, were not so much the premises on which the worker opposition rested its case, but rather the conclusions which it drew from them. "There is an opinion," he wrote,

> that only the most developed factory centers can provide the soil for agitational activity, [because] in handicrafts and workshop production . . . the profound gulf in the position of master and worker is absent; [because] apart from this, the worker can with relative ease, become a master or an independent producer and is willing to put up with certain sacrifices.[59]

But in fact, Kremer argued, it did not follow that the Social Democrats should write off the handicraft proletariat as a potentially revolutionary force. There were even advantages created by its particular situation. An artisan employed in a workshop did not have to fear dismissal as much as a factory hand, because there were innumerable other small shops where he could find work, and this was doubly true if he were fully skilled. If the worst came to the worst, he could even set up on his own. Further, as a class these skilled workers were better educated than the factory proletariat and were more easily organized. In sum, these arguments led, as Ezra Mendelsohn has accurately observed, "to the paradoxical conclusion that the very nature of the Jewish working-class might foster rather than impede the labour movement."[60]

Kremer also called in historical dynamics to justify the new program. True, he admitted, domestic and handicraft production was doomed and would ultimately be replaced by large-scale industry. But this fact made it doubly important that the workers in small-scale production face the harsh transitional period as a united entity. Otherwise, they would be exposed to limitless exploitation and degradation. The goal should be to provide the worker with the means of defense whether he remained where he was or moved to a new industrial setting. "We are lucky," he concluded, "that we live in an epoch where the process of change is so clear that we can foresee all the subsequent stages. To know that process and not to use that knowledge would be to commit a major historical error."[61]

In their statements, Gozhansky and Martov likewise placed great emphasis on the fact that, by stressing immediate economic demands, by making the movement "more materialist," the Social Democrats could organize the Jewish proletariat en masse. But, unlike Kremer, they did not stop there. They gave at least equal weight to the problem of political – and specifically of national – interests.

Gozhansky, in his *Letter to the Agitators,* which was probably written late in 1893, did not even attempt to deduce the political from the socioeconomic argument. The Vilna movement had to become more national, he insisted, because that was the most rational policy in the light of the recent Jewish experience in Europe.

There could be no doubt, he wrote, that in the foreseeable future the Russian Autocracy would fall and be replaced by a constitutional system, but it was no longer possible to assume that a more democratic regime would automatically bring with it political equality for the Jews. Recent history clearly demonstrated that even parliamentary systems could deprive minorities of their rights, either through legislation (as in Roumania) or through intimidation and privilege (as in Austria-Hungary). Indeed, "in constitutional Roumania, the Jews have fewer rights than in autocratic Russia."[62]

The position of minority nationalities in a parliamentary system depended, he argued, on a combination of "external" factors, on the relative power of the various classes and political parties in the country as a whole, and on "internal" factors, the ability of a given minority to assert and defend its own cause. "Those rights," he wrote,

> which the Jewish proletariat receives without a conscious and political struggle will be worth almost nothing. The fact that the Jews have lived in Russia without rights for so many years has taught the chinovniki how to treat the Jews barbarically without any resistance from them . . . If the Jewish proletariat does not reach the necessary [political] level, most of the laws which the constitution concedes will remain dead letters, so much paper . . . We Jewish Social Democrats must develop the political consciousness of the Jewish proletariat. Its consciousness must become sufficiently strong that it will be ready to win its rights and fight to defend those rights once it has gained them.[63]

In defense of this strategy, Gozhansky advanced two important supplementary theses which were inspired by the Marxist line of thought. First, he noticed that in Russian politics the urban centers were becoming crucially important, and this fact gave the Jews a potential power beyond their purely numerical strength. "The political struggle," he wrote, "will be conducted mainly by the city population, and in Russia the Jews constitute 36 percent of the urban inhabitants."[64] This same idea, applied to the Roumanian situation, was to reappear in the report sent by the Lumina group in Jassy to the London Congress of the Socialist International in 1896.[65]

Gozhansky buttressed his case with a second sociopolitical argument. The Jewish bourgeoisie, he wrote, had proved itself totally incapable of defending the rights of Russian Jewry. The most that the middle-class intelligentsia had ever done was to write articles and books in self-defense, but as a class the bourgeoisie had proved itself politically impotent, utterly unable to mount "a national-Jewish political struggle."[66] "Therefore," he concluded, "we can say categorically that if the Jews are ever to conduct a political struggle it will be the Jewish proletariat – and not the Jewish bourgeoisie – which alone will participate in it."[67]

From what is known about the Vilna Social Democratic group, it can be safely assumed that Gozhansky's declaration of faith, in contrast to Kremer's *On Agitation,* was considered too nationalistic by some of the members. Nevertheless, it probably did represent the majority opinion. John Mill later recalled that a conference held in Vilna in August 1894 adopted a position essentially identical to that of Gozhansky's. "This," Mill explained,

> was the first time that we declared our stand on the Jewish question so clearly, without any ambiguity whatsoever . . . ; that the Jewish worker suffers in Russia not merely as a worker but as a Jew; that in agitation all forms of national oppression should be stressed more and more; that, together with the general political and economic struggle, the struggle for civil equality must be one of our immediate tasks; and that this struggle can best be carried out by the organized Jewish worker himself. Closer cooperation with the Jewish labor organizations in other cities must, therefore, logically be the next step.[68]

According to Mill's account, Isai Aizenshtat and Timofei Kopelzon, who would probably have joined Leon Goldman in criticizing the majority, were not among the participants. Goldman reportedly argued that to place special emphasis on fighting for Jewish equality would "develop a harmful, nationalistic spirit among the Jewish workers, that through it they would be isolated from the Russian masses and that the united political struggle would be undermined."[69] It fell to Vladimir Kossovsky, like Martov a newcomer in the Vilna leadership, to counter Goldman's plea. "Kossovsky," Mill recalled, "gave a brilliant survey of the proposed theses . . . At no time later did I ever hear [him] . . . speak with so much fire and power of persuasion. I believe that this conference raised Kossovsky to the first ranks and helped make him an authoritative spokesman of the Jewish labor movement."[70]

Recalling the conflict with Gordon's opposition, Martov would later observe that "it would have been more than natural if the debates arising in such circumstances had led to the crystallization of two hostile tendencies – nationalism and internationalism. But that did not happen. At that time we approached the question of agitation and propaganda from the point of view of selecting the best weapons – and that was all."[71] Taken at its face value, this summary of the situation as it was in 1894 could be seriously misleading.

In a very real sense, the split between the intelligentsia and the worker opposition was specifically a conflict between nationalism and internationalism, or (to use less emotive terms) between a commitment to, and a denial of, Jewish politics.[72] What inspired and united the opposition was, above all, the idea that in becoming socialist, they had joined an international movement, a powerful fraternity, in which every member regardless of origin could play an equal role and share a common language (Russian or, in Poland, Polish).

Although the opposition in Vilna went into sharp decline in 1895 – given its emphasis on worker education, it could not survive without support from the intelligentsia[73] – its off-shoots reemerged here and there in later years too. Thus, in 1898, Moisei Lure and Ruvim Fridman played a central role in Belostok, running the underground press of the *Rabochee znamia* group. They, in turn, were linked to groups in Kharkov, Kiev, and Grodno that also included veteran members of the Vilna opposition. In 1900, a dissident group even organized itself in Vilna to run an illegal press in association with the Sotsialist movement in St. Petersburg. Little is known about these groupings, but a common thread running through their history was their repeated attempt to merge into a centralized, strongly political and mono-cultural party – be it the Russian (the *Russkaia* as opposed to *Rossiiskaia*) Social Democratic Party of 1898, the PPS, the *Iskra* movement, or the SR party.[74] (E. I. Levin, for instance, who as a Kharkov student had come to Vilna in 1894 to help Gordon, would be among the most bitter critics of the Bund at the Second Congress of the RSDRP in 1903.)

However, if Gordon's worker opposition undoubtedly defined itself as internationalist, the leadership group in Vilna during the years 1893–5 did not see itself as "nationalist." In that sense Martov was right. As Marxists, they insisted that their only concern was to create a strictly one-class movement, an organization of the Jewish proletariat. Although other classes among the Jewish people would benefit from equal civil rights, the proletariat alone was capable of fighting for those rights and it would do so on its own behalf and not on behalf of the nation as a whole.

Although this distinction might appear casuistic (and it was not always tightly drawn), it was undoubtedly of central importance in the credo of the leadership. It alone can explain the dispute in the years 1894–5 between Avrom Lesin (Valt), then an *ekstern* in Minsk, and the Vilna leadership. *Valtovshchina*, as it became known, has frequently been described – starting with the account published by Boris Frumkin in 1913[75] – as constituting "not a concrete program but a vague demand to stress the Jewish character and spirit of the movement."[76] So undefined a position, however, could not in itself have led to the break between Lesin and the leadership, which at that very moment was working without rest to create a Yiddish-speaking movement committed to the fight for Jewish civil rights.

Lesin was already a budding poet and it may well be that he formulated his thoughts in somewhat elliptical ways, but, judging from his own recollections, he had in fact developed a coherent and distinctive ideology of his own. He argued that neither sociologically nor politically did the situation of the Jewish people in Russia permit the Social Democrats to think in terms of an exclusively proletarian party. The true distinction in Jewish society was not that which divided the employer from the employee but that which divided the rich minority from the impoverished majority – in the workshops of the Pale, he used to say, the "fight between capital and labor is a fight between the beggar and the bankrupt."[77] Gordon, too, was urging this thesis, but Lesin drew opposite conclusions. The Social Democrats should seek to unite all the impoverished strata, the *bednota,* in a campaign for the defense of the elementary political rights of the Jewish people as a whole. A movement that would be as much nationalist as socialist was especially urgent, he frequently insisted, because "the great pogroms are still to come."[78]

In 1894 Lesin came from Minsk to Vilna in order to meet Arkadii Kremer, then the recognized head of the movement, and to plead his cause. "I argued," he recalled,

> that it is not Marxist to adapt life to suit brochures, especially when the brochures come from as far away as Geneva . . . Kremer threw me a withering glance and began to get angry. I shouted more loudly still that the Jewish worker is a fiction, that the worker in our cities as soon as he gets married becomes a small-scale employer, and that the movement must therefore give up its narrow economic character. It must become broader, more political, more national. One must work out Jewish national demands. Then we could appeal with our socialism to far broader masses of people – to all the impoverished strata. Of course, all my arguments bounced off Kremer like so many balls off a stone wall.[79]

Clearly, the central issue here was that Lesin categorically rejected the idea of proletarian self-sufficiency, of dividing the mass of the nation into mutually exclusive and hostile classes; even Social Democrats, he maintained, accepted the concept of national unity in wars of self-defense. For the Vilna leadership this line of reasoning was not Marxist, was unacceptable. In 1895 Lesin emigrated to the United States. "I was fed up," he wrote later, "with the minor disputes, and had heard rumor of the 30,000 organized Jewish workers – real factory workers [in New York]."[80]

At this stage in the discussion it is possible to reassess the place of Martov's lecture of 1 May 1895 in the evolution of Bundist ideology. It is clear that, in reality, he did not formulate a new political credo. Rather, he summed up and synthesized various ideas that had been accepted by the majority in the Vilna leadership since 1893. His personal contribution was to describe the "national-Jewish political struggle" (the concept enunciated by Gozhansky in 1893) as the necessary platform for a mass movement of the Jewish proletariat, the logical outcome of the economic agitation movement. However inaccurate it was as a description of historical fact, this theory, with its underpinning of Marxist orthodoxy, permitted Martov to proclaim the "new program" of 1893 with greater boldness than even Gozhansky had demonstrated.

In order to be truly socialist, he wrote, the Jewish proletariat had to be imbued with national pride: "that working class which can reconcile itself to the ill fate of a particular nation will never rise up against the ill fate of a particular class . . . The awakening of national and class consciousness should go hand in hand."[81] The creation of a separate organization of the Jewish proletariat committed to war against national oppression could not lead to the betrayal of internationalism because (here Martov followed Gozhansky) the Jewish bourgeoisie was "the most miserable and lowly in the world."[82] Thus, the Jewish socialists – in contrast to the Polish – had the arena to themselves in their fight against tsarism and therefore could not be infected by middle- or upper-class chauvinism.

At the same time, however, the Jewish working class could not rely on the Russian proletariat to fight for its interests. This was a question not only of principle ("everything through the people") but also of common sense; a group that did not defend its own interests could not expect others to take them into account. Here again, in repeating Gozhansky's concept, Martov spelled out its implications with greater sharpness. "Without the success of the Russian and Polish workers," he wrote,

> we will not achieve much, but on the other hand, we can no longer await everything from the Russian proletariat as our bourgeoisie expects everything from the Russian government and bureaucratic liberalism ... Clearly, when the Russian proletariat is forced to sacrifice certain of its demands in order to gain something, it will first give up those demands which concern only the Jews ... such as that for equal rights. Nor should we complain about this ... *The class which does not know how to fight for its own freedom is not worthy of it.*[83]

In his memoirs, Martov wrote that he soon came to regret having "nourished a lack of faith among the Jewish workers toward their fellows in the ruling nationality,"[84] and that he therefore took the first opportunity to present a more balanced view. However, the evidence he cites – a pamphlet written in the summer of 1895 – reveals that at that point he was still committed to the idea of a powerful and united organization of the Jewish proletariat which would fight to gain civil equality for the entire Jewish nation. He did not repeat the idea that the Russian proletariat might betray specifically Jewish interests, but otherwise his new statement was, if anything, bolder than his speech. "As workers," he now wrote,

> we suffer from the yoke of capital; as Jews we suffer from the yoke of inequality. Therefore we must do everything to win equal rights ... Everywhere the Jewish workers are beginning to fight ... When the Jewish workers are organized everywhere – when the worker who leaves his hometown shall find wherever he goes a union of comrades – then we shall have on our side a power such as cannot now even be imagined. That power will not be enough to master the Russian government, but we will have reliable allies: Russian, Polish, Lithuanian workers ... Fighting for our rights we will grow in strength: with that strength we are destined to gain equal rights ... [But] we cannot attain the abolition of all restrictions for ourselves alone. When – thanks to our fight – the chains holding us down fall away, they will fall not only from us, but also from those [Jews] who are astride our backs.[85]

If economic agitation was not the sole, or even the major, factor that induced the Vilna leadership to adopt the new program, to launch the campaign for a Jewish labor movement, then what did lie behind this decision? Further, if the change of policy in 1893 involved a sharp break, then what were its immediate, as distinct from long-term, causes?

In general terms, the emergence of a Yiddish-speaking socialist movement in the Pale of Settlement was in no way surprising. If socialist groups in Moldavia, Galicia, and on a smaller scale in Congress Poland undertook this experiment, then the Social Democrats in Lithuania and White Russia were almost bound sooner or later to do likewise. The Russian Jewish emigrants in London and especially in New York had proved that a Yiddish-speaking labor movement could succeed.

Moreover, their newspapers, journals, and pamphlets in Yiddish filtered into Russia from at least 1888, and in that year, too, the Yiddish edition of the brochure *What Do People Live By* was smuggled across the frontier in hundreds of copies.

The history of that brochure in itself provides an insight into the process by which apparently totally different movements interacted with, and influenced, each other. *What Do People Live By* was written in Polish by S. Dikshtein, a member of the Polish socialist movement, Proletariat, and first published under the pseudonym of Jan Młot in Geneva in 1881. In 1886 Shmuel Rabinovich (the son of the leading Palestinophile, S. P. Rabinovich), who was then an active member of a Polish socialist *kruzhok* in Warsaw, began to translate the brochure into Yiddish. He completed the translation in 1887 in western Europe, where his project gained the sympathy of Lavrov and the active support of the leading Polish revolutionary, Stanisław Mendelson. Eventually it was published at the expense of the Polish organization on the press of the *Arbeter fraynd* in London and in the name of the Jewish Workers' Library (a group Rabinovich was trying to establish in Zurich).[86] In his memoirs, Timofei Kopelzon recalled that the socialists in Vilna put the large number of copies that reached them to immediate use. "The booklet became a kind of Torah among us and we used to read it and debate it in all the workers' circles."[87]

This episode was not an isolated phenomenon but marked the beginning of a process. Socialist publications in Yiddish reached eastern Europe from London and New York in ever-increasing quantitites.[88] The "new program" of 1893, Martov recalled, was based on the premise that for the foreseeable future, the Vilna movement, in switching from Russian to Yiddish, could rely on imported material.[89] By 1896, a report from John Mill's Social Democratic group in Warsaw noted that among the reading matter distributed to the workers was "the entire American Yiddish socialist literature, especially *Di tsukunft.*"[90]

The decision to create a Yiddish-speaking labor movement in Lithuania can, then, largely be explained in terms of the overseas example. But – given their internationalist or assimiliationist ideology – the Yiddish-speaking socialists in London and New York clearly could not have inspired the Vilna leadership in its turn of 1893 toward a national policy. That aspect of the "new program" was the product primarily of the political situation in Russia, and here, too, there were long-term factors at work.

No group in Russian Jewry, perhaps, was more directly alienated by the policies of the tsarist regime than the students and would-be students. Huge numbers of candidates were kept out of the universities and high schools by the numerus clausus imposed in 1887, and even those who did gain a place were often unable to study where and what they wanted.[91] Direct victims of discrimination themselves, they became increasingly sensitive to the general policy of discrimination, whether it took the form of long-standing restrictions (the Pale of Settlement) or sudden blows (the expulsion from Moscow in 1891).[92]

But the Vilna program did not arise only out of hatred for the discriminatory policies of the regime. There was also a distrust – never fully enunciated but present nonetheless – of the Russian, and even international, socialist movement. The stand taken by the Narodnaia Volia during the pogroms of 1881–2 was well known, in outline if not in all its details, and that was a legacy from the past not easily to be ignored. Moreover, the Vilna group was familiar with, and held discussions on, the resolution of the Second International that in 1891 condemned not only antisemitism but also philo-semitism. Awareness of this resolution, and of the stand on Jewish disabilities taken by the Social Democrats in Roumania, may have undermined faith in socialist internationalism as a complete substitute for national self-help.

In turn, this concept of self-reliance which was central to the thought of the Vilna Social Democrats was no doubt partially derived from Palestinophilism. John Mill's assertion that among the socialists "Palestinophilism was of interest to nobody" and was treated with "total indifference"[93] is not exact. The truth is that the socialists were actively hostile to the Palestine movement, argued against it, regarded it as a threat, and in attacking it were influenced by its mode of thought. Lesin was nearer the truth when he asserted that even before the emergence of the Vilna Social Democratic movement, Palestinophilism had "to some degree halted the national betrayal by the *intelligenty* who . . . [previously] had sought individual salvation by escape from the Jewish masses into higher education . . . , [thus] casting off the ghetto and the legal restrictions."[94] It was in emphasizing the idea that the Jews should organize themselves to solve the Jewish question that Palestinophilism influenced the socialists. "Zionism," Lesin concluded, "gave the people an intelligentsia; Bundism gave the intelligentsia a people."[95]

When the well-known Palestinophile Vladimir Temkin came to Vilna in 1892, he was debated by Isai Aizenshtat, who caused a sensation by quoting at length from Rubanovich's article on the subject in the *Vestnik narodnoi voli* of 1886.[96] Pati Srednitskaia recalled a similar debate in 1895 between Arkadii Kremer and a leading *Palestinets* in Vitebsk.[97] Again, one of the workers who spoke on May Day 1892 devoted a large part of his address to the issue. He too followed Rubanovich in arguing that the Palestinophile idea was flawed because it was possible neither to settle all the Jews in Palestine nor to establish there "equality, brotherhood, and freedom."[98]

However, both this speaker (Gershovsky, a shoe worker) and Yogikhes in his introduction to the brochure, *Four Speeches by Jewish Workers,* readily admitted that Palestinophilism had a considerable following. "It is understandable . . . ," Gershovsky said, "that the poor Jewish people fall eagerly on this bait; there lives in it the desire to be liberated from the thousand-year harassment; the belief that some day the Messiah will come and lead all the Jews to Palestine."[99] And Yogikhes wrote that "educated Jews, Jewish student youth, have in recent years produced far fewer socialist revolutionaries than before," because so many of them were attracted to the idea of "an independent Jewish state" in Palestine.[100] The truth of the matter is that, however ineffectual Palestinophilism had proved, it was still the first modern political party to be created by the Jews in Russia and it could not but make an impact on subsequent movements, however hostile they might be.

All the factors considered so far – Yiddish-speaking socialism abroad; governmental antisemitism; distrust in majority socialism; Palestinophilism – were of long standing, had all been at work for about a decade, and therefore cannot adequately explain the sudden adoption of the "new program" in 1893. There were also short-term causes involved.

There can be little doubt, for instance, that personal changes in the Vilna socialist group were of decisive importance. In the period 1885–9, Lev Yogikhes had emerged as the leading figure in Vilna; his influence had grown particularly following the arrests that swept the city after the assassination attempt on Alexander III in 1887. (Józef Piłsudski was among those then arrested; I. V. Dembo escaped abroad). In his memoirs, Timofei Kopelzon has described how Yogikhes personally controlled the propaganda circles established in those years among the workers. Already then he revealed many of the characteristics for which he would become well known in later years as a leader of first the Polish Social Democratic movement and then the Spartakusbund in Germany: a penchant for centralized and highly conspiratorial forms of organization, a strong belief in socialist internationalism, an authoritarian inclination.[101] His personal influence over the organized workers in Vilna, judging from Avrom Gordon's account, was immense.[102]

However, in the years 1889–91 there was a turnover in the composition of the leadership. Yogikhes went abroad in 1889. Arkadii Kremer, expelled from St. Petersburg after a period in prison, arrived early in 1890. Among the other recruits at that time were Pati Srednitskaia and, in 1891, Shmuel Gozhansky. Although some veterans from the 1880s remained (or now returned from prison) – Aizenshtat, Kopelzon, Mill, Liuba Levinson – the dominant role rapidly passed to the new guard and they pressed for innovations. To Gozhansky belonged the idea of using the law of Catherine II to provide the strike movement with a legal base.[103] In the disputes with workers and the public debates against the opposition, Kremer and Gozhansky represented the leadership. And, of course, they also were the ones who defended the new ideas in written form.

The most enthusiastic support for the "new program" was to be found mainly among latecomers: Martov, who arrived in Vilna in 1893, Kossovsky, and Avrom (Gleb) Mutnik, who came in 1894. Of the veterans only John Mill seems to have committed himself to it wholeheartedly. Judging from their later statements on the issue, Aizenshtat and Kopelzon must have had major reservations about the national focus that Gozhansky and Martov were seeking to give the movement. Lev Yogikhes had the opportunity to state his opposition from Geneva when in 1893 he published his introduction (written with the help of Rosa Luxemburg)[104] to the May Day speeches of the previous year.

Yogikhes, of course, wrote with excitement of the political awakening of the Jewish workers in Russia. But, at the same time, he rejected by clear implication the two new strategies which had been adopted by the Vilna group since his departure. First, he attacked the way his successors were interpreting the economic agitation movement. It was absurd, he wrote, to expect the tsarist regime to tolerate the development of open trade unionism – here, of course, was his comment on the use of the 1789 law. And it was also wrong "to say that for the time being we will fight our direct enemies, the employers, and then when our forces are stronger we will begin the fight against . . . the tsarist regime."[105] Political and economic agitation should go hand in hand from the start; Jewish workers would no doubt be open to such an approach because "the restrictions and persecutions which they suffer in Russia, *as Jews* make them especially receptive to ideas of political freedom."[106] However – and here Yogikhes was making plain his reservations about the new national line in Vilna – the workers in fighting for freedom had no need for a separate organization. "The Jewish workers in Russia are consciously and

Figure 10. Isai Aizenshtat, 1867–1937.

decisively breaking away from the narrow traditions and views of the Jewish people [*narodnost*] in order to unite with the great international labor army . . .[107] [They proclaim] that they have no special Jewish tasks, that there are only the tasks and goals common to the workers of all countries and all peoples!"[108]

Thus Yogikhes was lending support to his one-time pupils, Avrom Gordon and the worker opposition; and it was only natural that, as Mill recalls, his introduction "did not please any of us."[109] In the summer of 1894, Mill met Rosa Luxemburg and Yogikhes in Zurich and discussed with them the decisions of the conference just held in Vilna. "I shall not mention their silly jokes about the conclusions of the conference," Mill wrote,

> but their furious criticism was directed against its general position which they represented as one hundred percent separatist, as a kind of PPS-ism in the street of Jewish labor, as a step which logically would bring us nearer to the ideology of the petty bourgeoisie. What we needed, they maintained, was not Yiddish and various Jewish organizations but the language of the surrounding people which leads to unity with the Christian proletariat. Any other way would only lead us into a nationalist swamp.[110]

With their reference to "PPS-ism" in Jewish form, Rosa Luxemburg and Yogikhes touched on what had undoubtedly become a crucial factor in the thinking of the Social Democratic group in Vilna. In the years 1892–3 the Polish socialist movement was dividing into two bitterly hostile camps, and the Jewish Social Democrats from the very first were caught in the resulting cross fire. While Rosa Luxemburg and Yogikhes were in the process of founding the Polish Social Democratic movement, pledged to an extreme form of Marxist internationalism, the majority of Polish socialists had moved toward an uninhibitedly nationalist position. The creation of an independent Polish state was declared their most immediate goal both at their congress held in Paris in November 1892 and at the founding congress of the Polish Socialist Party (PPS) in Vilna in the summer of 1893. Convinced that Russia as a whole was far more backward politically, culturally, and economically than Poland, the PPS argued that the Polish proletariat should rely on its own nation to carry through a successful revolution.[111]

The emergence of this new force in 1892 confronted the Jewish Social Democrats in Vilna with a genuine dilemma. Hitherto, they had equated internationalism with participation in the Russian movement. But, now, the PPS insisted that as citizens of the future Polish state (Lithuania had, after all, been part of the Polish kingdom until 1772–95) the Jews in the northwest region should act as such, should learn Polish rather than Russian, join forces with the Polish revolutionaries, and accept early Polish independence as in their own direct interest.

In 1892 Józef Piłsudski had returned to Vilna after five years' penal exile in Siberia and in May 1893 he published an open letter "To the Jewish Socialist Comrades in the Occupied Polish Provinces." (It appeared in *Przedświt,* the Polish socialist paper printed in London.) He criticized the tactics of the Jewish Social Democrats mercilessly and appealed to them to change course;

> In their negation of the political side of socialism the Jewish socialists in the occupied areas have carried things ad absurdum. In our region [*krai*], subjected to the yoke of the Muravevs and Kakhanovs, where the brutal power of tsarist despotism has reached its ultimate expression in the politics of "unification," there the Jewish socialists have begun their work among the Jewish proletariat by seeking to impose on it the Russian language as a path to culture.[112]

To this theme – the cancer of Jewish self-Russification – Pilsudski would constantly return, here and in subsequent articles. At times he warned the Jewish socialists that their Russian-oriented policy could provoke the Polish masses into a fury of indignation – a statement that sounded like a threat of pogroms. At other times, he preferred mockery:

> The Jewish socialists until recently were breaking their heads over the question of whether the Russian *obshchina* should be defended from capitalism . . . or subjugated to it; of how to turn the artel – which is of such importance – into a communist producer collective, etc. But over the last thousand years there have been no *obshchina* and artel in Lithuania, and so all their research had to remain in the realm of theory.[113]

The publication of his articles in *Przedświt* was only one of the methods, the most public but perhaps the least important, that he employed to influence the Jewish Social Democratic group. Thus, Kopelzon recalls that he and Kremer spent a number of evenings in ideological discussion with Pilsudski, who always accused them of pursuing the policy of Russification.[114] Conscious that the Lithuanian Jews felt, and were, remote from Polish culture, Pilsudski opted for the lesser evil and systematically encouraged the Jewish movement to substitute Yiddish for Russian as its primary language.

The fact that his movement was well equipped to aid the Jewish Social Democrats made this stance the more persuasive. The PPS was ready to purchase and transport Yiddish material from the West for the Vilna group[115] (albeit at the expense of the latter). Moreover, the Galician Social Democratic Party (the fraternal party of the PPS) supplied the Vilna Social Democrats with copies of its Yiddish paper, *Der arbeter,* and permitted them to print up their own Yiddish brochures on its press.[116]

In his memoirs, Martov wrote that by the end of 1894 "the Yiddish socialist journals from London and New York were being ordered in greater quantities, [but] the Galician Yiddish literature, to which we had also turned, was considered unsuitable because of the Polish national spirit in which it was conducted."[117] However, judging by Pilsudski's contemporary correspondence, Martov here gave an exaggerated impression of the hostility then prevailing between the Jewish Social Democrats and the PPS. Thus, a letter of September 1895 mentioned that manuscripts were then being sent by the Vilna group to Lemberg for printing, and Pilsudski in the years 1894–5 frequently raised the possibility of converting *Der arbeter* into a joint journal, shared by the Vilna Social Democrats and the affiliates of the PPS in Galicia.[118]

True, in public (in his articles in *Przedświt*) Pilsudski continued to berate the Jewish group even at that time. "It is extremely difficult," he wrote in 1894,

> to break with old habits, and our Jewish comrades, instead of drawing . . . spiritual nourishment from our [Polish] publications, therefore continue to draw on Russian revolutionary productions from the 90s, 80s and even the 70s . . . Still more remarkable is the fact that even Yiddish publications have been ill-received by some of them who – seeing in the use of Yiddish a turn toward a "national" standpoint – fear to leave the boundaries of messianic Russian [ideology]. And this is so despite the fact that – talking only of

socialist literature – the quantity available in Yiddish now equals, or surpasses, what there is in Russian.[119]

However, in private he reported in a different vein. He was particularly pleased by the fact that relations between the Vilna Social Democrats and the group of Rosa Luxemburg and Yogikhes had perceptibly cooled. In one letter he noted triumphantly that the Vilna group had even stopped its subscription to *Sprawa Robotnicza*, the journal published in Zurich by Luxemburg and Yogikhes[120] (who in 1894 had founded the Social Democratic Party of the Kingdom of Poland in direct opposition to the PPS). "A propos the Jews," he wrote on 9, July 1895,

> they have made enormous progress since Menia [Mendelson] talked with them . . . Some of them sometimes come out with "our ideas" so much that I wonder what is causing it. In any case, they permit themselves to be influenced strongly – in particular, the younger members, who refrain from actual unification with us often only because of the authority of the veterans who are too ultra-Social Democratic, although they too have become a good bit softer.[121]

Pilsudski here was probably overstating his case, too. The truth is that the Vilna Social Democrats were seeking through their "new program" to develop their own autonomous course. Against Yogikhes and the worker opposition, they had driven through the substitution of Yiddish for Russian as the official language of their movement, and here, momentarily at least, they could cooperate with Pilsudski. But there is no evidence to suggest that they sympathized with the political program of the PPS. On the contrary, they clearly continued to think in terms of a coordinated attempt led by Russian revolutionaries to overthrow tsarism, and they were critical of the priority given by the PPS to the fight for an independent Polish state. Here they were in sympathy with Yogikhes, Luxemburg, and their SDKP. Pilsudski no doubt was referring to this aspect of their thinking when he condemned their "ultra-Social Democratic" tendencies. The truth is that the "new program" adopted in 1893 was too Jewish to satisfy Yogikhes and too oriented toward the Russian revolutionary idea to appease Pilsudski.

Arkadii Kremer, the Russian movement, and the creation of the Bund, 1895–1897

On the face of it, the Vilna Social Democrats could have been expected, at least as early as 1895, to proclaim their movement officially the organization of the Jewish proletariat in the Russian Empire. By 1895, after all, they had defined an ideology, overcome the workers' opposition, and established close links with the fraternal organizations in Minsk, Kovno, and other cities of the northwest. They had a far more concrete achievement to their name than had Yogikhes and Rosa Luxemburg, for instance, when they decided to found the SDKP in 1893.

A joint conference of representatives from the Jewish Social Democratic group in Vilna and Minsk was held in June 1895. It decided in principle on the necessity to issue a Yiddish paper for all the organizations of the northwest region.[122] Frants Kursky even described it as "a kind of congress in miniature."[123] But the fact remains that another two years were to pass before the Bund was formally established.

The reasons for this delay are clear enough. The "new program" had been worked out by a very small group. Its best-known statement of principle, *On Agitation*, had studiously avoided all mention of the national issue. Despite the years of conflict with the worker opposition, not even the leadership group had yet developed a clear sense of its separate and cohesive identity. The first history of the movement, published in 1900, noted that even among its own members in 1895 there was "still a large section who doubted whether a separate organization was necessary."[124]

Thus, the exodus of activists to Russian-speaking areas was by no means brought to a halt by the ideological metamorphosis. In October 1895 Martov returned to St. Petersburg. At the same time Iudin (Aizenshtat) (never an enthusiast of the national orientation) moved to Odessa, reportedly because he was dissatisfied with the "small number of workers in Vilna."[125] M. Dushkan and M. Frankfurt settled in Ekaterinoslav. Dushkan was later joined there by A. M. Ginzburg and I. Vilensky from Vitebsk, and together, in 1899, they helped establish and run the underground paper, *Iuzhny rabochii.* A. Litvak was also active for some years in Ekaterinoslav.[126] In 1900 Zeldov (Nemansky) went to St. Petersburg, where he worked on the press of *Rabochaia mysl,* and in 1901–2 Leon Goldman was in charge of the clandestine press of *Iskra* established in Kishinev. Thus, there is much truth in Allan Wildman's judgment that "until the founding of the Bund in 1897 there was no fixed demarcation between the two movements [the Russian and the Jewish]: the Jewish Social Democrats worked simultaneously in both without the slightest conflict in loyalty [and] even after the founding of the Bund there was much moving back and forth."[127] Taken alone, this interpretation is overdrawn, but it does illuminate the other side of what was becoming a two-headed coin. For those who left the northwest in order to work in St. Petersburg, Ekaterinoslav, or Odessa, the central element in the Vilna program was seen not as the national concept (advanced by Gozhansky and by Martov) but the tactic of economic agitation (formulated in Kremer's brochure); not the particular but the universal.

The practical steps taken to make Yiddish the primary language of the labor movement did gradually contribute to the creation of a group identity, did reinforce at a day-to-day level what had initially been an abstract ideological decision. It was not just that the leaders, however uncertain their grasp of the language, now forced themselves to use Yiddish in their contacts with the workers. (Litvak later recalled Kremer's difficulties lecturing in the new language: "He tried to speak Yiddish 'as the people speak it,' but he thought that meant to scatter swear-words and curses through his speech.")[128]

More important was the fact that the shift in language brought the *polu-intelligentsiia* into key positions in the emergent movement. In the mid-1870s Aron Liberman had urged that the *eksterny,* run-away yeshiva students, the youth educated in the heder rather than in the Russian schools and universities, were potentially a major source of revolutionary manpower and leadership. Now this idea could become reality. From the first, men like Litvak, Max Tobiash, and Zeldov (Nemansky) – all *polu-intelligenty* – played a central role in the field of publication in Yiddish. From 1895, the Jargon Committee commissioned and supervised the production, legal and illegal, of popular literature in Yiddish – fiction, science, politics – and this Committee at once became a rallying point for the *polu-intelligentsiia*. Thus, Avrom Amsterdam and Khatskel Usyshkin, who arrived from Vitebsk in 1896, made it their main sphere of activity. Both had been Palestinophiles in earlier years, both were steeped in modern Hebrew and Yiddish literature, and it was natural for them to see the function of the Jargon Committee as an end in itself, a symbol of Jewish populism (*narodnost*). "When he was a Hovev Zion," Litvak wrote of Usyshkin,

> he decided to walk to Palestine. In order to prepare for the long journey he used at one time to walk from Vitebsk to the nearby shtetls and he carried this so far that he could walk 40 versts a day . . . In Vilna he became a member of the Jargon Committee and took it upon himself to distribute the new books in an old way. He became a peddler and . . . used to go around the shtetls near Vilna with a basket of books. His work caught the imagination of the student youth and the "book peddler" became a kind of legend.[129]

In the long run, the Yiddish language would become the symbol of the separate identity of the movement. But this was a gradual process; not until shortly before World War I would Yiddish replace Russian as the main language used, for instance, at Bundist conferences. In 1895, this development was still at an embryonic stage. Again, the *polu-intelligentsiia* was still just emerging onto the historical stage. The *polu-intelligenty* had little real power in the movement at that time, and, as Lesin pointed out, even as late as 1906 they had not gained full equality with the intelligentsia, the dominant political stratum in the Bund. (It was in the Palestinian immigration of 1904–14 that the *polu-intelligentsiia* really came into its own.)

Men like Litvak, Amsterdam, and Khatskel Usyshkin were thus unable to bring pressure to bear on the leadership. On the contrary, Litvak (as he made clear in his memoirs) deeply resented the fact that in the Jargon Committee he and those who shared his outlook were kept very much in their place. The dominant administrative position in the Jargon Committee was held by Pavel Rozental (An-man), an *intelligent* who would never reveal much sympathy for the national element in the emergent movement. Rozental and other *intelligenty* in the Jargon Committee, Litvak wrote, "regarded the new Yiddish literature merely as a means for agitation; they did not ascribe it any value in itself . . . The propagandized workers regarded Yiddish in the same way."[130] For the *polu-intelligentsiia* "soaked in Jewishness, the names of Peretz and Pinsky were holy."[131] But the Jargon Committee as a body took a very different position; and Litvak even hints that it was established at least partly as an attempt, if not to censor, then at least to keep some control over the new Yiddish writers and literature. "The pioneers of the Bund" he suggested, "saw it as necessary to take the entire matter into their own hands, because, in the last resort, they did not regard Peretz as entirely one of their own. His socialism was for them not sufficiently clear, too belletristic."[132] Divided from within, the Jargon Committee did not flourish, and in 1898 it transferred its functions in large part to a group of radical Jewish émigrés in Berlin, the Tsayt-gayst society.[133]

A leader of a type different from Arkadii Kremer might have decided that, despite internal dissension and doubts, the time had come for the Jewish Social Democratic movement in the northwest to unite formally and declare itself an autonomous political organization. But Kremer saw things differently. He had a profound belief in the power of economically determined and organic processes of growth, in the power of socio-historical law. He preferred to let the movement, of which he was the acknowledged leader, develop as an informal association bound together by common interests and mutual dependence rather than by a formal party framework. He was, after all, the man who first formulated what would come to be known as "the theory of stages" (according to which the mass movement develops at its own speed from economic to political militancy).

Kremer evidently felt that two preconditions were necessary before the Jewish Social Democrats in the Pale declared themselves a political entity. First, the agitation movement had to mature until it embraced large strata of the proletariat in the Jewish Pale. To further this end, some of the leaders of the Vilna group moved to other cities with the deliberate intention of organizing the Jewish proletariat. Thus, in 1895 Gozhansky transferred to Belostok, Noyakh Portnoi to Grodno, and Mill to Warsaw.[134] Accompanied or followed by other veterans of the Vilna movement, they were able to gain a foothold among the workers in those cities with remarkable speed. The methods well tested in Vilna—the distribution of leaflets in Yiddish summarizing concrete economic grievances, the foundation of strike funds, strikes—had a powerful impact elsewhere just because of their novelty. The existence in cities such as Warsaw and Belostok of large groups of workers who had migrated from Lithuania facilitated this process. Outsiders, speaking a different Yiddish dialect, possessed of their own (non-Chassidic) traditions and outlook, the Litvakes were more readily recruited than the local *Polyakn* by the Vilna Social Democrats.[135] In deciding to move to industrial centers with a large Yiddish-speaking working class, Mill and presumably Gozhansky were acting in accord with the logic of the new program of 1893 (as formulated by Gozhansky). Here was the other side of the coin.

Second, Kremer was determined that the Jewish movement should not advance in isolation from or too far ahead of the Russian movement. Whether he actually encouraged Martov to return to St. Petersburg or Dushkan and Frankfurt to move to southern Russia is not known, but it would not have been inconsistent with his general position. Alone, the Jewish movement could not act as a powerful political force. As an autonomous unit in an all-Russian party it could serve both the particular and the general interest to the maximal degree. In that sense, his *On Agitation*, with its extrapolation of a general law from the specific and the local, reflected his political philosophy exactly.

The Vilna Social Democratic group, with Kremer to the fore, sought to aid the Russian movement in a wide variety of ways. Throughout the mid and late 1890s, Vilna was a major center for the transportation and further distribution to the interior of illegal literature from abroad. Timofei Kopelzon moved to Berlin in 1897 and together with Bukhgolts coordinated this complex organization. In fact, he acted as the agent both of the Union of Russian Social Democrats Abroad (established in Switzerland in 1895 under the leadership of Plekhanov, Akselrod, and Zasulich) and of the Vilna movement. Kopelzon and Kremer met frequently with the leaders in Kiev, Petersburg, and Moscow in the years 1895–7 to discuss common interests and to plan the foundation of a united Social Democratic Party.[136]

Again, the Vilna group constantly sought to advance the cause of economic agitation among the Russian workers. Thus, in February 1895 Kopelzon participated in a conference held in St. Petersburg with Lenin, G. Krzhizhanovsky, Sponti (Nikitin), and Ia. Liakhovsky to discuss ways of increasing the publication of popular and agitational literature in Russian. According to Sponti, the initiative came from the Vilna group.[137] This meeting triggered off a series of deputations from the movement in Russia to the Group for the Liberation of Labor in Switzerland. Sponti and Lenin went in 1895, and they were followed during the next two years by Kremer, Takhtarev, and Mill. In response to their requests – in particular to Lenin's – the Group undertook to publish a journal and a news chronicle (*Rabotnik* and *Listok rabotnika*) for the movement in Russia. It likewise agreed to bring out Kremer's *On Agitation* under its aegis. Finally, it decided to set up the Union of Russian Social Democrats Abroad as a framework in which selected members of the revolutionary youth resident in the West could help in the publication and transportation of illegal literature.[138]

In 1896, the Jewish Social Democratic committees in Vilna, Minsk, Smorgon, and Warsaw sent their mandates for the London congress of the Second International to the Group for the Liberation of Labor. In turn, Plekhanov's Group in its report to the congress noted that the Jewish proletariat could "in some respects be considered the avant-garde of the workers' army in Russia."[139]

As long as the Vilna movement was able to grow unhindered and in organic fashion, Kremer would doubtless have preferred to maintain its informal character. True, Kossovsky, who (with Mutnik and Kremer) was a member of the central troika of the Vilna group in the years 1895–8, criticized this cautious policy. As editor of the *Der yidisher arbeter* (prepared for publication in Vilna but printed abroad), Kossovsky had the chance to express his own view. The editorial in the first issue of the paper, which came out late in 1896, argued that the enormous demand for socialist literature in Yiddish demonstrated the need for a single organization of the Jewish proletariat. "The time is already drawing near," it concluded, "when the individual groups of the Jewish proletariat – which now fight separately – will unite in one labor socialist organization . . . We hope that our organization will be the beginning of such a unification."[140]

But Kossovksy, however consistent and outspoken as an ideologist, lacked the political authority of Kremer. In his recollections of the period, he did not attempt to hide his reservations about Kremer's leadership. "By nature," he wrote, "[Kremer] was a little despotic and could not tolerate – or could little tolerate – one's opposing him . . . [However] Arkadii was by no means of a decisive nature. He wished to weigh every question from different angles and the more he considered it the more aspects he discovered, and so it was hard for him to decide."[141] Kossovsky's two natural allies on the nationality issues, Gozhansky and Mill, had both left Vilna in 1895, and alone he could not persuade Kremer that the time had come for the movement to proclaim itself a political entity. Only in mid-1897 did Kremer – under heavy pressure from two different sources – decide to speed up the pace of events, to take decisive action.

On the one hand, Kremer found himself in sharp disagreement with Plekhanov when he met him in May 1897. Despite the outward show of solidarity displayed in 1896, this clash had deep roots. It was partly psychological. Contemporary correspondence and memoirs reveal that the veteran émigrés, and their young confederate Ulianov, resented the fact that a provincial and non-Russian group had attained such a key position in the emergent Social Democratic camp.

Thus, in a letter of November 1895 Lenin reported to Akselrod that during a recent visit to Vilna he had been promised support for their proposed new journal, *Rabotnik*. But, he added, "in general their attitude was one of suspicion. (I remembered what you had to say about Pal[estinian] provincialism) – all right, [they said] we shall wait and see whether it is in accord with the tactics of agitational, economic, struggle. I emphasized, before all else, that this depends on us."[142] Again, in 1896 Vera Zasulich wrote to Plekhanov that while at an earlier stage she had "considered the [popular] publication work here to be of tremendous significance, now I think it is of none. For Peter[sburg] it has no interest and Vilna does not interest me."[143] In another letter of that year, this one to Lev Deich, Zasulich explained there was a cultural barrier that divided her from the new stratum of Jewish socialist youth from the Pale of Settlement: "Their level of development is terribly low, although, in the main, they are capable, but they are not acquainted with Russian, or any other, literature. All they have is what they learned in the *gimnaziia*. They often acquire a whole world-outlook from a few books, but it is so narrow, so stereotyped. I find them boring . . ."[144] Thus, from a psychocultural point of view it was not surprising that the meeting between Kremer and Plekhanov in the late spring of 1897 was nothing short of disastrous. In repeating the account of what had happened, Medem saw it specifically as a clash of differing temperaments and backgrounds:

> They met somewhere in a small wood outside the town [Zurich]. Together with Plekhanov was Akselrod and Vera Zasulich . . . Plekhanov, of course, liked good manners and was accustomed to being addressed with great respect. But Aleksandr and good manners were worlds apart. They got into an argument. Plekhanov became excited over some question and said: "I have already told you that it must be so." Aleksandr made one of his ironical gestures . . . and said: "Listen! He said so . . ." Without another word, Plekhanov left with his friends and Aleksandr remained alone . . . From that time on they were not on speaking terms.[145]

The psychological aspect, however, was compounded by an ideological difference (as suggested by Lenin's letter of 1895). Plekhanov and the Group did not accept Kremer's political strategy. In his appendix to *On Agitation*, published in 1897, Akselrod argued that excessive concentration on the conflict between labor and capital was more reminiscent of Bakuninist oversimplification than Marxist dialectic; that in semifeudal Russia, property-owning strata were certainly class enemies but were also potential allies in the political war against the Autocracy.[146] This was a blow at a basic doctrine of the Vilna movement, the thesis that the middle class and most specifically the Jewish bourgeoisie had permanently opted out of politics in Russia, leaving the oppositional cause in the hands of the socialists.

Now, when they met, Plekhanov told Kremer bluntly that the Social Democrats in Russia could not afford to remain a loose coalition of committees, that they had to unite in one ideologically defined organization. "The founder of Russian Marxism," Kremer recalled, "put a hard question to me: 'How can we represent you [at congresses abroad] when you are not united among yourselves? Formally, there is as yet nobody to represent.' . . . This question made a deep impression on me . . . And when I returned to Vilna at the end of August I spoke to my close comrades about it."[147]

In his reminiscences, Kremer nowhere mentions the failure of his talks with the Group for the Liberation of the Labor nor the clash with Plekhanov. But, in his account of events, Akimov did so. According to him, Kremer was not alone but together with Takhtarev (of the St. Petersburg organization) when he met the Group on the Zürichberg. The two representatives of the movement in Russia "expounded their plans and insisted with particular vigor that if unification were achieved the Union Abroad should not interfere with the internal affairs of the organization in Russia."[148] This, Akimov suggested, was how the dispute began.

Seen in this light, Kremer's decision finally to create the Bund (as it would soon become) has to be explained not so much as a positive response to a request from Plekhanov as an attempt to forestall possible attacks from the Group abroad (perhaps in alliance with potential allies inside Russia). The Vilna group knew that the Kiev committee under the leadership of B. L. Eidelman and N. A. Vigdorchik had been pressing for the creation of a united Russian Social Democratic party since 1896.[149] Hitherto, Kremer had preferred to put off positive action, but the clash with the Group for the Liberation of Labor must have brought home to him the dangers of further delay. The Jewish committees could now find themselves disunited and isolated in the face of a coalition of hostile forces.

At the founding congress itself, as reported in *Arbeter shtime*, Kremer hinted that this was a real consideration: "The point is drawing near for the creation of a general Russian workers' party. The Jewish proletariat will no doubt occupy a significant place in that party. But divided into separate, independent groups, it could not join such a party."[150] John Mill wrote in his memoirs that Kremer (who stopped in Warsaw on his return from Switzerland at the end of the summer) had employed this argument in their consultations: "The fear that our organizations would come disunited – with separate plans, without a general program – to the foundation [congress] of the Russian party had forced Arkadii to rethink the question and to conclude that it was especially important to call our own congress first."[151] Thus, immediately on his arrival in Russia, Kremer promised to make urgent preparations for the meeting of the foundation congress and he was as good as his word: The delegates were instructed to come to Vilna in the last week of September 1897.

However, according to Mill's account, even at the very last moment Kremer was not only hesitating but actually decided on the eve of the congress to cancel it. (He was afraid that police surveillance had become too effective in the recent period.) At this juncture only Mill's intervention saved the day. He apparently refused to lead his three-man delegation back to Warsaw empty-handed, and Kremer finally agreed to let the congress meet. On this occasion, as in 1893, the influence of the Polish issue was of great, even crucial, importance.

Mill recalled that he had been urging Kremer to found a united party of the Jewish proletariat for years, and this claim is certainly in accord with everything we know about his political ideology. The very choice of Warsaw as his field of action in 1895 was indicative of his single-minded determination to prove that the Jewish proletariat throughout the empire had to be seen as a single political entity. His decision to assign the Warsaw mandate for the London congress of the International to Plekhanov's Group rather than to the PPS or the SDKP was in itself a provocative declaration of independence from both the local parties. He was delib-

Figure 11. The site of the founding Congress of the Bund, Vilna, 1897.

erately entering the lion's den challenging the SDKP and, still more, the PPS on their home territory. His was undoubtedly the boldest attempt to carry the national aspect in the Vilna program to its logical conclusion.

In 1896 he succeeded in drawing the Yiddish-speaking workers' group led by Anastazy Rug away from the PPS (to which it had hitherto been exclusively linked) and into a new organization, the Jewish Labor Union in Poland. In a contemporary article, Mill explained that the language barrier alone was enough to prevent "the representatives of the Polish labor movement [the PPS] from doing anything among the Jewish workers even if they wanted."[152] In reality, the PPS not only imported *Der arbeter* from Lemberg but even commissioned Yiddish literature from prominent Russian-Jewish socialists in New York, most notably from the veteran revolutionary B. Feigenbaum.[153] When, early in 1897, Mill gave his new partners, the Rug group, an ultimatum – to recognize that the struggle for political freedom and equal civil rights had greater priority than the issue of Polish independence – they decided to return to the PPS. The "Litvak organization" now pointedly took as its new name the Jewish Social Democratic Labor Union in Warsaw.[154]

The failure to consolidate their early gains threw Mill and his group of Vilna comrades (Tsivye Gurevich, Mariia Zhaludskaia, and Leon Goldman) onto the defensive. In a letter of July 1897 Pilsudski could announce triumphantly to his comrades abroad that "the union of Lithuanian and Warsaw Jews has totally collapsed ... Now we hope we can undertake really serious Jewish work."[155] It was this development that made the creation of a Jewish proletarian union of such vital and urgent importance to the Vilna Social Democrats in Warsaw. In order to compete with the PPS, Mill argued at his meeting with Kremer, "the power and authority of a Jewish socialist *party* [was] essential – a party likewise well centralized and disciplined and also strong in the clarity of its goals, its program."[156] Already severely shaken by his encounter with Plekhanov, Kremer was ready in the autumn of 1897 to yield to this pressure.

When the congress met on 25 September, its composition bore clear witness to its origins: Of the thirteen delegates, six were from Vilna and three from Warsaw. (Of the others one, Pavel Berman, was from Minsk; two were from Belostok; and one, Noyakh Abramov, was counted as a delegate from Vitebsk but was actually then living in Vilna.) With only one or two exceptions, all the delegates were either then resident in Vilna or had originally been members of the Vilna group.[157]

The divergent attitudes of Mill and Kremer again made themselves felt during the congress itself (which lasted three days and was held in a small attic room in a worker's house). For his part, Mill proposed that the new organization be called the Union of Jewish Social Democratic Groups in Russia, while Kremer suggested the name, the General Jewish Labor Union in Russia. The Warsaw delegation was anxious to stress the political and ideologically committed nature of the new union. Kremer, on the other hand, remained true to his philosophy of organic development from below. "A Social Democratic group," so his views were summarized,

> is only a handful of people who adhere to Social Democratic principles and are the leaders of the labor movement of one town or another, of one region or another. A union of such groups would be a union of the "summits." . . . There would be no room in it for all the laboring masses and this would be deplorable, for the Union [Bund] will only become strong when all the working masses in the struggle join it.[158]

Kremer's opinion predictably prevailed, although at the suggestion of the Warsaw delegation, it was decided to add "Poland" to the name. The title as it finally came out – the General Jewish Labor Union in Russia and Poland – left no doubt that its goal was to organize the Yiddish-speaking proletariat throughout the western regions of the Empire, specifically including the strongholds of the PPS. The congress further defined its ideological standpoint by officially declaring itself in favor of unification with the Union of Russian Social Democrats Abroad (then still under the control of Plekhanov's Group).[159]

In the months following the foundation of the Bund, events unfolded as anticipated by Kremer. By acting swiftly in September 1897, he had gained the initiative, had implicitly refuted the accusations that the Jewish movement was insufficiently "political" (and too "economic"), and had insured it a key role in the long-expected creation of a general, or Russian, party. Thus, the *Listok rabotnika*, edited by Vera Zasulich, as well as *Vorwärts* (the organ of the German Social Democratic Party), both hastened to greet the new organization and to express the hope that its establishment was "the first step . . . to the creation of a general Russian labour party."[160] *Rabochaia gazeta,* the authoritative paper published by the Social Democratic committee in Kiev, also published a friendly report on the foundation of the Bund in which it was noted that "together with general political demands [it] lays a special stress on the *demand for equal civil rights for the Jews.*"[161]

The founding congress of the Russian party met in Minsk on 1 March 1898. It owed its existence to the joint initiative of the Bund and the Kiev committee, and six of the nine delegates came from those two organizations (Kremer, Mutnik, and Taras [Kats] from the Vilna group; Eidelman, Tuchapsky, and Vigdorchik from Kiev). St. Petersburg was represented by S. Radchenko, a veteran confederate of Lenin, renowned for his strict Marxist orthodoxy and his penchant for a political (as against an "economic") orientation. His presence symbolized the conscious effort made by the initiating groups to stress that their goal was the direct struggle for political freedom and the end of the Autocracy. (Like the Bund the new party declared itself at one with Plekhanov's organization, the Union of Russian Social Democrats Abroad.)

For the leadership of the Bund, the First Congress of the Russian party represented the realization of their "new program" of 1893, of their most cherished ambition: the integration of a Jewish revolutionary movement with its autonomy preserved and respected, into a general, international, framework. It was also a personal triumph for Arkadii Kremer, who had worked day in and day out for eight years in anticipation of that moment, restraining but not stifling his more ebullient comrades. Twenty years after Aron Liberman's arrest in Vienna, his dream had become a reality.

Reflected in the provisional constitution adopted by the congress was a clear preference for the concept of a loose association rather than a tightly knit, centralized organization. "The General Jewish Labor Union in Russia and Poland," it resolved, "enters the party as an autonomous organization, independent only in questions which specifically concern the Jewish proletariat."[162] Another clause stated that "local committees execute the directions of the central committee in the way which they find most suited to local conditions. Under exceptional circumstances the committees have the right to refuse to carry out the demands of the central committee."[163]

Moreover, in naming the new party, the congress adopted the Bundist proposal to use the term *Rossiiskaia* with its purely territorial connotations – "within the Russian Empire" – rather than *Russkaia,* which had a definite ethnic, Great Russian, implication. Kremer's very characteristic proposal to include the word "labor" in the title was rejected at the congress, but here, too, his view soon prevailed. As one of the two members of the newly elected central committee who survived the mass arrests immediately following the congress (Radchenko was the other), he had this decision revised, and the first publications of the new organization in April therefore carried the name The Russian Social Democratic Labor Party (RSDRP).[164]

In the wake of the congress, *Arbeter shtime* published an article, "Our Goals," which summarized the Bundist ideology as it had crystallized over the previous five years. Bearing the clear stamp of Kossovsky's style and line of thought, it caught the note of self-confidence characteristic of that moment. The Jewish people, and the proletariat as a section of that nation, had its own interests to defend. "And only a special Jewish organization can undertake to defend those Jewish interests – an organization which is completely free to act as it sees right." Of course, in those spheres which were unaffected by "religion or nationality, the Jewish Bund is a section of the party and is bound to follow the central committee." The Bund claimed no special privileges but only the rights within the party that logically belonged "to every labor organization which defends the special interests of the workers of an entire nation."[165]

The government sought to inflame "the hatred of the Christian population – both of the middle class and the workers – against the Jews." In order to perpetuate its power, in order to divide and rule, it made the Jews into a scapegoat, encouraged pogroms, assigned scarce jobs on an ethnic and therefore inflammatory basis. Thus, the proletariat as a whole, regardless of nationality, had "an interest in doing away with the civil inequality imposed on the Jews." But – and here was the crucial question – "does the party have the strength to undertake this [task] unless it can rely on a special organization of the Jewish proletariat? There can be only one answer to that question – no, it does not have the strength ... [it] cannot give the necessary attention to the special interests of the workers in the oppressed nationalities."[166] The party, with its own grandiose tasks, could not assign "the money and men"[167] needed for large-scale work among the subject nationalities. Thus, the conclusion was absolutely firm – the party was rightly and logically being formed as a voluntary and loosely knit union of separate constituents including, first and foremost, national proletarian organizations.

Emboldened by the fact that he could now write in the name of the Bund and the RSDRP, Kossovsky here and in a separate brochure struck back at the PPS, which not unexpectedly had launched a sharp attack on the new Jewish organization. In the press and at the Fourth Congress of the PPS (held in November 1897), the Bund was accused of "renouncing solidarity with the Polish and Lithuanian working class in its struggle for liberation from tsarist occupation" and, through its emphasis on the issue of equal rights for all Jews, of having adopted a nationalist position.[168]

In fact, Kossovsky replied, the demand for an end to discrimination was "purely proletarian"[169] because the proletariat suffered from it the most and because only the proletariat was willing to fight actively against it. (Here was the familiar thesis first advanced by Gozhansky.) But the real issue was different. "What," he asked the PPS, "did you do all this time for the Jewish workers? ... You were occupied with unsavory vituperation against the advanced section of the Jewish proletariat declaring that it contributed to the Russification of Lithuania – and this slander you continuously offered to your readers, thus sowing enmity between the Polish, Lithuanian, and Jewish proletariats."[170]

Party schism and Jewish national autonomism, 1898–1903

In the spring of 1898, the founding congress of the RSDRP was seen by the Bundist leadership as the opening of a new era full of hope. But, in retrospect, the year 1898 must be regarded from the point of view of the Bund not as a year of promise but as a fateful moment, foreshadowing later catastrophe.

Instead of party unity came dissension, bitterness, and schism. Instead of being integrated into a broader family, the Bund was forced to take sides in a fratricidal struggle. It had hoped to win a consensus in the party on how to solve the Jewish question; but just the opposite happened and the Jewish question ended up as a major issue of internal party dispute. While the Bund continued to develop its program in a more national direction, the most dynamic group in the RSDRP, the *Iskra* organization, moved toward militant assimilationism. At the Second Congress of the party in 1903, the Bund found itself with no choice but to leave the party it had done so much to found in 1898.

Although it reentered the RSDRP in 1906 with Bolshevik support, later developments served to underline the profound significance of the period 1898–1903 in Bundist history, as indeed in the history of Russia and the world in general. The Bolshevik Revolution, victory, and subsequent policies may or may not have been inevitable – like all such questions, this one has to be asked and can never be satisfactorily answered; but what can hardly be denied is the fact that the Bolsheviks came to power molded and shaped (albeit not as yet tempered in the furnace of civil war) by the prerevolutionary experience. In the Jewish question, there was a clear continuity between the ideological positions marked out by Lenin in the years 1902–3 and 1913–14 (in the latter period, with Stalin's collaboration) and the policy later implemented by the people's commissariat of nationalities (with Stalin as commissar).[171] Thus, the fate of the Bund and of the Jews in Soviet Russia was, if not actually decided, then at least, and to a large extent, foreshadowed in the years 1898–1903.

Between Plekhanov and Zhitlovsky, 1898–1901: toward the Belostok congress

A number of strands, ideological and organizational, which were originally not (or little) connected, finally merged in the years 1901–3 to make the status of the Bund and the Jewish question in general central issues of dispute in the RSDRP. First, the coalition formally established by the congress of the RSDRP in March 1898 began, like a mere pack of cards, to fall apart almost instantly. From April 1898, the Union of Russian Social Democrats Abroad became the scene of a violent clash of personalities that soon developed into a clash of principles. At one level all that was involved was a quarrel that erupted between S. N. Prokopovich and Plekhanov when, in April 1898, the former decided to draw up a critique of the program adopted by the Group for the Liberation of Labor in 1885. Plekhanov was deeply offended by Prokopovich's accusation that the Group was utopian in its expectation of the early overthrow of the tsarist Autocracy and irresponsible in its attempts to accelerate the transformation of the infant labor movement into an openly insurrectionary force.

An essentially private dispute was transformed into a public issue by Plekhanov's demand that Prokopovich be expelled from or somehow eased out of the Union.[172] And here the Bund became entangled in the conflict. Timofei Kopelzon (Grishin), who had come to play a key role in the Union since his arrival in Berlin in 1897, insisted that the demand for doctrinal homogeneity should not be enforced with excessive rigidity, lest the emergent Marxist party be reduced to a mere sect. "Who," asked Kopelzon in a letter of mid-1898, "is not guilty of exaggeration and theoretical excesses? This nonetheless does not prevent one from working together or from valuing a man as active and sincere."[173] Again, at the congress of the Union held in November 1898, he pleaded "that there can be disagreements among the [Russian] Social Democrats just as there are among the Germans."[174]

In taking this position, Kopelzon was relying on the tradition that had developed in the proto-Bundist movement under the leadership of Kremer. Sharing a common danger, united in one practical undertaking, the Vilna group had throughout been willing to tolerate the most diverse theoretical opinions so long as they did not affect the sphere of day-to-day action. To Plekhanov and Akselrod this lack of ideological uniformity smacked of a dangerous muddle-headedness.

"They, of course," Akselrod wrote to Plekhanov on 10 May 1898,

> do not want to speak of any but "practical" questions. Everything else is "theory," "program." There would be no great harm in this if it were not a

contagion in the Union and did not have a corrupting influence on the minds of our grown infants . . . *Praktika* means the composition and delivery of as great a number of . . . brochures and pamphlets as possible – only, so Koltsov tells me, not those published by the Gr. for the Lib. of Lab. . . . but those, if I may so put it, of a vulgar [*lubochnogo*] type.[175]

From 1898 to 1900, Grishin worked tirelessly to prevent a final schism among the Social Democrats abroad. In mid-1898 he proposed that the unrewarding work of collecting and editing agitational material be handed over to a group of the younger members who would work within the Union, leaving the Group free to concentrate on the theoretical and strategic questions that they considered of vital importance. Even after the veteran trio – Plekhanov, Akselrod, and Zasulich – had resigned demonstratively from all their responsible posts in the Union in November 1898, Grishin (now elected secretary) did not give up. His persistent attempts at reconciliation infuriated the ideologues on both sides, not only Plekhanov but also Kuskova and Prokopovich in 1898 and Akimov in the winter of 1899–1900.

Although he was held in contempt by the veterans, his position as the de facto representative of the Bund gave him a weight which he would otherwise not have had. Thus, Akselrod, in a letter of 1 June 1898 to the Plekhanovs, wrote that "Grishin (a member of the Jewish organization) should not be officially and irrevocably forced out of the Union without tangible and convincing reasons."[176] It was not just that the veterans placed high hopes on the new RSDRP and hence feared to antagonize the Bund as one of its central components. There was also on the part of Zasulich and Akselrod a feeling of guilt that they had failed to produce enough popular material for the labor movement in Russia during the years 1895–8 and that the younger generation (who took over the Union in November 1898 and brought out the journal *Rabochee delo*) was much more effective. ("In the last years," Akselrod wrote in one letter, "we have treated our functions more than listlessly for reasons beyond our control.")[177]

Iurii Steklov, who came abroad in this period directly from Siberian exile and was a committed supporter of Plekhanov, found himself unpleasantly surprised to discover that the veteran troika was antagonizing the entire new generation of revolutionaries, including the Bundists. "The misfortune," he recalled in his memoirs,

> was that the people who joined the Rabochedeltsy were from a practical point of view more serious than the so-called Plekhanovites . . . Among the latter were people such as Koltsov . . . who had long since left Russia and had no connections with the new movement . . . or else really young students. The Rabochedeltsy were people who had . . . gone through a practical school, full of energy, not divorced from Russia, traveling back and forth . . . Particularly valuable for them was the help of the Bund which "held open the frontier"; through whose hands passed the major transportation of illegal literature; through whom correspondence was conducted, connections with Russia maintained.[178]

However, there was still another factor which did not permit the Group to dismiss Grishin out of hand. An important – perhaps the most important – source of funds for the émigré Social Democrats had been the Russian-Jewish socialist community in New York. In 1897 *Rabotnik,* in an editorial note and in response to a message of support sent by the United Hebrew Trades to the great textile workers' strike in St. Petersburg, published a rare acknowledgement of this crucial aid:

> It is now more than ten years that almost annually they [in New York] have been giving hundreds of roubles for the publication of Social Democratic material meant for propaganda among the Russian [*russkikh*] workers . . . We are convinced that the revolutionary proletariat in Russia will remember with gratitude the sympathy and help given its liberation movement by the Russian-Jewish proletarians [in America].[179]

For the Group to precipitate an open and official schism in the movement was bound to endanger this steady flow of financial support, and this would be doubly true if the Bund were driven irreconcilably into the hostile camp. While the Group had a faithful ally among the New York socialists – Dr. Ingerman – the Bund could naturally count on enormous reserves of good will on the Lower East Side, and this was an intimidating thought for Plekhanov's beleaguered Group.

The result was that for two years, from April 1898 to early 1900, the dispute between the "veterans" and the "youngsters" was kept almost totally hidden from the public eye. This was a limited success for Grishin, who was constantly carrying draft agreements between the two camps in search of a final compromise. But from the correspondence of the Group, it is clear that their frustration was taking the form of deep resentment against Grishin, who had failed to give them unequivocable support, and against the Bund in general. "We have broken with the people here," Vera Zasulich wrote to Lev Deich early in 1899.

> Their main contingent are "patriots" from the Minsk-Vilna fatherland . . . They are now all singing the same song about [the revolution] in hundreds of years . . . and on that basis are trying to exploit absolutely everything in the interest of their own fatherland – that is, Minsk-Vilna . . . Heresies were also involved, but actually the "patriots" are little concerned with ideas only with *praktika.*[180]

In fact, apart from Grishin and John Mill (who arrived abroad in the autumn of 1898), the "youngsters" were not Bundists and by no means all were even of Jewish origin, but Zasulich here was giving vent to her resentment against the power accumulated by the Bund.

When Plekhanov finally decided to cut the Gordian knot, to publish an open attack on the "youngsters," he was essentially gambling on a dangerous but calculated risk. He was appealing over the head of the Social Democrats active in the Russian underground and the "colonies" abroad to the more distant faithful, who were unaware (except in the vaguest terms) of the actual facts. In particular, he had in mind many such as Lenin and Potresov, who had been shut off in prison and penal exile for years on end but would soon be returning to active political life; and Ingerman in New York, who could be expected to defend the Group through thick and thin if only provided with the necessary ammunition.

Money for the movement had reached Akselrod early in 1899 from Ingerman.

Whether it belonged to the Union and should therefore be handed over to Grishin or to the Group had in itself become a matter of bitter dispute. But by using this money to publish an attack on *Rabochee delo*, Plekhanov hoped to guarantee the Group its financial base in the United States. An open split, a public campaign, would permit Ingerman to present the issue in New York as one of orthodoxy against heresy; to depict the "youngsters" not only as "Economists" but as, in effect, members of Eduard Bernstein's revisionist camp.

"Do not forget," Akselrod wrote to Plekhanov in December 1899,

> that our "dear comrades" have been conducting agitation there [in New York]–both behind the scenes and through the Yiddish press–and have sent over their publications in Yiddish from which the New York journals have reprinted what was of use to our enemies. I (that is, we) did not fulfill our promise made in the spring–that is, that with the American money we would publish selected articles against Bernstein . . . In view of the New Year Ball . . . Ingerman–not having a list of our (recent) publications–is, of course, in great difficulties.[181]

However, in February 1900, Plekhanov finally did bring out his assault on the "youngsters," his famous *Vademecum*. In order to prove that there were deviations in the movement Plekhanov in this brochure included a series of private letters and manuscripts written by his opponents, even though for the sake of peace they had deliberately left them unpublished since 1898. Although he did not attack the Bund by name, he used Grishin's letters in order to prove that he had been not unsympathetic to some of Prokopovich's ideas in mid-1898:

> And all these are *comrades!* All these are *Social Democrats!* Is not this anarchy? Is not this chaos? Is not this infamous?[182] . . . The point is not which trend Mr. G. supports but that we have many people who call themselves Social Democrats and have not even learned the alphabet of contemporary socialism. This, too, explains the confusion which at present reigns among us thanks to which one will soon be able to say with truth that where there are two Russian Social Democrats there will certainly be three Social Democratic parties. I must admit that I never thought that I would live through such a disgrace.[183]

In selecting Grishin as a principal target, Plekhanov had taken a fateful step. A personal dispute between Prokopovich and Plekhanov had been transformed into a public conflict involving not only the émigré world but also (through the Bund) the movement in Russia. In April at a congress of the Union Abroad, Plekhanov and his followers formally withdrew from that organization and established their rival Revolutionary Social Democratic Organization.

Until this moment, the Bund had studiously refrained from all mention in its press of the tensions in the Union Abroad, but now *Der yidisher arbeter* (published since 1898 abroad) broke its silence. "People," it noted, "who could be expected . . . to devote all their energy to creating a disciplined and centralized party in Russia . . . have introduced divisions, fights, hatred, war into the ranks of Social Democracy."[184] It then reported an extraordinary incident in New York, where, according to the press in America, Dr. Ingerman had made the mistake of reading aloud at a public meeting a letter from Plekhanov and Akselrod "in which they begged for help in their struggle with the 'Minsk and Vilna *yidlekh*' who had introduced warfare and dissent into the Russian Union [Abroad]."[185] The truth, *Der yidisher arbeter* concluded, was just the opposite. The Bundists had been the first in the Union "to come out for peace, unity, discipline and centralization."[186]

Looked at in historical perspective, the outbreak of open hostility between Plekhanov's Group and the Bund can be seen to have had deep roots. After all, Grishin's fate had been foreshadowed by the dispute between Plekhanov and Kremer in May 1897. Kremer had then acted as Plekhanov urged. But this was not the essential issue. The basic point was that while in the Bund *teoriia* was prized, if anything, less than *praktika,* the veteran troika abroad held a scale of values exactly the reverse. They were deeply convinced that their superior intellectual sweep and their greater knowledge of Marxism and European politics of necessity gave them the right to lead. Between a movement which acted as a fraternity of partisans and a small elitist group who saw themselves as the chiefs-of-staff of a disciplined revolutionary army (albeit as yet unformed), there could be no easy peace.

In the late 1890s two leading Bundists were involved in the émigré politics of the Russian "colonies" in western Europe: Grishin and John Mill. Both had been active in the Vilna movement since the 1880s and now (in December 1898) together they formed the Committee of the Bund Abroad. Grishin's political philosophy typified the internationalist school of Bundist thought, while Mill throughout had supported the quest for a more nationalist theory. Ironically, it was Grishin who, in his unflagging quest for unity in the Russian Social Democratic movement, hopelessly and permanently antagonized Plekhanov. In contrast, John Mill's extraordinary efforts to provide the Bund with a far more nationalist program went unnoticed in the years 1898–1900 by the Group for the Liberation of Labor. The internationalist became the object of Plekhanov's terrible wrath, not the nationalist.

However, it was the dispute within the Union Abroad that provided Mill with the freedom he sought to press for a revision of the Bund's attitude to the Jewish question. His viewpoint was not accepted by the Group, by Grishin, or the Rabochedeltsy – the contrary was true – but they simply had no time or energy left to pay it attention. Moreover, to all intents and purposes, Mill was also totally free of restraint from the movement in Russia because in July 1898 the Bundist leadership group had been decimated by arrests, and among those caught in the net were both Kremer and Kossovsky. The central committee in the autumn of 1898 was reduced to one man, Dovid Kats (Taras), who was junior to Mill in revolutionary experience and inferior to him in ideological expertise.

There was probably no more startling publication in the history of the Bundist (and proto-Bundist) movement than *Der yidisher arbeter*, no. 6, which was dated March 1899, and was the first to be edited by John Mill after he came to the West. Most astonishing of all, perhaps, was Mill's decision to include the two articles signed by Ben Ehud. This was the pseudonym of no less a person than Chaim Zhitlovsky, not merely a self-avowed apostle of revolutionary populism but a man who had long achieved fame in the Russian "colonies" as a bitter and caustic opponent of Plekhanov. (Their public debates on Marxism and populism had been

Figure 12. John Mill, 1870–1952.

known to go on night after night for weeks on end.) The mere fact of his publication in a Bundist journal was in itself a sensational indication of Mill's determination to follow a boldly open-minded and exploratory editorial policy.

Zhitlovsky's role in the development of Jewish socialism will be described at length in the next chapter, and it will suffice here to give the barest summary of his ideas. In 1892, with his brochure *A Jew to the Jews,* he had gained the reputation of being the most passionate advocate in the Russian revolutionary movement of the view that a socialist of Jewish origin had no right to ignore the plight of his own people (or, at least, of the poverty-stricken majority within it). And now, in *Der yidisher arbeter,* no. 6, he argued that the Yiddish-speaking *folk* had its own national culture; that socialists should work to develop this folk culture into a full-fledged modern civilization; that they should think in terms of a network of Yiddish-speaking and secular schools and universities in Europe, the United States, and wherever else the east European Jews were concentrated; and that, as an immediate step, they ought to demonstrate their concern for the Jewish masses on a worldwide scale by establishing an International Jewish Labor Secretariat. This thorough-going commitment to the development of modern Jewish nationhood — world-wide in scope, socialist and secular in content, Yiddish-speaking in form — was completely without precedent in the revolutionary camp.

For years, Mill had been vainly urging Kremer to establish a Jewish party, both socialist and national, and now he clearly could not resist the sudden opportunity he had to publicize freely his own and closely related philosophies. True, he added an editorial note expressing reservations about the most controversial section of Zhitlovsky's article, which, he wrote,

> *expresses not our opinion but that of the author.* We stand firmly for the principle that all nations — including the Jewish — must have equal political, economic, and national rights. We even fight for that. But whether the Jewish folk language, the Jargon, will develop into a cultural language; whether . . . a special Jewish literature and science . . . , Jewish *gimnazii,* universities and other schools [will develop]; whether it is necessary to link the Jewish workers in different countries . . . all these are questions which it is as yet hard to answer definitely.[187]

In the context of contemporary Bundist ideology, the most striking aspect of this editorial statement was not that it expressed doubts but that it failed to reject Zhitlovsky's theses out of hand, and still more, that it disingenuously took for granted the necessity to fight for "national rights." This idea — so casually accepted as a fact of life — had hitherto not even been discussed in Bundist literature.

Der yidisher arbeter, no. 6, was given over almost in its entirety to the national and Jewish questions. Apart from Zhitlovsky's piece, there were articles on the Lithuanian Social Democratic Party and its conflict with the PPS; on antisemitism in Galicia; on the tsarist oppression of the Jewish, Armenian, Finnish, and Polish nationalities; and on the new Zionist paper, *Der Jude.* But perhaps the most revealing item in the paper was Mill's critique of the new Yiddish journal put out by the PPS (named like its Galician predecessor, *Der arbeter*). Here Mill set down in bleak terms his reasons for rejecting the argument of the PPS that the Jews could enjoy true liberty and equality not in barbaric and semi-Asiatic Russia (however "constitutional" its form of government in the future) but only in an independent, democratic, and western-oriented Poland. "What," he asked,

> can the Jewish proletariat expect from "the separation of Poland"? Can it expect that persecution against it *as Jews* will cease? Will it really receive

national equality? This is the entire question. Nobody can prove to us that we will really gain national rights. We will be the minority in free Poland and the future Polish regime can persecute us just as much as the present Russian regime. And in . . . [such a] Garden of Eden we may then have to fight for our civil and national rights as we do now.[188]

No less a person than Karl Kautsky, Mill noted, had recently argued in the name of Marxist principles that to divide the Austro-Hungarian Empire into independent national states would solve nothing, for the problem of oppressed minorities would live on in the new states. Indeed, Kautsky suggested, the fate of the Jews and the Ruthenians in an independent Galicia would not be an enviable one. The optimal solution, therefore, was a reorganization of the Hapsburg Empire which would grant each national group autonomy.[189]

In seizing on Kautsky's authority, Mill was clearly moved by a conviction that the Jewish people could hope for full equality only in a truly multinational state; there alone would it be in the self-interest of the powerful nations to encourage cultural pluralism. In such a state, the Jewish people could demand recognition as one national entity among many. "Every nation," Mill concluded, "should have equal rights in everything: to study as it wishes; to publish papers and write in the mother tongue etc. . . . There can be no other national program for the socialists.[190]

In sum, *Der yidisher arbeter*, no. 6, was nothing less than an outright manifesto of the nationalist wing of the Bund. But Mill was not satisfied with this. In the following two numbers of the journal, dated August and December 1899, he continued to hammer away relentlessly at what he saw as the fundamental issues: the danger inherent in the program of the PPS for the fragmentation of the empire (he even published an article by Rosa Luxemburg on this inflammable subject);[191] the fact that some leading Marxist theoreticians in the West (most notably Karl Renner) were moving toward a concept of the multinational state in which the territorial aspect of nationality would become politically irrelevant;[192] his belief that the Bund had to act as the true champion of Jewish national interests. Commenting on the recent pogrom in Nikolaev, he wrote that

> the struggle of the Jewish proletariat against absolutism, against the contemporary capitalist order, is also a struggle against antisemitism . . . When we have a broad, powerful, and independent organization of the Jewish proletariat we will be able to stand up against antisemitism both from the "higher" and "lower" classes.[193]

Above all, he seized on the opportunity – provided by the debate on the national question at the congress of the Austrian Social Democratic Labor Party held in Brünn in September 1899 – to buttress his case. Most congenial to Mill was the resolution introduced at Brünn by the South Slav delegation, which suggested that national self-government be constructed on the basis not only of the territorial unit but also on the nation as a sum total of individuals (a Czech in Vienna or a German in Prague would have the right to participate in the elections to their respective national assemblies). Although this resolution was not adopted, the congress did call for the reconstruction of the empire on the basis of linguistically defined cantons in place of the historically formed crown lands.

Mill chose to interpret the resolution adopted in a highly tendentious if not downright misleading fashion. The congress, he wrote,

> pronounced that nations have equal rights and that the proletariat is interested that national cultures, languages, and literature should develop. Second, it makes a great distinction between the territory and the nation and does not consider that only a people with a territory should be considered a nation and can demand national rights. According to the . . . resolution, the old rule that a nation is its territory has been replaced by another rule – that *a nation is its culture*.[194]

Given this fact, Mill argued, it was clearly anomalous and highly disadvantageous that, as yet, there was still no "autonomous, Jewish Social Democratic organization in Austria." As for the Bund, he concluded, "we must also give an answer to our national question . . . It is high time."[195]

In December 1899, John Mill returned briefly to Russia to attend the Third Congress of the Bund, which was held in Kovno. He went as the delegate of the Bundist committee abroad, secure in the knowledge that *Der yidisher arbeter*, no. 6, had been "enthusiastically received" by the Bundist student groups in Switzerland and Germany.[196] (Lesin had also sent him a letter from New York in praise of the issue, "a veritable love song," as Mill recalled, "a song of praise to the Bund for its effort to find an answer to the Jewish problems and to the Jewish national question.")[197] But he could have had few illusions about the cool reception awaiting him – or, rather, his ideological revisions – at the congress.

Since the arrest of Kremer and Kossovsky, the reconstituted Bundist leadership in Russia had moved in exactly the opposite direction from that taken by Mill and *Der yidisher arbeter*. Dovid Kats (Taras), Leon Goldman, Pavel (Piney) Rozental, and Zeldov (Nemansky), who emerged as the most articulate and powerful spokesmen in the period from mid-1898 to early 1900, all belonged to the "internationalist" wing of the Bund. Thus, at the Second Congress of the Bund held in September 1898 (that is, after the formation of the new central committee under Taras) the majority of the delegates had spoken out in criticism of the "very sharp tone" employed by Kossovsky in his brochure against the PPS.[198] Kremer would later recall that the brochure had been necessitated not only as an answer to the PPS, but "even for our own members themselves, who because of their poorly understood internationalism were in doubt about the very right of Bundism as such to exist."[199]

In mid-1899 Taras had met with Mill in Berlin and had protested sharply against the nationalism of *Der yidisher arbeter*, no. 6. "Our long debate led nowhere," Mill recalled. "We had reached no agreement."[200] At the same time the Warsaw committee of the Bund, now under the leadership of Rakhmiel (Veinshtein), actually decided to insert a note into those copies of the journal which it distributed, declaring that it could agree "neither with the attitude of [Zhitlovsky's] article, 'Zionism or Socialism?' nor with the opinions expressed about the Polish Socialist Party," and therefore disclaimed all responsibility for them.[201]

Given these set positions, it was no surprise that Mill found himself a minority of one at the Kovno congress. He pleaded for the immediate inclusion of a demand for Jewish "national rights" in the program of the Bund.[202] Experience had shown, he pointed out, that equal civil rights could be converted into a sham where a national minority was subject to collective coercion by the majority. Their civil liberties were of little use to the Poles in Posen, for instance, who were forbidden by the German authorities to use Polish at public meetings. "Freedom of assembly," he said, "would be just an empty phrase for the Jewish proletariat [in a constitutional Russia] if the Yiddish language does not enjoy equal rights with the Russian." The realistic view was that, far from being a short-lived organization needed only until the revolution, the Bund would have a major role to play even in a democratic Russia. Therefore, its program had to envisage the measures required to safeguard the basic interests of "the Jewish proletariat in the future, just as every party presents in its program demands which cannot be satisfied at the given moment."[203]

But Mill found no support among the delegates. They sharply attacked his policy as the editor of *Der yidisher arbeter* and to a man declared against any change in the program of the movement. To raise the demand for "national rights" (ran the counter-argument) might well divert "the attention of the proletariat away from its class, and toward its national, interests." The entire proletariat, regardless of nationality, should unite behind the crucial fight for political freedom: "We must not fragment our forces . . . by making national demands."[204] Some of Mill's opponents went farther, arguing that the Jewish workers would at no stage need anything more than individual freedom. After all, they pointed out – later, this would become a favorite theme of Lenin – the Jewish proletariat in England and the United States had not found it necessary to demand national (or group) rights over and beyond the civil rights guaranteed by the constitution.

The resolution adopted by the Third Congress stated laconically: "In its political demands, the Bund includes only civil – not national – rights."[205] To Mill, the one concession made was a resolution calling for an open discussion of the national question in *Der yidisher arbeter*.

Within slightly over a year, at its next congress, the Bund reversed its decision of December 1899. The resolution adopted at the Fourth Congress held in Belostok in April 1901 committed the Bund in principle to the idea of Jewish national autonomy. This epoch-making decision was formulated in two parts. The first was affirmative and strongly stated:

> The congress recognizes that the Social Democratic program condemns not only the oppression of one class by another; not only that of citizens by the government; but also the oppression of one nationality by another, and the imposition of one language upon another.
>
> The congress recognizes that a state such as Russia, which is composed of many different nationalities, must in the future develop into a federation of nationalities in which every nationality enjoys full national autonomy, regardless of the territory which it occupies.
>
> The congress recognizes that the term "nationality" is applicable also to the Jews.[206]

To this clear-cut statement the following saving clause was added:

> The congress regards it, however, as premature, in present circumstances, to put forward the demand for national autonomy for the Jews and, for the time

being, considers it sufficient to struggle for the repeal of all laws which discriminate against the Jews; to note and protest against the oppression of the Jewish nationality; and to avoid inflating national feelings, which can only obscure the class consciousness of the proletariat and create chauvinism.[207]

However, this qualification could not obscure the magnitude of the step which the congress had taken. To emphasize the cause of equal civil rights for every citizen, including the Jews, had meant simply to defend a plank in the universally accepted Social Democratic platform. In contrast, to come out in favor of federalism, of nonterritorial national autonomism, and of national self-government for the Jews as one nationality among the many in Russia meant to break entirely new ground in the Social Democratic world. In the light of the caution which the Bund (and proto-Bundist movement) had always revealed in defining its official stand on the national policy, the resolution of the Fourth Congress represented a remarkable departure from precedent.

The adoption of the new principles at Belostok presents the historian with something of an enigma. After all, it came hard on the heels of the explicit rejection of those same principles in December 1899; and, even more remarkable, at the Fourth Congress as at the Third, only one delegate out of a total of twenty-four defended an unequivocally national position. The role played by John Mill at the Third Congress now fell to Mark Liber. Essentially, he repeated Mill's arguments, although he did so with all the intense enthusiam which was his by temperament and youth (he was then twenty-one years old). He had evidently been influenced by Martov's speech of 1895, recently published in Yiddish by the Bund and in Russian by the Union Abroad, particularly by the idea that a decent national pride could only stimulate revolutionary and class war. "Our task . . . ," he said at the congress,

> is to *prepare* the Jewish proletariat for national autonomy, to develop its national self-consciousness. To a considerable extent, we have until now been cosmopolitans. We must become nationalists. There is no need to be afraid of this word. *National* is not *nationalistic* . . . [National agitation] can only raise political consciousness without in any way hindering class consciousness; likewise, it can in no way lead to isolation or exclusiveness.[208]

But Liber, who was only a recent recruit to the Bund, could not carry weight at the congress. His views, stated the official report, "did not meet with sympathy from the delegates. Nobody agreed with the practical conclusions to which he came."[209] During the debate on the resolution, he raised or supported close to twenty amendments, all but one of which was rejected. The decision of the congress to adopt the principle of autonomism certainly cannot be explained as his personal victory, the result of his powers of persuasion.

Again, there had been little preparatory discussion of the national program prior to the congress in the local committees or organizations in Russia. As a result, Kopelzon recalled in 1903, "the resolution arrived unexpectedly. Such a bold resolution had not been anticipated. The masses had taken little interest in the question."[210] The decision came as such a shock that, according to another contemporary source, "within a few months it was being said in many committees that the resolution should be repealed."[211] Thus, pressure from below was also not a factor in the decision.

In general terms, the breakthrough made by the Belostok congress has to be seen as a victory for John Mill and the Bundist student youth in Germany and Switzerland. Most of the Bundists involved in the endless debates and ideological ferment of the Russian "colonies" abroad saw the adoption of a bold national program as an absolute necessity. Under the dual influence of Herzl's Zionism – which could be opposed but not ignored – and of the Dreyfus Affair, they were passionately concerned that the Bund should once and for all mark itself off from the assimilationist tradition in socialism; should present its own, non-Zionist, but nonetheless national solution to the Jewish question.

The most outspoken nationalists in the Bund during the period before the Fourth Congress were to be found in Berne. John Mill (acting on the resolution of the Third Congress) published two major articles submitted to *Der yidisher arbeter* by members of the Berne Group, one by Y. Blumshtein (Frumin) and the other by Ben Tsiyon Hofman (Zivion). What these articles made evident was that on the Jewish question their authors followed the same line of thought as Chaim Zhitlovsky, who also lived in Berne. Thus, in reality, there was nothing intrinsically surprising in Zhitlovsky's offer made at that time to join the Bund, even though John Mill later described the incident as a comical anomaly.[212]

Frumin and Zivion introduced themes never before heard within the Bundist world. First, they struck out at those socialists of Jewish origin who denied Jewish nationhood and the importance of nationality problems in the name of internationalism. Hitherto this had been a taboo subject, too divisive to raise publicly. But the official schism in the Union Abroad, the failure of the Group under the influence of Guesde to respond forcefully to the Dreyfus Affair,[213] and its now well-publicized contempt for the "Minsk and Vilna *yidlekh*" all combined to break down old inhibitions. Zivion, following a theme of Zhitlovsky, now argued that internationalism (faith in the cooperation between nations) was the opposite of cosmopolitanism (the naive denial of national differences), and that the refusal of Jewish socialists to recognize the existence of a Jewish nation was a unique form of "bourgeois slavishness":[214] "A section of our socialists have still not liberated themselves from bourgeois ideas ... [It was] the Jewish bourgeoisie which found it necessary to shout in all the streets that the Jews are no nation, that they are simply true Russians."[215]

For his part, Frumin, in recalling a debate about the national question with Koltsov, Plekhanov's faithful lieutenant and himself a Jew, denounced what he called the "*hutspa* methods of our learned internationalist socialists (who are also, as it were, Jewish)."[216] It was incredible, Frumin stated, that so many Jewish socialists, including members of the Bund itself, had "got it into their heads once and for all that they are 'socialists', not 'Jews' ";[217] that "there are Jewish pogroms, with all that means, and Jewish socialists remain silent ... , [that] in Roumania ... *Jewish blood flows in the streets and the Jewish socialists look on and are silent.*"[218]

Frumin insisted that it was the duty of the Bund to put itself at the head of all the classes and groups in the Jewish world ready to fight against the tsarist regime. This plea in essence was a repetition of Lesin's heresy of 1894 and had never appeared before in a Bundist publication. "The more opposition both in quantity and quality," he pleaded, the better ... And "national demands" are one of the fighting methods which strengthen the opposition ... Almost the entire oppressed Jewish nation could sign under such demands including those classes, too, which have economic interests totally opposed to the interests of the proletariat ... Marx and Engels wrote that the proletariat can go hand in hand with bourgeois oppositional parties for a time.[219]

Here was the clear-cut demand that the Bund act as the vanguard of a national, not just of a class, revolt.

Zivion and Frumin stated explicitly that they wanted the Bund to compete with the Zionists for the support of the nationally minded intelligentsia. This was a repudiation of the long-entrenched doctrine that the Jewish bourgeoisie (including the Zionists) were so politically apathetic that they could be discounted as a factor in Russian politics. It could happen, Frumin admitted, that some Bundists would leave the movement if it became more nationalist. But he insisted that this loss would be more than compensated for by the influx of "those Jewish elements which meanwhile keep their distance from the Bund because their strong Jewish feelings are not satisfied when it demands [only] civil ... and, not national, rights."[220]

In a historical note written in 1917, Zivion, as noted above, stressed that the national program adopted in 1901 had been worked out and advocated exclusively by him and his comrades abroad who had to cross swords day in and day out with the new generation of Zionists: the Weizmanns, Abersons, and Feiwels, who were then momentarily imbued with a heady self-confidence as the result of Herzl's meteoric rise. "In the struggle with Zionism," Zivion wrote, "the Bund found itself, crystallized itself and became the really *Jewish* socialist organization of the Jewish proletariat in Russia – Jewish, not only because the organization was made up of Jewish workers ... but also because of its content, its program which sought to give an answer to the Jewish question in Russia."[221]

Zivion's analysis was undoubtedly correct in broad outline, but what he never sought to explain was how the program worked out abroad, above all in Berne, came to be accepted by the Fourth Congress. *Der yidisher arbeter*, no. 11 (where the articles by Frumin and Zivion were published), did not reach Russia until after the congress. Liber, who had recently returned to Russia after a lengthy visit to western Europe and was in effect the delegate of the "national" wing in the movement, was isolated at the congress. The leaders, most notably Taras and Rozental, who had presided over Mill's defeat at Kovno, were again present at Belostok, and they vehemently argued against any thought of ideological revision. "The attempts to force the Jewish labor movement into a national mold," they reportedly said,

originated abroad, where the question really is urgent and timely, while here in Russia *as of now* it is alien to the masses and to raise it now can do nothing but harm ... "In recent times, the proletariat has begun to free itself from the views which it had inherited and acquired in childhood; Social Democratic propaganda diverts it from the path of national separation; it is learning to believe and to feel that all proletarians without national or religious distinction are brothers. This among other things saves it from the pessimism of the Zionists... " [To add] the national element to Social Democratic propaganda means to [venture onto] a slippery slope where it is hard to keep one's balance. It *could* ... give the Bund the completely undesirable character of self-sufficiency, exclusiveness, and separation at that very time when, on the contrary, what is needed is the most amicable cooperation with the Christian proletariat and parties.[222]

Any explanation of what happened at Belostok, then, must include not only the ideological pressure from abroad (which although a necessary was not a sufficient cause) but also the mechanics of decision making at the congress. There, the key personality was undoubtedly Yekutiel Portnoi (Noyakh). A graduate of the Jewish Teachers Institute in Vilna, a member of the proto-Bundist movement in the early 1890s, Portnoi had been arrested in Kovno in 1895. Following his escape and flight from Siberia in 1899, he was almost immediately coopted onto the central committee of the Bund, which now had three members: Pavel Rozental, Taras, and Portnoi. An outstanding organizer, a master of conspiratorial planning, Portnoi was able in a remarkably short time to establish himself as the preeminent leader of the movement in Russia, thus filling the vacuum left by Kremer's arrest in 1898.

Both contemporary and memoir reports agree that the resolution on the national question adopted at the Fourth Congress resulted from a compromise, achieved after arduous negotiations between Rozental and Portnoi.[223] During the long and harsh debates, it had become clear that both men—each a veteran revolutionary and central committee member—could count on the support of a large number of delegates. The end product was the resolution that recognized Jewish national autonomism in principle while excluding it from the actual and official program of the movement.

From the evidence available there is no way of knowing with certainty what decided Portnoi to take up a centrist position at the Fourth Congress. All that can be done is to note those factors which could have persuaded him, as the new leader of the movement in Russia, to take the stand he did. There was no denying, for instance, that the national wing of the movement was stronger in early 1901 than it had been in December 1899. Vladimir Kossovsky was released from prison by Zubatov in April 1900 and in August he fled abroad. For many years he had been one of the most persistent advocates in the Vilna movement of a more national policy, and therefore it was not surprising that he identified himself immediately and whole-heartedly with the revisionists grouped around the committee abroad and *Der yidisher arbeter*. Moreover, according to Mill, the two other veteran leaders who came abroad in 1900, Mutnik (who entered Berne University) and Kremer, now also decided that the Bund should adopt the demand for Jewish national autonomy. Presumably they were won over (in part at least) by the ideological enthusiasts who dominated the Bundist groups abroad. And, in turn, their standpoint (to the extent that it was known in Russia) must have carried great weight with Portnoi.[224]

However, it is very possible that Portnoi saw the Belostok resolution not only as a natural concession to Bundist opinion abroad but also as an integral element in the transition from an "economically" to a "politically" oriented strategy. As shown above, this change of policy evolved gradually and can be traced back at least to the creation of the Bund in September 1897.

The Bund played a major role in the creation of the RSDRP, in the publication of its *Manifesto,* and in the plans to renew the publication of *Rabochaia gazeta* as its organ. At the Third Congress of the Bund, many of the delegates had attacked the *kassy* (the time-honored instrument of the strike movement) as tending to create "an aristocracy," a worker elite that looked down on the unorganized mass; and they demanded that greater emphasis be put on "illegal literature, proclamations, circulars."[225] An article in *Di arbeter shtime* of July 1900 added "open demonstrations"[226] to the list, and a subsequent account recorded the participation of thousands of workers in the May Day demonstrations of that year. In some cases, workers marched openly in the streets carrying red flags and shouting slogans – "Down with the Autocracy!" "Down with Capitalism!" Finally, the official report on the Fourth Congress stated that "not one voice was raised at the Congress against the view that at the present time it is essential to go over to more intensive political agitation."[227]

The slump in the Russian economy that began in 1899; the prolonged and sensational upheaval caused in the years 1899–1901 by the student strikes and demonstrations at the major Russian universities; the successful renewal of political terror tactics signaled by the assassination of the minister of education, Bogolepov, in February 1901; Zubatov's attempt initiated early in 1900 to create an officially sanctioned trade union movement in Minsk in direct competition with the Bund – all combined to accentuate the disenchantment with the economic policy.[228] But the more political the movement sought to become, the more it found itself in need of recruits from the intelligentsia and the students. They were required to produce insurrectionary literature on a now redoubled scale, to conduct classes in revolutionary theory, and to prepare the agitators for the transition from economic to political campaigns.

Thus, in 1900, Rozental wrote a brochure, *A Call to the Jewish Intelligentsia,* in which he admitted ruefully that "the educated section of Jewry ... so-called 'society' is hardly better informed about the character and dimensions of the Bund's activities than about the Boxers in China and rather less than about the Boers in Africa,"[229] and that those few (namely radical Zionists abroad), who were familiar with the Bund, often accused it of "cosmopolitanism, lack of interest in the Jewish people, its history, its traditions, etc."[230] This situation, Rozental concluded, was intolerable, for the only effective way in which the intelligentsia could demonstrate its opposition to tsarism was to merge with the proletariat, with the Bund.

Rozental put all the onus of responsibility on the intelligentsia. But, judging from his actions, Portnoi apparently felt that the Bund could not win over the revolutionary but nationally minded sections within the Jewish youth unless it radically improved its political image. He took it upon himself to make contact with Jewish student groups at the universities of Moscow, Petersburg, Riga, and Kiev. One of the members of the group in Kiev, which included a number of students (Zaslavsky, A. Zolotarev, Gisser, Geilikman) who would soon rise to prominence in the Bund, has described its ideological evolution up until the moment when it was contacted by Portnoi. "The pioneers of the Jewish national movement in Kiev," Zaslavsky wrote, were the Zionists. . . . Vigorous discussions used to take place at Dr. Mandelshtam's . . . The more active [student] circles remained estranged from it [Zionism]. But it made a breach in the totally cosmopolitan world-outlook which had dominated until then . . . The fact that the national question was presented so radically in Zionism had the advantage of provoking thought. We were not Zionists – on that we were clear. But the assimilationist ideology which was in essence nihilistic also could not satisfy us . . . [231] About the Bund we [in 1899–1900] knew little. Rather, we knew nothing. Two or three brochures, an odd number of *Poslednie izvestiia* – that was the sum of what [our] "Group of Jewish *Intelligenty*" had in its possession in order to glean its knowledge of the Bund. And because of that the halo around the Bund shone all the brighter . . . we not only respected it, we believed in it. We sought the Bund and the Bund was then seeking us out too.[232]

In the autumn of 1900, Portnoi came to Kiev and met with Zaslavsky and other leaders of his circle. He was dissatisfied with the fact that the "Group of Jewish *Intelligenty*" was formally a "nonparty" organization, but from then on, he returned frequently to Kiev to supply the Bundist supporters there with revolutionary literature.[233]

No pressure in favor of Jewish autonomism was exerted by the Kiev group – it was, in Zaslavsky's words, still "an unfamiliar term"[234] to them – but Portnoi's constant contact with students there and elsewhere in Russia must have brought home to him the enormous importance that they attached to ideological and programmatic issues. If the Bund were to attract the student youth in considerable numbers, it would clearly have to present itself more dramatically than hitherto as a third force in the Jewish world, clearly distinguished from, and in competition with, both socialist "cosmopolitanism" and Zionism. Was there any choice but to move at least some distance in the direction demanded by Mill, *Der yidisher arbeter,* the Berne Bundists, and at Belostok by Mark Liber?

Beyond doubt is the fact that the resolutions passed at the Fourth Congress, when taken as a whole, all pointed in one direction: toward the recognition of the Bund as a sovereign party, avowedly Jewish and political. This was true of the resolutions already described on national autonomism and political agitation. It was true, too, of the decisions to publish more material in Russian and Polish aimed explicitly at the Jewish intelligentsia; to send a message of support to the "entire student body in its struggle for academic freedom and against police barbarity"; and to announce that "under no circumstances should Zionists be allowed into either our economic or political organizations."[235] (This was, in fact, a call for the expulsion of Zionist workers from all branches of the movement.)

But the most telling expression of Portnoi's line of thought came in the momentous decision on the organization of the Russian Social Democratic movement: "The congress, which regards the RSDRP as a federal union of the SD parties in the Russian state, recommends that the Bund, as the representative of the Jewish proletariat, should enter it as a federative section, and instructs the central committee of the Bund to carry this resolution into effect."[236] Here was a clear-cut declaration in favor of recognizing de jure what had been the de facto situation since 1897 (or even in a sense since 1893). The Bund had developed as an autonomous movement, which, although Marxist and Social Democratic, had its own political interests and priorities. In the 1890s Kremer had preferred to play down this fact and present it in muted terms. Portnoi, as the new leader, chose to present it in unambiguous form. Given the multiple crisis then facing the Bund—the economic depression, the startling success of the Zubatov movement, the open split with the Group for the Liberation of Labor—he no doubt felt that a bold display of political self-confidence and ideological coherence had become a question of survival. Under his guidance the Vilna movement in April 1901 had declared itself of age.

Iskra and the Bund, 1901–1903: toward the Second Congress of the RSDRP

In the ten years leading up to the Belostok congress, the Vilna movement had developed its national ideology sure in the knowledge that on one flank, the Russian Social Democratic movement, it was secure from attack. Weak and disorganized; anxious to avoid at all costs any policy reminiscent of the antisemitic stand of the Narodnaia Volia in 1881; further distracted after 1898 by the dispute between Plekhanov and the "youngsters"; the Russian Marxists had left the Bund to handle the Jewish question as it saw fit. The one possible exception to this rule, the decision of the Rabochedeltsy in 1900 to bring out two important Bundist statements in Russian (Martov's speech of 1895 and Kossovsky's attack of 1898 on the PPS), only served to encourage the national wing in the Jewish movement.

But in 1901 this immunity came to an end and the Bund found itself under mounting pressure (at first mainly organizational but also and increasingly ideological) from the Russian Marxists, specifically from *Iskra*. For the Bund, the challenge from the Russian Social Democrats presented incomparably more difficult problems than did the conflict with the PPS or the Zionists. After all, the entire ideology of the Bund was based on the idea that the Jewish movement (albeit self-governing) formed an integral unit in the international but Russian-centered party. To have to decide between loyalty to the Russian party and to Bundism, as it had developed by 1901, was a cruel choice indeed.

That the Bund would be faced by this dilemma was (it can be seen retrospectively) actually decided in the latter half of 1899 when Lenin, then still in Siberia, made up his mind to throw his support behind the beleaguered Plekhanov in the internal party dispute. This highly crucial decision was first revealed in a letter that Lenin then sent to the editors of *Rabochaia gazeta* (or, more exactly, to Taras [Kats] and the central committee of the Bund, which was attempting to issue that paper as the official organ of the RSDRP). "From letters I have received," he wrote,

> I understand that in your estimate the "old trend is strong" and that there is no especial need for polemics again Bernsteinism and its Russian reflections. I regard that view as too optimistic. The public declaration of Bernstein that the majority of the Russian Social Democrats agree with him; the schism between the "young" Russian Social Democrats Abroad and the Group for the Liberation of Labor which founded, perpetuates, and most faithfully guards the "old trend"; the labors of *Rabochaia mysl* to say something

new; . . . finally the total chaos of legal Marxist literature . . . all this in my opinion clearly shows that to reinforce and energetically *defend* the "old trend" undoubtedly constitutes the order of the day.[237]

At this time, Lenin almost certainly did not realize that Grishin, a leading Bundist as well as secretary of the Union Abroad, and through him the Bund as a whole, had become a (perhaps the) bête noire of Plekhanov. In a polemic against *Rabochaia mysl*, also written late in 1899, Lenin specifically praised the Bund together with the St. Petersburg and Kiev committees for having "created the Russian labor movement" and for having "*united* with a group of other Russian organizations and . . . founded the Russian Social Democratic Labor Party . . . an enormous step toward the *coalescence* of the Russian labor with the Russian revolutionary movement."[238] Again, his confidence in the Bund at this time was reflected in the fact that with his letter to Taras he also sent him three important articles to be published.

For its part, *Rabochee delo*, too, was doing all in its power to reassure him and his fellow exiles in Siberia that it was opposed to Economism and in favor of a strong political orientation. It had published and associated itself with the Protest of the Seventeen organized by Lenin against Kuskova's "Credo"; attacked the ideological position of *Rabochaia mysl*; reviewed favorably Lenin's brochure published in 1898, *The Tasks of the Russian Social Democrats*; and even reached a formal settlement (negotiated by Grishin) with the Group for the Liberation of Labor on 9 January 1900 (even though, as it transpired, Plekhanov, then seeing the *Vademecum* through the press, had no intention of abiding by it).

In mid-May 1900 the indefatigable Grishin met Lenin in Pskov and did what he could to show him that the Economist heresy was not deeply entrenched in the movement, that it was fading away even where it did exist, and that it would prove disastrous if the schism abroad were now to disrupt the organizations in Russia. But Lenin had returned from penal exile to European Russia in January, had met with Vera Zasulich (who had come to St. Petersburg in the winter) and was by now familiar with the *Vademecum*. Thus it was hardly surprising that (as Grishin later recalled) "he acted with extreme reserve, spoke little of his plans and [merely] promised that he would soon be in Europe and would then decide finally the question of his relations to the groupings abroad."[239] At that point, he together with Martov and Potresov had already worked out in detail a plan for the creation of a new journal which would weld together the Russian Social Democrats through "firm ideological unity"[240] and act as the focal point of a communications network linking all the centers of the movement. Unknown to Grishin, the draft announcement for this journal (worked out by Lenin's troika in Pskov in April) had implicitly endorsed the *Vademecum*. It stated that "with all our heart we welcome the renewed literary activity of the Group for the Lib. of Labor and the fight which it has begun against the attempts to distort and debase Social Democracy."[241]

But, as Potresov and Lenin discovered in August when they met him in Switzerland, Plekhanov was by now an extremely angry man, and what he sought was not merely a declaration of support for himself and a condemnation of the out-and-out heretics (Kuskova and *Rabochaia mysl*), but also the excommunication of those who had not come out early enough or vehemently enough against the heretics (*Rabochee delo* and the Bund). The two younger men were dumbfounded by his attitude. Lenin wrote down an account of his impressions during the meetings. "Toward the *Soiuzniki*," this report reads,

> he revealed a hatred which passes the bounds of decency (hints of spying, accusations of *Geschäftsmacherei,* of rascality, declarations that he would "shoot" such "traitors" without the slightest hesitation, etc.). The most circumspect suggestions that he too had gone to extremes (e.g., my remark about publishing private letters and the inadvisability of doing this) got him terribly excited and really upset.[242]

Plekhanov was disdainful of the announcement proposed by the troika for the new journal. "It was written (from G.V.'s point of view)," Lenin noted, "too 'opportunistically': it permitted polemics between the co-editors, was modest in tone, suggested that a peaceful end to the argument with the Economists might be possible."[243] Plekhanov was so contemptuous of the document that he would not even suggest any corrections to it. His most bitter language he reserved for the Bund:

> He declared straight out that this is not a Social Democratic organization, but simply an organization of exploitation – to exploit the Russians. He felt that our goal is to kick the Bund out of the Party, that the Jews are all chauvinists and nationalists, that a Russian [*russkaia*] party must be Russian and not "give itself into captivity to the tribe of Gad," etc. . . . G.V. was not to be moved from this position. He says that we simply have no knowledge of the Jews, no experience of conducting affairs with them. No resolution on this question was adopted.[244]

It might have been expected that a few days of such an experience – and these are only a few examples in a long series of intolerant and arrogant outbursts – would have suggested to Lenin and Potresov that the majority in the Union Abroad had a real case; that the split in 1898 had perhaps been caused by a personality problem; that the subsequent attempts to ascribe the schism to deep-rooted deviationism was a device to maintain power when all else had failed. (Lenin's notes, after all, record his conviction that Plekhanov sought "total domination" in their proposed editorial board.)[245] But in reality, the two younger men drew a different conclusion. They patched up a compromise. "We decided not to tell anybody except our closest comrades what had happened, to keep up appearances, not to give our enemies cause to rejoice. Externally, everything will be as if nothing had happened, the entire machine must continue to move."[246]

This apparently incomprehensible attitude seemed natural enough to Lenin and Potresov and doubtless to Martov, too, when he joined them later in the year. While still in penal exile, they had made up their minds that the fragmentation of the RSDRP inside Russia was due not to organizational incompetence nor to the efficiency of the Okhrana under Zubatov's direction, but to a scorn for Marxist theory and deviations from Marxist orthodoxy. From this premise it followed that in order to create a united party it was essential first to restore ideological unanimity. The very symbol of orthodoxy, however, was Plekhanov, and it was at that stage unthinkable to Lenin and Potresov to launch a crusade without (and inevitably against) "the father of Russian Marxism."

For them, the paranoia and megalomania of their leader were not issues of moral or political significance, because they shared his assumption that without ideological discipline the Social Democratic movement was doomed. Late in 1900 Apolonariia Yakubova, one of Lenin's oldest friends from St. Petersburg, corresponded with Lenin, begging him to reconsider his plans to work with Plekhanov and in his spirit lest the

> disorders at the "summit" interfere with the practical work "down below" as did the fight between the *narodniki* and the Marxists . . . There are always few people to do *real* work while there are many ready for tongue wagging . . . For [real work] it is enough to be a decent [*poriadochnym*], upright human being who feels for the working class . . . I really have no idea if there are many "Credists" and if they are actually *doing anything.* If not, then it is not even worth talking about.[247]

However, Lenin was adamant and stated quite candidly that in his view an out-and-out, internal, ideological war could only advance the cause:

> Without a dismantling there cannot be a successful forward movement and there cannot be *firm unity* . . . A direct struggle against the Bernsteinians and Economists is . . . one of the necessary conditions for the *reestablishment* of unity . . . A unity in which we hide "Economist" documents from the comrades like some secret illness, in which we take offense when they are published . . . such "unity" is not worth a penny, such unity is real cant, it leads only to a deterioration of the illness, to its development into a malignant form.[248]

Martov and Potresov, of course, would later repudiate this conception of party organization. But in Lenin, Plekhanov had found a more receptive disciple. The Manichean analysis of Russian Marxism in which the orthodox had to fight a perpetual battle against the heretics, the saints against the sinners, the Mountain against the Gironde had struck a deep chord in Lenin's psychology. Throughout the rest of his life he would repeatedly launch doctrinal crusades to save the party, even against Plekhanov himself.[249]

In December 1900 the first number of *Iskra* appeared and the campaign for the control of the Russian Social Democratic movement was thus officially launched. The early issues (initially they came out less than once a month) clearly demonstrated that *Iskra* would be a Plekhanovite paper in the sphere of ideology but not in that of short-range political tactics. Centered in Munich, Lenin's troika wisely kept the day-to-day control of policy out of Plekhanov's hands. They charted their own course.

Since April 1898 Plekhanov had acted according to the dictum "Who is not for me is against me" and as a result by the summer of 1900 he had reduced his Group for the Liberation of Labor to a sorry state of almost total isolation. Lenin throughout was guided by the belief that whoever was not against him would eventually be for him. This meant that *Iskra* planned to concentrate its public attacks on one enemy at a time, to devastate the "right," while confusing and gradually winning hegemony over the "center," the "marsh."

In practice, the initial onslaught was concentrated on *Rabochaia mysl,* the organ of the St. Petersburg Union of Struggle, even though it had already abandoned the "Economism" that marked some of its earlier issues. It was accused of paving the way psychologically for Zubatov's police trade unionism. The Union Abroad (the Rabochedeltsy) were handled with kid gloves and even offered a few words of faint praise (*Iskra* "in no way denies the services of *Rabochee delo,* which has done a great deal to publish and transport [revolutionary] literature").[250] As for the Bund, it was picked out in an article by Martov in *Iskra,* no. 1, for its exemplary and swift condemnation of Zubatov's plot to establish official trade unionism in Minsk. ("The central committee [of the Bund] acted with the greatest possible wisdom in deciding to lance the ulcers and come out openly at the first sign of threatening internal dangers.")[251]

Over the next two-and-one-half years, *Iskra* followed this same order in its campaign against the anti-Plekhanovite forces – one by one, *Rabochaia mysl, Rabochee delo,* and the Bund would have to bear the brunt of the attack. However, *Iskra* throughout conducted the battle flexibly, not tied down to any rigid timetable or detailed plan.

For the years 1901–2, *Iskra*'s approach to the Bund was one of malign neglect.[252] This is to say, the journal for the most part refrained from polemicizing with or even mentioning the Jewish movement. This studied silence was the public facet of what (judging from the little documentary evidence available) must have been a well-calculated policy. The aim was to bring home to the Bundist leadership that in the long run it would have to choose between two alternatives: it could recognize *Iskra*'s hegemony in the RSDRP and make the ideological adjustments demanded of it; but, if it refused, it would eventually be forced out of the party. There was, *Iskra* conveyed, no third way.

On only one occasion (*Iskra,* no. 7, published in August 1901) did the journal publish an attack on the basic principles of the Bund, specifically on the resolutions of the Belostok congress. In a short article, Martov repudiated the idea of Jewish national autonomism, which he either did not – or pretended not – to understand. Ignoring the central idea of the resolution, nonterritorial self-government, he asked whether the Bund would not have to demand "the conversion of those shtetls where the Jewish population predominated into separate self-governing units . . . severing the urban population from the rural, [and also] . . . self-government . . . for every urban district populated by the Jews." He then stated that "for our part we can only regard as a major political mistake this aspiration to compress *quite artificially* the Jewish working masses within *the confines of nationalism.*"[253]

Far more ominous, though, were his comments on the resolution in favor of reconstituting the RSDRP as a federation into which the Bund should "enter" as one of its constituent national units. Such a statement, Martov insisted, had to be seen as a unilateral abrogation of the party constitution and was therefore "completely illegal"; and could only be interpreted to mean that the "Bund is leaving the party as it was constituted at the congress of 1898. An organization can only enter a party if it is first outside it."[254] The Bundist central committee sent a letter to *Iskra* explaining that the Belostok resolution had obviously been meant as a proposal, not as a fait accompli.[255] Following that, the name of the Bund all but disappeared again from the pages of *Iskra.*

The threat implicit in Martov's words had been harsh and unmistakable, but *Iskra* was not ready to pursue this challenge publicly at that time. By avoiding long-drawn-out polemics, Lenin and his group no doubt hoped to neutralize the Bundist committee abroad (Mill, Kossovsky, Kremer), to prevent it from publicly defending the *Rabochee delo,* and to reduce its importance in comparison with that of the less nationalist and ideologically self-conscious central committee in Russia (Taras, Rozental, Portnoi).

Behind the scenes, *Iskra* did what it could to intimidate the Bundist central committee. Writing to Akselrod in July 1901, Martov mentioned that he had been sending "very 'threatening' "[256] letters to the Bund in Russia and that these were soon to be followed up by a meeting between *Iskra*'s representative in Vilna (Sergei Tsederbaum) and the Bundists. The central committee would there be asked "to declare publicly the Bundist support of, and solidarity with, *Iskra* and the general Russian S.D. organs. Such a commitment should be countersigned by the committee of the Bund here ... What is important is that with such a declaration they disavow their delegates abroad."[257]

For his part, Lenin explained to Akselrod (in a letter of May 1901) that *Iskra* would probably seek to have the Bundist committee abroad specifically excluded from future negotiations between the Russian Social Democratic groups in the West, "on the grounds of section 1 of the decision of the congress of the RSDRP made in 1898 (according to this section, the Bund only has autonomy in questions that specifically affect the Jewish proletariat – and so it cannot enter as an independent side into negotiations)."[258] Although this demand was apparently not followed up – the Bund did take part in the "conciliation" talks of the émigré groups held in June 1901 and at their conference in September – it has to be seen as part of a systematic attempt to sow suspicion between the forces opposed to *Iskra*. On the day after the collapse of the September conference, where, in the words of Martynov, "one member of *Iskra* played the role of Papal Nuncio and solemnly read out the bull which excommunicated the Union Abroad from the Church,"[259] Lenin and Martov arranged to meet with Mill and Kremer. They invited the Bund to break with the Rabochedeltsy (who would now be attacked openly as heretics) and to join *Iskra*. "If you remain allied to the Union Abroad," Lenin reportedly warned, "you will only compromise yourselves."[260]

That a small, united, and determined group can often outmanoeuver, divide, and eventually dominate a numerically much larger but less homogeneous opposition is one of the basic laws of political life. True, this tendency can be countered by constitutional procedures if, in turn, those procedures are accepted by the participants in the political process as legitimate and necessary. But in the years 1901–3, constitutional safeguards were considered all-important by only a minority in the RSDRP. That minority was progressively undermined by the *Iskra* group, which appealed to the higher legitimacy of Marxist orthodoxy while at the same time paying lip service to the idea of fair play and party statute.

For its part, the Bund appears to have played the role assigned to it in the tactical plan of the *Iskra* group. Certainly, it did not agree to the proposal that it formally recognize *Iskra* as the central journal of the RSDRP, but then, as Sergei Tsederbaum suggests in his recollections, such a hasty capitulation had hardly been expected. "On instructions from abroad," he recalled, "I had to raise that demand for recognition which, before all else, *Iskra* was presenting to every organization. This was to be a sign of external hegemony. Of course, the Bund did not accept this approach and the talks were broken off."[261] At the meeting with Lenin and Martov, Kremer explained that the Union of Russian Social Democrats Abroad had been recognized by the party congress in 1898 as the only official party organization outside Russia, that the Bundist committee abroad was formally linked to the Union, and that these commitments were obviously binding. After three years of the closest cooperation between the Bundist committee and the Union Abroad, this was the only reply which could have been anticipated from a cautious and straightforward man like Kremer.

But, at the same time, it is striking that the Bund did not come out openly in criticism of *Iskra*'s political philosophy in the crucial initial stages of its campaign for hegemony, that is, during the years 1901–2. When, in May 1901, Lenin published his plan on party organization "Where to Begin?" with its call for the creation of "a network of [*Iskra*] agents" as the central core in the party and with its conception of the journal not "only as a . . . collective agitator but also as a collective organizer,"[262] the Bund remained silent. When the *Iskra* group walked out abruptly from the "unification" congress in September 1901, the Bund again remained silent. It was left to the *Rabochee delo* alone to state that "a journal, which stands *over* the party and *beyond its control* and independent of it thanks to its 'own network of agents,' can be the organ of an individual, of a separate group, of a conspiratorial society . . . but not of a Social Democratic party."[263]

In his history of the Social Democratic movement in Russia, published in 1904, Vladimir Akimov explained this passive attitude of the Bund toward such vital issues of principle as the result of its exclusive concern with *praktika* (day-to-day organizational concerns). "I regard this," he wrote,

> as an unquestionable shortcoming of the Bund: the Jewish proletariat lacks theoreticians. At the Second Congress of the Party [in 1903] the Bund delegation did not even try to contribute to working out the program . . . Although it instinctively sensed that its own organizational principles were in sharp contradiction to those of *Iskra* it proved incapable of formulating its opposition to *Iskra* in clearly defined terms . . . It moves forward itself but it does not lead.[264]

However, this explanation is clearly oversimplified. The Bund did have its *teoretiki*, but its leadership was not willing to unleash them in an assault on the political philosophy of *Iskra*. Bound together by loyalty to a common cause and organization but divided on basic ideological issues, the Bundists were able to unite against the nationalist Right (the Zionists or the PPS) with incomparably greater ease than against the internationalist Left (*Iskra* or the SDKP). As a result, in the dispute between the *Rabochee delo* and *Iskra*, the Bund gravitated naturally toward the role of mediator. Its own organizational cohesion had always depended on ideological compromise and ambiguity and it sought to reunite the Russian Social Democratic movement on this basis.

Only on the nationality issue did the Bund fire off a salvo against *Iskra*. In February 1902 it published a brochure written by Kossovsky which rebutted at length the points made by Martov in *Iskra*, no. 7. Kossovsky there adopted a sober

Figure 13. Vladimir Kossovsky, 1867–1941.

and reasoned stance. He pointed out that national problems and passions were politically too important to be ignored ("What can we do! Drive out nature through the door and it flies in through the window.");[265] that the Austrian Social Democrats had reorganized their party in 1897 as a federation of national organ-

234

izations and were seeking a conceptual solution to the national question in general; and that the Bund was therefore acting in an orthodox ideological context. True internationalism meant not to ignore the aspirations of the different nationalities but to reconcile them. ("Social Democracy wants to destroy national privileges, to create the conditions for the peaceful coexistence of nationalities; the bourgeois [nationalistic] parties seek the domination of one nation over others.")[266]

He dealt some shrewd thrusts at *Iskra* itself. So far, he pointed out, it had studiously avoided the national question (except for its brief assaults on the Bund). Its readers had no way of knowing whether it was for or against the federal organization of the RSDRP, for or against national autonomy in a democratic Russia. ("Does *Iskra* recognize national autonomy or not? Does it not recognize it for all people except the Jews?")[267] Caustically he suggested that a socialist movement, however ostensibly internationalist, could easily become "nationalistic" if it were "blinded by the 'general-Russian,' 'general-Polish' or 'general-German' cause which holds the rights of subject nationalities in contempt."[268]

In only one place did Kossovsky slip in a reference to *Iskra*'s attempt to establish hegemony in the party. Of Martov's statement that the Bund's organizational proposal was "illegal," he wrote: "Coming from *Iskra* the reference to legality involuntarily calls to mind the well-meaning figure of Chichikov [the anti-hero of Gogol's *Dead Souls*], who of course was fond of declaring: 'The law! I revere the law!' "[269] In its original form – a lecture (*referat*) delivered to the student colonies – Kossovsky's attack had presumably been far more explicit on this, the key issue. He would later recall that the central committee of the Bund in Russia had "censored my manuscript and smoothed out all the sharp edges in the . . . treatment of the national problem."[270]

If Kossovsky had hoped to provoke *Iskra* into a full-scale polemical battle he was to be disappointed. The only response was very brief, and came not in *Iskra* itself but months later, in its more academic sister journal, *Zaria*.[271] In the year following the abortive "unification" conference in September 1901, the Bund had in fact moved perceptively closer to *Iskra* and its relationship with *Rabochee delo* had become strained.

There were a number of straws in the wind indicating that the Bund was seeking to reach middle ground. *Der yidisher arbeter*, no. 13, which appeared early in 1902, contained, astonishingly, the translation of a recent article of Plekhanov that inter alia sought to prove that *On Agitation* was the "Bible of the 'pure' Economists."[272] This attack on the classic work of proto-Bundism was reproduced without comment. In the same number of the journal there were two articles by that stern guardian of internationalism – and no friend of the Bund – Rosa Luxemburg. This and subsequent issues of the journal were brought out by Kremer with the help of Kossovsky, and not a trace remained from the heterodox era of John Mill's editorship. In the same month, February 1902, *Rabochee delo*, no. 11, came out with a critical comment by Krichevsky on the new Bundist theory of Jewish national autonomy. Under existing conditions, he wrote, the idea was a "utopia" and, even in the long run, the fact could not be ignored that "the *essence* of the Jewish spirit" was not nationality but "religion."[273] Clearly, the alliance between the Union Abroad and the Bund was suffering under considerable strain.

In a desperate attempt to bridge the gulf between the two warring camps – *Iskra* and *Rabochee delo* – the central committee of the Bund in Russia undertook to organize a Second Congress of the RSDRP, Nemansky took it upon himself to gain the consent of the committees in the north (particularly in St. Petersburg, where he had been active for some years), and Portnoi went to the south to bring in the group associated with *Iuzhny rabochii*. Some ten delegates assembled in Belostok in March 1902. The *Iskra* delegate, Fedor Dan, brought with him a categorical demand that the assembly declare itself a conference and not a congress, a demand that, as Rozental later recalled, "we accepted without any great objections."[274]

During the conference, a clear voting pattern emerged. On nearly all the controversial issues on which the Union Abroad and *Iskra* clashed, the central committee of the Bund (represented by Portnoi and Rozental) either abstained or, more frequently, voted with *Iskra*. Generally, but not always, Kremer (representing the Bundist committee abroad) followed the same policy.[275] In the light of these developments it comes as no surprise to find Krupskaia in May 1902 writing to one of the *Iskra* "agents" in Russia that in the recent period "the Bund has changed front and has tipped toward *Iskra*."[276]

Throughout 1902 the trend within the Bundist movement in Russia, both in the central committee and at lower levels, was clearly toward an ever-growing identification with *Iskra*. Thus, the Fifth Conference of the Bund, held in September 1902, came out boldly in favor of a radical reorganization of the movement in order to emphasize the primacy of "politics" over "economics."[277] The article in *Di arbeter shtime*, no. 28, summarizing the decisions of the conference represented a startling shift toward – and indeed an almost word-for-word reflection of – Lenin's theory of party organization:

> The trade unions expend, in very large measure, the organization's strength ... No, our organization must consist primarily of revolutionaries, i.e., of people with the determination and ability to display constant revolutionary energy and activity. They must be au courant with everything happening at *all* levels both of the working class and of "society"; must know how always to seize on every sign of discontent and protest ... and how to unite the separate streams into one river.[278]

Late in 1902, on his release from prison in Belostok, Leyb Blekhman discovered that the central bureau of the Tanners Union (*Garber-bund*), which counted among its members such leading Bundists as Beynish Mikhalevich, was made up entirely of "supporters of Lenin," enthusiastic disciples of his *What Is To Be Done?* In order to avoid "constant conflicts,"[279] he relinquished his post as an organizer for the tanners.

Early in 1903 three of the leading Bundists in Russia – Pavel Rozental, his wife Anna, and Zeldov (Nemansky) – sent a letter from prison appealing to the leadership still at liberty to do everything within its power to avoid a collision with the majority of the Russian Social Democrats. The resolution on national autonomy, they wrote, had been adopted in 1901 "without enough thought, with a degree of haste completely unsuited to such important questions." Still worse was the decision in favor of a federal restructuring of the RSDRP:

> The question of federation [in the RSDRP] must be decided from the point of view not of a narrow organizational self-concern or pride but from that of

the *real concrete interests* of the Jewish proletariat and of the entire movement. And those interests, in our view, do not now – under the Autocracy – demand federation in any way . . . This proposal has *no hope* of going through the [coming] party congress . . . There are absolutely no grounds for fearing that the Jewish (or Polish) organizations will be dictated to by the Russian organization because there are not – and cannot be in the future – any tactical differences of opinion in the national sphere. Federation would provide only a very problematic broadening of the autonomy already enjoyed by the Bund now. The Bund has no right to demand an equal influence [in the RSDRP] . . . because (1) there is a real factory proletariat only among the Russians; (2) qualitatively it is incomparably larger than the Jewish workshop proletariat; (3) the industrial Jewish proletariat shows no tendency to grow in size, quite the contrary; (4) the revolutionary consciousness of the Russian proletariat is growing fast . . . and as a revolutionary factor is constantly reducing the role of the Jewish proletariat; (5) the emergence of the peasantry . . . pushes the Bund still further into the background; (6) the Bund knows very little about the Russian movement and is little competent [to judge its needs].[280]

Primarily this letter has to be seen as an extremely forceful presentation of the political philosophy long held by the "internationalist" wing of the Bund. But it also reflected the realities of the moment: the rising faith in political action (street demonstrations and terror or "organized revenge"),[281] the growing enthusiasm of many Bundists in Russia for the idea of a centralized Russian party, the increasing tendency to make peace with *Iskra* and even with *Iskra*-ism.

By the summer of 1902, Lenin had decided that *Iskra* could make good use of the fact that the Bund (in Krupskaia's words) "has even begun to take our side." The March conference of the RSDRP had elected an organizational committee (OK) of three to make the necessary preparations for the Second Party Congress; of those three only one (Portnoi from the Bund) had escaped arrest, and Lenin now proposed that the *Iskra* agents in Russia reconstitute the OK themselves inviting Portnoi to join them. The trappings of continuity and legitimacy would thus be maintained. "You must definitely form the Russian OK," Lenin wrote on 16 July 1902,

and take it into your hands – you . . . , [Krzhizhanovsky] & one of our people from the south – that is the idea . . . Toward the Bund act with great caution and reserve, do not show your cards, let it conduct the affairs of the Bund and *do not let it stick its nose* into Russian [*russkie*] affairs; remember it is an unreliable friend (*and even an enemy*).[282]

In October, at a meeting in Pskov, the new organizational committee was established even though the delegate from the Bund had not arrived (the invitation to Portnoi was unclear and arrived too late). "I was very, very pleased," Lenin wrote in November to Krasikov (in St. Petersburg),

to hear that you have pushed ahead fast with the OK affair and included six people in it. I was only surprised that you coopted people *before* it was formally constituted, *before* the Bund was invited . . . That, though, is not so important if you are convinced that no complications can arise. [Anyway] act as strictly as possible with the Bund.[283]

Encouraged, perhaps, by this letter, Krasikov proceeded on his own initiative to make public the statement announcing the establishment of the OK, thus breaking a specific promise to show the text to and consult with Portnoi before publication.

The response of the Bundist central committee in Russia to these manoeuverers was extraordinarily mild. Portnoi and Aizenshtat joined the organization committee and cooperated with the Iskrovtsy who controlled it. Thus, as one of Lenin's supporters described it in February 1903, Aizenshtat "at first was very dry and unyielding, but then everything worked out extremely well and we are all delighted with him."[284] Portnoi was described by Krzhizhanovsky as "very genial, [and as having] behaved very correctly; he has much respect for the party and understanding of party discipline." In a later letter, another Iskrovets, E. M. Aleksandrova, wrote suggesting that the Bundist representatives simply did not dare to cause trouble:

> The Bundist does not hinder us. Formally, for example, we do not actually have the right in the name of the OK to bring pressure to bear on the committees even on the issue of solidarity with *Iskra*. We are doing this and the Bundist knows that very well and keeps quiet and does not open his mouth on that account. I have the impression that they would go a long way (although not on everything) in order only to remain in the OK. Their presence in the OK will give them the chance to subdue their organizations in revolt: "You see [they can say] we are not isolated from Russia and are working together."[285]

But if Portnoi and Aizenshtat were doing their utmost to guarantee an amicable settlement with the *Iskra* group at the Second Congress of the RSDRP, Lenin was thinking along very different lines. In a letter sent to E. I. Levin (of the *Iuzhny rabochii* group) he proposed that the first item on the agenda of the congress should be a debate not on the new party program, not on the structure of party organization but on the Bund – "if only federation, then an immediate split and sessions apart."[286] From Lenin's point of view this plan had a double advantage. A concerted assault on a clearly defined "outside" group would permit the *Iskra* leadership to inspire its own followers with a sense of unity, a heightened esprit de corps, and, further, if the Bund did decide to walk out of the congress, the potential strength of any opposition would thereby be decimated. *Rabochee delo* and the Union Abroad – now anyway much weakened – were not to be discussed, according to Lenin, until almost the end of the congress.

Throughout the early months of 1903 Lenin bombarded his followers in Russia with letters explaining that the confrontation with the Bund would be assigned a primary place at the congress. "It is essential," he wrote to Krzhizhanovsky in April,

> to drive each and everyone mad, to ram into their heads that it is essential to prepare for war against the Bund if one wants peace. War with the Bund at the congress, right up to a split whatever happens. Only then will it yield beyond a doubt. But we absolutely cannot accept a nonsensical federation and never

shall. Autonomy according to the old constitution of 1898 – with the participation of a representative of the CC in the CC of the Bund is the very most.[287]

In her letter to Lenin, Aleksandrova objected to the tactics being employed against
the Bund. "The watchword of Ignat [Krasikov]," she wrote,

> (and he said it is yours too) is "To hell with the Bundist." I do not understand
> it at all. Why, in that case, did he have to be dragged into the OK? In order to
> observe formality? . . . I think that either we need not have had regard for
> formality or we should observe it until the congress. Otherwise we get a kind
> of "political trickery" [*politikanstvo*], the end of which I cannot see.[288]

She proposed that *Iskra* conduct a full discussion of the issues involved – the structure of the party organization and the nationality question – in its own paper. But
Lenin made it plain in his reply that he preferred to prepare for the clash behind
the scenes. "Formally, in my opinion," he wrote to her,

> it is essential to be correct and loyal with the Bund (not to knock its teeth in
> directly), but at the same time icily cold, buttoned up completely, and on a
> legal basis to drive it into a corner implacably and unremittingly – going
> fearlessly to the very end. Let them leave if they want but we must not put
> the slightest excuse into their hands, not the hint of an excuse for a split . . .
> on no account should we show our cards.[289]

Within the Bund, the only possible threat to Lenin's plans came, of course, from
the committee abroad and its supporters in the student colonies. It was there that
veteran spokesmen for the "national" wing of the Bund were now to be found
(Mill, Kossovsky, Frumin), and they were increasingly reinforced by new recruits
with similar views (Medem, Abramovich, Groser). From January 1903, the journal
of the committee abroad, *Poslednie izvestiia,* was clearly attempting to provoke
Iskra into a major ideological debate on the Jewish question and the role of the
Bund in the RSDRP. But they enjoyed only marginal success. Lenin and Martov
did publish three articles in reply to attacks from the Bund, but, as in 1901, they
preferred to concentrate primarily on immediate issues of loyalty and solidarity
rather than be drawn into more theoretical issues.

In February and March 1903, for the first time since *Iskra* had appeared, Kossovsky was given a free hand to write as he wished. The accumulated bitterness
against *Iskra* – for having openly acted as though the Bund did not exist while
secretly doing everything to encircle it by a wall of hostility – now at last appeared
in print. When, for instance, in *Iskra,* no. 33, Lenin attacked the Bund (in fact, the
committee abroad) for having complained publicly about the conduct of the Organizational Committee ("[This] conduct flies in the face of all the rules of com-
radely conduct in a *common* cause"),[290] Kossovsky responded that ever since the
conference of March 1902, *Iskra* had been blatantly

> striving for hegemony – not only theoretical but organizational – and the
> Bund is hindering you by its separate existence, its independence, so you are
> fighting against it; . . . with your open and your clandestine incitement you
> are working those revolutionaries who heed your voice into such a mood
> that they can blurt out the following remarkable words – "The task of the
> Second Congress is to destroy the Bund."[291]

Lenin accused the Bund of describing itself as an "independent [sic] political party," and to this Kossovsky replied that indeed this was exactly what the Bund had become over the years, through dint of revolutionary determination and in the absence of the RSDRP as anything but a fiction. As for Martov's statement that "life demands the victory of our 'imperialist' principles,"[292] this in Kossovsky's eyes was simply an example of "revolutionary assimilationism." "The Bund," he insisted, "does not exist for the general-Russian movement but for the Jewish proletariat."[293]

But the Bundist leadership in Russia (Portnoi and Aizenshtat) was not willing to permit the attacks on *Iskra* to continue unabated; the conflict over the Organizational Committee was declared a "misunderstanding";[294] and by April the polemics were once again at an end. By now the differences of opinion between the central committee of the Bund in Russia and its committee abroad had become impossible to conceal. Both Krzhizhanovsky and Aleksandrova reported independently that the Bundist representative to the OK openly disassociated himself from the policy of his comrades in London and Switzerland. Thus, it was not surprising that in a letter to the committee abroad, written in April, Liber described the approaching Fifth Congress of the Bund, which would have to thresh out a common policy for the entire movement, as of "colossal – one can say, decisive – importance."[295]

The Fifth Congress of the Bund met in Zurich in June 1903 and was followed almost immediately by the Second Congress of the RSDRP, which was held initially in Brussels and then in London. Each congress faithfully reflected the character of the two movements as they had developed since 1898 – on the one hand, the Bund, sharply divided ideologically but still united by an overriding common loyalty (or "organizational patriotism" as it was described in *Zaria*);[296] and, on the other hand, the RSDRP, finally reconstructed by *Iskra*, ideologically united but driven relentlessly by the urge toward an ever greater (and finally unattainable) unanimity.

According to strict logic, the Fifth Congress should have produced a schism in the Bund. Because the congress was held abroad, the nationalist wing enjoyed a much stronger position than in 1898 or 1901; it was numerically much larger and it had a chance to hammer out its position at a preliminary conference held in Geneva. Its leading spokesmen at the congress (Liber, Medem, Kossovsky, and Zhenia Hurvich) demanded that the Bund finally develop a totally coherent ideology – unequivocally for national autonomy, for national as well as class agitation, for the right of the Bund to represent and work among the Jewish proletariat throughout the empire. Angered by the arrogance of the Iskrovtsy ("The only thing that unites them all," Liber had written in a letter shortly before, "is their hostile attitude to the Bund"),[297] profoundly agitated by the still-fresh accounts of the Kishinev pogrom, convinced that a Jewish party had to have a specific answer to the Jewish question – they were in no mood for compromise.

But their opponents were no less outspoken or determined. Led by two of the founders of the Vilna movement, Aizenshtat and Grishin, a series of speakers argued that the resolution on national autonomy had been adopted in reckless haste in 1901 ("under the influence of the PPS and the Zionists," as Boris Frumkin put it);[298] that with the abolition of the Pale of Settlement the Jews would in all probability assimilate culturally and linguistically with the Russian and Polish

populations; that it was unwise to assume the existence of any long-term sociological difference between the situation of the Jews in eastern Europe and that in the
West. In many cases, there was nothing to distinguish their arguments from those
of the Iskrovtsy. "A material basis is necessary for culture," said Maks Vinokur
from Berdichev. "There is no Jewish culture in existence. Jews have no territory, no
independence and so no culture."[299] "The Jewish proletariat... ," Aizenshtat
declared, "possesses many petty-bourgeois attributes. Therefore we must be especially careful in handling the national question... The tendency of [historical]
development is to wipe out every difference... between a Russian and a Jewish
proletarian."[300] Very much aware that the Bund might soon be expelled from the
RSDRP, they were determined to avoid any needless provocation.

In the past, the key leaders had succeeded in working out an acceptable compromise behind the scenes. But by now, the disagreement was too clearly defined, too
sharp, and the major issue – whether to include the demand for national autonomy
in the Bundist program – had to be put to the vote. The result was a tie, and it was
decided, faute de mieux, to strike all reference to the long but inconclusive debate
from the published report on the congress.[301] Thus, on the national question, the
double-edged and hesitant resolution of the Fourth Congress stood unaltered.

Yet, point by point and often after fierce argument, the Fifth Congress did work
out the proposals it would present to the RSDRP. The tradition in the Bund of
compromise rather than schism again proved its remarkable strength. The Bundist
delegation was equipped with a series of maximal theses and, as a last line of
defense, with a minimal platform beyond which there was to be no retreat. The
most important of the expendable demands was that for the reconstruction of the
RSDRP on a federal basis. Of the ultimata, the central one was the demand for
recognition that "the Bund is the Social Democratic organization of the Jewish
proletariat, enters the RSDRP as its sole representative, and is not subject to any
geographical restriction."[302] This meant, inter alia, that the Bund considered itself
free to expand into southern Russia, an idea that had been specifically rejected at
the previous congress in 1901.

Even though the term "federal" was considered negotiable, the Bundist ultimata
included demands that implied a form of federalism in practice: Directives from the
central committee of the RSDRP to the Bund (and vice versa) were to be channeled
through the Bundist central committee; the Bund was to be represented in the
governing institutions of the RSDRP as one of its constituent members and on an
equitable basis; and the Bund was to have the power to veto any changes in these
basic points. As against this, however, the competence of the Bund was limited
(according to the narrow formula of 1898) to "all questions which specifically
touch on the Jewish proletariat" (this self-limitation was carried by 16 votes to 5
with 8 abstaining).[303] It was made clear also that the demand for equitable representation did not necessarily mean that the Bund expected to enjoy numerical
equality with other constituent sections in the higher party bodies. In sum, neither
side could claim a clear-cut victory at the Fifth Congress, and the Bundist delegation therefore went to the Second Congress of the RSDRP with a set of demands
which left it considerable room for manoeuver between provocative intransigence
and abject self-abnegation.

The Bundists (Medem, Kossovsky, Aizenshtat, Liber, Portnoi, and Kremer) arrived in Brussels at the end of July for the Second Congress expecting difficult negotiations, hard bargaining, with the leaders of the RSDRP. They were therefore stunned to discover that the first substantive item on the agenda was the place of the Bund in the party (Lenin, of course, unknown to them, had decided on this step late in 1902), and that this was to be a debate not about the details of an agreement but about the basic principles involved: centralism against federalism, international unity as against national separation.

For days on end, the fifty-nine delegates discussed the question of the Bund. The protocols of that opening debate reveal to the reader a situation, in itself perhaps not free of absurdity, but pregnant with future tragedy. The Iskrovtsy enjoyed an overwhelming numerical majority at the congress, which was hardly surprising, as they had organized it. Convinced that the RSDRP had finally entered an era of unity and power, that *Iskra* had been vindicated, that the original heresies threatening the movement – "Economism, Bernsteinism, and Millerandism" – had been thoroughly defeated, the delegates turned against the Bund in a mounting ecstasy of indignation. The assult was led by Iskrovtsy of three main types: the Jews (Martov, Trotsky, E. I. Levin), who appealed to the Bund to rise above its narrow parochialism; the Georgians (Zhordania, Topuridze, Knuniants), who clearly feared that the principle of national organization could undermine their control of the Trans-Caucasian movement; and the representatives from southern Russia (Odessa, Ekaterinoslav), who were determined to prevent the expansion of the Bund into their area. Guiding the assault was Lenin, aided by the occasional sarcasm from Plekhanov, who was the chairman.

Martov opened the debate on a relatively mild note arguing that while the "abnormal situation"[304] represented by the existence of the Bund could not be removed by "one heroic resolution," it also should not be ignored. "With whom are we dealing," he asked, "with a section of the party or a free agent?"[305] But few others shared even his small degree of self-restraint. Trotsky pointed out that he, Martov, and the other Jews, who alone had signed the resolution in favor of keeping the Bund within narrow constitutional limits, "also regard ourselves as representatives of the Jewish proletariat." "Among whom they have never worked,"[306] shouted Liber bitterly. From then on, Trotsky took the lead in baiting the Bundists:

> I listened with surprise when Comrade Liber spoke of the desire to destroy the Bund. What does that mean? Do we want to destroy physically those comrades who belong to the Bundist organization? Do we want to destroy [its] fruitful work in developing the consciousness of the Jewish proletariat? Or is what we want to destroy in the Bund only its special situation in the party? The Bund as the sole representative of the interests of the Jewish proletariat in the party and before the party – or the Bund as the special organization of the party for agitation among the Jewish proletariat? That is how the question must be put.[307] The statute [you] proposed to us has as its goal . . . to raise a wall between us and the Bund . . . Against that wall the congress must come out in total unanimity.[308]

"The demand of the Bund to set up a state within a state surprised me,"[309] Topuridze declared. "I consider," Knuniants said, "that the existence of the Bund

Figure 14. Mark Liber, 1880–1937?

has created separatism."[310] "So long as the Bund does not relegate the national question to the background," Stopani insisted, "conflicts [with it] are inevitable."[311] "You," Moshinsky said, "want to carry through a revolution in our party! And only thanks to the agenda decided upon did we discover [your] intentions so quickly . . ."[312] Today, comrades from the Bund, you revealed to us finally your true physiognomy."[313] In his speech, E. I. Levin recalled the struggle of Avrom Gordon's worker opposition—"Russian revolutionaries in the best sense of the word"—against the founders of the Bund, "who had made for themselves a special corner, retreated into their own national shell . . . It is of no interest to us what happens to the Jews, the Poles, the Russians, etc., as such. We believe that the interests of nationality will be satisfied automatically by the achievement of our ideal."[314] When, finally, Kossovsky complained that the Bundists were being hounded by a solidly hostile congress, Lenin chose to take his remarks as a compliment:

> In my opinion, we ought to be not ashamed but proud of the fact that there is a compact majority at the congress. And we would be still prouder if our party was one compact—a really compact—90 percent majority . . . Central-ism demands the *absence* of all barriers between the center and the most distant, the most isolated sections, of the party[315] . . . [But a] lack of faith runs through all the judgments of the Bundists.[316]

Thrown back onto the defensive by this prolonged onslaught, the Bundist dele-gation proved unable to rise to the occasion. Only three of the six Bundists—Kossovsky, Liber, and Portnoi—took the floor to counter the criticism. They showed themselves uncowed—Kossovsky sharp and often cuttingly ironical; Liber impassioned; Portnoi calm and determined to keep the facts straight—but they did not launch a counteroffensive. The only delegate that threw back at *Iskra* a real challenge was not a Bundist but Vladimir Akimov from the Union Abroad. He argued with remarkable cogency and courage that the political philosophy of *Iskra*—its elitism, its hyper-centralism, its willingness to use any means necessary to gain its ends—was bound to produce tragic consequences. The attempt of the Iskrovtsy to teach the Bund the principles of revolutionary Social Democracy was, he stated bluntly, "laughable" and would "contrary to the [general] opinion . . . only [lead to] a new era of strife."[317]

But Akimov spoke essentially as an individual (albeit one, in the words of Adam Ulam, "endowed with a prophetic sense").[318] The Bundists, though, were responsi-ble to an entire movement which had not been prepared in any way by its central committee to accept a split with the RSDRP; which was strongly revolutionary and internationalist; and which was accustomed to seeing violent ideological disagree-ments finally settled by compromise rather than schism. Thus, even the most effective thrusts of Kossovsky and Liber—when, for instance, they pointed out that the concept of a "general-Russian" [*obshcherusskii*] cause was repellent if it meant ignoring the parts that made up the whole, "founding international socialism with-out an international movement"[319]—were not integrated into a comprehensive counter-philosophy.

Rather, the Bundist delegation acted as though what was involved was a gro-tesque misunderstanding. In order to prove that the accusations of nationalistic separatism were false, they repeatedly and unilaterally discarded the demands worked out at the Fifth Congress. The maximal position, the federalist concept, was hastily withdrawn without ever being presented. "In order not to increase the hostile mood against the Bund," stated the Bundist report later in the year, "and to ease the possibility of agreement, we decided to exclude from the projected statute those points that sharply stressed our position in principle and so to move the weight of our argument more toward practice."[320] As the debate advanced, and the attacks on the Bund became more virulent, so the decision was taken to cut away at the minimal demands, the ultimata – instead of the power to veto any changes in the Bund's basic position, all that was now demanded was that such changes should be carried by at least a two-thirds majority of an RSDRP congress; the central committee of the Bund was no longer to have the right to act as sole intermediary between the movement and the RSDRP; and Bundist representation in the RSDRP was no longer necessarily to be on equitable lines.[321] These concessions were extraordinary in that they went against the specific instructions of the Bundist congress, which was the one sovereign body in the movement. (Without the presence of both Portnoi and Kremer in Brussels, such a step would surely have been inconceivable.)

When the revised proposal was presented to the Second Congress, it produced a sensation and momentary hesitation among the *Iskra* group but no change in its general line. Instead of discussing the Bundist plan immediately, as Kossovsky requested, the Iskrovtsy decided it should be considered much later with other organizational questions.[322] Meanwhile, Martov's resolution, which confined Bundist autonomy to "everything that concerns those particular problems of agitation among the Jewish population which are the result of its special language and particular living conditions," was voted through, 46 to 5.[323] An amendment proposed by Liber to reaffirm the decision of the First Congress of the RSDRP, granting autonomy "in all questions which particularly concern the Jewish proletariat," was rejected by 26 votes to 13.[324]

The Bundist organizational plan, or statute *(ustav)*, was not in fact voted on until weeks later at the twenty-sixth session, no longer in Brussels but in London. The crucial clause, which defined the Bund as the "sole representative of the Jewish proletariat" and as an organization unlimited by geographical bounds, was then defeated, 41 to 5 (with 5 abstentions).[325] The Bundist delegation finally announced its withdrawal from the congress – and by implication, from the RSDRP.

It must be presumed that the *Iskra* leadership delayed this final vote in the hope that, given time and subjected to sufficient pressure, the Bundists would make still further concessions in order to remain in the RSDRP. However, this hypothesis was never put to the test. The longer the congress lasted, the more cracks began to appear in the *Iskra* bloc. Thus the Bundists (together with the three "Economists") were able to add their weight in the critical votes against the "hards" led by Lenin and Plekhanov. Allied to the Georgian delegates, they took the lead in pushing through (after innumerable tied votes and endless delaying tactics by the "hards") a clause in the program of the RSDRP that, going beyond recognition of the right of national self-determination, spelled out safeguards for the minority nationalities. It stated that

the population has the right to be educated in its native language; that in order to guarantee this right, the necessary schools be established and financed by the state and by the organs of self-government; that every citizen has the right to express himself at public assemblies in his native tongue; and that the native language be given equal status with the state language in all local government and state institutions.[326]

In the years 1913–14, during his renewed polemics against the Bund, Lenin would frequently call in this clause of the party program in order to demonstrate Bolshevik generosity in the national question.[327] The grudging concession of today became the cause for self-congratulation on the morrow.

The Bundists also provided Martov's famous resolution on party membership with its clear majority over Lenin's proposal. By the time they finally departed, the congress was in total disarray and there was no longer any question of their being intimidated into making still further concessions. For their part, Martov and the "softs" who supported him were not prepared to keep the Bundists and "Economists" at the congress, even though without their vote his following was transformed from the majority to minority (*menshinstvo*).

Martov thus fell into the same trap that had ensnared the Bundists since 1901. He was not willing to ally with the Right against the Left within the Social Democratic movement. The fear of being tarnished by heresy was real and deep. Once having accepted the logic of Marxist reductionism, that all "right wing" deviations represented bourgeois or petty-bourgeois interests in a proletarian guise, it was well-nigh impossible to escape it. The Bundists had now left the RSDRP; but they did so on the narrow ground of self-preservation rather than in the name of general principle. The genius of their movement lay in compromise and common sense. And these were qualities which could not be effectively employed at the Second Congress nor, as it would ultimately prove, in twentieth-century Russia.

Only one man had the independence of mind and spirit to ask boldly how it was possible that the Social Democratic congress had been conducted in such a spirit:

> But what is this? Such things, then, can happen in our party! It is possible for party leaders . . . to deprive their opponent of the opportunity to reply and then to distort the latter's view before the eyes of all with a fantastic, incredible boldness, while no one, not a single comrade, is moved to rise in indignation, to interrupt them, to cry out that it is shameful . . .[328] It would not be rational to explain all this by individual traits of delegates who "know not what they do." It is essential to find the general principle.[329]

That general principle, Akimov stated, was the belief explicitly expounded by Plekhanov that the end justifies the means and that minority dictatorship was therefore acceptable to a Social Democrat. "Our answer to the problem of dictatorship," he concluded, "will affect every single step of our activity."[330] Akimov defended the Bund at the congress but its delegation did not defend him. He eventually drifted out of the Social Democratic movement altogether.

The Bund reenters the Russian Social Democratic Labor Party, 1906

At its Sixth Congress, held in Zurich in October 1905, the Bund finally included the demand for national autonomy in its program. The resolution adopted there defined this term much more specifically than had the Fourth Congress in 1901. What was demanded was national-cultural autonomy... those governmental-juridical insitutions which would permit each nation its free cultural development... The [governmental] functions connected with cultural questions (public education, etc.) should be removed from the state and from local and territorial self-government and be transferred to the nation, per se, to special institutions (both local and central) elected by all its members on the basis of universal, equal, direct, and secret suffrage.[331]

In 1906 the Bund reentered the Russian Social Democratic Labor Party. At the Stockholm congress of the RSDRP, held in April, a majority voted in favor of a reunification project, which in turn was ratified by the Seventh Congress of the Bund meeting in Lemberg in August. At Stockholm, 58 delegates voted for unification and 40 against; at Lemberg the majority was still larger – 47 in favor, 20 against.

On the face of it, these developments would appear to reinforce the established historiographical approach. Forced out of the RSDRP in 1903, the Bund defeated subsequent attempts by Mensheviks and Bolsheviks to "capture" its proletarian following; adopted a more national program in order to meet the demands of its mass membership (enormously augmented in 1905), and, finally, negotiating from a position of strength, won recognition of its legitimacy from and its rightful place in the mother party. This approach was implicit in Rozental's important study of the reunification published in Warsaw in 1922. The terms offered in Stockholm, he wrote, were (with one exception) such that even "the greatest optimist could not have hoped for such a success."[332] Its adoption by the Bund was inevitable because "even with point 6, the unification clauses worked out in Stockholm... were a great step forward."[333]

In reality, however, the Sixth and Seventh Congresses (the nationalist resolution of 1905, and the reentry into the RSDRP in August 1906) did not represent points on a rising curve of Bundist political growth. Just the opposite was the case. To pursue the metaphor, the Sixth Congress has to be seen as a high point on the graph of political and ideological self-confidence with the curve then descending to the Lemberg congress. To gloss over this basic fact is to ignore the extremely volatile nature of mass politics during the revolution of 1905–6. Interestingly enough, Abramovich, speaking in April 1906, decried the triumphantly determinist view of Bundist reentry into the RSDRP as "too 'Marxist' for me – they [Rozental, etc.] fall into the usual error of all ultra-Marxists, overestimating objective tendencies and underestimating the importance of consciousness and form."[334]

The decision of the Stockholm congress in favor of the reunification project hardly reflected a recognition that the Bund had emerged justified, still less triumphant, from the three years of schism. A Bundist reentry into the party would have been out of the question if Lenin, of all people, had not decided to throw behind it the full support of the Bolshevik faction. Of the 58 votes in favor of the project, 41 came from the Bolsheviks. (Among those voting for the proposal were Voroshilov and Stalin, who, as a Georgian, went out of his way to disassociate himself from Zhordania's hostility to the Bund.)[335] On the other hand, of the Mensheviks, who were not tied by factional discipline on the issue, 38 voted against and only 17 for the Bund.[336]

Lenin's calculation was clear enough. During the revolution, the Bund had consistently followed a tactical line which ran much closer to that of the Bolsheviks than to that of the Mensheviks. Thus, with the Bolsheviks, the Bund had come out for a boycott of the elections to the Bulygin and First Dumas, for party trade unions, for restricting the role of the Soviets and for planning toward an armed uprising. As the Bolshevik faction could not count on a majority in the RSDRP – it was outnumbered by the Mensheviks at Stockholm – it naturally turned to the nationality parties (the SDKPiL, the LSDRP, and the Bund) in order to shift the balance in its favor. Having abandoned the idea of consolidating the RSDRP into a monolithic movement, Lenin was ready to include the Bund within it. But this was a purely tactical move, a fact symbolically underlined by Lenin's decision to remain silent during the relevant debate.

However, the motives underlying the offer to the Bund were obviously less important than its terms, and the inescapable fact is that the terms were very harsh. The natural standard of comparison is the truncated statute presented as its last word by the Bundist delegation at the seventh session of the Second Congress in 1903.[337] The demand for recognition as "the sole representative" of the Jewish proletariat, which had been retained then, was now dropped by the Bund even before sending its delegation to Stockholm. Again, at the Second Congress, it had been proposed that any change in the constitutional agreement between the Bund and the RSDRP require at least a two-thirds majority at a party congress. The provisional instructions to the Bundist delegation in Stockholm went further still, demanding veto power over any change; but the agreement then worked out in the joint commission dropped all mention of any such provision. Finally, implicit in the statute presented to the Second Congress 1903 was the idea that the local Bundist organization was subject to only one regular chain of command, that leading down from the central committee of the RSDRP through the Bundist central committee. But in the joint commission at Stockholm it was agreed that in every city there be a supreme committee elected by all party members (Bundists, Bolsheviks, Mensheviks, and others) on the basis of proportional representation.

At the Stockholm congress, Abramovich explained to the plenary session just how much the Bund had given up. "[Our] slogan," he said, "is: workers, organize yourselves within one party but with national subdivisions [po natsionalnostiam]. We have waived that basic principle. Then again we have recognized that other [Social Democratic] organizations work and have the right to work among the masses of the Jewish proletariat. That is also a basic concession of principle."[338] But this is by no means all that the Bund was expected to yield. During the final voting of the Stockholm congress, the plenary session introduced drastic amendments to the preliminary agreement. Thus, clause 2 had recognized (as demanded in a Bundist ultimatum) that "the Bund has the right to preserve its program on the national question."[339] But the plenum amended this to read that "the national question remains open because it was not considered at [this] . . . congress."[340] As explained by the chairman, F. Dan, this meant that the Bund could keep its program until the next congress of the RSDRP.

During a scene of growing confusion and uproar, the congress next voted an amendment to clause 6, deciding that the urban committees be elected by direct majority vote and not (as agreed in the joint preparatory commission) by proportional representation. Abramovich rushed to declare that "the amendment is unacceptable to the Bund" and that "with all the noise in the hall resolutions are being carried which contradict the decision already taken."[341] But his efforts availed nothing because (whether so planned or not) the Bolsheviks had suddenly deserted the Bundist cause en bloc. The crippling amendment (proposed by Varsky of the SDKPiL) was carried by an overwhelming majority: 62 for and 6 against, with 18 abstentions.[342]

This decision, if realized in practice, was bound to lead to the disappearance of the Bund from all those areas where it did not control a majority of the Social Democratic membership—it would be rolled back to its original "Vilna-Minsk fatherland." Thus, in effect, it negated the first clause of the agreement which recognized that the Bund was "not confined within geographical limits." At the Lemberg congress of the Bund in August, the observers from the RSDRP (Leon Goldman and Martynov) made it unmistakably clear that this was precisely how they understood this clause; the urban committee of the party in Warsaw or Odessa, for instance, would now have complete control over the local Bundist organization. "This declaration," stated the report on the Lemberg congress, "had a dampening effect [on the delegates] and seriously depressed enthusiasm for unification."[343]

All in all, the terms on which the Bund reentered the RSDRP were considerably worse than those for the sake of which the Bundist delegation had walked out of the Second Congress in 1903. It was, then, only natural that for four months, from April until August, the question of reunification with the RSDRP became a matter of enormous controversy within the Bund. No holds were barred in the struggle for the soul of the movement. But, at the same time, the spirit of mutual tolerance which had always reigned in the Bundist leadership now truly came into its own. Both the "hards"—those in favor of rejecting the terms offered—and the "softs" were given access to the press of the movement and to meetings of the local organizations. Despite the harshness of the confrontation, most members seemed to have positively reveled in the opportunity to conduct a public debate legally and openly. There had never been anything like it before in the Russian Bund and never would be again.

To a large extent, the struggle between the "hards" and the "softs" in the spring and early summer of 1906 represented one more round in the conflict between what have been termed here the "nationalist" and "internationalist" wings of the movement. Thus, among the most vocal advocates of reunification were Pavel and Anna Rozental, Zeldov (Nemansky), and Taras (Kats), who of course had consistently opposed the increasingly national character of the Bund since the late 1890s. Similarly, among the "hards" were many who had fought for the idea of a Jewish Social Democratic party. Thus, predictably enough, Vladimir Kossovsky argued strongly against paying so high a price for reunification. Then there were the Bundists associated with the Warsaw movement: Mill, Pesakhzon and (from the new generation) Bronislav Groser, all of whom tended to feel that the Bund should be neither Russian nor Polish but just Jewish. Frumin, Zivion, and Ezra Rozin, from the group of "Berne Bundists," were likewise committed "hards" as were a number of veteran polu-intelligenty, most notably Lesin (who returned from New York to attend the Lemberg congress) and Litvak.

But for the first time since 1899, the advocates of the more "national" policy

Figure 15. From left: Shmuel Gozhansky, Maks Vinokur, Avrom Mutnik, John Mill, 1907.

now went down to defeat. At the Seventh Conference of the Bund held in Berne in March 1906, when the conditions for reunification were first formally debated, the two sides were still evenly balanced. The major decision of the conference, not to demand recognition of the Bund as the sole representative of the Jewish proletariat, was carried by the narrowest of margins: 19 to 17 with 1 absention.[344]

In early May, Litvak was still convinced that the "hards" actually represented the majority of the movement[345] and would succeed in having the reunification rejected at the coming congress of the Bund. Certainly, they had much the better of the debate in the *Folks-tsaytung*, where Pavel Rozental for a long time was left to defend reentry into the RSDRP almost single-handed. Nonetheless, at Lemberg in August the delegates, who had been democratically elected by the local organizations, voted overwhelmingly to accept the terms offered by the RSDRP.

The balance was tipped sharply against the "hards" as a growing number of key leaders came out unequivocally for ratification. In the past, Kremer and Portnoi, who if not charismatic leaders at least enjoyed a kind of paternal authority, had tended to favor the national wing of the movement; now they went the other way. More surprising, many of the key representatives of the young intelligentsia – Liber, Abramovich, Medem, and Zaslavsky – did likewise. Thus, a large majority of the central committee was publicly committed to reunification, and this in itself was a decisive factor. But why had these men, who hitherto had belonged to or supported the national orientation, now swung the other way?

Undoubtedly, their deep-rooted loyalty to the idea of an international, albeit Russian-centered, revolutionary movement moved them profoundly. Even a man like Mill has recorded that when he heard Medem report on the walkout from the Second Congress in 1903 he had "wept openly like child, without shame."[346] They had always seen their movement as bridging two worlds; and they were ready to do almost anything in their power to repair the bridge that had been abruptly cut down three years before. This, after all, had been Kremer's life work.

Moreover, many of the younger *intelligenty* may have been tempted by the opportunity now opening up before them to move into a larger arena where their talents would have full play. The subsequent careers of men such as Liber and Abramovich, who eventually became more associated with the Mensheviks than the Bund, tends to lend credence to this possibility. A number of outside observers who had some familiarity with life in the Bundist movement were struck by its gray earnestness, by its "narrow horizons,"[347] by its almost deliberate exclusion of "theory, philosophy, ethics, and esthetics."[348] Against this background, the vision of a powerful, reunited, multinational (but essentially Russian-speaking and intelligentsia-dominated) party must have shone brightly indeed. Certainly, Lesin had the feeling at the Lemberg congress that "the 'hards' came mainly from the yeshiva, while the 'softs' were predominantly from the russified school."[349] For those involved in Yiddish journalism or public speaking – Frumin, Zivion, Litvak, Lesin, Shakhne Epstein, Vladeck – reentry into the RSDRP promised few personal opportunities.

Lesin further recorded his impression that the *polu-intelligenty* carried relatively little weight at the congress because "they had never worn the brass *gimnaziia* buttons"[350] while, on the other hand, an absurdly exaggerated respect was shown to the two Mensheviks, Leontev and Martynov, who were present as representatives of the central committee of the RSDRP.

> [They were] the two representatives of the "goyim" – and both were Jews and both wore beards ... The congress had its fine and elevated moments ... But, in addition, it revealed the most typically Jewish complexes, enough typically Jewish self-denigration even toward their own great movement. To me it was comical to see how these two purely Jewish physiognomies with their two pure Russian names (not their real ones) attracted everybody's attention, ... demands, requests; they were the pillar on which the congress stood.[351]

Nevertheless, to suggest that the division between the "hards" and the "softs" was mainly between the *intelligentsiia* and the *polu-intelligentsiia* would be grossly to oversimplify. Not sociological but political factors were of predominant significance.

The decision of the Bund to ratify the humiliating terms offered by the RSDRP reflected, above all, a crisis of confidence within the movement. Until October 1905, the Bund had advanced from strength to strength; but that month was a watershed in its development, and thereafter, even though it retained or even increased its very large membership, it suffered a long series of setbacks. The fact that its failures were rarely of its own making did not lessen the sense of malaise, of loss of control.

Throughout the revolution, the Bund pursued an essentially consistent policy. It worked on the basic assumption that the proletariat was the one true revolutionary class and the Bund the only true revolutionary party in the Jewish world. As long as it enjoyed hegemony in the Jewish "street," it was prepared to welcome the emergence of other oppositional forces. It took credit not only for having stirred the somnolent bourgeoisie into action but also for having anticipated the growing call for Jewish national rights. "Times change," stated an important article in *Poslednie izvestiia* on 12 September 1905.

> It is not so many years since the Fourth Congress of the Bund formulated the principle of national-cultural autonomy, is it? We were then entirely isolated on this question ... How totally the picture has changed now. It is enough simply to glance at the Jewish legal press (both Yiddish and Russian) of the last seven to eight months in order to be convinced that an undoubted and clear revolution has taken place. A veritable deluge of articles, declarations, resolutions, petitions, an entire wave of public opinion has come out – in more or less disguised form – for that same Bundist national-cultural autonomy. Now it has become up to date, a fashionable political slogan ... [This] revolution ... is the best proof that we are dealing with a demand raised by the masses, which is required by the masses, which meets the needs of the masses.[352]

These sentiments were published in anticipation of the approaching Sixth Congress of the Bund and they expressed the self-assurance of a party then at the height of an undisputed authority, riding on the crest of the wave, united by and confident in its success. An exclusively class party, it was also in the vanguard of national politics.

But the wave began to break starting from early in October 1905. The Bund leadership fell victim to a series of major setbacks. When the great October strike movement began, the leaders almost to a man were in Zurich attending the Sixth Congress, and they were unable to return to Russia because the railways had closed down. Their enforced absence in those historic days and the resultant inactivity of the Bund simply underlined the fact that the final stages of the revolution were to be decided in the heartlands, not the borderlands, of the empire; by the Russian and not by the Jewish, Polish, or Latvian proletariat. Then from the 18 October came the anti-Jewish pogroms. The subsequent revulsion and fear inevitably struck hardest at the Bund if only because its prestige was inextricably linked in the Jewish world to that of the revolution as a whole. "Following the October Days," stated Ezra Rozin at the Lemberg congress, "the central committee completely lost control and for almost two months did not exist."[353] This and similar statements were received by the delegates as uncontroversial, a simple statement of a sad truth. Not until *Der veker* began to come out late in December 1905 did the Bund find its voice again.

But soon, another factor was to erode the foundations of the movement's power. At the height of the revolution, funds in unprecedented quantities had been collected for the Bund in the United States (and to a lesser extent in South Africa) – the committee abroad alone received 295,000 francs from these two countries in the period between the Sixth and Seventh Congresses.[354] But, in the words of the official report, "when the [revolutionary] movement began to die down the sums of money from America began increasingly to decline."[355] The smaller budget inevitably required a reduction in the corps of professional revolutionaries, which had grown into the hundreds in 1905.

It was not that the Bund suddenly began to disintegrate, but simply that the supremacy which it had established in the Jewish world since January 1905 now came under mounting challenge. The basic assumption of Bundist ideology, that the accentuation of class divisions and class warfare within the Jewish people was in the best interests of the nation, became the cause of bitter attacks from the "bourgeois" leaders of the Union for Equal Rights. The Bund, Dubnov wrote in December 1905,

> declares its pretensions to be the representative of our national interests . . . but the alienation of these Marxist fanatics was revealed in tragic form during the recent events. Together with their comrades from the Russian socialist organizations, they are profoundly convinced that the Russian people are called upon to carry through a revolution of the highest order which will enable it in one fell swoop to leap all historical barriers, even a democratic constitution, directly to a "people's government" or to a demo-cratic republic or even a little further – to social revolution . . . How has this mystical Russian [russkii] nationalism seized hold of you, gentlemen, the Jewish Social Democrats, you, brothers and sisters, who have just experi-enced on your broken skulls one of the historic "missions" of the Russian people, making 1905 analogous to 1648 (read 1648 not 1848)?[356]

Dubnov was convinced that in a time of emergency, what was required was na-tional unity and a collective reponse to the collective crisis.

But this argument neither the Bund nor the other Jewish socialist parties was in any way prepared to accept. The goal now was to unite all the active revolutionary forces, regardless of nationality, in one final assault against the tsarist system. There could be no talk of a Jewish *Seim* or National Assembly until the revolution was fully victorious, until Russia as a whole was liberated. The Bund had to follow its own separate path in the Jewish world, declared *Der veker* in January 1906: "The National Assembly will work out a national program – that is nonsense . . . Each class has its own political program . . . The Jewish proletariat does not have to go to your Seim in order to gain a political Torah; it has already received one from Karl Marx and his followers."[357] Besides, continued the argument, the Jewish proletariat "forms, after all, a minority in the Jewish people – true, an important and active minority but still a minority." The Bund could not permit others to dictate to it; would therefore have to walk out of a Jewish National Assembly; and so, why should it "go there in the first place?"[358]

Jabotinsky, of course, pounced on such pronouncements in order to expose what he described as the inconsistency of the Bundist position. If it advocated Jewish self-government, how could it deny the validity of majority rule in Jewish life? "What of cultural autonomy? What of the cultural Seim? Or did they have in mind here that the voters to the National Cultural Seim would be only proletarian and the remaining classes of the population would be deprived of voting rights?"[359] After all, insisted Jabotinsky, the Bund was committed to universal suffrage in the Jewish world and that commitment could hardly just be forgotten – it had either to be repudiated or reaffirmed. "We have known for a long time," he concluded, "that the Bund could not remain indefinitely at its present crossroads."[360]

It was not difficult for the Bundist spokesmen to hit back in answer to such attacks. ("I can assure Ahad Ha-Am, Dubnov, and their friends," Frumin wrote, "that what really involves the honor of the Jewish people is as holy and dear, if not more so, to the Jewish proletariat as to the Jewish bourgeoisie.")[361] But what was involved here was not just polemical sniping. The attacks were symptomatic of the gradual erosion of Bundist dominance in the Jewish world. Throughout the early months of 1906, the Bund (together with the other Jewish socialist parties) was trying to ensure a total boycott of the elections to the First Duma. The almost complete failure of this campaign to deter the Jewish voters was a major defeat for the Left as a whole, but above all for the Bund.

What for the Bund was an unmitigated disaster had its compensations for the new Jewish socialist parties (the SSRP, SERP, and the ESDRP-PZ). Advocating much more far-reaching solutions to the Jewish question – territorialism in various forms – they were able to make short-term gains from the discomfiture of the Bundists. Essentially, they sought to outbid or outflank the Bund by adopting positions at once more nationalist and more "proletarian." Thus, the SSRP came out, like the Mensheviks, for nonparty unions and for workers' soviets. At the same time, they asserted constantly that the Bund saw the Jewish situation through rose-tinted glasses and ignored the deep-rooted forces crowding the Jews out of the country's society and economy. "We are not surprised," stated an attack on the Bund by the Warsaw committee of the SSRP in 1905, "that the streams of blood shed by the Jews – revolutionaries and nonrevolutionaries – [in the pogroms] have not opened your eyes to the abnormal positon of the Jewish proletariat."[362]

For their part, the "internationalist" parties, the SDKPiL and the RSDRP, had by no means abandoned the hope of winning over to their side the rank-and-file membership of the Bund. In 1904 two organizations of the RSDRP, the Northwest and Polese committees, had been established essentially to carry the war against the Bund into Lithuania and White Russia. The Bund had more than held its own in this struggle for control in 1904 and 1905, but the rivalry continued unabated. Those Social Democrats who were involved in the anti-Bundist campaign were by and large convinced that their initial defeats were due to poor organization and that their "internationalist" position enjoyed much support among the workers. Typical of this view was the following speech made by G. L. Shklovsky from Minsk at the Bolshevik congress of April 1905:

> The idea of nationalism has had no success among the Jewish proletariat and all the nationalistic ideas of the workers were *inoculated into them in the most artificial way by the Bund* (Lenin and others: hear! hear!) . . . When the broad strata of the Bundist workers learned of the exit of the Bund from the party, there were serious disturbances in their organizations . . . The Bund mobilized its forces. At once the best Bundist orators began to tour its regions . . . they unleased a wave of demagogy . . . Our Party did not mobilize its forces against *this kind* of activity of the Bund . . . The Bund was victorious . . . [363] [But now] the mood of the masses has changed sharply in our favor. We have to thank the 9 January for that. When the real revolution began in Russia, the best Bundists and the broadest masses of the Bund understood the falsity of political separatism. Many have come over to us.[364]

The fact that the Northwest committee of the RSDRP had not published any material in Yiddish – "not one leaflet" – was, in Shklovsky's view, a major reason for its relative failure in 1905. But in the worsening situation of 1906, the Bund was plagued by the vision of being surrounded by a hostile ring of parties, with the other Jewish socialist movements drawing away the more national workers and the RSDRP and the SDKPiL (or even the PPS) attracting the internationalist masses. The fact that the SSRP often cooperated with the Mensheviks on an ad hoc basis against the Bund only heightened this fear. Again, the decision of Plekhanov late in 1905 to grant Jabotinsky an interview, in which he praised the Poale Zion as "far more consistent than the Bund"[365] and declared that the Bundists were simply "Zionists afraid of seasickness," was hardly reassuring.[366]

Thus, when the word spread early in 1906 that the Mensheviks and the Bolsheviks were planning to unite not only among themselves but also with the Polish and Latvian Social Democratic parties, the Bund felt itself profoundly menaced. This threat was formulated very bluntly by the delegate from the Vilna committee of the RSDRP at the Stockholm congress in April 1906. "The Bund and the Jewish proletariat," he said, "are two different things. The Jewish proletariat enters our organization ... and after the unification with the SDKPiL and the Latvians our organization ... will be everywhere where the Jewish proletariat lives. So I am convinced that our party has no grounds for making a compromise in principle with the Bund."[367]

If the "softs" constantly gained strength between March and August 1906 it was because reunification with the RSDRP, even on harsh terms, at least represented a positive step, a chance to escape ideological and organizational encirclement. As Taras (Kats) put it at the Seventh Conference: "If the R[SDR]P unites with the PSD and the Latvians the Bund will be *kaput* (laughter, protest). I am for unification at any price as long as we keep point 1, of course."[368] "We must recognize," Mikhalevich said, "that what is taking place is not a Jewish but a Russian revolution ... The Bund cannot exist without unification ... Any other attitude ... is unforgivingly doctrinaire [*doktrinerstvo*]."[369] "The unification of the RSDRP with the PSD and the Latvians, ..." Nemansky said, "would have a very demoralizing influence on our workers."[370]

Ultimately, the "hards" could not rebuff the harsh logic of these arguments. The deeply entrenched policy of nonalliance with other forces in the Jewish world, be it the Union for Equal Rights or the other socialist parties, made it impossible for the "hards" to advocate an "opening to the right" as a coherent counterstrategy. Essentially, they were left to defend the status quo, which meant increasing isolation in both the Jewish and the socialist worlds.

On the face of it, the "hards" could have been expected to adopt a Menshevik-type strategy in their Jewish politics – an attempt to rally all the oppositional forces on a common platform of equal rights, national autonomy, and support for radical or left-wing candidates in the Duma elections. At the Lemberg congress, Leon Goldman criticized the Bundist leadership for having failed to do this, but the only supporter he found among the delegates was Virgily Cohen, a "soft." In fact, this was typical. The "hards" generally advocated intransigent policies all along the line. Those who opposed reentry into the party – Groser, Litvak, Ezra Rozin – were usually also in favor of boycotting elections even to the Second Duma.

The "hards" won the battle of words. They were more single-minded, not the least hesitant, more eloquent. "Only an organization that has grown out of ... the Jewish masses," wrote Litvak in May 1906, which lives their life, feels what they feel . . . only such an organization can adapt to the psychology of the Jewish masses . . . only it can give the right answer to all the questions that Jewish life calls forth . . . [371] For three years we have been laughed at, mocked, called chauvinists, separatists, inconsistent Zionists and so on . . . But the three years have shown that we were right . . . [Then] there were no Jewish Social Democratic masses [in the south] . . . Now we are stronger among the Jews [there] than the RSDRP . . . Has the [Northwest committee of the RSDRP] won over the Jewish proletarian masses? No and no! . . . Did it prevent the Bund from growing? Again, no! . . . [372] The Russian party has learned nothing in the last three years . . . As before it does not recognize the right of the Bund to exist . . . It hopes that it will be easier to eliminate the Bund once it is inside the party.[373]

But these and similar arguments availed nothing. The "hards" were defeated because the situation of the Bund was deteriorating; because they had no alternative strategy; because the rank and file were opposed to isolation. In 1906, for the first time, the Bund had become a largely democratic organization and this too worked against the "hards." "The pressure of the Jewish workers for unification,"[374] Litvak later admitted, had become irresistible.

Conclusion

The Bund was the first, and throughout the period covered in this book the most important, Jewish socialist party. Its influence on other such parties founded in Russia, eastern Europe, and Palestine – as indeed on the Jewish labor movement in the USA – was profound. A revolutionary party with a mass labor, quasi-trade-union base; a strongly centralized and conspiratorial party which was not and did not seek to be monolithic, a popular party with strong emphasis on self-defense units armed against pogroms – this was the organizational model that others sought to reproduce or adapt to different circumstances. A Jewish party with a specific medium-range program to meet the Jewish question, an international party linked to the Russian revolutionary movement and Second International, a class party committed to the class war, a party of "scientific" socialism which saw itself as the instrument of historic necessity – this was the ideological model that influenced all the other parties even as they denounced it in varying degrees and for varying reasons.

Firmly rejecting sectarianism in its internal life, the Bundist (and proto-Bundist) movement escaped schisms and splits throughout the period from 1895 to 1919. Against the background of theocratic intolerance that came to dominate the Russian Social Democratic movement this was a remarkable achievement, a demonstration of human decency and common sense in a setting where those qualities were increasingly held in contempt. However, Akimov's hope that the Bund would lead the fight for democratic values in the Russian Social Democratic Labor Party was not realistic. Throughout the pre-1914 period, the Bund saw its role in the party as that of mediator, shunning polemics and seeking to reconcile the warring factions.

In taking this stand, the Bund was acting according to its own inner norms. The development of Bundist ideology had throughout required enormous investments of energy and ingenuity in order to reconcile opposing viewpoints or, at the very least, to find formulas that would not lead to open schism.

For within the Bund's leading strata there were groups that held totally contradictory views of what their movement was, should aim for, and become. While some saw it as the political avant-garde of the Jewish people in Russia – the proletarian base that would liberate the nation – others saw it as a branch of the general Russian revolutionary movement and assumed (with Lenin, Martov, or Trotsky) that the Jewish nationality would soon integrate totally into Russian society. The spiritual struggle of the Jewish socialist as an individual – torn (like Liberman and Hess) between loyalty to the Jewish people and loyalty to an all-embracing cause – thus in the case of the Bund became the burden of an entire movement.

As long as its principal rivals were on the right – the Zionists and the PPS – the leadership slowly moved toward the idea of a fully autonomous Jewish socialist party, combining class war with the defense of national interests. It saw the opportunity to preempt the cause of Diaspora nationalism, revolutionary and socialist, and by 1901 it had moved far and effectively to do so. But when, with the creation of *Iskra,* the challenge came from the "internationalist Left," the Bund was thrown into a deep inner crisis from which there could be no satisfactory escape. To the extent that pressure was exerted from below, from the organized workers (in 1902–3, and in 1906) it was in favor of "internationalist" positions. The Bundist leadership would not capitulate and would not split but it could only fight back when its very survival was directly threatened. It was a harsh reality; but, then, the situation of the Jewish people in the Russian Empire was in itself beset by impossible dilemmas. These the Bund faithfully reflected.

CHAPTER 5

Chaim Zhitlovsky

Russian populist and Jewish socialist, *1887–1907*

When he died in 1943 while on a lecture tour in Canada, Chaim Zhitlovsky was still a well-known figure in the Jewish world as he had been for some forty years, so much so that posthumously he at once became the object of a bitter and highly publicized controversy. Accused in articles and monographs by leading members of the *Forverts* group – Abe Cahan, Hillel Rogoff, and Chaim Liberman[1] – of having been a life-long Jewish antisemite, he was defended by the literary critic Shmuel Niger in a series of articles in *Der tog*[2] and in a book put out by his memorial committee, which included such prominent publicists on the pro-Communist left as Ben Zion Goldberg and Kalman Marmor.[3] By now, however, he is largely forgotten.[4]

Perhaps this fate is no more than poetic justice. A man who adopted, abandoned, or lost interest in so many different political programs and causes; who joined, left, or drifted away from so many parties was probably destined, at least in the short run, to oblivion. At varying times, he was a sharp opponent of Zionism and a Zionist, an antiterritorialist and a territorialist, a supporter of the Bund and one of its harshest critics, a Socialist Revolutionary and an apologist for Bolshevism. He was a kind of ideological nomad, forever on the move.

Such a man might, of course, have imposed himself on the imagination of posterity by his sheer creative power or the depth of his personality. But it would be hard to argue that he had in him the stuff of genius or tragedy. Indeed, as a human being, he must suffer by comparison with his lifelong friend and associate, An-sky, who immersed himself totally and long in every task he undertook, who tirelessly wore himself out in such causes as refugee relief during World War I, was more modest and is today better remembered both for his role as a Centrist SR in the October Revolution of 1917 and for his play, *The Dybbuk*.

Yet, however true all this is, the fact remains that Zhitlovksy played a central role in the development of Jewish socialist thought and politics. Indeed, his faults simply represented the reverse side of his strengths. Tied to no one movement, he was able to influence many, especially in their early formative periods. Constantly and irritatingly analyzing the place of his own works in history, at the same time he possessed a remarkable sense of the historical process in general, and this at a time when the great majority of his socialist comrades had eyes only for the present and a mythic future. He tended at moments to overplay the prophetic role, excoriating his people even when (as in the late 1930s) such bitter accusations could serve no useful purpose; and yet in his analyses of the Jewish predicament in the pre-1914 period he did at times reveal a profound and comprehensive awareness of impending tragedy.

Straining for originality, he really has proved to be among the most "modern" of his contemporaries, dealing with (and providing possible answers to) questions heatedly debated today in the Jewish world. To take just two examples from many, he devoted much attention even before World War I to the issue of "Who Is a Jew?"—anticipating in detail the argument of Father Daniel in his famous case before the Israeli Supreme Court—and to the problem of how a Jewish secular culture could absorb and transform the national heritage, despite its overwhelmingly religious character.

As early as 1912, An-sky anticipated the criticism that could be leveled against his friend and sought to rebut it. Judging from his career, he wrote even then,

> one might imagine that we are dealing with a man of burning, inexhaustible energy, with a man who throws himself in different directions, who takes on every possible job, who is always striving to be on top, who wavers between different ideological tendencies. It is hard to imagine anything less like Zhitlovsky. In his whole personality . . . he is a professor, a scholar, an observer . . . He dislikes the turmoil of public life, has absolutely no understanding for politicking . . . [5] Playing an important role in a number of parties, which were close to his ideas, he never put himself forward as the "leader" and always rejected all "command positions" . . . It would be still more erroneous to argue that Zhitlovsky wavers in his convictions . . . That which can be interpreted as ideological wavering is in him only a restless search for the right path to his goal . . .[6] The necessity for a synthesis between the national foundations and the general goals of humanity . . . inspired his . . . entire effort. One can say with complete confidence that in his conflict with Russian Marxism, in his dedication to the ideals of Russian *narodnichestvo,* he held the same position: the search for a harmonious interdependence between the populist foundations and the highest ideals of mankind as a whole.[7]

It is in fact true that at one level, Zhitlovsky was remarkably consistent, faithful throughout his near sixty years in public life to two basic concepts. First, he held that the life of the Jewish masses had to be radically reconstructed on new foundations, not through an exodus (which could never take place on a scale commensurate with the problem) but in the countries where they lived. Town dwellers, they should become primarily an agricultural people (both in eastern Europe and North America); a people of many tongues, they should opt for one national language, Yiddish. Once guaranteed against general assimilation by the perpetuation and reinforcement of Yiddish as the language of education and culture, the Jews would be free to develop a modern, secular, free-thinking, humanist ethos. To undermine the ancient religious faith would no longer be to endanger the national survival.

Second, in his numerous *referaty* and essays on the philosophy of history, he argued long and vehemently against the assumption that the triumph of socialism was guaranteed by, and dependent on, sociohistorical scientific laws. Against the determinism of the Marxists he advanced a voluntarist conception. Against their materialism, he insisted that ideas and ideals had an autonomous power of their own. Against their thesis that economics and the sociology of class ultimately determined all else, he proclaimed the independent force of politics and the individual. In the long run, he argued, hope and will were surer guarantees of success than faith in a necessarily imperfect science.

In many essential ways, Zhitlovsky always remained a man of the mid-1880s. The conflict between populism and Marxism, and the search for a higher synthesis between the positive in both doctrines, were of abiding concern to him. Again, in his double disillusionment with socialist assimilationism and with Palestinophilism – and in his conscious search for a third way – he stayed the archetypal representative of those transitional years. As a man from another age, time and again in the years 1893–1914, he became the rallying point for those who for one reason or another were alienated from the prevailing Social Democratic orthodoxy. To future leaders of the SR party (such as Chernov), to the national wing of the Bund (Mill, Frumin), to radicals among the Zionist youth (Zilberfarb, Fabrikant, Ben Adir), to ex-anarchists, Am Olam members, and social revolutionaries in New York (Vinchevsky, Raevsky, Zolotarov, Pavel Kaplan) he was at various times a natural ideological mentor and leader.

Nevertheless, An-sky overstated his case. True, Zhitlovsky was hardly a political weathercock. If anything, he disliked being a member of the majority, or echoing prevailing opinion. But he was a political barometer, sensitive to and quickly reflecting incipient changes in the atmosphere. He was a man of sharply differing moods. At times he interpreted his own basic concepts with a euphoric optimism, and then again, working from the same general premises, he could be the blackest pessimist. He always carried with him not only a number of first principles but also certain crucial dilemmas, doubts, and hesitations. Was the Jewish people capable of generating its own sociopolitical renaissance? Or would that reconstruction have to come from above? Was the populist path – for, and through, the people – the right one? Or was political elitism the only answer? As a Narodovolets and Communist sympathizer he gave one answer. As a would-be Bundist and Seimist he gave another. As a socialist Zionist he hesitated somewhere in between.

On prophets and parasites, 1887–1892

The biographies of Chaim Zhitlovsky and Shloyme Zanvl Rappoport (An-sky) demonstrate how, even after the pogroms of 1882 and by a paradoxical logic, a commitment to the tenets of Russian revolutionary populism could lead to a simultaneous involvement in Jewish life and politics. Both these men had arrived by 1905–6 at a similar position, members of the SR party and spokesmen for the revolutionary Left in the Jewish world. But they had followed very different paths in reaching that point.

Zhitlovsky and An-sky became close friends in 1878–80 while still in their teens in Vitebsk. Having both suffered terribly through their years in the heder with its twelve-hour day of Talmud study – "an absolute hell,"[8] as Zhitlovsky called it – they now threw themselves with abandon into the Russian radical classics, Chernyshevsky, Pisarev, Lavrov, Mikhailovsky. They felt a revulsion from the established Jewish world with its strict religious discipline, its all-pervasive traditionalism, its urban character, its dependence on trade. In Russian culture and the Russian countryside they saw a way of life freer, broader, more moral, healthier.

An-sky developed step by step from a yeshiva-bokher to a Russian *intelligent* and *narodnik*. In Vitebsk, while still at the high school, he organized a "commune" for runaway yeshiva students. In 1881 he was expelled from the Jewish shtetl of Liozno, where he had worked as a tutor and had been found lending his pupils a copy of Lilienblum's "nihilist" novel, *The Sins of Youth*. The rabbi there blamed him and his kind for the pogroms and ordered a public burning of all the nonreligious books in the shtetl.[9] In 1883 he left Vitebsk permanently, working now as a smith, now as a bookbinder in other towns of the northwest. His first piece of fiction, a realistic study of a Jewish family in transition to the modern world, was published pseudonomously (in translation from the original Yiddish) in *Voskhod* in 1884.[10] (In the winter of 1894–5, Litvak, unaware of who its author was, translated it back into Yiddish for the Jargon Committee in Vilna).[11]

At this stage, An-sky "went to the people"; he found work in coal and salt mines in southern Russia, lived among the peasants. He acted as radical propagandist, as observer of folk mores and psychology, as one of the people. Toward the end of the 1880s, he began to send carefully researched reports and fiction drawn from his experiences to the leading populist journals, *Russkoe bogatstvo* and *Severny vestnik,* and eventually some of his contributions were accepted for publication. In 1892 he went abroad, worked in Paris as a bookbinder, and in 1894 became Lavrov's private secretary and faithful assistant, staying with him until his death in 1900.[12]

On the face of it, here was a typical case of total self-immersion in the Russian world, the deliberate adoption of a Russian persona. And, in fact, An-sky did consciously cut himself off from all involvement in Jewish affairs for some twelve years. Zhitlovsky would later recall An-sky's having said to him in 1892, "It is good that you are not leaving your people."[13] Nonetheless, it would be erroneous to overemphasize his commitment to self-Russification. An-sky's populism was, rather, universalist in character. Thus, while he was in France he began to prepare a large-scale study of French peasant life.

With the rapid growth in the mid-1890s of a Yiddish-speaking revolutionary movement and of Yiddish belles-lettres, he turned again to literary themes drawn from Jewish folk-life. Of course, he was encouraged in this by Zhitlovsky, with whom he corresponded regularly. In 1896 he published a story (translated from the Russian) in one of Y. L. Peretz's famous almanacs, the *Yontev bletlekh*,[14] and henceforward he wrote increasingly on Jewish themes. When he moved to Berne in 1901 he was not unwilling to be persuaded by Zhitlovsky (with help from Viktor Chernov) that the Jewish workers needed their own political party with a program both national and socialist.[15]

Until the summer of 1883, when he was approaching the age of twenty, Zhitlovsky held the same ideas as An-sky, who was two years his senior. Thus, late in 1882 he moved to Tula (in central Russia), where he stayed with relatives of An-sky and entered the local *gimnaziia*. An-sky had long urged him to leave the "bourgeois atmosphere" of his Yiddish-speaking home in Vitebsk – Zhitlovsky's father was a successful timber merchant – and now in Tula he saw in the local Jewish community, which was made up largely of Cantonists and was well on the way to total assimilation linguistically and through intermarriage, an ideal example for Russian Jewry as a whole.[16]

In June 1883 Zhitlovsky was persuaded by his mother, who came specifically to

Figure 16. An-sky (right) and Zhitlovsky in Paris, 1900.

Tula for the purpose, to spend the summer with his family; they were going to visit his uncle in the shtetl of Ushachi. There his thinking first began to take a different turn. Reading through the Hebrew press, he came across some important articles by Lilienblum in defense of the Palestinophile cause and he was deeply stirred.[17] The radicalism of Lilienblum's program attracted him, the call for a total reconstruction of Jewish life in a new country and on a new economic basis. The refusal to justify the existent, the insistence on building afresh, the vision of a new world—all this had an irresistible appeal for the young Zhitlovsky, who, as he later described, was utterly repelled by the life of the Jews he saw around him:

> Samuil Solomonovich Poliakov builds railways in Russia. These railways, according to Nekrasov's famous poem which reflects the true socioeconomic fact, are built on the skeleton of the Russian peasantry. My uncle, Mikhail, brews spirits in his distillery for the Russian people . . . My niece, Liza, sells the spirits to the peasant. The whole shtetl lives from the *Russian* peasant. My father [in Vitebsk] employs him to cut down Russian woods which he buys from the greatest exploiter of the Russian muzhik—the Russian noble . . . Wherever my eyes rested, I saw only *one* thing . . . the harmful effect of Jewish tradesmen on the Russian peasantry.[18]

At the end of the summer, he did not return to Tula but went back with his parents to Vitebsk. That winter, he recalled, he hung a map of Palestine in his room in order to follow the progress of "the communist students of the Bilu who—so I believed—had taken to distant Arabia the seed of our new covenant, of *our* socialist Torah."[19]

It was in this same period that he suffered a traumatic shock reading a new fable of Saltykov-Shchedrin, "The Poor Wolf," which seemed to suggest that everywhere the Jews were damned to be an insufferable burden on their neighbors: "A storm of chauvinist nationalism beat at my head and heart. So! We are wolves . . . And that's how Shchedrin of all people regards me. We are men: better, more human, than you all. My assimilationist ideas disappeared like smoke."[20] When, later in 1884, his father brought him the protocols of the first Hoveve Zion conference in Kattowitz, he was enormously impressed by Pinsker's opening address with its call for a revolutionary turn in Jewish history.[21]

Nevertheless, although he found himself drawn to the idea of national self-liberation and self-renewal, the young Zhitlovsky could not identify himself with the Palestinophile movement. He could not forgive Pinsker and Lilienblum their willingness to work with the most orthodox and obscurantist rabbinical forces for the sake of their cause. And he was shocked by the fact that businessmen with most unsavory reputations were among the leaders of the movement in Vitebsk. The Palestinophiles, Zhitlovsky argued, could not pass the simple test demanded by Dobroliubov of every movement: "A clean cause needs clean hands."[22] Surely, the answer was to find a synthesis between the cause of national regeneration (advocated by the Palestinophiles) and the commitment to general human progress, to civilization, to the modern world, to socialism (advocated by the radical assimilationists).

In 1884 Zhitlovsky had joined a small circle of Narodovoltsy in Vitebsk—Vera and Nikolai Lokhov, Aleksandr Dukhovich, and Lukashevich—and in 1885 he proposed to them that he together with other Jewish socialists in the town bring out a newspaper in Yiddish on behalf of the party. It was to be called *Tshues yisroel* (The Salvation of Israel) and would be used for propaganda among both the student youth and the workers. The idea won the approval of the local Narodovoltsy but in 1886 it was rejected by the executive committee of the party (which by then had become almost nonexistent as an organized force). In 1906 Lev

Shternberg told Zhitlovsky that he had participated in the relevant meeting of the executive committee twenty years before, that the majority present were of Jewish origin, and that the negative decision had resulted "not from the centralism of the Narodnaia Volia [but] only [from] Jewish assimilationism."[23] At the time, though, the rejection of his plan came as a harsh blow to Zhitlovsky.

By now, however, he was emotionally committed to his search for a socialist form of Jewish self-emancipation and was not prepared simply to give up altogether. In 1886 he went to St. Petersburg in order to read more deeply on Jewish history than he could in Vitebsk and in order to formulate his ideas in some more coherent and comprehensive form. The result appeared in 1887 in the form of a short book printed for the twenty-two-year-old author at his father's expense. It was entitled *Thoughts on the Historical Fate of Jewry* and represented an attempt to distill the essence of Jewish history into slightly over a hundred pages.

As depicted by Zhitlovsky, that history could be reduced to two basic themes and their dialectical interaction: the struggle for social justice and the struggle for national survival. Until the destruction of Jerusalem in the year 70, the social issue was dominant. Against the growing disparities of wealth and class, against the growing exploitation of the have-nots by the haves, were pitted the ideals of equality and justice embodied in the Mosaic Code with its severe limitations on slavery, on excessive land acquisition, on usury. The Prophets had fought hard to preserve and restore "the Mosaic commune,"[24] had stood against "the jauntiness and self-assurance of the people,"[25] had held up the vision of the "brotherhood and unity of mankind."[26] "But no social compact could preserve that which had been delivered on Mount Sinai amidst thunder and lightning once it was destroyed by the natural unfolding of economic development."[27]

Aware that the primitive commune could no longer be restored, the Essenes had emerged with a program for a higher form of egalitarianism. Zhitlovsky argued that it was erroneous to see the Essenes as a monastic sect seeking isolation in the desert. In fact, they included men from all walks of life (except trade and seafaring), and their communal settlements simply represented the first phase in their plans for the total transformation of society: "They sought to destroy those aspects of it [the Mosaic *obshchina*] that led inevitably to its dissolution . . . ; from the Mosaic institutions all that they retained was the *principle of association* on which they built an entirely new program.[28] Enjoying the trust of "all the laboring masses,"[29] the Essenes confidently awaited the opportune moment to take their program to the people at large – they were waiting for the right leader, for the Messiah. With the coming of Jesus, who "sanctioned their contempt for wealth and property, their communalism,"[30] the time had arrived for them to work with the masses (the *am ha-arets*).

But then came the Jewish revolts of the years 70 and 135. The Essenes decided to join the war of national liberation while the early Christians shunned it, thus driving a permanent wedge between the two movements. And now, in order to ensure national survival in their period of defeat and exile, the Jews consciously subordinated themselves to Pharisaic (rabbinical) leadership. The Mishna, the Talmud, the Kabala – all were walls created to buttress the national existence of a people scattered and dispersed across the world. Nothing could be more erroneous than the general assumption that the rabbinical domination had been perpetuated by persecution from without. "The Jewish people ... *wanted* to be isolated in order to preserve itself."[31]

An entirely new philosophy of life was now created by the national genius. The Messiah was no longer seen as prophet, as national leader, but as a supernatural and miraculous force. In place of active politics came a passive waiting, limitless faith. Where competing ideologies and class conflicts had been seen as normal, now only maximal unity was prized. The heterodox and impatient had to submit or suffer expulsion. "All of Jewish history from the fall of Judea until Mendelssohn constitutes one almost unbroken epoch in which the individual was subjugated to the good of the nation."[32]

The Jews had survived down to the modern era, but the price had been high, perhaps too high. "It would be hard to imagine a sharper contradiction between the *goal* – self-preservation of Jewish [national] individuality – and the *means* which the nation chose, or was forced to choose, in order to attain it ... For the Jews to alienate themselves from others means to corrupt themselves, to degrade their own type."[33] Thus, from a nation dedicated to the highest standards of social justice and universality, they had become a nation of middlemen who exploited the labor of others. Honesty could not permit one to hide "the terrible picture of parasitism in an entire people."[34]

What, then, did the future hold? Since Mendelssohn, the Jews in the West, convinced that "a future independent national life is *impossible* ... [and] *undesirable*,"[35] had gone far toward assimilation. Under the open conditions existing there, this was a natural and unobjectionable process. But in the Russian Empire, the Jewish intelligentsia had generally ignored the special circumstances – governmental restrictions, linguistic isolation, the ignorance of the masses – that closed the Western path to the Jewish people there. The "best" among the intelligentsia had joined the revolutionaries, who saw in the Jews "not a nation but a class, a harmful class, which together with the Russian bourgeoisie had to pay for their sins."[36] And, indeed, if one accepted Lavrov's theory that "the educated minority" should repay the working *narod* for what it had lost through exploitation, then "the entire Jewish intelligentsia should have left its own people to its own devices and given itself over entirely to serving the Russian people."[37]

Nevertheless, given the pogroms of 1881 and subsequent persecution by the regime, it was understandable that a section of the intelligentsia should have thought in terms of a national solution; that "the first pioneers to Palestine were students who threw over their studies in order to take up agriculture ... agriculture 'as the only way to rise to the level of man.' " This movement should perhaps be seen as " 'a repentant Judaism,' as Mikhailovsky would put it."[38] But in recent years, it had become all too clear that Palestinophilism was passing into the hands of the "gray-bearded rabbis." "What is this movement?" Zhitlovsky asked. "The beginning of a new era in Jewish history or the last convulsions of the Jewish people before death?"[39]

Surely, he concluded his essay, there had to be a middle way between flight from civilization to the East – to some Fiji – and assimilation: "Will our nationalists be able to reconcile the principles of nationality and the principles of progress ... , to show that the preservation of the Jewish nationality is *desirable* from the point of view of the intellectual and moral progress of the Jews and is *possible* by means which do not contradict that progress—or should this be considered something impossible[?]"[40]

In his memoirs, Zhitlovsky wrote that in these years (1885–8) he had in fact worked out a definite political program. After the overthrow of tsarism and the seizure of power by the Narodnaia Volia, its Jewish section, which would be able to draw on all the resources of the new government, would settle the Jews en masse on the land. He identified himself fully with the Tikhomirov wing of the Narodnaia Volia, which argued that society should be transformed along socialist lines before the Constituent Assembly met. Such a revolution from above would permit a practical and socialist solution to the Jewish question.[41] In Zhitlovsky's description of the Essenes it is possible to discern the outline of this elitist scheme.

Nevertheless, in its discussion of the future, his book of 1887 was far more tentative and hesitant than his tidy recollections allow. In many ways, in fact, his *Thoughts on the Historical Fate of Jewry* was remarkably reminiscent of Hess's attitude to the Jewish question in the years 1837–40. Of course, Hess was working in a metaphysical and theological—and Zhitlovsky in a positivist—tradition of philosophy; but they both moved within similar historiographical frameworks. There was the same emphasis on the strand of social idealism running through Biblical legislation and the Prophetic utterance; the same view of Jesus as the supreme embodiment of that tradition; the same bleak attitude to the Jews in modern times—a people of an inglorious present and uncertain future, a ghost suspended miserably between resurrection and death.

Like the young Hess, Zhitlovsky in the mid-1880s was subject to conflicting pressures: hurt to the quick by the powerful antisemitic voice in Russian society (and even in the revolutionary movement), repelled by the stiff-necked immobility of the traditional Jewish world, anxious to build a bridge between the Prophetic past of the Jewish people and the messianic future promised by socialism. Like Hess, Zhitlovsky had received an intensive initiation as a boy into some of the major texts of classical Judaism, and he too was bound by strong ties of respect to his learned and close-knit family. Indeed, as he described in his recollections, it was his grandfather who in 1885 first forcefully pointed out to him the egalitarian elements in ancient Jewish thought: the reference in the Talmud to the "common purse" of the Essenes, the attacks by the Prophets on the avaricious rich ("woe unto them who add house to house and field to field"), and the universalism of the Jewish prayer ("And they will be one brotherhood throughout the whole world").[42] Zhitlovsky had set out to explain the basic tenets of socialism to the old man only to find the tables turned on him. This conversation inspired his sudden interest in Jewish history.

In the mid-1880s Zhitlovsky probably knew nothing of *Rome and Jerusalem* nor of its author, but in later years he would note with particular interest how great an influence the family had exerted on Hess's development. "His grandfather," Zhitlovsky wrote in 1912 in his long study of Hess, "was an established merchant but at the same time a learned man who in every free moment studied the Talmud. His belief in the Messiah went so far that he made no plans for the distant future lest the Messiah suddenly come."[43] Can there by any doubt that Zhitlovsky was also thinking of his own grandfather—who was forever initiating plans to move to Jerusalem—when he wrote these lines?

From 1841 until 1860, Hess had deliberately cut the threads tying him to the

Jewish world. In an earlier period, Zhitlovsky might well have done the same. He had the example of An-sky before him. He was shocked by the scathing reviews of his book in the Jewish press, most notably by Dubnov in *Voskhod*. (Dubnov not only considered the research careless – which it was – but also dismissed with an unwarranted asperity his attempts to open up new lines of thought in Jewish historiography).[44] In 1888 he and Vera Lokhova, a Russian girl, decided to marry – a step which was bound to antagonize his family.

Nevertheless, Zhitlovsky did not follow the path taken by Hess. On the contrary, he persisted in arguing that the solution to the Jewish question had somehow to be at once revolutionary, socialist, and national. By the 1880s, Jewish politics – a framework of competitive organizations and ideologies – had the power to hold the permanent, if not full-time, interest of a Zhitlovsky. Thus, when he decided to go abroad in the summer of 1888 (he had been warned that his arrest was imminent), he did so with the specific intention of directing the Jewish Workers' Library in Zurich, that is, the project for the publication of socialist material in Yiddish initiated in 1887 by Shmuel Rabinovich.[45] This project came to nothing, but in 1891 we find Zhitlovsky (then a student at Berne University) publishing Yiddish poetry in translation from the French in Vinchevsky's *Di fraye velt* in London.[46] In 1892 he was able to persuade the Russian Free Press (Kravchinsky, Chaikovsky) to publish his brochure *Evrei k evreiam* (*A Jew to the Jews*, which will be described below). And in 1893, during the Zurich congress of the International, he entered into negotiations (albeit unsuccessful) with Vinchevsky and Abe Cahan for the joint publication in Yiddish of socialist propaganda material for Russia.

A letter from An-sky to Zhitlovsky sent from Ekaterinoslav on 16 June 1888 throws much light on the state of mind of the two young men at that formative period in their lives and specifically goes far to explain why Zhitlovsky persisted in his search for an ideology of Jewish socialism:

> Dear brother! Let's sit down and talk. Your letter made a depressing impression on me . . . because you yourself regard your own cause with such a sickly scepticism . . . Nobody would talk about a cause dear to him in such a way unless he was either deceiving himself or had suffered many disappointments and defeats. At one time, when I saw the world as some paradise fed by the pure waters of Social Democracy, I held that the Jewish intelligentsia does not have the right to devote itself to the mere handful of its own people . . . to forget about everybody else. I felt that that was as much a sin as to forget all other people for the sake of one's own family . . . But . . . I have learned that the number of people capable of living for anything else but their own skin, let alone of devoting themselves to a good cause, . . . is very, very small . . . [and] now I no longer regard everybody who does not go hand in hand with me . . . as an enemy and fool . . . A man should devote himself to whatever good cause he has and [we] should love him and wish him well and not look forward into history to see what will become of this good cause in hundreds of thousands of years.
>
> It seems to me that you consider me much more of a cosmopolitan than I in fact am. There is a great deal of . . . patriotic feeling in me. And more than once my national nerve has jolted me in such a way that life was miserable.

But every such time ended in nothing. The fact is that I never found a suitable basis for action in Jewish life . . . I have moved into the Russian village to which I have already half given myself and hope soon to give myself entirely. I feel good here: I like the simple working life of the *narod*, its naiveté, poverty, truth, its lack of malice. Here I shall find a cause for myself. *You* can work on behalf of the Jewish people – that work appeals to you . . . I wish you every success and especially I wish for you a burning, all-consuming faith in your own cause . . .

A couple of words on your remarks about the forces lost to Jewry . . . Could these people [Lassalle, Marx, Börne] have remained in the Jewish people without losing a great part of their greatness? What makes them great is precisely their universality . . . Christ would not keep within the narrow Palestinian limits and so they threw him out. Thus . . . given an autonomous Jewish form of life these great men would leave, or else Lassalle would turn into some miniature Bismarck [etc.] . . . [47]

This letter, taken together with other available evidence, suggests that contrary to what he would later write in his memoirs, Zhitlovsky was not faced by a wall of indifference and apathy in the years 1885–95. True, in his dualism, his determination to give equal weight to the national and to the class factors, and in his view of national history as a political force in its own right, he stood alone among the Jewish socialists. Indeed, with the fast-rising popularity of Marxism, his ideological approach was bound to appear increasingly idiosyncratic and eccentric. As against this, though, the emergence of Yiddish-speaking socialism in London and New York; the plea by Rubanovich (published in Lavrov's *Vestnik narodnoi voli* in 1886) for the creation of a similar movement in Russia; the aid provided Shmuel Rabinovich by Lavrov and Stanisław Mendelson all show that in his most fundamental demand, that the socialists undertake to organize the Jewish masses, he was far from alone.

Thus, it is not surprising that by 1892, having spent over three years in Switzerland, he was ready to present an ideological statement that was unequivocal and startlingly sharp. His *A Jew to the Jews*, unlike his *Thoughts* of 1887, was clearly the product of much meditation. It was the statement of a man who had become thoroughly familiar at first hand with the arguments of Plekhanov against Russian populism, who had remained unconvinced on many basic issues, and who had defined his disagreements during countless nights of debate in the student colonies.[48] Thus, *A Jew to the Jews* was an attempt to form a higher synthesis over and beyond the extremes of Palestinophilism and socialist assimilationism, Tikhomirov's populism and Plekhanov's Marxism.

Zhitlovsky built up his case on four basic propositions. First, he clearly (albeit implicitly) repudiated his statement of 1887 that the Jewish nation in Russia was a people of parasites. On the contrary, he now wrote, they were in very large number "unskilled laborers, . . . porters, stonebreakers . . . [49] Yes, the Jewish people in Russia is a laboring people and the great majority are occupied in almost all branches of physical labor."[50] This complete turnabout could, perhaps, be explained by the fact that his earlier proposition had been criticized as grossly inaccurate even in the Russian radical press. Besides, his earlier position was clearly an extreme expression of Narodovolets elitism in the style of Tikhomirov, a position from which Zhitlovsky was now edging away.

Second (again in contrast to 1887), he denounced the Western model of Jewish development. Nothing, he wrote, could be more disastrous for the Jewish masses in Russia than to find themselves living under a liberal parliamentary regime. Under a system of laissez-faire economics, one large stratum of Jews would certainly rise to the ranks of the middle and haute bourgeoisie, thus arousing enormous antisemitism; the intelligentsia would rush to gain entrance into the dominant Russian or Polish cultures; and the masses would sink into an ever more abject poverty and superstition. As a result, he concluded, "the entire Jewish people will call down on itself an antisemitism even more terrible than that of today, for with the coming of political freedom, the Judaeophobes will have at their disposal all the means of unremitting free agitation."[51] This process could already be observed in all its viciousness in the Hapsburg Empire, particularly in Galicia and Bukovina.

With its repressive policies, the tsarist regime in Russia had slowed down the fragmentation and *embourgeoisement* of the Jewish people. The revolutionary intelligentsia could, therefore, still hope to save the Jews in Russia from the disastrous effects of capitalism. "Russia," he wrote,

> is now, in all probability, entering the epoch of capitalist development. This 4 percent of the population, with its commercial industrial genius, could do much to accelerate greatly this unhappy process: the rapid proletarianization of the masses. A brother would be filled with horror if his sister became a prostitute . . . ; but the Jewish revolutionary can look on while everything is paving the way for his people to become a parasite and he will not raise a finger on behalf of the morality, the honor, or the health of his own nation.[52]

Here, of course, we hear all the scorn of the populist for the Marxist faith in the capitalist road to progress.

On the basis of this analysis, Zhitlovsky turned to the socialist intelligentsia (to those of Jewish origin) with an impassioned plea – they should learn from the Palestinophiles who "have inscribed on their banner: the return of the intelligentsia to its own people."[53] The belief in "national self-renunciation"[54] was a concept first created by the Jewish bourgeoisie in the West in its unseemly haste to attain equal civil rights at any cost. Now, by some strange logic, it had been taken over by the socialists: "Whatever actions the Russian regime takes against us, the Jewish youth remains silent as though all these measures were directed against some Jesuit order."[55]

The Jewish socialists should fight "not only for the liberation of our common home – Russia – but also for the rebirth of our own people."[56] Working in unison with the Russian socialists, they should plan for the resettlement of the Jews on the land in Russia. Such a policy would put an end to "the ethical degeneration of the Jewish people – which is the necessary result of its urban trading life;"[57] sharply reduce antisemitism; and permit the Jews "to absorb the principles of European civilization without having to fear that they will cease to be Jewish and become 'adherents of the Mosaic persuasion.' "[58]

Thus – this was his final point – Zhitlovsky was suggesting that the very concept of Jewish self-Russification was fundamentally objectionable. It meant, de facto, to support "the Great Russian nationality in its russifying tendencies vis-à-vis the other nationalities that inhabit Russia [and] . . . that is no small matter."[59] Moreover, it ignored the fact that the Russian Empire was multilingual, that "transitional epochs" were bound to precede the millennium when there would be "neither Hellenes nor Jews," and that in the meanwhile "the 'Jews' and the 'Hellenes' must come to some agreement on how to live in one and the same state."[60] A commission of the Austrian Reichsrat had already declared the Jews are "as much a full nationality with full rights as the German or any other nationality."[61] And this was clearly the correct policy. Here, Zhitlovsky was clearly moving toward the theory of extraterritorial national self-government. The Jewish people, he wrote, should demand "an equal and independent alliance with all the other nations inhabiting Russia."[62]

A Jew to the Jews was, perhaps, Zhitlovsky's boldest work. At a time when socialists assumed that economic progress had rendered national problems obsolete, he stated bluntly that liberalism and capitalism threatened the Jews with unprecedented catastrophe. To rely on historical necessity was therefore an abdication of reason and will. If the Jewish intelligentsia did not act to avert the disaster nothing and nobody else could. Only one other socialist wrote in this vein in the pre-1914 period and that was Nachman Syrkin; but Zhitlovsky anticipated his major writings by almost ten years.

Tempora mutantur: Zhitlovsky and the rise of Jewish socialism in Russia, 1892–1906

In the early 1890s, Zhitlovsky stood on the periphery of the Jewish socialist "subworld" as it was forming in Europe and the United States. His *Thoughts on the Historical Fate of Jewry* and *A Jew to the Jews,* despite – or rather because of – their originality and highly personal vision, made very little direct impact at the time. Vinchevsky later recalled that he himself was becoming very much the Social Democratic "internationalist" when he met Zhitlovsky in 1893 and that his "Jewishness [*yidishkayt*] did not appeal to me; his anti-Marxism did not convince me; his [social-revolutionary] party activity for Russia seemed to me to be on a false track."[63] Lesin, who, on the face of it, might have been directly influenced by Zhitlovsky, had not even heard of him until late in 1894. It was Timofei Kopelzon who first told him of the existence of *A Jew to the Jews,* but he assured Lesin that its author was a mere "eclectic." "I asked no more," wrote Lesin. "I no longer had any desire to ask anymore. Among the Marxists, such a reference was enough to wipe a man out – to wipe him out without even bothering to use a knife. A man who jumbles together a world-outlook from the fragments of various philosophies – that was really an intellectual nothing of the first order."[64]

By 1905–6, however, Zhitlovsky enjoyed great intellectual prestige on the Jewish left. Sent in 1904 to the United States (together with the veteran revolutionary, Breshko-Breshkovskaia) on a fund-raising mission for the PSR, he rapidly gained a remarkable reputation among the Yiddish-speaking socialists in New York as a man of ideas and as a public speaker – his humiliating rout of Abe Cahan at a debate on Marxism in 1905 was remembered for many decades.[65] One of his critics in America could even write that "as a lecturer he had a hypnotic power – he

intoxicated his audiences, who followed him as though in their sleep."⁶⁶ In 1906
he was chosen as the candidate of the SERP for the Vitebsk district in the election
to the Second Duma. He was a leading member of both the SERP and the PSR and
was responsible for the establishment of the formal link between those two parties.
In short, he was then at the center of the stage.

This metamorphosis was, above all, the result of the enormous transformation in
Jewish politics in the intervening decade. The mounting demand from the politically minded Jewish youth for a synthesis of socialism and nationalism; the emergence of the Bund as a party both revolutionary and Jewish; the growth and
break-away of the socialist off-shoots of Zionism – all combined to transform Zhitlovsky from eccentric to mentor. The mountain had come to Mohammed. Nachman Syrkin benefited from this same rapid change of attitudes in the new generation. But unlike Syrkin, who would not bend to political fashion, Zhitlovsky
moved with the times. In his case, Mohammed also went to the mountain.

The Zhitlovsky of the period from the mid-1890s to 1907 sounded notes distinc-
tively different from those he had used in his books of 1887 and 1892. Then, he
was the historian of national decline, the scourge of his people (parasites or potential parasites), the prophet of disaster. Of course, he balanced this somber picture
with the promise of redemption. But salvation was an uncertain hope, dependent
on the foresight and will of the revolutionary few, the heroes, the latter-day Essenes. It required a sharp and total break with the past, the resettlement of the Jews
on the land, and the uprooting of an outworn religion. The message here was not
only elitist (albeit less so in 1892 than in 1887), but also highly pessimistic, tragic
in its implications.

There is little trace of any of this in the decade leading up to, and through, the
1905 revolution. Zhitlovsky became increasingly absorbed in what can perhaps best
be summarized as the theory and strategy of mass mobilization. He now concentrated not on the prediction of disaster but on questions of popular consciousness.
As the central theme in his writing, the agrarian was replaced by the cultural
revolution; "productivization" by "lingualism" – the necessity of transforming Yiddish from a "jargon" into the national language of the Jewish people. Emphasis
shifted from an ideology of sharp discontinuities to one positing a stage-by-stage
expansion of mass politics. Thus, the Zhitlovsky of 1905–07 could be described by
contemporaries – accurately enough – as the philosopher of a "deep optimism."⁶⁷

During the years 1895–98, Zhitlovsky was drawn for the first time into the mainstream of the new Jewish politics. He was sought out by those in the younger
generation who were then groping their way toward a synthesis of nationalism and
socialism. Few, or none, could accept his ideology in its entirety, but an ever-
increasing number were now ready to take him seriously.

Specifically, there were two groups on which Zhitlovsky now began to exert an
influence. One was the Yiddish publication society Tsayt-gayst, founded in Berlin
in 1896 by a group of Yiddish writers and enthusiasts, among whom were Pinsky,
Eliyohu Davidzon, and I. Eliashev (Baal Makhshoves). (In 1898 it was the Tsayt-
gayst society that was asked by the Bund to take over in part the functions of its
Jargon Committee.) Zhitlovsky early became one of the society's editors, a decision
warmly welcomed by An-sky in a letter of 2 June 1897.⁶⁸ Immediately following

the First Zionist Congress held in Basle in August 1897, the Tsayt-gayst held a public meeting there to explain its goals to those of the delegates willing to listen. According to Pinsky's account, Zhitlovsky was selected to present the case for Yiddish as the national language of the Jewish people. He did so with enormous enthusiasm and in Pinsky's words was "the hero and focus of the evening."[69]

More important, however, than Zhitlovsky's connections with the Berlin group was his growing influence from the mid-1890s on the Russian-Jewish students in Switzerland, particularly in Berne. His biting attacks on Zionism and, equally, on assimilationism – or cosmopolitanism, as he now began to call it – won him a small but dedicated following even among those who regarded his anti-Marxism as an outmoded anachronism. Thus, the Group of Jewish Socialists Abroad, of which Zhitlovsky and Y. Blumshtein (Frumin) were the most active members, was set up in Berne in 1896 and undertook the translation of a number of socialist books into Yiddish, including the first such translation of *The Communist Manifesto*.[70] The Berne group and the Bund naturally sought each other out. The Bund eventually published the Yiddish brochures prepared by the Group of Jewish Socialists, and it was to them that John Mill turned when he took over the editorship of *Der yidisher arbeter* in 1898.

In these years, Zhitlovsky suddenly felt himself on a rising wave, and the resultant mood of optimism, almost exaltation, permeated everything which he wrote then. He was excited by the changing attitudes of the socialist youth. In the five years since the publication of *A Jew to the Jews*, he wrote in 1897, "the entire situation has changed . . . Not only in London and America . . . but also in Galicia and Russia the Jewish socialists have set to work . . . with all their strength in order to organize the Jewish workers and to lead them into the great army of the European proletariat."[71]

The decision of the "younger generation"[72] to use Yiddish showed that it was determined to tie its fate to that of the Jewish masses. "The best teacher of socialism is the life of the workers – the fight for life, the conflict with the employers; and so long as we did not have that teacher . . . our socialism was left hanging in the air."[73] The socialist youth had learned its lesson. It was doing everything it could to defend the interests of the workers, to obtain marginal improvements in their standard of living, "not at that point when all the nations start the socialist revolution but *now*, at once."[74] There was little of the Tikhomirov Narodovolets, the elitist and "utopian" left here.

In his works of 1887 and 1892, Zhitlovksy had written with some ambivalence about the Palestinian movement, admiring the cataclysmic vision of its founders and their radical (albeit impractical) solutions. But now, in his "Zionism or Socialism?" published in *Der yidisher arbeter*, no. 6, he did not have a good word to say about it. The Zionist movement he wrote, was simply a middle-class response to antisemitism – "and just as there can never be peace between the bourgeoisie and the worker *so there can never be peace between socialism and Zionism*."[75] Palestine and its environs were already partially populated and there was not room there for more than a small percentage of the world Jewish population. And "with a tiny state of two million Jewish inhabitants one cannot help the entire Jewish people which in Russia, Poland, and Galicia alone is over six million people."[76] As for the idea of establishing a socialist society in Palestine (presumably he was thinking of Syrkin here), that was pure fantasy, because one could not "carry through in Turkey what is still impossible in Europe." Apart from anything else, the European Powers would simply not "stand aside and watch the Jews demonstrate the feasibility of socialism."[77]

Unfortunately, all this was not a mere harmless fantasy because the Zionists were causing active damage to the socialist movement. In their eagerness to kowtow to kings and ministers, they sought to discourage all political action by the Jews in the countries where they lived. "It has to be shown that the entire Jewish people is God-fearing, innocent and far–so help us–from today's revolutionary ideas; that the Jewish worker will not bring the terrible plague of socialism and the class war to Turkey–Heaven forbid!"[78] More, Zionism divided the politically minded youth against itself, drawing vitally needed reinforcements away from the revolution. Addressing himself to the Zionist youth (including the would-be socialists among them), he wrote, "Everything you do, you are doing together with the bourgeoisie and, in the last resort, for the bourgeoisie. Every step you take damages the holy cause of the Jewish worker! Every penny you can take from a poor Jew is a crime against him . . . and against the labor movement."[79] Zhitlovksy could employ such invective because he now felt confident that his idea of a third course–an acceptable alternative to Zionism and assimilationism–was becoming reality before his very eyes.

It was typical of his mood in this period that he saw the opening chapter of modern Jewish politics not as he did at other times in Pinsker and Lilienblum, with their deep-rooted pessimism, but rather in the optimistic Jewish socialists of the 1870s: "The last twenty-five years, since Liberman and Zundelevich [sic] first brought out the Hebrew *Ha-emet* in Vienna. . . . will be considered by the future Jewish historian as one of the most important periods in the life of the Jewish people. One can go still further and say that it is more important than the whole previous thousands of years which the Jews have lived in the Diaspora [*goles*]."[80]

Zhitlovsky was convinced that Liberman's only major error had been his use of Hebrew rather than Yiddish and that his successors of the 1890s, by reversing this policy, had guaranteed their success. Yiddish, he believed, was fast establishing itself as the national language of the Jewish people. It was already spoken by the great majority and was increasingly used for books, newspapers, and drama. The working masses, in contrast to the Zionists, were truly patriotic in their allegiance to the nation and its language:

> The majority of educated Zionists are so out of necessity, because they are not permitted to become non-Jews . . . Do they not argue that they would willingly become Russians, Germans, Poles . . . if this were not prevented by damned antisemitism . . . As against this, consider the simple Jewish worker. The idea never entered his head that he is not a Jew, but he has never stormed and wailed about the fact.[81]

Given the emergence of nations long submerged (and indeed of "new" nationalities), the Jews could expect to gain recognition as an official, albeit extraterritorial, nationality. And in the socialist period, they would be able to create a vast network of Yiddish schools and universities in many different countries. In the meantime, as a concrete step in this direction, the Jewish socialist movements throughout the world should unite to create an International Jewish Labor Secretariat. The immediate function of this secretariat would be to coordinate assistance to the waves of migrants moving from eastern Europe to new countries overseas. However, over and beyond this, Zhitlovsky clearly felt that such an institution could have an important symbolic function: recognition for the legitimacy of a new Jewish nationality, modern, Yiddish-speaking, socialist, capable of fighting for its rights wherever Jews lived.

The decision to publish Zhitlovsky's declaration of faith in the party journal was, of course, no aberration but rather a deliberate move in John Mill's campaign to turn the Bund into a clearly national movement, and over the next few years Berne became the center of the nationalist wing in the Bund. Among the young Bundists who spent long periods of time there during the years 1898–1904 were Medem, Frumin, Ezra, Mutnik, Liber, and Zivion. They acted as a filter through which certain elements of Zhitlovsky's thinking could seep into the ideology of the Bund. Having made up his mind early, he could effectively urge others to take a clear stand on the basic issues.

In Berne, from 1900 Zhitlovsky was reinforced by Viktor Chernov and An-sky. Chernov, who was to emerge as perhaps the most famous leader of the Socialist Revolutionary party, accepted Zhitlovsky's approach to the nationality question. He had come abroad in 1899 (after acting as a revolutionary agitator among the peasants in Tambov province), had suffered through the usual clash with Plekhanov (who, as he put it, had proved himself "very aggressively inclined"),[82] and had turned for guidance to An-sky in Paris and Zhitlovsky in Berne. Zhitlovsky gave him access to his library, acting as his guide in philosophy and political theory. "I looked on him as a teacher who stood on a higher level than me,"[83] Chernov would write later.

Even though Chernov was a Russian, not a Jew, he worked hard to persuade An-sky to take a more positive attitude to the Jewish national revival (as to other forms of nationalism). He believed that in this sphere An-sky had been unduly influenced by Lavrov, who since the 1870s had persistently advocated the assimilationist solution to the Jewish question. In general, he argued, Lavrov had remained a man of the strongly centralized First International. "Everywhere that Lavrov said 'no' on this subject," Chernov wrote of his conversations with An-sky, "I said 'yes.' The Second International is not regressive but progressive in comparison with the First. So long as it did not pass through the stage of 'national self-determination,' of socialism according to the particular conditions of every country, the International would have remained a house of cards, Jewish socialism must pass through its period of 'nationalization.' "[84] However, if An-sky now changed his stance, it was probably not so much because of the theoretical arguments thrust upon him by Zhitlovsky and Chernov but rather because he was drawn instinctively to the vital new world of Jewish socialism and Yiddish literature. "The atmosphere in the Jewish colonies abroad," An-sky recalled of Berne in 1901, "was daily becoming more nationalist. And in this Peretz played an important part. Nobody could reject Peretz, not even the most truculent Social Democrats. He became an argument, a banner ... On [his] account assimilated youngsters learned Yiddish. Rarely did a Jewish evening, whether Zionist or Bundist (both parties regarded Peretz as theirs), pass without a reading from Peretz."[85]

An-sky, ever ready to throw himself wholeheartedly into an authentic environment, could not resist the intense inner life of the student colonies in Switzerland
during the years 1901–4. He produced Yiddish plays. He chaired debates. On one
memorable occasion he was especially called in – when everybody else had failed –
to restore order during a debate between the Zionist Democratic Fraction (Weizmann, Aberson, Feiwel) and the Bundists. "The greatest success in the colony,"
Vladimir Medem recalled,

> was enjoyed by An-sky . . . He was then in his middle years – some 38 years
> old – but he looked much older. His hair was graying. His back was very
> bent and his intelligent, sympathetic face with its large, eagle-nose and small,
> pointed beard was marked by deep wrinkles – signs of great spiritual suffer-
> ing. He was, however, as fresh and lively as a youth. He was always sur-
> rounded by girls, constantly coming out with lightning flashes of wit, with
> stories, with tales . . . Everybody liked him.[86]

An-sky now wrote two Yiddish songs for the Bund, "The Oath ("Di shevue") and
"To the Bund" ("Tsum bund"),[87] which became extraordinarily popular in the
Pale – singing at clandestine meetings in the forests or, still more, in street demonstrations (with danger ever present) was, of course, a deeply emotional experience.
"Tsum bund" was composed in honor of the publication of the "jubilee" number
of Di arbeter shtime (no. 25), and An-sky gave its first public reading at a celebration of the "colony" in Berne. Its penultimate line – "Both God and the Messiah
are dead" ("Got un meshiekh in eynem geshtorbn")[88] – caught the self-confidence
of those days when (so it was felt) man was finally coming into his own, liberated
from oppressive divinity and superstitious hope.

Chernov has recalled that An-sky was greatly angered by the treatment of the
Bund at the Second Congress of the RSDRP in 1903 and took its side against the
Iskrovtsy. And of course, he added,

> Zhitlovsky spared neither time nor effort in order to lay under the organiza-
> tional "revolt" of the Bundists a more logical . . . ideological base. He forced
> somebody like . . . Liber, for instance, to take thought. But others such as . . .
> Grishin (under this pseudonym . . . Kopelzon-Timofei lived in Berne) feared
> nothing so much as that the "Zhitlovsky plague" should – Heaven forbid –
> infect the Bundist ranks.[89]

In 1904 the informal but important association of Zhitlovsky with the Bund
finally came to an end. In that year he added the following note to an article
published in the second issue of Vozrozhdenie:

> On the question of a territory, the author has radically changed his original
> standpoint. Previously a decided supporter of that view which sees a territory
> as only a desirable – but far from necessary – condition for the development
> of national life he was forced, after a more careful . . . consideration of the
> arguments pro et contra, to agree with those theorists of national action
> which see in a separate territory a conditio sine qua non for the healthy,
> unhindered, and independent progress of any particular nation.[90]

In the political context of the time, this statement meant that Zhitlovsky had
swung out of the ideological orbit of the Bund and into that of the amorphous

galaxy of Zionist and territorialist socialism. This was one of those remarkable voltes-face that would punctuate Zhitlovsky's political career until the very last years of his life. Coming from the man who had published the first, but by no means the last, attack on the territorialist idea in the Bundist press, this conversion was utterly unexpected. Nevertheless, it had its own logic.

The truth is that Zhitlovsky's flirtation with the Bund had always fallen far short of marriage, that relations between them had deteriorated since at least 1902, and that he would inevitably choose a more compatible partner if one were only to appear. Men such as Frumin or Zivion, with views very close to those of Zhitlovsky had joined the Bund. They accepted the fact that it had a collective ideology and that, regardless of the enormous internal dissensions, all members had to subscribe to the party program. But this Zhitlovsky was not willing to do. He insisted on regarding a party as an ad hoc organization seeking certain common goals rather than as a movement bound together by a common philosophy. In his important booklet of 1898, *Socialism and the Struggle for Political Freedom,* he stated: "Marxism is a complete world outlook that embraces practically all branches of human thought and it would be hardly practical to demand that all members of a given party be united in their attitude toward highly specialized and debatable points of philosophy and sociology."[91] Granted this premise, there was nothing surprising in his offer to join the Bund even though he was and would continue to be an outspoken critic of the Marxist determinism expounded by Engels, Plekhanov, and the Bundists themselves. This attempt to narrow the sphere of ideological uniformity to a bare minimum negated the most basic attitudes of the Russian Social Democrats. "Whoever continues to see in Marxism only a 'hypothesis' or only 'transient philosophical assumptions,'" wrote Boris Krichevsky in reply to Zhitlovsky, "severs himself entirely both from the Russian and west European labor movements."[92]

In his memoirs, John Mill wrote how he was constantly amazed by the way in which Zhitlovsky formulated his request for membership:

> He was one hundred percent in agreement with the practical work of the Bund. His social philosophy, his anti-Marxism, his attachment to the Socialist Revolutionaries—"What has all this," he used naively to ask, "got to do with the Bundist movement?" The agrarian question did not exist for the Jews. The employment of political terror by a Jewish movement in Russia he regarded as harmful. So what stood in the way of his joining the Bund?[93]

As an outsider, Zhitlovsky was soon denied access to the Bundist press. Moreover, a large section of his "Zionism or Socialism?" was omitted when it was published as a brochure by the party. And his article "Why Yiddish?" written in 1897 as an introduction to one of the booklets translated by Frumin, was likewise rejected. (Zhitlovsky eventually published it in *Forverts* in 1900.)[94] His nationalism, however generally acceptable to John Mill and the Berne group, was too much for the central committee of the Bund.

The fact that Zhitlovsky was a revolutionary populist also contributed eventually to his alienation from the Bund, but in the years 1897–1900 it seems to have affected the relationship surprisingly little. Since 1893, Zhitlovsky had been a founding and leading member of the Union of Russian Socialist Revolutionaries, which published the popular journal *Russkii rabochii* and had it smuggled into Russia. (Among its other members were Charles Rappoport, M. M. Rozenbaum, and An-sky.) Ideologically, this organization marked itself off from the Social Democrats in that (in principle) it endorsed a limited use of terrorism against the tsarist regime; considered the peasantry and the intelligentsia as classes essentially equal in revolutionary potential to the proletariat; and regarded Marxism more as a series of hypotheses than as scientific fact.[95]

However, for a long time the Union of Russian Socialist Revolutionaries was too small and ineffectual to be regarded as a serious threat by most Social Democrats. *Russkii rabochii* reached Russia and had its followers (Chernov among them), but it did so irregularly and in small quantities (it was financed until 1898 exclusively from the private funds of Rappoport's wife).[96] The younger Russian Marxists, at least, tended to see Zhitlovsky's Union as a rather harmless eccentricity.

And, of course, with the "Economist" crisis – the split between the Plekhanovite and anti-Plekhanovite Social Democrats – the revolutionary populists found themselves eyed as potential partners for a détente by both the warring sides (as well as by more peripheral Marxist groups). It was now that the Bundist committee abroad drew closest to Zhitlovsky, publishing articles by him and Yiddish translations prepared under his auspices. In a letter of March 1899 from Ingerman to Akselrod we read the following comment on this situation: "I have received a number of parcels of Russian and Yiddish literature from Berne – without a letter but signed by Zhitlovsky . . . Is [he] now a Social Democrat? And having become a Social Democrat . . . and within the Social Democratic ranks does he intend to continue in his old manner the war against the Social Democrats?"[97] For his part, Plekhanov had his *Vademecum* published on the press of the Group of Old Narodovoltsy and, in general, began suggesting that the time had come to return to the revolutionary élan of the populists in the 1870s and early 1880s. Zhitlovsky saw here a victory for his own ideology, writing in a publication of 1900 that "undoubtedly the Social Democrats have taken enormous strides recently toward our program, particularly on questions of the political struggle."[98]

Starting from 1901, however, this situation rapidly changed. On the one hand, the arrival abroad of Chernov and then of Grigorii Gershuny set in motion a movement toward the unification of the many fragmented populist groups in Russia and the emigration. Thus, the creation of the Agraro-Socialist League in 1899 was followed by the establishment in 1902 of the Party of Socialist Revolutionaries.[99] On the other hand, the *Iskra* group was determined to consolidate the Russian Social Democrats into a monolithic party and, despite ups and downs, to a large extent succeeded in doing so. The increasingly embittered rivalry between populists and Marxists was bound to inhibit Zhitlovsky in his role as gadfly to the Bund.

Among the Iskrovtsy, Plekhanov became the major advocate of the united front against the Socialist Revolutionaries. "I have been in Berne," wrote Plekhanov on 28 June 1901 to his fellow editors in Munich. "Zhitlovsky and Chernov are really in a rage about the possibility of a reconciliation with the *Rabochee delo*. You did well to make peace."[100] He returned to this theme again in 1902. "Our enemies now are the Social Revolutionaries."[101] Chernov states in his memoirs that Grishin (Kopelzon) was working tirelessly at this time to consolidate the Social Democratic camp against the populists. The acrimonious controversy over the policy of terror-ism drove a deep wedge between the PSR and the RSDRP, including the Bund, which (after its initial hesitation) joined *Iskra* in a total rejection of the assassin-ation policy. Relations between the Socialist Revolutionaries and the Bund deterio-rated so far that Ilia Rubanovich could choose the occasion of a fifth-anniversary celebration (held in Paris in November 1902) to attack the Bund publicly. "He ended his speech," reported *Poslednie izvestiia*, "with a call for heroic deeds to attract the masses."[102]

The split in the RSDRP at its Second Congress on 2 August 1903, and the walkout of the Bund, probably led (as Chernov has suggested) to a certain reconcil-iation between the Bundists (especially those living in Berne) and the Socialist Revolutionary trio (Chernov, An-sky, Zhitlovsky). But the party lines were now too firmly drawn to have permitted a return to the situation of 1897–1900; there was no role Zhitlovsky could now play in the ideological policy formation of the Bund. Or, as Vladimir Medem put it, recalling an encounter with Zhitlovsky during the Amsterdam congress of the International in 1904, "We had neither the time nor the inclination to carry on theoretical discussions with him."[103] Repelled from the Bund, he was naturally drawn to the rising force in Jewish politics – revolutionary territorialism with its dual commitment to the antitsarist war and to a Jewish state (in Palestine or elsewhere).

Until 1903 the Zionist movement had kept almost entirely clear of revolutionary action in Russia. This was true even of its radical and labor wing, often loosely termed Poale Zion. There were socialist Zionists who publicly advocated revolu-tion in Russia, but the most prominent among them, Nachman Syrkin, insisted that this could not be the task of the Zionist organization with its exclusive goals of emigration and colonization. Some Poale Zion groups – that in Dvinsk, for ex-ample – had a working-class membership and were prepared to go beyond the law, but only in order to conduct trade-union activity, while still other organizations (most notably that led by Y. Berger in Minsk) insisted that even this was too much, that rigid legality was essential in order to avoid police interference.

However, the strict refusal of the Zionist organization to interfere in internal politics became the cause of an increasing resentment among its student supporters. It could not be otherwise given the upward spiral of protest and repression at the Russian universities. Unrest was answered by the mass recruitment of students into the army; the ministers of education and the interior were killed in 1901 and 1902 respectively by student terrorists (Karpovich and Balmashev); and the net result was to convert the university into a veritable breeding ground for the revolutionary parties. Zionist student groups, such as the Kadima society in Kiev, came under increasing pressure to integrate a revolutionary plank into their program. As a tentative step in this direction, a number of the leading student Zionists, meeting in Rovno early in 1903, decided to call together a conference later in the year of all the major Poale Zion and socialist Zionist groups.[104]

The Kishinev pogrom of April 1903 brought the long-simmering self-criticism to the boil, turned doubt into certainty. While established figures in the Jewish world – Ahad Ha-Am and Dubnov, for instance – now called openly for the forma-tion of self-defense units, for the most part the Zionist youth was determined to go farther, to embrace the revolutionary cause. Pinhas Dashevsky, a Kiev student who had attended the meeting at Rovno, attempted to stab to death the editor of the two Kishinev papers, *Bessarabets* and *Drug*, that had openly incited their readers to attack the Jews. This act was promptly greeted by two other members of the Rovno group and Kadima society in Kiev, N. Shtif and B. Fridland, with a brochure entitled *What Is the Lesson of Dashevsky's Assassination Attempt?*[105] Independently, a similar document was produced by A. Rozin (Ben Adir) and V. Fabrikant in Kharkov.[106]

Herzl's visit to Russia in August 1903 only served to heighten the alienation of the youth from official Zionism. Desperately anxious to win the support of the tsarist government for the Zionist cause and to gain legal concessions for Russian Jewry, Herzl met with both Pleve and Witte. They each urged him to help neutralize the revolutionary forces at work among the Russian Jews. How could he expect support from the tsarist regime, Witte asked, when "the seven million Jews, among a total population of 136 million, comprise about 50 percent of the membership in the revolutionary parties."[107] It was presumably in response to these overtures that Herzl met privately with Zhitlovsky, hoping – quixotically – that he might help rein in the Jewish revolutionaries. And in his public address to the Sixth Zionist Congress in Basle, Herzl called on his followers in Russia to behave "calmly and legally."[108] This appeal, and the entire episode, was regarded as little short of treasonable by the Zionist left wing, and the day after Herzl's speech, Yaakov Leshchinsky, one of the leaders of the socialist youth at the congress, distributed a rebellious pamphlet entitled *Neither Calmly nor Legally.*[109] At the same time, Herzl was at least given credit for his new Uganda project, for his attempt to grapple with the immediate plight of the Russian-Jewish masses. The leaders of Russian Zionism, who clung exclusively to the Palestinian solution, were held in contempt by the majority of the Zionist youth.

Thus, when the conference, planned at Rovno in the spring, met in Kiev in September 1903, the delegates were determined to seek new formulas, to go their own way. It was typical of the prevailing mood that the chairman, Mark Ratner, was a member not of the Zionist movement but of the Party of Socialist Revolutionaries. Horrified by the Kishinev pogrom, he had decided that Jewish politics had to become his first priority. In reality, beyond certain very basic principles (a territorial solution to the Jewish question, revolutionary activism), there was little agreement at the conference.[110] The fundamental divisions of opinion, which would lead by 1906 to the creation not of one but of three major parties from the former Poale Zion, were already very much in evidence.

Nevertheless, a core group – Zilberfarb (Bazin), Vladimir Fabrikant, Avrom Rozin (Ben Adir), and Mark Ratner – set the guidelines for the conference. And it was the same group that from the first was able to control the journal, *Vozrozhdenie* (Rebirth), established by the conference. (*Vozrozhdenie*, no. 1, printed in Paris, came out early in 1904.)

They shared or had hammered out together a common program and a common philosophy. Thus, in concrete terms, the Vozrozhdentsy demanded the creation of a "fighting [*boevaia*] national party"[111] that (unlike the Zionist movement) would participate in the struggle for a free Russia, and (unlike the Bund) would advocate maximal solutions to the Jewish question. They were for the creation of a worldwide Jewish socialist organization (to be represented at the Socialist International), for the direction of Jewish emigration to a chosen area, and for the establishment of a "territorial center." "Yes," declared the editorial in *Vozrozhdenie,* no. 1, "we openly declare ourselves nationalists."[112] But they also proclaimed themselves socialists and saw the proletariat as "the avant-garde of the Jewish revolutionary movement." Yet, in contrast to the Bund, they did not shrink from the idea of a close alliance with "the best part of the Jewish bourgeoisie." ("The magnitude of our tasks . . . obliges us to attract a maximum of revolutionary energy wherever we find it.")[113] Again, the Vozrozhdentsy openly advocated the use of organized terror against those in the local administration and in the antisemitic press responsible for the outbreaks of pogroms.

The basic error of Bundists and Zionists alike, *Vozrozhdenie* argued, lay in the fact that they had still not emancipated themselves from a utopian view of politics. They believed that history advanced dialectically, with catastrophe acting as the midwife of progress; that it was their function to prepare for the day of judgment – be it the revolution or the exodus – and that any diversion from their single goal could only delay the salvation. They saw the class war and the struggle for national liberation as the one threatening the other.

But, in fact, insisted the Vozrozhdentsy, the key to effective change lay in the maximal mobilization and organization of political forces and political enthusiasm. And the way to achieve this was to supplement concrete action in the here and now with a vision of the ultimate liberation, both social and national. "The Zionists," the journal explained, "have indeed created a distant social *ideal,* but have not been able to create a matching sociohistorical *movement.*"[114] On the other hand, Dubnov and the Bundists, in denying the ultimate national goal of a Jewish territory, were cutting at the very root of the "national consciousness," were seeking "to break the barrel while keeping the wine inside."[115]

It was utterly self-defeating to cling to a cataclysmic view of history, to the idea that "the worse things are, the better"[116] (*chem khuzhe, tem luchshe*), to the *Zusammenbruchstheorie.* As there was no single, ultimate, factor generating historical causation, so there could be no single event that would solve all social problems. In reality, the process of national regeneration (*vozrozhdenie*) was cumulative, was dependent on the growth of experience, of self-confidence, and of power. Small victories would lead to greater victories. Self-defense against the pogroms, revolutionary action, the first steps in the colonization of a territory – all would complement and reinforce each other, open the way to new achievements. "National autonomy" in the Diaspora would act as the natural base for the ultimate attainment of national sovereignty in a separate territory.

"In order that the Jews," read one article in *Vozrozhdenie,* "shall not be caught unawares at the moment when we gain a territory, we have to make efforts to concentrate our energies not in a definite place but in a definite direction. We have to fix our national thought, our national effort, our national energies on one central idea – rebirth."[117]

In 1904, Zhitlovsky was asked and agreed to cooperate with the *Vozrozhdenie* group; a long article of his appeared in the second issue of the journal late in the year.[118] With the single exception of the territorialist issue, there could hardly have been a more natural alliance. In the equal weight they assigned to nationalism and socialism, in their endorsement of organized terrorism (or at least of reprisals), their hostility to Marxist determinism, their open preference for Mikhailovsky rather than Plekhanov, their call for a worldwide Jewish socialist alliance – the Vozrozhdentsy sounded like disciples of Zhitlovsky. Indeed, at times, they seemed to be simply paraphrasing him, as, for instance, when they wrote (in words almost identical with a memorable passage in *Evrei k evreiam*) that "our greatest misfortune lies in the fact that we always constitute a certain percentage of some whole and never 100 percent of ourselves."[119]

Both Zhitlovsky and Zilberfarb have left brief descriptions of the first meetings between the young leaders of the new venture and the veteran ideologue. According to Zilberfarb, Zhitlovsky was initially adamant in his rejection of the territorial plank in the program of the *Vozrozhdenie*. But, he added, "after long discussions and arguments he nevertheless did agree to cooperate with our journal, and that alone was a great political gain for us considering the popularity of Zhitlovsky in revolutionary-socialist circles."[120]

Clearly at some time in 1903–4 Zhitlovsky yielded on the territorialist principle. In his earlier days (until the mid-1890s), such a decision would have meant a total break in his ideology. Then he had seen the issue in terms of "either-or": either a revolution from above (which was a realistic possibility) or Palestinophilism (which was a mythic utopia and dangerous distraction). He then believed that for the Jewish people, time was running out and that its only hope lay in a swift coup by the revolutionary elite. But, given his more recent attitude, the adoption of territorialism did not present him with any fundamental dilemma. Long before the appearance of *Vozrozhdenie,* he had envisaged the solution to the Jewish question as a process of growth, mass mobilization, and cultural metamorphosis. A Jewish territory could fit into this framework not as the negation of *Gegenwartsarbeit*, of revolution in the Diaspora, but as an ultimate ideal, the culminating achievement of a people reborn. Thus, the messianic idea, which Zhitlovsky had written off in 1887 as having outlived its role in Jewish history, was now reintegrated into his ideology as secular territorialism, as the legitimate hope of an ancient nation. "I myself," he later wrote, "came to recognize in 1903 the limits of my pure Diaspora-nationalist standpoint and became a territorialist, but an abstract territorialist, a territorialist for the future, in principle."[121]

As he recalled it, Zilberfarb and Ben Adir asked him whether the *Vozrozhdenie* group

> should remain in the Zionist party or whether it should leave it and in the latter case what should be our central demands and what slogan should we take to the masses? I answered that we must certainly leave Zionism; found our own independent party with territorialism as the future goal; unite forthwith with the Russian revolutionary movement; and adopt a "Jewish Seim" as our central demand.[122]

Possibly Zhitlovsky was writing here with the benefit of hindsight, for these guidelines, which he apparently laid down in mid-1904, had become the official platform of the movement by 1906. He himself was in the United States during the revolution of 1905, initially on his fund-raising mission for the PSR and also, it seems, for the *Vozrozhdenie,* and he did not reach Russia until the autumn of 1906. Thus, to the extent that the Vozrozhdentsy adopted his strategy, it was not because of his personal influence but because of the overwhelming pressure exerted by the revolutionary realities. In fact, on some basic issues, the Vozrozhdentsy now put a healthy distance between themselves and Zhitlovsky's ideology (and, indeed, their own former standpoint).

The original function assigned the journal, *Vozrozhdenie,* at the conference of the Zionist left wing in September 1903 had been that of rallying point for all the scattered forces of the Poale Zion in Russia. But it became clear in the years 1905–6 that this was an impossible task. In the fierce light of the revolution, ideological differences were seen as unbridgeable chasms. Organizational consolidation, the formation of nationwide parties, proceeded apace, but it was accompanied by the parallel process of marking-off and schism. Thus, in February 1905, the SSRP was founded at a conference in Odessa. Although a representative of their group, B. Fridland, attended that conference and was elected to the central committee, the Vozrozhdentsy eventually decided not to join the new party. Early in 1906, those numerous Poale Zion groups that had not entered the SSRP crystallized out, forming two new parties, the ESDRP-PZ and the SERP. The Vozrozhdentsy played a central role in the creation of the latter organization.

The ideological impact of the revolution on the *Vozrozhdenie* movement can therefore be measured by a comparison of its original program with that of the SERP, which it helped to found and into which it merged. In the years 1905–6, the pressure on the Jewish Left was in favor of an abstract territory and against Palestine; toward a local, Yiddish-based nationalism and against the investment of effort in overseas colonization; toward proletarian hegemony and against compromise with the powers-that-be; toward internationalist-socialist solidarity and against national self-reliance.

As a result, by 1906 the Vozrozhdentsy had adjusted their position considerably. While in 1904 they had demanded that revolutionary and emigrationist politics be conducted simultaneously, they now held that, for the foreseeable future, the one excluded the other. As Mark Ratner put it in an important article in the party journal of SERP: "We will fight all territorialist projects and undertakings put forward at the present moment; will ignore all territorialist organizations that already exist, or are now being formed; but will at the same time advocate [territorialism] as our final national ideal and through it illuminate all the ulcers and defects of our present-day national life."[123] On the other hand, the idea of Jewish national autonomism in Russia became both the corner- and the headstone of the party's ideology. The creation of a national parliament, a Seim, with the control of a large, tax-based budget, was seen as the crucial first step toward the reconstruction and modernization of Jewish life. Indeed, the members of the SERP were increasingly known simply as "Seimists."

On these two issues (the reduction of territorialism to an abstraction and the elevation of Diaspora autonomism to an end in itself) the Vozrozhdentsy held the lead, anticipating the general trend. The SSRP and the Palestine-oriented Poale Zion followed along the same path reluctantly, hesitantly, and never went so far. Thus, it was only natural that in the elections to the Second Duma, the SERP – when it had to choose – "supported . . . the Bund against the SSRP."[124]

In contrast, in the spheres of socialist ideology and revolutionary strategy, it was the *Vozrozhdenie* group that had to trim its sails closest to the wind. In 1904 the Vozrozhdentsy had gloried in their voluntarist ideology, their emphasis on consciousness rather than being, on freedom rather than necessity. At the same time, they had demanded the creation of a revolutionary party that would be truly national in character and include sections of the bourgeoisie in its ranks (or at least in its orbit). However, little was left of this by 1906.

The draft program of the SERP was formulated in purely Social Democratic terms, placing great emphasis on class antagonism. "The bourgeoisie of the oppressed nationalities," it stated, for example, "uses its class privileges in an effort to place the entire weight of the national yoke on the propertyless classes. Moreover, with its propagation of a politics 'above class' and its denial of class contradictions in the face of the common enemy, it strives to becloud the class-consciousness of the proletariat and to divide its ranks."[125] In practical terms, this meant that the SERP was as enthusiastic as the other Jewish left wing parties in their boycott of the elections to the First Duma and in their rejection of a Jewish National Assembly to be called during the revolution. On the face of it, a party that made a Jewish Seim its central demand might have been expected to support the campaign on behalf of the National Assembly, especially as Mark Ratner participated actively in the Union for Equal Rights, but this was not to be. Socialist solidarity was the order of the day.[126]

The sharp swing away from the populist ideology was a natural response to the mood then prevailing among the Jewish socialists and organized workers. "In general sociological questions," admitted SERP, no. 2, "[*Vozrozhdenie* originally] wrote in the spirit of the Socialist Revolutionaries and of critical Marxism while the mass of the Poale Zion . . . took their stand on orthodox Marxism."[127] It is true that in 1907 a formal alliance was established between the Party of Socialist Revolutionaries and the SERP, but this reflected more the long-standing friendship between Zhitlovsky and Ratner, on the one hand, and Chernov, on the other, than the sentiment of the rank and file. "It became apparent," Chernov later recalled, "that many of the local Seimist organizations considered themselves to be Marxists and did not want any alliance with the SRs."[128]

Thus, on his return to Russia, Zhitlovsky had a choice. He might have adopted the stance of critic in his own party, the SERP, attacking its swing to orthodox Marxism, its excessive reliance on the wage-earning proletariat (a minority of the Jewish people). Again, as a veteran ideologist of proven independence, he might have undertaken a detached analysis of the long-term dangers facing Russian Jewry.

After all, in his answer to Dubnov, while personally defending the socialist parties, An-sky struck a sensitive balance between advocacy and doubt, romanticism and realism. There he made plain his belief that the prevailing view of class politics as a universal panacea was, however inevitable, still erroneous. "As far as I personally am concerned," An-sky wrote in March 1906,

> I fully recognize that class politics in no way contradict national politics of certain kinds . . . I consider that the entire accumulation of positive cultural treasures created by the Jewish national genius over a period of three thou-

Figure 17. Chaim Zhitlovsky, 1865–1943.

sand years . . . possess an enormous value not only for the Jews but for all mankind . . . and that . . . we must cherish its source – the creative national genius of the Jewish people . . . and, nonetheless, I would not find in myself the courage to turn to the Jewish laboring masses with the *demand* that – even at the expense of their own class interests – they undertake to defend the national interests . . . of the Jewish people.[129]

This was not the tone Zhitlovsky adopted. He exalted in the strength of the tide and let it carry him forward.[130] Looking back from 1912 on the revolutionary period, he chided the Zionist leadership for having treated the attainment of equal rights as an end in itself, adding, however, that actually they had had no choice because to have done otherwise would have "thrown the Jewish middle class into a terrible uproar and because [it was assumed] that any day all discrimination was about to be swept away by the powerful waves of the revolution."[131] In fact, this can be taken (whether consciously or not) as a comment, too, on his own attitude and euphoria in the years 1906–7.

His articles in the SERP paper, *Folks-shtime,* published in Vilna late in 1906 and during 1907, revealed him in his most optimistic mood. He had moved toward a position of romantic or "uncritical" populism. The participation of the Jewish workers in the revolution, he wrote in his "Letter from a Jewish Socialist," owed its impressive power to the spiritual impulses nurtured over the ages by Jewish faith and martyrdom. "That national Jewish energy," he wrote, "which has burst forth in such force in the revolutionary struggle of the Jewish proletariat and the Jewish socialist youth . . . has simply been transferred from the religious to the revolutionary sphere, without in any way losing its national . . . content."[132] The universal human passion for "truth," "beauty," and "justice"[133] that had sustained their orthodox forefathers now inspired the revolutionary socialists. "The holy word of the Baal-Shem – socialism – . . . has had the impact of the Messiah's sho-far."[134] The modern Yiddish writers, Peretz, Pinsky, and An-sky, had a much deeper understanding of the "life of the people [*folks-lebn*],"[135] specifically of Hasidism, than the academic historians such as Graetz. The socialist intelligentsia could no longer see the Jews and their history "through the eyes of our crudely atheistic fathers and grandfathers." They had to understand that they were not dealing with "the dry leaves fallen from a tree . . . but with a tree, very much alive and fresh, with living and supple roots even if it is planted in a poisonous swamp . . . [136] We must have a deep respect for a great people which lies enchained; an ardent and deserved love for it; the proud thought that we belong to it."[137] One cannot but wonder whether Zhitlovsky here was writing under the influence not only of the revolutionary experience but also of Moses Hess, whom he held in growing admiration.

The same almost mystic note sounded through his other writings of this period. He reminded his readers that the vision that had inspired Marx was a society where "wage labor" would be replaced by "human labor," the exploitation of man by his many-sided self-fulfillment. What this meant in practical terms, Zhitlovsky insisted, was the transfer of the urban masses to agricultural production or at least to a rural setting. He recalled that this had been the program of many Russian-Jewish *intelligenty* and maskilim in the late 1870s and had then been integrated into the Palestinophile program of the early 1880s. "That was the beginning of the Jewish *revolution* . . . and the final goal of the revolution was clear for all to see – a land of one's own which would bind the people [*folk*] to nature." It was now transparently obvious that this could not be achieved by "the transfer of the entire people from one place to another on 'the wings of eagles,' " but had to be undertaken in Russia. "The Jewish people must lay the foundation of its new life in the Diaspora [goles]."[138] This of course was a repetition of one of Zhitlovsky's oldest themes, but now he looked not to the elite, but to the masses to make it a reality. "The Jewish people now has a power which can take it upon itself to carry through the program of the Jewish revolution – that is, the Jewish working class that has emerged during the last twenty-five years."[139] Of course, the Jewish workingman had as yet only the haziest conception of the final goal of socialism.

> Through and through a needle-and-thread man, an awl-and-cobble man, it is hard for him to imagine . . . that the Jews will become land workers. And when he fantasizes about the near future he dreams not about the open fields and free work under the open skies but about the great steam factories which day-in and day-out belch forth black smoke and make the worker a cog in a machine.[140]

But he was sure that with the upsurge of the proletarian movement, the working class would come to understand the meaning of socialism, the goal of the Jewish revolution.

Conclusion

Chaim Zhitlovsky was an individualist. He often stood alone and his influence was historically most important when he could act as a rallying point for those Jewish socialists who were seeking new ways. In his individualism; in his attempt to see the present against the backdrop of Jewish history; in his abiding concern with the messianic and prophetic in that history; in his view of nationalism and socialism as naturally allied; in his hostility to determinism and materialism – he was, as he himself came to recognize, reminiscent of Moses Hess. "That Hess, as the Jew, became known so late," he wrote in 1912,

> was a great loss for our socialist generation which in the 80s broke its head over the basic problem of Jewish socialism – the great question of how to unite socialist principles with the ideal of Jewish rebirth.
> Familiarity with Hess's *Rome and Jerusalem* would have saved a great deal of theoretical effort. This does not mean that [his] . . . Jewish theories were sacred writ. But the manner of presenting the problem, the way in which Hess sought the answers, the new view of all of Jewish history presented *as only* a socialist could seriously think it through – everything which [our] generation had to work out . . . – that all in its main outline was illuminated and developed by Moses Hess.[141]

In some ways, Zhitlovsky had the advantage over Hess. The fact that he developed under the influence not of Hegel and German idealist philosophy but in the more down-to-earth school of Mikhailovsky and Lavrov tended to hold him within the bounds of reality. His early writings revealed a bold originality, a keen sense of impending Jewish tragedy, and an impatient urge to seek an escape route.

In those years he clearly was preparing himself to don the prophetic mantle, and he would return to this role in later years. But in fact he was not temperamentally suited to that part. A prophet must excoriate his people in its hours of triumph and console it in its despair.

Zhitlovsky tended to follow the reverse pattern. He himself was subject to the prevailing atmosphere, a creature of transient mood. True, throughout his life he remained loyal to certain key concepts (voluntarism, agrarianism, a synthesis of nationalism and socialism), but he applied these concepts to reality in startlingly different ways at different times.

He swung between two extremes. He could take his stand outside the Jewish situation and analyze the precarious role of the Jews as a nation of middlemen in a hostile social environment, threatened by its very competitive success and moving unawares toward an abyss. Only the most extreme countermeasures – agrarianization, national self-isolation – could prevent disaster. He wrote thus in 1892 (as a Narodovolets); in 1912 (as editor of *Dos naye lebn*); in 1937 (as an advocate of Biro-Bidzhan). In this role he reminds one of nobody so much as Lilienblum or Pinsker, who profoundly influenced him although without winning him in their lifetime to the Palestinian cause.

But, at other times, he was the complete optimist. When he felt that political and social forces had taken a clear upturn (Jewish socialism and Yiddish culture from 1897, the revolution of 1905, the Bolshevik revolution), his critical faculties ceased to function and he was carried along in an almost mystical ecstasy. At such times, nothing looked impossible: man was brother to man; and the people holy. The last word should go to Viktor Chernov, the third partner of the populist troika of the Berne years.

> Just like... An-sky, Zhitlovsky too was through and through the Jew, through and through the Russian *narodnik,* but with this possible deep distinction – with An-sky both his natures were whole, indivisible, each one its separate self. But Zhitlovsky during his life would often say: "Two souls live in my heart and each seeks to escape the other." The same was true, in fact, of other elements and forces in his being.[142]

CHAPTER 6

Nachman Syrkin

On the populist and prophetic strands in socialist Zionism, 1882–1907

In 1939 Berl Katznelson published his essay on Syrkin's early life (until 1903). It still stands as the most impressive memorial to him, characterized as it is by a broad historical sweep, a sensitive understanding of the man and his ideas, much humor and wit. However, partly no doubt for artistic effect, partly perhaps under the spell of a romantic view of party origins, Katznelson overemphasized one theme in Syrkin's life. Entitled "Alone in the Battle," his essay suggests a picture of Nachman Syrkin as virtually the sole advocate of socialist Zionism in the 1890s, a man who was cut off for years from his fellow men by his commitment to a new ideology, but who was then raised to leadership by the emergence of a new generation in the period of the Kishinev pogrom and the 1905 revolution. "Mad Nakhke," who had stood alone on the battlefield, found himself reinforced by an army of new recruits.

"He struggled for many years, arguing and preaching," wrote Katznelson of Syrkin's early tribulations, "before he finally succeeded in 1901 in organizing three people (he was a fourth) in a socialist Zionist society."[1] Here the historian was simply following his protagonist's own view of his role as described in his brief autobiographical sketches. "In the 1890s," Syrkin recalled, "I undertook the thankless task of being a socialist among the Zionists and a Zionist among the socialists and, of course, each side sought to shove and kick me over to the other."[2]

But, in reality, Syrkin was never an outsider in the sense that Moses Hess or even Aron Liberman had been. Equally, he never became an insider, a party man, even at those times when he was in the top leadership of the socialist Zionist (or territorialist) movements. For close to thirty years he participated actively in the Jewish politics first of Russia, then of America, and finally of Palestine, too. Yet although he threw himself unreservedly into his own times, he was never fully of them.

Syrkin did not have to suffer the isolation of a Hess because his life unfolded in the post-1881 period, within the developing framework of the new Jewish politics. He has to be seen as one of the many men who grew up in the shadow of the 1881 crisis and then acted in leading roles in the later periods of political upsurge, in the years 1897 to 1907 and again from 1915 to 1920. The political thinking of that generation had been shaped by the hopes and plans (taken singly or in various combinations) of 1881–82 (the "exodus," "auto-emancipation," a "going to the people") and by the utter failure of those hopes and plans. This was true alike of many leading Hoveve Zion (Ussishkin, Ahad Ha-Am, Temkin, Chlenov, Motskin) and of the founders of the American-Jewish labor movement (Abe Cahan, Bernard Weinstein, Philip Krantz).

Syrkin was of this generation. He too sought to build on the experience of 1881–82. He did so in cantankerous disagreement with most of his contemporaries, but nonetheless he was participating in a common debate conducted on the basis of many shared assumptions. Moreover, within the general world of post-1881 Jewish politics, he moved freely within the minority but influential circles that crystallized out during the 1890s on the radical periphery of Hoveve Zion and on the national periphery of the proto-Bundist movement—men such as Chaim Weizmann, Lev Motskin, Nathan Birnbaum, and Abraham Salz, on the one hand, and Dovid Pinsky, Isidor (Yisrael) Eliashev, Elyohu Davidzon, Chaim Zhitlovsky, and Y. Blumshtein (Frumin), on the other. Moreover, beyond these informal associations was the small group that shared Syrkin's socialist Zionism and like Syrkin battled for their beliefs on the floor of the early Zionist congresses, particularly the two important publicists, David Farbstein and S. R. Landau.

That there was throughout much of the "typical" in Syrkin can be illustrated by comparing him with Zhitlovsky. Just because they always differed sharply in temperament and nearly always in their politics, the parallels between these two men are all the more striking. So, for example, in their general philosophy, they shared the same determination to give as much weight to the national as to the socioeconomic factor; the same preference for Mikhailovsky over Plekhanov; the same fascination with the Second Temple period in Jewish history, particularly with its messianic and communistic sects; the same respect for Moses Hess as their major forerunner. Authors in the 1890s of highly controversial booklets on the Jewish question, they were both involved in the rising revolutionary and territorialist movements after 1903; were both associated with the Vozrozhdenie in 1904; both became leaders and Duma candidates of rival but similar Jewish parties in 1906; both left for the United States in 1908, where they edited competing socialist journals in Yiddish; both acted as leaders of the American Jewish Congress movement and Poale Zion party during World War I; and both appeared after the war as Zionists and simultaneously as enthusiastic (although nonparty) supporters of the Bolshevik regime.

Syrkin's importance in the history of modern Jewish politics (in Russia and beyond) cannot be measured primarily in terms of the role he played in any particular episode or party, be it as founding father or as politician. He was among the first socialists in the Zionist movement founded by Herzl, among the leaders both of the Zionist Socialist Labor Party (SSRP) in the years 1905–7 and of the world Poale Zion movement from 1909 to 1924. But in all these spheres he was never more than one of a group of able speakers, political organizers, ideologists, and publicists.

The unique impact made by Syrkin results, rather, from the combination of idiosyncratic doctrine and single-minded temperament, of eccentric ideology and personality. Fundamentally, what differentiated Syrkin from others of his generation was his attitude to the experience of 1881–2. While the overwhelming tendency among his contemporaries was to seek the roots of the great failure of 1882 in the sphere of objective reality and therefore to abandon or at least modify or reinterpret the plans of that period, he saw the failure as stemming from random political errors. As a result, while others became Marxists or advocates of a highly limited colonization in Palestine or disciples of Diaspora nationalism, Yiddishism,

Figure 18. Nachman Syrkin, 1868–1924.

and folkism (*narodnost*), he, on the contrary, sought to resurrect the program of 1882 in its most maximalist forms. He remained an advocate of the mass exodus from Europe, thought in terms of a broad popular movement that would organize that exodus, envisaged the colonization of the Jewish territory as taking place from the first on fully socialist foundations, and insisted on the revival of the Hebrew language as the essential condition for a national renaissance.

The one concession he was willing to make to the realities of the post-1882 era was his admission that such a program could only be executed over a prolonged period. But the conclusion he drew was also maximalist. As the Jewish masses could not immediately escape the Russian Empire en bloc, those who remained had no choice but to participate fully in the revolutionary movement. The idea that Zionism negated revolution was as erroneous as the idea that it negated socialism. Colonization overseas and insurrection on the spot had to enjoy equal priority.

For some thirty years Syrkin preached his version of socialist Zionism. It was unacceptable not only to the official Zionist organization but also to the great majority in the socialist Zionist and territorialist camps. His contemporaries and even more the younger generation, which emerged in 1905, sought to introduce a definite order of priorities into their program, subordinating nation to class, colonization to revolution, the exodus to the Diaspora – or, as the case might be, vice versa. But Syrkin demanded the maximalization of effort simultaneously in both directions, insisted on the complete divorce of the one sphere from the other, and asserted that there was no way of bridging the gap between the two.

He did nothing to sugar this pill for the benefit of party comrades, still less for political opponents. On the contrary, he presented his ideas in the most provocative way possible. Paradox was in his lifeblood. Indeed, his view of Jewish politics was essentially based on a series of paradoxical theses. First, he argued, the more fantastic the solutions appeared the more realistic they were often likely to be in fact. Second, the better the immediate situation of the Jewish people, the bleaker were its future prospects. Third, in the short run, national interest had to be sacrificed to national pride. In a period when Marxism was in the ascendant and left its stamp even on non-Marxist thinking, such theses were bound to appear to most of his comrades as sheer madness.

Whether he was in Berlin in 1898, in Russia in 1906, in America in 1914, or in Palestine in 1920, he spoke in the same vein, with the same passionate commitment to his own vision, with the same supreme self-confidence and angry scorn for those who could not, or would not, see the truth. In the sphere of Russian-Jewish politics, where everything was in constant flux, where parties were so often short-lived, where popular enthusiasms rose and fell with lightning speed, such unbending consistency over so long a period was bound eventually to win itself an audience. In the United States during and after World War I and even more in Palestine in the 1920s, his views gained a more attentive hearing. Ideas which had seemed absurd in the relatively stable world of the 1890s made more sense to many in the chaos that overtook Europe in the era of the World War and the October Revolution.

Essentially, then, Syrkin has to be seen not only as a pioneer and leader of socialist Zionism in the years after 1897, but even more as heir to the legacy of 1882; as the most important and committed disciple of Moses Hess; and as mentor to the leaders of Ahdut Ha-Avoda in the 1920s – to such men as Shneyer Zalman

Rubashev (Shazar), David Ben Gurion, and above all Berl Katznelson. Indeed, it is arguable that he had more in common with Hess (who died shortly after he was born) and with Katznelson (who rose to prominence after his own time) than with any of his contemporaries or disciples in Russia and America.

Syrkin's ideology: general theory

Contemporaries were rarely aware of the consistency which marked Syrkin's political stance over some thirty years. They noted that he was often as much out of step with his own following as with opposing parties and they concluded that he was governed more than anything else by caprice. So, for instance, Zivion could write in *Di tsukunft* in 1909 that "if there are men in this world who are to be envied then Dr. Syrkin is surely one of them. He has to be envied the speed, ease, and agility with which he changes his theories, opinions, and programs."[3] This was the comment of a Bundist, but party comrades writing in party journals – Moyshe Litvakov in 1906 or Avrom Revutsky[4] in 1924 – could write in a similar vein.

What contemporaries did not understand, and what his biographers have not sufficiently stressed, was the fact that Syrkin's ad hoc political positions were almost without exception deduced from an all-embracing schema, that this schema remained largely (although not totally) unchanged throughout his lifetime, and that it had been formed initially only through the most strenuous intellectual effort.

Throughout most of the period from 1888 until 1903, that is, from the age of twenty to thirty-five, he was enrolled as a student at the University of Berlin and later at the University of Berne. Outwardly, his life was typical of the Russian student abroad with much time devoted to political debate, to all-night discussions, and to the camaraderie celebrated in Russian tea or German beer. Even his marriage in 1898 and the birth of a baby daughter in 1899 did little or nothing to alter his peripatetic and gregarious student existence.

Nevertheless, those who knew Syrkin well were united in their opinion that in fact he was marked off from his contemporaries by the intensity with which he sought answers to the "accursed questions" of life. There was no limit to the time and energy which he was willing to spend studying works on philosophy, psychology, and history. The ascetic and unworldly side of Syrkin's character became something of a legend. Thus Chaim Weizmann described him in the 1890s as "definitely underfed" and recalled that

> at the beginning of every month he would turn up for a loan and I pinched off what I could from my allowance. Towards the end of the month, when cash was scarce, he would ask for a "pledge" . . . which could be pawned. I had two pledges: one was a wonderful cushion . . . and the other was my set of chemist's weights. At the end of the month I was generally without cushion and without weights.[5]

Shmarya Levin has described in his memoirs how when he first arrived from Russia at the Berlin railway station, Syrkin (a friend from his Minsk days)

> refused to let me take a droshky or a carriage: it cost too much money and was not fitting for a student. He had . . . ordered his landlady to come . . .

with a small cart drawn by a dog! . . . The dog pulled away at the cartful of luggage; the landlady drove the dog; and Syrkin and I strolled two or three miles through the streets of Berlin to his lodgings . . . Syrkin's room lay on the fifth floor of a typical workers' tenement: a vast building housing a huge swarm of lodgers.[6]

Of course, for Marie Syrkin, who spent her entire childhood and youth in a Micawber-like atmosphere of penury and imminent financial disaster, immersion in the world of ideas and politics at the expense of all else was a matter of a very different, even tragic, significance. In her biography of her father (which stands as a work of art in its own right), she does not conceal the nagging pain caused her by the thought that if only he had lived with his feet more on the ground, her mother might have escaped her premature death from tuberculosis.[7]

Syrkin's immense erudition in many fields and many languages both ancient and modern was likewise the subject of much comment. S. L. Tsitron has recalled that even in 1882 (that is, at the age of fourteen) he already impressed the youth in Minsk with his extensive knowledge of the Talmud, and of both medieval and modern Hebrew literature.[8] In later years, he would take it for granted that what interested him would be of equal interest to his family, and Marie recalls that "three books were the *bêtes-noires* of my early adolescence, the Bible in Hebrew, *Das Kapital* in German, and Spinoza's 'Ethics' in Latin."[9]

That his asceticism and erudition were only the outward signs of a highly systematic mind was little appreciated at the time. Even Berl Katznelson did not consider it necessary to devote any significant attention to his two doctoral dissertations – the one on the philosophy of history and the other on theories of epistomology – which were published in 1896 and 1903 respectively. Yet, these works, particularly the *Geschichtsphilosophische Betrachtungen*, reveal more perhaps than anywhere else the depth of his thinking.

He shared the belief common to most ideologists of the Russian Left that political theory had to be developed as only one facet of a general weltanschauung embracing at least philosophy, sociology, anthropology, psychology, and biology. This architectonic quality in his thought gave him the self-confidence to pursue so utterly an independent line in politics for over three decades.

The focal point in Syrkin's thought was, without a doubt, his belief that a grandiose act of the national will, of utopian construction, was a philosophical possibility and, in the case of the Jewish people, a political necessity. It was this belief that dominated his philosophy of history, in which he sought to liberate politics and subjectivity from domination by the sociological and economic; his psychology of politics, in which he argued that goals have a power independent of tangible facts; and his system of ethics, in which he insisted that values had to be seen as absolute and universal rather than relative, situational, or historically conditioned.

Thus he was even more opposed than Zhitlovsky to every attempt to explain historical development as predetermined. In his *Thoughts on the Philosophy of History* he attacked, in turn, the metaphysical theories that saw history as the unfolding of an a priori logic, the positivist and Social Darwinist theories that described society as analogous to a natural organism and subject to laws identical with those of natural science, and the materialist theories that sought by reductionist methodology to explain all human affairs ultimately in terms of economic relationships. Against Hegel and Fichte, Comte, Spencer and Buckle, Marx and Engels, he called in the contemporary German philosophy of Dilthey and Simmel as well as the Russian populists, Lavrov, Mikhailovsky, and Kareev.

He argued that historical monism in all its many different manifestations was fatally flawed. Thus, first and foremost, it stood in flagrant contradiction to historical experience. There was no empirical justification for assuming that a single or simple pattern was waiting to be discovered within the flux of human development. On the contrary, there was an irreducible multiplicity of factors governing human affairs. "The facts of history result from [various] totally autonomous processes which influence each other, interact and generally entangle the historical web."[10] Chance – the random and the contingent – was an element of real weight that in itself brought to nought every attempt to posit omnipotent laws. Further, the fact that man himself becomes increasingly a conscious participant in the social process meant that past experience could not provide a sure basis for prediction. "History is distinguished from nature by the fact that in nature the object observed is distinct from the observing subject while in history subject and object coincide."[11] In sum, "every attempt to conceive history according to one uniform plan or one law must be considered erroneous. To try to discover a few historical laws in the multifarious variety of historical reality is also a barren and unscientific undertaking."[12]

However, Syrkin's lifelong hostility to historical determinism was no doubt motivated at least as much by political and ethical as by purely philosophical considerations. Thus, he argued, the modern theories of inevitability encouraged a spurious self-confidence. It was in reaction to his political isolation and "impotence," Syrkin wrote in 1923, "that Marx caught hold of the wheel of world history . . . Marx was in reality the purest social voluntarist but he strengthened his will through his conviction that it coincided with that of the proletariat and that the proletarian will represents historical necessity."[13] But such a flight from reality could hardly be a source of human strength. "Vulgar optimism is . . . an impediment insofar as it permits a comfortable self-satisfaction, while in history nothing is won cheaply."[14]

Then again he insisted, all totalist theories of history led in one degree or another to justification of past wrongs and, more important, to the demand that the living be sacrificed to the putative welfare of their descendants. It was repellent, he wrote, "to see in the entire historical process only a means for the well-being of future generations," thus depriving the past and present of their "independent worth."[15]

In marshaling the case against the Hegelians and Marxists, Social Darwinists and Positivists, Syrkin had relied on arguments associated more with conservative than socialist thinkers, not only with Dilthey and Simmel but also with Dostoevsky and Schopenhauer. If there were no scientific laws governing social development, if there was no possibility of predicting the future with accuracy, if well-laid plans could be frustrated by chance events, then what guarantee was there that a new form of society would be preferable to the old? In asserting man's freedom did one not condemn him to a pessimistic quietism?

For Syrkin, with his consciously "utopian" outlook, it was essential to demonstrate that, on the contrary, the subjective premise could actually reinforce faith in radical change. He had no intention of throwing out the baby with the bathwater, teleology with determinism. The idea of progress, he urged, was not dependent on the concept of necessity but, on the contrary, had to be understood simply as an "empirically based generalization."[16] He drew a clear line between the theory of progress elaborated by a number of the leading figures in the eighteenth-century Enlightenment – Condorcet, Turgot, Kant, Herder – and the supposedly scientific theories developed by nineteenth-century thinkers. The former had noted a "tendency" toward human advance, proposed a hypothesis to explain observable facts, and suggested the final goals which mankind could logically attain. The latter had deviated from this approach by identifying "progress" – "a subjective, human, voluntaristic concept" – with "evolution," a "cosmic, objective and scientific concept."[17]

He argued that progress was an observable fact produced by a combination of objective and subjective, sociological and political factors. First, following Turgot and Condorcet, he noted that in the spheres of science and technology, as in fact of learning generally, knowledge and expertise tended to advance at an ever greater speed. Every discovery served as the basis for a series of further discoveries. The development of tools and language, writing and printing, gave each generation the chance to start at the level of proficiency attained by the previous one. Here, clearly, was the explanation of scientific advance hitherto and the guarantee of more rapid advance in the future.

But none of this, he readily admitted, had any intrinsic relevance to the social or ethical spheres. Indeed, it could be argued with much force that man as an ethical being had remained at the most primitive level. It was undeniable, after all, that "in social as in international life, ethics lack all power."[18]

If, nonetheless, Syrkin insisted that a theory of progress was also applicable to the moral sphere, it was because he placed such crucial emphasis on the role played in history by ideas and by faith. While ethical progress had still not transformed social or international relations, he argued, it had already exerted a profound influence on the dominant ideologies and on the "inner life of man."[19] "The morality of Christianity," he wrote for example, "differs from ancient Paganism no less than the modern Christian differs in his life and behavior from the Hellene of antiquity."[20] Even the most rabid reactionary, he wrote (here mirroring the optimistic conceptions of his age), would not suggest subjecting the workers in modern Europe to the cruelties suffered by the slaves in ancient Rome.

The process of human advance, he believed, was made possible first by ideological revolution among the few; then by the absorption of the new values into the collective consciousness and subconsciousness of the masses; and only as a final stage by the radical transformation of social institutions and relations. What moral advance there was in human society had been made possible by the reception of the prophetic message into the popular psyche. Once this process was truly understood – and taken as a basis for action – it would prove to be far more effective, all-embracing, and persistent. Knowledge was power.

In the spirit of Lavrov, Mikhailovsky, and their school, he was convinced that there could have been, and would be, no progress without the conscious intervention in history of the individual, the hero. For him, Thomas Carlyle, despite his many exaggerations, was nearer the truth than Herbert Spencer. "The view that

the great personalities are merely children of their time is false, for [such] personalities and geniuses often stand in contradiction to their own time."[21] A Moses, a
Christ, a Confucius had been compelled to formulate new modes of moral and
philosophical truths in direct opposition to prevailing opinion. "True heroism in
history is often a martyrdom."[22]

In his book of 1903 on epistomology, *Sensation and Idea,* he sought to provide a
psychological underpinning for his theory of the individual role in history. Against
the extreme school of sensationalist psychology, he called in the evidence of recent
medical research on hypnosis, trauma, and hallucination. Clearly, he argued, the
workings of the mind were not confined within the boundaries of actual experience. "Ideas which are linked to deep emotions and, above all, to strong interests,"
he wrote, "exercise a superiority in man's consciousness over sensations,"[23] and he
added that "the absentminded look of the dreamer sunk in his fantasies or of the
man absorbed in great plans are examples of the involuntary exclusion of sensation
and the greater potency of the idea."[24]

He was convinced that unless they were in some sense divorced from the surrounding world of tangible fact, moral and political leaders could never attain true
greatness. The following eyewitness account of Syrkin's remarks at a reception for
Chaim Weizmann in New York in 1921 again illustrates this point:

> One of the speakers had remarked that [ironically] it was the Russian Jew,
> Weizmann, who had freed Zionism from its impractical ways [*batlones*].
> Syrkin spoke next ... : "What! Weizmann is not hopelessly impractical
> [*batlen*]? He is the greatest, emptiest good-for-nothing that I have ever met. I
> have known him for the last twenty-five years and I know him well." The
> audience was all astir. Weizmann remained sitting bolt upright ... "Herzl
> was a good-for-nothing. So was Karl Marx and so was Moses. All great
> leaders and men who create ideas and movements have to be *batlonim* ...
> Practical ... men do not do those things."[25]

After the prophetic word, Syrkin argued, came the popular process. Radical
ideological change was adapted to the rhythms of social continuity. The new ideas
and values were taken into the bloodstream of the masses. Between sociology and
biology, he insisted, stood the autonomous sphere of psychology. Herein lay the
vital importance of the attempt by Lazarus and Wundt, the contemporary German
scholars, to develop the study of the collective and national psyche. They had
provided the necessary corrective to the one-sided theories of Karl Marx and
Herbert Spencer, for whom "consciousness, inner convictions, the psychic nature
of man, are not factors in history."[26]

National entities were so central to modern life precisely because over the centuries they had established a hold on mass sentiment and emotion. Every people had
gradually developed its own image of the world and of its role in history. Nations
changed with time; they were divided into subgroups and social classes but they
were, nonetheless, overarching communities possessed of a tangible existence, continuity, and reality. National memory transmitted the social norms – deep-rooted
but subject to periodic modification – from generation to generation and this
shaped the national consciousness. And in order to become a political force, in
order to transform society, radical ideology (and ideologists) had no choice but to

appeal to the *Volksgeist,* the traditional motivations, symbols, and demiurges of a given people.

Man, he asserted, was moved not only by considerations of material interest but also by religious and quasireligious drives, by visionary "goals." "The law of causation," he wrote, "posits that there is no effect without a cause; the law of ends posits that there is no will – or what is the same thing – no action without a goal."[27] Indeed, the more absurd a project might appear to the utilitarian mind, the more realistic it often was in fact. "In the actual world," he wrote, "Newton's *Principia philosophiae naturalis* have only a relative value. On the other hand, the absolute realization of the Utopia of a Thomas More or of a Bellamy is in itself no logical impossibility."[28] The real test of a political strategy was not the extent to which it accorded with present actualities but rather its potential power to penetrate the mass psyche and activate the popular will. In this sense, the best guarantee of progress itself was the fact that since the eighteenth century "the idea of progress has become for mankind an article of faith. What the 'end of days' once was for the Jews and Salvation – the 'Kingdom of Heaven' – for the Christians, the faith in progress is for contemporary humanity."[29] In assigning so central a role to the mass subconscious, Syrkin was clearly pursuing a line of thought that could lead to the relativism associated with the German historical school or even to a racialist chauvinism. If history could only advance through the medium of distinct national cultures, did it not follow that values had no distinct validity until adopted by the *Volksgeist,* that the only truth was that recognized by the national consciousness, that every race was bound to consider itself superior to the next?

But having already rejected the monistic methodology in all its manifestations, Syrkin did not feel compelled to assign dominance in the sphere of values to nationality and the *Volksgeist.* On the contrary, he asserted, popular recognition was of great importance politically and sociologically, but was no yardstick of truth. In the sphere of ethics, he turned not to the theories of collective psychology or historical relativism but to the philosophy of Reason as expounded by leaders of the eighteenth-century Enlightenment. The past and present had to be measured against human potentialities, the existent by the ideal, the particular by the general, the national by the universal. As Herder had put it: "The final end of history is humanity."[30] In this sense, the pre-Marxist Left, which had seen socialism as the creation of "man," had come nearer the truth than the Marxists who saw it as the work (initially at least) of the "proletarian," of class interest and class consciousness.

Viewed from the vantage point of Man rather than of men, all nationalities were to be seen as equal participants in a common drama, moving along separate paths toward a universal goal. Here Syrkin was consciously following in the footsteps not only of Herder but also of Hess. Of the latter he wrote in 1916 – and this was a self-defense, too – that

> Hess was an outspoken race theoretician . . . But [he] . . . was far from following . . . Gobineau, Chamberlain, or even the Slavophile theorists. For [them] there were worthy and worthless races and nations – races that have a right to history and races that stand in contradiction to [history] . . . But with Hess all nations are in fact chosen people. Every nation, like the Jewish people, must have a mission, a historical faith.[31]

As national creativity was not an end in itself but had to be measured by Reason, by its contribution to human progress, it followed in Syrkin's view that a national culture, *Volksgeist,* could not flourish either in isolation or as a homogeneous unity. A nation, in order to develop its own positive potentialities to the full, had to be open constantly to influences from without, from the surrounding world. And within such a nation there had to be a constant struggle for the soul of the people between competing values, groups, and classes. Thus, the *Volksgeist* was not the expression of some mystic or organic unity but, on the contrary, "it is the individual [members] who maintain the spirit of the nation and without them it has no existence."[32]

Thus, his populism involved a cult of the "people," of the mass, not as it actually was but only as it might become. True, the popular way of life based on physical labor was simpler, more egalitarian than that of the upper classes, and this difference was reflected in the "sayings, riddles, idioms, jokes, and opinions which exist among the people."[33] However, what was required from a true leader was not to romanticize the existent, but rather a relentless struggle to draw out the latent idealism of the masses, to distinguish between the "absolute values" to which the people could attain and the "historical dross" which it should slough off. The only values ultimately worthy of every nation were those that had passed through "the furnace of history and acquired a universal-human content recognized by all men ... The universal achievements, the progressive and universal values are at first the possession of one people, its particular historically selected characteristic, but in time they become the cultural possession of the entire world."[34]

Syrkin's ideology: the Jewish question

Syrkin's standpoint in Jewish affairs was fully integrated with his overall ideology. The general and the particular reinforced each other. In his approach to Jewish politics as in his philosophy as a whole, there was the same truculent insistence on a radical discontinuity between the objective and the subjective, sociology and politics, the subconscious and the rational, the realm of fact and the realm of ends.

On the one hand, his socioeconomic analysis of the Jewish situation was marked by the blackest pessimism. He consistently developed the somber themes first elaborated by Lilienblum in his articles of late 1881 (and later taken up, inter alia, by Zhitlovsky in his *A Jew to the Jews* of 1892). Essentially, he argued that powerful socioeconomic forces were inexorably undermining the position of the Jews in the world and that only strenuous political countermeasures could avert a final tragedy.

In eastern Europe, he maintained, contemporaries were witnessing that same pattern of exclusion that had uprooted all the major Jewish communities of western Europe during the Middle Ages. The Jews had been permitted entry, or even invited, into backward and feudal societies in order to fulfill certain specific economic functions which at that time were out of bounds to the indigenous population, whether nobles, peasants, or churchmen. They had acted as intermediaries between the warrior class and its serfs, between one branch of the society and another. Despised by the upper classes and hated by the lower, they had rarely lived anything but a precarious existence. The Khmelnitsky massacres of 1648 were only an extreme example of a chronic peril, a process which "runs through the whole of Jewish history like a scarlet thread."[35]

So long as there was little or no direct competition from within the ranks of the host nation, the Jews had usually been able to count on a measure of official protection against the popular wrath. But as soon as the indigenous nationality produced a capitalist and middle class of its own, the presence of the Jews became an historical anachronism. Sooner or later, the pressure to expel them from their positions in the economy and even from the country itself became irresistible. It was now the turn of the Jews in the Pale of Settlement, Galicia, and Roumania to suffer the fate that had overtaken the Jews in England, France, and Spain hundreds of years before. By means of legislation, boycott, discrimination, and violence, the rival groups within the indigenous nationalities were squeezing them out of the economic lifestream, creating a "million-headed poverty-stricken Jewish mass."[36]

> Eighty percent of the Jewish people ... is slowly losing its sources of liveli-
> hood and is doomed to disaster. The transfer to productive labor is full of
> obstacles and, for the most part, blocked entirely ... But apart from eco-
> nomic pressure, this ... mass also carries on its shoulders all the nightmare of
> antisemitism in the government, the police, the middle class, and the mob.[37]

And even those Jews who had become wage-earning workers were confined to the margin of the productive process, to domestic industry and sweat shops—a mere "national reserve army of the international proletariat."[38]

In the West, the situation on the surface was incomparably better, and many believed that democratization, the abolition of the Pale of Settlement, the removal of the numerus clausus in education, and the attainment of equal civil rights would solve the Jewish question in eastern Europe too. But, Syrkin insisted, there could be no form of self-deception greater than this. Political equality, in fact, represented a double threat to the Jews: acid-like corrosion within and mounting hatred without.

Once permitted to compete on an equal basis in a modern industrial society and a free-market economy, the Jews in large part could be relied upon to rise rapidly up the economic ladder. Liberated from legal and social restraints, they invariably concentrated, out of all proportion to their numbers, in the middle and upper sections of the bourgeoisie as merchants, traders, professionals, and academics. "The Jews in western Europe," he wrote in 1901, "were turned into a bourgeois class, directly after the Emancipation, and a similar process is now to be seen [among the east European Jewish emigrants] in England and America."[39] "If Jew-ish immigration from Europe were to be halted for ten years," he stated in Di tsayt in 1922, "the Jewish working class in America would be reduced to an insignifi-cant size and the Jewish labor movement would almost disappear."[40] In the same period, he noted a similar development "in Communist Russia, where ninety per-cent of the Jews are speculators, merchants, storekeepers, middlemen and now, when petty trade [the NEP] is to be permitted ... , we shall soon have an unadul-terated Jewish merchant people without any proletarian admixture. That is the law of Jewish social development everywhere when the pressure on the Jews is momen-tarily relaxed."[41]

The price to be paid for this advance up the economic ladder, he argued, was far too high. First, it was nearly always accompanied by a deliberate attempt on the part of the Jews to divest themselves of their national heritage, to abandon the ideal of an autonomous national existence or a national mission. A shameless assimilationism was the natural ideological stance of the new Jewish bourgeoisie, the instinctive attempt to pay for economic and social status in the coin of self-betrayal. "For how did the Shylock of the Middle Ages turn into the king of the Stock Exchange today, the ghetto money-lender into the arrogant banker of our times, the peddler into the independent merchant, the yeshiva student of old into the emancipated doctor and lawyer of today – through assimilation!"[42]

In support of this denunciation, Syrkin turned not only to Hess and Peretz Smolenskin (he admired the latter almost as much as the former) but also, with his characteristic penchant for paradox, to Karl Marx. Throughout his life, he took a savage delight in praising, quoting, or paraphrasing Marx's essay of 1844, "On the Jewish Question." Even though this piece has frequently and understandably been regarded as overtly antisemitic, he chose to see in it a brilliant analysis of the degenerate Jewish bourgeoisie and even of the potential corruption inherent in the Diaspora situation per se. The post-Emancipation Jewish middle class, he wrote in 1903,

> is revolutionary at heart, but conservative and loyal to the state in public; would-be orthodox in the synagogue but a modern man before the world. That is the money-psychology of the Jewish bourgeoisie in the goles. Marx rightly said that the Jews are an antisocial and anticultural element in the world – because he saw before him the Jewish bourgeoisie in the days of its assimilation.[43]

Commenting in 1922 on the pro-Zionist resolutions of the Second International, he spoke with still less restraint: "Marx's characterization of the Jewish goles – that it is by nature an antisocial phenomenon and that the Jews exist only in the nooks and crannies of society – this description of genius was bound to penetrate the consciousness of the ... international proletariat."[44]

The external consequences of Jewish *embourgoisement* were even more disastrous than the internal. For, the more the Jews benefited from the freedoms of a competitive society, the more they aroused hostility in the host nationality at all its levels, and the petty-bourgeois strata dangling in despair between capital and labor were the most virulently antisemitic of all. "Not the character of the Jews, even though it is a miserable and disgusting caricature ... but the open profit motive, the hunger for the wealth of the Jews, the desire to strike the ground from under a competitor, to confiscate his property, to expel him from the country – these are the factors that make them antisemitic."[45] In this form, he argued, antisemitism could well provide the basis for "a revolutionary movement of the Catilinarian type – that is, the revolt of one class against another and against the existing regime not out of high and general principles, but out of egoistic interest."[46] Thus, as the crisis of the capitalist system grew in dimensions, so in direct ratio did the danger to the Jews. "The more unstable the social classes," he wrote in 1898,

> the more difficult and insecure life becomes, the greater the danger of a proletarian rising ... – a rising directed against Jewry, capital, the monarchy and the state – the higher the waves of antisemitism will rise. The warring

forces . . . will draw together in the common struggle against the Jews, and the elements with real power in the property-based society – the great landowners, the monarchy, the church, and state – will seek to replace the social war by the religious and racial war. Antisemitism has the tendency to embrace the entire class society.[47]

However, as Syrkin foresaw the unfolding of events, what could finally seal the fate of European Jewry was neither the postfeudal crisis in the East nor the capitalist crisis in the West taken separately, but rather the tendency of these two phenomena to merge. The central feature of modern Jewish society, he wrote, was the mass emigration from eastern to western Europe and thence overseas, primarily to North and South America. Over a million Jewish immigrants, he noted in 1900, had entered the United States in the years 1882–97. This wave of newcomers, who moved first into the sweatshops, then (in large part) into the petty bourgeoisie, and finally (in significant numbers) into the higher levels of the middle class, carried the Jewish problem across the entire world.

The results were predictable. Mounting antisemitism in the recipient countries threatened the security of all the Jews living there, the native and the newcomer alike. In turn, public pressure was bound to bring about legislation restricting further immigration. "We see with our own eyes," he wrote in 1903, "that the democratic countries such as England and America are about to legislate against the entry of Jews."[48] The Aliens Bill was enacted into law in England in 1905 while the Immigration Act in the United States was not legislated until 1923. But throughout all that period, he constantly reiterated his conviction that with the closing of the doors against immigration from eastern Europe, the Jewish problem would enter a new and catastrophic phase. As he put it in 1923:

> The life of the Jews in Greek Alexandria in the first century before Christ, in Arab Bagdad in the ninth century, in Moorish Cordova in the eleventh century, in Polish Cracow in the seventeenth century, and in American New York in the twentieth is outwardly and inwardly the same – the same religion, the same customs, the same family ties, the same economics, the same class divisions, the same world-outlook . . . The *goles* does not develop, but from era to era the Jewish tragedy grows in classical dimensions.[49]

For Syrkin, of course, it was the task of sociology to define problems, not to seek their solution. He could speak with such passion as the prophet of doom because he believed that only an irredeemably pessimistic analysis of the future could provoke a revolution in Jewish attitudes to the world; that the exertion of will could avert that which otherwise was inevitable; that the politics of change had to be based ultimately not on prediction but on goals.

There could be only one solution to the Jewish problem, he insisted, and that was the transfer of the Jews from Europe to a national homeland. His analysis of the Diaspora situation did not allow room for any half-way measures or palliatives. The Jews had to create their own state while there was still time. Despite the importance he assigned to messianic impulses in shaping the collective psyche and despite his own emotional attachment to Palestine as the ancestral homeland, he was consistently ready to give preference to an alternative (or additional) territory. The overriding consideration was to find an area that would permit a massive and immediate colonization effort.

An eyewitness, looking back to the debates in Minsk in 1882, later recalled that "in the homeland question Syrkin came out from the first for America as the freest, most democratic country in the world."[50] In that period, he–like Pinsker and many others–eventually came to the conclusion that Palestine was more likely than any other country to attract Jewish colonization. But this was a pragmatic decision, and in his booklet of 1898 he could insist that if Palestine remained largely closed to the Jews, they should settle elsewhere, perhaps nearby, in Cyprus or Sinai, or alternatively somewhere in Africa. In his manifesto of 1901, he attacked the "pseudo-romantic intoxication which demands that we begin colonization only in the 'Holy Land' and on no account in one of the neighboring countries belonging to England."[51] With the schism produced in the Zionist movement by Herzl's East African proposal of 1903, he naturally joined the territorialist wing and launched into violent attacks on the *Palestintsy*. Even when he returned to the Zionist camp in 1909, he still argued–initially at least–that Palestine should be only one center of colonization in the Middle East and that Mesopotamia was far more suited to mass settlement.

Where Syrkin differed from Pinsker or Herzl was in his insistence that from the first the Jewish territory be constructed on fully socialist lines. In this sense, he saw himself as picking up the threads dropped by the youthful emigration movement of 1882. "The first Bilu group–that famous group of Russian students who were the first idealistic pioneers in the Jewish country–was," he wrote with considerable exaggeration, "a communist organization. The Bilu, who went to Palestine in 1882, wanted to live and work communistically and thus serve as an example for the further development of the country."[52]

In his *The Jewish Question and the Jewish Socialist State* (1898), he first sketched out the blueprint for this ideal society, a blueprint that over the next twenty-five years he elaborated but left essentially unaltered. His vision was consciously based on the utopian tradition in socialist thought and is reminiscent of that of Fourier, Proudhon, and Chernyshevsky. As he envisaged it, the settlers would organize in middle-sized communities, approximately ten thousand strong. The land would be "the communal property of the group that works it,"[53] and each would function as a "large industrial village in which industry and agriculture are contiguous. The contradiction between town and village is abolished."[54]

Every member would be free to choose how many hours per day he worked and would be paid according to the amount and type of work he did. Harder and more unpleasant tasks would carry higher rewards than the more attractive alternatives. With the pay chits he received, each member would be free to select the goods, the housing, and the schools he preferred. Certain services–theaters, institutions of higher learning, museums, banks–would be concentrated in quasi-urban centers, but their population would rotate with that of the villages. In such a society, he insisted in 1898, "the state becomes superfluous: in its place comes the union of free producers."[55] (During the period following World War I, and under the influence of the Bolshevik experience, he somewhat modified but did not abandon his commitment to this anarchist ideal.)

It was a basic axiom for Syrkin that the capitalist system and the bourgeois class should not be permitted any foothold in the new society. Only the working masses, or those who were prepared to toil for their living, could count on a future there. As he put it in his *referat* at the Stockholm conference of Poale Zion in 1919: "For the Jewish trading class . . . there is no future in Palestine. On the gates of Jaffa, the Jewish working class must inscribe [for it] Dante's famous words of despair: 'Abandon all hope!' "56

Following the Bolshevik example, Syrkin conceded the possibility of short-term concessions to capitalists but only on the condition that whatever they built be speedily nationalized. As against this, he encouraged the idea that those with relatively small capital sums – five hundred or a thousand dollars – should invest the money in cooperatives that they themselves would join. And whenever he could, he actively supported such projects, most notably the Ahava [Brotherhood] society, which from 1911 prepared itself to leave the United States and establish settlements in Palestine. For him, with his anarchist leanings, the cooperative principle represented a legitimate form of socialism and did not imply any surrender to bourgeois principles. "Palestine will be built up on social cooperative foundations and the exclusion of capitalism," he wrote in *Di tsayt* in 1921, "or it will not be colonized at all."57

In the main, the colonization effort would have to be financed by capital drawn from the Jewish people throughout the world, particularly from the Jewish haute-bourgeoisie. This capital would be administered by the elected representatives of the Jewish people as a whole or, failing that, by the Zionist or territorialist movement. Land purchase, credit institutions, and the construction of ports, railways, and roads would all be taken on itself by the national fund. That a totally socialist enterprise should be financed largely by the hated class of Jewish bankers and capitalists was, on the face of it, a hopeless contradiction. But Syrkin was convinced that it was in accord with the realities of Jewish life. And from the very first (through his speeches at the Second Zionist Congress on the Jewish Colonial Bank established in 1898, his articles on the National Fund set up at the Fifth Congress in 1901, and his campaign against ICA in 1901–3) he tried to prove this central point. Unrelenting and massive public pressure could force the vulnerable Jewish haute-bourgeoisie to pay for the socialist state in the making.

The overtly utopian and paradoxical nature of Syrkin's strategy was throughout the object of much amused comment and derisive attack. To the Bundists it symbolized all that was most absurd in Zionism. "Dr. Syrkin seeks to make adventurism into a principle," Zivion wrote in 1909.58 And even Lesin, who often felt at least a sneaking sympathy for him, eventually lost patience and declared in 1921 that "with him the world is always in labor and he is the midwife, mouthing his phrases . . . his problems, plans, cursings and all in an arrogant tone of contempt for everybody."59 The Marxist Zionists and territorialists all saw his mode of thought as outdated, a strange survival from the past.

Zhitlovsky, too, always regarded his colonization strategy as pure fantasy. In 1898 he assured the readers of *Der yidisher arbeter* that the Great Powers would never tolerate the creation of a hotbed of socialist unrest in the Middle East. And in 1921 he could still argue in a similar vein that it was absurd on Syrkin's part to deny the possibility of private investment in the up-building of Palestine. "It is a fact," he mocked his party comrade, that Baron Rothschild and the English capitalists are real "utopians" . . . while Dr. Syrkin, of course, is a tough-minded *real-politiker* . . . This alone means that in financial questions it is better to rely on Dr. Syrkin than on Baron Rothschild . . . But if those utopian "fantasists" want to throw away their money into building harbors and railways what can we do about it?[60]

Syrkin was unmoved by such criticism. His daughter, Marie, has recalled that at one meeting in New York her father, speaking of Zhitlovsky, declared: "We have divided the world between us . . . Zhitlovsky has taken everything that exists, I have taken everything that still does not exist. Zhitlovsky has chosen the Diaspora which we have; I the homeland which we still do not have."[61] It was his considered belief that, as he put it in 1898, "what elsewhere is a utopia, among the Jews is a necessity."[62]

In defense of this thesis he marshaled a number of technical arguments. He noted, in particular, that in undeveloped countries such as Palestine, the native labor was so cheap that it would always triumph in competition against the immigrant Jewish worker from Europe. The inevitable result would be the transfer of the socioeconomic pathology of the Diaspora to the prospective Jewish territory. The Jews would act as employers, go-betweens, managers, while the physical labor would become the monopoly of the indigenous population. To create a new Jewish capitalism fueled by Arab labor, he said on his arrival in Jaffa in 1920, would be a tragi-comic endeavor, a "new Kasrilevka."[63] Such an experiment was doomed to failure. "The Jews who have come to the country," he wrote of Palestine in 1898, "have [already] begun to leave it."[64]

At root, however, Syrkin believed that a "utopian" colonization program was essential because it alone could find a response in the collective psyche of the Jewish masses. It was in his attitude to the popular mind and the national mission that the influence of Moses Hess was most apparent. For, with Hess, he saw the construction of a socialist society as the essential culmination of the Jewish past and as the logical contribution of the Jewish people to human progress in general. As Varda Pilovski has pointed out,[65] Syrkin must have been familiar with *Rome and Jerusalem* at least by the late 1880s, if not earlier, for it was in 1888 that *Ha-magid* began to publish it in translation. Thereafter, Syrkin himself rarely missed an opportunity to acknowledge his debt to Hess. (Of course, in broader terms, both men belonged to that trend in European radical thought most prominently represented perhaps by Mazzini, Mickiewicz, and Herzen, who each believed that his own nation was allotted a messianic mission, a key role, in the self-redemption of mankind.)

In this context, Syrkin developed and elaborated on three themes central to *Rome and Jerusalem*. First, he too built his entire program on the idea that the Jewish masses in eastern Europe were organically linked to the national past and that, in contrast to the alienated Jews of the West, they would answer instinctively to the idea of a national rebirth. Over two thousand years the seed of hope had been preserved by the tradition-bound people, by the *folk*, the *narod*, and that seed could still germinate.

True, Syrkin tended generally to be far more critical than Hess in 1862 of the existing way of life in eastern Europe and indeed of the Jews throughout the entire

Diaspora period. "The external situation of the Jews, exile and enslavement," he wrote in 1898, "has made this remarkable people into a caricature . . . The universal Jewish morality has become the universal Jewish Stock Exchange and Panama; the creative powers of the nation have become crude mimicry of others; its language – a miserable jargon."[66] In the prewar period – much less so toward the end of his life – a violent anticlericalism formed an essential element in this negative appraisal of Jewish history since the year 70: "Practical ordinances; the idolatry involved in reducing faith to ritual; restrictions; fencing-in; religious customs – such became the only spiritual creation of the people. On the ruins of Jerusalem, Yavne was built – the total negation of national freedom; from Rabbi Yohanan Ben Zakai began the period of spiritual decline, the Talmudic era of the Jewish people."[67]

But, however great the fall, Syrkin argued, the Yiddish-speaking Jewish masses still formed a living link to the sources of national inspiration. Indeed, the very political impotence that had distorted so many aspects of Jewish life had also acted to preserve much that was positive. "As a persecuted and impoverished people that did not live by its sword but by its spirit . . . , " he wrote in 1903,

> it acquired in the Diaspora a spiritual content and special morality which left their mark on popular life . . . The feeling of freedom and equality among the people; spiritual exertion; a detestation of the everyday; the urge to greatness; the power to hope; contempt for the petty and vulgar – those are the national values which the Jewish people acquired in its history.[68]

Second, Syrkin shared Hess's conception of what constituted this heritage preserved since ancient times. For both men, the central strand in Jewish history was to be found in the development of the prophetic and messianic ideas, in their interaction, and their impact. "Hess," Syrkin wrote in his introduction to the Yiddish edition of *Rome and Jerusalem* published in New York in 1916,

> was the first to reveal the real content of Judaism, the interconnection between Jewish Biblical Prophecy and the creative spirit of human history in general. For Moses Hess was not only the founder of Zionism but also the discoverer of the socialist content of Judaism . . . *Rome and Jerusalem,* which was written one-half century ago, was not the outcome of that time, but a prophetic anticipation of our present period and its problems.[69]

Like Hess, Syrkin placed great emphasis on the contrast, so central to much nineteenth-century thought, between the Greek and the Jewish attitudes to life, between Hellenism and Hebraism. While the Greeks perceived the world as a "garden of art and play," the Hebrews saw life as a "holy place where the universal idea must triumph."[70] Historically, he argued, the commitment to social justice had been forged in the nomadic period of Jewish history. "In the desert, infinity, the universe, the sky and the stars speak to man . . . The spirit of the desert is a monotheistic spirit . . . And the spirit of the nomadic God is social. In the nomadic life there is no private land and the animals and goods belong to the tribe as a whole."[71] These early communalist attitudes were perpetuated by their inclusion in the Mosaic Code and the first Five Books of the Bible, and they became the central message the Prophets had sought to defend against the encroachment of the propertied classes and the oppressive state.

"What are the Jewish works—the Pentateuch and the Prophets," he wrote in 1900, "if not a literary memorial to the class war between the haves and have-nots?"[72] "It was this people," he declared in 1902, "that thousands of years ago said that 'there shall be no poor among you' and made social laws such as the Jubilee, the sabbatical year, and all the laws on gleaning in order that justice rule in the world."[73] "The Jewish people," he stated in a speech in New York in 1918, "is a socialist people not because it lives in want but because the revolution was declared on Mount Sinai."[74] "Remove the socialist creativity . . . from Jewish history," he declared in Jaffa in 1920, "and we are left without any reason for projecting Jewish history into the future."[75]

The historical significance of prophecy became fully apparent, he argued, only when its message became the object of messianic hope and when the national God, Yahweh, was replaced in the popular consciousness by a "universal" God. Thus, for him, it was in the period of the Second Temple that Jewish history reached its most dramatic moment. He was always fascinated by the parallels between the Jewish experience in Second Temple Palestine and that beginning to unfold in his own age. The fragmentation into parties, the struggle between the assimilationists and nationalsits, a messianic and socialist chiliasm had dominated the scene then and were all reemerging now. And just as it had long been characteristic of the non-Marxist socialists—Saint-Simonians, Russian Populists—to compare their movement with early Christianity, so Syrkin found it natural to see socialist Zionism as a new version of ancient Jewish messianism.

In describing the Second Temple period he concentrated particular attention on two phenomena: the role of the Essenes (which had so intrigued Zhitlovsky in the mid-1880s) and the national revolt against the Romans. As he described it, the Essenes were the key party in the moral revolution of the time. They had lived, he wrote in 1903, "on a communal basis; they held their property in common; their labor was socialized . . . It was from this sect that messianism, the new teaching emerged—a religious product of the Hebrew spirit under unusual sociopolitical conditions and under the prolonged influence of Greek culture."[76] In the uprising against the Romans, he saw "the last war for freedom in the ancient world," a war in which national and social motivations combined. "In Jerusalem itself," he wrote of the year 70, "the Essenes, the Zealots, the Sicarii, the remarkable messiahs such as Shimon Bar Giora took over power. They linked the struggle against Rome to the struggle against the internal aristocracy, against the rich, the priests, the middle-class Pharisees who wanted . . . shameful surrender."[77]

Jesus, Syrkin maintained, had to be seen as the personification of the messianic drive, of the urge for total social change, of the universalist vision so prevalent in Second Temple Palestine. But the early Christians had parted ways with the Jewish people irrevocably when they disassociated themselves from the anti-Roman revolt and substituted belief in future life for the vision of an earthly kingdom. And here, too, he called in the authority of Hess who, he wrote, had negated "Christianity but not that ur-Christianity which was revolutionary and communist Judaism in Palestine and sought to bring messianic redemption to the world . . . . [78] Christ [for him] was a Jewish social revolutionary, sprung from the loins of the Essenes."[79]

Finally, Syrkin shared with Hess the belief that the general upsurge of nationalism in nineteenth-century Europe made it both natural and imperative that the

Jewish people formulate its own strategy for political independence. His undivided support for national liberation movements and his conviction that the road to socialism lay through nationalism, again mark him as an essentially pre-Marxist socialist. Indeed, scattered throughout his writings are positive references to the nationalism of the European Left in the 1830s and 1840s and, in particular, to the examples of nascent Jewish patriotism in the biographies of Lassalle and Heine. Where Zhitlovsky tended to treat nations and nationalisms with a cautious empiricism – as facts of life not to be denied – Syrkin with Hess saw in them the central vehicle of historical change and, potentially, a major force for progress.

In his booklet of 1898, he looked forward to the day when the Jews, in Palestine and throughout the world, would come out openly against the Ottoman state, would "forge an alliance with the oppressed peoples of Turkey [Macedonians, Armenians, Greeks]; strive for a just division of that oppressive state; support the rebels with money from the National Fund and supply volunteers to the war."[80] As one of the legitimate successor nations to the defunct Empire, the Jews would then establish their state in Palestine.

During World War I, Syrkin believed that this vision was becoming reality, and especially after the fall of the tsarist government and American entry into the conflict, his enthusiasm for the struggle against the Hohenzollern, Hapsburg, and Ottoman Empires knew no bounds. Early in 1918, he volunteered for the recently formed Jewish Legion (only his age, forty-nine, prevented his enlistment). Like Hess at the time of the Italian Risorgimento, he was convinced that the outlines of a new and higher order were to be discerned through the smoke of battle. "It is almost," he wrote in 1916,

> as if Hess had foreseen this world catastrophe, this World War which is the terrible prologue to the world revolution . . . The historically oppressed peoples are awakening to a new national life; world power will be divided among the nations in a different way; a historical rebirth is taking place in Palestine and the Orient. The democratic and social revolutionary forces of the entire civilized world are awakening to a great and conclusive struggle against the reactionary forces of the old order.[81]

Perhaps in no other episode of his life did Syrkin find himself so bitterly reviled by the majority of his comrades as on this, the war issue. The antiwar policy dominated the Jewish labor movement in New York in the years 1914–18. In 1917 Syrkin even felt compelled to resign from the central committee of his own party, the American Poale Zion, which was opposed to the participation of the United States in the war.

Syrkin's political strategy, with its emphasis on an "exodus" and a "utopia," was consciously oriented toward the future. Nevertheless, he prided himself on his empirical approach to reality. He readily admitted that for the foreseeable future there was no chance of evacuating the majority of Jews from Europe, and that they would therefore long have to defend their own interests as a minority in the various countries of the Diaspora.

On the face of it, the logic of Syrkin's analysis pointed unmistakably toward a policy of nonintervention by the Jews in the politics of those states in which they lived. If to him equal rights meant to hasten the process of Jewish *embourgeoise-ment* and to fan the flames of antisemitism, then what justification could there be for seeking to change the status quo? (The fact that Syrkin frequently drew attention to examples of antisemitism in the socialist camp, above all, to the pogrom incitement of the Narodnaia Volia in 1881–2, could only lend weight to this line of reasoning.)

But Syrkin was not ready to submit to the dictates of his own sociological analysis. No people, he argued, could afford to submit passively to political humiliation, insult, and aggression. In the east European context, the Jewish socialists and masses alike had no choice but to support the revolutionary cause. Beyond that, there could never be any justification for not joining the forces of progress against those of reaction, whether it was the United States against Germany in 1917, or the extreme left wing against the center and right in the Russian revolutions.

In his attitude to the politics of the Russian and world socialist movements, his ingrained maximalism proved the dominant factor. In 1898 we find him condemning "the opportunism of Social Democracy [which] brings it into conflict with its own principles of socialism [and] revolution."[82] Similarly in 1905–6 and again during the Russian civil war he came down on the side of the Bolsheviks against the Mensheviks. Despite his concern for the liberty of the individual and his admiration for the political freedom prevailing in England and the United States, he found himself irresistably attracted to the Bolshevik venture. He felt that his own attitude to history, with its emphasis on the breakthrough to a higher social order, messianic leadership, mass enthusiasm, and constructionist socialism, had been reaffirmed by the Communist triumph. With many in or close to the anarchist camp, he put more emphasis on the popular than on the dictatorial aspects of the October regime. And he had no sympathy for the *Forverts* and other American-Jewish labor organizations that adopted an openly critical attitude to Soviet Russia and the Third International. "Capitalist domination is bankrupt," he declared in Jaffa in 1920, "and has collapsed throughout the entire world."[83]

Syrkin realized that there was a fundamental contradiction between his thesis that revolutionary change in eastern Europe could only aggravate the Jewish plight and his support for organized Jewish participation in the revolutionary cause, but he argued that there was no escape from this duality because "by its very essence Jewish reality is in fact highly complex."[84] What had to be done was to ensure that the two entirely different spheres of action, the territorialist and the revolutionary, did not detract the one from the other. Ideally, he felt, there should be two entirely different organizations, the one to represent labor and the socialist cause within the Zionist movement, the other to unify the Jewish masses as one branch of the general revolutionary movement in Russia. The goal of the Left in the territorialist (or Zionist) movement was to moderate class differences and mobilize all the resources of the Jewish people for the socialist colonization program. The goal of the revolutionary organization could only be to aggravate the class war in every sphere of day-to-day Jewish life within the Russian Empire. If it were not possible to create two parallel organizations, then even within one socialist-territorialist party the principle of a strict division of functions would have to be maintained.

It was in keeping with this dualist conception that Syrkin regarded Hebrew, not Yiddish, as the national language (the language of the past and future), remained a life-long opponent of Yiddishism, and yet used Yiddish in most of his writings and speeches. Again, he was always fiercely critical of Bundism, the assumption that democratization would improve the Jewish situation, and yet he admired the Bund. He was in favor of general representative bodies – the Zionist congress or even a broadly based elective Jewish congress – to organize migration and colonization but openly sympathized with Bolshevism in Russian politics. He was an enthusiastic supporter of Herzl in his resettlement projects, but vehemently opposed to his unabashed attempts to seek cooperation with the regimes of Nicholas II and Abdul Hamid.

His dualism was rarely understood in his own party and the story is told that in 1921 he would open his speeches – normally in Yiddish, of course – to the Poale Zion groups in Europe with the following statement: "To save unnecessary questions, let's get this clear: I am for participating in the Zionist congress *and* the Third International. I admire the Red Army *and* I believe in the Jewish Legion. I am for Hebrew and not for Yiddish."[85]

Syrkin and the Politics of Socialist Zionism, 1897–1907

Toward a movement

The image of Syrkin as a prophet in the desert is misleading, for, although his was undoubtedly the prophetic temperament, he did not in fact act in a political wilderness in the early years of Herzlian Zionism. He no more worked in an ideological vacuum than had the forerunners of the Bund in the Vilna of the 1890s, even though, in both cases, party mythology preferred to stress genealogical exclusivity. If he had little success as a would-be leader, it was because his idiosyncratic vision was unacceptable to his potential allies.

The fact is that the emergence of Theodor Herzl as a Jewish leader; the publication of his *Der Judenstaat* in 1896; the assembly of the First Zionist Congress in Basle in August 1897; and the creation there of a worldwide Zionist organization had the unintended effect of inspiring a commitment in limited circles but in many places toward the idea of proletarian or socialist Zionism. This development was hardly surprising.

First, Herzl revived the original hopes of the Palestine movement – hopes that had faded away over the long years of disappointment since 1882. Herzlian Zionism, in its early stage, envisioned a movement of the people for the people culminating in a vast exodus and a practical solution to the Jewish question as it existed in east and central Europe. The First Zionist Congress, with delegates arriving from all over the world, was an event dramatically new in modern Jewish life and was immediately seen as a form of national parliament. The quasi-democratic electoral system worked out for future congresses – everybody who paid a small sum (the shekel) had the right to participate in the selection of delegates – reinforced the belief that here was a movement radically different from the discredited Hoveve Zion. Thus, young Jews in various countries could arrive independently at the idea that as a democratic movement, pledged to a program of radical change in Jewish life, Zionism should make it a major priority to win over the Yiddish-speaking and working masses.

Parallel changes within the European socialist movement worked to encourage this same idea of proletarian or socialist Zionism. The increasing emphasis Social Democrats placed on immediate rather than ultimate goals, on the "minimal" rather than the "maximal" program, on changes within rather than the overthrow of the capitalist world – all combined to legitimize nationalist aspirations, or, as the Second International had put it in 1896, "the right of every nation to self-determination." If the Social Democrats, for the most part, supported the demand for Polish liberation, why should they oppose the idea of Jewish nationalism? This line of thought, which enabled the Bund to formulate its national program in 1901, inspired others to argue that Zionism and socialism were complementary, not contradictory: Zionism belonged to the sphere of the minimal program, partial solutions; socialism to the sphere of the maximal program, ultimate solutions.

It is not the purpose of this chapter to describe in detail the emergence of the left wing Zionist organizations (a subject which remains largely virgin soil for the historian), but in order to see Syrkin in perspective, it is essential to sketch out this process, however briefly. Within the space of a few years, 1898–1904, innumerable worker and socialist Zionist organizations sprang up in Austria-Hungary, the Russian Empire, England, and the United States. The most visible and coherent development came in the Hapsburg Empire. In 1898 three labor Zionist organizations were formed there: the Emuna group in Brünn, the Ivri in Lemberg and The Union of Jewish Workers and Clerical Employees, Ahva, in Vienna. A Yiddish biweekly, *Ivri,* was published in Lemberg and a German monthly, *Der Jüdische Arbeiter,* in Vienna. A conference held on 6–7 August 1899 decided to establish a country-wide Union of Jewish Workers and Clerical Employees with a clearly Zionist orientation and, early in 1900, a new journal, *Jüdische Volksstimme* published in Brünn by Max Hickl, was established by this organization. On 13 January 1901 its official founding congress was held in Cracow. In October 1903 a new journal, again *Der Jüdische Arbeiter,* appeared; at first published in German in Vienna, it soon went over to Yiddish and in 1906 moved to Galicia. In May 1904 a Congress of the Jewish Workers and Clerical Employees led by Nathan Gross and Shlomo Kaplansky set up the Poale Zion party in Austria-Hungary.[86]

In Russia the development was much more complex and its early stages remain little documented. But the existing material – memoirs, correspondence – reveal a definite pattern. In the years 1897–1901, worker Zionist groups were formed in a large number of towns throughout the Pale of Settlement, independently and, in some cases, without their even being aware of each other's existence. The group in Minsk was formed in the late 1890s, perhaps as early as 1897, and it was there that the name, Poale Zion – subsequently to be adopted by fraternal organizations throughout the Jewish world – was first coined. Similar societies of worker Zionists were formed throughout the northwest and White Russia, in Bobruisk, Vitebsk, Vilna, Grodno, Dvinsk, and Homel.[87] In the south, socialist Zionist societies also appeared, albeit slightly later. There was the student group, Kadima, in Kiev (which has already been described in the chapters on the Bund and Zhitlovsky); the organization headed by Kolia Teper in Odessa, a report on which, from the year 1899, was preserved in the Okhrana archives; and the group in Ekaterinoslav established late in 1900 by Shimon Dobin and Ber Borochov. Similar organizations were formed from the turn of the century in Warsaw, Belostok, and other cities in tsarist Poland.

The first attempt to unite at least some of these scattered groups into one organization was made at a conference held in Minsk in November 1901, where the major groups in northwest Russia drew up a national platform and established a joint coordinating committee. Subsequent efforts to create more all-embracing forms of unification – most notably at the conferences held in June 1903 in Vilna and in September 1903 in Kiev – enjoyed only partial success.[88] The movement continued to grow piecemeal and during the years of revolution, 1905–6, produced three major but rival parties.

In the Russian-Jewish student "colonies" abroad, a number of leading figures openly advocated a synthesis of socialism and Zionism: apart from Syrkin himself, there were, for example, David Farbstein (who adopted Swiss citizenship and became a leading member of the Social Democratic party in Switzerland), Roza Grinblat (who had been one of the delegates to the founding congress of the Bund but became a Zionist soon after), Kalman Marmor (who had been a member of Rezchik's worker opposition in Vilna), and Daniil Pasmanik. Other Zionists – Eliashev, Bukhmil, even Motskin[89] – also stood far to the left in their attitudes and sympathies. In 1900 a group of students marched in the May Day parade in Geneva carrying the national Jewish flag, an act bitterly resented by the majority of Russian-Jewish students, which ended in an angry scuffle.[90] And starting from 1901, various socialist-Zionist groups began to be formed in the "colonies."

Poale Zion organizations were in existence on the Lower East Side of New York as early as 1900. In the years 1902–3, the first left-wing and labor Zionist organizations – Maaravi, Poale Zion, and Forverts – were established in the East End of London.[91] Both in London and New York, the movement soon began to bring out journals in Yiddish.[92]

The more rapid and unified development in Austria-Hungary, as opposed to the fragmentation in Russia, can be explained primarily by the fact that Palestinophilism in the Hapsburg Empire had always placed greater emphasis than its Russian counterpart on activity in the Diaspora; that labor Zionism with a trade-unionist, welfare, and cultural orientation could therefore claim a full legitimacy there; and that, with the field long clear of any equivalent to the Bund, the Zionists could easily seize and hold the flag of nationalist socialism. It was the labor Zionists in Austria-Hungary who accused the Social Democrats under Victor Adler and Ignacy Daszynski of deliberately ignoring the collective interests of the Jewish proletariat, of avoiding direct confrontation with the rising wave of antisemitism, and of turning a blind eye to the Dreyfus Affair. As against this, in the tsarist Empire the existence of the Bund long complicated the development of labor Zionism, with some members arguing that the movement should seek to compete with the Bund as a revolutionary force, but with more insisting that, on the contrary – in the tradition of the Russian Zionists – it should steer clear of internal politics.

But at least as significant as the contrast between the different movements was the degree of interaction and mutual influence linking them together despite the geographical and political barriers. There were a number of channels through which information flowed and contacts were maintained. First, there was the Zionist congress itself, which met annually (usually in Basle) between the First Congress in August 1897 and the Fifth Congress in December 1901. For the left wing of the Zionist movement, the most important opportunities provided by the congress lay outside the formal sessions. At the time of every congress, members of the radical opposition gathered from all over Europe, held meetings and conferences, drew up programs, established organizations. *Referaty* were delivered at public meetings in hired halls, debates conducted. Kalman Marmor even recalls that representatives of the non-Zionist parties (the SRs, the Bund) would come to the congress in order to collect funds for their revolutionary activities from individual delegates.[93]

Those socialist Zionists who had been elected as delegates also used the official sessions of the congress to propagate their views, not so much to the assembled delegates as to the large body of students (mainly from Russia, of course) who were in the galleries. Just to take one example, at the First Congress, where Syrkin like Zhitlovsky was a mere spectator, David Farbstein, an elected delegate, made the most of the opportunity and delivered a speech that spelled out the basic elements of his socialist Zionist ideology.

Antisemitism, he argued, was reaching dangerous proportions because the indigenous population was ready to take over the intermediary position in the economy hitherto held by the Jews. There was no chance of their being absorbed into the factory proletariat (if only because of the Sabbath laws), and so even the grant of equal civil rights – the abolition of the Pale of Settlement – would do nothing to solve the problem but, on the contrary, would broaden its geographical dimensions. Therefore, there had to be massive resettlement of the Jews in their own territory, and Zionism had to break entirely with the tradition of the Hoveve Zion, who were proud of having settled seven thousand in Palestine over a period of seventeen years. Finally, he asserted that "Zionism is not only a national but also a sociopolitical and economic reform movement." He quoted Levanda's view that Zionism had to be "a movement toward physical labor, toward agriculture, toward earning one's bread by the sweat of one's brow"[94] and Hess's belief that "the healthy man like a healthy plant or animal needs free land in which to grow to full strength – otherwise he must fall to the level of a parasitic existence."[95] (The striking similarity between Farbstein's position and that of Syrkin was hardly coincidental; for many years, they had both been active members of the Russian-Jewish student debating society in Berlin.)[96]

A second channel of communication was formed by the labor Zionist press, most notably by that published in Austria-Hungary. Because of legal restrictions and its inner fragmentation, the movement in Russia, except in the years 1905–7, never succeeded in producing an effective party press. Thus, in the periods before and after the revolution, leading socialist Zionists in exile from Russia had no choice but to publish their articles in Vienna, Brünn, or Cracow, confident that from there they would find their way across the eastern frontier. Material also came directly from Russia.

One of the most fascinating items in S. R. Landau's *Der Jüdische Arbeiter* is an open letter sent from "the Zionist youth in Vitebsk" and published in June 1899. This letter, which revealed a detailed knowledge of recent developments in the Zionist movement and a familiarity with its publications, attacked both Herzl's leadership and also the socialist movement in Russia. Herzl's policies were threatening to turn Zionism into "a capitalist undertaking" and to produce "a Jesuit capitalist state," while the international socialists, "friends of the Jews but enemies of Judaism – forget that the Biblical laws defended the people, indeed were socialist, that we find the first communes among the Essenes and among their successors, the Jewish Christians." The traditionally educated (Hebrew-reading) youth in the shtetl, concluded the letter, should join the Russian-educated youth in the towns to form a party with both a national and social orientation, "a Zionist *Volkspartei*"[97]

The students who attended universities in the West but frequently returned home for their vacations acted as yet another conduit of information. They brought the latest news from the "colonies" abroad to Russia and vice versa. Kalman Marmor recounts in his memoirs, for example, how during his summer vacation from Berne University in 1900, he addressed a number of political meetings in Kovno. On one such occasion, he recalled, he gave a three-hour *referat* to an audience of workers and *intelligenty* in refutation of

> the arguments of Ben Ehud (Dr. Chaim Zhitlovsky in Berne) against the ideas of socialist Zionism and a Jewish state ... Against his assertions that every Zionist must stand with the bourgeoisie I brought up the existence of leading Zionists such as Dr. Farbstein in Zurich and Dr. Landau in Austria who were also socialist activists ... I also recalled what Kolia Teper had told me in Basle [at the 1899 Zionist Congress] about his activity in Odessa as a Bundist and Zionist equally.[98]

Finally, the rising waves of emigration in the early years of the century, reaching a peak in 1906, also worked to spread socialist Zionism from place to place and to forge ties between them. The fact that Vienna, London, New York, and from 1905 Jaffa became important centers of the fledgling movement is to be explained by the constant influx of Jewish migrants from eastern Europe. Many of them had been members of Poale Zion in Russia or Galicia and were eager to set up or join similar organizations in their new homes. This was true of Shlomo Kaplansky, who moved from Belostok to Vienna in 1902.[99] And it was equally true of A. Litvin, who in the mid-1890s had been among Lesin's disciples (an adherent of *Valtovshchina*) in the Minsk Social Democratic organization; who had then (together with others in that group) been among the founders of the Poale Zion in Minsk; and who, in 1901, had left for America (after meeting Syrkin in Berlin) with plans to found a branch of the movement in New York.[100]

Syrkin until 1897

It was almost certainly the emergence of Herzlian Zionism, and the left-wing opposition within it, that first inspired Syrkin to undertake a fully active role in politics. All the available evidence suggests that until 1897 or 1898 he did not believe there was any point in trying to launch a socialist Zionist movement, party, or even group, even though he had hammered out his ideological standpoint long before then.

Indeed, as described by Tsitron, the Syrkin of 1882 – then a teen-ager newly arrived from Mohilev – launched himself into the youth circles of Minsk with ideas that sound much like those of the mature man of twenty years later. "I remember," he wrote,

> that this first speech made an enormous impression on all of us ... It was ... as though a volcano had erupted before us ... He began with a

furious assault on the Petersburg Jewish plutocracy, the Gintsburgs, the Poliakovs, and the others who out of fear were attacking Jewish emigration
from Russia. He banged his fist on the table frequently and as though he had
them before him he shouted out furiously: "Traitors! Traitors!"[101]

At that stage, he defended America against Palestine with the characteristic argument that "only in America would it be possible to found a Jewish state on
healthy, social principles," and he grounded the program on a theoretical "mixture
of political economy, sociology, Marxism and philosophy."

Even then he was apparently in favor of revolution in Russia – Tsitron recalls
that it was dangerous to accompany him in the streets because "it was his wont to
talk on top of his voice, literally to shout, so that passers-by used to stop and stare
at us . . . He would . . . begin loudly attacking the unjust status quo and come out
with bitter truths of a kind for which in those days one could be sent to the coldest
places."[102] In 1885 he was arrested as the result of his revolutionary contacts and
was lucky to escape a long prison sentence.

In London in 1886, he contributed an article to Elyohu Volf Rabinovich's Yiddish paper, Di tsukunft, and here again its theme is reminiscent of his better-
known later works. "It is greatly to be regretted," he wrote in this, apparently his
first, article

> when a city like London with its over sixty thousand Jews is so indifferent to a
> movement [Palestinophilism] in which all the classes of our people participate
> and which represents our only hope for the future . . . So long as this [Pales-
> tine] idea has not been absorbed by the people itself, so long as the people has
> not come to realize why we are hated . . . ; that we will be hated wherever we
> go; and that this hate is caused not by our own faults but by the fact of our
> being aliens . . . so long . . . will our work be idle, leading nowhere.[103]

Again, articles of his published in Ha-magid in 1889 reveal another lifelong conviction, his belief that the Second Temple period provided a parallel to the modern era
opening up before the Jewish people.[104]

That Syrkin's views were already largely formed at this very early stage is likewise confirmed in their memoirs by both Elyohu Davidzon[105] and Shmarya
Levin.[106] But, despite this early maturing of his ideology, Syrkin confined his
political activity in Berlin during the decade 1888–98 to regular participation in
the meetings of the Russian-Jewish Academic Society, a Palestinophile organization
that included many talented students, among them Lev Motskin, Chaim Weizmann, and Shmarya Levin. The majority of its members defined themselves as
followers of Ahad Ha-Am and the socialists (Syrkin, Farbstein, Davidzon) were in
a minority. In those years, Syrkin's politics do not appear to have gone beyond
delivering the occasional lecture to the society – which treated his views with great
scepticism – and developing his gift for repartee.

It will suffice here to record just two of Syrkin's caustic interventions in the
innumerable public debates of that period between the nationalists and the internationalist Social Democrats. First, there was the time when, as described by Levin,

> Parvus was thundering – as only he could – against the meaninglessness of
> nationalism. He cited Marx, history, and philosophy . . . and then he

grabbed hold of his own coat and roared: "The wool in this coat was taken from the sheep which were pastured in Angora; it was spun in Lodz; the buttons came from Germany; the thread from Austria: is it not clear to you that this world of ours is *inter*national . . . ?" Hands were lifted to applaud and then something unexpected happened . . . In the fury of gesticulation he had ripped the right elbow . . . Syrkin, unable to contain himself, rose to his feet and shouted: "And the rip in your sleeve comes from the pogrom in Kiev."[107]

The second incident involved another Social Democrat, Itelson, who as Davidzon recalls it argued in a lecture that whether

> . . . "the Jews are a nation or not depends on how we define the term. In zoology books, the chicken is defined as belonging to the bird species . . . but the Russian proverb does not recognize that definition." At this point, Syrkin jumped up and shouted: "While the stupid, vain hens are crowing that they are not birds, the hawk will come and tear them to pieces."[108]

It is noteworthy that the first book Syrkin published (no doubt with great financial difficulty) was not a work on politics but—in 1896—his *Thoughts on the Philosophy of History*. In those days, Syrkin was seen more as the eternal student than the political activist. Davidzon has even recalled that he did not intend to go to the First Zionist Congress and only changed his mind at the very last moment.[109]

However, what he saw and experienced in Basle in August 1897 apparently exercised a decisive influence on him. He attended the conference of the radical and left wing elements that met on the eve of the congress—among those present were Zhitlovsky, Pinsky, Bukhmil, Motskin—and did his utmost to win it over to his own viewpoint. But, as recalled by Kogan-Bernshtein, "Motskin's authority in the group was very great and Syrkin tried in vain to overshadow it."[110] Then came the congress itself, and Syrkin saw how outside the hall "endless discussions about Zionism-socialism raged on" among the delegates and students.[111] He also saw how men like Farbstein, Birnbaum, and Landau, all delegates, were able to expound radical and even socialist ideas from the floor of the congress.[112] Finally, he had the chance to study Herzl at first hand, and he was without doubt deeply impressed not so much by his views as by his magnetic personality.

It was an axiomatic belief with Syrkin that the individual—in the right time at the right place—could play a decisive role in history. Herzl's meteoric rise to prominence could be seen as a remarkable example of this thesis, which he had just expounded in his *Thoughts on the Philosophy of History*, and over the years, he often dwelt on this chapter in Zionist history.

"Every great historical movement," he wrote in July 1906, "has its utopian forerunner, its poet, its dreamer, its prophet . . .[113] Herzl began to awaken the power of the Jews."[114] "In the year 1897," he wrote in 1915, "political Zionism appeared on the scene with the great Dr. Herzl as its leader . . . The call of the Messiah created wonders among the Jews and overnight there emerged a large Zionist movement that embraced Jews from all countries and all classes."[115] The last article he ever wrote, "The Messiah and the Convert" (published in *Der tog* on

23 August 1924), was devoted to Herzl, whose son had recently become a Christian. "Theodor Herzl felt himself to be the Messiah and his son, Hans, has converted. There is here an almost mystical necessity, the fate of the Messiah." (Syrkin had in mind, of course, the conversions of Shabbetai Zvi and Jacob Frank.) "Judaism is a heroic idea and every heroic idea swings between the mountain and the valley, between the most ardent enthusiasm and cold despair."[116]

That the Basle congress was of decisive importance in Syrkin's life is confirmed by the fact that he changed his plans to return to Berlin, stayed in Switzerland, and at once settled down to work on his major new treatise, *The Jewish Question and the Jewish Socialist State.* With this work he sought to go beyond Herzl, presenting his thesis that the program most likely to succeed was one that was openly utopian and revolutionary in spirit.

Henceforward, throughout the rest of his life, Syrkin devoted most of his energies to political activity. He sought to propagate his ideology as widely as possible and in this he quickly achieved considerable success. He also sought to win over a significant body of disciples, to create an effective organizational base, a party devoted to his program. In this he failed. However, if until 1903 his organizational failure was total, from 1903 it was only partial.

Syrkin and the movement, 1898–1903

Syrkin's work on the Jewish question was first published in article form in July 1898 in *Deutsche Worte,* the journal of Engelbert Pernerstorfer, a leading Austrian Social Democrat who, himself not a Jew, sympathized with the idea of Jewish nationalism and also published Zhitlovsky. It came out in book form in August 1898. The timing was not coincidental. The Second Zionist Congress was to meet in Basle at the end of August 1898. In preparation for it, a number of radicals and socialists had launched a highly active campaign: Landau had started his journal, *Der Jüdischer Arbeiter;*[117] Farbstein had brought out his speech of 1897 in book form under the title *Zionism and the Jewish Question (Economics and Ethics);*[118] and a concentrated effort was made to ensure that leading spokesmen of left-wing Zionism be elected to the congress.

Thanks mainly to the influence of the Zionist radicals in Galicia who were grouped around the long-established journal, *Przyszłość,* this campaign enjoyed considerable success.[119] When it came to the test, the left could muster some twenty-five votes at the congress. Among these delegates were the leading French anarchists, Bernard Lazare and Jacques Bahar; the radical group from Galicia, which included J. Thon, A. Korkis, D. Malz, and A. Salz; a worker from Odessa by the name of Shifrin; and an assortment of oppositionists who originated from Russia and Austria-Hungary but now gathered from all over Europe: Nathan Birnbaum, Yehoshua Bukhmil, Farbstein, Landau, and Syrkin himself.

The Left apparently hoped that they would succeed in winning Herzl over or at least in drawing him closer to their side. Syrkin would later point out that, in fact, Herzl did gradually move leftward in some spheres. At the Sixth Congress in 1903, he gave his backing to the idea (presented by Franz Oppenheimer) of cooperative settlements in Palestine, and his *Altneuland* of 1902 was much more egalitarian in spirit than *Der Judenstaat.* As the Left was in a small minority at the Second

Congress, however, it could hardly expect quick results and would have had to tread carefully if it were not to antagonize the great mass of delegates and the leader himself. "Do not forget," Bahar wrote to Landau on 15 August 1898, "that our people is, after all, a poverty-ridden people, that it is you who are founding the first paper of the poor and that therefore sooner or later you will overthrow the entire claque. That is only a question of time. But meanwhile the rich are stronger, so we must rely more on spirit than on might."[120]

In reality, the self-denying tactic advised by Bahar proved too much for at least two members of the group, Landau and Syrkin. Their initial moves were moderate enough. They sought to ensure a sizable representation by the Left on the various commissions elected at the start of the congress; but it did not take long before a series of highly disputatious confrontations began to follow each other in quick succession. When Herzl proposed sending the tsar a telegram that would express appreciation of his plans for a world peace conference, Syrkin rose in angry protest. The uproar produced was so great that Herzl threatened to close the session – he was clearly afraid of what could be seen as an act of hostility to the Russian government.

When the proposal to set up the Jewish Colonial Bank was put forward, the Left objected that the plan, as formulated, would give control over the bank to a handful of wealthy bankers, not to the Zionist congress. Syrkin took the opportunity to expound his view that Palestine should be developed along noncapitalist lines and that all classes in the Jewish people cooperate in such an idealistic enterprise. But he did not stop at that. "I do not in the least deceive myself," he said, "into thinking that my opinion will be accepted. We are waiting for a better opportunity, for a future congress which will more accurately represent the Jewish people."[121] Once again chaos was let loose. Shouts, hissing, and cries of "Social Democrat!" "That is an insult. Withdraw it!" were recorded in the protocols. And when S. R. Landau provoked Herzl by developing the theme of "class contradiction" in Jewish society (and by implication in the Zionist movement), Syrkin once more threw himself into the fray, or as the protocol put it: "There now occurred a sharp clash between the president, Mr. Herzl, and the delegate Syrkin amid uproar and whistles from many delegates."[122] The veteran Palestinophile, Maks Mandelshtam from Kiev, even took the opportunity at this point to propose that "all socialists be excluded from the Zionist congress." Herzl turned this suggestion down, but clearly the damage had been done.

The attempt to gain a foothold in the Zionist congress had failed. In the eyes of Herzl, the Left, by trying to draw the movement onto radical or even revolutionary paths, had aimed a direct blow at his own plans to win a hearing in the banking houses and palaces of the world. The attacks on the tsar, the rabbis, and the bankers had antagonized him. As a result, the left-wing opposition departed the congress in disarray. With Herzl's encouragement, the *Przyszłość* group was deprived in the closing stages of the congress of its large representation on the plenary (Greater) Actions Committee, the formal executive of the movement. Over the next year, matters went from bad to worse. S. R. Landau became involved in a lawsuit against Herzl and in 1899 closed *Der Jüdische Arbeiter*. Bernard Lazare and Jacques Bahar resigned from the plenary Actions Committee, publishing letters of protest against the nondemocratic character of the movement.[123]

Syrkin was expelled from the student Zionist society in Berne for having "slandered" the movement in a report on the Second Congress. Five members of the society resigned out of solidarity with him. (Among those responsible for the expulsion was Chaim Weizmann.) A letter to Herzl from Nahum Slousch, a Russian-Jewish student and Zionist who had followed the incident closely, described it thus:

> He [Syrkin] lectured on Zionism from the Social Democratic point of view and although his Zionism cannot withstand serious criticism, the Social Democratic students are no *more* serious. Anyway, Mr. Syrkin was of use ... a socialist needs courage to declare himself a Zionist ... I am surprised that it was possible to confuse my friend Weizmann to such an extent ... The question of the participation of socialists in our movement is very complicated – the special point of view of Syrkin, Farbstein, and of Bukhmil, too, cannot be satisfied [by us], but we have no right to expel them.[124]

When a report of the case was published in *Die Welt* (the official Zionist journal),[125] Syrkin wrote in to announce that "as a socialist Zionist, I have nothing to do with the Zionism of the Second Basle Congress."[126]

Clearly implied in this statement as in his noisy interventions at the congress itself was the belief that he could appeal effectively against the Zionist leadership to the gallery – the student world – and to the "street" – the mass of Jewish poor. But his efforts to do so ran into insurmountable obstacles until 1903.

His connections with the Zionist Left in Austria-Hungary proved to be of strictly limited value. Landau gave considerable publicity in his journal to Syrkin's article and book,[127] but he himself was rapidly sinking into oblivion. In the years 1900–1, Hickl's *Die Jüdische Volksstimme* opened its pages to Syrkin and he published many articles there,[128] but his maximalist, cataclysmic views aroused no visible interest among the local readers, who sent in neither protest nor comment.

It was among the Russian Jews that he hoped to gain a real following. Primarily to this end, he held a rival – socialist Zionist – meeting at the time of the Third Zionist Congress in 1899; founded thereafter a whole series of societies and organizations; and put out an increasing flow of manifestos, leaflets, and journals in Russian, Hebrew, and Yiddish during the years 1900–3. But two aspects of Syrkin's program produced adamant opposition in this early period.

First, there was his attitude toward revolutionary action. In his *Vozzvanie k evreiskoi molodezhi* ("A Manifesto to the Jewish Youth," published in 1901 in the name of the Group of Zionist Socialists) and in other direct appeals of that period, he forcefully developed his thesis that the Jewish proletariat should maintain two separate organizations which would work independently but in amicable coexistence: the one devoted to revolution, the other to the exodus. This strategy, however consistent with his overall philosophy, was hardly calculated to win widespread support. Those (such as the ideologists of the Minsk Poale Zion) who shared his belief that Jewish existence in the Diaspora was doomed under all circumstances, saw it as totally illogical to advocate Jewish participation in the revolution. Others (most members of the Democratic Fraction, for instance) who, on the contrary, held that the revolution might well lead to an improvement in the situation of Russian Jewry, nevertheless saw it as sheer folly for the Zionists to endanger their near-legal status by saying so publicly.

Equally out of step with the times was a second aspect of Syrkin's strategy, his insistence that the Zionist Left eschew all palliatives. Anything encouraging belief that Jewish life in the Diaspora could long survive without disaster had to be shunned like the plague. The Zionists should therefore have nothing to do with the establishment in Russia or Austria of trade unions, cooperatives, or insurance schemes—everything that went under the heading of *Gegenwartsarbeit*. No less suspect was any cultural activity, whether in the spirit of Ahad Ha-Am or of Yiddishist *folkism*, which assumed that Jewish life could develop along evolutionary lines rather than through a revolutionary break with past and present. As the great majority on the Zionist left saw it as their distinctive task to fight for immediate improvements, economic and cultural, in the life of the Jewish proletariat, Syrkin's stand here again repelled his potential following.

Implied in the *Manifesto* of mid-1901 was a division of labor between the Zionist Left, which would pursue the goal of a Jewish socialist state, and the Bund with its revolutionary policies. Syrkin had maintained close personal contact with many of the Bundist leaders abroad since the mid-1890s, and, given the growing nationalism of the Bund, some such coexistence might momentarily have seemed plausible. But the Fourth Congress of the Bund in April 1901 had, inter alia, called for the expulsion of all Zionists from its ranks and in effect had slammed the door in Syrkin's face before his *Manifesto* even appeared. Later in the year, in a new publication of the Group of Socialist Zionists, the *Programmatic Letter No. 1*, Syrkin threatened a change of strategy unless the Bund relented: "If Jewish Social Democracy will not change its attitude to Zionism ... the Zionist socialists will have to found another Social Democratic organization with a positive attitude to Zionism. And to us the time seems ripe for this."[129] In fact, here was an anticipation of a later development, the creation of the SSRP in 1905.

Even though all these proposals remained in the realm of theory, they were sufficient to undercut Syrkin's other organizational plans. This became apparent in the period before and during the Fifth Zionist Congress in December 1901. In anticipation of the congress, there was a flurry of activity by various radical factions as they sought new recruits and alliances. Syrkin (who for the first time since 1898 was again a delegate to the congress) believed the time ripe for the establishment of a strong socialist Zionist movement.

But his strategies and reputation now came home to roost. In a number of letters sent to Syrkin from Vilna, Aron Gurland reported on the lack of enthusiasm there for the "two-field" concept. Gurland had addressed the local worker Zionist society, the Bne Moshe (which had over a hundred members), and he was also in correspondence with Yitshak Berger, the leader of the Poale Zion in Minsk. "The workers," wrote Gurland, "understand Zionism differently [from you] and they really want it to embrace their lives entirely—and you mock at that, because of your dualistic views about tactics in the galut lands. I saw and felt this desire for *unity*, for wholeness, in all meetings of Bne Moshe."[130] In November 1901 all the worker Zionist groups of northwest Russia were due to hold their joint conference in Minsk, and Gurland correctly forecast that it would not come out in support of Syrkin.

Letters reached Berger from abroad warning him against an alliance with Syrkin's circle. Motskin, Weizmann, Aberson, and their group were then planning to establish a broad coalition of radical forces within the Zionist movement based on principles sharply opposed to those of Syrkin: *Gegenwartsarbeit* in socioeconomic affairs, Ahad Ha-Am's approach in the cultural sphere, and strict noninvolvement in Russian politics.[131] (Weizmann's reaction to the *Manifesto* was characteristic of this division. In a letter to Motskin in June 1901 he had written that "we are accustomed here to all kinds of pamphlets and are not particularly spoiled in this respect, but I have never read a pamphlet like this before... This is sheer madness... It makes me angry to think that it is possible to feed [the] 'youth' on such things.")[132]

In a letter to Berger in November, Motskin wrote in a similar vein:

> The organization of worker Zionists... should have its class interests in view... and not the special [revolutionary] struggle for the future of the galut lands... The formation abroad of the circle of so-called Socialist Zionists, who are of no significance here, should not because of its name and the distance be allowed to impress the workers' circles – particularly as its new program is radically different from the original one of a month ago... The harm which this miniscule group can do, and has already done to Zionism by its light-minded actions; its inattention to the real interests of the general organization and to the conditions in which it has to work; its crude denunciation of everything and everybody – all this compels me to warn the workers' circles that are so important for Zionism.[133]

From this struggle, Syrkin emerged the loser. The Poale Zion in Russia, under Berger's leadership, preferred an alliance with the new Democratic Fraction founded by the Weizmann-Motskin group. However, Syrkin was prepared to work at a number of different levels and through various ad hoc organizations at the same time. His full program had been set forth in the publication of the Group of Socialist Zionists, but other organizations that he initiated were assigned strictly limited goals.

His Hessiana and his Svobodnaia Iudeia (Free Judea) were both set up in 1901 with the single task of discussing, planning, and publicizing "collectivist" forms of settlement in Palestine.[134] (A meeting of Hessiana in November 1901 was addressed by Franz Oppenheimer.)[135] But even in this, its most modest incarnation, Syrkin's group was not permitted to participate in the conference that met in December 1901 and established the Democratic Fraction. "We have not written anything to Hessiana," Weizmann wrote to Motskin on 30 November 1901, "and have given no reasons... We shall of course reject Syrkin."[136]

The most promising of his ventures in this period was the Herut (Freedom) organization, which was established in 1901 and held its official foundation congress in December 1902 in Zurich. As he envisaged it, the function of Herut was to wage war on the major Jewish philanthropic organizations in the West: the Alliance israélite, the B'nai B'rith, and above all the Jewish Colonisation Association (ICA). In the first instance, the plan was to lead the Jewish immigrant masses from the East End to demonstrate outside the headquarters of ICA in London, to harry the ICA officials and board members incessantly, and to sustain a general campaign of protest in Jewish centers throughout the world – all this to persuade ICA to divert its funds from random undertakings to the Zionist enterprise in Palestine.

This project, with its emphasis on direct action, on mass participation, and on the urgency of colonization, was highly typical of Syrkin's approach, but it also appealed to a considerable number of others prominent on the Zionist Left such as Eliashev, Bukhmil, and Gurland. (Zilberfarb and Latsky were among the younger members of Herut.) Even Weizmann was strongly attracted to its plan of action, and he joined a delegation led by Syrkin that went to lay it before Herzl in December 1901.[137]

In his diary, Herzl recorded this visit and wrote laconically that he had rejected the proposals of "Syrkin's exultados."[138] As for Weizmann, he found that even this momentary, coincidental, and ad hoc cooperation with Syrkin was enough to lay him open to the most furious attacks from Motskin and the entire Berlin branch of the Democratic Fraction. In the end, he felt compelled to wash his hands of the whole affair and even to apologize in part.

> My secret alliance with S., as you put it, das Klingt gefährlich. But surely I don't have to repeat that you are exaggerating . . . Once again, you are right: Knowing S.'s attitude to you all . . . I had no right to talk to him at all . . . But . . . when I was invited I was hardly thinking of who was inviting me but rather for what purpose I was being asked . . . I acted rashly in discussing this whole matter with S., but God be my witness, es war gut gemeint.[139]

Syrkin did succeed in establishing a group of followers in London – it took the name of Forverts – but nothing came of the demonstrations against ICA. When the Herut organization held its official foundation congress in December 1902, it was already riven by dissent. Almost half the delegates, led by Eliashev, adamantly refused to accept the program that expressed Syrkin's philosophy (a specific rejection of Gegenwartsarbeit, for instance), and they left the organization there and then. As its hard-core membership was only about twenty, the walkout of "45 percent" was disastrous.[140]

Syrkin now came under repeated criticism from his associates. Kalman Marmor recalls that at a meeting of Herut in 1903 he took the opportunity to tell his "older and respected comrade [that he] had no knowledge of the Jewish masses in England in whose name he spoke,"[141] and in a letter of 16 June 1903, Gurland wrote to Syrkin that "Herut is an organization that was founded for a specific purpose and if in this respect you have displayed neither political tact nor organizational talent, I cannot believe very much in its future prospects."[142]

Syrkin in the period of pogroms and revolution, 1903–1907

Syrkin had failed to found a movement in the years 1898–1902, but he had made a name for himself; his views had become widely known; and his Manifesto of 1901 was eagerly read in youth circles in the Pale of Settlement. Thus, when the political situation changed overnight in 1903, it was natural that many, who had previously regarded him as a mere eccentric, should now turn to him with a new respect. His prestige in Russia never stood so high as in the period between the Kishinev pogrom and the 1905 revolution.

His ideology had always been rooted in the experience of the 1881 pogroms; now, with the new pogroms in Kishinev and Homel, the younger generation could grasp what he had been talking about for so long. His dual theme – that the Jews had to evacuate themselves from Europe and meanwhile, out of sheer self-respect, take up arms against oppression – looked less paradoxical and more realistic.

Kishinev, he wrote in 1903, was not just the work of the Russian government; it also represented accurately national feelings deeply rooted in the Russian masses. Even the revolutionaries, who now (in contrast to 1881) condemned Kishinev, spent far more time and effort attacking Zionism and the Bund than the pogroms. ("No sooner did they see that a liberation movement had emerged among the Jews, that they want to be a nation, to form a state of their own, to act as an end rather than a means – than they began with typical antisemitic impertinence to accuse this movement of being reactionary and bourgeois.")[143] His conclusion was clear:

> For the Jewish people, the Kishinev pogrom is the finger of history. It is one more proof that there is no solution to the Jewish question except in a Jewish territory ... [It] also shows that the Jews can rely on nobody and can expect defence from nobody but themselves ... The only defence against murder is to arm oneself and if blood is to be spilled, better that it be in open battle than by having one's throat cut in the cellar.[144]

When Herzl raised the East African project at the Sixth Zionist Congress in August 1903, Syrkin again found himself riding the tide of popular feeling on the Zionist left. He had always argued that the essence of Zionism was not the acquisition of Palestine but the resettlement of the great mass of Jews on their own territory. Now with the movement split down the middle, with most of the Democratic Fraction strongly opposed to East Africa, he effectively stood forth as the spokesman of "reason" against "romanticism," and this time he found himself siding with Herzl, whom he always regarded as a man of destiny. His major speech at the congress was one of the most powerful he ever made:

> I can well understand that these feelings come from the heart ... that this romanticism is rooted deeply in the soul of every Zionist ... [But] we must bear in mind that it is not treason to Palestine that draws us to choose another country ... but rather the fact that a need has matured within the Jewish masses ... It is essential to regulate emigration ... Every year the future of emigration becomes more critical. The receiving countries are closing their frontiers. It is a matter of life and death to answer this question.[145]

Never before had his words been received with such stormy and prolonged applause.

In the years 1903–4, the Poale Zion and socialist Zionists were wholly taken up, at the practical level, with the organization of self-defense units and, at the ideological level, with the East African and territorialist issue. Although important groups refused to abandon the Palestine cause, the majority was swept along by the territorialist hope. "There is such an utter disorder in people's minds," wrote Weizmann from Pinsk to Aberson in April 1904, "that no end is in sight. The only ones who work ... are the Poale Zion [and] they – with very few exceptions – are territorialists with such fanciful theories that one remains breathless. People have read of the existence of New Zealand from the encyclopedia and everything is being compared with it."[146]

As a result, Syrkin now found himself at the center of a powerful movement in the making. In 1903 larger sums of money reached him from the "colonies" abroad and from the groups in Russia than in earlier years. Thus, he was able to increase his publishing activities and it was now that he brought out the first (and only) issues of *Der hamoyn* (in Yiddish) and *Ha-shahar* (in Hebrew). They were adequately distributed and, because of their timing, made a profound impression on many readers.

A letter from a Poale Zion leader in New York assured Syrkin that his group was in total agreement with *Der hamoyn* regarding "the personality of Herzl, the East African question, and everything to do with the Russian regime." (He was in favor of "arming every Jew.")[147] Kalman Marmor wrote from London asking permission to translate Syrkin's book of 1898 into Yiddish for the Poale Zion there.[148] Rafalkes wrote from Warsaw inquiring about the role of the Narodnaia Volia in the pogroms of 1881. (When he had raised this issue in the presence of the Bundists, he told Syrkin, "A terrible row broke out and I was almost torn to pieces.")[149] "People are reading your *Hamoyn* over and over six or seven times." Latsky wrote. "People are being reborn and I too am learning from it . . . Through these journals you are making a name for yourself among the Jewish people which until now could not have any conception of you. If you manage to bring out a weekly in Yiddish in London I am sure that not a home will remain without it."[150] In his memoirs, Ben Zion Dinur recalled that a copy of *Der hamoyn* reached him, then a youth, in the small town of Priluki in mid-1903 (brought by a student from Heidelberg) and that

> it was an experience for me because of its content and because of its polemi-cal tone. I identified myself with every word in it as if it had taken the words from my own heart . . . The small journal crystallized the feelings, the out-look and ideas that had [long] excited me and given me no rest . . . I lectured on the importance of *Der hamoyn* to a group of friends and we even decided to try to work in the Zionist movement in the spirit of Syrkin.[151]

The left wing of the Poale Zion, marked by its revolutionary commitment in Russian and its territorialism in Zionist politics, increasingly divided off as a sepa-rate faction. At the Vilna conference in June 1903, the revolutionaries (or "PKs," *politishe kemfer*) had been in a minority but they dominated the Kiev conference that gave birth to the *Vozrozhdenie*. The assassination attempt by Pinhas Dashev-sky against Krushevan gave a powerful impetus to this process of political radical-ization,[152] and Nokhem Shtif's brochure on the incident enjoyed wide circulation. ("The first revolutionary swallows came to us from the south," recalled one mem-ber of the Poale Zion in Vilna. "I still remember the impression made on us by the manifesto of the Kiev group, Molodoi Izrail, and its [Shtif's] brochure *What Can We Learn from Dashevsky's Assassination Attempt?* which were impregnated with . . . a strong national spirit and a great revolutionary enthusiasm.")[153]

Syrkin had been invited to the Kiev conference, and although he did not attend, he was closely associated with the *Vozrozhdenie* group. A letter from Fabrikant written in Kiev early in October informed Syrkin that the conference ("the wedding") had been a success and it asked him for a contribution to their planned journal, some-thing "very strong and clear as you with your talent alone can do."[154] He promised to ensure wide distribution of *Der hamoyn* in the south and the dispatch of money as the copies were sold. Meanwhile, in London, a group closely associated with Syrkin began the publication and distribution of a whole series of brochures composed in Russia and abroad by the revolutionary-territorialist wing of Poale Zion, mostly material from the Kiev group of Shtif and Fabrikant and from the Warsaw group led by the Leshchinsky brothers.[155] (So conspicuous had Syrkin's antitsarist activities become that in 1904 he was expelled from Germany, and he moved to Paris.)[156]

In July 1904 the revolutionary-territorialist section of Poale Zion – the Warsaw, Kiev, Dvinsk, and *Vozrozhdenie* groups – held an organizational conference in Warsaw. This was followed up by a congress that met in Odessa in December and (after delays due to arrests)[157] declared the establishment of the Zionist Socialist Labor Party, the SSRP (better known by its initials, the SS). Although Syrkin again was not present in person, his views were faithfully represented here, as at the Kiev conference and in the Dvinsk Poale Zion organization, by Zeev Latsky (Bertoldi), one of his few fully committed disciples. Latsky was elected in Odessa to the central committee of the new party, and there can be no doubt that Syrkin saw himself and was regarded as a member of the SSRP from the day of its foundation.

When the Seventh Zionist Congress met in Basle in July 1905, the main spokesman for the SSRP delegation was Syrkin. The long-anticipated congress had to decide the outcome of the battle, which had already raged for two years, between the Palestinian and territorialist wings of the movement. Tempers ran extremely high. At the pre-conference of the Russian delegation there was a violent clash between the pro-Palestinian Poale Zion delegation led by Borochov and the SSRP delegation led by Syrkin. The territorialists, in the minority, wanted the praesidium elected by proportional representation, while the *Palestintsy* favored a direct majority vote. Syrkin accused the majority of "political mindlessness" and threw the meeting into utter confusion. ("Thumping, shouts, whistles prevent the speeches from continuing. In the middle of the hall one delegate openly waves his fist at Syrkin.")[158] But this, of course, did not prevent the majority from voting down the minority.

The same pattern repeated itself at the congress. Syrkin later recalled that the Left had hung "enormous red placards in the Congress Hall announcing Zionist Socialist meetings. This was at the time of the Russian revolution and the Zionists had to keep quiet in the face of this blasphemy."[159] He declared proudly to the congress that he was "speaking in the name of the Socialist Zionist Labor delegation, which is represented by 30 delegates and has 10,000 organized workers behind it." But on July 30 he nonetheless had no choice but to lead his delegation out of the congress. (They left together with the other territorialists.) With its Palestine-fixation, he declared angrily before departing, the majority "narrows the meaning and the content of our freedom movement; . . . stands in deep contradiction to the interests of the Jewish proletariat and broad masses of the people . . . ; [and appeals] only to the uneducated section of the . . . masses and to the reactionary-nationalistic section of the Jewish intelligentsia."[160]

In the autumn of 1905, Syrkin returned to Russia in order to participate actively in the revolution. When, starting in December, the SSRP began to bring out its party journal on a regular basis, he became a central contributor and, in the autumn of 1906, he was a party candidate in the elections to the Second Duma. He was then a member of the top party leadership. But it can clearly be observed from the pages of the party press that throughout the revolutionary period Syrkin was completely out of step on ideological issues with nearly all his comrades (Latsky, as usual, being a notable exception).

The SSRP shared Syrkin's dual belief in revolution à l'outrance and in the exodus, but here the agreement stopped. As the uprising unfolded, so the SSRP found itself competing directly with the Bund, which it sought (with considerable success, especially after the pogroms late in 1905) to outflank from the left; it tried to be more Marxist in theory and more revolutionary in practice. The *Vozrozhdenie* group, initially inclined to populism, broke away from the SSRP early in 1905, leaving it a purely Social Democratic party. It was determinist and monistic in its philosophy, arguing that the Jewish territory would be created by long-term socio-economic processes and that the predominant task of the Social Democrats was to conduct the class war here and now.

Its first public statement, a *Declaration* issued early in 1905, formulated the party doctrine in these words:

> We Zionist Socialists have as our aim a Jewish socialist society. Taking our stand on the general Social Democratic position and waging war on capitalist society, we are convinced that we can only realize our socialist ideal through unremitting class war against the other classes in the Jewish nation – which are also interested in the fulfilment of Zionism.[161]

In subsequent publications, the ideologists of the younger generation – Yaakov Leshchinsky, Moyshe Litvakov, L. Lvovich (Davidovich), Zvi Abrahami – set out to develop this thesis to its final conclusion. Their doctrine, which received official sanction at the party congress of March 1906 in Leipzig, can be summarized as follows.

The development of capitalism undermined the economy of the Jews in east Europe, undercut the middle class, and drove the great mass of Jews into poverty. As the result of historically determined conditions, the Jewish manufacturers were only able to maintain themselves on the margins of the modern economy; the Jewish proletariat could find employment only in the sweatshops; and hence there developed the syndrome of "nonindustrialization" (as Leshchinsky termed it). With the ever greater flow of Jewish migration, the same pattern developed in new centers overseas, or as it was stated by the party congress of March 1906, "Jewish emigration in its further growth comes into conflict with the forms of concentration that it itself creates and of necessity changes its direction."[162] As conditions in New York, Chicago, and London became as intolerable as those in Vilna, Warsaw, and Belostok, so the Jewish masses would have no choice but to seek refuge in underdeveloped countries and go over from an urban to an agricultural economy. (Increased emigration to South America suggested that this process had already begun.)

As this objective process developed with ever greater force, so all the classes in the Jewish people would realize that it was in their own interests to direct the flow of migration to a selected territory. The task of regulation would fall on the capitalist class, which for its own ends would develop the chosen territory, while the role of the proletariat was a secondary one: to safeguard the interests of the masses by means of a vigilant and critical opposition to the bourgeoisie. "Colonization for the Jewish masses," Lvovich wrote in *Der nayer veg* in May 1906, is now the way of least resistance . . . One cannot create a society unless it is in tune with the natural objective [*stikhish*] process . . . One has to think dialectically. What was a utopia under certain conditions can become a real historical necessity under different conditions . . . [163] Our task is . . . only to introduce consciousness into the unconscious historical evolution. To the extent that this is in accord with the interests of the Jewish proletariat and its class struggle, to that extent this is the task of Jewish Social Democracy.[164]

To those in the mainstream, Syrkin's viewpoint appeared ever more anachronistic and embarrassing. In the spring of 1906, Moyshe Litvakov published a major article in the party journal in which he undertook to draw a clear line between the ideology of the majority in the SSRP and that of Syrkin. Rather than launch a direct attack on a party comrade, he chose to analyze the standpoint of the Herut organization and its journal, *Der hamoyn* of 1903. Syrkin's journal, he argued, objectively reflected the interests and viewpoint of the petty bourgeoisie. Its standpoint was naive, primitive, and self-contradictory.

First, the petty bourgeois is "capable only of abstractions: he cuts the future away from its roots and turns it into a heavenly ideal toward which one must strive only because of its moral beauty." Second, he is "terribly pessimistic about the present: he does not hope to gain anything for himself here." Nevertheless, third, "one must fight for freedom here where we live."[165] But, fourth, according to this viewpoint, victory in the revolution would be positively dangerous, aggravating "some kind of objective process that supposedly leads the Jewish worker into the ranks of the bourgeoisie[166] . . . [and] makes him into 'an antisocial factor in the world.' "[167] In sum, for the petty bourgeois of *Der hamoyn*, "socialism is not bound up with Jewish life; it contradicts it. The ideal is not the accumulation of all the tendencies of reality but is its opposite."[168] Herut, he concluded, was "prehistoric."[169]

There is relatively little information available about the inner workings of *Der nayer veg* editorial board during 1906. (Marie Syrkin's childhood recollections only tell us that during the summer months the Syrkin family and Zeev Latsky shared a dacha outside Vilna that was always overflowing with comrades and chronically short of food.)[170] But it is clear from the contents of the journal (and its successor, *Dos vort*) that as the revolutionary tide ebbed from mid-1906, so the presence of Syrkin and Latsky made itself more strongly felt. The readers gained their first explicit knowledge of the division in the leadership when a debate developed in the journal between Latsky and Abramovich (Abrahami).

In an article published late in July devoted to the theme of historical necessity, Latsky (Bertoldi) stated bluntly: "To the question whether in our territorialism we have as certain a guide as Marxist historical determinism, we must answer in the negative."[171] Abrahami retorted angrily that Latsky's view was unacceptable to "the great majority of our members who take their stand on the Marxist conception of social development[172] [and that] . . . such a subjective belief cannot be the credo of a political party and the source of its political program."[173] In fact, he insisted, "the socioeconomic processes of Jewish reality . . . necessarily result in the territorialist ideology [and] *also organize* the Jewish masses and *prepare them for the direct conditions in which territorialism will be realized.*" [174]

For his part, Syrkin at first avoided outright polemics, preferring to present his viewpoint piecemeal and ad hoc. In a series of articles written in the summer and autumn of 1906 he ranged far and wide in his most impassioned mood. The only concession he made to his times was to place a somewhat greater emphasis on the "proletariat" rather than the "masses," as the avant-garde in Jewish politics. Otherwise, he was uncompromising.

He attacked the Zionist movement for having made a fetish of "equal rights" and for its tacit alliance with the Kadets. ("Here in Russia, Zionism no longer speaks about Jewish ethics . . . they [the Zionists] are simply Kadets . . . they simply await equal rights, the right to trade and do business in all of Russia.")[175] He attacked the Bund likewise for the narrowness of its goals and horizons. ("The Bund has raised the social and cultural *goles* to an ideal.")[176] He attacked ITO (the new Jewish Territorial Organisation led by Israel Zangwill) for acting as a lobbying group rather than becoming a mass movement. (This was "philanthropy from above rather than serious and intensive activity of the people itself.")[177] He devoted an article to the founder of the Zionist movement ("Herzl is the protest against *goles*; bourgeois Zionism is the product of *goles*.")[178] He surveyed the history of the Jewish people showing how "every period has its new God."[179] (The highest concept of God had come "at the end of the Second Temple . . . the Father of all men"; and the lowest in the Reform Temple of contemporary Western Jewry – "each in his individual insecurity needs a God . . . from whom he can beg for money and wealth for himself and, naturally, disaster and misfortune for the others.")[180]

In October, however, he came out with an onslaught against the ideology dominant in his party. The fact that the SSRP saw its role as secondary rather than primary in the territorialist movement and that it had hitherto avoided taking any action (other than verbal) to participate in the territorialist venture, plus the feeling that territorialism was in danger of becoming a purely abstract concept in the party, must all have prompted him to speak his mind without inhibitions. (Ben Zion Dinur later recalled his own impression that even when the party conference in December 1906 did "decide on the need to conduct large-scale propaganda for the foundation of a Territorialist Union . . . in reality it was a victory for those with faith in the 'historical process' and simply paid lip service to territorialist activism.")[181]

In his October article, "On the Realization of Territorialism," Syrkin ascribed the triumph of the determinist faction in the SSRP to the extremely limited intellectual horizons imposed on Jewish politics by life in the Pale of Settlement.

> A tendency emerged that linked territorialism to the class struggle in its most superficial, vulgar form. The class struggle of the street was seen as the only . . . historical form of proletarian creation. Every historical creativity . . . was conceived as the struggle between capital and labor . . . And as it is very difficult sociologically to link in one formula the destructive class struggle in one country with constructive territorialism in another country, so . . . dialectical tricks and inventions [were brought in].[182]

Although the SSRP had been guilty of such casuistry, he wrote, the worst offenders had been the Palestine-oriented Poale Zion. He summarized Borochov's thought caustically:

How should one conceive the creation of a Jewish state in Palestine? – through a revolution of the Jewish proletariat. How does the Jewish proletariat develop in Palestine? – like every proletariat everywhere, through class war. The proletariat also wages class war outside Palestine – so class war and territorialism coincide. The Jewish state is therefore a product of the proletarian class struggle.[183]

As against this "sharpening of minds," Syrkin advanced his own credo: "[The proletarian] role in territorialism cannot be critical, destructive, oppositional as in the existing society, but must be creative construction in the cause of building a new society."[184]

Syrkin remained in Vilna until 1907. By then the ideas defended by him and Latsky were clearly gaining ascendancy in the party journal. But this was hardly reassuring, for the ebb tide of the revolution was running fast and all the revolutionary parties were in a state of utter disintegration. In 1908 Syrkin joined the mass migration to the United States. He accepted the invitation to edit *Dos folk*, the journal of the socialist territorialist party in New York. The European period of his life had ended.

Conclusion

Syrkin did not play a decisive role in the formation or leadership of worker and socialist Zionism in Russia. The movement grew in a scattered, amorphous form – a natural mutation of Zionism, on the one hand, and socialism, on the other. But within that movement, his name became synonymous with a particular school of thought that combined in one organic synthesis the populist view of the Jewish people in eastern Europe and the prophetic vision of the Jewish socialist state (here he was consciously heir to Hess); a sociological prediction of disaster about to overtake the Diaspora (here he was unacknowledged heir to Lilienblum); a belief in the organized exodus of the Jewish masses to their own territory (here he maintained intact his faith of 1882); and a belief in the Russian revolution based not on the immediate economic or political interests of the Jews but on his theory of collective psychology (here he was entirely original).

He never saw a need to modify his ideology. At times, it gained a certain popularity (as after Kishinev); more often it was seen by the new generation as dangerous (1898–1902) or anachronistic (1905–6). In later years, he would again find himself in violent conflict with most of his party comrades over the issues of the war and Bolshevism, but he always made himself heard and he gradually acquired disciples. It was through them, perhaps, that he made his most important impact on modern Jewish politics.

When, in 1939, Berl Katznelson, then the dominant theoretician of Mapai, published his essay on Syrkin, he did so as an act of homage by a disciple to the master, long since dead. It was a just reward for a man who had never been captive to his own time but had held firm to his presentiment of tragedy and vision of redemption.

CHAPTER 7

Ber Borochov and Marxist Zionism

1903–1907

In contrast to Zhitlovsky and Syrkin, whose ideologies had been largely shaped by the drama of 1881–2, Ber Borochov underwent the decisive political experience of his life in the crisis of 1903–7. They had been born in the late 1860s; he was born in 1881 and belonged to a new generation. In fact, Borochov's early political development was to a large extent typical of the young leadership group that emerged on the Russian-Jewish Left during the 1905 revolution. As a leader of the ESDRP-PZ – The Jewish Social Democratic Labor Party (Poale Zion), a Palestine-oriented party founded in February 1906 – he was recognizably of the same vintage as his counterparts in the SSRP (Moyshe Litvakov, Yaakov and Yoysef Leshchinsky, Shmuel Niger) and in the SERP (Moyshe Zilberfarb, Nokhem Shtif, Yehude Novakovsky).

These men owed to the revolution their sudden rise to power (albeit a power confined within a narrow party circumference). They had the energy to travel constantly from one town to the next carrying their party message, the enthusiasm to inspire faith in their cause, the oratorical ability to sway *intelligentsiia* gatherings or worker crowds (or both), the acumen to prepare an impressive *referat* replete with statistical data; the strength to speak for hours on end, the ability to concentrate through party conferences that lasted for days or even weeks, and the debating skill to outmanoeuver hecklers, overwhelm opponents, and win over the undecided.

They were extremely young in 1905, utterly committed both to the cause of revolution and to that of armed Jewish self-defense against the pogroms. Almost to a man they had become fervent Marxists by 1906, and even those who had not (Zilberfarb, for instance) now advocated (philosophically) a monistic determinism and (politically) proletarian class war. By 1906, the revolution had absorbed their every waking moment, every ounce of strength and every hope. However, to them the revolution meant a struggle not only for social equality and political freedom, but also for national, for Jewish, liberation. They were party men through and through, convinced that their party program alone pointed the one inevitable way linking the present to the future, the "now" to the "then," the "here" to the "there," the class struggle to the Jewish territory.

By the spring of 1906, their new movements had grown so fast that they threatened the Bundist hold on the politicized Jewish masses. Even though the Bund produced its own champions in 1905 – Vladeck, Goldfarb, Maksim, Olgin – it was hard-pressed by these rival parties, which combined Marxist "orthodoxy" with bolder, more nationalist, formulas for the solution of the Jewish question.

Borochov, who was a latecomer to proletarian politics, embodied in quintessential form the trends prevalent during the latter stages of the revolution. His Marxist-materialist monism was more total than that of the Bund, his territorialism more concrete than that of the SSRP, his scheme for Jewish national autonomy in Russia no less far-reaching than that of the Seimists. He was the peripatetic agitator and *referant*, the ever resourceful *teoretik* and indefatigable *praktik*, the party champion relentlessly exposing the doctrinal errors of rival organizations.

However, even at the time, Borochov's position was in some respects atypical. Thus, the Bund, the SSRP, and the SERP had been created by collective leadership groups in which were represented different generations and differing ideological nuances, but the ESDRP-PZ was very much Borochov's personal creation. Its youthful members were derisively called *Borokhovtsy* by their opponents, but they themselves readily adopted this name as a badge of honor. The party doctrine, which came to be known as *Borokhovizm*, was likewise his own handiwork. All contemporary participants concur in their memoirs that without Borochov, the pro-Palestine fragments of Poale Zion would have disintegrated entirely under the impact of the revolution.

Subsequent events have served to augment Borochov's reputation while obscuring the role of his contemporaries in the parallel parties. It is as if some terrible flood had savagely swept away an entire forest leaving only one or two trees to dominate the landscape. The failure of the various territorialist schemes (be it in Uganda, Angola, or Canada); the ruthless elimination of the Jewish socialist parties, the Evsektsiia and the Yiddish cultural institutions in Soviet Russia; the destruction of the Jewish people in east-central Europe by the Nazis; and the rapid decline of Yiddish as a spoken language everywhere have all served to cast into obscurity the memory of such men as Zilberfarb, Vladeck, Litvatov, and Novakovsky.

In contrast, the fact that the Zionist enterprise in Palestine has gone from strength to strength and was for so long dominated by the socialist parties has lent Borochov – the sole *Palestinets* in that group – a certain heroic status. He himself died in Kiev in December 1917, following a short illness, at the age of thirty-six. But his followers and comrades from the Poale Zion party became dominant figures in the Yishuv, rising with the successor organizations, Ahdut Ha-Avoda and Mapai. Yitshak Ben Zvi, the second president of the State of Israel, and Zalman Rubashev (Shazar), the third president, had been among Borochov's closest personal associates in the Russian party in its year of foundation, 1906. Three prime ministers of Israel (David Ben Gurion, Moshe Sharett, and Golda Meir) were also veteran party members although not personally identified with Borochov. His works have been republished in innumerable editions in many languages, and starting in the early 1950s two of Israel's major kibbutz movements began jointly to publish in Hebrew translation a multivolume edition of all his writings complete with detailed annotation. Streets and city quarters have been called after him in Israel.

Borochovism has been treated as a relevant and living doctrine by various sections of the Zionist labor movement over the last seventy years. Those who saw themselves as dedicated *Borokhovtsy* have been outspoken in their commitment, while those who regarded Borochovism sceptically or even with hostility have tended to skirt the issue out of respect for Borochov, the founding father of the Poale Zion party. As a result, Borochov the legend and myth has persistently obscured Borochov the man, the historical reality. Shazar noted this in his introduction to an edition of Borochov's works published in 1944. "Among the theoreticians of the Jewish labor and Zionist movements," he wrote,

> there are few whose names are regarded with such true admiration by readers and disciples even years after their voices have fallen silent. And even when the movement split after his death, neither of the rival sections would surrender their claims to his heritage. And when the Zionist socialist oak many years later put out new branches, they too remained close to the trunk, drawing nourishment from those same roots. Some of his writings ... were raised to the level of a party canon ... And yet there are few admired figures in the movement who, whether deliberately or not, have been "buried" as he has. Even his orthodox followers, who were ready to lay down their lives for every letter in one of his works, did not trouble to examine what he himself had said on the same subject elsewhere even in a work chronologically proximate.[1]

Shazar himself, when he came to explain this paradox, ascribed it to technical causes (the fact that Borochov had written much in Russian rather than Yiddish, for instance). This, however, was something of a disingenuous evasion. The truth is that his followers preferred to see Borochov as a symbolic figure, monolithic and drawn in sharp outlines, rather than as the complex, complicated, and enigmatic man he actually was.

It was not until the 1960s, when Borochov became a subject of academic research, that the most striking feature of his development in his classical period (1904–7) was ascribed its due weight. There was not one Borochov in the revolutionary period but two, the general Zionist of 1904–5 and the proletarian revolutionary of 1906–7.[2] The one stage in his life could not be dismissed simply as the prologue to the other, a youthful diversion, but had to be seen for what it was: a period in which he developed an autonomous, coherent ideology that largely stood in direct negation to the theory he was to expound in the following period.

The task of the historian is not to explain the evolution of Borochov's thought toward its mature culmination in 1906 but rather to examine the contradiction that lies at the heart of his biography in the revolutionary period; to describe the two self-contained doctrines that, on crucial issues, refuted the one the other; and to seek the explanation for this sudden change of role and doctrinal volte-face.

Ussishkin's lieutenant, 1904–1905

Politics

Borochov's parents emigrated from Poltava to the United States in August 1903 and his letters to them in New York have been preserved. In one postcard sent from Minsk on 12 April 1905, he wrote that "I am hurrying, for I am terribly busy – as I have been all the time throughout the last seven months of my life."[3] Since October 1904 he had been acting as an "agitator" for the pro-Palestine wing of the Russian Zionist movement against the territorialist and pro-Uganda forces. The Seventh Congress of the World Zionist Organisation was due to meet in mid-1905, and Menahem Mendel Ussishkin was determined to ensure that the *Palestintsy* (or Zionists for Zion, Zione Zion, as they also called themselves) should dominate the Russian delegation to the congress. In October 1903 he, as the primus inter pares of the veteran Zionist leadership in Russia, had called together the Kharkov conference, which pledged itself to fight to the bitter end against any betrayal of, or deviation from, Zion. Among those committed to Palestine was Vladimir Jabotinsky, who now came into his own as a brilliant young firebrand and polemicist. But Ussishkin undertook in 1904 to recruit reinforcements, and among those who agreed to preach the cause was Ber Borochov, then twenty-three years old.

A letter of September 1904 sent to Ussishkin from Bograchov, who was visiting Poltava on a recruiting mission, gives us an insight into Borochov's induction as an agitator:

> Borochov is ready to do anything which you order. And in my opinion it is possible and necessary [for him] . . . to give lectures in the entire area. He is an educated young man, a marvelous dialectician. He has a name and many pupils and admirers . . . in the entire region and he has the power to influence them.[4]

In reality, Borochov's path as itinerant spokesman for the Zione Zion carried him far beyond the Poltava region; across the length and breadth of the Pale of Settlement, Congress Poland, and beyond, to such towns as Odessa, Warsaw, Elizavetgrad, and Vilna.

Wherever he went, he sent letters or postcards to Ussishkin giving progress reports and asking for further instructions. From them it is possible to gather some idea of the obstacle course he had to run. He rarely stayed more than a few days in each town and he could normally expect to address at least one meeting – of workers, *intelligenty, gimnazisty* or general Zionists – every day. Constantly on the move, he had to abandon his work as a tutor and was left without any source of steady income. Sometimes Ussishkin would supply him with the necessary funds to keep him going, but at other times, in order to make ends meet, he felt compelled to give a paid academic lecture on some theme popular with the educated public (most frequently on Nietzsche).[5]

Throughout the winter and spring of 1905, the constant railway strikes frequently left him stranded high and dry in one place when he was expected in another. The constant travel and speech-making in the thick of the Russian winter often made him desperately hoarse and hardly able to fulfil his engagements. In the northwest, he had to switch from Russian to "my abominable Yiddish."[6] As an active member of the Jewish self-defense organization, he also found himself diverted from his route by news of threatening pogroms. (Thus, for instance, on 15 February 1905 he wrote from Odessa that he was "considering going in the next few days to Elizavetgrad, where in view of the expected panic I would now be useful, for there are no people there at all.")[7]

Every town presented its own specific problem to Borochov, the pro-Palestine agitator. In Priluki, Berdichev, and Zhitomir, where he went in November 1904, he found that the Bund was going from strength to strength because it was undertaking to "organize the self-defence." ("One has to counteract their further agitation," he

Figure 19. Ber Borochov, 1881–1917.

wrote to Ussishkin, "and make use of the rising nationalist mood.")[8] In Vilna in January 1905, he addressed a mass meeting of over five hundred people. "Everything would have been all right except that the third of my opponents began insisting that the '*Palestintsy* are not Zionists.' That produced a terrible storm of outrage – a scandal; the windows of the synagogue were smashed, there was brawling, etc."[9] In Warsaw in June, he held some ten meetings but found that the territorialists "possess very strong forces." Moreover, his last debate there was ruined by Yitshak Grinbaum, himself a prominent pro-Palestinian but one who "does not like my Marxist argumentation as he is an opponent of historical materialism."[10]

Borochov came out of this ordeal with flying colors. His reputation as a remarkably original and enthusiastic spokesman for his cause was established through-out the Russian-Jewish world. One success leads to another and from February 1905, the leading Zionist journal, *Evreiskaia zhizn,* began to publish long articles by Borochov on an almost monthly basis. His name rapidly became a household word in the Zionist camp, particularly among the youth and on the left. But, throughout, he acted as Ussishkin's loyal field officer. "In accord with the rules of discipline," he wrote in October 1904, "I shall obey your order and go to Kiev tonight."[11] "Once you wrote," stated a letter of February 1905, "that I should ensure that the Zione Zion recognize the Vilna [conference] program, I am of course doing just that and will not leave Odessa until I get it done."[12] On his return from Elizavetgrad, he promised not long after, "I shall once more return to regular work under your leadership."[13]

As Matityahu Mintz has rightly pointed out in his excellent full-scale study of the early Borochov, neither the veteran Zionist leader nor his young lieutenant ever described the nature and scope of their intensive collaboration.[14] However, both of them have left very brief accounts describing episodes from an earlier period when their activities momentarily overlapped. In 1900, having graduated from the *gimnaziia* in Poltava, Borochov went to live in Ekaterinoslav, which was Ussishkin's home town, and there he became active in a Zionist youth club with which Ussishkin (as the leading figure in the movement) was also associated. Looking back from 1916 on this episode, Borochov wrote as follows:

> Just as Dr. Syrkin's thought developed at first independently of, without any connection to, the distant and forgotten philosophy of Moses Hess, so in Russia itself the socialist Zionist movement began independently and with-out any connection to Dr. Syrkin's propaganda abroad. The first group of socialist, class-conscious Poale Zion in Russia was formed in November 1900 in Ekaterinoslav. Its founders were the writer of these lines and Shimon Dobin ... From September 1900 to May 1901 this writer, who belonged to the Russian Social Democratic [Labor] Party in Ekaterinoslav, delivered a series of *referaty* on socialist Zionism to a club of young workers ... Dr. Shmarya Levin ... delivered a series of lectures against the new idea. The lengthy discussions ... resulted in the club accepting the new viewpoint and adopting the name, the Zionist Labor Union.[15]

For his part, Ussishkin in a conversation with Ben Zvi in the 1930s recalled that word had reached him in Ekaterinoslav of Borochov's debating exploits and philo-sophical expertise while the latter was still at high school in Poltava. "A short time afterwards," he recalled,

> a young *gimnazist* came into my room and asked me to arrange a lecture for him on a subject of Jewish, political, or philosophical interest. I asked him immediately: "Are you the Borochov of Avenarius?" And he replied that he was. I remembered what Professor Liashevich had told me about him, but still I answered that it was the first time that I had set eyes on him and would hardly arrange a lecture for him when it could easily be a flop. But Borochov talked me into it ... I invited all my friends, the Zionists and the best of the Ekaterinoslav intelligentsia in general ... ; his lecture made an extraordinary

impression on the whole audience, which was . . . astounded by the powerful mind of the youngster.[16]

A few months later, Ussishkin recommended Borochov as a contributor to *The Zionist Almanach,* and his first published article appeared there in 1902.

Thus, while Ussishkin took pride in having discovered the young prodigy from Poltava, Borochov sought to demonstrate that from the first he had pursued a strict class line independently of, and against, the Zionist establishment. In fact, Borochov's account is throughout marked by an extreme overschematization. The known facts suggest that, in reality, Borochov in Ekaterinoslav did not lay down the foundation of his future party – Marxist, revolutionary, fiercely class oriented – but, on the contrary, came increasingly under the sway of the two leading Zionists there, Shmarya Levin and Ussishkin.

When Borochov came to Ekaterinoslav, he joined the Russian Social Democratic Labor Party, and this was presumably his main reason for coming to that burgeoning industrial city. Soon after his arrival he was made a propagandist for the RSDRP and put in charge of a number of *kruzhki.* But, thereafter, he gradually severed his links with the revolutionary Left.[17]

His insistence on including pro-Zionist propaganda in his classes led to his expulsion from the RSDRP. His work in the Zionist club, according to Shmarya Levin, was conducted "under the direction of Ussishkin."[18] Although there he no doubt expounded Marxist ideas distasteful to the veteran leader, it is unlikely that he crossed the crucial borderline separating the majority of Poale Zion groups in Russia from the small minority that advocated active Zionist participation in the revolutionary cause. Certainly, Borochov took up Ussishkin's offer to publish his article, "On the Character of the Jewish Mind," in a legal and general Zionist book.

In 1902, when he returned to Poltava, Borochov made a conscious break with the Poale Zion movement, which was then spreading far and wide over the Pale of Settlement. Explaining this decision, Borochov later ascribed it to his rejection of the "theory of nonproletarianization," which was gaining a hold on the movement. Mintz suggests that at that stage he actually subscribed to this theory but believed that it made the autonomous existence of a proletarian organization such as Poale Zion redundant and self-contradictory.[19] Be that as it may, he had arrived in Ekaterinoslav as a revolutionary Social Democrat, had there briefly become a member of Poale Zion and returned to Poltava as a general Zionist.

Borochov throughout his youth had powerful ambitions to make his mark as a philosopher. No doubt he would have been willing to spend some years quietly in Poltava, reading voraciously, lecturing and debating to his small circle of friends, and eventually writing a book on his philosophical worldview. But here events intervened to draw him into active political life as an agitator for Ussishkin.

The Kishinev and Homel pogroms in April and September 1903, respectively, made an enormous impression on Borochov and his friends in Poltava. There, in the heart of the Ukraine, the threat of further pogroms and massacres was tangible in the extreme. It was now that his family left for America, a fact in itself indicative of the pervading atmosphere. His letters to them were throughout full of detailed information on the pogroms, threatened or actual, and on the self-defense. Writing in October 1903, he identified himself with the Bundists and the Poale Zion, who together had formed a self-defense force of five hundred in Homel and had prepared in advance "an adequate quantity of firearms and other weapons."[20]

On the other hand, he was bitterly angry at the central role played by the Russian railway workers in the pogrom and the failure of socialist propaganda demonstrated thereby:

> To the eternal shame of Russian Social Democracy it must be said that these workers had been exposed to Social Democratic agitation . . . And it must be added that those who introduced revolutionary ideas among the workers – who to the last man joined in the destruction – were Jews: Social Revolutionaries and Social Democrats of Jewish origin. Fine educational propaganda! Great successes! Marvelous results![21]

A letter of June 1904 described a pogrom threat in Poltava itself; Borochov's role in organizing the self-defense; the determination of the Zionists "to defend our national honor to the last drop of blood"; the fact that "the other Jews did not join us ('It is,' they say, 'Poltava after all and not Kishinev and Homel')"; and the fact that "the local socialists, who shout a lot and do nothing, did not want to join up with the Zionists and made fun of us."[22]

His letters were also replete with detailed descriptions of conflict within the government hierarchy and within the Russian nationalist camp – Pleve had circulated an internal memorandum demanding the preservation of order, but Krushevan and the antisemitic press were openly inciting to violence; in Homel the local police had been against permitting a pogrom but they had been overruled at higher levels; in Poltava the Cossacks, many of whom had Jewish girlfriends in tailoring families, had helped prevent a pogrom.

The underlying motif running through all these accounts was unmistakable – the tsarist regime could not be held alone responsible for the pogroms, and the Jews had no cause whatsoever to expect salvation from the revolution or revolutionaries. In adopting this position, Borochov was swimming against the tide that was fast carrying most of his contemporaries in Poale Zion, the *Vozrozhdenie,* and related groups toward active revolutionary commitment. Thus, it was natural enough that he was so eager in 1904 to join the standard raised by Ussishkin and the Zione Zion.

Since the Zionist conference in Minsk in 1902, Ussishkin had taken it upon himself to promulgate a Palestine-oriented program capable of attracting the Russian-Jewish youth. In its most complete version, entitled "Our Program," his credo was published in November 1904. But in all essential details his plans had long been widely publicized. Borochov had presumably become familiar with them while still in Ekaterinoslav, and he certainly would have received a detailed summary from Bograchov in September 1904.

Two points in "Our Program" were calculated to appeal to Borochov. First, there was the general strategy, which was designed, so Ussishkin believed, to avoid the errors made over the previous two decades by the Zionist (and proto-Zionist) movement; to assure rapid progress in the coming years; and guarantee the eventual establishment of "a Jewish state in Palestine."[23] Hitherto, Ussishkin argued, the movement had pursued a series of one-sided policies: land purchase and settlement until 1891, a cultural renaissance as advocated by Ahad Ha-Am in the mid-1890s, and Herzl's pursuit of a charter through a diplomatic effort since 1897. The fallacy at every stage had been the belief that one formula excluded the other.

In fact, all three paths – colonization, national education, diplomacy – had to be pursued simultaneously. The latent enthusiasm and energy of the rank-and-file membership would then be tapped; the reliance on "the chosen few . . . , or to be exact, only the one chosen individual"[24] would be set aside; and success on one front would reinforce the campaigns being waged on the other two. Above all, Ussishkin set out to prove that despite the restrictions imposed by the Turkish government and bureaucracy, land purchase and settlement remained a viable possibility, "difficult, unbelievably *difficult, but not impossible*. With difficulties, the Zionists must grapple. Our weapons . . . must be patience, time and money."[25]

Second, Ussishkin assigned a central place in this overall strategy to the youth. Past experience had demonstrated that nothing was to be gained by establishing colonies if most of the actual labor was assigned to Arab workers. The fact that there were hardly any Jewish laborers and many thousands of Arabs in the settlements meant that the cause of "Jewish colonization in Palestine is built on sand or, more accurately, on a volcano."[26] In order to escape this trap, Ussishkin proposed that young Jewish men and women volunteer to work as laborers in the Palestinian settlements:

> It is essential to create a worldwide Jewish workers' artel drawn from young, unmarried youth healthy in body and mind. It will be the duty of every member of this artel to go for three years to Palestine and to undertake military service to the Jewish people not with sword and rifle but with spade and plow. These thousands of youngsters will have to come to the Jewish colonies and offer themselves as hired laborers on the same terms as the Arab, to live an unprecedentedly hard life . . . After he has completed his three years' service such a worker can, if he wishes, settle in the country in the hope of obtaining a lease on a plot of land from ICA or else he can join a cooperative settlement (if he brings the requisite means from home) . . . If at the beginning of the 80s, we found dozens of Bilu, I sincerely believe that today we can find thousands like them. The young generation is awake, is thirsting for self-sacrifice. But it must be . . . shown the way.[27]

With his choice of the term artel (with its *narodnik* socialist connotations) and with his appeal to the prestige of the Bilu, Ussishkin was trying to tap the romantic vein in the psyche of the younger generation. For his part, Borochov responded with genuine enthusiasm. Obviously, what attracted him was the fact that Ussishkin's strategy assigned a key role to his age group, that (in contrast to Herzlian Zionism) it demanded of him and his contemporaries a high degree of personal commitment, self-sacrifice, and discipline; that it relied unashamedly on the voluntarist factor in history; and that (in contrast to the caution of Ahad Ha-Am) it was uncompromising in its formulation of ultimate goals ("a Jewish state in Palestine").

Borochov's letters of late 1904 and early 1905 reveal how completely he then identified himself with Ussishkin's strategy. "In Zionism," he wrote to his parents late in 1904, "a new encouraging tendency has emerged . . . Possibly 'soon in our time' the Jewish people will return to Palestine and have rest from its suffering. The old Bilu is being reborn but this time it is organized and possesses large forces. Possibly by the spring you will receive a letter from me from Palestine."[28] Yitshak Shimshelevich (Ben Zvi), who in 1904 went to Palestine for the summer, has recorded how on his return to Poltava, Borochov cross-examined him about his every impression and experience.[29] In January 1905 Borochov informed Ussishkin that he had finally finished an article on "Biluism."[30] In February he wrote to him announcing that he intended to send an article to *Evreiskaia zhizn* defending " 'Our Programme' (yours = *ours*)" against those critics who demanded a greater emphasis on *Gegenwartsarbeit* in Russia.[31]

In Poltava, Bograchov reported to Ussishkin, Borochov had "thirty people who on his orders will go through fire and water,"[32] and during his agitational tour, the latter sought to recruit additional members for the new Bilu. Thus, in November he wrote that he had "completed the organization of an active group of dedicated *Palestintsy,* young people, here in Kharkov, [although] unfortunately most of them (all in all there are ten) are students who will have to finish their studies before going to Palestine."[33] In Odessa, he visited a pioneer (He-Haluts) group that

> at the moment numbers twelve full members and three to four probationaries. They have turned away many who wish to join them for they are working for complete solidarity and the absolute spirit of comradeship. They are all exalted and naive youngsters, ... rich in faith. They live together, eat together and, with the general appearance of their commune, give as it were a preview of our future artels.[34]

In another letter from Odessa, he reported that he had won over "a *kruzhok* from the territorialists – one they had already organized. I have come together with He-Haluts [The Pioneer]: a very good beginning."[35]

Ideology

It is possible to gain a comprehensive insight into the ideology Borochov was advocating during his whirlwind tours from two articles which he published in 1905 in *Evreiskaia zhizn.* The longer of these articles, "On the Question of Zion and a Territory," published in parts from June until October 1905, was actually written during the period in which he was working as an agitator for Zione Zion. In letters and cards to Ussishkin sent during the period from February until April from Odessa, Minsk, and Poltava, he reported on its gradual completion. The other piece, "On Questions of Zionist Theory," was apparently written, in its first form at least, in the period 1902–3; but, in most basic respects, it complemented and reinforced the ideas presented in his other article. This is understandable enough, as he was hardly the man to permit the publication of a manuscript, whenever first written, with which he had come to disagree. In essence, what he sought to do in these articles (especially in "On the Question of Zion and a Territory") was to place Ussishkin's "Our Program" firmly within an intellectual frame of reference comprehensible to his own generation.

He constructed his case for Palestine and the pioneer concept on a dual foundation. His entire theory rested on the thesis that Jewish politics in the near future had to be radically different from such politics in the more distant future, that in this case the short run operated according to rules qualitatively different from those of the long run. Each stage, he argued, was dominated by "necessity," but this one term actually signified two opposing ideas.

Ultimately, he granted, the Zionists could depend for success on the flow of powerful sociological processes. At this level, the theoreticians of the territorialist movement, of the SSRP, had analyzed the future of the Jewish people correctly. Deep-rooted factors were working inexorably to force the Jews out of modern society, thus rendering a territorial solution to the Jewish question inevitable. This development, he argued (here following Lilienblum, Syrkin, and his contemporaries in the SSRP), was at root socioeconomic in character. The Jews had been able to find refuge in feudal societies but were relentlessly pressed to the margins by advancing capitalism. Russia was moving directly from feudalism to the higher stages of capitalism—therefore, "in east Europe the Jews are being rendered more thoroughly superfluous than in the West and no reform will save them from isolation."[36]

However, he continued (here reminiscent of Pinsker), it was erroneous to explain antisemitism in purely socioeconomic terms. It is "enmity to the Jews as such, for no fault of their own, for no cause; hatred for the Yid because he is a Yid." Education, far from solving the problem, was more likely to exacerbate both the violence of the hatred and the sensitivity of its victims.

> A calm critical attitude to an irrational emotion is almost impossible ... The intellectual progress of the Judaeophobic classes of society does not weaken antisemitism but, on the contrary, reinforces it. On the other hand, that same progress because of the Weber-Fechner law and the so-called hedonist paradox, renders the Jews more sensitive and discontented.[37]

Indeed, as democracy replaced feudalism, so the position of the Jews became more untenable. "The destruction of class barriers, universal suffrage, trial by jury, etc.," he wrote (following Syrkin),

> all these by weakening the differences between the upper and lower social strata, will lead to a union of the Judaeophobia from above with the Judaeophobia from below and will ... render the Jews ever more vulnerable to social antisemitism and boycott. The same prospect of growing isolation ... awaits, for example, the Negroes in the United States ..., awaits all groups that in the capitalist era ... do not possess their own territory, are treated as aliens.[38]

Forced to leave one country for another, the Jews simply carried antisemitism with them to new areas of the world. In despair, they were being driven "en masse into the ranks of the most extreme, the most destructive, parties (the followers of Stirner, Kropotkin, McKay, etc.) ... making the Jews still more hated by all social elements, both reactionary and progressive."[39]

Given the accuracy of this analysis, Borochov argued, it was absurd for the Jews to expect, as so many did, their collective salvation from the social revolution. It was indicative in this context that he specifically selected for praise "the ideology of the Minsk Poale Zion, both Zionist and territorialist"[40]—an ideology known primarily for its adamant and consistent opposition to Zionist participation in the "political struggle" against tsarism.

"The socialist cataclysm on which our optimists rest their hopes," Borochov wrote, "will not come so soon, if it comes at all."[41] But even assuming the contrary, the Jews could hardly expect to benefit even from the total victory of the progressive Left. First, as a marginal group of outsiders, they would beyond doubt find themselves caught in the cross-fire between the forces of revolution and counterrevolution. "As an example," he wrote,

> let us take the comparatively small number of Jews who live in Morocco . . . Progress cannot pass Morocco by: the European Powers after all are already sinking their claws into that barbaric country. And inevitably the advance of culture will bring about an uprising of the indigenous Moroccan population for whom everything alien and European is hateful. And is not such a revolution bound to bring destruction on the Jews there? Will not their fury turn against the Jews, who are defenceless, rather than against the European predators, who are well defended? . . . The same fate awaits the Jews in Persia and other countries of the Orient. These Jews will pay for the first steps of militant progress with their lives.[42]

Further, even if a socialist regime did somehow succeed in establishing itself, this fact per se could hardly guarantee a solution to a problem rooted not only in the sociopolitical order but also in the popular psyche. Antisemitism "as hate pure and simple"[43] could be excluded from the governmental and juridical system only to reemerge embodied in "new forms." "We do not put our trust in progress," he declared. "Progress has two aspects: the angel in man advances, but so does the devil."[44] Thus, he concluded, the one escape was that promised by the classic exodic solution (now taken up by the territorialists). The Jews had to resettle themselves en masse in a sovereign territory of their own.

At this point, however, Borochov parted company with the territorialists. Even at the level of socioeconomic law, he argued, Palestine would exert a greater pull on Jewish migration than the other alternatives hitherto suggested (Uganda, Angola, Canada, Manchuria). To prove this point in purely sociological, objective terms was no easy undertaking, but he was determined to take up this self-imposed challenge.

His initial thrust – directed against the territorialist projects – was undoubtedly perceptive and important. All colonization schemes in the modern era, he maintained, were bound to fall under the sway of the capitalist system and, in normal circumstances, this fact would enmesh Jewish settlement in a cruel trap. With its every economic advance, Jewish colonization would draw a large number of indigenous (or other non-Jewish) workers into its orbit. Because of their extremely low standard of living and greater familiarity with hard physical labor, the native workers would gain a monopoly on the manual jobs, thus undermining all projects for the formation of a Jewish proletariat. ("For unqualified work, the Negro, the Mongolian . . . will be preferable, for he is both more productive and incomparably cheaper.")[45]

The long-term results of this development would be fatal. Sooner or later, he argued, the native population would turn against the newcomers:

> What a revolution must inevitably come about in the general way of life of the natives as a result of the extraordinary invasion by the new people with

its unheard-of customs, habits, language and outlook, by a people which is energetic and restless ... Eventually it will not remain a secret to the natives that the Jews are coming with the aim of gaining possession of the country; and if they do not always – far from always – submit willingly to the ... almost imperceptible rule of a Power, which is sometimes quite nominal, how much more intense will be their wrath against the Jews who intend to seize their country in a way by no means nominal ... [46] Eventually, the natives seeing in the Jews their nearest ... enemy will be stimulated to develop and strengthen their [own] national ... consciousness.[47]

In the resulting struggle, victory would not be with the Jews, for an upper crust of settlers could not permanently dominate the native masses. For example, he noted, "there can be no doubt that the future of Uganda belongs not to the English but to the Ugandans ... [the latter] feel this even if they do not recognize it in sociological or juridical terms."[48]

It was Borochov's thesis that exceptional circumstances rendered Palestine relatively immune to this syndrome. He marshaled numerous arguments to prove this point. So, for example, he insisted that capitalism in Palestine would develop much more slowly than in most areas because it was under the rule of Turkey rather than England or some other Western power; because it possessed no gold deposits, diamond fields, or other natural treasures; and because it had a climate unattractive to the average European immigrant. Again, in Palestine there was already settled a medium-sized Jewish population, which in part was ready to enter the ranks of the proletariat.

What gave Palestine its decisive advantage, however, was the nature of the indigenous population, whom he described as *fellakhy* (felaheen). The *fellakhy*, he suggested, had to be seen as "direct descendants of the Judean and Canaanite population with a very small addition of Arab blood."[49] They could "in no way be distinguished" in appearance from the Sephardi Jews of the area. They were sufficiently cultured and rooted in their native villages that they would not move "too rapidly into a capitalist economy," but not of a culture high enough to resist Western influence.[50] In short, the Palestinian *fellakhy* would gradually be absorbed into the developing Jewish community, adopt its culture, and supply part but not all of the growing proletariat. The incoming Jews could thus hope to establish the same kind of symbiotic relationship with the Palestinian *fellakhy* as the American Negroes had attained with the natives of Liberia. Thus, Borochov concluded, "the only one of all the territories which we can consider seriously is Palestine."[51]

At this one level, then – in his analysis of the objective forces driving the Jewish people from the Diaspora to Palestine – Borochov was consciously following the ideological trends dominant at the time. Politics, in the view of his generation, had to reflect scientific law, had to move with the objective flow of history, had to be solidly grounded in sociology and economics. But, in fact, his primary purpose in 1905 was to stand against this orthodoxy. His key contention was that long-term sociological trends would dissipate themselves in aimless tragedy unless immediate political measures were taken to prepare the way for them, channels dug to harness and direct them.

To illustrate this point, he argued that a radical distinction had to be made between the Zionist movement in its early stages and the socialist movement. True, both were produced by the advance of capitalism, and both were guaranteed victory in their respective spheres by the crisis building up within the bourgeois order. But here the similarity ceased. The concentration of capital in the hands of a few, the proletarianization of the many, and the growth of modern industry were all preparing the way directly for the final expropriation of the expropriators. Therefore, the task of the socialist party was merely to ease the birth pangs of the new order, to hasten a process which anyway was progressing inexorably to its predestined end.

In contrast, the capitalist crisis provided a necessary, but decidedly not a sufficient, basis for Zionist strategy. Left to itself, the socioeconomic process could only lead to a catastrophe for the Jewish people. There was no intrinsic reason why the Great Powers, if driven far enough, should not "render harmless the Jews in their state of [advanced] degeneration – and do so in a way by no means to the good of the Jewish people."[52] Only conscious action by a minority could tip the balance in another direction.

To underline the difference between the two types of movement, he termed the one "evolutionary" and the other "therapeutic." The former could rely on forces "immanent" within the developing economic order; the latter was dependent on "transcendent" forces – a party that could discern the social abnormality and correct it as the doctor prescribes the appropriate cure for a given illness. "A therapeutic movement by its very nature faces *obstacles* and so, by definition, must be organized according to a previously elaborated *plan;* in an evolutionary movement neither *plans* nor *obstacles* play a substantial role."[53] "It is the very essence of the Zionist movement . . . , " he insisted, "that it can only *begin* through the mobilization of conscious and organised pioneers whose numbers will grow in accordance with the successes attained, and these, for the first long period, are not guaranteed us."[54] Only when the plan, the cure, had been successfully executed, could socioeconomic forces become the main factor in Zionist advance. Eventually, once the foundation of a Jewish society in Palestine had been laid, the masses would be drawn thither like flood waters seeking out the path of least resistance.

Armed with this concept of a two-stage development, he struck out at both the camp of Ahad Ha-Am, on the right, and the territorialists, on the left. In narrowing their goals to the idea of a small "spiritual center" in Palestine, the followers of Ahad Ha-Am had abandoned the central idea in Zionism: the necessity to rescue the Jewish people from the world of want and violence. All those who placed loyalty to Palestine above the plight of the masses had betrayed the Zionist ideal. "I confess," was one biting comment, "that my mind is not capable of grasping what benefit would redound to poor, hounded Yankel if a Spinoza were to write his works in Hebrew, a Meyerbeer compose his operas on strictly Jewish themes, and Ahad Ha-Am create a wonderful museum of Jewish antiquities in Jerusalem."[55] "Sometimes," he wrote again, "[I] . . . am seized by the urge to hate Palestine when [I] meet with those among its advocates who, whether fastidiously or ecstatically, push aside all thought for the people and its needs in order to devote themselves fully to some kind of national essence."[56]

But if a nationalism wholly absorbed with historical values was repellent, the "populism" of the territorialists was naive. They believed that their colonization projects had to be carried through not only for the people but also by the people, and this was patently impossible. In this sense, assimilationists such as Bikerman who mocked at Zionist reliance on the popular will were absolutely right. "We have to recognize the truth of his assertion," Borochov wrote,

> that the people as such, 90 percent of the Jewish nation, will make no sacrifices for auto-emancipation and cannot make such sacrifices, for it can only go where arrangements have been made for its reception . . . The people – that is 90 percent of it – would rather die of hunger and cold, sink hopelessly into the lower depths of society [bosiachestvo] rather than undertake difficult, creative work according to a long-term plan . . . If Zionism is absolutely and always to be a popular movement, then it is a mere chimera.[57]

Whether or not his attack was launched specifically at Syrkin, it certainly struck directly at one of his central beliefs. Syrkin, after all, was through and through a populist of the classical school, while the Borochov of 1905 had been influenced by Bolshevik political thought with its emphasis on the crucial role of the conscious elite. He specifically attacked those Social Democrats who believed it possible to build a socialist movement on nothing more than "the direct needs" of the working class – an approach that, he wrote, led to "a withered and confined trade-unionist movement" and to "the miserable reaction of the Revisionists."[58] Every movement of radical change had to combine the negative factor of social distress with some positive ideal. This, he insisted, was doubly true of the Zionist movement, which could not advance without the personal self-sacrifice of the pioneer youth.

For this reason it was absurd to treat Palestine, the ancestral homeland, as simply one more territory to be judged exclusively by the same criteria as any other. Its emotional appeal to the Jews, including the youth, gave it ceteris paribus a weighty advantage. The alacrity with which the territorialists had given up Palestine for the sake of what was still a purely hypothetical alternative revealed a contempt for the power of historical symbols in human affairs. That Jews in large numbers had willingly accepted this turnabout was hardly surprising, for

> the memory . . . of the degenerating Jewish lumpen-bourgeoisie does not go back even as far as grandfather, but is confined to the present day – this is the miserable class in whose shattered soul the moment about to come does not harmonize with that just passed; [and] the yesterday carries no obligation for today.[59]

In fact, so long as there was no more realistic alternative, Palestine was bound to become the focus of hope for those perceptive enough to foresee the impending tragedy. "We cannot but love our motherland once we are no longer allowed to feel that the Diaspora is our motherland . . . [60] The more this isolation takes on an oppressive, burdensome form, the more the Jew is forced to turn in on his own people, to its psychological content, to its past."[61] Thus, the pioneer youth was forced to look to Palestine by his objective situation, his alienation from Russia, his search for some ideal more concrete and historically rooted than an abstract populism or territorialism.

This reliance, ultimately, on socioeconomic factors but, immediately, on the idealistic pioneer youth would not, Borochov admitted, win a ready acceptance by his contemporaries.

> The critically disposed reader will see in the negative aspect of our conception a philanthropic approach and, in the positive, an aristocratic individualism . . . [62] If our theory annoys anybody because it lacks democratism then so much the worse for him. Believe me, we would be glad to see our movement a popular movement and it displeases us no less, perhaps, than it does you. But what is to be done! . . . the avant-garde elements are those who feel before others the necessity of exodus from the Diaspora, but this does not mean that they are the *select,* the *chosen.* [63]

The term "necessity" in this context, Borochov explained, was to be understood not as scientifically determined, but rather as a political imperative. Palestine represented the only positive alternative to catastrophe. "There have," he wrote, "been approximations to our ideal in history: the revival of the autonomous Jewish society of Judca after the Babylonian exile; Liberia, etc. But beyond *hope* there is also a *guarantee* – we are obliged to triumph."[64] In his attitude to Palestine, there was a note of urgency not characteristic of prevailing opinion in 1905. "The optimists advise us to wait . . . " he wrote in his February article. "But we Jews *must not* wait. We Zionists *cannot* wait."[65] "In order to survive," he declared later in the year, "the Jews must complete their Exodus from the Diaspora."[66]

In sum, Borochov in his Ussishkin period was politically in favor of immediate colonization and indifferent (or even hostile) to the revolution in Russia. He was organizationally an elitist who assigned a crucial role to the avant-garde and placed no reliance on mass action. He was philosophically a dualist who balanced determinism against voluntarism, materialism against idealism, the socioeconomic against the psychological, and the needs of the moment against the demands of history.

Borochov as revolutionary Zionist, 1906–1907

From July until November 1905 Borochov was abroad, first in Switzerland, at the time of the Seventh Zionist Congress, and then in Berlin. He returned to Russia after the October days and soon took it upon himself to rally the scattered and demoralized pro-Palestine Poale Zion into a new party. He threw himself into this undertaking with a ferocious energy.

In late December we find him at a regional Poale Zion conference in Poltava that was attended by Zvi Shimshelevich (Ben Zvi), Zerubavel, and other home-town friends of many years' standing. It was there during four days of excited work that the main ideological principles of their party, then still in the planning stage, were hammered out. From Poltava, Borochov traveled with Ben Zvi straight to Berdichev for a conference of Poale Zion in the southwest. He arrived, after a train journey much delayed by strikes, with a heavy cold but, nonetheless, he singlehanded conducted the battle against the Vozrozhdentsy led by Moyshe Zilberfarb. The contest raged, Zilberfarb later recalled, for an exhausting eight days, but always at a "high intellectual level";[67] and although most of the delegates remained loyal to the Vozrozhdenie, it was generally agreed that Borochov had more than held his own. The Poale Zion-*Palestintsy* had passed their first test unscathed.

The next step was the organization of the founding congress. As recalled by Zerubavel, the brunt of the work again fell on the one leader:

> The secretariat of the Organization Bureau was Borochov himself. He sent dozens of letters to organizations and individual comrades. There were letters, too, that did not deal only with pure organizational matters; there were also questions and answers on the basic issues of the Poale Zion world outlook . . . He quickly won the real trust of his comrades and became the recognised leader and rebbe of thousands of dedicated disciples . . . He aroused trust and security among his comrades. "Don't worry. Borye will soon provide the answer." . . . And he did so provide. Day and night he worked at his freely adopted task.[68]

The foundation congress of the new party, which took the name The Jewish Social Democratic Labor Party (Poale Zion), met in late February 1906 in Poltava. The thirty delegates, who came from centers all over the Pale of Settlement, first met in a girls' school (in the absence of the pupils), but most of the sessions were held in the two back rooms of a bakery. There, for one week, the delegates – made ghostlike by their perpetual cover of flour – worked through the agenda of the congress. Finally, fearing a police raid, they adjourned to a small hotel hastily "expropriated" from the terrified owner.[69]

An ideological commission was elected by the congress and its members immediately left Poltava for Simferopol (where the Poale Zion group under Feliks Menchikovsky was well organized) to prepare a full-length exposition on the new party's program. There Borochov drew up the outline of his most famous work, "Our Platform" (which began to appear over the following months in the party journal, published in Poltava, *Evreiskaia rabochaia khronika*). Ben Zvi, who was a member of the commission, later described how the piece had been prepared. "Borochov would lecture and then we held a discussion until we reached a conclusion. We noted everything down and so we went from subject to subject."[70]

From the first, the new party – the ESDRP-PZ – regarded itself as strictly proletarian. Coming so late to the revolutionary scene, it spared no effort to validate its credentials.[71] Of all the Jewish socialist parties, it was in fact the only one to include the term "Social Democratic" in its name, and at the Second Congress of the party in 1907 there were delegates who sought, albeit unsuccessfully, to have the words Poale Zion dropped altogether.[72] On tactical issues, the party usually took its cue from the Bolsheviks and was critical of the Mensheviks. Thus, it boycotted the elections to the First Duma and – as in the Bolshevik movement – there was a strong minority which demanded that the same policy be repeated in the case of the Second Duma. The party, most notably in Poland but also elsewhere, pursued an active policy of "expropriations."[73]

Its press was constantly predicting a violent climax to the revolution and the imminent overthrow of tsarism. "All are coming under the red workers' flag," declared the party paper in July 1906. "We shall have to offer up many sacrifices on the altar of the revolution; the pogroms will reoccur many times, as the last writhings of the dying monster, . . . but victory is not far off."[74] "Final victory," Aleksandr (Khashin) wrote at the same time, "[is] near."[75] "The day of total liberation," R. Goldin ((Rahel Yanait Ben Zvi) wrote in January 1907, "is not far off! The red flags, held in strong hands, give promise of the coming, the noble, dawn."[76]

The same radicalism marked the national program of the party. It demanded "Jewish personal political autonomy," in other words, a Seim with far-reaching authority, for the Jews as a national minority in Russia; and its maximal goal was "territorial autonomy" (a Jewish state). In this way, it absorbed the goals of both the Seimists and the SSRP into its program, outflanking them and far outbidding the Bund.

It was thus hardly surprising that "Our Platform" should have presented a doctrine utterly different in many important respects from that which Borochov had advocated in the previous year. True, the new party proclaimed its faith in the Palestinian solution to the Jewish question, and it saw in the current migration to Palestine, however miniscule, the first trickle destined with time to grow into a flood. These were the articles of faith that the Borochov of 1906 shared with the Borochov of 1905, that constituted the main distinguishing feature of the new party, and that marked it off unmistakably from both the SSRP (with its non-Palestinian territorialism) and from the Seimists (who were actively opposed to all territorialist projects until the victory of the revolution and the establishment of the Seim). But here the similarity ended.

In essence, what Borochov did in "Our Platform" was to cut away one-half of the dualistic synthesis he had so laboriously constructed in the earlier period. The pivot on which his original program had revolved was, of course, the project for a pioneer youth artel, a new Bilu, to go from Russia to Palestine. There was no trace of this idea in 1906, and with it went the concept of the "therapeutic" stage in Zionism, the "plan," the "avant-garde", the "transcendental" forces. There was no room for the appeal of Palestine, the ancestral homeland, to the psyche of the alienated youth, for "positive" ideals and "idealism." What remained was the other half of his doctrine, that which looked to long-term regularities, "evolutionary" trends, socioeconomic processes. Zionist and socialist strategy were here seen not as different in kind but as actually one and the same, an undifferentiated whole.

It is now the proletariat and its role in the class war that are described as the key factors in Jewish politics. "The first Russian Social Democrats," declared "Our Platform," "had the full right to say that the liberation of Russia would be won by the labor movement or not at all. That is what we say about territorialism – the liberation of the Jewish people will come about as a result of the labor movement or not at all."[77] Elsewhere in the same work, we read that "proletarian Zionism is possible only if its aims can be achieved through the class struggle."[78]

There were at least three apparent contradictions in the program of the ESDRP-PZ that Borochov set out to demonstrate were not contradictions at all, but part of an overarching logical conception rooted in reality. First, if the Jews, including the workers, were everywhere being forced out of the capitalist economy, what justification could there be for their participating in a revolution defined by the Social Democrats as "bourgeois"? What could they contribute to such a revolution and what could they possibly gain from it? Second, if, conversely, major political objectives were attainable in Russia – Jewish self-government (a Seim) was, after all, a demand of the ESDRP-PZ – then why did the Jews need a separate territory of their own? If the situation was potentially so good why was it so irredeemably bad? Third, how was it possible for the Jewish people to gain hold of a territory, as yet hardly settled, by means of class war?

In a pamphlet published late in 1904, the Minsk Poale Zion had in fact raised all these issues with a biting irony. A powerful revolutionary struggle, it declared, "can only be conducted by the healthy proletariat of a healthy nation with firm ground under its feet. And both elements are lacking in the Jewish people."[79] On the other hand, it was surely self-evident that "one could not be a good Zionist if one expected great things from the revolution in Russia."[80] Again, we read elsewhere in the same brochure, there had always been "historical materialists" in the Zionist movement but "it would never have occurred to them to conceive of Zionism as class war of all things. There can be no doubt that if the German Social Democrats had to fight alongside all the other classes in Germany for the unity of their country, they would not consider this a pure class struggle."[81]

Borochov had been in full agreement with these arguments of the Minsk Poale Zion in earlier years, as he had specifically stated at the time. Now he was on the other side of the fence. The "old-style Minsk Poale Zion," declared "Our Platform," "have nothing in common with a true proletarian ideology."[82] First, he insisted, although the situation of the Jewish proletariat was abnormal, that class still existed and would continue to exist in the lands of the Diaspora for the foreseeable future. The theories of nonproletarianization or nonindustrialization propagated by the SSRP and the Minsk Poale Zion distorted this reality and were false.

Where there was a proletariat there was ipso facto a class conflict, and it was the duty of the Social Democrats to organize that conflict, to lend it direction, leadership. "One must not take as the starting point," he wrote in a key passage, "the general future of the nation and deduce from this the future of the proletariat. On the contrary, one must take as the starting point the interests of the proletariat and from these reach the future of the people as a whole."[83]

Given this standpoint, it was natural enough that he paid generous tribute to the Bund, which had always advocated this same line of thought. Despite its many ideological errors, the Bund had

> accumulated enormous credit in work on behalf of the Jewish proletariat, and the name of the Bund is inscribed in golden letters in the history of the Jewish labor movement. The future generations of the Jewish proletariat will raise a fine memorial to it in Palestine. It developed the class consciousness of the Jewish workers, educated them to conduct an organized struggle in defence of their interests, tended the spirit of discipline within them and fostered their democratic ideas.[84]

In fact, he insisted, his party should recognize that it had its own genealogy leading back directly through the Bund.

> Zionism is not one but two movements: the development of bourgeois Zionism progresses from the Haskala via Hibat Zion and Ahad Ha-Am-ism to political [Herzlian] Zionism; while the development of proletarian Zionism

is quite independent, moving from primitive cosmopolitanism via Bundist autonomism and the territorialism of the SSRP to the realist territorialism of the Poale Zion.[85]

In 1905 Borochov, basing his theory on the analysis of the "general future of the nation," had written off Jewish involvement in the Russian revolution as a hopeless anachronism. Fated to exclusion from society, the Jews could not afford to squander energy in the fight for ephemeral political rights. Now, in 1906, making the class struggle his terminus a quo, he viewed this issue from a totally different perspective. The proletariat had to fight for any and every improvement in its position, however marginal or insecure that improvement might be. Where earlier he had placed exclusive emphasis on the uniqueness of the Jewish situation, he now insisted that the Jews should be seen as one battalion in the army of oppressed nationalities fighting for equal rights against the tsarist regime. The fact that the Jews are "dependent on the lives of those nations among which they dwell," he wrote in 1907, "is not exceptional. Neither the Polish nor Armenian proletariats could defend their specific national demands through their own strength alone without the aid of other elements . . . The difference [between the Jews and such nations] is not one of essence but of degree, basically one of quantity not quality."[86] It was incumbent on the party to make the boldest demands of the here and now in order not to forgo any possible improvement in the situation of the Jewish proletariat and in order not to neglect any chance to inspire revolutionary enthusiasm. So he now adopted the demand of the Vozrozhdentsy for a Jewish Seim (or "national political autonomy," as he termed it). Given the interest of all the oppressed nationalities in a reconstruction of the state, there was no intrinsic reason why such a Seim should not become a reality. Moreover, once in existence, the Seim might well be able to act in defense of Jewish interests at home and abroad, insisting, for instance, that Russia (following the example of the Western powers) extend protection to its Jewish citizens in Ottoman Palestine.

As against this, though, he insisted that the attitude of the Seimists – "the better, the better" – was in its own way as erroneous as that of the SSRP – "the worse, the better." Political advance, however superficially impressive, could not alter the underlying sociological realities, the forces steadily excluding the Jews from the economy and threatening their position in society. Democratization would make pogroms less common but could not put a final end to them. Even if a Jewish Seim were established, its effective powers would probably be severely limited and its future uncertain. "The Seimists," he wrote with great prescience,

> do not talk of the prior conditions that must mature before the attainment of national political autonomy . . . It is possible that in the hour of chaos, with the complete collapse of tsarism, in the period of preparing and convening the Constituent Assembly – as a result of a combination of convenient happenings – . . . autonomy for the Jewish people and for certain other national minorities might be won, . . . but the autonomy attained at such a time of revolution will be very short-lived.[87]

In selecting this middle path, Borochov was following the dictates of party interest, the necessity to mark off the new ESDRP-PZ from its more established rivals, from the pessimists (the SSRP) and the optimists (the Vozrozhdentsy) alike. But he was also giving genuine expression to the mounting ambiguity of much Jewish sentiment in the post-October days – a tenacious and even millennarian faith in the revolution combined with a nagging fear that perhaps the pogrom, vicious antisemitism, was after all endemic to Russia, ineradicable.

The linchpin in his new conceptual framework was the theory that the Jewish question would be solved primarily not by political action but by the workings of socioeconomic law. Reducing politics to a strictly secondary and auxiliary role, he had no difficulty in justifying his party's full-scale participation in the Russian revolution. True, the Jews could expect only marginal and insecure benefits from revolutionary victory. But this was not a futile diversion of forces, for territorialism in its early stages would be realized almost exclusively by sociological processes.

He thus reversed, stood on its head, his central thesis of 1905. So doing, he aligned himself in ideological method fully with the young Marxist theoreticians of the SSRP: Litvakov, Abrahami, Lvovich. Indeed, his territorial prognosis as presented in "Our Platform" must be seen as an elaboration on themes they had already defended at their Second Party Congress in March 1906. As a result, it was only natural that he too found himself crossing swords with the non-Marxist members of the SSRP leadership – Syrkin and Latsky – and that each side attacked the other's political philosophy in terms of unlimited scorn. Syrkin's comments on Borochov have been described above, and here it will suffice to quote from the latter's initial intervention in what was originally a strictly internal debate within the SSRP. "Many of the Zionist Socialists [SSRP]," wrote Borochov in response to the article of Latsky (Bertoldi) in *Der nayer veg*, no. 13,

> admit openly that they have no prognosis, that they cannot have one because they have no clear historical perspective and because such a perspective is impossible. Mr. Bertoldi . . . openly awards the SSRP a certificate of historical and social bankruptcy, is even proud of the fact that he has no prognosis; this absurd pride goes so far with Mr. Bertoldi that he even tries to accentuate the adventurism which impregnates so much of the SSRP ideology and makes a highly positive virtue of it.[88]

Nothing could be more erroneous, Borochov now wrote, than the belief that "it is possible to correct and cure a perversion within the sphere of economics by means of political institutions."[89] Again, nothing could be more utopian than socialist involvement in settlement projects such as those drawn up by Franz Oppenheimer – "as if a proletarian party could devote much attention to colonization programs."[90] Equally absurd was the importance assigned to the diplomatic sphere by the official Zionist and territorialist leaderships. "Diplomacy," he wrote, "is only of value where *everything* could be done without it. In such cases, [it] . . . eases the steady march of history."[91] In illustration of this latter point, he argued that

> the settlement of Algiers is not the result of the political rule of France in Algiers but, just the opposite, the need of the French farmer to emigrate because of the loss of his land . . . and the need of new French capital to broaden its national market forced France to conquer Algiers. Only the

bourgeoisie . . . makes a fetish of the state which, in fact, is nothing but a blind tool in the hands of undirected development.[92]

Where, in 1905, he had seen it as the task of the avant-garde to lay the groundwork for mass immigration to Palestine, he now argued that this function would be fulfilled by the natural flows of capital and labor. So long as the gates to the developed countries remained open, he wrote, "there is no basis for thinking in terms of the concentration of Jewish migration in one place [and] . . . territorialist colonization remains a mere idea."[93] But as soon as England, the United States, and South Africa restricted immigration, the Jews would have to move to an alternative destination. There was no possibility of their settling in the fast-developing agrarian countries such as Brazil or the Argentine, for they could not compete effectively as farmers with the peasant labor arriving from southern and eastern Europe.

The way of least resistance would lead to a semiagrarian country with an economy based on farming, an international transit trade, and agricultural exports. There alone could the Jews gain a foothold in the urban centers as merchants, factory owners, and industrial workers. "Other nationalities will not settle in Palestine because of its low political and cultural level."[94] "Only one country remains that can absorb the Jews – that is Palestine, where Jewish capital and the Jewish labor force are already, undirected, beginning to concentrate."[95] When in 1905 Borochov spoke of the "necessity" of Palestine as the Jewish territory, he was referring to an act of choice by a conscious minority; now the term referred to the predestined goal of History on its onward march.

The role of the Zionist movement in this process was a subordinate one, that of smoothing the path for full capitalist development. The kinds of tasks it could usefully undertake would be to establish scientific institutes to research the geographic and economic conditions prevailing in Palestine and information bureaus to disseminate the knowledge thus acquired. Insofar as the movement confined itself to this limited role, he argued in 1906–7, there was no reason why Poale Zion should not participate as a left-wing opposition in the Zionist congresses. At the same time, though, the world Poale Zion movement should also set up its own labor exchanges in Palestine, its own statistical bureaus, information offices, and labor funds. But it would be "a great error," he wrote, "to suggest that we call for emigration to Palestine. That . . . we leave to the natural [stikhiiny] process."[96]

In the last resort, he argued, the class war would bring about the establishment of the Jewish state (or "territorial autonomy") in Palestine. From the first, economic development would be accompanied by the struggle between capital and labor, between the bourgeoisie and the proletariat. "Even today," he noted with pride in "Our Platform,"

> a Jewish Social Democratic Labor Party is organized in Palestine. The Jewish proletariat (which at the moment is very small) has already entered into a bitter struggle with its employers . . . This year, already, the workers in Palestine celebrated the First of May and so entered the international family of the working class.[97]

As the Jewish population in Palestine grew, so the class war would take on ever more menacing proportions and force the Turkish state to intervene to restore order. What had started as a purely "economic" conflict would thus ignite "the national struggle of the Jewish population in Palestine (together with the local population) against the Turkish regime."[98] But the class difference would still remain.

> We have already learned the lesson of the Russian – and earlier – revolutions well enough. We know that in the Palestinian revolution to come we will have to fight on two fronts at the same time: against the Turkish bureaucracy and against the Jewish bourgeoisie. We will try to make the revolution that is democratic in kind, also democratic in results. We will fight for the complete and unlimited rule of the people in Palestine.[99]

Just as revolutionary victory in Russia, the establishment of a Seim, could aid the class struggle in Palestine, so political liberation there would redound to the benefit of the Jewish proletariat around the world, raise its class consciousness and militancy. Indeed, he concluded, there was no essential division between the policies to be pursued in the various countries where the Jewish proletariat was concentrated. All the constituent parties in the world union of the Poale Zion – which was founded in The Hague in the summer of 1907[100] – could thus be expected to pursue the same strategy, if not always the same tactics.

In all cases, "the only task of the Jewish S. D. Labor Party ... is to direct the class war."[101] In a capitalist society, "the proletariat cannot create anything because we are still not living in the period of the *socialist dictatorship of the proletariat*."[102] Capitalism, following its own laws of development, would construct the Jewish territory; the proletariat, pursuing its own interest, would win national independence for that territory. "Usually it is thought that much *money* is required to achieve territorial autonomy; ... that much will have to be *created*. But we say that much will have to be *liberated*."[103]

The volte-face

After-effects

The volte-face of late 1905 – from Palestinian pioneer recruit to revolutionary leader in Russia, from voluntarist to determinist, from advocate of the "plan" to theorist of the class war – was the central event in Borochov's early ideological development and cast its shadow over his subsequent political life. In the revolutionary and early postrevolutionary years, he was forced to polemicize against those of his party comrades who held to views which he himself had defended in 1905. Indeed, as he moved farther to the left, he even repudiated as nonproletarian some of the positions he had still advocated in 1906. Here again he clashed with some of his own followers, the most notable example being his demand of 1909 that all the Poale Zion parties henceforth withdraw from the Zionist congress and thus sever their last organizational links with bourgeois Zionism. In the subsequent period, in the immediate prewar years and even more during World War I, the reverse process took place. Shifting to the right, he had to attack the orthodoxy that went under his own name, Borochovism, and his self-proclaimed disciples, the *Borokhovtsy.*

At the Second Congress of ESDRP-PZ, which met in Cracow in August 1907, a major dispute developed between the leaders of the party in Poland led by Nahum Rafalkes (Nir) and the delegates from Russia, headed by Borochov. The Polish section (in which Yitshak Tabenkin and David Bloch were also prominent members) had long advocated what it called "principled" Zionism as against the "practical" and "prognostic" theories adopted by the Russian leadership. By "principled" Zionism they meant that Palestine (erets-yisrael) had a special hold on the Jewish people that differentiated it qualitatively – "in principle" – from any other potential territory. A Marxist could not ignore the fact that the Jews over a two-thousand-year period had been forced by economic marginality and political ostracism to develop a deep-rooted attachment to the idea of their own ancient homeland. To discuss Palestine in purely objective terms, simply as the most suitable semiagrarian country currently available, was absurd. The Polish group, Nir later recalled, condemned this approach of the Russian leadership as "not dialectical but metaphysical: the conditions required of a territory were analyzed ... [by the Brokhovtsy] in the context of the present time without making any analysis or inquiry into the historical aspect of the question."[104]

In 1905 Borochov had made precisely the same point with much force. But now he led the attack against the Polish position in the name of his theory of 1906. "Borochov spoke after me," Nir wrote,

> and with the full force of his erudition not only expounded prognostic Palestinism but also polemicized strongly against us, reducing us to nothing. He did so ... with scientific arguments in a comradely tone ... But Khashin ... spoke in bitter tones, with the sharpest polemical thrusts and deeply insulted us. We could not pass this over in silence and we announced that in protest we would not take any further part in the discussion.[105]

Borochov's role at the next, the Third, Congress of the party, which met in Kiev exactly ten years later (in August 1917) again involved a reversal of positions and was in every way highly dramatic. He arrived on the third day of the congress after his long journey from New York – a veritable obstacle course in that time of war and revolution. He entered the congress during the morning session. All the members on the platform rose to their feet and he was greeted by wild applause. The ovation lasted for many minutes. There were repeated shouts of "Long live Comrade Borochov, the founder of the party!" Bouquets showered down from the balcony and in no time, it was reported, "the platform looked like a veritable garden of flowers."[106] But the excitement of his entry was soon to be compounded by the statement of his views. Over the next few days, the delegates, in mounting bewilderment, heard him as he implicitly repudiated many of the central tenets of "Our Platform," the major source of orthodox Borochovism.

Point by point, he reverted to ideas he had defended in 1905. He came out powerfully against economic determinism. "I must remind you here of the words of the man of eternity, the leader of general Zionism [Herzl]: 'If you wish it, it shall be no dream.' "[107] He demanded that stress be put on the historical and emotional appeal of Palestine, not Palestina but Erets-yisroel: "Twelve years ago we were far removed from all romanticism, ornamentation, and decoration ... [But] now we feel the need for a new, a richer terminology. Now we can and must use the

Figure 20. Borochov with wife and child shortly before his death.

language of emotion also. Now we can and must say *erets yisroel – an eygenr heym* [our own homeland]."[108] He made an impassioned plea on behalf of the pioneers in Palestine, going beyond the concept of Ussishkin in 1904 and coming close to a full endorsement of Syrkin's socialist constructivism:

> Earlier we would always say that the process of Zionist fulfillment is an unconscious [*stikhish*] process. We had only to remove the obstacles from its path. And so we left all constructive work in the hands of the bourgeoisie . . . But the experience of work in Palestine [*erets yisroel*] has brought us to

Figure 21. Borochov's grave in the Kinneret cemetery. His remains were brought from Kiev with the permission of the Soviet authorities, 1963.

totally different ideas ... I am referring to the cooperative colonization in Palestine, in general, and that conducted according to Oppenheimer's system in particular ... We must begin constructive socialist work in Palestine.

Borochov was harshly attacked by those in the party leadership who for over ten years had seen themselves as his faithful disciples. However, a schism was averted at the congress, and it was not until 1920, some three years after his death, that the world Poale Zion movement split into two independent sections, the more pro-Comintern Left and the less pro-Comintern Right. In this and subsequent schisms in the socialist Zionist movement, the warring sides both drew on the canon of Borochov's works to buttress their positions.

It became standard practice on the left almost exclusively to reproduce, and rely on, "Our Platform" and the related works of 1906–7. This was true not only of the left Poale Zion in its various permutations but also of the Palestine Communist Party in its so-called "Yishuv" phase of the early and mid-1920s, and subsequently of Ha-Shomer Ha-Tsair in its Moscow-oriented years. In response, the right wing socialists tended to publish a greater range including (as in the volume brought out by Shazar) his works of 1905, and (as in the volume edited by Berl Locker) a selection of essays from the period of World War I.[109]

Perhaps the most interesting example of this esoteric battle of the texts was the issue of *Kuntres* (the Hebrew journal of the Ahdut Ha-Avodah party), edited by Berl Katznelson in 1927 on the anniversary of Borochov's death. In this collection of essays and translations, the Borochov of 1906–7 was all but totally ignored. Characteristically, the opening pieces were written by Syrkin (his speech on the occasion of Borochov's death) and by Shlomo Kaplansky – both men associated with a profound and lifelong opposition to the classical Borochovist ideology. Furthermore, long essays therein were devoted to Borochov's first article of 1902 and to his appearance at the Kiev party congress in 1917, two thoroughly "heterodox" chapters in his biography.[110] It is noteworthy, however, that even here, in the bastion of constructivist socialism, there was no explicit repudiation of "Our Platform," no outright analysis of the profound inner contradiction that characterized Borochov's ideological development.

Toward an explanation

Just how sharp a break Borochov made in his ideology in the winter of 1905–6 becomes even more apparent when one examines his first essay, published in 1902 in *The Zionist Almanach*. This study, "On the Character of the Jewish Mind," provides if not the key to Borochov's intellectual biography, then at least a number of crucial pieces in the jigsaw puzzle.

In this article (which was based on the lecture delivered in Ussishkin's home in 1900) he advanced the thesis that different nationalities possessed different modes of thought, that the mind of the nation found its overt expression in its men of genius, and that the Jewish people provided a striking example of this fact. The Jewish intellect, he argued, was inclined toward the most thoroughgoing, "absolute," forms of monism. This was a tendency running throughout the entire national history and could be observed alike in Biblical monotheism, in Philo and Maimonides, Spinoza and Solomon Maimon, Lazarus and Nordau, Ricardo and Marx.

The powerful predilection for "the ideal of total monism"[111] drove the Jewish thinker to work not empirically but subjectively, not building theory on fact but subordinating fact to abstract logic. The underlying inspiration was not scientific, the search for evidential truth, but social and ethical. Seeing others only as "variant expressions of his own self," the out-and-out monist was drawn naturally to altruism; to the imperative "Love your neighbor as yourself"; to an overriding concern with the practical consequences of theory and doctrine.[112] As a result, his concepts, based on deduction rather than induction and oriented toward practice rather than knowledge for its own sake, time and again exerted a powerful revolutionary effect. Against the world as it was, he set up a world based on logical principle.

The Jew, he wrote, is

> interested not so much in premises as in conclusions – that is the result of subjectivism . . . ; as his interest in consequences utterly overshadows his interest in proofs, he regards the latter either as a necessary evil or as an agile form of mental gymnastics. That is why the complex argument of the Jew always creates the impression of something terribly complicated, finely dialectical, something scholastic and even sophistical. [His] proofs do not con-

vince but trap . . . He prefers a roundabout argument carried ad absurdum to a direct proof; a play on words to a reconciliation of facts. Something rather strange results; arguments begin ab ovo in arbitrary logic, are conducted in the most abstract way, albeit with a mathematical precision, and in their content overpower and intimidate rather than convince – and yet the conclusion, like some sudden revelation, amazes one with its deep vital truth and enthusiastic conviction. I am sure that not one outstanding Jew ever arrived at his discoveries by ways ever resembling the method allegedly used to reach them.[113]

One consequence of this mode of thought, he suggested – quite inaccurately it can now be seen – was the fact that Jews never showed outstanding talent in spheres demanding respect for the objective world, such as the natural sciences and the plastic arts, while because of their subjective bent, they often excelled as lyric poets and musicians.

Nowhere in the article does Borochov define clearly his own attitude to the Jewish mind as thus depicted, and this has left the way open to differing historical interpretations. Matityahu Mintz believes that in this essay Borochov defined, as it were, his own predilections, his own ambition to take his place in a great tradition of radical thought stretching back through Marx and Spinoza into the distant national path.[114] Tabori emphasized, rather, the element of unconscious revelation involved. "We find in this article," he wrote in Kuntres, "a remarkable symmetry between the author himself and the psychology of the Jewish mind as he describes it to us."[115] And Shazar presented still a third interpretation, seeing the article as a strong condemnation of the Jewish role in the Diaspora, of the pathological effects resulting from chronic alienation and rootlessness.[116]

Each of these three interpretations reflects, in all probability, an aspect of the truth.[117] Borochov was no doubt powerfully attracted to what he called "total" or "abstract" monism, and, as Mintz and Tabori suggest, he here described a mode of thought which he himself would later adopt. But surely Shazar was also correct in his view that, at this stage in his life, he had ended up by rejecting the monistic mode of thought. What we witness here was the outcome of an inner drama, in which Borochov had weighed the possibility of adopting a strictly schematic and reductionist philosophy, only to reject it as intellectually arbitrary or even dishonest.

In the years 1902–5, he saw himself as committed both to the "historical materialism" of Marx and to the strict, natural scientific empiricism of Avenarius, with the one constantly confronting, modifying, and balancing the other. His essay of 1902, while granting a legitimacy to all categories of thought ranging from monism to pluralism, clearly suggests a preference for dualism. "An objective view of things," he thus wrote, "is dualistic at very root, for it contrasts subject to object, seeking to understand the object per se, unrelated to the subject."[118] As against this, he espied a quasi-religious, "fetishist," and illegitimate element in Marx's reductionism. "In every thesis of Marx," he contended, "is to be felt a mystical obeisance before the inner strength of the developmental process of the productive relations and of the class struggle – and likewise a contempt for everything else."[119] In his unpublished notes (examined with enormous care by Matityahu Mintz),[120] the same trend of thought revealed itself. He rejected Bogdanov's assertion that monism is ipso facto preferable to dualism; argued that "idealism is now more courageous than materialism and positivism";[121] and condemned what he called the "Marxist religion."[122]

Likewise, the dualist approach (as noted above) provided the ideological under-pinning for his major work of 1905, "On the Question of Zion and a Territory." He there spoke of the "psychological soil" and the "material subsoil" as two indepen-dent (although historically related) spheres; of a dual foundation for the movement, the one base being "shared suffering" the other "shared joy"; and of a "historical necessity [that] for us is conditional—the condition being that we ourselves become active."[123] "One-sided enthusiasms," he wrote there, "are more dangerous than is many-sided realism."[124] Or, as he put it elsewhere in the same work: "Zionism . . . cannot and must not be grounded one-sidedly . . . The theory must take into account both the needs of the people and the aspirations of the avant-garde elements . . . One should not . . . *simplify* the question instead of *solving* it."[125]

What these facts suggest is that in the winter of 1905–6, Borochov not only changed his political strategy and tactics but, even more remarkably, suddenly abandoned the philosophical position he had tenaciously held throughout his adult years. He now adopted that "absolute" monism which he had consciously rejected as unempirical, as subjectivity masquerading in the form of objectivity, and even (if we grant the validity of Shazar's insight) as the pathological manifestation of the Jewish mind warped by exile. His interpretation of historical development in terms of the one factor, economics, and his equally relentless reduction of all politics to a single form—the class war—thus involved a deliberate decision on his part to repudiate an entire weltanschauung. What prompted him to take this step?

The answer most frequently provided by party histories argues that the Boro-chov of 1906 was the product of a gradual evolutionary process. His growing contacts with the Jewish proletariat, first in Ekaterinoslav and then during his tour in the winter of 1904–5, brought him to a new view of the Jewish question, with the emphasis shifting from organized emigration to mass organization on the spot; from Hebrew (and Russian) to Yiddish; from southern Russia to Lithuania and the northwest. In his biography of Borochov (published in Warsaw in 1926), Zeruba-vel made this case as follows:

> Looked at from the outside, it can even seem strange that the same author wrote two such very different articles one after the other. It is enough to look somewhat deeper, however, to discern an entirely logical evolution from his earlier ideas. At the beginning there was only theory. Jewish life was lacking. But Jewish life, in all its naked harshness, intervened and initially negated the theory totally. A strenuous intellectual effort was required to adapt theory to life.[126]

Or, as he put it elsewhere: "In his journeys over the Pale, he met the great Jewish proletarian masses; here, too, he met the Bund and the theoreticians and activists of the Poale Zion. He underwent a long reevaluation of all values until there was gradually worked out his conception of Poale Zionism."[127]

This thesis, while reflecting the preconceptions underlying much Social Demo-cratic historiography, was not in accord with the facts. Borochov left Ekaterinoslav in 1902 as a general Zionist. He ended his tours of the Pale of Settlement in 1904–5 as much a follower of Ussishkin and disciple of "Our Program" as he had begun it. He spent the summer and autumn of 1905 not in the Pale of Settlement but in Switzerland and Germany, where he intended (as Matityahu Mintz has argued persuasively)[128] to spend a long period in further study. The decisions to return to Russia in late October and to lead the pro-Palestine Poale Zion on a new path speak not of an evolutionary process but of a sudden decision, a clean break with the past.

Even so, however, there remain two additional and alternative ways of explaining Borochov's change of front, both of which can be supported by the known facts. It is possible, first, to interpret it in terms of utilitarian political calculation. The tide of revolution was running so strong in the latter half of 1905 that it threatened to sweep away all the hard-won bastions established over more than two decades by the Russian Zionist (and proto-Zionist) movement. Those who retained their traditional loyalty to Palestine often decided that they had no choice but to modify their public stance radically in order to gain a hearing. Jabotinsky and Idelson were outstanding examples of this trend, which resulted eventually in the Helsingfors Program of December 1906.

Seen against this background, it is quite plausible to argue (as does Mintz, for example)[129] that Borochov reformulated his ideology in order to save the pro-Palestine remnant of Poale Zion from political extinction. The fact that the one central theme running throughout Borochov's entire life was his devotion to the Palestinian cause lends great weight to this thesis. As a schoolboy (once at the age of nine or ten and again in his early teens), he twice ran away from home to try to make his own way to the ancestral homeland.[130] A letter he sent to friends in Palestine in 1897 asked about agricultural conditions in that country. "This request may surprise you," he went on, "but it is easily explained by the fact that at the moment I want to settle in Palestine and am studying agronomy, particularly Palestinian . . . Please write about the state of the Jewish colonies. Describe Jerusalem and the attitude of the population to the Jews."[131] His commitment did not waver even during the Russian revolutions of 1905 and 1917. What was it, Shazar has asked, that produced

> this zealous loyalty to Zion? He never saw the country and did not drink from the wells of the Hebrew language . . . Was it the Hibat Zion atmosphere in his father's house? Or his flight from home as a child . . . ? Or the influence of the Ussishkin-Levin atmosphere in Ekaterinoslav? Or a deep realization that a popular liberation movement cannot be diverted . . . from the path marked out by the will of generations and historical fate?[132]

However we answer these questions, the fact itself is beyond doubt. As a *Palestinets*, Borochov could have felt that it was his duty to develop a new ideology fashioned to meet the demands of the revolutionary youth, the mass meetings. He himself, speaking at the Third Congress of the party in 1917, suggested that this had been a primary factor: "The fear of what others will say does not intimidate us any more . . . [But] twelve years ago . . . we fought on two fronts: against both the Bund and the general Zionists. And in order not to be misinterpreted and deserted we had to be extraordinarily careful in our terminology."[133] Syrkin (also writing in 1917) offered this same explanation, describing Borochov's determinist theory of

1906 as "the price paid to the ruling socialist ideology, particularly the Bund . . . In the ideological atmosphere dominant at that time, this system of Borochov was of great value to Poale Zionism."[134]

There is no doubt that the young *Palestintsy* in the Poale Zion were in urgent need of a theory that would justify Zionism in strictly Marxist terms and explain how it could be united with revolutionary activism. Even in memoirs written many years later, the relief and enthusiasm produced by Borochov's new message can be tangibly felt. Rahel Yanait (Ben Zvi) has explained the attraction of his "prognostic" theory in these terms:

> Borochov's doctrine strengthened the faith in our path: not just a blind faith, not some passive idea based on sentimental feelings for the distant past, but a necessity rooted in life . . . We believed that the masses of people would go to Palestine and we saw it as the task of the Party to work within this "elemental [*stikhi*] process," to accelerate and direct it.[135]

"Every page [of 'Our Platform']," recalled Zerubavel,

> was a revelation from on high [*gilui ha-shekhina*] of the proletarian creative spirit that brings light into the dark corners of the mind . . . It was not an abstract academic study but a Jewish proletarian fighting manifesto that set forth the iron laws governing the development of Jewish reality which proved the historical necessity of the elemental [*stikhish*] process, . . . and indicated a clear battle strategy for the Jewish proletariat.[136]

Throughout the winter of 1905–6 and even beyond, Borochov remained in touch with Ussishkin. This fact lends the greatest weight to the belief that his new doctrine was more a question of tactics than conviction. Certainly, this was the contention of the rival wing in the strife-ridden Poale Zion movement, the Vozrozhdentsy. Their propagandists argued, according to one report of early 1906, that "all the organizations have adopted Seimism apart from a certain 'B' around whom 500 members are grouped; that 'B' is an insignificant character, a petty bourgeois Zionist, and he has been bought by Ussishkin."[137] In a letter of February 1906, Borochov himself wrote of the constant accusations that "I am selling the proletariat to the bourgeoisie for money."[138]

The truth is that Borochov did frequently turn to Ussishkin with requests for the funds necessary to establish the new ESDRP-PZ and its party press. Without money from the general Zionist Organisation, he insisted, all his plans for the new pro-Palestinian party would be stillborn. "One can [in that case] forget about proletarian *Zionism* for a long time . . . ," he wrote to Ussishkin on the eve of the foundation congress in February.

> All that will remain are a few steadfast *teoretiki* and, no doubt, the Poltava region. I will then throw over all work and wait until a new Poale Zionism is reborn. In such a complicated time as the present revolution, those who are of a Palestine or, generally, of an anti-galut inclination can only carry on when there is literature, organization, and systematic agitation. Certainly the Zionist functionaries may not understand this, but you of course know that this is an important cause . . . As for Palestine, you know me well: in general,

to the extent that I take things upon myself and carry them through, it is in order, as far as within me lies, to contribute to the rebirth of the Jewish people in Palestine.[139]

In this context, it should also be recalled that, at this stage (1906–7), Borochov still advocated the participation of the Poale Zion in the world Zionist congress, a stand he himself repudiated in later years as inconsistent with a militant class war ideology.

There is, however, an alternative explanation of the volte-face. Evidence is available to suggest that we are faced here not by a political manoeuver, a brilliant holding action, but by a sudden reevaluation analogous to a religious conversion. Borochov was able to persuade others with such success because he had earlier convinced himself.

The fact that he was forced to stand by idly in Berlin at the time of the October strikes and the terrible pogroms could well have had a traumatic effect upon him. Certainly, when the news arrived, he and his group of friends in Berlin decided at once to hasten back to Russia, delaying only long enough to collect some money for the purchase of arms. Rahel Yanait (Ben Zvi) has described how, arriving in Russia, they found their comrades who had lived through the pogroms in a state of shock. "Terrible shame and deep self-accusation looked out of the eyes of all the youth in Kiev . . . We were in mourning and ashamed."[140]

Reaching Russia at such a moment, Borochov probably felt that he had been guilty of a tragic mistake. How had he permitted himself to place exclusive emphasis on the exodus – still so far away – and to urge a Zionist boycott of the revolutionary movement in Russia? Had he not revealed an unforgivable arrogance in adopting the elitist strategy of the pioneer avant-garde at a time when the Jewish proletariat in Russia was fighting for its rights and being cut down by the Cossacks? Was there not something repellent in his stubborn allegiance to the individualist philosophy of critical empiricism with its emphasis on scientific detachment, on individual judgment, on the alienation of the observer from the observed, the subject from the object, the psychological from the sociological?

The factual evidence supporting this explanation is to be found both in the philosophical study that Borochov wrote while in Liège in 1908 and in the letters that, likewise in the immediate postrevolutionary period, he sent to his parents and to Lunacharsky. The essay was rejected in 1908 by the Russian Marxist journal to which he had sent it, but in 1920 it was published in Moscow in book form under the title *Virtualism and the Religious-Ethical Problem in Marxism*. (It came out with an introduction by L. Berlinraut, a veteran leader of the Poale Zion party, which, in various quasi-Communist and "Borochovist" reincarnations, was to remain legal in the Soviet Union until 1928.)[141]

In this essay – which took issue with Lunacharsky's recent book, *Religion and Socialism*[142] – Borochov laid forth his own philosophy as he had reformulated it during the revolution. He there describes his final repudiation of empirio-criticism and his total identification with the proletariat in revelationary terms. In the late 1890s, he wrote, while still at high school, he had studied the theory of Avenarius and become an enthusiastic disciple. He described this and his subsequent mental development in the third person:

He [the author, Borochov] still remembers, as if today, the radical revolution called forth by his [Avenarius's] booklet in his feeling for the world: everything suddenly appeared extraordinarily clear and straightforward... he suddenly felt that in the world there are no "causes," "forces," "matter," "spirit"... that all these are a series of constantly changing processes. And the total cleansing of experience filled him with joy, released him... The provincial youth remained enthralled by this doctrine... until he became immersed in the seething cauldron of the class, national and party disputes... But [even then], for a long time, the sensationalist, purely descriptive – no, purely observant – strata of empirico-criticism resisted the pressure of labor and struggle. But finally, in the bright, red light... of the revolutionary conflagration, of class hatred, there developed before his eyes another, infinitely holding, deeply stirring, theory... The last sensationalist strata were swept away by the waves of social conflict... Life appeared in all the greatness of its terrible conflicts, the world again became heavy, again pressing. Resistance, struggle, tension, violence again took up their previous position... Drawing close to the working class the author became a Marxist, a virtualist.[143]

The empirio-critical approach to reality – as a form of sensationalist psychology – was incapable, he was now convinced, of overcoming the "dualism" dividing the "psychic" from the "physical," the "solipsistic" observer from the "thing in itself."[144] It was doomed to passivity: "it does not act, but only reacts to external stimulations."[145] It could not escape the realm of "pure experience" and was unable to bridge the gap between the "is" and the "ought."

Marxism was the highest form of "virtualism" because it constituted an integral element in the struggle of the mass, the proletariat, for its future, and the future of mankind. Nietzsche, although a "virtualist," had not gone beyond a strict individualism and his "split personality" in fact reflected the "division in society," the class barriers.[146] In the proletariat, Borochov wrote, "no room remains for the self-division of the healthy personality, for impotent worship. Out of the fragmentary particles of the past, a new man is being formed."[147] "The enthusiasm of the proletariat," he stated again, "is totally unlike that of romantically inclined individuals... [In it] there is none of the inhibiting activity of the cortical centers of the brain."[148] Only the proletariat was able "to reconcile life with the ideal... It posits miserable reality and the shining future in the limits of one unbroken *historic perspective*."[149] It alone was able "to flood the daily prose of life with the light of the final ideal."[150]

Throughout the work, this indeed was the central theme. The individual could not attain to a meaningful existence unless he merged himself with the class of the future, unless he threw himself into its battle. Active participation in the class war was itself the overriding bridge that would surmount the dichotomies of philosophic doubt: the "is" and the "ought," mind and matter, subject and object. True, an act of faith was demanded to discern within the proletariat the "new man" in the making, to see in the class war the matrix of a future society infinitely superior to that now existing. But life advanced through action, action demanded belief, and therefore belief was justified by life. Faith in the proletariat, however, was "scientific" rather than "religious." Predicting the socialist revolution was not as sure as predicting the eclipse of the moon, but it was still a supposition based on reasoned premises.

> Scientific faith does not pay attention to doubts because it finds them unfruitful ... Scientific faith willingly admits that it is not based on total proof ... but it also knows that it is irrefutable; it works in the sphere of probabilities. It prefers, above all, the maximal degree of probability, but makes do with a lower level if the higher is not attainable ... Scientific faith, faith in the historical prognosis ... is a theoretical gamble and the daring of such a gamble does not demand guarantees[151] ... We do not qualify ourselves with a cautious "perhaps" – we gamble with our prognosis and therefore place our entire life and all its meaning on that card.[152]

In these words – and in this work as a whole – Borochov was surely explaining, justifying, to himself his decision late in 1905 to abandon dualistic doubt, voluntarism, elitism, and to plunge into a monistic ideology of class war, economic determinism, and proletarian internationalism.

It could perhaps be argued that as a document meant for publication in a Russian Marxist journal this article does not necessarily present a complete picture of Borochov's true sentiments. But here the letters addressed to his parents in the immediate postrevolutionary period provided a further insight. In these letters which (inter alia) described the situation of the young couple in exile – penniless, grasping at ephemeral plans and false hopes, driven by circumstance to the edge of despair – Borochov set forth his inner thoughts as nowhere else. What we glimpse here is a man who has won through to a faith, a credo, and who is not prepared to surrender it without a struggle. He can no longer see the world simply in terms of the Jewish exodus from the Diaspora; he has gone beyond the ideas of the founding generation of Hibat Zion, of Ussishkin and of his own father; and even the failure of the revolution will not bring him back to the philosophy of his earlier years. "We lowly people," he wrote from Liège on 9 January 1909,

> can only *fight* politically, socially, economically, when the life of the society about us is boiling over – but we [must] *dream* when a deadly silence reigns around us. I dream of justifying the hopes placed in me by my parents, my friends, my comrades – to write that of which I would have been capable under satisfactory conditions ... But there will be ... no books. I will not write my books. I will not liberate the comrades from jail, from forced labor, from penal exile and the death sentence. I will not save my parents from worry; I will do nothing; and I will die not having achieved that for which you brought me up and for which my comrades, with their last strength, are supporting me. And all this – because we are proletarians. And therein lies my comfort.
>
> Yes, dear father, our misery is caused not only by the Jewish Diaspora, but also by the ugly chaos of capitalism. And if we are persecuted by exclusionary laws, antisemitism, pogroms; if we curse the Diaspora and welcome the emergent realization of Zionism, still it is with no less force that we give our blessings to socialism.

Not only you and I are gifted. I have seen and looked about me and I am convinced that with the exception of a very few, unfortunate halfwits, cretins, all so-called normal people, *all, all,* are gifted . . . But from all of us poor people nothing has come and nothing will come. But I find comfort in this—what you and I have not managed to achieve, others will do, others who are more fortunate—contemporaries or our descendents.

Every cause has its time . . . and does it make any difference *who* carries it through, I or somebody else? Yet, although all this gives me the consolation of history, it leaves the personal pain untouched. And here . . . words are powerless and reasoning impotent . . .

[When it comes to publishing] my Zionism is a drawback in the eyes of the socialists and my Marxism in the eyes of the bourgeois Zionists. And, besides, I have no particular desire to turn to the bourgeois Zionists. Here, dear father, you have a clear proof of how even an "educated" man can die of hunger, or commit suicide, or go mad without overcoming the obstacles erected by the chaotic methods of capitalism . . . All this says clearly and unmistakably: "Down with capitalism!" And in that cry lies my consolation, my hope, and the source of my courage. Do not think that *I have sunk into despair,* my dear ones. No, I shall always find ways—as much as in my strength lies—to inflict damage on capitalism.[153]

Conclusion

Because of his long association in the public mind with Borochovism—the principles laid down in "Our Platform" of 1906—Borochov has usually been regarded as something of a monolithic figure. In fact, he was a man struggling in a sea of doubt and grasping for the firm rock of faith. In 1904 he believed that he had found the rock in Ussishkin's plan for an avant-garde of Palestine pioneers. In the winter of 1905–6 he produced an alternative form of Palestinianism based exclusively on the proletarian class struggle, an immersion in the here and now, on the revolutionary moment. His contemporary articles and letters thus reflect the ideological quest of so many in his generation of politically minded Russian Jews. Eager to join, but suspicious of, the revolution; tied by a shared fate and populist sentiment to their own people and yet drawn to universal truths and universal solutions—these young men and women seized on Marxist determinism in order to reconcile that which had appeared irreconcilable.

III

Ideology and émigré realities

An extraordinarily high percentage, perhaps a majority, of those involved in the Jewish revolutionary parties left Russia in the years 1903–14. As a result, labor parties and ideologies that had formed themselves in the Pale of Settlement now developed strong offshoots overseas. There, subject to radically alien conditions, they underwent a process of constant mutation, while nonetheless retaining much of their original group identity. Thus, where in Part Two, the revolutionary experience was a culmination, here it is a starting point.

In many important ways, the problems facing the graduates of 1905 in Palestine and in America were analogous. In both countries, the newcomers faced institutions established and dominated by the political generation of the 1880's. Thus, in Palestine the national bank, the Hebrew press, Zionist functions and influence were largely concentrated in the hands of such men as Levontin, Ben Yehuda, Dizengof, Ha-Cohen, and Khisin. In America the labor organizations were likewise controlled by veterans, by Cahan, Weinstein, and Pine.

The new arrivals brought with them a faith in the party politics that they had experienced in Russia. They believed in centralization and discipline, doctrinal unity and orthodoxy. Many (mostly in the United States) were committed Marxists, advocates of a strict class war doctrine. They looked askance at the institutions controlled by the previous generation and were determined to purify them. In both countries alike, the natural result was generational confrontation and conflict.

At the same time, though, the Palestinian and American experience diverged radically. It could not be otherwise given the miniscule size of the parties in Palestine and the mass scale of the burgeoning immigrant organizations in America. In the United States, the labor movement offered the individual leader the chance to rise rapidly and far, but the generation found itself hemmed in politically. (This same irony, albeit in far harsher, tragic form, faced the Jewish socialists in the emerging Soviet state after 1917.)

In Palestine, the situation ultimately proved to be the reverse. The youth of 1905 fell back on itself, creating its own miniature politics, culture, and even economy. What follows is thus, inter alia, a study in the paradoxical political advantages of smallness and backwardness.

CHAPTER 8

The revolutionary ethos in transition

Russian-Jewish youth in Palestine, 1904–1914

The radical and left-wing Zionist youth who emigrated from the Russian Empire in the years 1904–14 played a decisive role in the history of Jewish settlement and politics in Palestine. It is improbable that a Jewish state could have been created without their intrusion into the Yishuv.

By 1914, they had arrived at a new strategy for Jewish settlement based on collective and smallholding models,[1] which enabled the kibbutz and moshav movements to burgeon into dominance in the interwar period. They had created the two labor parties, which, following their unification in 1930 as Mapai, attained political supremacy in the Yishuv, the World Zionist Organization, and subsequently in the State of Israel.

Before World War I, again, they had established the two agricultural labor unions, one in the south (Judea) and one in the north (Galilee), that were the prototypes of the Histadrut. The Histadrut (the General Jewish Labor Federation in Palestine) was founded in 1920 and soon came to fulfill an ubiquitous role in the economy of the Yishuv, uniting under one umbrella the functions, inter alia, of a trade union, a consumer cooperative, a producer cooperative, and a health insurance movement. Yet another venture of the youth in the prewar decade was the creation of a society of armed watchmen (Ha-Shomer) that was the forerunner of the Hagana – the defense organization of the Histadrut and, in effect, the unofficial army of Palestinian Jewry in the period of the British Mandate. Further, with their two party weeklies they had raised political and literary journalism in the Yishuv to a remarkably high level, rendering it a powerful source of inspiration and influence alike.

This eruption of political creativity in Palestine was of course directly linked to the disruption of Jewish life in Russia in the years 1903–8, the period of the revolution and the pogroms. The Second Aliya (immigration) was just as much the product of a deep crisis in Russian Jewry as the First Aliya, set in motion by the pogroms of 1881.

What made possible this intense political improvisation? Quantity clearly was not among the causes at work here. While close to 1,000,000 Jews left the Russian Empire for the United States alone in the decade before World War I, a mere 20,000–30,000 settled in Palestine,[2] and that is far from the whole story. No more than a third or perhaps a quarter of this number can be classified as youth. The majority were older people driven by traditional religious motives to come to the Holy Land. In many cases, indeed, the aim was not so much to live in the country as to ensure that one died and was buried there.

However, more remarkable than the low number of those coming was the huge percentage of the youth who left during the decade of the Second Aliya. On one occasion, Ben Gurion asserted that no more than 10 percent had remained in the country.[3] A survey made at Jaffa for the year 1912 produced the information that (the Yemenites apart) some 750 prospective immigrants under thirty had entered the country through that port while almost exactly the same number had left.[4]

Throughout the period, the press reported a more or less constant range of figures, 500–1,500 youngsters from the Russian Empire who were working on the land or in town. As this number was largely made up of a floating population it follows, however extraordinary the fact may seem, that the more or less permanent force of labor youth – the group considered synonymous in popular parlance with the "Second Aliya" – was no more than a few hundred strong.

The strengths of this group were thus exclusively qualitative. But here the most obvious hypotheses turn out to be the least relevant. In contrast to the Bolsheviks or the Narodovoltsy, the immigrant youth in Palestine did not succeed in creating strong organizations with a high degree of internal unity. The attempts made to do so, Ha-Shomer (The Watchman) and Legion Ha-Avoda (The Labor Legion), were in the one case partially and in the other totally unsuccessful. Indiscipline, individualism, and downright anarchy were the norm. None of the organizations created by the youth looked the least sound or permanent in 1914. On the contrary, it was widely feared that they might wither away in a few years.

Equally conspicuous by its absence was another motif much valued by the Russian Social Democrats and revolutionaries in general: ideological consistency. The history of the labor movement in Palestine during these years was, in fact, a history of the reevaluation of values, of ideological renewal and self-repudiation.

Nor, it turns out, should one seek a unique bravery in this generation of immigrants. Of course, they went hungry, came down with malaria, died anonymous deaths, in some cases were shot in feuds with neighboring Arabs. But they were rarely called upon to show the dogged tenacity in the face of disease, penury, and mass death demonstrated, in turn, by the middle-aged and deeply religious Roumanian Jews who came with their families to Zikhron Yaakov in 1882, by the Russian Jews who settled in malaria-infested Hadera in 1891, or by the Yemenite Jews who came to live in the colonies in the years 1908–12.

Ultimately, we are dealing here with a phenomenon best explained by a rather less tangible factor. The hard core within the immigrant youth, perhaps no more than two or three hundred, were charged to an exceptional degree with political energy – an energy drawing its force from the Russian revolutionary experience, on the one hand, and from Jewish messianism, on the other. The revolution had provided them, first, with a heightened belief in themselves, the youth, as the natural source of political leadership. Increasingly, in the period between the Kishinev pogrom and the assembly of the First Duma, the very young (as noted above) had come to dominate Jewish politics in the Pale of Settlement. Those who had grown up in those tumultuous times took for granted that not only the future but also the present belonged to the youth. Second, they brought with them from this contact with the revolution and with radical thought in Russia generally a sharp-cutting critical spirit, a profound urge to negate the existent, to damn every compromise or hypocrisy, every tradition as an obstacle to freedom and every sign of comfort as bourgeois.

Finally, they came committed to the conduct of ideological politics as such politics had been developed by two generations of the intelligentsia in Russia. The present had to be subjected to a total socioeconomic critique, the future sketched out in bold lines centered on an ultimate goal, and a strategy and organization developed to ensure the transition from the one sphere to the other, from the kingdom of necessity to the kingdom of freedom.

But if the revolutionary ethos shaped the political attitudes of the youth, it was specifically nationalism, the urge to national liberation, that kept the small pioneer group in Palestine despite the failure of their original plans, the apparent hopelessness of their situation and the harsh hostility of the environment (both physical and human). They were an anticlerical, often atheist generation, but their vision of the world remained largely messianic – shaped by the heder and yeshiva, by their Hasidic upbringing or by their deeply emotional involvement with Herzl as the harbinger of the long-awaited Redemption, the End of Days. Thus, the negation of the existent inculcated by the revolutionary experience was reinforced by the traditional belief that the galut (Exile) was a merely transient phenomenon to be terminated at the moment that the Jews had proved themselves worthy of the coming of the Messiah.

Those of the immigrant youth whose attachment to Zionism was rooted in socio-revolutionary concepts alone without the admixture of national myth rarely stayed in the country for more than a short time. A survey conducted in the 1930s revealed that about a third of the immigrant men had studied in a yeshiva or at least a heder and that over half had an excellent knowledge of Hebrew on arrival.[5] Almost 13 percent had been sons of rabbis, cantors, or other religious administrants[6] (as against an insignificant percentage of the total Jewish population). All this, of course, calls to mind Aron Liberman's thesis that the yeshiva would provide excellent ground for the recruitment of radical political activists. The *poluintelligentsiia* came into its own in the Second Aliya.

At this point it must be asked how the youth who went from Russia to Palestine in 1904–14 differed from their forerunners of the 1880s. In fact, a close parallelism marked their initial experience in the country, but the circumstances were radically different. Many in the Second Aliya saw themselves as heirs to the Bilu and some had even belonged to the New Bilu organization in Russia. But the youth who went to Palestine in the 1880s had been rapidly depoliticized, leaving the country (as in the case of Mints), driven out of the colonies by the Rothschild officials (as in the case of Belkind), or forced into a high degree of conformity in order to obtain at least minimal goals (as in the case of the Gedera settlers). The youth who arrived after 1905 entered established agricultural colonies, came in larger numbers and with much greater political experience. Taken together, these factors permitted them to preserve, even to sharpen, a militantly oppositional and hostile stance toward the established Yishuv, and often to the Jewish world in general.

The few hundred youngsters who now formed the kernel of the labor movement were by no means a homogeneous group but they had, after all, grown up under the impact of the same traumatic and dramatic episodes – the emergence of Herzl, the Kishinev pogrom, the Uganda crisis, the self-defense movement, the rising wave of revolutionary activity and (for most) the 1905 revolution. To a remarkable extent, those who were to play a key part in the movement in Palestine tended to be close in age, very young (in their teens or early twenties in 1905) and yet to have gained a political apprenticeship while still in Russia (often as second-rank or local leaders).

Yosef Busel (the moving spirit in the first communal farm, Deganya), was born into a Hasidic family in a shtetl in Minsk province in 1891, studied in the Slutsk yeshiva, had been a member of the New Bilu in Russia, and went to Palestine late in 1907.[7] Yitshak Ben Zvi (Shimshelevich) was born in Poltava in 1884, had been active since 1904 in Poale Zion, was a member of its central committee from 1906, went to Palestine in 1907, and would eventually end up as the second president of Israel. Yosef Barats, another founder of Deganya, was born in a shtetl in Podolia of a Hasidic family, studied in a heder, joined Zeire Zion in Kishinev, and went to Palestine in 1907. David Ben Gurion (Grin) was born in Plonsk in 1886 into a family of Hoveve Zion, received an excellent Hebrew education, was a leading agitator and organizer for Poale Zion in Poland during the 1905 revolution, arrived in Palestine in 1906, and was one day to become Israel's first prime minister.

Yisrael Giladi (Butelbroit), a key member of Ha-Shomer, was born in a shtetl in Bessarabia in 1886, was active in the organization of Jewish self-defense in Russia, and went to Palestine in 1905. Avraham Hartsfeld was born in 1888 in a shtetl in the Ukraine, studied in a yeshiva in Berdichev, was active in the Zionist Socialist Labor Party (the SSRP) in 1906, was sentenced to penal labor, escaped from Siberia following the Lena Goldfield uprising in 1912, reached Palestine in 1914, and rapidly became a dominant figure in labor settlement policy. Aleksandr Zaid was born in Siberia in 1886 (of a Subbotnik mother), moved to Vilna in his teens, joined Poale Zion there, went to Palestine in 1904, and was among the founders of Ha-Shomer. Yaakov Zerubavel was born into a Hasidic family in Poltava in 1886, became a member of the Poale Zion central committee in Russia, was imprisoned, went to Palestine in 1909 where he joined the editorial board of the party paper, *Ha-ahdut,* and after World War I became a leader of the Left, pro-Comintern, wing of Poale Zion in Poland.

Haya Sara Khenkin was born in 1886 in Homel, worked as a seamstress, joined the Bund at age fourteen, left it in 1902 for Poale Zion, was involved (together with her future husband, Yehezkel Khenkin) in the self-defense organization there, and together they went to Palestine late in 1903 following the notorious pogrom in the city. Yehezkel Khenkin was among the founders of Ha-Shomer. Yitshak Tabenkin was born in Bobruisk in 1887, was a member of the central committee of Poale Zion in Poland during the 1905 revolution, went to Palestine in 1910, and became a central figure in the kibbutz movement and labor politics until his death in 1974. Nahum Tversky was born in 1884 in a shtetl in the Ukraine of a Hasidic family, became a leading member of the Zeire Zion and Ha-Tehiya groups in Kishinev, went to Palestine in 1905, and became a well-known worker in the party press. Berl Katznelson was born in Bobruisk in 1887, studied in a heder, joined the SSRP during the 1905 revolution, and came to Palestine in 1909 where he soon became a labor leader; in later years he was recognized as the major ideologist of Mapai.

Of course, not everybody fitted this pattern. A. D. Gordon, perhaps the most striking personality in the labor movement as it had developed by 1914, was born in 1856. Yosef Aharonovich, the major spokesman of the Ha-Poel Ha-Tsair party, was born in 1876, while Levi Eshkol (Shkolnik), one day to become Israel's third prime minister, was born in 1895 and did not come to Palestine until 1913. But these were surely the exceptions that prove the rule.

Tabenkin would later describe the roots of his generation in the following terms:

> All were subject to one horizon, to one landscape – to that sum of circum-stances which encompass the man . . . One came from a Jewish shtetl, son of its rabbi . . . and was totally alienated from the Bund, saw in it a rabble, was shocked by the youngsters in the shtetl who wore red shirts . . . On the other hand, there were people who took part in the revolutionary movements, in self-defense, in the Russian revolution . . . However, the main thing is not how they responded, but that they lived throughout the same period, breathed its air . . .[8] Bialik was read not only by Zionists. In secret those Bundists who knew Hebrew also read his every new poem . . . And every devotee of Hebrew read the Yiddish works of Peretz, Sholem Aleichem or Nomberg . . . all were "for" or "against" but nobody was outside . . . The class and social question, the divisions within the people, found more expres-sion in Yiddish literature than in Hebrew . . . But the revolutionary attitude to the life of the Jews, to the Jewish individual, to all the foundations of his life and all his ways found its main expression in Hebrew literature.[9]

In this chapter, an attempt will be made to trace the transformation of the revolu-tionary ethos in the Palestinian labor movement, to examine the interaction of imported ideology and Palestinian reality in the decade following the Kishinev pogrom.

Party doctrine, 1906–9: orthodoxies

The interparty consensus

Late in 1905, two parties were established by rival groups among the immigrant youth in Palestine. One party was established, it seems, in October 1905 at a meeting in the home of a farmer in Petah Tikva, had only nine founding members (of whom four came from the small town of Plonsk in Congress Poland), and took the name The Organization of Young Workers in Palestine. It became known simply as Ha-Poel Ha-Tsair (The Young Worker).[10] The other party, established in November, called itself Poale Zion, the movement from which its members had graduated in Russia. A letter sent from Jaffa in February 1906 and published in the paper of Poale Zion in Poltava (*Evreiskaia rabochaia khronika*) reported that Ha-Poel Ha-Tsair had ninety members and the rival party, sixty.[11]

As these parties consolidated themselves organizationally in the years 1906–9, each striving to maintain its own journal and field its own team of propagandists, so they formulated two clearly defined and hostile (albeit rarely monolithic) ideolo-gies. At times, in 1907–8 and even more in 1912–13, the interparty polemics and rival manoeuvers reached heights of fury reminiscent of such feuds on the Russian Left. Faced by a totally new political situation after World War I, they still could not bring themselves to unite until 1930.

Nevertheless, in retrospect what impresses the observer most is the extent to which the leading theoreticians of the two parties shared a number of underlying and centrally important assumptions. In the last resort, the initial contact with the Jewish community (or communities) in Palestine tended to produce a similar response in the youth who had arrived straight from the Russia of the revolution. Differences of philosophy, conflicting self-images, and organizational competition kept the parties apart, but in their socioeconomic analysis and their overall political strategy the degree of convergence was remarkably high.

Above all, in both parties the dominant conception held that the Zionist enterprise in Palestine could succeed only as the result of rapid and ever-broadening capitalist development. The influx of capital in search of profit, the yeast of private enterprise, the expansion of the internal market and the growth of export – these alone could assure real advance. Entrepreneurial initiative would draw in its wake the working masses from eastern Europe who meanwhile were heading in their hundreds of thousands for North America.

This shared faith in the capitalist path was rooted in both the Russian and Palestinian experience. As described above, the pull of the Marxist creed had acted with magnetic power on the Jewish youth in the Pale of Settlement during the revolutionary period of 1905–6. A sociology, rather than a religion, of progress; a harshly realistic rather than a romantic mode of discourse; scientific materialism rather than utopianism – these had become both sword and armor for every self-respecting political activist under thirty. Even parties inclined to populism such as the SERP, with its SR connections, had been pulled along by the tide, and the theories of the 1880s that inspired such men as Syrkin and Zhitlovsky were cast aside as so much driftwood.

The year 1905 stamped its mark no less on the thought of the leading spokesmen for the two Palestine parties, whether they were avowed Marxists such as Yitshak Ben Zvi and Rahel Yanait or critics of Social Democratic orthodoxy such as Yosef Aharonovich and Nahum Tversky of Ha-Poel Ha-Tsair. Indeed, Tversky would later argue that only the revolution and its anticlimax in October 1905 transformed the youth immigration into a phenomenon of true historical importance. "There was a prologue," he wrote,

> marked by the immigrants from Homel [in 1903] and there was a follow-up
> ... for some years after but the Second Aliya in the real sense only lasted a
> few months in [the winter of] 1905–6. It was a kind of volcanic eruption
> following the first Russian revolution and the reaction against it – the terrible
> pogroms of late 1905. A stream of molten lava in the shape of a few hundred
> youngsters poured forth in a moment on to the fields of Palestine.[12]

Certainly, the men and women who ran the embryo party organizations, established and edited their journals, formulated their doctrines and strategies, had almost all lived through the year of 1905 in Russia. Those who had come before October 1905 generally yielded this sphere to those who came after. They sought other forms of activity and experiment. For the most part, they went north, to Samaria or Galilee. The main centers of both organization and membership – Petah Tikva, Rishon Le-Zion, Rehovot, Jaffa, Jerusalem – were left in the hands of those who sought to apply the doctrines and strategies acquired in revolutionary Russia to the Palestinian situation.

But this is only one side of the coin. At this stage, the history of Jewish coloniza-tion in Palestine since 1882 was generally interpreted as the best argument in favor of the capitalist path. For almost twenty years, Baron Edmond de Rothschild had dominated the settlement enterprise, investing in it at the very least £2 million sterling, steering existing colonies away from certain disintegration, and supporting the creation of new villages. But the net result had been disheartening. The empha-sis on one-crop agriculture, primarily viniculture, had rendered the farmers totally dependent on external aid until the vines had matured, whenever the plants became diseased (as occurred in catastrophic proportions), and when the prices on the European market fell (as happened with distressing frequency). Dependence on the baron's wealth, subservience to the baron's officials, and excessive reliance on cheap Arab labor were seen as the combined cause of the prolonged economic and social stagnation. As a result, in the years 1899–1900, Rothschild transferred many of the functions that he had fulfilled hitherto to ICA (The Jewish Coloniza-tion Association).

For its part, ICA sought to avoid previous errors. It put an end to the policy of outright grants and insisted that all financial assistance take the form of interest-bearing loans, that aid be cut to minimal proportions and that supervision over the existing colonies be progressively reduced. At the same time, it established new colonies in Galilee based on arable farming, which required much less initial invest-ment, no period of idling until the first yields came in, and (in theory at least) no hired labor. It was frequently said that if Rothschild saw the Jewish colonist in terms of the prosperous viniculturist he knew in his native France, so ICA hoped to make of him a simple plowman, a Russian muzhik. In 1899 ICA set up a training farm at Sejera in order to prepare potential colonists along these lines.

But this new policy had its own drawbacks. Extensive farming meant that large areas of land were required to settle a small number of farmers. By 1904, the five ICA settlements in Galilee had a total population of a mere 100 families, and it was estimated that to settle one colonist in this way cost 15,000 francs,[13] while at the end, he remained debt-ridden, the hapless victim of market fluctuations.

Moreover, the switch from baronial largesse to the penny-pinching of ICA pro-duced a major crisis in the veteran colonies during the years 1900–3. Many farmers left the country in despair, and the number of Jewish workers in the colonies, which had stood at some 500 in 1901, dropped to perhaps a third of that figure over the next two years.[14] With few prospects of regular employment and fewer still of being settled on the land by ICA, they too chose to reemigrate.

All in all, in the period 1881–1904, about 1 percent of the land in Palestine had been purchased by the Jewish settlement organizations and over twenty colonies had been founded. Living in those colonies there were perhaps 700 farming fami-lies and a total Jewish population of over 5,000.[15] Given the goals of Hoveve Zion and Zionism as expressed by such leaders as Lilienblum, Pinsker, and Herzl, this was little to show for the efforts of almost a quarter of a century. It is hardly surprising, therefore, that many of the most authoritative spokesmen of the na-tional movement in Palestine (including Eliezer Ben Yehuda and almost all the colonists in Rishon Le-Zion) turned out to be enthusiastic supporters of the Uganda project.

By 1904 the dominant trend of thought in Palestine held that one era in settlement politics was over. The policies of Rothschild and ICA had reached a dead end. Settlement based on philanthropy and supervision, it was argued, was bound to culminate in stagnation, in decline. Only the profit motive could generate dynamic growth.

This in large part was what Ahad Ha-Am had been arguing since 1891. And Rehovot, the colony founded in that year by immigrants from Russia who had capital to invest and who counted themselves in many cases as disciples of Ahad Ha-Am, was the most quoted example in favor of private initiative. But Rehovot was not the only case. Increasingly from 1904, the farmers in Petah Tikva, and to a lesser extent in Rishon Le-Zion, sought every means to make their farms self-supporting and profitable. Using commercial capital, they invested heavily in orange groves and almond orchards aimed at the lucrative European markets. It was estimated that an initial investment of 4,000 francs per acre could produce eventually an annual profit of 12–15 percent.[16]

In 1906 Rothschild made over his large wine cellars in Palestine to a syndicate of the farmers. Moreover, at this time, a number of small factories were founded and others greatly expanded on the private initiative of Jewish immigrants (particularly of the Vilbushevich family from Belostok)[17] – the Shtein machine works in Jaffa, for example, and the Atid olive-processing factories in Ben Shemen and Haifa.

Thus, the anti-utopian and often out-and-out Marxist attitudes that the youth brought with them after 1905 were strongly reinforced by the situation and prevailing opinion they found on arrival in Palestine. The hostility to paternalism, the belief in private enterprise were shared by all sections of the new (or post-1881) Yishuv in Judea, by the young labor leaders, by the veteran colonists, and by the officials of the major Jewish institutions in Jaffa.

The only hope, wrote Moshe Smilansky in 1907, was to rely on "the commercial and capitalist forces."[18] Smilansky was a veteran farmer in Rehovot, a Hebrew writer, a disciple of Ahad Ha-Am, and these sentiments were published in *Ha-poel ha-tsair*. Yosef Aharonovich, the editor of the paper and for some years a worker in the orange groves of Rehovot, lost no opportunity to support Smilansky's views. Modern farming was highly capitalized and required a large supply of wage labor. Peasant farming was outmoded and inefficient. Privately financed plantations geared to the export market represented the only kind of farming that could constantly generate profits, expansion, and work for large masses of men.

Der onfang, the Poale Zion paper, declared in 1907 that the entire settlement enterprise of Rothschild and the Palestinophiles has

> only provided us with yet one more generation of old men ... Thousands have fallen by the roadside while only the few have been "established" as farmers. And this is only a solution for them personally but does nothing to solve the general question ... The reason is quite obvious: they sought to go against the order of nature ... They believed that salvation would come when all Jews – property owners, petty traders, workers and just beggars – would become ... colonists. Obviously such a method was doomed from the first. The only truly vital element is that which has emerged from deep within life and is moved by life itself ... We regard [as such] ... an element, before all else, the newly arrived Jewish capitalist and the Jewish worker ...

The great majority [of the latter] are staying as workers and the employers are entrenching themselves as capitalists.[19]

Yaakov Rabinovich, looking back from the vantage point of 1912, wrote that "in the early period of the new immigration we were all under the influence of the doctrine that the intermediate class was destined to destruction. We dreamed only of capital and Jewish wage workers."[20] Likewise, Ruppin, in his famous address to the Eleventh Zionist Congress in 1913, recalled how during his first visit of 1907 prevailing opinion in Palestine held that "the be-all and end-all was private enterprise, which alone could advance agricultural settlement, while every act by an administrative body was totally worthless."[21] Sharing this basic premise – belief in the capitalist dynamic as the key to progress – the ideologists of the two labor (or more exactly, the youth) parties tended to interpret the world about them and their place in it along broadly similar lines. First, they were convinced that what was required at this stage in the development of the Yishuv was the creation of a Jewish working class that, however small in size initially, would be strong enough to grow together with the influx of capitalist enterprise. The idea that the status of wage worker was temporary, that the paid laborer would eventually become a farmer, was fiercely refuted by both parties alike. Without "capital and the exploitation of labor," as Aharonovich put it in 1909,[22] there was no hope. Any worker who became a farmer was therefore in danger of being "considered a traitor to the ideals of the organization."[23] Those members of the Ha-Poel Ha-Tsair who decided to settle in the new worker suburb of En Ganim (on the outskirts of Petah Tikva) were "forced to leave"[24] the party, even though the size of the individual plots was a mere four acres.

The two parties were united in the immediate post-1905 period in their hostility to the receipt of any aid that might be regarded as philanthropy. It was an axiom that the young Jew had to live from what he could earn at current wage rates. To fail in that endeavor would prove, it was felt, that the Palestinian labor market was unable to absorb European workers; that the immigrant youth was yielding to the norms of the older Jewish communities in Palestine, which were supported in varying degrees by charity (the haluka) and organized aid; that once again the Jews had failed to break into the onward march of history.

Ha-Poel Ha-Tsair even rejected in the winter of 1906–7 an offer of 600 roubles from the World Zionist Organization that would have enabled it to open an office with a paid secretary. Tversky, writing in 1912, explained this and similar decisions in the following terms:

> Their inner slogan was to stand on their own feet, to live off their own labor without a penny of outside support. And the reality which they found had converted this slogan into a sacred decision of the most extreme order. The terrible decay prevalent in the colonies which still depended on ICA and the Baron; the general flight from the country; the hatred most of the farmers felt for it [Palestine]; the Ugandism that swept all along with it; and, above all, the general contempt for all labor and for the worker – all this made a profound, an ineradicable, impression on those immigrants. The word "begging" [shnorerut] ... represented for them the greatest fall possible for a man and a nation. To eat even one meal at the table of a farmer, to take a

loan of any sum whatsoever, even to receive money from one's parents abroad – all this was despised and those guilty were not forgiven.[25]

The assumption was that the youth who had arrived in the years 1904–7 constituted only the first small wave in what would soon become a flood, a mass immigration. Both parties agreed that before long, Jaffa port would witness the arrival of an ever-growing number of Jewish proletarians, workers born and bred in laboring families, with strong arms, quick hands, and few demands. The "natural worker," as contrasted to the *intelligent* or *polu-intelligent* turned laborer, was confidently awaited. In its manifesto of 1908, Ha-Poel Ha-Tsair spoke of the "Jewish working masses who are destined to follow [the vanguard]."[26] The Ramle program of Poale Zion, drawn up in 1906, declared that the "broad masses of Jewry are being forced out of all spheres of production, are being compelled to emigrate . . . and it is inevitable that this Jewish migration will concentrate in Palestine, for in the highly developed countries it is meeting with ever greater obstacles."[27]

Not a tiny minority of insolent and alienated youngsters but a general staff sketching out the strategic plans for an army soon to be mobilized – this, then, was the self-image of the youth. Going through the party publications, the reader cannot but be impressed by the gap between the actual resources at the disposal of the organizations and the scope of their ambitions. Basing themselves not on tangible facts but on long-term prognoses, from the first they saw Palestine as the hub of Jewish politics throughout the world.

The fact that in the early years they had to bring out all their publications conspiratorially, including the two party papers, *Ha-poel ha-tsair* and *Der onfang*, for fear of the Turkish police reinforced the belief in their special role. *Ha-poel ha-tsair* was ostensibly put out in Cairo although, in reality, it was printed in Jerusalem. "That was really fine revolutionary work," recalled Barats. "All political life at that time sounded as it were with the echo from the revolutionary period in Russia."[28]

Again, from their earliest days both parties began competing with each other in the attempt to organize the workers within the old Yishuv. On the face of it, this was a strange use of their extremely limited manpower and resources. Most of the youth from Russia went to live as agricultural workers in the colonies and those who found jobs in town did so primarily in Jaffa, not in Jerusalem, the main center of the old Yishuv. Further, Ben Zvi estimated that there were no more than two thousand workers, mainly from the Oriental communities, out of a total population of over thirty thousand Jews in Jerusalem.[29]

For the immigrant youth, though, what counted was not actuality but potentiality. To organize the existing Jewish working class, however numerically small, meant to reach out to the "natural workers," to a rooted proletariat, without having to wait for their arrival from Europe. Much energy was therefore invested in the attempt to establish contact with the artisans from the Oriental Jewish communities, Yemenite, Kurd, Syrian, Persian. Trade unions were established among the printers and stonecutters in Jerusalem.

"Because the worker seeks to broaden his ranks . . . ," we read in the Poale Zion paper of 1907, *Der onfang,* "he turns to the local indigenous [people] and to his great joy he finds in them comrades! And not only among the Ashkenazim but also among the Eastern Jews, Yemenites, Sephardïm. They listen thirstily to the new Torah which links together the liberation of the workers with the liberation of the entire nation – and they are joining our ranks."[30] Again, Yosef Barats has described in his memoirs how Ha-Poel Ha-Tsair sent him in 1906 to Jerusalem to become a stonecutter and act as a party agitator. "There was a constant struggle," he recalled, "between Ha-Poel Ha-Tsair and Poale Zion, who were then preaching class war Rostov-style among the Yemenites . . . A union of artisans was founded that the Yemenites called Ahdut. We devoted many evenings to speeches and useless debate in that union."[31] Both Ben Zvi and Tversky made Jerusalem their home at this time, and when in 1908 the Printers Union called a general strike, the two youth parties were united in support of it, seeking to give it maximal publicity.

The organization of the Jewish working class in Palestine was envisaged as the foundation on which a far-ranging program of political action could be reared. Even before 1908, the outlines of such a program were clearly discernible in the publications of the two parties. But with the revolt of the Young Turks and the declaration of constitutional government in Istanbul, the strategy was clearly spelled out. As Tversky put it in *Ha-Poel ha-tsair* late in 1908, the movement had to become a political party in the full sense of the word: "The organization must enjoy great influence over the working masses . . . and those masses must be strong enough to influence the course of public life."[32]

Both parties demanded what was called the "democratization" of institutional life in the Yishuv. The workers – and the women – should be given voting rights in the agricultural colonies where they lived. As the Turkish system of government permitted the colonies a large degree of autonomy, such a broadening of the franchise would turn them into true cells of self-government. To achieve this goal, *Der onfang* declared, it was essential that the second generation, the farmers' sons in the older colonies such as Petah Tikva, "be as closely linked as possible to the labor organizations."[33] "The time has come," Tversky declared, "to enter the self-governmental institutions of the colonies and take up civil rights."[34]

Democratization was similarly expected to transform the urban Jewish centers, above all Jerusalem. The provisional program of Poale Zion drawn up in 1907 demanded "universal suffrage in all the institutions of self-government in town and colony [and] the democratic control of all the institutions in Palestine founded by public Jewish funds."[35] In this context, Ben Gurion took up a slogan first popularized by Herzl in 1898: "the conquest of the communities."[36] It was constantly pointed out that the Jews constituted a clear majority in Jerusalem, Safed, and Tiberias. In order to exploit this potential power base it was essential to persuade the Ashkenazi Jews to abandon their status as subjects of foreign powers and to apply for Ottoman citizenship. It was equally crucial to unite the Palestine Jews in one national and democratically elected body. "If one remembers," stated an article of 1908 in *Ha-poel ha-tsair*, "that the gentile population in our country likewise does not form one homogeneous unity but is divided into many and various national, linguistic, and religious groups, then it is obvious that a united Jewry numbering one hundred thousand organized Jews will constitute . . . a strong minority with often decisive influence."[37] Using the elections effectively, such a cohesive pressure group could win major concessions from the Ottoman parties competing for votes in Palestine.

But the political horizon was not limited to Palestine. There were perhaps as many as half a million Jews living throughout the Turkish Empire, and they too could be activated on behalf of the national cause. Indeed, the Turkish *millet* system had long recognized the Jewish population throughout the Empire as a self-governing religious community. "Jewish national autonomy is a real fact in Turkey," wrote Ben Zvi in *Der yidisher arbeter* (the paper of the Poale Zion in Austria). "It exists . . . It must be democratized."[38]

Underlying this approach was the belief expressed in the press of both parties that Zionism would best be served for the foreseeable future by the preservation of a strong Ottoman Empire. "It is laughable," wrote a correspondent (probably Yanait) in 1908 again, "to demand territorial autonomy for the Jews in Palestine, for in practice that means to demand it for the Arabs."[39] Thus, as with the Jewish parties in Russia, the clear preference was for a form of cultural, nonterritorial autonomy within the existing imperial boundaries. Equally central was the conviction that the diplomatic era of Zionist politics was over, bankrupt, and that power had to be built from the bottom upward. "Not all have grasped the fact," Ben Gurion wrote,

> that the attainment of political rights and the defense of political interests is the task of the citizens of the state in which they are living—in this case, of the Jews of Palestine and Turkey. That has to be the fulcrum . . . Political work is entirely outside the Zionist Organization's field of authority . . . It is the function of the Jews of Palestine themselves.[40]

The revolution of the Young Turks was greeted generally (albeit not unanimously) with enthusiasm by the spokesmen of both parties. Lengthy reports in the press reflected the excitement. "In Jerusalem," Ben Zvi wrote for *Der yidisher arbeter*,

> the Jews were the first to come out with their national flags in the celebration of freedom, with their own songs and many speakers. A similar development took place in Jaffa and some of the colonies. In these places, the new immigrant element undoubtedly played a leading role, setting the tone, influencing others. All the demonstrations were initiated among the Sephardi element by the Ashkenazi [Russian] youth . . . Only then did tens of thousands of Jews pour in from every corner of Jerusalem. They were followed by a mass of Arabs, Christians, and Muslims. This example shows to what a degree the supposedly dead masses can be called to life.[41]

In *Ha-poel ha-tsair*, the Jerusalem correspondent noted that while the established Jewish community had initially met the news of the revolt with apathy or fear,

> the reaction of the youth and workers who have arrived in the country recently has been different, totally different. For the most part, children of the great Russian revolution, active witnesses to the great and terrible October days . . . their joy in freedom for its own sake was enormous. Here too questions and doubts were heard . . . What will the effect be on our final

goal – the revival of our people in its own land? ... But if they could not answer the question from the theoretical point of view because of its suddenness and difficulty, they gave a clear and definite answer in practice – by their participation in all the processions, by their many speeches, their deep interest in the issue of the elections.[42]

A public meeting in Jerusalem, organized jointly by the two parties after the initial celebrations were over, was addressed by both Ben Zvi and Aharonovich. It attracted an enormous crowd. They spoke on "the importance of freedom in general and on its importance for the Jews of Palestine and the workers there in particular."[43]

The belief in capitalist development and mass proletarian immigration tended in the early years, then, to reinforce imported patterns of thought and action. Worker organization, trade unions, propaganda, agitation, the democratization of Jewish life, the hegemony of the youth, Jewish national autonomy in a multinational empire – all these were concepts familiar enough from Jewish politics in Russia. But in one important sphere, in the attitude to internationalism and Jewish nationalism, there was a clear tendency to diverge from the models developed in the Pale of Settlement.

It was obvious to the immigrant youth that unless preventive action was taken, the inflow of capital would produce a growth not in the Jewish but in the local Arab proletariat. Arab workers were in the main low paid, readily available, experienced in agriculture and in the building trades. Thousands of Arabs were employed in the Jewish colonies, and every expansion or intensification brought with it yet another increase in their number.

Given their penchant for prognosis and social analysis, the youth in both parties were equally convinced that such a trend could culminate in only one result – social conflict would merge with national conflict. The Jewish farmers would eventually be dispossessed by an Arab worker-peasant uprising. "One Jacquerie is enough to bring down the entire structure that we are building with Arab hands," declared *Ha-poel ha-tsair* in 1907,[44] and the manifesto put out by the party in 1908 called on the Zionist youth abroad to "remember the danger threatening us if all the branches of labor should fall into Arab hands, if they should be our workers at the point when they develop [politically] and take up the slogan: 'The land belongs to those who work it.'"[45] "It is now a secret open to all," we read in *Ha-poel ha-tsair* of 1909, "that the Jewish colonization in Palestine is more *Arab* than *Jewish*."[46] "If we do not manage to create a healthy working class in Palestine in time, then our country is lost to us for ever."[47]

Developing this same line of thought, a Palestine correspondent stated in *Der yidisher arbeter* in 1908 that "everything must be done in order to create a majority in Palestine."[48] Or, as Ben Gurion put it in *Ha-ahdut:* "Because there is not only a class difference but also a national difference between the workers and the farmers – the enmity between them takes on the form of national hatred and the national factor becomes more powerful than the class factor."[49]

This analysis encouraged the parties in Palestine to adopt a form of nationalism far more overt, more pronounced, and more militant than that of the mother movements in Russia. The fact that the established leadership in the colonies, and in the Yishuv generally, had long since tended to follow a path of extreme caution in relation to the local powers-that-be, both Turkish and Arab; that many in the Yishuv had despaired of Zionism as a solution to the Jewish problem, opting for territorialism; and that the Arab labor force continued inexorably to grow faster than the Jewish — all drove the youth parties to become increasingly vociferous in their nationalist pronouncements. Moreover, there was no entrenched antinationalist or cosmopolitan movement in Palestine to maintain that constant pressure from the left which had throughout forced the Jewish socialist parties in Russia to seek desperately a balance between the particular and the universal. Relatively (although not totally) unharried by the "internationalist" camp, the two youth parties were free to take up the national cause, which as they saw it had been betrayed by the Yishuv.

Here, it will suffice to illustrate this tendency with three of many possible examples. In 1907 an article entitled "An Unasked Question" was published in the Odessa journal founded by Ahad Ha-Am, *Ha-shiloah*. In it, Yitshak Epstein (who had been in Palestine on and off since the 1880s) argued that future Jewish settlement should be concentrated almost exclusively in those areas of the country which had hitherto been uncultivated (particularly the mountainous region); that if occasionally cultivated land were purchased, then on no account should the Arab population be moved away, even with the payment of compensation; that, on the contrary, the Jews should employ their funds to raise the level of the local Arab agriculture and education.

> One thing we have forgotten, that in the land of our hopes there is an entire nation [*am*] which has lived in it for hundreds of years and has never thought of leaving it . . . From the point of view of normal and formal justice we behave more than correctly and do more than is required . . . [But], in general, we have made a crude psychological error in our relationship to a large, determined and jealous people . . . Eventually, they will awaken to return by force what was taken from them by gold . . .[50] We shall sin a great sin against our own people and its future if we set aside lightly our best weapon: the rightness of our cause and the justice of our ways.[51]

The reactions in *Ha-Poel ha-tsair* to this article were diverse, but no voice spoke out there (or in the Poale Zion press) in defense of Epstein. A strongly hostile note was struck by Aharonovich and Moshe Smilansky. As for the question of right, wrote Smilansky,

> there are only two alternatives. If Palestine belongs — in the national sense — to the Arabs who have settled here in recent times, then we have no place in it and should say outright, the land of our fathers is lost to us. But if it belongs to us, the Jewish people, then for us the national interests of our people take precedence over everything else . . . One country cannot be the motherland of two peoples![52]

Besides, he continued, there was not one Arab people in Palestine, but many warring groups. "The Beduin hate the Fellahin . . . and they both hate the Metawileh . . . and all hate the Druze, who hate them all." And then there were three Christian sects, two Muslim sects, Cherkassy from the Caucasus, Arabs from Algeria, not to talk of the many Beduin tribes with their ancient internecine feuds. "And can one call them *one* great people? And is the nationalism of all of them tied to Palestine?"[53]

As for practical politics, nothing could be more naive, he wrote, than to argue that investment in Arab agriculture and education would guarantee good relations between the two peoples. If Arab nationalism were potentially as strong as Epstein suggested, then such assistance could only bring nearer the day of reckoning and prepare the Arabs "to take up the struggle for their national existence." "And who will be the first targets of their nationalism if not us?" Finally, where were the financial resources for such grandiose schemes? To intensify agriculture on the scale envisaged by Epstein "one needs billions and it is in the nature of billions that they only come to places which bring in profits of millions."[54] The public funds available to the Jews were laughably small and not adequate to cover even minimal needs. "Our main task," he concluded, "must be to attain the majority here in our country. Every act in hindrance of that goal is a national crime."[55]

A. D. Gordon, the father figure among the workers of the Second Aliya, refused to accept this either-or approach. "It is an established fact," he argued,

> that the country is ours so long as the Jewish people is alive and has not forgotten its land. But, on the other hand, one cannot rule that the Arabs have no part in it. The question is in what sense and to what extent is it ours, to what extent theirs, and how to adjust the demands of the two sides. The question is not simple and requires study, very great study.

But he too struck a note distinct from that of Epstein and very characteristic of the emerging labor movement in Palestine. "The country will belong more to that side which is able, willing, to suffer and work for it the more . . . And here again you see the place of labor in our revival and redemption."[56]

As described below, the two parties differed in their view of how the Jewish worker would establish a firm foothold in the economy despite the competition of Arab labor. But they were united in the belief that if he failed to do so, the Zionist enterprise was doomed, and on this shared ground, they were able at times to make common cause in the early years. Perhaps the most striking example of such cooperation was the agitational war waged over the school for girls built in 1908 in Jaffa. This enterprise was financed by the Odessa Committee of the Hoveve Zion, and the two labor parties insisted that as national funds were involved, preference be given to Jewish building workers even if they had to be brought in from Jerusalem. The contractors met this demand, but only for a few days (whether because they were unable or unwilling to do otherwise remains unclear), and so the issue became one of fierce dispute, pitting the youth against the school board on which sat the pioneers of yesteryear, Dizengof, Levontin, and Chaim Khisin.[57]

Even more heat was generated, however, by yet a third issue. On public occasions, the youth made a point of carrying the blue-and-white Jewish flag. The established leadership in the Yishuv frequently requested them not to do so for fear of bringing down the wrath of the Turkish administration on the colonies and on the Zionist movement generally. Given the miniscule size and political impotence of the new Yishuv, this request had a powerful logic behind it. But the youth of both parties acted in accord not with facts but with potentialities, not with the Palestine that existed then but with the one that they envisaged. As they saw it, if the Jews did not act as a group with national rights in the country, then those rights would be lost by default.

The result was that on numerous occasions, the youth raised the flag while the old-timers struggled to lower it or tear it down by force. Following one such incident in Jaffa in 1908, A. D. Gordon accused the leading figures in the Yishuv of seeking "to extinguish the last spark of the Rebirth,"[58] and commenting on another such incident in Petah Tikva, the Poale Zion paper, *Ha-ahdut,* wrote that "acts were committed here – not by bloodthirsty and wild beasts from the North – but by our own people, the Jewish people, which makes the blood freeze in one's veins."[59]

In such statements, of course, can be heard the bitterness of men who had lived through the period of the pogroms and the emergent Jewish self-defense groups. They saw in Palestine a country where the Jews were to be the majority and should act in accordance with that fact. "The desire for self-determination," Ben Gurion concluded in 1910, "is growing and the national question will not find a real solution without a difficult struggle and harsh competition between the different nations ... And if every nation has to organize and defend its affairs, then the Jewish people has still more need to do so."[60]

The interparty dispute

Granted the great stretch of common ground shared by the parties, what was it that kept them in a state of constant, often bitter, ideological warfare? The most straightforward answer, of course, is that the one party drew its recruits primarily from the Poale Zion movement in Russia, while the membership of the Ha-Poel Ha-Tsair came in the main from the youth sections of the general Zionist movement, particularly from the Zeire Zion and Ha-Tehiya groups. But this fact in itself, although crucial, does not tell the whole story, for all these movements had been thoroughly fragmented and in a state of constant flux in Russia during the years 1904–7. What is more, many of those who had been active members before emigration decided not to join the parties in Palestine, became passive members, or devoted their efforts to political enterprises outside or only peripherally linked to the parties.

Thus, the old labels per se counted for relatively little. Indeed, when the first steps towards political organization were taken in the summer of 1905, it had been assumed that there would be only one labor party, and the split that resulted from the creation of Ha-Poel Ha-Tsair in October 1905 apparently came as a surprise. Ben Gurion later recalled that when his friend Shlomo Tsemakh, a founding member of Ha-Poel Ha-Tsair, returned from Palestine for a visit to their native Plonsk in the winter of 1905–6, "we both came to see that even though we belonged to separate organizations, there was no difference of views dividing us."[61] They agreed that on arrival in Palestine they would work to unify the two parties.

Looking back on the period, contemporaries sometimes explained the party division as essentially sociological. The Poale Zion in Russia had been strongest in Lithuania, White Russia, Poland, and the south and had drawn its membership (as

Figure 22. *Ben Gurion (seated in center wearing white) in Plonsk on the eve of his departure for Palestine, 1906. On banner: the party name in Yiddish (YSDAP: Poyle tsien).*

its name indeed suggests) largely from the working class. This was supposedly reflected in the composition of the Palestinian party. The members of Ha-Poel Ha-Tsair, on the other hand, came more from the southwest, from Volhynia, Podolia, and Bessarabia; sons and daughters of the middle-class Hasidim, educated in the heder and yeshiva. As Shlomo Tsemakh put it:

> There was something else that stood in the way of unification. The Poale Zion people were physically strong, real heroes. In the colonies, they walked with their powerful muscles visible. They knew how to carry and use arms, were good shots . . . They were graduates of the Russian revolution and self-defense. In contrast, here were these soft youngsters overwhelmed by working with the hoe, weakened by malaria, with hands unused to work.[62]

However, a detailed analysis made by Yosef Gorni of the survey conducted in the 1930s among some nine hundred veterans of the Second Aliya failed to reveal any profound difference in the social origin of the membership.[63] The traditional impression is confirmed but only in very marginal terms. Some 17 percent of the Poale Zion membership had worked in Russia as artisans as against 10 percent in Ha-Poel Ha-Tsair; and some 12 percent of the Ha-Poel Ha-Tsair had been teachers in Russia as against 6 percent in Poale Zion. Some 22 percent of the Poale Zion members came from Poland as against some 16 percent of Ha-Poel Ha-Tsair; 6

percent as against just under 5 percent from Lithuania; and some 18 percent as against some 14 percent from Russia proper. On the other hand, close to 9 percent of Ha-Poel Ha-Tsair came from Bessarabia as against 6 percent of Poale Zion.

In both parties just over 60 percent reported that they had not been gainfully employed at all in Russia; they had gone to Palestine very young. And in both parties most members had come from trading and business families. Indeed, Gorni concluded that as reflected in the survey, the Poale Zion party in Palestine was in origin as much middle class (meaning, no doubt, primarily lower middle class) as Ha-Poel Ha-Tsair.

This does not mean that Tsemakh's impressionistic explanation was not based on fact. Rather, it suggests that what he described was the specific situation existing in the year 1905 in the Judean colonies, particularly in Petah Tikva. At that time, the Poale Zion in Palestine was almost synonymous with the group that had arrived from Homel following its participation in the self-defense against the pogrom of September 1903. It was Yehezkel Khenkin, his wife Haya Sara, and the other Poale Zion from Homel, together with only a very few individual immigrants from other towns (Aleksandr Zaid, Yisrael Shokhat), whom Tsemakh surely had in mind.

The truth is that as the impact of the revolutionary period in Russia made itself felt in Palestine in the years 1906–8, so the two embryonic organizations were forced apart. Each attracted to its leadership men determined to drive home what they saw as the essential lessons of the revolution. As the rival ideologies took clear shape, so many members who chose to differ drifted away from party activity, leaving only a hard core to make the crucial ideological and practical decisions. Conversely, those who sought to perpetuate the rough-and-tumble of the debates, the *referaty* and *kontr-referaty*, membership drives and organizational rivalries, were attracted to party leadership and party publication. Thus, a dynamic process was set in motion that reproduced in Palestine the tension characteristic of Jewish politics in revolutionary Russia.

The ideological watershed that separated the two parties corresponded with the line that had divided Russian Jewry in 1905–6. Thus, the Poale Zion party in Palestine saw itself as totally committed to the revolutionary cause. The mother party was identified with that cause in Russia and it felt bound to maintain that tradition in its new home, the Ottoman Empire. It defined itself as an orthodox Social Democratic party. In 1906 it adopted a name, The Jewish Social Democratic Labor Party in Palestine (Poale Zion), that emphasized its links with the party founded at Poltava in February 1906 and with the revolutionary Marxist movement in general. "[We] who proudly hold our banner aloft amidst the smoke and the fire of the revolution," declared *Der onfang* in 1907, "we who first introduced the correct synthesis of socialism and nationalism into the ranks of the Jewish working class across the world, cannot be frightened off by any obstacles."[64] "Poale Zion," wrote the party correspondent in Jerusalem to *Der yidisher arbeter* in 1908, "is the only party of the Jewish workers per se and the only Jewish revolutionary party in Palestine."[65]

As expressed in its journal, the attitude of Ha-Poel Ha-Tsair to the revolutionary cause in Russia was sharply different. The writers did not attack the revolution. On the contrary, the underlying note of admiration and even support came through time and again. But the note of reservation sounded clearer still and was usually dominant. For the Jews to throw their energies into the revolution in Russia was to divert those energies from the national cause. Poale Zion saw the revolution and Zionism as reinforcing each other. Ha-Poel Ha-Tsair believed that at the level of practical, day-to-day politics, the one movement tended to grow at the expense of the other.

The manifesto put out by the party early in 1908 calling on the youth in Russia to come to Palestine made this its central point:

> We call on you to cease your labor of Sisyphus in Exile, ... to be done with the dualism which is tearing you apart, to stop serving on two fronts, to stop discussing "real" work in Palestine and actually to work here! We, the Jewish workers in Palestine, were until recently active together with you abroad, dedicated ourselves to the Jewish self-defense groups, stood in the path of the pogroms ... We stood our ground until we saw that our work was in vain ... And we realized something very important: this is not the way![66]

Commenting on Chaim Zhitlovsky's suggestion that the task of Poale Zion was to "disseminate the socialist doctrine in the Orient," Yosef Chaim Brenner wrote in *Ha-Poel ha-tsair* in 1910:

> Those who live here and know the difficulties of life here ... even without having to preach to the Arabs, the Turks, the Armenians, the Greeks ... about social justice cannot but laugh, to say the very least, at such words ... We want at long last to stop being wandering preachers for others ... to give up the privilege of being a light to the nations.[67]

And, writing on Vitkin, shortly after his death, Yosef Aharonovich summed up what can be seen as his own outlook and that of their party:

> If Vitkin had belonged to another nation ... he would undoubtedly have been in the first rank of those fighting for social liberation. But he belonged to an ancient people ... forced by reality to forget the suffering of Man ... And the anguish caused by this contradiction – an anguish that affects the best youth of our nation – struck deep into his soul. It is easy to say, let us fuse the two questions and solve them as one. But what is one to do if deep down one does not believe in this fusion, does not see in it a solution ... ?[68]

Thus, even though both parties welcomed the revolution of the Young Turks in 1908, the nature of their response was far from identical. The comments from Poale Zion suggested that the upheaval had not been radical enough, "that the true revolution, made by the broad popular masses and characterized by a sharp class differentiation remains a task for the future ... [First] capitalism must develop."[69] Only between the lines, in the rejection of territorial autonomy for Palestine, did the underlying fear of Arab domination make itself felt.

In *Ha-poel ha-tsair,* in contrast, there was an open division of opinion, with some dissenting writers asking whether the party's enthusiastic participation in the celebrations, the processions, meetings and speech-making was wise, did not conflict with its own ideology: "We do not stand on firm ground," declared one such critic.

We do not know the language of the neighboring people [Arabic]. And Turkish, which is required of every member of parliament, is a closed book to us . . . We are outsiders in this celebration here in our own country just as we were abroad. And there is only one difference. There, we should not have rejoiced, while here we should not be outsiders.[70]

Those who defended the party's public stance argued that to fight for political freedom in the Turkish as opposed to the Russian Empire would not weaken the Jewish national cause:

When they [the youth and the workers] were in a similar situation in Russia and undertook work of this kind they felt a terrible inner division— at one and the same time they had to work for the revival of their own people in the future and for the improvement of its position in the present. And these two spheres existed in two different parts of the world and no amount of scholasticism [pilpul] could unite them. But that is not the case here and now. The feeling is that every step made for the present is also one for the future.[71]

As Ha-Poel Ha-Tsair saw itself as an affiliate of mainstream Zionism, with its ambiguous relationship to revolution, while Poale Zion declared itself a revolutionary party, the process of inner self-definition took on opposing forms within the two parties. Perhaps the most divisive issue for Ha-Poel Ha-Tsair was whether or not (and if so, how far) to accept financial aid from the Hoveve Zion in Russia and from the World Zionist Organization. Initially, as we have seen, the decision was to reject like the plague all outside financing. A true worker lived off his wages. But after a year or two, the nature of the debate changed, and the majority moved hesitantly to the position that some aid was legitimate. After all, if the proletariat in Europe could accept governmental insurance schemes, why should the working-class in Palestine not welcome cheap housing or a subsidized club from the national movement of which it was an integral part? However, there were critics of this volte-face, the most vociferous of whom was A. D. Gordon—his voice carried weight in the party even though he was no longer officially a member. The issue remained critical throughout those early years because it was far from simple to draw an acceptable line between charity and national aid to wage labor.

For Poale Zion, the key problem was of another order. It had to decide at what point on the left it should take its stand. In 1906 the revolutionary momentum was still powerful and there was a strong demand for a far-reaching internationalist program. Here, the lead was taken by the group, some thirty strong, that had arrived from Rostov-on-Don late in 1905. Russian-speaking, from an area far removed from the major centers of Jewish labor, thoroughly radicalized during the revolutionary year, they pressed for the creation of a trade union movement that would cut across national lines.

The issue came to a head at what came to be known as the First Party Congress, which was held in Jaffa at the Hotel Spektor (the hostel identified with Poale Zion) in the late summer of 1906. It was agreed that the party should work for the creation of a general trade union federation. But whether this organization should recruit only Jews or should seek to bring in Arab workers, too, became the subject of dispute. The Rostov group proposed the name, The General Labor Union in

Figure 23. The Third Congress of Ha-Poel Ha-Tsair, 1907.

Palestine, while Ben Gurion, speaking in the name of the more nationalist wing, demanded that the term, "Jewish," be specifically included in the title. After what was described as "an extremely stormy" debate,[72] Ben Gurion's argument won the day. In so deciding, of course, the party was following precedents established in the Pale of Settlement and, indeed, the adopted name corresponded almost exactly to that of the Bund.

Over the next year, the great majority of the Rostov group left the country, and when Ben Zvi arrived early in 1907 he became almost by default the major theoretician and publicist of Poale Zion in Palestine or, more exactly, in Judea. Known as a long-time associate of Borochov (like him from Poltava) and as a faithful exponent of Borochovism in the party press, he might have been expected to adopt a strictly internationalist position. But this did not prove to be the case. As long as capitalism and mass immigration were in an embryonic stage, he insisted, the Jewish proletariat had no choice but to organize along separate, national lines. Even now, individual activists still sought to create an internationalist labor organization that would include Jew and Arab, but they did so on the periphery, not in the mainstream, of the Poale Zion movement.

The open debate between the two parties was conducted exclusively on the verbal level in the period 1906–7. "Meetings went on day and night," Tversky recalled a few years later, "and the party rivalry even served to redouble the initiative and interest invested in public life. It was sufficient that a mere handful of workers arrive in a colony for organizational life to start up there – readings, lectures, parties and when possible, 'economic' [mutual-benefit] institutions."[73] Ben Zvi's debates against Aharonovich in the colonies developed into a major event in 1907. "A new leader has arrived in this, the year of the Eighth Zionist Congress," mocked *Ha-poel ha-tsair*, "a *teoretik* who wants to continue in Palestine along the path laid down by their Great Man [Borochov] – to ground Jewish history in all its various facets on historical materialism alone."[74]

In 1908, the debate went over into print, the one side publishing in *Ha-poel Ha-tsair*, the other (for want of an established local paper) forced to employ *Der yidisher arbeter* in Galicia. In outline, the arguments employed were familiar enough. The greatest heat, understandably, was engendered by the issue of most immediate importance to the youth: what steps should be taken to entrench the Jewish workers in Palestine prior to the mass immigration. Essentially, the positions corresponded, on the one hand, to that advanced by Borochov early in 1905 and, on the other, to that advanced by Borochov in 1906.

Thus, Ha-Poel Ha-Tsair insisted that during the transitional period, the role of the avant-garde, the pioneer, was of crucial importance.[75] The Jewish youth had to prove that it was possible to compete directly with Arab labor, to establish a bridgehead of wage workers in the colonies. This, of course, had long been a favorite theme of Ussishkin, and it comes as no surprise to discover that a number of graduates of the New Bilu movement which he had supported (with Borochov's help in the winter of 1904–5), should have ended up as key members of Ha-Poel Ha-Tsair.

For its part, Poale Zion insisted that the Jewish worker would establish himself from the first in accord with normal market forces. If wages were higher in town than in the country, then he would naturally leave the village. If he had a skill that was in demand, then he would establish himself as a relatively highly paid worker. As the economy developed, so the jobs that only European workers could handle would constantly expand in number. It was the task of the party not to create a working class but to organize the Jewish workers already in the country (including the indigenous and Oriental Jews). It defined its policy as one of "class entrenchment" [*bitsur ha-maamad*] as against the policy of Ha-Poel Ha-Tsair: "labour conquest" [*kibush ha-avoda*].[76]

In its manifesto put out early in 1908, Ha-Poel Ha-Tsair called on the Jewish youth abroad to act as "a vanguard coming ahead of the Jewish working masses."[77] This appeal was greeted with downright scorn by the spokesman for the Poale Zion in Palestine:

> There is no logic in a yeshiva student [*bokher*] suddenly becoming a farm laborer just as it is utopian to think of creating an agrarian working class from Russian *eksterny* and Hebrew teachers – after all, they are the ones in Russia who read [such] proclamations ... [They demand] endless sacrifice from the workers ... monasticism for its own sake.[78]

If it succeeded such a policy would create a proletarian "reserve army" helpless in the face of ruthless wage-cutting exploitation. What was required in reality were not "half-*intelligenty* who come here for an ideal but simple Jewish workers with strong muscles who sold their labor power abroad too. Only this type of immigration can create a healthy normal working class in Palestine."[79] It was in line with this policy that the Poale Zion (at the urging of Ben Zvi and to the disgust, inter alia, of Ben Gurion) decided to bring out its first party paper, not in Hebrew but in Yiddish – the language of the mass immigration then considered imminent. Again, the emphasis in party agitation and ideology was more on the urban than the agrarian worker. There were not only far more Jewish workers in the cities than in the colonies, but, as Ben Gurion put it, "the worker in town is more natural, more entrenched in his job."[80]

Anticipating a classic pattern of economic development, Poale Zion based their political program on the standard prognosis of Borochov. "Our minimal goal," *Der onfang* stated in 1907, "is the seizure of economic and political power here in the country. Our maximal goal is the total overthrow of oppression . . . the abolition of classes . . . The two goals are logically and historically linked like two steps on a ladder."[81] In organizing the working class for the trade union and political struggle, "we are creating the first healthy kernel of the future Jewish state."[82]

If Ha-Poel Ha-Tsair was accused of utopianism, it in turn saw in all this a total divorce from reality. Poale Zion blindly followed Marxist dogma, ignoring the writings of Bernstein, Vollmar, Jaurès, and other revisionist critics. They were determinists in a situation demanding a voluntarist response. It was "not natural," Aharonovich wrote in 1908, "for the worker from Lodz or Warsaw – however natural a worker – to leave large town life . . . Of all the thousands of workers who have come to Palestine over the last four years only the more educated have remained . . . while his [Ben Zvi's Poale Zion] comrades have all left the work and the country because they lack idealism."[83]

The class-war theme central to the Poale Zion ideology, he argued, made no sense for the Jewish cause in Palestine. There was virtually no industry. "If we want to count all [the factories] finger by finger many fingers will remain uncounted even if we use only one hand." And everywhere else, Arabs were ready to replace Jews if they caused trouble to their employers. To organize Arab labor, "to march arm-in-arm," was to oppose the national interest.[84] "A war of labor against capital," he wrote, "has started before either has established itself in the country and so, of course, its tactics take on strange and pathological forms."[85]

For Ha-Poel Ha-Tsair, the use of Hebrew rather than Yiddish in its publications and (increasingly) in its meetings was not a marginal issue. On the contrary, it symbolized all that was most radical in their approach. In their fierce commitment to Hebrew was reflected their rejection of Jewish life as it was lived abroad, in Exile, and their determination to begin everything afresh. In the acerbic note it struck, in its puritanical rejection of high-pitched rhetoric, in its apparently reckless portrayal of reality and failure, the party journal was without parallel in Russian-Jewish politics. Strongly felt was the influence of the most mordant and critical figures in modern Hebrew literature, Mendele, Lilienblum, the Ahad Ha-Am of the 1890s, and above all of Berdichevsky. And, of course, from 1908 Brenner, the writer who grimly hunted down hypocrisy and self-delusion,[86] joined the staff of the paper. Thus in its own way Ha-Poel Ha-Tsair, which rejected the class war doctrine and saw itself as a Zionist rather than a socialist party, was acting out a revolutionary role at least as much as Poale Zion.

Party Doctrine, 1906–1909: heterodoxies

In the period 1909–14, the ideology dominant in the years immediately following the Russian revolution gradually lost its primacy. The strategy that now gained ever more support relied not on private but on public or "national" capital; not on the creation of a permanent wage-earning proletariat but on the pioneer settlement of new lands; not on the political hegemony of the immigrant youth in the Yishuv as a whole but on the creation of an autonomous, perhaps even autarchic society minimally linked to the existing Yishuv. Here was a major doctrinal reversal.

The chroniclers and historians of the Second Aliya have often argued that this radical change of direction was dictated by the day-to-day confrontation with the realities of life in agrarian Palestine. It was the result of an organic process rooted in the local soil. This view was formulated in clear-cut terms by Yitshak Ben Zvi as early as 1911. Writing in *Ha-ahdut,* he compared the emergence of the new strategy in Palestine with that of Marxism in the nineteenth century. Theory and practice had for a long period developed quite independently. The utopian socialism of Fourier and Saint Simon, on the one hand, and British trade-unionism and Chartism on the other emerged on parallel lines. Only at a later stage were the two strands combined by Marx in "scientific socialism."

> So it has been among us with the idea of cooperative settlement: on the one hand, it emerged in the thought of a man of theory, Oppenheimer, as a pure idea, a link in an entire sociological chain without any connection to Jewish reality . . . or Palestine. On the other hand, this idea of cooperative settlement began to mature among the agriculture workers here in Palestine, who relied on the settlement experience of some years and who created in practice new models such as the worker kvutsot [cooperative groups], which are self-governing and rent land collectively from the National Fund. Now these two factors have met—the abstract idea . . . and the practical movement . . . and they stand face to face. The near future will reveal the nature of their union and merger.[87]

This analysis was clearly influenced by that major trend in Russian socialist historiography, both populist and Marxist, which saw ideology as emerging organically from "life" and independently of "theory." Thus, it is not surprising that Ben Zvi's conception recalls inter alia the way in which Bundist historians have usually explained the reversal of 1901 in their own party ideology. As in the case of the Bund, so in that of the Second Aliyah, the exclusive emphasis on "life," day-to-day practice, *stikhiia,* is misleading. The actual development was less neatly divided, more complex and interwoven than Ben Zvi's account would suggest.[88]

First, there is the fact that a small but by no means insignificant minority of the immigrant youths had throughout argued in favor of the strategy that would later become that of the majority. As early as 1906, this minority had begun to create its own organizations centered in northern Palestine, primarily in Galilee. Moreover, the first experiment by the youth in self-administered farming was launched in 1907 as the result not just of practical necessity but also and probably even more as the result of an overarching, a priori theory.

Second, while it is true that Franz Oppenheimer's blueprint for settlement cooperatives was developed in Berlin in the mid-1890s before he became a Zionist, it is also a fact that from 1901 he began to agitate actively on behalf of his scheme within the Zionist movement. He found allies in the German Zionist organization, and from 1903 they edged the movement toward active settlement policies in Palestine. By 1907, their influence was making itself felt increasingly in the form of concrete, albeit modest, experiments in Palestine itself.

What is more, among Oppenheimer's most active supporters was the Poale Zion party in Austria-Hungary. As early as 1905, the case for labor settlement cooperatives in Palestine was being argued vigorously in its party press. Given the fact that neither the Russian nor the Palestinian Poale Zion were able to produce a party paper regularly in these years, *Der yidisher arbeter* published in Cracow had to serve as the organ of the world movement and was widely read far beyond the frontiers of the Hapsburg Empire. The workers in Palestine may often have disagreed with its views, but they were certainly aware of them.

If the orthodoxies prevailing in the two Palestine youth parties were in large measure a direct legacy from the Russian revolution, so the heterodoxies that came to dominate the Zionist Left in Galilee and Galicia reflected pre-1905 modes of thought. Romanticism and utopianism, discredited during the revolutionary years, found a secure refuge there. In this case, as so often in the history of modern Jewish politics, the sequence of events can hardly be understood in the context of one movement, one country, or one short period of years alone.

Galilee

The objective conditions in Galilee were certainly more suited to the idea of settlement and less suited to the idea of wage labor than those prevailing in Judea. There were no capital-intensive plantations here, no irrigation systems, almost no livestock and consequently almost no fertilizer. This was an area of extensive agriculture, very low yields, and living standards barely above the subsistence level. Thought of a mass proletariat was clearly absurd when the average farmer employed no more than one full-time worker. Even in the two most developed of the northern settlements, Zikhron Yaakov and Hadera, the plantation system was still in its embryo stage and there were relatively few jobs available for wage workers. (And, of course, these villages were on the coastal plain of Samaria, not in Galilee proper.)

But if the prospects for proletarianization were strictly limited in the north, the same could not be said of settlements. The fact that this was an area of extensive, low-yield arable farming meant that the price of land was infinitely cheaper and the local Arab population much sparser than in Judea. It was this logic that had moved ICA to concentrate its efforts in Galilee and to establish some half-dozen new settlements there in the years 1900–2.

Nevertheless, in this case it was not existence that exclusively or even primarily determined consciousness. Many of the young immigrants who worked in Galilee continued to see the creation of a wage-earning proletariat, however small initially, as the primary goal. The demand for the creation of worker suburbs on the edge of the farming colonies was raised in the north as in the south. More significant, the proletarianization strategy was if anything more widely advocated in Galilee in

1908 and 1909 than in 1906 and 1907. There was no inexorable process at work here but rather an unceasing dialogue in which now one theory, now another momentarily gained the ascendant.

Certainly, there is much evidence to suggest that in many cases to go north was not a random decision. Those who went to Zikhron Yaakov and Galilee in 1906 tended to be relative veterans in the country, men and women who had left Russia in 1904 or the pre-October days of 1905. This was true in particular of those who emerged as central figures in the movement in the north. Yisrael and Eliezer Shokhat, Yisrael Giladi, Shlomo Tsemakh, Shlomo Lefkovich (Lavi), Sara Malkin, Aleksandr Zaid, and Saadia Paz all fit this pattern.[89] (Manya Vilbushevich was a unique case. She went to Palestine first in 1904 but then traveled extensively in Europe and the United States. She became a key figure in the purchase and shipment of arms from the West to the self-defense organizations in Russia after October 1905.)[90]

They had lived through the early phases of the revolutionary uprising in Russia but had not experienced the period of mass politics, teen-age hegemony, and Marxist supremacy. As the post-October political culture took root in Judea, so they tended to move on. In his memoirs, Yisrael Shokhat described how the Rostov group consolidated its hold over the party center in Jaffa and how the more national wing of the party concentrated in the north.

> They carried on their party life from Rostov . . . and they employed a left-wing phraseology. The comrades who had come to Palestine before the Rostovians, people from Lithuania, Plonsk, and Odessa who had put down roots in the [new] country, who were educated on the Hebrew language, . . . began to regard the Rostovians with suspicion and many threw off their party ties. In Samaria and in Galilee a group of Poale Zion was founded with its own center . . . with some twenty-five members who served as a counterweight to the Rostovians. So Poale Zion had two centers: one in Judea and one in Galilee.[91]

Contemporary accounts convey a similar picture. The youth who went to Galilee tended to look down on the way of life that they had put behind them in the south. A correspondent writing in Ha-Poel ha-tsair in 1908 noted that a new union (Ha-Horesh) had been set up in the north because "among all the workers in Galilee – or at least among the majority – an attitude of contempt for all the various established labor organizations is to be felt. They do not believe in their effectiveness."[92]

It was commonly felt that to leave Judea was in some degree to repudiate the prevailing belief in proletarianization. Thus, Shlomo Tsemakh, recalling the year 1906, could write that "Yosef Aharonovich was right that this ascent to Galilee was directed, consciously or unconsciously, against the idea of labor conquest [kibush ha-avoda] as defined in its [the party's] statutes and that [as he argued] it had to be stopped from the very outset."[93] Again, Yosef Veits remembered that when he decided to go north in 1909, "Munchik, the secretary of the party at that time . . . tried to divert me from my path."[94]

To set out for Galilee was seen as a conscious decision to leave civilization for the frontier. It meant to choose an existence far more lonely and physically wearing, but also more adventurous than that of the workers in the south. A letter of

Figure 24. Manya Vilbushevich (Shokhat), 1880–1961, in Paris, 1906.

1907 noted that people "point to the worker from Galilee as at some strange being. And, indeed, how difficult it is to stand the test – to stay a whole year away from Jaffa, far from the conferences, the speeches, the meetings, and the other pastimes of the worker in Judea."[95] And Zeev Smilansky, writing in *Ha-shiloah* in

1908, made the same point: "In order to mount the barricades one needs enthusiasm for a few hours or at most a few days. But how much courage . . . is needed to stay for years far from a large town in the small villages of Galilee which rarely see a new face, to sleep in the barn together with the livestock and to live under conditions far . . . worse than those in the Judean colonies."[96] "In Judea," Tsemakh recalled, "the two parties were already noisily locked in battle. Does the class war or 'labor conquest' have preference? Hebrew or Yiddish? Determinism [stikhiia] or will? But here in Galilee a great silence reigned."[97]

In the years 1906–8, the workers in the north established three experimental organizations: a farm labor union, a conspiratorial (would-be paramilitary) armed cell, and a wage and profit-sharing commune. Each organization was independent of the others, but there was a high degree of overlap in both ideology and membership. Yisrael Shokhat and Yisrael Giladi, for example, both played leading roles in all three organizations simultaneously. The common theme was innovation, and emancipation from the orthodoxies of the south.

Thus, the farm labor union declared itself a nonparty organization and many members of both parties were to be found in its ranks (even though it was originally founded in the winter of 1906–7 by a group belonging to Ha-Poel Ha-Tsair). "It is a known fact," M. Sheinkin wrote in 1909, "that most workers belong neither to Ha-Poel Ha-Tsair nor to Poale Zion. The workers in Galilee – that is the real workers – have united in a separate organization, Ha-Horesh."[98] Its very name carried overtones of deviation for, semantically, Ha-Horesh (The Plowman) could apply equally to wage worker and farmer. Even though the original statutes have been lost, those of 1908 as well as contemporary accounts and later memoirs leave no doubt that this ambiguity was deliberate.

Correspondents in Ha-poel ha-tsair reported that in 1908 the workers in Galilee were actively debating at least three alternative strategies (not to talk of possible mutations and syntheses). First, there was the orthodox concept of wage labor, but few regarded this, the established formula, as adequate any longer. Beyond it, most insisted, was the need "to organize settlement in the future so that [the work in it] be handled by Jews."[99]

Some believed that "only small-holding colonization can develop the Yishuv";[100] that national funds should constantly settle veteran workers on new areas of land; and that newcomers should meanwhile serve on a temporary basis as wage workers in the established colonies. A dynamic process fueled by public capital would thus ensure a constant supply of farm laborers, new colonies, and experienced hands to settle them. Finally, a third school of thought argued in favor of "large-scale and complex projects . . . in which the more intensive methods of agriculture can be concentrated." To the extent that private investment was not forthcoming, "national capital should also participate [in financing] cooperative undertakings."[101]

The statutes of Ha-Horesh, published in 1908, did not come out clearly in favor of any one of these theories. But reading between the lines, it is impossible not to see a repudiation of the party ideologies as hitherto formulated. Absolute priority had to go to farming rather than to urban work, "for land is the foundation of every state." At the same time, the program came out against reliance on the planter. "The plantation system has a capitalist character that cannot bind the settler to the land and to nature." Arable farming should be assigned preference, for it required minimal investment and only a few hands to work (and hold) very large areas. Further, unlike the plantation system, it was not dependent on world markets.[102]

Ha-Horesh sought to bring into its ranks all the immigrant workers in Galilee, and at its highpoint in 1908 it almost succeeded in doing so. Its specific goals were therefore kept within modest and relatively noncontroversial limits: the organization of Hebrew and Arabic lessons, of gymnastics and weapons-training, of worker kitchens and laundries. It was constructed (on paper at least) along democratic lines, with the central committee to be elected every six months by general meetings of the full membership. It aimed to "develop in our country an element of worker-felaheen, healthy in body and soul."[103]

The other two experiments centered in Galilee in the years 1907–8 were undertaken by small groups with programs much more sharply focused. Indeed, their membership and ideology overlapped to such a degree that they can hardly be studied apart.

In September 1907 a secret meeting in Jaffa attended by some ten members of Poale Zion created a clandestine, self-defense paramilitary organization. It was named after one of the heroes of the Jewish Revolt against the Romans in the years 66–73, Bar Giora. Immediately after the meeting, all except two of the founding members left for Galilee to launch an experiment in communal farming and living at the ICA training farm in Sejera.

The political strategy they advocated stood in polar opposition to the official party doctrine of Ha-Poel Ha-Tsair and still more of Poale Zion. The group in Sejera consciously invested its hopes in the frontier, in the areas of scattered and nomadic population, in national and philanthropic rather than profit-seeking capital, in the elite rather than the mass, and in clandestine rather than open politics.

First, the members saw themselves as the nucleus of a group that would eventually establish a large settlement some hundreds strong in the mountainous areas of Hauran, east of the Jordan. Rothschild had made large purchases there in the 1890s and the land still stood empty. The assumption was that this future settlement would be run on egalitarian or socialist principles. "There are those," read a report from the Sejera group in 1908, "who are dreaming of a collective farm and those who dream of a collective village."[104]

On the ICA training farm, the group, known as the "Collective" (*kollektiv*), had contracted to farm over two hundred acres of arable land on its own responsibility for one year. They were guaranteed a share of the profits (to the extent that there were any), and the management also agreed to pay the workers a minimal wage as well as to put all the necessary equipment and draft animals at their disposal. The workers in the "Collective" – there were some ten full members – shared all the basic living expenses on an equal basis during the year (even though they kept separate accounts on paper for each member).

The aim of the experiment, stated a report in *Ha-Poel ha-tsair*, was "to test to what degree the workers, on the one hand, and the conditions in Palestine, on the other, allow a more or less complete form of collective living." "On the basis of their small experience," concluded the correspondent writing when the experiment was some six months old, "the members of the Collective think that communal life is very difficult but not impossible. The main condition is to begin with great caution, little by little, and not to attempt too much all at once."[105]

Second, the group (or at least all those who were also members of Bar Giora) assigned great importance to its role as a clandestine armed force. "The Galilee is broad," a member reportedly said to his future wife as they looked over the hills, "and there is much room for settlement in it . . . , but our numbers are few and we have to create a strong force so that our neighbors stop thinking us . . . incapable of making a stand. That force is needed even before the mass of Jews come here seeking to settle."[106] The proposed colony across the Jordan was often compared in conception to a Cossack *sech*.

The existence of the conspiratorial unit was kept a strict secret not only from the management and local farmers but even from the other workers at Sejera. It was run on hierarchical lines with all control effectively in the hands of the top leadership. Her initiation, as she later remembered it, has been described by Esther Beker. She was warned in advance that "whoever enters the society cannot leave it alive— our actions must be kept secret." The ceremony took place at night in a dimly lit cavern with comrades waiting half hidden in the shadows.

> All this mystery cast a spell. I had seen and known the members before, but now they made a different, a special impression. Yisrael Shokhat conducted the meeting. His words were commands. And in the comrades—[one felt] discipline, admiration, obedience . . . from now on there was a different content in all that I did and every look of one of the members signified our common tie to the one goal, which only we knew. The feeling of unity added strength, courage . . . and faith.[107]

That the Poale Zion movement should have produced a mutation as exotic as this was, as suggested above, not so surprising as it might appear. First, there was the fact that since the Kishinev pogrom of April 1903, the Poale Zion in Russia had become ever more deeply engrossed in the organization of self-defense units. The slogan adopted by Bar Giora—"In blood and fire Judea fell, in blood and fire Judea shall rise"—had been employed in a Poale Zion leaflet put out in Russia as early as the spring of 1905.[108] (It originated in a poem by the modern Hebrew poet, Yaakov Cohen.) The members of Bar Giora almost to a man had been active in the self-defense units, and its highly conspiratorial style was no doubt brought in large part directly from Russia.

Second, the fact that the leaders had left Russia mainly in the years 1903–4 (or in the early months of 1905) meant that they had not lived through the era of open and mass politics. The influence of populism and the SRs was often greater than that of orthodox Marxism. Yisrael Shokhat referred specifically to the "slogans of the SR party in Russia, on whose legal and underground literature I was educated."[109] (He was a man whose entire subsequent life was in effect involved in conspiratorial undertakings.)

Manya Vilbushevich (who became Yisrael Shokhat's wife) had even been recruited briefly into the terrorist section of the SR party. She was the driving force behind the plans for a large-scale collective settlement, a project she had been pursuing actively ever since her first visit to Palestine in 1904. Modern farming, she insisted, required a high degree of mechanization that could be economical only in large-scale units. The Sejera Collective was set up primarily on her initiative.

A number of the Bar Giora members had been profoundly influenced while in the Russian Poale Zion of 1902–5 by Mikhael Halperin, a romantic and adventurer to his bones. He had worked in the early Palestine settlements in the 1880s, had been among the leading rebels against the Rothschild administration in Rishon Le-Zion, had organized a secret society in the early 1890s to plan an armed uprising against Ottoman rule, and had later returned to Russia, where he had toured the Pale of Settlement preaching the idea of Palestine pioneering. With his long years of personal experience and real first-hand knowledge, this bearded veteran had fired the imagination of such young Poale Zion members as Yehezkel Khenkin and Aleksandr Zaid (both founding members of Bar Giora). One of his favorite projects apparently envisaged the establishment of Jewish pastoral, Beduin-like groups in Sinai that, together with the British, would conquer Palestine in a future Anglo-Turkish war.[110]

That Ben Zvi was among the founding members of Bar Giora is, on the face of it, highly paradoxical. After all, he came to Palestine in 1907 as a leading disciple of Borochov. But, of course, he too had played a key role in the organization of self-defense in Poltava and, indeed, the discovery of an arms cache in his garden had led to the arrest (among others) of his own father. As an avowed revolutionary he could not object to the existence of an armed underground per se. Moreover – and this is surely the central point – he himself did not join the others in Galilee; he settled first in Jaffa, then in Jerusalem, and there concentrated on trade-union organization and the publication of the party's Yiddish journal, *Der onfang*.

By late in 1908, it was becoming increasingly obvious that the innovative experiments launched in Galilee over the preceding two years had run out of steam. The Sejera Collective was not renewed for another term nor was the system transplanted anywhere else for the agricultural year 1908–9. The existence of wheels within wheels during the period 1907–8, with the secret society trying to keep itself hidden even from some members of the Collective, had complicated still further what was anyway a tense trial period.

Yisrael Shokhat and his circle now changed course. They signed a contract with the village of Mesha (Kfar Tavor) in Lower Galilee to provide armed watchmen for the year 1908–9 on condition that the farmers agreed to employ a large number of Jewish farm laborers. The idea now gained ground that this package deal could be extended indefinitely, that the farmers in their eagerness to obtain reliable guards could be induced to go over from Arab to Jewish labor. In the spring of 1909 the founding congress of Ha-Shomer (The Watchman) was held in Mesha. This organization, described by Yisrael Shokhat as "the legal form of the secret order, Bar Giora,"[111] was established to pursue the new policy. Later in the year, yet another organization was added with the same goal, the Labor Legion (Legion Ha-Avoda).

Thus, by 1909 the strategy of proletarianization, of *kibush ha-avoda*, was reasserting itself in Galilee. But in the meantime, as shall now be described, the idea of cooperative settlement had found active support in the Zionist and Poale Zion movements abroad. By 1908 this support was beginning to make itself felt in the form of practical undertakings in Palestine. Ironically, the first result was a furious clash with the organized workers in Galilee.

Franz Oppenheimer, the Berlin Zionists, the Austrian Poale Zion, and the Daleika-Kinneret experiment, 1903–1908

In 1895 Franz Oppenheimer, a well-known Berlin intellectual, a doctor by training but an economist by calling, published his book *Freiland in Deutschland,* which was followed in 1896 by his *Die Siedlungsgenossenschaft* (The Settlement Cooperative). The subtitle of the latter work – "An Attempt to Supersede Communism along Positive Lines by Solving the Cooperative Problem and the Agrarian Question" – indicates neatly enough what the author was driving at in this lengthy work.

Cooperative settlement, he argued, was the highest form of social organization, superior to capitalism with its exploitation of man by man and superior to communism with its inherent tendency toward dictatorial, leveling egalitarianism. He saw himself as working in a long tradition going back to the "utopian" thought of Fourier, Cabet, and Owen, and more immediately to (inter alia) Lassalle and Schulze-Delitzsch. However, in his view, what he was proposing was neither an experiment in utopia nor one more social reform but a dynamic system that could lead to the reconstruction along new lines of society as a whole.

The first settlement cooperative, a pilot project, was to be financed by private or at least profit-seeking capital and peopled by recruits drawn from the impoverished urban mass. Initially, the members would concentrate on agriculture alone, would be trained and supervised by a qualified agronomist, and would receive a wage as well as a large share of the profit. Interest and the remainder of the profits would be paid over to the investment corporation and shareholders.

At the second stage, the members would repay the initial investment, take over control, and gain the freedom to decide on the future shape of their community. They could divide the land into individual plots, and in this case one-fifth of the area would revert to the investment corporation. But, hopefully, they would maintain the land as a single economic unit. If so, in the final stage, the settlement would extend beyond agriculture and put aside land for those (members and newcomers alike) who wished to develop manufacture, trade, and services. Meanwhile, having regained its capital and made a profit, the investment company could launch further such projects ad infinitum, thus gradually transforming society without revolution and without curtailing the freedom of the individual.[112]

In many ways, of course, Oppenheimer's conception is reminiscent of Syrkin's: his avowed adherence to the "utopian" tradition, his belief in cooperative settlement as a higher synthesis of individualism and communism, of rural and urban forms of life. The similarity became still more striking when, with increasing frequency, Oppenheimer argued that in essence his theory was a restatement of the principles that had inspired the Biblical land code and the Prophets. (He was the son of a reform rabbi.) Whether there was any direct influence of the one man on the other in the 1890s, when they both lived in Berlin, remains an open question, but it is known that in 1901 Oppenheimer accepted an invitation to lecture on his scheme to Syrkin's Hessiana Society in Berlin.[113]

Late in that year, Oppenheimer published a series of articles in the central Zionist paper, *Die Welt,* which appeared in Vienna under Herzl's guidance. Oppenheimer and Herzl now began to correspond, both men seeking in the other an ally for his own cause. Herzl was attracted in principle to the idea of cooperative projects (and had declared so in his *Altneuland* written in 1901), but he demanded complete loyalty from his followers. Oppenheimer was ready to devote his energies to the Zionist cause but, to all intents and purposes, only to the extent that it adopted his pilot project.[114]

In March 1903 Oppenheimer was quoted in *Die Welt* as saying, "the remedy that the leaders of the movement seek to employ is one I myself have proposed ... , namely, cooperative settlement on land publicly owned in perpetuity." He added that "I am a *Zionist* because, and to the extent that, I am a believing *socialist.*"[115] In June, Herzl informed Oppenheimer that "we are now planning to acquire land in Palestine ... If it will be possible to establish settlements there, I will do it according to your system."[116]

At the Sixth Zionist Congress in August 1903, Oppenheimer (at Herzl's invitation) delivered a key address on his scheme and its relevance to Zionism. The Uganda crisis intervened at this point and no formal resolution on cooperative settlement was adopted. But a step was now taken that aroused little interest in the midst of the storm then raging but can be seen in retrospect to have had the greatest significance. At the congress, Herzl permitted the establishment of a commission with the task of examining the possibilities for practical action in Palestine. There were three members elected to the Palestine Commission: Otto Warburg, Selig (Evgenii) Soskin, and Franz Oppenheimer.

A few years later, at the Eighth Congress held in August 1907, Warburg explained how in his view, at least, the Palestine Commission had originated. In the early years of the movement, Warburg had chosen to play a passive role in Zionist affairs because he did not share Herzl's faith in diplomacy as the all-but-exclusive instrument of Zionist policy. He himself had always advocated an evolutionary path, a series of small-scale but concrete projects in Palestine. However, he recalled, "the time came when Herzl began to experiment. Oppenheimer and I went to Vienna. We laid before him a part of what has now become a wide-ranging program. Herzl expressed agreement and the Palestine Commission was set up."[117]

All three members of the commission lived in Berlin, and Warburg, as chairman, rapidly converted it into the main vehicle for the implementation of his ideas. A leading scientist, professor, a member of the prominent banking family, a man of energy and political acumen, he lost no opportunity to advance his case and his cause. He saw in Oppenheimer a natural ally.

In April 1904 the Greater Actions Committee of the Zionist movement passed a resolution calling for the establishment of a settlement along the cooperative lines proposed by Oppenheimer. The Palestine Commission was unable to implement this resolution at the time – its annual budget was a mere 15,000 francs per annum – but it financed exploratory and survey expeditions, initiated projects for tree-planting (the Herzl forest and Olive Grove Fund), and encouraged the Jewish National Fund to purchase tracts of land in Palestine. It brought out a journal, *Altneuland.* It advanced plans, inter alia, for workers' housing estates, for an agricultural research station, for an agricultural training farm, and for cooperative settlement.[118] In 1907 it encouraged the promising young scholar and economist, Arthur Ruppin, to undertake an extended study tour of Palestine, and in that year it brought before the Eighth Congress the plan to establish a permanent office

(*Palastinaamt*) to represent Zionist interests in Palestine (it being understood that Ruppin would probably consent to run it, to act in effect as Warburg's man in Jaffa).

Increasingly, following Herzl's death in 1904, Warburg placed himself at the head of the opposition to the new president of the world Zionist movement, David Wolffsohn. Warburg saw the Russian Zionists with their Hoveve Zion traditions as leading allies, while Wolffsohn considered himself the faithful heir to Herzl's policy of diplomacy first. The Jewish Colonial Bank and its Jaffa branch, the Anglo-Palestine Company (headed by Z. D. Levontin), were counted in Wolff-sohn's camp, for they tended to oppose any project that smacked of waste, philan-thropy, and the erosion of the movement's financial power.[119] This division was variously described as that between "practical" and "political" Zionism and that between Berlin and Cologne (where Wolffsohn had his home and the Jewish Na-tional Fund its head office). At the Eighth Congress, Warburg summed up his position in the following terms: "Zionism must either become Palestine-centered or it will not survive at all (vigorous applause and clapping). Without economic foundations in Palestine political Zionism is and remains a house of cards (cries of assent) . . . Laissez-faire, laissez-aller is not suited to Palestinian conditions."[120]

It was as junior partners in the opposition associated with Warburg that the Austrian Poale Zion came to play an increasingly vocal and effective role. They took up Oppenheimer's project and made it their own. In fact, their leaders, particularly Shlomo Kaplansky and Nathan Gross, now replaced Syrkin (who from 1903 was moving toward territorialism) as the most persistent advocates of the idea that only large-scale cooperative settlement in Palestine could save the Zionist enterprise from disaster.

Of course, the more the Russian Poale Zion moved to the left and toward a purist class-war doctrine, so the gap dividing them from the Austrian party leader-ship became ever more sharply defined. Furthermore, Kaplansky and Gross found themselves faced with an internal opposition that, in step with the revolution of 1905, was drawn to the "orthodoxy" of the Russian party. "Something more concrete than territorialism," Gross declared at the Austrian Poale Zion conference of June 1905,

> divides us from our proletarian-Zionist brothers in Russia – that is, their theory of Zionist development constructed on orthodox Marxist lines . . . They say that . . . it is the task of Zionism to proletarianize the Jewish people . . . But we do not need any theories of proletarianization and pauper-ization in Zionism. According to the most recent scientific theory, we have the right . . . to ensure that our proletarians . . . should become settlers – not capitalists but free farmers living from the produce of their own labor on their own piece of land.[121]

In reply, the spokesman for the left wing insisted that

> we are workers first and only then Zionists . . . It has in no way been proved that agrarian cooperatives will succeed. What financial means are available for colonisation? – only capitalist. The [Zionist] congress can have no influ-ence on colonization. Besides, how does the speaker [Gross] imagine that the

congress will remain uninfluenced by class hatred . . . [He] has criticized the Russian Poale Zion and Marxism. I believe, though, that we must follow the same path as the Russian [party].[122]

Many of the Russian Poale Zion leaders found refuge in Austria-Hungary once the revolution went into decline, and they defended their position uncompromisingly in the local press and at party meetings. "The capitalist spirit," write Efraim Blumenfeld (Bloch) in *Der yidisher arbeter* in 1908,

> is a revolutionary spirit . . . Palestine will become one of the great revolutionary centers in Turkey . . . [and] the Jewish proletariat will stand at the head of the Palestine revolution . . . [The Austrian Poale Zion] exaggerate the real value that the farming class has for us [and] regard it as our most important party task to create such a class in Palestine . . . But [modern agriculture] produces a special type of wage worker who sells his labor . . . to the large-scale landowner . . . We must begin at once to plant the seeds of international socialism among the Jewish workers in Palestine . . . and to prepare against the future treachery of the Jewish bourgeoisie . . . We must in no way exclude the Arab working class from Jewish production (we ourselves have been too often and too long excluded) . . . We must render the Arab worker more capable of fighting against Jewish exploitation.[123]

But this viewpoint never won over more than a minority within the Austrian Poale Zion party. The fact that Austrian (in contrast to Russian) Marxism had long tolerated various forms of revisionism goes far to explain, no doubt, this almost flaunted independence of thought. What the exiles from revolutionary Russia saw as deviation, the local leaders regarded rather as sophistication.

At the Eighth Zionist Congress of 1907, Gross and Kaplansky spoke out vigorously in defense of the Oppenheimer project and Warburg's policies. The Zionist goal, Kaplansky said there, was not "to ensure that the leading, the strongest, the most capitalist elements in Palestine be Jewish but . . . to ensure that the working elements – and hence the country itself – be Jewish."[124] "Every one hundred Jewish families," declared Gross, "attract six thousand Arabs; if things continue thus, we shall fall victim to the same fate as the Germans in certain Slavic lands."[125] The Jews had to work their own land without hired labor. They would not lower their standard of living to that of the small-holding peasant. And so the only solution lay in the large-scale, mechanized and cooperative farming proposed by Oppenheimer.

For his part, Warburg made a point of praising the stand taken by the Austrian Poale Zion. It was still a small party but "it moves according to a logical line and . . . in those regions where practical work is possible . . . What Mr. Gross has said is . . . that this must be the way and that on this basis we can undertake an experimental venture . . . We welcome with great satisfaction the fact that an organization such as Poale Zion is working with us."[126] In practical terms, Warburg suggested that the agricultural experimental station be set up in Atlit and the training farm at Hittin. Further (here he was merely reiterating his plans as stated to the congress of the German Zionists in June 1906),[127]

> the cooperative farm at Daleikah-Umeljunn [Daleika Umm Juni], which is to be on the Jordan at the place where it leaves the Sea of Galilee, should first

be adequately prepared by a managing body and only converted into a leasehold worker-cooperative at that stage when a sufficient working capital for a rational farming system has been collected and deposited with the Bank.[128]

The resolution adopted declared that "the Eighth Congress resolves to found a settlement cooperative on the land of the National Fund."[129]

On 3 April 1908 Arthur Ruppin arrived in Jaffa to head the Palestine Office and the Palestine Land Development Company (PLDC), both newly established institutions of the Zionist movement. In his diary, he had noted that "my life's mission will be to create an autonomous Jewish community [Gemeinwesen] in Palestine."[130] One of his first actions in 1908 was to launch an experiment on the land owned by the National Fund at the southern end of the Sea of Galilee, at Daleika.

The PLDC established a farm there to be worked by young Russian Jews under the direction of an experienced agronomist. Initial investment was kept down to a bare minimum, and it was hoped that the project could bring in a profit in the first year. The aim of the scheme was to provide the workers with varied and responsible experience in arable farming on the assumption that they would later become self-sufficient farmers (elsewhere if not at Daleika), to ensure that national land be worked by Jews, and to prove that Jewish labor could be profitable.

During his visit of 1907, Ruppin would later recall, he had already concluded that only the youth from Russia could shake the Yishuv out of its creeping paralysis. Even though he knew no Russian or Yiddish, and they rarely spoke German, he was determined to establish a real working relationship with them. "From many points of view," he wrote,

(an excessive tendency to emotionalism, the proclivity for long debates, restlessness, an absence of order and of exactness in work), the workers were alien to my temperament; but for all this I concluded that their real enthusiasm for agriculture as the foundation stone of the Jewish national home was a precious asset that had to be husbanded in every possible way.[131]

Eight workers arrived in Daleika, henceforward to be known as Kinneret, on 8 June 1908, and they were soon joined by one woman, Sara Malkin, who acted as the cook. All but one of the nine were members of Ha-Poel Ha-Tsair. Three of them – Yisrael Bloch, Yosef Elkin, Tankhum Tanfilov – had come together to Palestine in 1907; were from the same home town, Romny; and had belonged to the Ha-Tehiya and New Bilu movements in Russia.

Bloch later recalled that they had formed themselves into a "commune" while on board ship en route to Jaffa, in his view "under the influence of the paragraph on collectivism in the program of Ha-Tehiya."[132] The truth is, though, that the youth in Palestine (regardless of present or past party affiliations) frequently formed such small communal groups in which income, expenditure, and living arrangements were shared. This made life much easier for these unmarried youngsters. Furthermore, it was in accord with that long tradition of Russian radical thought which assigned such key importance to egalitarian modes of life: to the mir or obshchina (the village commune); to the artel (the work cooperative); and to sobornost (community or communion). The trio from Romny later formed the nucleus of the group that in 1910 went to Umm Juni and gradually created the first communal farm settlement of Deganya – in effect and in present-day parlance (although not thus termed) the first kibbutz.[133]

Frequent reports in the press spoke of the enthusiasm that reigned initially in the small group at Kinneret. For the first time, the young immigrants had undertaken to farm land purchased by the Zionist movement, to demonstrate that those without any financial resources of their own could return a profit on public investment, to test and prove themselves.

But, paradoxically, the general labor organization in Galilee, Ha-Horesh, came out in the strongest terms against the Kinneret experiment. It went so far as to impose an official albeit "passive" boycott against the new enterprise. The reasons stated publicly were that the calculations projecting a profit were hopelessly exaggerated; that there would in fact certainly be a large deficit in the first years; that the agronomist in charge was incompetent and disloyal; and that the workers imported from Judea were totally inexperienced in arable farming.

However, two other factors were no doubt at work here. First, the group in Kinneret was almost solidly drawn from Ha-Poel Ha-Tsair, while Ha-Horesh in 1908 (even though officially nonparty) was led largely by members of Poale Zion. Second, and more significant, it was deeply resented that Ruppin had acted on his own initiative and had not turned for help or advice to the workers already in Galilee. Here was perhaps the earliest example of what was to become a constantly recurring pattern. The workers in Palestine were becoming more inclined to rely on public funds from abroad for the advancement of their cause, but they tended to rebel against outside direction even if it originated with the Zionist organization. "Of course," Ben Gurion recalled shortly thereafter,

> our bureaucracy took no notice whatsoever of all these protests. What is more, one of our writers [Radler-Feldman, then in Kinneret], the most devoted champion of the [official Zionist] leadership and especially of Warburg, came out with a protest against the rebellion within the camp . . . And, to our shame, some workers were found [in Judea] who chose to ignore the decision of the Galilee workers and went to work [there] . . . While the "nonnational" ICA farm in Sejera drew to it the best workers in Galilee, the "national" farm of the Jewish National Fund in Kinneret was regarded as little short of an atrocity . . . and no decent worker wanted to go there.[134]

As the months went by, malaria began to demoralize the group in Kinneret; the projected profit did indeed prove to be a mirage; and relations with the director, Berman, went from good to bad and from bad to worse. In 1909 a strike broke out and eight workers, including the Romny "commune," left for Hadera to work as wage workers in the village.[135]

In sum, then, the plans debated and the experiments launched in Galilee during the years 1906–8 had made little immediate headway. Neither the Sejera Collective (which had broken up), nor the national farm at Kinneret (which barely limped along) could be counted successful. It is, therefore, not surprising to discover that the leadership of the two parties in the south, in Judea, felt under no compulsion to modify their ideological stance in order to make room for the idea of worker settlement.

In the spring of 1908 Dr. Hillel Yoffe (the director of the small hospital in Zikhron Yaakov) published an article in *Ha-poel ha-tsair* arguing that the workers aided by public funds were duty-bound to establish agricultural colonies of their own. The workers should form groups (kvutsot) to take on this task. He left open the question of "whether these new settlements should opt for the individual or the collective forms of land use."[136] A similar case was made in a speech delivered to a congress of Ha-Poel Ha-Tsair in 1908 by Yosef Vitkin (a schoolteacher and writer who had lived for some years in Galilee): "Ha-Poel Ha-Tsair must . . . seek to attain its goal of conquering labor through the acquisition and settlement of the land."[137]

This speech, like Yoffe's article, appeared in the party journal accompanied by editorial notes critical of their content. The party conference did not adopt Vitkin's position and he withdrew from party life. When Aharonovich asked him to reconsider his position, he reportedly replied: "I have told you what my credo is. I have not abandoned it and will not abandon it. When the time comes that you can accept it, then call me in and I am with you."[138]

The position in Poale Zion was analogous. The party central committee in Judea maintained little contact with the Galilee. "Our party as such," noted Zerubavel, "stood apart from all these undertakings of the Jewish worker [in Galilee]. The comrades carried everything through alone or in small groups but outside the party, and often with the thought that it contradicted the party cause and goals."[139]

The failure of confrontation

The workers and the Yishuv, 1904–1911

In the years 1909–14, what had been the minority opinion became that of the majority. The two youth parties, and the labor movement as a whole, increasingly played down what had been the prevailing strategy – the reliance on capitalist development, on proletarianization (or labor conquest) and on the democratization of the Yishuv. The alternative concept based on labor settlement, "utopian" experimentation, and withdrawal into a self-contained world won ever more support. This reversal was neither sudden nor complete but it was far-reaching, encouraged by an increasing alienation from the established Yishuv and by a grim determination to create their own society.

Disillusionment with proletarianization as a primary goal was not produced by any change for the worse in the economic situation. On the contrary, the economy developed in the main as originally predicted. To a large extent, the decade before World War I was one of rapid growth for the Yishuv. It has been estimated that there was a net immigration of close to twenty thousand Jews. The Jewish population in the agricultural colonies rose to some twelve thousand, approximately double the number of 1904. As foreseen, the plantation system – citrus, almonds, and vines – advanced steadily as more sophisticated techniques were introduced, European markets opened up, and attractive returns on investment made possible. Tel Aviv was founded in 1909, proved remarkably popular, and had a population of over two thousand by 1914. Older centers also grew fast. In 1914, again, there were three thousand Jews in Haifa, ten thousand in Jaffa, and some fifty thousand in Jerusalem.[140] It was in these years that the Hebrew high schools (*gimnasyot*) were established in Tel Aviv and Jerusalem and that the Technion (or Technikum) was founded in Haifa.

There were, of course, times of economic recession and unemployment; the most severe case came in 1911. And work, especially in farming, was largely seasonal. All in all, though, the economic expansion brought with it a demand for manual workers both skilled and unskilled. Despite the severe Arab competition, wages rose sharply in this period. The most common plaint in the labor press was not that there were not jobs but that there were no immigrant workers to take up the places available.

It was the failure to exploit economic opportunity, not its absence, that defeated the orthodox strategy. Sociological and political factors intervened to frustrate proletarianization. There was in fact a crucial (and paradoxical) flaw in the orthodox prognosis. Those among the immigrant youth who were ready to adapt to local realities as they found them had every incentive to abandon the role of rank-and-file worker. On the other hand, the youth who insisted on remaining wage workers were precisely those whose unbending allegiance to their own way of life, whose stiff-necked pride, made them unacceptable to their potential employers. Driven to fury by the workers from Russia, the employers could always fall back on Arabs or Oriental Jews as replacements. There was a pattern here that runs through the history of the Second Aliya with a relentless regularity.

The development of the Yishuv opened up a whole range of opportunities for anybody willing to leave the ranks of the proletariat. Foremen were eagerly sought out to supervise the workers in the orchards and on the building sites. The modern schools now being established needed teachers. As various public institutions – banks, the Palestine Office, ICA, Ezra – grew in size, so did the demand for reliable officials. Anybody who was able to accumulate a small capital sum had a chance to acquire land in one of the colonies and become an independent farmer. Thus, to the extent that he had acquired some experience, the young radical from Russia, scorned and hounded as a worker, found himself under constant pressure to move one or two rungs up the socioeconomic ladder. "Bit by bit," we read in a letter from Berl Katznelson written in 1909,

> all the veteran and skilled workers become foremen and they do not even feel what kind of work that is. In Galilee, it seems, this type does not exist, but here [in Judea] you find it everywhere. Perhaps the only one who does not want to be a foreman is Gordon (no, there are others, definitely others). But Gordon is somebody who keeps himself and his family on sixty kopeks a day and says that he lacks for nothing.[141]

"Who," it was asked in *Ha-poel ha-tsair*, "are most of the farmers in Palestine if not the idealists of yesterday? . . . And who today is the foreman who drives away Jewish workers if not the idealist worker of yesterday?"[142]

Constantly depleted by defections and, even more, by the huge reemigration, the miniscule labor movement nonetheless remained obstinately loyal if not to its specific strategy then certainly to its overall way of life. The veteran Yishuv and the radical youth formed two different worlds, and the fact that the workers – the

"Moscovites," as they were often called—made no secret of their wish to remodel, "democratize," the Yishuv ensured that these were also two hostile worlds. The workers brought with them from Russia a code of behavior and set of values that provoked profound hostility among nearly all those who were not of their camp. A state of chronic ill-will, punctuated by periodic outbursts of open crisis, became the norm. There was hardly any sphere that did not produce its share of tension.

Thus, for example, the Yishuv as it had developed until 1903 was overwhelmingly committed to orthodox Judaism. True, there were within it nonobservant and free-thinking Jews, but they rarely flaunted the fact for fear of provoking furious retaliation. The Bilu group had only been permitted to settle in Gedera because it yielded so much ground on this issue to majority opinion. But the youth who now arrived from Russia were for the most part absolutely unwilling to hide their belief that the era of orthodox Judaism was over, that modern man had no need of religion at least in its established forms, and that compromise in this sphere was so much hypocrisy. They granted on occasion that there was much that was imposing and authentic in the rabbinic achievement, but the future would have to be built up on new, anthropocentric, principles.

In everyday life, this attitude produced constant friction. Aleksandr Zaid's "commune" of stonemasons had to leave its flat in the Bukharan Quarter of Jerusalem in 1906 "because of our heretic ways."[143] The attempts to recruit a following among the Oriental and Sephardi Jewish communities in Jerusalem were fatally damaged by the sight of the Russian youth boiling water for tea on the Sabbath.[144] In 1908, at Yavneel (or Yama), an ICA village in Galilee, the workers in the area were told to keep well away on Saturdays after a pistol shot had once disturbed the Sabbath peace.[145] Smoking and riding on the day of rest produced furious reactions. Farmers kept their daughters away from the radical youth, with their free and easy ways, "lest we ruin them" (as Sara Malkin put it).[146] "There are those [farmers] who say straight out," it was reported, "that for them there is no difference between a worker who desecrates the Sabbath and a Gentile and [so] . . . why should they prefer him to the Arab worker."[147]

The free man, it was felt, had not only the right but the duty to act and speak out in demonstratively nonconformist ways. To compromise was to betray. Nothing was greater anathema than attempts to adapt religion to modern ways. "Either the way of the past or the way of the future . . . , " we read in *Ha-poel ha-tsair*, "but not that synthesis of religion and life according to the liberal system, the golden rule."[148] "I am not a man of science . . . , " Brenner wrote in 1909 (attacking Berdiaev and his school),

> and not a rationalist nor a positivist . . . I know all the limited power of the human reason . . . and all the coldness of existence without God . . . [But] has the desire burning within us for liberation, for freedom in all its forms— despite the terror of irredeemable emptiness—been extinguished? Have we still not recognized that God, all the gods, have died, are dead? Yes, they have died, . . . are gone for ever and with them their laws, their commandments, their ordinances.[149]

As clearly suggested in this passage, the religious issue was merely symptomatic of a far wider conflict in attitude and outlook. Convinced that their values were those of the future, self-evident and more authentic than those of the Yishuv, the youth fast moved beyond simple opposition. Increasingly isolated and frustrated, they tended to adopt a prophetic stance, calling down fire and brimstone on the corrupt society around them. They measured the established norms not against their own achievements (which for a long time were marginal), but against their ideals, against their belief in simple manual labor, strict egalitarianism, absolute freedom, and national self-liberation.

Drawing heavily on the tradition of critical realism in both modern Russian and modern Hebrew literature (Saltykov, Dostoevsky, Mendele, Lilienblum), they were committed to speaking their minds with a brutal frankness. Yosef Aharonovich quoted approvingly Ahad Ha-Am's opinion that what distinguished the prophet above all was that he spoke out both as a "man of truth" and as a "man of extremes."[150] And he saw in Ahad Ha-Am's own uncompromising article of 1891 ("The Truth from Palestine") a model of the prophetic idiom. Brenner regarded Lilienblum as the giant of his, the previous, generation of Hebrew writers, above all because he was "a man of truth,"[151] and Radler-Feldman ("Rebi Binyamin") noted that the hatred for every false note, the quest for "extreme simplicity has reached in Brenner, it must be granted, almost pathological dimensions."[152]

One result was the frequent readiness of the youth to subject themselves to unflinching and often lacerating self-criticism. But there was a still greater readiness to denounce others. On one occasion, Aharonovich even wrote to Gordon complaining that "workers who cheat in their work . . . show contempt for everything sacred, cynicism about the country" were discussed behind closed doors but not in the party newspaper. "And I ask myself whether the comrades would pass by in silence if they saw such things not among workers but among other people . . . In this way, our paper no longer carries the truth in the full sense of the word but only a party truth which, generally, is not deserving of that word at all."[153]

What infuriated and embittered the youth, above all, was that the Yishuv they found awaiting them in Palestine was so reminiscent of what they had chosen to leave behind forever in the Pale of Settlement. Here, too, they felt, rabbinical theocracy ruled hand in hand with oligarchy. Here, too, non-Jews were workers and Jews employers. But now repugnance was reinforced by despair. Corruption in Exile, in the galut, was to be expected, but in the Promised Land it became a disaster terrible beyond measure, for it threatened a final end to hope. Terms of contempt drawn from Russian populism, from the Haskala, and once used to condemn the way of life in the Pale—*meshchanstvo,* parasitism—were now directed against the Yishuv. The labor journals painted reality ever more often in stark blacks and whites, contrasting the world of the present with that of the future, the slave to the past with the new man.

"You attack us, the new youth," wrote Aharonovich in 1907, "by saying that the first generation did not philosophize much and so it created something, while we criticize too much and so create nothing . . . True, we . . . are not creating in Palestine. But what can be done!"[154] "I have become accustomed," Gordon wrote in 1909, "to the idea that the flaws of the Exile are most pronounced here in Palestine of all places."[155] "Here," he wrote in 1911, "petty egotism reigns, the crudest materialism, which exceeds even that to be found in parts of the Exile."[156] "If I were an anti-Zionist," wrote Aharonovich at that time,

I would have no need for abstract theories but would simply draw attention to the biggest colony in Palestine – Petah Tikva . . . How does it differ from some small town in Exile except perhaps that there they devour one another while here they devour the last remaining resources of the nation for their own benefit.[157]

In the period of the Haskala, Brenner argued, again in 1911, the cry was "to be a Jew at home and a man outside"; for Hibat Zion it became "to be a Jew at home and a Jew outside"; but now a new call has gone out: "to be a man at home and a man outside."[158] Judaism had to be reduced to the common denominator shared by every healthy nationality: to do one's own work, to live in one's own land, to speak one's own language – no more but also no less. There were those among the workers from Russia who had grasped this truth. "They are few, these simple Jews, very few, but they do exist. They are new – a new type among the Children of Israel."[159]

"If at the end," Aharonovich wrote in 1912 (paraphrasing Vitkin but by now speaking for himself too), "we have here millions of workers at the mercy of a few predatory wolves, then what is all the effort for? . . . What Redemption is that?"[160] The basic issue, Brenner declared again in 1912, is that

the Jewish masses do not have work . . . and do not know how to work . . . that there is no constructive Jewish nation and perhaps never was such a nation; that we have always lived like gypsies scratching ourselves for the amusement of the indigenous population or like dogs, crawling before their masters; that we have always survived not despite the terrible persecutions, but because of them.[161]

"Judaism, after all," Gordon wrote in 1913,

grounded its ethics entirely on truth as opposed to Christianity, which based its ethics entirely on love. But truth knows no compromises with itself . . . And truth, simple truth, without evasions, says plainly that living on the labor of others, parasitism in any form, even the most aesthetic, even if justified by every possible theory, cannot serve as the basis for . . . right.[162]

This militant tone – it became ever more marked in the labor press – could not but strain still further the tense relationship of the radical youth with the established Yishuv. But the process of alienation owed even more to the everyday contacts, economic and political, between the workers and their employers. A vicious circle of mutual discontent and distrust fast developed. The farmer and the building contractor sought a system based on low wages, a stable core of experienced workers, and a large reservoir of casual labor for the peak seasons. But it soon became obvious that the immigrant workers could rarely meet any of these demands.

First, they tended to be forever on the move from one job to another, from one colony to the next. The reasons for their mobility are not hard to seek. They were for the most part very young, unmarried, and far from home. They were usually paid by the day, the week, or the month and so could move on at the shortest notice. They sought adventure, were restless, and did not adapt easily to the routine monotony of farm labor. "In many of the workers," we read in a report of 1908, "the wanderlust is strong. They cannot stay long in one place. They change their place of work every year and even in the middle of the year."[163] "From Galilee to Judea, from Judea to Galilee," wrote Vilkansky in 1910, "so the stream flows round and round."[164] Yaakov Rabinovich suggested that this phenomenon had ideological as well as psychological roots: "The worker of the revolutionary generation wants to be simply a worker living from nothing but his labor. He dreams for the time being only of freedom. For him, the main thing is absolute freedom: I work a set number of hours, receive my wages and have nothing more to do with you."[165] A survey undertaken by Zeev Smilansky in 1912 revealed that the majority of the Russian workers in Judea had been in their given place of residence for less than one year and only 15 percent had been in one place for more than three years.[166]

This trend, of course, antagonized the employers, who were reluctant to take on the aggravating task of training such volatile novices. But it also had another negative effect. The constant movement undermined every attempt to set up efficient self-help institutions, be it in colony or town. And as if this factor were not enough, a crippling influence was also exerted here by the party and other sectional rivalries; there were six overlapping organizations in Galilee alone in 1909. Kitchens, canteens, libraries, laundries, and shops were set up by the workers to make their life somewhat more bearable, but they rarely survived for longer than a few months, often collapsing in a ruin of unpaid debts. The many schemes "that were overambitious and failed," we read in a report from Petah Tikva in 1908, "have undermined their [the workers'] faith in their ability to do anything."[167] "We are big failures in organizing our lives," we read in a letter of Berl Katznelson to his brother in 1911. "And nobody is to blame but ourselves. We eat badly; we are dirty and from this follows the disorder, the neglect, and the frequent illness ... One is always getting ready for something; one is going to change one place for another ... and meanwhile one lives for the moment."[168]

Lacking the support that they would have gained from a network of mutual-benefit institutions, the workers had to press for higher pay. "True," wrote one observer in 1912,

> at one time Ussishkin did suggest that the Jewish youth ... offer to work for the same wages as the Arabs ... And, indeed, there were then Jewish workers who refused to receive higher wages ... so that it could not look as though they were in receipt of charity. But to live for a long time according to such harsh principles was impossible. When help from home no longer came (or when one tired of taking it), when one's trousers and shoes from home began to fall apart, one had to think about raising one's wages.[169]

In 1912 a Jewish worker was often paid as much as two francs a day, while an Arab (who usually had his own home and some land in a neighboring village) rarely received much more than one. In turn, this wage gap further exacerbated relations. The employer was reluctant to engage the more expensive labor unless he was sure of a commensurate return. The workers bitterly resented the vulnerability and insecurity of their position. If they were strongly enough placed to do so, they had resort to strikes. But this was usually a self-defeating tactic, given the ample supply of Arab replacements. The result was resentment and frustration.

They fell back on their political demands with a redoubled anger. A particular bone of contention was their claim that they were entitled to enfranchisement as equal–voting–members of the colonies. Predictably, this demand was invariably rejected by the colonists, who insisted that the right to vote had to be limited to property-owners or, at least, to permanent residents. Given the centrality of "democratization" in the political programs of the youth parties, this issue proved to be a constant source of irritation.

In the early days, when Ha-Poel Ha-Tsair was totally committed to the strategy of capitalist development and "labor conquest," the party leaders outspokenly condemned what they then regarded as examples of overreaction on the part of the workers. The war to be avoided at all costs, wrote Aharonovich in 1908,

> is neither K.K. [*Klassen-kampf*] nor the economic struggle but simply the war of words and whistles . . . , of curses and slander against everybody suspected of being bourgeois–a war with its origins in the Russian revolution, but one which has [by now] struck deep roots in our life in Palestine . . . It produces a terrible antagonism between the workers and the local inhabitants.[170]

Such admonitions became ever less frequent in later years as the policy of "democratization" gave way to that of self-sufficiency. But the relations of workers with employers and foremen remained as difficult as ever. A. Tsiyoni (Vilkansky), an agronomist who had been placed by Ruppin in charge of the experimental farm at Bet Arif (near Lod), gained first-hand experience of the problem and analyzed it in the pages of *Ha-poel ha-tsair*:

> What would be regarded by a normal free man, who has never born the yoke of class theory, as simple courtesy, he [the young worker] sees as subservience, sycophancy, crawling. In this class consciousness, which still stems from the revolutionary days in Russia, there is more . . . self-indulgence than the natural freedom which judges everything in its right context and acts by inner feeling with moderation, right measure and limits.[171]

Avshalom Feinberg, a native son of Zikhron Yaakov, who became a fierce opponent of the labor movement (and eventually a central member of the Nili spy group), spoke in similar terms to Yosef Klausner during the latter's visit to Palestine in 1912:

> I no longer know how to behave toward the Jewish workers! I tried to treat them in a friendly way, but they would shout: "We see what's going on! With all this sweet talk you are trying to weaken our class consciousness . . ." I tried to treat them as an employer, but then I was shouted at worse: "A farmer in Palestine is not entitled to be a bourgeois. He like us came for the sake of the same ideal! We will not tolerate this superior attitude . . . !"[172]

The situation was exacerbated still further by the conviction of the youth that the established Yishuv was indifferent to or at least pusillanimous in, the defense of the national interest. They insisted (as noted above) on carrying the national flag in demonstrations, thus provoking a number of public brawls. Similar incidents flared up when the youth (urged on initially by Ha-Poel Ha-Tsair but later by Poale Zion, too), protested against the use of languages other than Hebrew, be it Yiddish, French, Russian, or German, in public affairs. A French play put on by the school-children in Petah Tikva was shouted down by a group of some thirty workers. In turn, the furious parents heaped abuse on the hecklers: "Write about it in *Ha-poel ha-tsair*, but don't disrupt!" "Tramps! [*yehefim*]," "Hooligans!" "Loudmouths [*grobe yungen*]."[173] Such episodes became commonplace.

The more the young socialists took on work as paid guards in the colonies, the more they tended to emphasize their role as the champions of "national honor and pride" (as Ben Gurion put it in 1911).[174] They expressed an open contempt for those colonies which preferred to insure themselves against attack by hiring watch-men from the most predatory of the neighboring villages (Beduin, Cherkassy, or Metawileh, perhaps). To acquiesce in "protection," it was argued, served only to multiply the number of thefts, for if others were sometimes too afraid to rob, the hired guards certainly were not. In the long run, the colonists would be left with no choice but to hire Jewish guards. "The Arabs hate us," we read in *Ha-poel ha-tsair* in 1908, "and we are keeping deadly enemies in our homes, our farms, our fields . . . There are workers who do not want to succeed as the result [of such] negative factors . . . But we are dealing with a prognosis of vital significance, the symptoms of which will become more and more apparent."[175] "You, [the col-onists]," wrote Zerubavel in *Ha-ahdut* in 1911, "are too comfortable, too moder-ate, in placing Arab heroes – well-known thieves and robbers – over you and in letting them rob and plunder . . . The root of our problems lies not in a lack of tolerance, but in the fact that tolerance has rooted itself too deep in many of us."[176] He quoted with approval a rebuke cast by a young Jewish watchman at one of the farmers who had not resisted the theft of his horses until the bitter end: "How is it that your horses are gone and you are still alive? Shame on you." (The watchman in question was Yehezkel Nisanov, who in 1905 had been active in a Poale Zion self-defense group in Baku and who in 1911 was killed in Galilee in just such another incident.)

In many cases the colonies did switch, at least on an experimental basis, to Jewish guards, but this did not long improve relations. Wage and other monetary disputes became frequent, and neither side was prepared to trust the other to handle negotiations and diplomatic ties with the surrounding Arab villages. Where the colonists saw prudence, the workers saw cowardice. What the workers held to be a matter of honor was recklessness in the eyes of the colonists.

A related cause of friction was the chronic fear of the established Yishuv that the young workers, if thwarted, might resort to violence. The revolutionary and class war rhetoric employed in the early years by Poale Zion – above all, by the Rostov group – did much to encourage this belief. However, there were also actual cases of intimidation.

In Petah Tikva in 1908 a group of twenty-seven workers, who felt that they had been underpaid, ignored the findings of an arbitration committee, marched into the farmer's house, and forced him to pay over the disputed sum. "You workers, who come here to 'conquer labor'," wrote one of the most respected of the farmers, Zalman Gisin, "do you really expect to do so by such methods?"[177] In a similar case, Yaakov Chertok (who had first come to Palestine in 1882 with the Bilu) was forced to accept arbitration by an armed delegation from the Jerusalem committee of Poale Zion.[178] During the strike at the Shtein tool works in Jaffa, the workers reportedly "sought to take over the factory and act as though they were the owners. They would not permit anything to be removed from the factory, saying that it and all the machinery in it belonged to them."[179] They posted guards at the gate and searched everybody leaving, including the owners.

In 1909 a group was formed in Jaffa to enforce the employment of Jewish labor in the construction of Tel Aviv (Ahuzat Bayit), "by all and every means conceivable."[180] A few members of Ha-Poel Ha-Tsair joined this organization, and the party felt compelled to condemn officially the employment of terror as an instrument of "labor conquest." Apart from anything else, it was argued, terrorism "could give others who are stronger than we are the right to use the same methods against us."[181] It was also noted ironically that while terrorism had gone out of fashion in Russia it had now found its last advocates in Palestine.

Themes of violence and coercion recurred in all the most dramatic crises of the early years, 1905–8. When, late in 1905, the farmers in Petah Tikva (urged on by the rabbinical establishment in Jerusalem) decided to ban a public performance and party organized by the youth, they sent four mounted Beduin guards to try to enforce their order. When the majority of the workers subsequently refused to accept the conditions laid down by the colony – to observe the Sabbath ordinances; to obey the village committee; to refrain from inviting the village youth to their meetings – they were ordered out of the settlement. For their part, the workers refused to leave. "We stand before a new expulsion," Gordon reportedly said, "not from Spain but by our own brothers from our own country . . . We must not move from here."[182]

A concerted effort was made to deny the rebels work, lodging, medical assistance, and even to extend this boycott to other colonies. The youth was now accused (as Gordon recalled a few years later) "of wanting to trick the farmers out of their land . . . , to introduce 'terror', to destroy the Yishuv."[183] Lilienblum in Odessa wrote condemning the "Marxist children barely out of the kindergarten [marksistishe kheyder yinglekh.]"[184] One by one, the workers yielded ground, scattering to other colonies both in Judea and in the north.

The same pattern of development unfolded when the workers in the wine cellars of Rishon Le-Zion went out on strike early in 1907. Picketing led to blows and furious reactions on both sides. The strikers were defeated and the youth had no choice but to move to other colonies. But, we read in Der onfang, the farmers in Rehovot refused to employ "the Russian kramolnikes [incendiaries] who have done their best to ruin the wine cellars in Rishon."[185] Ha-Poel Ha-Tsair put the blame for this episode on Poale Zion. "The Rostov doctrine," read one ironic commentary, "began to develop into a guide for action, and . . . the first of the new pioneers arrived in the oldest of the colonies and raised barricades—yes, real barricades as befits twentieth-century pioneers!"[186]

Violence, more rhetorical than real in the Petah Tikva boycott and Rishon strike, became serious enough in the Jaffa incident of March 1908. Following a number of instances in which Jews there had been harried by Arab youth, the Poale Zion party resolved that henceforward in such cases it would retaliate. The situation, it was reported in Der yidisher arbeter, "forced us to decide once and for all – force against force!"[187]

Brawls twice ensued. In the second case, bottles were thrown from a building, the Jewish workers pursued their opponents into a shop, and in the fracas an Arab received a serious knife wound. At this stage, the Turkish authorities intervened. Five workers were arrested in the Hotel Haim Barukh, which was frequented by members of Ha-Poel Ha-Tsair. When the Turkish soldiers entered the Hotel Spektor (associated with the Poale Zion) they were greeted by a shot and, in a fury of rage, they set upon all about them, shooting at the workers indiscriminately, smashing furniture. All in all, thirteen residents were wounded.[188]

Analyzing the incident immediately thereafter, Ben Zvi argued that it had been caused not by Arab nationalism but was "a pogrom [instigated] by the lower echelons of the Turkish administration." "We have always anticipated as inevitable," he wrote,

> a conflict between the incoming Jews, on the one hand, and the Turkish regime, on the other. We have never fooled ourselves into thinking that the Jewish forces in Palestine could grow through a process that is always calm and slow. On the contrary, this process is bound to involve those longtime revolutionary factors that will solve the problems of the people not by paper rights but by iron and blood.[189]

Unfortunately, the revolutionary camp had now been caught off guard – "the blow fell at a time when our forces had still not developed enough to parry it." But he rejected out of hand the accusations of those "fools [who] blame the youth, especially Poale Zion, for the blood-letting – they do not, or cannot, understand people who stand up against bullying."

As against this, Moshe Smilansky, writing in *Ha-shiloah,* argued that even though the radicals had not initiated the fighting, they were by no means free of blame.

> We have brought to Palestine some of the "good manners" that held sway in Russia a year or two ago, and are now out of date even there. Youngsters who spoke openly in Jaffa of "barricades and bombs," who frightened the farmers in Petah Tikva by talk of *ekspropriatsiia* and *revoliutsiia,* who tried to introduce coercion into Jerusalem of all places, and held a strike for its own sake in Rishon Le-Zion . . . could, of course, hardly grasp that the time was not ripe to order our relationship with the Arabs on the basis of strict reciprocity. The shouts about "freedom", about "conquering the land" and so on – much noise and little action – went to their heads. In their fantasies, they saw themselves as already rulers of the country. The prejudice . . . that the Arab only respects the strong . . . led many of our youngsters to demonstrate their "strength" to the Arabs. And, of course, the Arabs showed them that when it comes to force they are much the more powerful and have the Turkish government on their side.[190]

Nobody, he concluded, expected the young workers to "lower their heads," but "caution was required, greater caution and more tact."

It was in the wake of this debacle and for fear of further arrests that Ben Zvi decided to transfer himself (and hence the Poale Zion central committee) from Jaffa to Jerusalem. Efforts to organize the workers there were now renewed and –

following the successful coup of the Young Turks—were pursued with such enthusiasm that it culminated in yet another bitter crisis in the relationship of the radical youth with the established Yishuv.

A strike was called in the Levy printing shop in December 1908, after one of the owners had hit out at a worker; pickets were posted; a strike breaker was attacked; and in the resulting melee a shot was fired by one of the workers. "The owners," reported *Ha-poel ha-tsair*, "used the shot . . . to raise a hue-and-cry—'the anarchists are taking over!' "[191]

The workers were now bluntly told that if they did not leave the trade union at once they would lose their jobs. In retaliation, the Printing Workers Union called a general strike, closing most of the printing works in Jerusalem. Morale was initially high and, on the third day, the strikers organized a march through the streets of the old and new cities. But, at this point, the leaders of the community intervened.

The rabbis issued a religious ban, a herem, against the strikers, and many prominent men (including Yehiel Mikhael Pines and David Yellin) publicly condemned the strike. Requests, it seems, were even directed to the foreign consuls asking for their intervention against "the Russian revolutionaries, terrorists, who because of their crimes were forced out of Russia."[192] Mordekhay Ben-Hillel Ha-Cohen and Zalman David Levontin arrived from Jaffa to mediate the conflict, but they, too, were accused of joining the antistrike coalition. The strike lasted eleven days but it ended in a humiliating defeat. The strikers were compelled to accept the demands of the employers, thirteen workers lost their jobs, and the Printing Workers Union was left in ruins.

As with the shooting incident in Hotel Spektor, so in this case, too, the labor leaders sought to minimize the extent of their own responsibility. It was untrue, wrote Tversky in *Ha-poel ha-tsair*, that "the [party] organizations had sought the opportunity to win popularity among the workers." On the contrary, they had been subject to pressure from below, from the workers (who were drawn from the old Yishuv and the Oriental communities)—this was "a protest strike against the strong-arm regime that still rules in the Jewish community despite the constitution in Turkey . . . ; an attempt to overthrow the yoke of tyranny in Jerusalem."[193] It failed, Ben Zvi concluded, because the workers (family men) depended for their survival on charity (the haluka) to supplement their absurdly low income of eight to ten francs a week. "Thus, the masses in Jerusalem are enslaved to those in control of these handouts."[194]

The frequent repetition of such incidents and the chronic tension dividing the radical youth from the rest of the Yishuv led the local press to devote ever more space to discussion of what was termed "the worker question."[195] Men who had come from Russia and established themselves in the country in the years 1880–1900 subjected this new generation of immigrants to bitter criticism.[196] The Bilu and other early pioneers, wrote one such veteran,

> were also well versed in the theories of Chernyshevsky, Lassalle, Owen, Fourier, Marx, etc., but when they undertook the work of construction, they decided to forget everything [else] . . . The solution of economic and social questions . . . all this was a problem for future generations . . . But you . . . came to us bringing along various platforms, economic theories, and these . . .

for you, or many of you, were of higher value than settling the country . . . just as though [here were] . . . textile workers in the large factories of Lodz or Moscow . . . It would be comic if it were not so painful![197]

"You are waging a war with the entire Yishuv, both the old and the new," declared Meir Dizengof (once a *narodnik* and Russian revolutionary himself, soon to become well-known as mayor of Tel Aviv), "as if after the flood of *embourgeoisement* you alone remain true to the flag of Rebirth. You have set yourselves the goal of conquering labor, but you cannot attain that goal and the war has become an end in itself, a holy war, war for its own sake."[198] "Here was a hall full of young men and women . . . ," wrote Mordekhay Ben-Hillel Ha-Cohen, describing a labor meeting in Jaffa,

> and nowhere in the entire hall did I see . . . people who really work. And this is understandable. Real workers would not stay until after midnight . . . to hear speeches and statements about everything under the sun when they have to get up next morning to work . . . They have filled their bellies with Marxist doctrine . . . They do not constitute the material with which to build the country. We need . . . simple laborers.[199]

The statement that caused the greatest resentment among the youth, however, came from Ben Yehuda: "From conversations with the best of the farmers . . . it has become clear to me that in a few years not one Jewish worker will remain in the colonies. And nothing in the world will help against this."[200]

These attacks did not go unanswered, of course. "All these people," wrote Gordon, "would like to see young workers here . . . who, like little lambs, do not make themselves heard, who only work . . . , express gratitude to their . . . [employers]; and do nothing else!"[201] What was being asked of the youth, insisted Vilkansky, was nothing less than "self-obliteration."[202] "In reality," declared M. Sheinkin (the Jaffa representative of the Russian Hoveve Zion) this was "not a class war . . . but the war of age against youth in its prime . . . Many of the employers in the country were the first pioneers . . . But decades have passed since then . . . Worn out by a life's work, they make do with short-term calculations. They [the youth], though, demand that thought for the future underly every action."[203]

When Sheinkin made this strong case in defense of the youth late in 1908, he was doubtless speaking not only for himself but also for the Odessa Committee of the Hoveve Zion (which was led by Ussishkin politically and identified with Ahad Ha-Am in the cultural sphere). In the early years, certainly, the Odessa Committee maintained a highly benevolent attitude to the labor movement in Palestine, particularly to Ha-Poel Ha-Tsair, in which it saw something of a daughter organization. But in 1910 this relationship, too, entered a severe crisis from which it was never fully to recover.

The immediate cause of the trouble was an article published by Brenner in *Ha-poel ha-tsair*. He argued there in his usual scathing style that the frequent conversions from Judaism to Christianity that had outraged Russian Jewry were of only the most marginal interest, that his own thinking was "secular, atheistic, atheological," that what counted was "to find a place of productive work" for the "sick" Jewish people. The baptism of Jews, he concluded, "is not an issue, not even a joke."[204]

This treatment of a highly sensitive issue was (as so often with Brenner) meant to shock and it succeeded. The Odessa Committee decided to cut off entirely the subsidy that it had been paying to the journal, and it demanded that the editorial board formally disassociate itself from Brenner. This Aharonovich refused to do, and the labor circles in Palestine protested, arguing against what was described as a concerted attempt to curtail the freedom of the press.

For his part, Ahad Ha-Am published an article in *Ha-shiloah* that demonstrated beyond a doubt that he was reconsidering his attitude to the young radicals. "Various signs suggest." he wrote,

> that this deliberately outrageous cynicism is now a "system" spreading in Palestine. People drunk on words have come from abroad, bringing with them the phraseology to which they were accustomed there . . . And they are trying to influence the younger generation in their own spirit, to liberate it not only from religious observance, but from everything that links generation to generation in national life. And if you refuse to be a partner in this "national effort" they wheel out . . . the deadly weapon against which nobody can stand – the great principle of "tolerance and free speech" . . . Abroad, in "those days," the Jewish youth used to come to the synagogues and in the name . . . of free speech take over the pulpit . . . to abuse and curse religion . . . And in Palestine they have now broadened . . . their interpretation [of this principle]; not only am I entitled to . . . destroy everything which you have built, but you are obliged to help voluntarily in the work of destruction.[205]

Aid to which strings were attached, Gordon retorted, was worse than nothing at all. "You have no right to worry about us. We will not let you trample on our human dignity, our labor in Palestine, in exchange for pennies, for small deeds [given in] mean spirit."[206] By making extraordinary efforts, the editors managed henceforward to maintain the journal without a subsidy.

In 1911 Ahad Ha-Am visited the country and on his return to Europe published a report on what he had seen. In general, he was very impressed by the economic and cultural progress that had taken place in the Yishuv since his last visit twelve years before. He was particularly struck by the change that had raised the farmer from his subordinate status, dependent on Baronial financing and officials, to independence. He saw the colonist becoming "a modern-day Boaz who earns his living from farming, understands it . . . , goes out every morning to supervise his workers . . . but, at the same time, lives the life of an educated man . . . whose existence is not entirely absorbed by the land."[207]

However, he took a much less sanguine view of the role played by the workers. The attempt to establish a Jewish working class in the colonies had to all effects and purposes failed utterly. "The weak-willed among them leave the country in bitterness. The obstinate . . . remain and you see them wandering from colony to colony . . . not to find better working conditions but because their spirit is restless and there is no peace in them."[208] For men like Yosef Aharonovich, who had always seen himself (in part at least) as a disciple of Ahad Ha-Am, this report was particularly galling. But then, again, this was only one among the many angry separations that were forcing the youth to reassess their role in those years.

The truth is that by the years 1909–10 a deepening depression had them in its grip. The dual policy of democratization and proletarianization had beaten in vain against the walls of reality. Almost nothing had changed in the politics of the Yishuv following the proclamation of the Turkish constitution. The miniature working class formed by the radical youth was in constant flux, and the hopes of a mass proletarian immigration – "natural" workers – had proved to be illusory.

In the journals and conferences, attention turned constantly to the apathy and "despair" (yeush) that had hold of the members. "A sad, thoroughly depressing picture is now presented by the workers in the colonies," Tversky wrote in 1909, "and without any exaggeration we can say that a period of collective decline, in the full sense of the word, has set in."[209] "How will it all end? – that is now the gnawing question, such is the mood," A. D. Gordon noted. "There is . . . despair in the heart."[210] "People," Zerubavel noted in 1911,

> almost take pride in the fact that the period of profound enthusiasm and exalted idealism is over, that they have begun to push aside the final ideal and to take only everyday interests into account. It is as if the holy spirit of great deeds has passed. The dreamers are laughed at . . . Never, perhaps, has such despair reigned in the workers' camp in Palestine as now. Many are leaving the country . . . And even those who remain . . . work without faith.[211]

"For over three years," declared Ben Gurion later in that same year, "total political apathy and, even worse, an inner contempt for all public work, for every attempt at organization, have taken hold of the workers in Judea who previously formed the most vital and active group."[212]

Some (particularly in Poale Zion, of course) explained the crisis of confidence as the inevitable result of an excessive idealism shattering itself against material existence. The youth, Ben Zvi wrote in 1910, "are not capable for the most part of living as workers."[213] Others tended to blame the fact that the reinforcements arriving after 1908 were much less public minded and dedicated than those who had come in the years of the revolution. "Most of the new youth," Tversky wrote in 1909, "come from a Russia where political life has declined totally in recent times and the emphasis on private life has taken on extreme proportions . . . and it is thus no wonder that they have yielded to the dead atmosphere which they find here."[214] "A few years ago," we read in Ha-ahdut of 1912, "great men, men of vision, were formed in the revolution and men with mighty goals and enormous will came here too. Now, everything is small and bodiless there; and ordinary people, without the holy spark, without horizons are arriving here. We here are frozen."[215]

New tactics, old strategy, 1909–1914

Even though the "orthodox" strategy had thus clearly reached a point of extreme crisis by 1909, there was an understandable reluctance simply to write it off as a failure. The Yishuv was being built up rapidly not by Jewish but by Arab workers. The labor parties could not reconcile themselves to this development even though they had proved powerless to halt it. Rather than abandon the policy of proletarianization, of "labor conquest," a desperate search was made for ways to salvage it.

New tactics were called in and only as they proved unsatisfactory in the years 1909–14 did a growing body of opinion arrive reluctantly, hesitantly, at the idea that the strategy itself was false.

A number of leaders believed, for example, that the Gordian knot could be cut by encouraging a large Yemenite immigration. Jews from the Yemen had begun arriving in Palestine in the 1880s and had settled for the most part in Jerusalem.[216] However, in the years 1908–9, a few dozen families who had recently arrived were encouraged, by *Ha-poel ha-tsair* among others, to try their luck as workers in the established Jewish colonies.

Housed for the most part in dilapidated outhouses and barns, they suffered terribly from malaria and other contagious diseases. The death rate, especially among the infant population, was staggeringly high. Unskilled and often puny workers, they were paid wages on the very lowest scale. But they proved to be industrious and extraordinarily long-suffering. Groups settled themselves mainly in Rehovot, Rishon Le-Zion, Petah-Tikva; and, however terrible their plight, nothing could bring them to leave.

In his survey of 1912, Zeev Smilansky recorded that some fifty-eight Yemenite workers (and they were usually heads of families) had been settled permanently in one place since 1908–9. Their wives found work in domestic service. And their punctilious observance of the religious ordinances favorably impressed the farmers. In fact, there were some colonists who felt that they carried things too far when they cut short their work early in order to hurry home on Friday afternoons or when they came late after their communal prayer at dawn.[217]

Their story was considered enough of a success to persuade Shmuel Yavneeli, one of the leading immigrant workers from Russia, to undertake a hazardous journey to the Yemen. (He was provided with the necessary funds by Arthur Ruppin's Palestine Office.) He spent over a year traveling by donkey from one mountain fastness to another in search of the remotest Jewish communities. The arrival of the young emissary from the Holy Land had an extraordinary effect on this devout and isolated people. In 1912 a large number of Yemenite Jews arrived via Aden in Palestine, many of them (over a thousand, it was estimated) heading straight for the colonies.[218] Ruppin and Warburg now pushed through an appropriation from the Jewish National Fund for the year 1912–13 of close to 100,000 francs with which to build them homes.[219]

As early as 1909, voices were to be heard in the labor parties arguing that the Yemenite Jew had all the essential attributes of the long-awaited "natural" worker. He took easily to monotonous physical labor, could live on a subsistence wage, and was a family man eager to settle down in one place. In short, he was possessed of just those attributes so conspicuously absent in the Russian-Jewish youth.

Perhaps the most enthusiastic advocate of the idea that the Yemenites would form the mass Jewish proletariat was David Ben Gurion. The young "idealists" from Russia, he argued, were able to open up new areas, act as a vanguard, but – in contrast to the Oriental Jews – they could not be expected to stay settled in one place. "The arrival of the Yemenites in the colonies," he wrote in 1912 in a passage typical of many, "which began three years ago . . . is a phenomenon of the utmost importance in the life of the Yishuv; for here lies the key to the *radical* solution of the Jewish labor question in the colonies."[220] The same case was made

Figure 25. Yemenite Jews in Ben Shemen.

in *Ha-poel ha-tsair* by Zeev Smilansky, who insisted that "we must make every effort to ensure that their [the Yemenite] numbers increase continuously in all the colonies in Palestine, . . . [for] we all know that the pioneers [from Russia] have . . . long ceased to work with their former enthusiasm."[221]

However, by no means everybody in the youth parties shared this view. The Yemenites, ran the counterargument, could only depress wages still further and thus make it harder still for the Russian-Jewish youth to gain a foothold in the colonies. "The main thing," declared Rahel Yanait in opposition to Ben Gurion at the Poale Zion congress of 1910, "is not to replace Arabs by Jews but to entrench the class of Jewish agricultural workers, to permit their survival and development. The Yemenite does not raise – on the contrary, he lowers – the level of the agricultural workers."[222]

Yosef Aharonovich consistently argued along these same lines, for he long believed that capitalist development would eventually create a demand for higher-paid workers from Europe and that, in the meantime, the idealistic vanguard had to have priority. "Is it desirable under present conditions," he asked in 1912, "that the Yemenite worker take the place of the young Ashkenazi and is an organization such as ours justified in expending so much energy to introduce the Yemenites into the colonies, so closing them off to the youth? . . . We base our work-plan on the immigration of pioneers [*halutsim*] to Palestine."[223]

It was this latter view that, in practice even more than in theory, won out in this period, especially in the years 1913–14. Much was made of the fact that the Yemenites, with their slight build, were only able to compete against the Arabs in marginal and light jobs, not in heavy agricultural work such as hoeing. Moreover, the cultural gulf dividing the radical camp from the ultratraditional Yemenite families proved unbridgeable. Attempts to organize, or even to help, them proved beyond the already overstrained resources of the labor movement. "The youth," read a report on the Third Congress of the Agricultural Labor Union late in 1912, had revealed a "total indifference" in this sphere. "We can only feel shame, hide our faces, when we see workers educated on the ideals of national and proletarian solidarity alienating themselves in this strange way from their brothers in labor."[224] Beyond these factors, however, was the growing realization in these years that the Oriental Jews could be used by the employers in their efforts to break the organized power of the labor movement.

This fact emerged with ever greater force as the youth, in their efforts to entrench themselves as wage workers, became increasingly dependent on the organization Ha-Shomer (The Watchman) and on the national farms. In contrast to Bar Giora, the existence of which was kept secret, Ha-Shomer was organized partially in the open. Its leadership was essentially the same as that which had created Bar Giora, and its membership likewise was drawn primarily from the ranks of the Poale Zion movement. But it negotiated public contracts with individual colonies to provide them with armed (and often mounted) guards.

From the first, it sought to make the supply of the watchmen dependent on the willingness of the colonies to employ more Jewish workers. With varying degrees of reluctance and to a varying extent, the colonies were inclined to accept this condition. So great was the theft from the fields, plantations, and barns that it was financially worth their while to pay heavily and concede much in order to obtain reliable guards.

For its part, Ha-Shomer in 1909 encouraged the establishment of the Labor Legion (Legion Ha-Avoda), which was assigned the task of directing the workers to the colonies selected. Like Ha-Shomer, the Legion demanded strict discipline of its members (and even had a uniform). They had to put themselves at its disposal for at least two years. They were paid on the basis of strict equality and in kind (food, clothing) rather than in cash.

There was much paradoxical in the decision of Yisrael and Manya Shokhat, Yisrael Giladi, and the other leaders of Bar Giora to opt for a wage labor or proletarian strategy in 1909. After all, they had been the first to take practical measures for the advancement of the alternative plan: labor and cooperative settlement. But now, when the Zionist Organization was about to adopt this "heterodox" concept as the basis for a pilot project, they went over at least temporarily to the "orthodox" tactic of proletarianization, or "labor conquest." As Ruppin turned to Galilee, they began leaving for the south.

After its initial experience in the small colonies of the north–Sejera, Mesha (Kfar Tavor), Rosh Pina–Ha-Shomer transferred more and more of its energies to the vine and citrus growing areas, to Hadera, Zikhron Yaakov, and Rehovot. In the contract with Rehovot, drawn up in 1911, the organization undertook to supply twenty-seven guards (six of them mounted) during the fruit season and

Figure 26. A group of Ha-Shomer, mounted.

eighteen (five mounted) out of season.[225] In a report of that year, Ben Gurion noted triumphantly that Ha-Shomer was moving into the biggest colonies (albeit not, "of course," because of a growing "national consciousness" on the part of the farmers but because of their calculated self-interest).[226] "If only you could see our guards with their rifles and Mausers lashed to the saddles of their galloping horses," wrote Berl Katznelson admiringly to his brother abroad.[227]

But as so often in the history of the Second Aliya, preliminary and partial success was only the prelude to later decline. In this case, too, a number of familiar factors combined to frustrate the broader plans of Ha-Shomer. First, the Labor Legion soon became the cause of angry controversy among the workers themselves and even within the Poale Zion party. Its existence as a closed, secretive order naturally aroused the resentment and suspicion of those who had been excluded.

It had failed "to show consideration for the other workers," declared one delegate at a Poale Zion conference of 1910. "Most of its members have left the parties and have stopped working outside the narrow circle of their own group."[228] A correspondent in *Ha-poel ha-tsair* described its out-and-out egalitarianism as disastrous: "Attempts to realize the doctrine of communism . . . have all failed utterly and have proved its worthlessness. [But] it is this doctrine that has now found a following among, of all people, the sworn adherents of the materialist outlook."[229]

By 1911 the Labor Legion had collapsed and Ha-Shomer was left without its organized reservoir of workers. This development, of course, emphasized its paramilitary character still further and thus contributed to the crises now to come. The

Figure 27. Members of Ha-Shomer. From left: M. Khazanovich, S. Hefter, Y. Nakhmani, Y. Nadav.

watchmen were relatively well paid and could afford to spend money to fit themselves out in style. In contrast to their comrades, the farm laborers, whose barefooted and ragged appearance had become a byword, the guards tended to dress smartly and cleanly. Very often they sported Beduin clothing, particularly the headdress. They cut fine figures mounted on their horses and had ample free time as theirs was primarily night work. They became the idols of the village girls and, in like measure, were deeply resented as arrogant by the native-born and other young men in the colony.

In Zikhron Yaakov (where the settlers were mainly of Roumanian, not Russian origin) the local youth, led by Aharon Aaronsohn and Avshalom Feinberg, eventually reacted in 1913 by establishing their own rival organization of armed guards, the Gideonites. (It was from this kernel that the espionage organization, the Nili, would develop during World War I, again in violent opposition to the labor movement.)[230]

Even in the labor press, critical remarks began to creep in here and there. Yosef Aharonovich complained that the watchmen were alienating themselves from the new Hebrew culture, dressing as Arabs and speaking only Yiddish. "The moral state of the organization [Ha-Shomer]," he concluded, "is totally unsatisfactory."[231] Coming from the editor of *Ha-poel ha-tsair,* the negative tone was hardly surprising.

But Zerubavel, who for the most part was eager enough to champion Ha-Shomer, had already expressed grave doubts about its role late in 1911. The organization had not been able to maintain its initial policy of imposing Jewish labor wherever it contracted to guard. In Rehovot, he wrote, "our Jewish guards will only be protecting what the Arabs have produced. It would certainly have been better if Jewish labor had been brought in even if others had then guarded the produce."[232] "What is so wonderful for us," he asked, "if we have a few dozen youth who in, and for, their job have learnt to ride well and to shoot straight and fearlessly? Do we not have such people in Exile too?"[233]

However, in the conflict of guards and colonists, a strong element of politics was also involved. The fact that in Ha-Shomer the immigrant youth – specifically the Poale Zion – had at its disposal a relatively well-armed and well-trained force could only produce the gravest misgivings among the farmers. It could hardly be otherwise given their perennial fear that the revolutionaries, or even ex-revolutionaries, from Russia would attempt to impose their will by force.

This situation clearly called for the exercise of great tact on the part of Ha-Shomer. In many ways, the organization did act with caution and discretion. In their day-to-day relations with the neighboring Arab villages they tried to respect local custom and feelings. Its members not only showed a liking for Arab dress but also in many cases learned to speak Arabic. They entertained neighboring Arab dignitaries and were received by them in turn. Above all, they sought conscientiously to avoid having to fire their weapons in the frequent scuffles with the marauders for fear of involving the colony in all the terrible nightmare of a blood feud.

But all this was not enough to win over the farmers for long. They generally rejected the persistent demand of Ha-Shomer that it be made responsible in whole or in part for the conduct of negotiations between the colony and the neighboring Arabs; and they naturally resented suggestions of the kind made by Yisrael Shokhat in a memorandum sent to Ussishkin in 1912, that Ha-Shomer be empowered to organize the entire network of colonies in a militia under its own control. ("We are now at a political moment," Shokhat had written there, "when the need for the defense of the Yishuv is doubly urgent... The Ottoman Empire is somewhat weakened and perhaps further changes will come in the near future... Our goal is not a transient one born of momentary chance, but a great historic goal, a permanent goal, set for generations.")[234]

Above all, however, the colonists feared that the bravery of the guards could too easily become (or at least be interpreted as) provocation. The slightest error of judgment could set off a round of killing and involve the village in all the enormous expenses (fines, bribes, compensation) required to make "peace." In vain, Zerubavel pointed out that in the armed clashes over the years seven Jews had been killed and only two Arabs.[235] The farmers of Yesud Ha-Maala, for example, were quoted as saying that "those places in which the guard duty has been given over to the Russians are the only ones to witness fights, death, etc. – why should they become involved?"[236]

This simmering conflict eventually came to a head in Rehovot. In a series of clashes in July 1913, a guard (Shmuel Fridman) and an Arab assailant were killed outright, while a farmer and two guards were wounded (one fatally). Far from bringing the workers and the colonists together in shared grief or united self-defense, this incident only served to deepen the gulf dividing them. The workers demanded that the colony cease to employ, at least temporarily, anybody from the neighboring village of Zarnuka in which the marauders were apparently concentrated. Local custom and concepts of honor, so they argued, demanded that, once blood had been spilled, normal relations between the two villages had to be severed. But the farmers rejected this demand outright. As far as they were concerned, this case (as other such cases in the past) would have to be settled through litigation and a financial settlement, however long-drawn-out and expensive they might prove to be.[237]

Thus it was that Shmuel Fridman's funeral turned into a demonstration of protest by the Jewish workers against Rehovot. Among those who delivered funeral orations were Mendel Portugali (a leader of Ha-Shomer) and the impassioned veteran of many such disputes, Mikhael Halperin.[238] The speakers attacked the colony vehemently for its reliance on the labor of Arabs and in effect blamed the Rehovot farmers for the death of their comrade. This attack enraged the colonists, who reciprocated by accusing Ha-Shomer of irresponsibility, of having brought in "young guards who do not know the local language [Arabic] or local customs."[239]

Ill feeling eventually reached the point of no return. The village committee presented Ha-Shomer with an ultimatum. Unless its members signed an agreement to maintain the Sabbath ordinances their contract would not be renewed. Ha-Shomer refused (in the words of *Ha-poel ha-tsair*) "to accept the yoke of Jesuitism,"[240] and the guards left Rehovot.

This setback was in fact part of a pattern, now clearly emerging. Ha-Shomer was no longer wanted on a permanent basis in the colonies. It lost its foothold not only in Rehovot but also in Hadera and in many of the Galilee colonies. The period 1911–12 turned out to have been the high point of its geographical expansion. In search of replacements, the colonies now often turned not to Beduin guards but to Jews unattached to Ha-Shomer. Rival organizations and contractors – "private enterprise" – now stepped in to fill the breach, and in many cases, the new Jewish guards were of Oriental origin, most often members of communities that had originated in northern Syria and Kurdistan.

The Rehovot incident (as will be discussed further below) was a major landmark in the process of disillusionment with the proletarianization strategy. However, this strategy was also losing credibility at this time in yet another crucial sphere. Since 1906, an increasing number of jobs had become available in land development, tree planting, and other agricultural melioration projects. Some of these enterprises were privately financed by ad hoc investment groups formed by Jews abroad (Migdal, Poriya, Ruhama); others were supported by the Zionist Organization and the Jewish National Fund, or by ICA (Sejera, Ben Shemen, Hulda, Kinneret, Merhavya). For the young immigrants from Russia, the chance to work in such projects was very attractive. The competition of Arab labor was relatively little felt here because it was considered natural to give preference to Jews in what (whether privately or publicly owned) were regarded as national enterprises. Wages were therefore higher, the tempo less frenetic, the hours of work clearly defined, and the leisure time greater.

As early as 1908, reports from Galilee noted that of 82 workers there, 45 were concentrated in Sejera, where ICA had its training and experimental farm,[241] and this trend maintained itself thereafter as new sites were taken over for development. By 1910, only 10 of the immigrant youth were left working in the established colonies of Galilee.[242] In 1912 Aharonovich estimated that of the 500 Jewish agricultural workers then in the country, as many as 300 were employed on national farms and other large-scale melioration projects.[243] But this system, too, fell victim (inter alia) to the militant independence and self-assertiveness of the youth from Russia.

In nearly all cases, the public projects were directed by managers or supervisers. Unlike the farmers of Petah Tikva or Zikhron Yaakov, these men were often in sympathy with the aims and aspirations of their young workers. There was no kulturkampf here. But the managers were held responsible by the societies abroad for the efficient development of their land and they were eager to show a profit whenever possible or, at least, to keep deficits within manageable proportions.

Of course, in principle, the workers shared this goal. However, they resented the fact that the managers were paid wages many times higher than their own and were expected (as befitted European gentlemen in the Orient) to live in many-roomed, handsome houses. They saw these expenses as in no small measure responsible for the chronic budgetary deficits. Their own living conditions were primitive in the extreme, and a psychological barrier naturally came to divide them from the managers.

Indeed, in many cases the youth saw here a simple case of the exploitation of labor by capital. Those who rejected this interpretation, related Sara Malkin of Kinneret in the years 1908–9, were "accused of being too right wing, too dedicated to the farm, too careful of national money – one should, rather, be introducing the eight-hour day."[244] "In its relationship to the Jewish worker in Palestine," A. Reuveni (Ben Zvi's brother) wrote in 1911, "the Zionist Organization acts as the representative of Property. In all its enterprises . . . [including] the national farms, the same bourgeois relationship . . . reveals itself . . . Exploitation is unavoidable in the present-day system of property."[245] "Workers are always workers," Ben Zvi wrote in Ha-ahdut, "and when they work they are exploited whether for the benefit of the individual or of the community . . . and what the worker does he does not as a free man but under coercion from without."[246]

Thus, ironically enough, the national farms (and other projects financed from abroad) became the last refuge for the philosophy and tactics of confrontation. Strikes, collective walkouts, and threats of violence had acted as a boomerang in the colonies, the few factories, and the urban workshops. There, the labor movement had found itself undermined by the employment of Arabs and Oriental Jews in place of the "Russians," by boycotts and lockouts, and by the exertion of financial pressure.

The managers of the public farms were, of course, severely restricted in the use of these weapons. The result was that in the years 1909–14, these farms became the scene of every type of labor dispute. There were strikes in Kinneret and Sejera in 1909; again in Kinneret in 1911; and again in Sejera in 1914. Most of these strikes ended in collective resignations and walkouts by the workers. This form of action was also taken at Ben Shemen, as a protest against the manager, Y. Vilkansky (Tsiyoni) in 1910; at Sejera in 1912; and at Kfar Uriya in 1914.

There were frequent reports that the managers in Migdal, Poriya, Ruhama, Sharona, and Bitanya were seeking every means to dismiss some or all of their Russian workers.[247] That such dimissals were limited in number was only due to the fear of a public outcry in the labor press in Palestine and in Zionist circles abroad.

The issues involved in these disputes fall into three different categories. First, there were the power struggles in which the manager, eager to impose discipline, was pitted against young men too proud and independent to accept orders unquestioningly from above. Often, in such cases, personal prejudices and antagonisms were of central importance. Berman, the manager of Kinneret, twice found himself and the farm under boycott by the labor union, Ha-Horesh. The manager at Ruhama was accused of selecting the Poale Zion members for dismissal from the farm, and Dyk at Merhavya was known for his efforts to rid himself of the "revolutionary workers."[248]

Following the strike in Kinneret of 1911, Ben Gurion came out with a furious attack on the system developed by Ruppin. "It [the Baronial officialdom]," he wrote,

> is being reborn in its new form now called The Palestine Office ... Our new "colonizers" have not grasped the simple fact that the Yishuv cannot be built up only by orders from outside[249] ... How many times have we heard from the "friends" of the workers ... that they must surrender their class interests for their national interests. But ... in reality there is no contradiction at all between the class politics and the national politics of the workers ... If officialdom tramples down workers' rights as happened in Kinneret and partially in Lod [Ben Shemen] ... then the workers must *at once* seize on the appropriate means to put an end to the evil at its embryonic stage.[250]

A second cause of friction, of course, was economic. The workers, aware of the strength inherent in their situation, frequently demanded what were known as "European" wages, an eight-hour day, and improved living conditions. For fear of the looming deficits, the managers often felt compelled to resist such demands, so further alienating the workers. They in turn responded by working to rote. Even in the labor press, articles critical of the workers on the national farms appeared with growing frequency. "The Jewish worker at root," wrote Yaakov Rabinovich in *Ha-poel ha-tsair* in July 1912,

> remains by nature a wanderer. You all know the type who today is a worker, tomorrow a guard, the day after a hiker and always hungry ... Such people come to a national farm and the disputes begin at once as if such farms were not their own and as if the National Fund were some kind of capitalist exploiter. And there, too, he remains only a worker – that is, a man who is involved neither with the work nor with the responsibility ... If they [the national farms] do not become profitable, then there is no point in maintaining them and if despite that they are kept up, then in practice they become philanthropic institutions.[251]

The factor that produced the most bitter controversies, however, was neither the personal nor the economic but the national. No question was so explosive as the employment of Arab labor on these farms. At least here, the youth felt, all the work – and of course all guard duty – should be in Jewish hands. If proletarianization, "labor conquest," had failed in the colonies then it was doubly important that they become the norm on the public farms.

In one way or another, this complex of questions was involved in nearly all the major disputes and was often the key issue. Thus, the outburst of anger against Vilkansky in Ben Shemen was caused by his adamant refusal to make the workers responsible for guarding the farm against Beduin marauders. The brusque terms he employed were quoted in identical form in both labor journals: "This is not Galilee. You don't need weapons here! This is none of your business. I am in charge here and, if I want, I'll let the Arabs destroy the whole farm and you have not a thing to say about it!"[252] This incident decided most of the workers to leave Ben Shemen in collective protest. A similar decision on the part of Krause, the manager of the ICA farm at Sejera, led to the walkout by the workers in 1912.[253]

Far more serious were the conflicts that overtook Sejera and Merhavya in 1914. Both cases involved the employment of Arab labor on a seasonal basis – to help, in the one case, in tree planting and, in the other, in harvesting a crop of sesame. Franz Oppenheimer, following his visit to Palestine of 1913, had already reported that in Merhavya "almost the entire body of laborers steadfastly adhered to the principle that such work [Arab labor] cannot be tolerated under any circumstances ... [they] fear a development such as has taken place in the planters' colonies in Judea."[254] Oppenheimer had argued then that the "principle here ought not to be carried to extremes," but he failed to change their mind. (In a letter to Bodenheimer, discussing the Arab issue, he had stated that "with the exaggerated nationalism of the Russian terrorists we shall soon come to a sorry plight.")[255]

In the dispute of 1914, Ruppin was called in to adjudicate. He ruled that the issue be decided by the governing committee abroad, that meanwhile Dyk remain as manager, that five of the rebel workers leave the farm at once, and that Arab labor, if absolutely required, be permitted until new instructions come from overseas. In his letter to Cologne, he disassociated himself from Dyk's view that the total opposition to Arab labor constituted a "chauvinist principle consuming our national workers like a plague."[256] When the dust finally settled a few months later, Dyk found himself with no choice but to abandon his post.

The conflict in Sejera took on a still more extreme form. The farm had been run since 1913 by Agudat Netaim (The Plantation Company), a shareholding association that undertook to establish orchards and plantations for eventual sale and parcellation. The Jewish workers there decided to call a strike in protest against the employment of Arab labor, following the murder of one of the guards, Yaakov Feldman. As in Rehovot, they tended to blame the death of their comrade on the failure of the management to demonstrate unequivocally that this was a Jewish settlement. ("It was hard to accept the idea," we read in *Ha-ahdut*, "that the murderers and their comrades should come to work in this place as they had done before.")[257]

As the strike wore on, a militant group within the local Ha-Shomer organization (which included such members as David Fish and David Tselbich) sought to coerce the director of the Sejera farm, Kantorovich, into submission; he was threatened with death unless he agreed to a system based entirely on Jewish labor. The same group also advocated resorting to a blood feud as the most effective method of revenging Feldman's death.

In both these cases, the labor leadership as a whole and that of Ha-Shomer in particular disassociated itself from the extremists. But the damage was done. The management decided to resist the strike to the bitter end and eventually it was defeated. The strikers left the farm. The Agricultural Labor Union imposed a boycott on it, and the management maintained it by the employment of Kurdish and other Oriental Jews (as well as Arabs) in place of the Russians.

A major factor in the defeat of the strike was undoubtedly the largely hostile reception given it in the Hebrew press both in Palestine and abroad. The Plantation Company, noted Moshe Smilansky, for instance, in *Ha-olam,* had spent close to a million francs in Palestine and employed almost three hundred Jews in its work.

> On the face of it the leaders of Jewish labor should treat the Company with respect and gratitude. But nothing of the sort! Not a month passes without a new attack on this Company . . . And it is not surprising that this "system" ended up – because fifteen non-Jews were employed alongside the fifty-five Jewish workers – in the strike and the cases of violence in Sejera.[258]

At this point, Smilansky raised an argument which was being heard with growing frequency and insistence in this, the immediate prewar period. To refuse to employ Arabs at all in the Jewish villages and on the Jewish farms could only unite the local population and the Turkish administration against the Yishuv. "If the workers remained in the world of reality," Smilansky wrote,

> and did not always float off into the heavens of fantasy, they could never have arrived at this demand . . . Can one seriously entertain the idea that in our colonies we should declare a state of war and not let the "alien" cross the frontier? And even if we had the ability to do this, would it be right? Can we use unclean methods even for the purest ends?[259]

Smilansky could write with such scorn because he felt that the tide of public opinion was flowing strongly against the workers in their confrontation with management. It is true that in the case of Merhavya, Dyk eventually was forced out, but this resulted from the decision of the governing committee abroad. Furthermore (this was the crucial factor, as will be described below), Merhavya was designed from the first to remain under a manager for only a limited period. It was planned as a worker cooperative that would transform the proletarians into owners and farmers. The defeat of Dyk was thus victory not for the strategy of proletarianization but for that of settlement.

The Parallel Society, 1909–1914

The adoption of the Oppenheimer project: the Poale Zion World Congress and the Zionist Congress, 1909

To the extent that the policies of proletarianization and confrontation proved ineffective, so the leaders of the labor movement in Palestine became more willing to consider not only alternative tactics but also alternative strategies. This trend received dramatic illustration in December 1909, when the Second Congress of the World Union of Poale Zion assembled in Cracow.

In anticipation of this event (and of the Ninth Zionist Congress which was due to meet immediately thereafter), the Poale Zion party in Austria had for many months been waging a vigorous propaganda campaign on behalf of Franz Oppenheimer's plan for cooperative settlement. Scarcely an issue of *Der yidisher arbeter* went by without support for the idea. ("We must believe," declared one article, "that all the capitalist filth will not be transferred thither [to Palestine] from Europe.")[260]

At the invitation of the party, Oppenheimer went to Lemberg and other cities in Galicia to lecture on his project.[261] At its conference, held in the summer, the party renewed its long-standing commitment to fight for his plan within the world Zionist movement. It was the Poale Zion party in Austria, moreover, that ensured Oppenheimer's election from a Galician constituency to the Ninth Zionist Congress.

Oppenheimer (writing in 1914) described the crucial support that he had received from the Poale Zion in Austria and contrasted their attitude with the doctrinaire stance of the youth who had lived through 1905 in Russia. The "communistic groups of laborers" in Palestine, he wrote,

> lacked the knowledge of agricultural science, and these Marxists reared in the school of the Russian Revolution were altogether too keen theoreticians to place themselves under an administrator. There were, nevertheless, labor leaders, strange to say, who after the movement had come to a standstill, brought it again into motion: namely, the leaders of the Poale Zion in Austria ... It was owing to their indefatigable agitation that the [Zionist] congresses at the Hague [in 1907] and Hamburg [in 1909] decided to take up the work of cooperative settlement again ... The same leaders of the Poale Zion compelled me to emerge from my retirement.[262]

While the Austrian party was thus strengthening its ties with the Berlin group in the general Zionist leadership, the Russian Poale Zion were moving in the opposite direction. In September 1909 the Russian party held a conference that was attended by thirteen delegates, some of whom represented committees within the Russian Empire and others the committee abroad. Although Kaplansky came as an observer, Borochov dominated the conference. At his urging, a series of resolutions were adopted that in important respects carried the party even farther to the left than during the revolutionary years of 1906–7.

It called for the unification of all Jewish socialist parties in Russia, including the Bund, into one revolutionary organization that would work "hand in hand with the entire Russian proletariat" and seek entry to the International. Most significant, it reversed its previous position regarding the participation of the Poale Zion movement in the world Zionist congress. "The deeper the class consciousness of [our] members has become," read the resolution, "and the more we emphasize the role of the proletariat in the fulfilment of territorialism—so the more have we divided off from bourgeois Zionism ... therefore, the conference considers that the time has come finally to break all organizational ties with bourgeois Zionism, with the congress and all its other institutions."[263]

The conference did not find time to discuss the Oppenheimer plan, but its resolutions on Palestine followed strictly "orthodox" lines, with the emphasis on the democratization and Ottomanization of the Yishuv, trade unionism, and agitation. Moreover, in calling for peaceful relations with the Arab population of the country, it protested against "the senseless agrarian politics of certain Jewish colonization societies which provoke national incitement."[264] (The reference was presumably to policies such as those implemented by the Rothschild organization and ICA at Metula.)

Kaplansky's reaction to the left wing turn taken by the conference, not surprisingly, was negative in the extreme. He maintained that the decision to boycott the Zionist congress had resulted from improper manipulations of the voting "by party functionaries and coopted individuals who represent nobody."[265] Much more remarkable, however, was the reaction of Ben Zvi writing from Jerusalem.

Ben Zvi, of course, had come to Palestine with a well-established reputation as Borochov's right-hand man and ideological disciple. This fact had enabled him to take over leadership of the party immediately on his arrival. But now (for the first time in his life) he launched a public attack on Borochov and the ideological line of the Russian party. Its revolutionary rhetoric, he argued, bore absolutely no relation to the realities of life in contemporary Russia. The party membership, after all, had dropped from some twelve thousand in 1907 to a mere three or four hundred now. "All the events of past and present, " he wrote,

> should have been enough to open the eyes of even the most obstinate people, to force our comrades in Russia to undertake a deep analysis of their own "Platform," of all their positions ... To the great regret and confusion of every friend of the Russian Poale Zion, such an analysis was not forthcoming ... How long are we going to fool ourselves with ringing phrases and empty illusions!

What offended him more than anything else was that the resolution calling for unification with the Bund made no mention of Palestine. This omission, he insisted, "smacked of opportunism ... and [reveals] the readiness with which our Russian comrades surrender their most basic principles in order to gain the blessing of such great rabbis as the Bund."[266]

In his reply, Borochov was no less scathing. Ben Zvi's article, he argued, revealed a remarkable lack of interest in the political situation prevailing in the Russian Empire.

> Let him remember for a moment that this was a conference not of the Palestinian but of the Russian Poale Zion. If for comrade Avner [Ben Zvi] and the other Palestine comrades, Russia's political situation has no significance, for us it is of the greatest importance imaginable! ... We are a party not for Palestine but of the Jewish proletariat.[267]

Thus, when the congress of the Poale Zion World Union met in December 1909, it inevitably became the forum for a full-scale debate between the two major and opposing ideological schools within the movement. The Oppenheimer project now emerged as a central issue in the clash of opposing theories.

What lent this occasion particular interest was the fact that Nachman Syrkin had now arrived in Cracow as a member of the American delegation. He had made his peace with the idea of Palestine as the most suitable Jewish territory and had returned to Poale Zion at the Fourth (the so-called Unification) Congress of the American party held in Chicago in June 1909. This was the first encounter between Borochov and Syrkin since the furious collision at Fribourg on the eve of the Seventh Zionist Congress in August 1905.

Kaplansky, opening the debate, demanded that the congress officially take a stand in favor of the Oppenheimer project and urge the general Zionist movement to implement it immediately. His view was rejected by all the spokesmen for the Russian party, by Borochov, Revutsky (Shlimovich), Blumenfeld, and Zerubavel. Borochov lectured on the subject for over an hour and argued that the idea of converting proletarians into farmers was totally opposed to the class ideology of the party. "He came out sharply and decisively," we read in the report,

> against Oppenheimer's project generally, comparing it with many theories of "do-gooders" who seek to introduce socialism artificially and at once. He argued categorically that this project was utterly unsuited to agrarian conditions in Palestine. In conclusion, he spoke specifically about the fact that this project actually seeks to make workers into nonworkers, to turn them into employers. We, however, are the representatives of the working class and we must only conduct activity aimed at defending its interests as a class and must lead its struggle in all spheres.[268]

Syrkin, who of course had been defending the case for large-scale cooperative settlement since at least the 1890s, took up the cudgels on the side of Kaplansky. "Comrade Dr. Syrkin," reported the summary, "polemicized particularly against Comrade Shtendiger [Borochov]. He ironized at the expense of the Russian Poale Zion, who stand so ironclad for the principle of class struggle. He believes that in Zionism one can stop talking about the class war for a moment."[269] This line of attack provoked Zerubavel (who had stayed in Russia after the revolution and been imprisoned) into a furious response. But Ben Zvi now adopted a very different position, ostensibly intermediate but in practice close to that of the Austrian and American delegations. The Poale Zion movement, he argued, should support the Oppenheimer plan – not, granted, as a step towards socialism, but at least as an ad hoc pilot project applicable to Galilee and inapplicable to Judea. It was an issue not of ideology, but of improvization. "This is, meanwhile, only an experiment . . . no more. We should not fool ourselves into thinking that in cooperative colonization lies the entire cure for the Jewish agrarian question in Palestine."[270]

The Russian leadership was outvoted on yet another significant question. Shortly before the Cracow congress, a decision had been taken by the leaders of the world movement to establish a Palestine Labor Fund. As its name suggests, it was designed to collect money abroad to reinforce Poale Zion and working-class policies in Palestine. But, it was now asked, should there be a specific resolution permitting the use of these funds to organize the proletariat of the Ottoman Empire without regard to nationality or should it be left understood that this was a fund of and for the Jewish working class.

Borochov and Zerubavel – this time supported by the delegation from Palestine – argued strongly that "where it is required for the strengthening of the Jewish proletariat, the Palestine Labor Fund should also organize workers belonging to other nations" and that the congress should adopt an internationalist statement of intent. However, the majority rejected this view as smacking of apologetics and of "sychophancy toward International Socialism." "Solidarity," so ran prevailing opinion, "exists between those who have equal rights . . . When we are organized and strong, then our solidarity will have practical, real significance."[271]

Yosef Aharonovich, the ideological leader of Ha-Poel Ha-Tsair, attended the Cracow congress as a guest and observer. Paradoxically but not unpredictably, his subsequent reports reveal that on key issues, his sympathies were with Borochov and the Russian party. He felt that the adoption of the Oppenheimer scheme had dealt a blow at the campaign to create a wage-earning working class in Palestine. Once the Poale Zion movement

> declares the bankruptcy of the "worker qua worker," [it] destroys the entire structure reared by the new workers [in Palestine] over the last five years . . . At the moment that it decided to work in this [the settlement] field, it transformed itself into a poverty-stricken Colonization Society which in the practical sphere will do no good and in the moral sphere will do much harm.[272]

He likewise expressed support for the boycott of the Zionist congress, albeit not for reasons of class war, but because the official Zionist movement had proved so ineffectual for so long. (He even saw strict logic, although a total lack of common sense, in Borochov's internationalist view of the Palestine Labor Fund: "Otherwise, it [Poale Zion] has no right to knock on the doors of the International and tell it of the light which it is bringing to the Middle East.")

In general (he made an exception of Kaplansky), he poured scorn on the Austrian Poale Zion party, which "even in the most enthusiastic periods of worker immigration . . . produced no forces for Palestine . . . and was [concerned with] nothing but debates against the PPS and the ŻPS, and excursions, parties, and dances."[273]

He found the delegates from the Russian party much more impressive: "Youngsters familiar to us with their ardent temperament, their total dedication to a given idea, but also with their twisted and scholastic ways of thinking; and with their theories in which they have invested so much effort that they have emptied them of life." He expressed satisfaction with the fact that the delegates from Palestine (Ben Zvi and Rahel Yanait) had finally begun to emancipate themselves from the thraldom of their original ideology with its Yiddishist and revolutionary orientation. "Whoever remembers them – before their lapse – when they first arrived in Palestine, their attitude to Hebrew, etc., cannot but rejoice at the transformation . . . and, if I were not afraid of insulting them, I would say that they have become pure and simple Hoveve Zion."[274] The period of the "red-shirt, 'revolutionary' Poale Zion" in Palestine, he declared elsewhere, was clearly over.[275]

When the Ninth Zionist Congress met in Hamburg on 21 December 1909, the Oppenheimer project had a prominent place on the agenda. As in 1903, Oppenheimer again presented his theories in a major address, and among those speaking in favor of his plan were now the representatives of the Poale Zion party in Palestine, Ben Zvi and Rahel Yanait. This time, at last, the congress decided that steps should be taken immediately for the implementation of the project.

Figure 28. Merhavya.

A Cooperative Settlement Fund was established with the goal of collecting the capital sum required to launch the plan, 100,000 francs – of which 40,000 were pledged by donors at the congress itself. It was decided that the cooperative would be established on the land of, and with help from, the Jewish National Fund. The governing body was to include representatives of Jewish labor[276] and when it was eventually established in 1911, it included not only Franz Oppenheimer, Otto Warburg, and Arthur Ruppin but also Nathan Gross and Shlomo Kaplansky.

In the period following the congress, Franz Oppenheimer launched a personal campaign to ensure the success of the project. He visited Palestine in the spring of 1910 and then went on a fund-raising tour of Austria and Germany. By the end of that year over 100,000 marks had been collected, and in 1911 Ruppin arranged for the first group of workers to occupy a site purchased in the Jezreel Valley. The area of the farm was some thirty-five hundred dunams and the name chosen for it was Merhavya.

Breaking away: Labor collectivism and settlement in Palestine, 1909–1914

While the theory of worker settlement, in general, and cooperative settlement in particular, was being debated in Cracow and Hamburg, Arthur Ruppin had taken another practical albeit little publicized step in this same direction. In 1908 (as noted above) he had initiated the establishment of the national farm at Kinneret under the direction of the agronomist, Berman. Now, in December 1909, he launched a further experiment.

The Palestine Office decided to assign a part of the Kinneret land – thirteen hundred dunams – to a group of six workers who would farm it entirely on their own responsibility. In the contract (which was reminiscent of the agreement made by the ICA manager with the Sejera Collective in 1907) the workers were promised a daily wage and a share in the profits. The contract was made initially for a one-year period. The land set aside for the experiment was known then as Umm Juni but would soon be called Deganya.

Despite the small scale and the initially limited duration, it was regarded from the first as highly significant by all those involved. It will be recalled that at least since 1906 Otto Warburg had assumed that the cooperative settlement associated with Oppenheimer would be established in this area, "Daleikah-Umeljunn." And even though another site would eventually be chosen, Ruppin undoubtedly saw in this new experiment of 1909 a variant on the Oppenheimer idea.

Here, first, workers who had no capital of their own were being encouraged to lease land belonging to the Jewish National Fund. Second, they were to manage their own affairs without any outside supervision. All the men in the group were experienced workers, hand-picked and drawn from both parties. Eliezer Shokhat himself was one of the six. Finally, it was known that the workers would run the farm on collectivist lines, sharing all profits and basic expenditures equally.

The historical sources cannot be reconciled when it comes to deciding who first raised the idea of leasing the land at Umm Juni to a cooperative worker group. An article of 1912 published in *Ha-poel ha-tsair* stated that it was Ruppin (acting through Berman) who initiated the plan.[277] (In a letter of 1908, Berman referred approvingly, albeit in a somewhat different context, to the "Sejera Collective.")[278] As against this, Thon wrote to Warburg in September 1909 that "the workers who originally offered to lease the land of Umm Juni have not given up the idea and they want to get ready to carry out the plan next year."[279]

The truth of the matter is that from the moment of Ruppin's arrival in the country, a dynamic process of interaction had developed between the settlement-oriented wing of the World Zionist Organization and sections of the labor movement in Palestine. Therefore, it is not always possible to ascertain who first influenced whom in specific cases such as this.

What is clear is that in 1908 the workers had preferred for the time being, at least, to remain as paid laborers under supervision, but that following the strike at Kinneret in 1909 they decided to take up the Umm Juni option. They considered this an important but fragile pilot project. "The explicit wish of the workers as of ourselves," Ruppin wrote to Germany in 1909, "is that this first modest attempt to create a cooperative settlement group in Palestine should be allowed to proceed quietly at least during the first year and not be publicized initially."[280]

The first year, 1910, proved to be a financial success. Instead of the chronic deficit that plagued the national farm at Kinneret, the kvutsa (collective labor group) at Umm Juni was able to show a 4,000-franc profit following the harvest. The group of six did not renew the contract and most of them moved on to join the recently established worker kvutsa at Merhavya. However, the experiment at

Umm Juni did not come to an end. A new work group took over the farm on the same terms. Among its members, nine in all, there were veterans of various previous experiments in collective living: the Jerusalem Stone Cutters Commune, the Romny Commune, and the Hadera Commune.

With their arrival, the policy of nonpublicity was set aside. A conscious attempt was made to present the experiment at Umm Juni, despite the enormous problems involved, as the way of the future. "Here," read a report of January 1911, "we are both the workers and the administration . . . Apart from the actual work, we have all kinds of duties . . . such as buying tools and livestock, management, the upkeep of various buildings and also bookkeeping . . . If, nonetheless, we are able to cope, it is only thanks to a really exceptional effort."[281]

An article of May 1911 published in *Ha-poel ha-tsair* argued that in contrast to the national farms such as Kinneret, which had failed, the experiment at Umm Juni was proving itself a success:

> There are no quarrels, no bitterness. There is only unlimited dedication to work . . . and the Palestine Office has also grasped this idea. It has begun to take an interest itself in the creation of kvutsot founded on cooperative labor and on self-responsibility. If the Palestine Office sees in this idea only . . . a saving in expenditure—which also has great value—we see a much more important gain in that it will involve the workers more in their work . . . and it will draw new contingents from abroad, because they will find here a chance to participate in the effort of construction not as instruments but as a creative force—an advantage which tips the balance decisively in favor of this idea.[282]

At this stage, in the years 1910–12, the term kvutsa was applied with little distinction both to the idea of a temporary, ad hoc labor association, the equivalent of the Russian artel, and to the idea of a permanent cooperative or collective settlement. This lack of clarity was natural given that these were years of transition in which the model of the wage worker, without ties and always on the move, was gradually giving way to the model of the laborer as pioneer farmer. What was seen as most important at the time was that the workers in the kvutsa had freed themselves from the foremen and had won the right to play an autonomous role in the settlement process.

"All the workers in Galilee and many in Judea," noted an article of July 1912 summing up the first three years at Deganya,

> followed the new experiment with great attention and, when it succeeded, they could breathe more freely: they felt that [henceforward] they could serve not only as clay in the hands of the settlement authorities but also as men capable of running broad settlement projects quite independently. Those in charge of Palestine Office also drew satisfaction [from the experiment] . . . And the faith grew to such an extent that when immediately afterwards a very important and responsible new enterprise had to be launched . . . at Merhavya . . . it was handed over from the first to a worker kvutsa. And now, three years since the beginning of the first experiment in independent work by Jewish laborers, we find kvutsot in Deganya, Merhavya, Sejera

(associated with the ICA administration), Ben Shemen, and Hulda ... The perspectives for the immediate future of settlement work are entirely linked to the possibility of such kvutsot.[283]

While in Galilee attention was thus increasingly focused on Deganya and on the kvutsa, in Judea a rival center of interest was emerging: En Ganim. The village of En Ganim had been founded in 1908 as a worker suburb of Petah Tikva. The initiative had come from the Odessa Committee of the Hoveve Zion, and it had been regarded as ideologically suspect not only by Poale Zion but also by Ha-Poel Ha-Tsair. The plots assigned to each family were modest in size but still too large to permit their owners to cultivate them in their spare time, and they therefore did not work, as originally envisaged, on a regular basis as wage laborers in Petah Tikva. Thus, En Ganim from the first developed as a village of small holding farmers.

However, a number of features distinguished it from the old established settlements. The early introduction of irrigation permitted the rapid development of more intensive forms of agriculture—vegetable gardens, for instance—than had been customary hitherto. Second, the farmers (who had been recruited for the most part from the post-1905 worker immigration) worked their own land with their own hands. And, finally, when they did need seasonal reinforcements, they brought in Jewish workers from Petah Tikva rather than rely on the cheaper Arab labor.

As the proletarianization strategy began to lose its credibility, so En Ganim became more attractive as a possible model for the workers. Wage labor did not rule there but then neither did Arab labor, and that at least was seen as a step forward. "From the stifling atmosphere of the hotel and the stifling morality in Petah Tikva," wrote Berl Katznelson in a letter of late 1909, "we entered the small, free republic which has sprung up beside it. Whatever cannot find its place in the religious orthodoxy of Petah Tikva finds refuge here. Here, it is a free world."[284] "Our sworn pessimists," wrote a correspondent in Ha-poel ha-tsair in December 1911, "prophesied that [with En Ganim] one more ruin was being set up in Palestine. And, nonetheless, in three years the colony has grown and reached such a level that even the doubters have to admit that where there is a will, energy, a wish to work and an inner tie to the country all is possible."[285]

If Deganya came to be seen in the years 1911–14 as the model kvutsa, so En Ganim, for all its well-publicized problems, was regarded more and more as the archetypal smallholding settlement for workers (or moshav ovdim, as it was soon to be called). Nobody in this period was more active than Berl Katznelson in arguing for the need to reproduce many villages of this type.

After many years of battling in vain to recast the established Yishuv, knocking their heads against a stone wall, the workers involved in these various experiments could find new inspiration in breaking away, starting everything from scratch. In the veteran colonies and in the towns, they had been overwhelmed numerically, politically, and above all morally—there had been a constant desertion from the ranks of labor to those of the "bourgeoisie" or, at least, of the petty bourgeoisie, the *meshchanstvo*.

In the kvusta and to an extent, even in smallholding villages such as En Ganim, they could live their own life, without interference. True, the kvutsa provided a harsh environment. There were few women and almost no children to soften the excessively masculine existence. Asceticism reigned supreme and it could hardly be otherwise given the desperate efforts to avoid financial deficits. Vegetarianism at times became almost de rigueur. (" ' You no doubt are a vegetarian,' " was the way in which the girl from the kitchen apparently greeted one newcomer to Deganya. "In this question there was a note of [such] certainty that, not wanting to disappoint her, I replied, 'Of course,' and so became a vegetarian.")[286]

Workers not involved in the new experiments often resented what they saw as the moral arrogance of the pioneers. "The young people who come to Palestine," wrote a correspondent with some bitterness in *Ha-ahdut* in 1911,

> are [held] duty bound to become vegetarians, hermits and to join some kvutsa in Galilee for the sake of "conquering" the country [*kibush ha-arets*]. And if some young man decides that the "conquest" is not for him and he enjoys decent clothes and a decent flat ... then he and his like are not idealists ... and their place is not here. Let them go wherever they choose. We do not need them! ... Say what you like but I see here an inheritance from the Exile, from a life of self-deprivation, fasting, flagellation, the self-torture of body and soul.[287]

The strain on the young men, and the few young women, in the kvutsot was intense. Aliza Zhidlovsky (who was to spend her life as a pioneer in the Jordan Valley) argued that even the singing and dancing, so often recalled in memoirs, should rightly be seen as a sign less of joie de vivre than of extreme psychological tension. "Since those days," she wrote of Deganya in 1913,

> I have never heard people sing like that. The singing provided an outlet for the feelings of loneliness suffered collectively and individually by this small group (our number was twenty-four). There was no link with any other settlement. The paper, *Ha-poel ha-tsair,* came rarely. The few books people had brought with them remained unpacked in their cases. There was a real feeling of being cut off from Europe, from the world, from one's previous existence ... And into that singing went all one's doubts and the fear that there would be no tomorrow ... very often, this singing ended in a circle dance, the hora, which was also very strange – people danced until they fainted ... This was not just a dance, but a kind of inarticulated scream, a release for all that was bottled up in the heart ... It was a period of cruelty toward the individual. The people were living in difficult conditions and they demanded that the individual give everything he had regardless of his ability, or inability, to do [what was demanded].[288]

The relative success of the kvutsa in these years was made possible, surely, not despite but because of this high tension. In many cases the members were clearly inspired by a sectarian enthusiasn, by the belief that they were creating something entirely new, a moral counterweight to, even a negation of, the existing Yishuv. This fact emerged, for instance, when the time came to recruit support from the ranks of the workers in Galilee for Franz Oppenheimer's project.

A strict and tenaciously held egalitarianism was increasingly seen in the kvutsot as a fundamental principle of the social order that they were seeking to build. And when, in 1911, Shlomo Dyk called on the members of Deganya to join him in launching the Oppenheimer scheme, they replied that

> they have just as much faith in the success of the kvutsa as they have in that of the cooperative settlement, and see no reason why they should give up one in order to join another. Furthermore, they are opposed to two specific principles in Oppenheimer's doctrine: (a) the fact that all the workers do not receive equal wages and (b) that a group of [experienced] ... workers should have an official director as their superintendent.[289]

In response to this decision, the directors of the settlement cooperative retorted from Germany that they regarded "pessimistically the chances of the development of this group [in Deganya], which constitutes a kind of communist experiment aiming to triumph over the Oppenheimer project."[290]

Writing in *Ha-ahdut* in 1911, Ben-Zvi argued that the Jewish National Fund should support any experienced worker kvutsa seeking to settle on the land even if "it deviates marginally from the Oppenheimer doctrine. The goal of cooperative settlement must be wider than the scientific settlement experiment ... All the experiments of various kinds are important for us. All are of value as expressions of the independence and originality of the worker."[291]

The fact is that in the period 1909–14 the various forms of labor settlement – the small-holding village with En Ganim as a concrete example; the settlement kvutsa with Deganya as a model; the Oppenheimer project taking shape at Merhavya – developed through a process of constant interaction between theory and practice, ideology and experiment. With growing frequency and in greater numbers, contributors to the labor press and speakers at the labor conferences argued that the future of the movement lay less in proletarianization than in settlement.

One of the most cogent and authoritative advocates of this viewpoint was Y. Vilkansky, agronomist, member of Ha-Poel Ha-Tsair, and (from 1909) manager of the national farm at Ben Shemen (Bet Arif). As early as the winter of 1908–9, he insisted that in the Yishuv, as it had developed hitherto, there was no room for the Jewish working youth from Russia; that the youth could make "all the sacrifices in the world" but could not submit to the "self-negation" demanded of them;[292] and that "here everything – everything – has to be built from scratch. And much, very much, has to be destroyed."[293]

The weight of evidence, he argued in October 1909, no longer favored the view that the capitalist latifundium was more economic or progressive than the small-scale farm. Kautsky had been refuted by David and Bernstein. It was therefore absurd to write off En Ganim as regressive, for with irrigation such settlements could develop highly efficient market gardening and other forms of intensive agriculture.

> We have to create the small-scale farmer in every way and by all means – training farms, agricultural schools, colonization societies. That is the case even if the means are philanthropic. We have to seek [financial support] among all sections of the people. And it is not for us to measure in the scales the amount of money spent on the farmer.[294]

In 1910 he came out in strong support of the Oppenheimer scheme. The planned cooperative settlement would make possible mechanization and economies of scale without stifling individual inititative or responsibility. The young worker from Russia, he wrote,

> had been created, as it were, for the role. His ready enthusiasm for radical change [tikun ha-olam] which hampers our cause in other cases, in this instance can only advance and enhance it ... All for one and one for all ... Here, he [the worker] always remains a pioneer and in building his own world, he is building ours and, still more, is renewing mankind as a whole![295]

This latter theme recurred frequently in the labor press. In joining a kvutsa or a settlement, the worker (so it was argued) had lost the freedom of the proletarian and rebel, but had won for himself a more responsible role, was creating his own future. "Between those [workers] who are established or are involved in the kvutsot and those who lack all permanence," wrote Yaakov Rabinovich in *Ha-poel ha-tsair* in July 1911,

> there is both an overt and a hidden opposition ... The root of the opposition is the division between a positive and a negative attitude to construction ... If the Jewish worker manages to build a national cooperative settlement, he will have created something great, without precedent ... Here there is no room for negation and destruction ... Here a total reevaluation of values is required ... [in contrast], the liberated and unmarried worker remains a severed limb outside life and all development, stranded on the ruin of his own world, preserving the last spark of absolute freedom and negation ... [And] total freedom becomes anarchy.[296]

"Over the last few years," said Berl Katznelson in a speech of 1912,

> many experiments of both a social and a settlement character have been launched and nearly all have succeeded. Are we going to exploit these seeds of Rebirth in order to turn the wheels of progress; or are we going to leave everything to others who will do what they do by chance? ... The workers must become a vital and active force that influences the entire enterprise here.[297]

An editorial published in *Ha-ahdut* in 1912 (presumably written by Zerubavel) declared that what the worker now needed most was "the inner awareness, the emotion, required *to change oneself* ... Only those ideals that rest on tangible subjective needs can live and survive."[298] The kvutsot, moshavim, and other such undertakings were producing "an enormous and basic change in the attitude of the worker to his work."[299]

The metamorphosis visible here – after all, Zerubavel had been an outspoken disciple of Borochov at the Cracow congress of 1909 – was by no means an isolated phenomenon. One by one, the most unbending advocates of proletarianization, of "labor conquest," went over to the strategy of settlement, construction, and parallel development. Those who had placed the greatest faith in the capitalist path now often came out as its bitterest critics.

Thus, in an article of July 1911, Yosef Aharonovich maintained that the farmers of Petah Tikva had launched yet another campaign against En Ganim because they were in fear of the "new methods of settlement in which the principle will be not business and exploitation, but Jewish labor." They, the colonists, had therefore concluded that they had no choice but to "pursue the workers and destroy them utterly."[300]

Again, writing in 1912, he contrasted the Bilu pioneers, who had established Gedera, with the founders of Rishon Le-Zion (petty bourgeoisie, *"meshchane"* and *"meshchanstvo"*)[301] and with the founders of Petah Tikva (who were motivated by a single-minded "pursuit of wealth and by a reactionary spirit."). "Gedera . . . had to wait while, itself included, the Yishuv passed through all seven circles of demoralization, until at last it saw its heirs in the new pioneers and a start to the realization of its goal . . . in Deganya."[302]

In October 1913, following the departure of Ha-Shomer from Rehovot, he quoted with much sympathy (although not in full agreement) the view that "our accounts with the old colonies are already finished; that we have no hope in them; that we have to leave them entirely, and devote all our forces to the building of a new structure in which we can preserve the purity of the Yishuv from the very beginning."[303]

If Aharonovich still hesitated to endorse so total a concept of separation, A. D. Gordon did not. Following the strike at Sejera against Agudat Netaim (The Plantation Company), he came out in April 1914 with a far-reaching declaration of independence: "We say that national construction cannot be based on private enterprise . . . but only on national land and national labor . . . What do we have in common with the existing colonies and all who follow that system? . . . We must pursue our own path and seek new ways to fulfil our goals."[304] The efforts of the National Fund and of the Palestine Office should be directed exclusively to worker settlement, for experience had shown that to stimulate private enterprise meant to increase the scale and scope of Arab labor. "We take one step forward and two steps backward – toward 'labor conquest' and private capital."[305]

Zerubavel (with the Merhavya dispute in mind) could write, again in 1914, that

> only thanks to our propaganda did the Zionist congress at Hamburg [in 1909] give its agreement to the creation of the first cooperative settlement, based on the Oppenheimer system, in Palestine. We have never seen the cooperative as the key to the solution of the worker question in the world, but we have seen it as the solution to the Jewish labor question, to the question of mass settlement in Palestine.[306]

Zerubavel, of course, had strongly opposed the Oppenheimer scheme in 1909. And Gordon, too, had moved a long way since the days when he furiously denounced all aid, be it from private or public sources, as so much charity.

Again, worker settlement was seen increasingly as the most acceptable way of ordering the Arab-Jewish relationship. First, it was argued, as the Jews in the new settlements worked the land themselves, they had eliminated the social dimension from the national conflict. Hatred for the intruder was no longer exacerbated by hatred for the employer. Arabs visiting En Ganim, wrote Yaakov Rabinovich in 1914, "regard it as a normal sight. In their own village, the farmer works with his family and so it is in En Ganim. Among them, the work is done by members of their own faith and race, and so it is with us."[307]

Second, the settlement strategy, it was hoped, would permit the labor movement to escape from the cul-de-sac into which it was being led by the policies of Ha-

Shomer. The more the watchmen found themselves guarding crops produced by Arab labor for Jewish owners, the less attractive their life became. The question asked over and over again by members of Ha-Shomer was whether their work was not in direct conflict with their socialist principles.

> Socialism makes international fraternity and solidarity its goal, but we are acting on behalf of national interests. Is there not a contradiction here – especially when our interests clash with the national interests of others? . . . [More], the watchman [shomer] guards private property. Can a socialist do such a thing?[308]

In a series of lectures and articles in the years 1909–12, Ben Zvi sought to demonstrate that these dilemmas were illusory; that internationalism demanded the equality of national groups; that to perpetuate discrimination against the Jewish working class was to negate the socialist ideal; that Ha-Shomer was contributing to the consolidation of the national proletariat; and that it was therefore acting in accord with party principle.[309] However, the frequent recurrence of the debate suggests that not all in Ha-Shomer were fully convinced by these theses.

Moreover, the problems of Ha-Shomer (as noted above) went beyond ideology. There were the constant disputes with the colonies and the settlement societies; the monotony and mental fatigue involved in their long hours of night duty; the failure to impose the principle that where they guarded, Jews should be the workers.

Once it created its own settlements, the labor movement (so the argument now went) could dispense with a separate paramilitary organization. The workers would rotate as guards. This in fact was the policy adopted from the first at Deganya, and it was particularly attractive to the Ha-Poel Ha-Tsair party. "The fact is," Aharonovich wrote in November 1912, "that Jewish guarding in its present form is not to be seen as ideal for the future. When we have real worker settlements, they will arrange to have the guarding done by the workers themselves."[310] In 1914 Shprintsak declared that "the time has come for a more cautious and adult approach – the sphere of 'defense' and national 'politics' here [in this country] should not be left neglected as a kind of sport for irresponsible and self-appointed groups." It was essential, he concluded, "to fix bounds between the two peoples."[311]

In Ha-Shomer itself there was a rising demand to think in terms of settlement. And in 1913 (the year in which Ha-Shomer had to leave Hadera and Rehovot), the organization formally decided to establish a colony of its own, and a site was chosen near Merhavya at Tel Adas (Adashim). "There is much poison in guarding," we read in a letter of 1913 from Mendel Portugali, to his wife,

> and much, very much, must change in the life of the guards. The moral satisfaction from guarding is perhaps there only in the early period when everything is new, but afterwards . . . the emptiness brings with it arrogance and demoralization . . . there is nothing better than labor . . . The ideal of the guard is power; of the worker, brotherhood. Guarding says: Take that which is not yours. Labor says: Live from the fruit of your hands . . . So we must link guarding with labor . . . [Our] settlement should be modeled on that of the Cossacks . . . The work in the colony will be collective: everybody will take part according to his ability.[312]

Portugali had been among the founding members of Bar Giora and the Sejera Collective in 1907, and in his letter can be seen a return to, a renewal of, the ideas current in those early days. He and those of like mind in the organization – Aleksandr Zaid, Yisrael Giladi, Chaim Shturman, Shmuel Hefter – were seeking to bring Ha-Shomer round full circle.

One of the most remarkable indications of the metamorphosis taking place in the years 1909–14 was the changing attitude in the Palestine labor movement toward the leading ideologists abroad. In the period 1906–8, the theories developed by Borochov during the revolution had dominated the official thinking of the Poale Zion party in Palestine. At that time, Ahad Ha-Am (thanks to his reports of the 1890s on Palestine) was also still considered something of a moral authority in Ha-Poel Ha-Tsair.

But then, in the years 1909–10, the Palestinian Poale Zion had come out openly against Borochov at Cracow; while for its part, Ha-Poel Ha-Tsair found itself in bitter dispute with Ahad Ha-Am and the Odessa Committee. This, of course, was not a random development. In their very different ways, Borochov and Ahad Ha-Am were both advocates of the capitalist path, private enterprise, and wage labor; and as the movement edged away from this conception, so it naturally turned to other authorities.

On the pages of *Ha-poel ha-tsair*, respect for the Berlin school of German Zionism rose in direct proportion to the decline in the prestige of the Russian Hoveve Zion. This volte-face reached its climax in 1913, the year of the Eleventh Zionist Congress. Otto Warburg (who had replaced Wolffsohn as elected leader of the World Zionist Organization in 1911) was now described as the indispensable head of the movement. No longer did Ha-Poel Ha-Tsair see Ussishkin as the natural candidate for that role. "The Warburg-Ruppin system of work, for all its weaknesses," Yaakov Rabinovich wrote, "is the central pillar on which all settlement in Palestine, if it is to be both modern and Jewish, must rest."[313] "If there had been a time," Yosef Aharonovich wrote of the congress, "when we distinguished between Zionists from the East and those from the West, it was now quite impossible to do so. It was as if the borders between East and West had been blotted out."[314]

Ruppin chose this occasion to make his first public report to a Zionist congress. In the midst of his largely statistical and strictly factual speech, this understated man for a moment struck an almost mystical note. "More than once," he said, surveying the work of the Palestine Office since 1908, "I felt that it was too audacious to try to create something permanent with 300,000 marks alone when . . . the Baron Rothschild had already spent more than 50,000,000 on the Yishuv. But optimism gradually won out. I said to myself: in the beginning was the Deed. And the name of the deed was Kinneret."[315]

Ruppin's long report was reproduced in full not only in *Ha-poel ha-tsair* but also in the paper of Poale Zion, *Ha-ahdut*. This was an unprecedented sign of respect for the Berlin leadership, but it was not surprising. "In his speech," argued Rabinovich, "Dr. Ruppin gave not what is German in him but what he has taken from the sectarians – he gave of us. It is not by chance that [his] opponents say that his speech could have been an ideological article taken from *Ha-poel ha-tsair*. It is true."[316]

The reversal of ideological alliances was even more pronounced in the pages of *Ha-ahdut* than in *Ha-poel ha-tsair*. At the so-called Unification (Fourth) Congress of 1909 in Chicago, Nachman Syrkin and Chaim Zhitlovsky had entered the American Poale Zion party. And in the years 1912–14, Syrkin, writing from New York, became a frequent contributor to *Ha-ahdut*. Zhitlovsky, who visited Palestine in 1914, published a number of major articles in the journal. Prominent coverage was likewise given to the standpoint of Shlomo Kaplansky during his stay of 1912. In contrast, the views of Borochov and the Russian school of Poale Zion now went all but unheard.

Syrkin clearly felt elated by the new trends in the Palestine labor movement, and he eagerly sought the macrocosmic solutions of the future in the microcosmic experiments of the present. "The mission of the socialist party in Palestine," he wrote in a characteristic passage, "cannot be compared to that of such parties elsewhere which is usually confined to the class war . . . Its main task is to demonstrate to the Exile all the forms of socialist action and construction in Palestine."[317]

It was essential to think on a large scale. "The present period in which we are now living," he declared in 1912, "is pregnant with world revolution." The Jewish people had to prepare itself for total change. "The revolution in Russia has lifted the burden of suffering, shame, and fear which for centuries weighed down the masses of the people,"[318] and the potential strength thus liberated had to be mobilized for the cause of national liberation.

In article after article, he returned to those same basic themes that he had first developed in the 1890s. The Jewish people had to raise huge sums of national capital – "hundreds of millions." This money should be used to ground "the entire settlement enterprise [on a] . . . collective, cooperative, and socialist basis."[319] There could be no other way, for "the Arab workers will of economic necessity always form the great majority in all enterprises based on private capital, be it in town or country."[320]

What for so long had remained abstract theses, Syrkin insisted, were at last taking on concrete form. "The cooperative principle has conquered in Zionist theory. Worker kvutsot, the cooperative colony [at Merhavya], the farms of the National Fund, the immigration societies, Bezalel and the cooperatives within it – these are the seeds . . . of the future."[321] In 1913 he described in *Ha-ahdut* the formation of a society, Ahava (Brotherhood), which "will organize the emigration of workers [from America] to Palestine [and] establish . . . garden cities, factories, urban districts, shops, restaurants – all on cooperative foundations so that there will be no room for capitalist exploitation."[322] Even though this society did not grow into the mass movement that Syrkin had characteristically envisaged, it gained support not only in the United States (it had a hundred members there in 1914), but also in Palestine. A branch of Ahava was founded by a group of workers in Petah Tikva, who contracted to cultivate orchards and orange groves entirely on their own responsibility. The core group were members of the Poale Zion party.

They rented a house in En Ganim and lived on a communal basis. One member recalled later that Syrkin's articles on cooperative socialism had inspired the creation of the society. "His simple words clarified the idea, deepened it, and showed the way."[323] (In the 1920s, members of this Ahava group were among the founders of Kibbutz Yagur.) In a letter of 1913, Berl Katznelson wrote to his brother Chaim

Figure 29. Zhitlovsky (in center holding straw hat) among the workers in Petah Tikva, 1914. (AMJLM)

in New York asking to be remembered to Syrkin: "He is the one man abroad who has a feel for the affairs in this country and also has a profound historical understanding, even though he lacks all practical grasp of the present. Of all the crowd, he is the only one for whom I feel affection."[324]

The "utopian" or constructivist, as against the "scientific" or class war school of socialism, was again represented on the pages of *Ha-ahdut,* although in less totalist form, by Kaplansky and Zhitlovsky. "The worker," Kaplansky declared at the May Day rally of 1912 in Jaffa, "creates new social values . . . and he is destined . . . to create the new social milieu. Here in this country there arose the great Prophets who reached the highest values of mankind . . . and the spirit of Prophecy will awaken again thanks to the Jewish worker in the settlements of Galilee and Judea."[325] In contrast to Syrkin, however, Kaplansky did not expect the cooperative system to sweep aside the existing system of private enterprise in the foreseeable future. "It is clear," he was reported saying in 1913, "that we shall not jump over the capitalist period in Palestine. But the settlement experience until now proves that socialism is not a dream for the morrow but a necessity for today."[326]

During his visit in the summer of 1914, Zhitlovsky managed to stir up a veritable storm of protest because of his argument that Yiddish and not Hebrew was destined to become the dominant language of the Yishuv. On one occasion, high school students in Tel-Aviv surrounded the house in which he was staying and would not permit him to reach the public meeting at which he was to speak – in Yiddish.

Zhitlovsky also did some frank talking about some of the attitudes to Arab labor prevalent in the movement. The entire concept of "labor conquest" (*kibush ha-avoda*), he argued, was erroneous. There was no possibility of competing with the cheap and plentiful Arab labor in unskilled jobs, and in skilled roles, the worker from Europe anyway had a clear advantage. "From the practical point of view," he wrote in *Ha-ahdut*, "the slogan of 'Jewish labor' is not viable and from the socialist-internationalist standpoint, there is hardly any need to demonstrate how incorrect and distorted it is. We who fight in every place against every kind of boycott and chauvinism . . . are not entitled to support a slogan that distinguishes *in principle* between the Jewish and non-Jewish worker."[327]

The way out of this dilemma, he argued, was to create a new agricultural Yishuv based on the national ownership of land and the nonemployment of wage labor. As a kvutsa of the Deganya type intensified its agricultural methods, it should make over its surplus land for the establishment of new settlements. "Thus, one should not fight for 'Jewish labor,' but construct the Yishuv on Jewish labor."[328]

The struggle for hegemony

The fact that both the labor parties shared in the ideological reevaluation of 1909–14; that both placed an increasing emphasis on settlement; and that both were involved in constructivist" enterprises – Deganya, Merhavya – inevitably cast doubt on their continued right to exist as rival and separate organizations. Of the new arrivals who came to the country as workers after 1908, very few joined the parties. At the same time, many of the veterans had become passive, nominal, or past members. This decline in active participation, however, came in a period when the party policies required the existence of stable, broadly based, and representative institutions.

As long as financial aid from abroad had been rejected as a corruptive influence, the labor movement had been able to make do with the most skeletal institutions. But once it was seen that proletarianization was not a self-generating process, once settlement and the kvutsa became of central importance, it was no longer possible to spurn financial aid. Without public funds there could be no labor settlements, suburbs, housing, no stabilization of the labor force, and the entire effort of the Second Aliya would wither away without trace.

That this change of line had fateful implications was realized from the first. Those institutions that channeled the aid from abroad, or could influence its use, would clearly gain enormously in power. Broadly speaking, three schools of thought emerged on this issue.

There were those who wanted public funds from abroad to remain the sole responsibility of the Zionist Organization, specifically of the National Fund and the Palestine Office. The only workers involved would be the small group directly and contractually responsible for a given project. As against this, another school argued that the workers had to create their own institutions representative of the entire labor movement, above party divisions, entitled to play a central role in shaping the policies of public expenditure. Finally, a vociferous body of opinion argued that there was no reason why a party per se could not legitimately raise funds abroad and dispose of them for the benefit of the labor movement in Palestine as a whole.

In short, the turn to constructivism produced a strong centripetal tendency and gave a powerful impetus to the idea of labor unity; but it likewise strengthened countervailing and centrifugal forces, for the influx of funds from abroad could infuse the languishing party system with a new lease on life. It could even provide the basis for a full-blooded localism, every settlement or kvutsa, as it were, an "anarchist" microcosm. Thus, the prewar years became, paradoxically, a period not only of ideological convergence but also of bitter organizational strife.

The year 1911 saw the establishment of the two Agricultural Labor Unions, the one in Galilee and the other in Judea. This step was a logical outcome of the growing recognition that the parties alone were not capable of grappling with the problems of financial aid and public capital.

When the First Congress of the Galilee Union met at Deganya in the spring of 1911, the Oppenheimer project was a central point on the agenda. Work at Merhavya was about to begin and, according to the decision of the Ninth Zionist Congress, the representatives of organized labor had to be included in the farm committee. The assumption was that the Galilee congress would select the labor members of the Merhavya committee. But, in fact, the seventeen delegates (representing some 140 workers) proved unable to reach any meaningful agreement on this issue.[329]

The establishment of the farm was welcomed among other things because it aimed, as one speaker put it, to make "the worker his own man in his own work." But the principle of differential wages and the appointment (even though temporary) of a manager, aroused opposition and doubts. It was made evident in the debates that in all probability, "those workers who had become accustomed in the kvutsot to free, independent work, would not join the settlement."[330]

Although the congress established the Agricultural Labor Union on a permanent basis, it refused to take on any direct responsibility for Merhavya. Ultimate control remained with Dyk, Oppenheimer, and the committee abroad. The kvutsa that went to Merhavya did so on an autonomous, temporary, and contractual basis without any share in the management. Behind this decision lay the suspicion of one party (Ha-Poel Ha-Tsair) in the face of a project associated with its rival (Poale Zion), the determination of the local workers not to lose their independence to organizations abroad, and the acute difficulty experienced in deciding on the correct institutional response to the influx of development funds.

The result of this nonparticipation was to strengthen the hand of the manager, who (as noted above) entered in 1914 into a head-on and prolonged conflict with the workers on the farm and with the Union. Only the intervention of the committee abroad (of which Kaplansky was a key member) finally decided the day against Dyk. "[Here is] a good lesson," concluded Zerubavel in 1914, "not to trust others, not even the representatives of other [national] institutions."[331]

In the years 1911–14, the Galilee Union acted primarily as a go-between, seeking out suitable projects that could provide employment for the available kvutsot and mediating in disputes between workers and management. This proved to be a frustrating and very modest role. In 1914 Eliezer Yoffe suggested that the Union should itself act as a contractor, employing labor and accumulating capital. It would thus act on a larger scale and create far more work than could the miniscule kvutsot.[332] But, as with so many projects and ideas of the Second Aliya, this concept would only come into its own in the 1920s. In the meantime, the power of the Union was kept within narrow bounds by the fear (expressed at the First Congress in 1911) that it would "seek to inherit the role of the parties and put an end to the ideological conflict between them."[333]

However, it was in Judea that the organizational tensions and conflict reached the boiling point. What added fuel to the fire there was the introduction of an extraneous factor that did not become an issue in Galilee: the Palestine Labor Fund. This fund (as noted above) had been established in 1909 by the World Union of Poale Zion to enable it to initiate or underwrite select projects in Palestine. For a time, its aims remained ill-defined and the sums collected minimal. But by 1911 – the year of the Third Congress of the World Union – it was apparent that the fund would soon become an active force in Palestine. (The party in the United States proved to be the one effective contributor.)

Henceforward, the fund became a major source of conflagration, the center of a furious, albeit diffuse, political conflict. The factors in dispute were clarified in the opposing decisions adopted in 1911 by three separate congresses. At the Seventh Annual Congress of the Palestine Poale Zion party, which met in Galilee in the spring, it was decided that the practical management of the fund should be assigned to the labor movement in Palestine and that "the World Congress is not entitled to lay down in concrete form the plan of action in Palestine."[334]

A few weeks later, the First Congress of the Agricultural Labor Union in Judea met at Petah Tikva. The question of the fund was the central point on the agenda. Ben Zvi explained that the Poale Zion party did not desire monopoly control of this money and, if pressed, would even seek alternative sources of finance for the party journal. "I repeat, the fund will not be in the hands of some bureaucrat ... It will be in entirety the property of the workers of Palestine and dependent on their will."[335] But the delegates at Petah Tikva adopted a decision directly hostile to the fund. The Agricultural Labor Union would finance projects only by the "self-taxation" of the workers in Palestine and rejected aid from abroad.[336]

This decision was promptly denounced in Ha-ahdut as "the result of obstinacy and hypocrisy."[337] The leaders of the Union were willing, it was claimed, to take money surreptitiously from the Zionist Organization and the Hoveve Zion, drawing the line only when it came to aid from fellow workers overseas. In reality, of course, what had motivated the negative decision was the fear that the Poale Zion party would use its financial power to dominate the Union and the labor movement in Palestine, as a whole.

The Palestine Poale Zion party suffered yet another reversal at the Third World Congress of their movement, which met in Vienna in the summer. Ben Zvi and Ben Gurion, the party spokesmen, found their arguments swept summarily aside. The congress resolved that control of the Palestine Labor Fund should be kept firmly in the hands of the world Poale Zion movement. Leaders should be sent from abroad to establish a labor office and a labor exchange to oversee the affairs of the fund in Palestine. "The World Congress," read the resolution,

Figure 30. Poale Zion leaders associated with Ha-ahdut, 1912–14: Seated from left: (1) Zerubavel; (2) Ben Gurion; (4) David Bloch. Standing: (4) Ben Zvi.

rejects the decision of the Seventh Congress of the Jewish Social Democratic Labor Party (PZ) in Palestine which sought to remove the work of the Palestine Labor Fund . . . from the competence of the World Congress . . . Such aspirations (which also found expression in *Ha-ahdut*) to make proletarian activity independent of the united will of the World Jewish Socialist Labor Union (Poale Zion) can cause nothing but harm.[338]

This resolution infuriated Ben Gurion particularly and (parodying it) he wrote shortly afterwards that the attempt "to make the Zionist proletarian enterprise independent of the united will of the Labor Unions in Palestine can cause nothing but harm."[339]

If the Poale Zion party in Palestine had in fact decided to defy the world movement, it might well have gained in local popularity but would have faced financial bankruptcy, a consequent decline in real influence, and a loss of its ideological legitimacy as a section of an international socialist movement. The party central committee chose, rather, to yield ground. It resolved "to accept the decision regarding the establishment of a labor exchange" and at the same time insisted that "the other concrete undertakings of the Palestine Labor Fund should be undertaken in accord with the decisions of the Seventh Congress."[340]

Ben Zvi and Ben Gurion left Palestine shortly thereafter for Istanbul and Salonica respectively. They had decided to study law and, at the same time, to try to

Figure 31. Ben Gurion and Ben Zvi as students at Istanbul University.

give concrete form to the Ottoman orientation of their party program, to forge links with the socialist and Jewish movements in the heartlands of the empire. By 1912 Ben Zvi, Ben Gurion, and Yisrael and Manya Shokhat were all living as students in Istanbul. Zerubavel remained as the sole authoritative leader of the party in Palestine.

In 1912 Shlomo Kaplansky and Efraim Blumenfeld (David Bloch) arrived in Palestine as representatives of the world movement to oversee the establishment of the new institutions, the labor exchange and the labor office. Ben Gurion and Ben Zvi in Istanbul (as well as the central committee in Palestine) had objected strongly to Kaplansky's visit as "a waste of large sums of money,"[341] but once again they were overruled.

The new line found expression at the Eighth Annual Congress of the Palestine Poale Zion in the spring of 1912, which decided that the fund had to be under party control. "It was a mistake on our part," declared *Ha-ahdut,* commenting on the congress,

> to seek to win the sympathy of the workers for the Palestine Labor Fund before it began to do anything. And it would have been a still greater mistake to have removed the ... fund entirely from the aegis of our party ... The work of the fund must be in the hands of its founders. And others, insofar as they recognize the need for it and its principles ..., should participate in running it.[342]

Clearly, the decision of the Third World Congress of Poale Zion and the subsequent acquiescence (however grudging) of the Palestine party constituted a direct challenge to Ha-Poel Ha-Tsair and to the authority of the Agricultural Labor Union. A fierce struggle for hegemony in the labor movement was the inevitable result. At the Second Congress of the Union, held late in 1911, Poale Zion managed to push through, by a vote of 13 to 12, a resolution abrogating the earlier rejection of all direct financial aid from abroad.

But there was a proviso that made the possibility of cooperation almost impossible. "The congress," read the key resolution, "recognizes the necessity of a fund common to the workers in Palestine and to those abroad who are interested in action in Palestine . . . The fund must be entirely in the hands of a general, nonparty union of the workers in Palestine."[343]

Open polemics appeared in the press. Zerubavel argued that those opposed to the fund were guilty of a narrow provincialism, of "Bundism" and of "elitism."[344] The leaders of the Agricultural Labor Union, Berl Katznelson and Meir Rotberg, refused in effect to cooperate with the new labor exchange, because (in their words) it was a "party institution by origin and in its management."[345] Kaplansky took it upon himself to warn "certain fanatics"[346] that their noncooperation with the labor exchange was an act of self-destruction.

At this stage, the long-dormant ideological conflicts of 1905–8 began to reemerge with surprising force. Thus, in a furious article of August 1912 published in Ha-poel ha-tsair, Berl Katznelson revived all the fears of domination by orthodox Social Democracy. If those who opposed dictation from abroad were guilty of Bundism, he declared, then Poale Zion was acting in the manner of Iskra and the Polish Social Democrats, seeking to oppress dissent in the name of proletarian internationalism. "There is apparently one thing in common to all the sole representatives of the proletariat everywhere. They cannot accept that . . . a section, some minority, should suddenly emerge that does not see itself as either a section or a minority, but as an independent, autonomous whole."[347] With its emphasis on the proletarian masses, the Palestine Labor Fund was an anachronism.

> There is no hope of redeeming our country . . . without individuals, men of will, men who seek great things . . . The past of the "natural" worker does not ensure that he will remain a worker here; and a privileged family background does not destine a man to leave the working world . . . Individuals are needed . . . They will build their lives and they will build the country.[348]

Katznelson was accused, in turn, of betraying the material and class interests of the worker in the name of national solidarity. "They fear," wrote N. Vagman (Reuveni) in Ha-ahdut, "that under such [Poale Zion] influence, the workers will become egoists, will begin to think only of their own interests, will kick out at the . . . exploitation by the employers, who take refuge in nationalism."[349]

But then again, declared Tversky in Ha-poel ha-tsair, what did all this emphasis on class division mean if not an attempt to split the Zionist movement in half: "Every class comes to Zionism with its own interests and so organizes in a separate organization." Such a viewpoint was totally unacceptable to the majority of workers in Palestine, who "see the Zionist movment as one whole, undivided, the movement of the Jewish people . . . And . . . they see no reason for the creation of the Palestine Labor Fund but, on the contrary, are opposed to it as an alien intrusion that can only divide the great movement needlessly."[350]

The years 1911–13 witnessed coups and countercoups within the labor organization in the colonies. In Petah Tikva, for instance, the opponents of Poale Zion established their own rival labor exchange. The cooperative kitchen and workers' house there witnessed furious struggles for control. Meetings were hastily assembled and momentary majorities trumpeted forth.

"Those who were close only yesterday," Tversky wrote, "are now estranged. Friends have become enemies."[351] "In our small world," Aharonovich concluded, "the 'war of ideologies' has long ended and because that is lacking it has been replaced by another kind of war, a war of fists."[352] "What is needed now for the success of the labor exchange," Khashin declared, "is fanaticism."[353] And members of Ha-Shomer reportedly rapped their whips on the table during one meeting in Hadera, shouting that "we will force you to accept the Palestine Labor Fund."[354]

In this struggle, the cards were stacked against the World Union of Poale Zion. Blumenfeld could not run the labor exchange without the cooperation of the Agricultural Labor Union and Ha-Poel Ha-Tsair, and the fiscal weapon was not powerful enough to force their cooperation. In the National Fund and the Palestine Office they possessed, after all, an alternative and ampler source of capital. Thus, when the Fourth World Congress of Poale Zion met in Cracow in August 1913, the assembled delegates had no choice but to reconsider their decision of 1911.

True, Borochov undertook a tenacious rearguard action at the congress in defense of a clear-cut class and Marxist position. This was true of his attitude to cooperative settlements and kvutsot ("Socialism does not rely on projects, on programs ... Socialist settlement is impossible in the capitalist order; and in Palestine, too, the socialist order will come as the result of the class war.")[355] It was true, too, in his approach to the National Fund. ("At the root of the National Fund lies the idea that one can nationalize the land without class war [and] as that is impossible ... it is inevitable that it ... expend its money on the enterprises of private capitalists.")[356] Finally, it was true of his attitude to the Palestine Labor Fund. "We cannot," he said, "take into account the nonparty or nonorganized workers, for they have no permanent viewpoint ... And, of course, we cannot pay attention to the arguments of Ha-Poel Ha-Tsair. We have a distinct viewpoint and we shall work in Palestine in accord with its spirit."[357]

But on all these issues, Borochov found himself in a minority. As for the Palestine Labor Fund, the majority now inclined to the view that an erroneous decision had been taken in 1911 and had now to be corrected. "At the Third [World] Congress," declared Ben Zvi, "the comrades from Palestine explained that it would be impossible to work there without total agreement with the nonparty workers. Unfortunately, our advice was not heeded and, as a result, an important section of the workers treats us with enmity ... If we have made mistakes hitherto, the responsibility falls on the comrades who came from abroad."[358] "We must give due weight," said Ben Gurion, "to the work of our opponents and to the demands of the workers."[359]

It was decided that Poale Zion should abandon the idea of an independent labor exchange in Palestine. The search for places of work should be assigned to the Agricultural Labor Unions alone. The Palestine Labor Fund would remain in existence but would not trespass on the sphere of the Unions. This decision did not put an immediate end to the embittered relations between the parties. Zhitlovsky's visit and his defense of Yiddish as the national language rekindled the flames of controversy in 1914. Nonetheless, the major point of dispute had been settled.

By 1914 the lines along which the labor movement would seek to advance were clear. Worker settlements would be financed by the Zionist Organization, acting through its National Fund, the Cooperative Fund, and other similar institutions. Formal representation of the labor movement was assigned to the nonparty Agricultural Labor Unions, and they would be responsible for the defense of the economic interests of the worker, including settlement.

However, the party system was to remain intact. The sphere left to the parties was political, ideological, and social. They remained as surrogate families. Unable to supplant each other, they could compete for influence in the Unions. They, too, would be reinforced by financial assistance from abroad but – as with the capital invested in settlement by the Zionist Organization – this was to be aid without strings. In the years 1911–14, it was clearly established that in the new society labor was seeking to create, he who paid the piper should not be allowed to call the tune.

Conclusion

The youth who went from Russia to Palestine in the years 1905–8 took as their goal the radical transformation of the existing society, the Yishuv. They expected that capitalism would create a mass proletariat. The ideal was the wage worker. They established trade unions and a clandestine press, called for strikes and demonstrations. They sought the replacement of oligarchy by democracy; of theocratic rule by secular rule; of religious autonomy by national autonomy. Their horizons were wide, embracing the politics of the Ottoman Empire and international socialism.

This prognosis and this strategy received momentary encouragement from the revolution of the Young Turks in 1908. But by the years 1909–10, their failure (at least in terms of their original goals) was becoming nakedly obvious. Proletarianization beat in vain against the rock of subsistence wages, and the policy of confrontation produced a furious reaction in the Yishuv against the "anarchists" and "Moscovites." Unable to change society, the radical youth found themselves alienated and isolated.

Many left the country and many others abandoned their role as physical laborers. The minuscule labor movement undertook in the years 1909–14 a major ideological revision. Private capital was denounced and national capital called in to replace it. The ideal was no longer to work for the farmer or planter but, on the contrary, to be free of all outside control by employer or manager, to join a cooperative or collective group, a settlement society, a smallholding village, a mobile labor platoon. This strategy envisaged not confrontation but separation, a new society built outside the existing social framework.

This process was marked not only by a high degree of change but also, at different levels, by a high degree of continuity. First, the "orthodoxy" of the late period had existed as the "heterodoxy" of the revolutionary years. To start a new life on the frontiers of civilization was an idea which had circulated among the

Zionist youth in Russia before 1905, and it clearly exerted an influence on the groups that moved north to Galilee in the years 1906–8. Such experiments as the Sejera Collective formed links, however small, in a chain that would later encompass an ever greater following.

Second, even in the years 1912–14, the accepted doctrine of the previous period persisted as a muted but alternative conception. The "capitalist path" had been blocked by the competition of Arab labor, but the direct road to socialism could be rendered impassable by its enormous expense and by the shortage of funds available to the Zionist movement. Perhaps, after all, there was no real substitute for private capital, class differentiation, and even class war? Here were two conceptions that were to prove not so much mutually exclusive as, faute de mieux, complementary.

Third, the political parties lived on to link the two periods. For the most part, they failed to recruit the post-1908 immigration. But, despite many hopes to the contrary, they were not swallowed up by the nonparty and all-embracing Agricultural Labor Unions. Rather, they reached a modus vivendi with the Unions, permitting the latter a large part in settlement policies but seeking for themselves an independent financial base and a political role. (In the years 1912–14, after all, Ben Zvi, Ben Gurion, and Yisrael Shokhat were to be found not in Galilee but in Istanbul seeking the keys to an Ottoman strategy.)

Finally, there was psychopolitical continuity. The tenacious belief in national liberation, the importance assigned to national honor, self-defense, and self-respect acted throughout as a major source of energy. It was nationalism, above all, that prevented the disintegration of the labor movement in its moments of crisis.

Again, the concept of the alternative society was deeply rooted in the values, the way of life, the subculture the youth had brought with them from Russia. To build from scratch on a new basis, in open defiance of the society round about – here too was a challenge of youth to age, an act of negation, a doctrine of rebellion, a revolutionary mutation.

Eventually, the parallel society, complete with its political parties, settlements, labor federation, and paramilitary forces, would gain hegemony over the Yishuv as a whole. That far its strength, built on the alliance of pioneer youth and Zionist capital, could reach. But to recreate the Yishuv in its own image – that was a task which hitherto has proved beyond its grasp.

CHAPTER 9

Class war and community

The socialists in American-Jewish politics, 1897–1918

The internationalism of the American-Jewish labor movement and its limits

The Russian-Jewish socialists generally became more nationalist after their arrival in Palestine. But in the United States, the trend was toward internationalism. As described above, the youth who came over from Russia in the 1880s, imbued with theories in part populist and in part Jewish nationalist, largely ended up as orthodox Marxists and strict anarchists,[1] in both cases, firmly hostile to nationalism in any shape or form. This evolution was illustrated by the names they chose – the earliest group came in 1881–2 as members of Am Olam (the Eternal People); the first radical Yiddish journal in New York was *Di yidishe folks-tsaytung* (*The Jewish People's Journal*) of 1887; but later journals were given titles that emphasized a class, not a national commitment: *Di arbeter tsaytung* (*The Labor Journal*), *Di fraye arbeter shtime* (*The Free Labor Voice*), *Forverts* (*Forward*), *Di tsukunft* (*The Future*).

However, from the late 1890s and more dramatically from 1903 this tendency became less all-embracing. The factors that encouraged counterforces (a more national current in the Jewish socialist mainstream; nationalist groupings on the socialist periphery) were for the most part not locally engendered, not American in origin. Rather, events in Europe imposed themselves from without, forcing ideological and organizational change upon the American movement. The larger the Jewish problem loomed across the Atlantic Ocean, the more it forced its way into the consciousness of the American Jew, both in its European form (modern antisemitism) and in its American (the mass influx of immigration from the Russian Empire).

In the wake of these pressures, the problem for the ideologists and leaders of the Jewish socialist movement now became how far, if at all, to modify their hard won internationalist – or more exactly antinational – orthodoxies. Would the veterans who had arrived in the 1880s be ready to retrace their steps, address themselves again specifically to the Jewish question, and risk the accusation of nationalist deviation?

Could they bring themselves to ally with the generation of Jewish socialists carried in by the large wave of immigration after the Russian revolution of 1905? Was Bundism a permissible variant of Marxism? If so, was it applicable at least in modified form to American-Jewish politics? Again, should the irreconcilable barrier, which divided the socialist Zionist from the Bundist camps in Europe, remain standing or was it anachronistic in the United States?

Finally, should the socialists in America (following the Bundist example) insist on a strict class war doctrine in Jewish politics? Or, on the contrary, was there room here for a policy of *Burgfrieden* ("class peace"), for full socialist participation in the American-Jewish community? And if so, should the socialists confine themselves to ad hoc demands or rather insist on a complete reorganization – the full-scale democratization of the community, or "autonomism" in American form?

On the face of it, of course, the reemergence of Jewish political consciousness, even of Jewish nationalism, in the American ("Yiddish-speaking") socialist movement, was clearly opposed to the "objective" or "natural" run of things. First, the mere fact of emigration from eastern Europe to the United States was widely regarded in the Jewish world, and often by the emigrants themselves, as implying a sharp break with the traditional way of life. It has been noted, for instance, that there were almost no ritual baths on the Lower East Side at the turn of the century.[2] Sabbath observance there was in rapid decline. If the mass of immigrants regarded such change as inevitable, perhaps, but painful, the socialists and their sympathizers were naturally inclined to see their arrival in America as a total liberation from the past, a radical commitment to the modern world.

Their faith in modern education, in science, in enlightenment; their rebellion against religion, against tradition, against national particularism; their vision of a united mankind – all combined to make Americanization particularly attractive to them. True, they were at war with the American system of free enterprise. But this was a dialectical hostility, qualified by their belief that socialism would result from the full fruition of capitalism and that in this process America, together with Germany, was leading the world. They took to their hearts the American public school system, based as it was on a monolingualism and on the separation of church from state. The "melting pot," for all its hardships and cruelties, was seen as a manifestation of progress, of historical inevitability.

Until 1897, at least, the development of the socialist movement in the United States served to legitimize still further the assumption that internationalism implied an out-and-out Americanization. The Socialist Labor Party of America permitted the publication of literature and the establishment of local branches employing the immigrant languages. It could thus hardly be accused of any gross insensitivity toward the incoming workers. But this tolerance went hand in hand with a strict adherence to orthodox Marxism, to an unbending class-war ideology. When it came to "internationalism," the SLP and the anarchists outdid one another.

The foreign-language organizations were regarded as mere way stations receiving the immigrant only until he knew enough English to join the mainstream. This process of Americanization was personally exemplified by such members as Morris Hillquit (Hilkovich) and Henry Slobodin, who, starting on the "Yiddish-speaking" Lower East Side, had risen to nationwide prominence in the upper, "English-speaking," echelons of the party. In its leader, Daniel De Leon, the SLP had a strong advocate of organizational centralism who was determined to prevent the emergence of any particularist or localist deviation.

Moreover, the Jewish party organizations – the Yiddish-speaking branches and the Yiddish press (*Di arbeter tsaytung, Dos abend-blat,* and *Di tsukunft*) – were reinforced in their internationalism by the nonparty socialist organizations, which had likewise been created in the decade 1887–97. The United Hebrew Trades (Di Fareynikte Yidishe Geverkshaftn) was established in 1888 and the Workmen's

Circle or Arbeter Ring in 1892. These institutions (both party and nonparty) developed in practice as a firm alliance committed to Marxist socialism against anarchism.[3]

In the years of massive immigration after 1905, they were to grow to enormous dimensions. They met the manifest needs of a large proportion of the new immigration, of the working class, of the radicalized *polu-intelligentsiia,* and even of many traditional Jews eager to familiarize themselves with the modern world. No labor organization founded later outside the framework of these early institutions succeeded in attracting such mass allegiance. This in itself provided the veteran, the "internationalist," generation with a preeminent power base denied to the second, post-1905 (or post-1903) socialist immigration.

The strong pull toward universalism was also reinforced (at least initially) by the encounter between the Russian-Jewish immigration and the German-Jewish community that since 1848 had established itself in the United States. On the one hand, in the last decades of the nineteenth century, German Jews had developed a far-reaching version of Reform Judaism that was designed to purify the religion of everything national and particularist. Perhaps the most famous statement of this creed was the declaration issued by the rabbinical conference held in Pittsburgh in 1885. "We hold," read this document,

> that all such Mosaic and rabbinical laws as regulate diet, priestly purity and dress . . . are in our days apt rather to obstruct than to further modern spiritual elevation . . . We recognize in the modern era of universal culture of heart and intellect the approach of the realization of Israel's great messianic hope for the establishment of the kingdom of truth, justice and peace among all men. We consider ourselves no longer a nation but a religious community.[4]

If such was the dominant opinion of the American rabbinate, it was not surprising that the immigrant socialists should have equated progress with the overthrow of everything traditional.

On the other hand, at the socioeconomic level, the early contacts between the immigrant from Russia and the veteran of German-Jewish origin were ideally suited to fuel a class-war ideology. The German Jews were established not only in the realms of high finance – among them were the founders of famous banks and department stores – but also much lower down the economic ladder, as landlords and manufacturers. While the Russian-Jewish immigrants provided the manual labor in the fast-growing, ready-to-wear clothing industry of New York, the employers (in the initial stages at least) were primarily German Jews. They, of course, were the first to be blamed for the terrible conditions of overcrowding in the tenements as well as for the cutthroat pay and endless hours in the sweatshop.

The fact that the German Jews had established a wide range of philanthropic institutions (hospitals, welfare and educational organizations) served, if anything, to exacerbate the relationship between the two groups, for the recipients deeply resented having to take charity second hand from what (as they experienced it) was a heartless bureaucracy. The class division thus coincided with a profound psychological division in which each side was inclined to regard the other with contempt, suspicion, and even hatred.

All the factors enumerated here were deep-rooted and would long exert a dominant influence on the Jewish socialist movement in the United States. But that movement developed along far less monolithic, internationalist, and orthodox lines than might have been predicted in the mid-1890s. In fact, what came to characterize the immigrant Left in New York was an ever broader range of opinion and wider variety of groupings. There were, in fact, a number of reasons why the founding fathers failed to maintain ideological uniformity.

First, and this was of key importance, the structure of the Jewish labor movements in the United States was entirely different from that in the Russian Empire or Palestine. In the Pale, the political parties at their height exerted control over a broad range of labor institutions: the trade-union movement, the socialist press, the mutual benefit organizations. Politics dominated, and were reinforced by, economics. Furthermore, the supply of money from abroad, primarily from America, was channeled to the party leaderships. With imported funds and the party press at their disposal, they could normally maintain a high measure of ideological orthodoxy. Of course, the illegal and conspiratorial nature of all nongovernmental labor organizations further strengthened every centralizing tendency.

In Palestine a similar structure had developed in less pronounced form, leaving the parties relatively weaker, and initially, the development in America was analogous. The socialist intelligentsia took upon itself the organization of trade unions, a labor press, worker insurance. These institutions thereafter maintained a socialist orientation (in marked contrast to the apoliticism of the dominant trade-union movement in the United States). But here the similarity with the Russian model ends. In the American-Jewish labor movement, the social and economic organizations flourished, while the political parties atrophied.

This fact finds its most dramatic illustration, perhaps, in statistics. In 1880, it has been estimated, there were about 250,000 Jews in the United States of whom some 85,000 were in New York City; while in 1914 there were over 3,000,000 Jews in the country of whom some 1,335,000 were in New York.[5] Over 500,000 Jews were then concentrated on the Lower East Side alone – an area described by Morris Hillquit as containing "a larger number of human beings than any similar area in the world with the exception, perhaps, of the most densely populated sections of China."[6]

By the time of World War I the socialist paper, the *Forverts,* was selling almost two hundred thousand copies daily[7] and the United Hebrew Trades (which had begun with 40 members in 1889) reported that there were now some 250,000 workers in its affiliated trade unions.[8] The *Forverts* was then reportedly making a profit of well over $50,000 a year,[9] while the Joint Board of Cloakmakers was able to lend other sections of the trade-union movement sums of $500,000 or more.[10] The Arbeter Ring had a membership of less than 1,000 as late as 1900, but that number had risen to almost 50,000 by 1914.

Yet amid all these figures of growth, the remarkable fact was that the socialist vote among the Jews of New York City remained all but static throughout the twenty years before World War I. In the Ninth Congressional District, on the Lower East Side, the socialist candidate could normally expect to win no more than three or four thousand votes,[11] and it was only by the narrowest of margins that the Socialist Party candidate, Meyer London, was finally elected in a three-cornered contest to the United States Congress in 1914.

Figure 32. Orchard Street looking south from Hester Street, 1898.

Membership in the socialist parties, the SLP and the SP, was subject to much greater fluctuations but was never high. Following the 1905 revolution in Russia, there were some five hundred members in the downtown branches of the Socialist Party, but in 1911 Salutsky could report that the number was down to a few dozen. ("Speaking openly without covering up, we must admit that we have almost no organized socialists despite the fact that the influence of socialist thinking is rather high.")[12] The Jewish Socialist Federation established in 1912 (as a Yiddish-language subsection of the SP) had reached a countrywide membership of no more than two thousand by 1914.

The reasons for this extraordinary disparity between the socioeconomic and the political arms of the Jewish socialist movement in America were varied. Some commentators tended to blame the coercive power of Tammany Hall, the legendary (or notorious) Democratic Party machine in New York. "Tammany," declared *The Worker* in 1903,

> has reduced political rascality to a science and an art. One almost forgets to be shocked at its infamy in admiring its efficiency. . . . A fearfully large proportion of the people have always some personal interest at stake in old party politics – the hope of a job, public or private (for political "pull"

counts even in private employment), the hope of a contract, the hope of exemption from . . . police regulations; . . . hope or fear, if not for one's self, then for some relative or friend.[13]

Others regarded the two-party system as primarily responsible. The reluctance of the average man to "waste" his vote on a hopeless candidate produced a vicious circle, permanently reducing the chances of any third-party politician. This was doubly true of the socialist parties, which, because of their class-war policy, despised "fusion" tactics. The Jewish voter was still further constrained by the fear that his vote for the socialists could be seen as an un-American act, an affirmation of the separate and subversive status of the ghetto. Speaking at the Socialist Party congress in 1910, Meyer London described this as a factor of major importance. "Why," the would-be socialist voter was asked, "send a Jewish immigrant to Congress when the American working men do not . . .? If you should send a socialist to Congress, they will exclude the Jews from America and adopt a strong immigration law."[14]

Yet another explanation was sought in the fact that new arrivals could not vote during their first years in the country, and by the time they did have citizenship they were very probably living in the less compact areas where the socialist parties carried little or no weight. The wage workers were the first to leave while the shopkeepers mostly remained. "The Reds move out," we read in *Di tsukunft* of 1908.[15]

In reality, however, a more all-encompassing process was involved here. The immigrants who poured into America in their tens of thousands every year sought out (or created) those organizations that could help them directly in establishing themselves in their new country. The newcomer joined up with his family and other immigrants from his home town or district. Together with them it was easier to overcome the economic and emotional barriers that blocked his path from the moment of arrival. Jews from the same town (or shtetl even) united to set up small congregations or synagogues, clubs (landsmanshaftn), and burial societies.

It has been estimated, for instance, that in the prewar period there were some five hundred religious congregations on the East Side alone. "They represented," in the words of Arthur Goren, "the map of Russian-Jewish settlement with all its sectional rivalries and regional peculiarities."[16] The daily newspapers in Yiddish and the great insurance societies (of which the Arbeter Ring was only one and by no means the largest) were likewise seen (together with the public schools) as essential to survival in the urban jungle.[17]

In contrast, the trade unions had a much more uphill struggle. The immigrant workers were normally willing enough recruits when it came to a strike for improved working conditions, and the strikes in the textile industry of New York in the period 1890–1914 became legends in their own time, pitting hungry pickets – often young women – against manufacturers, police, and judges. But when it came to paying regular dues to the unions, it was a very different story. Unions expanded at breathtaking speed during the strikes and contracted to nothing once a settlement had been made.

The Jewish workers, Salutsky wrote in 1910, were considered "very bad unionists . . . but good strikers."[18] Only in the immediate prewar period, when the em-

Figure 33. A shoemaker in a Ludlow Street cellar.

ployers began to cooperate in the regular collection of dues, could the trade unions grow into the permanent and powerful organizations which they then became.

Of course, no such system of automatic (and in part coercive) payment was open to the socialist parties. Geared (like all American parties) primarily to fighting the annual election campaign, they had little appeal to the immigrant (who, anyway, did not have the vote for years). Even the committed socialists were reluctant to dip into their hard-earned and meager resources in order to become dues-paying party members. This was particularly true if they wanted affiliation with the Jewish Agitation Bureau (after 1907) or with the Jewish Socialist Federation (after 1912) – and not all Yiddish-speaking branches permitted their members such a step – because they then had either to pay far higher dues than normal or else forgo their right to vote in inner-party elections.

What is more, the desperate scramble to escape the sweatshop produced a rapid turnover as veterans left and new immigrants entered the class of manual wage workers. Thus, although the Jewish proletariat in New York grew constantly in size in this period, it did not provide the socialists either psychologically or socio-logically with a firm political base. "In the Jewish trades," wrote A. Rozenberg, a leader of the International Ladies Garment Workers Union, "a new element comes in every three years and the old-timers become storekeepers, peddlers or sweatshop owners."[19] Or, as Chaim Zhitlovsky wrote in 1912 (four years after he had settled permanently in New York): "The Jew looks on his work only as a transitional stage and all he thinks about is not how to strengthen his position as a worker . . . [but] on the contrary, how to free himself, or at least his children, from the chains of wage labor."

> This results from the entire "psycho-physique" of the Jews; their inborn "anarchism," which cannot tolerate any master . . . ; their restless, nervous temperament, which finds intolerable the monotony of the working life; their passion to take the initiative, to do "as I choose"; their competitive urge . . . ; their will to gamble on the chances of life . . . ; their alert always active mind, which easily seizes on opportunities; their determination and thrift in the early stages when "one must have the first few pennies of capital."[20]

Constantly eroded by this outward flow, both the actual and the potential, the parties remained simply too weak to impose ideological discipline on the socialist intelligentsia. The press, the unions, and the insurance organizations towered over the political movements. The organizational structure was thus polycentric or quasi-feudal. And, in this respect, the labor movement simply reproduced the general institutional pattern characteristic of American Jewry, a pattern described by Daniel Elazar as "federalist" rather than "Jacobin."[21]

Within the autonomous principalities, there was room somewhere for every ideologist however eccentric his particular version of socialism. From the first, for instance, Lesin wrote regular columns for the *Forverts* and indeed was even appointed editor at various periods. Immediately after his arrival in America in 1908, Syrkin began publishing articles in *Di tsukunft* (the leading journal of orthodox Marxism). Chaim Zhitlovsky was not only able to maintain his own journal, *Dos naye lebn*, but also played an active, though oppositional, role in the Arbeter Ring; while Borochov, when he arrived during the war, was provided with a permanent platform in Louis Miller's independent nationalist, radical (but no longer socialist) newspaper, *Di varhayt*.

But more than a far-reaching freedom of speech was involved here. The entire relationship between the socialist leadership, the party membership, and the great mass of Jews, both wage-earners and petty bourgeoisie, was utterly different from that prevailing in Russia (not to talk of Palestine). The labor parties in Palestine appealed to a numerically microscopic audience, to the pioneer workers themselves and to their few active sympathizers abroad. Poale Zion recognized this fact, of course, when it replaced Yiddish with Hebrew as the language of its party journal.

In Russia, the socialist press addressed itself primarily to the party cadres (who were few in number) and to the large periphery of "organized workers" who were committed by the conspirational nature of their trade unionism to the revolutionary cause. Only in the years 1906–7 did this situation change as the parties began to compete openly for a mass following, readership, and electoral support. But even then the parties depended, in the main, on outside financial support, above all from the United States.

It was in America, as nowhere else, that the socialist intelligentsia found itself appealing to, and dependent on, the great mass of Jews, not hundreds or thousands, but hundreds of thousands. This fact goes a long way to explain the lack of authority wielded by the party leadership in ideological matters, the eclecticism that became ever more pronounced even in orthodox Marxist circles, the declining importance of fixed doctrine in the movement. The party cadres were too small, too transient in every sense – geographically, sociologically, and even politically – to remain the focal point of socialist attention.

This fact first became cruelly evident, perhaps, with the split of 1897 in the New York ("Yiddish-speaking) membership of the Socialist Labor Party. The subsequent struggle between the daily newspaper of the SLP, *Dos abend-blat,* and the breakaway *Forverts* developed into a battle to the death for supremacy in the field of mass circulation. The victory of the latter not only led in 1902 to the disappearance of the former, but it also contributed decisively to the decline of the SLP as a force on the Lower East Side.

Socialist activity – publishing, trade unionism, insurance, election campaigns, fund raising, lectures – all became in varying degrees subject to the laws of the marketplace. In 1907, when the Vilna daily of the Bund, *Folks-tsaytung,* ran into financial difficulties, it became the object of much ironic comment from the New York socialists, who prided themselves on their ability to popularize and sell newspapers. ("Twenty-five years have passed since the first emigration to America . . .," Zametkin wrote, "and we have learned in those . . . years that we must lay aside the student uniform and the student psychology entirely if we want the worker not only to hold us in respect but also to understand us.")[22] Similarly the *Forverts* demanded that Max Goldfarb, the leading Bundist, give a test lecture in a small hall before it would consent to launch (or "boom") his first fund-raising tour of the United States in 1913 – a demand that he, newly arrived from Europe, indignantly rejected.[23]

Under these circumstances, ideological debate and political activity naturally took on forms characteristically American. In Russia (and Palestine) doctrinal controversy had a clear object – to change the party platform – and it was the overt expression of factional competition. In America, ideological divisions flared up in ad hoc response to a given political crisis or event (a pogrom in Russia, a war, an election campaign).

Public interest and concern were fed, stimulated, by saturation campaigns in the press, on the streets, in the meeting halls. Eventually, interest gave way to apathy, and the campaign sank, often without trace. The star system followed a similar cycle. Massive publicity, for example, was used to boost the fund-raising, countrywide tour of a given revolutionary personality who, however little known in Russia, was now briefly rocketed to fame. The mass circulation press also had its stars – Cahan, Baranov, Lesin – who enjoyed very much of a free hand in what they chose to write.

Newcomers from Russia, of course, found all this frenetic activity and publicity seeking very hard to take. "America lives fast," reported one observer back to the Poale Zion paper in Vilna in 1907,

America lives in the street. America loves noise and especially noise based on bluff . . . Every Monday and Thursday, Roosevelt undertakes to abolish the

Trusts; every Tuesday the brothels are cleaned out . . . ,[24] and every day dozens of people shoot themselves, hang themselves, drown themselves . . . And the yellow press carries the noise from city to city . . .[25] Our own little world is no less noisy – the world of sweatshops, poverty and dirt; of shuls, burial societies, and landsmanshaftn, of trade unions on matchstick legs . . . , of progressive movements which have not progressed at all in twenty years . . . We also have murders and suicides . . . We have our yellow press . . . Every day, dozens of lectures are delivered by men who have never held a book in their hand . . . Every day new movements and unions are founded – and on the morrow they have to be founded again . . . ; and every year, we have elections and we socialists grow, conquer and triumph – until the votes are counted . . .[26] And our own yellow press sells itself like a whore and kicks up a rumpus like a drunken Russian officer and fawns before the public and bows and scrapes like a Polish *yidl* of yesteryear to his highness, the Polish *pan.*[27]

The fierce competition to attract mass interest was in itself a factor encouraging ideological multiplicity – nationalist sentiments side by side with internationalist – in the socialist press. Once a paper like the *Forverts* was raising its circulation by tens of thousands a year, it had to assume that it was being read not only by socialists, atheists, and wage workers but also by Zionists, traditional Jews, shopkeepers, and other members of the petty bourgeoisie. News of interest to such sectors of the public could not be ignored nor could their sentiments be too scornfully dismissed on the editorial pages. After all, it was locked in a relentless battle for readership with the Zionist and religiously oriented Yiddish dailies. Thus, through their control of a mass circulation press, the orthodox Marxists were forced to practice a kind of ad hoc populism from which it was only one step to an ad hoc nationalism.

Yet such internal, organically American factors, however much necessary, were not a sufficient cause of ideological reappraisal. The decisive issues, after all, were all centered (or at least originated) in Europe, and ultimately it was European nationalism, in its various manifestations, that tempered the internationalism of the melting pot.

The Lower East Side was adequately informed by the daily press about the various triumphs of the antisemitic movement in western and central Europe, about the administration of Karl Lueger, for example, as mayor of Vienna. As for the Dreyfus Affair, it was given saturation coverage over long periods by the Yiddish papers.

From 1897, the new Jewish national movements – Herzl's Zionism and the Bund – also began to attract attention. Every paper considered it essential to have its own correspondent to report directly from the annual Zionist congress, and the socialist dailies now chose (or felt compelled) to publish news and documents originating from the Jewish revolutionary movement in the Pale of Settlement.

All this was nothing compared to the explosion of concern and involvement sparked off by the Kishinev pogrom in 1903. In 1905 even this peak of excitement was surpassed as the immigrant community responded first to the revolutionary victories and then to the news of the October pogroms.

But, of course, over and beyond this, every year between 1904 and 1907 witnessed the arrival of over 100,000 new Jewish immigrants, the great majority from the Russian Empire. In the peak years, 1905–6, the number reached some 150,000. Among the immigrants, there were, according to all accounts, a very large number who had been involved in the labor and revolutionary movements, both as rank-and-file members and as "officers." This high percentage apparently remained constant even in the post-revolutionary years, when the scale of immigration returned to lower levels.

"If one glances over the history of the Jewish labor movement in Russia," wrote P. Libman, a leading Bundist, in 1913,

> and asks where now are all the intelligentsia activists, one discovers that not all have sunk into their own private affairs, but that many, very many – perhaps more than have remained in Russia and left the movement – are now in America. Leaf through the *Folks-tsaytung*, for instance, and note who were its writers and correspondents [in 1906–7] . . . I assure you that at least three quarters are in America . . . And, today, this emigration of the socialist intelligentsia (which over the recent period has consisted almost exclusively of the worker intelligentsia) is, it seems, no less than it was a few years ago.[28]

This great wave of immigration, perhaps 1,000,000 between 1900 and 1914, brought with it the political movements and theories that had first taken shape in the Pale of Settlement before or during the revolution of 1905. But the impact of the immigration on Jewish politics in America went beyond the direct transfer of members, parties, and ideologies across the Atlantic.

The fact is that immigration, in general, and Jewish immigration, in particular, now as never before, became a major source of political controversy in American politics. Pressure to cut down, or even put an end to immigration from eastern and southern Europe now mounted fast and culminated in the Dillingham and Burnett Immigration Bills of 1912–15. Here was an issue that challenged the Jews of America head-on; that provoked various forms of active response from within the Jewish community; and that could not be ignored by the Jewish socialists, who every year had to fight yet another election campaign.

When it came to the immigration and other similar issues, the German-Jewish leadership, in marked opposition to stereotype, mounted surprisingly effective campaigns. Indeed, it is one of the paradoxes of this subject that the German-Jewish establishment, as represented by such figures as Jacob Schiff, Louis Marshall, and Judah Magnes, created political institutions to defend Jewish interests (meaning, above all, Russian-Jewish interests) long before the "Yiddish-speaking" socialists were ready to follow suit.

Thus, Schiff, Magnes, and their associates played a key role in founding the American Jewish Committee in 1906 and the New York Jewish Community (or Kehila) in 1908. Schiff was also crucially involved in the reestablishment in 1902 of the Jewish Theological Seminary, which, under the direction of Solomon Schechter, was soon to become the recognized center of Conservative Judaism. Taken together, all these initiatives reflected a new line of thinking within the German-Jewish elite.

There was to be felt here a measure of disillusionment with the concept of inexorable progress. Across the ocean, the tsarist and lesser reactionary regimes were proving unexpectedly obdurate in their refusal to liberalize themselves. In the United States (such were the second thoughts), a breakneck Americanization was ruthlessly uprooting the immigrants from their traditional soil leaving them neither genuine Jews nor genuine Americans; exposing them defenseless to the temptations of crime and thus encouraging hostility to further immigration.

It was, perhaps, the time to build bridges between Uptown and Downtown; between the radical Reform Judaism of the established community and the orthodox religion of eastern Europe; between the philanthropists and the masses; even, somehow, between oligarchy and democracy. Arthur Goren has written of the Kehila experiment, "no less instructive than the breakdown of community was the endeavor to reconstruct one."[29]

In sum, the climate of thought prevailing in American-Jewish affairs changed greatly in the decade 1897–1907. The many nationalist-socialist ideologists who arrived in the United States during or after the 1905 revolution thus found the Jewish world, in general, and the labor movement, in particular, not unreceptive to their ideas.

Their synthesis of socialism and nationalism, their involvement in Jewish self-defense (both physical and political), their concern with problems of Jewish national survival in the modern world – all found a willing, often sympathetic audience in Downtown New York and, on occasion, Uptown. They – the Zhitlovskys, Syrkins, Zivions, and Goldfarbs – found each his own niche in one of the many principalities of the labor movement. Local variants of the Poale Zion (the Jewish Socialist Labor Party–Poale Zion); of the Bund (the Jewish Socialist Federation); of the SSRP and SERP (the Jewish Socialist Territorialist Labor Party) managed to consolidate themselves in America. Funds flowed back to the maternal parties in Russia and, in the case of the Poale Zion, to the fraternal party in Palestine.

But the question still remained whether they could go beyond these limited achievements, whether they could expand these beachheads and actually take control at least ideologically of the American-Jewish labor movement. Could the recurring crises that overtook European (above all, Russian) Jewry suffice to bring about a truly fundamental change in the American-Jewish labor movement, indeed, in the American-Jewish community as a whole? What was the impact of the Dreyfus Affair, of the Kishinev pogrom, of the 1905 revolution, and finally, of the mass expulsions from the Eastern Zone in World War I?

The party split of 1897 and the Dreyfus Affair

Nowhere, Zivion wrote in 1909 (he had arrived in the United States in the previous year), "has socialism been so confused with cosmopolitanism as by the Jewish socialists in America. Cosmopolitanism that looks forward to the amalgamation of all the different nations into one mankind has everywhere been warmly received by the Jewish socialists but nowhere with more warmth than by those in America."[30] At the time that this passage was published, it referred to only one aspect of reality. (Its very publication in Di tsukunft bore witness to the existence of a powerful contrary trend.) However, applied to the previous decade, specifically to the years 1890–6, it was true with little or no qualification.

Those were the years when, on the Lower East Side, the Social Democrats and the anarchists were locked in all-compassing conflict. In that period, before the establishment of the Bund, before Herzl and the Dreyfus Affair, pressure from the nationalist camp was minimal. The two left-wing movements were thus free to outdo each other in revolutionary and internationalist zeal. Then, as Lesin later put it, the socialists, the *genosn,* "dreamed of the social revolution . . . They . . . intended to win over to socialism – in one fell swoop – the entire Quarter, the entire Jewish mass."[31] The struggle between the two movements was waged in the trade unions, in the experimental cooperatives, in the press, in the printing shops of the rival papers (*Di arbeter tsaytung* and *Di fraye arbeter shtime*), everywhere within reach.

Support for the anarchists gradually declined, but the socialists did not gain as much from the discomfiture of their rivals as they had hoped. The unions provided a highly fragile foundation, and electoral victories eluded them. The socialists were thus compelled to concentrate their efforts primarily on the propaganda front. They began to publish a weekly, *Di arbeter tsaytung,* in 1890; a monthly, *Di tsukunft,* in 1892; and a daily, *Dos abend-blat,* in 1894.

In April 1892 Louis Miller explained in *Di tsukunft* why, as he believed, it was essential to provide the immigrant with a thorough socialist education. The majority of the Jewish workers (including the trade-union members) had been in Europe

> university students, *gimnazisty,* salesmen, clerks, merchants, factors, wagoneers, sextons, tefilin scribes, yeshiva students, soldiers who have completed their service and others who have not . . . Arriving in the American Jerusalem, they do not find the milk and honey they had expected . . . and it is no wonder that they all became radical . . . adopting socialism, communism, anarchism and whatever other "ism" you like.[32]

But a group so motley in its sociological origins could not long sustain its initial enthusiasm. "Many unions were formed, many stamps sold, many strikes called and still the Messiah did not come."[33] No choice remained, therefore, but to build from the bottom up, to prepare cadres of highly motivated and well-informed agitators.

Di tsukunft was in fact designed specifically to meet this need of socialist education. Its readers were provided with a vast quantity of articles on revolutionary history, socialist theory, materialist philosophy, atheism, and natural science. On its pages in these years appeared all the material which in Russia would have been considered ideal for revolutionary "propaganda" in the conspiratorial worker circles (*kruzhki*). "We want him," stated the editor, "to understand Darwin's theory of the struggle for survival as well as Karl Marx's theory of surplus value; . . . the emergence and development of religion as well as the emergence and development of private property."[34]

In the first number of the journal there were articles by M. Hilkovich (Hillquit) on "Karl Marx," by Philip Krantz on "God, Religion, and Morals," by Daniel De Leon on "The Rise of the Proletariat in America," by Abe Cahan on Darwinism, by H. Schlueter on the Reichstag elections in Germany, and again by Krantz on "Malthusianism and Darwinism." Every month at least one biographical article was published, and representative of the subjects selected were Babeuf, Chernyshevsky, Engels, Fourier, Bebel, Lavrov, Liebknecht, William Morris, Paul Singer, Victor Hugo, Sofiia Perovskaia, Garibaldi, and Spinoza. The annual index contained the following sections: biography, politics, economics, society, religion and religious institutions, the history of socialism and the class war, psychology, pedagogy, peoples and races, astronomy, natural history, physiology, physics, literature and art, poetry, and fiction.

The articles on religion were antireligious and those on Jewish history antinational. (An interesting exception was Vinchevsky's semi-autobiographical article on the socialist journals that Aron Liberman and he had published in Hebrew in the 1870s.)[35] Only in the literary sections were there any echoes of Jewish nationalism or (more correctly) of the Hebrew and Yiddish cultural renaissance. There, the reader could find short stories by Gordin and Fin, poetry by Rosenfeld and Vinchevsky, criticism by Gorin and Cahan. But very little space was devoted to any of this.

Above all, the goal of the monthly was to bring the worker into the modern world. Writing as editor in 1896, Cahan clearly implied that he saw it as both heir to the Haskala – devoted to the "enlightenment of the Jewish people [folk] " – and as rebel against the Haskala. "The maskilim there [in Russia]," he insisted, "cannot believe their eyes seeing this thoroughly scientific journal in which physics, astronomy, the theories of Karl Marx, etc., are explained in plain Yiddish [mame-loshn]."[36]

Jewish nationalism in any shape or form was to be rejected out of hand. "We are no patriots of a special 'Jewish labor movement,' " Miller explained. "We would like the Jews to be members of the American unions."[37] The socialist aim, Cahan wrote in 1896, was a "more rapid Americanization – healthy propaganda in Yiddish will bring the Jewish workers to socialism and to [English,] the language of the country."[38] The Jewish capitalists, Peskin wrote in 1897,

declare that the "socialist" is worse than a convert to Christianity [meshumed]. The American Jews hate the Russian Jews, i.e., the socialists . . . Yes, the Jewish worker has rejected his brothers, the "Israelites" . . . We have a new Torah . . . and new brothers, the proletariat of all countries . . . and the more we help each other, the quicker the world will be rid of all its problems . . . including the fat-bellied "Israelites," antisemitism, and the Jewish question.[39]

At the annual convention of the Jewish sections of the SLP, which was held from 1891 to 1895, a banner was always put on display. "We are not Jewish socialists," it read, "but Yiddish-speaking socialists."[40]

It was in 1897 that the first irreparable cracks began to break up the monolithic surface of the Marxist movement in New York. On 7 January of that year, a meeting of the *Arbeter tsaytung* Publishing Association became the scene of what was to develop into a formal split in the Social Democratic ranks. A large minority group of fifty-two walked out en bloc, established their own organization, and on 22 April 1897 started to bring out a new daily, the *Forverts*.[41]

This rebellion has been explained, then and subsequently, in different ways. At one level, it was seen as a final act of defiance by a group of party dissidents against the leadership of Daniel De Leon, against his dictatorial methods and against his strategy of splitting the trade-union movement in order to undermine the American Federation of Labor (this aspect of the dispute was the one emphasized in Cahan's memoirs).

At another level, it was seen as an uprising within the Jewish labor movement against domination of the Yiddish press by a self-perpetuating and bureaucratic clique. It was well-nigh impossible, so the opposition argued, for a new member to enter the Publishing Association that controlled both *Di arbeter tsaytung* and *Dos abend-blat*. (An applicant had to be sponsored by at least five members and attend a minimum of three consecutive meetings.) Abe Cahan had written in 1896 that the Association, which should be "controlled by all the Jewish members of the Socialist Labor Party," was in fact no more representative than the British House of Lords.[42]

But, at yet a third level, the entire episode was explained as a crucial stage in a naked struggle for control of the daily press. Certainly this was how I. H. Hourwich would describe it in 1909 (on the pages of Zhitlovsky's journal, *Dos naye lebn*). As Hourwich argued, Cahan and Miller could not reconcile themselves to the fact that Philip Krantz, with his old-fashioned, European style of journalism, was the editor of *Dos abend-blat*. Both the opposition leaders, he argued, had come to the United States in the 1880s extremely young, graduates of clandestine *narodnik* circles, with little formal education, and once in New York had developed a totally uncritical admiration for the American newspaper world. The real issue, in this view, was whether or not to open up the socialist press to "American commercialism, which nowhere manifests itself so clearly as in American yellow journalism."[43]

However disputable the causes of the split, its concrete results were clear enough. The majority group that remained in control of *Dos abend-blat* – Philip Krantz, Jacob Milch, Joseph Schlossberg, Benjamin Feigenbaum – enjoyed the full backing of De Leon and the National Executive of the SLP. And the opposition, now the *Forverts* group – Miller, Cahan, Vinchevsky, Lesin, Mikhl Zametkin, Max Pine – was formally expelled from the SLP in June 1897. Its immediate reaction was to join the new socialist party led by Eugene V. Debs, the Social Democracy of America.[44] (Established at a convention in Chicago in June, it had already won the support of such maverick figures on the Lower East Side as Isaac H. Hourwich and Joseph Barondess.)

Thus, by the summer of 1897, the stage was set for a battle royal between the two Social Democratic Yiddish dailies, the one "loyalist," the other "oppositional," each linked to a different socialist party, both competing for the same readership, the one determined to eliminate the other. To an important extent, this press war was fought out in ideological terms, as *Dos abend-blat* entrenched itself in the more "orthodox" Marxist positions and the *Forverts* moved toward what was not so much revisionism as latitudinarianism. But even in *Dos abend-blat* and the other Yiddish publications of the SLP, ideological uniformity was far from total.

The two papers took up opposing ideas on the issue of the Spanish-American War in 1898. The *Forverts* argued that whatever the predatory capitalist goals of the United States, its victory would objectively serve the cause of progress. After all, the Cubans were seeking the political independence of their island. And, besides, America was a far more advanced country – and so historically nearer to socialism – than Spain.

For its part, *Dos abend-blat* insisted that no genuine socialist could support the aggressor in such a war; that the Berlin *Vorwärts,* the SLP, and even the English-language press of the Social Democracy of America had all condemned American intervention; and that the only principle motivating the *Forverts* was its determination to gain readers – "to swim with every stream of mass enthusiasm, to play those tunes that can win a mass following."[45]

It indignantly rejected charges that its antiwar stand could encourage antisemitism. On the contrary, it declared, repeatedly, that the courageous participation of Jews in the socialist and revolutionary cause could only serve to refute the antisemitic slander that every Jew was a capitalist, parasite, and coward.

However, even *Dos abend-blat,* as a daily newspaper, felt obliged to run banner headlines announcing the progress of the war and the American military victories. This inspired a cartoon in *Forverts* showing a two-headed figure: the one head was that of Uncle Sam, representing the front page; the other that of a scruffy intellectual, representing the editorial page (written for the "conscious" readers, as the caption put it).[46]

But, it was the Dreyfus Affair that produced the most tense division of opinion. From the summer of 1898 until the spring of 1899, the two papers took their stand on opposite sides of the fence dividing socialist opinion in Europe. *Dos abend-blat* remained faithful to the line laid down by the French socialist deputies in their manifesto of January 1898, which had dismissed the Affair as "a struggle between two factions of the bourgeoisie."[47] (In so doing, the paper was following the lead of Jules Guesde and, indeed, of the majority in the French socialist movement.)

Its front-page reporting for a long time was definitely scanty, and what there was clearly suggested that the whole case was being blown up out of all proportions. Typical headlines read: "A Death Blow to Dreyfus," "The Dreyfusards in Confusion," or "Esterhazy Again Telling Stories." The editors often added acid comments to the news stories, explaining, for instance, that there "can no longer be any hope of salvation for the prisoner on Devil's Island"[48] or that the publicity given to Esterhazy's confessions in the London press was so much "bluff."[49]

A front-page article in February 1899 reported that "the members of the Dreyfus Syndicate are beginning to admit that the verdict of the military court . . . will not be reversed."[50] It described the attacks by the strongly anti-Dreyfusard *Le Soir* on the chief rabbi of France, Zadoc Kahn, and noted with satisfaction that its editor, Gaston Pollonais, was a Jew. "This shows," stated the editors of *Dos abend-blat* in an addendum, "how false is the antisemitic slander that all the Jews are in the Dreyfus Syndicate."[51]

In contrast, the *Forverts* placed itself wholeheartedly in the camp of Jean Jaurès, who in the summer of 1898 had come out strongly in defense of Dreyfus. The fact that the editors were now Miller and Lesin (Cahan had resigned the year before) probably explains why the paper went to such lengths in this direction. The Dreyfus Affair provided Miller with a perfect opportunity to expose and outsell the rival paper, while it enabled Lesin for the first time to present the public at large with his ideas on the Jewish question.

It reported on the case earlier, more extensively, and more prominently than *Dos abend-blat.* Its headlines read "Justice for Dreyfus," "Dreyfus' Innocence," "Antisemites Defeated." When in May 1899 the army tribunal ordered a new trial – thus in effect overturning the original verdict – Miller came out with a furious attack on *Dos abend-blat* (which since April had been hurrying to change sides). "It quite simply and openly insinuated," he wrote, "that the Dreyfus agitation in France was arranged by a Jewish Syndicate and financed by Jewish money. It always showed the news in such a way as to [suggest] . . . that Dreyfus was guilty . . . Imagine a Jewish paper that almost openly spreads antisemitic slander, lies, and falsehood."[52]

In a long reply, *Dos abend-blat* insisted that the vindication of Dreyfus had, in fact, justified its belief that the Affair had been needlessly inflated; that the overreaction on all sides had only delayed Dreyfus's release; that the inevitability of progress had throughout guaranteed a just dénouement:

> The extreme Jewish "patriots" . . . strove to recruit the Jews in just the same way . . . that the Patriotic League [and] Drumont . . . managed for a time to attract sections of the French public . . . [They] worked up the Jewish masses with the hysterical claim that the Jews no longer have the right to live anywhere, that even in France they are helpless victims of antisemitism . . . [But] unrest in the streets is not the spirit of the people . . . and such uproar is transitory . . . It was our healthy *socialist* conviction that assured us, like all socialists, that a pathological and momentary turmoil cannot be interpreted as the solid march of development – a development powered by forces totally different and a thousand times stronger.[53]

When Millerand, with Jaurès's support, entered the government of Waldeck-Rousseau in July 1899, the two papers again took up differing positions. With its choice of quotation from Liebknecht and Kautsky, *Dos abend-blat* made clear (at least implicitly) its opposition to this unorthodox move. On the pages of the *Forverts,* Jaurès remained the central hero of the French drama.

Beyond the Dreyfus Affair, the papers again divided in their evaluation of the conflict between the Bund and the PPS, which (with the harsh polemics of 1898) had now come into the public eye. In an article of February 1899, *Dos abend-blat* reported extensively on the new Yiddish paper of the PPS, *Der arbeter,* and praised its determination to combat "the race hatred that has existed for hundreds of years [in Poland]."[54]

Dos abend-blat announced that it had not detected any sign of undue Polish nationalism, of "patriotism," in *Der arbeter* and that it would therefore remain "neutral" in the ideological conflict between the Bund and the PPS. In practical terms, as it explained, this meant that it was ready to offer the PPS every support in publishing and distributing its Yiddish organ. For its part, the *Forverts* came out wholeheartedly in support of the Bund.

As these cases suggest, the policy of the *Forverts* was not only more popular with the broad, nonparty, reading public, but was also presented in bolder terms than that of the rival camp. For the Yiddish-speaking sections of the SLP, the years 1898–9 became increasingly a period of inner dissension. Thus, for example, in

October 1898, Baranov had published a review in the SLP journal, *Di naye tsayt*, that astonishingly went a long way toward defending the book just published in Switzerland by Nachman Syrkin (*Die Judenfrage und der sozialistische Judenstaat*).

What appealed to Baranov in this book was its uncompromising insistence that a man who was both socialist and Jew could not escape from, but had to grapple with, the Jewish question. It was universally accepted on the left, wrote Baranov, that "a Jewish socialist must everywhere love all mankind at once . . . except that he can permit himself to be a German patriot if he lives in Germany or a Russian patriot in Russia (as his bones are being broken there)."[55] For that matter, in America, he could be "a Yankee patriot on Christie Street."[56] But Ben Elieser (Syrkin) was "the first Jewish socialist whom I have come across who is not ashamed to be a Jewish patriot."[57] And Syrkin had logic on his side, for "we are everywhere regarded as a nation, a separate nation, . . . and we are held to a greater or lesser degree in contempt as a nation . . .[58] Is it not natural that your own nation should be dearer to you than other nations, . . . that you would defend it when it is held up to contempt?"[59] Syrkin was not motivated by "religious-nationalistic-messianic-patriotic" motives, but simply by a determination to solve the Jewish question. "This is not nationalism . . . but philanthropy . . . [which] is not in contradiction to scientific socialism."[60]

The editor, apparently Philip Krantz, rejected Baranov's arguments outright. The socialists acted as Jewish patriots, in the best sense, when they united "to establish Jewish sections, to write and speak Yiddish."[61] But if patriotism meant to seek the political unity of all classes within a given nation, then no true socialist could have truck with it. A socialist could support the Polish struggle for independence because the attainment of this goal would in itself contribute to the revolutionary, anti-tsarist cause. Zionism, on the contrary, by its very nature could only divert forces away from that cause. What meant most to the masses was "the wish to be freed not from their special suffering, as Jews, but from the much more real oppression of poverty."[62]

Yet another striking example of the tension within the SLP was the decision of *Dos abend-blat* in June 1899 to publish a lengthy and positive review of the Bund's *Der yidisher arbeter*, no. 6 (edited by John Mill), a review that put the major emphasis on Zhitlovsky's articles, particularly his "Zionism or Socialism." The concept of a Yiddish-based nationalism, it was stated there, had "never attracted much attention from the Jewish socialists in America."[63] But the time had now come to appraise it with due seriousness.

Even more surprising, perhaps, was a note appended by Philip Krantz in which he declared that he, too, was considering plans for the formation of an "international Jewish socialist committee not for the purposes proposed by Ben Ehud [Zhitlovsky], but specifically to link together the Jewish socialists themselves, and to help the Jewish workers in Russia more effectively and systematically."[64] He hoped that such a committee could be set up during the Paris Congress of the International in 1900.

While *Dos abend-blat* thus revealed signs of deep inner confusion, Lesin was publishing frequent articles in the *Forverts* that in contrast presented a coherent political conception. In essence, the themes that he developed there were similar to those being elaborated contemporaneously by Zhitlovsky and Mill in *Der yidisher*

Figure 34. Avrom Lesin, 1872–1938. YIVO Archive

arbeter. (How much this was a case of direct influence, how much of parallel development is not clear.) First, he insisted, socialism did not demand that the Jews abandon their nationality at this stage in history. "The Jewish working masses . . . join other peoples not in order to assimilate and disappear into other nationalities as the bourgeoisie . . . has sought to do . . . So long as other nations exist, so long

471

will the Jews exist. The Jews should not become Russians, Germans, etc., only men."[65] However, and this was Lesin's second point, the commitment to national survival (at least until the socialist epoch) by no means implied an attempt to unite the entire nation in one political camp. Class division ran too deep and the Jewish middle class was too cowardly to permit any form of national unity.

> Even antisemitism is incapable of creating solidarity between the wealthy bourgeoisie and the . . . masses; . . . the Jews have lost not only their Abrabanels, who were ready to abandon all their wealth to join their poor brothers and go into exile, but even their Crémieux, who among their other interests still found time to worry now and then about their poor people.[66]

True, one could not but admire the "first pioneers of Zionism, the socialist-inclined youth from the intelligentsia . . . who dreamed of a socialist society in the future Jewish home."[67] And, equally, it could not be denied that Marxism permitted all classes to unite in defense of the nation against external aggression. But the Zionist movement of Herzl and Nordau was now moving toward an alliance with the most reactionary groups, with the rabbis and plutocrats. Socialists could have no part in such an unholy alliance.

The only solution to the Jewish question lay in the victory of the progressive forces. This fact, Lesin complained bitterly, had been obscured by the behavior of Guesde's school of socialism, which had betrayed the spirit for the letter of the socialist law, had opted for cheap popularity rather than fight for justice. This was nothing new, he wrote, recalling (apparently for the first time in the Yiddish press of New York) the fate of Abe Cahan's resolution against antisemitism at the International Congress of 1891. Then, too, French socialists had refused to condemn antisemitism, using arguments which "before that I had heard only from the Jewish cosmopolitans who . . . fear every good word on the Jewish side."[68]

But, in the last resort "Jaurès, with the other Dreyfusard socialists, saved socialism from shame . . . This French Lassalle with all the strength of a noble soul threw himself into the fight – not against an ancient aristocratic family on behalf of a beautiful woman – but against the entire world for a hated and unfortunate Jew."[69] For Lesin, Jaurès in France and the Bund in Russia were two beacon lights brilliantly illuminating the road ahead. The Jewish masses had to form their own national unit, but within the ranks of international socialism.

Lesin was apparently the first man to describe in detail the ideology and achievements of the Bund to the New York public. He attacked the PPS for founding its nationalism on historical rather than ethnic concepts and boundaries, thus denying to others what it demanded for itself. And he justified the Bund, which had "made Yiddish [zhargon] the language of agitation, created an entire literature for the masses and in a short period of time, called forth a powerful mass movement in the Jewish provinces [guberniyes]."[70] The Bund, he believed, could draw strength from the unique historical experience of the Jews as a nation in exile. "The remarkable history of the Jewish people," he wrote, "will never lose its significance as a demonstration of the power of martyrdom."[71] In sum, socialism alone could solve the Jewish question. "The modern epoch, which has produced antisemitism, has also at the same time produced socialism, which demonstrates with every step . . . how groundless . . . Zionist theory is."[72]

While the *Forverts,* then, presented a bold face to the world, the problems within the SLP were destroying *Dos abend-blat.* In July 1899, a major schism split the SLP asunder and the division reached from the National Executive down into the Yiddish-speaking branches. *Dos abend-blat* remained in the hands of De Leon's supporters, but many of its leading associates including Feigenbaum and Krantz now left the paper. Two rival parties both claiming the title SLP – and both, at one stage, issuing papers with the same name, *The People* – maintained themselves until 1901. In July of that year, the anti-De Leon wing (of which Morris Hillquit was a leading member) united with the Social Democratic Party to form the Socialist Party.[73]

In 1902 the Yiddish press of the SLP, *Dos abend-blat* and *Di arbeter tsaytung,* had to close down. In that year, too, *Di tsukunft* (which had ceased to appear in 1897) was reopened. Like the *Forverts,* it supported the Socialist Party.

Thus, when the next crisis of European Jewry, the Kishinev pogrom, crashed down on the Lower East Side in 1903, the Jewish socialist movement was no longer what it had been at the time of the Dreyfus Affair. The *Forverts* remained as the only socialist daily and was growing fast in popularity. The era of Daniel De Leon was over, and the now dominant Socialist Party was less centralized and less authoritative than the SLP of yesteryear. The precedent of 1898–99, when the attacks of *Dos abend-blat* on the "Jewish Syndicate" had proved such a debacle, in itself guaranteed that this time the internationalists would have to act with greater circumspection.

Kishinev

The Kishinev pogrom of April 1903 had a far more shattering impact than the Dreyfus Affair on American Jewry in general and on the Jewish socialist movement in particular. This was the first time that the new immigrant community in the United States (over half a million Jews had arrived from the Russian Empire since 1881) found itself observing from afar a major crisis in the mother community, in *der heym.* Jews from Bessarabia waited anxiously for weeks to hear whether their own relatives had fallen victim to the pogroms, and immigrants from other areas could not escape the fear that, as in the year 1881–2, the pogroms would spread like a plague across the Pale of Settlement.

At the time of the Dreyfus Affair, the New York socialists had found themselves caught up in a purely doctrinal controversy, the one wing identifying with Guesde, the other with Jaurès. However, from the first it was obvious that the Kishinev pogrom was an issue which called not only for a theoretical but also for a practical reaction. A whole series of projects, ranging from short-term financial relief to the resettlement of Russian Jewry in East Africa, had now to be weighed up as real possibilities demanding active participation or active opposition.

Again, once the socialists found themselves drawn into the area of practical politics and plans, they had inevitably to face up to a new question. Did the Kishinev pogrom justify collaboration, at least on an ad hoc basis, with nonproletarian organizations?

The reaction on the Lower East Side to the news of the Kishinev pogrom was immediate and extremely intense. For the first two weeks it stood in remarkable contrast to the silence in the English-language press, to the (at least outward) calm of the German-Jewish community, to the apparent indifference of the American public at large.

Starting on 27 April, the Yiddish papers day-in day-out carried enormous head-lines on Kishinev that were followed by detailed reports on the fate of the Jews in the town, on the repercussions throughout the world, and on the various forms of action undertaken or contemplated in response. On the first day, relief funds were launched, and thereafter innumerable protest meetings and fund-raising events were hastily organized. Plans – not always realized – were made for mass petitions and street demonstrations.

When in mid-May, *The New York Times* finally began to take note of the entire affair, it devoted considerable space to the turmoil Downtown. "The extent to which the Kishinoff outrages have wrought up the population of the East Side," reported an article on 16 May, "may be gathered from the largely increased sale of the various local Jewish papers, the offices of which are besieged all day by eager throngs seeking scraps of information over which to speculate upon the possible fate of relatives or friends."[74]

The initial silence of the established Jewish community was the cause of much angry comment on the Lower East Side. However, as time went on, it became apparent that the German-Jewish elite could not escape the Kishinev issue. Its increasingly vigorous response (combined with the ceaseless stir Downtown) led many observers to conclude that for the first time the hegemony in world Jewish affairs, in the sense of fund-raising and the mobilization of diplomatic influence, was passing from Europe to America.

At the beginning of May, the Alliance israélite universelle called on the major Jewish communities in the Western World to contribute to a common relief fund. In response, on 14 May, a committee of Uptown Jews – of which Jacob Schiff, Emanuel Lehman, Joseph Bloomingdale, Isaac Seligman, Isidor Straus, and Daniel Guggenheim were members – sent out an appeal to a select list of potential subscribers.[75]

The amount thus collected was kept discreetly hidden from the public eye, but within days rumor on the Lower East Side reported sums of up to $500,000.[76] Most of the fund was kept in reserve, but on 17 May *The New York Times* was able to report that this, the so-called Bankers Committee, had already dispatched $10,000 to Paris.[77] An official report, issued in June, noted that American Jewry, as a whole, had despatched $100,000, an amount that constituted a quarter of the total sum collected across the world and that totally overshadowed the less than £4,000 sterling contributed by the Anglo-Jewish community.[78]

At the same time, two important protest actions were organized by leading German-Jewish circles. On 27 May a large meeting was held in Carnegie Hall in demonstration against the Kishinev pogrom. In the chair was the mayor of New York, Seth Low, and among the speakers were Grover Cleveland, Archbishop Farley, Jacob G. Shurman (the president of Cornell University), as well as Jacob Schiff. The audience, reported the *Forverts* (under a large front-page headline), was largely made up of leading "representatives of the political, financial, scientific and literary institutions of New York . . . and of the entire country. Their protest is, therefore, powerful . . . and will echo in Washington and in Petersburg."[79]

Meanwhile, the B'nai B'rith (which was led primarily by German Jews from outside New York, particularly from the Midwest and the West Coast) had acted independently to draw up a petition addressed to the Russian government. On 15 June a delegation of its leading members was received by the President of the United States, Theodore Roosevelt, who told them that

> never in my experience of this country [have] I known of a more immediate or deeper expression of sympathy [than in the Kishinev case] . . . I may say that the United States is that country in which . . . most has been done in acknowledging the debt due to the Jewish race and of endeavoring to do justice to those American citizens who are of Jewish ancestry and faith.[80]

After a delay of some two weeks, Roosevelt agreed to pass on the petition (which had been signed by some ten thousand citizens) to the tsarist government – although, in the end, it did not go beyond the American chargé d'affaires in St. Petersburg, who had been warned that it would be summarily rejected if actually delivered to the Russian Ministry for Foreign Affairs. Roosevelt met a delegation made up of Simon Wolf, Oscar Straus, and Leo Levi (the B'nai B'rith president) to explain that no more could be done. "It would have been the height of folly," concluded *The American Hebrew* on 24 July, "for us to insist on our government going any further."[81]

Observers noted that, in yet another reaction to Kishinev, German Jews were showing a new interest in Zionism and joining the Federation of American Zionists in greater numbers. "I noticed," read a report in *The American Hebrew* on a Zionist meeting in Pittsburgh,

> that the theater was crowded from pit to dome. Never before had I seen such an audience . . . [It] was not made up entirely of Russian Jews. The most cultured specimens of the German Jews were there, the followers of all sorts of schools and fads sat side by side with the bearded Jew. What a triumph it was for the latter . . .[82] Was it Zionism that wrought this miracle, or Kishinev? Chiefly the latter, I think.[83]

In the summer of 1903, the American Zionist leadership, which included such prominent German Jews as Richard Gottheil and Harry Friedenwald, came out strongly in support of Herzl's East African project.

By that time, too, the complaint was frequently being made that the organized response to Kishinev had been too haphazard and uncoordinated. *The American Hebrew* spoke of the "aimless way of our institutions,"[84] and a leading rabbi declared that "we often present the spectacle of a house divided against itself."[85] Some prominent personages such as David Philipson (a key leader of Reform Judaism) now called for a full-scale American Jewish Congress.[86] Rabbi Silverman (the president of the Union of American Hebrew Congregations) called for a looser federative form of union, possibly "a central board consisting of the executive committees of the various orders and national organizations, said board to have full authority to act for all constituent societies in matters of general interest to all Israel."[87]

Nothing, in fact, came of these plans at this time and the issue of political unity went into abeyance until the new crisis of 1905–6. But *The American Hebrew* was nonetheless expressing a widespread opinion when it stated on 17 July that "Kishinev will mark a decided turn in Jewish history ... Kishinev has made American provincialism impossible with self-respect and Jewish dignity. American Jewry has emerged and stretched out its hands to its brothers."[88]

The action of the German Jews in America was made to look all the more impressive by the almost total inaction of the Jewish establishment in England. This time, the roles of 1882 had been reversed. The fact that England was just recovering from the ordeal of the Boer War while America had emerged unscathed from the Spanish War was no doubt a factor here – the Foreign Office was reluctant to deepen British isolation in the world by antagonizing Russia.

For its part, Anglo-Jewry was living under the cloud of the anti-alien campaign and saw the investigation of the Alien Immigration Commission at the time as nothing less than a "trial of the Jew" (in the words of the *The Jewish Chronicle*).[89] Over and above all this, the Lord Mayor of London, Marcus Samuel (later Lord Bearsted), was unwilling as a Jew to use his office as his predecessor had done in 1882.

The result was a bitter controversy in the Anglo-Jewish community in which an opposition group led by Herbert Bentwich and Joseph Prag accused the leadership (Lord Rothschild, Samuel Montagu, Claude Montefiore, D. L. Alexander) of cowardice and betrayal. In response, they argued that demonstrative action could only be counterproductive. Lucien Wolf even insisted that the public protests of the 1880s had then provoked the tsarist regime into its policy of renewed anti-Jewish legislation.[90]

In the end, the immigrant Jews of the East End organized their own mass march from Whitechapel to Hyde Park, where they were addressed, inter alia, by the veteran Russian revolutionary, N. Chaikovsky – an action described by Sir Samuel Montagu as "a danger to the Russian Jews." ("He did not believe," he said, "that the Jews in Russia were revolutionary.")[91] Surveying this entire development, *The Jewish Chronicle* declared on 12 June that "in America the manifestation of public opinion can only be described as remarkable ... England alone remains dumb so far as the platform's concerned."[92]

Despite the fact that by now most of the active Jewish socialists in America supported only one party, the SP, they were almost as divided by Kishinev as they had been by the Dreyfus Affair. Within the SP, three different camps emerged, each associated with a different journal: the *Forverts, Di tsukunft,* and the English-language paper of the party in New York, *The Worker.*

The *Forverts* from the first threw itself fully into the whirlwind of news reporting, protest, and activity that Kishinev had unleashed on the Lower East Side. At this juncture, the editors were Lesin and Raevsky, who on the Kishinev issue received full support in the paper from Miller, Cahan, Hourwich, and Peskin.

On the day that the news of the pogrom was first published, 27 April, the *Forverts* immediately called for a massive response, including "a monster demonstration."[93] On the twenty-eighth, it announced that it was opening its own fund for the relief of the victims and it called for contributions no matter how small. At the same time, the *Forverts* Association took part in a meeting of "progressive" organizations – among them, trade unions, Arbeter-Ring and SP branches, the

Friends of Russian Freedom (Druzia Russkoi Svobody), the *Tsukunft* Press Federation – to discuss joint action.

Louis Miller there declared that the Left was strong enough to act independently and to spurn all forms of cooperation with the conservative forces in the Jewish world.[94] A committee of fifteen (which included Lesin) was elected and, as its first step, organized a protest rally at Cooper Union on 4 May that was addressed by (among others) Abe Cahan, Joseph Barondess, and William Edlin. In mid-May, the *Forverts* drew up its own mass petition to Theodore Roosevelt, calling on its readers to return it signed to the editorial offices.

The *Forverts* was torn in its attitude to the campaigns organized Uptown. As news items, the Carnegie Hall protest or the meetings with Roosevelt won enthusiastic coverage, but analysis and editorial comment tended to be critical and sarcastic. On 11 May the paper noted that "the rich Jews Uptown are doing nothing."[95] And when, a day later, word of the "Bankers Committee" came in, it declared that it was only "our unceasing and successful work which finally forced the Uptown Jewish notables to make [their] large contribution [of $500,000]."[96]

It condemned the leadership of the B'nai B'rith, which in mid-May had called on the American Jews "to preserve our calm, ... [to] do nothing and say nothing that will cut us off from the right to make a dignified and manly appeal ... to the dignity and manhood of the Czar."[97] ("We say," declared the *Forverts,* "that there is no human heart in these smooth and sated executive members, but only cold stone or ice.")[98]

In fact, during the Kishinev crisis, the *Forverts* group as a whole moved over to the position that Lesin had formulated in 1898. Forming an autonomous unit in the socialist army, the Jewish labor movement could act as the true champion of Jewish interests. Class war, revolution, and socialism offered the only long-term solution to the Jewish question, but these goals could best be served by national self-affirmation rather than by national self-abnegation.

The themes sounded in the *Forverts* at this point were thus somewhat reminiscent of those heard in the Bund in the year 1897–1901 in that the call for national self-defense was not extended to include national demands or a national program. But this analogy cannot be carried too far. The ideological consistency so characteristic of the party press in Russia was heavily diluted in the *Forverts* by the individualism, freedom, and often flamboyant inconsistency of the New York newspaper columnists.

Louis Miller insisted that socialist dogma could not be permitted to stifle the natural, emotional protest called forth by Kishinev. "A Jewish socialist bears within him not only socialism but also humanity and Jewishness, and when a contradiction between them occurs, one cannot simply bury the one under the other ... We must give the answer ourselves and on this answer ... depends our future success or failure in the advance and progress of the Jewish people."[99] Abe Cahan constantly referred back to the crisis of 1881–2 and argued that now as then the Jewish question demanded its own urgent solutions. In Brody in 1882, he recalled

> we debated, but the word "pogrom" united everybody. The one was heading for Palestine, the other for America; one wanted Jewish communes which would serve as an example to the whole world; another wanted nothing of

that. But we were united. All shared the same feeling, the same idea: "The Jews in Russia go daily in danger of their lives. We must help the Jews of Russia find a home." . . . And as far as possible we worked for our bloodied people together.[100]

For his part, I. H. Hourwich rebuked Miller for seeing a contradiction (albeit one to be reconciled) between socialism and Jewish emergency action: "This means that if a socialist takes an interest in the victims of inhuman barbarism, then he is inconsistent as a socialist; . . . [that] if a socialist wants to be 'uncompromising,' he must keep his distance even in such a matter."[101]

However, it was left to Shmuel Peskin to describe in the most black-and-white terms the impact wrought by Kishinev on the Jewish socialist movement across the world.

I doubt if our Jewish movement in all its [various] countries will remain what it has been hitherto. All the veteran Jewish comrades in America remember the permanent poster which used . . . always to be displayed at every Jewish convention: "We are not Jewish socialists, but Yiddish-speaking socialists." And this sign really expressed the spirit of the movement here as it was then and to a considerable extent in Russia, too. We were not Jews but it so happened that we and the masses spoke Yiddish . . . No national question existed for us . . . The entire world was divided for us into two classes . . . [and] we divided antisemitism into two classes too . . . as a means by which the ruling classes sought to deceive the people . . . ; [and] worker antisemitism, which we explained away primarily as the result of ignorance . . . Once somewhat enlightened, these antisemites would become the best socialists . . . [Anyway] we knew that the entire question would soon become defunct . . . once the red flag began flying over every parliament . . .

But gradually this all changed and now it is about to change permanently. First of all, it became apparent that antisemitism was not lessening in the slightest. One should not judge by America, but by Russia, Austria, and Roumania . . . The Kishinev massacre is . . . only a great explosion that reveals the profound turmoil raging in the hearts of millions . . . The Russian regime is blamed for everything but it is false to assert that the people are guiltless because the regime is guilty. An innocent man, even a hardened criminal, cannot on command go and cut people up limb by limb.[102]

Top priority, he concluded, had to go to armed self-defense in Russia. At the ideological level, the Jewish socialists should openly declare their support for nationalism, albeit militantly secular, "free-thinking," and "progressive."

Why should we not see that the Jews too, will remain a nation . . . In addition to being socialists, we want to support the maintenance of the Jews as a nation. We know what difficulties such a standpoint causes the Jewish socialist movement. But one does not overcome difficulties by shutting one's eyes to them.[103]

Undoubtedly, the most divisive ideological problem looming up before the *Forverts* group was that of possible cooperation between the proletarian and the bourgeois camps. Ironically, at the time of Kishinev, Lesin (the "nationalist") pursued a much more consistent class-war line than Cahan (the "internationalist"). Lesin wrote mainly in support of the Bund, endorsed its synthesis of national and class politics, and held it up as a model. Given a natural increase in Russian Jewry of 120,000 per annum, not emigration but only revolution could solve the Jewish question in eastern Europe. "The Jews of the Bund . . . ," he wrote, "are the new Maccabees who after eighteen hundred years of Exile have taken up the fight for liberation . . . If we fight together with the Russian people, they will be on our side . . . The tsar will make ever fewer pogroms."[104]

On the other hand, Cahan was urgently seeking immediate forms of action (apart from fund raising or newspaper publicity) in America and, time and again, he suggested the need for cooperation with nonsocialist forces. "If all the papers worked together," he wrote on 10 May, "we could ensure that on a set day as great a mass would march as at the funeral of the rabbi of the Kolel – with black flags and funeral music."[105]

But, beyond this, the American community, or at least the more than one million Russian Jews now in the United States, should take it upon itself to ensure the resettlement of the emigrants now fleeing Russia in unprecedented numbers. Cahan believed the obvious solution to be the planned and organized dispersal of the immigrants across the United States. The Russian Jews of 1903 had to avoid the errors of omission and commission made by the German Jews in 1881–2. "We need a good organization over the entire country," he wrote on 4 June, "with sections in every city or region, with congresses, with information committees. The Jewish socialists, with their intelligence and seriousness, could do much to assist such an organization." As for sources of finance, he added, "it turns out that the rich Jews of all countries are ready to give considerable sums for emigration."[106] When in August, news of Herzl's East African plan came in, Cahan was even ready to give that a tentative endorsement. "Today, who has anything against such a plan – as long as there is even a possibility of Jews making a living there, as long as there are new places in which the unfortunate Jews from Russia and Roumania can find a home."[107]

It now emerged that Cahan made a clear distinction between national unity at the moment of acute emergency and class division as the norm at all other periods. This was his formula for the reconciliation of support for far-reaching nationalist (or at least, national) projects with support for an equally far-reaching form of Marxist internationalism. "A few days later, we are again divided from each other; the Jewish factory owner again sucks the blood of his Jewish employees; they cannot be brothers. And when the Kishinev Jews . . . arrive here they will receive charity from the rich Jews, but no hand of brotherhood."[108]

Di tsukunft in 1903 adopted a midway position, opposed to the *Forverts* group but much less extreme in its criticism than *The Worker*. The group in control of *Di tsukunft* – Philip Krantz, Benjamin Feigenbaum, and Jacob Milch – had remained in the SLP in 1897, had broken away with the anti-De Leon split of the party in 1899, and had entered the newly formed Socialist Party in 1901. They and their faction were often termed derisively the "Kangaroos."

They did not enforce a monolithic line in their monthly journal (which was heavily subsidized by the Arbeter Ring). In the years 1903–4, articles by A. Litvin (who had been one of the founders of Poale Zion in Minsk in the late 1890s) and Frumin (who wrote as a Bundist from Switzerland) followed a consistently nationalist line of thought. Indeed, Frumin was so outspoken that the Bundist Committee Abroad felt compelled to disassociate itself officially from his viewpoint. (He had written, for instance, that with the Bund, "the Jewish nation came back to life from the dead . . . [Here is] the revival of the . . . Jewish proletariat as a *class* . . . , of the Jewish people as a *nation* . . . a beginning of the Redemption . . . , of the end of the Jewish Exile.")[109]

However, Krantz, the editor, and his veteran associates persistently criticized what they regarded as an epidemic of nationalist hysteria in the movement. They rejected outright the plea put forward by Miller and Cahan that at such a moment the dictates of natural emotion could not be stifled. "A fire is raging," Milch wrote, "and we have lost our heads. Instead of doing what is needed, we go around wringing our hands, shouting and screaming."[110] The simple truth, they insisted, was that the Kishinev pogrom was an attempt by the tsarist regime to divide the opposition camp, to intimidate the Jewish revolutionaries, to divert the venging forces of insurrection. In 1881, Milch wrote again, Lilienblum in his famous article had blamed the pogroms on popular hatred. But since then "the world has learned something . . . Even though it is the muzhik who strikes at the Jews, it is the regime . . . that is really responsible."[111] To act as though it were otherwise, was to fall directly into the trap. "That is just what the regime wants! That is the goal of the pogroms!"[112]

It was false to suggest that the downfall of tsarism would not ameliorate the lot of the Jews in Russia. Political freedom did help. Despite the Dreyfus Affair, the Jews in France were infinitely more secure that those in Russia. "Ask our Zionists if they are considering the removal of French Jews to Palestine and they will look at you as if you are mad." To see this truth it was enough to look around and watch how politicians in America – William Randolph Hearst, for example – were now courting Jewish support by making Kishinev into a cause célèbre. Even the German Jews had been forced to follow suit. "And the *yahudim*? They, too, are some kind of reformers. They are for Mayor Low, after all. How can they keep quiet? Still, it took them three weeks to wake up. What does this demonstrate? It shows that where Jews have political rights, they have political power."[113]

But power in America did not bring with it power in Russia. "With protests from outside Russia," Krantz wrote,

> one can do very little to help the Jews [there]. And, actually, one can even say that nothing can be done. The Russian regime mocks at such protests and the Russian people knows nothing about them. It is stupid and laughable to think that . . . protest meetings in western Europe and America . . . can have any impact on the Russian regime. Even protests in parliament will not bring them to shame.[114]

The increasing support for Jewish nationalism in the movement both in Russia (the Bund) and in the United States (the *Forverts* group) was irrational. Civil liberties were all that the Jews required, insisted Milch, to attain full political freedom.

The Jews should be satisfied to define themselves as Americans by nationality, with the right to remain Jewish by religion if they so chose. Anyway, he asked, "who stops the Jews in New York from having six daily newspapers [in Yiddish] and four Yiddish theaters?"[115] "The narrow 'Jewish spirit'," declared Feigenbaum, "has not produced any value that could not have been created – and created better – by the universal human spirit."[116]

As for the brave-sounding Bundist declaration that "the liberation of the Jews is the cause of the Jews themselves," Milch wrote – this was little more than dangerous rhetoric. "The Jews alone cannot liberate themselves, for they are weak and powerless."[117] Only the maximal solidarity of the international proletariat could ensure a revolutionary victory.

As for the *Forverts* group, or as Krantz described them – "The 'Jewish socialists'..., an entirely new sort of people who have suddenly appeared since the Kishinev pogrom" – "they have begun to arouse an undefined 'Jewish feeling,' to laud Jewish ways as the best... and to proclaim that Jewish socialists must be Jews before all else. What actually do they mean by this? What should one do, what should one strive for as Jews? This they have never explained."[118] Krantz defined himself as a "socialist internationalist." He did not demand assimilation and he wrote in Yiddish. But nationalism was not the central problem: "The workers should not worry themselves with all these issues... Their main task is to unite themselves internationally in the struggle for their share in the world's wealth."[119]

However, it fell to the English-language party paper, *The Worker,* to mount the major offensive on behalf of the internationalist camp. Like the *Forverts* and *Di tsukunft, The Worker* was brought out by an autonomous publishing association. It was edited by two leading socialists, Algernon Lee and Courtenay Lemon. But on Kishinev, the paper was in all probability speaking above all in the name of the leading Jewish members of the party in New York, the men who were naturally regarded as authorities on the problem. In 1903 Henry Slobodin was secretary of the New York State Party organization; Morris Hillquit was a representative from New York on the National Executive Committee;[120] and U. Solomon was a member of the party Executive Committee for New York City (and was appointed acting organizer in the summer).

In the debates within the party on problems of nationality and organization, Hillquit and Solomon consistently took a stand hostile to "foreign-language" interests within the party. Hillquit, for instance, led the attack at the SP convention of 1904 against the proposal for "foreign-language" federations with "the right to organize a national executive committee for that nationality." Such a step, he declared, would mean the creation of "a party within a party."[121] Solomon adopted a similar approach as Organizer for New York City and as chairman of the committee on "foreign-speaking organizations" at the convention of 1908.[122]

Again, in the period 1904–7 Hillquit was among those in the leadership who demanded that the socialist movement come out formally against the principle of unrestricted immigration (meaning, in the American context, against free immigration from the Far East). At the Stuttgart Congress of the International in 1907, the resolution introduced by Hillquit in the name of the American party came up against a counterresolution proposed by the Bund in favor of free immigration and was heavily defeated.[123]

On both the organizational and the immigration issues, Hillquit and Solomon were compelled by the same logic. They sought a truly American party, English-speaking, centralized (at least up to the state level), with a direct appeal to the native-born, and with the recent immigrant population as a peripheral rather than a central force; a party able to win elections across the country.

For a month, *The Worker* (a weekly) chose to ignore Kishinev entirely. But it broke its silence on 24 May. The pogrom, it declared, had to be seen as one more act in the desperate campaign of the exploiting classes to shore up their crumbling defenses. "Nothing is cheaper than denunciation and condolence," it declared.

> All official and propertied Christendom condemns the crime ... He [the tsar] knows where are the real sympathies of the rulers and owners of the world. He has been their partner ... less than three years ago in committing still bloodier outrages in China for no less infamous ends ... There is but one power that Nicholas and partners in this guilt fear. It is the same power that the Kaiser fears, that the Rothschilds fear, that the Morgans and Rockefellers fear. That foe is the revolutionary movement ... It alone can protest, for it alone has clean hands not stained with the blood of Chinese, of Filipinos, or of Boers.[124]

On 7 June *The Worker* quoted in full the resolutions on Kishinev carried by a mass meeting of the party held on Clinton Street. It condemned "antisemitic as well as other movements based on race prejudice [as] one of the greatest evils caused by the present order of society." But, at the same time, it deplored the fact that Kishinev had diverted "part of the Jewish laboring and intelligent classes ... from the revolutionary propaganda of which they have been a very potent factor and tends to drive them into a nationalistic movement of their own."[125] On 21 June, it reproduced in full a translation of Plekhanov's article from *Iskra,* "Times Change."

On 12 July, it published yet another party resolution, this time carried by a New York City convention, that was particularly outspoken in its condemnation of the public uproar produced by Kishinev:

> We brand the pretended indignation of the capitalist class and its press about the Kishineff massacre as insincere and hypocritical in view of the fact that the Russian government is daily dependent on the help of the capitalist class in Europe and America for their financial support. We brand the interposition of our government on behalf of the Jews of Russia as disingenuous and doomed to failure because of its own policy of fostering race-hatred.
>
> We call upon the Jewish working class to remember that the Jewish capitalists are in the forefront of those who keep the Russian government alive by their ready financial aid and that the only solution of the so-called Jewish problem lies in the abolition of all racial ... distinctions between the working men of all countries ... through the struggle of the working class for its emancipation ... from ... capitalism.[126]

The *Forverts* group was not prepared to accept in silence the condemnation of its stand implicit in statements of the New York party leadership and of *The Worker.* Cahan, Miller, and Lesin were determined to hit back. The long-standing resentment of those who had remained in the Jewish Quarter and the Yiddish press against those who had moved out and up – into the higher, English-speaking sections of the party – added a note of bitterness to the controversy. (In fact, this confrontation in many ways anticipated the drama that was to unfold a few months later at the Second Congress of the RSDRP in Brussels, when Martov and the other Jewish members of the *Iskra* group led the assault on the Bund.)

Cahan took it upon himself to defend the emotional response of the *Forverts* to Kishinev. It was right, he insisted, to react most strongly to wrongs done one's own kith and kin. "Whoever cannot feel," he wrote on 26 May,

> that these are his brothers, his people who have been torn to bits is not needed by socialism ... [The Jews] were slaughtered or raped in Kishinev because they are exactly what I am ... Sentimental socialism alone is not right; but the socialism of the head alone is a thousand times worse. Can a man who suffers nothing when people with his blood, with his looks, are hacked to pieces, really suffer with the problems of mankind?[127]

"Just as the Germans are a nation," he wrote on 23 June, "in that they have their own homeland, just so – indeed more so – are we a special nation in that we have no homeland ... Jewish mourning – that is our homeland! ... The pogroms and the Dreyfus Case – they are our Holy Land!"[128]

For his part, Lesin concentrated on what he saw as a pathological tendency of Jews in the radical camp to take up every cause except that of their own people. Writing on 20 May, he noted angrily that, so far, *The Worker* had not so much as mentioned Kishinev. "Some of our socialists," he wrote,

> say that we are hysterical ... They are Pharisees who argue that the Sabbath was not given for man, but man for the Sabbath ... These free Jews are slaves ... when it comes to their own people. This is the great curse placed on us by the Exile ... They are prepared to go over the Mountains of Darkness to find and defend oppressed nations, but if you point out to them the most oppressed ... nation of all – their own – then they want to debate with us whether the Jews constitute a nation; to call on us to wait until the Messiah comes; until the salvation of all mankind.[129]

Miller, in turn, chose to direct his counterattack primarily against the thesis that Kishinev was simply one example of the class war no different in principle from any other, that it was analogous to the great strikes and lockouts in the United States. "In Homestead and Coeur d'Alène," he wrote,

> it was a war between two armies of society ... a chapter in the eternal class war that we preach, prepare for, and welcome ... [In Kishinev] all the classes of one nation united against all the classes of another nation. And there was no war, no battle, between the two peoples but a slaughter, a butchery, the brutal murder of unarmed, defenceless, old people, young children and sick women ... Homestead and Coeur d'Alène were battles of the twentieth century ... Kishinev of the sixteenth century.[130]

Thus, the *Forverts* gave as good as it got. But, like American Jewry as a whole, it did not translate its emotional reaction to Kishinev into permanent organizational form. It had collected some $8,000 during the emergency and forwarded them – through the offices of the St. Petersburg Jewish paper, *Voskhod* – to the victims in

Kishinev. It had contributed much to the volume of public protest. It had taken part in the joint committee to plan the mourning march (the plans for which proved abortive). It had renounced socialist indifference and "cosmopolitanism." It had spoken in terms of Jewish nationhood and self-defense. But it had not come out clearly in favor of labor participation in any general, communal, action. Nor had it brought itself to establish an American equivalent of the Bund nor even to pronounce such a step necessary.

The politics of the Pale in America, 1905–1907

The response of American Jewry and of the Jewish socialists to the pogroms of October 1905 was qualitatively different from their response to Kishinev (and, of course, to the Dreyfus Affair). It was not only speedier and more intense, it also culminated in the creation of new and permanent political organizations: the American Jewish Committee, on the one hand, and the Jewish Agitation Bureau, on the other.

In the years 1903–7, the structure of the Jewish socialist world in America was transformed. The massive new immigration brought with it socialist movements that had formed themselves in the Pale of Settlement since the 1890s. These movements – the Bund, the Poale Zion, the socialist territorialists – combined a commitment to socialism (often in its strict class-war form) with a commitment to Jewish self-defense and nationalism. In America, they at first saw their primary task as raising funds for the mother parties in the Russian Empire (and, in the case of Poale Zion, for the fraternal party in Palestine). But nonetheless, they were at once drawn into the web of American-Jewish, or at least East Side, politics.

As a result, the *Forverts* – which in 1898 and 1903 (under Lesin's leadership) had represented the most national wing of the labor movement – was now outflanked from the "right." Faced by a bloc of socialist forces calling for maximal national unity, it formed a coalition with the Bundist organizations in America that were pledged if not to class war then at least to class division. The *Forverts* had not become less nationally oriented – the contrary was probably true – but in the new constellation of forces it now found itself a standard bearer of "internationalism" (if only in the relative sense).

This did not mean that the out-and-out "cosmopolitan" ideology had withered away. It still remained (according to all accounts) the dominant credo of most Jews in the English-speaking sections of the Socialist Party and, indeed, in many key Yiddish-speaking sections, too. But the outspoken militancy displayed by the "orthodox" Marxists in 1898 and 1903 had now given way to an almost total silence.

To persist in minimizing the specific tragedy of the pogroms was, after all, hardly calculated to win votes in the annual elections that the SP had to fight every year on the Lower East Side. (Morris Hillquit, for example, ran regularly in this period as socialist candidate for the U.S. Congress from the Ninth District.) The "cosmopolitan" socialists no doubt felt that the power of the melting pot was so great that the nationalist varieties of socialism could anyway not long survive on the American side of the Atlantic.

The Worker, in speedy response, made do with one uncontroversial editorial published on 11 November 1905. It laid the blame for the bloodshed squarely on the Russian government and added that "while there is apparently no aid for these unfortunates from outside, there is at least the consolation of knowing that the revolution in Russia is ultimately irresistible."[131] For its part, *Di fraye arbeter shtime,* the anarchist weekly, virtually ignored the pogroms for some six weeks. Only in December did it note drily that in the sphere of "the protest meetings, marches, the appeals to the mighty of the world – all is quieter, calmer." The root cause of the pogroms, it added, was religion and one answer was the antireligious campaign. It concluded with the general slogan: "Down with the plague of religious faith!"[132]

The fact is that the framework of American-Jewish politics as it was to stand until 1918 first took shape (albeit in skeletal form) during the period of the 1905 revolution. From now on, four distinct camps faced each other in a complex interrelationship of shifting hostilities and alliances.

On the left stood the powerful but uneasy bloc of the veteran *Forverts* group and the new Bundist forces. To this coalition, the *Forverts* brought its mounting influence on the Lower East Side, its growing financial success, and its close ties with the other long-established Jewish labor organizations: the United Hebrew Trades, its constituent trade unions, and the Arbeter Ring. In turn, the Bundists were more coherent than the *Forverts* in their conception of Jewish politics, more devoted to the Yiddish language and literature, more nationalist, perhaps, but also more doctrinally consistent, committed to a strict Marxism, to class division and to anti-Zionism.

This was strictly a marriage of convenience. From the first, the *Forverts* had identified itself with the Bund as an anti-tsarist revolutionary movement in Russia. This support was nourished alike by the anti-De Leonism of the *Forverts,* by its populist instinct, and by its fight for mass circulation – the heroism of the Bund in Russia had, after all, a natural appeal on the Lower East Side. For their part, the Bundists in America were dependent on the *Forverts.* This was true of their organizations (the Central Federation of Bundist Organizations in America and the Friends of the Bund, both established in the winter of 1903–4), which were concerned primarily with fund raising on behalf of the movement in Russia. It was equally true of individual leaders, immigrants seeking key positions in the labor press, the trade unions and the Arbeter Ring.

In 1907 the Jewish Agitation Bureau was established as an affiliate organization of the Socialist Party with the support of both the *Forverts* and the Bundist forces in America. But the Bundists suspected that the *Forverts* was in reality hostile to any new organization that might one day challenge its total independence and untrammeled power. And the *Forverts,* with Abe Cahan as its editor, suspected in turn that the younger generation, with its new brand of party and ideological politics, would eventually seek to take control of the entire Jewish labor movement, including its press. To forestall this development, Cahan chose to coopt individuals into the labor establishment while giving only nominal encouragement to such political experiments as the Jewish Agitation Bureau and (from 1912) the Jewish Socialist Federation. While there was no love lost here, however, neither side could afford a final separation and divorce.

At the second corner of the political quadrangle stood the general Zionist camp, the Federation of American Zionists, which had been established in 1898. The FAZ remained a small organization with limited funds, but its impact on American

Jewish politics was greater than the bare figures suggested.[133] It brought together in its ranks native-born Americans, Russian Jews from the post-1881 immigration, and new arrivals. Numbered among its leadership were distinguished intellectuals and professionals: Israel Friedlaender, Judah Magnes, Richard Gottheil, Harry Friedenwald; and a number of the German-Jewish magnates, such as Cyrus L. Sulzberger, were known as sympathizers (until they went over to the territorialist movement in 1906). The Jewish Theological Seminary (with Schechter's encouragement) became de facto a focal center of the new movement.

The fact that it was the first political organization in American Jewry to address itself directly to the Jewish question in its modern form gave it a head-start over rival parties. Again, the fact that its leaders were inclined to a cultural nationalism, were in part disciples of Ahad Ha-Am, and developed theories of "ethnic pluralism," also added to its prestige in a period when the philosophy of the melting pot was coming under challenge.

Third was the camp of the non-Bundist Left, or the nationalist wing of the Jewish socialist movement, specifically the Poale Zion and the socialist territorialists. (The Socialist Organization Poale-Zion of America was established in 1905, and the Socialist Territorialist Organization of America in 1906).[134] Denied the patronage of the *Forverts* and the established labor movement, they had no organizational power and little day-to-day influence beyond their own limited membership. (Poale Zion had some one thousand members at its height.)

An article of 1907 in the Poale Zion journal *Der yidisher kempfer*, spoke of a "Chinese Wall" erected by "the Jewish socialist movement here" to exclude the nationalist (non-Bundist) camp.[135] In reaction, the nationalist socialists in America tended to work together and even unite, setting aside the ideological barriers brought over from Russia. A most striking example of this trend was the decision of Syrkin, Zhitlovsky, and other well-known territorialists in 1909 to identify themselves officially with the Poale Zion party.

In times of crisis, in the period 1905–6 and again during World War I, this marginal force was able to exert an extraordinary influence, partly because it had always advocated a clear-cut, radical plan to solve the Jewish question, partly because the rival political organizations – the Jewish Agitation Bureau, later the Jewish Socialist Federation – were for all their ties with the SP and the *Forverts* also numerically weak. By taking up the cry of Jewish unity in the hour of need, it was able to gain the mass hearing normally denied it.

Finally, there was the American Jewish Committee, which was established in 1906 by the German-Jewish leadership headed by Jacob Schiff and Louis Marshall. It took as its goal the coordination of political pressure on behalf of the Jews overseas (above all, of course, in the Russian Empire). Liberal and emancipationist, not Zionist, it applied to the problems of world Jewry an ad hoc rather than overall strategy.[136]

In this respect, the AJC was closest to the *Forverts*-Bundist bloc. In 1903 the *Forverts* had dispatched its own relief funds directly to Russia, sponsored its own petition to the President, and denigrated the parallel activities Uptown. But in 1905 the *Forverts* no longer sought to match every effort undertaken elsewhere and it preferred a division of labor that would assign some spheres of activity to the bourgeois organizations, others to the proletarian. This approach mirrored that of the AJC, which had little desire to share the power bestowed by wealth and influence with the Downtown world. The call for democratization, for the institutionalization of national unity was thus left to the nationalist forces, to the Zionists and nationalist-socialists, to those who represented neither capital nor labor, to the outsiders who hoped to move in.

In 1903 the collection and transmission of funds had been disunited, haphazard, and in large part shrouded in discreet secrecy. In 1905 it was decided from the first that this example should not be repeated. The Uptown Jews no longer shunned publicity and were now ready to give the lead in a broadly based, popular fundraising campaign. The Russian Jews, in turn, seeking to avoid duplication, agreed that all the funds be channeled to Europe through one central clearing committee. On all sides it was agreed that Jacob Schiff should act as treasurer.

On 7 November 1905, a large meeting was held at Temple Emanu-El, the famous Fifth Avenue synagogue. Oscar Straus was in the chair and all the major sections of New York Jewry were represented. "There were the 'native born', the German element," wrote an eye-witness, "Nationalists, Zionists, Reformers, Orthodox, Social Revolutionaries – in short there was a united Jewry present."[137] (Abe Cahan was among the speakers.)

For all the initial good will, the meeting did not go smoothly. Schiff and Straus insisted that the relief funds should be available to "Jew and Gentile alike." Given the circumstances, this ultimatum was incomprehensible to the Russian Jews present. Straus, it was reported, had resort to "parliamentary tactics worthy of Tom Reed . . . , recognised only safe persons and ignored radicals . . . It was with difficulty that the 'radicals' restrained themselves from making a scene."[138] But there was no walkout. Schiff's conception was allowed to stand; a committee of fifty was selected to establish the American Committee for the Relief of Russian Jews (known for short as the National Relief Committee); and all sectors agreed that it alone should handle the relief funds.

The money was forwarded via the Rothschilds in London to Baron Gintsburg in St. Petersburg, who (with the consent of the tsarist government) put it at the disposal of the local relief committees. The *Forverts* openly associated itself with this arrangement, which for all its plutocratic overtones had the advantage of unity, simplicity and despatch. The target set by the committee was $1,000,000, and this amount had in fact been passed by early December, with almost half the sum coming from New York City, the remainder from some six hundred and seventy towns. The total collected by world Jewry at that point was estimated at $4,000,000.[139]

In the years 1905–6, two separate attempts were made to establish unity not only in the sphere of relief (where it was now first being applied with success) but also in that of politics. Clearly, both fund raising and pressure politics on behalf of Russian Jewry could be rendered far more effective by a united front, and this fact explains the recurring demands that the Jews in America close ranks. As against this, in Russia the politics of revolution tended to exacerbate division within the Jewish community, pitting the socialists against the nonsocialists.

On 2 November 1905, a number of prominent radicals on the Lower East Side issued (under the name of the New York Group of Socialist Revolutionaries) a call inviting delegates from "all Jewish federations, unions, societies, and lodges" to an emergency meeting to be held at Clinton Hall. Among the signatories were Chaim Zhitlovsky (who had been in New York for a year), M. Katz (a socialist territorialist), and two well-known New York radicals (who had been members of the Am Olam in 1882), Ezra Raevsky and Pavel Kaplan. The aim was to discuss ways of organizing a "mighty protest" against the pogroms.[140]

At the meeting some forty people spoke (among them Zhitlovsky, Cahan, and Barondess) and a committee of fifty-nine was established to coordinate a protest campaign.[141] It was this committee that on the following day established the Jewish Defense Association. In mid-November the Association announced the establishment of a special fund (complementary to that of the National Relief Committee) that was to purchase weapons for the Jewish self-defense forces in Russia. In its manifesto it called for the creation of local branches across the United States: "The Jewish people is arming itself. We must create the means."[142]

Among the signatories were not only the original group headed by Zhitlovsky but also leading general Zionists and territorialists – Louis Lipsky, Abe Goldberg, B. G. Richards – as well as other public figures (Abe Cahan among them). Barondess was secretary and, most important, Judah L. Magnes, chairman. Magnes was then a young but fast-rising Reform rabbi as well as secretary of the Federation of American Zionists. Very much a member of the establishment, closely related by marriage to Louis Marshall, soon to be appointed rabbi at Temple Emanu-El, he clearly regarded it as a personal mission to bridge the gap between the German-Jewish and the immigrant communities. The Jewish Defense Association was an opportunity and challenge that he was eager to take up.

With Magnes at its head, the Jewish Defense Association became the first political organization to gain the support of Uptown and Downtown, socialist and nonsocialist, nationalist and antinationalist. The Federation of American Zionists announced that "every Zionist society is herewith called upon to join the Jewish Defense Association."[143] Schiff sent in a nominal donation ($100), Marshall a larger one ($500). "Whatever doubts I have hitherto had," he wrote, "have disappeared on reading the reports of the unspeakable outrages . . . [Yet] under normal conditions the Russian Jew, if afforded the means of self-defense, will be able to protect himself. The possession of arms will of itself develop the spirit which is essential to the working out of his destiny."[144]

Established immediately after the October pogroms, the Association became the natural channel for the mounting waves of popular anger and fear. On 26 November it organized a mass meeting at the Grand Central Palace that was attended by some six thousand, and crowds were turned away. It was addressed, inter alia, by Dr. Lyman Abbott (a leading protestant clergyman), Judge Samuel Greenbaum (a member of the New York Supreme Court), Corporation Counsel Delaney (who "as an Irishman [said that] he understood what self-defense meant"),[145] by Miller, Barondess, and Zhitlovsky. The key address was delivered by Magnes. "We should rise as heroes," he declared,

> but we are weak and fawn and bend the back. We of all the Europeans have . . . turned the cheek when smitten. That we have bent to the whip of the Cossacks is as much a reproach to you and to me as is the self-defense of

our brethren in Russia an honor to them. Is not the lesson to be learned from the founders of this great country? Are we not too inclined to look patronizingly upon those of our race in Russia and call them slaves while we congratulate ourselves that we are free?[146]

The high point of the Association's campaign, however, came on Monday, 4 December, when, at its initiative, a great march of mourning wound its way through the streets of the Lower East Side up Broadway to Union Square. It was estimated that some two hundred thousand people marched. On arrival at Union Square, they dispersed to eight theaters to be addressed by such speakers as Abe Cahan, Nicholas Aleinikoff, Chaim Zhitlovsky, Pavel Kaplan, Baruch Zuckerman, Boris Tomashevsky, and the Reverend Z. H. Masliansky. Their theme was self-defense.

Eye-witnesses noted that, for all the expressions of unity, the march was peopled strictly by residents of the Lower East Side, with Uptown Jews and even the immigrant middle class conspicuous by their absence. "It would have been no shame to our judges, our lawyers, our great merchant princes, our bankers, our litterateurs, and playwrights ... ," wrote a correspondent to the long-established *American Hebrew,* "to have lent the dignity of their combined might and presence to this great marching line of protest."[147]

Nonetheless, the march made a deep impression. *Dos yidishe tageblat* stressed its spontaneity, a popular initiative with "no parallel in the history of any nation ... The mourning march was not organized by anybody ... The people organized itself."[148] The reports in the *Forverts* noted that the shops on the Lower East Side started closing at ten o'clock and that by then all the pushcarts had left the streets. "A deathly hush reigned in the streets. Everybody held his breath as though anxious not to disturb anybody else by his presence. The wind unfurled the black and red flags ... and the air was heavy with sadness."[149] "A strange procession was this," wrote a correspondent in *The American Hebrew,*

> that emerged from the dark narrow street into the wide sunlit square. Feeble women, pale as death, with eyes that glisten as burning coals, bearded men with bowed backs, little children with large eyes and pinched faces, frail youths with hollow cheeks – hand in hand, shoulder to shoulder – thousands on thousands, surging silently forward ... And now a thin quavering voice begins to sing, soon another ... and now the melancholy chant swells into mighty tones.[150]

The march of 4 December proved in fact to be the single triumph of the Jewish Defense Association. By then, it had already become apparent that the Association had failed in its bid to draw the entire immigrant leadership – and indeed, American Jewry as a whole – into one united political campaign.

At the preliminary meeting in Clinton Hall on 5 November, the Central Federation of Bundist Organizations in America had been represented and some of its delegates were elected to the committee of the fifty-nine. But thereafter the Bund refrained from participation in the Association. At the critical moment, it drew back from an organization specifically grounded on the principle of interclass cooperation, or *klal-yisroel politik.*

This fateful decision was taken hesitantly. Abe Cahan, as editor of the *Forverts,* tried to persuade the Bundists to change their minds. He himself, after all, was an active member of the committee of the fifty-nine. But the Association at that point (in the second week of November) made a decision that reinforced the resolve of the Bund to keep its distance. The money collected, it was decided, was to be divided between the Poale Zion (40 percent), the Bund (40 percent), and the Socialist Revolutionaries (20 percent). As the larger party, the Bund could hardly acquiesce in this equality of status granted the Poale Zion, and it was not clear why, if the SRs were included, the Russian Social Democrats (who had their own fund-raising organization in New York headed by Dr. S. Ingerman) should be excluded.

What was initially a tentative act of separation fast developed into a public battle, each side seeking to consolidate itself at the expense of the other. On 19 November, Y. Abrahams (Golovchiner) published a statement in the name of the Bund calling on its supporters to donate for self-defense directly to the Bundist party fund, not to the Jewish Defense Association. A week later, the Central Federation of Bundist Organizations demanded that it receive its share of the funds collected by the Association in the thirteen days (14–26 November) when the public had been under the misapprehension that the Bund was to be a beneficiary. In turn, the Association denounced as absurd the idea that the Bundists should boycott its campaigns, raise funds independently, and then demand a large part of its budget. It refused to hand over a single penny.[151]

As the dispute grew increasingly acrimonious, so an ever-widening circle of organizations and public figures was forced to take sides. The Bund appealed to the Poale Zion – as a real revolutionary and Jewish party in Russia – to leave the Association and set up a joint fund-raising campaign. But the Poale Zion refused to break ranks.

On the other hand, the *Forverts* slowly but surely moved away from the Jewish Defense Association and toward the Bund. It supported the mourning march of 4 December (which was boycotted by the Bundist organizations), but on 10 December it came out with an editorial upholding the right of the Bund, as by far the largest Jewish revolutionary party, to maintain its own self-defense fund.

For its part, the Jewish Defense Association could count on the support not only of the two nonsocialist dailies, *Der morgn-zhurnal* and *Dos yidishe tageblat,* but also increasingly – as the lines of battle were drawn – on the new socialist daily, *Di varhayt.* This paper was launched in November 1905 by Louis Miller in open opposition to the *Forverts,* or, to be more exact, to Abe Cahan. (Friends since the 1880s, joint founders of the *Forverts* in 1897, they had fallen out finally and bitterly in 1904.)

From the first, *Di varhayt* proclaimed a policy of "free speech," gave a considered hearing to the Poale Zion and the socialist territorialists, and called on the Bund to rise above separatism. "Bundists," declared an editorial of 17 November,

> it is to you that we turn! You are the strongest Jewish organization, the most powerful! On you falls the responsibility, the greatest responsibility ever placed by history on a section of the Jewish people. Everybody . . . is making the same call . . . "Arm the Jewish people!" But to arm is not enough . . . We must also unite. You must help unite the Jews. For the time being, forget what divides you from the others.[152]

By the 30 November *Di varhayt* was writing that the refusal of the Bund to join a united front was an error that "the Jews here and in Russia will never forget."[153] For its part, the *Forverts* now called on the socialists in the Jewish Defense Association to break all ties with its right wing, as represented above all by the conservative *Morgn zhurnal.*

The polemics ranged ever farther afield. The Bund claimed that at those points where it was well established in the Russian Empire, it had been strong enough to prevent the outbreak of pogroms.[154] But Isaac H. Hourwich (writing in *Di varhayt*) rejected this argument scornfully, pointing out that in 1881–2 (when there had been no Bund), Poland and Lithuania had likewise been virtually untouched by pogroms.[155]

Zhitlovsky declared that it was, in reality, the presence in the Jewish Defense Association of the SRs – not of the "religious and capitalist Jews" – that had alienated the Bund. "The Bund is ... an orthodox Marxist organization ... and its main goal is the dictatorship of the proletariat ... Like every organization that seeks autocratic rule, the Bund is fanatical, narrow, and brutal toward all other parties."[156] Taking up the challenge, Abe Cahan compared the Bund ("a mighty army for the Jewish people") with Zhitlovsky, an isolated individual, driven by a rage to destroy what others built, an "anarchist," an SR trying to push his way into Jewish politics, a man who "in order to found a new movement in Russia has come from Geneva to New York."[157]

Perhaps the most violent note was struck by J. Kopeloff (a leading figure in the Jewish Defense Association who was also in charge of the SR fund-raising drive in New York). "The Bund," he wrote, "knows full well that in these pogroms it did absolutely nothing ... Who has made [it] ... master of the entire Jewish people and given it a patent monopoly on fund-raising for the self-defense of all Jews?"[158] In reality, he insisted, the Bund used its weapons as much to intimidate the Jewish bourgeoisie as to defend the Jews against the *pogromshchiki.* "No, not all the donors to self-defense intended that the Bundists use their money to buy revolvers with which to shoot at Zionist Jews in Pinsk ... or at a Jewish factory owner in Warsaw."[159]

In response to such criticism (which of course echoed the anti-Bundist reaction in the Pale at the time), Y. Abrahams insisted that the Bund was not only a revolutionary but also a Jewish party fighting for national rights: "Do you really believe that it will not defend the honor and life of all Jews?" No other Jewish organization in Russia could compare with the Bund when it came to mobilizing the youth and workers to fight. "The Bundist who knows how to handle a revolver in the time of a demonstration will be able to use that same revolver to best effect in time of a pogrom." The fact was that the movement in Russia simply did "not want the Bund here in America to compromise itself [by association] with all kinds of charlatans."[160]

Of course, more than a war of words was involved here. The fund-raising campaigns of the Central Federation of Bundist Organizations in America and of the Jewish Defense Association were in direct competition. As it turned out, the Bund succeeded in raising the larger sums. From November 1905 until the summer of 1906, it collected at least $50,000 (some estimates being much higher).[161]

In the same period, the Jewish Defense Association took in a sum of some $26,500, most of it in the months of November and December 1905.[162] The money was used for the purchase of arms in Europe, with Manya and other members of the Vilbushevich family playing a key role in their transportation to various Poale Zion factions in the Pale of Settlement.[163]

Perhaps the most publicized episode in this financial war was that involving the Bundist, "Maksim" Klevansky, who arrived in New York in April 1906 and was launched – as the hero of the Riga "republic" – on a coast-to-coast fund-raising campaign. Hardly had he arrived, however, when the Poale Zion and Di varhayt came out with the accusation that he was an imposter, that he had not been in Riga at all when the city was taken over by the revolutionaries. This charge produced a public scandal of the first order, but it could not be substantiated and probably added still more to Maksim's remarkable success (he reportedly collected tens of thousands of dollars).

However, Maksim was by no means the only well-known revolutionary to arrive from Europe on such a mission. Every party despatched its own emissaries, among them, Gorky, Chaikovsky, Gershuny, Danieli, and Liber. Large sums of money were also raised at the public balls that were particularly popular in late December and on New Year's Eve. "Never," wrote Baranov sardonically in January 1906,

> has one danced as much in the Russian colony in New York as during this last year. One danced for the Bund; one danced for the free-thinking Socialist Revolutionaries; and one even danced for the scientific Social Democrats. One danced for the Jewish widows and orphans in Odessa; for the revolutionary sailors in Sebastopol; for the Latvian socialists and the Polish socialists ... The more they went on strike and went hungry in Europe, the more one danced in New York. The more the shooting over there, the more the quadrilles danced over here.[164]

As interest in the Jewish Defense Association waned, so the idea of an American Jewish Congress (raised transiently in the summer of 1903) was revived. Once again, the absence of a body representative of American Jewry as a whole was widely regarded as a crippling defect that hindered every attempt to help the Russian Jews, be it politically or be it economically. It was on these grounds that as early as September 1905, The Maccabean, the Zionist monthly edited by Jacob De Haas, had attacked the delegation of Jewish notables (Schiff among them) that went to see Witte, who was then in the United States for the Portsmouth Peace Conference: "The five men who called on M. Witte are each in their own way representative Jews, but they are not Jewish representatives, and their right to act on behalf of the Jews had no other sanction than their own consciences."[165]

Only in December, however, was the cry for a full-fledged Congress taken up. "We must call a Congress of all the Jews in America, consult together, work out plans," Dos yidishe tageblat then declared.

> And all Jews from all classes, be it Orthodox or Reform or Freethinking should take part in this Congress. It must be a people's congress, not an assembly of self-appointed "representatives." The people which were able to bring out a march two hundred thousand strong ... without the help of leaders or organizers should create the Congress to decide how to help those who are suffering in Russia.[166]

Nicholas Aleinikoff (the leader of the Kiev Am Olam in 1881) likewise expressed his confidence that "the Congress of American Jews ... now planned will certainly devise the proper plans ... for the reception and distribution of the Jewish refugees."[167]

The American Hebrew took up the same theme: "It is our duty to send a message of hope to our brethren abroad, to inspire them with the belief that we are doing our utmost to make impossible a repetition of massacre; and this can only be done by a united Israel speaking in a representative capacity."[168] In a letter published on 29 December, Dr. David Philipson recalled that he had raised this issue in 1903 and expressed the hope that its hour had now finally come.[169]

The fact that an international Jewish conference was due to meet in Brussels in January 1906 (on the initiative of David Wolffsohn, Herzl's successor as head of the world Zionist movement) provided an argument for the immediate convocation of an American Jewish Congress. Thus, on 18 December *Dos yidishe tageblat* declared that "We, the American Jews, must have a Congress in order to transmit to Brussels a clear answer as to what we can and must do on behalf of our brothers in Russia."[170] As against this, however, *The American Hebrew* insisted that there be no undue haste: "It is more important that our Congress be established on firm ground, if it is to become an actuality, than that we be represented at the European Congress."[171]

In reality, caution won the day. Attempts by Magnes in December to call an immediate preparatory conference were frustrated by the leadership of the National Relief Committee. No American delegation was sent to the Brussels conference. However, public interest did not decline. At an open debate in January, Magnes declared that "it is necessary that the Jewish people itself have a voice in the conduct of its own affairs ... , [that it] have a democratic constitution and not a bureaucratic institution."[172] But, significantly, he there came under sharp attack from the leading Reform rabbi, S. Schulman: "By making nationalism a dogma, Zionism has made it impossible for the two million Jews in Europe and America, who have no national aspirations, to cooperate with it in any work on behalf of Jews and Judaism."[173]

Finally, on 4 February 1906, a meeting of Jewish leaders drawn from across the United States met in New York to discuss the issue of organizational unity. The initiative had come from a small ad hoc committee, headed by Louis Marshall, that sent out invitations to fifty-five people, of whom thirty-four actually came.

The list of participants read like a "who's who" of the German-Jewish establishment: Among them were Oscar Straus, Schiff, Harry Cutler, Cyrus Adler, Simon Wolf, Jacob Gimbel, Cyrus L. Sulzberger, and Judge Mayer Sulzberger. The meeting was not open to the public and every effort was made to permit it to proceed in discreet confidence.

However, the attempt to shun publicity proved counterproductive. *Dos yidishe tageblat* called on its readers to go uninvited to the meeting (at the United Hebrew Charities Building on Second Avenue at Twenty-first Street). All the Jewish parties, the Poale Zion, Territorialists, Bundists, Zionists, it asserted (albeit without any authority to do so), "are going to call ... on their followers to come to the 'confidential' meeting in order to force those invited to hear all the opinions ... existing among the Jewish people, and if a committee is formed on the Jewish question let it represent all Jewish classes."[174]

The meeting found itself besieged by a crowd of hundreds, but nonetheless proceeded as planned to conduct its proceedings in camera. ("We can in no way understand what kind of a secret our *yahudim,* the millionaires, are making of the Jewish question," reacted the *Tageblat.*)[175] The decision taken behind the closed doors was to reject the idea of an American Jewish Congress but at the same time to appoint a committee of seven headed by Louis Marshall that would work out a less radical form of organizational unity for American Jewry.

Three months later, on 19 May 1906, the committee of seven submitted its findings to the ad hoc conference of notables that had appointed it. Its proposals went far to meet the demands for the democratization advanced by Magnes (who was one of its members). American Jewry was to elect a representative assembly. The elections were to be indirect with the synagogue as the primary electoral unit, but nonaffiliated Jews would also have voting rights if they registered for that purpose in advance. The assembly was to be committed by its charter to "the cause of Judaism."[176]

The blueprint, in fact, proved to be too democratic for important sectors of the German-Jewish community and too cautious for most representatives of the Russian-Jewish world. The leaders of B'nai B'rith (Adolf Kraus and Simon Wolf) sent in a letter rejecting the plan of the seven in the sharpest terms. If adopted, it could "threaten the religious liberty of the Jews and the autonomy of the existing congregations and fraternities." The proposed electoral process was hopelessly complex and dangerously popular.

> Unless the proposed new corporation or conference be composed of the most conservative men, the standing of the Jews in the American nation will be severely affected for the worse. With the machinery for elections as outlined [the] conservative elements... will be crowded to the rear and the new organization will fall into the hands of radical theorists.[177]

From the other flank, Aleinikoff (as a spokesman for the immigrant community) declared that we are "Jews by nationality ... and there is absolutely no occasion for the promotion of Judaism." The only goals of a representative assembly should be to "aid in obtaining civil rights for Jews overseas and to help those fleeing persecution."[178]

Louis Marshall and Cyrus Adler fought hard in defense of their conception. "To make a committee that would command respect," said Marshall, "it must be based on a democratic representation."[179] And Adler saw their proposal as deeply rooted in history, part of the "effort made on the part of the Jews of the United States for the past forty to sixty years to get some kind of concert in public opinion ... You may be sure that an organization of Jews in the United States will be effected; it will represent large numbers, it will be powerful and it will be composed of radical men."[180]

But the tide of opposition was too strong. "The arrogant assumption of the so-called East Siders that numbers give wisdom," declared Judge Mayer Sulzberger, for example, "ought to be treated as nil. There is more to American Jewry than is comprised within the Ghettos."[181] The final decision was to make do with a permanent select committee that, in essence, would be self-appointing.

A committee of five, headed by Mayer Sulzberger, was chosen to appoint the membership (originally set at fifty and later raised to sixty). This body assembled on 11 November 1906 and took the name of the American Jewish Committee. Its raison d'être was formulated in the tersest terms: "The purpose of the committee is to prevent infringement of the civil and religious rights of Jews and to alleviate the consequences of persecution."[182]

The dominant element in the committee was the circle of Uptown Jewry associated with Schiff, Marshall, and Temple Emanu-El. Kraus and Wolf of the B'nai B'rith eventually declined the membership offered them. The idea of democratic unity was barely kept alive Downtown by Abraham Schomer, who in 1907 established an obscure organization called the International Jewish Congress. The Jewish socialists did not play an active role in the movement for an American Jewish Congress. At least until the summer of 1906, their attention was riveted almost exclusively on the Russian revolution. The Jewish Defense Association was important to them because it was directed to the purchase and delivery of arms to Russia. In contrast, an American Jewish Congress was seen as an irrelevant, or at most a peripheral, issue.

However, within the Jewish socialist world itself developments closely paralleled those at the general Jewish level. There, too, the upheaval caused by the revolution and the pogroms encouraged a widespread demand for thorough-going organizational reform – specifically, within the framework of the Socialist Party. And there, too, the powers-that-be eventually succeeded in keeping change within strict limits.

Two major trends impressed observers of the socialist world in the years 1905–6. First, there was an even stronger swing than in 1903 toward nationalism, toward a positive evaluation of the Jewish past and even of the Jewish religion. This trend found expression at many levels; in the consolidation of the Poale Zion and socialist territorialist groups into nationwide parties; in the appearance of their new journals (*Der yidisher kemfer, Dos folk*); in their mass meetings; in the popularity of Zhitlovsky; in the sudden rise of the Jewish Defense Association; in the support of *Di varhayt* for schemes of Jewish colonization in Africa.

"People who have always laughed out loud at talk of a special Jewish spirit, . . . of Jewish national aspirations," mocked F. Rozenblat in January 1906 in *Di tsukunft*, "– such people have suddenly repented and have begun shouting that the Jew must leave the Exile, must have his own home and that we, living in America, must create this home for him."[183] "We have here," wrote Jacob Milch caustically, "pure-and-simple Zionists, and we have pure-and-simple territorialists; and we have Poale Zion, Zionist Socialists, Socialist Territorialists, socialist-revolutionary territorialists and just anarchist-national-territorialists."[184]

Even *The American Hebrew* took note of this trend. An article published there on Zhitlovsky noted that he had "made Jewish nationalists of many radicals whose leading idea had been assimilation . . . The cosmopolitan views of Karl Marx . . . he combated at every opportunity. As a result of his propoganda, he has made nationalists of such men as Barondess, Dr. Solotaroff [Zolotarov], M. Katz and many others in the radical groups of the East Side."[185]

But much attention was also given to the reverse side of the coin, the inchoate and disorganized state of the moderate "internationalist" camp as represented by the Bundist wing, on the one hand, and by the *Forverts, Di tsukunft,* the *Arbeter Ring* and the UHT, on the other. This bloc, which on paper was enormously powerful, had no unified political organization to speak in its name, to launch a counterattack against the rising forces of socialist territorialism and Zionism.

The veterans blamed the disorganization on the new arrivals. The only subject of interest to the newcomers, so the argument went, was Russia, *der heym*, the revolution, and the pogroms. This was a theme on which Peskin, in particular, constantly elaborated in the *Forverts*. "How much energy and time," he wrote for instance on 2 February 1906, "is devoted to Russian parties and their tactical questions, while the movement here is totally neglected. The impression is that most of the 'greeners' have come here only temporarily and are about soon to return ... The fund-raising is actually run by a few dozen people. The other hundreds and perhaps thousands of comrades bustle endlessly around with their Russian party disputes."[186]

From their side, the new immigrants complained that the Socialist Party branches were lifeless, geared only to the annual election campaigns; that the press was dominated by the system of sensations and stars; that the trade unions were socialist only in name and were concerned with nothing but the narrow economic interests of their members.

But there were still other factors working against the creation of a unified organization of Jewish socialists within the SP. Abe Cahan had good reason to fear that such an organization would threaten the independence, the hegemony, of the *Forverts*. Many other old-timers (with no less reason) feared that it would serve as a Trojan horse, permitting Bundist nationalism to take over the "Yiddish-speaking" movement in America.

The first attempt to create a unified Jewish section within the SP, in fact, came to nothing. On 3 March 1906, a conference of the Yiddish-speaking organizations identified with the SP in New York was called together to consider this crucial organizational issue. The notice of invitation contrasted the potential power of the Jewish movement – the UHT, the Arbeter Ring, the Bundist organizations, the press – with its actual impotence, "not organized and not disciplined." This situation was nothing less than a "condemnation of socialism."[187]

When the conference met, however, it served to emphasize rather than overcome the divisive group interests. It turned into a confrontation between Abe Cahan and a hostile coalition of Bundist newcomers and old-time opponents who had been associated with *Dos abend-blat* in the years 1897–9.[188] The conference made do with the establishment of a committee of seven that was to prepare for a country-wide, Jewish socialist (SP) convention. This turned out to be a neat way of burying the issue, at least momentarily. The trouble, declared the *Forverts* with evident *Schadenfreude*, was the verbosity of the Jewish comrades who, unlike the German or American comrades in the SP, mistook words for action. "Twenty speakers say the same thing and every speaker repeats his speech twenty times."[189]

As the revolutionary tide in Russia ebbed away, the idea of creating a nation-wide Jewish section within the SP was revived, now, with a greater sense of urgency. A many-sided debate on the issue was conducted in the months of January–February 1907 on the pages of *Tsayt-gayst* (the weekly journal associated with the *Forverts,* but which enjoyed a measure of editorial autonomy).

The demand for a Jewish federation within the SP was advanced by relatively little-known members, in the main no doubt recent immigrants. Without a "strong,

well-disciplined party,"[190] went the argument, Jewish socialists would remain politically impotent, unable to reply coherently to the Poale Zion and Socialist Territorialists. They were careful to deny charges of importing Bundism: "We have no
Jewish demands, but must have a Jewish section of the Socialist Party."[191]

All the talk of a Jewish socialist "federation" or even a "party" provoked a
furious response from a number of well-known veterans, above all, from Herts
Burgin and Mikhl Zametkin, but also (in somewhat milder form) from Shmuel
Peskin. No case could be made, they insisted, for re-creating the Bund in any shape
or form in America. "If there is a specially Jewish organization in Russia," wrote
Burgin, "it results from . . . the special situation [there]. But here in America, there
is no special Jewish question . . . No, let us remain, rather, international socialists!
Let us remember once and for all that our national feelings, traditions, customs,
etc., have nothing to do with the politico-economic struggle of the working
class."[192] In the United States, Zametkin argued repeatedly, the Jews were equal
citizens in a parliamentary and constitutional democracy. As Jews, they had nothing to fight for in America. Socialism, the class war pure and simple, had to remain
the single cause. "Separatism in all its forms," he wrote, "is a sickness which must
be healed. The infected have only to be kept in quarantine; the carriers have to be
left outside the camp."[193] A work such as Medem's *Social Democracy and the
National Question,* he insisted again, reflected a pathological way of thought:
"One feels as if one is in the torture room of the Inquisition . . . My God, how sad
it is! . . . It is an excellent example of a deep, heart-breaking moan – in scientific
style. Read it, comrades, and you will realize that the distance from Russia to
America is hundreds of years long."[194]

Peskin came out against any form of federation (not to talk of a party), but he
granted the need for a nationwide Jewish socialist convention. He was enraged by
a decision of U. Solomon, M. Oppenheimer, and other SP leaders, who in May
1907 used their key positions in the New York party organization to forbid a
convention of a far more limited nature, one representative of the Greater New
York area. (Perhaps, he wondered ironically, the convention should meet across
the Hudson in Hoboken, New Jersey.) However, he did insist that a major convention should admit only those active in the American movement – representatives of
the Yiddish-speaking SP branches, of the Arbeter Ring and the unions, but not of
the "Bundist branches, landslayt organizations, Russian socialist parties, Latvian
organizations, Socialist Territorialists, Socialist Revolutionaries, and all other similar organizations."[195]

In reality, the control of events now slipped momentarily out of the hands of the
Forverts group and of New York City generally. On 1 September 1907 a convention of Jewish socialists, drawn from across the country, met in Rochester. There
were eighteen delegates of whom four alone represented major organizations of the
labor movement: the Arbeter Ring, the UHT, and the *Forverts* (Lesin and Feigenbaum were the representatives of the *Forverts*). There was one delegate from a
Bundist organization, and the remaining thirteen represented the Yiddish-speaking
party branches of a large number of cities.

The convention was very much a coup for the provinces, and the driving force
behind it was Max Kaufman of Rochester. In September 1905 he had inspired the
creation of the Jewish Agitation Bureau of Upstate New York. The result of the

convention in 1907 was to convert this Bureau from an institution strictly local in scope into one designed to work on a national scale. The goal it adopted was "to organize the Jewish workers in the Socialist Party . . . and to agitate for the principles of the party orally and in writing."[196] Among other activities, it henceforth convened annual conventions.

From the first, the strictly internationalist (or "cosmopolitan" wing) of the Jewish socialist movement in New York City boycotted the Rochester convention. The major Yiddish-speaking branches in Manhattan and Brooklyn refused to affiliate themselves to the Jewish Agitation Bureau, which they regarded as separatist, as nationalistic.[197] In so doing, of course, they received the full support of the New York General Committee and its Organizer, U. Solomon (who, in the words of *Tsayt-gayst*, was always ready to wield a "big stick" on such issues).[198]

In contrast, the *Forverts* initially assured the new organization of its support and praised the Rochester convention in fulsome terms: "We have had many conventions, but we have never seen a convention before that accomplished so much real, tangible work . . . The Bureau is now certainly the base for the mighty fighting power of Jewish labor in America."[199] But this positive attitude was more apparent than real. The *Forverts*, from the first, starved the Bureau of publicity.

In retaliation, the Bureau at its fourth convention, held in Chicago in 1908, criticized the *Forverts* for "devoting very little attention to the organizational work of the Socialist Party and the trade unions." Still more daring, it recognized at the same time a new Chicago weekly, *Di yidishe arbeter velt*, as "the official organ of the Jewish Agitation Bureau."[200] (Its editor was A. S. Zaks, a recent arrival from Russia, where he had written for the Bundist *Folks-tsaytung* and elsewhere.)

It strongly supported the demands for a full-scale Jewish federation within the Socialist Party. "The American labor movement," stated a typical editorial, "consists of various nationalities . . . [Each nationality must have] special nationwide institutions that enjoy a definite autonomy and are free to decide independently how to implement party decisions. [Otherwise] . . . all the party work could prove barren."[201] In January 1909 the Bureau engineered something of a coup when the National Executive Committee of the Socialist Party appointed its nominee, S. Litman of Chicago, as national organizer for the Yiddish-speaking movement.

The immediate outcome was an open attack by the *Forverts* on the Bureau and *Di yidishe arbeter velt*. In the longer run, the result was the decision of the *Forverts* and its allied organizations in New York to take over the Bureau. At the convention of 1909 a large delegation arrived from New York and was able to gain the majority. In consequence, a decision was carried to move the headquarters of the Bureau from Chicago to New York, to elect an executive made up of New York residents (seven out of eight), and to replace Kaufman by Shiplacoff as secretary.[202]

Thus, the incipient revolt – described by the *Forverts* as that of "the west" against "the east," and of "the greeners" against "those no longer green"[203] – had been nipped in the bud. The Bureau was now conceived not as "a party within the party" (the aim ascribed to Zaks and Kaufman by their critics) but as a technical organization in charge of party propaganda in Yiddish. Speaking at the Socialist Party Convention of 1912, Jacob Panken described the Jewish Agitation Bureau (of which he was the representative) as organized on an entirely different basis from any of the other foreign-speaking organizations. The membership is affiliated with the Socialist Party in the respective states . . . paying the same dues as the English-speaking members . . . The branches of the Bureau are in every respect similar to the ordinary party locals or branches excepting that they use and speak the Jewish language.[204]

In sum, the Jewish Agitation Bureau of the Socialist Party, like the American Jewish Committee, emerged eventually on a basis far narrower than that demanded by the maximalists. Just as the idea of an American Jewish Congress had been shunted aside, so now the plans for a powerful Jewish socialist federation (or party) within the SP had been thoroughly truncated. Nonetheless, the four points making up the institutional quadrangle of American-Jewish politics were now in place: the Federation of American Zionists; the American Jewish Committee; the Jewish Agitation Bureau; the Poale Zion and Socialist Territorialist parties.

The postrevolutionary years, 1907–1914

The period between the 1905 revolution and World War I did not witness any further crises in Europe to throw American Jewry into turmoil. It was then, however, that the organizations established in the years 1905–7 consolidated themselves.[205] They put down roots. The concept of American-Jewish politics – the defense of Jewish interests in the world and in the United States – was now increasingly taken for granted, gained legitimacy. Interaction between the opposing camps became more commonplace. They influenced each other. The result was a greater sense if not always of Jewish nationalism (a highly controversial concept) then at least of Jewish solidarity.

A number of factors combined to sustain this trend. The continuous flow of immigration at a high level (although never again as high as in the years 1905–7) kept the Jewish question in the public eye. Here, after all, was a problem European in origin but American in its effect. The anti-immigration movement, aimed at restricting free entry from eastern and southern Europe, was increasingly perceived by Jewish leaders (German earlier than Russian perhaps) as a threat to Jewry that had to be resisted both directly, through pressure politics, and indirectly, by encouraging the immigrant community to organize, to present a more acceptable face to the outside world.

In reality, of course, the forms of organization developed by the immigrants were not always to the liking of Uptown. These became the years of mass trade unionism, of mammoth strikes, of unprecedented circulation for the *Forverts*. But however disturbing these developments might seem, they could not be ignored by the German-Jewish establishment, which above all during the strikes was brought face to face with the leaders of the Jewish labor movement. The millionaires and corporation lawyers often developed a natural respect for the practical and powerful men who spoke for the new unions.

But there was yet another factor involved here. The period of reaction witnessed a swing toward Jewish nationalism in Russia, a crisis of faith in the camp of revolution and socialist internationalism. It was a time of introspection, and this trend in Russia coincided with a deepening criticism of crude Americanization in the United States. The past was increasingly called in to balance what was now seen as an overcommitment to an undefined future. Thus, in this, the cultural and philosophical sphere, too, there was greater readiness to lower at least marginally the barriers separating Russian Jew from German Jew, Zionist from non-Zionist, socialist from nonsocialist.

Here, it will suffice to mention a few examples characteristic of this development. On 27 February 1909, a constituent convention met to establish the Jewish Community (or Kehila) of New York City. A climate of opinion favorable to the establishment of the Kehila had been created by the charge of Police Commissioner Bingham, that most criminals in the city were Jews. A single representative institution, it was felt, would be able to rebut unfounded accusations and, more important, act to prevent the growth of criminality and corruption in the immigrant districts.

The convention in February was the final outcome of negotiations over a period of months between the representatives of the American Jewish Committee (AJC) and an ad hoc committee of twenty-five that had emerged from a Downtown conference held in October 1908. Included in this committee (which Magnes had been authorized to select) were Barondess, Gedaliah Bublick, Louis Miller, Abraham Schomer, Solomon Schechter, Samuel Dorf, Dovid Pinsky, and the Reverend Z. H. Masliansky.[206]

Both sides had been forced to compromise in order to make the agreement possible. The AJC was to have as its sphere the defense of Jewish interests at the national and international levels. The Kehila was to concentrate on the local problems of New York Jews. However, the leaders of the AJC took the opportunity to introduce a measure of democracy into its hitherto oligarchic structure. The Kehila conventions were to elect an executive committee of twenty-five members who at the same time would serve as the New York section of the AJC. The Kehila convention itself was to be a representative institution with delegates elected by synagogues, fraternities, lodges, and other Jewish societies.[207] Thus, Uptown Jewry had agreed to submit itself for election by Downtown Jewry.

The executive committee, when elected, contained ten members of the AJC (as hitherto constituted). Schiff received the most votes. "The Kehila," Magnes wrote to Friedenwald on 3 March 1909, "is blossoming . . . The meetings were, I believe, the first of the kind in which all sections of the community came together for a common purpose."[208]

Democratization was far from total, however. Only American citizens could be elected as delegates to the convention. This clause excluded Syrkin, for example, who had been an early supporter of the Kehila. Another provision barred political office holders from election and banned political activity within the Kehila. Moreover, its statement of purpose contained the precise clause that had aroused such a furor in 1906: "to further the cause of Judaism."[209] This phrase, with its suggestion of a religious commitment, was bound to antagonize the secularist nationalists.

Thus, Magnes who (as in the Jewish Defense Association) was again the driving force behind this experiment had attained only a partial unity. The more conservative leaders of Downtown Jewry had entered into an alliance with the German-Jewish establishment, but the radicals and socialists (both Zionist and non-Zionist) were for the most part excluded, be it de jure or de facto.

Zhitlovsky, nonetheless, welcomed the experiment as nationalist in spirit if not in letter (even if "the radical elements in the Jewish Quarter are almost entirely keeping their distance.")[210] For its part, the *Forverts* chose (as so often in such cases) simply to ignore the issue. But Fornberg, writing in *Di tsukunft* in January 1910, declared that the Kehila looked "still-born,"[211] and Zivion was of much the same opinion three years later.

> For an entire year, the Kehila sleeps quite calmly. Nobody hears anything about it . . . But when the annual convention is held, things become a bit livelier . . . there is an opposition available, caucus meetings are held, there is a fight . . . And one might imagine that there is something there, that it is alive, that it exists . . . I am convinced that a Kehila built on democratic foundations could be very useful . . . One does not have to be a heretic on the class-war question or a nationalist in order to hold that the Jewish population has common Jewish interests and that there are certain moments in Jewish life when all classes and all parties have something in common and should come together in common action . . .[212] [But] meanwhile the Kehila is maintained by a few "German" *yahudim*. They pay the piper and they call the tune. And one has to grant that they . . . stand head and shoulders over all the representatives of the various shuls, societies, and lodges [in the Kehila].[213]

As Zivion pointed out, Magnes at this stage, in the years 1913–14, was actively seeking to bring a sizeable representation from the labor movement into the Kehila. But the response was decidedly lukewarm. The major activities of the organization – aid to Jewish education, the supervision of kashrut, crime-fighting – had little appeal to most socialist leaders. The Kehila also concerned itself with labor relations, but, as Goren has put it, "mediation failed to lead to affiliation."[214] Unity, if it was to come, would be created not by local Jewish affairs but by a common involvement with Russian Jewry.

Indeed, it was in defense of the Russian Jews that the American Jewish Committee made its greatest impact. It was Louis Marshall, acting on behalf of the AJC, who directed the campaign for the abrogation of the Russian-American Commercial Treaty. This demand was grounded on the fact that the tsarist government frequently denied entry visas even to Jews holding American citizenship, but it was inspired more by the desire to strike back at the antisemitism officially sanctioned in Russia.

Articles and letters on the issue were produced in the press, public meetings called, politicians lobbied, and interviews obtained with President Taft. On 13 December 1911, the House of Representatives voted, 301 against 1, to terminate the treaty. Shortly thereafter, Taft announced that the treaty would cease to be operative at the end of the year.[215]

Writing in *Di tsukunft* in April 1914, Lesin explained that this triumph of the AJC – "a group of influential Jews with Louis Marshall at the head" – was to be explained in part by American irritation at the joint Russo-Japanese closed-door policy in the Far East. This left President Taft "free to estimate that his chances of a second term would be much better if he somehow won over the mass of Jewish citizens in the great ghettoes of New York, Chicago, Cleveland, and Cincinnati . . . the abrogation of the treaty was really a moral triumph of Jewish America over the

Figure 35. KEEP BLOWING. For all their experience with the bellows, Dr. Magnes, Rabbi Jaffe, and Louis Marshall are getting nowhere. Without the breath of life, the bones stay as dead and dry as ever.
(Magnes is holding the bellows labeled "The Annual Speech." The bones are the "Delegates to the Kehila Convention." Marshall is on the left. 3 March 1911. This and all the following cartoons are reproduced from Der groyser kundes [The Great Prankster], *an independent satirical journal published in New York by Yankev Marinov. Its English title was* The Big Stick. *It was socialist but violently hostile to the* Forverts *and sympathetic to Jewish nationalism.)*

forces of the tsar."[216] The passport case, Lesin argued, should serve as a model for future action by American Jewry against the tsarist regime. No other country provided such opportunities for pressure politics of this type as did America.

The United States is not compelled to seek Russian friendship at any price as are France and England. And we, the Jews of America, can fight the influence of the Russian regime much more decisively . . . But we . . . — millions who are bitter enemies of the Russian regime — have hitherto done nothing. A few *yahudim* have done something, but not our great masses. Even our radicals have not done their duty in any systematic way.[217]

The AJC could not achieve any comparable victory in its campaign of these years (1911–14) to prevent the passage through Congress of legislation restricting immigration. But on this issue, too, it fought hard, joining forces on the one hand with parallel Jewish organizations (the B'nai B'rith, in particular) and on the other with organizations representative of various immigrant nationalities (primarily Germans and Italians). In 1912 President Taft vetoed the anti-immigration bill sponsored by Burnett and Dillingham. (In 1915, Woodrow Wilson followed suit, vetoing the next such bill to reach the White House.)[218]

In an article in *Di tsukunft* in December 1912, Karl Fornberg noted the central role played by the German-Jewish leadership in the campaign against immigrant restriction and deplored the fact that this, too, was an "issue that is thrown entirely upon their shoulders."[219] Reflected in such statements was the conviction shared by Fornberg, Lesin, Zivion, and other leading socialists that the labor establishment centered on the *Forverts* Publishing Association had not done anything like enough to defend Jewish interests.

The Jewish Agitation Bureau had not developed into an effective organization since the coup of 1909 had brought it to New York. Its membership was no more than a "few hundred" in 1912,[220] and its influence even within the SP was minimal. And this was true at a time when the AJC was thus successfully directing public campaigns against the tsarist regime, on behalf of free immigration, and for a united Jewish front (the Kehila).

This was a time, too, when the Zionist movement had recovered at least in part from the crisis created for it in the years 1905–7 by the upsurge of enthusiasm for the revolution and for territorialism. In the era of Otto Warburg, the Federation of American Zionists gained in importance if only because of its potential ability to raise substantial funds for colonization and other specific projects in Palestine. Here, again, the ubiquitous Magnes played a key role, finding large sums (with Schiff as usual a primary donor) for Aaron Aaronsohn's Agricultural Experimental Station at Atlit and for the Haifa Technikum (or Technion). In 1914 Franz Oppenheimer (assisted by Magnes) came to the United States in search of funds on behalf of his cooperative settlement project in Merhavya.

In May 1913 *Di tsukunft* published an article (satirical in tone, but serious in intent) that contrasted the Russian immigrant community, so deficient in organizational efficiency, with the German-Jewish establishment, so deficient in vision:

> Formally, "they" are the givers and "we" the takers . . . They give us charity; we, though, give them political weight and social influence . . . They are active, busy . . . but not creative; "we" create new gods, new movements, new cultural values deep within the life of the people . . . but, en masse, we are not . . . organized and chaos reigns among us . . . They react more to the great events and happenings in the life of the Jewish world. While we, for example, conduct discussions and party feuds about the future of the Jewish people, they have a whole series of institutions . . . occupied with the fate of the Jewish immigrant masses . . . While we clarify the problems of Jewish education, they are educating a large percentage of our children in their spirit. When the Kehila question was just becoming an issue for the Social Democratic movement in Russia – and was not even that for us here – they go

Figure 36. THE TOMCAT IS BACK! Wilson: "Amazing. We've drowned the cat so many times and here he is back again!"
(Twice, the cat, labeled respectively the "Dillingham Bill" and the "Burnett Bill," has been drowned with weights: "Taft's veto" and "Wilson's veto." But here he is, "The Anti-Immigration Bill," to confront Wilson again. 19 January 1917.)

and set up [a] Kehila. . . . But a curse lies on all their organizations . . . they have fine bodies but no soul.[221]

However, the failure of the Jewish Agitation Bureau was thrown into still greater relief by the relative success of other immigrant labor organizations, both Jewish and non-Jewish. Even the Poale Zion, for example, although likewise small in numbers, had more to show for itself. In 1909 the party had been joined by break-away groups from the territorialist movement (among the new members being Syrkin, officially, and Zhitlovsky, de facto). In 1910 the party was the moving force behind the establishment of the Jewish National Workers Alliance (or Farband), a mutual-benefit organization of Zionist-territorialist orientation that proved able to withstand the competition of the powerful Arbeter Ring.

The Alliance, in turn, became the pivot for yet another new experiment, the development of the national-radical school movement. In the immediate prewar years, such schools (which were supplementary to the public school system) were opened in many cities. Their approach was Yiddishist, secularist, and socialist-nationalist. Their relative popularity with parents stemmed from fears and frustrations well described by Zolotarov in *Di tsukunft*:

> With few exceptions, the children . . . of the socialists, anarchists, and free-thinkers do not belong to them, do not share their ideas and ideals. And what, for example, would happen to the immigrant Jews in the United States if the doors were closed? . . . In a few generations, they would forget their language, leave their literature, give up their way of life and become – what? Americans? That perhaps, would not be too bad . . . They will become that strange androgynous type represented by the assimilated Jew everywhere in Europe.[222]

But, of course, a true success story of the immediate prewar period was that recorded by the trade-union movement and the socialist press (specifically, the *Forverts*). It was now that the *Forverts* reached a circulation of almost two hundred thousand and that it built its multi-story office building to tower over East Broadway.

These, too, were the heroic years of the mass strike – in 1910, of the cloak-makers; in 1912–13, of the furriers, of the men's tailors, of the ladies' waist- and dressmakers. At one point in 1912, an estimated 175,000 workers in the "Jewish trades" were out on strike. Now, for the first time, the key unions stabilized themselves, winning recognition from the manufacturers and some form of closed (or "preferential") shop – a breakthrough that permitted the Joint Board of Cloak-makers (affiliated to the ILGWU) and the Amalgated Clothing Workers to accumulate real power.[223]

During the complicated and much publicized negotiations between the unions and the employers, such prominent figures as Marshall, Magnes, and Schiff were engaged as mediators or peacemakers. It was thus, too, that the prominent Boston attorney, Louis Dembitz Brandeis, first became crucially involved in the affairs of the Lower East Side. It was as union lawyers that Hillquit and still more London gained mass popularity (permitting the latter to be elected as a socialist to the U.S. Congress in 1914 and again in 1916).

Observers explained this upsurge of mass action partly as a direct result of the fact that the workers and still more their leaders had lived through the revolutionary years, 1905–7, in Russia. "It is a well-known fact," A. Rozenberg wrote of the ILGWU in 1910, "that our Jewish masses are, to a greater or lesser extent, revolutionary minded."[224] "The socialist movement [in Russia], particularly the Bundist movement . . . ," Lesin wrote in 1913, "taught the Jewish workers how to maintain a strike and how to hold scabs in contempt – this was work of the greatest importance for us in America."[225] But if the class war was real enough, it was not total. However bitter the strikes, the subsequent settlements created a complex network of interdependence linking worker and manufacturer, labor leader and patrician. It was against this background that the decision was taken in 1912 (at the seventh annual convention held in Paterson, New Jersey) to replace the Jewish Agitation Bureau by the Jewish Socialist Federation. (Like the Bureau, the Federation was a subsection of the Socialist Party.) The forces advocating this step had been much strengthened by the outcome of the debate on the foreign-language organizations at the congress of the Socialist Party in Chicago in May 1910.

At Chicago, the delegates had been impressed by the example of the Finnish National Socialist Organization, which, founded as a subsection of the SP in 1906, had reached a membership of 6,000, spent over $100,000 annually on agitation, and despatched large sums to the revolutionary movement in Finland, even though there were only 300,000 Finns in the United States. The resolution carried at the congress of 1910 did not relieve foreign-language organizations of their higher per capita dues but it did state clearly that "this congress recommends strongly to all respective state organizations that they grant charters to locals and branches of foreign-speaking organizations, on conditions which shall return to the latter 50 percent of the state and local dues."[226]

As more and more fully fledged foreign-language federations (or sections) were established – Italian, Scandinavian, Bohemian, Polish, South Slavic – so the constitutional status of the Jewish Agitation Bureau, with its strictly limited goals, powers, and achievements, had become increasingly anomolous. By 1912 its transformation into a Federation had thus become all but a foregone conclusion.

Nonetheless, its establishment was something of a victory for the Bundist group – Zivion, Fornberg, Salutsky, Shakhne Epstein – which for years had been arguing that the Socialist Party (the Jewish Agitation Bureau included) had failed to recruit the Jewish masses because it systematically ignored Jewish life and Jewish interests. *Di tsukunft,* under the editorship of Morris Vinchevsky, had long provided a platform for this group, which was in undeclared opposition to the *Forverts* and its implicit defense of the status quo.

Zivion and Fornberg had consistently argued there that the assimilationist ideology of the veteran generation had proved disastrous. It had encouraged the socialists to alienate themselves from their own people. "Having no link to his own nation, unfamiliar with its past, not believing in its future," wrote Zivion in 1909,

Figure 37. LAMENTATIONS OF THE PROPHET. Karl Marx: "There is cause to weep! Under this ten-story capitalist eyesore lies buried the socialist movement of the New York Jews." (*The flag and the various floors of the* Forverts *building carry such labels as* "The Forverts Job-Holders Association," "Smut Manufacturers," "The Black List Dept." *28 April 1911.*)

the Jewish *intelligent* could feel nothing but the chains shackled on him . . .
by his Jewish past . . . The "Yiddish-speaking socialist" is a purely American
creation . . . as is the American Jewish "free-thinker" – that privileged person
who is free of all duties, because of the great sacrifice he has offered mankind by eating pork sausage on buttered bread on Yom Kippur.[227]

Divorced from their origins, they inevitably antagonized the immigrant workers of
the second generation. "Propaganda and agitation," wrote Shakhne Epstein in
1912, "can only have an effect if they have Jewish content . . . This fact has been
entirely ignored by many of our party leaders because they wanted to assimilate the
Jewish workers by force and make them true Yankees as quickly as possible."[228]

However, if the establishment of the Jewish Socialist Federation in 1912 was
certainly a victory for this school of Bundism, it was far from a total victory.
Old-time leaders such as Benjamin Feigenbaum (who could count on the backing
of the *Forverts*) were not prepared to step aside without a fight. Feigenbaum came
to the Paterson convention and resisted doggedly every attempt to ground the
Federation on a nationalist ideology.

He did succeed in rallying a majority of the delegates against a proposed reference to "the specific conditions of the Jewish proletariat."[229] (His view was upheld
by a narrow, two-vote, margin). There was no room, he insisted, for ideological
revision or fundamental organizational change:

> Yiddish papers? We have them! Yiddish speakers? We have them! Special
> Yiddish socialist branches? We have them! A unity of the Jewish branches in a
> country-side federation? We have that! . . . My dear friends, what actually do
> you want? . . .[230] What "Jewish interests" are they dreaming about? What
> concerns the Jewish masses more than their . . . shop slavery or material wor-
> ries? . . .[231] The socialist movement has always encouraged *assimilation*.[232]

Feigenbaum was determined to work within the Federation and to counter
(when necessary) what he regarded as excessive Bundist influence. And this, albeit
with still greater circumspection, was the official attitude of Abe Cahan and the
Forverts leadership. In contrast, as in 1907, when the Jewish Agitation Bureau had
been in question, the largest Yiddish-speaking party branches in New York –
Brownsville and the East Side – refused outright to affiliate themselves with the
Federation. To them it was a clear expression of nationalism.

In reality, over the next two years and until the World War, the Federation did
develop its own policy and style, which were at variance with precedent. Indeed, it
soon became apparent that in practice the Paterson convention had opened the
way to the reversal of the coup engineered by the *Forverts* in 1909. With J. B.
Salutsky, a Bundist, as its secretary and organizer, it did not remain simply the
Jewish Agitation Bureau under a different name. It brought out its own journal,
Der yidisher sotsyalist (initially in Chicago). The view there developed was that
Jewish politics – the defense of Jewish interests – could not be held in abeyance until
the periodic crisis but demanded constant involvement.

In the winter of 1913–14, the Federation organized (together with many Arbeter Ring branches) a public campaign in favor of free immigration, even though
it involved a direct clash not only with the AFL but also with the National

Executive Committee of the SP, which was openly accused by *Der yidisher sotsy-alist* of pursuing "double-faced diplomacy" on this issue.[233] At its convention in 1913, the Federation voted to permit its local branches to establish Yiddish socialist ("national-radical") schools.[234] It even made hesitant moves toward co-operation with the Poale Zion, a step that produced a furor among the rank-and-file membership and, following a referendum, had to be abandoned.

This policy predictably led to an open clash with the *Forverts*, which was as wary of the new journal as it had been of its predecessor, *Di yidishe arbeter velt*, in 1908–9. Cahan accused Salutsky of turning his organization into a refuge for all the enemies of the *Forverts*, and Salutsky accused Cahan of seeking to destroy the Federation by witholding the publicity essential for its growth. He looked forward to the day when "a healthy, disciplined organization" would be able to take control of the *Forverts*, "which belongs to all of us and make it into what it should be."[235]

The Jewish Socialist Federation did not become a mass organization. In 1913, it claimed some two thousand members in seventy branches. But, in it, the Bundist school at last had a political organization that (despite opposition from within and without) could be shaped in its own image. It was, wrote Fornberg in 1913, "the first step in a *new* direction."[236] The graduates of the Bund, Salutsky declared in 1914, had "helped build the mighty trade unions here; they strengthened and reinforced the Arbeter Ring, and now they are in the forefront of the Jewish Socialist Federation."[237]

The American Jewish Congress and the socialists, 1914–18

During World War I public pressure in favor of Jewish unity built up with an unprecedented force. To a real degree, this was simply the culminating stage in a trend that can be traced back (as has been described here) to Kishinev and even (as Cyrus Adler argued) to the mid-nineteenth century. In the summer of 1903 and again in the winter of 1905–6, the pogroms had prompted demands for united political action and specifically for an American Jewish Congress. With the mass expulsions from the Eastern War Zone by the Russian army, the debate was taken up again in the winter of 1914–15 where it had been halted in 1906. The rival organizations were already established and determined to defend their respective positions.

For all that, however, the balance of forces was radically different in 1915 than in 1905. Then, the Zionist camp, small at the best of times, had been thrown onto the defensive as popular interest focused on the Russian revolution and (to a lesser extent) on territorialism. The call for a permanent democratic and representative organization had produced little popular enthusiasm in 1905–6 and was then rejected by the German-Jewish leadership with its creation of the American Jewish Committee.

The tide of opinion in the war period flowed in the opposite direction. For the first time the Zionist movement became a major political force within American Jewry. The war with its anti-Jewish brutalities, with its militant nationalism, with its promise of shattered empires and new mono-national states encouraged a change of perception – carrying Zionism, as many saw it, from the realm of fantasy to that of possibility.

It was natural under these circumstances that the demand for democracy, for mass participation, for political unity became the rallying cry of the Zionist camp and in equal measure, was treated with the utmost suspicion by the non-Zionists. Indeed, the prolonged campaign for an American Jewish Congress (which finally met, albeit in truncated form, in December 1918) can be seen as a struggle of the outsiders to overwhelm the powers-that-be and, failing that, at least to join those inside.

Thus, the official Zionist organization challenged the authority of the American Jewish Committee in the Jewish community at large. And for its part, the Poale Zion launched its campaign to win over the labor movement to the cause of a permanent Jewish Congress and against the doctrine of class division as upheld by the Jewish Socialist Federation.

On the face of it, there was something highly quixotic in such a challenge by the Zionists, whether at the general or at the socialist level. They were few in number, financially weak, and until 1914, at least, widely regarded as eccentric. But the fact that amidst the vast mushrooming of Jewish institutions in the United States political organization had remained stunted and secondary now left the way open for the Zionist assault.

The American Jewish Committee and the *Forverts*-Bundist bloc, however powerful on paper, were not mass organizations and could not count automatically on popular support. In a period of crisis, when the fate of Russian Jewry was seen as hanging in the balance, the reaction of the post-1881 immigrants proved to be unpredictable, explosive, ideologically unstable.

With the outbreak of World War I and the almost immediate disruption of Jewish life in the Eastern War Zone and in Palestine, the machinery of financial relief was fast assembled. As in 1905, there was general acceptance that the funds should be despatched overseas through a single channel, and in November 1914 the Joint Distribution Committee was established. Collection, on the other hand, was organized along sectional lines.

The American Jewish Relief Committee, aimed in the main at the German-Jewish establishment, was directed primarily by Schiff, Magnes, and Felix Warburg. The Central Relief Committee (established like the AJRC in October 1914) was based on the more conservative and synagogue-affiliated sections of the Russian-Jewish community, and the People's Relief Committee was formed belatedly in August 1915 to reach out to the labor movement. These organizations were politically nonpartisan – Brandeis (now a militant Zionist) was, for instance, a prominent member of the AJRC, while Zuckerman, of the Poale Zion, served together with Meyer London and Abe Cahan on the executive committee of the People's Relief.[238]

In the winter months of 1914–15 the call for political unity and specifically for the American Jewish Congress was taken up once again. The immediate catalyst here was the news arriving piecemeal that the Russian army was expelling hundreds of thousands of Jews as potential spies from their homes in the War Zone.[239]

If united (so the argument went), the Jews of America could perhaps exert enough pressure to force the tsarist regime to halt the indiscriminate waves of destruction. But beyond this, there were those already thinking of the postwar settlement, the presentation of claims and demands to an eventual peace congress.

Figure 38. CATALEPSY. European Jewry: "Fire! Fire! Brother, save me!"
Her brother, American Jewry, snores.
*(The sleeping brother is surrounded by "appeals," "war letters," "news from
his town," "letters from home." European Jewry is engulfed in the smoke of
"Jewish destruction." 6 August 1915.)*

Jewish interests, it was now recalled, had been effectively advanced at the Congress of Berlin.[240]

The initial moves were made by veterans of the 1905 campaigns in New York. Thus, the leading members of the Jewish Congress Organization Committee founded in March 1915 were Joseph Barondess (now a Zionist), Gedaliah Bublick of *Dos yidishe tageblat* (which had led the Congress agitation in 1905–6), and Bernard G. Richards (then a leading territorialist, now also a Zionist).[241] In the labor camp, the call for united action was issued by an ad hoc committee of five prominent men representative of different ideologies and parties: Lesin, Syrkin, Zhitlovsky, Schlossberg, and London. This committee in February 1915 addressed a letter to all major sections of the Jewish labor movement inviting them to cooperate in preparing a joint political conference.[242]

Predictably, Magnes was likewise involved from the first in these exploratory moves. In February 1915 a committee of the New York Kehila, under his guidance, passed a resolution "demanding" that the American Jewish Committee "invite to a conference the representatives of all the Jewish national organizations of the country for the purpose of considering the necessity of forming a united Committee which can represent a united American Jewry."[243]

All these moves were part appeal and part threat. They left the way open to the American Jewish Committee and to the *Forverts*-Bundist bloc to take the lead, but also made it clear that if they failed to do so alternative leaderships were ready to appeal directly to public opinion. Magnes hoped passionately that Marshall and Schiff would yield to pressure and place the American Jewish Committee at the head of a mass protest movement. Similarly, Lesin expected the Jewish Socialist Federation (in alliance with the *Forverts*) to unite the entire labor movement on behalf of Russian Jewry. They were the natural advocates of compromise.

But unity was not to come easily. For their part, the leaders of the Jewish Socialist Federation – Salutsky, Goldfarb, Shakhne Epstein, Olgin – were determined not to provide the Poale Zion and the nationalist fringe of the labor movement with the mantle of legitimacy. In this stand, they were supported by A. Litvak, who early in 1915 arrived in New York, then regarded as a secure neutral center, to handle the affairs of the Bund's Committee Abroad.

The exploratory talks among seven leading labor organizations – the Arbeter Ring, the *Forverts* Association, the United Hebrew Trades, the Jewish Socialist Federation, the Jewish Socialist Labor Party (Poale Zion), the Jewish National Workers Alliance, and the Jewish Socialist Territorialist Labor Party of America – ended inconclusively. On 2 April 1915, the *Forverts* announced that the first four (the most powerful) of the above organizations had come together to form a joint political committee: the National Workmen's Committee on Jewish Rights in the Belligerent Lands (known more simply thereafter as the National Workmen's Committee [NWC]). This sudden move represented a triumph for the Jewish Socialist Federation, for it clearly implied that the veteran socialists – above all, Abe Cahan – had thrown their support to the Bundist group, headed by Salutsky and Litvak, rather than to Lesin and his committee of five.

The full meaning of this decision became apparent at the official foundation conference of the National Workmen's Committee, which, attended by some 370 delegates, met in New York on 18 April. The nationalist wing (the Poale Zion and the Territorialists) was consistently outvoted and its attempts to gain representation on the NWC were rebuffed. Amid mounting uproar, the minority (estimated by their opponents as less than 40 delegates and by their supporters at over 70) walked out of the conference.

Max Goldfarb summed up this development frankly: "A miracle happened. They [the Poale Zion and Territorialists] all walked out of the conference. All seemed well – they had corrected our error [of letting them attend]."[244] Or as Olgin put it in an earlier analysis:

> A great part of the utopianism and dreams which we have been fed lately will disappear . . . [It will become clear] that to create at this point a general Jewish [klal-yisroel] organization is untimely because even if it were possible it would at the best take years to achieve; . . . that if we want to do something for the Jews in Russia (to the extent that anything can be done) we must now, at this stage, use all the existing organizational forces . . . This means that the idea of a Jewish Congress, of a Jewish parliament, of an all-embracing Jewish organization [kerpershaft] has faded before it has flowered.[245]

Like the Jewish Socialist Federation, the American Jewish Committee under the direction of Louis Marshall refused doggedly to come out in support of a Congress. At work here were fear of a Zionist coup, the belief that noisy public campaigns could provoke the Russian and Turkish governments into savage reprisals against their Jewish subjects, and the determination to abide absolutely by President Wilson's call for strict neutrality in every sphere.

The clash of ideology and will emerged in all its bitterness at the annual convention of the New York Kehila that assembled on 25 April. Magnes had hoped that this convention would be the scene of a dramatic reconciliation between all sections of the community and had ensured that the labor movement was better represented there than ever before.

But Marshall refused to bend. All that the American Jewish Committee was prepared to offer was a conference of Jewish national organizations to consider how best to provide political aid to the victims of the war. As for a representative and open Congress, that was out of the question:

> The ebullitions of passion, the expression of emotion, the theories of the propagandist, and the dreams of a visionary will lead either to misconstruction, to ridicule, or to antagonism, in those quarters where above all things it is necessary to look for sympathy, and to appeal to reason and to considerations of expediency . . . [A Congress] will have no more effect, except for evil, upon the concert of the European Powers than a pebble cast in the Atlantic Ocean would have on the European coast-line.[246]

For all its inner conviction, however, Marshall's plea failed to win over the delegates. The East Side Jews, the yidn, strongly suspected that the Americanized leaders, the yahudim, were ready to sacrifice Russian Jewry on the altar of pro-Allied sentiment in the United States. The resolutions committee delivered a majority report calling for a Congress to be held "subsequent and supplementary to the conference called by the AJC."[247] This demand was taken up in open debate by Louis Miller, Zuckerman, Barondess and–most violently–by Isaac H. Hourwich. "It is time," he declared, to set aside the Jew's traditional policy of meekness in matters of grave concern to them. The situation calls for action . . . We have nothing to lose. What are we afraid of? Will one more rabbi be hung without trial or a few more women violated? Why have we not a right to cry and weep against the outrages perpetrated against our brothers and sisters on the other side? It is a question of maintaining the dignity and rights of the Jewish race.[248]

The debate ranged back and forth for five hours and a roll-call vote at the end produced a majority resolution in favor of a Congress. This decision produced something of a constitutional crisis, because although the Kehila elected a third of the AJC membership (by now seventy-five strong) it had no de jure control over it. Marshall refused to be bound by the vote. "I have," he announced angrily, "no fear for anyone but God above and indiscreet men below. If you persist and insist on calling a Congress, I'll have none of it." This, in turn, was too much for Magnes: "As the people have faith in the American Jewish Committee, so the Committee should have faith in the people."[249]

To avoid a final split, it was decided to reconvene the convention a month later following consultations. By then, as announced by Hourwich to the reassembled delegates on 23 May, a draft agreement had been reached. There would not be a "Congress" after all, only a "conference." On the other hand, a concession was made to democracy in that the delegates were to be elected by the members (not by the officers) of the national Jewish organizations. Hourwich proposed the resolution and Schiff seconded it.

Even this dramatic display of unity, though, did not settle the issue. Zuckerman now introduced a proposal to make the resolution binding on the twenty-five representatives of the Kehila in the AJC. Despite Marshall's vehement protest, this "imperative mandate" was carried by 118 to 87 votes. Magnes, now at his wits' end, implored the delegates to think again: "I am heart and soul for a Congress. But you cannot command the delegates [to the AJC] how to vote . . . I could appeal to your passion and prejudice; instead, I appeal to your reason."[250] Magnes's counterresolution on "freedom of conscience" was carried by 102 votes to 91, and then, on a second vote, defeated, 93 to 82. He saw here a personal vote of no confidence and declared that as president of the New York Kehila, "I feel a great deal of my usefulness is at an end."[251]

Clearly, this final vote was bound to antagonize the Uptown leadership, and when the AJC met in full executive session on 20 June it repudiated the agreement negotiated in May. The national conference, it now decided, would not be selected by the "membership" of the national organizations but, rather, "each organization should choose its delegates in such manner as it may deem advisable." The conference, to be organized by the AJC, was to be attended by no more than 150 delegates and "for the sole purpose of considering the Jewish question as it affects our brethren in belligerent lands." It was to meet in Washington on 24 October.[252]

Thus, by June 1915, the belief that unity could be attained by simple compromise and good will had proved a total illusion. Just as Abe Cahan, Salutsky, and Litvak were in no mood to compromise with the Poale Zion, so Marshall and Schiff were not ready to meet halfway with Miller, Barondess, Zuckerman, and Hourwich in the New York Kehila.

However, the assumption that the Congress movement would simply fade away in the face of firm resistance was now to prove equally erroneous. Frustrated in their attempt to reach a compromise with the powers-that-be, the outsiders turned to the public. The appeal at the general (or "bourgeois") level of the community was to the mutual benefit societies, to the federations of landsmanshaftn and synagogues, to their rank and file as much as to the upper echelons. In the labor movement, the goal was to win over significant sections of the trade-union and Arbeter Ring membership, to seek out and broaden the latent fissures within the veteran (pre-1905) leadership, and thus to bring about the isolation of the Bundist group that now stood at the head of both the Jewish Socialist Federation and the National Workmen's Committee.

In the summer of 1915, the Congress movement grew into a major force. Many factors combined to lend it strength, but above all there was the decision of Louis D. Brandeis to place himself at its head. Since the outbreak of war, when he had accepted the chairmanship of the Provisional Executive Committee for General Zionist Affairs, Brandeis had emerged as the outstanding leader of American Zionism.

But it was only much later, in the months of May and June 1915, that he decided to take up the cause of the Congress in open defiance of the American Jewish Committee. Once the decision was taken, he fought hard. Among the country's leading lawyers, a brilliant speaker, he had the ability and standing to challenge Marshall and Schiff. A Bostonian, a Wilsonian Democrat, for long a marginal Jew but now a convert to Zionism, he also had the will to contend with the New York oligarchy, predominantly Republican and hostile to the concept of Jewish nationhood as it was.[253]

The Poale Zion and Territorialist bloc likewise found itself much reinforced in the summer of 1915. In particular, the arrival of Pinhas Rutenberg from Europe in June proved to be of major importance. A veteran SR, associated with the field execution of Gapon in 1906, a recent convert to Zionism, an active advocate of a Jewish Legion to fight with the Allies, Rutenberg was ideally suited to arouse maximal public interest on the Lower East Side, and indeed throughout the Russian-Jewish immigrant world as a whole.

Zhitlovsky and Rutenberg now became the star speakers of the National Socialist Agitation Bureau, which was founded in July 1915 to rally support for a Jewish Congress. The two men toured the United States addressing rallies on behalf of the cause and were scathingly dubbed the "flying squadron"[254] by their opponents. The Agitation Bureau brought out its own journal, *Der yidisher kongres,* which likewise benefited much from the influx of newcomers from Europe, publishing articles not only by Rutenberg but also, inter alia, by Borochov (who had recently arrived from Italy) and from late in the summer by Ben Gurion and Ben Zvi (who had been expelled from Palestine by the Turkish authorities).

The Congress movement was carried forward on the tide of hostility to the Russian regime. With its constant flow of atrocity stories, the daily press brought anti-tsarist sentiment to a fever pitch. Abe Cahan's despatches from Europe, which began to appear in the *Forverts* from April 1915, contributed much to the rising tension, thus paradoxically (but by no means atypically) rendering less popular the ideological stance adopted by the paper. The violent anti-Russianism easily turned against the opponents of the Congress, above all, of course, against the German-

Jewish oligarchs, the *yahudim,* but also against the socialist "cosmopolitans." Two of the daily newspapers, *Di varhayt* and *Dos yidishe tageblat,* were fully committed to the Congress idea and did their utmost to build up this public pressure.

In appealing to the more direct forms of democracy, the Congress movement could count for its popularity in part on the Russian experience, on the long-standing sentiment in the Pale of Settlement in favor of thoroughgoing representative government, on the commitment of all the Jewish parties in Russia to one form or another of national autonomism. But American influence also played its part. This, after all, was the period of the Wilsonian reform movement, with its drive for popular participation and political primary elections.

The first move against the American Jewish Committee was taken shortly after its decision of 20 June to reject the compromise adopted by the Kehila convention. Meeting in Boston on 27 June, the Provisional Executive Committee for General Zionist Affairs came out with the demand for "an American Jewish Congress which shall consider the proper steps to be taken to obtain full civil status for the Jews in all lands and further development of a homeland for the Jewish people in Palestine."[255]

Magnes argued vehemently against this resolution, which, as he rightly foresaw, was bound to lead to a head-on collision with the American Jewish Committee. He advocated, rather, a division of labor that would permit the Zionists to devote all their efforts to the Palestinian cause and leave other international issues to the AJC. But Louis Lipsky would have none of this: "We cannot go hand in hand with the AJC who are anti-nationalists and anti-Zionists . . . If we set the lead, the Jews of the United States will follow us."[256] Brandeis supported Lipsky's position and Magnes was defeated by 66 to 11 votes.

On 12 July Brandeis met with Dr. Cyrus Adler to ascertain, albeit at the eleventh hour, whether there was any room for compromise. (Professor Felix Frankfurter kept the minutes of this meeting.) Brandeis proposed that the AJC drop its planned conference and instead join with the other leading Jewish organizations to call a pre-conference, which in turn would decide what kind of assembly should represent American Jewry. On 13 July the Executive Committee of the AJC rejected this proposal out of hand.[257]

The correspondence between Brandeis and Adler was now published. Brandeis there attacked the AJC for its "system of self-election and perpetuation in office"; for its deep suspicion of democracy; and for its insistence on a closed conference — "secrecy necessarily breeds suspicion and creates misunderstanding."[258] For his part, Adler insisted that the AJC was the only existing organization specifically created to defend Jewish interests overseas; that it therefore could not be equated with other organizations; that it was as representative as possible given the fragmentation of Jewish life; that "the direct proportionate representation of organizations based upon numbers seems to me neither fair nor wise"; and that secrecy was essential for fear "of intemperate and even ill-considered speech . . . [which could] risk injury to our unhappy brethren abroad."[259]

Huge public meetings were now organized across the country in favor of a Congress. A meeting at Cooper Union on 19 August was attended by some 20,000 and addressed by Barondess, Syrkin, and Shmarya Levin. Brandeis spoke in Baltimore in September, where he proclaimed that the Congress was to be not "an exalted mass meeting [but]... the effective instrument of organized Jewry in America."[260] Rabbi Stephen Wise, addressing the Free Synagogue at Carnegie Hall, declared that "the Jewish masses are determined at all costs to become masters of their own fates."[261]

By August the Congress movement could claim a respectable list of endorsements from, among others, the Independent Order B'rith Abraham, the Independent Order B'rith Sholom, the Galician Varband, the Federation of Roumanian Jews, as well as eighteen branches of the YMHA. Moreover, the B'nai B'rith refused to endorse either Congress or conference (thus upholding the independent role it had adopted in 1906). True, the AJC likewise had the support of many organizations, including the Conservative and Reform synagogue movements. But that was not enough. Early in October, it decided to postpone its Washington conference, which in fact never met.

The mounting enthusiasm for a Congress that was to be observed on the Lower East Side and in other major immigrant quarters similarly upset the balance of forces in the labor movement. On the purely polemical level, *Der yidisher kongres* was no doubt well matched by its rival, *Di naye velt* (which had replaced *Der yidisher sotsyalist* as the journal of the Jewish Socialist Federation). The basic lines of division, after all, were the same as in 1905, when the Jewish Defense Association had been kept at arm's length by the Bundists.

On the one hand, there was the appeal for unity, for a concerted effort to solve the Jewish question, for a national territory in Palestine. And, on the other, there was the determination to maintain proletarian independence, to remain free of national romanticism and fantasy, to reject the politics of class peace (*klal-yisroel politik*).

But the war situation lent an added force and fire to the arguments for unity. "It depends on the Jews," Syrkin could now write,

> how, to what extent and how seriously, the international peace congress will concern itself with the situation of the Jews in the world and with the Jewish nation... [262] To represent the Jewish people, to speak in its name, to conduct its politics, to organize it, to raise it up, to liberate and restructure its entire life – this cannot be done by self-appointed groups of shtadlonim, by a party, by a faction or an organization, but only by the people organized as such, working through its democratically elected representatives.[263]

The few hundred thousand Montenegrins, asserted Borochov, had more political influence than the thirteen million Jews, "because the Montenegrins do not depend on assimilation and on the progress of all humanity, but on their own meager forces."[264] "We Jews," declared Rutenberg, "built up socialism, but we have also poisoned it with our cosmopolitanism. All European socialists... have become patriots. Only the Jewish socialists, driven from Russia and other countries, have remained true to cosmopolitanism."[265]

Against all this, the leaders of the Jewish Socialist Federation pointed out that there was little chance of gaining Palestine at a peace congress; that promises made at such a moment were rarely kept; that the Jews, anyway, would continue

Figure 39. THREE IN ONE – DR. N. ŚYRKIN. *(Captions from right to left.)*
(1) His friends say that he is the modern Isaiah. (2) His enemies say that he is
just mixed up. (3) In fact, he is a bearded baby playing with his toys.
*(Syrkin, the baby is surrounded by objects and toys variously labeled "Col-
onization," "Hebrew," "Congress," "Cooperative Hat Stores," and "Socialism." 22 October 1915.)*

to emigrate to America, certainly not to the Middle East; and that the true socialists in Europe – Liebknecht, Mehring, Bernstein – had rejected class peace and national defensism.

However, these counterarguments now fell on deaf ears. It was the Nationalist
Socialist Agitation Bureau that was able to attract the big crowds to its meetings
(the largest, held at Cooper Union on 5 August, was addressed by, among others,
Zhitlovsky, Hourwich, Zuckerman, Syrkin, and Rutenberg). And it was the Nationalist Socialist Agitation Bureau, again, that sounded the most confident as it
accused the American Jewish Committee of cowardice and the Bundists of secret,
back-stairs cooperation with the Wall Street oligarchs of the AJC.

In contrast, the National Workmen's Committee remained surprisingly passive,
and within its own ranks many now emerged as openly hostile to its strict proletarian strategy. Lesin and Zivion were particularly outspoken. What was needed,
declared Lesin, was not so much a Congress – although that would be better than
nothing – but rather "one imposing protest rally, like the historic meeting [at
Carnegie Hall] after the Kishinev pogrom or one imposing protest demonstration
like the Mourning March after the Odessa pogrom [in 1905]."[266]

"The spokesmen of the so-called revolutionary struggle . . . ," declared Zivion,
"have driven the entire Congress movement into the hands of the Zionists . . . This
is not a question of class struggle, not of revolutionary struggle, but only of rescue:
a people is drowning in blood and we must save it."[267] And, for its part, *Fortshrit*,
the weekly paper of the Amalgamated Clothing Workers of America, deplored the
"split that came about at the labor convention of [18 April] . . . Instead of considering who was right and who was wrong, we express the hope that the errors
will be corrected and the work advanced with united forces."[268]

The pressure eventually began to tell. As Salutsky later wrote: "Much as it may amuse our 'comrades' [*khaveyrim*] from the *Kemfer* [the Poale Zion journal], they were able to terrorize the leadership of the organized labor movement. Yes, terrorize."[269] Reluctantly, a series of concessions were made. First, in the early summer, representatives of the Zionist-Territorialist bloc were permitted to join the NWC (a reversal of the April decision). Then, on 1 August, the executive committee of the Jewish Socialist Federation issued a statement condemning the Congress movement with its "openly Zionist-party content," but expressing support for "an assembly of all Jewish organizations that will fight sincerely and in a nonparty spirit for full rights for the Jews in belligerent lands, . . . that will be based on democratic foundations; and that will have a businesslike character, not that of a mass meeting."[270] This statement was immediately endorsed by the *Forverts*. Its meaning was clear. There could be a measure of class cooperation, a democratically elected conference, as long as the agenda excluded any possibility of a Zionist coup.

Still another concession came on 29 August at the labor conference held in the *Forverts* hall to elect the one hundred New York representatives to the coming National Workmen's Convention. The pro-Congress forces, as a minority, feared that they would be totally excluded from the delegation. But, this time, the leadership of the National Workmen's Committee acted on the principle of proportional representation, permitting the nationalist wing to elect some 30 percent of the delegation.

In its summer campaign the Nationalist Socialist Agitation Bureau had certainly benefited from the parallel success of the general Congress movement directed by Brandeis. But it was by no means a mere appendage of the Jewish Congress Organization Committee. In the variety, talent, and energy of its members – Zhitlovsky, Rutenberg, Syrkin, Borochov, Cherikover, Hourwich, Ben Gurion, Ben Zvi, Kaplansky (who was also in America in 1915) – it seemed to overshadow the general leadership with its excessive dependence on Brandeis and Wise. In fact, Magnes in his belated letter of resignation from the Provisional Executive Committee for General Zionist Affairs, sent to Brandeis in September, even suggested that the entire movement was falling into the hands of the socialists:

> I am pained to observe that the presentation and interpretation of the Palestine ideal seems to have been taken out of the hands of the American Zionist organization by the more "radical" elements who have come to be associated with the Zionists in the so-called "Congress." Many of these radicals, for whom personally I have much regard, are among those who during the Russian revolution were not content with securing political emancipation but who insisted on bringing about at the same time the great "Social Revolution." As a result, Russia gained neither political emancipation nor social revolution. Some of these extra-organization Zionists are now, by the intemperance of their utterance, the "radicalism" of their demands . . . endangering the Jewish inhabitants of Palestine and the international Zionist organization.[271]

It was at the National Workmen's Convention, which assembled at Cooper Union on 4 September 1915, that the pro-Congress socialists – and, indeed, the Congress movement as a whole – reached the crest of the upward wave. (There were some two hundred delegates from across the United States, selected for the most part by local conferences representative of virtually all the Jewish socialist and labor organizations in the given area.) The three-day convention was throughout punctuated by crisis and threatened with schism. But, in the last resort, both sides had too much to lose by open failure at a time when the public demand for united action had reached unprecedented heights.

On Monday, 6 September, the resolutions committee, which was composed of representatives from both camps, presented its compromise formula to the assembled delegates. In general terms, it called for a concerted campaign on behalf of Jewish rights. Where the give-and-take became evident was in the definition of those rights. Here the Bundists implicitly acknowledged that Palestine was a major center of Jewish life, while the Zionists, in turn, did not insist that Palestine be recognized as unique in its importance.

Thus, for example, the resolution called for "state-recognized and internationally guaranteed juridical institutions that will make possible national self-determination and unhampered national development for the Jewish people in all lands where it finds itself (Russia, Galicia, Roumania, Palestine, etc)." Or, again, it demanded an end to all anti-Jewish "social, economic and cultural restrictions – for example, the Pale of Settlement and numerus clausus in Russia, the restrictions on the use of the mother tongue in Galicia, the nonrecognition of the Jews as citizens in Roumania, the restriction on immigration and property acquisition in Palestine etc."[272] In short, here was a virtuoso performance on the ideological tightrope, withholding recognition of Zionist doctrine while granting it to Zionist practice.

It was a formula that made possible the entire settlement. On this basis, the majority felt able to grant a major concession – its agreement to support an American Jewish Congress: "The National Workmen's Convention instructs its Executive to take part in a conference of national Jewish organizations that will call together a general Jewish Congress to which the delegates will be elected democratically by local organizations." The counter-concession from the nationalist wing was the agreement that the program of the Congress would have to be formulated in advance and would have to correspond with the compromise now drawn up, "otherwise, the National Workmen's Committee as such will not take part in the Congress and will leave the conference."[273]

More threatening from the Zionist point of view was a resolution proposed by Jacob Panken, the SP leader, that called for negotiations with the American Jewish Committee in order to ensure a truly united front. A committee of seven – Goldfarb, Rozenblat, Shiplacoff, Vladeck, Sholem Asch, and Dovid Pinsky – was elected to conduct the negotiations. It was left unclear what would happen in case no agreement was reached with the AJC. Would a Congress be held without, against, it? Or would the majority of the newly elected National Workmen's Committee prefer to use such a deadlock to postpone, or even repudiate, the Congress?

However, for the moment, all such doubts were put aside. The atmosphere was one of high excitement. Here, surely, was the first time that the Bundist and Zionist-Territorialist wings of the Jewish labor movement had been able to unite behind one program. The speakers conveyed the prevailing feeling that they were witnessing an event little short of miraculous.

"At this convention," declared Zhitlovsky, "a great historical event has occurred—the united Jewish socialist party has been formed." "We, the Jewish workers," declared Max Pine, the veteran leader of the UHT, "will first win rights and then we shall win Palestine, too!" Frank Rozenblat said that "this side did not win, that side did not win. The Jewish people has won." And Olgin confessed that "today for the first time I saw what good socialists the nationalists are."[274]

And the euphoria outlived the Convention. Writing in *Di naye velt*, Goldfarb stated that it had been "wonderfully productive . . . a common platform was created for all the different shades of Jewish labor."[275] For his part, Ben Gurion stated that the compromise formula contained "almost everything which we can demand for Palestine at this time."[276] In a letter of 13 September to Cyrus Adler, which reported on a private meeting with Goldfarb, Magnes likewise struck an optimistic note:

> The majority which Dr. Goldfarb represents is as much opposed to the demogagy and irresponsibility of those who have had the Congress question in hand up to the present time as is the American Jewish Committee. It seems to me that the opportunity is now offered the American Jewish Committee to take up negotiations with a group now practically in control of the Congress movement. The Zionists cannot now move without this group in as much as a number of Zionists, greatly to the surprise of many persons, accepted the resolutions adopted by the National Workmen's Convention. With the re-tirement of the Zionists into the background—something that has already been affected by the resolutions of the National Workingmen's Convention—the other organizations which have been following the Zionists' lead will fall into line.[277]

In retrospect, it is clear that the National Workmen's Convention represented the climax of the pro-Congress campaign. In six months, the movement had gone from strength to strength, transforming what had been a marginal concept into the central issue of American-Jewish life. But from now on many of the factors that had served to raise it up began to work against it.

The fragmented structure of American Jewry had permitted the new movement to make extraordinarily rapid progress, but it also set strict limits to that progress. Many major organizations—the B'nai B'rith, the AJC, the synagogue federations—were determined to stand firm against what they interpreted as demogogic pressures. They would not, could not, be moved.

Again, the crisis-centered campaign, with its maximal press coverage, could arouse mass emotion but was by its nature unable to sustain it for long periods of time. The ferociously competitive daily press had eventually to seek new issues and stories in the internecine fight for readers. And the star system was of similarly short-ranged effectiveness. Rutenberg's appeal had been so great largely because he was newly arrived from Europe, and it fast declined with familiarity.

The extreme dependence on Brandeis proved a veritable double-edged sword. He tended to make major, and sometimes contradictory, decisions alone and unexplained. After January 1916, with his acceptance of a seat on the Supreme Court of the United States, he tended more and more to avoid the limelight, directing his forces erratically from behind the lines.

More, the movement had risen with the news of catastrophe in the Eastern War

Zone and it lost momentum as that news gradually improved. In August 1915, the tsarist government decided to permit temporarily the free movement of Jews into the interior of Russia. This move came partly as a genuine attempt to alleviate the disastrous refugee problem. But it was also a response to the pressure created by Jacob Schiff, who had coordinated the effort to exclude Russian war loans from the United States. The importance of this factor, little appreciated by the general public at the time, was fully revealed years later with the publication after the revolution of the proceedings of the tsarist government.[278] But enough was known by initiates to strengthen the leadership of the American Jewish Committee in its determination to follow its own independent path. The virtual abolition of the Pale combined with the extensive German conquests to reduce the fear that Russian Jewry was about to suffer wholesale destruction.

In essence, the Congress movement had two alternatives in September 1915. It could reach a compromise with the American Jewish Committee surrendering the ideal of a democratic and sovereign Congress but nonetheless achieving a degree of united action. Alternatively, it could set a strict time limit to further negotiations and, with their failure, proceed to call a Congress independently – without, indeed against, the American Jewish Committee and the majority in the National Workmen's Committee. In fact, it wavered between these alternatives, falling hard between two stools.

Negotiations among the three organizations – the American Jewish Committee, the Jewish Congress Organization Committee, and the National Workmen's Committee – were conducted by a tripartite committee of nine (Magnes among them) established at the end of September. The negotiations were difficult or, as Zuckerman put it: "Nine Jews got together; some of them are looking for any and every way to escape the 'mob' and erect a barrier against the newly awakened popular will; a second group, on the other hand, is seeking to organize this awakening and to direct it toward concrete action; and the third group tries by various means, open and covert, to help the first."[279] Nevertheless, a tentative agreement was initialed in the second week of October and accepted on 10 October by the executive committee of the American Jewish Committee (a conditional decision that had still to be endorsed by the annual, plenary meeting of the AJC on 14 November).

But on 12 October the Jewish Congress Organization took the extraordinary step of rejecting the pact. Instead, it decided to call its own pre-conference of all the "national Jewish organizations that are for a Congress and of the central committees in the cities that have already organized themselves."[280] The conference, of course, was to decide how and when to assemble the American Jewish Congress.

This decision, on the face of it, suggested that Brandeis had decided to appeal over the heads of the established organizations to the Jewish people in America.[281] This policy, if pursued with sufficient unity, speed, and determination, might have enjoyed considerable success. But the magnitude of the task apparently induced second thoughts, for on 19 October the Jewish Congress Organization Committee again reversed itself and acceded to an appeal by the National Workmen's Committee to renew negotiations. As a result, a new draft agreement was drawn up.

Now, finally, it seemed that Magnes was to have his triumph and achieve the compromise settlement for which he had been working tirelessly since early in the year. But this was not to be. At the annual meeting on 14 November not only Cyrus Adler but also Louis Marshall argued against the adoption of the proposed peace treaty, and the majority followed their lead.

The central phrase in the three-cornered agreement laid before the AJC read "That a Conference of national Jewish organizations be held for considering the rights of Jews in belligerent lands and in Roumania and that it call a Congress on a democratic basis at such time, in such place and in such manner as it may deem best to secure such rights."[282] In contrast, the resolution actually adopted at the annual meeting amended this statement, changing the last clause to read that the proposed conference "take steps to call a Congress on a democratic basis after the termination of hostilities."[283] Whatever the objective merits of this decision, it could only be interpreted as a repudiation of Magnes and a gesture of contempt for the Congress movement.

In a letter to Schiff, written before this latest debacle, Magnes had already described his view of this fluctuating and endlessly frustrating search for common ground:

> Many of your strictures on the Zionists are all too true. Yet it must be said of them that they have zeal, and that Jewish affairs are to them of primary importance. They have an organization built up after much sacrifice. They have a devoted following. What is of great importance, they look at the Jewish question as a whole and, in accordance with one of the great lessons of the War, as affecting the Jews as a minority People. What do we find on the other side? A handful of serious, large-minded, exceedingly busy men of affairs for whom, to be sure, Judaism is of primary concern. But as for their followers – almost complete indifference to Jewish affairs, except perhaps to Jewish physical charities ... I have been trying to persuade the American Jewish Committee to take the lead in unifying the Jewish forces of America in view of the historic crisis presented by the War ... When, finally, the Committee got ready to act, the opportunity had been lost ... I have been trying with just as little success to persuade the Zionists that they must act in conjunction with the ... Committee ... We are a sick, individualistic people, unused to self-discipline and unable to co-ordinate our activities. We are like a man afflicted with locomotor ataxis. First, you try hard to get one leg to move. When at last you succeed, there is another leg lagging behind.[284]

Within the Congress camp, there were those who hoped that the socialist majority in the National Workmen's Committee would now decide to throw its weight firmly against the American Jewish Committee and its high-handed action of 14 November. But this was an illusion. Goldfarb and Salutsky, as the central strategists of the NWC, saw in the decision of the AJC an ideal opportunity to escape the net woven around them by the pro-Congress socialists. "If we are to have a Congress," *Di naye velt* now stated, "let it be with everybody, not only with a part of the people."[285]

The National Workmen's Committee insisted that the negotiations had, therefore, to be renewed. But, as against this, the Congress movement saw its strength eroded relentlessly by every further day of indecision. "We accuse the National Workmen's Committee of passive resistance to the Congress idea ..." Borochov wrote. "If the majority [of the NWC] held the interests of the people dearer than the interests of the Wall Street magnates they would have broken off all negotiations with the American Jewish Committee as soon as it had the audacity to give the people an ultimatum – the demand that the Congress be delayed until after the war."[286]

Finally, on 23 December the Jewish Congress Organization Committee decided to revert to its plan of 12 October, to organize its own pre-conference, and to mobilize the rank and file of American Jewry against the powers-that-be.[287] Once again, as in the summer of 1915, a series of mass meetings were addressed by Wise and Brandeis. Speaking at Carnegie Hall on 24 January 1916, Brandeis called on Jewry to avoid the error of 1878 with its naive trust that the Berlin Treaty would be self-enforcing: "Had there existed the machinery of organized Jews, Roumania would have been compelled to keep her word. Through the Congress, we must secure that power in men, in ability and influence, and in money necessary to maintain any gains that may be made." He concluded on a high note of optimism: "Unity will develop because the minority will cooperate with the majority to attain the common end, when the judgement and will of the majority have been democratically ascertained. That is in accordance with American methods."[288] But four days later, Brandeis was appointed by President Wilson to the Supreme Court. And, that fateful step apart, his strategy was in all probability based on a misreading of the political map.

The most that the Congress movement could realistically expect now was to demonstrate that it had a genuinely mass following, and this it did. Electoral conventions were held across the country to select delegates to the pre-conference. The largest, the Manhattan Congress Convention, which met on 22 February, was attended by 677 delegates representing 488 organizations.

On 26 March 1916, the pre-conference assembled in Philadelphia in an atmosphere of veritable euphoria. Three hundred and fifty-seven delegates had been sent by congress committees across the United States and by those national organizations that had pledged their support to the Jewish Congress Organization Committee. In all, it was estimated, over a million Jews were represented at Philadelphia.

Under these circumstances, it was all too easy to forget that this was a conference not of the entire Jewish people in America, but of only one section within it. *Di naye velt* was not far from the truth in its ill-tempered comment: "It was a Zionist convention [in Manhattan]. On 26 and 27 March there will be a Zionist pre-conference in Philadelphia, and later will come a Zionist Congress."[289]

The socialists at Philadelphia, Zuckerman and Rutenberg among them, tended to urge moderation and the adoption of resolutions that would leave the leadership free to negotiate an agreement later with the American Jewish Committee and the National Workmen's Committee. But they were consistently overruled. Stephen Wise and Jacob De Haas (who no doubt spoke for the absent Brandeis) took the line that the era of negotiation had now been replaced by the era of direct democracy. "There is nothing to negotiate . . . ," declared De Haas. "We have written our constitution as best we can and our invitation is extended to all Jews to come into the fold."[290] "Negotiations," said Wise, "means compromise and surrender."[291]

In its final form, the resolution adopted laid down that if the executive committee were subsequently to allow additional organizations into the movement, it could then broaden its ranks by no more than 20 percent – or, in other words, add at most fourteen new members to its existing membership of seventy. This move could, of course, only be regarded by the AJC and the NWC as an insult.

A similarly hard line was taken on the issue of the electoral system for the Congress; direct and universal suffrage was chosen rather than elections within the existing Jewish organizations (as favored by Isaac H. Hourwich). Yet another crucial decision of the Philadelphia conference permitted only citizens of the United States to be elected to the executive committee of seventy. This move at one stroke excluded the great majority of the socialist leaders, who with a few exceptions (such as Hourwich, Syrkin, and Zuckerman) were still Russian citizens.

The line laid down at Philadelphia logically demanded an immediate drive to organize the elections to an American Jewish Congress.[292] But the committee of seventy proved to be an unwieldy mammoth. Wise was no substitute for Brandeis as a leader. Rutenberg (as a noncitizen) was not even a member. The months of April, May, and June 1916 were allowed simply to slip by without any significant action. The Philadelphia conference had left the movement in a state of euphoric passivity.

Meanwhile, the opponents of the Congress movement did not stand by idly. The National Workmen's Committee had organized its own rival convention in March 1916 at the Beethoven Hall in New York. It adopted a conciliatory stance, calling for renewed efforts to unite all the rival parties in a common effort. Acting on this decision, Max Goldfarb now sent out letters to the AJC and to the Jewish Congress Executive inviting them to reopen negotiations on an equal footing. Prohibited by the Philadelphia Conference from further negotiation, the Congress executive was left with no choice but to reject this overture, thus laying itself open to charges of intransigence and schism.

In the American-Jewish world the atmosphere became increasingly bitter and frustrated during these months, when accusation and counteraccusation followed each other in fast succession. Speaking at the Kehila Convention in June 1916, Schiff expressed his disgust with the Yiddish press, which "launched against me a campaign, maligned me, even threatened me."[293] Magnes in his formal address spoke in terms of despair:

> We find a leadership of [the] masses that is in large measure irresponsible. We find a Jewish press, sensation-loving, out for circulation alone ... We find other men who are endeavouring to rise politically upon the body of the Jewish people and who do so rise. We find the blatant rhetoricians, ... and also a residuum of well-meaning, sincere young men and women who are obsessed with the notion that all Jews not in absolute agreement with them must be damned for ever ... And, on the other side, ... we find a handful of leaders who have given their lives ... to the cause of the Jews ... yet are so far away from the life of the people that they do not fully understand it ... So that we are crushed between these two millstones – you and I.[294]

The final act in this, the second, period of public confrontation between the Congress movement and its opponents came at a conference held at the Astor Hotel on 16 July. This meeting, organized jointly by the American Jewish Committee and the National Workmen's Committee, was attended by the representatives

Figure 40. THE HERO WIELDS HIS SLIPPERS. "Mr. Schiff, you're wasting your time. You can't stop the tide with your slippers."
(*Jacob Schiff is trying to drive back the wave, the "Congress Movement," with his slippers marked respectively "Forverts" and "The American Jewish Committee." 3 March 1916.*)

of the major (or "national") Jewish organizations that had boycotted the Philadelphia pre-conference in March. Thus it marked the formal proclamation, as it were, of a re-alliance of alliances, bringing together the leaders of the "internationalist" wing of the labor movement with the German-Jewish establishment. This development was of course the natural outcome of the hard-line policy adopted by the Congress movement at Philadelphia.

Nonetheless, it aroused much critical, and often scathing, comment even from within the ranks of the *Forverts*-Bundist bloc itself. Lesin, for example, now decided to publish a bitter attack by "an old Bundist" in *Di tsukunft*. What an extraordinary picture, he wrote, was made by this alliance of socialists, committed to "national rights" with "our *yahudim* [who] have always fought bitterly against the idea that the Jews are a people with a culture."

> Instead of a mass movement, we have got caught up in *shtadlones*, politics, diplomacy . . . We have danced to their tune . . . Was this the time for settling accounts with Zionists?[295] . . . To hobnob with the great men of the AJC is easier, more pleasant, more acceptable than to devote oneself to such

Figure 41. ALL AWHIRL. American Jewry: "Nu, I no longer have any idea of what kind of world I'm in."
("American Jewry" is reduced to a state of dizziness by the surrounding whirl: "plans," "bazaars," "speeches," "relief." Over his head the "Philadelphia Conference" and the "New York Conference" are fighting. 31 March 1916.)

banal subjects as simple Jewish workers. Would people who really want to work behave in such a manner? . . .²⁹⁶

It was the fear of being totally isolated, however, that had driven the two en-trenched leaderships together. As Goldfarb put it: "The *yahudim* and the *yidn* would sooner or later have made peace, and any peace between them would, in practice, have been a union against us."²⁹⁷ Or, as Schiff had written to Marshall on 10 March 1916:

> I am very much convinced that unless we do something very positive and very promptly to revive the proposed convention, those who are making a Golden Calf of a Congress will very soon say: "This man Moses is dead, these are your Gods, O Israel!", substituting the American Jewish Committee for Moses and the proposed Congress for these are your Gods.²⁹⁸

An additional consideration (at least for the socialists) was the impending No-vember election, when hard contests, including Meyer London's fight to hold his U.S. Congressional seat, were expected. A number of leading Democrats – Judge Aaron Levy, Henry Goldfogle, Leon Sanders – had been associated from the first with the Jewish Congress movement. But now, the socialists had a chance to turn the tables, to take up the cause of Jewish unity abandoned (as it were) by the Zionists at the Philadelphia pre-conference. The alliance of the National Workmen's Committee with the American Jewish Committee was thus, at one level, a not unnatural alliance of Socialists and Republicans against Democrats.

On behalf of the Jewish Congress executive, a delegation of three, with observer status alone, attended the Astor Hotel conference. It was led by Brandeis. The proceedings were not published at the time, but the protocol is available today and reveals that a bitter personal clash between Brandeis and Magnes overshadowed all else. Brandeis appealed for unity on the basis laid down at Philadelphia: "I am commissioned by the Executive Committee to say to you that you will be just as welcome as if you had come in three or four months [ago]."[299] In turn, Magnes proposed that the Astor Hotel conference elect its own executive to unite, on a basis of parity, with the Congress Committee. "We shall have thereby achieved unity," he said. "We create a body equal to the Congress organization so that these two equal bodies may come together."[300]

In response, Brandeis adopted a formalistic position. The Congress executive committee, he insisted, had no right to go beyond the decisions adopted at Philadelphia (which would allow the Astor Hotel coalition only a 20 percent representation.) "I feel," he said, "that I ought at this time to call your attention to these facts, that is, to what has been done and which our Executive Committee has no power whatever to alter in any respect."[301] This stance infuriated Magnes:

> In plain words, that means this: That Mr. Brandeis, that Mr. Justice Brandeis and his colleagues come to this meeting and say to us, either you will come into our organization or you will not be with us at all . . . No, Mr. Brandeis and gentlemen, no Jewish organization at this time can say of representatives of old, established and important institutions of this country, that you will do as we have laid it down that you shall do or you cannot cooperate with us.[302]

"Facts," replied Brandeis, "are facts . . . Mr. Magnes must know . . . that we are the committee of the Philadelphia Conference and believe in democratic matters and believe in the Law." But Magnes would not let him have the last word. "Mr. Chairman," he said, "the only Jewish gathering I know of that has never revoked the decision it has come to was at Mt. Sinai. Even the Constitution of the United States can be amended."[303] Magnes, of course, received the support of the socialists present and, indeed, in some cases they outdid him in the harshness of their attacks on Brandeis and the Congress executive.

In this contest of will and policy, Magnes now had the better of it. The Astor Hotel conference adopted his proposals. Most notably, it did not make support for an American Jewish Congress dependent on its being held after the war. Louis Marshall thus tacitly abandoned the principle (adopted by the AJC in November 1915) that had produced the second period of bitter confrontation.

For his part, Brandeis decided that he could no longer permit himself to play so public a part in the Congress movement. His role at the Astor Hotel conference had been promptly criticized by an editorial in *The New York Times* which stated that "Justice Brandeis might with very great propriety have avoided taking part in such

Figure 42. MAGNES IS A PUPPET. The voice of Magnes is the voice of
Marshall.
*(Magnes, "President of the Kehila," faithfully echoes Marshall, "President of
the American Jewish Committee," and mouths: "The Kehila cannot bother
itself with the Jewish Congress." 9 June 1916.)*

a controversy."[304] In a confidential letter to Judge Hugo Pam on 21 July, he announced his resignation as temporary chairman of the executive organization committee for the American Jewish Congress. "The fact . . . ," he wrote "that the attack [by Magnes, Vladeck, etc.] was made without any conceivable provocation. . . . suggests that [it] . . . may have been not only malevolent, but premeditated . . . I feel that respect for the high court of which I am a member and also the future of our cause demand that so far as humanly possible I should guard against a repetition of such incidents."[305]

Brandeis had been withdrawing progressively from leadership since January, but his formal resignation put the seal of bankruptcy on the policy adopted at Philadelphia in March. Where Brandeis had failed, Wise, Lipsky, and Mack could hardly expect to succeed. Despite the rigid guidelines laid down by the Philadelphia conference, a compromise would once again have to be sought.

In fact, negotiations between the two sides began in July. Understandably, given the general state of exhaustion, a peace treaty was drawn up and ready by August. It was immediately approved by the two parties involved, the executive committee for an American Jewish Congress and the executive committee of the Conference of National Jewish Organizations (that is, the Astor Hotel alliance).

The proposed settlement was actually very similar to that proposed in November 1915. Thus the agenda of the Congress was to be formulated in advance and strictly limited (so excluding any chance of a sectional takeover). It was to meet "exclusively for the purpose" of securing "full rights for the Jews of all lands," such rights being defined as "civil, religious and political." In those countries where national minority status was recognized, the definition could be extended to include "group rights." An additional clause spoke of the "security and protection of Jewish rights in Palestine."

Elections to the Congress were to be on the basis of "a democratic and universal suffrage," but additional delegates would also be selected by "the various Jewish National Organizations." The details of the system were to be worked out by the executive committee, which was to be doubled in size by the addition of seventy members to be chosen by the Astor Hotel group. Finally, the pact declared that "the Congress shall be held at such time before the cessation of the present European War as shall be fixed by the [new] Executive Committee [of 140]."[306]

Here was a genuine compromise and, with both camps exhausted, it was expected to receive rapid endorsement. On 10 August the Jewish Congress executive committee did vote it through "with only three negative votes."[307] It was now submitted for approval by postal vote to all the delegates to the Philadelphia pre-conference, a move regarded at first as a pure formality.

But, this time, it was the Poale Zion which balked. It issued a manifesto, "To the Jewish People in America," which in strongly emotional terms called for the outright rejection of the proposed settlement as "illegal" – "it reduces to nothing all the work done in Philadelphia." "The Jewish Congress must be only free and democratic. The Jewish Congress must be only a national congress."[308] In order to lead the public campaign against the settlement, a Jewish Congress League, with David Ben Gurion as secretary, was established.

On the face of it, the step taken by the Poale Zion was extraordinary. After all, the party had consistently urged compromise ever since the National Workmen's

Convention of September 1915. What prompted this sudden rebellion, however, was probably not so much the terms of the agreement itself as the dawning realization that the labor movement had been consistently shunted to the sidelines ever since the Philadelphia pre-conference. Noncitizens had there been excluded from the executive committee and in July not one socialist had been included in the subcommittee that had negotiated the peace pact. On the other side of the fence, the "orthodox" socialists had been poorly represented at the Astor Hotel conference (where they had had only twenty-six delegates out of a total of eighty-nine).

If the socialists had been able to consolidate the united front of September 1915, they could no doubt have maintained themselves as a powerful political force in American Jewish life, the most imposing voice from within the immigrant world. But, divided, they could sustain neither credibility nor popular interest, and their influence inevitably declined. The peace pact of August 1916 was in fact a settlement between the Zionist leadership (effectively without Brandeis) and the German-Jewish establishment. The socialists found themselves left with a mere supporting role, and this they proved unwilling to accept without protest.

In the referendum, the Poale Zion won a partial victory. The clause on the restricted competence of the Congress was rejected by 127 votes to 119, and that on the selection of delegates by 129 votes to 113. The Jewish Congress League triumphantly called on the Congress executive to "begin at once to prepare the direct arrangements for the Congress and to organize the elections."[309] In *Di naye velt*, Zivion now wrote an obituary on the entire Jewish Congress, blaming its demise on the Poale Zion, who throughout "took it upon themselves to be the pacemakers in the Jewish street, to dictate their will to parties and groups incomparably greater and stronger and more influential than themselves ... The more they wailed and shouted about the Congress, the more impossible they made it."[310]

But, in reality, power by this stage was no longer with the socialists. Jacob De Haas, on the one hand, and Louis Marshall, on the other, now had the reins firmly in hand. They had decided that there would be a compromise and a compromise there was. The original agreement was amended in response to the referendum. The agenda was broadened to include (if so desired) "economic reconstruction" (for postwar European Jewry). The controversial term, "group rights," was dropped, although it was replaced not by "national rights," but by a reference to the rights of "peoples" (including those of "the Jewish people"). Finally, it was agreed that 75 percent of the delegates to the Congress would be elected on the basis of one man, one vote.[311]

That this amended proposal would be endorsed in a new referendum was a foregone conclusion. Even the Poale Zion had decided that this was the end of the road and put up no further resistance. The new pact, declared Zuckerman (putting the best face on the fait accompli), meant that on the essential issues, "beyond doubt, we have won."[312] Salutsky's judgment was probably the more accurate, though. "The agreement now reached," he wrote, "means in practice that the Congress movement has renounced its essence, its basic objective for a momentary goal, for a by-product."[313]

As the détente between the American Jewish Committee and the general Zionist leadership cemented itself, it induced a growing sense of alienation among the socialists. Anger and suspicion developed now on the nationalist wing of the labor movement, among the Poale Zion, now on the "internationalist" wing, in the National Workmen's Committee.

Thus, at the conference called to put the final seal of approval on the peace treaty, it was the turn of the "internationalists" to feel the sharp pinch of the new realities. On 25 December 1916, the Philadelphia and Astor Hotel executives met at the Savoy Hotel in New York. Of the one hundred and forty members of the newly combined executive committee, only fourteen represented "orthodox" labor, a percentage denounced by *Di naye velt* as "a crying injustice."[314] As Borochov put it bitingly: "Although it [the NWC] was responsible for the success of the American Jewish Committee, still the latter does not have too much time for gratitude."[315]

But worse was to come when the nominees for the administrative committee were announced at the conference by the appropriate subcommittee – of thirty-five proposed members only four were from the camp of "internationalist" socialism. In retaliation, these four, among whom were two important union leaders, Ben Schlesinger and Joseph Schlossberg, refused the proffered membership. As Shakhne Epstein described the situation: "After almost two years . . . peace was achieved and at the last moment the two sides with the blessing of Poale Zion betrayed the National Workmen's Committee."[316]

Tempers reached boiling point when Syrkin launched a bitter attack on the Left, describing them as "false prophets" and "not Jews at all."[317] It was only with the greatest effort that Magnes managed to cool tempers somewhat and prevent a walkout. In the end, the subcommittee drew up a new proposal that provided the "orthodox" socialists with eleven of the fifty-five members on the administrative committee. The Poale Zion representation went up from three to five.

So now, at last, peace appeared to have been made. "The National Workmen's Committee," declared the *Forverts*, "won its victory in a civilized and just way."[318] Similarly, *Fortshrit* (the journal of the Amalgamated Clothing Workers) praised "a meeting in which were united all classes and strata of American Jewry, labor and capital, orthodox and nonorthodox."[319]

"You are doubtless aware," wrote Magnes to Norman Bentwich at this juncture,

> that all parties in American Jewry have come to an understanding as to a Jewish Congress . . . It can help us in creating public opinion in America and in influencing the statesmen and peoples of Europe . . . It will be declared out of order if any . . . organization presents for voting a party platform. This was one of the quarrels I had with the Zionist organization here . . . They desired to commit American Jewry by majority vote to the Zionist platform . . . [It] is questionable if they could have secured a majority . . . [and] even if they could it is not by a majority vote that Jewry are committed to Zionism . . . The Palestine question will of course receive special consideration . . . I am glad that everything seems hopeful for a real American Congress.[320]

However, even the modest settlement achieved in December 1916 was by no means as final as it then seemed and it did not stand up well in the coming storms. It had been assumed that the Congress would finally assemble early in 1917. But it was not until March that the electoral system – broadly similar to that used in the elections to the U.S. House of Representatives – was formally adopted by the Jewish Congress administrative committee, and the date then chosen for the elections was 10 June 1917.

In turn, this delay of almost half a year produced second thoughts in the National Workmen's Committee. It failed to exploit the interval in order to ensure success in the elections, but on the contrary entangled itself in a web of inner conflict and confusion.

On 11 February 1917, it called together the second National Workmen's Convention, partly in order to lay the groundwork for the elections. In reality, though, the convention became a battle ground, pitting the veteran leadership of the labor movement against the Bundists of the post-1905 immigration grouped in the Jewish Socialist Federation. This long-standing division had been submerged since 1915 by a common hostility to the pro-Congress forces and by a common fear of a Zionist coup. But, now, with the Congress issue apparently settled, it erupted with a new ferocity.

The leaders of the Jewish Socialist Federation – Litvak, Goldfarb, Salutsky, Olgin, Epstein – ill-advisedly took the opportunity to propose that the National Workmen's Committee be converted from a temporary, ad hoc, one-issue body into "a permanent, organic union of all those Jewish organizations that stand for the class struggle in all its forms."[321]

In so doing, they were of course reasserting a long-standing ambition. They were seeking to unite the mass of fragmented and sovereign organizations known loosely as the American-Jewish labor movement – trade unions, publishing associations, the Arbeter Ring – under one political and ideological roof. The fact that the Poale Zion had walked out of the National Workmen's Committee in 1916 seemed to provide an ideal opportunity to translate the nominally Marxist and class-war commitment of the movement into institutional forms, into political power.

This had always been the goal of the Bundist activists in America and had always been feared by the pre-1905 leadership. The sudden revival of the idea now, however, simply served to disrupt the convention. The veteran president of the United Hebrew Trades, Max Pine, adamantly refused to accept the proposal to perpetuate the National Workmen's Committee, and he led a walkout of dozens of delegates when the proposal, albeit only in principle, was put to the vote.

The disarray increased in the aftermath of the convention. *Di naye velt* published a scathing attack on the labor establishment by Shakhne Epstein, who compared "two trends . . . one the obsolete trend that is afraid of every new wind, of every new reform, because they could – heaven forbid – tear the rudder of power from its hands; and the other, the trend that seeks ever new ways . . . Comrade Goldfarb was right when he said that we are ready to measure forces . . . Those who do not reckon with the 'spirit' of the times must leave the stage, that is the law of life."[322] But the leaders of the Jewish Socialist Federation had severely miscalculated. Their two-year leadership of the National Workmen's Committee had been made possible not by any radical change in the balance of power, but by the reluctance of the veteran generation to involve itself in the exhausting, complex tangle of Jewish politics. Lesin now came to the defense of "Max Pine [and his like] who with twenty-five years of work have formed the movement and its very great newspapers for these same 'youngsters' just off the ship and have given them every opportunity to feel so much at ease in America."[323] And Borochov noted with satisfaction the discomfiture of the Jewish Socialist Federation, suggesting acidly that "they parade before us in the name of the unions; and before the unions in the name of national politics."[324]

The United Hebrew Trades and the Arbeter Ring both assembled their executives to vote against perpetuation of the National Workmen's Committee. The coup de grace was delivered when the *Forverts* Association, after some delay, did likewise. As Zivion now put it: "When the *Forverts* so wishes, it acts as though [the JSF] does not even exist."[325] The second, the Bundist, generation had in fact failed in its boldest bid to establish a new political order in the American-Jewish labor movement.

Precious time had meanwhile been lost in preparing for the Congress elections. Caught up in its internal divisions, the leadership of the National Workmen's Committee had even failed to bring its weight to bear in the choice of the electoral system. Isaac H. Hourwich had fought for some form of proportional representation that would ensure minority groups their fair share of delegates. But when the crucial vote was taken in the Jewish Congress administrative committee on 11 March, few members of the "orthodox" labor movement were present. Among those missing were Olgin, Morris Hillquit, Meyer London, Sholem Asch, Benjamin Schlesinger, and Joseph Schlossberg. Their votes could have ensured the adoption of a system far more favorable to socialist interests.

The nominating conventions, at which candidates had to be confirmed, were due to be held as early as 10 May. On 27 April *Di naye velt* was still urging its readers to organize themselves, however belatedly, for the election campaign. "True," it argued, "the electoral system is not sufficiently democratic to guarantee labor a proportionally just representation, but what is possible must be achieved."[326] But then on 8 May 1917 – at the very last minute – the National Workmen's Committee met and voted to call on all its affiliated organizations, on the entire labor movement, to boycott the elections to the American Jewish Congress.

In justification of this extraordinary step, *Di naye velt* advanced two major arguments. First, the electoral system would not be sufficiently representative: "In practice, it is anti-democratic throughout."[327] Second, the February Revolution in Russia rendered the entire concept of the Congress obsolete. Its only justification had been the exertion of political pressure on the tsarist regime and, with Russia a democracy, it had lost its one raison d'être. The Palestine issue would now take first place. But, asked *Di naye velt*, "Why should we take a Zionist Congress and make it look like a People's Congress?"[328]

The February Revolution certainly produced a wave of genuine enthusiasm in the immigrant world. Hundreds of socialists returned to Russia. Among the first to leave were Goldfarb and Litvak. Borochov had even opposed momentarily the calling of a nationalist socialist convention in February 1917 to prepare for the Jewish Congress elections, lest it detract "from the greatness and holiness of the new revolution in Russia."[329] He himself left for Russia in the summer of 1917, as did Rutenberg. (Zhitlovsky, too, sought to go back, but he failed to raise the necessary funds.)

Thus, if the National Workmen's Committee had called for the boycott in March or April, its case could have had the power of consistency. But coming so late in the day, its decision was inevitably interpreted as a sign of weakness, as fear

Figure 43. FROM HEART TO HEART. "Da zdrastvuet svobodnaia Rossiia!" ("Long live free Russia!")
(The "refugee" in America greets "Russian Freedom." 23 March 1917.)

of electoral defeat. By walking out at the eleventh hour, it laid itself open to ridicule.

"If one considers," wrote Zuckerman, for example, "that in the opinion of the NWC it represents half a million organized workers, then it had the possibility of electing *all* three hundred delegates."[330] But perhaps the most scathing criticism came in *Di naye velt* itself. M. Tsipin (who was soon to return to Russia) there pointed out that much of East European Jewry was still in grave danger and that even in Russia itself the future was cloudy: "Nicholas provoked pogroms; but the pogroms were made by the Russian people." As for the electoral system, there had been ample time to amend it in the administrative committee, but "one does not protest against this sort of thing so late . . . The impression remains – once good and honorable leaders led, but what can one expect any more from the machine people! . . . Terrified by the specter of Palestine, you began to plan how to be rid of the entire matter. But it was too late. The masses have spoken too much about the Congress."[331]

When taking its decision, the National Workmen's Committee had undoubtedly assumed that the elections would prove anticlimactic. The triumphant Russian revolution and the entry of the United States into the war had totally captured the newspaper headlines. Anxiously, the public waited for governmental decisions on a military draft. Even the most ardent supporters of the Jewish Congress felt that the elections were coming at the worst possible moment.

But, in reality, the elections, well-publicized by advertisements in the press, proved to be remarkably successful. True, worker participation was relatively limited. One observer in *Der yidisher kemfer* admitted openly that "the great labor masses *do* let themselves be led by the National Workmen's Committee; . . . the greatest percent of the workers did *not* take part in the Congress elections."[332]

All in all, though, over 300,000 people went to the polls. In New York 125,000 voted; in Philadelphia, 25,000. "We underestimated our forces," wrote Yoel Entin on *Di varhayt:*

> As soon as the Sabbath was over [on 9 June], large groups of Jews thronged around the voting place . . . There were many old people, Jews with beards, women in wigs and shawls . . . There were socialists, young and old, union people, and Arbeter Ring Jews . . . There were American Jewish girls who – judging by their manners and behavior – think, one could imagine, of nothing but enjoying themselves and dancing.[333]

Of the one hundred delegates elected in New York, thirty-one had run on the nationalist-socialist ticket, among them, Pinsky, Syrkin, and Zuckerman. "What remains," Zuckerman now asked scornfully, "of the assertion of the National Workmen's Committee that the workers had no possibility of electing their candidates?"[334] It was his estimate that 75,000 workers had taken part in the elections in Greater New York.

For the National Workmen's Committee, the result was of course a disaster. Having done so much in 1916 to make the elections possible, it had now thrown away in one false move all the credit that it had accumulated. "Let us speak frankly," wrote Zivion. "Can one imagine confusion more confounded than that displayed by the leaders of the Jewish Socialist Federation in the Congress question? They tie themselves up in their own confusion."[335]

This moment of triumph for the Poale Zion, however, proved to be short-lived. The American Jewish Congress, which logically should have met shortly after the elections, was in fact constantly postponed. The date was shifted by the administration committee from 17 June to 2 September and then, again, to 18 November. Finally, at a plenary meeting of the committee of 140 on 14 October, it was decided by 73 to 31 votes to postpone the Congress until after the war.

A clear voting pattern emerged in these committee meetings. The Zionist leadership (with a few notable exceptions) joined with the leaders of the American Jewish Committee in order to defeat the Poale Zion and other nationalist socialists who demanded the immediate assembly of the Congress. Stephen Wise, Julian Mack, and Nathan Straus united on this issue with Marshall, Schiff, and Morgenthau. Of the well-known general Zionist figures, only Lipsky and Magnes consistently voted with the socialists.

That the American Jewish Committee urged the postponement of the Congress was, of course, readily understandable. Marshall had always considered it preferable that the Congress come at the end of the war. And now that the United States was itself involved in the hostilities, he was doubly convinced. It was his view that American Jewry had now to devote itself solely and single-mindedly to the war effort. He was appalled by the fact that the Jewish labor movement in New York – including not only the Jewish Socialist Federation but also the Poale Zion and the United Hebrew Trades – was overwhelmingly associated with the antiwar organization, the People's Council of America for Democracy and Peace.[336] (Syrkin had to resign from the Poale Zion central committee because of his vehemently pro-Allied stance and his view of the struggle as a "revolutionary war.")

All that could now be done, Marshall felt, was to prove beyond all doubt that the majority of Jews, at least, were unwavering patriots ready to set aside all sectional interests for the duration of the war. A Jewish Congress was the last thing required. As for Magnes, the fact that he had stepped forth as a leader of the peace movement totally disqualified him in his traditional role of mediator between the Downtown and Uptown Jews. Typical was Marshall's comment on the mayoral elections of November 1917: "Every vote for Hillquit is a vote for the Kaiser, for ... autocracy ... and militarism ..., for the obliteration of small nationalities ... The American people will be rightly outraged against those who have shown themselves the enemies of our liberty and democracy."[337]

The motivation of the general Zionists was more complex. The Zionist camp had won a decisive victory in the Jewish Congress elections and, with the religious Zionists (the Mizrachi) and the Poale Zion included, could confidently expect to dominate the Congress. Why, then, did the leadership agree to its indefinite postponement?

First, there was the financial aspect. The Zionist organization had invested much money to make the Congress elections possible. The Congress itself would likewise involve heavy expenditure. "The question that will arise," wrote De Haas to Brandeis as early as May, "will be whether or not we will spend $20,000 necessary to run the Congress from our side, with the whole situation in our hands."[338] Perhaps the Zionist movement should rest on its laurels, confident that it had been immensely strengthened by its election victory.

Second, since the entry of the United States into the war, the Zionist leaders – most notably Brandeis and Wise – had been involved in the highly confidential negotiations which in November 1917 were to culminate in the publication of the Balfour Declaration. Brandeis met a number of times with Mr. Balfour when he visited Washington in April 1917, and he followed up these talks in subsequent meetings with Woodrow Wilson. The American Zionists transmitted funds to Weizmann to help sustain the organizational effort in England.

Weizmann, who was seeking a pro-Zionist British protectorate in Palestine, could count on the support of Brandeis and the other leading American Zionists.[339] In radical and Poale Zion circles, however, the tendency was to advocate a Jewish republic in Palestine under joint Great Power guarantees. To call together the Jewish Congress under such circumstances was to risk publicizing profound internal disagreements not only within the Jewish world as a whole but even within the Zionist movement.

Finally, there was yet another consideration. The Allied governments were negotiating on the Palestine question directly with the Zionists in Britain and America. As it turned out, the Balfour Declaration was addressed to Lord Rothschild, as the most prominent of British Zionists. If the Jewish Congress were to meet, a clash of authority could well result. Not the Zionist movement but the Congress executive would become the natural spokesman for American Jewry. Perhaps, after all, Magnes had been right in 1915 when he called for a division of labor between the American Jewish Committee and the Zionist movement, with the latter devoting its efforts all but exclusively to the Palestine cause.

The public commitment of the Zionist movement to the idea of a Congress as the standing, representative, and sovereign body of American Jewry had been so total that its change of front was hard to explain and downright embarrassing. Indeed, whenever possible, the Zionist leadership let the American Jewish Committee take the lead in calling for the postponement of the Congress. But it could not conceal the fundamental change of front for long, nor could it escape the inevitable criticism from many of its most committed supporters.[340]

Above all, in the Poale Zion party, the sense of betrayal aroused real bitterness. They fought hard against every vote in favor of postponement, but could not muster the necessary support in the relevant committees. From that point of view, the departure of the National Workmen's Committee from the Congress organization in May proved disastrous for the Poale Zion, which lost thereby a potential ally against the now dominant coalition.

They toyed with the idea of calling together the Congress without, indeed against, the majority in the executive committee. But, bereft of allies, the nationalist socialist bloc was too weak to initiate such a revolution. All it could do was to protest and this it did vigorously. Entin, describing the meeting of 7 July 1917, when the Congress was again postponed, wrote that

> Rabbi Wise . . . gave the *polkovnik* Cutler [of the AJC] the wink . . . The Zionist machine had power firmly in its hands . . .[341] If anyone still doubted that the Zionists want to kill off the Congress, abort it, he can no longer have any doubts. Our way is clear, a fight, a bitter fight . . . All the power that we previously turned against the *yahudim* and the *genosn* must now be directed against them.[342]

"We accuse the Zionist leaders," wrote Zuckerman, "of wanting a monopoly on Palestine . . . They are afraid of the elected representatives of the people, because the people could take out of their hands the sole responsibility for Palestine."[343]

However, following the Balfour Declaration, dissenting voices made themselves heard within the ranks of the Poale Zion. David Ben Gurion, above all, now demanded a complete revision of the long-standing commitment to the American Jewish Congress. The time had come, he argued, to cut the party's losses. Not an American, nor even a world, Jewish Congress, but the World Zionist Organization would represent Jewish national interests in Palestine. That was a fait accompli, and Poale Zion should seek to work within that framework. "The first thing," he wrote,

> that we must throw out—because it is small, everyday, typical of Exile—is the old, servile Congress, the Congress born in impotence and shame, which ... erased the word "nation" and renounced the proud hope of a Jewish Palestine ... We are marching back into our own land ...[344] Our historic task ... is to devote all forces to the *exclusive* goal of mobilizing Jewish labor for Palestine ... and in Palestine ...[345] The Zionist Congress will now become ... the preparatory parliament of the future Jewish home in Palestine ... [There, Jewish labor must try] to force the entire Zionist Organization to build the Jewish home on those social foundations that alone can guarantee the national and democratic character of the Jewish country.[346]

The majority in Poale Zion rejected Ben Gurion's position out of hand. They remained loyal to the concept of an American Jewish Congress. *Der yidisher kemfer* (of which Pinsky was then the editor) accused him of inconsistency: "Can Ben Gurion deny that he rejoiced at the outcome of the Congress elections?"[347]

But Ben Gurion had simply recognized that the defeat was irreversible. The Congress was not going to be the dominant force in American Jewish life nor the cornerstone of a world Jewish congress. The decision he now took to return to Palestine with the Allied forces, as a soldier in the Jewish Legion, followed logically from his view that the Balfour Declaration marked the opening of a totally new epoch.

The American Jewish Congress did finally assemble almost immediately after the end of World War I, as Louis Marshall had always hoped that it would. But even at this late stage, there was a startling turn of events. In a last-minute flurry of controversy and confusion, the National Workmen's Committee overrode its boycott of May 1917 and negotiated the terms of its participation in the Congress.

This volte-face was executed in kaleidoscopic haste. In late October 1918, the Jewish Socialist Federation sent a letter to many of the labor leaders calling for the revival of the National Workmen's Committee, which had been out of action since mid-1917. On the assumption that the American Jewish Congress would never meet, the letter expected the National Workmen's Committee to "approach all the recognized Jewish organizations without differentiation of ideology ... and together with them [to] convene a competent and effective Jewish forum which shall transmit the will and hopes of the great masses of the Jewish people to the peace negotiations."[348]

Early in November, the National Workmen's Committee was in fact reconstituted, and at its first meeting it decided to convene a labor conference in New York. But, by the time the conference met on 17 November, it had become apparent that there was a strong movement afoot to convene the American Jewish Congress immediately and that the only choice left was either to perpetuate the boycott or else to negotiate entry into the Congress as elected in June 1917.

Two prominent socialists, J. Panken and J. Baskin, argued vehemently against a return to the Congress. It could well turn into an anti-Soviet demonstration and in any case, represented the hostile classes. ("We have nothing to do in common with the bourgeoisie.")[349] "In the entire world," said Panken, "a social revolution is coming and we are expected to go together with the reactionary, Jewish bourgeoisie."[350]

However, most of the leaders – Schlossberg, Pine, and Zivion, as to be expected, but also Salutsky and Olgin – spoke in favor of entry into the Congress. It could serve, argued Salutsky, as an effective platform for the socialists. They would be in a minority and could act as an opposition without responsibility for the decisions taken: "If I had the chance of having majority . . . in all likelihood I would not go at all . . . I am afraid to have a majority . . . Of all the possible and thinkable parliaments, the Jewish Congress will be incomparably the most impossible and unthinkable – a parliament without power, without a treasury, and therefore without significant influence."[351] Again, Salutsky noted that the situation in Russia and eastern Europe had changed beyond recognition since mid-1917. The Jews there were now faced by the proliferation of small national states and chronic civil war. Insofar as the American Jewish Congress could intervene, however marginally, on their behalf at the Peace Conference, it deserved socialist support.

To a great extent, though, the turn about made by Olgin and Salutsky reflected the weakness of the Jewish Socialist Federation at this stage. Eroded by the return of many of its members to Russia; humiliated by its attempt to perpetuate the National Workmen's Committee in 1917; divided on the Palestine and anti-war issues; perplexed by the Bolshevik takeover in Russia and division in the world Social Democratic movement, it was simply not strong enough to exclude itself from the American Jewish Congress. The majority of the 774 delegates at the labor conference voted, often with undisguised reluctance, in favor of participation (191 delegates voted against).

Now it proved well-nigh impossible to agree on what terms the prodigal son should be permitted to return. A delegation from the National Workmen's Committee appeared before the Jewish Congress administrative committee on 26 November and proposed that it be allowed to nominate 100 delegates, raising the total from 400 to 500. The Poale Zion, who had been smarting under the Zionist yoke for over a year, were (together with Magnes and Schiff) ready to accept some such proposal – perhaps 60 delegates.

The Zionist leadership, though, would have none of it. The National Workmen's Committee and its affiliated organizations, as nationwide Jewish bodies, were entitled to a total of 14 delegates. No more should be allowed. "I do not believe in their sincerity," said Judge Aaron J. Levy. "I think that they are playing a political game, executing political manoeuvers. They realize that the Congress will be held, they see that the Jewish popular masses are for Palestine; they see that all who stand aside will be regarded as traitors to the Jewish people, and so they have come here."[352] In a letter to Brandeis, De Haas described what had happened. "The critical incident," he wrote, was the attempt of the Forward group to get back into the Congress with one hundred delegates. We stood on the legality of the Constitution and offered to reseat them on the basis of what they were originally allotted and no other. This they will probably refuse. I saw in the whole scheme (which was supported by Mr. Schiff and the Poale Zion and Magnes) a trick to get control of the Congress thru the Bolshevik element . . . This was defeated.[353]

The delegation from the National Workmen's Committee was shocked to find the door thus shut firmly in its face. "In the decades of my public work," wrote Schlossberg, "I have never suffered such bitter insults as on that evening of 26 November . . . [It will now be] a bourgeois, Zionist Congress."[354] "Those who spoke to us," declared Olgin in the *Forverts* on 2 December,

> were not men and citizens . . . but Tammany slaves who are afraid of honest competition . . . ; bourgeois party politicians who need the Jewish Congress to show their gentile party comrades that they are a power among the Jews; . . . aristocratic reactionaries . . . who wondered how the workers dare interfere in community affairs; . . . self-satisfied *alrightniks* who will come to the Congress as a picnic and are afraid that the workers will make trouble . . . ; people from the bourgeois Yiddish press who saw in us . . . competition from the *Forverts* . . . ; orthodox rabbis and reform ministers who are afraid lest our educational work among the poor and oppressed bring a little light into their minds; . . . Zionist chatterboxes and chinovniki [bureaucrats] . . . in short, the Jewish bourgeoisie in all its glory.[355]

It was widely assumed that "orthodox" labor would hold a rival convention to coincide with that of the "bourgeoisie" as it had done at the time of the Philadelphia pre-conference in March 1916. But, on both sides, there were now many determined to force through an agreement. The last-minute formula proposed to bridge the gulf was that the National Workmen's Committee, over and above its fourteen places, be assigned all the seats that had fallen vacant (due to death, ill health or travel abroad). This would bring their number up to twenty.

On 7 December Joseph Barondess came in person to a meeting of the National Workmen's Committee in order to urge that it adopt this proposal. He was strongly supported by Schlossberg and Rozenblat, opposed by Panken and Schlesinger. The voices of compromise carried the day. As summarized in the *Forverts,* the position of Schlossberg and Rozenblat was that "the main thing, after all, is the demonstration that the Congress can make at the moment and if the participation of Jewish labor in a Jewish Congress can make that demonstration stronger, then let us take part."[356]

At 2:30 P.M. on 15 December 1918, the American Jewish Congress was called to order by Colonel Cutler. The opening session was in the opera house in Philadelphia. Five thousand people were seated inside and some ten thousand milled around outside. The Jewish neighborhood was hung with banners, and the blue and white flag of the Jewish national movement was raised over Independence Hall.

On the day, the *Forverts* carried two major articles on the Congress. The editorial expressed muted support:

Figure 44. AN EMBARRASSING SITUATION FOR THE LADY. American Jewry: "Hurry, hurry. Do me up, Mister. I have to get to Philadelphia!" *(The man, "Poale Zion," is struggling to hook the lady, "American Jewry," into her "Congress dress." The two parts of the dress are labeled "Labor" and "the general Jewish community." 6 December 1918.)*

We do not believe that the impression should be formed by anyone that the Jewish people has anything real to expect from the Congress . . . But [if it] can do something, if the great Jewish demonstration for rights and equality and for the national existence of the Jewish people will have any impact, the Jewish labor movement will have played its part in the results attained.[357]

In contrast, Sholem Asch struck a note of high emotion:

You are coming together, you Jews . . . When Abraham . . . recognized the one God . . . you were all in him! You were all together on the night of the exodus from Egypt. You were all together at Mount Sinai. And the last time you were together was on the walls of Jerusalem fighting the enemy. And now, after thousands of years, you are again coming together, you Jews in a land of which our ancestors had never heard and knew nothing.[358]

Faithfully reflected in these two articles was the inner tension which had characterized the *Forverts* at every such moment since the Dreyfus Affair.

The National Workmen's Committee did not, in fact, send the twenty delegates to which it was entitled to the Congress. Only a symbolic delegation of nine arrived. Reporting on the first day of the Congress, Zivion wrote in the *Forverts* that the "labor group feels very outside things, like strangers at a wedding."[359] Or, as *Der tog* put it, they acted "like spies come to spy out a foreign land."[360] But the powers-that-be (anxious, no doubt, to avoid yet another walkout) did everything they could to involve the minuscule delegation in the workings of the Congress, and Zivion was soon reporting that "we have almost more posts of honor than we have delegates."[361]

It was the nationalist socialist wing of the labor movement, led by Zhitlovsky, Zuckerman, and Syrkin, that made itself highly conspicuous at the Congress. They proposed a praesidium rather than a president; put up their own candidate for president (Yehoash, the poet) against Judge Julian Mack; and with their bloc vote of seventy played the role of a loyal but noisy opposition.

Zhitlovsky took it upon himself to state the general ideological standpoint of the nationalist socialist caucus. He proclaimed "the fundamental principle of the separation between state and religion" and called for "a clear-cut separation of the Jewish religious conception from the Jewish national idea."[362] His speech worked the Mizrachi into a fury for they saw in it an attempt to replace religion by nationality as the basis of Judaism. All the "gray beards," as one report put it, jumped to their feet proclaiming "The faith! The faith! (*"Di emune! Di emune!"*)[363] Zhitlovsky was forced to stop talking and in the end the police had to intervene to restore order.

"For the first time in Jewish history . . . ," wrote Yoel Entin, "at a major Jewish assembly, there came a declaration that we Jews are a nation, very simply a nation, whether we are a religion or not a religion. Here, . . . for the first time, was the secularization of Jewishness [*yidishkayt*]."[364] Sholem Asch, writing in the *Forverts*, described how watching Zhitlovsky talk, "my fantasy conjured up before me a Jewish country where all the Jews were gathered to work out the constitution for the Jewish people. Imagine Dr. Zhitlovsky—an Uriel da Costa—standing on the platform, pale, with wild eyes, one hand stretched up in the air, the other holding

Figure 45. Dr. Zhitlovsky as Uriel da Costa the Second *(20 December 1918).*

the document on which is written the new Torah . . . : 'The Jews are not a religious sect, but a nation' "[365]

Zhitlovsky would later declare that to the extent that there was a "Zionist machine" at the Congress, it was put out of action by energetic harassment from the nationalist socialist caucus.[366] This, however, was a gross exaggeration. The Congress was dominated throughout by the same alliance of the Zionist leadership and the AJC that had controlled events since late in 1916. Jacob De Haas was accurate when he telegraphed to Brandeis on 16 December that "the session ended last night in [a] scrap between Mizrachi and Poale Zion. Coalition [between them, against us] therefore practically broken."[367]

It was only when the dominant alliance was internally divided that the socialists were able to bring their weight to bear. Then, in the closed committee meetings, where the resolutions had to be hammered out, there were true contests of will and ideology. In all probability, the Zionists had the strength, unaided, to drive their opinion through the Congress, but the wish for unanimity was so great that some committees worked all night in search of compromise.

The resolution on Palestine, reported out of committee unanimously on 17 December, called for a British trusteeship in Palestine that was to be developed as a Jewish national home. Compared with the Savoy Hotel agreement, which had spoken only of the "securing and protection of Jewish rights in Palestine," this statement represented a radical shift in the official position of the American Jewish Committee and, to the extent that its representatives did not publicly dissent, of the National Workmen's Committee, too. Read out by Israel Friedlaender, the resolution was greeted with extraordinary enthusiasm. At one point, Nathan Straus, the leading philanthropist and Zionist, appeared on the platform, shouting over the tumult: "The Jewish people lives!"[368] Suddenly, everybody, it seemed, was singing "Ha-tikva."

Not until the last day of the Congress was a resolution worked out that endorsed "national rights" for Polish and East European Jewry. Louis Marshall had fought "tooth and nail"[369] to maintain the exclusion of this term. Among those who did battle with him in committee were Hourwich, Zhitlovsky, and Zuckerman. The *Forverts* declared the result "a victory, a great victory, for the supporters of national rights."[370] Marshall read out the resolution to the Congress, a dramatic gesture that again produced a wave of excitement among the delegates.

Other significant decisions attracted less public attention. The nationalist socialist bloc slipped through a resolution in favor of a world Jewish congress – despite the wishes apparently of De Haas. As against this, the dominant coalition (the Zionists and the AJC) successfully headed off all moves to make the American Jewish Congress a permanent institution.

The composition of the delegation to be sent to the Paris peace talks was also decided behind the scenes, although De Haas and Marshall were careful to produce a politically representative group. (Only the large Orders were left without a place in the delegation). Ten men were chosen to go to Paris on behalf of the American Jewish Congress: Julian Mack, Stephen Wise, Jacob De Haas, Bernard G. Richards, and Joseph Barondess (all Zionists); Louis Marshall and Colonel Cutler (of the American Jewish Committee); B. L. Levinthal (a rabbi); Nachman Syrkin (from the nationalist socialist bloc); and Morris Vinchevsky (the delegate of the Jewish Socialist Federation).

Vinchevsky accepted his place in the delegation to Paris without prior consultation with the leaders of the Jewish Socialist Federation, who had sent him to Philadelphia in the erroneous expectation that he would fulfill a symbolic rather than a political function. Olgin, Salutsky, and many others in the camp of "orthodox" labor were infuriated by Vinchevsky's insistence on going to Paris as well as by the speeches that Max Pine and he made at the final session of the Congress. Vinchevsky there declared that "Palestine no longer has any opponents in the socialist camp" and that he hoped to die as a socialist but in "our own land."[371]

Di naye velt accused him of "a breach of trust" and "hysterical ultra-Zionism."[372] Angered by these and subsequent attacks and by the persistent anti-Zionism of a majority in the Jewish Socialist Federation, Max Pine again led the

United Hebrew Trades out of the National Workmen's Committee in February 1919, thus dealing that organization a final death blow.

Writing from London, Vinchevsky published a rejoinder in *Di tsukunft* in which he defended himself against the accusations of his comrades. Despite "Marxism, Vilna-style," he wrote, he would continue to work in order that "those principles for which we have fought all our lives shall triumph in our homeland, too."[373]

Vinchevsky and Syrkin were already in Europe when the delegation met, on behalf of the American Jewish Congress, with President Wilson in Washington in March 1919 (only Mack, Marshall, Wise, and Richards went). But the two men actively lobbied European socialists and labor leaders on behalf of the Congress program, which to a large extent was written into the various postwar treaties and agreements. The treaty with Poland, in particular, was seen as a diplomatic triumph. Marshall described it as "literally a charter of liberty, and the final act of emancipation of those who for centuries have been bereft of elemental human rights."[374]

On 30 May 1920 the American Jewish Congress was called back into session to hear the report of its delegation to the peace talks. It voted approval of what had been done in its name and dispersed "sine die."[375]

Conclusion

Politics were the hub of the Jewish labor movement in the Pale. But, in America, politics were at best a seasonal phenomenon attracting public attention once a year at the time of the November elections. Only a major crisis threatening the Jews overseas—primarily, of course, in Russia—was capable of arousing mass involvement in Jewish politics. The central theme of such politics in Russia became self-liberation. But in America, Jewish politics were the politics of "philanthropy," or perhaps of self-liberation at many thousands of miles' remove.

What resulted, of course, was paradoxical. The Jewish labor movement in America was predominantly "internationalist" in its official ideology. But, at times of emergency, the normal balance of forces was reversed and the more nationalist wing could go over to the offensive. Thus, in 1898, it was the *Forverts* that demonstrated the greater self-confidence while *Dos abend-blat* was hard put to defend itself. The same pattern recurred in 1903 when the *Forverts* clashed with *The Worker* (and less violently with *Di tsukunft*).

In the years 1905–6, it was the Zionist-Territorialist bloc that benefited from this trend. The Bundist organization in America was hard pressed to withstand the demands for unity and was fortunate to gain the eventual backing of the *Forverts* against what it dismissed as the politics of "class peace." The goal that the Bundist leaders in America set themselves was to unite not the Jewish people but the Jewish proletariat, to place a strong political roof over the loosely-knit socioeconomic conglomeration known as the American-Jewish labor movement.

The mass enthusiasm engendered by momentary crisis tends to be short-lived. It was not sufficiently sustained either in 1903 or in 1905–6 to produce those representative institutions then widely held to be the necessary precondition for political unity. At the level of establishment (or "German"-Jewish) politics, the B'nai B'rith led the resistance to democratization, and the American Jewish Committee was created in 1906 as a merely self-appointed institution. Again, the Bund refused to join the Jewish Defense Association (initiated by Magnes and Zhitlovsky), which was left with the mourning march of 4 December 1905 as its single greatest achievement. In turn, the Bundist projects for proletarian unity (in effect, an American version of the Bund) were cut down to size by the *Forverts* – the Jewish Agitation Bureau (established in 1907) and even the Jewish Socialist Federation (which replaced it in 1912) languished as peripheral organizations until 1914.

However, with the outbreak of World War I, with the catastrophic expulsions in the Eastern War Zone, new and highly dramatic variations were played on the now familiar theme of unity and democratization. The campaign for a representative and permanent American Jewish Congress was taken up by the Zionist movement under the leadership of Brandeis. In the labor world, it was conducted by an alliance of nationalist socialists grouped around the Poale Zion party, which was headed by an effective group of immigrant leaders, among them Zhitlovsky, Syrkin, and Borochov.

The powers-that-be – the American Jewish Committee at the "bourgeois," the *Forverts*-Bundists bloc at the proletarian, level – doggedly resisted. But, under pressure, they shifted ground, agreeing to an American Jewish Congress as an ad hoc body to deal with the immediate problems of war and peace. On this basis, an unprecedented display of unity was achieved at the National Workmen's Convention, which in September 1915 brought together on a common platform the Zionist-Territorialist wing of the labor movement and the *Forverts*-Bundist alliance.

It was on this basis, too, that the American Jewish Congress in fact met in December 1918. The Congress as a temporary institution was a success, and it dispatched a seven-man delegation (among whom were Syrkin, Vinchevsky, and Barondess) to the Paris peace talks. But the four-year conflict that had preceded its convocation left the balance of forces in American Jewish politics permanently changed.

Most notably, the Zionists at one level and the labor Zionists at another had achieved a new degree of recognition and legitimacy. In contrast, the Jewish Socialist Federation, owing primarily to a series of abrupt and ill-timed about-turns, had failed to establish its claim to leadership in the American-Jewish labor movement. Its alliance with the *Forverts* and the veteran generation had been reduced to disarray.

This development no doubt hastened the entry of many of its members, including Olgin and Salutsky, into the new Communist movement. There, Yiddish-speaking "internationalism" and class-war doctrine took on a new lease of life in the interwar period.[376] On the other hand, the *Forverts* and many of the founding fathers – Cahan, Lesin, Schlossberg, Pine – displayed a growing sympathy for labor Zionism and its pioneering projects in Palestine.

Beyond this, it is true that, as in 1905, the movements for the centralized political unity of American Jewry (and of American-Jewish labor) had been beaten back. In contrast to the radical immigrants who arrived in Palestine in the period 1903–14, the post-1903 generation in America did not succeed in transforming the basic structure of Jewish life that they had found on arrival. The pattern of fragmentation, grassroots and mushroom organization, polycentrism – characteristic of the labor movement as of the entire American-Jewish community – proved highly resistant to revolutionary change. The "Jacobin" episode in American-Jewish history had to give way to emergent "federalism."

The American Jewish Congress and Russian Jewry, 1915–1919

The movement for an American Jewish Congress was given broad and detailed coverage in the Russian-Jewish press. Despite the hesitant response of the Bund to the actual issues involved, this was true even of its publications. In December 1915, for example, Vladimir Kossovsky published an attack in the Russian-language bulletin of the Bund abroad on the "two SRs" leading the Congress agitation in New York: Zhitlovsky and Rutenberg ("the one-time terrorist").[1] In 1916 Olgin sent over a series of articles for the *Evreiskie vesti* in Petrograd on the National Workmen's Committee and the Congress movement.[2]

Of the Bundist leaders, Rafes (then in Petrograd) was the most enthusiastic supporter of the Congress idea. He was largely responsible, no doubt, for the fact that a Bundist conference held in Russia in the spring of 1916 decided to give serious consideration to the idea of a world Jewish congress.[3] An unsigned "Letter from Russia," written at the time, argued that proletarian "class solidarity" did not demand a policy of "boycottism," "a refusal to participate in the general [Jewish] organizations created during the struggle for equal rights."[4]

As against this, Erlich (likewise in Petrograd), in response to the Savoy Hotel agreement of December 1916, insisted that the National Workmen's Committee had conceded far too much in permitting the term "national rights" to be supplanted by mere "group rights." In his view, two or three parallel, class-based congresses would have been preferable to this facade of unity: "Real political defense, the defense of real interests, can only be undertaken by groups, by classes."[5]

With the February Revolution, the idea of a Russian-Jewish Congress became an immediate issue. The Poale Zion called for a Congress with an open agenda, but the Bund and the Zionists, as in America, both insisted that hard-and-fast guidelines be laid down in advance. Thus, the Zionists demanded that the Palestine issue constitute a separate item on the agenda (as it did in the Savoy Hotel pact). For their part, the Bundists were only willing to take part in a Congress if it restricted itself in advance to domestic concerns and excluded world Jewish affairs.[6]

The decision in May 1917 of the National Workmen's Committee ("headed by our Bundist comrades now in America")[7] to boycott the elections to the American Jewish Congress cast its shadow over the negotiations in Russia, which now ground to a halt. An article of 6 July by Max Weinreich in the Bundist paper, *Di arbeter shtime*, suggested that a Russian-Jewish Congress would in all probability never meet. "We have constantly said and written," he explained there, "that in *political questions* we do not recognize a national will."[8]

However, an all-party conference was now called in a last attempt to break the stalemate of mutually exclusive ultimata. It met on 18–21 July 1917 and succeeded in hammering out an agreed agenda. The key clause was strikingly reminiscent of the compromise reached at the Workmen's Convention of September 1915 in New York: "The guarantee of the civil and national rights of the Jews (1) in independent Poland (2) in Palestine (3) in Roumania."[9] The pact was accepted, reluctantly, by the Bund, which feared that to do otherwise could lead to its total isolation in the Jewish world. As in America, the Zionist movement was incomparably stronger in 1917 then in 1905.

The elections to the Russian-Jewish Congress were held in the winter of 1917–18, but the new Bolshevik regime never permitted it to meet.[10] However, a Jewish National Council was formed ad hoc by a group of elected delegates living in the Bolshevik-controlled areas, and in July 1918 it appealed to the executive committee of the American Jewish Congress for aid in "the furtherance of the national interests of our people in this land."[11]

The nearest thing to the Congress ever to meet in Soviet Russia was a conference held in Moscow in July 1918 attended by 149 representatives of the new, democratically elected community boards (kehilot). With the consolidation of the Communist regime as a one-party dictatorship, the repetition of this experiment soon became unthinkable.

Initially, at least, events followed a different path in the Ukraine. As that region, led by the socialist parties in the Central Rada, moved fast toward autonomy and then toward independence, far-reaching political concessions were made to the minorities, including the Jews. The Bund was assigned a seat in the Ukrainian government (which was filled first by Rafes and then by A. Zolotarev). In July 1917 Moyshe Zilberfarb of the United Jewish Socialist Labor Party (or Farenynikte) was appointed vice-secretary for Jewish affairs, a post that in January 1918 was raised to the level of minister.

On 9 January 1918, the Rada approved unanimously a law on "national personal autonomy" that granted the three chief minorities in the Ukraine – Russians, Poles, Jews – the right to their own national assemblies and national councils. These bodies were to be granted legislative and executive functions (within limits to be defined by the future constituent assembly of the Ukrainian Republic).[12] This law was something of a personal, albeit fleeting, triumph for Zilberfarb (one of the founders of the Vozrozhdenie group in 1903 and of the SERP in 1906), who had chaired the drafting committee.

Some months earlier, in October 1917, a provisional Jewish National Council (natsional-rat) had been established as an advisory body by the vice-secretary for Jewish affairs. Its membership was made up of representatives from the various Jewish parties. Initially, however, the assigned places were only taken up by the left wing, as the Zionist and other "bourgeois" parties refused to accept the system of appointment from above – Zilberfarb being, of course, the nominee of the Ukrainian socialist government.

Not until April 1918, after the successive Bolshevik and German invasions – when Zilberfarb was replaced as minister by Latsky-Bertoldy (now of the Folkspartey) – did the Zionists agree to enter the National Council. As a condition of entry, they insisted that the Provisional Jewish Congress (for-parlament), then at the advanced planning stage, be composed entirely of delegates from the newly reorganized, democratically elected community boards (kehilot). The previous plan had called for a Congress to be made up in part by community delegates and in part by the existing (predominantly socialist) membership of the National Council (*natsional-rat*).

The Provisional Congress in fact did not meet until 3 November 1918, after the Skoropadsky regime (now deprived of German support) had been replaced by the Ukrainian socialist Directorate. The Zionists in alliance with the religious bloc (a coalition described scornfully on the left as "Black-Blue")[13] held a clear majority at the Congress. And they used the majority to vote through their policies.

On 11 November 1918, a delegation was elected by the Congress to represent "the three million [Ukrainian] Jews" at the Paris peace talks. They were instructed, among other things, to work for a Jewish "national political center" in Palestine, and for the admission of the world-wide "Jewish nation" into the projected League of Nations. The delegation of five was headed by Ussishkin and included Ahad Ha-Am.[14]

In protest, all the Jewish socialist parties announced their resignation from the Provisional Congress. There were no socialists in the delegation to Paris. But the minister for Jewish affairs (a post restored by the Directorate), was now once again a socialist: Avrom Revutsky of the Poale Zion. Thus, the Jewish Ministry and the Provisional Congress, each claiming legitimacy from different sources, faced one another with open suspicion and hostility. All that "national autonomy" had brought with it, declared an article of February 1919 in the Bundist *Folks-tsaytung*, were "constant conflicts with the Zionists . . . a deepening of the abyss between the two cultures – the Hebrew and the democratic. Our friends have been Russian and Ukrainian socialists. From the point of view of both pedagogy and psychology they have been much closer to us than the Jewish majority in the kehilot and the National Council."[15]

By this time, however, the Red Army was once again on the march into the Ukraine. The days of the National Council and of the Jewish Ministry alike were numbered. The Jewish socialist parties were in the process of rapid polarization as one wing (led by Rafes and Litvakov, among others) moved toward Communism and the other wing (which included Litvak and Liber of the Bund, Rozin of the Fareynikte, Revutsky of the Poale Zion) rejected the Bolshevik dictatorship.[16]

Only the delegation from the Ukraine, safe in Paris, was able to live out its days unmolested. It entered the main bloc of Jewish delegations – Le Comité des Délégations juives auprès de la Conférence de la Paix – and Ussishkin played a major role in its deliberations. The delegation selected by the American Jewish Congress (led by Marshall and Mack) likewise joined this bloc, a move that left only the French Alliance and the British Conjoint Committee unaffiliated. Loyal to the decisions of the American Jewish Congress, Marshall was now ready to advocate "national rights" for the Jews of eastern Europe – a demand with which the Jewish delegations from England and France could not identify themselves.[17]

The Jewish populations of Poland, Lithuania, and Latvia were all brought under the purview of the Paris treaties and the other international instruments guaranteed by the League of Nations. According to these agreements, "educational committees, appointed locally by the Jewish communities" were granted the right to run primary schools in the language of their choice and at state expense.[18] The Lithuanian government went much farther, pledging itself in 1919 to establish national autonomy and a ministry for Jewish affairs.[19]

No such treaty arrangements, of course, applied to the new Soviet Republics of Russia, the Ukraine and White Russia. There, the Communist Party used its Jewish section (Evsektsiia) and the Jewish commissariat, both established in 1918, in order to implement its policy of "the proletarian dictatorship in the Jewish Street."

Conclusion

In general terms, this book has examined the role of Jewish socialism in the emergence of modern Jewish politics. Specifically, it has concentrated on the clash between socialist internationalism and Jewish nationalism; on the attempts to reconcile the one with the other in some form of synthesis; and on the subsequent interrelationship of movements and ideologies that were in varying degrees both socialist (or at least proletarian) and nationalist (or at least national). Throughout, it has emphasized the constant interaction of the ideological and the political.

It was argued in the Introduction that Jewish socialism could be regarded as a political subworld or subculture. By 1914, this subworld was in existence in every major center of Russian-Jewish life – not only in the Pale, Galicia, London, and New York but also (on however small a scale) in Paris, Canada, South America, and South Africa.

Its constituent movements did not share a common ideology: far from it. But certain shared assumptions, a lowest common denominator of belief, did exist. Thus, they all accepted that there was room within Jewish society for at least an autonomous (if not an independent) labor or socialist movement; that such a movement could contribute to the solution of the Jewish question; and that its right to exist was no less than that of parallel organizations among other minority peoples. They all put their faith in a radically new society and in the new man (however differently envisaged he might be). And for the sake of the future order, revolutionary change, they were alike determined to cast off totally the yoke of established religion, be it traditional, be it reformed.

With the exception of the movements in Palestine (which opted primarily for Hebrew), they employed the same language, Yiddish. They appealed, albeit with varying emphasis, to the same strata of society, sought out the same constituencies: the proletariat, the poor, the intelligentsia (including the *polu-intelligentsiia*) and the youth. So doing, they engaged in constant polemic and competition, attacking – and influencing – each other. The political borders of this subworld cannot be drawn with exactitude, but it has been taken that they included (if only as a kind of no-man's land), at the one extreme, such anarchist journals as the *Arbeter fraynd* or *Di fraye arbeter shtime* and, at the other, such aspiring labor organizations as Ha-Poel Ha-Tsair (which in this period, at least, defined itself as nonsocialist).

Now, in the light of the case studies undertaken here, it is necessary to go further, to enumerate the factors that appear to have been of dominant importance in the ideological history of this subworld.

First, and of key significance, was the fact that Jewish socialism emerged at a very late stage in the modernization of Jewish life. It was, as suggested in the

CONCLUSION

Introduction, a postliberal phenomenon. What is more, it only developed in a period when socialist internationalism and Jewish nationalism alike were already firmly established as possible options for the posttraditional Jew. Indeed, Jewish socialism crystallized in the space between these two forces, in opposition (of varying extent) to both and yet dependent upon them.

This bipolar framework was an essential precondition for the emergence of Jewish socialism but, equally, a cause of the high tension that characterized so much of its subsequent development. The potentialities inherent in this situation were first demonstrated in the lives of Hess and Liberman. Thus, in 1840, at the time of the Damascus Blood Libel, Hess quickly abandoned his half-formed plans to devote himself to the cause of Jewish national revival and, in so doing, he was merely reacting to the inchoate state of Jewish politics at the time. Montefiore and Crémieux themselves did not follow up their intervention in Syria by the creation of a permanent institution to defend Jewish interests. As against this, left Hegelianism in Germany and socialism in France were then at a stage of high creativity and self-confidence. They naturally acted like a magnet on the young Hess, who, abruptly severing his ties with the Jewish world, threw himself into that of radical and revolutionary politics.

In 1860, on the other hand, the Left had still not recovered from the debacle of 1848; nationalism was on the rise throughout Europe; and there were subtle signs of rethinking in the Jewish world. Hess was impressed by the establishment of the Alliance israélite universelle; by the protonationalism of Graetz's *History of the Jews;* by Kalischer's schemes for Palestinian colonization. He could now write his *Rome and Jerusalem* in the hope of reaching out not just to a responsive audience but to a nationalist camp in the making. In this, of course, he was disappointed. And, in his later years, he lived something of a double life, a would-be Jewish activist and, at the same time, a German socialist leader (thus acting out in person what Syrkin would treat as general theory forty years later with his "twofold" strategy of socialist Zionism).

Liberman, from the first, sought to span the gap dividing the nationally conscious – Smolenskin – wing of the Haskala from the revolutionary populism of Lavrov. He ended up accused by the one side of reckless radicalism and by the other of Jewish nationalism, of deviation from the internationalist code. He was almost literally torn apart by the bipolar forces he had taken it upon himself to reconcile.

What was true of Hess and Liberman at the individual level was equally true of Jewish socialism as a sociopolitical phenomenon, as an emerging subworld. Thus, it took the crisis of 1881 to create the preconditions necessary for its viability. For, it was then, with the establishment of the Hoveve Zion (or Palestinophile) movement, that Jewish nationalism first took on permanent organizational form and could act as a counterweight to socialist internationalism. And, at the other extreme, it was in the 1880s, too, that the percentage of Jews recruited into the general Russian underground movements (both populist and Marxist) began to mount rapidly and out of all proportion to the size of the Jewish population. Finally, it was in this period that Yiddish-speaking socialism began to put down roots in London and New York, the work in large part of young people who had left Russia during the post-1881 crisis, many of them members or sympathizers of the Am Olam movement, advocates of a "going to the people," in conscious search for a middle way, both socialist and Jewish.

Given this bipolar division in Russia and the existence of an intermediate alternative overseas, it could only be a question of time (as Rubanovich and Zhitlovsky argued in the 1880s) until a third force, a Jewish socialism in its various forms, was created in the Pale, too. But it was equally true that by moving into the space between Jewish nationalism and socialist internationalism, the new movements would be forever pulled now in one direction, now in the other, depending on the relative strength of the antipodes at any given moment.

Of course, there were other major factors that contributed to the oscillating character of the Jewish socialist ideologies. Thus, of key importance was the fact that in the Pale, the party leaderships, the intelligentsia, were relatively insulated from the built-in institutional pressures normally associated with party politics (the pressures exercised by economic interest groups, by electoral constituencies, by an assertive rank-and-file membership). The conspiratorial nature of the party there, the funding from abroad, the erratic and sudden fluctuations in mass support, the eagerness for charismatic leadership, the deep need felt for doctrinal unity – all tended to make the ideologists, the *teoretiki,* into something of a self-contained caste that in the very act of fighting the interparty wars transcended party barriers.

Certainly, as they often argued, they were influenced by local economic realities, by grassroots opinion, by "life." But, equally, they were caught up in the constant debate conducted in both the socialist and Jewish worlds, in Russia and abroad, about nationality, internationalism and national rights, about the strategies of liberation – political, social, and national. The programs of the parties in Russia were at least partly evolved in the lectures, the *referaty,* delivered to interparty audiences in the émigré and student colonies in Switzerland or Germany. In turn, those programs influenced each other. And thence they were soon carried to every center in the subworld of Jewish socialism, where they were again subject to transformation. (In the United States and Palestine, the intelligentsia found itself increasingly restricted by institutional commitments, by "life," but this was a gradual process hardly discernible in America before the 1890s or in Palestine before 1910).

Granted this political structure, on the one hand, and the overwhelming intractability of the Jewish question, on the other, it was thus not surprising that – especially at moments of crisis, of political upsurge – new strategies, new movements, were thrown up in quick succession; or that men and parties frequently changed front with an extraordinary abruptness. There were, after all, a remarkable number of theoretically feasible solutions, each of which combined means and ends in a different permutation – ends here meaning not final goals, not the "maximal" program (a world socialist order) but the intermediate targets of the "minimal" program.

First, of course, there was the fundamental division between the two grand strategies, the revolution and the exodus. But that was only a beginning. If an organized exodus were the choice, should the destination be Zion or some other more hospitable territory? And, in either case, should the chosen country follow the capitalist, or the direct, path to socialism?

Again, assuming that revolution in Russia was to be the way, should the Jews demand civil rights, individual equality and liberty alone, or–over and beyond that–also national rights? And granted that national autonomy in the Diaspora was a legitimate goal, should it be maximalized (to include health, welfare, religion, politics, diplomacy) or should it be minimalized (limited strictly to cultural and educational affairs)? And if it were minimalized, was the educational aim to be the preservation of the Jewish people or, rather, the overthrow of every tradition and the creation of a new proletarian culture, socialist in content and national only in the use (very probably transient) of Yiddish?

Moreover, it was possible to treat such alternatives as complementary rather than as mutually exclusive. This possibility became increasingly attractive as experience produced a growing disenchantment with the two monistic alternatives (social revolution or a total evacuation). The new generation that came into politics in the decade 1895–1905 increasingly opted for various forms of synthesis, combining revolution, national autonomy, and even in many cases some type of territorialism.

The problem of means was no less vexing than that of ends. Those who entered politics in the 1880s naturally tended to think in terms familiar from the populist (narodnik) movements. Thus, some opted for an elitist policy that would permit the intelligentsia to act alone in the initial stages of the given strategy. Such an approach was clearly spelled out by Zhitlovsky in the period 1887–92, when he still pinned his hopes on the Narododnaia Volia. It also underlay the plans of the Bilu and Am Olam (and was explicitly formulated by their members on occasion). It was taken up again by the followers of Ussishkin in the years 1904–6, by the early Borochov, by the New Bilu, by Ha-Poel Ha-Tsair, all of whom thought in terms of a voluntarist avant-garde.

But, again, as in the history of the narodnik movement, elitism was often rejected in favor of a mass strategy that would mobilize the entire Jewish people or, at the very least, all its lower strata. Syrkin, of course, always insisted that this was the only feasible policy. Zhitlovsky thought in such terms increasingly from the mid-1890s as, for that matter, did An-sky (and the Lesin of 1894, then a member of the proto-Bundist movement in Minsk). When Zhitlovsky sought support in New York in 1905–6 for the Jewish Defense Association, for the Socialist Territorialist organization, and for its journal, Dos folk, he found his most enthusiastic supporters among veterans from the 1880s who had retained (or now returned to) their early populist allegiances–among them, Moyshe Katz, J. Kopeloff, Pavel Kaplan, Ezra Raevsky.

Characteristic of both the narodnik schools of thought was their frequent appeal to the Bible, particularly to the Mosaic Code and the Prophets, as well as to other selected chapters in Jewish history: the Maccabees, the Essenes, martyrdom, messianism. Such themes, it was assumed, had an important place in the collective memory, the folk psyche, and could serve to mobilize support for the national and socialist cause. The attempt to reach back over the liberal experience to traditional society, albeit in order to transcend it, was of key importance in the thinking not only of Hess and Syrkin (the latter, after all, was the avowed disciple of the former) but also to a considerable extent in that of Liberman, Zhitlovsky, and even Lesin.

The third possibility was to ground strategy on the power, actual or potential, of the proletariat. The attractions of the proletarian option were many and extraordinarily persuasive. In contrast to the populist programs, it could free the movement from the embarrassing pressures to cooperate with the bourgeoisie. In trade unionism and the "economic" struggle, it provided a broad field for action that produced impressive results in the here and now. Again, in its Yiddish-based policies of popular education it could see itself as the legitimate, albeit more radical, heir to the most critical and modernizing forces of the Haskala with all their withering criticism of Jewish tradition. Finally, in its stress on the proletariat as a class transcending national barriers, it guaranteed internationalism (without negating the right of separate national parties to exist as constituent members of the Second International).

True, even here, there was room for fundamental division of opinion, with one wing advocating class war as an absolute principle and the other ready to modify that principle in favor of interclass cooperation on an ad hoc basis – in parliamentary or quasi-parliamentary situations or in times of national emergency. But, nonetheless, increasingly from the 1890s, the Jewish socialist movements developed along Social Democratic lines, and Marxism was embraced with fast-mounting enthusiasm by ever broader circles of the new generation.

The factors so far enumerated here can be seen as a general (a necessary but not sufficient) explanation for the many ideological reversals that have provided a central theme in this work: the swing, for example, from emancipation to auto-emancipation in the years 1881–2, which inspired the Bilu and Am Olam and reached deep into the world of socialist internationalism to touch such veteran revolutionaries as Pavel Akselrod; the subsequent reversal, which led so many of the generation once in England or the United States to adopt a militantly "internationalist," assimilationist (albeit Yiddish-speaking), reading of Marxist or anarchist doctrine; and the about-turns executed by the Bund between 1899 (its Third Congress) and 1901 (its Fourth); by Syrkin the ardent Zionist in 1900 and the territorialist in 1905; by Borochov, the voluntarist (Ussishkin's man) in 1905 and the determinist, the proletarian revolutionary, in 1906; by Ben Zvi, an out-and-out Borochovist in 1907 and an advocate of Franz Oppenheimer's cooperative settlement in 1909; by Ben Gurion, champion of the American Jewish Congress in mid-1917, its bitter critic at the end of that year; by Zhitlovsky, who changed position so often on so many fundamental issues.

However, this emphasis on the dynamics of interaction between the constituent parts of the Jewish socialist subworld is not meant to imply that the specific, the local, time and place, did not play a central role in its history. All the movements examined in this study, after all, were founded by Jews in or from the Pale of Settlement, but nonetheless, they developed along very divergent lines in each different country. This fact emerges clearly enough from the comparison undertaken here between the three major centers: Russia, America, and Palestine.

Thus, in the Pale of Settlement, the Bund successfully established itself in the period 1897–1905 as the dominant socialist movement. It was able to exploit to the full the vacuum created, on the one hand, by the reluctance of the Zionist movement (with its strong emigrationist and Palestinian bias) to engage in Russian politics and, on the other, by the unwillingness or inability of the Russian and Polish parties to organize the Jewish workers.

It took upon itself (when no other movement was ready to do so) to marshal the Jewish working class for open warfare against both their employers and the tsarist authorities; to champion the idea of national autonomy in the Diaspora; to encourage the production of Yiddish literature for the masses. With its conspiratorial network gradually fanning out from Lithuania across the Pale; its remarkable fusion of intellectuals, *polu-intelligentsiia,* and workers into one cohesive, centralized movement; its underground publications printed in Russia or smuggled from abroad; its conferences and congresses; its high degree of doctrinal loyalty (despite profound ideological disagreements); its party-controlled trade unions; its large periphery of supporters both proletarian and nonproletarian; its ability to raise funds on a large scale abroad, particularly (aided by the *Forverts*) among the Russian Jews in America – it became a model which was bound to inspire imitation.

In the period 1905–6, three important parties (the SSRP, the SERP, the ESDRP-PZ) were founded in direct competition with the Bund. They sought to outflank it by adopting a stance not only more national but also more revolutionary. They outdid one another to prove their orthodox Marxism, their right to join the Second International, and their proletarian and Yiddish-speaking character. Even the general Zionist organization in Russia found itself drawn belatedly far toward the left, demanding at its Helsingfors conference of 1906 not only the full democratization of Russia but also national autonomy for the Jews.

However, this upsurge of enthusiasm for the revolution, for Marxism and Diaspora nationalism proved unable to sustain itself. When the tide ebbed, the Jewish Left crashed down with even greater force than the Russian revolutionary movements. The memory of the October pogroms; the huge, unprecedented, emigration; the sudden drop in the funds from America; the prolonged economic depression in the northwest reduced it to the barest shadow of its former self. It recovered rapidly in 1917 but then found itself facing a real rise in the popular enthusiasm for Zionism – a fact that prevented a repetition of 1905 in the Jewish world.

Arriving in Palestine in the years 1905–8, the radical youth from Russia initially assumed that they would be able to recreate a labor movement in their new country on the model familiar from the Pale. As in Russia, the generation of 1881 had failed in the attempts to establish a Jewish socialist or labor movement. (Mints and his circle in the Bilu had left the country; Gedera was indistinguishable in its social structure from the other early colonies; Halperin had been driven out of Rishon Le-Zion and spent much of his time in the Pale as a peripatetic advocate of labor Zionism). And the new arrivals expected that they could fill this gap by the employment of imported strategies.

The two parties, Poale Zion and the Ha-Poel Ha-Tsair, differed on many issues. The one in 1906–7 was Marxist, Borochovist, and determined to publish in Yiddish; the other was voluntarist, worked in the tradition of Ussishkin and Ahad Ha-am, and was strongly Hebraist. But both argued that Palestine would follow the capitalist path and that the future lay with the large Jewish working class, which, it was confidently believed, would develop there no less than in the Pale or New York. The task of the parties was to organize the wage workers, to form trade unions and to defend their interests, both economic and political. For its part, Poale Zion looked forward to the anti-Turkish and proletarian revolutions that would lead directly to the creation of the Jewish state.

However, in reality, the growing labor force was supplied primarily by Arabs, and the youth from Russia went over to a strategy of cooperative or communal settlement. Unable to change the existing society, they fell back on the creation of a miniature society in their own image. This new social order was to be financed not by private but by "public" capital (primarily funds from the World Zionist Organization), founded on principles of equality, and sustained by manual labor and self-defense, which were to be in the hands of Jews alone.

The political parties in Palestine lost the absolute hegemony that they had enjoyed at their height in the Pale, but they survived to represent the ideological and political aspirations of the labor movement – they coexisted uneasily with the new Agricultural Labor Unions and the largely autonomous farming settlements. As their programs changed, so old allegiances were loosened and new ones formed. The Poale Zion in Palestine in practice dropped its Borochovist line, drawing closer to the fraternal parties in Austria and America. Syrkin was published frequently in Ha-ahdut, Borochov hardly at all. Zhitlovsky and Kaplansky visited the country, Borochov did not. Ha-Poel Ha-Tsair entered a bitter public dispute with Ahad Ha-Am and allied itself closely to the Warburg wing of the German Zionist movement, which had Arthur Ruppin as its de facto representative in Palestine.

The actual achievements of this new strategy by 1914 were minuscule and of uncertain future. They were all but destroyed by the depredations of the war period. But the nucleus formed in the decade prior to 1914 found itself in an excellent position to establish a high degree of control over the new wave of pioneers who arrived in their many thousands in the 1920s.

In the United States, Jewish socialism developed along yet a third path. The generation of the 1880s had there succeeded in erecting a firm institutional framework which stood ready to take in the huge immigration of workers (actual or potential) that poured into America in the years 1903–14. The leadership of the labor movement had become predominantly Social Democratic and owed its allegiance in the main to the Socialist Party (although in its ranks were also supporters of the SLP and even anarchists). But its success throughout was far greater in the socioeconomic sphere associated with immigrant absorption than in party politics. The socialist press, insurance societies, and trade unions grew, while the Yiddish-speaking party branches stagnated.

As a result, a highly dichotomous policy toward the Jewish question was developed. In normal times, the movement was strongly internationalist, in favor of rapid Americanization, committed firmly to the class war and against any form of interclass cooperation or Jewish solidarity. But at times of crisis – the Dreyfus Affair, the Kishinev pogrom – all this changed. The Forverts gave unlimited space to Jewish issues and (together with its associated organizations) launched funds, sponsored petitions, organized demonstrations, and advocated a variety of resettlement (or even territorialist) projects. Increasingly, at such moments, the keynote was interclass cooperation rather than class war. Given its mass audience, its anxiety to increase circulation and the impotence of the Yiddish-speaking party branches, this responsiveness to public opinion at large was natural enough. And it was seen at the time both as a throwback – on the part of Cahan and Miller – to their narodnik origins and also as an adaptation to the competitive ethos of American popular journalism (then epitomized by William Randolph Hearst).

CONCLUSION

The socialists, who began to arrive in large numbers after 1903, generally found themselves repelled by what they found and were determined to rebuild the movement along the lines familiar to them from Russia. Above all, they believed that the political arm should predominate in the labor movement and that the Jewish question should be treated with greater ideological consistency. In practice, however, the second generation, for all its revolutionary experience and links to the new mass immigration, was able to force through relatively little change. It was the established organizations that absorbed the immigrant workers and now grew by leaps and bounds.

What frustrated the attempts at reform, above all, was perhaps the profound inner conflict within the new generation itself. The Bundists, on the one hand, and the Poale Zion (and socialist territorialists), on the other, were usually to be found on opposite sides of any given issue. Thus, the generational conflict was to a great extent overshadowed by the internecine struggle between the two new groups – each side eagerly seeking support within the veteran leadership. Until the war, the Bundist forces (which in 1912 established the Jewish Socialist Federation) enjoyed an overwhelming advantage in this tug-of-war, among other reasons because of the historic alliance between the *Forverts* and the Bund, which dated back to 1898.

But during World War I, the Poale Zion and their allies went far to restoring the balance of forces. In calling for Jewish solidarity on behalf of the Russian Jews in the war zone – for an American Jewish Congress – they struck a responsive chord in public opinion. The Bundist reliance on the class-war strategy (as against interclass cooperation, *klal-yisroel politik*) proved to be far less popular in the United States (at least in such periods) than in the Pale. By 1918, many of the veteran leaders were edging their way toward a rapprochement with labor Zionism.

A fundamentally new era in the history of the Jewish socialist movements was in fact reached with the two events of November 1917: the Bolshevik revolution and the Balfour Declaration. The net effect of these developments was to strengthen enormously the attraction of the two poles between which Jewish socialism was held in balance. Lenin and (to an extent) even Weizmann now became central actors on the world stage. The new Moscow and the promise of a new Jeruslaem loomed large over Jewish politics.

In the Soviet areas, all the Jewish socialist parties (the Bund, the Poale Zion, the Fareynikte) split asunder in the years 1919–21, with large sections going over to Communism and, in many cases, to the Evsektsiia (the Jewish section of the Communist Party). The non-Communist rump parties were suppressed and their members in part managed to escape the country. A left-wing (Borochovist) Poale Zion party survived in truncated form (albeit with its own journal) until 1928, when it, too, was closed down.

As against this, in independent Poland (as in Lithuania) the established socialist parties remained to play a significant role in Jewish life. But the space in which they could move was drastically narrowed. On one side, they were hemmed in by the Communist camp, which now included a powerful Yiddish-speaking section (a new phenomenon). And, on the other, they faced an enormously strengthened Zionist movement which, under the leadership of Yitshak Grinbaum, was actively involved in Polish politics and which included a burgeoning camp of pioneer youth (so marginal a factor in 1905). The Poale Zion split into right-wing and left-wing parties, the latter, like the Bund, unsuccessfully seeking entry into the Comintern. Only in the 1930s, with the decline of general Zionist popularity, did they regain something of their former political weight.

In Palestine, the veterans of the Second Aliya, with their constructivist ideology, formed the Histradrut and the Hagana. And the Poale Zion merged with other factions to form a new umbrella party, entitled Labor Unity (Ahdut Ha-Avoda). These were the institutions that permitted the prewar generation, numerically so insignificant, to exert a predominant influence over the expanding labor movement of the 1920s. It was not until the mid-1920s, during a period of major economic slump, that there emerged a real opposition to the veteran Histradrut leadership – an opposition that found expression partly in the PKP (the Palestine Communist Party) and partly in a resurgence of Borochovist, class-war, theories of Zionism.

Predictably, the schismatic blade cut a much deeper swathe through the Jewish labor movement in the United States. There, it was not the Poale Zion but the Jewish Socialist Federation (with its Bundist background) that split, a large section entering the emergent Communist movement of America. Out-and-out internationalism and class-war doctrine, in its Yiddish-speaking form, enjoyed a powerful resurgence there. In the anti-Communist camp, there were moves toward a détente – and even active cooperation – with labor Zionism.

Given its central position on a bipolar continuum, it was hardly surprising that Jewish socialism was thus progressively pulled apart. After all, its constituent movements, each in its own way, sought to combine extreme modernization with involvement in a people which then was still (in large part) highly traditional; internationalism with the use of national languages and literatures that at the time were arguably dead or dying; universalist aspirations with a particularist context extraordinarily confined in its political potentialities. Ideological tension was therefore inherent in the development of the various parties as in the individual lives of those who led or manned those parties.

Their attempts to span worlds so alien, to create something so new and so great within a setting so narrow, was the source of both extraordinary political energy and of profound political weakness; of genuine tragedy and genuine farce. In the last resort, though, what was mirrored – with remarkable accuracy – in this search for total solutions to problems that could be resolved only in part, was the predicament of the Jewish people as it entered the twentieth century.

Notes

Abbreviations

AB: Abend-blat
Ah: Ha-ahdut
AH: American Hebrew
AIU:*BM* Alliance israélite universelle: *Bulletin mensuel*
AJA: American Jewish Archives
AJHQ: American Jewish Historical Quarterly
AJYB: American Jewish Year Book
AMJLM: Archives and Museum of the Jewish Labor Movement (Tel Aviv)
AS: Arbter shtime
Cahiers: Cahiers du monde russe et soviétique
CAHJP: Central Archives for the History of the Jewish People (Jerusalem)
CZA: Central Zionist Archive (Jerusalem)
EL: Evreiskaia letopis
ERKh: Evreiskaia rabochaia khronika
ES: Evreiskaia starina
EZ: Evreiskaia zhizn
FTs: Folks-tsaytung
HS: Historishe shriftn
IRS: Istoriko-revoliutsionny sbornik
IRSH: International Review of Social History
JC: Jewish Chronicle
JJS: Jewish Journal of Sociology
JSS: Jewish Social Studies
KA: Krasny arkhiv
KhEZh: Khronika evreiskoi zhizni
KiS: Katorga i ssylka
KL: Krasnaia letopis
LBIYB: Leo Baeck Institute Year Book
LR: Letopis revoliutsii
LS: Leninskii sbornik
NV: Nayer veg
NVe: Naye velt
NYT: New York Times
PAJHS: Publications of the American Jewish Historical Society
PG: Proletarisher gedank
PI: Poslednie izvestiia
PR: Proletarskaia revoliutsiia
PTs: Ha-poel ha-tsair
RE: Russkii evrei

RP: Royter pinkes
SEER: Slavonic and East European Review
SR: Slavic Review
ST: Sotsyalistisher teritoryalizm
VIL:*PSS:* V. I. Lenin, *Polnoe sobranie sochinenii*
VS: Volnoe slovo
YA: Yidisher arbeter
YAJSS: YIVO Annual of Jewish Social Science
YAP: Yidisher arbeter pinkes
YK: Yidisher kemfer
YKon: Yidisher kongres
YS: Yidisher sotsyalist
ZAL: Zionist Archives and Library (New York)

Items listed in the Bibliography appear in the Notes in abbreviated form.

Chapter 1. Dilemmas of the messianic conscience

1. Cornu, p. 8.
2. On Hess's childhood and youth see Silberner, *Moses Hess,* pp. 1–21; Zlocisti, pp. 16–22.
3. [Hess], *Moses Hess: Briefwechsel,* p. 48. For an extraordinarily complete listing of Hess's works see Silberner, *Works of Moses Hess.*
4. Silberner, *Moses Hess,* p. 31.
5. [Hess], *Die heilige Geschichte.* On *The Sacred History* and *The European Triarchy* see Cornu, pp. 8–49; Silberner, *Moses Hess,* pp. 31–49, 66–90; Goitein, pp. 12–18; I. Berlin, pp. 7–18; Weiss, pp. 10–22.
6. [Hess], *Die heilige Geschichte,* pp. 189–90.
7. Ibid., p. 80.
8. Ibid., pp. 22, 89, 237.
9. On Hess's enthusiastic identification with Spinoza see Liebeschütz, "German Radicalism" in Altmann (ed.), *Studies,* p. 161.
10. Hess, *Die europäische Triarchie,* p. 28.
11. In the twelfth century, Joachim of Fiore (or Flora) developed this concept of a three-stage historical development in which the first era was that of the Father, the second that of the Son, and the third that of the Holy Ghost, the messianic age or world Sabbath. Liebeschütz has suggested that a possible source for Hess's familiarity with this historiographical tradition could have been J. A. Neander (Liebeschütz in Altmann, ed., *Studies,* p. 162).
12. Hess, *Die heilige Geschichte,* pp. 328–9.
13. On the originality of this emphasis on technological progress as a condition of socialism see Cornu, pp. 10, 42 (he sees in Hess an "intuition of genius").
14. Hess, *Die heilige Geschichte,* pp. 105, 137.
15. Ibid., pp. 339–40.
16. Hess, *Die europäische Triarchie,* p. 139.
17. Ibid., pp. 111, 112.
18. Hess, *Die heilige Geschichte,* p. 344.
19. The Damascus Affair created a furor throughout the Jewish world. It produced a strong reaction not only in Hess but also, for instance, in Lassalle and Heine. On the Affair see Graetz, *History of the Jews,* V, 632–71. (He described the case as an "unforeseen event, insignificant at the beginning, but of vast importance in its results"; ibid., p. 632); Posener, I, 198–247; Wolf, pp. 71–100.

20. Hess, *Rom und Jerusalem*, pp. 26–7.

21. Ibid., pp. 27–8.

22. Quoted in Silberner, *Moses Hess*, p. 63.

23. On plans for a Jewish restoration to Palestine publicized in England at this juncture see Hyamson; Sokolow, I, 101–40. For a general survey of the English relationship to Palestine and the Jewish claim see Tuchman.

24. Quoted in Silberner, *Moses Hess*, p. 63.

25. A proto-Zionist group, drawn from the young Jewish intelligentsia, was created in Vienna in the wake of the Damascus Case, but it failed to gain effective backing: see Baron, "Abraham Benisch's Project."

26. Silberner, *Moses Hess*, p. 63.

27. On this MS., "The Poles and the Jews" now in the Zionist Archive in Jerusalem, see ibid., pp. 62–4.

28. Hess, *Die europäische Triarchie*, p. 140.

29. Ibid., p. 177.

30. Ibid., p. 86.

31. Hess, *Rom und Jerusalem*, p. 23.

32. Hess, *Die europäische Triarchie*, p. 13.

33. Among the more recent works in English on the evolution of the young Hegelians see Avineri, *Social and Political Thought of Karl Marx*; McLellan, *Marx before Marxism*; Tucker. For the specific role of Hess see Lukacs, "Moses Hess"; Mielcke.

34. For a reference to Young Germany see Hess, *Die europäische Triarchie*, pp. 162–3.

35. [Hess], *Moses Hess: Briefwechsel*, p. 81.

36. Ibid., p. 83.

37. Silberner, *Moses Hess*, pp. 110–11.

38. [Hess], *Moses Hess: Briefwechsel*, pp. 97–98.

39. Ibid., pp. 98, 99.

40. Hess's commonlaw (and in 1851, formal) marriage to Sibylle Pesch probably also contributed to this development. She was a working-class girl, German and Christian by origin, often described as having been at one time a prostitute. In the winter of 1843–4, she was living with Hess in Paris as his wife (Silberner, *Moses Hess*, pp. 166–71). The decision to enter into this marriage could not have been easy given Hess's background. That it was of great symbolic importance for him is suggested by the passage in *Rom und Jerusalem* where he described the crucial role played in his life by women in distress.

41. [Hess], *Moses Hess: Briefwechsel*, p. 103 (cf. Engels's statement in a letter of 1843 that in his circles it was Hess who "made plausible the idea that communism was the necessary doctrine of the Young Hegelians"; Zlocisti, p. 99; Mayer, I, 103).

42. Silberner, *Moses Hess*, p. 121.

43. [Hess], *Moses Hess: Briefwechsel*, pp. 79–80.

44. Engels wrote in the 1880s that Feuerbach's *Essence of Christianity* (1841) exerted a decisive influence on the Young Hegelians. But recent studies have emphasized Bauer's role in the onslaught on Christianity, theism, and existing society. See Engels, *Ludwig Feuerbach und der Aufgang der klassischen deutschen Philosophie* (Berlin, 1886) (in Marx and Engels, *Werke*, XXI, 272); and e.g., Rosen; McLellan, *Young Hegelians*.

45. "Philosophie der Tat," p. 312.

46. Ibid., pp. 313, 315.

47. Ibid., pp. 315–16.

48. Ibid., p. 316; cf. the essay on the attitude of the Left Hegelians to Judaism in Ettinger, *Ha-antishemiyut*, pp. 89–98.

49. Bauer first published his "Jewish Question" in 1842; it came out enlarged and in book form a year later. He took up the issue again in his "Die Fähigkeit der heutigen Juden

und Christen frei zu werden," *Einundzwanzig Bogen aus der Schweiz* (ed. G. Herwegh) pp. 56–71. Marx in his critique reviewed the latter two publications (on this episode see Rotenstreich).

50. Hess, *Die heilige Geschichte*, p. 236.

51. "Die Judenfrage," *Deutsche Jahrbücher* (22 Nov. 1842), no. 278, p. 1111.

52. Ibid. (21 Nov. 1842), no. 277, p. 1108; ibid., (24 Nov. 1842), no. 280, p. 1120.

53. The *Einundzwanzig Bogen* was published in July 1843, but Hess's "Socialism and Communism" was submitted in November 1842, the month when Bauer's essay was first published (see Silberner, *Moses Hess*, p. 124). He may have used the interval to make certain additions, or else he was familiar with Bauer's stand on Jewish emancipation from elsewhere. He attended Bauer's lectures in Bonn.

54. [Hess], "Sozialismus und Kommunismus," p. 90.

55. Ibid., p. 87.

56. "Ökonomisch-philosophische Manuscripte (1844)," in Marx and Engels, *Werke*, I, 468.

57. "Zur Judenfrage," *Deutsch-Französische Jahrbücher* pp. 212, 213, 211, 209.

58. For a full-scale study of the nature and subsequent impact of Marx's "On the Jewish Question" see Carlebach. On Marx's relationship to Judaism and his Jewish origins, see also Künzli; Massiczek; Avineri, "Marx and Jewish Emancipation"; Bloom, "Karl Marx and the Jews"; Feuer; Silberner, "Was Marx an Anti-Semite?"

59. Hess completed his "On the Nature of Money" not later than early 1844 and then submitted it to the *Deutsch-Französische Jahrbücher,* which did not publish it. It is not clear whether Marx had already seen the MS. – and was influenced by it – when writing his essays on the Jewish question. For a thorough examination of the issue see Carlebach, pp. 110–24. He argues that Marx probably had not seen the MS. For the opposing view see Silberner, *Moses Hess,* pp. 184–92, and McLellan, who writes that "the similarities between Hess's articles and Marx's 'Judenfrage' . . . can only be accounted for on the supposition that Marx copied heavily from Hess's essay" (*Young Hegelians,* pp. 154–5).

60. "Fortschritt und Entwicklung" (*Neue Anekdota,* 1845), in Hess, *Philosophische und sozialistische Schriften,* p. 284. Other editions of Hess's socialist works are *Sozialistische Aufsätze 1841–1847, Ausgewählte Schriften,* and *Ktavim klaliyim.*

61. "Über das Geldwesen," *Rheinische Jahrbücher zur gesellschaftlichen Reform,* I (1845), 30.

62. Ibid., p. 29.

63. Silberner, *Moses Hess,* p. 211.

64. [Hess], *Moses Hess: Briefwechsel,* p. 111.

65. Zlocisti, p. 179.

66. Silberner, *Moses Hess,* pp. 247–8; cf. W. Mönke, "Über die Mitarbeit."

67. [Hess], *Moses Hess: Briefwechsel,* p. 157.

68. Quoted in Zlocisti, p. 240 (cf. Marx and Engels, *Briefwechsel,* I, 84–121).

69. "Kommunistisches Glaubenskenntnis in Fragen und Antworten," *Rheinische Jahrbücher zur gesellschaftlichen Reform,* II (1846) (reproduced slightly altered from *Vorwärts,* 21 and 28 Dec. 1844); and *Rother Katechismus für das deutsche Volk* (1849/50), both in Goitein, pp. 128–38, 146–57.

70. "Die Folgen einer Revolution des Proletariats" (*Deutsche-Brusseller-Zeitung,* nos. 82, 89, 90, Oct.–Nov. 1847), in *Philosophische und sozialistische Schriften,* p. 443.

71. Ibid., p. 440.

72. *Rother Katechismus,* in Goitein, p. 147.

73. Silberner, *Moses Hess,* p. 198.

74. *Briefwechsel,* pp. 240, 242.

75. "Naturwissenschaften und Gesellschaftslehre, Briefe aus Paris." (*Das Jahrundert: Zeitschrift für Politik und Literatur,* I–II, 1856–7). See Silberner, *Moses Hess,* pp. 336–47.

76. Quoted in Silberner, *Moses Hess*, p. 340.

77. Ibid., p. 385.

78. Cf. I. Berlin, who described Hess's adoption of a "universal" in place of a national religion as "the prototype of the story of many a Jewish socialist and communist since his day" (*Life and Opinions*, pp. 19–20).

79. Quoted in Silberner, *Moses Hess*, p. 335n.

80. Hess, *Rom und Jerusalem*, pp. v–vi, 24.

81. Silberner, *Moses Hess*, p. 420.

82. Hess, *Rom und Jerusalem*, p. 1.

83. Ibid., pp. 183–4.

84. [Hess], *Moses Hess: Briefwechsel*, pp. 368, 366.

85. A. Ruge.

86. Hess, "Doctore Graziano's Werke" (*Deutsche-Brusseller Zeitung*, Aug. 1846), in *Philosophische und sozialistische Schriften*, pp. 417, 422 (cf. Hess's letter to Marx, 17 Jan. 1845 in [Hess], *Moses Hess: Briefwechsel*, p. 107). Hess was also irritated by Ruge's description of him as a "tall, gaunt man with a benevolent look and a neck bent forward in cocklike fashion. His gray cowl completed his priestlike look" (*Zwei Jahre*, I, 31).

87. Hess, *Rom und Jerusalem*, p. 23.

88. Ibid., p. 42.

89. [Hess], *Moses Hess: Briefwechsel*, pp. 306, 307–8. For an important study of the intellectual circles in Paris that influenced Hess in the 1850s see M. Graetz.

90. Ibid., p. 364.

91. Ibid., p. 368.

92. Hess, *Rom und Jerusalem*, p. 2.

93. Silberner, *Moses Hess*, p. 403; [Hess], *Moses Hess: Briefwechsel*, p. 374n. (At this point, Hess was separated from his wife, who was periodically unfaithful to him. They were later reconciled.)

94. Cf. I. Berlin: "Everything that had been suppressed by Hess for over twenty years now came welling up. He constantly returns to beliefs instilled in him by his father and grandfather" (*Life and Opinions*, p. 35).

95. Hess, *Rom und Jerusalem*, pp. 28, 29.

96. Ibid., pp. 144, 161.

97. Ibid., pp. 45, 236, 41, 114.

98. Ibid., pp. 29, 116.

99. Ibid., p. 210 (cf. I. Berlin: "But what is remarkable is that an émigré communist agitator should have heard of this movement at all and have realized at so early a date that the founder of this movement – the Baal Shem – was destined in the end to triumph over Moses Mendelssohn"; *Life and Opinions*, p. 33).

100. Hess, *Rom und Jerusalem*, p. 110.

101. Ibid., p. 95.

102. [Hess], *Moses Hess: Briefwechsel*, pp. 386–7.

103. The "discovery" of Hess in proto-Zionist circles apparently does not date back beyond the late 1880s. The first translations from *Rom und Jerusalem* appeared in *Ha-magid*, nos. 26, 27, 32, 35, 36 (1888), and nos. 8, 9, 11, 13 (1889); a booklet on Hess was published on Ussishkin's initiative in 1894 (M.E., *Moisei Ges*), and the first full translation came out five years later (*Roma vi-[ye]rushalayim; sheelat ha-leom* [trans. David Tsemakh] [Warsaw, 1899]). In 1905 Zlocisti published the first edition of his biography and a volume of selected works on Jewish themes, both in German. Zhitlovsky and Syrkin wrote their biographical essays in Yiddish later (Zhitlovsky, "Moyshe Hes," *Dos naye lebn* [1912]; Syrkin, "Mozes Hes," in *Roym un yerusholayim* [1916]).

104. [Hess], *Moses Hess: Briefwechsel*, p. 376.

105. Silberner, *Moses Hess*, p. 441.

106. [Hess], *Moses Hess: Briefwechsel*, pp. 386, 387.

107. Silberner, *Moses Hess*, pp. 596–609.

108. Ibid., p. 576.

109. *Sinai et Golgotha ou les origines du judaisme et du christianisme suivi d'un examen critique des Evangiles anciens et modernes* (traduit et mis en ordre par Maurice Hess) (Paris 1867). On the friendship of Hess and Graetz see [Hess], *Moses Hess: Briefwechsel*, pp. 523–30; Michael.

110. [Hess], *Moses Hess: Briefwechsel*, p. 532.

111. "Das Gottvertrauen der Anawim in dem Stürmen unserer Zeit," in Hess, "*Jüdische Schriften*, pp. 122–3; *Ktavim tsiyoniyim*, pp. 235–8.

112. Silberner, *Moses Hess*, p. 606.

113. [Lavrov], *Russkoi sotsialno-revolutiutsionnoi molodezhi*, pp. 53, 54.

114. Lavrov, *Narodniki-propogandisty*, p. 20.

115. Liberman was born in 1843, graduated from the pedagogical section of the Vilna Rabbinical Seminary in 1867, then served for two years as a teacher in Suvalki. He studied graphics and engraving in St. Petersburg in 1870–1 and then returned to Vilna, where he worked as an insurance agent. On his life see Krol; J. Klausner, VI, 243–306; Sapir, "Liberman"; Tsitron, *Dray literarishe doyres*, 3–49.

116. On the Vilna circles (of which Y.A. Finkelshtein was apparently the original founder) see Cherikover, "Der onheyb," pp. 469–76; idem, "Yidn-revolutsyonern," pp. 124, 155–60; Yokhelson, "Dalekoe proshloe"; Frumkin, "Iz istorii revoliutsionnogo dvizheniia," pp. 221–35. On the Rabbinical Seminary in Vilna see Slutsky, "Bet ha-midrash le-rabanim."

117. Sidirov, "Statisticheskie svedeniia." The Jews made up 6.5 percent of the political arrestees in 1873–7 (ibid., p. 43).

118. For works in English on the Haskala see Raisin, *Haskalah Movement*; Dubnov, *Jews in Russia and Poland*, II; Greenberg, I. On the Haskala and the concept of "productivization," cf. M. Levin.

119. Daniel Ish Hamudot, "Hazut ha-kol," *Ha-shahar*, VI (1874–5), no. 1/62, pp. 42–57; no. 2/63, pp. 105–19; no. 3/64, pp. 145–52.

120. There were some eight hundred subscribers in Russia (M. Berkovich, "Mi-maerekhet 'ha-emet'," *Ha-tsfira*, 1919, no. 40/137, p. 12).

121. *Ha-shahar*, VI, 118, 56–57.

122. Ibid., pp. 50, 146.

123. Ibid., pp. 108, 57, 107n.

124. Ibid., pp. 147, 57.

125. On these literary circles see J. Klausner, IV (Pt. 2), V, VI; Tsitron, "Di ershte yidishe sotsyalistn in der hebreyisher literatur," in *Dray literarishe doyres*, II, 104–33. For a study of Smolenskin in English see Freundlich.

126. The two key supporters of Liberman in Berlin were Grigorii Gurevich and Khasia Shur. Among the others were Moisei Aronzon and the brothers Gerasim and Maksim Romm. They lived in a "commune" during the period 1875–6 and helped in the transportation of revolutionary literature via Koenigsberg to Russia. This operation was directed by Zundelevich. See, e.g., Gurevich, "Zikhroynes," pp. 233–9; Weinryb, pp. 16–36; Kamensky; Deich, pp. 232–54 (Yiddish: pp. 226–47).

127. [Liberman], *Arn Libermans briv*, pp. 41, 47.

128. On Lavrov see Pomper; Venturi, pp. 429–68. Lavrov's most influential work, *Historical Letters*, has been translated. On the national question and the Jews in history see ibid., pp. 211–22.

129. "Nasha programma," *Vpered* (1873), no. 1, p. 10.

130. "Schety russkogo naroda," ibid., p. 59.

131. "Iz Vilno," *Vpered* (1 Sept. 1875), no. 16, p. 504. For a Hebrew translation of Liberman's articles in *Vpered!* see [Liberman], *A. S. Liberman: katavot.*
132. *Vpered* (1 Sept. 1875), no. 16, p. 505).
133. Ibid.
134. Ibid.
135. Lavrov, *Narodniki-propagandisty 1873–77 godov*, p. 76.
136. Ya. N. [Yantsin] to Smirnov, quoted in *HS*, I, 513; cf. the letter from S. Podolinsky to Smirnov (19 June 1876), where he wrote that "in my view Yidophobia is as indispensable for every Russian socialist as is hatred of the bourgeoisie" (Sapir [ed.], *"Vpered"* 1873–77, II; 466). Mishkinsky has argued that there was a direct line leading from this conception to the 1881 proclamation of the Narodnaia Volia in support of the pogroms but that, nonetheless, in the late 1870s Dragomanov was considering cooperation with Jewish revolutionary forces ("Al emdata shel ha-tnua ha-mahpkhanit"). Cf. Lavrov to Lopatin (7 April 1878): "How the Ukrainians [*khokhly*] get along with the Jews–that's the problem. They say that Dragomanov is very well disposed to Liberman, and it is to be hoped that the Jews [*zhidy*] will manage the transportation [of revolutionary literature] better" (Sapir [ed.], *Lavrov*, II, 528). A long article, not published at the time, was sent to *Vpered!* in 1876 from the Ukraine attacking the Judaeophobic views prevalent among many revolutionaries ("Predrassudki").
137. [Liberman], *Arn Libermans briv*, p. 68. Cf. a letter from L. S. Ginsburg to Lavrov and Smirnov in 1875 which vouched for Liberman's integrity and ability but criticized his plan to "found socialist doctrines on religious ideas–a concept from which he must be disabused" (Sapir, "Liberman," p. 59). In a speech of 1886 to the Jewish Labor Society (Evreiskoe Rabochee Obshchestvo) in Paris and in an open letter of 1892 to *Der veker*, a Yiddish journal edited by M. Baranov in London, Lavrov elaborated on his view that an unbridgeable gulf separated socialism from traditional religion and from nationalism. At the same time, though, he suggested that Jewish history and messianism had perhaps made the Jews unusually receptive to socialism. In his letter of 1892, he seemed to be consciously paraphrasing key themes from Liberman's first article in *Vpered!* and yet doing so more cautiously (for both documents see Cherikover, "Peter Lavrov"). The speech of 1886 was published as a separate pamphlet in Yiddish (*Peter Lavrov un di yidishe arbeter*, London, 1887). The translator was Vinchevsky; see his article, "Eyn eydler kharakter," *Arbeter fraynd* (11 April 1887), no. 21, p. 2.
138. [Liberman], *Arn Libermans briv*, p. 67.
139. Ibid., p. 68.
140. Ibid.
141. Vinchevsky, "Erinerungen," *Gezamlte verk*, X, 94.
142. "Iz Belostoka," *Vpered* (3/15 Feb. 1876), no. 27, p. 81.
143. Lavrov, *Russkoi sotsialno-revoliutsionnoi molodezhi*, p. 20.
144. "Iz Belostoka," *Vpered* (3/15 Dec. 1875), no. 23, p. 721.
145. Ibid., no. 27, pp. 81, 85; ibid. (19/31 Dec. 1875), no. 24, p. 754; ibid., no. 27, p. 81.
146. Ibid., p. 82.
147. Ibid., pp. 83–84.
148. Ibid., p. 84.
149. Ibid., p. 83. Weinryb argues that Liberman increasingly came under the influence of Marx and emancipated himself from that of Lavrov (*Be-reshit ha-sotsyalizm ha-yehudi*, pp. 75–106). But Lavrov himself was much influenced by Marx–both men, after all, were strongly opposed to Bakunin and Tkachev–and the later division between Russian populism and Russian Marxism was not yet clearly drawn (cf. Mishkinsky, who likewise sees Weinryb's thesis as exaggerated, in his introduction to *A. S. Liberman: Katavot*, p. 50, n. 26).
150. "Evreiskoi intelligentnoi molodezhi," *Vpered* (20 July/1 Aug. 1876), no. 38, pp. 475–6. Liberman tore up the original version of the manifesto because Lavrov and Smirnov

felt that it was too absorbed with "his favorite theme – the Bible and the rabbis" (see the letter from Smirnov to Rozalia Idelson, 25 Nov. 1875, in Sapir, "Liberman," p. 60).

151. With the opening of the tsarist archives, it became known that in January 1876 Liberman had also drawn up a "statute for the organization of a Social Revolutionary Union among the Jews in Russia." It was seized with the arrest of the Vilna circle, led by L. Davidovich, in April 1876. It proposed that the Jewish "sections federate among themselves and with similar organizations abroad or else with sections of other nationalities in Russia and abroad" (for this document see Bukhbinder, "Iz istorii revoliutsionnoi propagandy," pp. 44–51; also in his *Di geshikhte*, pp. 30–41).

152. *Vpered* no. 38, p. 474n.

153. Ibid., pp. 474, 475.

154. Ibid., p. 475.

155. [Liberman], *Arn Libermans briv*, p. 50.

156. Berkovich in *Davar (musaf)*, III (9 Sept. 1927), no. 47, 2.

157. Gurevich, "Protsess," p. 163.

158. M. Vinchevsky, "Erinerungen," *Gezamlte verk* IX, 159.

159. See HS, I, 479; and Halperin, p. 16.

160. On this Union in London see e.g., Gartner, *The Jewish Immigrant*, pp. 100–106; and Fishman, pp. 97–134. On L. Goldenberg see Sapir, "Jewish Socialists around 'Vpered,' " pp. 370–1, 380.

161. Cherikover published the minutes in full: "Pinkas," HS, I, 533–94 (with an introduction, pp. 469–532).

162. Ibid., pp. 541, 543, 583.

163. "Osnovanie Sotsialno-revoliutsionnogo obshchestva evreiskikh rabotnikov v Londone," *Vpered* (1876), no. 37, p. 364 (this article was written by Smirnov in part as a deliberate rebuff in the face of Podolinsky's protests against *Vpered!*'s support for Liberman; see his letter to Rozalia Idelson, July 1876, quoted in Sapir, "Liberman," p. 41).

164. HS, I, 569, 570.

165. This view was that disseminated by *The Jewish Chronicle*, for example: "Seeing that these conversionist agents . . . invite a breach of the peace, we should think that the law could be enforced which prevents such meetings" ("Another Conversionist Trick," JC [8 Sept. 1876], p. 364).

166. HS, I, 582, 575.

167. For example, ibid., pp. 580, 592.

168. Ibid., p. 558.

169. Ibid., p. 582.

170. [Liberman], *Arn Libermans briv*, pp. 74, 79n. (on the crisis in the editorial offices see Sapir [ed.], *"Vpered" 1873–1877*, I, 337–63; Pomper, pp. 192–200).

171. [Liberman], *Arn Libermans briv*, pp. 80–81.

172. Ibid., pp. 100, 114.

173. On Liberman's fund-raising efforts in Berlin in mid-1876, see his letter to Rozalia Idelson (Sapir, "Liberman," p. 63). As planned in 1875–6, the paper was to be called "The Hammer" (*Ha-patish*) (Krol, pp. 7–13).

174. "Ha-yehudim be-london," *Ha-emet* (1877), no. 3, pp. 45–6 (all references are to Krol's re-publication of 1938).

175. "Petiha li-sheelat ha-sakin ve-hamazleg," ibid., pp. 39, 40.

176. "Maase satan–hazon," ibid., pp. 53, 52.

177. "Shitat Makiaveli," ibid., p. 49.

178. "Milhemet ha-kiyum," ibid., no. 2, p. 21.

179. "Sheelat ha-yehudim," ibid., no. 1, p. 4.

180. Ibid.

181. Berkovich in *Davar (musaf)*, III (25 Nov. 1927), no. 8, p. 3.

182. Ibid. (9 Dec. 1927), no. 10, p. 2.

183. Quoted in Krol, p. 17.

184. Berkovich in *Ha-tsfira* (1919), no. 41/138, p. 11.

185. Lilienblum's piece was eventually published not in *Ha-emet* but in Vinchevsky's successor journal, *Asefat hakhamim*.

186. Ben-Nets [Vinchevsky], "Ben-Moshe ve-haemet," *Asefat hakhamim* (1878), no. 6, p. 106. Vinchevsky cooperated in the publication of this monthly with E. V. Rabinovich, and financial backing was provided by M. L. Rodkinson, the publisher of a Hebrew newspaper, *Ha-kol*. Both journals came out in Koenigsberg (Vinchevsky, *Gezamlte verk*, IX, 192–324, and Klausner, VI, 323–50.)

187. "Khaim Spivak," in Reizen, II, 687.

188. In the prospectus for *Ha-emet* (Krol, p. 2). Smolenskin's rejoinder is in "Daat sofrim: 'ha-emet'," *Ha-shahar*, VIII (1876–7), 470–2 (also in Krol, pp. 115–16).

189. Krol, p. 16.

190. Berkovich in *Ha-tsfira* (1919), no. 41/138, p. 13.

191. Ibid.

192. Ibid.

193. Ibid., no. 43/140, pp. 10, 13.

194. [Liberman], *Arn Libermans briv*, p. 130.

195. Ibid., p. 141.

196. Ibid., pp. 141, 145.

197. Ibid., p. 143.

198. Ibid., pp. 184, 186.

199. For the indictment and verdict (in the original German) and for a full description of this episode see Weinryb, pp. 36–72; cf. Gurevich, "Protsess."

200. On this period in Liberman's life see Vinchevsky, *Gezamlte verk*, I, 94–112.

201. Sapir, "Liberman," p. 82 (Liberman's letters of 1880 to Smirnov are also in [Liberman], *Arn Libermans briv*).

202. Yokhelson writes that it was L. Gartman who decided against Liberman, considering him "too expansive and little suited for the discipline and self-control required by conspiratorial conditions." Yokhelson retrospectively disagreed arguing that the Narodnaia volia had lost in him "a brave and selfless fighter" ("Dalekoe proshloe," p. 60).

203. *HS*, I, 159.

204. Ibid., p. 136. On the political attitudes of Jews in the Russian revolutionary movement see, e.g., Schapiro, "The Role of the Jews"; Kiel.

205. Sapir, "Liberman," p. 81.

206. Ibid., pp. 84–85.

207. See, e.g., Ivensky, p. 6.

208. Buber, p. 148. As a supporter of the non-Marxist wing of Jewish labor in Palestine, specifically of Ha-Poel Ha-Tsair, Buber was drawn to Hess. In a recent essay, Avineri also favorably contrasted Hess's attitude to nationalism with that of Marx: for Hess, "nationalism constitutes a mediating factor, analogous to the family, between the individual and the universal commonality . . . Hess's view enables us to transcend the non-dialectical one dimensionality appearing in Marx" (Avineri, "Socialism," p. 43).

209. Herzl added: "The only bothersome thing is his Hegelian terminology. Wonderful the Spinozistic-Jewish and nationalist elements. Since Spinoza, Jewry has brought forth no greater spirit" (*Complete Diaries*, V, 1090).

210. Ben Nets [Vinchevsky], "Toldot Ludvig Berne [Ludwig Börne]," *Asefat hakhamim* (1878), no. 5, p. 72 (this piece was dedicated to Lilienblum).

211. [Hess], *Moses Hess: Briefwechsel*, p. 375.

212. In an important article, Jacob Katz argues that Jewish nationalism should be regarded in this period (the 1860s and 1870s) as an emergent movement rather than as a purely individualist phenomenon: "The common idea became a basis of social unity . . . not the need created the idea but the idea created the social unit." However, he too sees 1881 as a turning point (J. Katz, "The Jewish National Movement" in his *Emancipation and Assimilation*, pp. 129–47, esp. p. 141). Katz discusses Hess but not Jewish socialism, which, it has been suggested here, was at an earlier, more inchoate, individual stage of development than Jewish nationalism in the period 1862–81.

Chapter 2. Emergence of the new politics

1. Estimates of the Mansion House Committee and the Alliance for the period September 1881–2: (*a*) 12,000–15,000 Russian Jews aided to go to the United States; (*b*) 8,000 went at own expense; (*c*) 8,000 repatriated to Russia; (*d*) 2,000 dispersed to various centers in Europe. The fact that 2,749 "new cases" fell on the support of the Jewish Board of Guardians in England in 1882 suggests a much higher figure for category (*d*). Samuel Joseph gives a lower estimate for categories (*a*) and (*b*) ("Mansion House Russian Jews Relief Fund," *JC* [24 Oct. 1882], p. 6; AIU:*BM* [Sept. 1882], no. 9, p. 180; Gartner, "Notes"; Joseph, *Jewish Immigration*, p. 162).

2. Leshchinsky, "Di yidishe imigratsye," in Cherikover (ed.), *Geshikhte*, I, 39.

3. Cherikover, "Revolutsyonere un natsyonale ideologyes," in ibid., p. 149.

4. On the pogrom of 1881–2 see *Materialy*, II; *Judenpogrome*, I, 12–96; Slutzky, "Hageografya." On the sociopolitical background to the pogroms see Rogger, "Jews, Peasants."

5. E.g., Levin, "Mi-tokh tazkir." On the intellectual roots of Russian antisemitism in this period see Ettinger, *Ha-antishemiyut*, pp. 99–167. On the reaction of the Russian press to the pogroms, see idem, "Ha-nitsul."

6. Ha-Cohen, *Olami*, I, 159–60.

7. Quoted in Akselrod, "O zadachakh evreisko-sotsialisticheskoi intelligentsii," in *Iz arkhiva P. B. Akselroda*, p. 219.

8. Cahan, *Bleter*, I, 435.

9. Nidah, "Ha-sofrim ha-ivriyim," *Ha-tsfira* (16 Aug. 1917), no. 25, pp. 9–10.

10. E.g., "Oy, me haya lanu!" *Ha-melits* (7 July 1881), no. 26, p. 540; "Rusland," *Ha-magid* (1 June 1881), no. 21, p. 174. On Alexander III's negative reaction to the pogroms (1881–3) see Kantor, "Aleksandr III." On governmental attitudes in general see Aronson, "The Prospects."

11. "Rusland," p. 174 (see n. 10).

12. "Oy, me haya lanu," p. 540 (see n. 10).

13. E.g., the confidential report of the governor of Poltava (7 May 1881) in *Materialy*, II, 51–2. On evidence that the pogroms were not spontaneous but were stimulated by itinerant agitators see Sonin, "Vospominaniia"; Dubnov, "Anti-evreiskoe dvizhenie"; for the suggestion that they were directed by the Holy Brotherhood (Sviashchennaia Druzhina, a Russian nationalist organization formed in March 1881 to combat the revolutionary movement) see Dinur, "Tokhniyotav," pp. 12–19.

14. "Poslednie izvestiia," *RE* (21 May 1881), no. 21, p. 838.

15. Nidah, in *Ha-tsfira* (23 Aug. 1917), no. 26, p. 10.

16. *RE* (4 June 1881), no. 23, p. 885.

17. M. [M. I. Rabinovich], "Vliianie protivuevreiskikh bezporiadkov na evreev," *VS* (15 May 1882), no. 37, p. 11.

18. *Materialy*, II, 65.

19. "The Persecutions of the Jews in Russia," *JC* (13 Jan. 1882), p. 9.

20. *VS* (15 May 1882), no. 37, p. 11.

21. M. [M. I. Rabinovich] "Brozhenie v evreiskoi masse pod vliianiem krovavykh sobytii poslednogo vremeni," *VS* (1 June 1882), no. 38, p. 19.

22. Ibid.

23. On this movement see Menes, "Am Oylom Movement"; Turtel, "Tnuat 'am-olam'."

24. M. [M. I. Rabinovich], "Brozhenie," p. 19 (see n. 21).

25. Ibid., p. 20.

26. Rombro would become best known as one of the pioneers of the Jewish labor movement in England and the United States under the name Philip Krantz.

27. I. Rombro, " 'Alliance' i radeteli," *Razsvet* (1 Feb. 1882), no. 5, p. 186.

28. Cahan, *Bleter,* II, 18.

29. M. [M. I. Rabinovich], "Brozhenie," p. 20 (see n. 21).

30. I. Petrikovsky, "Masa midbar luiziana," *Ha-melits* (7 Nov. 1883), no. 86, p. 1363.

31. AIU:*BM* (Nov. 1881), no. 11, p. 174.

32. Quoted in L. Blank, "K pereselencheskomu voprosu," *Razsvet* (27 Nov. 1881), no. 48, p. 1882.

33. S. M. Dubnov, "Kakaia samoemantsipatsiia nuzhna evreiam?" *Voskhod* (May–June 1883), no. 5–6, pp. 219–46; ibid. (July–Aug. 1883), no. 7–8, pp. 3–30.

34. M. [M. I. Rabinovich], "Talmud li, ili zhizhn prepiatsvuet evreiam zanimatsia proizvoditelnym trudom?" *VS* (15 Aug. 1882), no. 43, p. 11.

35. Ha-Cohen, *Olami,* I, 97–99.

36. Ibid., p. 164.

37. Ibid., p. 166.

38. E.g., "Va-tehi la-dal tikva," *Ha-magid* (18 May 1881), no. 19, pp. 151–3; "Bin ba-davar ve-haven ba-mare," *Ha-melits* (26 May 1881), no. 20, which expressed the hope that given Jewish colonization, "the states of Europe . . . will come together to form a Jewish state as they did in Roumania, Serbia and Bulgaria" (p. 410).

39. "Kievskii pogrom," *RE* (8 May 1881), no. 19, p. 737.

40. Oksman, "Otlik."

41. *RE* (10 June 1881), no. 24, p. 924.

42. AIU:*BM* (July 1881), no. 7, p. 116.

43. E.g., Szajkowski, "The Alliance"; Kohler, "Board of Delegates" (Appendix), pp. 90–2.

44. *Bulletin de l'Alliance,* III (1881), 55.

45. Ibid., p. 56.

46. "Zaiavlenie 'Evreiskogo souiza,' " *Razsvet* (14 Aug. 1881), no. 33, pp. 1300–1; Erez [Tsederbaum], "Dori nasa ve-nigla," *Ha-melits,* (18 Aug. 1881); no. 32, p. 671.

47. "Arur ose mlekhet ha-shem rmiya," ibid., (6 Oct. 1881); no. 39, pp. 802–3.

48. "The Russian Fugitives at Brody," *JC* (2 Dec. 1881), p. 11; *Bulletin de l'alliance,* III (1881), 57. On the mass emigration of 1881–2 see Szajkowski, "Mass Migration"; Cherikover, "Jewish Immigrants," pp. 157–67; 'Plite praot."

49. ***[Y. L. Gordon], "Nahamu, nahamu ami!" *Ha-melits* (25 July 1881), p. 611: cf. *RE* (29 July 1881), no. 31, p. 1204. On the emigration debate of 1881–2 see Turtel, "Pulmus."

50. Erez, "Dori," *He-melits* (11 Aug. 1881), no. 32, p. 672.

51. "Za nedeliu," *RE* (12 Aug. 1881), no. 33, p. 1290.

52. Ibid.

53. Ben-rabbi [Bogrov], "Chto delat?" *RE* (19 Aug. 1881), no. 34, pp. 1326–31; "Pismo v redaktsiiu," ibid. (3 Sept. 1881), no. 36, pp. 1408–9; Dubnov, "Vopros dnia," *Razsvet* (21 Aug. 1881), no. 34, pp. 1348–50; ibid. (28 Aug. 1881), no. 35, pp. 1384–8.

54. Ben-rabbi [Bogrov], in *RE* (2 Sept. 1881), no. 36, p. 1408.

55. Ibid., no. 34 (19 Aug. 1881), p. 1330.

56. *Razsvet* (21 Aug. 1881), no. 34, p. 1349.

57. On these ties see e.g.; the letter from Y. L. Levin to Dr. Asher in Droujanoff, III:390–5; Lifshits, *Zikhron Yaakov* III, 20–89; [Levin], *Yehuda Leb Levin*, p. 71. On Mandelshtam's role in the 1880s see Slutsky, "Dr. Maks Mandelshtam."

58. Droujanoff, I, 2.

59. Ha-Cohen, *Olami*, I, 167–8 (cf. the memorandum submitted by leading Kiev Jews to Count Kutaisov, 16 June 1881, in *Materialy*, II, 425–9).

60. "The Jews in Russia" (letter from Louis Cohen and Sons), *JC* (16 Sept. 1881), p. 10.

61. Droujanoff, I, 2.

62. On the Palestine movement 1881–2 see, e.g., Tsitron, *Toldot hibat tsiyon*, pp. 81–226; Y. Klausner, *Be-hitorer am*, pp. 91–328; Yavnieli (ed), *Sefer ha-tsiyonut* pp. 1–78; Vital, pp. 49–147. On Hibat Zion in historical perspective see Halpern, *Idea of the Jewish State*, pp. 3–130.

63. Smolenskin, "Derekh laavor geulim," *Ha-shahar*, X (1879–82), no. 7, 329–56.

64. Ibid., p. 338.

65. Ibid., pp. 352–3.

66. Ibid., pp. 353–4.

67. Ibid., p. 355.

68. Ibid.

69. Ibid., p. 356n.

70. Ibid., p. 355.

71. Ibid.

72. On the conference (Sept. 1881) see Dinur, "Tokhniyotav," pp. 37–44.

73. "The Jews in Russia," *JC* (23 Sept. 1881), p. 7.

74. Ibid.

75. Dubnov, *Jews in Russia and Poland*, II, 269–75. Mandelshtam, one of the two Jewish representatives on the commission in Kiev, later described how it functioned ("Ignatevskaia komissiia," *Perezhitoe*, IV [1913], 46–64).

76. "The Jews in Russia," *JC* (14 Oct. 1881), p. 5.

77. Bulletin de l'Alliance, III (1881), 55–6. On the Board of Delegates in general see Kohler, pp. 75–135.

78. "Relief of Russian Hebrews," *AH* (8 Sept. 1881), p. 33. The organization initially took as its name the Russian Emigrant Relief Committee.

79. AIU:*BM* (Oct. 1881), no. 10, p. 161.

80. *AH* (8 Sept. 1881), p. 33; *JC* (7 Oct. 1881), p. 7.

81. "Israélites de Russie," AIU:*BM* (Oct. 1881), no. 10, p. 153.

82. Ibid., p. 155.

83. Ibid., p. 161; ibid. (Nov. 1881), no. 11, p. 173.

84. Ibid., no. 11, p. 157.

85. "Hebrew Emigrant Aid Society of the U.S.," *AH* (2 Dec. 1881), p. 28.

86. *Bulletin de l'Alliance*, IV (1882), 12.

87. "Israélites en Russie," AIU:*BM* (Dec. 1881), no. 12, p. 193. On the confused reactions of American Jewry to the new migration see Szajkowski, "Attitude of American Jews."

88. "Israélites en Russie," AIU:*BM* (Nov. 1881), no. 11, p. 174.

89. Ibid., (May 1882), no. 5, p. 97; cf. O.K., "Dvizhenie v polzu emigratsii," *Razsvet* (4 April 1882), no. 14, p. 515.

90. "Inostrannaia khronika," *RE* (22 Jan. 1882), no. 4, p. 142.

91. "Ustav pervoi zemledelcheskoi kolonii russkikh izrailtian v Amerike," ibid. (12 Feb. 1882), no. 7, pp. 273–4.

92. I. Petrikovsky, "Zagranichnaia khronika," *Razsvet* (13 June 1882), no. 24, p. 920.

93. "Niu Iork," *RE* (2 April 1882), no. 14, p. 523.

94. Ibid., pp. 523–4.

95. Ibid., p. 525.

96. Greenberg, II, 29.

97. "Soveshchaniia sezda," *Re* (11 Aug. 1882), no. 32, p. 1238. For Shvabakher's position, cf. his memorandum to Count P. I. Kutaisov (12 July 1881), *Materialy*, II, 304–12.

98. On Ignatev's meetings with the Kiev delegation see Droujanoff, I, 2; with A. Tsederbaum see "Keren ora," *Ha-melits* (29 Sept. 1881), no. 38, pp. 790–1; with Orshansky see *Razsvet*, (22 January 1882), no. 4, pp. 125–6; with Drabkin see *Materialy*, II, 526, and Nidah in *Ha-tsfira* (20 Sept. 1917), no. 30, pp. 7–8. For two sharply conflicting interpretations of Ignatev's policies see Dinur, "Tokhniyotav" and Aronson, "Attitudes."

99. *Razsvet* (22 Jan. 1882), no. 4, p. 125.

100. E.g., Sliozberg, *Dela minuvshikh dnei*, I, 254.

101. "Za nedeliu," *RE* (28 Oct. 1881), no. 44, p. 1731.

102. On the Warsaw pogrom see Shatsky, III, 95–109; Gelber, "Ha-praot."

103. "Pogromy na iuge: baltskii pogrom," *RE* (16 April 1882), no. 16, pp. 581–9.

104. Ianki, "Iz vsekh stran sveta: Niu Iork (iz pisma emigranta)," *RE* (9 Dec. 1881), no. 50, p. 1986.

105. "Hebrew Emigrant Aid Society of the U.S.," *AH* (2 Dec. 1881), p. 28; cf. Osofsky.

106. "Notes of the Week," *JC* (27 Jan. 1882), p. 4; "The Emigration of Russian Jews," ibid., p. 11.

107. "The Jews in Russia," ibid. (7 Oct. 1881), p. 7.

108. "The Conference: Important Meeting of Delegates from all Parts of North America," *AH* (9 June 1882), p. 43.

109. A sum of £8,337 had been collected by mid-1881 ("The Russian Jewish Relief Fund," *JC* [12 Aug. 1881], p. 7).

110. For the protocols of the parliamentary debate and the meeting with Lord Grenville see ibid. (20 May 1881), pp. 12–13; ibid. (27 May 1881), pp. 12–14.

111. "The Jews in Russia: Important Conference," *JC* (11 Nov. 1881), p. 7; cf. ibid. (18 Nov. 1881), p. 7; ibid. (2 Dec. 1881), p. 9.

112. "The Russian Emigrants," ibid. (11 Nov. 1881), p. 8.

113. "The Answer to the Jewish Question," ibid. (21 Oct. 1881), p. 9.

114. "The Jews in Russia," ibid (29 July 1881), p. 9.

115. Jurisconsultus, "The Russian Crisis," ibid. (11 Nov. 1881), p. 9.

116. "The Persecutions of the Jews in Russia," *The Times* (11 Jan. 1882), p. 4.; ibid. (13 Jan. 1882), p. 4.

117. "The Jews in Russia: Provincial Meetings," *JC* (27 Jan. 1882), p. 12.

118. "The Mansion House Meeting," ibid. (3 Feb. 1882), p. 9.

119. Ibid. (17 Feb. 1882), p. 14.

120. "Israélites de Russie," *Bulletin de l'Alliance*, IV (1882), 14.

121. "The Mansion House Relief Fund," *JC* (24 Feb. 1882), p. 14.

122. E.g. AIU:BM (May 1882), no. 5, p. 82; A. Onufrovich, "Krakov," *RE* (26 May 1882), no. 21, p. 806.

123. "Raznie izvestiia," *RE* (4 March 1882), no. 10, p. 383.

124. M.S., "Zhitomir," ibid. (26 Feb. 1882), no. 9, p. 337.

125. Peer [S. P. Rabinovich], "Varshava," ibid. (16 April 1882), no. 16, p. 595.

126. "Nam pishut," ibid. (7 May 1882), no. 19, pp. 712–13.

127. Cahan, *Bleter*, II, 45–7.

128. On these policies, particularly that of the French-Jewish leadership; see Szajkowski, "European Attitude."

129. "The Berlin International Congress," *JC* (12 May 1882), p. 9.

130. A. Onufrovich, "Krakov," *RE* (18 June 1882), no. 24, p. 924.

131. "The Mansion House Committee," *JC* (30 June 1882), p. 4.

132. On the changing attitudes and role of the intelligentsia, particularly the maskilim, see Breiman, "Ha-mifne"; Sosis, *Di geshikhte*, pp. 153–72; Slutsky, *Ha-itonut ha-yehudit-rusit ba-mea ha-tsha-esre*, pp. 121–41.

133. Lifshits, III, 21–2.

134. Ibid., p. 38.

135. Ibid., pp. 57–8.

136. Droujanoff, I, 13–14.

137. Erez, "Ha-yesh tikva le-aharitenu," *Ha-melits* (26 Jan. 1882), no. 4, pp. 60–2.

138. *Razsvet* (22 Jan. 1881), no. 4, p. 125 (the interview was first reported in a special supplement to no. 3).

139. Ibid., pp. 125–6.

140. A. F-r (Flekser), p. 133; Ha-Cohen, *Olami*, II, 9; cf. the letter of the St. Petersburg Jewish leadership to Ignatev in *Materialy*, II, 526.

141. *RE* (22 Jan. 1882), no. 4, p. 131.

142. Droujanoff, III, 363.

143. I. Orshansky, "Po adresu 'zlobstvuiushchikh'," *Razsvet* (22 Jan. 1882), no. 4, p. 128.

144. *Razsvet* (1 Feb. 1882), no. 5, p. 165.

145. Akselrod, *Iz arkhiva P. B. Akselroda*, p. 228.

146. M. Aizman, "Ezrat sofrim: or la-goyim," *Ha-melits* (20 July 1882), no. 28, p. 565.

147. B. Brandt, "Stolitsa i provintsiia," *Razsvet* (27 April 1882), no. 17, p. 620.

148. Ibid., p. 621.

149. Yehalel [Y. L. Levin], "Yakiru ve-yedu," *Ha-melits* (9 March 1882), no. 10, p. 173.

150. Ibid., p. 172.

151. Ibid., p. 171.

152. Ibid., p. 173.

153. Nidah in *Ha-tsfira* (20 Sept. 1917), no. 30, pp. 7–8.

154. Ibid.

155. Akselrod, *Iz arkhiva P.B. Akselroda*, pp. 228–9.

156. "The Jews in Russia (a Narrative from the Borders)," *JC* (24 March 1882), p. 10.

157. Droujanoff, III, 364.

158. Ibid., I, 15.

159. Ibid., III, 360.

160. Y. Klausner, *Be-hitorer am*, p. 170.

161. Droujanoff, I, 12.

162. Nidah in *Ha-tsfira* (27 Sept. 1917), no. 31, p. 12.

163. "Raznie izvestiia," *RE* (7 May 1882), no. 19, p. 615.

164. "Soveshchaniia sezda," in ibid., (31 Aug. 1882), no. 35, p. 1319. For a Hebrew translation of the protocol of the April conference see appendix to Dinur in *He-avar*, X, 61–82.

165. Dubnov, *Jews of Russia and Poland*, II, 307.

166. *Razsvet*, (27 June 1882), no. 26, p. 979.

167. M.O., "Za proshly god," *Voskhod* (March 1882, sec. 2), p. 42.

168. Droujanoff, III, 397.

169. Ibid., I, 63

170. Y. Klausner, "Mi-yamim rishonim," *Ha-olam* no. 24 (20 March 1941), p. 383.

171. Droujanoff, I, 33.

172. "Iz vsekh stran sveta; Avstriia," *RE* (23 April 1882), no. 17, p. 642.

173. Droujanoff, III, 399.

174. Ibid., I, 23.

175. Smolenskin, "Tshuva," *Ha-shahar*, X (1879–82), no. 5, 248. This response was part of an exchange between Smolenskin and Ben Yehuda which began with the former's "Sheelat ha-yehudim–sheelat ha-hayim," ibid., no. 2, pp. 57–65; no. 3, pp. 105–14; no. 4, pp. 153–

60 and included Ben Yehuda's critique: ibid., no. 5, pp. 241–5. Ben Yehuda emigrated from Russia to Palestine in 1881.

176. *Ha-shahar*, X (1879–82), no. 5, p. 247.

177. Ibid., p. 248.

178. Smolenskin, "Hotsi am iver?" ibid., XI (1882–3), no. 1, p. 9.

179. Ibid., p. 12.

180. Smolenskin, "Lehashiv davar," ibid., X (1879–82), no. 8, p. 405.

181. Smolenskin, "Im lo akhshav ematay?" ibid., no. 10, pp. 524–5. For the text of a memorandum stating the Palestine case which Smolenskin sent to the Alliance at this time see "Tazkir," *He-avar*, IV (1956), 40–6; V (1957), 18–28. For Y. Klausner's introduction see ibid., IV (1956), 37–40.

182. Smolenskin, "Sheelat ha-yehudim–sheelat he-hayim," ibid., XI (1882–3), no. 8, 305. According to contemporary estimates, some £285,000 (the equivalent of over 7,000,000 francs) had been collected by mid-1882 (*JC* [30 June 1882], p. 3; ibid. [7 July 1882], p. 5).

183. "Harimu mikhshol miderekh ami," *Ha-shahar*, XI (1882–3), no. 2, 77–8n.

184. On the issue see, e.g., Tsitron, *Toldot hibat tsiyon*, p. 21; Freundlich, p. 148.

185. "Yerushalayim, taale al levavkhem," *Ha-melits* (1 Dec. 1881), no. 47, p. 946.

186. "Lemaan tsiyon lo eheshe?" ibid., (15 Dec. 1881), no. 49, p. 983.

187. Ibid.

188. Ibid. (1 Dec. 1881), no. 47, p. 947.

189. M. Aizman, "Pne ha-lot ha-lot," *Ha-melits* (18 May 1882), no. 19, p. 394.

190. ***[Y. L. Gordon], "Geulatenu u-fdut nafshenu," ibid. (22 March 1882), no. 12, p. 215.

191. ***"Ha-halom ve-shivro," ibid. (1 June 1882), no. 21, p. 409.

192. *RE* (7 May 1882), no. 19, p. 697.

193. Ibid., p. 699.

194. Dubnov, "Sabbatai tsevi i psevdomessianizm v XVII veke," *Voskhod* (July–Aug. 1882), pp. 136–63; ibid. (Sept.–Oct. 1882), pp. 13–44 On Dubnov's politics in the 1880s see Y. Klausner, "Shimon Duvnov," *He-avar*, VIII (1960), 32–42; Slutsky, "Kritikus."

195. Scholem, p. 144.

196. Frug, "Evreiskaia melodiia," *Razsvet* (5 Jan. 1882), no. 1, p. 3. The Biblical quotation (Exodus 14:15) reduced to an acronym was soon adopted by the Palestinophile youth group in Kharkov as its name, although the final choice of title went, of course, to another acronym: Bilu.

197. Lilienblum, "Al yisrael ve-al artso," *Ha-shahar*, X (1879–82), no. 8, p. 402.

198. Ibid., p. 403.

199. Ibid., p. 400.

200. Lilienblum, "Obshcheevreiskii vopros i Palestina," *Razsvet* (16 Oct. 1881), no. 42, p. 1642.

201. Ibid. (9 Oct. 1881), no. 41, p. 1597. For an excellent summary of Lilienblum's position see Vital, pp. 111–22.

202. Lilienblum's socioeconomic theory of cyclical antisemitism was probably influenced by the German historian Wilhelm Roscher, whose essay on the subject (1875) was published in Russian translation in *Evreiskaia biblioteka*, VI (1878), no. 2, 37–60. For an English translation, introduced by G. Kish, see *Historica Judaica*, VI (1944), no. 1, 1–26.

203. *Razsvet* (9 Oct. 1881), no. 41, p. 1600.

204. Ibid. (16 Oct. 1881), no. 42, p. 1639.

205. On Stöcker and political antisemitism in Germany, 1879–82 see e.g., Pulzer, pp. 88–107; Massing, pp. 21–47. On political antisemitism as an emerging international movement, see J. Katz, *Sinat yisrael*, pp. 231–97.

206. *Razsvet* (16 Oct. 1881), no. 42, p. 1638.

207. Ibid. (9 Oct. 1881), no. 41, p. 1599.
208. Ibid., p. 1641.
209. Ibid.
210. Ha-Cohen, *Olami*, I, 195–6.
211. On the attitudes of the Russian-language Jewish press prior to the pogroms see Sosis, "Na rubezhe," *ES*, VIII (1915), 324–37.
212. L.L. [Levanda], "Privislianskaia khronika," *Razsvet* (1 Jan. 1882), no. 1, p. 29.
213. Yehalel, "Mikhtav el ha-mol," *Ha-magid* (6 Oct. 1881), no. 39, p. 322.
214. ***[Y. L. Gordon], "Geulatenu u-fdut nafshenu," *He-melits* (22 March 1882), no. 12, p. 215.
215. Gamzefon [Zamenhof], "Chto zhe nakonets delat?" *Razsvet* (22 Jan. 1882), no. 4, p. 133.
216. Ibid. (1 Feb. 1882), no. 5, p. 170.
217. Y. L. Levin, "Le-masa ha-mahanot (mikhtav el ha-mol)" *Ha-magid* (17 May 1882), no. 19, p. 152.
218. A. S. Fridberg, "Hazon la-moed," *Ha-melits* (2 March 1882), no. 9, pp. 158–9.
219. Lilienblum, "Le-yoshve ketsavot," *Ha-melits* (20 July 1882), no. 28, pp. 558–61.
220. I.Y., "V Palestinu," *Razsvet* (5 March 1882), no. 10, p. 385.
221. Lilienblum, "Ezrat sofrim: mikhtav la-mol," *Ha-melits* (8 June 1882), no. 22, p. 436.
222. Zalman Epstein, "Ale nidaf: li-flagot maskilenu," ibid. (22 June 1882), no. 24, p. 477.
223. Dubnov, "Kakaia samo-emantsipatsiia nuzhna evreiam," *Voskhod* (July–Aug. 1883), p. 30.
224. Ha-Cohen, *Olami*, I, 192.
225. Exodus 15:9.
226. B. Z. Dinaburg [Dinur], "Me-arkhiono," *Kiryat sefer*, I (1924), 81. For a vivid description of the psychological impact made by news of the pogroms on a Lithuanian shtetl see S. Levin's autobiography, *Youth in Revolt*, pp. 3–47.
227. Ha-Cohen, *Olami*, I, 192.
228. "The Jews in Russia: From Our Correspondent (Kieff)," *JC* (3 March 1882), p. 12.
229. Akselrod, *Iz arkhiva P. B. Akselroda*, p. 228.
230. Droujanoff, III, 343.
231. Ibid., p. 345.
232. Ibid.
233. Ibid., p. 348.
234. E. Khisin, "Iz dnevnika palestinskogo emigranta," p. 228. The diary has been published in slightly incomplete form in English and in Hebrew.
235. Droujanoff, I, 52.
236. Ibid., p. 53.
237. Ibid., p. 54.
238. Ibid., pp. 54–65.
239. Ibid., III, 356–7.
240. Ibid., p. 352.
241. Ibid., pp. 352–3.
242. Raevsky, "Mayn ershte bagegenish," in *Yubileum shrift*, p. 15.
243. Ibid., p. 23.
244. Spivak, "Erinerungen fun Kahan's grine tsaytn," in ibid., p. 30.
245. Raevsky, in ibid., p. 24.
246. Cahan, *Bleter*, I, 506.
247. Ibid., p. 507.
248. Ibid., pp. 507–8.

249. A. Onufrovich, "Krakov," *RE* (18 June 1882), no. 24, p. 924.

250. Cahan, *Bleter,* II, 130.

251. On Cedar Valley and similar experiments among the Russian populists see Hecht.

252. Droujanoff, III, 394–5.

253. Ibid., I, 19.

254. Ibid., p. 20.

255. Ibid.

256. Ibid., I, 33.

257. Cahan, *Bleter,* II, 50.

258. I. Petrikovsky, "Zagranichnaia khronika," *Razsvet* (20 June 1882), no. 25, p. 964.

259. Idem, "Vse uvelichivaiushchiisia pritok emigrantov," ibid. (27 June 1882), no. 26, p. 1006.

260. Av. Kagan [Abe Cahan], "Niu Iork," *RE* (7 Oct. 1882), no. 40, p. 1507.

261. Droujanoff, III, 497.

262. "Kitve bilu," *Mi-yamim rishonim,* I (Sept. 1934), no. 4, 78. On the Bilu, see Laskov's major studies, *Ha-biluim* and "Livte."

263. See n. 196 and Droujanoff, I, 56n. On the emergence of the Bilu see e.g., Y. Klausner, *Be-hitorer am,* p. 170; Belkind, pp. 127–64.

264. Droujanoff, I, 57; Y. Klausner, *Be-hitorer am,* p. 170.

265. Droujanoff, I, 57.

266. Ibid., p. 58.

267. Ibid., p. 36.

268. Ibid.

269. Ibid., p. 40.

270. Ibid.

271. "Iz chastnoi perepiski," *RE* (23 Dec. 1882), no. 51, p. 906.

272. Droujanoff, I, 41.

273. Belkind, "Pismo v redaktsiiu," *Razsvet* (30 Nov. 1882), no. 48, p. 1849.

274. Droujanoff, III, 495.

275. Valk, "G. G. Romanenko," pp. 50–2. For a Hebrew translation of this proclamation see Maor, "Ha-kruz."

276. Volk, p. 138n.

277. Bogucharsky, p. 222.

278. Valk, "G. G. Romanenko," p. 52.

279. "Vnutrenee obozrenie," *Narodnaia volia* (23 Oct. 1881), no. 6, p. 12 [in *Literatura partii "Narodnoi voli"* (Moscow, 1930), p. 138].

280. Ibid., p. 13 [p. 139].

281. Ibid., p. 14 [p. 140].

282. Ibid., note (i.e., "The author here is merely repeating the view expressed by the executive committee in the proclamation of 30 August to the Ukrainian people").

283. "Pismo s iuga," *Cherny peredel* (Sept. 1881) (in *Cherney peredel* [Moscow, 1923], p. 304).

284. Ibid., p. 306.

285. "Proklamatsiia vziataia pri obnaruzhenii tainoi tipografii v g. Kieve, v noch na 28-3 aprelia 1881 goda," in *Materialy,* II, 225. For a definitive study of the proclamation see Mishkinsky, "Igud ha-poalim."

286. "Russkaia zhizn," *Zerno: rabochii listok* (June 1881), no. 3, in *IRS* II, 361.

287. *Materialy,* II, 225.

288. *Shvut,* I (1973), 68–9.

289. *IRS,* II, 360.

290. Deich, *Rol evreev,* pp. 325–6.

291. See n. 9.

292. "The Jews in Russia: a Narrative from the Borders [Lyck]," *JC* (16 Dec. 1881), p. 11.

293. Lesin, "Epizodn," *HS*, III, 204.

294. [Levin], *Yehuda Leb Levin*, pp. 65–6.

295. Kursky, "Di zhenever 'grupe'," *HS*, III, 557–62; and Ch. [Cherikover], "Nokh vegn der zhenever grupe."

296. "Ot gruppy sotsialistov-evreev," ibid., p. 572. The manifesto is there republished in Yiddish translation: ibid., pp. 568–76. (Hebrew: A. Rudin, *Me-et havurat sotsyalistim-yehudiyim*. A publication of the Research Project on the Jewish Labor Movement, Hebrew University. Jerusalem, 1966).

297. Ibid., p. 570.

298. Ibid., p. 574.

299. After 1917, it became known that a Yiddish version of the *Rabochaia gazeta,* no. 1 (a publication of the Narodnaia Volia) had been published in January 1881. For the text and a commentary see [Cherikover], "Di narodovolishe *'arbeter tsaytung'* "; cf. Kantor, " 'Arbeiter tseitung.' " Cherikover discounts the theory that Lazar Tsukerman was responsible for the publication.

300. Zaslavsky, p. 109 (cf. *HS*, III, 559–62).

301. On Kropotkin's lecture in which he spoke on "the socioeconomic causes" of the pogroms see Dragomanov, "Iz voprosov tekushchei zhizni," *VS* (13/25 Feb. 1882), no. 28, p. 3.

302. Gurevich, "Sredi revoliutsionerov."

303. M., "Vliianie protivuevreiskikh bezporiadkov na evreev," *VS* (15/27 May 1882), no. 37, p. 10.

304. Dragomanov, "Iz voprosov tekushchei zhizni," p. 4.

305. Dragomanov, "Evreiskii vopros na Ukraine," ibid. (15/27 July 1882), no. 41, p. 6.

306. Ibid.

307. Ibid., note.

308. Dragomanov, "Iz voprosov tekushchei zhizni," p. 4.

309. M., "Vliianie," ibid., (15/27 May 1882), no. 37, p. 10.

310. Ibid.

311. Dragomanov, "Evreiskii vopros," p. 5.

312. Ibid.

313. *VS* (15/27 May 1882), no. 37, p. 10n.

314. Gurevich moved from Berlin to Zurich in the winter of 1880 and lived there in the home of the Akselrods (*EL*, IV [1926], 98).

315. On Akselrod's attitude to Jewish issues (in 1881–2, during the Dreyfus Affair and later) see Ascher's major biographical study, *Pavel Axelrod and the Development of Menshevism*, pp. 69–78, 144–9, 339–40, and his article: "Pavel Axelrod." Cf. Akselrod's unfinished autobiography, "Perezhitoe i peredumannoe," pp. 17–73.

316. Akselrod, "O zadachakh evreisko-sotsialisticheskoi intelligentsii," in *Iz arkhiva P. B. Akselroda,* p. 217. This article and the manifesto "From a Group of Socialist Jews," 1880, have been published together in Hebrew translation. See n. 296.

317. Ibid., p. 218.

318. Ibid., note.

319. Ibid., 218.

320. Ibid., pp. 218–19.

321. Ibid., p. 221.

322. Ibid., p. 223.

323. Ibid., pp. 223–4.

324. Ibid., p. 225.

325. Ibid., p. 226.

326. Ibid.
327. Akselrod, "Pogromen," p. 550.
328. *Gruppa "osvobozhdenie truda,"* I, 153.
329. Ibid., p. 160.
330. Ibid.
331. Ibid., p. 151.
332. Akselrod, *Iz arkhiva P. B. Akselroda,* p. 30.
333. Ibid., p. 31.
334. *Gruppa "osvobozhdenie truda,"* I, 160.
335. Ibid.
336. Akselrod, *Iz arkhiva P. B. Akselroda,* p. 31.
337. E.g., Dubnov, *Jews in Russia and Poland,* II, 308–12; Cherikover, "Di tsarishe politik," in *Geshikhte,* I, 106.
338. Dubnov, *Jews in Russia and Poland,* II, 310–11.
339. Ibid., p. 314.
340. *RE* (1882), no. 26, pp. 978–9.
341. Droujanoff, III, 415.
342. "The Russo-Jewish Refugees," *JC* (14 April 1882), p. 11.
343. "The Russian Refugees," ibid. (21 April 1882), p. 12 (the letter was from Lionel L. Alexander).
344. Ibid. The secretary of the Mansion House Committee, N. S. Joseph, soon denied the authenticity of the memorandum as published in the press (ibid. [April 1882], p. 6).
345. AIU:*BM* (May 1882), no. 5, p. 90.
346. "The Emigration of Russian Refugees to America," *JC* (23 June 1882), p. 12.
347. "The American Hebrew Emigrants' Aid Society," ibid. (30 June 1882), p. 9.
348. "Plain Talk," *AH* (23 June 1882), p. 66.
349. Letter from J. Abrahams, Cincinnati, *JC* (4 Aug. 1882), p. 6.
350. M. Dropsie, "Philadelphia and the Russian Refugees," ibid. (8 Sept. 1882), pp. 5–6.
351. N.N., "Niu Iork," *RE* (18 June 1882), no. 24, p. 925.
352. Z., "Niu Iork," ibid. (7 July 1882), no. 26, p. 1041.
353. "The Russo-Jewish Conference at Vienna," *JC* (1 Sept. 1882), p. 12.
354. Ibid. For a previous international Jewish conference, that on Roumanian Jewry in 1872, see Gartner, "Roumania."
355. "5642," *JC* (15 Sept. 1882), pp. 10–11.
356. Letter from J. Abrahams, Cincinnati, ibid. (29 Sept. 1882), p. 5.
357. *Razsvet* (25 July 1882), no. 30, p. 1137.
358. Ibid. (18 July 1882), no. 29.
359. *RE* (21 July 1882), no. 29, p. 1099.
360. Droujanoff, I, 39.
361. *Ha-melits* (18 May 1882), no. 19, p. 377.
362. Droujanoff, III, 409.
363. G. Gurevich, "Po vozvrashchenii iz Palestini (Aleksandriia)," *Voskhod* (April–May 1882, sec. 2), p. 33.
364. A. Levshenzed, "Koloniia 'Rishon Letsion' v Palestine," *Razsvet* (12 Dec. 1882), no. 50, p. 1945.
365. For the memoirs of an emigrant stranded in Constantinople at this time see Krippe.
366. E.g., *Ha-tsfira* (3 Aug. 1882), no. 30, p. 236.
367. *Razsvet* (28 Sept. 1882), no. 39, p. 1489.
368. "Pismo v redaktsiiu," *Razsvet* (30 Nov. 1882), no. 48, p. 1849.
369. Droujanoff, III, 507.
370. "Our St. Petersburg Letter," *JC* (18 Aug. 1882), p. 6.

371. Droujanoff, I, 51.
372. Ibid.
373. Ibid., p. 66.
374. A. F-r [Flekser], p. 133.
375. Gurevich, "Po vozvrashchenii," *Voskhod* (1882, sec. 2), p. 36.
376. "Avto-emantsipatsiia," *Razsvet* (31 Oct. 1882), no. 44, p. 1689.
377. "Eder adonay (likhvod L. P-r baal ha-hoveret 'oytoemantsipatsion')," *Ha-shahar*, XI (1892–3), 184–5. This poem was dedicated to Pinsker, who responded in a personal letter to Gordon with the suggestion that its all but total despair was exaggerated ("Pismo d-ra L. S. Pinskera k L. O. Gordonu," *Perezhitoe*, III (1911), 392–3).
378. E.g., Akselrod's letter to Deich (22 May 1882) complaining that the brochure was still not ready: "I am embarrassed vis-à-vis the Jews; they undoubtedly think that we just promised to do this for show alone" (*Gruppa "osvobozhdenie truda,"* V, 82).
379. For the possible effects that clandestine financing by the counterrevolutionary Holy Brotherhood may have had on *Volnoe slovo* see Galai and cf. Ben-Ami.
380. Dragomanov, "Evreiskii vopros," VS, no. 41, p. 5.
381. M., "Talmud li," VS, no. 43, p. 13.
382. Ibid., p. 11.
383. M. Dragomanov, "Evreiskii vopros," ibid. (15 Sept. 1882), no. 45, p. 3.
384. Ibid., p. 5.
385. Sh-t, "Pervy antisemiticheskii kongress," ibid. (15 Nov. 1882), no. 49, p. 11.
386. "Po povodu evreiskikh besporiadkov," *Prilozhenie k "listku narodnoi voli"* (1883), no. 1, p. 5 [in *Literatura partii "Narodnoi voli,"* 1930, p. 199].
387. Ibid., p. 6 [p. 200].
388. Yosef Feinberg. Rabbi S. Mohilever, from Belostok, had met with Rothschild three weeks earlier than Feinberg in order, likewise, to plead the cause of settlement in the Holy Land. Y. Klausner, *Be-hitorer am*, pp. 269–74; Schama, pp. 53–6.
389. On the crucial role played by Rothschild in sustaining the settlements of the 1880s see Giladi, "Ha-baron."
390. Droujanoff I, 138–9. S. Hirsch was director of the Mikve Yisrael agricultural school at this period.
391. Ibid., p. 163. Michel Erlanger, a Paris banker and close associate of Edmund de Rothschild, made frequent visits to Palestine in order to inspect the latter's enterprises there.
392. On the establishment of Gedera see Belkind, pp. 169–94.
393. On the Kattowitz conference and the subsequent development of Hoveve Zion see Y. Klausner, *Be-hitorer am*, pp. 440–74; idem, *Mi-katovits ad bazel;* Vital, pp. 147–86; Apel, pp. 171–95.
394. Droujanoff, II, 55.
395. On the United Hebrew Trades see H. Frank; Schappes, "Political Origins."
396. On the early years of the Jewish labor movement in the United States see Epstein, *Jewish Labor,* I, 108–238; Burgin, pp. 68–184.
397. For Cahan's report to the congress of the Second International, see "Referat vegn der sotsyalistisher arbeter bavegung tsvishn di yidish-redende proletarier in amerike," *Di fraye velt* (Oct. 1891), no. 5, p. 20.
398. Cahan, *Bleter,* III, 48–9.
399. "In nyu york," *Di arbeter tsaytung* (May 1890), no. 10, pp. 1–2.
400. Cahan, *Bleter,* III, 96.
401. P. Krantz, "Byalestok un nyu york," *Di arbeter tsaytung* (5 Sept. 1890), no. 27, p. 1.
402. I. Iliashevich [pseud.], "Chto delat evreiam v Rossii," *Vestnik narodnoid voli* (Dec. 1886), no. 5, p. 125. (Hebrew: *Ma al yehude rusya laasot?* A publication of the Research Project on the Jewish Labor Movement, Hebrew University, Jerusalem, 1967).

403. On the movement in London in the 1880s see Fishman, pp. 134–84; Gartner, *The Jewish Immigrant*, pp. 106–40; Cherikover, "London."

404. Cherikover (ed.), *Geshikhte*, II, 195.

405. G. Voltke, "Prosveshchenie," *Evreiskaia entsiklopediia*, XIII, 57–8. On the growth in the Jewish student population, cf. Cherikover, *Istoriia Obshchestva dlia rasprostraneniia prosveshcheniia*; Slutsky, "Tsmihata." Of course, Voltke's figures do not include the Russian-Jewish students at universities abroad, whose number climbed rapidly after 1887.

406. "O zadachakh deiateln. partii v narode," *Narodnaia volia* (Sept. 1884), no. 10, p. 10 [in *Literatura partii "Narodnoi voli*," p. 221].

407. *Vestnik narodnoi voli* (Dec. 1886), no. 5, p. 103.

408. Cahan, *Bleter*, II, 165.

409. On Yanovsky as editor of *Arbeter fraynd* see Fishman, pp. 197–214; Gordin, pp. 159–77; Rocker, *London Years*, pp. 128–31.

410. See Pollak, pp. 205–20. On the fate of one such colony see, e.g., "A Colony in Kansas – 1882"; Rudin; Feld.

411. Br., "Niu Iork," *RE* (12 Nov. 1882), no. 45, p. 1708.

412. Av. Kagan, "Niu Iork," ibid., (1 Dec. 1882), no. 48, p. 1790.

413. On the New Jersey colonies founded in the 1880s see Brandes.

414. I. Petrikovsky, "Evreisko-russkie emigranty i stachka niu iorkshikh zhelezno-dorozhnykh rabochikh," *Razsvet* (1 Aug. 1882), no. 31, p. 1203.

415. Ibid.

416. For the text of the handbill see Lifschutz and Cherikover, p. 261. Cf. Weinstein, pp. 41–5.

417. See e.g., Goldberg, pp. 297–318.

418. Cahan, *Bleter*, II, 432–3.

419. See e.g., Goldberg, pp. 319–45.

420. On Finkelshtein see Reizen, III, 95–9; Vinchevsky, "Erinerungen," in *Gezamlte verk*, X, 220–4.

421. I. Rombro, "Alians i Palestina," in *Palestina* (1884), p. 127.

422. Droujanoff, III, 556.

423. Ibid., pp. 556–7.

424. Ibid., p. 557.

425. Ibid., p. 559.

426. "Mikhtav le-or: mi-ze ehad u-mize ehad," *Ha-magid* (23 May 1883), no. 20, p. 164.

427. Ibid., pp. 164–5.

428. "Nayes fun der yidisher velt," *Der poylisher yidl* (15 Aug. 1884), no. 4, p. 17.

429. "Farmishte nakhrikhtn," ibid. (6 Feb. 1885), no. 29, p. 219. The reference was to the journal of Nathan Birnbaum, *Selbst-Emanzipation*.

430. "An di lezer," ibid. (25 July 1884), no. 1, p. 1.

431. "Yidishe akhdes," ibid. (22 Aug. 1884), no. 5, p. 21.

432. "Yidish," ibid. (8 Aug. 1884), no. 3, p. 9.

433. "Ver iz der meyukhes?" ibid. (29 Aug. 1884), no. 6, pp. 29–30.

434. "Kitve bilu," *Mi-yamim rishonim*, I (Sept. 1934), no. 4, 79.

435. Ibid., p. 78. Cf. Horvits, "Mi-rshimotav," ibid., no. 9–14, pp. 248–9.

436. On this journal see Lifschutz, "Ha-'yidishe folks-tsaytung'." Cf. Kopeloff, p. 189.

437. "A shtikl geshikhte far khonuke," *Nyu yorker yidisher folks tsaytung* (31 Dec. 1886), no. 28, p. 1.

438. "Dos yidntum un di n.y. yidisher folks tsaytung," ibid. (1 April 1887), no. 41, p. 1.

439. Ibid.

440. Droujanoff, I, 126.

441. Ibid., pp. 148–9.
442. Ibid., p. 164.
443. Ibid., p. 165.
444. Ibid., II, 223n. Cf. Belkind, pp. 85–126; Kellner.
445. Droujanoff, II, 291.
446. Ibid., p. 271.
447. [Ben Yehuda], "Divre yeme ha-shavua," *Ha-tsvi* (25 Sivan 5647/17 June 1887), no. 14, p. 2.
448. Ibid., p. 262.
449. Ibid., p. 282.
450. Ibid., p. 414.
451. Ibid., p. 302.
452. Ibid., p. 454. On religious observance as a source of conflict between the old Yishuv and the First Aliya see Abramov, pp. 38–54.
453. Ahad Ha-Am, p. 23.
454. Droujanoff, II, 414.
455. *HS*, III, 768–9.
456. "Chto delat evreiam v Rossii," *Vestnik narodnoi voli* (1886), no. 5, p. 107.
457. Ibid., p. 111.
458. Ibid., p. 110.
459. Ibid., p. 108.
460. Ibid., p. 84.
461. Ibid., p. 109.
462. Ibid., p. 112.
463. Ibid., p. 113.
464. Ibid., p. 114.
465. Ibid.
466. Ibid.
467. Ibid., p. 123.
468. M. Yoeli, p. 119.
469. *Vestnik narodnoi voli* (1886), no. 5, p. 125.
470. On the increasing polarization between socialist and Hovev Zion in London which found expression from 1886 in the rivalry of the *Arbeter fraynd* and *Di tsukunft* see Orren; cf. Marmor, *Moris Vintshevski*, pp. 94–145.
471. J.J., "Natsyonalizmus un stosyalizmus," *Arbeter fraynd* (5 Aug. 1887), no. 27, pp. 2–3.
472. Ibid., p. 3.
473. Ibid., (19 Aug. 1887), no. 29, p. 3.
474. Ibid.
475. Hapgood, p. 34.
476. "Vi kumt a sotsyalist tsu politike," *Di arbeter tsaytung* (20 June 1890), no. 16, p. 4.
477. "Emet me-erets yisrael," in Ahad Ha-Am, pp. 28–9.
478. K. Liberman, "Di yidishe arbeter in england un di yidishe sotsyalistn," *Di fraye velt* (Sept. 1892), no. 4, p. 94.
479. "Program dem sotsyalisten arbeter fareyn," ibid. (Nov. 1892), no. 5, p. 120.
480. "Rabochee dvizhenie v 1891 godu," *Sotsial-Demokrat* (1892), no. 4 (sec. 2), p. 105.
481. Ibid., pp. 107–8. E.g., "The congress could have pointed out that *philo*-semitism can in no way be equated with *anti*-semitism. If there were a Jewish state in which special rights were assigned the Jews *as Jews* then the amendment . . . would have been fully appropriate" (p. 107).

Chapter 3. Politics of Jewish liberation

1. Einhorn, "Vladek'n," in Jeshurin (ed.), p. 117.
2. I. Brutskus, "V poiskakh za programmoi," *KhEZh* (22 March 1906), no. 11, p. 1.
3. On Jewish politics in 1905 see Slutsky, "Shnat 1905." For some works in English on 1905 see Harcave; Sablinsky; Schwarz; Trotsky.
4. On the pogroms of 1903–6 see *Die Judenpogrome*, I, 187–223, and II; *Materialy*, I; and the annual reports in *AJYB*.
5. "From Kishineff to Bialystok: A Table of Pogroms from 1903 to 1906," *AJYB*, VIII (1906–7), 34–69.
6. A. Linden, "Die Dimensionen der Oktoberpogrome (1905)," in *Die Judenpogrome*, I, 189–92.
7. Joseph, p. 93; cf Leshchinsky, *Di yidishe vanderung*, pp. 8–9.
8. "Sezd delegatov 'Soiuza polnopraviia,'" *Voskhod* (23 Feb. 1906), no. 8, p. 30.
9. Ibid.
10. Ibid. (2 March 1906), no. 9, p. 27.
11. Dubnov, "Uroki strashnykh dnei," *Voskhod* (1 Dec. 1905), no. 47–8, p. 3. (For a partial English translation see idem, *Nationalism and History*, pp. 200–14).
12. "Uroki strashnykh dnei," *Voskhod* (1 Dec. 1905), p. 4.
13. Ibid., p. 5.
14. On the East African project see Heymann; Weisbrod; Bein, pp. 411–503.
15. On opposition attitudes to the Jewish problem see Maor, *Sheelat ha-yehudim*.
16. Plekhanov, "Vremena meniaiutsia," *Iskra* (May 1903), no. 39, p. 3 (a translation appeared in *The Worker*, New York, 21 June 1903). For a later article of Plekhanov on the 1881 pogroms see "Neudachnaia istoriia Partii narodnoi voli," *Sovremenny mir* (1912), no. 5, pp. 147–76.
17. *Iskra*, no. 39, p. 3.
18. On self-defence units against pogroms see *Sefer toldot ha-hagana*, I, 155–75; Y. Halpern (ed.), *Sefer ha-gvura*, III, 1–229.
19. "Akt 17 oktiabria," *KhEZh* (28 Oct. 1905), no. 41–2, p. 5.
20. "Politicheskaia reaktsiia," ibid. (10 Jan. 1906), no. 1, p. 3.
21. On the revolutionaries from the Tsederbaum family see Martov, *Zapiski*; Levitsky; Getzler.
22. According to official statistics, in the years 1900–3 there were 2,269 Jews among the political arrestees, or 29.1 percent of the total; in 1905 the percentage reached 34. In that year it was estimated that of the political prisoners held in Siberia, 37 percent were Jews (Slutsky, *Ha-itonut ha-yedudit-rusit (1900–18)*, pp. 17–18; Maor, *Sheelat ha-yehudim*, p. 48).
23. E.g., Herzl's report on his interviews with both Pleve and Witte (*Complete Diaries*, IV, 1525, 1530). Cf. the angry reaction to an implied threat of Witte toward Russian Jewry, "V komitete ministrov," *Voskhod* (4 March 1905), no. 9, pp. 6–7. On the policies of the tsarist regime to the Jews in this period, cf. Löwe.
24. [Weizmann], *Letters and Papers*, II, 307.
25. Korzec.
26. [Weizmann], *Letters and Papers*, I, 208.
27. Ibid., II, 305.
28. Ibid., p. 307. L. Gartner has suggested, in conversation, that demographic factors– the preponderant percentage of the younger age groups in the Jewish population–probably account in part for the important role played by the youth in 1905.
29. "Sezd Souiza polnopraviia," *KhEZh* (23 Dec. 1905), no. 48–9, p. 37. The reference here was to the so-called Bulygin constitution, published on 6 August 1905, which included provisions for elections, on a restricted franchise, to a state duma.

30. An-sky, "Uroki strashnykh vekov," *Voskhod* (23 Feb. 1906), no. 8, p. 6.

31. Bialik's famous poem, "Masa nemirov" ("A Tale of Nemirov"), was first published in *Ha-zman: measef le-sifrut u-l[e]mada* III (July–Sept. 1904), 3–15. His preferred title, "The City of Slaughter" ("Ir ha-harega"), was not used to avoid censorship.

32. An-sky, "Uroki," *Voskhod* (23 Feb. 1906), no. 8, p. 8.

33. A. Feigenzon, "Vegn di ratn fun di arbeter deputatn," *NV* (28 Aug. 1906), no. 16, pp. 8–9.

34. The ICA report of 1904 gave the number of Jewish artisans as 500,986; of unskilled workers as 105,000; and of workers in industry as 33,933. The census of 1897 reported 1,530,307 Jews as gainfully employed. In neither work was there an overall division into the categories of employer, employee, and self-employed, but in the 1920s, Leshchinsky estimated that the wage-earners constituted 27.8 percent of the gainfully employed Jewish population in Poland. Assuming that a similar percentage applied to the situation in the empire as a whole twenty years earlier, the Jewish wage-earning class would then have been approximately 400,000 strong. Estimates of party membership in 1906 were: ESDRP-PZ, 16,000; SSRP, 24,000; SERP, 7,000 (alternatively, 15,000); Bund, 35,000 (see ICA, I, 421, 423, and II, 208–9; [Pervaia vseobshchaia perepis], II, 334–5; Martov et al., *Obshchestvennoe dvizhenie*, III, 333; [SERP], "Materialy," *SERP*, II, 387, 393; Bukhbinder, *Istoriia*, pp. 350–3).

35. On the Jewish revolutionary parties and labor movement in the period 1905–7 see Bukhbinder, *Istoriia*; Kirzhnits and Rafes (eds.), I–II; Rafes, *Ocherki po istorii Bunda*, pp. 121–202; *1905 yor in barditshev*.

36. Dimanshtein. "Di revolutsyonere bavegung," p. 11.

37. I. G. Eizenberg, "Po mogilevskoi gubernii," *Voskhod* (18 Nov. 1905), no. 46, p. 39.

38. Ibid.

39. On the low representation of the Jews in the mechanized factories, see Mendelsohn, *Class Struggle in the Pale*, pp. 112–15, 156–8.

40. Dimanshtein, "Di revolutsyonere bavegung," p. 21.

41. "Revoliutsiia v Rossii," *PI* (19 Jan./1 Feb. 1905), no. 212, p. 1.

42. Ibid.

43. Ibid.

44. Ibid., p. 2.

45. Ibid., p. 1.

46. "Sobytiia v Rige," ibid., (16 Feb./1 March 1905), no. 217, p. 6.

47. "Revoliutsionnye dni na okrainakh," ibid., p. 1.

48. Ibid., p. 2.

49. "Sobytiia v Minske," ibid. (19 Feb./4 March 1905), no. 218, p. 4.

50. "Krovavoe stolknovenie v Varshave," ibid. (7/20 April 1905), no. 227, p. 1.

51. "Krovavaia nedelia v Lodzi," ibid. (14/27 June 1905), no. 238, pp. 1–3.

52. *AJYB*, VIII (1906–7), 47; cf. *PI* (21 June/4 July 1905), no. 239, p. 1, where the number of killed and wounded was given as 1,300.

53. "Rabochee vozstanie v Lodzi," *Iskra* (15 June 1905), no. 102, p. 5.

54. "Odesskoe vozstanie," *PI* (4/17 July 1905), no. 241, p. 2.

55. "Odesskoe vozstanie," *Iskra* (21 June 1905), no. 103, p. 4.

56. "Chrezvychainye mery," *Voskhod* (29 June 1905), no. 26, p. 3.

57. "Pervoe maia i pogromy," *PI* (5/18 May 1905), no. 231, p. 2.

58. Litvak, "In der yidisher veltl," *Der veker* (1/14 Jan. 1906), no. 7, p. 3.

59. Ibid.

60. E.g., Virgily, "Byalestok," ibid. (12/25 Jan. 1906), no. 15, p. 4.

61. Akimov, "Stroiteli budushchego," *Obrazovanie* (1907), no. 4 (sec. 2), p. 116.

62. Idelson, "O evreiskoi sotsial demokratii," *EZ* (Dec. 1905), no. 12, p. 111.

63. Ibn-Daud [Idelson], "Novy kurs Bunda," *KhEZh* (10 May 1906), no. 18, p. 13.

64. Chemerisky, p. 1.
65. D., "Korrespondents i soobshcheniia: pismo iz Pinska," *Voskhod* (8 Oct. 1905), no. 40, p. 29.
66. Ibid.
67. Ibid., p. 30.
68. Iulii V., "Tri preduprezhdeniia (k istorii oktiabrskikh dnei v Minske)," *Voskhod* (11 Nov. 1905), no. 44–5, p. 15.
69. Litvak, "In der yidisher veltl," p. 3.
70. Dubnov, "Uroki," *Voskhod* (16 Dec. 1905), no. 49–50, p. 11.
71. An-sky, "Uroki," ibid. (23 Feb. 1906), no. 8, p. 7.
72. Blekhman, p. 229.
73. "Sezd Soiuza polnopraviia," *Voskhod* (30 Dec. 1905), no. 51–2, p. 4.
74. Ibid., pp. 5–6.
75. I. Brutskus, "Ekonomicheskii krizis," *KhEZh* (23 Dec. 1905), no. 48–9, p. 10.
76. Ibid., p. 11.
77. T., "Obzor evreiskoi pechati," *Voskhod* (3 Feb. 1906), no. 5, p. 17.
78. P. Bogrov [Zaslavsky], "Briv fun VII tsuzamenfor," *FTs* (11 Sept. 1906), no. 157, p. 5.
79. "Bobroysk," *Der veker* (12 Jan. 1906), no. 15, p. 4.
80. Virgily, "Byalestok," ibid.
81. Ibid.
82. "Undzere anarkhistn," *FTs* (26 Feb. 1906), no. 7, p. 1. On the Jewish anarchists in Russia in 1905–6, cf. I. H. Hourwich's despatch to New York: "Di anarkhistn in rusland," *Tsayt-gayst* [7 Sept. 1906], no. 54, pp. 2–3; on the anarchist movement generally see Avrich.
83. "Fun partey-lebn," *FTs* (24 Feb. 1906), no. 6, p. 3.
84. Peretskys A Veber, "Korespondentsn," ibid. (27 April 1906), no. 51, p. 6; (28 April), no. 52, p. 6.
85. M., "Byalestok," ibid. (22 June 1906), no. 96, p. 2.
86. An Alter Bekanter [Pesakhzon], "A nayer peyrush oyfn byalestoker pogrom," ibid.
87. Gavriel [Liliput], "Di shrekn un byalestok-yidishe pogromen un ekspropriyatsyes," ibid. (12 June 1906), no. 87, p. 2.
88. M. Sukennikov, "Evreiskaia samooborona," *Voskhod* (27 Oct. 1905), no. 42–3, p. 59.
89. Jabotinsky, "Nabroski bez zaglaviia," *KhEZh* (10 Jan. 1906), no. 1, p. 14.
90. Ibid.
91. Dimanshtein, "Di revolutsyonere bavegung," p. 10.
92. "Der byalestoker pogrom in der duma," *NV* (7 July 1906), no. 11, p. 45.
93. "Di zelbst-shuts," ibid. (22 June 1906), no. 9, pp. 381–2.
94. A.L. [Litvak], "Vegn di pogromen," *FTs* (11 June 1906), no. 86, p. 1.
95. On the trade-union movement among the Jewish workers in this period see Kirzhnits, *Di profbavegung*.
96. Anna Rozental, "Vladek," in Jeshurin (ed.), p. 110.
97. Lesin, "B. Vladek amol in itst," ibid., pp. 21–2.
98. Blekhman, pp. 219–20.
99. Litvak, "Di organizatsyons frage," *Der veker* (29 Dec. 1905), no. 5, p. 1.
100. "In der yidisher veltl," ibid. (1 Jan. 1906), no. 7, p. 3.
101. Shazar, *Or ishim*, I, 85.
102. Ibid., p. 86.
103. Y. Klebanov, "Rezultaty sezda v Tsiurikhe," *Razsvet* (15 March 1913), no. 11, p. 9.
104. A member of the working class could only vote if he was employed in a factory with at least fifty workers. On the system used for the election of the First and Second Dumas see Mehlinger and Thompson, pp. 241–88; Haimson, *Politics*, pp. 1–29.

105. Frumin, "Di duma, di pogromen un di yidishe rekhtn," *FTs* (23 July 1906), no. 117, p. 1.

106. On the Jewish deputies and Jewish issues in the First Duma see Harcave, "The Jews"; idem, "Jewish Question in the First Duma,"; B. Z. Katz, "Ha-parlament ha-rishon"; Maor, "Yehude rusya"; Levin, *Arena*, pp. 291–5.

107. "Proklamatsiia tsentralnogo komiteta Bunda," *PI* (12 Jan. 1905), no. 209, p. 1.

108. [Weizmann], *Letters and Papers*, III, 229–30.

109. Jabotinsky, "Nabroski bez zaglaviia," *KhEZh* (2 Jan. 1905), no. 1, p. 6.

110. "V redaktsiiu postupilo sleduiushchee obrashchenie k sionistam ot chlenov sionist-skogo Actions-Comité v Rossii," ibid (22 May 1905), no. 19, p. 3.

111. "O vserossiiskom sezde sionistov," ibid. (8 April 1906), no. 13, p. 1.

112. N. Pereferkovich, "Nedelia o zhargone," *Voskhod* (9 Feb. 1906), no. 6, p. 42.

113. An-sky, "Uroki," ibid. (9 March 1906), no. 10, p. 11.

114. Ibid.

115. "Ekstrennoe sobranie 'Obshchestva rasprostraneniia prosveshcheniia,'" ibid. (4 March 1905), no. 9, p. 13.

116. E.M., "Obshchee sobranie kievskogo Ob-va prosveshcheniia," ibid. (13 Oct. 1905), no. 41, pp. 8–9.

117. 27 February; Klausner file, Ussishkin archive, CZA.

118. Ibid., 20 May 1905.

119. Ibid., 15 January 1906. On the crisis in Hebrew publishing cf. Y. Klausner, "Ha-mashber."

120. On the political tactics of the Zionists and liberals in the period 1905–6 see Maor, *Ha-tnua ha-tsiyonit* pp. 303–19; Slutsky, "Menahem Usishkin"; Sliozberg, *Dela minuvshikh dnei*, III, 168–280.

121. "Sezd delegatov 'Soiuza polnopraviia,'" *Voskhod* (23 Feb. 1906), no. 8, p. 28.

122. I. G. Eizenbet, "Po mogilevskoi gubernii," ibid. (18 Nov. 1906), no. 46, p. 37.

123. On the Union of Unions and its role in the 1905 revolution see Galai, *Liberation Movement*, pp. 245–72.

124. "Sezd Soiuza polnopraviia," *KhEZh* (23 Dec. 1905), no. 48–9, p. 34.

125. Cf. Schechtman, I, 110–25.

126. "Sezd Soiuza polnopraviia," *KhEZh* (23 Dec. 1905), no. 48–9, p. 36.

127. Jabotinsky, "Eshche o Bunde," *KhEZh* (28 Feb. 1906), no. 8, p. 8.

128. Idem, "Bund i natsionalnoe sobranie," ibid. (17 Feb. 1906), no. 2, p. 5.

129. "Sezd Soiuza polnopraviia," *Voskhod* (30 Dec. 1905), no. 51–2, p. 6.

130. Ibid., pp. 7–8.

131. Jabotinsky, "Nabroski bez zaglaviia," *KhEZh* (10 Jan. 1906), no. 1, p. 10.

132. Levin, *Arena*, p. 289.

133. Jabotinsky, "Avtonomiia," *KhEZh* (23 Dec. 1905), no. 48–9, p. 18.

134. Idem, "Eshche o Bunde," p. 8.

135. Idem, "Nabroski bez zaglaviia," ibid. (10 Jan. 1906), no. 1, p. 14.

136. Idem, "Eshche o Bunde," p. 11.

137. 15 Jan. 1906; Klausner file, Ussishkin archive, CZA.

138. Dubnov, "Evrei," p. 412. Cf. Maor, *Ha-tnua ha-tsiyonit*, pp. 315–9; Grinbaum.

139. "Sezd Soiuza polnopraviia," *KhEZh* (23 Dec. 1905), no. 48–9, p. 36.

140. Jabotinsky, "Nashi zadachi," *KhEZh* (20 July 1906), no. 28, p. 15.

141. Olgin, "Yunge zkeynim," *FTs* (11 April 1906), no. 38, p. 2.

142. S. [Syrkin], "Di yidishe gas far di valn," *NV* (10 Jan. 1907), no. 25, p. 2.

143. Ibid., p. 3.

144. G-'. [Liliput?], "Di frishgebakene sotsyal-demokratn," *FTs* (27 March 1906), no. 32, p. 3.

145. Jabotinsky, "Pole 'brani'," *KhEZh* (30 Dec. 1905), no. 50, p. 5.
146. "Sezd Soiuza polnopraviia," ibid. (23 Dec. 1905), no. 48–9, p. 36.
147. E.g., Spector.
148. Jabotinsky described the movement for Jewish autonomy in Austria-Hungary as part of a broad historical trend, and he went to Galicia in 1906 to study Zionist policy there (see his "Avtonomiia," pp. 18–22; Gelber, *Toldot ha-tnua ha-tsiyonit*, II, 528).
149. From M. Broide's reminiscences as quoted in Gelber, *Toldot ha-tnua ha-tsiyonit*, II, 539.
150. M. Kleiman, "Sezd avstriiskikh poalei tsion," *Evreiskii narod* (18 Oct. 1906), no. 1, p. 31.
151. On the origins of this party, usually known by the initials of its name in Polish (the ŻPS), see Grossman.

Chapter 4. The Bund

1. Mishkinsky, "Yesodot leumiyim," pp. 116–31. For two other major histories of the Bund in tsarist Russia see Tobias, *Jewish Bund;* and *Di geshikhte fun Bund*, I–II. For a shorter work on the early Bund and socialist Zionism see Patkin.
2. G. V. Plekhanov, *O zadachakh*, p. 58.
3. On these early strikes see Menes, "Di yidishe arbeter bavegung," pp. 9–36.
4. *Pervoe maia 1892 goda*, p. 3.
5. Trunk, "Di onheybn," *Di geshikhte fun Bund*, I, 68.
6. [Martov], *Povorotny punkt*, pp. 11–12.
7. Ibid., pp. 17–18.
8. Ibid., p. 18.
9. Ibid., p. 19.
10. [Rozental], *Vozzvanie*, p. 3.
11. [Kossovky], *K voprosu*, p. 13.
12. Ezra [Rozin], "Tsu der diskusye vegn der fareynikungs frage," *FTs* (23 June 1906), no. 97, p. 3.
13. Olgin, "Tsen yor," p. 12.
14. Lesin, *Zikhronot*, p. 125.
15. In my Ph.D. thesis, I described the period 1892–7 although not that of 1897–1903 in terms of this argument (J. Frankel, "Socialism," pp. 87–121).
16. [Pesakhzon], p. 28. There is doubt regarding the date of this manifesto. Cf. Shvarts, p. 528, and Mishkinsky, "Kruz," where he argued cogently for 1893.
17. Grossman, pp. 16–17.
18. Kisman.
19. Grossman, pp. 16–17.
20. Ibid., p. 18.
21. Cf. Bross.
22. Kisman, p. 460.
23. Ibid., pp. 465–6.
24. Ibid., p. 470.
25. [Herzl], IV, 1543–4. Cf. Bein, *Theodore Herzl*, pp. 447–52.
26. S. Levin, *The Arena*, pp. 131–2.
27. Weizmann, *Letters and Papers*, III, 64.
28. Ibid.
29. P. Libman [Hersh], "Likht un shotn in der bavegung," *Tsayt* (23 Jan. 1914), no. 4/43, p. 2.

30. E-r [Ester], "Vi azoy darf men shteln bay undz di shulfrage," ibid. (30 Jan. 1914), no. 5/44, p. 2.

31. Litvak, p. 140. This essay, "Kharakter-shtrikhn fun der yidisher arbeter-bavegung," is thought-provoking throughout, see ibid., pp. 116–47.

32. "Di diskusye," *Undzer tsayt* (Dec. 1927), no. 3, p. 88.

33. S. An-sky, "Uroki," *Voskhod* (9 March 1906), no. 10, p. 11.

34. [Akimov], *Vladimir Akimov*, p. 230.

35. Akimov, "Stroiteli budushchego," *Obrazovanie*, XVI (1907), no. 4 (sec. 2), 113–4.

36. Ibid., p. 114.

37. Ibid., p. 117.

38. Zivion, "20 yor 'bund'," p. 627.

39. Marx and Engels, "Manifest der kommunistischen Partei," *Werke*, IV, 479.

40. Ibid., p. 473.

41. Ibid., p. 479.

42. On the attitude of Marx and Engels to the national question see Bloom, *World of Nations*.

43. According to Medem's theory of "neutralism," first fully formulated in 1904, the Bund should adopt a position neither for nor against assimilation. This issue would ultimately be decided by long-term socioeconomic factors. But, nonetheless, the Bund had to demand that the state permit its contituent nationalities, including the Jewish people, genuine choice. Anything less than cultural-national autonomy would mean, in reality, sociopolitical coercion ("Sotsial demokratiia i natsionalny vopros," *Vestnik bunda*, 1904, no. 4, pp. 1–10; no. 5, pp. 7–14). Cf. Pinson, pp. 246–63; Tobias, *Jewish Bund*, pp. 272–8.

44. Martov, *Zapiski*, p. 224; [Srednitskaia], "Zikhroynes," p. 51; Gordon, pp. 58–66; [Bund], *Di geshikhte*, pp. 10–11. Mill (I, 101–5) dated the beginning of the crisis in May 1892.

45. Kopelzon gave 150 as the number of workers in propaganda circles alone in 1891. Gordon estimated the total number of workers in the movement in 1892 as 1,000, and the first party history gave the figure of 500 organized workers in 1895 (Kopelzon in Dimanshtein, *Revoliutsionnoe dvizhenie*, p. 70; Gordon, p. 42; [Bund], *Di geshikhte*, p. 20).

46. Gordon, p. 54.

47. Ibid., p. 64. The reference is to Liuba Levinson (Aizenshtat).

48. Ibid.

49. Gozhansky in Dimanshtein, *Revoliutsionnoe dvizhenie*, p. 85.

50. Martov, *Zapiski*, p. 233.

51. [Srednitskaia,] "Zikhroynes," p. 53.

52. [Kremer], *Ob agitatsii*, p. 3.

53. See the speech delivered by Fania Reznik for May Day, 1892, quoted above. She spoke there as if the entire strategy of economic agitation was already well familiar to her (cf. Mishkinsky, "Me-huge").

54. Kopelzon in Dimanshtein, *Revoliutsionnoe dvizhenie*, pp. 70–1. Yogikhes led a strike of some 30 printing workers in a Vilna printing works in 1888 (Menes, "Di yidishe arbeter bavegung," p. 38).

55. Kopelzon in Dimanshtein, *Revoliutsionnoe dvizhenie*, pp. 71–2; cf. idem, "Di ershte shprotsungen," pp. 66–7; Rabinovich, pp. 335–6.

56. Gordon, pp. 42–58.

57. Kremer, "Mit 35 yor tsurik," p. 83.

58. Gordon, p. 66. Apart from Gordon's own memoirs and publications, there are reminiscences of the Vilna "worker opposition" by two other of its members: Blum, "Zikhroynes," pp. 352–60; Marmor, *Mayn lebens geshikhte*, I, 314–65.

59. [Kremer], *Ob agitatsii*, pp. 23–4.

60. Mendelsohn, *Class Struggle*, p. 60. On the Vilna movement in the 1890s see ibid., pp. 1–81.
61. [Kremer], *Ob agitatsii*, p. 25.
62. "A briv tsu agitatorn," *HS*, III, 629. Cf. Mishkinsky, "Mekoroteha ha-rayoniyim."
63. *HS*, III, 630–1.
64. Ibid., p. 630.
65. "Bericht der jüdisch-sozialdemokratischen Gruppe 'Lumina' unterbreitet dem 'Internationalen Socialistischen Arbeiter Gewerkschafts Congress–London 1896'" (Yiddish: *HS*, III, 480–1).
66. "A briv tsu agitatorn," ibid., p. 631.
67. Ibid.
68. Mill, I, 216.
69. Ibid.
70. Ibid., pp. 216–7.
71. Martov, *Zapiski*, p. 232.
72. Marmor recalled that as a sympathizer with Gordon's "opposition," he regarded *On Agitation* as insufficiently "internationalist" – adequate, perhaps, "to win the twelve-hour day but not to overthrow the tsarist Autocracy" (*Mayn lebns geshikhte*, I, 321).
73. Marmor asserted, moreover, that Kremer's group, by warning falsely of an "imminent" police raid, had gained control of the movement library (ibid., p. 316).
74. For some of the fragmentary information on these opposition groups see B. Eidelman, pp. 35–7, 57–8; Gelman; Gershanovich; Broido; Pietkewicz.
75. Frumkin, "Ocherki," p. 260.
76. Mill, I, 111.
77. Lesin, "A por verter tsu gen. Tsivyon's artikl," *Di tsukunft* (Nov. 1917), p. 630.
78. Idem, *Zikhronot*, p. 124.
79. Idem, "Mayn ershte bagegenish," p. 305.
80. Idem, *Zikhronot*, p. 131.
81. [Martov], *Povorotny punkt*, p. 20.
82. Ibid., p. 17.
83. Ibid., pp. 18–19.
84. Martov, *Zapiski*, p. 246.
85. [Martov], "Evreiskie rabochie protiv evreiskikh kapitalistov," *Rabotnik* (1896), no. 1–2 (sec. 2), pp. 87–8.
86. Rabinovich, "Mit 50 yor tsurik," pp. 329–36. Cf. Zhitlovsky, *Zikhroynes*, III, 145. Zhitlovsky at one time planned to join the projected group in Switzerland.
87. Kopelzon, "Di ershte shprotsungen," p. 67.
88. For example, in 1886 Shmuel Rabinovich sent ten copies of each of the *Nyu yorker yidishe folks-tsaytung* and of the *Arbeter fraynd* from Paris to Russia, where they were distributed to revolutionaries in Brest-Litovsk, Belostok, Vilna, and Minsk (*HS*, III, 329). Cf. [Bund], *Di geshikhte*, p. 20.
89. Martov, *Zapiski*, p. 227.
90. [Mill], "Varshe (detsembr, 1896)," *YA* (Feb. 1897), no. 2–3, p. 21.
91. On the numerus clausus, which restricted the number of Jews in the *gimnazii* and universities to 10 percent in the Pale, 3 percent in Moscow and St. Petersburg, and 5 percent elsewhere see e.g., Dubnov, *History of the Jews*, II, 348–53.
92. *He-avar* (1971), vol. XVII, contains a large number of articles on the expulsions from Moscow of 1891; e.g., Maor, "Ha-reka," ibid., pp. 25–34.
93. Mill, I, 107.
94. Lesin, "Der vikhtikster," p. 272.
95. Ibid.

96. Mill, I, 107.
97. [Srednitskaia], "Zikhroynes," p. 54.
98. *Pervoe maia 1892 goda*, p. 24.
99. Ibid., p. 23.
100. Ibid., introduction, p. v.
101. Kopelzon, "Di ershte shprotsungen," pp. 55–60; cf. Rappoport, pp. 213–14, 224–5.
102. Gordon, p. 13.
103. Gozhansky, in Dimanshtein, *Revoliutsionnoe dvizhenie*, pp. 86–7.
104. Mill, I, 98.
105. *Pervoe maia 1892 goda* (introduction), p. xviii.
106. Ibid., p. xxi.
107. Ibid., p. ii.
108. Ibid., p. vi.
109. Mill, I, 98.
110. Ibid., pp. 224–5.
111. On the two Polish socialist parties and their nationality policies see Haustein, pp. 137–277; Nettl, I, 63–111; Strobel, pp. 71–203; Wasilewski, pp. 180–202, 323–38.
112. "Do towarzyszy socyjalistów żydów w polskich zabranych prowincyjach," *Przedświt* (1893), no. 5, p. 9. The decision to publish this appeal to "the Jewish socialist comrades" in Lithuania had been taken at the congress of Polish socialists held in Paris, November 1892. On the relations between the Jewish socialist movement and the Polish socialist parties see Mishkinsky, "Tnuat ha-poalim ha-yehudit"; Zeira; and finally, Hertz, "The Bund's Nationality Program."
113. Czasowy [Piludski], "Wilno we wrześniu," *Przedświt* (1894), no. 9, p. 26.
114. In Dimanshtein, *Revoliutsionnoe dvizhenie*, pp. 72–3; Gozhansky recalled that discussions on the national question were also held in Vilna at this time with two of the future leaders of the Lithuanian Social Democratic Party, S. Trusiewicz and A. Domaszewicz (ibid., p. 84). Moreover, in January 1893, Mendelson, the PPS leader, came to Vilna and conducted formal negotiations with the representatives of the Jewish group (Shvarts, *Yuzef Pilsudski*, p. 36).
115. In Dimanshtein, *Revoliutsionnoe dvizhenie*, p. 72.
116. Shvarts, *Yuzef Pilsudski*, pp. 109–30. On Pilsudski's role in the publication and transportation of Yiddish literature cf. "Di 'tsukunft' in untererdishn rusland," in Kursky, *Gezamlte shriftn*, pp. 252–4.
117. Martov, *Zapiski*, p. 240.
118. Shvarts, *Yuzef Pilsudski*, p. 130.
119. Czasowy [Pilsudski], "Wilno we wrześniu," *Przedświt* (1894), no. 9, p. 27.
120. May 1894; quoted in Shvarts, *Yuzef Pilsudski*, p. 130; (Polish: "Listy Józefa Piłsudskiego," *Niepodległość*, XII [1935], 306.)
121. Shvarts, *Yuzef Pilsudski*, pp. 126–7; (*Niepodległość*, XII [1936], 145).
122. E.g., Dushkan in Dimanshtein, *Revoliutsionnoe dvizhenie*, pp. 241–2.
123. Kursky, "Arkadi un zayn tkufe," p. 86.
124. [Bund], *Di geshikhte*, p. 24.
125. Vilensky-Sibiriakov et al. (eds.), V (1–2), 35.
126. Rubach (ed.), pp. 80–4, 98.
127. Wildman, "Russian and Jewish Social Democracy," p. 76.
128. Litvak, *Vos geven* p. 98.
129. Ibid., pp. 105–6 (Litvak's article ["Di zhargonsihe komitetn," ibid., pp. 70–116] remains the major first-hand source of information on the Jargon Committee in Vilna.)
130. Litvak, *Vos geven*, p. 98.
131. Ibid., p. 83.
132. Ibid., p. 96.

133. Ibid., pp. 108–9. Among those associated with the Tsayt-gayst society were Dovid Pinsky, I. Eliashev, E. Davidzon (later an Iskrovets), and Zhitlovsky.

134. E.g., Mill, I, 230; Martov, *Zapiski*, pp. 253–4.

135. For a discussion of the very significant regional differences that characterized the formation of the Jewish socialist movements, see Mishkinsky, "Regional Factors"; Brym. For a sociological analysis of Bundist leadership see Woodhouse and Tobias, "Primordial Ties" and Tobias and Woodhouse, "Political Reaction."

136. E.g., Kopelzon, "Stranichka"; cf. Levitsky, pp. 27–8.

137. E.g., Sponti, p. 71.

138. "P.B. Akselrod o vstrechakh s E. I. Sponti i V. I. Ulianovym-Leninym," in [Plekhanov], *Perepiska G. V. Plekhanova i P. B. Akselroda*, I, 265–75.

139. *Doklad predstavlenny delegatsiei russk. sotsialdemokratov mezhdunarodnomu rabochemu sotsialisticheskomu kongressu v Londonu v 1896 godu;* quoted in *Di geshikhte fun bund*, I, 92.

140. "Fun der redaktsyon," *YA* (1896), no. 1, p. 2.

141. Kossovsky, "Zubatov," p. 182.

142. VIL: *PSS*, XLVI, 8.

143. *Gruppa "osvobozhdenie truda,"* V, 158.

144. Ibid., IV, 252.

145. Medem, "Di tsentrale figur," p. 234.

146. P. B. Akselrod, "Posleslovie," in [Kremer], *Ob agitatsii*, pp. 35–42.

147. Kremer, "Osnovanie Bunda," p. 52.

148. Akimov, "Pervy sezd RSDRP," p. 133.

149. E.g., B. Eidelman, pp. 31–3.

150. "Der yidisher sotsyal-demokratisher tsuzamenfor," *AS* (17 Oct. 1897), no. 6, pp. 3–4.

151. Mill, I, 261.

152. "Varshe," *YA* (1896), no. 1, p. 37.

153. Shvarts, *Yuzef Pilsudski*, pp. 145–6; cf. Cherikover, "Di onheybn," pp. 559–600; Haustein, pp. 246–51.

154. Trunk, in *Di geshikhte fun Bund*, I, 84. On the relations of Mill's group with that of Rug see Kaufman, pp. 341–7; Piasecki, pp. 21–35.

155. Shvarts, *Yuzef Piłsudski*, p. 141; *Niepodległość*, XVIII (1938), 289–9.

156. Mill, I, 268.

157. D. Kats, in Dimanshtein, *Revoliutsionnoe dvizhenie*, pp. 139–40.

158. "Der yidisher sotsyal-demokratisher tsuzamenfor," *AS* (17 Oct. 1897), no. 6, p. 4.

159. Ibid., p. 5.

160. *Listok rabotnika* (Nov. 1897), no. 3–4, p. 48.

161. "Po Rossii," *Rabochaia gazeta* (Nov. 1897), no. 2; reproduced in [RSDRP], *Pervy sezd*, p. 284.

162. [RSDRP], *Pervy sezd*, p. 82.

163. Ibid., p. 83.

164. D. Kats, in Dimanshtein, *Revoliutsionnoe dvizhenie*, p. 156.

165. "Undzere tsiln," *AS* (2 Dec. 1898), no. 11, p. 5.

166. Ibid., p. 6.

167. Ibid.

168. "Czwarty zjazd naszej partyi," *Robotnik* (13 Feb. 1898), no. 26, p. 2. Cf. "W kwestyi żydowskiej," ibid., pp. 2–4. On the hostile reaction of the PPS to the creation of the RSDRP see Haustein, pp. 232–9.

169. "Undzere tsiln," *AS* (2 Dec. 1898), no. 11, p. 7.

170. [Kossovsky], *Borba*, p. 13.

171. On the attitude of the Bolshevik regime toward the Jewish population in the post-1917 period see e.g., Gitelman, pp. 105 ff.; M. Altschuler, "Maamada."

172. For a fuller development of the views presented here on the "Economist" crisis see J. Frankel, introductory essay in [Akimov], *Vladimir Akimov*, pp. 3–98. On Plekhanov see Vaganian; S. H. Baron. Cf. J. Frankel, "Voluntarism"; idem, "Party Genealogy."

173. Letter published in Plekhanov (ed.), *Vademecum*, pp. 35–6.

174. "Materialy k istorii pervogo sezda," *PR* (1928), no. 3/74, p. 166.

175. [Plekhanov], *Perepiska G. V. Plekhanova i P.B. Akselroda*, II, 23.

176. Ibid., pp. 35–6.

177. Ibid., p. 19.

178. Steklov, "V ssylke," *PR* (1923), no. 5/17, pp. 211–12.

179. Editorial note to "Adres russko-evreiskikh rabochikh Niu Iorka peterburgskim stachechnikam," *Rabotnik* (1897), no. 3–4, pp. 169–70.

180. *Gruppa osvobozhdenie truda*, IV, 264.

181. [Plekhanov], *Perepiska G.V. Plekhanova i P.B. Akselroda*, II, 111.

182. Idem (ed.), *Vademecum*, p. li.

183. Ibid., p. lii.

184. "Fun der prese," *YA* (1900), no. 9, p. 76.

185. Ibid., p. 77.

186. Ibid.

187. *YA* (March 1899), no. 6, p. 11n.

188. Chaim [Mill], " 'Der arbeter' numer 1," ibid., p. 45.

189. Ibid., pp. 45–6. The reference is to Kautsky, "Der Kampf der Nationalitäten und das Staatsrecht in Oesterreich," *Die Neue Zeit* (1898), no. 17, 516–24; no. 18, 557–64. On the Social Democrats in Austria and Germany and the Jewish question see Wistrich, *Revolutionary Jews*, pp. 59–129 and his articles cited here in the bibliography; Massing, pp. 151–206.

190. *YA*, no. 6, p. 46.

191. R. Luxemburg, "Der sotsyalizmus in poyln," ibid. (Dec. 1899), no. 8, pp. 15–18. On the relationshp between the Bund and the SDKP in the years 1897–1901 see Strobel, pp. 137–9.

192. "Di natsyonale frage oyf dem kongres fun der estraykhisher sotsyal-demokratye in brun," *YA* (Dec. 1899), no. 8, pp. 23–7.

193. B. Chaim [Mill], "Di pogromen in nikolayev," ibid. (Aug. 1899), no. 7, p. 21.

194. "Di natsyonale frage," ibid. (Dec. 1899), no. 8, p. 27.

195. Ibid.

196. Mill, II, 54.

197. Ibid., I, 111.

198. D. Kats, in Dimanshtein, *Revoliutsionnoe dvizhenie*, p. 168.

199. Kremer, "Der ershter ts. k. fun bund," p. 389.

200. Mill, II, 51.

201. "Sotsyalistishe nakhrichtn," *YA* (Dec. 1899), no. 8, p. 32. The existence of this note was first publicized by the PPS "Protest," *Przedświt* (1899), no. 11, p. 21.

202. "Der driter tsuzamenfor fun dem algemaynem yidishn arbeter bund in rusland un poyln," *YA* (1900), no. 9, p. 5.

203. Ibid., p. 6.

204. Ibid., pp. 6–7.

205. Ibid., p. 7.

206. "Der ferter kongres fun algemaynem yidishn arbeter bund in rusland un poyln," *YA* (1901), no. 12, p. 99.

207. Ibid., pp. 99–100.

208. "Chetverty sezd," in [Bund], *Materialy*, pp. 115–16.

209. Ibid., p. 116.
210. [Bund], "Di diskusye," *Undzer tsayt* (15 Nov. 1927), no. 2, p. 87.
211. Boris Frumkin's speech in ibid. (15 Dec. 1927), no. 3, p. 87.
212. Mill, II, 40. Among the leading members of the Bundist group in Berne were also Y. Tiumin, S. Efros, and Marusiia Reinus. Kursky recalled that his own group in Berlin was much less nationally oriented than that in Berne, but that it was also less influential ("Di oyslendishe organizatsye fun bund," in Kursky, *Gezamlte shriftn*, pp. 206–24).
213. E.g., Ascher, "Pavel Axelrod," pp. 260–1.
214. Ish-tikve [Zivion], "Natsyonalizmus un natsyonal rekht," *YA* (1901), no. 11, p. 97.
215. Ibid., p. 96.
216. Rebi Kurev [Frumin], "Der driter kongres fun algemaynen yidishn arbeter bund un di natsyonale frage," ibid., p. 88n.
217. Ibid., p. 92.
218. Ibid., p. 93.
219. Ibid., p. 91.
220. Ibid., p. 90.
221. Zivion, "20 yor 'bund'," *Di tsukunft* (Nov. 1917), p. 626.
222. "Chetverty sezd," in [Bund], *Materialy,* pp. 118–19.
223. E.g., Mill, II, 94.
224. Ibid., p. 81.
225. "Der driter tsuzamenfor," *YA* (1900), no. 9, p. 4.
226. "Vegn undzere noenste oyfgaben," *AS* (July 1900), no. 18, p. 2.
227. "Chetverty sezd," p. 107.
228. On Zubatov's attempts in the period 1900–3 to establish state-sponsored trade unionism with Minsk as a major testing ground see Ainzaft; Bukhbinder, "Nezavisimaia evreiskaia rabochaia partiia"; "O zubatovshchine"; Frumkin, "Zubatovshchina"; Mishkinsky, "Ha-'sotsyalizm hamishtarti' "; "Novoe o zubatovshchine"; Pospielovsky; Schneiderman; Tidmarsh; Zaslavsky, "Zubatov."
229. [Rozental], *K evreiskoi intelligentsii,* p. 3.
230. Ibid., p. 9.
231. Zaslavsky, "Tsu der geshikhte fun bund," pp. 71–2.
232. Ibid., p. 75.
233. Ibid., pp. 75–6.
234. Ibid., p. 75.
235. "Der ferter kongres fun algemaynem yidishn arbeter bund in rusland un poyln," *YA* (1901), no. 12, p. 101.
236. Ibid., p. 98.
237. "Pismo k redaktorskoi gruppe 'Rabochei gazety,' " VIL:*PSS,* VI, 180.
238. "Popiatnoe napravlenie v russkoi sotsial-demokratii," ibid., p. 243.
239. Kopelzon, "Stranichka," p. 27.
240. "Zaiavlenie redaktsii 'Iskry'," in VIL:*PSS,* IV, 357.
241. Ibid., p. 356.
242. "Kak chut ne potukhla 'Iskra'?" ibid., p. 337.
243. Ibid., p. 338.
244. Ibid., pp. 338–9.
245. Ibid., p. 342.
246. Ibid., p. 351.
247. *LS,* XIII, 104–5.
248. Ibid., pp. 96–7.
249. There are a number of important books in English analyzing the Russian Social Democratic movement (1895–1914): Dan, *The Origins of Bolshevism;* Haimson, *The Rus-*

sian Marxists; Keep, *The Rise of Social Democracy*; Meyer, *Leninism*; Pipes, *Social Democracy*; Schapiro, *The Communist Party*; Treadgold, *Lenin and His Rivals*: Wildman, *Making of a Workers' Revolution*; Wolfe, *Three Who Made a Revolution* (cf. Geyer).

250. "Raskol v zagranichnom Soiuze russkikh sotsial-demokratov," VIL:*PSS*, IV, 385.

251. [Martov], "Novye druzia russkogo proletariata," *Iskra* (Dec. 1900), no. 1, p. 3.

252. For the most complete study of the relationship between the Bund and the *Iskra* group (1901–3) see Shukman.

253. [Martov], "Iz partii," *Iskra* (Aug. 1901), no. 7, p. 6.

254. Ibid.

255. Ibid., (10 Sept. 1901), no. 8, p. 6.

256. [Akselrod], *Pisma P.B. Akselroda i I.O. Martova*, p. 46.

257. Ibid.

258. VIL:*PSS*, XLVI, 111–12.

259. [Martynov], p. 28.

260. Mill, II, 102.

261. [Akselrod], *Pisma P. B. Akselroda i I. O. Martova*, p. 47n.

262. "S chego nachat?", VIL:*PSS*, V, 11.

263. B. Krichevsky, "Printsipy, taktika i borba," *Rabochee delo* (Sept. 1901), no. 10, p. 30.

264. [Akimov], *Vladimir Akimov*, p. 233.

265. [Kossovsky], *K voprosu o natsionlnoi avtonomii*, p. 6.

266. Ibid., p. 15.

267. Ibid., p. 14.

268. Ibid., pp. 14–15.

269. Ibid., p. 20.

270. Kossovsky, "V. Medem un di natsyonale frage," p. 131.

271. K.K., "O evreiskom rabochem dvizhenii, *Zaria* (Aug. 1902) (sec. 2), no. 4, pp. 40–54. K.K. was the pseudonym of Elyohu Davidzon, who had been active in the emergent Yiddishist movement of the 1890s and had now moved to the "internationalist" Left.

272. "Nokh a mol der sotsyalizm un der politisher kamf," *YA* (Feb. 1902), no. 13, pp. 1–29. From the Russian: *Zaria* (1901), no. 1, pp. 1–32.

273. Krichevsky, "Po povodu IV sezda Bunda," *Rabochee delo* (Feb. 1902), no. 11–12, p. 120.

274. Rozental, "Byalestoker peryod," p. 68.

275. "Zametki Alesksandra Kremera o belostokskoi konf.," Archives of the Bund, New York.

276. *LS*, VIII, 238.

277. "5-aia konferentsiia Bunda," *PI* (4 Oct. 1902), no. 88, pp. 1–4.

278. "Undzere noenste organizatsyons-oyfgabn," *AS* (Aug. 1902), no. 28, p. 2.

279. Blekhman, p. 150.

280. Quoted in A. Kirzhnits, "Bund in RSDRP," p. 70.

281. On Hirsh Lekert's attempted assassination of General Viktor von Wahl, his execution, and the response of the Bund see Tobias, *Jewish Bund*, pp. 147–56; Kazdan, pp. 231–57.

282. VIL:*PSS*, XLVI, 202–3.

283. Ibid., 232.

284. "Iz perepiski 'Iskri,' " *PR* (1928), no. 77–8, p. 127.

285. *LS*, VIII, 351.

286. VIL:*PSS*, XLVI, 235.

287. Ibid., 284.

288. *LS*, VIII, 351.

289. VIL:*PSS*, XLVI, 287.

290. "Po povodu zaiavleniie Bunda," ibid., VII, 96.

291. " 'Iskra' o Bunde," *PI* (13/26 Feb. 1903), no. 109, pp. 2–3.

292. "Edinaia russkaia sotsialdemokratiia i interesy evreiskogo proletariata," *Iskra* (15 March 1903), no. 36, p. 3.

293. [Bund], *Avtonomiia ili federatsiia,* p. 3.

294. *PI* (3/16 April 1903), no. 138, p. 4.

295. Kirzhnits, "Bund un RSDRP," p. 73. On the Fifth Congress of the Bund and the preliminary conference held earlier in Geneva see Abramovich, I, 104–17.

296. K.K., "O evreiskom rabochem dvizhenii," *Zaria,* no. 4, p. 54.

297. Kirzhnits, "Bund un RSDRP," p. 73.

298. [Bund], "Di diskusye," *Undzer tsayt* (Dec. 1927), no. 3, p. 87.

299. Ibid., (15 Jan 1928), no. 1, p. 90.

300. Ibid., (15 Nov. 1927), no. 2, p. 96.

301. Medem, II, 20.

302. [Bund], *V sezd,* p. 6.

303. Ibid., p. 17.

304. [RSDRP], *Vtoroi sezd,* p. 56.

305. Ibid.

306. Ibid., p. 57. On Trotsky's attitude to the Jewish question see Nedava; Howe, *Leon Trotsky,* pp. 173–7; Knei-Paz, pp. 533–55; Deutscher, *Prophet Armed,* pp. 72–6; Wistrich, *Revolutionary Jews,* pp. 189–207.

307. [RSDRP], *Vtoroi sezd,* p. 71.

308. Ibid., p. 73.

309. Ibid., p. 61.

310. Ibid., p. 67.

311. Ibid., p. 65.

312. Ibid., p. 74.

313. Ibid., p. 76.

314. Ibid., pp. 94–5.

315. Ibid., pp. 88–9.

316. Ibid., p. 90.

317. Ibid., pp. 84–5.

318. Ulam, p. 189.

319. [RSDRP], *Vtoroi sezd,* pp. 91–2.

320. [Bund], *II sezd Rossiiskoi SDR partii,* p. 7.

321. Ibid., pp. 15–16.

322. [RSDRP], *Vtoroi sezd,* pp. 96–107.

323. Ibid., p. 107. For the text of Martov's resolution see ibid., p. 57n.

324. Ibid., pp. 106–7.

325. Ibid., p. 321.

326. Ibid., p. 421. For the debate on this issue see pp. 182–92.

327. Lenin's articles of 1913–14 on the national question are to be found in vols. 23–5 of his collected works (*PSS*). For an analysis of Lenin's national policy as developed until World War I see, e.g., Pipes, *Formation of the Soviet Union,* pp. 34–48; Boersner, pp. 32–49; Carr.

328. [Akimov], *Vladimir Akimov,* p. 178.

329. Ibid., p. 179.

330. Ibid., p. 153.

331. "Fun partey-lebn: der VI tsuzamenfor fun algemaynem yidishn arbeter bund in lite, poyln un rusland (bund)," *Der veker* (25 Dec. 1905), no. 1, p. 4.

332. P. Rozental, "Di fareynikungs frage," p. 19.

333. Ibid., p. 21.

334. [Bund], *K voprosu ob obedinenii*, p. 37.
335. [RSDRP], *Chetverty sezd*, p. 442. Stalin spoke under the pseudonym of Ivanovich.
336. Ibid., p. 447.
337. Compare the amended statute of 1903 (*Vtoroi sezd*, pp. 96–7n) with the statute adopted in 1906 (*Chetverty sezd*, pp. 532–3).
338. Ibid., p. 438.
339. Ibid., p. 122.
340. Ibid., p. 449.
341. Ibid.
342. Ibid., p. 450.
343. P. Bogrov [Zaslavsky], "Briv fun VII tsuzamenfor," *FTs* (18 Oct. 1906), no. 173, p. 3.
344. [Bund], *Vegn der fareynikung*, p. 89.
345. Litvak, "Der eyntsiker forshteyer," ibid. (2 May 1906), no. 55, p. 1.
346. Mill, II, 119.
347. Levitsky, p. 73. He attributed these remarks to Lydiia Tsederbaum, later Mrs. Dan.
348. Akimov, "Stroiteli budushchego," *Obrazovanie* (1907) no. 4 (sec. 2), p. 118.
349. Lesin, "B. Vladek amol," p. 18.
350. Ibid., p. 15.
351. Ibid., p. 19.
352. "Sovremenny politicheskii moment i nashi natsionalnye trebovaniia," *PI* (12/25 Sept. 1905), no. 250, p. 1.
353. Bogrov [Zaslavsky], "Briv fun VII tsuzamenfor," *FTs* (11 Sept. 1906), no. 157, p. 5.
354. Ibid., (12 Sept. 1906), no. 158, p. 2. This was the sum reported in the official statement of the central committee: 270,000 francs were sent from the U.S.A. and 21,500 from South Africa. The total sum received by the Bund in Russia and abroad (Oct. 1905–Sept. 1906) has been officially estimated at 524,000 francs. ([Bund], *Der bund in revolutsye*, pp. 118–9).
355. *FTs* (12 Sept. 1906), no. 158, p. 2.
356. Dubnov, "Uroki," *Voskhod* (1 Dec. 1905), no. 47–8, p. 9.
357. "Der yidisher seym," *Der veker* (8 Jan. 1906), no. 12, p. 1.
358. Ibid., p. 2.
359. Jabotinsky, "Bund i natsionalnoe sobranie," *KhEZh* (17 Jan. 1906), no. 2, p. 7.
360. Ibid., p. 9.
361. K. Frumin [Blumshtein], "Der 'bund' un zayne bashuldiger," *FTs* (22 Feb. 1906), no. 4, p. 2.
362. " 'Majofis-singer' sotsialisty (Varshavskii komitet Sionistskosotsialisticheskoi rabochei partii)," *KhEZh* (30 Dec. 1905), no. 50, p. 13.
363. [RSDRP], *Tretii sezd*, pp. 366–7.
364. Ibid., p. 368.
365. Jabotinsky, "Nabroski bez zaglavikh: beseda s G.V. Plekhanovym," *KhEZh* (28 Oct. 1905), no. 41–2, p. 31.
366. Ibid., p. 30.
367. [RSDRP], *Chetverty sezd*, p. 425.
368. [Bund], *K voprosu ob obedinenii*, p. 13.
369. Ibid., pp. 16–17.
370. Ibid., p.32.
371. Litvak, "Der eyntsiker forshteyer," *FTs* (4 May 1906), no. 57, p. 1.
372. Ibid., p. 2.
373. Ibid., (7 May 1906), no. 59, p. 6.
374. A. Litvak, p. 144.

Chapter 5. Chaim Zhitlovsky

1. E.g., C. Liberman, *Yidn un yidishkayt;* H. Rogoff, "Dr. Zhitlovskis farloymdungen oyfn yidishn folk," *Forverts* (30 Jan. 1944) (sec. 2), p. 5; Cahan, "Zhitlovski – an umangenemer frage-tsaykhn," ibid. (5 Feb. 1944), p. 4.

2. Niger's response was published in *Der tog,* starting from 27 February 1944. ("Iz Dr. Khaim Zhitlovski geven, hayst es, a 'vilder anti-semit'?", sec. 2, p. 1). The subsequent articles appeared on 29 February and on 2, 5, and 7 March.

3. *Kegn di onfaln oyf Dr. Khaim Zhitlovski.* There was a further counterresponse: C. Liberman, *Dr. Khaim Zhitlovski un zayn farteydiker.*

4. A doctoral dissertation on Zhitlovsky was recently completed: Dresner, "Hayim Zhitlovski." For assessments of Zhitlovsky in English see Epstein, *Profiles of Eleven,* pp. 295–322; Howe, *World of Our Fathers,* pp. 240–1, 504–7; Goldsmith, pp. 161–81.

5. "Khaim Zhitlovsky (als mensh un gezelshaftlekher tuer)" (lecture delivered in 1912) in An-sky, X, 192.

6. Ibid., p. 193.

7. Ibid., p. 194.

8. Zhitlovsky, *Zikhroynes,* I, 15.

9. On An-sky's life in the 1880s see "Khatas neurim," in An-sky, X, 5–16; Zhitlovsky, "Shloyme Zanvl Rapoport Anski (zayn lebn un shafn)," in *Zikhroynes,* I, 9–14; "S. An-ski Rapoport," in Chernov, *Yidishe tuer,* pp. 52–90; Z. Reizen, "S. An-ski," *Lebn* (1920), no. 7–8, pp. 43–7 (this number of the journal, published in Vilna, was given over entirely to articles on An-sky).

10. Psevdonim [An-sky], "Istoriia odnogo semeistva (povest)," *Voskhod* (1884), no. 9, pp. 126–41; no. 10, pp. 6–30; no. 11, pp. 65–88; no. 12, pp. 29–53.

11. Litvak, pp. 88–9.

12. "P. L. Lavrov," in An-sky, X, 67–87.

13. Zhitlovsky, *Zikhroynes,* I, 75.

14. S. Rappopor[t], "Di ksuvim," *Oyneg shabes* (Yontev bletlekh: 2nd ser. 1895–6), pp. 17–26 (this story had been written in the 1880s).

15. Chernov, *Yidishe tuer,* pp. 79–86.

16. Zhitlovsky, *Zikhroynes,* I, 205–87.

17. Ibid., II, 35–6. On Zhitlovsky's changing attitudes to Zionism (and proto-Zionism) see Dresner, "Hayim Zhitlovski ve-hatsiyonut."

18. Zhitlovsky, *Zikhroynes,* II, 38.

19. Ibid., p. 45.

20. The crisis of this tale comes when the bear says to the captive wolf: "I cannot condemn you even though I know that I am taking much on my conscience in liberating you. One thing I must add. In your place I not only would not value life but would see death as a blessing" (N. Shchedrin, "Bedny volk," *Otechestvennye zapiski* [1884], no. 1, p. 278).

21. Zhitlovsky, *Zikhroynes,* II, 95–6.

22. Ibid., p. 42.

23. Ibid., p. 207.

24. Zhitlovsky, *Mysli,* p. 17.

25. Ibid., p. 11.

26. Ibid., p. 12.

27. Ibid., p. 19.

28. Ibid., p. 27.

29. Ibid., pp. 23–4.

30. Ibid., p. 34.
31. Ibid., pp. 47–8.
32. Ibid., p. 70.
33. Ibid., p. 104.
34. Ibid., p. 106.
35. Ibid., p. 111.
36. Ibid., p. 117.
37. Ibid., p. 118.
38. Ibid., p. 126n.
39. Ibid., p. 124.
40. Ibid., pp. 126–7.
41. Zhitlovsky, *Zikhroynes,* II, 142–5, 171–6.
42. The term "common purse" (*kis ehad*) appears in Proverbs 1:14 and was later used in rabbinic literature. Zhitlovsky's specific reference, however, remains obscure. The other two references are to Isaiah 5:5 and to the Amida prayer on Rosh Ha-Shana and Yom Kippur; e.g., *Service of the Synagogues: Day of Atonement* (Under the sanction of Herman Adler) (London, 1924), II, 45.
43. Zhitlovsky, "Moyshe Hes," *Dos naye lebn* (March 1912), p. 9.
44. Kritikus [Dubnov], "Literaturnaia letopis: ostatki literaturnoi zhatvy 1887 goda," *Voskhod* (Dec. 1887), pp. 6–13.
45. See Chapter 4.
46. "Der kholem fun a leydiger" (trans. C. Zhitlovsky), *Di fraye velt* (1891), no. 4, p. 21. Cf. "Der shkalfn shif," (trans. from Heine by S. Khasin [Zhitlovsky]), ibid. (1892), no. 4, pp. 106–7.
47. Letter in the An-sky file, Zhitlovsky archive, YIVO Archives, New York.
48. The Marxist-populist debate in Zurich during the winter of 1889–90 apparently went on for seventy-two nights, from nine in the evening until two or three in the morning (C. Zhitlovsky, "Di antshteyung," introduction to Rozenbaum, I, xxxiv.)
49. [Zhitlovsky], *Evrei k evreiam,* p. 9.
50. Ibid., p. 10.
51. Ibid., p. 55.
52. Ibid., p. 48.
53. Ibid., p. 49.
54. Ibid., p. 46.
55. Ibid., p. 44.
56. Ibid., p. 57.
57. Ibid., p. 51.
58. Ibid., p. 56.
59. Ibid., p. 47.
60. Ibid., p. 46.
61. Ibid., p. 35.
62. Ibid., p. 47.
63. Vinchevsky, "An erinerung," *Dos naye lebn* (Dec. 1912), p. 6. This issue of the journal was given over entirely to articles by and about Zhitlovsky on the twenty-fifth anniversary of his first publication.
64. Lesin, "Mayn ershte bagegenish," *Di tsukunft* (May 1922), pp. 305–6.
65. On the Cahan-Zhitlovsky debate see e.g., Milch, "Farvos shendn zey kvorim," in *Kegn di onfaln oyf Dr. Khaim Zhitlovski,* pp. 37–8.
66. C. Liberman, *Yidn un yidishkayt,* p. 115.
67. H. Ehrenreich, "Di virkung," *Dos naye lebn* (Dec. 1912), p. 33.

68. Letter in An-sky file, Zhitlovsky archive, YIVO Archives.
69. Pinsky, "A zhargon farzamlung," *Dos naye lebn* (Dec. 1912), p. 38.
70. *Dos manifest fun der kommunistishe partey* (a Bund publication) (Geneva, 1899).
71. "Far vos davke yidish?" Zhitlovsky, *Gezamelte shriftn*, V, 32–3.
72. Ibid., p. 42.
73. Ibid., p. 43.
74. Ibid.
75. Ben Ehud (Zhitlovsky), "Tsienizmus oder sotsyalizmus," *YA* (March 1899), no. 6, p. 6.
76. Ibid., p. 9.
77. Ibid., p. 6.
78. Ibid., p. 8.
79. Ibid., p. 10.
80. Ibid., p. 3.
81. Ibid., p. 12.
82. Chernov, *Yidishe tuer*, p. 281.
83. Ibid., pp. 283–4.
84. Ibid., p. 82.
85. "Yitshok Leybush Perets," in An-sky, X, 154.
86. Medem, *Fun mayn lebn*, I, 282–3.
87. "Dos yidishe arbeter lid," in Litvak, pp. 237–9.
88. Ibid., p. 238.
89. Chernov, *Yidishe tuer*, p. 83.
90. Ben Ehud [Zhitlovsky], "Predislovie," to "Natsionalny vopros i sotsializm," *Vozrozhdenie* (1904), no. 3–4, p. 42.
91. [Zhitlovsky], *Sotsializm i borba*, p. 81.
92. B. Krichevsky, "Prezhdevremenny naslednik sotsialdemokratii," *Rabochee delo* (1898), no. 1, p. 138.
93. Mill, II, 40.
94. Zhitlovsky, *Gezamlte shriftn*, V, 31–43.
95. On the Union of Russian Socialist Revolutionaries see Rozenbaum, II, 89–107; Zhitlovsky's introduction to those memoirs, "Di antshteyung," ibid., I, xlii–lviii; Chernov, "Khaim Zhitlovski," pp. 91–149; Rappoport, pp. 225–30.
96. Menshchikov (ed.), I, 21–2.
97. Letter in the Ingerman file, Akselrod archive, International Institute for Social History, Amsterdam.
98. [Zhitlovsky], *Nashi zadachi*, p. 64.
99. On the establishment and ideology of the Party of Socialist Revolutionaries see Radkey, pp. 3–87; Martov et al. (eds.), *Obshchestvennoe dvizhenie*, III, 89–107; Perrie.
100. LS, VIII, 191.
101. [Plekhanov], *Perepiska G. V. Plekhanova i P. B. Akselroda*, II, 182.
102. *PI* (26 Nov. 1902), no. 96, p. 4.
103. Medem, *Fun mayn lebn*, II, 66.
104. On the Rovno conference and Vozrozhdenie group see M. Zilberfarb, "Di grupe 'vozrozhdenye,'" *RP*, I, 113–16; Ben Adir, "Tsum oyfkum," in *ST*, pp. 9–56; Greenbaum.
105. [Shtif and Fridland]. Inter alia, this brochure declared: "The evil in Kishinev was not that a few dozen Jews fell . . . but that only two in the enemy camp were killed . . . That is shameful, terrible. Who, after that, can dare talk of the rebirth [*vozrozhdenie*] of the Jewish people?" (pp. 7–8).
106. Ben Adir, pp. 21–2.

107. [Herzl], IV, 1530.

108. For Zhitlovsky's account of his meeting with Herzl in August 1903 see "Aynike sho mit Dr. Teodor Hertsl," Zhitlovsky, IX, *Gezamlte shriftn*, IX, 5–39. Herzl reportedly told Zhitlovsky that he had been assured of outright Russian governmental support for the Zionist cause on condition that the Jews refrained from revolutionary action (ibid., p. 11). For Herzl's statement at the congress see Zionist Congress (VI), p. 9.

109. Zilberfarb, "Di grupe 'vozrozhdenye'," *RP*, I, 117. Cf. Ap-r [Ben Adir], "Koe chto o VI-om kongresse sionistov i o sionisticheskom dvizhenii voobshche," *Vozrozhdenie* (Jan.–Feb. 1904), no. 1–2, pp. 9–13, and the scathing Bundist commentary: [Medem], *VI-oi sionisticheskii kongres*, p. 16.

110. An official report on the conference including protocols of the debates was published at the time: [Vozrozhdeniia], *Otchet konferentsii*.

111. "Nashi zadachi," *Vozrozhdenie* (Jan.–Feb. 1904), no. 1–2, p. 7.

112. Ibid., p. 4.

113. Ibid., p. 8.

114. Ap-r [Ben-Adir], "Koe chto o VI-m kongresse sionistov," p. 10.

115. Ben-Adir, "Ograblennaia tema," *Vozrozhdenie* (Nov. 1904), no. 3–4, p. 57.

116. "Nash ratsionalny ideal i nashe natsionalnoe dvizhenie," ibid., p. 41. This article was directed particularly against Syrkin's views as expressed in *Der hamoyn*.

117. "Nashi zadachi," *Vozrozhdenie* (Jan.–Feb. 1904), no. 1–2, p. 6.

118. Ben Ehud [Zhitlovsky], "Natsionalny vopros i sotsializm," ibid. (1904), no. 3–4, pp. 42–7. This article had originally appeared in Engelbert Pernerstorfer's *Deutsche Worte* (1899), no. 8–9, pp. 305–43, under the title "Der Sozialismus und die Nationalitätenfrage."

119. "Nashi zadachi," *Vozrozhdenie* (Jan.–Feb. 1904), no. 1–2, p. 7.

120. Zilberfarb, "Di grupe 'vozrozhdenye'," p. 125.

121. Zhitlovsky, *Fun asimilatsye*, p. 5.

122. Ibid., pp. 5–6.

123. M. Borisov [Ratner], "Nashi zadachi," *SERP*, I (1907), 53.

124. "Materialy k istorii evreiskogo rabochego dvizheniia," ibid., II (1908), 392.

125. "Proekt programmy Evreiskoi sotsialisticheskoi rabochei partii," ibid., I (1907), 263.

126. On Vozrozhdenie in late 1905 see Mintz, "Shalosh teudot."

127. "Materialy k istorii evreiskogo rabochego dvizheniia," *SERP*, II, 384.

128. Chernov, *Yidishe tuer*, p. 308.

129. An-sky, "Uroki," *Voskhod* (9 March 1906), no. 10, p. 10.

130. Chernov perceptively suggested that Zhitlovsky felt himself to be "an unbridled and elemental force" ("Khaim Zhitlovski," in *Zhitlovsky zamlbukh*, p. 129).

131. Zhitlovsky, "Der anti-semitizm un di yidishe parteyen," *Dos naye lebn* (1912), no. 6, p. 15. This long essay was published there over the period December 1911–September 1912 and was republished under a new title in the collected works: "Der biterer emes," *Gezamlte shriftn*, VI, 163–251.

132. Zhitlovsky, "Briv fun a yidishn sotsyalist," *Folks-shtime* (Dec. 1906), no. 1, pp. 58–9.

133. Ibid., p. 59.

134. Ibid., p. 57.

135. Ibid., p. 58.

136. Ibid., p. 69.

137. Ibid., p. 70.

138. Zhitlovsky, "Mi-koyekh erd-arbet," *Folks-shtime* (18 July 1908), no. 12, p. 36.

139. Ibid.

140. Ibid., p. 37.

141. Zhitlovsky, "Moyshe Hes," *Dos naye lebn* (March 1912), pp. 8–9.

142. Chernov, *Yidishe tuer*, p. 297.

Chapter 6. Nachman Syrkin

1. Katznelson, "Ha-ehad be-maarakha," in [N. Syrkin], *Kitve Nahman Sirkin,* p. 84 (henceforward: *Kitve Sirkin*).

2. "Tsu der forgeshikhte fun sotsyalistishn tsienizm (erinergungen)," in [N. Syrkin], *Geklibene tsientishe-sotsyalistishe shriftn,* I, 133 (henceforward: *Geklibene shriftn*). On Syrkin, Borochov, and socialist Zionism in Zionist history generally see Hertzberg, pp. 15–100; Laqueur, pp. 270–337; Avineri, *Ha-rayon,* pp. 145–81.

3. Zivion, "Teritoryalizm oder avanturizm?" *Di tsukunft* (July 1909), p. 419.

4. Revutsky, "Dr. Nakhmen Sirkin," ibid. (Oct. 1924), p. 584.

5. Weizmann, *Trial and Error,* I, 38.

6. Levin, *Youth in Revolt,* p. 222.

7. M. Syrkin, pp. 135–56.

8. Tsitron, "Mayne bagegenishn," *Der tog* (Vilna) (1924), no. 229, p. 5.

9. M. Syrkin, p. 154.

10. N. Syrkin, *Geschichtsphilosophische Betrachtungen,* p. 34.

11. Ibid., p. 69.

12. Ibid., p. 31.

13. "Natsyonale kultur un natsyonale shprakh," *Dos naye lebn* (March 1923), no. 6, p. 27 (*Geklibene shriftn,* II, 202).

14. *Geschichtsphilosophische Betrachtungen,* pp. 85–6.

15. Ibid., p. 80.

16. Ibid., p. 31.

17. Ibid., p. 105.

18. Ibid., p. 77.

19. Ibid.

20. Ibid., p. 78.

21. Ibid., p. 115.

22. Ibid., p. 118.

23. N. Syrkin, *Empfindung und Vorstellung,* p. 77.

24. Ibid.

25. A. Volyner [Eliezer Landau], "Sirkinizmen," *Der yidisher arbeter* (New York), (9 Sept. 1927), no. 18, p. 8.

26. *Geschichtsphilosophische Betrachtungen,* p. 112.

27. Ibid., p. 106.

28. Ibid., p. 34.

29. Ibid., pp. 65–6.

30. Ibid., p. 8.

31. N. Syrkin, "Mozes Hes," p. 49.

32. *Geschichtsphilosophische Betrachtungen,* p. 99.

33. Ben-Elieser [Syrkin], "Etvos iber natsyonalizm," *Der hamoyn* (1903), no. 1, p. 33 (*Kitve Sirkin,* p. 204).

34. N.S. [Syrkin], "Min ha-hutsa ha-ohela (fragmentim)," *Ha-shahar* (1903), no. 1, pp. 47–8 (*Kitve Sirkin,* p. 171).

35. "Der letster meshiekh," *Geklibene shriftn,* II, 126.

36. "Di yidnfrage," *YK* (19 Aug. 1910), no. 22, p. 4 (*Geklibene shriftn,* I, 198).

37. [Syrkin], *Vozzvanie,* p. 3 (*Kitve Sirkin,* pp. 64–5).

38. "Di yidnfrage," *YK* (2 Sept. 1910), no. 24, p. 3 (*Geklibene shriftn,* I, 202).

39. "Der tsienizm un der hamoyn," *Der hamoyn* (1903), no. 1, p. 10 (*Kitve Sirkin,* p. 184).

40. "Der bund un der tsienizm," *Di tsayt* (27 Feb. 1922), p. 6 (*Geklibene shriftn,* I, 111).

41. "Utopish, reformistish, kontr-revolutsyoner," *Di tsayt* (2 Nov. 1921), p. 4 (*Geklibene shriftn*, II, 236).

42. "Der tsienizm un der bund," *Der hamoyn* (1903), no. 1, p. 47 (*Kitve Sirkin*, p. 218).

43. Ibid., *Der hamoyn*, p. 48 (*Kitve Sirkin*, p. 219).

44. "Der bund un der tsienizm," *Di tsayt* (2 March 1922), p. 4 (*Geklibene shriftn*, I, 115).

45. [Syrkin], *Die Judenfrage*, p. 24 (*Kitve Sirkin*, p. 21).

46. Ibid. (*Kitve Sirkin*, p. 22).

47. Ibid., pp. 25–6 (*Kitve Sirkin*, pp. 22–3).

48. "Der tsienizm un der hamoyn," *Der hamoyn*, p. 10 (*Kitve Sirkin*, pp. 183–4).

49. "Natsyonale kultur un natsyonale shprakh," *Dos naye lebn* (March 1923), no. 6, pp. 27–8 (*Geklibene shriftn*, II, 203).

50. Tsitron, "Mayne bagegenishn," *Der tog* (Vilna) (1924), no. 229, p. 5.

51. [Syrkin], *Vozzvanie*, p. 13 (*Kitve Sirkin*, p. 73). On Syrkin's attitude to territorialism see Elichai.

52. "Kooperativn in der kolonizatsye fun erets yisroel," *Geklibene shriftn*, I, 285–6.

53. Syrkin, *Die Judenfrage*, p. 61 (*Kitve Sirkin*, p. 54).

54. Ibid., p. 65 (*Kitve Sirkin*, p. 57).

55. Ibid., p. 63 (*Kitve Sirkin*, p. 56).

56. "Der konstruktiver sotsyalizm in erets-yisroel," *Geklibene shriftn*, II, 306 (a *referat* delivered at the Stockholm conference of the world union of Poale Zion, September 1919).

57. "Nokh dem tsienistishn kongres," *Di tsayt* (25 Sept. 1921), p. 7.

58. Zivion, "Teritoryalizm oder avanturizm?" *Di tsukunft* (July 1909), p. 419.

59. Lesin, "Bemerkungen tsu di 'notitsn fun a gelen'," ibid. (Aug. 1921), p. 494.

60. Zhitlovsky, "Vi tsu kolonizirn erets yisroel," *Di tsayt* (3 April 1921), p. 7.

61. M. Syrkin, p. 158.

62. N. Syrkin, *Die Judenfrage*, p. 67 (*Kitve Sirkin*, p. 59).

63. "Sotsyalizm – di shafung fun yidishn gayst," *Geklibene shriftn*, I, 307 (a speech delivered in Jaffa, 1920).

64. *Die Judenfrage*, p. 54 (*Kitve Sirkin*, p. 48).

65. Pilovski "Nahman Sirkin," pp. 15–17. This thesis is the definitive study of Syrkin's early political and intellectual development.

66. [Syrkin], *Vozzvanie*, pp. 6–7 (*Kitve Sirkin*, pp. 67–8).

67. "Min ha-hutsa ha-ohela (fragmentim)," *Ha-shahar* (1903), p. 34 (*Kitve Sirkin*, pp. 144–5).

68. Ibid., *Ha-shahar*, p. 49 (*Kitve Sirkin*, p. 170).

69. "Mozes Hes," pp. 8–9.

70. "Epokhn in der yidisher geshikhte," *Geklibene shriftn*, II, 31.

71. Ibid., p. 11.

72. N. Syrkin, "Die 'Jüdiche Volksstimme,'" *Die Jüdische Volksstimme* (Feb. 1900), no. 1, p. 2 (*Kitve Sirkin*, p. 256).

73. "Ha-am be-milkhama le-herut," *Kitve Sirkin*, p. 80 (Yiddish, original: *Dos folk in kamf far zayn frayhayt*, a Herut publication, 1901). The Biblical reference is to Deuteronomy 15:4.

74. "Der gaystiger sholem," *Geklibene shriftn*, I, 298 (a speech delivered 6 June 1918).

75. "Sotsyalizm – di shafung fun yidishe gayst," ibid., p. 306.

76. "Min ha-hutsa ha-ohela," *Ha-shahar*, p. 33 (*Kitve Sirkin*, p. 142).

77. "Epokhn in der yidisher geshikhte," *Geklibene shriftn*, II, 54.

78. "Mozes Hes," p. 47.

79. Ibid., p. 59.

80. *Die Judenfrage*, p. 60 (*Kitve Sirkin*, p. 53).

81. "Mozes Hes," p. 9.

82. *Die Judenfrage*, p. 42 (*Kitve Sirkin*, p. 48).

83. "Sotsyalizm," *Geklibene shriftn*, I, 306.

84. [Syrkin], *Vozzvanie*, p. 4 (*Kitve Sirkin*, p. 66).

85. M. Syrkin, p. 210.

86. On the emergence of labor Zionism and Poale Zion in Austria-Hungary see Landau, *Sturm und Drang*, pp. 147–58; Gelber, *Toldot ha-tnua ha-tsiyonit be-galitsya*, II, 737–79; Singer, *Shlomo Kaplanski*, I, 28–54.

87. E.g., Y. Berger to Motskin (6 March 1902); Motskin archive, CZA: A/126: 24/7/1.

88. On the origins of Poale Zion in Russia see Singer, *Be-reshit ha-tsiyonut ha-sotsyalistit*, pp. 20–102, 292–381; Gutman, pp. 152–60; Zilberfarb, "Di grupe 'vozrozhdenye,' " pp. 113–30; Ben Adir, pp. 9–43; Nir; Kivin; Mintz, *Ber Borokhov* pp. 25–53; Mishkinsky, "Tsmihat."

89. Kursky (*Gezamlte shriftn*, p. 208) recalled that in the 1890s, Syrkin and Motskin were both regular guests at the conspiratorial *referaty* organized by his own Bund-oriented circle.

90. *Protest* (Geneva, 1900) (published by the Gruppa Evreiskikh Studentov-Sotsialistov) in the Aberson archive, CZA: A 139/6.

91. On the emergence of Poale Zion in New York see Shpizman, I, 96–149; in London see Marmor, *Mayn lebens geshikhte*, II, 566–657. Cf. Singer, *Be-reshit*, pp. 382–94.

92. I.e., *Der koysl maaravi* (London, 1902–3), edited by Marmor and published by the Zienistn Fareyn "Maaravi"; *Di naye shtime: a radikal-tsienistishe tsaytshrift* (New York, 1904), published by the Poale Zion in New York.

93. Marmor, *Mayn lebns geshikhte*, II, 421–2.

94. Zionist Congress (I), p. 95.

95. Ibid., p. 105.

96. For Zhitlovsky's recollections of Syrkin and Farbstein, as of Franz Oppenheimer, see "Aynike sho mit Dr. Teodor Hertsl," *Gezamlte shriftn*, IX, 31–4.

97. "Die zionistische Jugend von Witebsk an den 'Jüdischen Arbeiter,' " *Der jüdische Arbeiter: Organ für die Interessen der jüdischen Arbeiterschaft* (1 June 1899), pp. 10–11.

98. Marmor, *Mayn lebns geshikhte*, II, 465.

99. Singer, *Shlomo Kaplanski*, I, 16–25.

100. For Litvin's numerous reminiscences of this period, see e.g., "Tsulib dem emes fun geshikhte," *Der yidisher arbeter* (26 March 1926), no. 6, pp. 13–14, no. 7, pp. 11–12; "In yener teg (tsu der geshikhte fun di ershte poyle tsienistishe krayzlekh in minsk un in nyu york)," ibid., no. 21 (29 Oct. 1926), pp. 9–10; "Mayn bagegenish mit Dr. Sirkin," ibid., no. 18 (9 Sept. 1927), pp. 5–6.

101. Tsitron, "Mayne bagegenishn," *Der tog* (Vilna) (1924), no. 229, p. 5.

102. Ibid.

103. Ben Eliezer [Syrkin], "Tsum miting iber yishev erets yisroel," *Di tsukunft* (6 July 1886), no. 3, p. 22.

104. E.g., N. Syrkin, "Divre pi hakham," *Ha-magid* (12 Sept. 1889), pp. 282–3.

105. Davidzon's reminiscences of Syrkin have been published (from the MS.) in Pilovski, "Nahman Sirkin," pp. 165–74.

106. Levin, *Youth in Revolt*, pp. 183–4.

107. Ibid., pp. 248–9.

108. Pilovski, "Nahman Sirkin," p. 170–1.

109. Ibid., pp. 172–3.

110. Bernshtein-Cohen, p. 120.

111. "Tsu der geshikhte fun sotsyalistishn tsienizm (erinerungen)," *Geklibene shriftn*, I, 131.

112. On the radical group at the 1897 Congress see Y. Frankel.

113. "Teodor Hertsl," *NV*, (7 July 1906), no. 11, p. 445.

114. Ibid., p. 446.

115. N. Syrkin, "Der sotsyalistisher tsienizm," *Der tog* (14 Nov. 1915), p. 14 (*Geklibene shriftn*, I, 269).

116. N. Syrkin, "Meshiekh un shmad," *Der tog* (23 Aug. 1924), p. 6 (*Geklibene shriftn*, II, 311).

117. In 1898, Landau also published his *Unter jüdischen Proletariern*.

118. *Der Zionizmus und die Judenfrage*; cf. his earlier and related work, *Das Recht der umfreien und der freien Arbeiter*.

119. E.g., Gelber, *Toldot ha-tnua ha-tsiyonit be-galitsya*, I, 378–96.

120. Landau, *Sturm und Drang*, p. 129.

121. Zionist Congress (II), p. 164.

122. Ibid., p. 226.

123. Silberner, "Bernar Lazar," p. 360 (Hebrew: 342–3). Cf. Wilson, pp. 222–52.

124. Quoted in Singer, *Be-reshit*, pp. 84–5.

125. "Die zionistische Bewegung: Bern," *Die Welt* (20 Jan. 1899), p. 11.

126. "Tribune," ibid. (10 Feb. 1899), p. 8.

127. E.g., the review of Syrkin's book: S. Landsberger, "Zum proletarischen Zionismus," *Der jüdische Arbeiter* (1 Jan. 1899), no. 1, pp. 1–3.

128. Articles by Syrkin appeared there (*Jüdische Volksstimme: Central organ der jüdischen Arbeiter und Handelsangestellten*) in nos. 1, 5, 16, 17, 19, 20, 22 (1900); nos. 4, 8 (1901).

129. *Programmnye pisma* (izdanie Sionistov-sotsialistov), (July 1901), no. 1, (Aberson archive, CZA: A/139).

130. Letter of 7 November 1901 in Syrkin archive, AMJLM: III, 103/20.

131. On the Democratic Fraction established by Motskin, Weizmann, et al., see Klausner, *Opozitsiya le-Hertsel*; cf. Yaakov Leshchinsky's identification with Ahad Ha-Am in 1901 (Pilovski, "Agudat halutsim").

132. [Weizmann], *Letters and Papers*, I, 133.

133. Letter of 27 Nov. 1901 in Motskin archive, CZA A/126.

134. *Statuten des Vereins "Hessiana"* (Syrkin archive, AMJLM: III, 103/17). A copy of the statutes of Svobodnaia Iudeia is in the Aberson archive, CZA:A/139. On Svobodnaia Iudeia see Y. Klausner, "Ha-histadrut."

135. The lecture on cooperative settlement, was held 9 Nov. 1901 (see the notice published by the Zionistische Verein "Hessiana"; Motskin archive, CZA: A/126).

136. [Weizmann], *Letters and Papers*, I, 211.

137. E.g., Y. Klausner, *Opozitsiya le-Hertsel*, pp. 157–63.

138. [Herzl], *Complete Diaries*, III, 192.

139. [Weizmann], *Letters and Papers*, I, 222–3.

140. See "Di organizatsyon 'kheyrus'," *Der hamoyn*, pp. 20–1 (*Kitve Sirkin*, pp. 192–3); and the letters on the conference from Mirkin and Perelman in the Syrkin archive, AMJLM: III/103.

141. Marmor, *Mayn lebns geshikhte*, II, 675.

142. Syrkin archive, AMJLM: III, 103/20.

143. Kheyrus [Syrkin], "Yidishe kronik," *Der hamoyn*, p. 80 (*Kitve Sirkin*, p. 243).

144. Ibid., *Der hamoyn*, pp. 82–3 (*Kitve Sirkin*, p. 246).

145. Zionist Congress (VI), pp. 177–8.

146. [Weizmann], *Letters and Papers*, III, 233.

147. Letter from S. Lure in Syrkin archive, AMJLM: III, 103/25.

148. 7 July 1903, ibid., III, 103/21.

149. 8 Nov. 1903, ibid., III, 103/22.

150. N. d. ibid., III, 103/25.

151. Dinur, *Be-olam she-shaka*, pp. 173-4.

152. On the swing toward a revolutionary ideology in the Poale Zion movement see *Di farsheydne shtremungen;* Likhtenstein, pp. 134–53; Katznelson, "Darki la-arets," pp. 67–79; Yanait, *Anu olim,* pp. 261–84; Nir, *Ershte yorn,* pp. 48–95; Guterman, "Ha-miflaga ha-tsiyonit ha-sotsyalistit," *M'asef,* IX (1977), 97–140.

153. Gutman, pp. 162–3.

154. 10 Oct. 1903, Syrkin archive, AMJLM: III, 103/22.

155. I.e., the Tsienistisher Arbeter Fareyn "Forverts," which published, inter alia, Dr. H. Zolotarov, *Ernste fragen* (1903); *Undzer tsukunft,* no. 2; and N. Syrkin, *Der tsienizm un der bund.* (The address provided was: J. Naroditsky, 48, Mile End Road.)

156. M. Syrkin, pp. 91–2.

157. On the organization of the founding congress of the SSRP in Odessa see Latsky-Bertoldi, "Ha-maasar," *Yediot ha-arkhiyon* (1938), no. 3–4, pp. 52–7; Bregman.

158. "Bazelskii kongress (forkonferentsiia)," *Voskhod* (21 July 1905), no. 29, p. 24.

159. "Tsu der geshikhte fun sotsyalistishn tsienizm (erinerungen)," *Geklibene shriftn,* I, 145.

160. Zionist Congress (VII), p. 136.

161. [SSRP], *Deklaratsiia,* p. 13 (Yiddish: in *ST,* p. 146). On the politics of the SSRP during the revolution see Guterman, "Ha-miflaga," *M'asef,* X (1978), 13–62.

162. "Fun partey lebn," *NV* (April 1906), no. 2, p. 81. The congress resolutions were published in nos. 1–2 and in Russian: *Rezoliutsii i postanovleniia.*

163. Da-vich [Lvovich], "Sotsyal-demokratn oder nit kayn sotsyaldemokratn," *NV* (May 1906), no. 6, pp. 221–2.

164. Ibid., p. 225.

165. Nitsots [Litvakov], "Vegn oytonomizn," ibid. (April 1906), no. 2, p. 57.

166. Ibid., (May 1906), no. 7, p. 263.

167. Ibid., (April 1906), no. 2, p. 57.

168. Ibid., (May 1906), no. 7, p. 263.

169. Ibid., (April 1906), no. 2, p. 58.

170. M. Syrkin, pp. 111–14.

171. Bertoldi Latsky, "Gedanken vegn teritoryalizm: 'historishe noytvendigkayt' und asimilatsyons-ideologye," *NV* (30 July 1906), no. 13, p. 549.

172. Z. Abrahami [Abramovich], "Tsu der frage vegn der historishe noytvendigkayt fun teritoryalizm," ibid. (23 Aug. 1906), no. 16, p. 10.

173. Ibid., pp. 11–12.

174. Ibid., p. 19.

175. Syrkin, "Di revolutsye un di yidishe burzhuazye," ibid. (30 June 1906), no. 10, p. 405.

176. [Syrkin?], "Der bund," ibid. (5 Oct. 1906), no. 20, p. 5.

177. S. [Syrkin], "Di YTO Konferents," ibid. (16 Aug. 1906), no. 15, p. 3.

178. S., "Yomim neroim," ibid. (19 Sept. 1906), no. 19, p. 8.

179. Ibid., p. 9.

180. Ibid., p. 15.

181. Dinur, *Be-olam she-shaka,* p. 297. On the second party conference of the SSRP see Nadezhdin, "Konferents-ayndrike," *NV* (10 Jan. 1907), no. 25, pp. 14–27; for the resolutions adopted see ibid., pp. 42–5. The decisions of the conference did reflect (as Dinur writes) a swing back toward a more activist concept of territorialism since the March congress.

182. "Iber di realizirung fun dem teritoryalizm," *NV* (5 Oct. 1906), no. 20, p. 7.

183. Ibid., p. 9.

184. Ibid., p. 11.

Chapter 7. Borochov and Marxist Zionism

1. Shazar in Borochov, *Ktavim nivharim*, p. 19.
2. J. Frankel, "Socialism and Jewish Nationalism," pp. 355–94; and Mintz's many publications culminating in *Ber Borokhov* (1976).
3. Borochov archive, AMJLM: III, 103.
4. Quoted in Mintz, *Ber Borokhov*, p. 91.
5. Borokhov file, Ussishkin archive, CZA:A 24, 125/14. Borochov's communications to Ussishkin have been published by M. Mintz in the Russian original and in Hebrew translation: "Igrot Boroknov," *Ha-tsiyonut* II, 237–300.
6. 24 Jan. 1905, ibid. (*Ha-tsiyonut,* II, 262).
7. Ibid. (*Ha-tsiyonut,* II, 273).
8. 30 Nov. 1904, ibid. (*Ha-tsiyonut,* II, 253).
9. 24 Jan. 1905, ibid. (*Ha-tsiyonut,* II, 262).
10. 3 June 1905, ibid. (*Ha-tsiyonut,* II, 284).
11. 1 Oct. 1904, ibid. (*Ha-tsiyonut,* II, 256).
12. 10 Feb. 1905, ibid. (*Ha-tsiyonut,* II, 271). The Vilna conference was held in January 1905 and endorsed Ussishkin's political line.
13. 15 Feb. 1905, ibid. (*Ha-tsiyonut,* II, 273).
14. Mintz, *Ber Borokhov,* pp. 35–7.
15. "Zikhroynes," in *Yidisher arbeter yor-bukh,* p. 181.
16. Ben Zvi in Borochov, *Ktavim nivharim,* p. 10.
17. Mintz, *Ber Borokhov,* pp. 27–37.
18. Levin, *Arena,* p. 262.
19. Mintz, *Ber Borokhov,* pp. 59–63.
20. 28 Sept./10 Oct. 1904, Borokhov archive, AMJLM: III, 103 (Hebrew: Mintz, "Shalosh igrot," in *Sefer Rafael Maler,* p. 175).
21. Autumn 1904, ibid. (date unclear) (Hebrew: *Sefer Rafael Maler,* p. 175).
22. Ibid. (*Sefer Rafael Maler,* pp. 180–1).
23. Ussishkin, "Nasha programma," p. 81 (English: p. 4).
24. Ibid., p. 82 (English: p. 6).
25. Ibid., pp. 94–5 (English: p. 19).
26. Ibid., p. 102 (English: p. 27).
27. Ibid., pp. 102–3 (English: pp. 27–8).
28. Borochov archive, AMJLM: III, 103 (Hebrew: *Sefer Rafael Maler,* p. 183).
29. Ben Zvi in Borochov, *Ktavim nivharim,* p. 11.
30. 24 Jan. 1905 in Borochov file, Ussishkin archive CZA: A24, 125/14 (*Ha-tsiyonut,* II, 263).
31. 10 Feb. 1905, ibid. (*Ha-tsiyonut,* II, 272).
32. Quoted in Mintz, *Ber Borokhov,* p. 66.
33. 30 Nov. 1904 in CZA: A24, A125/14 (*Ha-tsiyonut,* II, 253).
34. 10 Feb. 1905, ibid. (*Ha-tsiyonut,* II, 271).
35. 1 Feb. 1905, ibid. (*Ha-tsiyonut,* II, 265).
36. "K voprosu o Sione i territorii," *EZ* (June 1905), p. 103 (*Ktavim,* I, 41).
37. Ibid., pp. 98–9 (*Ktavim,* I, 37).
38. Ibid., p. 99 (*Ktavim,* I, 37–8).
39. Ibid., p. 105 (*Ktavim,* I, 43).
40. Ibid. (Aug. 1905), p. 54 (*Ktavim,* I, 93).
41. "K voprosam teorii sionizma," *EZ* (Feb. 1905), p. 135 (*Ktavim,* I, 15). (English: "On Questions of Zionist Theory," in Hardan, ed., *Sources,* II, 45–6).
42. Ibid., pp. 124–5 (*Ktavim,* I, 4; English: pp. 25–6).

43. Ibid., p. 135 (*Ktavim*, I, 15; English: p. 46).
44. Ibid., p. 123 (*Ktavim*, I, 3; English: p. 24).
45. "K voprosu o Sione i territorii," *EZ* (Oct. 1905), p. 33 (*Ktavim*, I, 140).
46. Ibid. (Sept. 1905), pp. 56–7 (*Ktavim*, I, 131–2).
47. Ibid., p. 58 (*Ktavim*, I, 133).
48. Ibid., p. 5.
49. Ibid. (Oct. 1905), pp. 42–3 (*Ktavim*, I, 148).
50. Ibid., p. 42 (*Ktavim*, I, 147).
51. Ibid., p. 45 (*Ktavim*, I, 149).
52. Ibid. (June 1905), p. 106 (*Ktavim*, I, 44).
53. Ibid. (July 1905), p. 71 (*Ktavim*, I, 49).
54. Ibid., p. 75 (*Ktavim*, I, 53).
55. Ibid., p. 83 (*Ktavim*, I, 59).
56. Ibid., (Aug. 1905), p. 55 (*Ktavim*, I, 93).
57. Ibid., (July 1905), pp. 76–7 (*Ktavim*, I, 54).
58. Ibid., p. 87 (*Ktavim*, I, 63).
59. Ibid., (June 1905), p. 87 (*Ktavim*, I, 26).
60. Ibid., (July 1905), p. 96 (*Ktavim*, I, 70).
61. Ibid., p. 99 (*Ktavim*, I, 72).
62. Ibid., p. 101 (*Ktavim*, I, 74).
63. Ibid., pp. 102–3 (*Ktavim*, I, 75–6).
64. Ibid. (Oct. 1905), p. 49 (*Ktavim*, I, 153).
65. "K voprosam teorii sionizma," ibid. (Feb. 1905), p. 122 (*Ktavim*, I, 2; English: p. 23).
66. "K voprosu o Sione i territorii," ibid. (June 1905), p. 106 (*Ktavim*, I, 44).
67. Zilberfarb, "Undzere ershte bagegenishn," *ST*, p. 78. On the Berdichev conference see "Iz protokolov iugo-zapadnoi konferentsii poale-tsion," *ERKh* (12 May 1906), no. 2, pp. 40–57.
68. Zerubavel, *Ber Borokhov*, p. 56.
69. On the creation of the new party in the winter 1905–6 see Yanait, *Anu olim*, pp. 285–92; Zerubavel, "Der grindungsperyod," *RP*, I, 138–48; Ben Zvi, *Ktavim*, IV, 57–63.
70. Ben Zvi, *Ktavim*, IV, 64.
71. On the efforts of the ESDRP-PZ (as of the SSRP and the SERP) to join the International see Mendelsohn, "The Jewish Socialist Movement."
72. Zerubavel, "Fun poltava," p. 110.
73. E.g., Nir, *Ershte yorn*, pp. 134–45.
74. P. Palestinets, "Reaktsiia i pogromy, " *Molot* (July 1906), no. 2, p. 5.
75. In *ERKh* (23 June 1906), no. 3, p. 8.
76. R. Goldin [Yanait], "Tsum historishn tog," *PG* (17 Jan. 1907), no. 1, p. 52.
77. Postoianny [Borokhov], "Nasha platforma," *ERKh* (23 April 1906), no. 1, p. 32 (*Ktavim*, I, 210).
78. Ibid., p. 33 (*Ktavim*, I, 211).
79. *Di farsheydne shtremungen*, p. 2.
80. Ibid., p. 1.
81. Ibid., p. 8.
82. "Nasha platforma," *ERKh* (23 April 1906), no. 1, p. 36 (*Ktavim*, I, 213).
83. Ibid. (12 May 1906), no. 2, p. 28 (*Ktavim*, I, 240).
84. Ibid., p. 14 (*Ktavim*, I, 226).
85. Ibid. (23 June 1906), no. 3, p. 21 (*Ktavim*, I, 261).
86. "Di rol fun dem arbeter klas in dem realizirung fun dem teritoryalizm," *Forverts* (Vilna) (4 May 1907), no. 1, pp. 43–4 (*Ktavim*, I, 336).

87. "Nasha platforma," *ERKh* (23 June 1906), no. 3, p. 27 (*Ktavim*, I, 267).
88. "Di rol," *Forverts* (Vilna) no. 1, p. 18 (*Ktavim*, I, 320).
89. "Nasha platforma," *ERKh* (23 June 1906), no. 3, p. 11 (*Ktavim*, I, 251).
90. Ibid., no. 2, p. 38 (*Ktavim*, I, 249).
91. Ibid., *Molot* (July 1906), no. 2, p. 33 (*Ktavim*, I, 296).
92. "Di rol," pp. 31–2 (*Ktavim*, I, 327–8).
93. Ibid., *PG* (28 Feb. 1907), no. 3, p. 16 (*Ktavim*, I, 313–4).
94. "Nasha platforma," *ERKh* (23 June 1906), no. 3, p. 47 (*Ktavim*, I, 284).
95. "Di rol," *PG* (28 Feb. 1907), no. 3, p. 16 (*Ktavim*, I, 314).
96. Ibid., *Forverts* (Vilna) (4 May 1907), no. 1, p. 24 (*Ktavim*, I, 323).
97. "Nasha platforma," *ERKh* (23 June 1906), no. 3, p. 55 (*Ktavim*, I, 292).
98. "Di rol," *PG* (28 Feb. 1907), no. 3, p. 17 (*Ktavim*, I, 314).
99. Ibid., *Forverts* (Vilna) (4 May 1907), no. 1, p. 37 (*Ktavim*, I, 331).
100. On the establishment of the world Poale Zion movement see Kener; Feldman.
101. "Di rol," *PG* (28 Feb. 1907), no. 3, pp. 19–20 (*Ktavim*, I, 316).
102. Ibid., p. 18 (*Ktavim*, I, 315).
103. "Nasha platforma," *Molot* (July 1906), no. 2, p. 41 (*Ktavim*, I, 302).
104. Nir, *Ershte yorn*, p. 126 (Hebrew: p. 97). Cf. Mintz, "Ha-mahloket," and idem, *Veidat krakov*.
105. Nir, *Ershte yorn*, p. 162 (Hebrew, p. 123). On the Poale Zion movement in Poland in this period, see also idem, "Der onheyb"; Mintz, "Ha-'farband' ha-polani."
106. Her, p. 26.
107. Ibid., p. 30. (*Ha-veida ha-shlishit*, ed. M. Mintz, p. 44).
108. Ibid. (*Ha-veida ha-shlishit*, pp. 45–7).
109. Borochov, *Geklibene shriftn*.
110. I.e., Tabori; and Her.
111. "O kharaktere evreiskogo uma," *Illiustrirovanny tsionistskii almanakh 1902–3*, p. 316.
112. Ibid., p. 323.
113. Ibid., pp. 331–2.
114. Mintz, *Ber Borokhov*, p. 48.
115. Tabori, pp. 9–12.
116. Shazar in Borochov, *Ktavim nivharim*, pp. 28–9.
117. For a recent discussion of this issue see the exchange between M. Mintz and the author: *Yom iyun*, pp. 31–2, 58.
118. "O kharaktere," *Illiustrirovanny sionistskii almanakh 1902–3*, p. 330.
119. Ibid., p. 336.
120. E.g., Mintz, "Mi-hagige Borokhov"; idem, *Mafteah le-hativat ha-hagigim*.
121. Notation 1877, quoted in Mintz, *Ber Borokhov*, p. 83.
122. Notation 1388, quoted in ibid., p. 84.
123. "K voprosu o Sione i territorii," *EZ* (Aug. 1905), p. 67 (*Ktavim*, I, 103).
124. Ibid., p. 56 (*Ktavim*, I, 94).
125. Ibid. (July, 1905), p. 88 (*Ktavim*, I, 65).
126. Zerubavel, *Ber Borokhov*, p. 45.
127. Idem, "Der grindungs-peryod," p. 135.
128. Mintz, *Ber Borokhov*, pp. 181–2.
129. Ibid., pp. 218–59.
130. M. A. Borochov, "Zikhroynes," in B. Borochov, *Geklibene shriftn*, pp. xix, xxi.
131. Letter to Ezrakhi, Borokhov archive, AMJLM, 2425/5/1.
132. Shazar in Borochov, *Ktavim nivharim*, p. 36.
133. Her, pp. 29–30.
134. N. Syrkin "B. Borokhov ve-torato," p. 5.

135. Yanait, *Anu olim,* p. 291.
136. Zerubavel, *Ber Borokhov,* pp. 65–6.
137. "Chto govoriat i pishut," *ERKh* (23 April 1906), no. 1, p. 62.
138. 18 Feb. 1906 in Ussishkin archive, Borokhov file, CZA:A 24/125/14.
139. Ibid.
140. Yanait, *Anu olim,* p. 284.
141. On the Poale Zion in Soviet Russia 1920–8 see, e.g., Z. Abramovich; Gurevitz; Nir, *Vanderungen;* Petrazil, *Ha-maavak,* I.
142. A. V. Lunacharsky, *Religiia i sotsializm* (St. Petersburg, 1908).
143. Borochov, *Virtualizm,* pp. 16–7. On Borochov's philosophical development cf. Mintz, "Borokhov ve-Bogdanov." Mintz argues that Bogdanov, as Marxist and Bolshevik, exerted a major influence on Borochov. On Bogdanov's thought see, e.g., Yassour, *Mi-likhe,* pp. 141–80.
144. Borochov, *Virtualizm,* p. 12.
145. Ibid., p. 5.
146. Ibid., p. 74.
147. Ibid., p. 78.
148. Ibid., p. 111.
149. Ibid., p. 105.
150. Ibid.
151. Ibid., pp. 64–5.
152. Ibid., pp. 65–6.
153. 9 Jan. 1909 in Borochov archive, AMJLM: III, 103.

Chapter 8. Revolutionary ethos in transition

1. For the fullest. and most important study of the ideological development of the Second Aliya see Kolatt, "Ideologya u-metsiut." See also Katznelson's remarkable analysis *Prakim* in *Kitve,* vol. XI. For general histories of the Jewish labor movement (a) in Palestine see Braslavsky; Slutsky, *Mavo;* (b) world-wide see Aizenshtat; Tartakover.
2. Ruppin (*The Jews,* p. 55) reckoned the annual immigration rate to be 2,000–3,000 in the period 1900–14 and the rise in the Jewish population to be 30,000 (from 55,000 to 85,000).
3. Ben Gurion, "Be-hag," p. 17.
4. C. Ridnik, "Ha-hagira ha-ivrit derekh hof yafo bi-shnat 1912," *PTs* (31 Jan. 1913), no. 18, p. 12.
5. Gorni, "Ha-shinuim," p. 215. Cf. Kolatt, "Ideologya u-metsiut," p. 86.
6. Gorni, "Ha-shinuim," p. 218.
7. For biographical sketches of prominent personalities in the Yishuv see Tidhar (ed.). For a popular sketch of the Second Aliya see Elon, pp. 106–35.
8. Tabenkin, "Ha-mkorot," pp. 23–4.
9. Ibid., pp. 27–8.
10. E.g., Shapira, pp. 28–9.
11. "Pisma iz Palestiny" [15/28 Feb.1906], *ERKh* (23 April 1906), no. 1, pp. 51–2. Here the Ha-poel Ha-Tsair party is called Zeire Zion.
12. N. Tversky, "Imo," *PTs* (6 April 1937), no. 27–8, p. 9.
13. Y. Slutsky, "Rishonim," *Sefer toldot ha-hagana,* I, 39; M. Ingberman, "Hearot li-sheelat ha-poalim," *Ah* (28 Shvat 5672/16 Feb. 1912), no. 19, p. 5.
14. On the workers in the pre-1904 period see Kressel, "Ben aliya la-aliya," in Habas, pp. 51–64; and idem, "Histadrut ha-poalim."

15. Ruppin, *Shloshim shnot binyan*, p. 1; Bein, *The Return*, pp. 4–11; Slutsky in *Sefer toldott ha-hagana*, I, 30–44. Cf. Nawratzki.

16. Oppenheimer, *Merchavia*, p. 1.

17. E.g., Avitsur, on Nahum Vilbushevich.

18. Heruti [Smilansky], "Me-inyene ha-yishuv," *PTs* (Shvat–Adar, 5668/Jan.–Feb. 1908), pp. 9–10.

19. "Undzere oyfgabn," *Der onfang* (15 Tammuz 5667/27 June 1907) no. 1, pp. 3–4.

20. Y.R., "Reshimot," *PTs* (1 Nov. 1912), no. 5–6, p. 9.

21. Zionist Congress XI, p. 195.

22. Aharonovich, "Le-verur ha-matsav," *PTs* (26 Nov. 1909), no. 4, p. 4.

23. "Tamtsit ha-vikuhim shel asefatenu ha-shnatit," *PTs* (11 Nov. 1910), no. 1–2, p. 25.

24. M. Sheinkin, "Al ha-shtika," ibid. (7 May 1913), no. 28–9, p. 14.

25. N.T., "Ha-hitnagdut ve-siboteha," *PTs* (2 Sept. 1912), no. 24, p. 4.

26. "Le-khol ha-tsiyonim ha-tseirim asher ba-galut," *PTs* (Tevet 5668/Dec. 1907–Jan. 1908), cover page.

27. "Ha-platforma ha-ramlayit" [Oct. 1906], in Ben Zvi, *Poale tsiyon* p. 210. First published: *PG* (28 Feb. 1907), no. 3, pp. 63–5. For a comparison of this with other early party platforms, etc., see Kalay, pp. 29–54.

28. Barats, p. 248.

29. Avner [Ben Zvi], "Matsav ha-poel ha-erets yisreeli ve-histadruto," *Ah* (2 Heshvan 5671/4 Nov. 1910), no. 1, p. 3.

30. "Undzere oyfgabn," *Der onfang,* no. 1, p. 5.

31. Barats, p. 248.

32. N. Tversky, "Ha-mishtar he-hadash be-turkiya," *PTs* (Tevet 5669/Dec. 1908–Jan. 1909), no. 6, p. 7.

33. Betser, "Petah-tikva," *Der onfang,* no. 1, p. 12.

34. Tversky, "Ha-mishtar," *PTs* (Tevet 5669), p. 6. (On the organizational structure of the Yishuv, see Kolatt, "The Organization.")

35. "Hatsaat tokhnit" [Jan. 1907], in Ben Zvi, p. 210. First published: *PG* (1907), no. 3, pp. 65–6.

36. Ben Gurion, "Li-sheelat ha-yishuv ha-yashan," *Ah* (Av 5670/Aug.–Sept. 1910), no. 2, p. 55.

37. Idem, "Al ha-perek," *PTs* (Tammuz–Av 5668/July–Aug. 1908), no. 10–11, p. 20.

38. Avner [Ben Zvi], "Palestiner politishe fragn (a briv fun yerusholayim)," *YA* (Galicia) (9 October 1908), no. 36, p. 2.

39. Palestinait [Yanait?], "Iber palestine politik," *YA* (Galicia) (13 Nov. 1908), no. 41, p. 1.

40. Ben Gurion, "Avodatenu ha-hevratit mdinit," *Ah* (9 Heshvan 5671/11 Nov. 1910), no. 2–3, pp. 1–2.

41. Avner, "Palestiner politische fragn," ibid. (9 Oct. 1908), no. 36, p. 1.

42. "Yerushalayim," *PTs* (Tammuz–Av 5668/July–Aug. 1908), no. 10–11, p. 18.

43. Ibid., p. 27.

44. [A.Turkenich], "Ha-avoda ha-realit be-erets yisrael," *PTs* (Heshvan 5668/Oct.–Nov. 1907), pp. 1–2.

45. "Le-khol ha-tsiyonim ha-tseirim," ibid. (Tevet 5668/Dec. 1907–Jan. 1908), cover page.

46. Ben Hava, "Ha-poel ha-glili," ibid. (Nisan–Iyar 5668/April–May 1908), no. 7–8, p. 3.

47. Ha-vaad ha-merkazi, "La-tsiyonim be-tsiyon," ibid. (Sivan 5668/June 1908), no. 9, p. 1.

48. Palestinait [Yanait?], "Iber palestine politik," *YA* (Galicia) (13 Nov. 1908), no. 41, p. 2.

49. Ben Gurion, "Le-verur matsavenu ha-mdini," *Ah* (Elul 5670/Sept.–Oct. 1910), no. 3, pp. 89–90.

50. Y. Epstein, "Sheela neelama," *Ha-shiloah*, XVII (July–Dec. 1907), 193–4.

51. Ibid., p. 196.

52. Heruti [Smilansky], "Me-inyene ha-yishuv," *PTs* (Shvat–Adar 5668/Jan.–Feb. 1908), pp. 5–6.

53. Ibid., p. 7.

54. Ibid., p. 8.

55. Ibid., p. 9.

56. A. D. Gordon, "Pitron lo ratsyonali," *PTs* (1 July 1909), no. 17, p. 5. On this debate see Gorni, "Shorasheha." Cf. Ro'i, "The Zionist Attitude." For a recent study of Gordon's thought in general see Schweid.

57. E.g., Dizengof's letter in *Hosafa le-hatsvi* (7 Tishre 5669/2 Oct. 1908), no. 4.

58. A. D. Gordon, "Al dvar mosro ha-tov shel ha-adon Dizenhof," *Ha-tsvi* (2 Heshvan 5669/27 Oct. 1908), no. 14.

59. "Al ha-perek," *Ah* (Tammuz 5670/July–Aug. 1910), no. 1, p. 28. On the foundation and policies of *Ha-ahdut* see Zerubavel, "Prakim."

60. D. Ben Gurion, "Le-virur matsavenu ha-mdini," *Ah* (Elul 5670/Sept.–Oct. 1910), p. 88.

61. Ben Gurion, *Zikhronot*, I, 23.

62. Tsemakh, *Be-reshit*, pp. 39–40.

63. Gorni, "Ha-shinuyim."

64. "Undzere oyfgabn," *Der onfang*, no. 1, p. 6.

65. Avner [Ben Zvi], "Palestiner politishe fragn," *YA* (Galicia) (2 Oct. 1908), no. 35, p. 1.

66. "Le-khol ha-tsiyonim ha-tseirim," *PTs* (Tevet 5668/Dec. 1907–Jan. 1908), cover page. The phrase, "this is not the way," had been made famous as the title of an article by Ahad Ha-Am, 1889. On the relationship of Ha-Poel Ha-Tsair to the Zionist youth in eastern Europe see Munchik, pp. 7–34.

67. Yosef Haver [Brenner], "Ba-itnout u-vasifrut," *PTs* (23 Dec. 1910), no. 5–6, p. 9. For indexes to *Ha-poel ha-tsair* and *Ha-ahdut* see Kressel (ed.), *Mafteah*.

68. Y. Aharonovich, "Yosef Vitkin z.l.," *PTs* (11 Feb. 1912), no. 9–10, p. 1.

69. "Palestiner politishe fragn," *YA* (Galicia) (2 Oct. 1908), no. 35, p. 2.

70. Man-dehu [K.L. Silman], "Al da ve-al ha," *PTs* (Tammuz–Av 5668/July–Aug. 1908), no. 10–11, pp. 23–4.

71. "Yerushalayim," ibid., p. 18.

72. E.g., Y. Shokhat, p. 12.

73. N.T., "Hayenu ha-tsiburiyim," *PTs* (23 April 1909), no. 12, p. 3.

74. Ohev Rina, "Zikhronot (me-hahove u-meheavar)," *PTs* (14 Sept. 1909), no. 23–4, p. 21.

75. On the ideology of Ha-Poel Ha-Tsair until 1914 see e.g., Kolatt, " 'Ha-poel ha-tsair' "; Gorni, " 'Ha-poel ha-tsair' ve-yahaso."

76. Ben Zvi, *Poale tsiyan* p. 33.

77. "Le-khol ha-tsiyonim ha-tseirim," *PTs* (Tevet 5668/Dec. 1907–Jan. 1908), cover page.

78. Khanibal [Ben Zvi?], "Der 'ha-poyel ha-tsair' in e.y.," *YA* (21 Aug. 1908), no. 29, pp. 3–4.

79. Palestinait [Yanait?], "Iber palestine politik," ibid., (13 Nov. 1908), no. 41, p. 2.

80. Ben Gurion, "Ha-k.p.e.y. ve-hamisrad ha-poel tsiyoni be-erets yisrael," *Ah* (16 Heshvan 5671/18 Nov. 1910), p. 4.

81. "Undzere oyfgabn," *Der onfang*, no. 1, p. 2.

82. Ibid., p. 6.

83. Y. Aharonovich, "Kibush ha-avoda o kibush ha-karka," *PTs* (Elul 5668/Aug.–Sept. 1908), no. 12, pp. 1–2.

84. Idem, "Milhemet ha-maamadot u-milhemet ha-kiyum," ibid., (Sivan 5668/June 1908), no. 9, p. 7.

85. Ibid, p. 5.

86. On Brenner's weltanschauung see, e.g., Gorni, "Ha-tikva she-beyeush."

87. Avner [Ben Zvi], "Sheelat ha-hityashvut ha-shitufit," *Ah* (11 Tammuz 5671/7 July 1911), no. 35, p. 1.

88. On the roots of "labor settlement" *(ha-hityashvut ha-ovedet)* and of the kibbutz see the debate in Slutsky, "Mkoma"; Kolatt, "Li-mkoma"; Slutsky, "Ha-idea." Cf. Gorni, "Behevle tmura"; R. Frankel.

89. On the attempts by leaders of Ha-Poel Ha-Tsair in 1905–6 to bring workers to Galilee see the letters of E. Shokhat and R. Sverdlov: Shokhat, "Shlosha mikhtavim," *Asupot* (1945), no. 1, pp. 38–9; Shapira, pp. 471–2. Sverdlov arrived in Palestine in 1904.

90. On Manya Vilbushevich (Shokhat) see e.g., I. H. Hourwich, "Der politsaysker sotsyalizmus in rusland," *Tsayt-gayst* (14 Sept. 1906), no. 55, p. 3; Shva; Yanait, *Manya Shohat*.

91. Y. Shokhat, p. 11.

92. Ben Hava, "Ha-poel ha-glili," *PTs* (Nisan–Iyar 5668/April–May 1908), no. 7–8, p. 6.

93. S. Tsemakh, "Eliezer Shohat," in E. Shokhat, p. 10.

94. Veits, p. 357.

95. Ivn Nisan [Mikhael Nisenbaum], "Mikhtavim me-hagalil," *PTs* (Heshvan 5668/Nov. 1907), p. 9.

96. Z.S. [Smilansky], 'Poalim ivriyim o arviyim," *Ha-shiloah*, XIX (July–Dec. 1908), 468–9.

97. Tsemakh, *Be-reshit*, p. 64.

98. M. Sheinkin, "Dvarim ke-havayatam," *PTs* (12 Nov. 1909), no. 3, p. 13.

99. Ben Hava, "Ha-poel ha-glili," ibid. (Nisan–Iyar 5668/April–Amy 1908), no. 7–8, p. 3.

100. Ibid. (Sivan 5668/June 1908), no. 9, p. 2.

101. Ibid., pp. 2–3.

102. "Tokhnit 'ha-horesh'," ibid. (Kislev 5669/Nov.–Dec. 1908), no. 5, p. 14.

103. Ibid.

104. Ben Hava, "Ha-poel ha-glili," *PTs* (Nisan–Iyar/April–May 1908), no. 7–8, p. 6.

105. Ibid.

106. E. Beker, "Me-haye mishpahat shomer," in Habas, p. 510.

107. Ibid., p. 511.

108. "Briv an di redaktsya," *YA* (Galicia) (1 July 1905), no. 10, p. 7. On the ideological roots of Bar Giora and Ha-Shomer cf. Gorni, "Ha-yesod."

109. Y. Shokhat, p. 7.

110. E.g., Zaid, pp. 24–30. Cf. Slutsky, "Ha-raayon ha-halutsi," pp. 12–13.

111. Y. Shohat, p. 20. For the program of Ha-Shomer see *Kovets "ha-shomer,"* p. 35.

112. Oppenheimer, *Die Siedlungsgenossenschaft*, pp. 469–567. Cf. idem, *Erlebtes*, pp. 136–68.

113. See the announcement in the Motzkin archive: CZA: A26/24/7/1.

114. E.g., Bein, "Franz Oppenheimer"; Kressel, *Frants Openhaymer*, pp. 25–40.

115. "Franz Oppenheimer über Zionismus," *Die Welt* (6 March 1903), no. 10, p. 4.

116. Bein, "Franz Oppenheimer," p. 107.

117. Zionist Congress VIII, pp. 315–6.

118. E.g., Warburg's report, ibid., pp. 128–45. On Warburg see the introduction to Thon (ed.), pp. 9–74.

119. See Levontin, II, 53–252; M. Eliav.

120. Zionist Congress VIII, p. 142. For a Hebrew translation of Warburg's major speeches at the Zionist congresses see Thon (ed.), pp. 114–55.

121. "Iber program un taktik," *YA* (Galicia) (15 Oct. 1905), no. 17, pp. 4–5.

122. "Der farbandstog fun poyle tsien estraykhs," *YA* (Galicia) (15 July 1905), no. 11, p. 3.

123. E. Blumenfeld [D. Bloch], "Tsu der frage vegn der realizirung fun der teritoryal.-polit. oytonomye in palestine," ibid., (28 May 1908), no. 18, p. 2.

124. Zionist Congress VIII, p. 115.

125. Ibid., pp. 308–9.

126. Ibid., pp. 316–7.

127. "Bericht über den zehnten Delegiertentag der deutschen Zionisten," *Die Welt* (8 June 1906), no. 23, p. 8.

128. Zionist Congress VIII, pp. 140–1.

129. Ibid., p. 328.

130. Ruppin, *Pirke hayay*, II, 42.

131. Ibid., p. 59.

132. Bloch, "Ole romni," in Habas, p. 155.

133. Deganya is officially entitled a kvutsa to this day.

134. Ben Gurion, "Ha-pkidut ve-hapoalim," *Ah* (24 Adar 5671/24 March 1911), no. 22, pp. 2–3.

135. E.g., "Bi-fnim ha-arets," *PTs* (4 Nov. 1909), no. 2, pp. 14–15.

136. H. Yoffe, "Ha-avoda ha-karkait shel ha-yehudim be-e.y.," *PTs* (Shevat-Adar 5668/Jan.–Feb. 1908), p. 11.

137. Y. Vitkin, "Kibush ha-karka ve-kibush ha-avoda," ibid., (Tammuz–Av 5668/July–Aug. 1908), no. 10–11, p. 3.

138. Y. Aharonovich, "Yosef Vitkin z.l.," ibid., (11 Feb. 1912), no. 9–10, p. 6.

139. Shimshon [Zerubavel], "Lifne veidat ha-miflaga," *Ah* (2 Nisan 5671/31 March 1911), no. 23, p. 11.

140. *Sefer toldot ha-hagana*, I, 132–4.

141. [Katznelson], *Igrot*, I, 122.

142. "Asefatenu ha-shnatit ha-shviit," *PTs* (13 Oct. 1912), no. 3, p. 3.

143. Zaid, *Haye rishonim*, p. 46.

144. Y. [Yehuda] Burla, "Le-matsav ha-tsdadim," *Ah* (12 Adar 5673/19 Feb. 1913), no. 23, p. 6.

145. "Yama (yavneel)," *PTs* (Sivan 5668/June 1908), no. 9, p. 13.

146. Sara M. [Malkin], "A.d. ha-poalot be-kineret," ibid. (5 March 1912), no. 11, p. 14.

147. Yaakov Levin, "Sheelat ha-poalim be-erets yisrael," *Ah* (3 Elul 5672/9 Aug. 1912), no. 42, p. 9.

148. Y. L-n, "Shvil ha-zahav," *PTs* (19 June 1914), no. 35, p. 14.

149. Y.H.B. [Brenner], "Regashim ve-hirhurim," *PTs* (1 July 1909), no. 17, pp. 4–5.

150. Y. Aharonovich, "Al ha-'sakh ha-kol'," ibid., (19 May 1912), no. 16, p. 3.

151. Bar Yohai [Brenner], "Mi-tokh ha-pinkas," *Ah* (29 Elul 5671/22 Sept. 1911), no. 47–8, p. 24.

152. "Me-asefat ha-sofrim," *PTs* (20 Feb. 1911), no. 9–10, p. 22.

153. [Aharonovich], *Kitve*, II, 234–5.

154. Y. Aharonovich, "Mikhtavim me-e.y.," *PTs* (Kislev 5668/Nov.–Dec. 1907), p. 14.

155. A. D. Gordon, "Tshuvat poel al divre ha-adon Ben Yehuda 'el ha-poalim'," ibid. (Tevet 5669/Dec. 1908–Jan. 1909), no. 6, p. 11.

156. Idem, "Meat hitbonenut," ibid. (10 Aug. 1911), no. 21, p. 4.

157. A., "Nishke milhama shel p.t.," ibid. (27 June 1911), no. 18, p. 3.

158. Y. H. Brenner, "Tsiyunim," ibid. (28 Aug. 1911), no. 22, p. 8.

159. Ibid.

160. Y. Aharonovich, "Yosef Vitkin," ibid. (11 Feb. 1912), no. 9–10, p. 3.

161. Y.H.B. [Brenner], "Mikha-Yosef Berdichevski," ibid. (25 Sept. 1912), no. 2, p. 14.

162. A. D. Gordon, "Universita ivrit," ibid. (18 Aug. 1913), no. 43–4, p. 8.

163. Ben Hava, "Ha-poel ha-glili," ibid. (Nisan–Iyar 5668/April–May 1908), p. 5.

164. A. Tsiyoni [Vilkansky], "Shitat ha-hityashvut shel Openhaymer," ibid. (4 Sept. 1910), no. 22, p. 6.

165. Y.R. [Rabinovich], "Reshimot," ibid. (11 July 1911), no. 19, p. 6.

166. Z.S. [Smilansky], "Ha-poalim ha-ivriyim be-moshvot yehuda," ibid. (31 Dec. 1912), no. 14, p. 4.

167. "Petah tikva," ibid. (Kislev 5668/Nov.–Dec. 1907), p. 12.

168. [Katznelson], Igrot, I, 222.

169. Y. Levin, "Sheelat ha-poalim," Ah (26 Av 5672/9 Aug. 1912), p. 10.

170. Y. Aharonovich, "Milhemet ha-maamadot u-milhemet ha-kiyum," PTs (Sivan 5668/June 1908), no. 9, pp. 7–8.

171. A. Tsiyoni, "Shitat ha-hityashvut shel Openhaymer," ibid., (4 Sept. 1910), no. 22, p. 6.

172. Y. Klausner, "Olam mithave," Ha-shiloah, XXIX (July–Dec. 1913), 54.

173. "Hag ha-yeladim be-fetah tikva," PTs (23 April 1909), no. 12, p. 14.

174. Ben Gurion, "Le-sidur poale ha-moshavot," Ah (28 Iyar 5671/24 May 1911), no. 28–9, p. 16.

175. Ben Hava, "Ha-poel ha-glili," PTs (Sivan 5668/June 1908), no. 9, p. 3.

176. Zerubavel, "Sovlanut," Ah (11 Tammuz 5671/7 July 1911), no. 35, p. 14.

177. S. Z. Gisin, "Mikhtavim la-maarekhet," PTs (Nisan–Iyar/April–May 1908), p. 29.

178. Ha-vaad ha-yerushalmi shel mifleget ha-poalim ha-sotsyalistim be-palestina (poale tsiyon), "Mikhtav la-maarekhet," Ha-tsvi (8 Heshvan 5669/2 Nov. 1908), no. 21, p. 3.

179. Letter from M. Dizengof in Hosafa le-hatsvi (7 Tishre 5669/2 Oct. 1908), no. 4.

180. "Ba-miflaga," PTs (27 Aug. 1909), no. 22, p. 13.

181. Haver ha-merkaz, "Emtsae avodatenu," ibid. (7 Dec. 1909), no. 5, p. 4.

182. Even Tov, "Be-fetah tikva," in Habas, p. 185.

183. A. D. Gordon, "Al dvar mosro ha-tov shel ha-adon Dizengof," Ha-tsvi (27 Tishre 5669/22 Oct. 1908), p. 2.

184. Quoted in "Tshuva," PTs (11 July 1911), no. 19, p. 7.

185. M.B., "Rekhovyes," Der onfang (1907), no. 1, p. 11. On the reaction to the Rishon Le-Zion strike see Slutsky, "Diyun."

186. Ohev Rina, "Zikhronot," PTs (14 Sept. 1909), no. 23–4, p. 21.

187. Avner [Ben Zvi], "Der yafeer lektsyon," YA (Galicia) (14 April 1908), no. 12–13, p. 3.

188. On the Jaffa incident (March 1908) see Eliav, "Meorot yafo."

189. Avner in YA (1908), no. 12–13, p. 3.

190. Ha-mashkif [M. Smilansky], "Hashkafa ivrit," Ha-shiloah, XVIII (Jan.–June 1908), 381.

191. Ton [Tversky], "Korespondentsyot–yerushalayim," PTs (Kislev 5669/Nov.–Dec. 1908), no. 3, p. 5.

192. Y. N-i [Yosef Nakhmany], "Li-tnuat poale ha-dfus bi-[ye]rushalayim," Ah (15 Kislev 5671/16 Dec. 1910), no. 8, p. 5.

193. Ezrah, "Yerushalayim" PTs (Kislev 5669/Nov.–Dec. 1908), no. 4, p. 9.

194. Avner [Ben Zvi], "Be-ikve ha-imur ha-klali bi-[ye]rushalayim," Ha-tsvi (28 Kislev 5669/17 June 1909), no. 59, p. 3. On the haluka as a source of conflict between the old and new Yishuv see Abramov, pp. 23–4.

195. Cf. Drori, "Hishtakfuta," Cathedra, II (1976), 69–80; Giladi, "Emdat ha-ikarim."

196. E.g., the letter from Levontin to Wolffsohn (10 April 1906): "Mi-teudot," Asupot (1954), no. 4, p. 12.

197. M. Ben Zvi, "Mikhtav la-poalim ha-tseirim be-e.y.," *PTs* (Tevet 5669/Dec. 1908–Jan. 1909), no. 7, pp. 4–5.
198. Letter of Dizengof in *Hosafa le-hatsvi* (7 Tishre 5669/2 Oct. 1908), no. 4.
199. M. Ben Hillel Ha-Cohen, "Ha-poalim ha-btelim," *Ha-tsvi* (4 Heshvan 5669/29 Oct. 1908), p. 1.
200. Avi [Ben Yehuda], "El ha-poalim," ibid. (15 Kislev 5669/9 Dec. 1908), no. 48, p. 1.
201. A. D. Gordon, "Al dvar mosro ha-tov shel ha-adon Dizenhof," ibid. (27 Tishre 5669/22 Oct. 1908), no. 11, pp. 1–2.
202. A. Tsiyoni, "Sheelot ha-yom," *PTs* (Adar 5669/Feb.–March 1909), p. 5.
203. M. Sheinkin, "Li-sheelat ha-poalim," ibid (Shvat 5669/Jan.–Feb. 1909), no. 8, pp. 4–5.
204. Yosef Haver [Brenner], "Ba-itonut u-vasifrut," *PTs* (24 Nov. 1910), no. 3, p. 8.
205. Ahad Ha-Am, "Yalkut katan: tora mi-tsiyon," *Ha-shiloah*, XXIV (Jan.–June 1911), 364–5.
206. A. D. Gordon, "Al ha-dvarim ha-noraim," *PTs* (9 May 1911), no. 14–15, p. 8.
207. Ahad Ha-Am, "Sakh ha-kol," *Ha-shiloah*, XXVI (Jan.–June 1912), 282.
208. Ibid., p. 285.
209. N.T. [Tversky], "Hayenu ha-tsiburiyim," *PTs* (23 April 1909), no. 12, p. 3.
210. A. D. Gordon, "Pitron lo ratsyonali," ibid. (17 June 1909), no. 16, p. 5.
211. Zerubavel, "Hahlatot u-maasim," *Ah* (27 Tevet 5671/27 Jan. 1911), no. 14, pp. 9–11.
212. Ben Gurion, "Le-sidur poale ha-moshavot," ibid, (28 Iyar 5671/21 Sept. 1911), no. 28–9, p. 15.
213. Avner [Ben Zvi], "Matsav ha-poel ha-erets yisreeli ve-histadruto," ibid. (2 Heshvan 5671/4 Nov. 1910), no. 1, p. 5.
214. N.T. [Tversky], "Hayenu ha-tsiburiyim," *PTs* (23 April 1909), no. 12, pp. 4–5.
215. –n [Zerubavel], "Veidat poale tsiyon bi-[ye]huda," *Ah* (10 Elul 5672/23 Aug. 1912), no. 43–4, p. 9.
216. E.g., Nini, "Ole teman," *Cathedra*, V (1977), 30–82.
217. Z.S. [Smilansky], "Ha-poalim ha-ivriyim be-moshvot yehuda," *PTs* (31 Dec. 1912), no. 14, p. 3.
218. "Ba-miflaga (tamtsit ha-vikuhim me-asefatenu ha-shviit)," *PTs* (29 Nov. 1912), no. 10, p. 16.
219. Cf. Ruppin, *Memoirs*, pp. 109–10.
220. Ben Gurion, "Huka ahat," *Ah* (14 Nisan 5672/1 April 1912), no. 25–6, p. 1.
221. Z.S. [Smilansky], "Berur dvarim" *PTs* (12 April 1910), no. 12, p. 5.
222. "Din ve-heshbon shel moetset ha-miflaga be-sukot 5671," *Ah* (9 Heshvan 5671/11 Nov. 1910), no. 2–3, p. 19.
223. "Ba-miflaga (tamtsit ha-vikuhim me-asefatenu ha-shviit)," *PTs* (29 Nov. 1912), no. 10, p. 16.
224. "Al ha-perek: ahare ha-veida," *Ah* (17 Tevet 5673/20 Oct. 1912), no. 11, p. 5.
225. Ben Garni, "Mikhtav me-rehovot," *PTs* (22 Oct. 1911), no. 1, pp. 15–17.
226. Ben Gurion, "Ha-shana ha-holefet be-haye ha-poalim," *Ah* (29 Elul 5671/22 Sept. 1911), no. 47–8, p. 5.
227. Katznelson, *Igrot*, I, p. 144.
228. "Din ve-heshbon me-haveida shel histadrut poale tsiyon ba-galil," *Ah* (Elul 5670/Sept.–Oct. 1910), no. 3, p. 112.
229. Barkai, "Mikhtav me-hagalil," *PTs* (10 May 1910), no. 13–14, p. 18.
230. On the Nili group see Aaronsohn; Engle; Livne, *Aharon Aronson; idem, Nili; Sefer toldot ha-hagana*, I, 353–79.
231. Y. Aharonovich, "Klape pnim," *PTs* (1 Nov. 1912), no. 5–6, p. 4.

232. Zerubavel, "Shmira ve-avoda," *Ah* (26 Heshvan 5672/17 Nov. 1911), no. 5, p. 4.
223. Ibid., p. 2.
234. *Sefer toldot ha-hagana*, I, 236.
235. Zerubavel, "Sovlanut," *Ah* (11 Tammuz/7 July 1911), no. 35, p. 11.
236. M. R. Cohen, "Mikhtav mi-[ye]sud ha-maala," *PTs* (27 June 1911), no. 18, p. 10.
237. On Rehovot's relations with the neighboring Arab villages see Ro'i, "Yahase rehovot." On the Arab attitude to Zionism generally see N. Mandel.
238. E.g., Kolar, "Meora zarnuga," in Habas, pp. 288–90.
239. Tsdadi, "Mikhtav me-rehovot," *PTs* (15 Oct. 1913), no. 12, p. 18.
240. Ibid., p. 19.
241. Ben Hava, "Ha-poel ha-glili," *PTs* (Nisan–Iyar 5668/April–May 1908), p. 4.
242. "Asefat ha-poalim ha-haklayim ba-galil," *Ah* (7 Shvat 5672/26 Jan. 1912), no. 16, p. 10.
243. "Ba-miflaga (tamtsit me-asefatenu ha-shviit)," *PTs* (29 Nov. 1912), no. 10, p. 16.
244. Malkin, "Darki," in Habas, p. 498.
245. A. Reuveni [Shimshelevich], "Ha-poalim ve-hakongres," *Ah* (11 Tammuz 5671/7 July 1911), no. 35, p. 9. Reuveni, like the Russian Poale Zion, was opposed to party participation in the Zionist congress.
246. Avner [Ben Zvi], "Ha-knesia be-bazel," ibid. (29 Elul 5671/22 Sept. 1911), no. 47–8, p. 10.
247. E.g., Ben Pori, 'Mikhtav mi-poriya," ibid. (28 Shvat 5672/16 Feb. 1912), no. 19, pp. 21–3; N. Vatik [Zerubavel], "Mikhtav mi-migdal," ibid. (15 Av 5673/18 Aug. 1913), no. 41–2, pp. 26–9; N.G., "Mikhtav mi-kfar uriya," ibid. (28 Nisan 5674/24 April 1914), no. 26, pp. 26–9.
248. Poel, "Mikhtav mi-merhavya," ibid. (26 Nisan 5674/22 April 1914), no. 34, p. 28.
249. Ben Gurion, "Ha-pkidut ve-hapoalim," ibid. (24 Adar 5671/24 March 1911), no. 22, p. 1.
250. Ibid., pp. 4–5.
251. Y.R. [Rabinovich], "Reshimot," *PTs* (11 July 1911), no. 19, p. 6.
252. E.g., "Mikhtavim la-maarekhet," ibid. (4 Sept. 1910), no. 22, p. 16.
253. Sh. N-n., "Mikhtav mi-sedzhera," *Ah* (25 Heshvan 5673/5 Nov. 1912), no. 4, p. 22.
254. Oppenheimer, *Merchavia*, p. 24.
255. Quoted in Kressel, *Frants Openhaymer*, p. 106.
256. Dyk's memorandum (p. 17) and Ruppin's letter (21 June 1914): CAZ: Z3/1527.
257. Shimshon [Zerubavel], "Ha-shvita be-sedzhera," *Ah* (1 Adar 5674/27 Feb. 1914), no. 20, p. 18.
258. M. Smilansky, "Ba-moledet (li-sheelat ha-poalim)," *Ha-olam* (10 April 1914), no. 14/370, p. 8.
259. Ibid., p. 9.
260. "Tsu der itstiker situatsye," *YA* (Galicia) (19 July 1909), no. 27, p. 1.
261. E.g., M. Rosenfeld, "Frants Openhaymer: tsu sayn 50 geburtstog," ibid. (10 April 1914), no. 9, p. 2.
262. Oppenheimer, *Merchavia*, preface.
263. "Di konferents fun der yid. sots. dem. arb. partey (poyle tsien in rusland)," *YA* (Galicia) (22 Oct. 1909), no. 37, p. 3. The protocols of this conference were first published in the 1920s; see *YAP*, pp. 172–279. For Borochov's speeches there, see his *Ktavim*, II, 171–213.
264. Ibid.
265. S. Kaplansky, "Di kongres frage," ibid. (Galacia) (10 Dec. 1909), no. 43, p. 2.
266. Avner, "Vegn der letster konferents fun di rusishe poyle tsien," ibid., pp. 2–3. On the first signs (in 1907) of the widening gap between the Poale Zion in Russia and in Palestine see Mintz, "Borokhov ve-nitsane."

267. Donin [Borochov], "Vegn der bayzer kritik un yuristisher argumentatsye," *YA* (Galicia) (17 Dec. 1909), no. 44, p. 3. (Hebrew: *Ktavim*, II, 224.)
268. "Di tsveyte konferents fun alveltlikhn yid. sots. arb. ferband poyle tsien in krakoy," ibid. (7 Jan. 1910), no. 1, p. 3.
269. Ibid.
270. Ibid.
271. Ibid.
272. Y.A. [Aharonovich], "Ha-veida ha-krakoit shel poale tsiyon," *PTs* (29 Feb. 1910), no. 9, p. 5.
273. Ibid. (11 Feb. 1910), no. 8, p. 14.
274. Ibid. (29 Feb. 1910), no. 9, p. 5.
275. Avtalyon, "A briv fun yerusholayim," *YA* (Galicia) (25 Feb. 1910), no. 8, p. 3.
276. Zionist Congress IX, pp. 195–212, 509.
277. Poel, "Dganya," *PTs* (9 Jan. 1912), no. 7, pp. 16–17.
278. 14 July 1908: CZA (Kinneret file): KKL 3/100, alef.
279. 12 Sept. 1909 (p. 3) CZA (PLDC files) L1/96; Cf. Ruppin, *Memoirs*, pp. 98–105.
280. 10 Dec. 1909 (p. 3): CZA: L1/96. [English: Ruppin, *Memoirs*, pp. 103–4.]
281. "Um el-dzhuni," *PTs* (15 Jan. 1911), no. 7, p. 17. On the development of Deganya see Dayan, *Hatsi yovel*.
282. Ben Sara, "Ha-pkidut ha-hadasha be-e.y.," *PTs* (9 May 1911), no. 14–15, p. 11.
283. Zmani, "Mikhtav me-hagalil," ibid. (12 July 1912), no. 19–20, p. 16.
284. [Katznelson], *Igrot*, I, 118–9.
285. Levyi, "En ganim," *PTs* (27 Dec. 1911), no. 6, p. 11. On the emergence of the moshav ovdim see Dayan, *Moshve ovdim*, pp. 7–53. cf. Harizman.
286. Y. Tunis, "Mi-yishuv le-yishuv," in Habas, p. 449.
287. Tsdadi, "Meat higayon," *Ah* (15 Elul 5671/8 Sept. 1911), no. 44–5, p. 6.
288. Zhidlovsky, "Hevle klita," in Habas, pp. 556–7.
289. Quoted in full: Bein, "Franz Oppenheimer," pp. 86–7.
290. Quoted in Kressel, *Frants Openhaymer*, p. 87.
291. Avner [Ben Zvi], "Sheelot ha-hityashvut ha-shitufit," *Ah* (17 Tammuz 5671/13 July 1911), no. 36, pp. 7–8.
292. A. Tsiyoni, "Sheelat ha-yom," *PTs* (Adar 5669/Feb.–March 1909), p. 5.
293. Ibid., p. 8.
294. Idem, "Ha-tsipiya le-kapitalizm," ibid. (22 Oct. 1909), no. 1, p. 6.
295. Idem, "Shitat ha-hityashvut shel Openhaymer," ibid. (4 Sept. 1910), no. 22, p. 7.
296. Y.R., "Reshimot," ibid. (11 July 1911), no. 19, pp. 6–7.
297. Shimshon [Zerubavel], "Ha-veida ha-shniya shel poale yehuda," *Ah* (12 Tevet 5672/2 Jan. 1912), no. 11–12, p. 16.
298. "Ha-veida ha-shminit," ibid. (6 Iyar 5672/23 April 1912), no. 27, pp. 1–2.
299. Ibid., pp. 2–3.
300. Y. Aharonovich, "Mehol ha-stanim," *PTs* (11 July 1911), no. 19, p. 4.
301. Idem, "Li-tkufat ha-shloshim," ibid. (18 Sept. 1912), no. 1, p. 7.
302. Ibid., p. 8.
303. Idem, "Le-inyene ha-shaa: dea meshabeshet," ibid. (31 Oct. 1913), no. 3, p. 3.
304. A. D. Gordon, "Mi-kotser ruah," ibid. (24 April 1914), no. 27, pp. 5–6.
305. Ibid., p. 8.
306. Zerubavel, "Be-mi ha-asham?" *Ah* (1 Av 5674/24 July 1914), no. 38–9, p. 25.
307. Y. Rabinovich, "Al ha-avoda ha-meorevet," *PTs* (20 March 1914), no. 22, p. 4.
308. Sh. [Zerubavel], "Me-haveida ha-miflagtit," *Ah* (6 Iyar 5673/13 May 1913), no. 27–8, pp. 18–19.

309. E.g., Avner [Ben Zvi], "Hagana leumit ve-hashkafa proletarit," ibid. (23 Shvat 5673/31 Jan. 1913), no. 16, pp. 1–7.

310. Y. Aharonovich, "Klape pnim," *PTs* s(1 Nov. 1912), no. 5–6, p. 4.

311. Y. Shprintsak, "Tkufat maavar ba-avodat ha-misrad ha-e.y.," ibid. (7 Aug. 1914), no. 41, p. 5.

312. Portugali, p. 21.

313. Y. Rabinovich, "Reshimot," *PTs* (28 Feb. 1913), no. 21, p. 5.

314. Y. Aharonovich, "Ha-kongres ha-ahad asar," ibid. (1 Oct. 1913), no. 49–50, p. 3.

315. Zionist Congress XI, p. 198.

316. Y.R. [Rabinovich], "Ba-itonut," *PTs* (7 Nov. 1913), no. 4, p. 12.

317. N. Syrkin, "Tkufat ha-maase," *Ah* (10 Elul 5672/23 Aug. 1912), no. 43–4, p. 3. On Syrkin's growing influence see Kolatt, "Ideologya u-metsiut," pp. 183–8.

318. Syrkin, "Tkufat ha-maase," p. 2.

319. Idem, "Li-sheelat ha-teritoryaliyut," ibid. (7 Heshvan 5673/18 Oct. 1912), no. 2, p. 3.

320. Idem, "Ha-hityashvut ha-kooperativit ve-ha'ahva'," ibid. (4 Sivan 5674/29 May 1914), no. 31, p. 3.

321. Idem, "Hityashvut hamonit ve-kooperatsya," ibid. (16 Shvat 5673/24 Jan. 1913), no. 14–15, p. 7.

322. Idem, "Ahva," ibid. (8 Sivan 5673/13 June 1913), no. 33, p. 2.

323. Y. Eidelman, "Li-dmuta shel kvutsat 'ahva'," in Habas, p. 267.

324. [Katznelson], *Igrot*, I, 527.

325. "Hag ha-avoda be-artsenu," *Ah* (23 Iyar 5672/10 May 1912), no. 29–30, p. 35.

326. Sh-n [Zerubavel], "Ha-veida ha-olamit ha-rviit bi-krakoy," ibid. (24 Elul 5673/26 Sept. 1913), no. 44–5, p. 24.

327. C. Zhitlovsky, "Li-sheelot yishuvenu," ibid. (9 Tammuz 5674/3 July 1914), no. 36, pp. 8–9.

328. Ibid., p. 9.

329. Shimshon [Zerubavel], "Moetset poale ha-galil ve-totsoteha," ibid. (14 Iyar 5671/12 May 1911), no. 25–6, pp. 15–22.

330. Mikri [Y. Shprintsak], "Mi-veidat poale ha-galil," *PTs* (26 May 1911), no. 16, p. 17.

331. Zerubavel, "Be-mi ha-asham?" *Ah* (1 Av 5674/24 July 1914), no. 38–9, p. 26.

332. E. Yoffe, "Bsis ha-histadrut shel poale ha-galil," ibid. (24 Adar 5674/22 March 1914), no. 22–23, pp. 15–16. Yoffe did try, without long-term success, to realize elements in this program during World War I.

333. Mikri, "Mi-veidat poale ha-galil," *PTs* (26 May 1911), no. 16, p. 16.

334. "Ha-veida ha-shviit," *Ah* (21 Iyar 5671/19 May 1911), no. 27, p. 1. On the attitude of Poale Zion in Palestine to the Labor Fund see Gorni, "Yahasa."

335. Avner [Ben Zvi], "Ha-k.p.e.y. ve-hapoalim," *Ah* (22 Sivan 5671/23 June 1911), no. 32, p. 4.

336. Shimshon [Zerubavel], "Veidat poale yehuda," ibid. (27 Sivan 5671/23 June 1911), no. 33, p. 9.

337. Ibid.

338. "Ha-veida ha-olamit ha-shlishit be-vina," ibid. (8 Elul 5671/1 Sept. 1911), no. 43, p. 14.

339. Ben Gurion, "Ha-tseadim ha-rishonim," ibid. (22 Elul 5671/15 Sept. 1911), no. 46, p. 9.

340. "La-avoda!" ibid. (12 Heshvan 5672/3 Nov. 1911), no. 3, p. 2.

341. "Mi-moetset ha-vaad ha-merkazi," ibid. (23 Elul 5672/5 Sept. 1912), no. 45–6, p. 38.

342. "Ha-veida ha-shminit," ibid. (6 Iyar 5672/23 April 1912), no. 27, p. 4.

343. "Me-hahlatot ha-veida ha-shniya shel poale yehuda," ibid. (1 Tevet 5671/22 Dec. 1911), no. 10, p. 23.

344. Zerubavel, "Be-ikvot ha-metsiut," ibid. pp. 3–4.

345. Vaad poale yehuda, "Mikhtav hozer (3)," ibid. (27 Sivan 5672/12 June 1912), no. 34, p. 21.

346. Kaplansky, "Lishkat ha-avoda u-mitnagdeha," ibid. (13 Tammuz 5671/28 June 1911), no. 36, p. 6.

347. Katznelson, "Mi-bifnim," *PTs* (16 Aug. 1912), no. 22–3, p. 5.

348. Ibid., pp. 5–6.

349. N. Vagman [Shimshelevich], "Sakana la-histadrut," *Ah* (26 Tammuz 5672/11 July 1912), no. 37, p. 5.

350. N.T. [Tversky], "Ha-hitnagdut ve-siboteha," *PTs* (2 Sept. 1912), no. 24, pp. 3–4.

351. Ibid., p. 3.

352. Y. Aharonovich, "Klape pnim," *PTs* (1 Nov. 1912), no. 5–6, p. 3.

353. –n [Zerubavel], "Veidat poale tsiyon bi-[ye]huda," *Ah* (10 Elul 5672/23 Aug. 1912), no. 43–4, p. 12.

354. Y. Rabinovich, "Reshimot," *PTs* (6 Dec. 1912), no. 11, p. 13.

355. Sh-n [Zerubavel], "Ha-veida ha-olamit ha-rviit bi-krakoy," *Ah* (29 Elul 5673/1 Oct. 1913), no. 46, p. 16.

356. Ibid., pp. 16–17.

357. Ibid. (9 Tishre 5674/10 Oct. 1913), no. 47–8, p. 30.

358. Ibid. (29 Elul 5673/1 Oct. 1913), no. 46, p. 19.

359. Ibid., p. 20.

Chapter 9. Class war and community

1. Cf. Mendelsohn, "The Russian Roots."

2. Liebman, *The Ambivalent American Jew*, p. 56.

3. On the character of the Jewish labor movement in America see Epstein, *Jewish Labor;* Hillberg; Hardman; Berman, "A Cursory View." On the Arbeter Ring see Hurwitz; Zaks.

4. Plaut, *Growth of Reform Judaism*, p. 34. The full text is on pp. 33–4.

5. Joseph, pp. 159–75; Oppenheim; Goren, pp. 17–18; Blau, Glazer, et al., pp. 11–29.

6. "On the East Side," *The Worker* (13 Oct. 1901), p. 1.

7. Epstein, *Jewish Labor*, I, 323.

8. Lesin, "Editoryele notitsn: tsum 25-yorikn yubileum fun di fareynikte yidishe geverk-shaftn," *Di tsufunft* (Feb. 1914), p. 115.

9. A. Caspe, "Undzer 'tsukunft' un undzer 'forverts'," ibid. (Feb. 1912), p. 154.

10. Vinchevsky, "Der kamf bey di klouk-makher," ibid. (Jan. 1914), p. 25.

11. Cf. Gorstein; Dubofsky.

12. Salutsky, "Undzer arbeter bavegung un di sotsyalistishe organizatsyon," *Di tsukunft* (Oct. 1911), p. 557.

13. "Socialism in New York," *The Worker* (1 May 1903), p. 3.

14. [SP of A], *National Congress* (1910), p. 128.

15. "Redakstyonele notitsn: vegn Dr. Sirkin's artikl," *Di tsukunft* (Dec. 1908), p. 52/769.

16. Goren, p. 77.

17. On the Russian-Jewish immigrant experience see Rischin, *The Promised City;* Feingold, pp. 113–78. (On the Russian Jews in France in this period, cf. Hayman.)

18. Salutsky, "Di lern fun dem klouk meyker strayk," *Di tsukunft* (Oct. 1910), p. 614.

19. A. Rozenberg, "Metodn un taktik fun der yidisher arbeter bavegung (diskusyon)," ibid. (Nov. 1910), p. 704.

20. Zhitlovsky, "Der antisemitizm un di yidishe parteyn," *Dos naye lebn* (Aug. 1912), p. 8. For an important study of immigrant mobility see Kessner. Cf. Sombart.

21. Elazar, *Community and Polity,* pp. 143–79; idem, "What Indeed is American Jewry?" (a response to Halpern, "What Is American Jewry?").

22. Zametkin, "Ver iz gerekht," *Tsayt-gayst* (19 April 1907), no. 86, p. 13.

23. Salutsky, "An ofener brif tsu Ab. Kahan," *YS* (15 March 1914), no. 8, p. 6.

24. A. Volyner [Eliezer Landau], "Loz gerusn fun amerike," *PG* (31 Jan. 1907), no. 2, pp. 5–6.

25. Ibid., p. 7.

26. Ibid., pp. 8–9.

27. Ibid., p. 10.

28. Libman, "Di arbeter un di sotsyalistishe inteligents (tsum gegnvartikn matsev fun der yidisher arbeter bavegung in rusland)," *Di tsukunft* (April 1914), pp. 247–8.

29. Goren, p. 4.

30. Zivion, "Di yidishe agitatsyons byuro," *Di tsukunft* (May 1909), p. 275.

31. Lesin, "Di geshikhte fun 'arbeter ring,' " ibid. (May 1904), p. 62/270.

32. Miller, "Vos zol men ton?" ibid. (April 1892), p. 17.

33. Ibid.

34. "Undzer tsukunft," ibid. (Jan. 1892), pp. 1–2. On the evolution of *Di tsukunft* (1892–1905) see B. H. Bloom.

35. Vinchevsky, "Mit a dor tsurik: Zundelevitsh un Liberman," *Di tsukunft* (Dec. 1894), pp. 1–6.

36. "Tsu di finftn yor-gang 'tsukunft'," ibid. (Jan. 1896), p. 18.

37. Miller, "Vos zol men tun?" ibid. (April 1892), p. 18.

38. Cahan, "Di tages frage in di yidishe abtaylung fun der sotsyalistisher bavegung," ibid. (July 1896), p. 50/354.

39. Peskin, "Di yidn frage," ibid. (Sept. 1897), p. 14.

40. Idem, "Vi fun yidish-shprekhnde sotsyalistn vern mir yidishe sotsyalistn," *Forverts* (3 June 1903), p. 4.

41. Hertz, *Di yidishe sotsyalistishe bavegung,* pp. 71–80.

42. Cahan, "Di tages frage," *Di tsukunft* (July 1896), pp. 44–5/348–9.

43. Yitskhok Ayzik Ben Arye Tsvi Ha-leyvi, "Di yidish-amerikanishe gele prese," *Dos naye lebn* (June 1909), p. 20/394.

44. Epstein, *Jewish Labor* I, 239–72; Cahan, *Bleter,* III, 425–58.

45. "Oyfn shand-klots," *AB* (4 May 1898), p. 4.

46. "Unter eyn yarmelke: oder di bayde ponemer fun 'abend blat'," *Forverts* (8 May 1898).

47. Quoted in Marrus, p. 210.

48. "A toyt klap far Dreyfusn," *AB* (8 July 1898), p. 1.

49. "Esterhazi vet vider dertseyln mayses," ibid. (3 March 1899), p. 1.

50. "Halt es shmol mit Dreyfusn," ibid. (2 Feb. 1899), p. 1.

51. Ibid.

52. L.M., "Dreyfus un 'ab. blat'," *Forverts* (31 May 1899).

53. "Zig fun varhayt iber alerley patryotn shkorim," *AB* (3 June 1899), p. 4.

54. " 'Der arbeter': yidisher organ fun di poylishe sotsyalistishe partey," *AB* (2 Feb. 1899), p. 4.

55. Baranov, "Di eybige frage; vegn dem bikhl 'Di yidnfrage un di sotsyalistishe yidn-shtat fun Ben Eliezer'," *Di naye tsayt* (6 Oct. 1898), p. 39.

56. Ibid., p. 42.

57. Ibid., p. 40.

58. Ibid., p. 41.

59. Ibid., p. 42.

60. Ibid., p. 44.

61. "Ken a yidisher sotsyalist zayn a yidisher patryot," ibid., p. 45.
62. Ibid., p. 48.
63. "Der 'yidisher arbeter' no. 6," AB (12 June 1899), p. 2.
64. Ibid.
65. Lesin, "Gedankn vegn dem yidishn folk," Forverts (9 Oct. 1898).
66. Idem, "Sotsyalizmus un di yidn frage," ibid. (5 Aug. 1899).
67. Idem, "Fun 3-tn tsienistishn kongres in bazel," ibid. (21 Aug. 1899).
68. [Idem], "Di frantseyzishe sotsyalistn oyfn brisler kongres," ibid. (10 Sept. 1899).
69. A.L., "Zhores un Dreyfus," ibid. (2 Sept. 1899).
70. Idem, "Di tsonkerayn tsvishn di yidishe un poylishe sotsyalistn," ibid. (11 June 1899).
71. Idem, "Erinerungen," ibid. (6 Sept. 1899).
72. Idem, "Sotsyalizmus un di yidn frage," ibid. (5 Aug. 1899).
73. On the SP and American socialism generally. See Bell; Hillquit, History of Socialism; idem, Loose Leaves; Kipnis; Shannon.
74. "New York Sends Aid to Kishineff Victims," NYT (16 May 1903), p. 3.
75. AIU:BM (May 1903), p. 94.
76. "A shaliekh kayn kishinev," Forverts (2 May 1903), p. 1.
77. "Money Pouring in for Kishineff Victims," NYT (17 May 1903), p. 2.
78. Adler, Voice of America, p. 468; "Board of Deputies," JC (19 June 1903), p. 26.
79. "Der protest in karnegi hol," Forverts (28 May 1903), p. 1.
80. "The Kishineff Massacres," JC (26 June 1903), p. 8.
81. "The Kishinev Incident Closed?" AH (24 July 1903), p. 302. On the official response of the U. S. government to the pogroms (1903–61) see Adler and Margalit, pp. 261–98.
82. Rebecca Altman, "An Evening with the Zionists," AH. (3 July 1903), p. 211.
83. Ibid., p. 212.
84. "The After Effects," ibid. (17 July 1903), p. 270.
85. "President Silverman to the Central Conference," ibid. (3 July 1903), p. 210.
86. E.g., "Yidisher velt kongres," Forverts (25 Sept. 1903), p. 1.
87. "President Silverman," ibid. (3 July 1903), p. 210.
88. "The After Effects," ibid. (17 July 1903), p. 270.
89. "Finis," JC (29 May 1903), p. 18.
90. "Anglo-Jewish Association," ibid. (19 June 1903), p. 17.
91. "Board of Deputies," ibid. (3 July 1903), p. 10.
92. "Dumb Dogs," ibid. (12 June 1903), pp. 19–20.
93. "Di flikht: vos yidn muzn itst ton," Forverts (27 April 1903), p. 1.
94. "Hilf far di leydende," ibid. (28 April 1903), p. 1.
95. "'Sibirya' morgn ovnt in talye teater," ibid. (11 May 1903), p. 1.
96. "A sheliekh keyn kishinev," ibid. (May 1903), p. 1.
97. "President Levi's Advice," NYT (18 May 1903), p. 2.
98. "A shande far yidn," Forverts (27 May 1903), p. 1.
99. M. "Di flikht fun yidishe sotsyalistn in de itstike mehume," ibid. (13 May 1903), p. 41.
100. Cahan, "Kishinev! Kishinev!" ibid. (19 May 1903), p. 4.
101. Yitskhok Ayzik Ben Arye Tsvi Ha-leyvi, "Stosyalizmus un de rasnfrage," ibid. (30 May 1903), p. 4.
102. S.P., "Vi fun yidish-shprekhende sotsyalistn," ibid. (3 June 1903), p. 4.
103. Idem, "Muzn mir zayn yidn, oder mir kenen oykh veln blaybn yidn?" ibid. (12 June 1903), p. 4.
104. Lesin, "Di pedler fun kol-yisroel verter," ibid. (9 May 1903), p. 4.
105. Cahan, "Vi ken men filozofirn in oza tsayt," ibid. (10 May 1903), p. 4. (The rabbi of

the Kolel: Jacob Joseph, chief rabbi of the Russian-Jewish orthodox congregations in New York. His funeral was attended by tens of thousands.)

106. Idem, "Emigratsyons arbet velkhe men tut nit," ibid. (4 June 1903), p. 4.

107. Idem, "Yidn-frayndshaft: tsienistishe un sotsyalistishe," ibid. (29 Aug. 1903), p. 4.

108. Idem, "Der yidisher veytog," ibid. (30 May 1903), p. 4.

109. Frumin, "Der 'bund' un zayne gegner," Di tsukunft (Dec. 1903), p. 16/614.

110. Milch, "Tsayt fragn: vos iz tsu ton," ibid. (June 1903), p. 5/271.

111. Ibid., p. 6/272.

112. Ibid., pp. 7–8/273–4.

113. Ibid., p. 8/274.

114. Krantz, "Kishinev, pogromn un der 'bund'," ibid. (Feb. 1904), pp. 3–4/55–6.

115. Milch, "De natsyonale programe fun bund," ibid. (May 1904), p. 31/239.

116. Feigenbaum, "Perln fun yidishkeyt," ibid. (Aug. 1904), p. 12/408.

117. Milch, "Di natsyonale programe," ibid. (May 1904), p. 32/240.

118. [Krantz?], "Yidishe natsyonale frage," ibid. (Sept. 1903), p. 45/481.

119. Ibid.

120. On Hillquit's attitude to Jewish issues see Pratt, pp. 83–98.

121. [SP of A], Proceedings of the National Convention (1904), p. 282.

122. Ibid. (1908), p. 313.

123. [Second International]. VII Congress socialiste, pp. 230–54. Giser, of the Bund, there described the position of the "American comrades" as one of "corporate egoism." Ibid., pp. 253–4.

124. "Kishineff – One Act in a World Drama of Crime," The Worker (24 May 1903), p. 1.

125. "Lessons of Kishineff," ibid. (7 June 1903), p. 1. Cf. the similar resolution adopted by the General Committee of the Party in New York: ibid. (30 May 1903), p. 2.

126. "Charles L. Furman for Mayor," ibid. (12 July 1903), p. 1.

127. Cahan, "Gefil un gefilekhts," Forverts (26 May 1903), p. 4.

128. Idem, "Yidishe sotsyalistn un sotsyalistishe yidn," ibid. (23 June 1903), p. 4.

129. Lesin, "Undzere fortgeshritne goles yidn," ibid. (20 May 1903), p. 4. The Mountains of Darkness: a popular theme of Jewish legend and mysticism associated with the lost ten tribes and the messianic coming.

130. M., "A vorenung," ibid. (29 May 1903).

131. " 'Law and Order' in Russia," The Worker (11 Nov. 1905), p. 2.

132. "Alkhet shekhotonu be-emune," Di fraye arbeter shtime (16 Dec. 1905), p. 4.

133. On the FAZ see Friesel, Ha-tnua ha-tsiyonit; Urofsky, American Zionism, pp. 81–116.

134. Both parties soon adopted new names: The Jewish Socialist Labor Party–Poale Zion and the Jewish Socialist Territorialist Labor Party of America. On the development of Poale Zion in America see Shpizman.

135. "Vokhntlikhe iberblik," YK (20 Sept. 1907), no. 25, p. 4.

136. On the AJC, Schiff, and Marshall see Cohen, Not Free to Desist; Rischin, "The American Jewish Committee"; Adler, Jacob H. Schiff; Rosenstock; Reznikoff.

137. A. H. Fromenson, "Notes on the Conference," The Jewish Daily News [an English-language supplement to Dos yidishe tageblat] (24 May 1906).

138. Ibid. On Oscar Straus's role in Jewish Affairs see Cohen, A Dual Heritage, pp. 121–44.

139. "The Relief Fund," AH (22 Dec. 1905), p. 175. Cf. "Editorial: 5666," ibid. (21 Sept. 1906), p. 381.

140. "Yidn, brider!" Forverts (4 Nov. 1905), p. 5.

141. "Di konferents in klintn hol," ibid. (6 Nov. 1905), p. 1.

142. "Oyfruf tsu di yidn fun amerike," Di varhayt (17 Nov. 1905), p. 5.

143. "Appeal for Funds," The Maccabean (Nov. 1905), p. 252.

144. "The Defense Idea Prevails," *The Jewish Daily News* (10 Dec. 1905).
145. "Jewish Defense," *AH* (1 Dec. 1905), p. 32.
146. Ibid.
147. "The Street Demonstration on Dec. 4," ibid. (15 Dec. 1905), p. 136. On the American-Jewish response to 1905 see Szajkowski, "The Impact."
148. "Der historisher troyer martsh," *Dos yidishe tageblat* (5 Dec. 1905), p. 41.
149. "Der grester yidisher martsh oyf der velt," *Forverts* (5 Dec. 1905), p. 1.
150. "The Street Demonstration on Dec. 4," *AH* (15 Dec. 1905), p. 136.
151. E.g., letters from Kopeloff: *Di varhayt* (29 Nov.) and *Forverts* (14 Dec. 1905).
152. "Der bund, poyle tsien un dos folk," *Di varhayt* (17 Nov. 1905), p. 41.
153. "Dos 'tageblat' un der bund," ibid. (30 Nov. 1905), p. 41
154. [Cahan], "Plonters oder knoyln," *Forverts* (17 Dec. 1905), p. 4.
155. "Farvos makht men keyn yidishe polk?" *Di varhayt* (19 Dec. 1905), p. 4.
156. Zhitlovsky, "Shayles-tshuves," *Forverts* (16 Dec. 1905), p. 4.
157. "Plonters oder knoyln," *Forverts* (17 Dec. 1905), p. 4.
158. "Shtimen fun folk," *Di varhayt* (29 Nov. 1905), p. 5.
159. "Fun folk tsum folk," *Forverts* (14 Dec. 1905), p. 5.
160. Ibid., *Forverts* (10 Dec. 1905), p. 5.
161. See above, Chapter 4. But Maksim alone was reported to have collected $40,000 on his U. S. tour. ("Maxim and His Opponents," *AH* [20 July 1906], p. 177.)
162. Treasurer's Report (Jewish Defense Association), Magnes archive, CAHJP: P3/979.
163. On the type, cost, and transportation of the weapons, see ibid.: P3/622.
164. Baranov, "Tvishn undz redndik," *Tsayt-gayst* (12 Jan. 1906), no. 20, p. 2.
165. "Representation," *The Maccabean* (Sept. 1905), p. 161–2.
166. "A yidisher kongres muz farrufn," *Dos yidishe tageblat* (8 Dec. 1905), p. 4.
167. N. Aleinikoff, "Will Emigration Solve the Jewish Problem in Russia?" *AH* (12 Jan. 1906), p. 238.
168. "Editorial," ibid. (15 Dec. 1906), p. 129.
169. "American Jewish Congress," ibid. (29 Dec. 1906), p. 212.
170. "Vos amerikaner yidn darfn zogn dem yidishn kongres in brisel," *Dos yidishe tageblat* (18 Dec. 1905), p. 4.
171. "Editorial," *AH* (22 Dec. 1905), p. 165.
172. "The Judeans: a Discussion on the American Jewish Congress," *AH* (2 Feb. 1906), p. 345.
173. Ibid., p. 348.
174. "Geyt helfn lezn di yidishe frage," *Dos yidishe tageblat* (2 Feb. 1906), p. 1.
175. "Zey muzn fregn dos folk," ibid. (4 Feb. 1906), p. 4.
176. "The Marshall Scheme Rejected," *The Jewish Daily News* (22, 23 May 1906).
177. Ibid. (22 May 1906).
178. Ibid. (23 May 1906).
179. "The American Jewish Conference," *AH* (25 May 1906), p. 808.
180. Ibid., p. 807. On earlier attempts to create a central political representation for U. S. Jewry see Jick, pp. 150–73; Korn.
181. *AH* (25 May 1906), p. 808.
182. "Act of Incorporation–Laws of New York," in American Jewish Committee, *Fifth Annual Report*, p. 24. On the formation of the AJC see Cohen, *Not Free to Desist*, pp. 3–36.
183. Rozenblat, "Di pogromn un di amerikaner yidn," *Di tsukunft* (Jan. 1906), p. 46.
184. Milch, "Tsienizmus, teritoryalizmus un sotsyalizmus," ibid. (May 1906), p. 15/275.
185. "Chayim Schitlowsky," *AH* (29 June 1906), p. 98.
186. Peskin, "A ruike diskusye iber ernste fragn," *Forverts* (2 Feb. 1906), p. 4.
187. "Oyfruf fun der konferents komite," ibid. (8 Feb. 1906), p. 4.

188. Cahan, *Bleter,* IV, 515–8.

189. "Vos iz aroyskumen fun konferents?" *Forverts* (7 March 1906), p. 4.

190. V. Tsukerman, "Iz a yidishe sotsyal-demokratishe partey noytvendik?" *Tsayt-gayst* (1 Feb. 1907), no. 75, p. 14.

191. Ibid.

192. Burgin, "Vegn a yidisher sotsyalistisher partey," ibid. (18 Jan. 1907), no. 73, p. 3.

193. Zametkin, "Opgezunderkeyt in di arbeter bavegung," ibid. (1 Feb. 1907), no. 75, p. 6.

194. Idem, "Fun iberal un fun ergets nit," ibid. (22 Feb. 1907), no. 78, p. 15. The reference is to Medem, *Sotsialdemokratiia i natsionalny vopros.*

195. Zametkin, "Fun undzer velt: darf men hoben a yidishe sotsyalistishe partey in amerike," ibid. (18 Jan. 1907), no. 73, p. 10.

196. "Ofitsyele barikht fun di yidish-sotsyalistishe konvenshon," *Forverts* (8 Sept. 1907), p. 5. On the origins of the Jewish Agitation Bureau see Zivion's article in *Di tsukunft* (May 1909).

197. Hertz, *Di yidishe sotsyalistishe bavegung,* pp. 105–6.

198. Peskin, "Di general komite shtert di konferents fun di yidishe sotsyalistn," *Tsayt-gayst* (26 April 1907), no. 87, p. 10.

199. "Undzer nayer 'arbeter bund' in Amerike," *Forverts* (11 Sept. 1907), p. 4.

200. "Agitatsyons konvenshon nemt on vikhtike beshlise," *Di yidishe arbeter velt* (11 Sept. 1908), no. 9, p. 1.

201. "Di yidishe agitatsyons byuro," ibid. (8 Jan. 1909), no. 26, p. 4.

202. "Konvenshon fun di yidishe agitatsyons byuro," *Forverts* (6 Sept. 1909), p. 3; (7 Sept.), p. 8.

203. "Der eyndruk fun der filadelfyer konvenshon," ibid. (10 Sept. 1909), p. 4.

204. [SP of A], *Proceedings: National Convention* (1912), p. 244.

205. Cf. Feingold, pp. 158–257.

206. Goren, pp. 30–56.

207. "The Jewish Community of New York City," *AJYB* (1909–10), pp. 44–54.

208. Magnes archive, CAHJP: P3/1006.

209. *AJYB* (1909–10), p. 50.

210. Zhitlovsky, "Nokh simonim fun a nayem lebn bay yidn," *Dos naye lebn* (May 1909), p. 55/369.

211. Fornberg, "Dos yidishe lebn," *Di tsukunft* (Jan. 1910), p. 69.

212. Zivion, "Di nyu yorker kehile un ir konvenshon," ibid. (May 1913), p. 489.

213. Ibid., p. 490.

214. Goren, p. 207.

215. Cohen, "The Abrogation."

216. Lesin, "Rusland un amerike," *Di tsukunft* (April 1912), p. 338.

217. Ibid., p. 339.

218. On the immigration issue in American politics in 1905–15 see Higham, *Strangers in the Land,* pp. 158–93; idem, *Send These to Me,* pp. 29–66. On the Jewish stance see Cohen, *Not Free to Desist,* pp. 37–53; Panitz, "The Polarity"; idem, "In Defense"; M. Berman.

219. Fornberg, "Vos di yidishe imigratsyon hot oyfgeton?" *Di tsukunft* (Dec. 1912), p. 812.

220. Idem, "Der yidisher sotsyalizmus in amerike (tsu der konvenshon fun der yidisher sotsyalistisher federatsyon)," ibid. (Sept. 1913), p. 893.

221. Bar-Kamkha, "Fun der yidisher velt," ibid. (May 1913), pp. 520–1.

222. Zolotarov, "Di yidishe aynvanderung far di letste 20-30 yar," ibid. (Sept. 1907), p. 19/514.

223. On the rise of the needlework and other leading "Jewish" trade unions see H. Berman, *Era of the Protocol*; Epstein, *Jewish Labor,* I, 362–420; Foner, pp. 18–77; Levine, pp. 99–319; Seidman, pp. 79–137; Zaretz, pp. 68–104.

224. Rozenberg, "Metodn un taktik fun der yidisher arbeter bavegung," *Di tsukunft* (Nov. 1910), p. 706.

225. Lesin, "Di groyse yunyons un di groyse strayks in yidishn kvartal," ibid. (Feb. 1913), p. 93.

226. [SP of A], *National Congress* (1910), p. 260.

227. Zivion, "Di yidishe agitatsyons byuro," *Di tsukunft* (May 1909), p. 275.

228. Epstein, "Di oyfgabn fun der yidisher arbeter bavegung in amerike," ibid. (May 1912), pp. 334–5.

229. Fornberg, "Der yidisher sotsyalizmus in amerike," ibid. (Sept. 1913), p. 894.

230. Feigenbaum, "Yidishkayt in der sotsyalistisher bavegung fun amerike," ibid. (June 1912), p. 393.

231. Ibid., p. 395.

232. Ibid., p. 396.

233. "Editoryels," *YS* (30 Jan. 1914), no. 5, p. 7.

234. A. M-ri [Merison?], "Khronik," *Dos naye lebn* (Nov. 1913), p. 57/601.

235. Salutsky, "An ofner briv tsu A. Kahan," *YS* (15 March 1914), no. 8, p. 7.

236. Fornberg, "Der elter un nayer veg fun yidishn sotsyalizmus in amerike," *Di tsukunft* (Oct. 1913), p. 974.

237. [Salutsky?], "Tsvey tsuzamnforn 1908–1914," *YS* (15 July 1914), no. 15, p. 5.

238. On American-Jewish relief in World War I see Szajkowski, "Concord and Discord"; idem, "Private American Jewish Overseas Relief."

239. A number of contemporary booklets described the expulsions from the War Zone: National Workmen's Committee, *The War*; American Jewish Committee, *The Jews in the Eastern War Zone*; Kossovsky, *Razgrom*; idem, *Der yidisher khurbm.*

240. For a recent study of the Jewish issue at Berlin (1878) see Stern, pp. 350–93.

241. Yitskhok Ayzik Ben Arye Tsvi Haleyvi, "Der bavegung farn yidishn kongres," *YKon* (6 Aug. 1915), no. 1, p. 5; Borochov, "Di khronologye fun dem yidishn kongres," *YK* (29 Dec. 1915), no. 35, pp. 5–6. For a fuller, but somewhat different, description of the socialist role in American Jewish politics, 1914–18 see J. Frankel, "The Jewish Socialists."

242. "A konferents fun yidishe sotsyalistn vegn der milkhome," *Der tog* (25 Nov. 1914), p. 3. The committee of five was selected by a nonparty meeting on 23 November, attended, inter alia, by Kaplansky and Zivion.

243. "Kehillah Urges United Action to Solve Jewish Problems," *AH* (26 Feb. 1915), p. 446.

244. Goldfarb, "Undzer kempeyn far yidishe rekht," *NVe* (20 Aug. 1915), no. 16, p. 4.

245. Olgin, "Undzer bavegung far yidishe rekht," *Forverts* (9 April 1915), p. 4.

246. Marshall, "War and the Jewish Question," *AH* (30 April 1915), p. 732.

247. "The Kehillah Convention," ibid., p. 737.

248. Ibid.

249. Ibid., p. 738.

250. "Kehillah Votes for Conference," ibid. (28 May 1915), p. 81.

251. Ibid.

252. American Jewish Committee, *Ninth Annual Report*, p. 28.

253. On Brandeis as Zionist see De Haas; Shapiro, "American Jews in Politics;" idem, *Leadership*; Urofsky, *A Mind of One Piece*, pp. 93–116; [Brandeis], *Letters*, III–IV (the years 1913–21); Gal; W. Berlin, pp. 21–45.

254. "Tsu di valn fun natsyonaln arbeter konvenshon," *NVe* (20 Aug. 1915), no. 16, p. 2.

255. "Zionist Convention in Boston," *AH* (20 Aug. 1915), p. 2.

256. "The Conference of the Provisional Executive Committee," *The Maccabean* (June 1915), p. 12.

257. "Conference vs. Congress," *AH* (13 Aug. 1915), p. 355.

258. Ibid., p. 362 (letter of 11 Aug. 1915).

259. Ibid., p. 358 (letter of 3 Aug. 1915).

260. Brandeis, "Jewish Unity and the Congress," ibid. (1 Oct. 1915), p. 604.

261. "Dr. Wise Urges Congress," ibid. (8 Oct. 1915), p. 631.

262. Syrkin, *Yidisher kongres in amerike,* p. 7.

263. Ibid., p. 18.

264. Borochov, "Natsyonale onmakht un natsyonale rekht," *YKon* (6 Aug. 1915), no. 3, p. 3.

265. "Groyse kongres demonstratsye in kuper yunyon," ibid. (13 Aug. 1915), no. 2, p. 2.

266. Lesin, "Zol undzer geshrey derhert vern," *Di tsukunft* (Aug. 1915), p. 679.

267. Zivion, "Der 'revolutsyonere kamf' in amerike far yidishe rekht in rusland," *NVe* (27 Aug. 1915), no. 17, p. 4.

268. "Notitsn," *Fortshrit* (30 April 1915), no. 5, p. 6.

269. Salutsky, "Di natsyonale arbeter komite," *NVe* (27 Oct. 1916), no. 43, p. 6.

270. "Vikhtike," ibid. (6 Aug. 1915), no. 14, p. 11.

271. 2 Sept. 1915; Magnes archive, CAHJP: P3/SP2/8.

272. "Di natsyonale arbeter konvenshon," *YKon* (8 Sept. 1915), no. 6, p. 6.

273. Ibid.

274. Ibid. (17 Sept. 1915), no. 7, p. 6.

275. Goldfarb, "Der skhakl fun der natsyonaler arbeter konvenshon," *NVe* (10 Sept. 1915), no. 19, p. 3.

276. Ben Gurion, "Erets-yisroel oyf der arbeter konvenshon," *YKon* (8 Sept. 1915), no. 6, p. 2.

277. Magnes archive, CAHJP: F46/L21/6.

278. Minutes of the Russian Council of Ministers in Cherniavsky, *Prologue to Revolution,* pp. 56–72.

279. Zuckerman, "Ven farmitler vern a tsad," *YKon* (18 Feb. 1916), no. 18, p. 2.

280. "Pshore vegn kongres-frage tsurikgevizn," *Di varhayt* (13 Oct. 1915), p. 1.

281. Cf. Brandeis to Richards (13 Oct. 1915), *Letters,* III, 604.

282. American Jewish Committee, *Ninth Annual Report,* p. 65.

283. Ibid., p. 66.

284. 10 Aug. 1915; Magnes archive, CAHJP: F46/L21/b.

285. "Di hilfsarbet in 1915," *NVe* (14 Jan. 1916), no. 2, p. 2.

286. Borochov, "A sof tsu der obstruktsye," *YKon* (10 Dec. 1915), no. 17, p. 3.

287. Brandeis, absent from the meeting of 23 December, opposed its resort to an ultimatum (*Letters,* III, 681–2).

288. Brandeis, "Jewish Rights and the Congress," *AH* (28 Jan. 1916), p. 320.

289. "An eygene simkhe," *NVe* (25 Feb. 1916), no. 3, p. 2.

290. "The Philadelphia Congress Conference," *AH* (31 March 1916), p. 590.

291. Ibid., p. 591.

292. Cf. Brandeis to Lipsky, Richards, and Wise (29 March 1916; *Letters,* IV, 134–5, 137–8).

293. "Mr. Schiff's Declaration, *AH* (9 June 1916), p. 139.

294. Magnes, "The Work of the Kehillah," ibid., p. 141.

295. Fun an altn bundist, "Di natsyonale arbeter komite," *Di tsukunft* (July 1916), p. 596.

296. Ibid., p. 597.

297. Goldfarb, "Di fareynikte kongres familye," *NVe* (22 Dec. 1916), no. 51, p. 7.

298. American Jewish Congress files, American Jewish Committee Archives.

299. *Conference of the AJC–Hotel Astor (16 July 1916): Stenographic Report;* p. 51 (typescript in American Jewish Committee Archives). For Brandeis's position, cf. his letter to Lipsky (31 May 1916), *Letters,* IV, 200–4.

300. *Conference of the AJC,* pp. 68–9.

301. Ibid., p. 76.
302. Ibid., p. 88.
303. Ibid., p.91.
304. "Out of Place," *NYT* (18 July 1916), p. 8.
305. [Brandeis], *Letters*, IV, 250–1.
306. *Report of the Sub-Committee Appointed by the Executive Organization Committee of the American Jewish Congress on July 14 to Confer with a Sub-Committee of the Conference of National Jewish Organizations* (American Jewish Congress files, YIVO Archive).
307. "Preliminary Statement" (signed by Barondess and Richards), in *Referendum Submitted by the Executive Organization Committee for an American Jewish Congress,* ibid.
308. "Tsum yidishn folk in amerike," *YK* (18 Aug. 1916), no. 17, p. 1.
309. "Oyfruf fun der yidisher kongres lige," *YK* (22 Sept. 1916), no. 22, p. 1.
310. Zivion, "Vegn vos meg men shraybn," *NVe* (3 Oct. 1916), no. 40, p. 4.
311. The Executive Committee for an American Jewish Congress, *Minutes of Meeting 10 October 1916* (American Jewish Congress files, YIVO Archive).
312. Zuckerman, "Der nayer opmakh in der kongres bavegung," *YK* (11 Oct. 1916), no. 25, p. 7.
313. Salutsky, "Di natsyonale arbeter komite," *NVe* (10 Nov. 1916), no. 45, p. 6.
314. "Di kongres komite," ibid. (22 Dec. 1916), no. 51, p. 2.
315. Borochov, "Di geeynikte kongres-komite," *Di varhayt* (23 Dec. 1916).
316. Epstein, "Der yidisher kongres un di yidishe arbeter," *Glaykhayt* (29 Dec. 1916), no. 52, p. 5.
317. Quoted by Schlossberg, "Di yidishe arbeter un der yidisher kongres," *Fortshrit* (19 Jan. 1917), p. 4.
318. "Yidisher kongres vet opgehaltn vern in vashington nit shpeter vi dem ershtn may," *Forverts* (26 Dec. 1916), p. 8.
319. "Der amerikaner yidisher kongres," *Fortshrit* (29 Dec. 1916), p. 5.
320. 26 Nov. 1916; Magnes archive, CAHJP: F7/L65.
321. "Di natsyonale arbeter konvenshon," *NVe* (9 Feb. 1917), no. 6/118, p. 2.
322. Epstein, ibid. (16 Feb. 1917), no. 7/119, pp. 4–5.
323. Lesin, "An entfer tsu gen. Olgin," *Di tsukunft* (March 1917), pp. 138–9.
324. Borochov, "Di konvenshon in 'forverts' hol," *YK* (16 Feb. 1917), no. 7/42, p. 6. Trotsky was invited to speak at this convention and – as reported by Borochov – "made fun of the Jewish Congress and of national aspirations"; ibid.
325. Zivion, "Di yidishe sotsyalistishe federatsye," *Di tsukunft* (June 1917), no. 6, p. 345.
326. "Di valn tsum yidishn kongres," *NVe* (27 April 1917), no. 17/219, p. 2.
327. "Tsum yidishn kongres," ibid. (11 May 1917), no. 19/131, p. 2.
328. Ibid.
329. Borochov, "Likht un shotn oyf arbeter-yontev," *Di varhayt* (29 March 1917).
330. Zuckerman, "Far vos zey geyen nisht tsum yidishn kongres," *YK* (18 May 1917), no. 25/55, p. 1.
331. Tsipin, "Vegn undzer shtelung tsum yidishn kongres," *NVe* (18 May 1917), no. 20/132, p. 3.
332. Menakhem, "Far vos nisht?" *YK* (24 Aug. 1917), no. 29/69, p. 5.
333. Entin, "Vi veynik mir veysn undzere koykhes," *Di varhayt* (12 June 1917).
334. Zuckerman, "Der groyser erfolg fun di kongres valn," *YK* (22 June 1916), no. 25/60, p. 6.
335. Zivion, "Teorye un faktn," *NVe* (18 Jan. 1917), no. 3/167, p. 4.
336. On the attitudes of American Jewry and the Jewish socialists to the war issue see Szajkowski, *Jews, War and Communism,* I, 3–382; Schappes, "World War I"; Rappaport. On the Left and the war in general see Grubbs; Marchand; Peterson and Fite.

337. Marshall, "Der Hilkvit-sam far di yidn," *Di varhayt* (31 Oct. 1917).

338. In De Haas archive, ZAL: 2:51:2:272–763.

339. On Zionist diplomacy in 1917 see Friedman; Parzen; Stein; Friesel, *Ha-mdiniut ha-tsiyonit.*

340. Cf. Brandeis to De Haas (29 Sept. 1917), *Letters,* IV, 312 and note.

341. Entin, "A pogrom oyfn yidishn kongres," *YK* (13 July 1917), no. 28/63, p. 1.

342. Ibid., p. 6.

343. Zuckerman, "Vi azoy tsu ratevn dem yidishn kongres," ibid. (27 July 1917), no. 25/26, p. 4.

344. Ben Gurion, "Vos un vi azoy," ibid. (30 Nov. 1917), no. 41/81, p. 1.

345. Ibid., p. 2.

346. Idem, "Kongres, tsienizm un di yidishe arbeter," ibid. (11 Jan. 1918), p. 6.

347. "Der yidisher kongres," ibid. (30 Nov. 1917), p. 4.

348. "Di yidishe frage oyf der togsordenung," *NVe* (1 Nov. 1918), no. 43/207, p. 3.

349. Paraphrased in Salutsky, "Vegn undzer bateylikung in yidishn kongres," ibid. (22 Nov. 1918), no. 46/210, p. 3.

350. Quoted in M. Epstein, "Vos hot di kongres bavegung gevunen fun der arbeter konferents," *Der tog* (19 Nov. 1918), p. 5.

351. Salutsky, "Vegn undzer bateylikung in yidishn kongres," *NVe* (22 Nov. 1918), no. 46/210, p. 3.

352. "Yidishe kongres gerufn in filadelfye 15-tn detsember," *Di varhayt* (27 Nov. 1918), p. 1.

353. De Haas archive; ZAL: microfilm, Rec. 3.

354. Schlossberg, "Loy yavoy be-kool," *NVe* (13 Dec. 1918), no. 49/213, p. 5.

355. Olgin, "Mir hobn geton undzer flikht," *Forverts* (2 Dec. 1918), p. 5.

356. "Natsyonale arbeter komite nemt on nayen forshlag fun kongres komite," *Forverts* (9 Dec. 1918), p. 8.

357. "Tsu der erefnung fun dem yidishn kongres," ibid. (15 Dec. 1918), p. 8.

358. Sholem Asch, "Derkent aykh!" ibid.

359. Ben-Tsien [Zivion], "Sheyne ayndruksfule erefnung fun dem yidishn kongres," *Forverts* (16 Dec. 1918), p. 3.

360. "Farshlag far a shtendikn alveltlikhn yidishn parlament," *Der tog* (17 Dec. 1918), p. 2.

361. Zivion, "Kongres notitsn," *Forverts* (18 Dec. 1918), p. 5.

362. [Am. Jew. Cong.], *Report of the Proceedings,* p. 32.

363. Asch, "Di zeydes un di eyniklekh," *Forverts* (17 Dec. 1918), p. 1.

364. Entin, "Der yidisher kongres," *Di varhayt* (21 Dec. 1918).

365. Asch, "Di zeydes," *Forverts* (17 Dec. 1918), p. 1.

366. "Arbeter kongres bashprekht zayn batsiyung tsu dem algemaynem yidishn kongres," *Der tog* (18 Jan. 1919), p. 2.

367. De Haas archive; ZAL: 61:3:147–208.

368. Y. Slonim, "Yidisher shtat in erets-yisroel unter dem protektorat fun england," *Di varhayt* (18 Dec. 1918).

369. "Yidisher kongres geshlosn," *Der tog* (19 Dec. 1918), p. 1.

370. "Der yidisher kongres," *Forverts* (20 Dec. 1918), p. 4.

371. "Sheyne redes un erhoybene begaysterung," *Der tog* (19 Dec. 1918), p. 2.

372. "Editoryele notitsn," *NVe* (20 Dec. 1918), no. 50/214, p. 2.

373. Vinchevsky, "A goy, a tsienist," *Di tsukunft* (Aug. 1919), p. 471.

374. American Jewish Committee, *Thirteenth Annual Report,* p. 21.

375. Idem, *Fourteenth Annual Report,* p. 58.

376. On the exodus of the Jewish Socialist Federation from the SP and the mergers with the Communist movement see Epstein, *The Jew and Communism;* Draper; Glazer; J. Weinstein.

The American Jewish Congress and Russian Jewry

1. V. Kossovsky, "Evreiskii 'aktivizm'," *Informatsionny listok zagranichnoi organizatsii Bunda* (Dec. 1915), no. 9–10, p. 12. On the Bund in the war period see Gelbard, "Ha-'bund'."

2. Olgin, "Kongressnoe dvizhenie sredi evreev v Amerike," *Evreiskie vesti* (2 Dec. 1916), no. 6, pp. 23–7; (8 Dec. 1916), no. 7, pp. 26–9; (15 Dec. 1916), no. 8, pp. 25–30; (22 Dec. 1916), no. 9, pp. 34–7.

3. "Izveshchenie o soveshchanii pri tsentralnom komitete Bunda," *Biulletin zagranichnogo komiteta Bunda* (Sept. 1916), no. 1, p. 2.

4. "Pismo iz rossii," ibid., p. 6.

5. H. Erlich, "K amerikanskomu kongressu," *Evreiskie vesti* (9 Feb.), no. 6/15, p. 28.

6. For an analysis of the debate on a Jewish Congress in Russia (1917) see Janowsky, *Jews*, pp. 211–30.

7. "Di yidishe arbeter un der amerik. yidisher kongres," *AS* (25 May/7 June 1917), no. 15, p. 2.

8. M. V. [Weinreich], "A tayere hamtsoe," ibid. (6/19 July 1917), no. 27, p. 2.

9. A. L. [Litvak] "Di yidishe konferents," ibid. (27 July/9 Aug. 1917), no. 33, pp. 2–4; Janowsky, *Jews*, p. 221.

10. On these elections see Altshuler, "Ha-nisayon," *He-avar*, XII (1965), 75–89.

11. Janowsky, *Jews*, p. 228.

12. On the movement for Jewish autonomy in the Ukraine 1917–20 see e.g. Goldelman; Revutsky, *In di shvere teg; Di yidishe avtonomye;* Zilberfarb, *Dos yidishe ministeryum.*

13. "Undzere kandidatn: Moyshe Rafes," *FTs* (6 Nov. 1917), no. 20, p. 3.

14. *Di yidishe avtonomye*, pp. 311–12.

15. K-r [Yekhezkl Kantor], "Di yidishe avtonomye," *FTs* (15 March 1919), no. 24/285, p. 2.

16. On this process of polarization see Z. Abramovich *Be-sherut*, pp. 180–234; Dinur, *Bi-[ye]me milhama;* Gitelman, pp. 151–232; Nir, *Vanderungen*, pp. 9–212; Petrazil, I, 54–166; Rafes, *Dva goda.*

17. Janowsky, *Jews*, pp. 235–319.

18. Ibid., p. 363; cf. idem, *Nationalities*, pp. 110–34.

19. On Jewish autonomy in Lithuania see Gringauz; Gurfunkel; Laserson.

Bibliography

Only works mentioned in the text or notes are listed here. Articles in the contemporary press, with a few exceptions, are not included.

[Aaronsohn, Aharon]. *Yoman Aharon Aharonson 1916–1919* (ed. Y. Efrati). Tel Aviv, 1970.
Abramov, Zalman S. *Perpetual Dilemma: Jewish Religion in the Jewish State.* New York, 1976.
Abramovich, Rafail A. *In tsvey revolutsyes: di geshikhte fun a dor.* 2 vols. New York, 1944.
Abramovich, Zeev. *Be-sherut ha-tnua.* Tel Aviv, 1966.
Adler, Cyrus. *Jacob H. Schiff (His Life and Letters).* 2 vols. New York, 1928.
  The Voice of America on Kishineff. Philadelphia, 1904.
  and Aaron M. Margalith. *With Firmness in the Right (American Diplomatic Action Affecting Jews 1840–1945).* New York, 1946.
[Ahad Ha-Am.] *Kol kitve Ahad Ha-Am.* Jerusalem, 1947.
[Aharonovich, Yosef]. *Kitve Yosef Aharonovich.* 2 vols. Tel Aviv, 1941.
Ainzaft, S. *Zubatovshchina i gaponovshchina.* Moscow, 1925.
Aizenshtat, Shmuel. *Prakim be-toldot tnuat ha-poalim ha-yehudit.* 2 vols. Tel Aviv, 1944.
Akimov [Makhnovets], Vladimir Petrovich. "Stroiteli budushchego," *Obrazovanie,* XVI (1907), no. 4, pp. 91–118; no. 5, pp. 66–98; no. 6, pp. 54–88.
  "Pervy sezd RSDR partii," *Minuvshie gody* (Feb. 1908), no. 2, pp. 128–68.
  Vladimir Akimov on the Dilemmas of Russian Marxism: Two Texts in Translation (ed. and introd. J. Frankel). Cambridge, 1969.
Akselrod, Pavel Borisovich. *Iz arkhiva P. B. Akselroda (Materialy po istorii russkogo revoliutsionnogo dvizheniia* II) (ed. V. S. Voitinsky, B. I. Nikolaevsky, et al.). Berlin, 1924.
  Pisma P. B. Akselroda i I. O. Martova (ed. F. Dan and B. I. Nikolaevsky). Berlin, 1924.
  "Pogromen un di revolutsyonere bavegung mit 43 yor tsurik," *Di tsukunft* (September 1924), no. 9, pp. 550–5.
Altshuler, Mordechai. "Ha-nisayon le-argen kinus klal-yehudi be-rusya," *He-avar,* XII (1965), 75–89.
  "Maamada ha-politi ve-hairguni shel ha-sektsya ha-yehudit ba-miflaga ha-komunistit shel br. ha-m. (1918–30)." Ph.D. thesis, The Hebrew University of Jerusalem, 1971.
American Jewish Congress. *Report of the Proceedings of the American Jewish Congress (December 1918).* New York, [1919?].
American Jewish Committee, The. *Fifth Annual Report.* New York, 1912.
  Ninth Annual Report. New York, 1916.
  Thirteenth Annual Report. New York, 1919.
  Fourteenth Annual Report. New York, 1920.
  The Jews in the Eastern War Zone. New York, 1916.
An-sky, Shloyme Zanvl. *Gezamlte shriftn.* 15 vols. Warsaw, 1920–5.
Apel, Yehuda. *Be-reshit ha-tehiya.* Tel Aviv, 1936.

Arkadi: zamlbukh tsum ondenk fun Arkadi Kremer. New York, 1942.

Aronson, I. Michael. "The Attitudes of Russian Officials in the 1880s toward Jewish Assimilation and Emigration," *SR*, XXXIV (1975), no. 1, 1–18.

"The Prospects for the Emancipation of Russian Jews during the 1880s," *SEER*, LV (1977), no. 3, 348–69.

Ascher, Abraham. "Pavel Axelrod: a Conflict between Jewish Loyalty and Revolutionary Dedication," *Russian Review*, XXIV (1965), 249–65.

Pavel Axelrod and the Development of Menshevism. Cambridge, Mass., 1972.

Avineri, Shlomo. "Marx and Jewish Emancipation," *Journal of the History of Ideas*, XXV (1964), no. 3, 445–50.

Ha-rayon ha-tsiyoni li-gvanav: prakim be-toldot ha-mahshava ha-leumit ha-yehudit. Tel Aviv, 1980.

"Socialism and Nationalism in Moses Hess," *Midstream*, XXII (1976), no. 4, 36–44.

The Social and Political Thought of Karl Marx. Cambridge, 1968.

Avitsur, Shmuel (ed.). *Haroshet ha-maase: le-zekher poolo shel Nahum Vilbush.* Tel Aviv, 1974.

Avrich, Paul. *The Russian Anarchists.* Princeton, 1967.

Barats, Yosef. "Mi-tkufat kibush ha-satatut bi-[ye]rushalayim," in Habas, pp. 246–9.

Baron, Salo Wittmayer. "Abraham Benisch's Project for Jewish Colonization in Palestine (1842)," in S. W. Baron and A. Marx (eds.), *Jewish Studies in Memory of George A. Kohut* (New York, 1935), pp. 72–87.

Baron, Samuel Haskell. *Plekhanov: the Father of Russian Marxism.* Stanford, 1963.

Bauer, Bruno. "Die Judenfrage," *Deutsche Jahrbücher fur Wissenschaft und Kunst* (17–26 Nov. 1842), nos. 274–82, pp. 1101–26; also in enlarged form: *Die Judenfrage.* Brunswick, 1843. (English: *The Jewish Question.* Cincinnati, 1958.)

Bein, Alex. "Franz Oppenheimer and Theodor Herzl," *Herzl Year Book*, VII (1971), 71–127.

The Return to the Soil (a History of Jewish Settlement in Israel). Jerusalem, 1952. (Hebrew: *Toldot ha-hityashvut ha-tsiyonit mi-tkufat Hertsel ve-ad yamenu.* Ramat Gan, 1970.)

Theodore Herzl: A Biography. London, 1957.

Belkind, Yisrael. *Di ershte shrit fun yishev erets yisroel.* New York, 1917.

Bell, Daniel. *Marxian Socialism in American Life.* Princeton, N.J., 1967.

Ben Adir [Rozin, A]. "Tsum oyfkum fun der yidisher sotsyalistisher arbeter partey (YS)," in *ST*, pp. 9–56.

Ben-Ami [M. I. Rabinovich]. "Moi snosheniia s M. Dragomanovym i rabota v 'Volnom slove,' " *ES*, VIII (1915), 347–66.

Ben Gurion, David. "Be-hag hatsi ha-yovel," in Habas, pp. 15–19.

Zikhronot. 3 vols. Tel Aviv, 1970–3.

Ben Zvi, Yitshak. *Ktavim.* 4 vols. Jerusalem, 1965 (IV: *Zikhronot ve-reshumot me-haneurim ad 1920*).

Poale tsiyon ba-aliya ha-shniya. Tel Aviv, 1950.

Berkovich, M. "Lilienblum ve-sofre ha-'emet'," *Ha-tsfira* (24 July 1919), no. 30/127, pp. 12–14; (31 July 1919), no. 31/128, pp. 12–13.

"Mi-maarekhet ha-'emet'," ibid. (2 Oct. 1919), no. 40/137, pp. 10–12; (7 Oct. 1919), no. 41/138, pp. 11–13; (23 Oct. 1919), no. 43/140, pp. 9–13; (30 July 1920), no. 160, p. 4; (6 Aug. 1920), no. 166, p. 4; (21 Jan. 1921), no. 18, p. 4; *Musaf le-"davar"*, (28 Av 5687/26 Aug. 1927), no. 45, p. 2; (5 Elul 5687/2 Sept.), no. 46, pp. 2–3; (12 Elul 5687/9 Sept. 1927), no. 47, pp. 2–3; (25 Elul 5687/22 Sept. 1927), no. 48, pp. 2–3; (25 Tishre 5688/21 Oct. 1927), no. 3, pp. 2–3; (2 Heshvan 5688/28 Oct. 1927), no. 4, pp. 2–3; (9 Heshvan 5688/4 Nov. 1927), no. 5, pp. 2–3; (16 Heshvan 5688/11 Nov. 1927), no. 6, pp. 3–4; (1 Kislev 5688/25 Nov. 1927), no. 8, pp. 3–4; (15 Kislev 5688/9 Dec. 1927), no. 10, pp. 2–3; (13 Tevet 5668/6 Jan. 1928), no. 14, pp. 2–3; (20 Tevet/5688/13 Jan. 1928), no. 15, p. 3.

Berlin, Isaiah. *The Life and Opinions of Moses Hess.* Cambridge, 1959.

Berlin, William S. *On the Edge of Politics: the Roots of Jewish Political Thought in America.* Westport, Conn., 1978.

Berman, Hyman. "A Cursory View of the Jewish Labor Movement: an Historiographical Survey," *AJHQ,* LII (1962–3), no. 2, 79–97.

"Era of the Protocol: a Chapter in the History of the International Ladies Garment Workers' Union, 1910–16." Ph.D. dissertation, Columbia University, 1956.

Berman, Myron. "The Attitude of American Jewry toward East European Jewish Immigration." Ph.D. dissertation, Columbia University, 1963.

Bernshtein-Cohen, Y. "Zikhronot," *Sefer Bernshtein-Kohen* (Tel-Aviv, 1946), pp. 37–212.

Blau, Joseph, N. Glazer, et al. *The Characteristics of American Jews.* New York, 1965.

Blekhman, Leyb (Avrom der Tate). *Bleter fun mayn yugnt.* New York, 1959.

Bloch, Yisrael. "Ole romni," in Habas, pp. 152–5.

Bloom, Bernard H. "Yiddish-Speaking Socialists in America 1892–1905," *AJA,* XII (1960), no. 1, 34–70.

Bloom, Solomon F. "Karl Marx and the Jews," *JSS,* IV (1942), no. 1, 3–16.

The World of Nations; a Study of the National Implications in the Work of Karl Marx. New York, 1941.

Blum, Hillel Kats. *Zikhroynes fun a bundist.* New York, 1940.

"Zikhroynes," *HS,* III, 348–68.

Boersner, D. *The Bolsheviks and the National and Colonial Question.* Geneva, 1957.

Bogucharsky [Yakovlev], V. I. *Iz istorii politicheskoi borby v 70-kh i 80-kh gg. XIX veka.* Moscow, 1912.

Borochov, Ber. *Geklibene shriftn* (ed. Berl Locker). New York, 1928. (Published as Vol. II taking as Vol. I: *Poyle tsien shriftn.* New York, 1920.)

"Igrot Borokhov le-Usishkin" (ed. M. Mintz), *Ha-tsiyonut,* II (1971), 237–300.

Ktavim (ed. L. Levite, D. Ben-Nahum, *et al.*). 3 vols. Tel Aviv, 1955–66.

Ktavim nivharim (ed. Z. Shazar [Rubashev]). Tel Aviv, 1944.

"O kharaktere evreiskogo uma," in *Illiustrirovanny sionistskii almanakh* 1902–3 (ed. A. A. Freidenberg) (Kiev, 1902), pp. 316–37.

Virtualizm: religiozno-eticheskaia problema v marksizme (introd. L. Berlinraut). Moscow, 1920.

"Zikhroynes (tsum yubileum fun rusishe poyle tsien)," [1916] in *Yidisher arbeter yor-bukh un almanakh* (ed. B. Locker) (New York, 1928), pp. 180–6.

Borochov, M. A. "Zikhroynes fun B. Borokhovs kinder un friye yugnt-yorn," in B. Borochov, *Geklibene shriftn* (1928), pp. xi–xxix.

Brandes, Joseph. *Immigrants to Freedom: Jewish Communities in Rural New Jersey since 1882.* Philadelphia, 1971.

[Brandeis, Louis Demibtz.] *Letters of Louis D. Brandeis* (ed. M. I. Urofsky and D. W. Levy). 5 vols. Albany, N.Y., 1971–8.

Braslavsky, Moshe. *Tnuat ha-poalim ha-erets yisreelit: korot u-mkorot.* 4 vols. Tel Aviv, 1956–73.

Bregman, Y. "Fun di ershte yorn fun proletarishn tsienizm, loyt arkhiv materyaln," *RP,* I, 174–94.

Breiman, Shlomo. "Ha-mifne be-mahshava ha-tsiburit ha-yehudit be-reshit shnot ha-shmonim," *Shivat tsiyon,* II–III (1951–2), 83–227.

"Ha-pulmus ben Lilienblum le-ven Ahad Ha-Am ve-Dubnov," *Shivat tsiyon,* I (1950), 138–68.

Broido, Eva Lvovna [Gordon]. "Gruppy 'Sotsialist' i 'Rabochaia biblioteka' 1899–1901 gg.,"
  LR (1923), no. 1, pp. 126–33.

Bross, Jacob. "The Beginning of the Jewish Labor Movement in Galicia," *YAJSS*, V (1950),
  55–84. (Yiddish: *HS*, III, 484–511.)

Brym, Robert J. *The Jewish Intelligentsia and Russian Marxism.* London, 1978.

Buber, Martin. "Moses Hess," *JSS*, VII (1945), 137–48. (Hebrew: *Ben am le-artso.* Jerusalem, 1944, pp. 112–26.)

Bukhbinder, Naum Abramovich. "Evreiskie revoliutsionnye kruzhki 80-kh i nachala 90-kh
  godov," *EL*, I (1923), 52–8.

Istoriia evreiskogo rabochego dvizheniia. Moscow, 1925. (Yiddish, revised: *Di geshikhte
  fun der yidisher arbeter bavegung in rusland.* Vilna, 1931.)

"Iz istorii revoliutsionnoi propagandy sredi evreev v Rossii v 70-kh godov," in *IRS,* (ed. V.
  I. Nevsky), I (1924), 37–66.

"Nezavisimaia evreiskaia rabochaia partiia," *KL* (1922), no. 2–3, pp. 208–84.

'O zubatovshchine," *KL* (1922), no. 4, pp. 289–325.

The Bund (The General Jewish Labor Union in Lithuania, Poland, and Russia). *Avtonomiia
  ili federatsiia.* London, 1903.

Der bund in der revolutsye fun 1905–1906; loyt di materyaln fun bundishn arkhiv. Warsaw, 1930.

"Di diskusye vegn der natsyonaler frage oyfn V tsuzamenfor fun bund yuni 1903 tsirikh
  (fun di protokln fun tsuzamenfor)," *Undzer tsayt* (November 1927), no. 2, pp. 87–96;
  (December 1927), no. 3, pp. 82–91; (January 1928), no. 1, pp. 83–96.

Di geshikhte fun der yidisher arbeter bavegung in rusland un poyln. Geneva, 1900.

*K voprosu ob obedinenii Bunda s Rossiiskoi sotsialdemokraticheskoi rabochei partii: iz-
  vlechenie iz protokolov VII konferentsii Bunda.* St. Petersburg, 1906.

Materialy k istorii evreiskogo rabochego dvizheniia. St. Petersburg, 1906.

V sezd Vseobshchego evreiskogo rabochego soiuza v Litve, Polshe i Rossii. London, 1903.

Vegn der fareynikung fun bund mit der ruslender sotsyaldemokratishe arbeter partey. St.
  Petersburg, 1906.

II sezd Rossiiskoi SDR Partii: otchet delegatsii Bunda. London, 1903.

Bunzl, John. *Klassenkampf in der Diaspora: zur Geschichte der jüdischen Arbeiterbewegung.*
  Vienna, 1975.

Burgin, Herts. *Di geshikhte fun der yidisher arbeter bavegung in amerike, rusland un england.* New York, 1913.

Cahan, Abe. *Bleter fun mayn lebn.* 5 vols. New York, 1926–36.

Yubileum-shrift tsu Ab. Kahans 50-stn geburtstog. New York, 1910.

Carlebach, Julius. *Karl Marx and the Radical Critique of Judaism.* London, 1978.

Carr, Edward H. "The Bolshevik Doctrine of Self Determination," in idem, *The Bolshevik
  Revolution,* I, 410–28. London, 1950.

Chemerisky, Aleksandr. "In lodz in 1905," *Royte bleter,* I, 1–3. Minsk, 1929. (Articles
  numbered separately.)

Cherikover, Elyohu (ed.). *Geshikhte fun der yidisher arbeter bavegung in di fareynikte shtatn.*
  2 vols. New York, 1943–5. (English, abr.: *The Early Jewish Labor Movement in the
  United States,* transl. and rev. A. Antonovksy. New York, 1961.)

Istoriia Obshchestva dlia rasprostraneniia prosveshcheniia mezhdu evreev v Rossii. St.
  Petersburg, 1913.

"Jewish Immigrants to the United States 1881–1900," *YAJSS*, VI (1951), 157–76.

"London un ir pyonerishe role in der bavegung," in Cherikover, *Geshikhte,* II, 76–137.

"Di narodovolishe 'arbeter tsaytung,' " *HS*, III, 604–9.

"Naye materyaln vegn di pogromen in rusland onheyb di 80-er yorn," *HS*, II, 446–65.

"Nokh vegn der zhenever 'grupe sotsyalistn-yidn,' " *HS*, III, 536–7.

"Der onheyb fun der yidisher sotsyalistisher bavegung (Libermans tkufe)," *HS*, I, 469–532.

"Di onheybn fun der umlegaler literatur in yidish," *HS*, III, 577–603. (Hebrew: idem, *Yehudim*, pp. 307–38.)

"Peter Lavrov and the Jewish Socialist Émigrés," *YAJSS*, VII (1952), 132–45.

"Revolutsyonere un natsyonale ideologyes fun der rusish-yidisher inteligents," in Cherikover, *Geshikhte*, II, 138–202. (Hebrew: idem, *Yehudim*, pp. 366–420.)

"Di tsarishe politik un di yidishe emigratsye," in Cherikover, *Geshikhte*, I, 88–112.

Yehudim be-itot mahpekha (introd. B. Z. Dinur). Tel Aviv, 1957.

"Yidn-revolutsyonern in rusland in di 60-er un 70-er yorn," *HS*, III, 60–172. (Hebrew: idem, *Yehudim*, pp. 127–306.)

Cherniavsky, Michael (ed.). *Prologue to Revolution: Notes of A. N. Iakhotonov on the Secret Meetings of the Council of Ministers, 1915.* Englewood, N.J., 1967. (Russian: in *Arkhiv russkoi revoliutsii*, XVIII, 1926, 15–136.)

Chernov, Viktor. "Khaim Zhitlovski un der 'farband fun rusishe sotsyal revolutsyonern (1900–1903)," in [Zhitlovsky], *Zhitlovski-zamlbukh*, pp. 91–149.

Yidishe tuer in der partey sotsyalistn revolutsyonern: biografishe eseyen. New York, 1948.

Cherny peredel: organ sotsialistov-federalistov 1880–1881 g. (pamiatniki agitatsionnoi literatury I) (ed. and introd. V. I. Nevsky). Moscow, 1923. (A republication of the original journal by the Petrogradskoe biuro Komissii oktiabrskoi revoliutsii i RKP.)

Cohen, Naomi W. "The Abrogation of the Russo-American Treaty of 1832," *JSS*, XXV (1963), no. 1, 3–41.

A Dual Heritage: the Public Career of Oscar S. Straus. Philadelphia, 1969.

Not Free to Desist: the American Jewish Committee 1906–1966. Philadelphia, 1972.

[Cohen-Virgily, Borekh Mordkhe]. *B. Kohen-Virgily: zamlbukh tsu zayn biografye un kharakteristik.* Vilna, 1938. (A YIVO publication.)

"A Colony in Kansas–1882," *AJA*, XVII, (Nov. 1965), no. 2, 114–39.

Cornu, Auguste. *Moses Hess et la gauche hégélienne.* Paris, 1934.

Dan, Theodore [F. I. Gurvich]. *The Origins of Bolshevism.* New York, 1964. (Russian: *Proiskhozhdenie bolshevizma.* New York, 1946.)

Davidzon, Elyohu [K. K.]. "O evreiskom rabochem dvizhenii v Rossii," *Zaria* (Aug. 1902), no. 4, sec. 2, pp. 40–54.

Davis, Moshe. "Israel Friedlaender's Minute Book of the Achavah Club 1909–1912," in the *Mordecai M. Kaplan Jubilee Volume* (New York, 1953), pp. 157–214.

Dayan, Shmuel. *Hatsi yovel shanim shel dganya.* Tel Aviv, 1935.

Moshve ovdim be-erets yisrael. Jerusalem, 1945.

De Haas, Jacob. *Louis Dembitz Brandeis. A Biographical Sketch.* New York, 1929.

Deich, Lev Grigorevich. *Rol evreev v russkom revoliutsionnom dvizhenii.* Berlin, 1923. (Yiddish: *Yidn in der rusisher revolutsye: zikhroynes vegn yidn revolutsyonern.* Berlin, 1924.)

Deutscher, Isaac. *The Non-Jewish Jew and Other Essays.* Oxford, 1968.

The Prophet Armed: Trotsky 1879–1921. Oxford, 1954.

Dimanshtein, Shimen. "Di revolutsyonere bavegung tsvishn di yidishe masn in revolutsye fun 1905–tn yor," *Royte bleter*, I (Minsk, 1929), 1–42.

(introd.) *Revoliutsionnoe dvizhenie sredi evreev.* Moscow, 1930.

Dinur [Dinaburg], Ben Zion. *Be-olam she-shaka; zikhronot ve-reshumot mi-derekh hayim 5644–74 [1884–1914].* Jerusalem, 1958.

Bi-[ye]me milhama u-mahpekha 5674–81 [1914–21]. Jerusalem, 1960.

"Me-arkhiyono shel Perets Smolenskin," *Kiryat sefer*, I (1924), 77–84.

"Tokhniyotav shel Ignatev le-fitron 'sheelat ha-yehudim' u-veidat netsige ha-kehilot be-peterburg bi-shnot 1881–2," *He-avar*, X (1963), 5–82.

"Dokumentim mi-gniza shel ha-mishtara ha-vilnayit al boo shel Hertsel le-sham ve-al ha-tsiyonut bi-khlal," *Mi-yamim rishonim*, I (Aug. 1934), no. 3, 63–72.

Draper, Theodore. *The Roots of American Communism*. New York, 1957.

Dresner, Camillo. "Hayim Zhitlovski – teoretikan ha-leumiyut ha-galutit be-zikata le-sotsyalizm." Ph.D. thesis, The Hebrew University of Jerusalem, 1975.

"Khayim Zhitlovski ve-hatsiyonut," *M'asef*, VIII (1976), 31–70.

Drori, Yigal. "Hishtakfuta shel ha-aliya ha-shniya ve-hamaavak la-avoda ivrit ba-itnonut ha-erets yisreelit ha-klalit," *Cathedra*, II (1976), 69–80.

Droujanoff [Druianov], Abraham Adler. *Ktavim le-toldot hibat-tsiyon ve-yishuv erets yisrael*. 3 vols. Odessa, 1919; Tel Aviv, 1932.

Dubnov, Shimen, "Anti-evreiskoe dvizhenie 1881–82 g.," *ES*, I–II (1909), no. 1, 88–109; no. 2, 265–76.

"Evrei" in A. I. Kasteliansky (ed.), *Formy natsionalnogo dvizheniia v sovremennykh gosudarstv: v Avstro-vengriia, Rossiia, Germaniia* (St. Petersburg, 1910), pp. 399–423.

History of the Jews in Russia and Poland. 3 vols. Philadelphia, 1916–20.

Nationalism and History: Essays on Old and New Judaism (ed. and introd. K. S. Pinson). Philadelphia, 1958.

Dubofsky, Melvyn. "Success and Failure of Socialism in New York City 1900–1918: A Case Study," *Labor History* IX (1968), no. 3, 361–75.

Dushkan, M. N. (Moyshe). "Minskaia konferentsiia 1895 g.," in Dimanshtein, *Revoliutsionnoe dvizhenie*, pp. 238–43.

Ehrenreich, H. "Di virkung fun Dr. Khaim Zhitlovski's optimizm oyf der yidisher yugnt," *Dos naye lebn* (Dec. 1912), pp. 31–5.

Eidelman, Boris Lvovich. 'K istorii vozniknoveniia RSDRP," *PR* (1921), no. 1, pp. 20–67.

Eidelman, Yehudit. "Li-dmuta shel kvutsat 'ahva'," in Habas, pp. 266–9.

Einhorn, Dovid. "Vladek'n," in Jeshurin (ed.), *Vladek*, pp. 117–18.

Elazar, Daniel J. *Community and Polity: the Organizational Dynamics of American Jewry*. Philadelphia, 1976.

"What Indeed Is American Jewry?" *Forum* (1978), no. 28–9, pp. 147–59.

Eliav, Mordechai. *David Volfson: ha-ish u-zmano (ha-tnua ha-tsiyonit bashanim 1905–1914)*. Tel Aviv, 1977.

"Meorot yafo be-furim 5668 (1908)," *Ha-tsiyonut*, III (1973), 152–97.

Elichai, Yosef. "Ha-konseptsya ha-teritoryalistit ha-sotsyalistit shel Sirkin," *M'asef*, X (1978), 5–12.

Elon, Amos, *The Israelis, Fathers and Sons*. London, 1971.

Engle, Anita. *The Nili Spies*. London, 1959.

Epstein, Melech. *The Jew and Communism: the Study of Early Communist Victories and Ultimate Defeats in the Jewish Community, U.S.A. 1919–1941*. New York, 1959.

Jewish Labor in USA: an Industrial, Political and Cultural History of the Jewish Labor Movement. I: *1882–1914*; II: *1914–1952*. New York, 1950–3.

Profiles of Eleven (Men Who Guided the Destiny of an Immigrant Society and Stimulated Social Consciousness among the American People). Detroit, 1965.

[ESDRP-PZ]. *Ha-veida ha-shlishit shel poale tsiyon be-rusya 1917 (teudot)* (ed. and introd. M. Mintz). Tel Aviv, 1976.

Ettinger, Shmuel. *Ha-antishemiyut ba-et ha-hadasha; pirke mehkar ve-iyun*. Tel Aviv, 1978.

"Ha-nitsul ha-yehudi be-daat ha-kahal ha-rusit shel reshit shnot ha-shmonim la-mea ha-tsha-esre," in the Festschrift for Jacob Katz (forthcoming).

Even Tov, Eliyahu. "Be-fetah tikva bi-tkufat ha-herem," in Habas, pp. 179–87.

Farbstein, David. *Das Recht der umfrein und der freien Arbeiter nach jüdisch-Talmudisch Recht, verglichen mit dem antiken, speciell mit dem römischen Recht*. Frankfurt-am-Main, 1896.

BIBLIOGRAPHY

Der Zionismus und die Judenfrage, ökonomisch und ethisch. Berne, 1898.

[*Di*] *farsheydne shtremungen bay poyle tsien.* 1904. A publication of the Minsker Komitet Fun Poyle Tsien. (Hebrew: *Ha-zramim ha-shonim be-kerev poale tsiyon.* A publication of the Research Project on the Jewish Labor Movement, Hebrew University. Jerusalem, 1968.)

Feingold, Henry L. *Zion in America: The Jewish Experience from Colonial Times to the Present.* New York, 1974.

Feld, Lipman Goldman. "New Light on the Lost Jewish Colony of Beersheba, Kansas (1882–1886)," *AJHQ,* LX (1970–1), 159–68.

Feldman, B. "Di ershte velt-konferents," *YAP,* pp. 164–71.

Feuer, Lewis S. "The Conversion of Karl Marx's Father," *JJS,* XIV (1972), no. 2, 149–66.

Fishman, William S. *Jewish Radicals from Czarist Stetl to London Ghetto.* New York, 1974. (British title: *East End Jewish Radicals 1875–1914.*)

Foner, Philip S. *The Fur and Leather Workers Union.* Newark, N.J., 1950.

F-r, A. [Akim Lvovich Flekser]. "Dela minuvshikh dnei ('Razsvet', organ russkikh evreev, 1882 g.)," in *Palestina: sbornik statei,* pp. 128–40.

Frank, Herman. "Di fareynikte yidishe geverkshaftn un di yidishe arbeter federatsye," in Cherikover, *Geshikhte,* II, 395–417.

Frankel, Jonathan. "The Jewish Socialists and the American Jewish Congress Movement," *YAJSS,* XVI (1976), 202–341.

"Party Genealogy and the Soviet Historians (1920–1938)," *SR,* XXV (1966), no. 4, 563–603.

"Socialism and Jewish Nationalism in Russia 1892–1907." Ph.D. thesis, Cambridge University, 1961.

"Voluntarism, Maximalism and the Group for the Emancipation of Labor (1883–1892)," in Alexander and Janet Rabinowitch with L. D. Kristof (eds.), *Revolution and Politics in Russia (Essays in Memory of B. I. Nicolaevsky)* (Bloomington, Ind., 1972), pp. 55–74.

Frankel, Rafael. "Yosef Busel, ha-komuna ha-haderatit, ve-hivatsrut ha-kvutsa," *Ha-tsiyonut,* IV (1975), 114–45.

Frankel, Yosef. "Halifat ha-mikhtavim ben Natan Birnbaum le-ven Zigmund Verner erev ha-kongres ha-rishon," *Shivat tsiyon,* II–III (1951–2), 275–99.

Freundlich, Charles. *Peretz Smolenskin: His Life and Thought (a Study of the Renascence of Jewish Nationalism).* New York, 1965.

Friedman, Isaiah. *The Question of Palestine 1914–18.* London, 1973.

Friesel, Avyatar. *Ha-mdiniyut ha-tsiyonit le-ahar hatsharat Balfur 1917–1922.* Tel Aviv, 1977.

Ha-tnua ha-tsiyonit be-artsot ha-brit ba-shanim 1897–1914. Tel Aviv, 1970.

Frumkin, Boris. "Iz istorii revoliutsionnogo dvizheniia sredi evreev v 1870-kh godov," *ES,* IV (1911), 221–48, 513–40.

"Ocherki iz istorii evreiskogo rabochego dvizheniia v Rossii (1885–1897)," *ES,* VI (1913), no. 1, 108–22; no. 2, 245–63.

"Zubatovshchina i evreiskoe rabochee dvizhenie," *Perezhitoe,* III (1911), 199–230.

Gal, Allon. "Brandeis, Progressivism and Zionism; a Study in the Interaction of Ideal and Social Background." Ph.D. dissertation, Brandeis University, 1975.

Galai, Shmuel. "Early Russian Constitutionalism, 'Volnoe Slovo' and the 'Zemstvo Union': a Study in Deception," *Jahrbücher fur Geschichte Osteuropas,* XXII (1974), no. 1, 35–55.

The Liberation Movement in Russia 1900–1905. Cambridge, 1973.

Gartner, Lloyd P. *The Jewish Immigrant in England 1870–1914.* London, 1960.

"Notes on the Statistics of Jewish Immigrants to England 1870–1914," *JSS,* XX (1960), no. 2, 97–102.

"Roumania, America and World Jewry: Consul Peixotta in Bucharest 1870–1876," *AJHQ,* LVIII (1968–9), 25–117.

Gelbard, Arieh. "Ha-'bund' bi-[ye]me milhemet ha-olam ha-rishona," *M'asef,* XI (1979), 50–81.

Gelber, Natan Mikhael. "Di rusishe pogromen onheyb di 80-er yorn in shayn fun estraykhisher diplomatisher korespondents," *HS,* II, 466–96.

"Plite praot shnot ha-shmonim be-vrodi," *He-avar,* IX (1962), 67–77.

"Ha-praot be-varsha 1881," *He-avar,* X (1963), 106–17.

Toldot ha-tnua ha-tsiyonit be-galitsya 1875–1918. 2 vols. Jerusalem, 1958.

Gelman, S. "Pervaia podpolnaia tipografiia gruppy 'Rabochee znamia,' " *KiS* (1926), no. 6/27, pp. 44–56.

Gershanovich, D. L. "Vospominaniia o gruppe 'Rabochego znameni': o Moisee Vladimiroviche Lure," *K dvadtsatipiatiletiiu pervogo sezda partii (1898–1923)* (Moscow, 1923), pp. 165–74. A publication of the Komissiia po istorii oktiabrskoi revoliutsii i RKP (b).

[*Di*] *geshikhte fun bund* (ed. G. Aronson, J. S. Hertz, et al.). 4 vols. New York, 1956–68.

Geshikhte fun der tsienistisher arbeter bavegung in tsofn amerike. 2 vols. New York, 1955.

Getzler, Israel. *Martov: a Political Biography of a Russian Social Democrat.* Cambridge, 1967.

Geyer, Dietrich. *Lenin in der russischen Sozialdemokratie.* Cologne, 1960.

Giladi, Dan. "Ha-baron, ha-pkidut ve-hamoshavot ha-rishonot be-erets yisrael: haarakha me-hadash," *Cathedra,* II (1976), 59–68.

"Emdat ha-ikarim la-avoda ha-ivrit ba-aliya ha-shniya," *Ba-derekh,* VI (1970), 69–73.

Gitelman, Zvi Y. *Jewish Nationality and Soviet Politics: the Jewish Sections of the CPSU 1917–1930.* Princeton, 1972.

Glazer, Nathan. *The Social Basis of American Communism.* New York, 1961.

Goitein, Irma. *Probleme der Gesellschaft und des Staates bei Moses Hess* (Beihefte zum Archiv fur die Geschichte des Sozialismus und der Arbeiterbewegung, V). Leipzig, 1931.

Goldberg, N. "Di yidishe sotsyalistishe bavegung in di 80-er yorn – der 'yidisher arbeter fareyn'," in Cherikover (ed.), *Geshikhte,* II, 276–96.

Goldelman, Solomon I. *Jewish National Autonomy in the Ukraine 1917–20.* Chicago, 1968.

Goldsmith, Emanuel S. *Architects of Yiddishism at the Beginning of the Twentieth Century: a Study in Jewish Cultural History.* Cranbury, N.J., 1976.

Gordin, Aba. *S. Yanovski: zayn lebn, kemfn un shafn.* Los Angeles, 1957.

Gordon, Avrom. *In friling fun yidisher arbeter bavegung.* Vilna, 1926.

Goren, Arthur A. *New York Jews and the Quest for Community: the Kehillah Experiment 1908–1922.* New York, 1970.

[Gorenstein]. "A Portrait of Ethnic Politics: the Socialists and the 1908 and 1910 Congressional Elections on the East Side," *PAJHS,* L (1960–1), no. 3, 202–38.

Gorni, Yosef. "Be-hevle tmura: le-hitpathut raayon ha-hityashvut ha-ovedet," *Ba-derekh,* II (1968), 71–87.

" 'Ha-poel ha-tsair' ve-yahaso el ha-sotsyalizm bi-tkufat ha-aliya ha-shniya," *Ba-derekh,* VI (1970), 74–83.

"Ha-shinuyim ba-mivne ha-hevrati ve-hapoliti shel ha-aliya ha-shniya ba-shanim 1904–1940," *Ha-tsiyonut,* I (1970), 208–45.

"Shorasheha shel todaat ha-imut ha-leumi ha-yehudi-aravi ve-hishtakfuta ba-itonut ha-ivrit ba-shanim 1900–18," *Ha-tsiyonut,* IV (1975), 72–113.

"Ha-tikva she-beyeush: al-hashkafato shel Yosef Hayim Brener," *Asupot* (1971), no. 2/15, pp. 5–29.

"Yahasa shel mifleget poale tsiyon be-erets yisrael la-gola (bi-tkufat ha-aliya ha-shniya)," *Ha-tsiyonut,* II (1971), 74–89.

"Ha-yesod ha-romanti ba-ideologya shel ha-aliya ha-shniya," *Asupot* (1966), no. 10, pp. 55–74.

Gozhansky, Shmuel. "A briv tsu agitatorn (1893)," *Historishe shriftn,* III, 626–48. (Hebrew: *Mikhtav el ha-agitatorim, vilna [1893–1894.]* A publication of the Research Project on the Jewish Labor Movement, Hebrew University, Jerusalem, 1968.)

"Evreiskoe rabochee dvizhenie nachala 90-kh godov," in Dimanshtein, *Revoliutsionnoe dvizhenie,* pp. 81–95.

Graetz, Heinrich Hirsch. *History of the Jews.* 6 vols. Philadelphia, 1891–8. (German, annotated: *Geschichte der Juden von den ältesten Zeiten bis auf die Gegenwart.* Leipzig, 1897–1911.)

Graetz, Michael. "Le-shivato shel Moshe Hes la-yahadut–ha-reka le-hibur 'romi vi-[ye]rush-alayim'," *Zion,* XLII (1980), no. 2, 133–53.

Greenbaum, A. "Mifleget ha-saymistim–vozrozhdeniya," *M'asef,* VI (1974), 82–90.

Greenberg, Louis. *The Jews in Russia: the Struggle for Emancipation.* 2 vols. New Haven, Conn., 1944–51.

Grinbaum, Yitshak. "Yovel she-nishkakh: hamishim shana li-veidat helsingfors," *He-avar,* V (1957), 11–17.

Gringauz, Samuel. "Jewish National Autonomy in Lithuania (1918–1925)," *JSS,* XIV (1952), 225–46.

Grossman, Henryk. *Der bundizm in galitsye.* Cracow, 1908.

Grubbs, Frank L. *The Struggle for Labor Loyalty: the A.F. of L. and the Pacifists 1917–1920.* Durham, N.C., 1968.

Gruppa "osvobozhdenie truda" (iz arkhivov G. V. Plekhanova i L. G. Deicha) (ed. L. G. Deich). 6 vols. Moscow, 1923–8.

Gurevich, Grigorii (Gershon Badanes). "Protsess evreiskikh sotsialistov v Berline (1878–1879 g.)," *ES,* X (1918), 151–74.

"Sredi revoliutsionerov v Tsiurikhe," *EL,* IV (1926), 98–103.

"Zikhroynes (1873–1880)," *HS,* III, 224–255.

Gurevitz, Baruch. "Un cas de communisme national en Union soviétique: le Poale Zion 1918–1928," *Cahiers,* XV (1974), 333–71.

Gurfunkel, L. *Di yidishe natsyonale avtonomye in lite.* Kovno, 1920.

Guterman, Aleksander. "Ha-miflaga ha-tsiyonit ha-sotsyalistit be-rusya (SS)," (1): "Hitha-vuta ve-gibusha ha-ideologi (1905–1906)," *M'asef,* IX (1977), 97–115; (2): "Peiluta ha-mdinit ve-hatsiburit ba-shanim 1905–6," ibid., X (1978), 13–62.

Gutman, M. "Tsu der forgeshikhte fun SS." *RP,* I, 152–73.

Habas, Brakha (ed.) *Ha-aliya ha-shniya.* Tel Aviv, 1947.

Ha-Cohen, Mordekhay Ben Hillel. *Olami.* 5 vols. Jerusalem, 1927–9.

Haimson, Leopold H. *The Politics of Rural Russia 1905–1914.* Bloomington, Ind., 1979.

The Russian Marxists and the Origins of Bolshevism. Cambridge, Mass., 1955.

Halperin, Georg. *Die jüdische Arbeiter in London.* Stuttgart, 1903.

Halpern, Ben. *The Idea of the Jewish State.* Cambridge, Mass., 1961.

"What Is American Jewry?" *Forum* (1977), no. 26, pp. 97–104.

Halpern, Yisrael (ed.). *Sefer ha-gvura: antologya historit sifrutit.* 3 vols. Tel Aviv, 1949–50.

Hapgood, Hutchings. *The Spirit of the Ghetto* (ed. M. Rischin). Cambridge, Mass., 1967.

Harcave, Sidney Samuel. *First Blood: the Russian Revolution of 1905.* New York, 1964.

"The Jewish Question in the First Duma," *JSS,* VI (1944), 155–76.

"The Jews and the First Russian National Election," *American and Slavic East European Review,* IX (1950), no. 1, 33–41.

Hardan, David (ed.) *Sources of Contemporary Jewish Thought,* no. 2 (introd. E. Schweid). Jerusalem, 1971.

Hardman [Salutsky], J. B. S. "The Jewish Labor Movement in the United States: Jewish and Non-Jewish Influences," *AJHQ,* LII (1962–3), no. 2, 98–132. (Followed by comments from E. Lifschutz and W. Haskett, pp. 133–51.)

Harizman, M. *En ganim*. Tel Aviv, 1930.

Haustein, Ulrich. *Sozialismus und nationale Frage in Polen; die Entwicklung der sozialistischen Bewegung in Kongress-Polen von 1875 bis 1900 unter besonderer Berücksichtigung der Polnischen Sozialistischen Partei (PPS)*. Cologne, 1969.

Hayman, Paula. *From Dreyfus to Vichy. The Remaking of French Jewry 1906–1939*. New York, 1979.

Hecht, David. *Russian Radicals Look to America*. Cambridge, Mass., 1947.

Her, Shmuel. "Im shuvo le-rusya," *Kuntres* (2 Tevet 5688/26 Dec. 1927), no. 322, pp. 24–32.

Herberg, Will. "The Jewish Labor Movement in the United States," *AJYB*, LIII (1952), 3–74.

Hertz, Jacob S. [Yankev Sholem]. "The Bund's Nationality Program and Its Critics in the Russian, Polish and Austrian Socialist Movements," *YAJSS*, XIV (1969), 53–67.

(ed.). *Doyres bundistn*. 3 vols. New York, 1956–68.

Di geshikhte fun bund in lodzh. New York, 1958.

Di yidishe sotsyalistishe bavegung in amerike. New York, 1954.

Hertzberg, Arthur. *The Zionist Idea: a Historical Analysis and Reader*. New York, 1959.

[Herzl, Theodor]. *The Complete Diaries of Theodor Herzl* (ed. R. Patai). 5 vols. New York, 1960.

Hess, Moses. *Ausgewählte Schriften* (ed. and introd. Horst Lademacher). Cologne, 1962.

Die europäische Triarchie. Leipzig, 1841.

Die heilige Geschichte der Menschheit. Von einem Jünger Spinoza's. Stuttgart, 1837.

Jüdische Schriften (ed. and introd. Theodor Zlocisti). Berlin, 1905.

Ktavim klaliyim (ed. and introd. M. Buber). Jerusalem, 1956.

Ktavim tsiyoniyim ve-yehudiyim (ed. and introd. M. Buber). Jerusalem, 1954.

Moses Hess: Briefwechsel (ed. E. Silberner). The Hague, 1959.

Moshe Hes u-vne doro: igrot mimenu ve-elav (ed. T. Zlocisti). Tel Aviv, 1947.

"Philosophie der Tat," in G. Herwegh (ed.), *Einundzwanzig Bogen aus der Schweiz* (Zurich, 1843), pp. 309–31.

Philosophische und sozialistische Schriften 1837–1850 (ed. A. Cornu and W. Mönke). Berlin, 1961.

Rom und Jerusalem: die letzte Nationalitätsfrage. Leipzig, 1862. [Yiddish: *Roym un yerusholayim*. New York, 1916.]

"Sozialismus und Kommunismus," *Einundzwanzig Bogen aus der Schweiz* (Zurich, 1843), pp. 74–91.

Sozialistische Aufsätze 1841–1847 (ed. T. Zlocisti). Berlin, 1921.

Heymann, Michael. *The Uganda Controversy*. Tel Aviv, 1970.

Higham, John. *Send These to Me. Jews and Other Immigrants in Urban America*. New York, 1975.

Strangers in the Land. New Brunswick, N.J., 1955.

Hillquit, Morris. *The History of Socialism in the United States*. New York, 1903.

Loose Leaves from a Busy Life. New York, 1934.

Historishe shriftn (ed. E. Cherikover et al.) 3 vols. Warsaw-Vilna, 1929–39. (A publication of the Historical Section of YIVO.)

Horvits, Zvi. "Me-rshimotav shel ehad mi-sride ha-biluim," *Mi-yamim rishonim*, I (Feb.–March 1935), no. 9–14, 241–54.

Hourwich [Gurvich], Isaac H. "Di anarkhistn in rusland," *Tsayt-gayst* (1906), no. 54, pp. 2–4.

Howe, Irving. *Leon Trotsky*. London, 1978.

(With the assistance of Kenneth Libo). *World of Our Fathers: the Journey of the East European Jews to America and the Life They Found and Made*. New York, 1976.

Hurwitz, Maximilian. *The Workmen's Circle. Its History, Ideals, Organization and Institutions*. New York, 1936.

Hyamson, Albert Montefiore. *British Projects for the Restoration of the Jews*. London, 1917.

BIBLIOGRAPHY

ICA [Jewish Colonisation Association]. *Recueil de matériaux sur la situation économique des Israélites de Russie*. 2 vols. Paris, 1906–8.

Ivensky, M. *Arn Shmuel Liberman – zayn shturmisher lebn un tragisher sof*. New York, 1934.

"Iz perepiski 'Iskri' s mestnymi organizatsiiami" (ed. T. Bobrovsky), *PR* (1928), no. 6–7/77–78, pp. 93–178.

Janowsky, Oscar I. *Jews and Minority Rights (1898–1919)*. New York, 1933.

Nationalities and National Minorities (with Special Reference to East-Central Europe). New York, 1945.

Jeshurin, Ephim H. (ed.). *Vladek in der opshatsung fun zayne fraynd*. New York, 1936.

Jick, Leon A. *The Americanization of the Synagogue 1820–1870*. Hanover, N.H., 1976.

Joseph, Samuel. *Jewish Immigration to the United States*. New York, 1914.

Die Judenpogrome in Russland (ed. L. Motskin). 2 vols. Cologne, 1910.

Kalay, David. *Ha-aliya ha-shniya*. Tel Aviv, 1946.

Kamensky, Moshe [M.K.]. "Nihilistim ivriyim bi-shnot ha-shivim (reshimot ve-zikhronot)," *Ha-shiloah*, XVII (September 1907), no. 3, pp. 257–63.

Kantor, R. M. "Alexandr III o evreiskikh pogromakh 1881–83 gg. (novye materialy)," *EL*, I (1923), 149–58.

" 'Arbeiter tseitung' 1881 goda," *EL*, III (1924), 197–204.

Kats, Dovid [V. Tsoglin (Taras)]. "Mezhdu pervym i tretim sezdami Bunda," in Dimanshtein, *Revoliutsionnoe dvizhenie*, pp. 149–81.

"Pervy sezd Bunda," in Dimanshtein, *Revoliutsionnoe dvizhenie*, pp. 131–48.

Katz, Ben Zion. "Ha-parlament ha-rishon be-rusya: ha-duma ha-mamlakhtit," *He-avar*, V (1957), 3–10.

Katz, Jacob. *Emancipation and Assimilation: Studies in Modern Jewish History*. Farnborough, England, 1972. Includes "The Jewish National Movement: a Sociological Analysis," pp. 129–45.

Sinat yisrael: mi-sinat ha-dat li-shlilat ha-geza. Tel Aviv, 1979.

Katznelson, Berl. "Darki la-arets," in B. Habas (ed.), *Ha-aliya ha-shniya*, pp. 67–85.

"Ha-ehad be-maarakha (reshito shel Nahman Sirkin)," in *Kitve Nahman Sirkin*, pp. 4–132. (Yiddish: *Eyner kegn alemen: Nakhmen Sirkins ershte kamf-yorn*, transl. V. Latsky-Bertoldi. Tel-Aviv, 1940.)

Igrot B. Katsnelson 1900–1914 (ed. Y. Sharet). Tel Aviv, 1961.

Kitve B. Katsnelson. 12 vols. Tel Aviv 1945–50. (XI: *Prakim le-toldot tnuat ha-poalim.)*

Kaufman, Mojżesz (Mojsie Mezryczer). "Początki roboty żydowskiej PPS," *Niepodległość*, VII (1933), 335–50.

Kazdan, Chaim Shloyme. "Der bund – biz dem finftn tsuzamenfor," *Di geshikhte fun bund*, I, 107–279.

Keep, John L. H. *The Rise of Social Democracy in Russia*. Oxford, 1963.

Kegn di onfaler oyf Dr. Khaim Zhitlovski: zamlung fun artiklen. New York, 1944. Articles by N. Maizil et al.; published by the Dr. Ch. Zhitlovsky People's Committee.

Kellner, Jacob. "Mered ha-mityashvim be-rishon le-tsiyon u-mered ha-mehagrim ha-yehudim be-nyu york be-1882," *Cathedra* V (1977), 3–29.

Kener, Y. "Vos hot gebracht tsu der antshteyung fun velt farband?" *YAP*, pp. 151–63.

Kessner, Thomas. *The Golden Door: Italian and Jewish Immigrant Mobility 1880–1915*. New York, 1977.

Khisin, E. [Chaim]. "Iz dnevnika palestinskogo emigranta," *Voskhod* (1889), no. 1–2, pp. 227–56; no. 3, pp. 20–32; no. 4, pp. 98–112; no. 5, pp. 3–18. (Hebrew: *Mi-yoman ahad ha-biluim*. Petah Tikva, 1977; English: Chissin, *A Palestine Diary. Memoirs of a Bilu Pioneer 1882–1887*. New York, 1976).

Kiel, Mark. "The Jewish Narodnik," *Judaism*, XIX (1970), 295–310.

Kipnis, Ira. *The American Socialist Movement 1897–1912*. New York, 1968.

Kirzhnits, Avrom. "Bund un RSDRP erev dem tsveytn partey tsuzamenfor," *Visenshaftlekhe yorbukher*, I (1929), 59–89.

Di profbavegung tsvishn di yidishe arbeter in di yorn fun der ershte revolutsye. Moscow, 1926.

and Moyshe Rafes (eds.) *Der yidisher arbeter: khrestomatye tsu der geshikhte fun der yidisher arbeter, revolutsyoner un sotsyalistisher bavegung in rusland.* I–II: *Di yorn 1904–7.* Moscow, 1925.

Kisman, Yoysef. "A kapitl geshikhte fun der yidisher arbeter bavegung in rumenye," *HS*, III, 447–83.

"Kitve bilu (1) megilat takanot shel bilu," *Mi-yamim rishonim*, I (Sept. 1934), no. 4, 73–80.

Kivin [Kopelushnik], Shloyme. "Baym vigele fun der partey," in *YAP*, pp. 31–46.

Klausner, Joseph [Yosef]. *Historiya shel ha-sifrut ha-ivrit ha-hadasha.* 6 vols. Jerusalem, 1930–50.

Klausner, Yisrael. *Be-hitorer am: ha-aliya ha-rishona me-rusya.* Jerusalem, 1962.

"Ha-histadrut 'yehuda ha-hofshit' mi-[ye]sodo shel Nahman Sirkin," *Asupot* (1961), no. 7, pp. 187–97.

"Ha-mashber ba-sifrut ha-ivrit bi-shnot ha-mahpekha ha-rishona be-rusya," *He-avar*, XXII (1977), 24–33.

Mi-katovits ad bazel. Jerusalem, 1965.

"Mi-yamim rishonim: mi-zikhronotav shel Moshe Kamyonski," *Ha-olam* (20 March 1941), no. 24, pp. 383–4; (27 March 1941), no. 25, pp. 396–7.

Opozitsya le-Hertsel. Jerusalem, 1960.

"Shimon Dubnov u-tnuat 'hibat tsiyon,' " *He-avar*, VII (1960), 32–42.

Knei-Paz, Baruch. *The Social and Political Thought of Leon Trotsky.* Oxford, 1978.

Kohler, Max J. "The Board of Delegates of American Israelites," *PAJHS*, XXIX (1925), 75–135.

Kolar, Avraham Moshe. "Meora zarnuga," in Habas, pp. 288–90.

Kolatt, Yisrael. *Avot u-meyasdim.* Jerusalem, 1975.

"Ideologya u-metsiut bi-tnuat ha-avoda be-erets yisrael." Ph.D. thesis, The Hebrew University of Jerusalem, 1964.

"Li-mkoma shel ha-idea be-hithavut ha-kvutsa ba-arets," *Ba-derekh*, III (1968), 161–4.

"The Organization of the Jewish Population of Palestine and the Development of its Political Consciousness before World War I," in Moshe Ma'oz (ed.), *Studies on Palestine During the Ottoman Period*," (Jerusalem, 1975) pp. 211–45.

" 'Ha-poel ha-tsair' – mi-kibush ha-avoda le-kidush ha-avoda," *Ba-derekh*, I (1967), 29–61.

Kopeloff, J. *Amolike yorn.* New York, 1931.

Kopelzon, Timofei M. "Di ershte shprotsungen (zikhroynes)," *Arbeter luekh*, III (Warsaw, 1922), 49–70.

"Evreiskoe rabochee dvizhenie kontsa 80-kh i nachala 90-kh godov," in Dimanshtein, *Revoliutsionnoe dvizhenie*, pp. 65–80.

"Stranichka iz vospominanii," in N. L. Meshcheriakov (ed.), *O Lenine*, III, 20–7.

Korn, Bertram W. *The American Reaction to the Mortara Case: 1858–1859.* Cincinnati, 1957.

Korzec, Pawel. "Three Documents of 1903–6 on the Russian Jewish Situation," *Soviet Jewish Affairs*, II (1972), no. 2, 75–95.

[Kossovksy, V.] *Borba "Polskoi sotsialisticheskoi partii" protiv "Evreiskogo rabochego soiuza."* Geneva, 1898. (A Bund publication; unsigned.)

K voprosu o natsionalnoi avtonomii i preobrazovanii Ros. sots.-demokr. rabochei partii na federativnykh nachalakh. London, 1902. (A Bund publication; unsigned.)

Razgrom evreev v Rossii. Geneva, 1915. (A publication of the Bund's Committee Abroad.)

"V. Medem un di natsyonale frage," in *Vladimir Medem*, pp. 13–40.

Der yidisher khurbm in rusland. New York, 1915. (A publication of the Tsentral Farband fun Bund in Amerike.)

"Zubatov 'likvidirt' dem bund," *Arkadi zamlbukh*, pp. 175–207.

Kovets "ha-shomer": teudot, zikhronot ve-divre haarakha ktuvim bi-[ye]de vatike "ha-shomer." Tel Aviv, 1937.

Kremer, Arkadi. "Der ershter ts. k. fun bund: epizod Zubatov," *Arkadi zamlbukh*, pp. 380–94.

"Mit 35 yor tsurik," *Undzer tsayt* (February 1928), no. 2, pp. 83–7.

Ob agitatsii (with an afterword by P. B. Akselrod). Geneva, 1897 (dated 1896).

"Osnovanie Bunda," *PR* (1922), no. 11, pp. 50–56.

Kressel, Getzel. *Frants Openhaymer, poolo ha-tsiyoni, u-merhavya: ha-kooperatsya bi-[ye]me ha-aliya ha-shniya.* Tel Aviv, 1972.

" 'Histadrut ha-poalim' bi-fros ha-aliya ha-shniya," *Asupot* (1959), no. 6, pp. 53–87.

(ed.). *Mafteah le-"haahdut."* Tel Aviv, [1961].

and Iza Kressel (eds.) *Mafteah le-"hapoel ha-tsair"* 5668–5717 [1907–57]. Tel Aviv, 1968.

Krippe, L. "Iz zapisok emigranta 1881 g.," *ES*, III (1911), 372–88.

Krol, Zvi. "Toldot Aharon Shmuel Liberman," in *Ha-emet: ha-iton ha-sotsyalisti ha-rishon be-ivrit* (Tel Aviv, 1938) pp. 5–48.

Künzli, Arnold. *Karl Marx: eine Psychographie.* Vienna, 1966.

Kursky, Frants. "Arkadi un zayn tkufe," *Arkadi zamlbukh*, pp. 73–111.

Gezamlte shriftn. New York, 1952.

"Di zhenever 'grupe sotsyalistn-yidn' un ir oyfruf (1880)," *HS*, III, 557–62.

Landau, Saul Raphael. *Sturm und Drang im Zionismus: Rückblicke eines Zionisten.* Vienna, 1937.

Unter jüdischen Proletariern: Reiseschilderungen aus Ostgalizien und Russland. Vienna, 1898.

Laqueur, Walter. *A History of Zionism.* London, 1972.

Laserson, Max M. "Jewish Minority Rights in the Baltic Countries," *JSS*, III (1941), 273–84.

Laskov, Shulamit. *Ha-biluim.* Tel Aviv, 1979.

"Livte tnuat 'bilu' be-reshit darka (tsha-esre teudot)," *Ha-tsiyonut*, V (1978), 263–98.

Latsky-Bertoldi, Volf. "Ha-maasar shel veidat ha-hagana ha-atsmit be-odesa bi-shnat 1904 (le-fi teudot department ha-mishtara be-rusya)," *Yediot ha-arkhiyon ve-hamuzeon shel tnuat ha-avoda* (1938), no. 3–4, pp. 52–7.

Lavrov, Petr Lavrovich [P. Mirtov]. *Historical Letters* [1870] (trans. and introd. J. P. Scanlan). Berkeley, 1967.

Narodniki-propagandisty 1873–77 godov. Geneva, 1895–6.

Russkoi sotsialno-revoliutsionnoi molodezhi. London, 1874.

Leninskii sbornik (ed. L. Kamenev et al.). 35 vols. Moscow, 1924–45. (A publication of the Institut Lenina pri Ts. K. P. (b.).)

Leshchinsky, Yaakov (ed.). *Shriftn far ekonomik un statistik* I. Berlin, 1928. (A YIVO publication.)

"Di yidishe imigratsye in di fareynikte shtatn (1870–1900)," in Cherikover, *Geshikhte*, I, 27–40.

Di yidishe vanderung far di letste 25 yor. Berlin, 1927.

Lesin [Valt], Avrom. "B. Vladek amol un itst," in Jeshurin, *Vladek*, pp. 14–31.

"Epizodn," *HS*, III, 173–223.

"Mayn ershte bagegenish mit Dovid Pinski," *Di tsukunft* (May 1922), no. 5, pp. 305–7.

"Der vikhtikster fun di ershte," *Arkadi zamlbukh*, pp. 270–6.

Zikhronot va-havayot (ed. and introd. B. Katznelson). Tel Aviv, 1943.

Levin, Emanuel. "Mi-tokh tazkir al ha-praot bi-shnot 1881–1882," *He-avar*, IX (1962), 78–81.

Levin, Mordechai (Marcus). *Erke hevra ve-kalkala ba-ideologya shel tkufat ha-haskala.* Jerusalem, 1975.

Levin, Shmarya. *The Arena.* New York, 1932.

Childhood in Exile. New York, 1929.

Youth in Revolt. New York, 1930.

[Levin, Yehuda Leb.] *Yehuda Leb Levin: zikhronot ve-hegyonot* (ed. Y. Slutsky). Jerusalem, 1968.

Levine, Louis. *The Women's Garment Workers. A History of the International Ladies Garment Workers' Union.* New York, 1924.

Levitsky, V. [Vladimir Osipovich Tsederbaum]. *Za chetvert veka.* Moscow, 1926.

Levontin, Zalman David. *Le-erets avotenu.* 3 vols. I: *le-toldot avodat hoveve tsiyon mi-shnat 5642 ad shnat 5649;* II: *le-toldot avodat ha-histadrut ha-tsiyonit mi-shnat 1901 ad 1914;* III: *ibid.*, 1915–27. Tel Aviv, 1924–8.

Liberman, Aron Shmuel. *A. S. Liberman: katavot u-maamarim be-"vperyod" (1875–1876)* (ed. and introd. M. Mishkinsky). Tel Aviv, 1977.

Arn Libermans briv (ed. K. Marmor). New York, 1940.

Liberman, Chaim. *Dr. Khaim Zhitlovski un zayn fartaydiker: nokh a vort vegn dem gaystikn bankrot fun a dor.* New York, 1944.

Yidn un yidishkayt in di shriftn fun Dr. K. Zhitlovski: gedanken vegn a farblondzhetn dor. New York, 1944.

Liebeschütz, Hans. "German Radicalism and the Formation of Jewish Political Attitudes during the Earlier Part of the Nineteenth Century," in A. Altmann (ed.), *Studies in Nineteenth Century Jewish Intellectual History* (Cambridge, Mass. 1964), pp. 141–70.

Liebman, Arthur. *Jews and the Left.* New York, 1979.

Liebman, Charles. *The Ambivalent American Jew.* Philadelphia, 1973.

Lifshits, Yaakov Ha-levi. *Zikhron Yaakov.* 3 vols. Frankfurt, 1924.

Lifschutz, Ezekiel. "Di amerikaner interventsyes vegn di pogromen in rusland in di 1880-er yorn," *HS*, II, 497–516.

"Ha-'yidishe folks-tsaytung' be-nyu york," *M'asef*, VII (1975), 4–48.

and E. Cherikover, "Di pyonern-tkufe fun der yidisher arbeter bavegung," in Cherikover, *Geshikhte*, II, 239–75.

Likhtenshtein (Weizmann), Haya. *Be-tsel koratenu: zikhronot mi-bet aba.* Tel Aviv, 1948.

Literatura partii "Narodnoi voli" (ed. A. V. Yakimovaia-Dikovskaia et al.). Moscow, 1930. (Republications of *Narodnaia volia* and other party papers.)

Litvak, A. [C. Y. Helfand]. *Vos geven: etyudn un zikhroynes.* Warsaw, 1926. (A selection of essays in Hebrew: *Ma she-haya: zikhronot al tnuat ha-poalim.* Tel Aviv. 1945.)

Litvin, A. "Tsulib dem emes fun geshikhte," *Der yidisher arbeter* IV (26 March 1926), no. 6, pp. 13–14; no. 7, pp. 11–12. For other memoirs by Litvin under different titles see ibid., no. 21, pp. 9–10; V (1927), no. 18, pp. 5–6.

Livne, Eliezer. *Nili: toldoteha shel heaza mdinit.* Jerusalem, 1961.

Aharon Aharonson: ha-ish u-zmano. Jerusalem, 1969.

Löwe, Heinz-Dietrich. *Antisemitismus und reaktionäre Utopie. Russischer Konservatismus im Kampf gegen den Wandel von Staat und Gesellschaft 1890–1917.* Hamburg, 1978.

Lukács, Georg. "Moses Hess und die Probleme der idealistischen Dialektik," *Archiv für die Geschichte des Sozialismus und der Arbeiterbewegung*, XII (1926), 105–55.

M.E. *Moisei Ges: stranitsa iz istorii sionskogo dvizheniia.* Ekaterinoslav, 1894.

McLellan, David. *Marx before Marxism.* London, 1970.

The Young Hegelians and Karl Marx. New York, 1969.

Malkin, Sara. "Darki ba-arets," in Habas, pp. 488–500.

Mandel, Irving Aaron. "Attitude of the American Jewish Community toward East-European Immigration as Reflected in the Anglo-Jewish Press (1880–90)," *AJA*, III (1950), no. 1, 11–36.

Mandel, Neville J. *The Arabs and Zionism before World War I*. Berkeley, 1976.

Mandelshtam, Maks Emanuil. "Ignatevskaia komissiia v Kieve 1881 g.," *Perezhitoe*, IV (1913), 46–64.

Maor, Yitshak. "Ha-reka le-gerush ha-yehudim mi-moskva," *He-avar*, XVIII (1971), 25–34.
  Sheelat ha-yehudim ba-tnua ha-liberalit ve-hamahpkhanit be-rusya 1890–1914. Jerusalem, 1964.
  "Ha-kruz ha-anti-shemi shel 'narodnaya volya,' " *Zion*, XV (1950), 150–5.
  Ha-tnua ha-tsiyonit be-rusya me-reshita ve-ad yamenu. Jerusalem, 1974.
  "Yehude rusya bi-[ye]me ha-dumot," *He-avar*, V (1957), 3–10.

Marchand, C. Roland. *The American Peace Movement and Social Reform 1898–1918*. Princeton, 1972.

Marmor, Kalman. *Mayn lebns geshikhte*. 2 vols. New York, 1959.
  Moris Vintchevski: zayn lebn, virkn un shafn (published as vol. 1 of M. Vinchevsky, *Gezamlte verk*). New York, 1928.

Marrus, Michael R. *The Politics of Assimilation; a Study of the French Jewish Community at the Time of the Dreyfus Affair*. Oxford, 1971.

Martov, L. [I.O. Tsederbaum] et al. (eds.). *Obshchestvennoe dvizhenie v Rossii v nachale XX veka*. 4 vols. St. Petersburg, 1914.
  Povorotny punkt v istorii evreiskogo rabochego dvizheniia. Geneva, 1900. (Hebrew: *Nkudat ha-mifne be-toldot tnuat ha-poalim ha-yehudit [vilna*, 2 *be-may]*. A publication of the Research Project on the Jewish Labor Movement, Hebrew University. Jerusalem, 1968).
  Zapiski sotsial-demokrata. Berlin, 1922.

[Martynov (A. S. Piker)]. *Dva sezda: tretii ocherednoi sezd Soiuza i "obedinitelny" sezd*. Geneva, 1901.

Marx, Karl. *Briefwechsel zwischen Karl Marx und Friedrich Engels*. 4 vols. Berlin, 1949–50.
  "Zur Judenfrage," *Deutsch-Französiche Jahrbücher* (Paris, 1844), pp. 182–214.
  and Friedrich Engels. *Werke*. 39 vols. Berlin, 1958–68.

Massiczek, Albert. *Der menschliche Mensch: Karl Marx' jüdischer Humanismus*. Vienna, 1968.

Massing, Paul W. *Rehearsal for Destruction; a Study of Political Anti-Semitism in Imperial Germany*. New York, 1949.

Materialy dlia istorii anti-evreiskikh pogromov v Rossii. I: *Dubossarskoe i kishinevskoe dela 1903 goda* (ed. S. M. Dubnov and G. Y. Krasny-Admoni); II: *Vosmidesiatye gody (15 aprelia 1881 g. –29 fevralia 1882 g.)* (ed. G. Y. Krasny-Admoni). Petrograd, 1919–23.

"Materialy k istorii pervogo sezda," *PR* (1928), no. 3/74, pp. 152–69. (Includes letters of T. Kopelzon.)

Mayer, Gustav. *Friedrich Engels: eine Biographie*. 2 vols. Berlin, 1923.

Medem, Vladimir. *Fun mayn lebn*. 2 vols. Warsaw, 1929. (English: *The Life and Soul of a Legendary Jewish Socialist*, introd. and trans. S. A. Portnoy. New York, 1978.)
  VI-oi sionisticheskii kongres v Bazele. London, 1903. (A Bund publication; unsigned.)
  Sotsialdemokratiia i natsionalny vopros. (A Bund publication; unsigned.)
  "Di tsentrale figur," *Arkadi zamelbukh*, pp. 232–5.
  Vladimir Medem: tsum tsvantsikstn yortsayt. New York, 1943.

Mehlinger, Howard D., and John M. Thompson. *Count Witte and the Tsarist Government in the 1905 Revolution*. Bloomington, Ind., 1972.

Mendelsohn, Ezra. *Class Struggle in the Pale: the Formative Years of the Jewish Workers Movement in Tsarist Russia*. Cambridge, 1970.

BIBLIOGRAPHY

"The Jewish Socialist Movement and the Second International 1889–1914: The Struggle for Recognition," *JSS*, XXVI (1964), no. 3, 131–45.

"The Russian Roots of the American Jewish Labor Movement," *YAJSS*, XVI (1976), 150–77.

Menes, Avrom. "The Am Oylom Movement," *YAJSS*, IV (1949), 9–33.

"Di yidishe arbeter bavegung in rusland fun onheyb 70-er bizn sof 90-er yorn," *HS*, III, 1–59.

Menshchikov, L. P. (ed.). *Russkii politicheskii sysk zagranitsei.* Paris, 1914.

Meyer, Alfred G. *Leninism.* Cambridge, Mass., 1957.

Michael, Reuwen. "Graetz und Hess," *LBIYB*, IX (1964), 91–121.

Mielcke, Karl. *Frühsozialismus: Gesellschaft und Geschichte in den Schriften von Weitling und Hess.* Stuttgart, 1931.

Mill, John [Y. Mil]. *Pyonern un boyer.* 2 vols. New York, 1946–9.

Mintz, Matityahu. *Ber Borokhov: ha-maagal ha-rishon (1900–1906).* Tel Aviv, 1976.

"Borokhov ve-Bogdanov," *Ba-derekh*, I (1967), 96–122.

"Ber Borokhov ve-nitsane ha-imut al odot ha-palestino-tsentrizm ben poale-tsiyon le-ven poale-tsiyon be-erets-yisrael," *Shorashim*, I (1979), 320–35.

"Ha-'farband' ha-polani u-mekomo be-mifleget ha-poalim ha-yehudit ha-SD 'poale tsiyon' be-rusya," *Asupot* (1972), no. 3/16, pp. 320–35.

"Ha-mahloket al mahut ha-palestinizm be-kerev mifleget ha-poalim ha-yehudit ha-SD poale tsiyon be-rusya (1906)," *Asupot* (1971), no. 2/15, pp. 53–73.

Mafteah le-hativat ha-hagigim: filozofiya u-mahshava hevratit leumit (1902–1904, 1907–1910). Tel Aviv, 1975.

"Me-hagige Borokhov," *Ha-tsiyonut*, III (1973), 502–19.

"Perek ha-siyum ha-ganuz shel hibur Yitshak Ben-Tsvi al nedidat ha-yehudim," *Cathedra* XIII (1979), 131–41.

"Shalosh igrot mi-shel Ber Barukhov le-aviv Moshe Aharon Barukhov," in *Sefer Rafael Maler: kovets mehkarim le-toldot yisrael,* (ed. S. Yeivin) (Tel Aviv, 1974), pp. 159–83.

"Shalosh teudot mi-[ye]me pulmus vozrozhdenye, erev veidat poltava shel mifleget ha-poalim ha-yehudit ha-sotsyal-demokratit poale-tsiyon," *Ha-tsiyonut*, V (1978), 310–41.

(ed. and introd.) *Veidat krakov shel mifleget poale tsiyon be-rusya, 1907 (teudot).* Tel Aviv, 1979.

Miron, Dan. *A Traveller Disguised: a Study in the Rise of Modern Yiddish Fiction in the Nineteenth Century.* New York, 1973.

Mishkinsky, Moshe. "Al emdata shel ha-tnua ha-mahpekhanit ha-rusit le-gabe ha-yehudim bi-shnot ha-70 shel ha-mea ha-19," *He-avar*, IX (1962), 38–66.

" 'Igud ha-poalim ha-drom rusi' ve-hapogrom be-kiyev bi-shnat 1881," *Shvut*, I (1973), 62–73.

"Kruz ha-ehad be-may ha-rishon le-poalim yehudiyim," *Ba-derekh*, I (1967), 3–6.

"Mekoroteha ha-raayoniyim shel tnuat ha-poalim ha-yehudit be-reshita," *Zion*, XXXI (1966), no. 1–2, 87–115.

"Mi-huge hasbara ve-limud li-tnuat poalim yehudiyim," *M'asef*, III–IV (1972), 13–33.

"Regional Factors in the Formation of the Jewish Labor Movement," *YAJSS*, XIV (1969), 27–52.

"Ha-'sotsyalizm ha-mishtarti' u-mgamot bi-mdiniyut ha-shilton ha-tsari le-gabe ha-yehudim (1900–1903)," *Zion*, XXV (1960), no. 3–4, 238–49.

"Tnuat ha-poalim ha-yehudit be-rusya ve-hatnua ha-sotsyalistit ha-polanit," *Asupot* (1970), no. 1/14, pp. 81–131.

"Tsmihat ha-tsiyonut ha-poalit be-rusya," *Shorashim*, I (1979), 270–319.

Yesodot leumiyim be-hithavuta shel tnuat ha-poalim ha-yehudit be-rusya (me-reshita ve-ad 1901)." Ph.D. thesis, The Hebrew University of Jerusalem, 1965.

"Mi-teudot ha-aliya ha-shniya," *Asupot* (1954), no. 4, pp. 10–43.

Mönke, Wolfgang. "Über die Mitarbeit von Moses Hess an der 'Deutschen Ideologie,' " in *Annali* (Instituto Giangiacomo Feltrinelli), VI (1963), 438–509.

Munchik, Eliyahu. *Le-toldot tseire tsiyon, ha-poel ha-tsair, he-haluts ve-hahistadrut.* Tel Aviv, [1943].

National Workmen's Committee for Jewish Rights. *The War and the Jews in Russia.* New York, 1916.

Nawratski, Curt. *Die jüdische Kolonisation Palästinas.* Munich, 1914.

1905 yor in barditshev: notitsn un zikhroynes. Berdichev, 1925.

Nedava, Joseph. *Trotsky and the Jews.* Philadelphia, 1972.

Nettl, J. P. *Rosa Luxemburg.* 2 vols. Oxford, 1966.

Nevsky, Vladimir Ivanovich (ed. and introd.). " 'Zerno': Rabochii listok," in *IRS* (ed. V. I. Nevsky), II (1924), 350–88. (Includes a republication of *Zerno*.)

Nidah [Ezriel Naton Frenk]. "Ha-sofrim ha-ivriyim u-fulotehem bi-[ye]me ha-pogromim ha-rishonim be-rusya," *Ha-tsfira* (16 Aug. 1917), no. 25, pp. 9–10; (23 Aug. 1917), no. 26, pp. 1–12; (20 Sept. 1917), no. 30, pp. 7–9; (27 Sept. 1917), no. 31, pp. 11–12; (4 Oct. 1917), no. 32, pp. 10–11; (18 Oct. 1917), no. 34, pp. 9–12.

Nikolaevsky, Boris I. [B.N.]. "Iz epokhi 'Iskry' i 'Zari'," *Katorga i ssylka* (1927), no. 6/35, pp. 7–35; no. 7/36, pp. 83–100.

Nini, Yehuda. "Ole teman be-erets yisrael ba-shanim 5642–5674 (1882–1914)," *Cathedra*, V (1977), 30–82.

Nir (Rafalkes), Nahum. *Ershte yorn: in rod fun dor un bavegung.* Tel Aviv, 1960. (Hebrew: *Pirke hayim: be-maagle ha-dor ve-hatnua 1884–1918.* Tel Aviv, 1958.)

"Der onheyb in poyln," *YAP,* pp. 114–50.

"Tsu der opshtamung fun poyle tsienizm," *YAP,* pp. 17–30.

Vanderungen. Tel Aviv, 1966.

"Novoe o zubatovshchine," *KA,* I (1922), 289–328.

Oksman, I. G. "Otlik moskovskikh promyshlennikov na anti-evreiskie besporiadki," *KA,* XIV (1926), no. 1, 258–60.

Olgin [M. Novomisky]. "Tsen yor: tsum yubileum fun bund," *Di tsukunft* (December 1907), no. 12, pp. 3–14.

Oppenheim, Samson D. "The Jewish Population of the United States," *AJYB* (1918–19), pp. 31–74.

Oppenheimer, Franz. *Erlebtes, Erstrebtes, Erreichtes: Lebenserrinnerungen.* Düsseldorf, 1964.

Merchavia: a Jewish Cooperative Settlement in Palestine. Cologne and New York, 1914.

Die Siedlungsgenossenschaft. Versuch einer Positiven Überwindung des Kommunismus durch Lösung des Genossenschaftsproblems und der Agrarfrage. [1895.] Jena, 1922.

Orren, Elhannan. "Ha-publitsistika ha-yidit be-mizrah london ba-shanim 1883–1887," *Ha-tsiyonut,* II (1971), 47–63.

Osofsky, Gilbert. "The Hebrew Emigrant Aid Society of the United States 1881–1883," *PAJHS,* XLIX (1959–60), no. 3, 173–87.

Palestina: sbornik statei i svedenii o evreiskikh poseleniiakh v sv. zemle. St. Petersburg, 1884.

Panitz, Esther. "In Defense of the Jewish Immigrant (1891–1924)," *AJHQ,* LV (1965–6), no. 1, 57–97.

"The Polarity of American Jewish Attitudes toward Immigration (1870–1891)," *AJHQ,* LIII (1963–4), no. 2, 99–130.

Parzen, Herbert. "Brandeis and the Balfour Declaration," *Herzl Year Book,* V (1963), 309–50.

Patkin, Aaron L. *The Origins of the Russian-Jewish Labour Movement.* Melbourne, 1947.

Perrie, Maureen. *The Agrarian Policy of the Russian Socialist Revolutionary Party from Its Origins through the Revolution of 1905–1907.* Cambridge, 1976.

[Pervaia vseobshchaia perepis naseleniia rossiiskoi imperii 1897 g.], *Obshchii svod po imperii rezultatov razrabotki dannykh pervoi vseobshchei perepisi naseleniia.* 2 vols. St. Petersburg, 1905.

Pervoe maia 1892 goda: chetyre rechi evreiskikh rabochikh [introd. L. Yogikhes]. Geneva, 1893. (Hebrew: *Arbaa neumim shel poalim yehudim: vilna ha-1 be-may 1892 (1893).* A publication of the Research Project on the Jewish Labor Movement, Hebrew University, Jerusalem, 1967.)

Pesakhzon, Yitskhok Mordkhe [An' alter Bekanter]. "Der onfang fun der yidisher arbeter bavegung in varshe (zikhroynes fun a yidishn sotsyalist)," *YA* (1900), no. 10, pp. 27–36.

Peterson, H. C., and G. C., Fite. *Opponents of War 1917–18.* Madison, Wis., 1957.

Petrazil, Yaakov. *Ha-maavak ba-zira ha-proletarit ha-benleumit.* I: *1907–27; II: 1928–47.* Jerusalem, 1954–5.

Piasecki, Henryk. *Żydowska organizacja PPS (1893–1907).* Wroclaw, 1978.

Pietkewicz, Kazimierz. "Mojżesz Lurjei i 'Raboczeje Znamia,'" *Niepodległość,* VI (1932), 26–40.

Pilovski (Bar Shalom), Varda. "Agudat halutsim–shalosh teudot al reshit darko ha-tsiburit shel Yaakov Leshchinski," *Ba-derekh,* II (1968), 122–32.

"Nahman Sirkin: haguto ha-leumit ve-hahevratit u-filuto ha-tsiburit-mdinit me-reshit darko ve-ad ha-kongres ha-tsiyoni ha-sheni." Ph.D. thesis, The Hebrew University of Jerusalem, 1974.

[Pilsudski, Józef]. "Listy Józefa Piłsudskiego" (ed. Leon Wasilewski and Władysław Pobóg-Malinowski), *Niepodległość,* XII–XX, 1935–9.

"Pinkas agudat ha-sotsyalistim ha-ivrim be-london (di protokoln funem yidishn sotyalistishn fareyn in london in 1876)," *HS* I, 533–94. (Hebrew: ibid. A publication of the Research Project on the Jewish Labor Movement, Hebrew University. Jerusalem, 1968.)

Pinsky, Dovid. "A zhargon farzamlung," *Dos naye lebn* (Dec. 1912), pp. 37–9.

Pinson, Koppel S. "Arkady Kremer, Vladimir Medem and the Ideology of the Jewish Bund," *JSS,* VII (1945), 233–64.

Pipes, Richard. *The Formation of the Soviet Union: Communism and Nationalism 1917–1923.* Cambridge, Mass., 1964.

Social Democracy and the St. Petersburg Labor Movement 1885–1907. Cambridge, Mass., 1963.

Plaut, W. Gunther. *The Growth of Reform Judaism. American and European Sources until 1948.* New York, 1965.

Plekhanov, Georgii Valentinovich. *O zadachakh sotsialistov v borbe s golodom v Rossii.* Geneva, 1892.

Perepiska G. V. Plekhanova i P. B. Akselroda (ed. P. A. Berlin et al.). 2 vols. Moscow, 1925.

(ed.) *Vademecum dlia redaktsii "Rabochego dela": sbornik materialov.* Geneva, 1900.

Pollak, Gustav. *Michael Heilprin and His Sons.* New York, 1912.

Pomper, Philip. *Peter Lavrov and the Russian Revolutionary Movement.* Chicago, 1972.

Portugali, Mendel. "Tsror mikhtavim," *Kovets "ha-shomer",* pp. 14–26.

Posener, S. *Adolphe Crémieux (1796–1880).* 2 vols. Paris, 1933–4. (English: S. V. Pozner: *Adolphe Crémieux: a Biography.* Philadelphia, 1940.)

Pospielovsky, Dmitry. *Russian Police Trade Unionism: Experiment or Provocation?* London, 1971.

Pratt, Norma Fain. *Morris Hillquit: a Political History of an American Jewish Socialist.* Westport, Conn., 1979.

"Predrassudki nashikh sotsialnykh revoliutsionerov protiv evreev (neopublikovannaia korrespondentsiia)," in B. Sapir (ed.), *Vpered,* II, 497–510. (Yiddish: ed. F. Kursky, *Undzere tsayt* [1929], no. 1, pp. 37–46; no. 2, pp. 50–7; no. 3, pp. 50–7; Hebrew: ed. M. Mishkinsky, *He-avar*, XXI [1975], 20–34.)

Pulzer, Peter G. J. *The Rise of Political Anti-Semitism in Germany and Austria.* New York, 1964.

Rabinovich, Shmuel. "Mit 50 yor tsurik – fragmentn fun zikhroynes," *HS*, III, 314–47.

Radkey, Oliver H. *The Agrarian Foes of Bolshevism: Promise and Default of the Russian Socialist Revolutionaries February to October 1917.* New York, 1958.

Raevsky, Ezra "Mayn ershte bagegenish mit Ab Kahan," in Cahan, *Yubileum-shrift*, pp. 15–24.

Rafes, Moyshe. *Dva goda revoliutsii v Ukraine; evoliutsiia i raskol "bunda".* Moscow, 1920. *Ocherki po istorii Bunda.* Moscow, 1923.

Raisin, Jacob S. *The Haskalah Movement in Russia.* Philadelphia, 1913.

Rappaport, Joseph. "Jewish Immigrants and World War I. A Study of American Yiddish Press Reactions." Ph.D. dissertation, Columbia University, 1951.

Rappoport, Charles. "The Life of a Revolutionary Émigré (Reminiscences)," *YAJSS*, VI (1951), 206–36. (Yiddish: *HS*, III, 283–312.)

Reizen, Zalmen. *Leksikon fun der yidisher literatur, prese un filologye.* 4 vols. Vilna, 1926–9. "S. An-ski (biografishe notitsn)," *Lebn* (1920), no. 7–8, pp. 43–56.

Revutsky, Avrom. "Dr. Nakhmen Sirkin: oyfn frishn keyver," *Di tsukunft* (Oct. 1924), no. 10, pp. 583–5. *In di shvere teg oyf ukraine: zikhroynes fun a yidishn minister.* Berlin, 1924.

Reznikoff, Charles. *Louis Marshall, Champion of Liberty* (introd. O. Handlin). 2 vols. Philadelphia, 1957.

Rischin, Moses. "The American Jewish Committee and Zionism, 1906–1922," *Herzl Year Book*, V (1963), 65–81. *The Promised City: New York's Jews 1870–1914.* New York, 1970.

Rocker, Rudolf. *The London Years.* London, 1956.

Rogger, Hans. "Jews, Peasants and Land in Russia," *Cahiers*, XVII (1976), no. 1, 5–21; no. 2–3, 171–211.

Rogoff, Harry. *An East Side Epic: the Legend and Work of Meyer London.* New York, 1930. (Yiddish: *Meyer London: a biografye.*)

Ro'i, Yaacov. "Yahase rehovot im shkheneha ha-aravim," *Ha-tsiyonut*, I (1970), 150–204. "The Zionist Attitude to the Arabs 1908–1914," *Middle Eastern Studies*, IV (1967–8), 198–242.

Rosen, Zvi. *Bruno Bauer and Karl Marx: the Influence of Bruno Bauer on Karl Marx's Thought.* The Hague, 1977.

Rosenstock, Morton. *Louis Marshall. Defender of Jewish Rights.* Detroit, 1965.

Rotenstreich, Nathan. "For and against Emancipation: The Bruno Bauer Controversy," *LBIYB*, IV (1959), 3–36.

Royter pinkes: tsu der geshikhte fun der yidisher arbeter bavegung un sotsyalistishe shtremungen bay yidn. 2 vols. Warsaw, 1921–2. (A publication of the Kultur Lige.)

Rozenbaum, Menakhem M. *Erinerungen fun a sotsyalist-revolutsyoner.* 2 vols. New York, 1924.

Rozental, Anna. "Vladek hot oyfgeshturmt gants vilne in 1905 un iz nokh biz itst nit fargesn gevorn," in Jeshurin, *Vladek*, pp. 109–13.

Rozental, Pavel [An-man]. "Byalestoker peryod in lebn fun ts. k. fun bund," *RP*, I (1921), 45–69. "Di fareynikungs-frage oyf der VII konferents fun bund," *RP*, II (1922), 5–21. *Vozzvanie k evreiskoi molodezhi.* London, 1901 (A Bund publication; unsigned.)

RSDRP [Russian Social Democratic Labour Party]. *Chetverty sezd RSDRP: protokoly.* Moscow, 1959. *Pervy sezd RSDRP: dokumenty i materialy.* Moscow, 1958.

Tretii sezd RSDRP: protokoly. Moscow, 1959.

Vtoroi sezd RSDRP: protokoly. Moscow, 1959.

Rubach, M. (ed.). *Istoriia Ekaterinoslavskoi sotsial-demokraticheskoi organizatsii 1899–1903.* Ekaterinoslav, 1923.

Rudin, A. James. "Beersheba, Kan. God's Pure Air on Government Land," *Kansas Historical Quarterly,* XXXIV (1968), no. 3, 282–98.

Ruge, Arnold. *Zwei Jahre in Paris: Studien und Erinnerungen.* Leipzig, 1846.

Ruppin, Arthur. *Arthur Ruppin: Memoirs, Diaries, Letters* (ed. and introd. A. Bein). London, 1971.

   The Jews in the Modern World. London, 1934.

   Pirke hayay (ed. A. Bein). 3 vols. Tel Aviv, 1968.

   Shloshim shnot binyan be-erets yisrael. Jerusalem, 1937.

Sablinsky, Walter. *The Road to Bloody Sunday: Father Gapon and the St. Petersburg Massacre of 1905.* Princeton, 1976.

Sadikov, P. A. "Obshchestvo 'Sviashchennoi druzhiny,' " *KA,* XXI (1927), 200–17.

Sanders, Ronald. "Moses Hess: the Hegelian Zionist," *Midstream,* VIII (1962), no. 1, 57–69.

Sapir, Boris. "Jewish Socialists around 'Vpered,' " *IRSH,* X (1965), 365–84.

   (ed. and introd.) *Lavrov: Years of Emigration: Letters and Documents.* Dordrecht, 1974.

   "Liberman et le socialisme russe," *IRSH,* III (1938), 25–88.

   (ed. and introd.). *"Vpered" 1873–1877: from the Archives of Valerian Nikolaevich Smirnov.* 2 vols. Dordrecht, 1970.

Schama, Simon. *Two Rothschilds and the Land of Israel.* New York, 1978.

Schapiro, Leonard. *The Communist Party of the Soviet Union.* London, 1960.

   "The Role of the Jews in the Russian Revolutionary Movement," *SEER,* XL (1961–2), 148–67.

Schappes, Morris U. "The Political Origins of the United Hebrew Trades," *Journal of Ethnic Studies,* V (1977), 13–44.

   "World War I and the Jewish Masses," *Jewish Life* (February 1955), pp. 16–19; (March 1955), pp. 21–5.

Schechtman, Joseph B. *Vladimir Jabotinsky Story.* 2 vols. New York, 1956–61.

Schneiderman, Jeremiah. *Sergei Zubatov and Revolutionary Marxism. The Struggle for the Working Class in Tsarist Russia.* Ithaca, N.Y., 1976.

Scholem, Gershom G. *The Messianic Idea in Judaism.* New York, 1971.

Schwarz, Solomon M. *The Russian Revolution of 1905.* Chicago, 1907.

Schweid, Eliezer. *Ha-yahid: olamo shel A. D. Gordon.* Tel Aviv, 1970.

Second International. *VII Congress socialiste international (tenu à Stuttgart du 16 au 24 août 1907). Compte rendu analytique.* Brussels, 1908.

Sefer ha-shomer (ed. Y. Ben Zvi, Y. Shokhat, et al.). Tel Aviv, 1957.

Sefer toldot ha-hagana (ed. B. Z. Dinur, Y. Slutsky, et al.). 3 vols. in 8 books. Tel Aviv, 1954–72.

Seidman, Joel. *The Needle Trades.* New York, 1942.

[SERP]. "Materialy k istorii evreiskogo rabochego dvizheniia," *SERP,* I (1907), 248–60; II (1908), 381–403. (Contains draft program of the party, report on SERP presented to the 1907 congress of the Second International, etc.)

Shannon, David A. *The Socialist Party of America: a History.* New York, 1955.

Shapira, Yosef. *Ha-poel ha-tsair: ha-raayon ve-hamaase.* Tel Aviv, 1968.

Shapiro, Yonathan. "American Jews in Politics: The Case of Louis D. Brandeis." *AJHQ,* LV (1965–6), no. 2, 199–211.

   Leadership of the American Zionist Organization 1897–1930. Urbana, Ill., 1970.

   "Ha-mahloket be-yahadut artsot ha-brit bi-sheelat kongres yehudi amerikani," *Hatsiyonut,* II (1971), 90–104.

Shatsky, Yankev. *Geshikhte fun yidn in varshe.* 3 vols. New York, 1947–53.

Shazar, Zalman [Rubashev]. "B. Borokhov u-morashto (kavim li-dmuto u-ldarkhe torato," in B. Borochov, *Ktavim nivharim* (Tel Aviv, 1944), pp. xix–xl.

Or ishim: divre masa ve-zikaron al pgishot she-tamu. 2 vols. Jerusalem, 1964.

Shokhat, Eliezer. *Bi-ntive avoda: reshimot, dvarim, mikhtavim* (ed. Y. Shapira). Tel Aviv, 1967.

Shokhat, Yisrael. "Shlikhut ve-derekh," *Sefer ha-shomer,* pp. 1–79.

Shpizman, Leyb. "Etapn in der geshikhte fun der tsienistisher arbeter bavegung in di fareynikte shtatn," in *Geshikhte fun der tsienistisher arbeter bavegung,* I, 81–292; II, 297–444.

[Shtif, N., and B. Fridland.] *Chemu nas uchit pokushenie Pinkhusa Dashevskogo?* London, 1903. (A publication of Molodoi Izrail.)

Shukman, Harold. "The Relations between the Jewish Bund and the RSDRP 1897–1903." D.Phil. thesis, Oxford University, 1961.

Shva, Shlomo. *Shevet ha-noazim: korot Manya ve-Yisrael Shohat ve-havrehem be-"hashomer."* Tel Aviv, 1969.

Shvarts, P. "Di ershte yidishe oysgabes fun der PPS," *HS,* III, 527–39.

Yuzef Pilsudski: zayn batsiyung tsu der yidn-frage un zayn kamf kegn bund (1893–1905). Warsaw, 1936.

Sidirov, N. I. "Statisticheskie svedeniia o propagandistakh 70-kh godov v obrabotke III otdeleniia," *KiS* (1928), no. 1/38, pp. 27–56.

Silberner, Edmund. "Bernar Lazar ve-hatsiyonut," *Shivat tsiyon,* II–III (1953), 328–63.

Moses Hess. Geschichte seines Lebens. Leiden, 1966.

Ha-sotsyalizm ha-maaravi u-sheelat ha-yehudim. Jerusalem, 1955. (German: *Sozialisten zur Judenfrage.* Berlin, 1962.)

"Was Marx an Anti-Semite?" *Historica Judaica,* XI (1949), no. 1, 3–52. (Also in *Ha-sotsyalizm ha-maaravi.*)

The Works of Moses Hess: an Inventory of his Signed and Anonymous Publications, Manuscripts and Correspondence. Leiden, 1958.

Singer [Zinger], Mendl. *Be-reshit ha-tsiyonut ha-sotsialistit; prakim u-dmuyot.* Haifa, [1957].

Shlomo Kaplanski: hayav ve-poalo. 2 vols. Jerusalem, 1971.

Sliozberg, Genrikh Borisovich. "Baron G. O. Gintsburg i pravovoe polozhenie evreev," *Perez-hitoe,* II (1910), 94–115.

Dela minuvshikh dnei. 3 vols. Paris, 1934.

Slutsky, Yehuda. "Bet ha-midrash le-rabanim be-vilna," *He-avar,* VII (1960), 29–48.

"Diyun bi-veayot yahase avoda be-reshit yeme ha-aliya ha-shniya," *Ha-tsiyonut,* III (1973), 198–213.

"Dr. Maks Mandelshtam," *He-avar,* IV (1956), 56–76.

"Ha-geografya shel praot 1881," *He-avar,* IX (1962), 16–25.

"Ha-idea ve-hakvutsa (le-mikhtavo shel Dr. Y. Kolat)," *Ba-derekh,* IV (1969), 164–6.

Ha-itonut ha-yehudit-rusit ba-mea ha-tsha-esre. Jerusalem, 1970.

Ha-itonut ha-yehudit-rusit be-reshit ha-mea ha-esrim 1900–1918. Tel Aviv, 1978.

"Kritikus," *He-avar,* VIII (1960), 43–9.

Mavo le-toldot tnuat ha-avoda ha-yisreelit. Tel Aviv, 1973.

"Menahem Usishkin – ha-tkufa ha-rusit," *He-avar,* XII (1965), 20–1.

"Mkoma shel ha-idea be-hithavut ha-kvutsa ba-arets," *Ba-derekh,* II (1968), 137–45.

"Ha-raayon ha-halutsi u-tnuot halutsiyot lifne milhemet ha-olam ha-rishona," *Asupot* (1968), no. 12, pp. 7–18.

"Shnat 1905 be-hayehem shel yehude rusya," *He-avar,* XXII (1977), 3–23.

"Tsmihata shel ha-inteligentsya ha-yehudit-rusit," *Zion,* XXV (1960), no. 3–4, 212–37.

Smolenskin, Peretz. "Tazkir le-alians ha-yisreelit be-nidon yehude rusya" (ed. Y. Klausner), *He-avar,* IV (1956), 40–6.

Sokolov [Sokolow], Nahum. *History of Zionism 1600–1918*. 2 vols. London, 1919.
Sombart, Werner. *Why Is There No Socialism in the United States?* [1905]. New York, 1978.
Sonin, P. "Vospominaniia o iuzhnorusskikh pogromakh 1881 g.," *ES* I (1909), no. 4, 206–18.
Sosis, Yisroel. *Di geshikhte fun di yidishe gezelshaftlekhe shtremungen in rusland in XIX y.h.* Minsk, 1929.
"Na rubezhe dvukh epokh: natsionalny vopros v literature kontsa 70-kh godov," *ES*, VIII (1915), 324–37.
Sotsyalistisher teritoryalizm: zikhroynes un materyaln fun di partayen SS, YS un fareynikte. Paris, 1934.
[SP of A]. *National Congress of the Socialist Party.* (15–21 May 1910). Chicago, 1910[?].
Proceedings of the National Convention of the Socialist Party of America (1–6 May 1904).
Proceedings of the National Convention, Socialist Party (10–17 May 1908). Chicago, 1908[?].
Proceedings: National Convention of the Socialist Party (1912). Chicago, 1912[?].
Spector, Ivar. *The First Russian Revolution: Its Impact on Asia.* Englewood Cliffs, N.J., 1962.
Spivak, Charles. "Erinerungen fun Kahans grine tsaytn," in [Cahan], *Yubileum-shrift*, pp. 30–5.
Sponti, Evgenii I. [Nikitin]. "Vstrechi s Leninym," *Zapiski Instituta Lenina* (1928), no. 3, pp. 71–3.
Srednitskaia, Pati. "Zikhroynes vegn Arkadin," in *Arkadi zamelbukh*, pp. 23–72.
[SSRP]. *Deklaratsiia Sionistsko-sotsialisticheskoi rabochei partii* (1905). (Yiddish: in *ST*, pp. 139–48; Hebrew: in B. Borochov, *Ktavim*, I, 367–72.)
Rezoliutsii i postanovleniia, priniatye na I-om ocherednom sezde Sionistsko-sotsialisticheskoi rabochei partii. 1906.
Stein, Leonard. *The Balfour Declaration.* London, 1961.
Steklov [Nakhamkes], Iurii Mikhailovich. "V ssylke i v emigratsii: ideinye konflikty," *PR* (1923), no. 5/17, pp. 193–250.
Stern, Fritz R. *Gold and Iron: Bismarck, Bleichröder and the Building of the German Empire.* New York, 1977.
Strobel, Georg W. *Die Partei Rosa Luxemburgs, Lenin und die SPD. Der polnische 'europäische' Internationalismus in der russischen Sozialdemokratie.* Wiesbaden, 1974.
Syrkin, Marie. *Nachman Syrkin: Socialist Zionist (a Biographical Memoir).* New York, 1961. (Includes key works by Syrkin, abridged, in translation.)
Syrkin, Nachman. "B. Borokhov ve-torato," *Kuntres* (2 Tevet 5688/26 Dec. 1927), no. 322, pp. 4–6.
Empfindung und Vorstellung. Bern, 1903.
Geklibene tsienistish-sotsyalistishe shriftn. 2 vols. New York, 1925–6.
Geschichtsphilosophische Betrachtungen. Berlin, 1896.
[Ben Elieser]. *Die Judenfrage und der sozialistische Judenstaat.* Berne, 1898. (Hebrew: *Kitve Sirkin*, pp. 1–59; English: abridged, in M. Syrkin, pp. 255–93.)
Kitve Nahman Sirkin (ed. and introd. B. Katznelson). Tel Aviv, 1939.
"Mozes Hes: zayn lebn, zayn virkung un zayn filozofye." Introduction to M. Hess, *Roym un yerusholayim* (New York, 1916), pp. 7–65.
Vozzvanie k evreiskoi molodezhi. London, 1903. (Izdanie sionistov-sotsialistov.) (Hebrew: *Kitve Syrkin*, pp. 63–76).
Yidisher kongres in amerike. New York, 1915.
Szajkowski, Zosa. "The Alliance israélite universelle and East European Jewry in the 60s," *JSS*, IV (1942), 139–60.
"The Attitude of American Jews to East European Jewish Immigration (1881–1892)," *PAJHS*, XL (1950–1), 221–80.

"Concord and Discord in American Jewish Overseas Relief 1914–24," *YAJSS*, XIV (1969), 99–158.

"The European Attitude to East European Jewish Immigration (1881–1893)," *PAJHS*, XLI (1951–2), 127–62.

"How the Mass Migration to America Began," *JSS*, IV (1942), 291–310.

"The Impact of the Russian Revolution of 1905 on American Jewish Life," *YAJSS*, VII (1978), 54–118.

Jews, Wars and Communism. 2 vols. New York, 1972–4.

"Private American Jewish Overseas Relief and Immigration (1914–38)," *AJHQ*, LVIII (1967–8), no. 1, 52–106; no. 2, 191–253.

Tabenkin, Yitshak. "Ha-mkorot," in Habas, pp. 23–30.

Tabori, A. "Borokhov u-maamaro ha-rishon," *Kuntres* (2 Tevet 5688/26 Dec. 1927), no. 322, pp. 9–12.

Talmon, Jacob L. "Jews between Revolution and the Counter-Revolution," in idem, *Israel among the Nations* (London, 1970), pp. 1–87.

The Myth of the Nation and the Vision of Revolution – the Origins of Ideological Polarisation in the Twentieth Century. Forthcoming.

Political Messianism: the Romantic Phase. London, 1960.

"Uniqueness and Universality," in idem, *The Unique and the Universal* (London, 1965), pp. 64–90.

Tartakover, Arye. *Toldot tnuat ha-ovdim ha-yehudit*. 3 vols. Warsaw, 1929.

Thon, Yaakov (ed.). *Sefer Varburg: korot hayav, divre haarakha, mikhtavim, neumim u-maamarim*. Herzliya, 1948.

Tidhar, David (ed.). *Entsiklopedya le-halutse ha-yishuv u-vonav*. 19 vols. Tel Aviv, 1947–71.

Tidmarsh, K. "The Zubatov Idea," *American Slavic and East European Review*, XIX (1960), no. 3, 335–46.

Tobias, Henry J. *The Jewish Bund in Russia: from its Origins to 1905*. Stanford, 1972.

with C. E. Woodhouse. "Political Reaction and Revolutionary Careers: the Jewish Bundists in Defeat 1907–10," *Comparative Studies in Society and History*, XIX (1977), 367–96.

Treadgold, Donald W. *Lenin and His Rivals: the Struggle for Russia's Future 1898–1906*. London, 1955.

Trotsky, Leon. *1905*. New York, 1971.

Trunk, Isaiah. "Di onheybn fun der yidisher arbeter bavegung," *Di geshikhte fun bund*, I, 11–105.

Tsemakh, Shlomo. *Be-reshit: le-toldot ha-hityashvut ha-ovedet*. Jerusalem, 1946.

"Eliezer Shohat," in E. Shokhat, *Bi-ntive avoda*, pp. 7–14.

Tsitron [Citron], Shmuel Leyb. *Dray literarishe doyres: zikhroynes vegn yidishe shriftshteler*. 4 vols. Vilna, 1920–8.

"Mayne bagegenishn mit Nakhmen Sirkin," *Der tog* (Vilna) (28 September 1924), no. 229, p. 5.

Toldot hibat tsiyon. I: *Me-reshit yeme ha-tnua ad she-nitasher vaad hoveve-tsiyon be-odesa*. Odessa, 1914.

Tuchman, Barbara W. *Bible and Sword: England and Palestine from the Bronze Age to Balfour*. New York, 1965.

Tucker, Robert C. *Philosophy and Myth in Karl Marx*. Cambridge, 1972.

Turtel, Hasiya. "Pulmus ha-hagira mi-rusya ahare 'ha-sufot ba-negev' bi-shnat 1881," *He-avar*, XXI (1962), 43–65.

"Tnuat 'am olam,' " *He-avar*, X (1963), 124–43.

Ulam, Adam B. *The Bolsheviks: the Intellectual and Political History of the Triumph of Communism in Russia*. New York, 1965.

Urofsky, Melvin I. *American Zionism from Herzl to the Holocaust*. New York, 1975.

A Mind of One Piece. Brandeis and American Reform. New York, 1971.

Ussishkin, Menahem M. "Nasha programma," *EZ* (December 1904), no. 12, pp. 78–111. (English: *Our Program.* New York 1905. A publication of the Federation of American Zionists).

Vaganian, V. *G. V. Plekhanov: opyt kharakteristiki sotsialnopoliticheskikh vzrenii.* Moscow, 1924.

Valk, Sigizmund Natanovich. "G. G. Romanenko (iz istorii 'Narodnoi voli')," *KiS* (1928), no. 48, pp. 36–59.

Veits, Yosef. "Ha-galila," in Habas, pp. 356–63.

Venturi, Franco. *Roots of Revolution: a History of the Populist and Socialist Movements in Nineteenth Century Russia.* London, 1960.

Vilensky-Sibiriakov, V., et al. (eds.). *Deiateli revoliutsionnogo dvizheniia v Rossii: bio-bibliograficheskii slovar* I(1–2); II(1–4); III(1–2); V(1–2). Moscow, 1927–34. (A publication of the Vsesoiuznoe obshchestvo politicheskikh katorzhan i ssylnoposelentsev.)

Vinchevsky, Morris. "An erinerung, an obshatsung un an oyffoderung," *Dos naye lebn* (Dec. 1912), pp. 3–9. (On Zhitlovsky.)

Gezamlte verk. 10 vols. New York, 1927–8. (IX–X: Vinchevsky's memoirs.)

Vital, David. *The Origins of Zionism.* Oxford, 1975.

Volk, Stepan Stepanovich. *Narodnaia volia 1897–1882.* Moscow, 1966.

Volyner, A. [Eliezer Landau]. "Sirkinizmen: opgerisene erinerungen," *Der yidisher arbeter* (9 Sept. 1927), no. 18, pp. 6–8.

Vozrozhdenie. *Otchet konferentsii "Vozrozhdeniia": prilozhenie k no. 1 "Vozrozhdeniia."* London, 1904.

Wasilewski, Leon. "Walka o postulat niepodległci w polskim obozie socjalistycznym," *Niepodległość,* X (1934), 1–20, 180–204, 323–49.

Weinryb, D. [Bernard]. *Be-reshit ha-sotsyalizm ha-yehudi: A. S. Liberman u-vne doro.* Jerusalem, 1940.

Weinstein, Bernard. *Fertsig yor in der yidisher arbeter bavegung.* New York, 1924.

Weinstein, James. *The Decline of American Socialism, 1912–1925.* New York, 1967.

Weisbrod, Robert G. *African Zion: the Attempt to Establish a Jewish Colony in the East Africa Protectorate.* Philadelphia, 1968.

Weiss, John. *Moses Hess: Utopian Socialist.* Detroit, 1960.

Weizmann, Chaim. *The Letters and Papers of Chaim Weizmann.* 14 vols. London, 1968–. *Trial and Error.* 2 vols. Philadelphia, 1949.

Wildman, Allan. *Making of a Workers' Revolution; Russian Social Democracy 1891–1903.* Chicago, 1967.

"Russian and Jewish Social Democracy," in A. and J. Rabinowitch with L. D. Kristof (eds.), *Revolution and Politics in Russia* (Bloomington, Ind., 1972), pp. 75–87.

Wilson, Nelly. *Bernard-Lazare: Antisemitism and the Problem of Jewish Identity in Late Nineteenth Century France.* Cambridge, 1978.

Wistrich, Robert S. "Anti-Capitalism or Anti-Semitism? The Case of Franz Mehring," *LBIYB,* XXII (1977), 35–54.

"German Social Democracy and the Problem of Jewish Nationalism 1897–1917," *LBIYB,* XXI (1976), 109–42.

Revolutionary Jews from Marx to Trotsky. London, 1976.

"Socialism and Anti-Semitism in Austria before 1914," *JSS,* XXXVII (1975), 323–32.

Wolf, Lucien. *Sir Moses Montefiore: a Centennial Biography.* New York, 1885.

Wolfe, Bertram. *Three Who Made a Revolution.* Boston, 1948.

Woodhouse, C., and H. J. Tobias. "Primordial Ties and Political Process in Pre-Revolutionary Russia: the Case of the Jewish Bund," *Comparative Studies in Society and History,* VIII (1965–6), 331–60.

BIBLIOGRAPHY

Yanait (Ben Zvi), Rahel. *Anu olim: pirke hayim.* Jerusalem, 1959. (English, abr.: *Coming Home.* Tel Aviv, 1963).
Manya Shohat. Jerusalem, 1976.
Yasny, A. Volf. *Geshikhte fun der yidisher arbeter bavegung in lodzh.* Lodz, 1937.
Yassour, Avraham. *Mi-likhe mahpekhat 1905 be-rusya: tsmihato shel ha-bolshevizm.* Ramat Gan. 1972.
Yavnieli, S. (ed.). *Sefer ha-tsiyonut.* II: *Tkufat hibat tsiyon.* Tel Aviv, 1942.
Di yidishe avtonomye un der natsyonaler sekretaryat in ukraine; materyaln un dokumentn. Kiev, 1920.
Yidisher arbeter pinkes (tsu der geshikhte fun der poyle tsien bavegung) (ed. Zerubavel). Warsaw, 1928.
Yoeli, Mordekhay (ed. and introd.). *L. Pinsker: mevaser ha-tehiya ha-leumit.* Tel Aviv, 1950.
Yokhelson, Vladimir. "Dalekoe proshloe: iz vospominaniia starogo narodovoltsa," *Byloe* (1918), no. 13, pp. 53–75.
Yom iyun: al sifro shel Matityahu Mints, "B. Borokhov: ha-maagal ha-rishon." Efal, 1978.
[Zaid, Aleksandr]. *Haye rishonim: mi-yomane Aleksander Zayd* (ed. E. Smoli). Tel Aviv, 1942.
Zaks, A. S. *Di geshikhte fun arbeter ring 1892–1925.* New York, 1925.
Zaretz, Charles Elbert. *The Amalgamated Clothing Workers of America: A Study in Progressive Trades-Unionism.* New York, 1934.
Zaslavsky, Dovid. *M. P. Dragomanov; k istorii ukrainskogo natsionalizma.* Moscow, 1934.
"Tsu der geshikhte fun 'bund' in kiev," *RP,* I (1921), 70–79.
"Zubatov i Mania Vilbushevich," *Byloe* (March 1918), no. 3/31, pp. 99–128.
Zeira, Asher. "Ben ha-PPS ve-habund," *M'asef,* I (May 1971), 165–84.
Zerubavel. *Ber Borokhov: zayn lebn un shafn.* Warsaw, 1926.
"Der grindungs-peryod fun der YSDAP-poyle tsien," *RP,* I, 131–51.
"Fun poltava biz kroke," *YAP,* pp. 62–113.
"Prakim al 'ha-ahdut'," *Asupot* (April 1954), no. 4, pp. 68–89; (June 1957), no. 5, pp. 121–33.
Zhidlovsky, Aliza. "Hevle klita," in Habas, pp. 554–8.
Zhitlovsky, Chaim [E. Khasin]. "Di antshteyung fun dem soyuz ruskikh sotsyalistov revolutsyonerov," introduction to M. M. Rozenbaum, *Erinerungen fun a sotsyalist-revolutsyoner,* pp. vii–lviii.
Evrei k evreiam. London, 1892. (Yiddish: *Gezamlte shriftn,* VI, 13–55; Hebrew: *Yehudi li-gydhhudim.* A publication of the Research Project on the Jewish Labor Movement, Hebrew University. Jerusalem, 1967).
Fun asimilatsye biz poyle tsienizm: di ontviklungs-epokhen fun dem yidish-sotsyalistishn gedank. New York, 1919.
Gezamlte shriftn. 15 vols. Warsaw, 1928–35.
"Moyshe Hes – der sotsyalist, der filosof, der yid," *Dos naye lebn* (1912), no. 3, pp. 1–12; no. 4, pp. 1–16; no. 5, pp. 1–14. (Also in *Gezamlte shriftn,* III, 195–231.)
Mysli ob istoricheskikh sudbakh evreistva. Moscow, 1887.
[S. Grigorovich]. *Nashi zadachi: osnovnye polozheniia programmy Soiuza sotsialistov-revoliutsionerov.* London, 1900.
[S. Grigorovich]. *Sotsializm i borba za politcheskuiu svobodu: istoriko-kriticheskii ocherk.* London, 1898.
Zhitlovski-zamlbukh: gevidmet Dr. Khaim Zhitlovski tsu zayn zekhtsikstn geburtstog fun zayne fraynd, khaveyrim, talmidim. Warsaw, 1929.
Zikhroynes fun mayn lebn. 3 vols. New York, 1935–40.
Zilberfarb, Moyshe. "Di grupe 'vozrozhdenye' (vi zi iz antshtanen un zikh antviklt)," *RP,* I, 113–30.

BIBLIOGRAPHY

Dos yidishe ministeryum un di yidishe avtonomye in ukraine (a bletl geshikhte). Kiev, 1919.

Zionist Congress (I). *Zionisten Kongress in Basel (29–31 August 1897: officielles Protokoll*. Vienna, 1898.

(II.) *Stenographisches Protokoll der Verhandlungen des II Zionisten Kongresses gehalten zu Basel (21–31 August 1898)*. Vienna, 1898.

(VI). *Stenographisches Protokoll: Verhandlungen VI Zionisten Kongresses in Basel (23–28 August 1903)*. Vienna, 1903.

(VII). *Stenographisches Protokoll der Verhandlungen des VII Zionisten Kongresses und des ausserordentlichen Kongresses in Basel (27 Juli–2 August 1905)*. Berlin, 1905.

(VIII). *Stenographisches Protokoll der Verhandlungen des VIII Zionisten Kongresses im Haag (vom 14 bis inklusive 21 August 1907)*. Cologne, 1907.

(IX). *Stenographisches Protokoll der Verhandlungen des IX Zionisten Kongresses in Hamburg vom 26 bis inklusive 30 Dezember 1909*. Cologne, 1910.

(XI). *Stenographisches Protokoll der Verhandlungen des XI Zionisten Kongresses in Wien vom 2 bis 9 September 1913*. Berlin, 1914.

Zivion. "20 yor 'bund' un 5 yor federatsye," *Di tsukunft* (Nov. 1917), no. 11, pp. 625–9.

"Di yidishe agitatsyons byuro," *Di tsukunft* (May 1909), pp. 274–81.

Zlocisti, Theodor. *Moses Hess, Der Vorkämpfer des Sozialismus und Zionismus 1812–1875*. Berlin, 1921. (Hebrew: *Moshe Hes*, introd. N. Rotenstreich, 2 vols. Jerusalem, 1945.)

INDEX

autonomism, 169, 587n148; Jewry, 2, 26, 57, 72, 95, 189, 218, 269, 307, 478; socialist organizations in, 176; Zionism and labor Zionist organizations in, 159, 310, 311, 312–3, 318, 390, 399–400, 428–32; *see also* Brody; Galicia

Austrian Reichsrat, 169, 270

Austrian Social Democratic Labor Party, 177, 218, 234–5

auto-emancipation, *see* self-emancipation

autonomism (Jewish national), 555; and American Jewry, 171, 454, 516; in Austria-Hungary, 169, 587n148; Borochov and the ESDRP-PZ, 330, 346–7, 348, 351; and Bund, 171, 181, 184, 185, 217–24, 226, 235, 236, 240–1, 246–7, 252, 253, 557, 588n43; and Dubnov, 164, 171; and *Iskra*, 231, 235; and Jabotinsky, 164, 253; and labor movement in Palestine, 376–7, 381, 451; popularity of, 162–7, 252, 282, 516; adopted by *Vozrozhdenie* and SERP, 280–2, 283; and Zhitlovsky, 171, 217, 270, 280–1

Avenarius, Richard, 356, 360–1

Avner, *see* Ben Zvi, Y.

Baal-Shem, (Israel Ben Eliezer Baal Shem Tov; Besht), 285, 565n99

Babeuf, Francois-Noël, Gracchus, 466

Babylonian exile, 10

Badanes, Gershon, *see* Gurevich, Grigorii Evseevich

Bahar, Jacques, 316–7

Bailey, Shneyer, 55

Bakst, Nikolai Ignatevich, 74

Bakunin, Mikhail Aleksandrovich, 27, 28, 567n149

Bakuninism, 40, 101, 106, 205

Balfour, Arthur James Balfour (from 1922, First Earl), 537–8

Balfour Declaration, 537–8, 539, 559

Balmashev, Stepan Valerianovich, 278

Balta, 77, 94; pogroms in, 69–70, 74, 107

Bar Giora, 394–6, 419, 441

Baranov, M. (Moyshe Gormidor), 119, 131, 461, 470, 492, 567n137

Barats, Yosef, 369, 375, 376

Barbès, Armand, 20

Barondess, Joseph, 467, 477, 488, 495; and American Jewish Congress (proposed), 512, 513, 514, 516, 541, 545, 547; and Kehila experiment, 500; as union leader, 118

Baskin, Joseph, 540

Bauer, Bruno, 14, 15, 16, 17, 18, 563n44, 563–4n49, 564n53

Bazin, M., *see* Zilberfarb, Moyshe

Bebel, August, 466

Becker, Johann Philipp, 27

Beduin, 279–80, 410–11, 421, 423, 426

Beker, Esther, 395

Belaia Tserkov, 58

Belgium, 20

Belkind, Yisrael, 90, 93, 95, 97, 111, 126, 368

Bellamy, Edward, 297

Belostok, 3, 51, 325; Bund Congress in, 220, 224, 226, 231; conference of RSDRP in, 236; expanding textile town, 36, 173; pogroms in, 135, 153–4, 155; strikes and revolutionary movement in, 152–3, 172, 191, 203; Hoveve Zion and Labor Zionism in, 116, 310

Ben Adir, *see* Rozin, Avrom

Ben Avuya, Elisha, 43

Ben Ami (Mark Iakovlevich Rabinovich; pseud. Reish Galuta), 54, 55, 56, 57, 90, 102–3, 112–13

Ben Ehud, *see* Zhitlovsky, Chaim

Ben Gurion, David (David Grin), 3, 330, 369, 416; and American Jewish Congress (proposed), 519, 521, 539, 556; on formation of Jewish working class, 388, 417, 425, 539; on hegemony of Yishuv in Zionism, 377, 402, 425, 539; on history of Second Aliya, 367, 381; nationalism and Jewish-Arab relations, 378, 386, 388, 410, 420, 425; and Ottoman orientation of, 376, 377, 447–8, 452; on Palestine Labor Fund, 446–7, 450; and Syrkin, 292; and Yemenite Jews, 417

Ben Shemen, 373, 409, 423, 424, 425, 426, 435, 437

Ben Yehuda, E. (Eliezer Yitshak Perlman), 50, 82, 85, 127, 160, 365, 372, 574-5n175

Ben Zakai, Yohanan, 305

Ben Zvi, Y. (Yitshak Shimshelevich; pseud. Avner), on Arab-Jewish relations and guarding, 396, 412, 440; and Borochov, 330, 334, 338, 344, 345, 429, 556; on cooperative settlement, 389, 430, 431, 437, 556; Ottoman orientation, 447–8; in Poale Zion (Palestine), 369, 371, 375, 376, 377, 378, 386–8, 389, 396, 412–3, 416, 424, 429, 431, 450, 519; and Poale Zion (Russia), 330, 338, 344, 345, 369, 429; in U. S., 515, 519; World Poale Zion and Palestine Labor Fund, 430, 431, 446, 450;

Bentwich, Herbert, 476

Bentwich, Norman, 532

Berdiaev, Nikolai Aleksandrovich, 405

Berdichev, 58, 332

Berdichevsky, Mikha Yosef, 388

Berger, Yitshak, 278, 319–20

Berliavsky, Yaakov, 96–7, 111, 125

Berlin: and emigration (*1881–82*), 66, 74; Haskala, 82; Russian-Jewish intelligentsia in, 38, 41, 43, 202, 219, 271–2, 291, 292, 312, 313, 360, 593n212; Warburg and Zionism in, 397–401, 428, 441

Berlin, Naftali Zvi Yehuda, 127

Berlin Treaty, 524

Berlinraut, Leyb, 360

Berman, M. 402, 425, 433

Berman, Pavel, 207

Berne, 40, 292, 313, 318; Bundists in, 222, 223, 224, 226, 249, 272, 274, 275, 276, 278, 593n12; Zhitlovsky and SRs in, 222, 261, 267, 272, 274–8, 287, 313

Berner Street Club, London, 121

Bernhardt, Sarah, 69

Bernstein, Eduard, 214, 388, 437, 518

Bernsteinism, 227, 230, 242

Bernstein, Karl, 66

Bessarabets, 279

Bessarabia, 50, 382, 383, 473

Bet Arif (place), *see* Ben Shemen

Bezalel, 442

Bialik, Chaim Nachman, 143, 160, 370, 584n131

Bible, 6, 7–8, 9, 16, 23, 44, 54, 56, 112, 160, 293, 355; ordinances on land use and distribution, 33, 63, 264, 266, 305–6, 397, 555; use of

Heilikman, T., *see* Geilikman, Tevye
Heilprin, Michael, 67, 95, 121
Heine, Heinrich, 15, 307, 562n19
Helfand, C. Y., *see* Litvak, A.
Helsingfors, conference, 166, 358, 557
Herder, Johann Gottfried, 295, 297
Herder, Moyshe, 55
Herut (Freedom) organization, 320–1, 326
Hersch, Pesach-Liebman (pseud. P. Libman), 180, 463
Herzen, Alexander (Aleksander Ivanovich), 20, 304
Herzl, Theodor, 140, 289, 296, 337, 352, 372, 465; death (*1904*), 158, 399; and Hess, 47; impact on Russian-Jewish students/youth, 222, 223, 309, 368; left-wing opposition to, 279, 312, 313, 316–17; myth in lifetime, 178–9, 315–16, 368; and Oppenheimer, 397–8; and Syrkin, 302, 313, 315–17, 321, 322, 327; and Uganda project, 137, 158–9, 279, 302, 322, 479; visits Russia (*1903*), 178, 279, 600n108
Herzl forest, 398
Herzlian Zionism, 148–9, 222, 289, 309, 313, 337, 347, 352, 372, 398, 462, 472
Hess, Moses, 6–28, 183, 257, 288; alienation from Jewish community, 14–19, 21, 266–7; and antisemitism, 12, 14–15, 23; and assimilation, 6, 10–11, 14, 26; biographical details, 6, 8, 13, 20–1, 266, 563n40; character and search for identity, 3, 5, 6–7, 21–4, 48, 257; *The European Triarchy*, 10–11, 13–14; and Germany, 11–12, 13, 21, 22–3, 24, 27, 28; Hegel and Hegelianism, 8, 13–14, 24; hope in east European Jewry, 3, 26, 304; Jewish role in history, 7, 9–11, 16–17, 24–6, 27–8, 304–7; on Jewish return to Palestine, 12, 24, 26, 28; Marx and Engels, 6, 14, 15, 16, 17–20, 23, 27, 28, 29, 564n59, 569n208; middle years (*1841–8*), 13–20, 564n53; nationalism and role of nation states, 7, 10, 12, 13, 21, 22, 24, 28, 297, 306–7, 569n208; philosophical assumptions, 7–8, 13, 16, 19, 21, 22, 48; posthumous reputation and influence, 5, 6, 27, 47–8, 83, 266–7, 285, 286–7, 291–2, 304–7, 328, 334, 565n103, 569n208; *Rome and Jerusalem* 21–2, 23, 24, 25–7, 28, 48, 83, 266, 286, 305; *The Sacred History*, 7, 8, 9–10, 13, 17, 24, 26, 27; and socialism, 6, 7, 12, 15, 18, 19–20, 22, 26, 27, 28, 47, 48, 286, 305; and Syrkin, 48, 291, 297, 304, 328, 334; and Zhitlovsky, 266–7, 285, 286–7
Hessiana Society, Berlin, 320, 397
Hibat Zion, *see* Hoveve Zion
Hickl, Max, 310, 318
Hildebrand, *see* Gregory VII (Hildebrand), pope
Hillquit, Morris (Hilkovich), 118, 454, 456, 465, 473, 481, 484, 505, 534, 537
Hirsch, Emilie, 24
Hirsch, Josephine, 24
Hirsch, Maurice de, Baron, 71, 179
Hirsch, Samuel, 97, 116, 127, 580n390
Histadrut (General Jewish Labor Federation in Palestine), 366, 560
Hittin, 400
Hofman, Ben Tsiyon (Zivion), *see* Zivion
Hohenzollern Empire, *see* Germany

Holy Brotherhood (Sviashchennaia Druzhina), 570n13
Homel: Jewish socialists and self-defence in, 310, 336, 369, 371, 383; pogroms in, 321, 335–6, 369
Homestead (strike in), 483
Horesh, Ha- (union), 391, 393–4, 425; opposed Kinneret Experiment, 402
Hourwich, Isaac H. (Yitskhok Ayzik Ben Ayre Zvi Ha-Leyvi), 467, 491; and American Jewish Congress (proposed), 513–14, 518, 519, 525, 534, 545; and *Forverts*, 476, 478
Hoveve Zion (Palestinophilism), 158, 289, 317, 369, 372, 553; and Bund, 182, 183, 195, 202; early period (*1880s*), 102, 114–17, 123–30, 131, 140, 260, 262–3, 265, 285–6, 288; ideology/intelligentsia create movement, 182, 195, 269, 570n212; influenced by populism, 126, 161; Odessa Committee of, 116, 380, 414–15, 435; and post-1897 Zionism, 309, 312, 347, 362, 399, 441; and Second Aliya, 369, 380, 385, 407, 414–15, 435, 441; and socialism/socialists, 102, 123–6, 128–30, 195, 202, 553; and Zhitlovsky, 260, 262–3, 265, 268, 269, 281, 285–6
Hromada (The Commune), 101
Hugo, Victor, 72, 466
Hulda, 423, 435
Hungary, 86, 122; *see also* Austria/Austria-Hungary
Hurvich, Shaul Yisrael (Shay), 27
Hurvich, Zhenia (Evgeniia Adolfovna Gurvich), 240

ICA, *see* Jewish Colonisation Association
ILGWU, *see* International Ladies Garment Workers Union
ITO, *see* Jewish Territorial Organisation
Idelson, Abram Davydovich, 117, 139, 159–60, 161, 166, 358
ideology, 49–51, 134–5, 444; and American Jewish socialist movements, 453–64, 546–7; as autonomous factor in historical process, 5, 47–8, 53, 182, 223–4, 286–7, 291–2, 295–6, 328, 330, 367, 370, 389–90, 437, 554; and Bolshevism, 210–11; in development of Bund, 171–85, 192–200, 209–10, 217–27, 233, 256–7, 272, 389; in development of Zionist movements, 182, 195; function of, in Jewish socialist parties, 2, 7, 169, 256, 276, 358–60, 368, 456, 461; limited and influenced by socio-political context, 5, 47–8, 53, 178, 182–3, 233, 266–8, 271–2, 282–7, 288–92, 329–30, 357–63, 370, 437, 552–60; socio-economic theories of origin, 174–5, 178, 193, 326, 334, 357–8, 389
Ignatev, Nikolai Pavlovich, Count, 53, 58, 62, 68–9, 75, 108, 109; replaced by Count Tolstoy, 108, 109
Iliashevich, *see* Rubanovich, Ilia
immigrants, Russian-Jewish, *see* Russian-Jewish community, U. S.; *specific countries*
immigration, *see* emigration
Independent Order of B'nai B'rith, *see* B'nai B'rith
Independent Order B'rith Abraham, 517
Independent Order B'rith Sholom, 517
Ingerman, Sergei Mikhailovich, 213–15, 277, 490

Marxism/Social Democracy (cont.)
  Austrian Poale Zion, 169, 399–400; and Boro-
    chov, 133, 327–8, 329–31, 335, 341–3, 346–
    51, 355–7, 359–63; in conflict with anarchism
    (U. S.), 120–3, 455, 465; emergence in Russia
    (until 1892), 45, 132, 171–2, 268; influence of
    German (in Russia/U. S.), 67, 123, 468, 518; and
    Jewish youth (Russia), 45, 140–1, 371; national-
    ism/internationalism in, 130–1, 183–5, 191–3,
    217–19, 222–3, 227, 233–5, 241–6, 253–5,
    257, 267–8, 346, 385–6, 454, 478–83, 484–5,
    556; in Palestine (1905–1914), 350–1, 365, 371,
    383–4, 387–8, 389, 391, 411, 413, 428, 449;
    predominant influence on Jewish left (1903–),
    133, 140–1, 168–9, 253–5, 282–5, 291, 325–8,
    329–31, 341, 358–60, 363, 371, 383–4, 391,
    399–400, 557; and pogroms/antisemitism, 120,
    132, 138–9, 183, 227, 482; problems of "here-
    sies" in, 168, 211–15, 227–8, 229–30, 232,
    242–4, 246; Revisionism/Bernsteinism in, 214,
    227–8, 230, 242, 308, 343, 388, 400; and Syr-
    kin, 289–91, 293, 294, 296, 297, 300, 303, 308,
    314, 325–8; and war question, 467–8, 517–18,
    537; weak Russian organization of (until 1900),
    183, 227, 229; and Zhitlovsky, 259–60, 268,
    276, 277, 285; see also specific parties, individu-
    als, and topics
Masaryk, Tomas Garrigue, 81
Mashbir, Eliezer, 70
maskilim, see Haskala
Masliansky, Zvi Hirsch, 489, 500
May Day, 118, 176, 195, 196, 225, 311; 1892,
    172, 173; 1905, 147
Maze, Yaakov, 117
Mazzini, Guiseppe, 81, 304
Medem, Vladimir, 3, 205; on An-sky, 275; Bund
    and RSDRP, 241, 250; in national wing of
    Bund, 239, 240, 274; and theory of "neutral-
    ism," 185, 497, 588n43; and Zhitlovsky, 274,
    278
Mehring, Franz, 518
Meir, Golda (Meyerson), 330
Melbourne, Australia, 26
Melitopol, 147
Melits, Ha- (The Advocate), 53, 59–60, 77, 83, 116
melamdim, see heder
Memel, 62, 74
Menchikovsky, Feliks, 345
Mendele Moykher Seforim (Shoylem Yankev
    Abramovich), 31, 42, 388, 406
Mendelsohn, Ezra 188
Mendelson, Stanisław (Menia), 194, 200, 268,
    590n114
Mendelssohn, Moses, 265
Mennonites, 71
Mensheviks, 146, 157, 184, 185, 251, 254, 308,
    345; and Bund, 247–8, 255
Merhavya, 423, 425, 426, 427, 432, 434, 437,
    439, 440, 442, 444, 445, 503
Mesha (Kfar Tavor), 396, 419
Mesopotamia, 302
Messiah, 3, 32, 50, 81, 84, 128, 195, 264, 265,
    266, 285, 315, 316, 368
messianism/millenianism, 622n129; as cause of
    Herzl mystique, 178–9, 315–16; during 1881–
    2 crisis, 50, 81, 83–5, 96, 110–11, 112, 114,

128; and Hess, 10, 17, 24, 25, 26, 28, 266,
    304, 305, 306, 562n11; and Liberman, 32, 34,
    36, 37, 38, 567n137; modern/secular, 2–3, 4,
    134; and Palestine, 81, 83–5, 96, 128–9, 195,
    301, 368; in revolution (1905–6), 134, 169;
    Rubanovich on, 128–9; Russian, attacked by
    Pilsudski, 199; and Second Aliya, 368; and Syr-
    kin, 297, 301, 304, 305–6, 315–16; and Zhit-
    lovsky, 264–5, 270, 281, 285
Metawileh, 379, 410
Metula, 429
Mickiewicz, Adam, 304
Migdal, 423, 425
Mikhailovsky, Nikolai Konstantinovich, 85, 260,
    265, 281, 286, 289, 294, 295
Mikhalevich, Beynish (Yoysef Izbitsky), 236, 255
Mikve Yisrael, 28, 65, 70, 82, 97, 115, 116, 126,
    127, 580n390
Milch, Jacob, 467, 495, 479–81
Mill, John (Yoysef Shloyme Mil), 204; and Bund-
    RSDRP relations (1898–1903), 213, 232, 235,
    239; on Bundist history, 190, 195, 198, 206,
    224, 250, 276; for national ideology in Bund,
    190, 194, 196, 204, 206–8, 215–20, 222, 224,
    226, 235, 239, 260, 272, 274, 470; in Warsaw/
    PPS and PSD, 194, 203, 206–7, 208, 249
millenium, see messianism
Miller, Louis E. (L. Bandes), 118, 488; and Ameri-
    can Jewish Congress (proposed), 513, 514; and
    Forverts, 467, 468–9, 476–8, 480, 482–3; on
    Jewish workers and socialism, 465, 466; and
    New York Kehila, 500, 514; and popular journal-
    ism, 118, 460, 467, 468–9, 558; and Di varhayt,
    460, 490
Millerand, Alexandre, 469
Millerandism, 242
Minor, Osip Solomonovich, 140
Minsk: fires/pogrom in, 52, 149; Hoveve Zion/Zi-
    onism in, 79, 116, 292, 293, 313–14, 336, 338,
    369; Jewish life in, 3, 6, 131, 152, 369; Poale
    Zion in, 278, 310, 311, 313, 318, 319, 339,
    347; proto-Bundism/Bundism in, 171, 191–2,
    200, 204, 207, 213, 249, 254, 313; revolution-
    ary activity in, 100, 146, 171, 254; Zubatov
    movement in, 225, 231
Mints, Moshe Yitshak: and Bilu, 90, 95–7, 111,
    125, 126, 368, 557; in U. S., 125–6
Mintz, Matityahu, 334, 335, 356, 358
Mishkinsky, Moshe, 100, 171, 567n136
Mizrachi, 543, 544
Młot, Jan, see Dikshtein, Shimen
Mohammed, 10
Mohilev, 31, 70, 93, 94, 144
Mohilever, Shmuel, Rabbi, 117, 127, 580n388
Moldavia, 183, 193
Moleschott, Jacob, 20
Molodoi Izrail (group), 323
Monatsschrift für Geschichte und Wissenschaft
    des Judentums, 28
Montagu, Samuel, 73, 74, 476
Montefiore, Claude Joseph, 476
Montefiore, Moses, 553
Montefiore Agricultural Aid Society, 121
Montenegrins, 517
More, Thomas, 297
Morgenthau, Henry (Sr.), 537

Nikolaev, 81, 83, 218
Nili (organization), 409, 421
Nir, N. (Nahum Rfalkes), 323, 352
Nisanov, Yehezkel, 410
Nomberg, Hersh David, 370
Nordau, Max (Simon Maximilian Sudfeld), 355, 472
Novakovsky, Yehude, 329, 330
Novoe vremia (The New Times), 52, 53, 69, 73
Novosylkov, 149
Nyu yorker yidishe folkstsaytung (The New York Jewish People's Journal), 123, 125, 453, 589n88

OPE, *see* Society for the Dissemination of Enlightenment among the Jews in Russia
ORT, 51, 61, 97
Odessa, 51, 73; Am Olam in/from, 55–7, 64, 66, 67, 90, 94, 95, 121; Bund in, 242, 249, 313; emigration/embarkation for Palestine, from, 73, 81, 92, 96, 110; Hoveve Zion/Zionism/Poale Zion in, 116, 127, 310, 313, 324, 332, 338, 414–15, 441; Lilienblum/Pinsker in, 61, 81, 86, 127, 411; pogrom/looting (1881) in, 52, 54, 55, 69, 86; pogroms in (1871/1905), 54, 135, 136, 149; revolutionary movement/action in, 54, 99, 104, 146–7, 201, 242, 249; self-defense groups in, 54–5, 154
Okhrana, 119
Olam, Ha- (The World), 427
Olgin, Moyshe (Moissaye; Moyshe Yosef Novomisky), 168, 175, 329, 548; and American Jewish Congress (proposed), 512, 513, 521, 533, 534, 540, 541, 545; in Communist movement, 547
Oliphant, Laurence, 50, 70, 73, 74, 80–1, 83, 96–7, 110–1
Olive Grove Fund, 398
Onfang, Der (The Beginning), 373–4, 375, 376, 383, 388, 396, 411
Operators and Cloakmakers Union (No. 1), 118
Oppenheimer, Franz: Ben Zvi and Poale Zion (Palestine) on, 389, 431, 439, 556; Borochov and ESDRP-PZ on, 349, 354, 400, 430–1, 439; Herzl/Sixth Zionist Congress (1903), 316, 397–8; The Palestine experiment/Merhavya, 426, 427, 432–3, 436–7, 437–8, 442, 445, 503; and Poale Zion (Austria), 389, 399–400, 427–8, 429–31, 432; supported by Warburg/Zionists in Germany, 390, 398–401, 432, 433; and Syrkin, 320, 397, 399, 429–30, 442; theory of co-operative settlement, 389–90, 397
Oppenheimer, M., 497
Oregon, 67, 94, 121
Orel, 68
Organization of Young Workers in Palestine, The, *see* Ha-Poel Ha-Tsair
Oriental Jewish communities (Palestine): cultural gap dividing from Second Aliya, 405, 419; employed as workers/guards, 404, 417–19, 423, 424, 427; in Jerusalem, 375; organization of, planned by Second Aliya, 375–6, 377
Orsha, 162
Orshansky, Ilia Grigorevich, 68, 75, 76, 77
Ossovetsky, O. (Yehoshua), 126–7
Osvobozhdenie (Liberation), 138
Ottoman Empire, *see* Turkey
Owen, Robert, 397, 413

PKP, *see* Palestine Communist Party
PLDC, *see* Palestine Land Development Company
PPS, *see* Polish Socialist Party (PPS)
PPSD, *see* Polish Social Democratic Party (PPSD)
Pale of Settlement, 48, 61, 74, 141, 152, 157, 158, 174, 310, 327, 335, 357–8, 473, 492, 552; activist youth in/from, 144, 205, 367, 371; economic conditions in, 36, 134, 172, 191, 203, 299, 312; educational restrictions in, 589n91; effects of abolition (anticipated), 299, 312; influence abroad of politics/life in, 3, 169–70, 365, 378, 386, 406, 456, 463, 484–7, 516; mass organization/psychology in, 117, 119, 133, 134, 156, 162, 203, 275, 386, 462; politics in, influenced by emigrant communities/émigrés, 3, 51, 193–4, 396, 554, 557; resented by its non-Jewish population, 68, 103; structure of politics in, 456, 546, 554, 557, 559; as reservoir of revolutionary propagandists, 187; restrictions imposed by/expulsions into, 68, 75, 138, 149, 299, 520; restrictions on eastward migration relaxed (1915), 522; *see also* Russian Jewry
Palestine/Yishuv, 3, 49, 158–9, 161, 291, 320, 328, 330, 332–3, 348, 366–452 *passim*, 510, 549, 554, 556, 558, 560; and American Jewish Congress movement, 516, 517–18, 519, 520, 521, 532, 534, 538–9, 545, 547; colonies established in (until 1902), 28, 114–17, 126–8, 131, 137, 312, 367, 368, 372–3, 390; economic development of, 373–4, 367–8, 390, 393–4, 398–401, 403–4, 423, 426–7; ideas of Jewish state/settlement in, 6, 12, 24, 26, 58, 59, 62–4, 65, 68, 70, 80–1, 82–97, 106, 110–12, 123–6, 128–30, 272–3, 278, 301–4, 314, 317, 322, 324, 336–8, 340–4, 350–1, 352–4, 358–60, 363, 553; industry in, 373, 388, 411; Jewish population in/immigration to, 51, 366–7, 403–4; offices/institutions in, 365, 380, 404, 414–15, 423, 435; orthodox/traditional Jewish community in, 88, 89, 93, 95, 127–8, 131, 374, 405, 411, 417; Second Temple period in, 10, 264, 266, 289, 306, 314, 327; societies for the colonization of (1881–84), 49, 77, 79, 94–5; Turkish government and, 80–1, 88, 96–7, 110, 114, 125, 377–8, 412, 515; *see also* Bilu; emigration; Hoveve Zion; Poale Zion (Palestine); Ha-Poel Ha-Tsair; Second Aliya; Zionism; *specific individuals*
Palestine Commission, 398–9
Palestine Communist Party, 354, 560
Palestine Labor Fund, 430–1, 446, 449–51; control of, 446–7, 448
Palestine Land Development Company (PLDC), 401
Palestine Office (World Zionist Organization), 401, 404, 417, 425, 433, 434, 439, 441, 444, 450
Palestintsy, see Hoveve Zion (Palestinophilism); Zione Zion (Zionists for Zion)
Pam, Hugo, judge, 530
Panama Canal scandal, 305
Panken, Jacob, 498–9, 520, 540, 541
Paris, 74, 118, 127, 552; émigré socialists in, 55, 119, 128, 261, 274, 278, 324; Hess in, 16, 19, 23; Jewish Labor Society in, 128, 567n137; *see also* l'Alliance israélite universelle; France; Rothschild, Edmund de

675

681

Yavneel (Yama), 405
Yavneeli, S. (Shmuel Varshavsky), 417
Yehoash (Solomon Bloomgarden), 543
Yellin, David, 413
Yemenite Jews, 367, 375–6, 417–19
yeshiva (yeshivot)/yeshiva students, 127, 260; and Bund, 201–2, 251; Liberman on, 37, 38, 44, 48, 201, 368; and Second Aliya, 368, 369, 382, 387
Yesud Ha-Maala, 115, 422
Yiddish language, 6, 555; attitude of Jewish workers to, 180–1; in crisis of *1881–2*, 54, 91, 103; Dragomanov's support of, 101–2, 103; enthusiasm for (*1905–6*), 160–1, 166, 282, 357; Liberman's attitude to, 31, 39, 41, 43–4, 101, 273; and Pilsudski/Polish socialists, 177, 199–200, 207, 217; as predominant language of east European Jews, 1, 3, 552; and proto-Bund/Bund, 173–4, 180, 186, 187, 188, 193–4, 200, 201–2, 204, 207, 217, 220, 251, 272, 275, 277, 472; and Second Aliya, 388, 410, 421, 443–4, 451, 460, 557; and socialists in Galicia/Roumania, 176, 177, 193; in Soviet Russia, 171, 330; Syrkin's attitude to, 308–9, 319; in U. S. (after *1890*), 466, 470, 472, 481, 485, 505, 508, 509; used by emigrant socialists in West (*1880s*), 118–19, 121, 122–3, 124–5, 131, 176, 178, 193–4, 553–4; "Yiddish-speaking" socialism/Communism (U. S.), 454, 463, 466, 478, 481, 508, 547, 559; and Zhitlovsky, 217, 259, 263–4, 267, 271–2, 273–4, 276, 277, 285, 443–4, 451; see also Hebrew language, as opposed to Yiddish; press, Yiddish
Yiddish literature, 6, 267, 370; An-sky as writer, 258, 261, 275, 285; links of Peretz/Pinsky with Bund/Left, 173, 202, 261, 271–2, 274, 285, 370; published in *Di tsukunft* (U. S.), 466; translations of classics, 160
Yidishe arbeter velt, Di (The Jewish Labor World), 498, 509
Yidishe tageblat, Dos (The Jewish Daily Chronicle), 489, 490, 492, 493, 494, 512, 516
Yidishe tsukunft, Di (The Jewish Future), 161
Yidisher arbeter, Der, 204, 214, 215–18, 219, 220, 222, 223, 224, 226, 235, 272, 303, 470
Yidisher arbeter, Der (Galicia), 377, 378, 383, 387, 390, 400, 411, 428
Yidisher Arbeter Fareyn (New York), 122–3
Yidisher kempfer, Der (The Jewish Combatant), 486, 495, 536, 539
Yidisher kongres, Der (The Jewish Congress), 515, 517
Yidisher sotsyalist, Der The Jewish Socialist), 508, 509, 517
Yishuv, the, *see* Palestine; Second Aliya
Yoffe, Eliezer Lipe, 446
Yoffe, Hillel, 403
Yogikhes Lev (pseuds. Tyshko; Grozovsky), 195, 196–8, 200
Yokhelson, Vladimir Ilich (Veniamin), 29, 38, 45, 569n202
Young Germany (movement), 14
Young Men's Hebrew Association (YMHA), 517
youth, Russian-Jewish: role of (*1881–2*), 53, 54–7, 60, 78, 84–5, 89–90, 120–3; *see also* Am Olam; Bilu; Borochov, for pioneer vanguard; intelligent-
sia; *polu-intelligentsiia;* revolution, Russian (*1905–7*), youth in leadership of; revolutionary activity/ strategy, attraction for Russian-Jewish youth; Second Aliya, characteristics of; students; Zionism, youth as radicalizing force in

Zaid, Aleksandr, 369, 383, 391, 396, 405, 441
Zak, Abram Isaakovich, 52, 57
Zaks, Avrom Simkhe, 498
Zamenhof, Ludwig Lazar (pseud. Gamzefon), 88
Zametkin, Mikhl, 461, 467, 497
Zangwill, Israel, 327
Zaria (The Dawn), 235, 240
Zarnuka, 423
Zaslavsky, Dovid, 225–6, 250
Zasulich, Vera Ivanovna, 6, 98, 101, 104, 106, 132, 203, 205, 208, 212, 213, 228
Zealots, 306
Zeire Zion, 369, 381
Zeldov, Sergei (Sender; pseud. Nemansky), 201, 219, 236, 249, 255
zemstva, 58, 138
Zerno (The Seed), 100
Zerubavel (Yaakov Vitkin): in Palestine (*1909–14*), 369, 403, 410, 416, 422, 438, 439, 445, 448, 449; in/on Poale Zion (Russia), 344, 345, 357, 359, 369, 430, 438, 439; in Poland (*1920s*), 369
Zhaludskaia, Mariia, 207
Zheliabov, Andrei Ivanovich, 45, 120
Zhidlovsky, Aliza, 436
Zhitlovsky, Chaim (pseud. Ben Ehud), 310, 316, 534, 554; and American Jewish Congress movement, 289, 512, 515, 518, 519, 520–1, 543–4, 545, 547, 548; advocates Jewish autonomism, 171, 270, 273–4, 275–8, 281; agrarianism of, 259, 266, 272, 281, 285–6, 287; attacks "cosmopolitanism," 222, 272, 495; and Bund, 215–17, 219, 258, 260, 272–4, 275, 277–8, 313, 470, 491, 548; changes to optimistic prognosis (*1897–1907*), 271–2, 286–7, 555; character/biographical details, 140–1, 258–60, 261–4, 266–8, 281–2, 286–7, 329, 556, 589n86; and Communism/Bolshevism, 258, 260, 287, 289; and Hess, 266–7, 286–7, 565n103; *A Jew to the Jews*, 217, 267, 268–70, 272, 290; and Marxism/Plekhanov, 215–16, 259–60, 268, 269, 270, 276, 277, 285, 289, 491, 495; for modernized Jewish nation (secular/Yiddish based), 217, 259, 273, 470, 543–4; and Narodnaia Volia, 263–4, 266, 268–9, 287, 555; and Palestine movement/Zionism, 219, 258, 262–3, 265, 272–3, 279, 287, 289, 303–4, 312, 313, 315, 384, 442, 443–4, 451, 486, 505, 558; as populist/voluntarist, 133, 215, 259–60, 268, 269, 276–7, 285, 286–7, 289, 555; posthumous controversy re, 258, 287; role in revolutionary period (*1905–7*), 133, 162, 270, 271, 281–2, 285–6, 287, 289, 371; as Socialist Revolutionary, 140–1, 258, 260, 270, 271, 274, 276, 277–8, 281, 488, 491, 548; and Syrkin, 270, 273, 289, 298, 303–4, 306, 307, 315, 316; *Thoughts on the Historical Fate of Jewry*, 264–6, 268, 270, 306; in U. S. (as SR/nationalist socialist), 260, 270–1, 281–2, 442, 460, 464, 467, 486, 488, 489, 495, 501, 505, 547, 555; and *Vozrozhdenie*/SERP, 271, 275–6, 280–2, 283, 289; warnings against western type devel-